THE

NEW-ENGLAND

Historical and Genealogical Register.

PUBLISHED QUARTERLY, UNDER THE DIRECTION OF THE

New=England Historic, Genealogical Society.

FOR THE YEAR 1876.

VOLUME XXX.

BOSTON:

PUBLISHED AT THE SOCIETY'S HOUSE, 18 SOMERSET STREET.

PRINTED BY DAVID CLAPP & SON.

1876.

Committee on Publication,

1 8 7 6.

ALBERT H. HOYT,

JOHN WARD DEAN,

WILLIAM B. TOWNE,*

LUCIUS R. PAIGE,

H. H. EDES,

JEREMIAH COLBURN.

Editor,

JOHN WARD DEAN.

Facsimile Reprint

Published 1995

HERITAGE BOOKS, INC.
1540E Pointer Ridge Place
Bowie, Maryland 20716
1-800-398-7709

* Mr. Towne died April 10, 1876.
ISBN 0-7884-0239-0

A Complete Catalog Listing Hundreds of Titles
On History, Genealogy, and Americana
Available Free Upon Request

GENERAL INDEX.

[Index of NAMES of Persons at the end of the Volume.]

Abstracts of the earliest wills in Suffolk, 78, 201, 432 ; in Middlesex, 457
Acadians, Papers relating to, 17
Adams, Rev. Hugh, church records of, 59
Adams, Samuel, Memoir of, 279
Alger, Genealogy of, 484
Allan, Col. John, sketch of, 353
Allen, Genealogy of, 444
Allyn, Matthew, query, 110
America, passengers and vessels to, 39, 459
American Chronicles of the Times, query, 390
American Antiquarian Society, report of council, 269 ; portraits and busts of, 22 ; Transactions, vols. v and vi., 253
American Flag, plagiarism from Commodore Preble's History of, 238
American History, Notes on, 231, 299, 410
American Revolution, documents and papers of actors in, 331
American State Universities, their origin and progress, 269
American Shakespeare Bibliography, 486
Ancient wills, 37
Arms. (See *Coats of Arms*.)
Atkinson, N. H., church choir of, 240
Aubrey, note, 15
Autographs, of Samuel Adams, 279 ; William A. Buckingham, 9 ; Robert Daniels, 448 ; Jesse Glover, 27 ; William Lowndes, 141 ; Charles W. Moore, 399
Axtel, Daniel, note, 239
Ayres, Capt. John, 421

Bagnall, Benjamin, note, 466
Baker, note, 464
Baptisms and births. (See *Records*.)
Bacon's Early Bar of Oneida, 481
Barrett, Samuel, query, 234
Bason of alchimy, query, 240 ; reply, 462
Bibliotheca Munselliana, 271
Blanchard, Claude, journal of, 396
Berkeley, William, note, 232
Bill contracted by Gov. Dudley's government, 239
Biographical sketches—
    William Alexander, 338
    John Allan, 353
    William B. Astor, 139
    Francis Bassett, 246
    James M. Beebe, 244
    John Carter Brown, 139
    Clarissa Butler, 139
    Jacob Chapman, 221
    George Clinton, 336
    David Cobb, 232
    Ellen W. Coolidge, 487
    McLaurin F. Cooke, 139
    Curtis Cutler, 122
    Francis Dane, 242

Biographical sketches—
    Mary M. Dean, 278
    John L. Devotion, 278
    Thomas DeWitt, 117
    Jonathan Edwards, 139
    William Eustis, 340
    Albert A. Folsom, 228
    Charles Folsom, 227
    George Folsom, 228
    John Folsom, 212
    Jonathan Folsom, 229
    Joseph L. Folsom, 218
    Joshua Folsom, 230
    Josiah Folsom, 216, 224
    Nathaniel S. Folsom, 227
    Samuel Folsom, 223
    Simeon Folsom, 220
    John Glover, 332
    Mordecai Gist, 340
    Joshua Green, 126
    Walter C. Green, 123
    William Heath, 334
    Peter Hobart, 278
    John Jeffries, 487
    Day O. Kellogg, 114
    Harriet M. Kidder, 140
    Charles Lowndes, 146
    Rawlins Lowndes, 147, 164*l*
    Hannah Merrill, 488
    John G. Nichols, 118
    Amos Otis, 124
    Samuel Paine, 369
    Laura H. Park, 140
    Rhoda K. Porter, 278
    George W. Pratt, 246
    William Prescott, 241
    Rufus Putnam, 338
    Charles A. Ranlett, 116
    Joseph Reed, 341
    William S. Robinson, 278
    Mary H. Rowe, 488
    Frederic W. Sawyer, 112
    John S. Sleeper, 222
    Thomas Smyth, 120
    David Snow, 242
    Solomon R. Spaulding, 245
    Joseph Spencer, 337
    John Thomas, 332
    Henry T. Thornton, 488
    Jonathan Trumbull, 337
    John S. Tyler, 243
    William Tyler, 243
    Henry Waldron, 488
    Thomas Waterman, 119
    Joseph F. Wentworth, 140
    Mark Wentworth, 278
    John S. Wright, 117
Blague, reply to query, 103

Book Notices—

Abbott's History of Maine, 270
Alger's Alger Genealogy, 484
Andrew's Hart Genealogy, 269
Arnold's History of Rhode Island, second edition, 134
Bacon's Early Bar of Oneida, 481
Batchelder's History of the Eastern Diocese, 482
Bell's Exeter in 1776, 398
Bibliotheca Americana, Library of John Carter Brown, 256
Bibliotheca Munselliana, 271
Blanchard, Claude, Journal of, 396
Boston, Celebration of the Centennial Anniversary of its Evacuation, 395
Brevoort's Verrazzano the Navigator, 130
Brown's Coasting Voyages by Champlain in the Gulf of Maine, 268
Buchanan's Roberdeau Genealogy, 484
Buck's Chronicles of the Land of Columbia, 486
Bunker Hill, Centennial Celebration of the battle by the city of Boston, 138
Bunker Hill Monument Association, Proceedings July 4, 1875, 138
Cambridge in the Centennial, 394
Canton, Proceedings on Memorial Day, 277
Capen's History of Democracy, 134
Centennial Orations, Published by the New England Historic, Genealogical Society, 134
Champlain's Voyages in the Gulf of Maine, 268
Chapman's Bulkeley Family, 262
Chase's Lowndes Genealogy, 484
Chester's Marriage, Baptismal and Burial Registers of Westminster Abbey, annotated, 479
Clapp Memorial, 484
Colesworthy's School is Out, 485
Comte de Paris's History of the Civil War in America, 258
Concord Fight, Proceedings at the Centennial Celebration, 394
Connecticut Colonial Records, edited by Hoadly, Vol. ix., 276
Craig's Olden Time, a Monthly Repository, second edition, 482
Cutter Family, Supplement to, 262
Devens's Oration at the Centennial Celebration of the Battle of Bunker Hill, 394
Dexter's As to Roger Williams, 480
Drake's Bunker Hill, the Story as told by British Officers, 136; Gen. Israel Putnam, the Commander at Bunker Hill, 136
Duyckinck's Cyclopædia of American Literature, edited by Simonds, 267
Ellis's Third Supplement to Notices of the Ellises of England, Scotland and Ireland, 262
Fowler's Essays, Historical, Literary and Educational, 261
Freeman Genealogy, 135
Frothingham's Battle Field of Bunker Hill, 270
Fullonton's History of Raymond, N. H., 137
Genealogist, The, 137, 487
Georgia Historical Society, Proceedings at the dedication of Hodgson Hall, 483
Goodell's Address at the Centennial Celebration of the meeting of the Massachusetts Provincial Assembly at Salem, 135
Goodrich's Character and Achievements of Christopher Columbus, 273
Goss's Historical Address at Melrose, 483
Grand Lodge of Free and Accepted Masons, Proceedings, 1875, 260
Green's Historical Address at Groton, 483
Green, Percival and Ellen, Descendants of, 262
Green's Report of the Council of the American Antiquarian Society, 269
Hazen's Historical Discourse at the Centennial Celebration of the Congregational Church at Plymouth, N. H., 277
Hingham in the late Civil War, 265
History, Why is it so little read? 274

Book Notices—

Homes on Historical Societies in the United States, 486; State and Territorial Libraries, 486
Jenness's Historical Sketch of the Isles of Shoals, 274; Original Documents in the English Archives relating to New Hampshire, 265
Jones's Address on Sergeant William Jasper, 398
Key stone State, History of this appellation, 276
Knortz's American Shakespeare Bibliography, 486
Leicester, Mass., Centennial Proceedings in 1876, 483
Lexington, Proceedings at the Centennial Celebration of the battle, 138
Long's The Names we Bear, 277
Loomis Genealogy, 272
Lossing's Outline History of the United States, 274
Maine Genealogist and Biographer, 137, 487
Miscellanea Genealogica et Heraldica, 487
Mitchener's Ohio Annals, 277
Moore's Record of the Year, 395
Morris' History of the First Church in Springfield, 266; Early History of Springfield, 266
Munsell's Bibliotheca Munselliana, 271; Reminiscences of Northfield, 275; Reprint of New England Primer, 271; Webster's Almanac, 271
Murphy on The Voyage of Verrazzano, 130
Nason's Life of Henry Wilson, 272
New England Primer, reprint by Munsell, 271
New Hampshire Documents and Records, edited by Bouton, Vol. viii., 273; Vol. ix., 394
New York Genealogical and Biographical Record, 487
Northfield, Mass., Temple and Sheldon's History of, 275; Munsell's Reminiscences of Men and Things in, 275
Odiorne Genealogy, 262
Parker's Col. William Prescott, the Commander at Bunker Hill, 136
Patterson's Stoddard Genealogy, 262; Booge Family, 262
Perkins, The Names as found on Essex Records, 484
Peyton's Memoir of William M. Peyton, 481; Over the Alleghanies, 481; Sketch of Anne M. Peyton, 481
Poole's The Ordinance of 1787, and Dr. Manasseh Cutler as a gent in its Formation, 482
Potter's American Monthly, 259, 394
Quincy, Josiah, Jr., Life of, 397
Randall's History of Chippewa Valley, 272
Rawson Genealogy 262
Rupp's Collection of Thirty Thousand Names of German, Swiss and Dutch Immigrants in Pennsylvania, 1727 to 1776, 276
Salem Centennial Celebration of Leslie's expedition, 1775. 138
Salisbury's William Diodate and his Italian Ancestry, 484
Scull's Genealogical Notes on the Family of Scull, 484
Smith on The Authenticity of Documents concerning Verrazzano, 130
Stearns's History of Rindge, N. H., 264
Stone's History of the Rhode Island Institute of Instruction, 277
Stickney's Kinsman Genealogy, 484
Sudbury Bi Centennial, 486
Sullivan, Gen., not a Pensioner of Luzerne, 138
Tarbox's Life of Gen Israel Putnam, 393
Ten Brook's American State Universities, their Origin and Progress, 268
Tenney Genealogy, 262
Thayer Genealogy, 484
Thomas's History of Printing, second edition, 253

Book Notices—
  Tuttle, J. F., on God's Work in the World the
    last Fifty Years, 273 ; C. R., Illustrated His-
    tory of Wisconsin, 270
  Valentine Family in America, 262
  Vilas, Peter, Descendants of, 262
  Warren Family, descended from Richard of the
    Mayflower, 262
  Webster's Almanac, 271
  Wentworth's Early Chicago, 487
  West Springfield Centennial Celebration, 266
  Wheildon's New History of the Battle of Bunker
    Hill, 136
  Williams's History of St Paul, Minn., 260
  Winthrop's Washington, Bowdoin and Franklin,
    and other Occasional Addresses, 398
  Worcester in the War of the Revolution, 395
  Wright's Principia or Basis of social Science, 485
Boston, arrivals in 1712, 39 ; donations to people,
  suffering under the port bill, 373 ; fire (in 1762),
  237 ; Huguenot church records, query, 109 ; old
  elm on common, 237 ; record of Committee of Cor-
  respondence, Inspection and Safety, 380, 441 ;
  schools, 236 ; Town Meeting for granting leave to
  erect Faneuil Hall, 368
Brabrooke, note, 465
Bradbury. John M., bequest of, 462
Brastow, Thomas, note, 391
Brewers of Essex County, Mass., 422
Brigham, note, 467
Brooks, note, 466
Buckingham, William A., memoir, 9

Calef, Robert, query, 461
Cape Fear Island, wreck on (1695), 200
Centenarianism, notes on, 107, 111, 240, 392
Centennial Celebration of the Declaration of Inde-
  pendence at Groton, Leicester and Melrose, 483
Centennial Exhibition, opening of, 391 ; education
  at, 233
Charlestown, Mass., church records, 178
Coats of Arms—
  Lowndes, 141
Cook, query, 239
Comer, note, 108
Cooper, Rev. William, interleaved Almanacs, 435
Committee of Correspondence, Inspection and Safety,
  380, 441
Continental Congress, first session of, 285
Congress of authors in Philadelphia, 461
Conquest of the Wilderness, note, 468
Corliss genealogy, note, 469
Cotton, note, 111
Cudworth, James, maternal ancestry of, 464

Dartmouth, Mass., records, 56
Davies, note, 361
Deaths, current, 139, 278, 487
Depositions of—
  Elizabeth Hasket, 110
  Alexander Lillington, 235
DeWolf, note, 465
Diaries—
  Timothy Connor, 175, 343
  William Cooper, 435
  Henry Knox, 321
  John May, 45
  William D. Williamson, 189, 429
Did the American colonists desire independence, 326
Documents and letters by actors in American Revo-
  lution, 331
Documents relating to Port Royal (1711), 196
Donations to people of Boston suffering under the
  Port Bill, 373
Douglass genealogy, note, 464
Dover, N H., baptisms in, 455 ; note, 468
Drake, Samuel G., sales of library, 238, 469
Durham, N. H., church records of, 59
Dynn, note, 108

Eastman, note, 463

Easton, dignitaries of, 103
English maids for Virginia planters, 410
Errata, 105, 398, 488
Essex County, emigrants from, to South Carolina, in-
  structions to, 64
Extracts from the diary of William D. Williamson,
  189, 429

Facsimiles of the stamps of 1765, note, 468
Faded writing, restoration of, 103, 467
Falmouth, Me., query, 240
Farrars of Essex County, Mass., 422
Fawne, name of, 108
Felton, deaths of aged persons of the name, 463
Fields, genealogy of, 406
Fillmore, note, 467
Fiske, note, 465
Flagg, family sketch of, 112
Fosom, query, 207
Fo(r)ster, genealogy of, 83
Foster, note, 462
Franklin, note, 234
Free Masonry, opposition to, 401
Furness, genealogy of, 63

Garrison, genealogy of, 418
Genealogies and Pedigrees—
  Allen, 444   Hayes, 105
  Axtell, 239   Hobart, 278
  Brewer, 422   Jeffries, 487
  Brigham, 467   Langdon, 33
  Brooks, 466   Low, 102
  Devotion, 278   Lowndes, 141
  De Wolf, 465   Machel, 464
  Eastman, 463, 488   Morgan, 108
  Farrar, 422   Mott, 104
  Felton, 463   Parker, 236
  Fields, 406   Pell, 236
  Flagg, 112   Penn, 32
  Folsom, 207   Tyler, 243
  Fo(r)ster, 83   Wells, 488
  Furness, 63   Willoughby, 67
  Garrison, 418   Wooster, 104
  Hall, 109   Young, 465
  Hammond, 28
Gerrish manuscripts, 82
Gibbons, note, 234
Gleanings, Whitmore's, 421
Glover. Josse, sketch of, 26
Great Seal of Maryland, note, 466

Hall, note, 109
Hammond, genealogy of, 28
Harrison, Me., note, 468
Harvard College graduates, ages of, 235
Hawley, query, 106
Hayes, note, 105
Hayfield, note, 110
Hill, note, 110
Historical Societies, proceedings of—
  Connecticut, 472 ; Delaware, 130 ; New England
  Historic, Genealogical, 126, 247, 469 ; Maine, 472 ;
  New London County, 129, 252 ; New Jersey, 473 ;
  Rhode Island, 129, 250, 471 ; Virginia, 252, 472
Hollis, N. H., in the War of the Revolution, 288
Hunt, query, 464

Illustrations—
  Arms of Lowndes, 141 ; seal of Robert Daniell, 458
  (See also Portraits.)
Independence, did the colonists desire it ? 326
Indian deserter, note, 234
Inman, note, 466
Instructions for emigrants from Essex County to
  South Carolina, 64

Jamestown, Virginia, ships arriving at, 414
Jenkins, note, 467

Kittery, Maine, Quakers in, 106
Knowles, note, 463

Knox, Gen. Henry, diary during his Ticonderoga expedition, 321 ; letter of H. G. Otis, relative to, 360

Lane, Samuel, extract from diary of, 107
Lang, query, 463
Langdon, genealogy of, 33 ; note, 109
Letters from—
John Adams (1774), 306 ; (1776), 310 ; (1821), 329
Samuel Adams (1776), 310
Ethan Allen (1781), 58
Charles Apthorp (1756), 18
John Armstrong (1776), 315
Abraham Clark (1776), 314
David Cobb (1780), 342
Elias Dayton (1776), 334
Silas Deane (1776), 315
William Eustis (1779), 340
William Floyd (1776), 311
Francis Foxcroft (1752), 82
Thomas Gage (1765), 303
Horatio Gates (1778), 319
Timothy Gerrish (1752), 82
Elbridge Gerry (1776), 312
Mordecai Gist (1779), 340
John Glover (1776), 332
John Gooch (1776), 334
Thomas Hancock (1756), 18
Cornelius Harnett (1777), 316
William Heath (1776), 334
Francis Hopkinson (1770), 314
Robert Howe (1773), 304
John Jay (1821), 326
John Langdon (1776), 309
Charles Lawrence (1755), 17
Richard H. Lee (1777), 316 ; (1776), 335 ; (1779), 339
Francis Lewis (1776), 335
Philip Livingston (1776), 335
James Lockwood (1776), 333
Thomas Mighill (1776), 302
James Monroe (1817), 164a
Robert Morris (1776), 335
Daniel Moulton (1775), 307
Thomas Nelson (1781), 320
Francis Nicholson (1710), 198
Harrison Gray Otis (1843), 361
Samuel Paine (1775), 371
John Penn (1778), 316, 320 ; (1777), 316
William Penn (1683), 15
Robert Pigot (1775), 352
Jedidiah Preble (1756), 19
John Preble (1780), 359
Rufus Putnam (1779), 338
Edward Randolph (1684), 20, 21
Joseph Reed (1774), 305 ; (1780), 341
J. Rutledge (1776), 313
Joseph Spencer (1777), 337
Lord Sterling (1778), 338
John Sullivan (1788), 105
John Thomas (1776), 332
Jonathan Trumbull (1778), 337
Joseph Warren (1775), 307
George Washington (1775), 300
William Whipple (1778), 317, 319 ; (1775), 308
William White (1776), 335
Isaac Winslow (1775), 354
John Witherspoon (1776), 313
David Wooster (1776), 333
Letters of signers of the Declaration of Independence, military men and others, during the Revolutionary War, 303
Lillington, note, 235
Lovering, note, 111
Low, Lieut. Jonathan, note, 102
Lowndes, genealogy of, 141
Lowndes, William, memoir of, 157

Marriages (1773), note, 106
Martin, Joseph P., memoir of, 330

Maryland, letter of Jesuit missionaries, note, 112
Maryland, great seal of, note, 466
Masonic periodicals, 401
May, John, journey of to Ohio country, 43
Mayflower People, the, 412
Members of the New England Historic, Genealogical Society, obituaries of. (See Necrologies.)
Memoirs—
Samuel Adams, 399
William A. Buckingham, 9
Thomas Lowndes, 152
William Lowndes, 157
Joseph P. Martin, 330
Charles W. Moore, 399
Francis Willoughby, 72
William Willoughby, 69
Memoranda from the Rev. William Cooper's interleaved almanacs, 435
Middlesex County, abstracts of wills, 457
Mighill, Thomas, sketch of, 301
Mitchell, Mary, query, 390
Moore, Charles W., memoir of, 398
Morgan, note, 108

Navy uniforms, note, 391
Necrologies of the New England Historic, Genealogical Society—
Francis Bassett, 246
James M. Beebe, 244
George G. Brewster, 475
Curtis Cutler, 122
Francis Dane, 242
Thomas DeWitt, 118
Abijah W. Draper, 478
Nathan Durfee, 477
Joshua Green, 126
Walter C. Green, 123
Day Otis Kellogg, 114
Henry W. Lee, 476
Theron Metcalf, 474
Beamish Murdoch, 474
John Gough Nichols, 118
Amos Otis, 124
George W. Pratt, 246
William Prescott, 241
Charles A. Ranlett, 116
William B. Reed, 477
Frederic W. Sawyer, 112
Thomas Smyth, 120
David Snow, 242
Solomon R. Spaulding, 245
Earl Stanhope, 475
John S. Tyler, 243
William Tyler, 243
Thomas Waterman, 119
John S. Wright, 117
Newbury, Mass., second foot company, 434
New England Historical and Genealogical Register, brief history of, 184
New England Historic, Genealogical Society, necrologies of, 112, 241, 474 ; number of genealogies in library, 187 ; President Wilder's annual address, 165 ; proceedings of, 126, 247, 469
Noble genealogy, note, 238
Notes on American history, 231, 410
Notes and queries, 102, 233, 389, 461

Obituary notices. (See Necrologies.)
Ohio, Col. May's journey to, 43

Paine, Samuel, letter of, 369 ; sketch of, 369
Palmer, note, 462
Papers relating to the Acadians, 17
Passengers and vessels to America, 41, 459
Parker, John, note, 299
Parker, note, 236
Parmelee, answer to query, 464
Pedigrees. (See Genealogies.)
Peirce, note, 104
Pell, note, 236
Philbrook, note, 103

Poole, note, 109
Port Royal, documents relating to, 196
Porter genealogy, note, 464
Portraits and busts in American Antiquarian Soc., 22
Portraits of—
    Samuel Adams, 278
    William A. Buckingham, 8
    William Lowndes, 140
    Charles W. Moore, 397
Pratt, William, note, 239
Preble, Jedidiah, note, 109 ; John, letter of, 359
Price, William, petition of, 237

Queries. (See *Notes and Queries.*)

Records, Charlestown, 178 ; Dartmouth, Mass., 56 ;
    Dover, N. H. baptisms, 455 ; Oyster River Parish,
    now Durham, N. H., 59 ; Stratham, N. H., 426 ;
    West Springfield, 50, 194
Record of the Boston Committee of Correspondence,
    Inspection and Safety (1776), 380, 441
Reed, note, 469
Register, brief history of the, 184
Restoring old deeds, note, 467
Revere, Paul, note, 468
Revolutionary War, history and genealogy of, note,
    106
Root, Joshua, note, 240
Rose, Robert, query, 237
Russell, John, query, 237
Russell, Mrs. Mary F. W., sketch of, 478

Seals, copying of, query, 463
Second foot company of Newbury, Mass., 434
South Carolina, emigration to, 64
Southington, Conn., history of, note, 107
Spooner genealogy, note, 107
Standish, note, 462
Stark, General, horse lost at Bennington, 366
Starr, John, note, 235
Stiff, note, 467
Stratham, N. H., deaths in, 426
Sudbury Canada grant (1741), proprietors of, 192
Suffolk County Probate files, abstracts of, 78, 201, 432

Talcott, note, 234
Thomas, note, 234
Thompson, Daniel, query, 390
Tibbetts, query, 469

Ticonderoga expedition, 321
Town records. (See *Records.*)
Treacle fetched out of a viper, note, 462
Transportation of homeless London children, 413
Trumbull, Jonathan, note, 10
Twelves, note, 469

Vessels and passengers to America, 41, 459

Waldron, Isaac, marriage certificate, 109
Waller family, note, 107
Ware, William, query, 465
Washington, autograph letter and portrait of, note,
    238 ; character of, 389
Watson, Jonathan, query, 238
Webber, note, 109
West Springfield, early settlers, 50, 194
White, note, 465
Willey family, destroyed by a land-slide, 468
Wigglesworth, Edward, note, 240
Wilder, Marshall P., address of, 165
Williamson, W. D., diary of, 189, 429
Willis, note, 463
Willoughby genealogy, 67 ; query, 103
Wills and other Probate records, abstracts of—
    Richard Barbour, 201
    Richard Cruse, 80
    Robert Daniels, 457
    Margery Elliot, 205
    William Frothingham, 206
    Samuel Holly, 81
    Robert Hunt, 80
    Thomas Lechford, 201
    John Lovering, 79
    Oliver Mellowes, 78
    Mary Newmarch, 37
    Henry Pease, 202
    Thomas Satell, 204
    Judith Smead, 79
    Jeffery Stapell, 201
Withington, note, 235
Wooster, note, 104
Worcester Co. Mechanic Association, portraits and
    busts of, 22

Yankee privateersman in prison in England (1777–
    79), 174, 343
York, Me., note, 390
Young, Rowland, query, 236 ; note, 465

THE

HISTORICAL AND GENEALOGICAL REGISTER.

JANUARY, 1876.

MEMOIR OF
THE HON. WILLIAM A. BUCKINGHAM, LL.D.

By Noah Porter, D.D., LL.D., President of Yale College, New-Haven, Ct.

WILLIAM ALFRED BUCKINGHAM was born in Lebanon, Connecticut, May 28, 1804. His father Samuel was born in Saybrook, and was a descendant in the direct line from the Rev. Thomas Buckingham, the minister of Saybrook (1665–1709), one of the ten founders of Yale College, and one of the moderators of the synod which framed the Saybrook Platform. Thomas was the son of Thomas, one of the original members of the New-Haven Colony, but soon removed to Milford, where he was one of the "seven pillars" of the church at its organization. His mother, Joanna Matson, was born in Lyme, Ct., Jan. 25, 1777, died Dec. 9, 1846. The parents began their married life at Saybrook, but soon removed to Lebanon, where they died and were buried. William was the second of six children, the others being Abigail, born March 26, 1801, died June 27, 1861; Lucy Ann, born Oct. 25, 1806, died Sept. 2, 1853; Samuel Matson, born July 12, 1809, died Nov. 26, 1810; Samuel Giles, born Nov. 18, 1812; Israel Matson, born Aug. 5, 1816.

Lebanon is a quiet, pleasant country town,—scarcely a village,—eleven miles from Norwich, on the high road to Hartford. Its broad and grassy street is bordered by a few farm houses, comfortable and neat rather than elegant, which are distributed at convenient distances for the uses of the more than usually comfortable farmers who own them. Near the meeting-house are a few dwellings a little more distinguished, as the former residences of the Governors Trumbull, with the "store" which during and ever since the war of the revolution has been dignified by the name of the "Old War Office." Lebanon had been for nearly fifty-four years—from December, 1722, to February, 1776—trained and honored by the ministry of Solomon Williams, D.D., brother of Elisha Williams, Rector of Yale College, and himself a leader among the Connecticut divines. Here was born in 1710, the first Jonathan Trumbull, who graduated at Harvard College in 1727, and was chosen governor of Connecticut annually from 1769 to 1783—which office he resigned after fifty years of public service. His son Jonathan, born at Lebanon, graduated at Harvard College 1759, was paymaster to the army, 1776–1778; secretary and aid to Washington, 1780–1783; in 1789, member of congress; in 1791, speaker of the lower house; in 1794, senator; and from 1798 to 1809, governor of Connecticut. An academy also graced the village green, and had been sustained for many years with more or less regularity.

Here were all the conditions for the training of a character like that of Senator Buckingham. A small population all known to one another; nearly enough upon a level to be animated by a common sympathy, and yet sufficiently varied in position and culture to be able to give without condescension, and to receive without servility; all devout in their habits, and worshiping with simple rites in the one church which their fathers had planted; all laboring for a livelihood, and therefore industrious in habits and simple in manners; all believing in intelligence and courtesy as only inferior to godliness. No thoughtful youth could live in such a community without special incitements to public spirit and the love of country. The traditions of the *old war office* would stir the heart of any aspiring boy who saw with his own eyes the marks of the spurs left by orderlies and *aides de camp* as they sat waiting for despatches, and listened with bated breath to the stories of the revolution which fell from the lips of all the elders of the town, and heard them describe, as they had seen, the persons of Washington, Lafayette, Knox, and Rochambeau. Nor could such a boy stand before the Trumbull tomb in the old burying ground, where was garnered the sacred dust of the two governors, of Joseph the first commissary-general of the United States, of David a deputy commissary in the war of the revolution, and of William Williams one of the signers of the Declaration of Independence, without imbibing some of that patriotism. Living from his earliest years under such influences, the dignity of a life of public duty and of sacrifice for God and country could not but be impressed upon a nature so sensitive and high-minded as was that of young Buckingham. Most influential of all was the atmosphere of his own home, over which the grave but gentle father presided with unpretending dignity, and which was pervaded by the cheerful sunlight of an active and loving mother, whose ministries of love and blessing filled the whole community. Besides the education of his home, with its lessons of industry and duty, of self-sacrifice and courtesy, and the education of the community with its patriotic memories and pride, Mr. Buckingham had the best advantages of the public schools and academy at Lebanon, and of the

Bacon Academy at Colchester, which at that time was much resorted to. One of his schoolmates at Colchester, from a distant part of the state, has described him as being in his youth what he was in manhood, singularly manly, earnest, noble, and attractive. He labored upon the farm with a willing heart and with strong hands. He taught a district school at Lyme a single winter, when eighteen years old, with great success. When twenty years of age he entered a dry-goods house in Norwich as clerk. After two years' experience there and a few months in a wholesale house in New-York, he opened a dry-goods store in Norwich. In 1830 he engaged in the manufacture of ingrain carpets, which he continued for eighteen years. In 1848 he relinquished both these occupations and embarked in the manufacture of India-rubber goods, and was made the treasurer and an active director in the Hayward Rubber Company. Subsequently he became interested in several important manufacturing enterprises. As a man of business he was distinguished for industry, integrity, and promptness. He uniformly fulfilled his engagements, and his credit was unquestioned for any sum which he required for himself or for his country.

In 1830, September 27, he was married to Miss Eliza Ripley (daughter of Dr. Dwight Ripley, of Norwich, Ct.), who was eminently fitted to make his life cheerful and public spirited, and whose hospitality was as cordial and liberal as his own. Mrs. Buckingham died April 19, 1868, leaving his home and heart desolate. His only son, William Ripley, died in early childhood, and his surviving daughter, Eliza Coit, born Dec. 7, 1838, was married August 28, 1862, to William A. Aiken, who served upon his staff as quartermaster general during the war, and since his marriage has made his home in Norwich.

In 1830 he became a communicant in the second Congregational Church, and was prominent in the organization of a new church in 1842, of which he was a deacon and a conspicuous and most zealous friend and benefactor. He was a Sunday-School teacher for the last thirty-seven years of his life, excepting four years during the war. He was principal chairman of the National Congregational Council in Boston in 1865. He was always in public and private pronounced in the avowal of his christian faith, and always fervent and decided in the expression of christian feeling. The prayers which hallowed his home and edified many christian assemblies, will not soon be forgotten by those who heard them. His christian liberality was from the first to the last uniformly generous, cheerful, and systematic. He was in principle and in practice a decided friend of temperance, and from the beginning to the end of his public life, which was distinguished for lavish and refined hospitality, he never deviated, in public or in private, from the letter or the spirit of his avowed pledges and principles. His interest in education was intelligent, constant, and most liberal. He was foremost in all the movements of his fellow citizens for the improvement of the public schools; was active and generous from the first in the endowment and management of the Norwich Free Academy, and was a princely benefactor of Yale College, especially of the Theological Department. Some of his most liberal contributions were the spontaneous offerings of his conscientious and willing generosity. He was not content with giving himself, but was active in prompting others to contribute, and always with refined courtesy. His benefactions were by no means confined to public societies and institutions. To the poor and unfortunate he was a sympathizing and tender-hearted friend, giving with a cheerful heart, with wise discretion, with a delicate regard to the feelings of those whom he helped, and with unfeigned modesty. Before he entered political life, he was known as a quiet and modest citizen, unobtrusive in manners though firm in principle, rarely if ever participating in public discussion; conspicuously intelligent, courteous, and refined, and as conspicuously unobtrusive in the public manifestation of his opinions.

Though decided in his political sympathies and opinions, and though not infrequently solicited to be a candidate for a seat in the legislature of the state, he consented but once and was defeated. In 1849, '50, '56, and 57, he was Mayor of Norwich. In 1858 he was elected Governor of Connecticut, not so much on the ground of his eminent political services or any special gifts of statesmanship, as on account of the universal confidence which was reposed in his good sense, his integrity, his courtesy, and his eminent moral worth. He had not been known to the people of the state as a public leader. He had been least of all prominent as a manager or leader in any party relations, although he had been decided and zealous at home in the councils of the republican party from its first organization, as he had previously been in the whig party before it. He had never had the opportunity of being known to the leading men of the state as a speaker in a legislative assembly, or in any other than small assemblies of men, and in them only except as they were gathered for some philanthropic or religious object. But he was well known and thoroughly respected in Norwich and in all the eastern parts of the state, as an honest, single-minded, firm-hearted, public-spirited christian gentleman, who united in himself a rare combination of those qualities which are fitted to command the respect and to win the confidence and love of his fellow men. He was elected by a small majority, and for eight years was continued in the office till he resigned its duties and honors.

At the time of his election to the office of governor, neither he nor his friends anticipated what was before him. Had either known or even dimly foreboded, that the office from being little more than a place of easy routine and formal administration, would be suddenly transformed into a post of the most serious responsibility, involving perplexity, toil, and anxiety, both he and his friends would have hesitated in thinking that he was the fittest man to fill the place and to fill it so long. No one would have dared to predict that he would meet all its responsibilities with such distinguished success. But in the review it may be confidently affirmed, that from the time when the first mutterings of war were heard to the moment when they died into silence, no citizen of the state was ever thought of as in any respect superior to or comparable with the noble "war governor" who represented the state of Connecticut. Whether his relations are considered to the executive of the United States, to the governors of the other states, to the party in Connecticut opposed to the war, to the soldiers and officers from Connecticut, to the men who were recruited or drafted, who were sick or in prison, to the banks and men of business all over the country, to the American people as far as they knew of him, his fitness for his place was unquestioned. Whether on horseback at an election parade or in a public reception, whether reading his own messages or speaking at a sudden call, often under very trying circumstances, whether writing stirring letters to President Lincoln, or addressing regiment after regiment as each was hurried away to the field, whether conferring with his staff or trusted friends in sudden exigencies, he was always heroic, patient, self-controlled and courteous. He met the demands of every public occasion with dignity and self-possession. At the time when he was elected he had been little accustomed to public speaking or to writing anything more than letters of business. Though familiar with political topics, he had not been trained to write or speak of them in public, because the necessity of defending and enforcing his political opinions had never been imposed upon him.

His friends could never doubt that he would successfully meet all the practical demands of his office, while they might reasonably question whether he would meet its intellectual requisitions with any special *éclat*. It was interesting to see how quickly he came up to the requirements of his position in these respects; how well from the first he wrote and spoke on the many occasions in which he was called upon. It was still more interesting to notice, when the country was first aroused to defend its life, how clearly his mind was enlarged and his heart glowed with patriotic feeling, and how nobly he spake and wrote. His messages and correspondence were not only important documents in the history of the war, but they reflect the highest honor on the mind and head of their author. His own clear and practical intellect discerned earlier than many practised statesmen what the issues were, and how stern and lasting the struggle would be. His decisive and ringing words bespoke serious and painful forebodings on the one hand, but they breathed only courage and triumph on the other. He wrote and spoke as a prophet, because he wrote and spoke from those firm convictions which were inspired by his faith in the right, and in the God who had defended the right in the past and could not desert it in the present. The people of Connecticut believed in him, because they recognized in his measured yet fervent words, and read in his consistent character and acts, their own strong convictions and their unshaken purposes. Whatever might have been thought of single acts of his, no Connecticut man who believed in the war failed to believe in Governor Buckingham. He reflected so perfectly the wishes and resolves of his fellow citizens that they did not hesitate to accept him as their leader. In multitudes of households his portrait was conspicuously displayed, and his name is still pronounced with love and honor. The services rendered by him to Connecticut and to the Union were also self-sacrificing and laborious. His private business was to a great extent transferred to others. His days and nights were spent in unremitted labor. His mind was oppressed by public care and his heart was tried by ready sympathy. While it was true that he had grown in intellect and character under the noble opportunities to which he so nobly responded, it was also true that he had given to others the best strength and the best days of his life. It was not surprising that after he resigned his office in 1866, he was elected in May, 1868, to fill the first vacancy which occurred in the Senate of the United States. In this office he continued till his death, which occurred one month before his term expired. As a senator he was dignified, courteous and conscientious, and won the respect and affection of men of all parties. In debate he was always clear, pointed and brief.

He comprehended with great clearness the political and financial difficulties incident to the processes of reconstruction, and he endeavored to meet these difficulties with entire fidelity to his convictions. No man ever doubted his honesty or his uprightness during the years of experiment and doubt in which he filled his high position. If it is premature to pronounce upon the wisdom of every measure which he supported or of every individual action which he performed while a senator, it is not premature to assert that he retained his personal and his political integrity from the beginning to the end. His home in Washington was elegant and hospitable, and it was hallowed by domestic worship; and in his public duties he never overlooked or lightly esteemed his duties to God or to his own christian profession. In the summer preceding his death he showed symptoms of debility. These increased as the winter came on. In the anticipation that his life might soon be terminated, he was entirely serene, and on the night of February 4, 1875, he died.

The solemnities of his funeral will not soon be forgotten by any one who was present. Though the day was exceptionally inclement, the city of Norwich was in sorrow for the honored citizen who was at once the pride and the idol of its entire population. The streets and public buildings were arrayed in mourning. Crowds of sincere mourners streamed to the house in which his remains were lying, the house to which many had resorted for counsel, sympathy and assistance, and from which no man ever failed to receive what he had a right to ask. The public services were conducted by clergymen of different denominations, and were singularly impressive and elevating. Gentlemen from all parts of the state were present, with a deputation of senators from Washington. The demonstrations of love and honor were unaffected and earnest from all parts of the country. The usual manifestations of public respect were paid in the Senate of the United States to the memory of its distinguished member, and an able and eloquent eulogy was pronounced by his colleague from Connecticut, the Hon. Orris S. Ferry.

Senator Buckingham was especially remarkable for the symmetry of his constitution and character. In person, in bearing, in manners, in disposition, in intellect, in industry, in patience, in reserved energy, in the knowledge of affairs, in an affectionate and sympathizing nature, in scrupulous conscientiousness, in fervent and enlightened religious feeling, he was harmoniously endowed and moulded into a rare example of human perfection. In his own home this example shone most brightly. To his relatives he was generous and true. To his friends he was frank and open-hearted. To the poor and friendless he was ever sympathizing and helpful. To his fellow citizens he was the soul of probity and honor. To the community he was eminently public-spirited and generous. To the state and the country he gave all that he was and all that he could perform. To God he gave a filial and trusting heart and an obedient and conscientious life, in which he followed his Great Master in meek and humble discipleship.

The writer of this sketch knew Senator Buckingham from before the beginning of his public career to the end of his life, and had frequent opportunities to judge of him in almost every one of the relations which have been named. After abating all that might be required from the partialities of personal friendship, he can honestly give his testimony that a conscientious sincerity and a graceful symmetry gave the strength and beauty to a character which other generations may reasonably hold in the highest honor.

LETTER OF WILLIAM PENN FROM PHILADELPHIA IN 1683 TO JOHN AUBREY, THE ANTIQUARY.

Communicated by GEORGE B. CHASE, A.M., of Boston.

THE following letter from Penn to Aubrey has been copied for me from the second volume of Aubrey's Letters in the Bodleian Library, Oxford, England, by the kind permission of the librarian, Dr. H. O. Coxe. I think it has never been printed. When this letter was written, Philadelphia, which William Penn, its writer, founded, was in its infancy; and he, himself, had been in America less than eight months, having landed at Newcastle on the 24th of October, 1682. It was not till two months later, August 16, 1683, that his letter to the committee of the Free Society of Traders of Pennsylvania residing in London, giving interesting facts in the early history of Pennsylvania, of a like character,[1] was written. A good account of Aubrey will be found in Allibone's "Dictionary of Authors." The meetings of the Royal Society were, in 1683, held at Gresham College, Bishopsgate Street, London.

Esteemed Friend

I value myselfe much upon ye good opinion of those Ingeneous Gentlemen I know of ye Royall Society, and their kind wishes for me and my poor Province: all I can say is That I & It are votarys to ye prosperity of their harmeless and usefull inquierys. It is even one Step to Heaven to returne to nature, and Though I Love that proportion should be observed in all things, yett a naturall Knowledge, or ye Science of things from Sence and a carefull observation and argumentation thereon, reinstates men, and gives them some possession of themselues againe; a thing they have long wanted by an ill Tradition, too closely followed and ye foolish Credulity So Incident to men. I am a Greshamist throughout; I Love — Inquiry, not for (inquiry's sake, but care not to trust) my Share in either world to other mens, Judgmets, at Least without having a finger in ye Pye for myself; yet I Love That Inquiry should be modest and peaceable; virtues, that have Strong charmes upon ye wiser and honester part of ye mistaken world. Pray give them my Sinceer respects, and in my behalfe Sollicite ye continuation of their friendship to my undertaking. we are ye wonder of our neighbours as in our coming and numbers, so to our selves in or health, Subsistance and Success: all goes well, blessed be God, and provision we Shall have to Spare, considerably, in a year or Two, unless very great quantitys of People croud upon us. The skies heat and Cold Resemble ye heart of France: ye Soyle good, ye Springs many & delightfull: ye fruits roots corne and flesh, as good as I have comonly eaten in Europe, I may Say of most of them better. Strawberry's ripe in ye woods in Aprill, and in ye Last Month, Peas, beans, Cherrys & mulberrys. Much blackwalnutt. Chesnutt, Cyprus, or white Cedar and mulberry are here. The Sorts of fish in these parts are excellent and numerous. Sturgeon leap day and night that we can hear them a bow Shot from ye Rivers in our beds, we have Roasted and pickeled them, and they eat like veal one way, and Sturgeon ye other way. Mineral hore is great Store, I shall send Some Soddainly for Tryall. Vines are here in Abundance every where, Some may be as bigg in the body as a mans Thigh. I have begun a Vineyard by a French man of Languedock and another of Poicteu, near Santonge. severall people from other Colonys are retireing hither, as Virginia, Mary Land, New England, Road Island, New York &c: I make it my business to Establish virtuous Economy and therefore Sett twice in Councell every week with good Success, I thank god. My Reception was with all ye show of Kindness ye rude State of ye Country could yeild; and after holding Two Genrll Assemblys, I am not uneasy to ye People. They to express their Love and gratitude gave me an Impost that might be worth 500*l.* per an,

---

[1] This Letter is printed in Proud's History of Pennsylvania, vol. i. pp. 246-64. See also a valuable Letter of Robert Turner, from Philadelphia, August 6, 1685, in the Register, vol. xiii. pp. 223-4.

and I returned it to Them with as much Creditt.   This is our p^{r}sent posture.
I am Debtor to thy Kindness for Two Letters wether this be pay or no, or
but wampum against Sterl: mettle, pray miss not to Continue to yeild that
Content And Liberality to   Thy very True Friend
                                                            WM. PENN

    Philadelphia | 13th of ye 4th Month | called June | 1683
    Particularly, pray give my Respects to Sr Wm Petty, my friend Hook,
Wood, Lodwick and D^r. Bernard Though unknowne, whose skill is a great
Complem^t VALE

    [On the back] W. Penn's l're
    [Addressed] For my esteem'd | Fr^d John Auberry | at Gresham |
Colledge

PAPERS RELATING TO THE ACADIANS.

T HE documents printed below, numbered I., II. and III., are copied
from the HANCOCK MANUSCRIPTS, presented to the New-England Historic, Genealogical Society by CHARLES L. HANCOCK, Esq.,
of Boston.   That numbered IV., namely a letter from Gen. Jedidiah Preble dated April 24, 1756, which was probably addressed to
William Shirley, governor of Massachusetts, is contributed by Commodore GEORGE HENRY PREBLE, U. S. N., of Philadelphia.   The
original, he informs us, is in the possession of John S. Barnes, Esq.,
of Elizabeth, N. J.

I.—*Letter of Gov. Lawrence to Thomas Hancock.*

Halifax 10th September 1755.
Sir
    I am to acknowledge the receit of your favour of the 30th of August
with the Letters you was so good as to take out of the Post Office, as also
your other Letter of the 1st instant.
    I should certainly have communicated the Destination of the French In-
habitants before now to your Government, had it not been absolutely necessary that it should remain a secret (to the Inhabitants at least) as long as
possible, as His Majesty's Council were apprehensive they might take some
extraordinary step upon receiving Intelligence of it, which might give the
Government not a little trouble.   In making the Distribution all possible
regard was had by the Council to make yours as easy as the nature of the
thing would bear : I believe you will have very few old Men (if any) and
as for the Children although they should be a little expensive at first,
you will the easier have it in your power to make them as they grow up
good Subjects.
    I am greatly obliged to you for your care in sending me what Intelli-
gence you receive of the Motions of the Armies.   I pray God they may
have the success we desire.   I received the Intelligence you make mention
of about the two ffleets being at Sea, but I can scarce think the French
Fleet would Sail for North America so late in the Year.

I am glad the Expedition Acco[ts] are in such forwardness, and shall expect them soon. You must be reffered to the Companys Letter of this date for what relates to the Victualling the Provincial Troops which contains all I can Say on that Subject.

I am Dear Sir

your most obliged humble

Servant

Thomas Hancock Esq.   CHA[s]. LAWRENCE.

II.—*Letter of Messrs. Apthorps and Hancock to Capt. Thomas Church, and his Declaration.*

Boston 8 May. 1756

Capt: Thos: Church

We having hired the Schooner Leopard whereof You are Master to carry off the French Inhabitants brôt here from Cape Sables which this Governme[t] refuse to take & Gov[r] Lawrence has recommended them to be sent to N. Carolina and deliver'd to his Excell[cy] Arthur Dobbs Esq Governor there : You are therefore to proceed from hence to North Carolina and deliver them to the Order of s[d] Gov[r] Dobbs delivering him inclosed Letter and on producing his Receipt we will pay You Ten shillings & eight pence a month p̃ Tun for your Vessell's hire and Three pounds p̃ month for a Pilott—to commence from their delivery at North Carolina, with a further allowance of [*torn*] time to return here; would advise to caution to prevent their rising—and recommend your treating them with humanity   we are

If Gov[r] Dobbs should not   Your Friends, &c
receive them, follow his   CHA. APTHORP & SON.
orders for your further proceedings.   THOMAS HANCOCK.

Recorded per R Jennys.

Boston May 11th 1756

These Certifie that in Consequence of the within Orders Rec'd from Charles Apthorp & Son & Thomas Hancock Esq[rs] having Rec'd Gov[r] Phips's Letter to Gov[r] Dobbs, my Provision on bo[d] & every thing necessary for y[e] aforementioned Voyage, & having the French Inhabitants on board I ordered my people to hall off the Wharff in order to proceed y[e] Voyage within mentioned, upon which there arose a Great Dissention among s[d] French, & they all arose Forc'd their way on shore with their Baggage and it was not in my power to proceed the Voyage, as they said they would sooner suffer the pains of Death upon the Wharff in Boston than be carried to N. Carolina, but were very Desirous and willing to be sent to the Northward, or stay in this Province & work for their Living, upon which I Returned the within Orders & the Letter to Gov[r] Dobbs to Thomas Hancock.

THOMAS CHURCH.

Recorded p̃ R[d] Jennys.

Suffolk ss :   Boston May the 13th 1756

Appeared Thomas Church the Subscriber to the above & beforegoing declaration, and made Oath to the truth thereof.

Before   WM. STODDARD, Just: pacis

Province of the   }
Massachusetts Bay. }   I Richard Jennys Notary and Tabellion Publick by Royal Authority duly admitted & sworn dwelling & Practising in Boston New England Do hereby Certify that William Stoddard is one of His Majestys Justices of the Peace for ye County of Suffolk within the Province afores^d duly Commissioned & sworn and that to his Attestations (as above) full faith & intire Credit is & ought to be given both in Court and without. Witness my Notarial firm & Seal this 13th day of May 1756.

RICH^dus JENNYS, Not: Pub:

[Notarial seal.   *Arms*—Erm. a bend cotised gu.]

1756

III.—*Action of the Massachusetts Council, May* 14, 1756.

At a Council held at the Council Chamber in Boston on Fryday the fourteenth of May 1756.

Mr. Hancock appearing before his Honour and the Board, informed that he had prepared a Vessel for the Transportation to North Carolina of the French Families last imported into this Province, And that after embarking, they came ashore by Force, and refused to reimbark, he therefore desires that he may be enabled to compel them to go on board, Or that they may be allowed to remain in the Province, or at least to tarry for fourteen days ; And if at the Expiration of the fourteen days it shall be the Mind of the Governm^t that they should be sent out of the Province, he will then provide a Vessel for their Transportation, without any Charge to the Government.

Advised that the French Families be allowed to remain the Term of fourteen days, on the proposed Condition, Provided also that Mr Hancock will take care for their Support without Expence to the Government.

Attest   THO^s CLARKE, Dp^ty Secry.

IV.—*Letter from Gen. Preble.*

On board the Vulture in Bacarow Passage,
April 24. 1756.

Sr

     I have the pleasure to inform your Excellency, that after A tedious passage we arived in Port Latore the 21 instant, Landed 167 men, officers included, marched overland in the Night, surprized the french people in their Beds, have since embarked them on board one of the transports you ware pleased to appoint for that purpose, the number and names of which I herewith send you enclosed.

The number of buildings we Burnt ware Forty-four, in the executing of which Capt. Scarft contributed everything in his power.

Nor can I forbare mentioning to your Excellency the kind treatment and respect I have received from that gentilman.

In justice to Capt Rogers I must beg leave to say he has contributed everything in his power for the good of the service.

Should have proceeded to Pugnico, but had advice which I could rely on that there was but two families there and could not think it would be for the good of his majesties service to carry such A number of Troops whare there was no Prospect of doing any considerable service.

I have the troops now all imbarkt and design to sail this Night for New-England.

And am, may it please your Excellency, your Excellencys most obedient and much obliged

Humble Servt.

JEDIDIAH PREBLE.

LETTERS OF EDWARD RANDOLPH, 1684–1685.

Communicated by Mr. WALTER LLOYD JEFFRIES, of Boston.

THESE letters are among a valuable collection of manuscripts, recently discovered in Faneuil Hall, partly official and partly private, belonging to David Jeffries, of Boston, who held the office of Town Treasurer, and was also County Treasurer for some years. Among the manuscripts is the following receipt in the autograph of Randolph :[1]

BOSTON Dec. 5ᵗʰ, 1683 ;

Then received of Mʳ. Benjamin Davis of Boston Mercᵗ by vertue of a letter of Atturney from Mʳ. Robert Holden late of Carolina Collector of his Ma. Customs there bearing date July yᵉ 15ᵗʰ day 1683 the Sū̅m of thirty pounds, New Engᵈ Money, in part of sixty eight pounds eleven shillings six pence three farthings, all N. Engᵈ Money. I say received by me.

ED. RANDOLPH, Coll.

The private manuscripts have been delivered by the city authorities to John Jeffries, M.D., of Boston, grandson of David Jeffries.

Sʳ.   Whitehall Janʳʸ 20ᵗʰ, 84.

I have not yet seen Mr Armitage, as yet being very busy at Whitehall : & am preparing for my voyage & bringing over with me a very good wife who will supply the loss of the former to all her friends. I question not but you abound in News. Sʳ I must confess we hear abundance relating to N. Engᵈ but the Greatest part fictitious. you may know that his Maᵗʸ has Judgmᵗ. against yʳ Chartr by default : & Coll Kerk is made your Gouʳ. Some progress is made & his Commission & Instructions & [are ?] preparing. & such of your Lawes as relate to yᵉ publick benefitt will be preserved & all others of none effect : who are so blind as those who will not see. but

---

[1] The editor of the REGISTER is indebted to Charles W. Tuttle, Esq., of Boston, for the following notice of Mr. Randolph :

Edward Randolph, the writer of these letters, is too well known among students of American colonial history to need any introduction in this place. The memorable part which he took in the overthrow of the first New-England Charters, and in the establishment of Episcopacy in the heart of the Puritan settlements, makes his name conspicuous in the history of that period. Considering his agency in these matters, and in others of hardly less historic interest, it is strange we know so little of his personal history. That he was of an ancient Kentish family, living in the archiepiscopal city of Canterbury, I have recently made certain. He had two wives, and several daughters; but had no male issue. Sir Egerton Brydges (*ante*, xxix. 236) is mistaken in making him the ancestor of the Virginia Randolphs. I have already collected some materials for a biography of Edward Randolph; and, as soon as I can find leisure, hope to complete the undertaking of writing an account of him.

the Eyes of your Magistrates are blinded as the Aramites were who could not See till they were in ye midst of Samaria; Mr Cranfeild has repealed his letter of Attorney given me. & his Gov^t. will expire upon Gou^r Kerks arrival; then Mr Vaughan & your brother Waldern may bring their Actions against him for false imprisonm^e & recouer Great damages: you may depend upon hauing liberty of Conscience. & my kindnes to your Country has made me not well thought of some how : my wife desires me to give your wife her hearty respects. & assures her she will be in all acts of friendship very ready to serve her & Mrs Betty. I have no account of your receit of what I sent you. they came all by Mr Stoddar & I hope you have long since received all those things you gave me in charge. I have not further to add only that I am S^r   Your most obliged

To M^r Jo: Usher: friend ` ED. RANDOLPH

Indorsed, "Edward Randolph 20 Janu 1684" [i. e. 1684–5]. Direction torn off.

S^r. I wrote you about 14 dayes ago since which by my daughters letters: I find you have accomodated them with money for their present occasions : now that it has pleased god to take away his late Matie: all things here are in great peace & order & his present Matie will act with all tenderness to peoples libertyes & proprietyes. I thank you for taking care of my Commission : I have that restored here & ye Office of Secretary & Register of your Country which will some what countervail the Charge I have been at: I have money to receive which his late Matie ordered me not above 14 dayes before his death : I will take care at my Coming over to see all accounts evened which is only that of gratitude for all your favors: It was reported since his Matie being proclaimed that Coll Kerk did not come to your parts: but I heare now that he is to be your Gou^r: the King will heare all Complaints ag^t his Gou^rs. & if Mr Vaughan whom (for your sake) I carried to ye E: of Clarendon: would have taken my assistance I would haue obtained satisfaction for him ag^t Gou^r Cranfeild and also ag^t ye french for their ketches and mens tyme and Costs: I now think of your Colony but with great grief to think they should be so vnhappy as to force a ruine upon themselves : I cannot see how you can avoid it, vnlesse they take the opportunity and by ye next ship addresse to his Matie and beg his Royall pardon : with a confirmation of your libertyes Sacred and Ciuill: but I know your people cannot think of Submission: and therefor they are broken because they will not bend: pray be kind to my landlord Harrison who has my poor Bro Gyls Son: I giue you my hearty respects and am your obliged friend and humble Servt

Mr Jo: Usher   ED. RANDOLPH
                                              ffeb: ii: 1684.

The following was on the outside of the letter: "Its probable you may haue another Gen^t for your Gou^r than yet named
    Tyme will order all things"

Address. "To Mr John Usher Mer^t in *Boston.*" Indorsed, "Edward Randolph 11th ffebu 1684" [i. e. 1684–5].

PORTRAITS AND BUSTS IN POSSESSION OF THE AMERICAN ANTIQUARIAN SOCIETY, AND OF OTHER ASSOCIATIONS IN WORCESTER, MASS.

Communicated by NATHANIEL PAINE, Esq., of Worcester.

AMERICAN ANTIQUARIAN SOCIETY.

Portraits.

1. ISAIAH THOMAS, LL.D., founder and first president of the American Antiquarian Society, author of "The History of Printing," &c. Born Jan. 19, 1749, O. S. ; died April 4, 1831. Painted from life by E. A. Greenwood.

2. THOMAS LINDALL WINTHROP, LL.D., second president of the Antiquarian Society, and Lieut. Governor of Massachusetts, 1826–32. Born in New-London, Conn., March 6, 1760 ; died Feb. 22, 1841. Painted by Thomas Sully.

3. JOHN DAVIS, LL.D., fourth president of the Antiquarian Society, and Governor of Massachusetts, 1833–35, and 1840–41. Born in Northboro', Mass., Jan. 13, 1787 ; died April 19, 1854. Painted by E. T. Billings, from a daguerreotype.

4. Rev. INCREASE MATHER, D.D., president of Harvard College 1685–1701. Born in Dorchester, Mass., June 21, 1639 ; died Aug. 23, 1723. Painted from life. This and the four following were presented to the Society by Mrs. Hannah Mather Crocker, of Boston.

5. Rev. COTTON MATHER, D.D., minister in Boston, 1684. Born Feb. 12, 1663 ; died Feb. 13, 1728. Painted by Pelham.

6. Rev. RICHARD MATHER, minister in Dorchester, Mass., 1636–69. Born in England, 1596; died in Dorchester, April 22, 1669. Painted from life.

7. Rev. SAMUEL MATHER, D.D., son of Cotton Mather. Born Oct. 30, 1706; died June 27, 1785. Painted from life.

8. Rev. SAMUEL MATHER, son of Richard Mather. Born in England, May 13, 1626 ; died in Dublin, Ireland, Oct. 29, 1671.

9. JOHN ENDECOTT, first Governor of Massachusetts Bay. Born in Dorchester, England, 1588; died March 15, 1665. Painted from an original, by Southland, of Salem, Mass. Presented to the Society by Judge William Endicott, of Salem. A memorial of Gov. Endecott was presented at a meeting of the Antiquarian Society, October, 1874, by Stephen Salisbury, LL.D. There is also a smaller portrait of Endecott, poorly executed and very old, probably painted from the original.

10. JOHN WINTHROP, second Governor of Massachusetts, 1629–33. Born in Groton, co. Suffolk, England, Jan. 12, 1588; died March 26, 1649. Painted from life.

11. Rev. WILLIAM BENTLEY, D.D., minister in Salem, 1783. Councillor of the Antiquarian Society from 1812 to 1820. Born in Boston, June 22, 1759 ; died in Salem, Dec. 29, 1819.

12. Rev. AARON BANCROFT, D.D., minister in Worcester, Mass., 1786–1839. Vice-president of the Antiquarian Society, 1816–31. Born in Reading, Mass., Nov. 10, 1755 ; died in Worcester, Aug. 19, 1839. Painted by Chester Harding.

13. CHRISTOPHER COLUMBUS BALDWIN, Librarian of the Antiquarian Society, 1827–30. Born Aug. 1, 1800 ; died Aug. 20, 1835. Painted by Harding.

14. EDWARD D. BANGS, Secretary of State, Mass., 1825–36. Born in Worcester, Mass., Aug. 22, 1790 ; died in Worcester, April 3, 1838.

15. WILLIAM BURNET, Colonial Governor of New-York and New-Jersey, 1720; of Massachusetts and New-Hampshire, 1728. Born 1688; died in Boston, Sept. 7, 1729.

16. Rev. THOMAS PRINCE, minister of Old South Church, Boston, 1718–58. Born in Sandwich, Mass., May 15, 1687 ; died in Boston, Oct. 22, 1758.

17. Rev. ELLIS GRAY, minister of the New Brick Church in Boston. Born 1717 ; died 1753.

18. CHARLES PAXTON, loyalist, Commissioner of the Customs at Boston. Born 1704; died in England, 1788. Supposed to have been painted by Copley.

19. JOHN ROGERS, said to be a portrait of the Martyr, or, if not of him, of a John Rogers his cousin.

20. JOHN CHANDLER, "the honest refugee," Sheriff, Judge of Probate and Treasurer for the County of Worcester. Born in New-London, Conn., 1720 ; died in London, Eng., 1800.

21. JOHN MAY, of Boston, in his uniform as Colonel of the "Boston Regiment of Militia." Born in Pomfret, Conn., Nov. 24, 1748; died in Boston, July 13, 1812. Painted by Gullag. Presented by Mary D. and C. Augusta May.

22. HANNAH ADAMS, author of History of New-England, &c. Born in Medfield, Mass., 1755 ; died in Brookline, Mass., Nov. 15, 1831. Painted by Alexander. Presented by Henry W. Miller.

23. EDWARD RAWSON, Secretary of Mass. Colony, 1650–86. Born in Gillingham, Dorset, Eng., April 16, 1615 ; died in Boston, Aug. 27, 1693.

24. REBECCA RAWSON, daughter of Secretary Rawson. Born in Boston, May, 1656 ; died at Port Royal, Jamaica, June 9, 1692.

25. ROBERT B. THOMAS, editor of the "Old Farmer's Almanac." Born 1766; died in West Boylston, Mass., May 19, 1846. Full length portrait, by a local artist.

26. JOHN LEVERETT. Governor of Massachusetts, 1673–78. Born 1617 ; died March 16, 1679.

27. COLUMBUS. A copy from an original by Francesco Mazzuoli (Parmigianino), in the Royal Museum at Naples. Painted by Antonio Scardino. Presented by Hon. Ira M. Barton.

28. VESPUCIUS. From an original by Parmigianino, at Naples—Scardino. Presented by Hon. Ira M. Barton.

29. JOHN DAVIS, Governor of Massachusetts. Crayon portrait, life size.

30. JAMES SULLIVAN, Governor of Massachusetts. Portrait in wax.

31. PIUS VII. Engraved by Raphael Morghen.

32. COLUMBUS, full length engraved portrait.

33. HIGGINSON. This is an old portrait, originally presented to the Society as that of Rev. Francis Higginson, minister in Salem 1629, but it is now considered to be of some other member of the family, perhaps of his son Rev. John Higginson.

There are also the rare engraved portraits of the four kings of Canada:

1. Tee-Yee-Neen-Ho-Ga-Rron, Emperor of the Six Nations. 2. Sa-Ga-Yeath-Qua-Pieth-Ton, King of the Naguas. 3. Eton-Oh-Koam, King of the River Nation. 4. Ho-Nee-Yeath-Tan-No-Rron, King of the Generethgarich.

In addition to the engraved portraits above named, there are upwards of one hundred, of eminent men of ancient and modern times, many of which are quite rare. There are also a few original engravings by William Hogarth, and several lithographs, photographs, &c., of interest in the hall and ante-rooms of the Society.

Statues and Busts.

1. Statue of CHRIST, in plaster, from the original by Michael Angelo in the Church of Sta. Maria Sopra Minerva at Rome. Presented to the Antiquarian Society by the Hon. Stephen Salisbury.
2. Statue of MOSES, from Michael Angelo's colossal statue in the Church of S. Pietro in Vincolo at Rome. Presented by the Hon. S. Salisbury. The remarks of the donor in presenting the statues have been published in the Proceedings of the Society, 1859–1861.
3. ISAIAH THOMAS, LL.D., publisher of the Massachusetts Spy, &c. Bust in marble, by B. H. Kinney.
4. JARED SPARKS, LL.D. A fine bust in plaster, by Hiram Powers. Presented by Mrs. Sparks.
5. Gov. JOHN DAVIS, of Massachusetts. Bust in plaster. By Henry Dexter.
6. GEORGE WASHINGTON. Bust in marble. This and the following one were presented by Mrs. Ira M. Barton.
7. BENJAMIN FRANKLIN. Bust in marble.
8. JOHN ADAMS, second President of the U. States. Bust in plaster.
9. ALEXANDER HAMILTON. Bust in plaster, from the original by Jos. Ceracchi.
10. ANDREW JACKSON. Bust in plaster.
11. HENRY CLAY. Bust in plaster, by Clevenger.
12. DANIEL WEBSTER. Bust by Clevenger.
13. VOLTAIRE and RACINE. Plaster busts, presented by Hon. Benjamin F. Thomas.
14. CATHERINE II., Empress of Russia, and Prince POTEMKIN, a Russian statesman and soldier.
15. JOHN WINTHROP, Governor of Massachusetts. Small bust in wood.
16. Rev. JAMES WALKER, D.D., President of Harvard University. Small bust in plaster, by J. C. King.
17. Baron PIETRO ERCOLE VISCONTI, of Rome, antiquary, &c. Small bust in plaster.
18. Medallion in plaster, life size, of Gov. JOHN DAVIS.

WORCESTER COUNTY MECHANICS' ASSOCIATION.

In the possession of this Association are the following portraits in oil:

1. GEORGE WASHINGTON. Full length portrait from the original by Stuárt in Faneuil Hall, Boston. Painted by Thomas Badger. Presented by Ichabod Washburn and Stephen Salisbury.
2. ABRAHAM LINCOLN, President of the U. S. A full length portrait by E. T. Billings. Presented by friends of the Association, as were the two following portraits.

3. JOHN A. ANDREW, Gov. of Massachusetts. Painted by E. T. Billings.
4. WILLIAM LLOYD GARRISON, reformer. By E. T. Billings.
5. ICHABOD WASHBURN, president and benefactor of the Mechanics' Association. Painted by Wight.
6. GEORGE H. WARD, Colonel of the 15th Mass. Regiment, killed at the battle of Gettysburg. Painted by E. T. Billings. Presented by 15th Mass. Regiment Association.
7. JAMES B. BLAKE, Mayor of the City of Worcester. Presented by citizens of Worcester. Painted by W. H. Willard.
8. WASHINGTON. A portrait from Stuart's in the Boston Athenæum. Painted by Eliza M. Judkins.

The Mechanics' Association also have busts of ICHABOD WASHBURN, in marble, and WILLIAM A. WHEELER, in plaster, former presidents. B. H. Kinney, artist.

OTHER SOCIETIES OR INSTITUTIONS IN WORCESTER.

SAMUEL B. WOODWARD, M.D., Superintendent of the State Lunatic Asylum. Painted by Frothingham.

GEORGE CHANDLER, M.D., Superintendent of the State Lunatic Asylum. Painted by Wight.

SAMUEL B. WOODWARD, M.D. A fine bust in marble, by J. C. King.

The three last named are in the office of the Superintendent at the Lunatic Asylum.

CHARLES DEVENS, Jr., Maj.-General, Judge of the Supreme Court of Massachusetts, in the hall of the Grand Army of the Republic. Painted by W. H. Willard.

JOHN MILTON EARLE, Editor of the Massachusetts Spy, and a prominent horticulturist, in the Library of the Worcester County Horticultural Society. Painted by Lincoln, of Providence.

Rev. AARON BANCROFT, D.D., and Rev. ALONZO HILL, D.D., both former pastors of the Second Congregational (Unitarian) Society, in the Vestry of the Church.

JOHN GREEN, M.D., founder of the Free Public Library at Worcester. A full length portrait, by William H. Furness, painted by order of the City Council, and a life-size statue, by B. H. Kinney, are in the Green Library Hall of the Public Library.

ISAIAH THOMAS, LL.D., and WILLIAM A. SMITH, Esq., prominent members of the Order of Free Masons, are in the Masonic Hall. Both painted by Billings, the latter from life.

There is also a portrait of BENEDICT J. FENWICK, R. C. Bishop of Boston, 1825-46, by J. Pope, at the College of the Holy Cross.

In the City Hall is a marble bust of Hon. CHARLES ALLEN, and plaster busts of Hon. EMORY WASHBURN, Hon. ISAAC DAVIS, and Hon. ICHABOD WASHBURN—all by B. H. Kinney. In St. Paul's Church, marble bust of Rt. Rev. P. T. O'REILLY, by Andrew O'Connor.

In the Orphan's Home, portrait by Harding, of Hon. JOHN W. LINCOLN, its founder.

In the new Court House, portrait of Judge PLINY MERRICK, by Healy, and of Judge B. F. THOMAS, by Wight.

At the Central National Bank, portrait by Healy of Hon. THOMAS KINNICUTT, formerly Judge of Probate for the County of Worcester.

In the Old Ladies' Home, a plaster bust of Hon. ICHABOD WASHBURN, its founder.

THE REVEREND JOSSE GLOVER.

AT the semi-annual meeting of the American Antiquarian Society, held in Boston, April 28, 1875, J. Hammond Trumbull, LL.D., made a communication in regard to the "christian name of the Reverend Mr. Glover, whom Thomas (History of Printing, i. 222) styles the 'Father of the American Press.'" By permission, we reproduce from the published Proceedings of that meeting, some extracts from Dr. Trumbull's communication; and by his liberality we are enabled to give a *facsimile* of Mr. Glover's signature to his will.   A. H. HOYT.

Thomas, after mentioning the fact that the name was "variously spelled in the ancient records," adopted *Jesse* as "in all probability, the true name." The histories of Harvard University, Peirce and Quincy, both professing to quote the college records, name "Mr. *Joseph* Glover," and their authority is accepted by Mr. Bancroft, Dr. Palfrey, and by the editors of the Society's new edition of Thomas's History. Mr. Savage, in his Genealogical Dictionary, finds that "the stranger name of *Josse* prevails." In my edition of Lechford's "Plain Dealing," printed in 1867, I gave in a note on page 123 some account of "Mr. *Josse* Glover,"—my principal authorities for the christian name being the Court Records (extracts from which had been accurately printed by Mr. Thomas) and entries in Lechford's MS. Journal; but I mentioned the monument erected to his first wife, in Sutton church, Surrey, on which his name appears as *Joseph*, if the copy of the inscription printed in Manning and Bray's History of Surrey is to be trusted, and so too in an extract from the parish register of Sutton, printed in the same work (ii. 483, 487). Mr. John Ward Dean, in the N. E. Historical and Genealogical Register (vol. xxiii. 135), hesitates between *Joseph* and *Josse;* and Mr. Sibley, with characteristic caution, names (Harvard Graduates, i. 208) "the Reverend *Jose, Josse,* or *Joseph* Glover." The strongest evidence I have found for *Jesse* is in the printed Calendar of British State Papers (Dom. series, 1634–35), in the abstracts of a petition addressed to Archbishop Laud by Edward Darcey, patron of the living of Sutton, for the appointment of a successor to "Jesse Glover, clerk," and of Laud's answer to this petition, in which this name is repeated (p. 355, doc. 45). . . . . For *Joseph,* the authorities are the printed extracts from the College Records, and the Sutton inscription printed by Manning and Bray. Mr. Sibley, having at my request examined the MS. Record of Donations quoted by Peirce and Quincy, gives me the extract *literatim:*

"Mr. *Joss:* Glover gave to the College a ffont of printing letters."

Mr. Sibley has also sent me several extracts from papers in the Court Files of Middlesex county, relating to the settlement of Mrs. Dunster's (formerly Mrs. Glover's) estate, in 1656, in which the name is written "Josse," and once, "Joss," but nowhere "Joseph."

Thomas Lechford, in his professional Journal, made copies of two instruments drawn for Mrs. Glover's signature, in which the name also appears as "Josse," and in one instance as "Joas."

Suspecting that Manning and Bray had taken the same liberty in copying the inscription on the monument erected by Mr. Glover to his first wife, as had been taken in printing extracts from the college records, I applied to the present rector of Sutton, a well known scholar and antiquary, the Rev. John A. Giles, D.D. He very obligingly complied with my request, by informing me that the name on the monument is " Jos. Glover"—not " Joseph," and that the entry in the register, of which he sends me a certified copy, is *Jose*. This entry is as follows :

Henry Wyshe being a Nonregent Maister of Arts in the University of Cambridge was inducted by Thomas Pope into the Rectorie of Sutton June 10th, An. Dom. 1636 ; after a Resignation made of the same Rectorie by *Jose* Glover, who was much beloved of the most if not all & his departure much lamented of the most, if not of all.

This is the first entry in our Register, which begins June 10, 1636.

This disposes of all the authority for " Joseph." For the correction of " Jesse," in the printed Calendar of State Papers, I addressed an inquiry to William Douglas Hamilton, Esq., F.S.A., who succeeds the late Mr. Bruce as editor of this series of the Calendars. He favors me with the following reply :

In reply to your note of the 18th ult., I can only say that I have looked carefully at the documents you mentioned, and find that the name is clearly written as you suggested, *Josse Glover*, both in the body of the petition and in Archbishop Laud's reference at the bottom of the petition.   *   *   *

There is then, so far as appears, *no* contemporary authority for either *Joseph* or *Jesse*. All the record evidence favors *Josse* or *Jose*. The Middlesex county records seem to prove that *Josse* was the spelling generally adopted by his widow, her second husband, President Dunster, and his son, Dr. John Glover. That he himself sometimes, if not always, wrote his name *Jose*, I am now able to prove on the authority of his autograph signature to his will, dated May 16, 1638.

A copy of this will, without date or signature, is in the Court Files of Middlesex county, and was printed in the N. E. HISTORICAL AND GENEALOGICAL REGISTER (vol. xxiii. p. 136), with a note by Mr. J. Ward Dean. Knowing that the original will must have been executed in the spring or early summer of 1638, and that it must have been proved in London before the payment of the legacies, I applied to Col. Joseph L. Chester, of London, for assistance to discover it. The following extract from his reply, dated Jan. 30, 1875, shows how promptly and successfully he prosecuted the search :

Mr. Glover's will, dated 16 May, 1638, was proved in the Prerogative Court of Canterbury, 22 December in the same year, and is recorded in Book " Lee," folio 176. The original is preserved and is now in the principal registry of Probate. It is holograph, which makes it most important for your purpose, as the man's own orthography must be accepted as conclusive.

The will commences : " I *Jose* Glover," and there are three signatures in the course of it, the spelling in each case being distinctly *Jose*.

. . . . . . In no instance is there a dot after the final letter *e*, which might indicate a contraction for Joseph. The man's name was clearly *Jose*, as he wrote it. . . . .

I may add that the arms on the seal are : a fess ermine between 3 crescents.

Comparison of the forms *Josse* and *Joas* with the autograph *Jose* shows that the name was pronounced as a monosyllable, and that the first vowel was moderately long. The name *Josse*, though a very uncommon one in England in the last half of the 16th and beginning of the 17th century, was not absolutely unknown.[1] Josse Hond, the designer and map engraver, better known as "Jodocus Hondius," a native of Flanders, was living in 1585, and after.

DESCENDANTS OF BENJAMIN HAMMOND.

Communicated by PHILIP BATTELL, Esq., of Middlebury, Vt.

AN authentic trace of Benjamin Hammond is given by Farmer (*Genealogical Register*, p. 186), that he came from London, married in Sandwich in 1650, and removed to Rochester. The record of marriage has not been found at Sandwich, but that of the death of Rose, a daughter of Benjamin and Mary Hammond, Nov. 20, 1676, is certified (courteously) by the town clerk. In referring the parentage of Benjamin to William and Elizabeth (Penn or Payne) Hammond, of Watertown, the sagacity of Farmer, and other genealogists, has been misled by a singular identity of names of the emigrant parents of two branches of the Hammonds, and a divided claim between them to the same family surname for the emigrant ancestress of each. Another coincidence is developed, also, in the emigration of the two Elizabeth (Penn or Payne) Hammonds in the same year, 1636, in different ships indeed, but each without her husband, a William Hammond, and each with several children. The tradition of circumstances so similar was likely to become complicated, and to be referred for explication to the first accessible record in which its threads might unite; which in Bond's Watertown, with but a little strain of adaptation, was found to answer the demands of all the name, except the descendants, otherwise provided for, of Thomas and Elizabeth (Cason) Hammond, first of Hingham. In this solution, to which Savage and the family generally seem committed, the line of Benjamin Hammond, in the Idumean border of the old colony, was least considered, and it was but practical justice that a rod out of its own stem should vindicate its history.

The summary in Dr. Bond's invaluable record of Watertown families, includes the English register, credited to Mr. S. Hammond Russell, of the birth of William and Thomas Hammond, which is copied here, as indicating a locality of the name.

THOMAS[1] HAMMOND, of Lavenham, co. Suffolk, married, May 14, 1573, Rose Trippe. He was buried, Nov. 26, 1589. Children:

    i.   ELIZABETH, bapt. April 1, 1574.
    ii. WILLIAM, bapt. Oct. 30, 1575; " settled in New-England."
    iii. ROSE, bapt. April 22, 1578.
    iv. MARTHA, bapt. Nov. 6, 1579.
    v. MARIE, bapt. July 7, 1587 (?).
    vi. SUSAN.
    vii. THOMAS, bapt. Jan. 9, 1586; of Hingham, afterwards of Newton.

WILLIAM[2] HAMMOND married, June 9, 1605, Elizabeth Payne (Penn?). Children:

---

[1] The surname Jose and Josse appears in New-Hampshire from about the middle of the 17th century.—A. H. H.

    i.   WILLIAM, bapt. Sept. 20, 1607.
    ii.   ANNE, bapt. Nov. 19, 1609.
    iii. JOHN, bapt. Dec. 5, 1611.
    iv. ANNE, bapt. July 14, 1616.
    v.   THOMAS, bapt. Sept. 17, 1618.
    vi. ELIZABETH, b. about 1619 (aged 15 in April, 1634[1]).
    vii. SARAH, b. about 1624 (aged 10, April, 1634).
    viii. JOHN, b. about 1627 (aged 7 in April, 1634).
    ix. BENJAMIN (see Farmer); probably not the youngest child ; not mentioned
        in his father's will.

A record of fine genealogical interest exists in the Memorandum Book
of Capt. Elnathan Hammond, of Newport, R. I., who lived an esteemed
citizen of that town, and died there May 24, 1793, at the age of 90. His
descendants cherish his memory with peculiar regard, retain his portrait,
point to his former residence still standing in Thames Street, recall his
character as a sea captain in the best commercial period of the town, and his
active interest in the congregational church.   The book is a reverend relic,
preserved in Vermont in the family of the grandson and namesake of the
original owner, now in the keeping of his only surviving great-grandson here,
at the age of eighty.   Its leather binding and metallic clasp and uneven margins indicate age and wear, its contents recall a historical period, and special
and various personal tastes.   It is a pocket memorandum book, of which
this is the first inscription in respect to date :

   Elnathan Hammond, his Memorandum Book, Feby 1755.   Memorandum of some
things I have observed, y^t. I think remarkable, and of some things I have thought
so in course of my reading.

Observations, extracts, statistics, recipes and memoranda, in a hand-writing both distinct and graceful, are supplemented by excerpts or documents
in print, pasted or folded in, of which Dr. Stiles's list of clergymen and
churches in New-England, and an early copy of the Declaration of Independence, are noticeable specimens.   On an initial fly-leaf is formally
inscribed :

   This Memorandum Book I have given to my grandson, Elnathan Hammond,
May ye 15th, 1781, and I desire that he may have the possession of it after my Decease : Witness my Daughter Eliz^th Sprague.   ELNATHAN HAMMOND.

The portion of the book which with genealogists has gained in vitality by
time, is of course that in which the family history is disclosed, nor in this
probably is the spirit misrepresented, which in a patriarchal way provided
that mode of preserving it.   The grave of Capt. Hammond, in the old burying ground, is with those of members of his family, finding their peace in dust
with his own, while the traces of his filial spirit in this record restore the
place of his ancestral line in remembrance, and that of his venerated ancestress who brought it over.

   A short Record of our Family, by Elnathan Hammond, copied from a Family Record
of my Father's, Mr. John Hammond, of Rochester, 1737, and continued, beginning the year at the 1st of January.

   William Hammond, born in the city of London, and there married Elizabeth Penn,
sister of Sir William Penn, had children : Benjamin their son born 1621, Elizabeth,
Martha and Rachel their daughters, all born in London.   William Hammond died
there and was buried.   Elizabeth Hammond, widow of William Hammond, with

---

[1] In Drake's lists of Founders of New-England, printed in the REGISTER, vol. xiv. pp. 331
and 332, are the names of Elizabeth Hammond and children.   Elizabeth aged 15, Sarah
aged 10, and John aged 7, passengers in the Francis of Ipswich, April, 1634.

her son Benjamin and three daughters, all young, left a good estate in London, and with several godly people came over to New England in troublesome Times in 1634, out of a conscious desire to have the liberty to serve God in the way of his appointment. They had with them the Rev. Mr. Lothrop, their minister, A.D. 1634.[1] Settled in Boston, and there died 1640, had an honorable burial and the character of a very godly woman.

Benjamin Hammond, their son, removed to Sandwich and there married Mary Vinsent, daughter of John Vinsent. She was born in England in 1633. Benjamin Hammond married to Mary Vinsent 1650. Had born :

> SAMUEL, their son, 1655.
> JOHN, their son, Nov. 30, 1663.
> NATHAN, their son, 1670.
> BENJAMIN, their son, Nov. 1673.
> Had two daughters, died young.

Benjamin Hammond, with his wife and four sons, moved to Rochester and there died, aged 82 years, 1703. Mary his widow died 1705.

John Hammond married Mary Arnold, eldest daughter of the Rev. Mr. Samuel Arnold, first minister of the gospel that was settled in Rochester, 1691. Mary Arnold born May, 1672.

John Hammond and Mary Arnold married 1691. Had seven sons and four daughters. Had born to grow up :

> BETHIAH, their daughter, Aug. 11, 1693.
> SARAH, their daughter, Dec. 23d, 1695.
> JABEZ, their son, Feb. 26, 1699.
> ELNATHAN, their son, March 7, 1703.
> BENJAMIN, their son, Dec. 1, 1704.
> ROWLAND, their son, Oct. 30, 1706.
> ELIZABETH, their daughter, January 5, 1709.
> ABIGAIL, y[r] daughter, March 27, 1714.
> JONATHAN, son, Sept. 4, 1716.

Bethiah Hammond, married to Mr. Joseph Haskell, had many children and died March the 17, 1757.

Sarah Hammond, married to Noah Sprague, of Rochester, had many children.

Jabez Hammond, married Sarah Lothrop, had a son and daughter. She dying, he married Abigail Farwel, and had many children.

Benjamin Hammond, married Priscilla Sprague, and had 2 sons and 3 daughters, and died July the 19th, 1758.

Rowland Hammond, married Ann Winslow, had two sons. She dying, married ——— Southward. She had no children.

Elizabeth Hammond, married to Ebenezer Lothrop ; had children.

Abigail Hammond, married to Ebenezer Perry ; had one son and died May 16, 1753 New Stile.

John Hammond, married to Mary Ruggles ; had many children.

John Hammond, my father, died April 19, 1749 O. S.

Mary Hammond, my mother, dyed Aug. 3, 1756 N. S.

Bethiah Haskell, my sister, died March 17, 1757.

Sarah Sprague, my sister, died

Jabez Hammond, my brother, died March 1786.

Benjamin Hammond, my brother, died July the 19th 1758.

Abigail Pery, my sister, died May 16, 1753.

Elnathan Hammond, son of John Hammond, born at Rochester March ye 7th 1703. Married Mary Wignall, widow, who was daughter of Mr. John Rogers of Newport, who was born August 24, 1700. Who were married Dec. 27th 1728. Had children born :

> JOHN ARNOLD, their son, Feb. 9, 1731.
> ABIGAIL, y[r] daughter, Sept. 20, 1733 ; d. Jan. 15, 1734.
> ELNATHAN, son, Jan. 17, 1736, who d. Dec. 4, 1737.
> ABIGAIL, a daughter, Feb. 15, 1737.

---

[1] The ship Griffin, with 200 passengers, including the Rev. Mr. Lothrop, Mr. and Mrs. Hutchinson, arrived Sept. 18, 1634. See Drake's "Boston."

ELNATHAN, a son, May 11, 1738.
JOSEPH, a son, April 13, 1739.
NATHANIEL, a son, June 2, 1740.
MARY, a daughter, Septem: 22, 1741, who dyed May ye 7, 1767.
ELIZABETH, a daughter, May 25, 1743.
SUSANNAH, a daughter, June 18, 1744.

Mary Hammond, wife of Elnathan Hammond, departed this life Oct. ye 20th 1749.
Elnathan Hammond married his second wife Elizabeth Cox, widow, Sep^t. ye 5th 1750 O. S. who was daughter of Samuel Vernon, Esq. was born in Newport, Aug. 5th 1709. Had a son still born, July 21, 1753, New Stile.
Elnathan Hammond Junr died Sept. 22, 1763.
Elizabeth Hammond the wife of Elnathan Hammond departed this life May the 11 1775.
Nathaniel Hammond died master of a ship in the London trade; died in Jamaica March 1777.
John Arnold Hammond taken by the English European Enemies and carried a prisoner to New York and died in the hospital some time June 1781.
Rowland Hammond my brother died June 16, 1788.
John Arnold Hammond married Mary Scot June 6, 1754.
Abigail Hammond married to Jacob Richardson Sept. 13, 1759.
Susanna Hammond married to Caleb Lyndon January 29, 1767 and died at Rehoboth August 24, 1780.
Nathaniel Hammond married to Betty Peabody Novr. 27, 1769 had two sons and one daughter.
Elizabeth Hammond married to Nathaniel Sprague of Rochester January ye 20, 1773.

Newport May ye 15, 1762.

My son John Arnold Hammond with his wife and two children a son and daughter, a negro boy and negro girl, with all his household goods, provision and some stock, removed from Hence and sailed for Cornwallis, in Minis in Nova Scotia to begin a settlement there, having the last summer lived and taken up a right of land there and made some preparation for a settlement.

This paragraph following his marriage and death in the record, contains the only allusion to the children of John Arnold Hammond; it is continued for a line or two in cipher. His wife, Mary Scott, is spoken of by the descendants as a niece of Benjamin Franklin. He returned from Nova Scotia, and engaged on the patriot side in the revolution, was captured aboard a ship, taken to New-York and died a prisoner. The record of his descendants at Middlebury is preserved in a family bible.

ELNATHAN HAMMOND, son of John A. Hammond and grandson of Elnathan Hammond, of Newport, R. I., was born at Newport, R. I., December 16, 1760. Deborah Carr, daughter of John Carr, Jr. and granddaughter of John Carr of North Kingston, R. I., born June 10, 1760. They were married at North Kingston, November 5, 1790. Children:

i.	LUCINDA, b. at Lanesboro', Mass., May 8, 1798; m. Leonard Whedon, of Bridport, Vt.; d. Jan. 19, 1853.
ii.	JOHN ARNOLD, b. at Middlebury, Vt., July 18, 1794; m. Fanny B. Keeler, of M., Nov. 11, 1824. Children: Martha H., Helen, Mariatt, Helen Jane. Mrs. F. B. H. d. April 3, 1870.
iii.	JANE, b. Oct. 27, 1795; m. Levi Sperry, of Cornwall, Vt.; d. March 19, 1850.
iv.	WILLIAM, b. April 2, 1797; m. Sally Olmsted, of M., Dec. 1835. Ch.: Henny W., Elizabeth. W. H. d. May 27, 1858; Mrs. S. H., Dec. 13, 1873.
v.	EMMA, b. May 4, 1799; m. Elijah Birge, of M., Sept. 13, 1832. Ch.: Cyrus.
vi.	EDWIN, b. May 20, 1803; m. Alpa Olmsted, of M., Dec. 29, 1828. Ch.: Edwin Seymour, George. E. H. d. Dec. 31, 1870; Mrs. A. H., May 1, 1871.
vii.	ABIGAIL, b. June 30, 1803.

Mrs. Elizabeth Penn Hammond.

Following the family record in the memorandum book, a note is made as follows :

Newport the 25th day of Feb. A.D. 1772. By our family record my Great Grand-Mother Elizabeth Hammond, with her son Benjamin Hammond aged 13 years and 3 daughters all young, came over to New England in the same ship or vessel with that worthy Minister Mr. John Lothrop, A.D. 1634 and by an ancient Manuscript Record found in the hands of the R[d]. Mr Elijah Lothrop of Gilead in Connecticut, in the handwriting of Mr John Lothrop, a copy of which taken by Doctor Ezra Stiles of Newport I have now before me, I find that Mr John Lothrop was at Scituate soon after his arrival in New England, viz. : " The 28 of September 1634, on the Lord's Day, spent my first Labors forenoon and afternoon.''
" January 8, 1634-5, were joined in covenant together as many of us as had been in covenant before, to wit (the names being mentioned)—9 men and 4 women. January 19th, I was chosen Pastor and invested into office.'' The church increased by additions from time to time until the 33d person joining is mentioned as follows : " Elizabeth Hammond, my Sister, having a dismission from the Ch. at Watertown was joined April 16, 1638." Rev John Lothrop with 30 men and 11 women members of his Ch. removed to Barnstable between the 26th of June and 11th of October in the year 1639. Now I suppose my Great Grandmother Elizabeth Hammond after Mr John Lothrop left Scituate removed to Boston, as it appears by our Family Record that she died and was buried at Boston A.D. 1640. This written by Elnathan Hammond Feb[y] 1772.

The Pastoral Journal of the Rev. John Lothrop, reprinted in full in the Register (vol. ix. pp. 279–87 ; x. pp. 37–43), including baptisms, burials and marriages, at Scituate and Barnstable, has no entry of Elizabeth Hammond's name but that quoted above. Her dismission from Watertown indicates a connection with the family there. The term " my Sister " implies a family relationship with her pastor, perhaps as a sister-in-law. Her name has not been found in the Probate or other records of Boston, nor a trace of her young daughters anywhere. As to her maiden name, that of Payne by the parish register of Lavenham is assigned to her competitor. In the pedigree of the Penns,[1] daughters are not named. Her son was nineteen at her death, and to that time the remembrances of home had been kept alive to him. Ten years later, his marriage with Mary Vincent at Sandwich, herself of English birth, would renew and assure them for transmission by their son, who always living near his parents, was forty at his father's death. The grandson made the record, when a subsequent collateral distinction might mislead him, but his ancestress ennobled the line in the sacrifice and silence of exile.

---

[1] William[1] Penn, of Minety, co. Gloucester, and of Penn's Lodge in Wiltshire, who died in 1591, had a son *William*,[2] who died before his father and left two sons, (1) *William*,[3] whose line is extinct, and (2) *Giles*.[3]

Giles[3] Penn was a captain in the Royal Navy, and held for some time the office of consul in the Mediterranean. He married Miss Gilbert, and had two sons—(1) *George*,[4] envoy to Spain, who died unmarried; and (2) Sir *William*.[4]

Sir William[4] Penn, born in Bristol 1621, entered the navy, where he distinguished himself and attained the rank of vice-admiral. He died at Wansted, Essex, in 1670. He married Margaret, dau. of John Jasper, of Rotterdam, by whom he had a son *William*,[5] the founder of Pennsylvania, and *Margaret*,[5] who m. Anthony Lowther, of Mask, Yorkshire.— *See Burke's Landed Gentry*, pp. 1021-2, and the *Heraldic Journal*, vol. iii. pp. 135–40.

DESCENDANTS OF PHILIP AND JOHN LANGDON, OF BOSTON.

By Arthur M. Alger, of Boston.

AMONG the early inhabitants of Boston were several families bearing the name of Langdon. The relationship, if any, existing between them we have failed to discover. John Langdon, a sailmaker, was the first comer, his name appearing in Boston as early as 1648. He married Sarah, daughter of the widow Alice Vermaes, of Salem, and had issue. Next came three brothers, Edward, Philip and John Langdon, and to them this sketch will be confined. Edward Langdon was a mariner, probably unmarried. His estate was settled by his brother John in 1704.

1. Philip[1] Langdon, who was also a mariner, and whose old oaken sea chest is still in the possession of his descendants, died Dec. 11, 1697. Mary, his wife, died Feb. 14, 1716. They had the following children :—

    i. Philip, an innkeeper.*
    ii. Susanna, b. Oct. 23, 1677: m. Samuel Gray.
    iii. John, b. Aug. 27, 1682. Probably the J. L. who m. Eliz. Indecot, March 8, 1713. Oct. 6, 1725, an inventory was taken of the goods of Eliz. Langdon, widow of John Langdon, mariner, deceased.
    iv. James, b. Aug. 15, 1685 ; d. young.
2. v. Samuel, b. Dec. 22, 1687 ; m. Esther Osgood, Aug. 8, 1712.
    vi. Mary, b. March 24, 1689 ; m. John Thwing, Sept. 2, 1713.
3. vii. Paul, b. Sept. 12, 1693 ; m. Mary Stacy, Aug. 18, 1718.

2. Samuel[2] Langdon (*Philip[1]*), a housewright, m. Esther Osgood, Aug. 8, 1712. He d. June 15, 1723, and she m. John Barnes, Nov. 30, 1725. The children of Samuel and Esther Langdon were:

    i. Samuel, b. June 16, 1713 ; d. Oct. 23, 1721.
    ii. Esther, b. May 12, 1715 ; m. John Gold, Nov. 4, 1736.
    iii. Mary, b. March 15, 1716.
    iv. Hannah, b. Aug. 8, 1719 ; d. June 5, 1721.
    v. Philip, b. June 9, 1721 ; d. Oct. 24, 1721.
4. vi. Samuel, b. Jan. 12, 1722 ; m. Elizabeth Brown.

3. Lt. Paul[2] Langdon (*Philip[1]*), a carpenter, millwright and farmer, m. Mary Stacy, Aug. 18, 1718. He removed to Salem, and thence to Wilbraham, where he d. Dec. 3, 1761. He was a man of great energy and enterprise. His children were :—

    i. Mary, b. Aug. 20, 1719 ; m. Henry Badger.
5. ii. Lewis, b. May 16, 1721 ; m. a Cooley.
    iii. Hannah, b. Feb. 22, 1723 ; m. a Meacham.
6. iv. Paul, b. Dec. 16, 1725 ; m. Thankful Stebbins.
7. v. John, b. June 1, 1728 ; m. Sarah Stebbins.
    vi. Elizabeth, b. July 1, 1730 ; d. Sept. 23, 1740.
    vii. Anna, b. Sept. 21, 1732 ; d. Sept. 12, 1740.

4. Rev. Samuel[3] Langdon, D.D., A.A.S. (*Samuel,[2] Philip[1]*), m. Elizabeth, dau. of the Rev. Richard Brown, of Reading, Mass. He graduated at H. U. 1740, taught school for a short time in Ipswich, Mass., and then went to Portsmouth, N. H., where he had charge of the grammar

---

* June 25, 1689, Paul Simmons, being bound to sea, appoints his trusty and well loved cousin, Philip Langdon, his attorney.

school, and was assistant to Mr. Fitch, minister of the First Church.   He was a chaplain at the capture of Louisburg in 1745.   Feb. 4, 1747, he was ordained as the successor of Mr. Fitch, and remained in that position until his appointment to the presidency of Harvard University, Oct. 14, 1774. Lacking the firmness and dignity necessary for the maintenance of discipline among the students, he resigned Aug. 30, 1780.   In 1781, he was installed over the church at Hampton Falls, N. H., where he d. Nov. 29, 1797, his extensive knowledge, hospitality, patriotism and piety having secured to him the affection and respect of his people.   In politics he was an ardent whig, and distinguished himself as a member of the New-Hampshire convention which adopted the federal constitution.   He published a number of essays, sermons, &c.

Dr. Langdon had by his wife Elizabeth nine children, four of whom died in infancy.   The other five were:—

> SAMUEL.   Had a family.
> PAUL.   Graduated at H.C. 1770.   Was the first preceptor of the academy in Fryeburg, Me., where Daniel Webster afterward taught.   Married, had children, and removed to New-York.
> RICHARD.   Had a family.
> ELIZABETH, m. the Hon. David Sewall, LL.D., of York, Me.
> MARY, m. the Hon. John Goddard, of Portsmouth.

5.   LEWIS[3] LANGDON *(Paul,[2] Philip[1])*, m. a Cooley, of Monson.   He erected the first saw-mill in Wilbraham, and invented a machine for turning cider-mill screws.   Children:—

> i. LEWIS.   ii. JOHN.   iii. PHILIP.   iv. CHRISTOPHER, m. Polly Walker. v. RACHEL.   vi. SARAH.

6.   Capt. PAUL[3] LANGDON *(Paul,[2] Philip[1])*, m. Thankful Stebbins, May 5, 1757, and d. June 23, 1804.   He was a sergeant in the French war, and commanded a company from Wilbraham in the war of the revolution.   Children:—

> i.   SAMUEL, b. May 10, 1758 ; d. Feb. 20, 1822.
> ii.   THANKFUL, b. July 4, 1760 ; m. a Burt.
> iii.   PAUL, b. Aug. 18, 1764 ; m. Azubah King.
> iv.   LOVISA, b. Nov. 13, 1768 ; m. (1) Abdiel Loomis ; (2) Joseph Wood.
> v.   MARY, b. Oct. 12, 1770 ; m. Jacob Wood.
> vi.   WALTER, b. June 22, 1779 ; m. Sophia Badger.

7.   JOHN[3] LANGDON *(Paul,[2] Philip[1])*, of Wilbraham, m. (1) Sarah Stebbins, Feb. 1755 ; (2) Eunice Torrey, Dec. 29, 1757.   He d. Oct. 10, 1822.   Said to have been a man of great energy.   He served as a sergeant in the revolutionary war.   By first wife he had:—

> i.   SARAH, b. July 12, 1755 ; m. Ebenezer Crocker, of Kinderhook, N. Y.

By second wife he had:—

> ii.   JOHN-WILSON, b. March 11, 1759 ; m. an Ashley.
> iii.   ARTEMAS, b. May 25, 1760 ; d. Oct. 2, 1760.
> iv.   JAMES, b. March 27, 1762 ; m. Esther Stebbins.
> v.   JOSIAH, b. Jan. 12, 1765 ; m. Sally Hall.
> vi.   JOANNA, b. June 21, 1767 ; m. Preserved Leonard.
> vii.   OLIVER, b. Oct. 9, 1769.
> viii.   EUNICE, b. March 7, 1772 ; m. Asa Merritt.
> ix.   SOLOMON, b. July 19, 1777.

Of these five brothers, three were methodist preachers, John W., Oliver, and Solomon; and one was an "exhorter," James.   Their descendants reside in Cincinnati, Ohio, and vicinity.   The other brother, Josiah, was a man of literary taste, and wrote considerable poetry in his day. His " Song of the Hoe " is the best known.

For further information concerning the Langdon family in Wilbraham, see Dr. Stebbins's History of that town.

---

1. JOHN[1] LANGDON, in the year 1672, lay sick in the Island of Barbadoes. Thinking, perhaps, that his end was near, he executed a will, bequeathing to his brother, Philip Langdon, of Boston, all his property, to wit : money, wearing apparel, sea instruments, one barrel of sugar, and two hogsheads of molasses, in the ship " John and Sarah of Boston ;" the master of the ship promising to deliver them, if it pleased God to send him well to Boston. But the sick man recovered, returned to Boston, married, and settled down as an innkeeper. He died, Dec. 6, 1732, aged 82. By Elizabeth, his wife, he had the following children :—

    i. ELIZABETH, b. 1686 ; m. —— Pitman, whom she survived. He may have been her second husband ; for an Eliz. Langdon m. William Symmes, June 13, 1706.

2. ii. JOSIAH, b. Jan. 28, 1687 ; m. Elizabeth Saxton, Sept. 2, 1708.

    iii. EPHRAIM, b. Jan. 25, 1689 ; m. Sarah ——, had Josiah, and d. before 1728.

    iv. MARY, bapt. Nov. 15, 1691 ; m. Samuel Hunt, April 24, 1712.

    v. JOANNA, b. Oct. 22, 1693 ; m. in Salem, March 14, 1711, Grafton Feveryear, a wealthy baker, of Boston.

3. vi. NATHANIEL, b. Sept. 14, 1695 ; m. Abigail Harris, Nov. 23, 1738.

4. vii. EDWARD, bapt. Oct. 23, 1698 ; m. Susanna Wadsworth.

    viii. MARGARET, b. Oct. 23, 1697 ; d. young.

    ix. JOHN, b. Oct. 17, 1698. John Langdon (No. 1) and John Hunt were sureties on a bond given June 14, 1722, by Mary Langdon, as administratrix of the estate of her husband, John Langdon, mariner, deceased.

    x. MICHAEL, d. Aug. 26, 1701.

    xi. MARGARET, b. Aug. 10, 1703 ; m. Benj. Proctor, a tanner, Feb. 28, 1721.

2. Deacon JOSIAH[2] LANGDON (*John[1]*), an innkeeper, married Elizabeth Saxton, Sept. 2, 1708, and died Nov. 5, 1742, leaving an estate which was inventoried at £5488. 18. 4½. He was one of the building committee for, and in 1737 was ordained deacon of the New North Church. He resided in Fish street. Children :—

    i. ELIZABETH, b. July 1, 1721 ; m. Oct. 5, 1742, the Rev. Andrew Eliot, D.D., who for thirty years was pastor of the New North Church. They were the parents of, *inter alios*, the Rev. Andrew Eliot, minister at Fairfield, Conn., graduated at H. U. in 1762 ; Ephraim Eliot, who graduated at H. U. 1780 ; and the Rev. John Eliot, S. T. D., who graduated at H. U. in 1772, and in 1778 succeeded his father as pastor of the New North Church.

    ii. EPHRAIM, b. Aug. 7, 1733 ; graduated at H. U. 1752, studied divinity, and was a decided Socinian, but insuperable constitutional timidity prevented him from preaching. For a number of years he was assistant master of the north latin grammar school, when Mr. Wiswall, the principal, was laboring under the infirmities of age. He was a rigid disciplinarian. He was unmarried, and died Nov. 21, 1765, aged 33.

3. NATHANIEL[2] LANGDON (*John[1]*), an innkeeper, married Abigail Harris, Nov. 23, 1738. He died Dec. 27, 1757, aged 63, and was buried on Copp's Hill. His estate was inventoried at £3354. 5. 10½. Children :—

    i. NATHANIEL, b. March 2, 1741 ; d. unmarried, about 1819.

    ii. ABIGAIL, b. Aug. 9, 1743 ; m. Thomas Bumstead, Nov. 17, 1767.

    iii. ELIZABETH, b. Dec. 17, 1744 ; d. young.

5. iv. Josiah, b. March 3, 1746 ; m. Dorothy Brintnall, Jan. 18, 1775.
6. v. John, b. July 28, 1747 ; m. Mary Walley, June 2, 1771.
     vi. Mary, b. July 11, 1748 ; m. Stephen Williams, Dec. 12, 1771.
    vii. Elizabeth, b. Oct. 8, 1749 ; d. unmarried, aged about 30.
   viii. William, b. Sept. 28, 1750 ; privateer—lost—never heard from.
     ix. Samuel, b. Oct. 6, 1752 ; d. young.
      x. Ephraim, b. Dec. 29, 1754 ; shipwrecked.
     xi. Joanna, b. March 28, 1755 ; m. Ebenezer Frothingham, March 9, 1779,
            and was mother, *inter alios*, of the Rev. Nathaniel Langdon Froth-
            ingham, D.D. ; and of Ephraim Langdon Frothingham, who was
            joint author with his son Arthur of a work on " Philosophy as Ab-
            solute Science," &c.
    xii. Priscilla, b. July 28, 1756 ; d. unm. at a good old age.

4. Deacon EDWARD[2] LANGDON (*John[1]*), a tallow chandler, married
Susanna Wadsworth, who died Sept. 3, 1760, aged 65.   He was a deacon
of the Second Church.   He died May 25, 1766, and was buried on Copp's
Hill.   Children:—

7. i. John, b. Jan. 17, 1722 ; m. Mary ———.
8. ii. Edward, b. June 10, 1724 ; m. Mary Parkman.
    iii. Susanna, b. May 3, 1727 ; }
     iv. Timothy, b. Feb. 17, 1732 ; } probably d. young.

5. Dr. JOSIAH[3] LANGDON (*Nathaniel,[2] John[1]*), graduated at H. U. 1764,
and succeeded Mr. Wiswall as principal of the north latin grammar school ;
but did not remain long, being deficient in the spirit of government.   He
married Dorothy, dau. of Paul Brintnall, of Sudbury, Jan. 18, 1775, and,
having studied medicine, settled in that town as a practising physician.
There he died in or about 1779.   His widow, perhaps, married again ; for
Dorothy Langdon and Daniel Eaton were published in Weston, Sept. 8, 1788.
Josiah and Dorothy Langdon had one child, viz. :—

      i. Josiah, d. July 23, 1793, a. 15 yrs. 5 mos. 3 days.

6. Captain JOHN[3] LANGDON (*Nathaniel,[2] John[1]*), married June 2, 1771,
Mary, dau. of Thomas Walley, one of the wealthiest merchants of Boston.
He served an apprenticeship with Wharton & Bowes, booksellers (the
firm in which Henry Knox, afterwards major-general, served).   In 1770,
he commenced business for himself, on Cornhill, but relinquished it on the
outbreak of hostilities, and raised a volunteer company, which was in active
service during the campaign in Rhode-Island.   At the close of the war he
obtained a position in the Custom House of Boston, in which city he died
Aug. 1793.   Children :—

      i. John-Walley, bapt. March 8, 1772 ; m. Rebecca Cordis, of Charles-
            town, Aug. 26, 1794, and had issue.   He was a merchant in the
            Smyrna trade.
     ii. Mary, bapt. July 18, 1773 ; m. Dr. William P. Greenwood, July 23,
            1796, and was the mother of the Rev. F. W. P. Greenwood, D.D.
            (H. U. 1814), and the Rev. Alfred Greenwood (H. U. 1824).   She
            was the author of a dialogue on female education in Bingham's
            " American Instructor."
    iii. Elizabeth, bapt. July 3, 1774 ; m. William Lovett, Esq., Nov. 22,
            1795.
     iv. Abigail-Harris, b. 1776–7, at Bolton ; m. Giles Lodge, Esq., 1799, and
            was the mother of Dr. Giles Henry Lodge (H. U. 1825), translator
            of Wincklemann's " History of Ancient Art among the Greeks,"
            and of an art novel from the German of Baron von Sternberg, entitled
            " The Breughel Brothers."
      v. Sarah, bapt. April 12, 1778 ; m. Andrew Aitcheson, Esq.
     vi. Anne-Hurd, bapt. Sept. 2, 1781 ; m. Aug. 1817, John Bellows, Esq.,
            president of the Manufacturers' and Mechanics' Bank.   He was the

father, by a former wife, of the Rev. Henry W. Bellows, D.D., of New-York.

vii. THOMAS-WALLEY, bapt. Oct. 5, 1783; m. Aug. 31, 1833, widow Jane Weaver Ross, only dau. of Dr. John Greenwood, of New-York, and d. without issue Dec. 17, 1861. He was for many years a merchant in the Smyrna trade in Boston, with his brother John.

viii. CATHARINE-AMELIA, bapt. Dec. 25, 1785; m. Samuel Cook, Esq.

ix. CHARLOTTE-AUGUSTA, bapt. Dec. 31, 1801, at the age of 13; d. unm.

7. JOHN³ LANGDON (*Edward*,² *John¹*), a merchant, married Mary ——, and died about 1783. Children:—

i. JOHN, b. Nov. 19, 1745. One of the "Sons of Liberty."

ii. TIMOTHY, b. Feb. 7, 1746. He graduated at H. U. 1765, and studied law with Jeremiah Gridley. Commencing practice in that part of Pownalboro', Me., which is now Wiscasset, he was appointed a Crown Lawyer before the Revolution; was a representative to the Provincial Congress in 1776; and in 1778 Admiralty Judge for the District of Maine. He was a man of brilliant talent, but of unstable character. He died in the year 1808. Mr. Willis, in his "Law, Law Courts, and Lawyers of Maine," erroneously states that he was a brother of Governor John Langdon of Portsmouth.

iii. EDWARD, b. May 3, 1749. Not mentioned in his father's will, 1780.

iv. SUSANNA, b. Feb. 15, 1750; m. Joseph Procter, June 11, 1773.

v. JOSEPH, b. Nov. 30, 1757.

vi. MARY, b. June 27, 1759; m. Dr. William Coffin, March 31, 1778.

vii. ELIZABETH, b. Oct. 30, 1760; d. soon.

viii. ELIZABETH, b. July 20, 1762; m. Henry Skinner, March 13, 1780.

ix. NATHANIEL, b. Sept. 15, 1763.

8. EDWARD³ LANGDON (*Edward*,² *John¹*), a tallow chandler, married Mary Parkman, Nov. 16, 1752, and died in 1755. His widow married Joshua Winter, Feb. 13, 1760.

Edward and Mary Langdon had one child, viz. :—

i. MARY, b. Dec. 14, 1753; d. Sept. 8, 1771.

The will of Elizabeth Langdon, of Malden, widow, dated Oct. 20, 1744, proved Aug. 5, 1745, mentions "only grandchild Eliz. Barry." On the back of the will appears the request of Eliz. Barry, and James Hovey, the executor, that the will be not admitted to probate, but that Deacon Edward Langdon, of Boston, be appointed administrator. This fact tends to show that the widow Elizabeth Langdon was related to the Boston Langdons.

ANCIENT WILLS.

Communicated by N. J. HERRICK, Esq., of Lawrence, Mass.

[MRS. MARY NEWMARCH.]

THE last Will and Testament of Mʳˢ Mary Newmarch the wife of the Revᵈ. John Newmarch of Kittery in the County of York in the Province of the Massachusetts Bay in New England Clerk made this thirtieth Day of August Anno Domini 1743. Whereas I the said Mary Newmarch did by my Contract or Agreement made with the said John Newmarch before marriage, to my Self (among other things) full Power and Liberty to dispose of that Estate which I had by my former Husband the Revᵈ. Mʳ. Theophilus Cotton late of Hampton Decᵈ. by Will or otherwise during our State of Wedlock. I do therefore make this my last Will and Testament to dispose of the Same in manner following, with the Consent of my s⁴. Husband viz⁵.

Impᵉ. I give and bequeath unto my beloved Husband Mʳ. John Newmarch that Bond or Debt due to me from Clement Hughs or the Land which was made over to my former Husband for Security for said Debt in Dover or Elsewhere, and my Silver Bowl.

Item 2ᵈˡʸ. I give to my Kinsman Caleb Cushing Junʳ. of Salisbury and Theophilus Cotton of Plymouth all the remaining part of my Right and Interest in yᵉ Town of Chester which I had by my former Husband Mʳ. Theophilus Cotton to be equally divided between them.

Item 3ᵈˡʸ. I give to my Cousin Mary Parker the Wife of Benjamin Parker of Kittery all my Plate or Silver Vessels (except the aforesᵈ Bowl and my Silver Porringer) and all my Household Stuff or Goods of all Sorts after my Husbands Death, and all my Wearing Cloaths Linnen and Woolen, and my Picture or Effigies, and Mʳ. Burkits notes on the N. T.

Item 4ˡʸ. I give to my Cousin James Cushing Mʳ. Flavels 2 Volumns and the morning Exercises 4 Volumns after my Husbands Death.

Item 5ˡʸ. I give to Sarah the Daughter of Caleb Cushing Junʳ. my Gold necklace, and I give to Mary yᵉ. Daughter of my Brother Samuel Gookin my Silver Porringer mark'd M: C:

Item 6ˡʸ. My Will is that what shall remain of my Cash Money Bills or Bonds due to me after the Payment of my Debts and Funeral Expences and Five pounds to Elizabeth Moody the Wife of Joshua Moody the same shall be equally divided between the aforesaid Theophilus Cotton of Plymouth and Mary Parker of Kittery.

And Finally I do constitute and appoint my beloved Husband to be Sole Executor of this my Will to whom I give any Book, or Estate that shall remain undisposed of in this my Will or otherways.

Witness my Hand and Seal the Day and Year first above mentioned August 30. 1743.

MARY NEWMARCH [Seal].

Signed Sealed and Delivered by the said } Mary Newmarch to be her last Will and } Testament. In presence of us }
    Caleb Cushing
    W:ᵐ Bradbury
    Judith Norton

N: B: That I the above named John Newmarch do Consent to the above written Will. Witness my Hand this 30th of August 1743.

JOHN NEWMARCH.

At a Court of Probate held at York Octᵒ. 21. 1746.

The within written Instrument being presented by the Revᵈ. Mʳ. John Newmarch Executor therein named on the Eighth of September last, and then the Revᵈ. Mʳ. Caleb Cushing and Judith Norton within named appeared and made Oath that they were present and did see the within named Mʳˢ. Mary Newmarch sign and seal and heard her declare the said Instrument as her last Will & Testament and that she was then of a sound disposing mind to their best discerning, and that they together with William Bradbury, Esqʳ. subscribed the same as Witnesses thereto in the Testators presence. And I do allow and approve of the same accordingly.

JER: MOULTON, Judge.

    Recorded from the original.
Pr. Simon Frost, Regr.
[Records of co. York, Book 7, p. 8.]

PASSENGERS TO AMERICA.

UNDER this head we propose to print lists of passengers and memoranda of the arrival of vessels in America. Contribu tions to this series of articles are solicited from our friends.

No. I.

ARRIVALS IN BOSTON, MASS., MAY TO JUNE, 1712.

From Manuscripts belonging to the New-England Historic, Genealogical Society.

Massachusets   Impost Office, Boston.

Vessells Entered in ye Month of March, 1711–12

8th John Row ye Sloop Dorcas & Mary from Fyall
    No Passengers
10th John Mathews ye Sloop Content from South Carolina
    No Passengers
    Ebenez^r Swan ye Brig^{tt} Fraternity from Turtuda
    No Passengers
24th Allexeand^r Duncan ye Swallow from Mary Land
    No Passengers
    John Gardner ye Sloop Seartryall from Virginia
    No Passengers
    John Mitchell ye Sloop Hanah & Mary from N Carolina
    No Passengers
    Henry Cally ye Bark Seaflower from Fyall
    No Passengers
    Thomas Bell ye Sloop Mary from Pocomoke Verginia
    No Passengers
    Nathan^{ll} Harris ye Sloop Vergin from Maryland
    No Passengers
    Moses Abbott ye Sloop Swallow from N Carolina
    No Passengers

Dated Boston, March 31st 1712.

p' DAN: RUSSELL, Com^{er}

Massachusets   Impost Office Boston.

Vessells Entred in ye Month April 1712

ye 4th John Dimon ye Sloop Aduenture from S^{tt} Christoph^r
    No Passengers
    Arthur Rexford ye Sloope Rose from Antigua
    No Passengers
    Michall Gill ye Ship John Gally from Turtuda
    No Passengers but Marreners
5th James Killying ye Sloop Mary from North Carolina
    No Passengers
    Thomas Ienkins ye Sloop Vnion from Virgina
    No Passengers

John Venteman y⁰ Ship Han⁰ & Eliz⁰ from Turtuda
  No Passengers
Wᵐ Marsh y⁰ Sloop Wᵐ & Sarah from New York
  Joseph Thorn ⎱
  John Wright ⎬ Planters
  Danˡˡ Lawrance ⎰
7ᵗʰ Joseph White y⁰ Ship Sheppard from Turtuda
  No Passengers
John Breet y⁰ Brigᵗᵗ Katherine from Holland
  No Passengers
8ᵗʰ Peter Papillon y⁰ Ship Sarah from London
  Twenty Nine Marriners
  James Gouge Gentleman
William Carkett y⁰ Sloop Endeavor from Virgina
  No Passengers
John Tuffton y⁰ Sloop Tryall from Surenam
  No Passengers
Benjᵃ Juery. y⁰ Sloop Endeavor from Sᵗᵗ Christophers
  No Passengers
9ᵗʰ John Petty y⁰ Sloop Dubertus from North Carolina
  No Passengers
William Cook y⁰ Sloop Dimond from Mounseratt
  No Passengers
John Royall y⁰ Sloop Speadwell from North Carolina
  No Passengers
10ᵗʰ Joseph Jenkins y⁰ Sloop Vnity from North Carolina
  No Passengers
12ᵗʰ Andʳ Gibson y⁰ Brigᵗᵗ Succes from Glasgow
  John Alron ⎱
  Patrick Cheap ⎬ Tradors
  Robert Clarke ⎰
  George Seiruin A Youth for Education
  Peacock A Cordwainer
14ᵗʰ Amos Story y⁰ Sloop Friends Aduenture from Turtuda
  No Passengers
Thomas Dalling y⁰ Sloop Dragon from Fyall
  No Passengers
Richard Fifield y⁰ Ship Eliz⁰ from Turtuda
  No Passengers
Francis Norris y⁰ Brigᵗᵗ Martha & Hanah from Mounseratt
  Allexeander Baker Marinʳ & his Seruant
          Haynes ⎱
          Scott ⎰ belonging to New York
Thomas Lathrop y⁰ Sloop Johan⁰ & Thankfull from N. york
  No Passengers
Robert Sanders y⁰ Sloop Daniel from Virginia
  No Passengers
15ᵗʰ John Cooper y⁰ Sloop Black Cock from Virginia
  No Passengers
Andrew Meade y⁰ Sloop Macy from Virginia
  No Passengers
19ᵗʰ William Thomas y⁰ Ship Succes from Surenam
  Johanes Vanharbergreen Merchᵗᵗ

26th Phillip Callender ye Sloop Ann from New York
    No Passengers
    Francis Biluton ye Sloop Fisher from Philedelpha
    No Passengers
28th Nath^{ll} Mason ye Sloop Eliz^a from S^{tt} Georges
    No Passengers but Marreners
    Thomas Vernam ye Barque Vnion from Barnstable
    No Passengers
    Thomas Landell ye Sloop Betty from Antigua
    No Passengers
    George Huntington ye Brig^{tt} Macy from London
    No Passengers but Marriners
    Edward Tyng ye Brig^{tt} Hope from Fyall
    William Wilson Merch^{tt}   ·
    and Six Marreners
29th Lewis Hunt ye Barque Hopewell from Surenam
    John Seylor A Saylor
            Dated Boston April 30th
                    p' DAN: RUSSELL Com^{er}

Massachusets   Impost Office Boston

       Vessells Entered in ye Month of May 1712

1st John Foster ye Sloop Maulborough from Antigua
    No Passengers
3^d William Alden ye Brig^{tt} S^{tt} John Battis from Anopolis
    No Passengers
5th Thomas Miors ye Ship Friendship from South Carolina
    John Jorden, A Merch^{tt}
    John Wakefield ye Brig^{tt}. Lisbon Merch^{tt}. from Lisbon
    No Passengers but Marriners
    Daniel Marshall ye Brig^{tt}. Lepard from Nevis
    No Passengers
12th Joseph Penwell ye Sloop Orringtree from Newf^d Land
    No Passengers
13th John Jenkens ye Brig^{tt} Jer^a & Thom^s from Madera
    No Passengers
    Jon^a Bull ye Sloop Two Brothers from Anopolis
    No Passengers
15th John Secomb ye Sloop Swallow from Madera
    No Passengers
17th John Hayes ye Ship Marcy & Sarah from Barbados
    Sarah Blanchard A Marryed Woman
    Aibel Macumber ye Sloop Speadwell from Jamaica
      Brattle Oliver Merch^{tt}
      John Rogers Phissihon
      David Jones Seruent
    Thomas Simpson ye Sloop Succes from Barbados
    No Passengers
19th Peter King ye Ship John & Mary from Barbados
    No Passengers
    William Euerton, ye Brig^{tt} Releaf from Madera
    No Passengers

20th Newcomb Blaque y[e] Ship Neptune from Barbados
    Benj[a] Wright ⎫
    Josiah Jackson ⎪
    Sam[ll] Hill ⎪
    Sam[ll] Rooke ⎬ Merch[tts]
    Thomas Jones ⎪
    Smith ⎭

21st George Phillips y[e] Brig[tt] Aduenture from Surenam
    No Passengers

23[d] Charles Howell y[e] Sloop Dubertus from New London
    Zacharia Rogers Cordwainer
    Two Marriners

29th John Pumroy y[e] Sloop Sarah & Mary from N:F[d] Land
    No Passengers
    Joseph Atkins y[e] Pink Sarah from Newfound Land
    No Passengers
    William Euerton y[e] Sloop Anna from Bristoll & Fyall
    Eleazer Armitage
    William Hutton y[e] Ship Jamaica Gally from Jamaica
    Lenord Vassell Esq[r] & his Sone & Dafter
    David Preshaw y[e] Ship Expedition from North Brittan
    John Nicolls Chrgeon
    James Nerne Gentleman
    Robert Cuningham & Two Marrenirs

31st Tho[s] Wenmouth y[e] Ship Eueling from Biddyford
    W[m] Dumer & Two Seruents, Indimion Walker & 4 Seruents
    Francis Wainwright & one Seruent
    Jeffry Farmer Merch[tt] John Irwin Curgeon

        Dated Boston May 31st 1712

                p' DAN[l] RUSSELL, Com[r]

Massachusets   Impost Office Boston
        Vessells Entred in y[e] Month of June 1712

17th Richard Loue y[e] Ship Peter & Phillip from London

John Channing	Peter Whalton
Mary Anthram	Christian Snowman
Ann Anthram	Isac Varenne
M[rs] Selby and her Child	Cap[t] John Woodward
Abra[m] De Senne	Edward Mobeley
Henry Whitton	M[r] Payne
M[r] Bayley his Wife & Two Child[n]	John Coats & his Sone
Madam Proctor	M[rs] Shad
Lydia	John Brewstow the Negro

                p' DAN[l] RUSSELL, Com[r]

No. II.

ARRIVAL ABOUT 1685.

Communicated by ARTHUR M. ALGER, of Boston.

IN the Colonial Records in the State House, Boston, vol. 61, p. 288, is a petition to the Hon. Simon Bradstreet, signed by Thomas Banister, Thomas Cobb, James Thornbeck, George Clarke, Ralph Killcup, bearing date Aug.

12, 1685. We gather from it that they with their families were passengers in a ship which had lately arrived from England, and, on account of a false report that they had brought the small-pox with them, were confined on an island in the harbor, where they had no shelter and were without fresh water. The petition set forth that they had all had the distemper in Old England many years ago, with the exception of four persons who had it on board ship, but had been well six weeks and upwards. They therefore prayed to be admitted within bounds, that they might provide for themselves and families.

Leave was given them to come ashore on the following day.

Two of the petitioners, Thomas Banister and George Clarke, settled in Boston; the latter afterward removing to Roxbury.

A FEW WORDS ADDITIONAL RELATIVE TO COL. JOHN MAY, OF BOSTON, AND HIS JOURNEYS TO THE OHIO COUNTRY IN 1788 AND 1789.

Communicated by the Rev. RICHARD S. EDES, of Bolton, Mass.

IN the REGISTER for January, 1873, appeared an article on the "Journal and Letters of Col. John May," said journal and letters having been written by him during two journeys which he made to the "Ohio Country," one in 1788, the other in 1789. Later in the same season of 1873, Robert Clarke & Co., of Cincinnati, under the auspices of the Ohio Historical Society, published the Journal in full, together with such letters from the same hand as had been preserved. Readers must have noticed, however, that while there is, in the book, quite a full and minute journal relating to the year '88, there is none of '89, but only some few letters, which, although sufficiently expressive, give but in brief and general terms the experiences of that year.

When the Journal and Letters were published, at the times mentioned, it was the belief of the present writer that he had in his possession all papers bearing on that portion of Col. May's life. In that impression he was mistaken. There was then in existence, in the library of Prof. Edward Tuckerman, of Amherst College, a grandson, a journal kept by Col. May in '89; and though at times Mr. T. had entertained thoughts of publishing it, the multiplication of other cares and duties and absorption in scientific pursuits prevented. Accordingly the MS. was left unused, locked up in a cabinet—a circumstance to be regretted, since a work of the kind could not have fallen into hands more competent to issue it. Meantime, illness supervened, necessitating a suspension of all literary labor, and again compelling Mr. Tuckerman to seek in European travel the relief which a tired brain required.

Thus it happened he was out of the country when the article above mentioned appeared, and also when the book referred to was issued from the press at Cincinnati. On returning home, later in the season, Mr. Tuckerman did not long delay to inform the present writer of the MS. in his possession, nor fail, in the exercise of his wonted kindness, to offer it to be used in any manner that might be deemed advisable. In this way he who writes these lines found himself in possession, altogether unexpectedly, of papers, which in 1873 he did not know to exist; and was thus enabled to trace Col. May's journeyings and experiences in '89 with as much distinctness and detail as those of '88.

The Journal of '89—except as it shows the workings of the same mind, and its peculiar cast of thought and modes of expression—is dissimilar almost entirely from that of '88, and relates to an experience wholly different. The sorely disappointed writer of it was thwarted in all his plans, not only by the peculiarity of the season, which was a very cold one, the lowness of the rivers, and a succession of disasters, but also by the almost utter disorder of the currency and other business arrangements throughout the country, and so found himself, as time wore on and circumstances changed, in positions as much unlike anything he had been expecting as could well be. Could he have come into possession of it earlier, the present writer would probably have attempted to publish the Journal of '89 as a supplement to that of '88; but as so many months have intervened since the latter was first introduced to the public, and attention is now diverted to other directions, he must relinquish all plans of that sort, and content himself with a few words of explanation and correction which appear to be needed, such as, by the courtesy of the editor of the REGISTER, and new light furnished, he is enabled to give.

Imprimis, he would like to corect an error into which he fell—naturally enough perhaps—in the absence of all tradition and all testimony, excepting such as could be gathered from the insufficient documents then in his possession. The error referred to occurs on page 119 of the Cincinnati publication, and originated in a letter written in '89, from Baltimore, by Col. May, the date of which is *April 9th* (another letter, which to appearance ought to follow it, being dated New-York, April 29th), when, as by comparison with the MS. Journal since brought to light is plainly shown, it should have been *May 9th.* The theory, therefore, which is introduced to explain the supposed journeyings of Col. May in the early part of that season must be entirely set aside.

Another error, found at the end of the second paragraph of the Biographical Sketch, may as well be corrected here as anywhere. It is there stated, erroneously, that Jonathan Sabin, who married Mary, sister of Col. John, was brother to Silas Sabin, who married Prudence, another sister, whereas the relationship between them was so slight that what it was they neither of them knew.

In two instances in the publication referred to, the wrong insertion of a comma has produced important mistakes, in one giving to Dr. George W. May, of Washington (youngest son of Col. John) three daughters, instead of two; and in the other, on page 147, converting three individuals into four. *Lucretia Dana* is the name of *one* individual, and should not be made into two, as it is in the place mentioned. Col. Richard Hatt turns out to be Col. Richard Platt (page 20); and for Sir John Temple (page 114) should be read St. John Temple. There are other slight, and perhaps unimportant errors; but we will not take up space with mentioning them, but pass to other matters.

Certain words used in the Journal, it has been found, have attracted attention, and in answer to inquiries the present writer has had a little private correspondence respecting them. " Cantsloper " is one of these. It occurs on page 54 of the Journal of '88, and is found again in that of '89, and also in a copy of the Journal made by the original writer's oldest daughter, Abby; but it is spelled differently, "*Kentsloper, khansloper.*" The suggestion is ventured that it was a slopper, or outside garment, for rough and wet weather, named, possibly, after the county of Kent in England, Kent-slopper, or, from one fancy or another, after the khan, and so khan-slopper.

We venture the suggestion also, that the word "waggloper," found on page 40, might be changed to wagon-loper, meaning the same as wagoner, or one who strides along side a wagon.

Since the book was published, two years ago last fall, the decease of Miss C. Augusta May, the last survivor of Col. John's children, has taken place; and, following that event, the breaking up of her household. In looking over old papers found in the house, scraps turned up here and there throwing a degree of light, however small, on portions of the colonel's earlier career, or possessed of interest in other points of view. Thus, for instance, a mutilated fragment of an "orderly book" was discovered; and thereby we are able to state that, somewhere in 1775 or '76, he was serving in the forces then stationed in and about Boston, with the rank, apparently, of orderly sergeant. We find the following in the book just referred to, in his hand-writing:—

Head-Quarters, Boston, August 16th, 177–.

Parole York.   Countersign War.

The officers and soldiers of the newly raised regiments will strictly conform themselves to the Rules and Regulations of the Continental Army.

A Sergeant's guard must be kept in each of the Forts on Dorchester Heights, which will be daily relieved at 8 o'clock in the morning.

All the men off duty are to fatigue eight hours a day, Sundays and rainy days excepted. The officers will choose those hours for working which best suit them.

The rolls of each company will be called every morning and evening; and delinquents (if there should be any) noticed. Each regiment will exercise at least one hour in a day, at such hour as the Commanding Officer shall order. As soon as the regiments are formed, the *réveille* is to be beat at day-break, the troop at 8 in the morning, the retreat at sunset, and the tattoo at 8 o'clock in the evening.

The drum and fife major of each regiment will pay particular attention to the improvement in martial musick.   (No signature.)

The above were, probably, general orders for the day, and copied by the several orderlies into their books. To the above citation from the "orderly book," and such scraps as were rescued from his old papers, and printed in the article in the January 1873 issue of the REGISTER, there is nothing, to our knowledge, which can be added to the record of Col. May's military life.

During both the journeys of Col. May to the West in '88 and '89, his wife at home in Boston was keeping a brief diary of occurrences, chiefly domestic, there. A quotation or two—as throwing light on the usages of the times, and in other respects—may not be without interest.

1788, April 14. Monday morning, precisely at 6 o'clock, Mr. May set out on his grand tour, in tolerable health and spirits. Breakfasted, then went to hackling flax.

Wednesday . . . . . . broke my wheel.

Thursday, the Publick Fast. Attended worship in the forenoon at the Chapel, at the brick in the afternoon. Dined with brother Joe, drank tea with sister Dawes.

[Another] Thursday. The children continue sick and cross. Sent for Warren, he came, &c. [Dr. John Warren, H. U. 1771, died 1815.] . . . . Mr. Ticknor (teacher) called in the evening, &c. &c.

This diary is continued but little farther, and breaks off abruptly.

That for '89 commences thus :—

April 23d. At 7 o'clock, Mr. May and Mr. Breck started on their journey for the West, not in the best health or spirits, leaving us very dull.

24th. A heavy old fashioned Southerly storm, wind very heavy . . . rained hard all night, . . . day dark, dull, and long. Mr. West [Rev. Dr. West, of Hollis St. Society] called on us, and daddy several times. He, daddy [Samuel May, her father], has sent me three cords of wood, sawed and piled it for me, put up my bacon, &c. . . . . In the afternoon brother came, and brought me the image of my friend [portrait of her husband, Col. John, in the military dress of the period, supposed to be by Stuart, since the death of Miss C. A. May deposited in the Antiquarian Hall at Worcester]. What a present! the most welcome he could have made me, unless it had been the original himself. With it [came] brother Shandy's, which, he says, may serve as a sort of foil to the other. Much praise is due to the painter. He has done his work well, and I don't wonder he says his hall is stripped of its greatest ornament. Brother has promised he shall have it again, after it has made me a visit.

Tuesday [May] 5th. Dark dull morning. Rose early to help Ruth warp, and put a piece in the loom. . . . .

Wednesday 6th. Mr. West called to see me and my picture.

Thursday 7th. Fast-Day. Attend all day. Mr. Eckley led our devotions, and in a very serious engaging manner. In the afternoon entertained by the divine West, whom it is a pleasure to see and musick to hear—from whose lips drop serious and important truths with so much ease, and yet with so much energy that they must turn a deaf ear who are not entertained. . . . . .

Sunday, 10th. Brother Joe . . . . brought me a letter which had laid in the office since Wednesday evening, when Mrs. Breck got hers. Brother Isaac [Davenport] sent for mine, but the post-master denied there was one.

Saturday [May] 16th. Mr. Cobb called to tell me of the safe arrival of my friend in Baltimore.

Monday, 18th. Engaged in baking and hackling yarn.

Tuesday, 19th. . . . . . At 7 Mr. P. Parker arrived at our wharf loaded with fresh and corned salmon, and the gentlemen from far and near flocked around the boat like flies about a molasses hogshead in August. . . . . . . Daddy sent for me to take an airing with him. I cheerfully accepted. A delightful ride round the [Jamaica] Pond. . . . . . . My good neighbors Tuckerman and Cunningham and Major Davis called to see me. . . . . . . Preparing the children for election . . . they crazy after they know not what.

Friday, 29th. A long web of mine to whiten and weave.

Monday, June 1st. [Artillery Election-day.] Sent Hannah to carry the little girls to the common. They returned safe, but tired out, and that we all are. . . . . . . Have received another letter which has done me good, and determined me to write at all events.

Friday [June] 5th. President Wheelock [of Dartmouth Col. where her son Frederick then was], his handsome nephew, and Mr. Ticknor here in the evening. . . . . . . Cut out my girls' gloves, set them to work, and left them to take care of the house.

Sunday, 14th.   Afternoon, all hands went, and the house was locked. After reading and catechising the children, went into mammy's, and drank tea with brother Joseph and aunt Williams.

. . . . . . 17th.   Mr. Ticknor came and breakfasted with me.   Sister Dawes dined with me, and towards evening we adjourned to Polly's [Mrs. Davenport] and drank tea.

. . . . . . Afternoon, we had father ——— of ——— who rolled and bellowed as if he had the *ma-lé-grubbles*, or, as many thought, as if he were in liquor.

Saturday, July 4th.   The day ushered in by ringing of bells as usual, and concluded with demonstrations of joy and hilarity to which we are accustomed.   Our girls attend the orations.

Wednesday, 8th.   Getting the boys ready for visitation, which came in proper time, and was attended by a large company of our first characters; and those who speak their impressions say that Mr. Ticknor and his scholars bore away the laurels of the evening. . . . . . The girls making gloves for their aunt Archbald. . . .

Sunday, 12th.   Agreeably entertained by Mr. Stillman.

July 16th.   Spent the forenoon in writing to President Wheelock and Fred,* by Mr. Kirkland who brought me letters.

Saturday, 18th.   A gentleman came in who said he had a letter for me from Marietta.   Oh, how my heart leaped for joy!   Disappointment, instead of a cordial from my friend, I find an old letter from Col. Batelle!

July 29th.   All meet with Misses Byles.   Had an agreeable visit. . . . . On my return, found a letter, to my great joy.   But am distressed when I think of the hardships and dangers he has encountered; but will strive to possess my soul in calmness, recommending him to the care of that universal parent whose arm is not shortened, nor his ear heavy—an ever present help in time of trouble.

30th.   Girls at Noddle's Island.

Aug. 14th.   Mrs. Breck has a letter which she sent me to read.

Monday, 17th.   Sitting busy with my needle, who should come in but Mr. Leach, with a packet that afforded me a feast indeed.   Mrs. Breck, after dinner, came up with hers, and we enjoyed our letters together.

20th.   Brother Cravath brought me a letter which gave me very mixed sensations.   Was rejoiced to know my friend was well but twenty days before; but deeply grieved he should be kept in ignorance of the state of his family, which is so dear to him,—especially when I had taken so much pains and pleasure in forwarding particulars to him.

August 26th.   Harry W[illiams] called to tell me Mr. Walcott is going to Marietta.   Gladly embrace the opportunity to write to my friend.

September 1st.   A large kettle of yarn to attend upon.

September 2nd.   Lucretia [Dana] and self rinse out through many waters, get out, dry, attend to, bring in, do up, and sort 110 score of yarn . . . . this with baking and ironing.

The journal ends as abruptly as the other, with Friday, September 5th.

Meanwhile, Col. John, on his journey to Marietta on the Ohio, across the

---

* Frederic May grad. H. C. 1792, died in Washington, D. C., 1847.   Mr. Kirkland was afterwards the Rev. Dr. Kirkland, president of Harvard College.

then wilderness of Pennsylvania, with his partners Messrs. Breck and Downer, on horseback most of the time, so ill he could not eat, after encountering any amount of fatigue from roads so bad that the horses were mired up to their bellies, and infinite trouble from the almost impossibility of procuring wagons to transport their merchandise; finding the season about 20 days later than it was the year before, when he was in that region; hearing on the road of fearful outrages and massacres by the Indians in the region to which his steps are bent; in short, after every imaginable experience from bad fare, bad air, and bad lodging; but having had "one notable breakfast at least of coffee, bacon, mackerel, bread and butter, and buckwheat cakes"; after these and diverse other experiences and adventures, Col. John had passed the "Forks of Yah," and arrived at Redstone, a place about 16 miles up the Monongahela. In crossing the Laurel Mountains, the snow two inches thick, and the ground very frosty every morning. It was now Saturday, May 23d, and arriving at Kirkendall's, thoroughly tired out, he was obliged to take for a sleeping place an old log house, with three beds on the floor, and eight people to sleep there as they could; but whatever he might think of his lodging, he was soothed to sleep by the barking of dogs and the howling of wolves. Talking with the people he finds them much frightened by the cold weather.

And now comes the culminating disaster of the season. He had arrived out at Pittsburg, but there, hearing nothing of his partners or of the wagons, after a while, all sick and weary as he was, he threw himself on horseback, and retraced a considerable portion of the way to find them and hurry them forward. On the 3d of June, having found them, and stopping to feed after a stage of the journey, news comes of an appalling nature;—"a violent hurricane near the Redstone last Saturday"—"half the trees on the Alleghany Mountains blown down," they learn. By and by, on the next day, ahead of the wagons he reaches the "outskirts of the devastation"— "such a scene as it was!" "what had been a dense forest of lofty trees thrown down, half of them, in a thousand ways"—a "black walnut tree that was 136 feet high, three feet through, sound and thrifty as tree could be, broken short off 5 ft. 3 in. from the ground, the small limbs mere crumbles, and the larger ones broken into fire wood"—near by a house unroofed, and the orchard and other trees in the vicinity prostrate. He tries to force a passage through, a farmer of the region going ahead, and endeavoring to clear the way with an axe; but after penetrating a quarter of a mile, they find it will be of no use to make further attempts—they could not work through without long delay; and so "the prospect of all his plans failing, his nerves are shook to pieces, and he goes to his bed sick, sick." He "stood, looked, then turned," lifted up his voice and wept, "O God, how infinite art thou, how frail and weak are we!" "Forty-three days of wearing anxiety, of almost incessant fatigue, and here at last shut out."

The result is, all their plans must be changed. They turned down to a place called Little Redstone, purchased an old "Kentuck boat," put their goods aboard, and there, owing to the lowness of the waters, were obliged to stay for weeks. After a time, finding there is not enough for them all to do, they dissolve partnership, and Col. May working along little by little as he is able, brings up at last at Wheeling, Virginia, on the Ohio; and there taking ginseng and skins of various kinds for money, stays till late in the Fall, when he once more retraces his way homewards, and 16th December arrives back again in Boston. He had had a hard, at times almost desperate, struggle in trying to "hold Colley by the tail" [melancholy by the tail], sick most of the time, three months and more from home before he got his first letter, making one excursion through the woods on foot, with others, the crowing of the cocks, signals made by the Indians, on every side apprised them that bands of savages were surrounding and watching them; but he was not to be conquered; he might be "cast down," like the apostle, but was of too tough stuff to be "subdued."

Near the close of this season of trials and disappointments, musing in the solitude of the night in his lonely shanty by the banks of the Ohio, we find him indulging in the following train of meditation:

"But I will not complain of my lot; for was I not like the rest of my race, born to trouble, even as the sparks fly upward? Whither can I flee from the hurry of business, or whither shall I go from anxiety and care? If I go to the Western waters, behold it is there; if I return to Boston, lo it is there; if I take the wings of a ship, and escape to the uttermost parts of the sea, even there still its hand will lead me, and its right hand shall hold possession of me. So, on the whole, it is best to keep on attending to duty, not fretting with what cannot be helped, and seeking to be content with what is allotted. However, it is much easier to talk about resignation than to practise it.

Col. May lived nearly twenty-three years after this, dying at his home at the North End, in the midst of the war of 1812, at a time of complete prostration of business in Boston, when ships were literally "rotting at the wharves," but continuing an indefatigable worker to the very last.

On the morning of his last day alive, he arose earlier than his wont, and, in rather better spirits than usual, washed, went to the barber's and to the market, and sent home his purchases. After breakfast, of which he partook with good relish (so wrote his widow to her daughter Mrs. Edes, then living in Providence), "he went into the garden, pulled up weeds, and cut down some tansy he found growing there. After that he went out again, and made more purchases, sending home vegetables, strawberries and cherries. Thence (being one of the Selectmen) he went to lay out a street for the pavers to work on; and was here joined by a number of friends and associates, who invited him to go up to Faneuil Hall with them (it being then about 11 o'clock). He replied, he must first go to the wharf, and then would join them. W. R. [William Rufus, one of his sons] was employed there with laborers dismantling a brig, and putting a roof over the decks. He stood and talked with them some time, and then retired to his counting room." In half an hour more he was found by his son lying under his desk insensible. Help was rallied at once, and he was sent home in a carriage. Dr. Ingalls, who happened to be near at hand, plied him with restoratives suitable to the case, and Dr. Warren, his family physician, was at once sent for; but to no favorable result. He continued to sink, and at 2½ on the morning of July 16th breathed his last.

Thus ended a life of great activity and energy, not crowned with so great success as many, but having its hearty enjoyments and satisfactions for all that; never degenerating into moping and despondency, let what would happen. Thus passed away from the world a man, who if,—like our New-England climate,—having rigors and rough points which might try those who approached him sometimes, had also his many virtues, not the least of which was his kindly and generous nature.

EARLY SETTLERS OF WEST SPRINGFIELD.

Transcribed from the Parish Records of the First Congregational Church, by
LYMAN H. BAGG.

[Continued from vol. xxix. page 289.]

17. The 17th Lot is to Francis Ball. Quantity ten acres　Length 80 Rods Bredth 20 Rods. bounded on the North by Pelati. Jones.

18. The 18th Lot to Captt Ball ten acres, length 80 Rods Bredth 20 Rods, bounded Notherly by Francis Ball.

19. The 19th Lot is to Jams Tailer Senr ten acres　Bredth 20 Rods length 80 Rods　Bounded notherly by Captt Ball, Southerly by a highway four Rods wide.

Then lyeth the high way four Rods wide.

20. The 20th lot Is to John Ely　Quantitye ten acres　Length 80 Rods Bredth 20 Rods. bounded North by the high way.

Att a meeting of the proprieters Legaly warned Janur 16th $17\frac{20}{21}$ Left. John Day chosen Moderator　Att this meeting It was voted that the lot which was drawn by Christian Vanhorne & by him Released (bounded Northerly by John Ely south by Jnº Lenord and in Number the 21 lot) should be & is given to Samll Ely　And shal be to him in lew of the lot that he Drew which land is in the Division at the top of the hill which lot is in Quantitye ten acres　And the Last lot is to John Lenord　Bounded on the North by Samll Ely : And containeth all the Remainder of the land belonging to that division which is yet undisposed off of the land granted to be laid out into whom lots.

Jany 16th $17\frac{20}{21}$. Att a meeting of the propriety It was voted that Ebenr Scot have his lot which is belongeing to him In that Division att chickely on the east side of the way on the Brook next to his own whom lot.

Voted that Mr Patrick Marshal have a lot provided for him according to the condition in the grant made by the town to provide for such as Came to us.

Voted that John Bag junr have his lot on the north side of his fathers lot on the east side of the Comon Rhoade in Chickely tear of division.

Voted That the land that is to be divided to those persons for whom we are to provide lots for : be distributed by a comitey.

And Serjatt Bag Wm Scot and Captt Downeing ware chosen to be the Comitey for the worck to divide the sd land to them for whom we are to provide lots for.

Voted That The heyres of Richard Excel have a lot divided to them.

Memorandum.　Febr 28, $17\frac{20}{21}$. Ebenezer Scot hath his lot or his ten acres laid out to him according to the Above vote　it is Bound Easterly By his own land westerly by lands of John Fowler & James Tailer : Northerly by the high way & Southerly by the top of the hill so as to Include & take all the swamp on dorbeys Brook Ranging with Fowlers land.

Memorandum ; Haveing drawn for the Lots.

Ano Jan. 30th $17\frac{20}{21}$. The lots in the first divisions ware laid out by the town Measurer : But the Rest of the land was laid out by the Commitey according to the vote of the proprieters who chose men to lay out & divide the land according to their order.

And all the lots folowing ware appointed and laid out by the s^d comitey who to gether with the Town Measuerer have laid out the s^d land in manner as is hereafter Recorded.   And the lots are divided first to the petitioners : and then to Such as Come to Inhabite & dwel in this precinct according to to the vote of the town; And every lot Respectively is laid out according to the order and appointment of the commitey.

An Acount of the Divideing of the Land Below Aggowam River Janu^y 21 17$\frac{2}{3}\frac{1}{0}$.

And first with Respect to the high ways   There is a highway Ten Rods wide that Runs away south east acros the land which is to be laid out. for the conveniency of out let from Sam^ll Coopers—And the lots west to aggowam will But on the said high way   And from the s^d Cros high way ther is laid out a highway twenty Rods wide which goeth from aggowam toward westfield and the lots But on each side the high way : by the Commitey : Ordered.

1. and the first lot on the east side of the said small high way is divided to Left John Day And is in Quantity ten acres About seventeen Rods wide bounded on the north west Partly by the high way and Comon land & partly by the land now Sam^ll Bodorthas, and is in length about one hundred Rods extending from the old grants or whom lots belongeing to aggowam and buts on the said small high way.

2. And the Next lot Is to John Day Jun ten acres bounded by his father on the northwest side and is in length about one hundred Rods Bredth sixteen Rods   the land is In length from the high way to the whom lots att aggowam.

3. The third lot is to Sam^ll Day Junr ten acres being in length about one hundred Rod from the way to the lots att aggowam : & in width It is sixteen Rods. bound by John Day Northwest.

4. The Next Lot is to Deacon Barber Deceased ten acres   In length from the way to the whomlots A bout one hundred Rods, & sixteen Rods wide bounded by Sam^ll Day on the northwest.

5. The fifth Lot is to Thos Barber Deceased ten acres   In Length from the whom lots to the high way one hundred Rods, width sixteen Rods.

6. The sixth lot is to Joseph Lenord ten acres.   Length from the highway to his own land 56 Rods width from —— to the top of the hill below the bro brook att the end next the way about 38 Rod wide.

Ther is three lots that ly west which are divided to Joseph Bodurtha jun^r Thos Bodurtha and Benjamin Bodurtha each ten acres which extend to the end of that division.

One that side of the great high way which is Southerly the lots begin to Number next to aggowam ; or easterly & goe westward.

1. The first lot is to James Stevenson Senr & is in Quantitye ten acres : lyeing in length 100 Rods by the little highway & 16 Rods wide by the great high way that goeth toward westfield.

2. The second lot is to James Stevenson Junr & is in Quantitye ten acres 100 Rods long & 16 wide.

3. The third lot is to Gersham Hail Senr ten acres one hundred Rod long from the street to the Comon and sixteen Rod wide.

4. The fourth lot is to Benjam^n Hail ten acres one hundred Rod long and Sixteen Rod wide.

5. The fifth lot is to John Barber ten acres one hundred Rod long & Sixteen Rod wide.

6. The Sixth lot is to Josiah Lenord John Hail ten acres one hundred Rod long and sixteen wide.

7. The Seventh lot is to Isack Frost ten acres from the highway to Sam[ll] Coopers land it is in length sixtey Rod & in width twenty seven Rod.

8. The eighth lot is to Sam[ll] Cooper ten acres In length sixtey Rods & in Bredth twenty seven Rods.

9. The ninth lot is to Joseph Coulton ten acres In length sixtey Rods & In Bredth twenty seven Rods.

10. The tenth lot is to John Fowler jun[r] ten acres In length eighty Rods & In Bredth twenty Rods.

11. The eleventh Lot is Eben[r] Lenord jun[r] ten acres In length eighty Rods and in Bredth twenty Rods.

12. The twelfth lot to Benjam[n] Ball ten acres In length eighty Rod and in width twenty Rods.

13. The thirteenth lot is to John White ten acres In length eighty Rods & in width twenty Rods.

14. The fourteenth lot is to Dan[ll] Coley ten acres In length eighty Rods & in width twenty Rods.

15. The fifteenth lot is to John Stevenson ten acres In length eighty Rods & in width twenty Rods.

16. The 16th Lot is divided to John Frost ten Acres 80 Rods Long 20 Rods Broad fronting on the Rhoad that goeth to Westfield.

17. The Next lot is to Richard Excel Ten acres 80 Rods Long 20 Rods Broad.

18. The eighteenth lot is to Caleb Parsons ten acres Butting on the great highway that goeth to westfield.

Memorandum That the Comittey order that the highway which is specified on the other side to be Between Sam Millers 2 lots Is wrong and the highway is to ly Below Booth those lots between Sam[ll] Frost & Sam[ll] Miller.

Jan[y] y[e] 21 17$\frac{29}{20}$. 1. The first Lot on the North side of the street which is twenty Rods wide and goeth towards westfield Is Divided And Ordered by the Comitey to be unto Joseph Lenord Sen[r] Deceased Quantity ten acres Bounded by the highway on two sides (viz.) Notherly or rather North east & Southerly or South east. on the easterly side 40 Rods on the southerly side About 54 Rods And westerly 22 Rods.

2. The Second lot is to Sam[ll] Lenord Deceased Quantity ten acres; By the high way 44 Rods and in length [About] the high way to the hill.

3. The third lot Sam[ll] Bodurtha Sen[r] Ten acres fronting on the high way. And bounded on the Reear by the Brow of the hill or Land Belongeing to the Lenords.

4. The fourth lot is to Jams Mireck jun[r] ten acres In length 50 Rods. Bredth 32 Rods.

5. The fifth lot is to Patrick Marshal ten acres bounded easterly by James Mirek In length from the highway to Benjam[n] Lenords land 54 Rods and in width 30 Rods.

And in the next Place the lots are turned faceing westerly.

1. And the Lot Next the Corner is to Joseph Bodurtha jun[r] Deceased Ten acres In length lyeing easterly 30 Rods Butting against a high that lyeth Notherly 20 Rods wide The high way that the lot fronts against runeth a Cros the Plain Notherly & Southerly this lot is 80 Rods long and 20 Rods wide.

2. The next lot is to Joseph Miller ten acres fronting on s^d high way Runeing easterly to Benjam^n Lenords land In length 80 Rods & is in width 20 Rods.

3. The third lot from the Corner is to Ensighn John Miller ten acres 80 Rods long & 20 Rods wide Buting on the s^d highway & Runeing easterly to Benjam^n Lenords land.

4. The fourth lot to Robert Old Senr Ten acres 80 Rods long and 20 Rods wide.

5. The Next Lot Is to Jonathan Ball Junr ten acres 80 Rods long 20 Rods wide.

6. Next is Eben^r Lenord Senr his lot ten acres 80 Rods long 20 Rods wide.

7. Thos Miller Senr hath the Next Lot 10 acres 80 Rods long 20 Rods wide. lyeing next to the highway goeing westerly from Benjam^n Lenords.

In the next Place are the lots that ly on the westerly side of the way that Runs across ye Plain.

1. And the first Lot Next to westfield Rhode is to Benjamin Miller 10 acres Butting easterly on the s^d highway Runeing westerly 80 Rods in length And 20 Rods wide.

2. the Second lot from the Corner is to John huggin 10 acres 80 Rods long & 20 Rods wide.

3. next is Jona^th Old his lot 10 acrs 80 Rods long 20 wide.

4. then Sam^ll Huggins his lot 10 acrs 80 Rods long 20 Rod wide.

5. next Joseph Ball his lot 10 acrs 80 Rod long 20 wide.

6. John Younglove his lot is 10 acres 80 Rods Long 20 wide.

Next Abel Lenord Senr his lot 10 acres 80 Rod long 20 D.

Then a high way eight Rods wide Runeing westerly And on the North side of the said high way is laid out 2 lots each 10 acres to Hezekiah Day And to Milse [?] Morgan extending from s^d high way to the Lenords land Hezekiah Days lot to ly next to Jonses dingle.

Memorandum. Josiah Lenords land Runs up with a narow slip to his own land: But this land is originaley to John Haill as is his proper Right & coms to Josiah Lenord by exchang & so is John Hails proper lot And Josiah Lenords Proper lot is in that division of Land against chickebey field and Is accordingly Recorded to him. And it was a mistake that the sixth lot on the other side was entered to Josiah Lenord.

The Land att Chickeby is Divided and Distributed as foloweth It is to Bee Remembred that ther is a high way twenty Rods wide from Dorbeys Brook to the upper end of chickeby field thru the midest of the land to be divided and the lots on Booth sides the way but on the street and the lots are Numbred begineing at the east side of the way going Northward from dorbey Brook.

1. And the first lot in that division is to Sam^ll Frost which is fortey Rods wide att that end next the high way and is in length eighty Rods but is very Narow & comes almost to a point att the east end. Quantity ten acres.

2. The second is to Sam^ll Miller jun^r Quantity ten acres In length eighty Rods and in Bredth twenty Rods In the next place is a high way twenty Rods wide.

3. The next lot on the north side of the high way is to Sam^ll Miller Senr and is in length from the high way to the whom lots belongeing to chickebey. In width seventeen Rods Conteineing ten acres.

4. The fourth lot is to Sam[ll] Bodortha jun[r] ten acres Seventeen Rods in width and in length from the high way to the top of the hill.

5. The fifth lot is to Sam[ll] Tailer jun[r] Quantity ten acres In width seventeen Rods. And in length from the high way to the tope of the hill.

6. The sixth is to Jonathan Bag conteineing ten acres and is In length from the high way to the tope of the hill and is in width sixteen Rods.

7. The Seventh lot is to Sam[ll] Kent ten acres In length one hundred & twelve Rods and in width It is fifteen Rods.

8. The eighth lot is to Nath[ll] Morgan sen[r] ten acres In length on hundred & twelve Rods width fifteen Rods.

9. The ninth lot is to Serja[t] John Bag. ten acres In width thirty Rods & a half, and fifty Rods in length.

10. The tenth lot is to John Bag jun[r] ten acres In length thirty Rods & a half. Bredth. I am wrong The length is fiftey Rods. Bredth is thirtye rod & a half These two lots are in length from the high way to the Lands formerly given to John Bag In the next place is a high way twenty Rods wide.

11. The next lot on the north side the high way is to Natha[ll] Sykes and is in Quantitye ten acres in length nintey Rod—Bredth eighteen Rods.

12. The twelfth lot is to Pelatiah Morgan ten acres In length nintey Rods. Bredth eighteen Rods.

All these lots are on the east side the great high way. And stil continueing on the east side the way.

13. The next lot which is in Number thirteen from the begineing of this division is to Sam[ll] Barker conteineing ten acres length one hundred Rods Bredth sixteen Rods.

14. The fourteenth lot is to Jams Barcker ten acres In length one hundred Rods: Bredth sixteen Rods.

15. The fifteenth lot is to John Petey ten acres In length from the high way to the field one hundred Rods and Bredth sixteen Rods.

16. The sixteenth lot is to Josiah Lenord ten acres In length from the field to the high way one hundred Rods Bredth sixteen Rods.

17. The seventeenth lot is to John Rogers ten acres. Length on hundred Rods Bredth sixteen Rods.

18. The eighteenth lot is to Henry Rogers Sen[r] ten acres which is thirtey two Rods wide next the high way But at the end next the field it is very narrow It is about one hundred Rods in length.

And then ther is a high way eigh Rods wide on the North side of the high way ther is a tract of About or near thirty acres which is divided by the comity to Natha[ll] Morgan jun[r] Sam[ll] Morgan and Eben[r] Morgan. each of them equaly to have his lot which land is bounded easterly By Nath[ll] Morgan Sen[r] westerly the high way Notherly By William Scot and Southerly By that high way that coms from the field.

In the Next place is William Scots lot ten acres Bounded by his own land Easterly By the high way westerly By Morgans southerly and by Samuell Millers Land Notherly Including a slipe of land pointeing Notherly Between Sam[ll] Millers land and his own land.

There is two Lots divided by the Comitey to Gersham Hail jun[r] And to Nathaniel Bancroft each lot conteining ten acres Being the two last lots on the east side of the way or east tear lyeing at the upper end of the field By or on the Brook. It is to be Remembred that ther is a high way of four Rods wide on the Southerly side or below the s[d] two lots which high way Runneth from the field to the great high way.

In the next place is an a Count of the divideing of that tear of lots on the west side of the high way or street And the Number begins from that end next dorbeys Brook going Notherly.

1. and the first lot is bounded by Sam^ll Ball Southerly and is in width twenty Rods & In length Eighty Rods And is to Benjamin Stebbins Quantity ten acres and Then a high way twenty Rods wide.

2. The next lot on the North side of the high way is to Charls Fery and is the second lot on that tear eighty Rod long. twenty rod wide ten acres.

3. The third lot is to Benjam^n Parsons ten acres In length eighty Rods Bredth twenty Rods.

4. The fourth lot is to Thos Miller jun^r In width twenty Rods Bredth : Length eighty Rods.

5. The next lot which is the fifth in that tear ten acres and by the Comity ordered to The Revd Mr Sam^ll Hopkins : Length eighty Rod : Bredth twenty Rods.

6. The sixth lot is to Henry Rogers jun^r ten acres In length eighty Rods Bredth twenty Rods.

7. The seventh lot is to Joseph Bodurtha sen^r ten acres Length êighty Rods from the street to the Comon. width 20 Rod.

8. Joseph Barcker hath a lot divided to him which lyeth on the South side of the high way a three cornered peice Bounded on the high way or street easterly. westerly on his fathers land. formerly [?] Clement [?]

And Then the lots are interupted by the land Now belongeing to the Barckers and ther is a high way twenty Rods wide on the Northerly side of the said Barcker land And now the lots shall be Numbred from the Notherly side of that high way : goeing Notherly.

1. and the first lot on the north side of the said high way is to John Miller jun^r ten acres In length eighty Rod Bredth twenty Rods.

2. The second lot is to Cap^tt Nath^ll Downeing ten acres in length eighty Rods. In Bredth twenty Rods.

3. The 3^d lot is to Ebenezer Ashly Deceased ten acres Length eighty Rods. Bredth twenty Rods.

4. The fourth lot is to Joseph Ashly Deceased ten Acres Length eighty Rods. Bredth twenty Rods.

5. The fifth lot is to Oliver Barcker ten acres length eighty Rods Bredth twenty Rods.

The Number is wrong The Seventh lot is the sixth & ye 8th ye 7th & so on.

7. The seventh Lot is to Sam^ll Fery ten acres In length from the high way to the Comon 80 Rods and in width twenty Rods.

8. The 8th lot is to Jona^th Bag jun^r Quantity ten acres In length eighty Rod. Bredth twenty Rods.

9. The ninth Lot is to Benj^m Ashly ten acres In length eighty Rods. Bredth twenty Rods.

10. The tenth Lot is to Josiah Miller ten acres In length eighty Rod. Bredth twenty Rods.

11. The eleventh Lot is to Mark Fery ten acres In length eighty Rods. Bredth twenty Rods.

12. The twelfth Lot is to John Hooker Bredth twenty Rods Length eighty Rods Ten acres Bounded Southerly by a high way twenty Rods wide

13. The next Lot is to John Bodurtha Ten acres which is narow att that end next the high way & wider next the woods : & is bounded easterly partly By John Bag Senr and partly By the high way : Length westerly eighty Rods.

It is to be Remembred that the lots are wrong Numbred the 6ᵗʰ lot is omitted & the seventh Put in the Place of the sixth and the 8 should have been the seventh lot & the 9ᵗʰ the 8ᵗʰ & the 10ᵗʰ the 9ᵗʰ & yᵉ 11ᵗʰ yᵒ 10ᵗʰ & yᵉ 12ᵗʰ yᵉ 11ᵗʰ & the 13ᵗʰ lot is But the 12ᵗʰ lot.

Memorandum. That ther is a highway twenty Rods wide Between Mark Ferys lot and John Hooker to Run from the great high way westerly into the woods.

———————

BIRTHS, MARRIAGES AND DEATHS, FROM THE RECORDS OF THE ANCIENT TOWN OF DARTMOUTH, MASS.

Transcribed for the REGISTER by JAMES B. CONGDEN, Esq., of New-Bedford.

[Continued from vol. xxii. page 69.]

BIRTHS.

Spooner, Simson,	s. of Isaac		Jan. 12, 1699
" Edward,	s. of "		Dec. 27, 1701
" Mercy,	d. of "		April 22, 1707
Waite, John,	s. of Thomas		Nov. 30, 171–
" Reuben,	s. of "		Feb. 7, 1713
" Thomas,	s. of "		Feb, 29, 1715–16
" Mary,	d. of "		April 5, 1718
" Meribah,	d. of "		July 20, 1720
" Mehitable,	d. of "		Nov. 18, 1722
" Martha,	d. of "		April 6, 1725
Slade, Ruth,	d. of Joseph and Deborah		April 14, 1762
Pequit, Thomas,	s. of James and Alice		June 23, 1773
" Lydia,	d. of " "		Aug. 17, 1775
Claghorn, Prince,	s. of Joseph and Elizabeth		Aug. 22, 1752
" Elizabeth	d. of " "		May 4, 1754
Mosher, William,	s. of James		March 24, 1715
" Timothy,	s. of "		Oct. 27, 1716
" Jonathan,	s. of "		May 9, 1718
" David,	s. of "		March 29, 1720
" Jeremiah,	s. of "		June 16, 1722
Sog Sarah,	d. of John and Rebecca		April 25, 1729
" Thomas,	s. of " "		Feb. 25, 1730–31
" Hannah,	d. of " "		June 6, 1733
" Mary,	d. of " "		Oct. 26, 1735
" Timothy,	s. of " "		Oct. 23, 1738
Tripp, George,	s. of John		June 16, 1716
" Timothy,	s. of "		Feb. 22, 1717
" Ruth,	d. of "		April 4, 1720
" Elizabeth,	d. of "		Aug. 23, 1722
" Rebeccah,	d. of "		July 27, 1724
" Hannah,	d. of " and Hannah		Aug. 25, 1738
" Mary,	d. of " "		March 20, 1741
Gifford, Silas,	s. of Adam and Ann		Nov. 4, 1747
" Peace,	d. of " "		Oct. 25, 1750
" William,	s. of " "		July 28, 1755

Tripp,	Thomas,	s. of James		Oct. 9, 1710
"	William,	s. of "		Feb. 27, 1712–13
"	Timothy,	s. of "		Oct. 22, 1716
"	Mary,	d. of "		Oct. 14, 1720
"	Isaac,	s. of "		Jan. 2, 1726–7

Taber, Jonathan, Grand-
son to Philip Taber, } s. of Jonathan and Robey   March 20, 1735
of Coaksit, minister,

Taber,	Margaret,	d. of Jonathan and Robey		July 10, 1740
"	Gardner,	s. of "	"	May 20, 1742
"	Benjamin,	s. of "	"	Feb. 20, 1747
"	Peleg,	s. of "	"	Jan. 27, 1751
"	Eseck,	s. of "	"	Nov. 5, 1755

[Note.—With each of these records the fact is connected that they were grand children of Philip Taber, of Coaksit, or Acoaksit, minister.]

Taber,	Thomas,	s. of * * Taber		Oct. 22, 1668
"	Esther,	d. of "		April 17, 1671
"	Lydia,	d. of "		Aug. 8, 1673
"	Mary,	d. of "		March 18, 1677
"	Joseph,	s. of "		March 7, 1679
"	John,	s. of "		Feb. 22, 1681
"	Jacob,	s. of "		July 26, 1683
"	Jonathan,	s. of "		Sept. 22, 1685
"	Bethiah,	d. of "		Sept. 3, 1687
"	Philip,	s. of "		Feb. 1689
"	Abigail,	d. of "		May 1693
"	Sarah,	d. of "		Jan. 1674

[Note by recorder—the 4th is last by mistake.]

[The record is so worn that the name of the father of the foregoing twelve children cannot be ascertained. The name of the first (?) child is obliterated, but the entry that follows the above gives Thomas Taber the son of Thomas *above*.]

Taber,	Pricilia,	d. of Thomas		June 28, 1701
"	Jonathan,	s. of "		Feb. 24, 1702–3
"	Amaziah,	s. of "		July 9, 1704
"	Esther,	d. of "		March 6, 1709–10
"	Mary,	d. of "		Nov. 12, 1711
"	Samuel,	s. of "		Dec. 4, 1714
"	Seth,	s. of "		July 5, 1719
"	Peace,	d. of Thomas (son of Joseph) & Ruth		Nov. 5, 1745
"	Ruth,	d. of "	"	May 7, 1748
Akin,	Davin (?)	s. of John		Sept. 1689
"	Susan,	d. of "		Jan. 1, 1691
"	Deborah,	d. of "		Dec. 30, 1692
"	Timothy,	s. of "		Jan. 1, 1694
"	Mary,	d. of "		Jan. 23, 1697
"	Hannah,	d. of "		March 12, 1699
"	Thomas,	s. of "		March 29, 1702
"	Elizabeth,	d. of "		May 23, 1704

Aken, James,	s. of John	Aug. 1, 1706
" Judith,	d. of "	Oct. 17, 1708
" Benjamin,	s. of "	May 18, 1715
" Ebenezer,	s. of "	Dec. 2, 1717
" Susanna,	d. of John and Hannah	Sept. 27, 1718
" Elihu,	s. of " "	Aug. 6, 1720
Spooner, Jemima,	d. of William	Dec. 7, 1700
" Jane,	d. of "	May 12, 1703
" Elizabeth,	d. of "	May 22, 1705
" Micah,	s. of "	April 2, 1707

A LETTER OF COL. ETHAN ALLEN.

Communicated by C. R. BATCHELDER, of Claremont, N. H.

THE history of the following letter of Col. Ethan Allen, so far as it is here known, is short. Prior to the date of it, Col. Allen had, by the permission of Congress and the consent of the legislature of New-York, exerted himself to form a regiment of Rangers. Naturally he expected to command it. When the officers were elected, however, Seth Warner was made the colonel. Allen was offended. Under the influence of passion, he wrote to the governor of New-York. Not wishing to employ him, his brother and others, he enclosed the letter to Governor Chittenden, of Vermont. In some way this letter came into the hands of Benjamin Sumner, of Claremont, N. H., and has been preserved among his papers.

"Ap^l: 14th 1781.

" SIR,

This with the intelegence of Capt: Putnam will give your Exellency to understand that Col^o: Ebenezer Allen, Capt: Jesse Sawyer, Lt. Nathaniel Holmes and myself are put out of Military Command in the state of Vermont—we are so Conceited as to Immagin that Vermont has not timber to supply our places—however this is a task Which Belongs to those Gentlemen in power to determin . . in the mean time propose to your Exellency not only for my self but those Gentlemen before Mentioned to engage in the service of New-York . . we think the proposals honorable wheather Complied with or no. Not withstanding the heretofore disputations which have subsisted between us and the Government of New-York we shall Esteam it the greatest happiness of our lives (lastly) to Defend the state of New-York against all her Cruel Envadors.

I am sir with due Respect,

To his Exellency
  Henry F. Clinton
  Governor of the state
  of New-York.

Your Exellencys most
  Humb^l & Obed^t
  Servt
  ETHAN ALLEN."

CHURCH RECORDS OF THE REV. HUGH ADAMS.

PRINCIPALLY AT OYSTER RIVER PARISH (NOW DURHAM), N. H.

Communicated by the Hon. SAMUEL C. ADAMS, of West Newfield, Me.

[Continued from vol. xxiv. page 29.]

1719.   BAPTISMS, &c.

Nov. 1st. Elizabeth Davis, wife of L* Col. James Davis; James Davis, her
   eldest son; Ephraim Davis, her youngest son.
" " Sarah Hicks.
" " Hannah Chesley, wife of Philip.
" " Hannah ⎫
" " Elizabeth ⎬ Davis, Maidens.
" " Phebe ⎭
" 8. Joseph Kent, son of Joseph Kent.
" 15. John Doe; Abigail Davis, wife of John; Mary Perkins, wife of
   Samuel, Francisca Perkins, their 2d Daughter.
" 22. Thomas Footman; Elizabeth Footman, his wife; Francis, Thomas [and] Elizabeth Footman, their children.
" 29. At the New Meetinghouse I baptized the children of John Doe
   and wife, namely:

     Daniel ⎫
     John   ⎪ Doe. Adult
     Joseph ⎬ their sons
     Benjamin ⎭
     Mary   ⎫ . Adult
     Elizabeth ⎬ Doe, their daughters
     Martha ⎭ a child in minority.

" " Martha Doe, the adult daughter of Samson.
Dec. 17. At a Lecture at Loverland, on account of her faith and engagement for its education, our sister Sarah Bennick, having an
   infant maid servant born in her house of a Negro father and
   Indian mother, had her baptized
         Mary Robinson.
" 20. Elizabeth Davis, sister of David Davis.
" 27. At Stratham, Joseph Merrill.
1719–20.
Jan'y 3. At Oyster River in Dover, Josiah Dun.
" 11. At the Garrison House, second Falls, James Tilley, the infant
   son of James Tilley.
" 17. Robert Huckins.
Feb'y 7. Samuel Perkins.
" 14. Jonathan Woodman and Elizabeth his wife, with John, Jonathan [and] Joshua Woodman, their adult sons; Edward,
   Downing, [and] Archelaus, sons in nonage; Mary, adult;
   Alice, in nonage.
" 28. Susanna Smith, wife of L* John Smith, and her children:—
   John Smith Junr ⎫ of age
   Joseph Smith ⎭

Samuel
Benjamin
Ebenezer } Smith in Nonage
Winthrop

Feb. 28.   Hannah Smith, of age.
" "   James Gooden, of age.
March 6.   John Crommet and Mary his wife and their young children: Philip [and] Elizabeth Crommet, twins; Margaret.
" "   William Pitman and Joanna his wife and their little children, Abigail, Dorcas and William Pitman.
" "   Samuel Willey and Sarah Willey his wife and their little children, Samuel and Sarah Willey, and Sarah Williams, her sister's little daughter in their family; William Willey, Mary Willey.
" 17.   Anne Knock, inf* dau* of James.
" "   Elizabeth Davis, inf* dau. of David Davis.
" 20.   Sarah Chesley, an aged Widow.
" "   Sarah Footman, Elderly wife of John.
" "   Margaret Stevenson, wife of B* Joseph Stevenson; Joseph Stevenson, their infant son.

1720.
April 10.   John Willey, son of Wm. Willey.
" 24.   William Turner, formerly a strong Quaker, as his parents and education influenced him in Old England, but now a Christian (I hope), servant to Philip Chesley.
" 10.   Abigail Hill, inf* dau* of Samuel Hill.
May 1.   James Head, illegit* son of Sarah Blanchard.
Dec. 25.   Nath* Meder, Batchelour.
" "   Elizabeth Meder, his sister, Maiden.
" 29.   William, servant of Ruth Williams.
" "   Eliphalet, Patience and Abigail Hill.

1720–1.
Jan'y 1.   James Huckins, John Huckins.
" 8.   Daniel Misharvey, Sen*; Daniel, Elizabeth, Mary [and] John Misharvey.
" "   John Rennolds.
" 22.   Jonathan Crosbey son of Jon*.
" "   Peter Dembo.
" 28.   John, Joseph, Nathaniel, Hannah, Elizabeth, Abigail, [and] Judith Davis, children of John Davis and wife.
" "   Wm. Jennison, 3 days old.
Feb'y 9th   Clement, Anne [and] Tamsen Misharvey.
" 12.   Mary Peveh, wife of Edward.
" 19.   Christian Willey, wife of John, Jun*.
March 2.   Anne Eliot, dau* of W** and Anne.
" 5.   Peter Mason and his daughters Hannah, Sarah and Mary Mason; Isaac Mason, his little brother.

1721.
April 30.   Samuel Chesley.
May 21.   Caleb [and] Mehitabel Wakeham, children of Edward Wakeham and wife.
" "   Thomas Jenkins, inf* son of Stephen.

May 21. Deliverance Davis.
" " George (killed by the Indians, 1724) [and] Elizabeth Chesley.
" " Sarah, Rebecca and Moses Davis.
July 16. Mary Tompson.
" " Temperance Follet, wife of Ichabod, and Abigail Follet her daughter.
" 30. Joseph Hix, and Sarah his infant dau.
Augt 6. Nathan Allen, infant of John.
" " Jamima Small, W. of Jos., and Joseph Small her infant son.
" " Judith Tasker, wife of John Tasker ; William Tasker, her inf^t son ; Elizabeth Tasker, her daughter.
" " Lydia Davis, maiden D. of David.
" 13. Joseph Drew, Jacob Wormwood.
" 14. Theodore, Thomas, Christian [and] Joanna Willey, children of John Willey Ju^n and wife.
" 27. At Portsm^o Old Meeting H. There and then I baptized Mary Sherburn, Infant dau^r of James Sherburn.
Septr 10. Aaron Edgerly, Inf^t son of Samuel.
" " Azariah, alias Hezekiah Boodey, son of Zechariah Boodey.
" 16. At Lower Falls, Lampereel River, Margaret Macdonel, Infant dau^r of Robert Macdonel.
" 17. Joshua Ambler, son of Eld. John A.
" " Joseph [and] Abigail Perkins, ch^n of Samuel P.
" " Edward Small, ye first born child of Joseph and Jamima Small.
" 28. John Rennolds, the little child of John Rennolds, his wife a Quakeress, not consenting.
" " Mary Willey, Infant of Samuel Willey.
Oct^o 8. John Sias, Junr.
" 13. Samuel Hill, Inf^t of Samuel Hill.
" 24. Elizabeth Durgin, wife of Wm. Durgin, in her childbed sickness, whereof she died about twelve hours after, had her infant baptized William Durgin.
" 29. Wm. Wormwood and his wife Martha Wormwood.
Nov. 19. Margaret Stevenson, Inf^t of Joseph Stevenson.
" 29. James Bafford, son of James Bafford.
Dec. 3. Edward Leathers ; Thomas Leathers.
" 21. Joseph [and] Hannah Catland, ch^n of Lydia Catland.
" 24. George Chesley ; Wm. Rendal, Batchelours.
" 31. Robert Huckens, Jr. ; Sarah Huckens, his sister.
1721-2.
Jan'y 28. Benjamin Davis, John Buzzell.
" " Elizabeth Bell ; Shadrach Bell her infant son.
" " Margaret Buzzel.
Feb. 11. Thomas Bickford.
" 18. Henry Tibbits.
" 25. Sarah Burnum, Dau. of John and Lydia Burnum.
Mar. 12. Abigail Laskey, Dau. of John and Abigail Laskey.
" 25. Thomas Willey, Frances Willey his wife ; Thomas [and] Stephen Willey, their children in minority.
1722.
April 1. John Buzzel, Senr.
" 8. Job Rennolds and Abigail his inf^t child.

April 15.   Sarah Williams, Dau^r of John Buzzel.
"   "   Love Nock, Infant of Eld. James Nock.
"   "   John York, Infant of John York.
"   26. Solomon Davis, a single man 26 years of age, being sick, son of
            Moses Davis.
May 13.   Joseph Jones; Joseph, Benjamin, John [and] Anthony Jones,
            adult sons; Elizabeth, Samuel [and] Richard Jones, their
            children in nonage.
"   "   Jonathan Chesley and his Infant son Jonathan Chesley.
"   "   Sarah Warner, Inf^t of Daniel Warner.
July 22.   Mary Langley, dau. of James.
"   "   Ezekiel Pitman, Inf^t of William.
"   "   Mercy Conner, Wid^w of Job.
"   "   Eleazer Davis, Inf^t of Samuel Davis.
Augt 12. Thomas Drew and Tamsen Drew his wife, they both being so
            (but profanely and idolatrously) baptized by a Popish Priest
            or Friar in their captivity, for which I had the warrant of
            Acts 19–3–5.
"   19. Joseph Bickford, John Smith.
Oct^o   7. Elizabeth Willey, Inf^t dau^r of William.
Nov. 4.   Samuel Williams.
"   8.   William Hill, Senr.
Dec. 21.   Thomas Miller, Mary Greiers.
"   "   Mary Elliot, wife of Francis; John [and] Francis Elliot, Inf^t
            sons of Francis.
"   30. Eleazer Bickford.
      1722–3.
Jan'y 2.   At Loverland, Elizabeth Doe, Infant Dau. of Samson Doe.
"   "   Jeremiah Drisco, son of Cornelius.
"   "   Hubartus Matoon, son of Richard.
"   27. James Davis, Widower.
"   "   Susanna Durgin, Maiden Dau. of James.
"   "   Samuel Mathes, Inf^t son of Benjamin.
"   28. Mary Gypson, dau. of James.
"   30. At funeral of Lt John Smith's (at Loverland) youngest son Win-
            throp, I baptized Jonathan [and] Trueworthy Durgen, sons
            of Susanna Durgin, wife of James.
      1723.
April 14.   On a fair, sunshining Lord's day, my infant Daughter, born on
            the 5th day (alias Thursday) of the week, being the 11th day
            of the second month, April, was after the name of her father's
            Godly Mother and her own Grandmother, baptized Avis
            Adams.
"   28. Sarah Pilsberry, Inf^t Dau^r of Nathan.
May   5.   Ebenezer Burnum, Inf^t son of Lydia Burnum, the wife of John
            Burnum.
"   19. Elizabeth Small, Inf^t of Joseph and Jamima Small.
"   26. John Stevenson, Inf^t of Joseph S.
"   "   Joseph Bickford, Inf^t of Joseph and Alice Bickford.

THE FURNESS PEDIGREE.

Communicated by Mrs. CAROLINE H. DALL, of Boston.

HAVING just discovered the following pedigree in a very frail condition, I copy it and send it for publication, if it should prove unpublished. This pedigree is an original brought from the old country, and made out in circles.

The possible future value of such papers is so great that I always hasten to put them in print. The original was among the papers of the late Dr. Morney, of Providence, and is now in the possession of Albert P. Ware, of Andover.

Sir HENRY FURNESS of Waldershare, Co. Kent.

I. GEORGE FURNESS, of London, merchant.
I. ANNE FURNESS, m. Mr. Williams, London, woolen draper.
I. ELISABETH FURNESS, m. Mr. John Branch, of Sandwich.
I. Sir HENRY FURNESS, m. 1st and had :
  ii. Sir ROBERT, who m. three wives and had issue by his first wife Mrs. Balaam :
    iii. ANN, who married the Lord Viscount St. John and is since dead, leaving issue :
      iv. Lord BOLINGBROKE.
      iv. Col. HENRY ST. JOHN.
      iv. JOHN ST. JOHN.
      iv. LOUISA, now wife of Sir Wm. Bagot, Baronet.
  ii. Sir ROBERT FURNESS, m. 1st, Mrs. Balaam ; 2nd, Lady Arabella Watson, by whom he had :
    iii. HENRY, afterwards Sir Henry Furness, who died under age and unmarried.
    iii. KATHARINE, who m. the earl of Rockingham and afterwards the earl of Guildford, and has since died without issue.
  ii. Sir ROBERT FURNESS, m. 1st, Mrs. Balaam ; 2nd, Lady Arabella Watson ; 3d, Lady Anne Shirley. By his third wife he had :
    iii. ANN, d. in infancy.
    iii. SELINA, m. Edward Doring, Esq., and since dead, leaving children :
      iv. Edward Doring.
      iv. Selina Doring.
I. Sir HENRY FURNESS, m. 1st [as above] ; 2nd, ———, by whom he had :
  ii. MATILDA, m. Lord Edgcumbe, who had issue :
  iii. Lord EDGCUMBE, d. s. p.
  iii. Commodore EDGCUMBE, now Lord Edgcumbe.
I. GEORGE FURNESS, of London, merchant, had issue :
  ii. HENRY, d. int. and s. p.
  ii. ELIZABETH, m. Pierce, d. s. p.
  ii. GEORGE, d. s. p.
I. ANNE FURNESS, m. Mr. Williams, woollen draper, of London, and had :
  ii. ANNE, m. Richard Arnold.
  ii. MARY, m. Samuel Storke.
  ii. ELIZABETH, m. Mr. John Overing, Boston, N. E.
  ii. REBECCA, d. in infancy.

II.   RICHARD ARNOLD and ANNE FURNESS had:

   iii.   ANNE ARNOLD, m. Benjamin Barlow, who had:
      iv.   ELIZABETH BARLOW, m. Mr. John Watkins, of Neuman st., Oxford Road. Also,
   iii.   RICHARD, ⎫
   iii.   JOHN, ⎬ all d. s. p.
   iii.   HENRIETTA, ⎪
   iii.   JAMES, ⎭

II.   SAMUEL STORKE and MARY FURNESS had:

   iii.   SAMUEL, who had:
      iv.   SAMUEL, d. s. p.
   iii.   ANN, m. Thomas, in Token House yard.
   iii.   MARY, living in Token House yard.

II.   JOHN OVERING and ELIZABETH FURNESS, of Boston, N. E., had issue :

   iii.   JAMES, d. s. p.
   iii.   ELIZABETH, m. Dr. John Wilson, at Hopkinton, near Boston, N. E. She has a son and a daughter.
      One of these Wilsons m. Dr. Morney. There were more than two children.

I.   ELIZABETH FURNESS, m. Mr. John Branch, of Sandwich, and had:

   ii.   ANN, wife of Mr. Laythropp, d. s. p.
   ii.   DEBORAH, wife of Dr. Braggs.

INSTRUCTIONS FOR EMIGRANTS FROM ESSEX COUNTY, MASS., TO SOUTH CAROLINA, 1697.

Copied by HENRY F. WATERS, A.B., of Salem, Mass., for the REGISTER, from the original in his own possession.

INSTRUCTIONS, given [1][by a Company of such Persons in Essex in N.-Eng[d]; who Intend to Remove themselves and ffamilies into South-Carolina][1] unto M[r] Nicholas Chattwil: Lev[t] Thomas Rayment, M[r] Richard Walker, Will[m] Haskol, Jn[o] Edwards, Isa[c] Evleth, Adventurers.

Gentlemen & Friends!

You being Intended to Adventure in to South-Carolina, w[th] a Designe to Accomodate y[r]selves and ffamilyes w[th] Lands for Settlement, in that Countrie: (And we being engaged by y[e] same subscription w[th] yourselves, in order to a Remove; But your Concerns and Inclinations, Exciting you to Adventure now at this Time: we all wish Gods Blessing upon you, and Rejoice in your forwardnesse: hoping the Opp[r]tunitie may Prove a Benefit to the whole Companie.)

Therfore Reposing Confidenc in your Love, ffidelitie and Prudence: We do now Propose, That in your Attending upon your P[r]sonall Likeing and Settlement, you will Also have a Regaurd to such Incouragments as may Promoat the Remove of y[e] whole Company of Subscribers.

The Recompenc you must Expect from us, must be but such a small Purse of Mony, as is now put into your hands, as may Enable you, in some Measure, to do the Businesse of y[e] Companie, w[n] you shall Arive in Carolina, as to your Transacting wth the Goverment there, w[ch] we Suppose will not be very Expensive.

---

[1] These brackets are in the original document.

You must not Expect that we can Ingage to defraye the whole Charge of ye voiage of your P^{r}sons and Expences, but what money we now put into your hands, you must take up Contented wth itt: And as it will be Some Ease to your Travels, so we do Expect it shall be as a Comon Purse, and only for such Expences as shall Arise by service for the Company w^n you are together; Or in any case, as you w^n ther shall think Meet, by a Major Vote, to Appoint any One or More of y^r Persons, to the dispatch of Any such Service as may be for ye Generall Good and Benefit of ye Subscribers.

And for our own [illegible] and your Guidance in this Voiage, we think it meet and Convenient to Lay before you thes following Instructions.

Imprimis.

We do Pray and Request, that you Indaivour (and Let God help you) to Carry, and behave yourselves as good and Sober men: wch we hope you Will: And that you will not Err from your former conversation, wch we have observed to be Adorned wth Prudence, and Sobrietie: Indeed we do the Rather Propose this Caution, In that we have been Informed, y^t many of N-Eng^d going into that Countrie, have so Demeaned themselves, as that they have been a Scandal to N-Eng^d And have been an offenc to the Sober and well minded in Carolina, and an Ill-Example unto others. Therfore we pray you will Remember you are in this voiage concerned not only for a worldly Interest, But (tho Remoatly yet Really) for the translating Christs Ordinances, and Worship into that Countrie: Therfore Hon^r your God, your [   ] and y^r Persons, by a good Behaviour.

Item: When you are Arrived (and God send you a Safe Voiage) into Carolina, Take Exact Notice of the Countrie, so that you may be able to make a true Report.

1: Take good Notice of the Mann^{r}s of ye People, and how they stand affected for ye Promoating, and Advanc of the Gospell Worship of God in their Countrie; and so far as you can observe, whether the Body or any Considerable Number of ye Inhabitants seem to comply wth the Designe of ye Right Hon^{r}able ye Gov^{r}n^r, and other Principle p^{r}sons in the Collony in that Affaire ; if you find that they do, it will much Incourage o^r Remove.

2: We would have you Curious in informing y^{r}selves how ye Countrie is for Health: and whether ye Climate does Agree well wth the Bodyes of o^r N-Eng^d People.

To think any Countrie on this side Heaven should have a Writ of Ease, and Securitie against Diseases or Death is but a vanitie: But whether that Countrie ma'nt be more Incident to Sicknesse, and the Decrease of ye Inhabitants then ours.

3: We would also have you Informe y^{r}selves what you can, of such wholsome Lawes as are ther Established: and what Civil means may be used for ye Restraining of Vice, and Ill-Manners; because some have Reported, that ther is no other Moral Evill ther punished, unlesse it be, Murther: But you finding Good and sufficient Lawes for the Terrour of Evill Doers, and the Gov^{r}ment Zealous for ye Prosecuting Law for the Advancing vertue, and Soberitie Amongst the Inhabitants, it will be no small Argument in what steps we are yet to take towards a Remove.

4: Take an Exact Surveye of the Countrie.

1: As to the Soyle, whether it be Rich or Barren in itself: or whether here and ther some Rich Spot, and the Barrens are farr the Greater in Quantitie, or how it may be? for tho we have had very Credible Information of yis and of many other p^{r}ticulars yet ye Adventure being Darkned wth so many Contrarie and we suppose false Reports, we are Desirous that you will be criticall and Also Judicious Observers; that ye Collony may not be wronged, nor we mislead, nor wthout Sufficient Reason discouraged from our Adventure.

2: As to the Element of Water. What Depths ye Rivers and Inlets may be off; and what ships for Burden may Trade ther: Also be Exact in observing the fall of the tides; and what probabilitie ther may be for Mills, both for Saws and Grists. Dont forget to take Notice what Supply of water ye Inhabitants have for their dayley use: whether they are Blest wth sweet, clear, and flowing streams and springs, or wth good and wholsome wels; Be carefull in this Point; because some have been so Confident to say they have not any good water in the Countrie: and Indeed good and wholsome and Plentifull water is so great a Blessing for the Life of Man; that ther cannot be Expected any Long time of Life and health without it.

3: As to ye Productions of the Countrie. We think our selves and all men must be very full of humane Distrust if we or they should not Believe Carolina to be a Rich and Plentifull Countrie by what we have heard of it; yet you being on this errant to satisfie your selves and us more fully in ye Matter; Informe yourselves, whether all sorts of English Grains will thrive ther: And whether it is a Countrie that is likely to cheirish Propagate, and Maintaine English Grass: And Also whether any or all of thos great and considerable staples, of Indigo, Cotten, Silk, Wine and Oyle, will yeild such a good Increase, as will sufficiently Repay the paines, and Profit the Labourers: ffor tho the Country may have an Aptnesse to produce thes and such other Rich Comodities: yet the soyle may be so faint; and ye Climate so disord^rly that Nature may faile mens hopes: Or whether y^{se} things are Like to be but the happie chanc of some few by Reason of a Luckie Settlement? or whether they may be Likely to be univ^rsall Blessings as the Result of good husbandrie, and of a sutable soyle and climate?

4: As to Conveniencie for settlement. Whether ye Countrie will Admit such a manner of settlement of townships for neer-Neighb^rhood, as in N-Eng^d.

That is: supposing that men will be contented wth a competent Quantitie of Land, and a comfortable Livelyhood, whether this may be expected wth ye Injoyment of neer-Neighbours? And that up in the Countrie wher men must expect to Live upon Stocks, Trades, and husbandrie.

5: We Advize that you take a perticular and peculiar Account how that Place called the Read-Banks is settled, or what condition that neck is in: if it may be sufficient for about one hundred ffamilies, more then what may be settled ther already wth our ffriend and Neighb^r Benj. Singleterry; then let us know it: and if you shall Judge it meet for y^rselves, and us to settle ther then we are Contented: But if that and all other Places near the Sea, be filled or Straitned by Settlements; then Let two or more of you go up into the Countrie to the higher Lands; and if thos high and Mountenous Lands have the Benefit of Rivers ffor Transportation, and ther be good falls for Mils, and a heartie Soyle, and good Timber tho it be Threscore Miles up, Look out some good Tract ther, near some Navigable River.

6: When you have sufficiently vewed the Countrie; and see Cause to determine upon a Settlement and a Remove for yourselves and families, and you Judge it meet and Behoofull for y^rselves and us, then wⁿ you have made Choice of a Good and Sufficient Tract, That you obtaine of the Right Hon^rable ye Gov^rn^r; that ye sd tract may be Reserved for us till 12^{ve} or 20^{tie} Months shall Exspire. In wch space we may Accomodate o^r Affaires for a Remove.

7: Having so done if any of your selves or any others of o^r Subscribers now In Companie wth you, shall see cause to stay in the Countrie and Begin a Plantation, before the Body of us Remove, you shall wthout offence to the Rest of us, have Libertie to take up your home Lots, not exceeding fourtie Acres: But in such a manner as may Least Prejudice the whole: That is you must not cross wth your Lots upon ye ffront of a River: neither must you Straiten any grand outlet, &c. But w^n you shall be together, and Judge most Convenient as shall be for the Good of the Whole, and for the Comfort of such as do stay, so proceed, and it will not hinder but Encourage o^r Remove and Settlement ther Also.

8: To conclude, hoping that you will Indaivour to satisfie us in all thes severall p'ticulers; and Also y^t you will Carefully Regaurd any thing else, wch may be Materiall for ye gaining a True Carecter of ye Countrie, wch we have not here Inserted, being Loath to Incumber you wth too Large discourses; we Therefore Leave all (und^r Divine Providenc) unto your ffidelitie and Discretion.

And so we have done, w^n we have told you; that we expect that you shall Esteeme and Respect Mr Nicholas Chattwil, Cheif in all your Agitations; and yet Also we expect and hope you shall p'forme the whole voiage in great ffriendship and Love one to an other, and to and wth the Rest of our Subscribers in the voiage wth you, both in your Ordinary Conv'sation, As Also upon the Disaster of any one P'son by Sicknesse or Any other Means.

So Joyning wth you in our Constant and Most Ardent Prayers, to the King of Heaven, whose Service we trust you are now upon; for all mann^r of Sutable Blessings upon ye P'sons, and Affaires in all your Travells, and on your ffamilies in your Absenc.

we Rest y^r ffriends
J^{no} Wise
In the name & wth ye Consent of the Companie

This Memorandū
To Wm Haskol Senr
    Purser for ye Company of Subscribers for ye voiage
    [Ipsw^{ch} In?] N-Eng^d
        This: 9th: 12°: 1696-7

THE WILLOUGHBY FAMILY OF NEW-ENGLAND.

By Isaac J. Greenwood, A.M., of New-York.

"The Willoughbys, now in the United States, I have reason to believe are the heirs of the dormant Barony of Willoughby of Parham," is a state-ment* which, though made by so excellent an authority as the late Hon. James Savage, it would be doubtless very difficult, if not impossible, to sub-stantiate. Glancing hastily over the descent of this family, we find that Sir Christopher[1] Willoughby, who was knighted in 1483 and died 1498, had five sons: William,[2] who succeeded to the title of eighth Lord Willoughby of Eresby, Sir Christopher,[2] George[2] who married, Sir Thomas[2] ancestor of the Lords Middleton, and John[2] who also married. The second son Sir

---

* Mass. Hist. Soc. Coll., S. III., vol. viii. 310.

Christopher[2] Willoughby, Knt. of Parham, co. Suffolk, was father of William,[3] created in 1547 Lord Willoughby of Parham, whose only son and successor Charles[4] matriculated at Magdalen College, Oxford, in 1551, being under 14 years of age, and died in 1603, having had six sons as mentioned below:

    i. WILLIAM,[5] ob. v. p., whose son William,[6] knighted 1603 at Belvoir Castle, succeeded as third Lord Willoughby of Parham, lived at Knath, near Gainsborough, co. Lincoln, and died Aug. 28, 1617, leaving three young sons the oldest not five years of age. The line terminated in his grandson Charles,[7] tenth Lord Willoughby, who died Dec. 9, 1679.

    ii. Sir AMBROSE,[5] of Matson, co. Glouc., knighted 1603. His descendants being absent in the Colonies, failed to receive notice of the elder line's having terminated. In May, 1733, his gt. gt. grandson, Henry[9] Willoughby, Esq., claimed the title, but it was not until March, 1757, that he succeeded as 16th Lord Willoughby of Parham. This nobleman, who died Jan. 29, 1775, aged 79, was twice Master of the Company of Brewers, London, a Justice of Peace, and Colonel of 2d Regiment of Militia of the Tower Hamlets. The line terminated on the decease of his nephew and successor George[10] Willoughby, Oct. 28, 1779,* aged about 31 years. In the petition presented to the House of Lords and claiming the title, it was stated that Sir Ambrose[5] Willoughby had an only son and heir Edward,[6] whose only son and heir Henry[7] went to Virginia about 1676, and there died at Hull's Creek, Nov. 26, 1685, aged 59, leaving an only son and heir Henry,[8] aged about 20 years, of whom the petitioner was the eldest son.

    iii. EDWARD,[5] whose son Edward,[6] ob. s. p.

    iv. CHARLES,[5] ob. s. p.

    v. FRANCIS.[5]

    vi. Sir THOMAS,[5] knighted at Belvoir Castle, 1603. His son Thomas,[6] claiming the title on the decease of Charles,[7] tenth Lord Willoughby of Parham, was summoned to Parliament as his successor in 1680, and died Feb. 29, 1694½, æt. 89, leaving Hugh,[7] Francis,[7] Jonathan,[7] and four other sons. Hugh[9] Willoughby, grandson of Francis,[7] was Pres. of the Soc. of Antiq., and F. R. S., he died Jan. 21, 1765, unmarried, the fifteenth Lord Willoughby, and the title passed to his kinsman, the descendant of Sir Ambrose,[6] as above stated.

From the above, it does not seem at all probable, that the father of the American progenitor of Willoughbys, who must have been born as early as 1587, was at all connected with the titled family of Parham. There is a tradition, however, preserved in the family on this side of the Atlantic, that one of their race was a kinswoman and maid of honor to Queen Elizabeth. In the "Nugæ Antiquæ," may be seen some laudatory verses to the six gentlewomen attending the Princess Elizabeth at Hatfield House, during the reign of her sister Mary (1553–'58), and whose names are given as Grey, Willoughby, Markham, Norwich, St. Loo and Skipwith. The latter was Bridget, daughter of Sir William Skipwith (Sheriff of Lincoln, 1526); Miss St. Loo was probably connected with Sir William Saintlow, one of the Princess's household; while Isabella Markham became the second wife of the enraptured poet.† There existed at this time a family of Willoughbys in Nottinghamshire, of some importance, and entirely distinct from the one we have previously considered: they were related to the Markhams and the Skipwiths, and through the Grey family were allied to the Princess Elizabeth, whose second cousin Anne Grey, daughter of the Marquis of Dorset, married Henry Willoughby of Wollaton, son and heir of Sir Edward Willoughby, and nephew of Sir Hugh Willoughby, the Arctic navigator. It

---

* The title has not since been claimed.
† Sir John Harrington.

would seem therefore that the American line of descent must be sought for in the records of this family, a pedigree of which, though very imperfect, may be found in Thoroton's History of Nottinghamshire.

Francis Willoughby, who came to New-England in 1638, with his wife Mary and young son Jonathan, is alluded to by Hutchinson as "a gentleman from England;" he was a son of William Willoughby, who, we learn from Winthrop, "was a Colonel of the City," i. e. of London; while from other sources* we learn that he was a native of Kent, and had been for some time commander of a vessel. This latter person appears to be identical with William Willoughby, who was a purveyor for ship-timber in co. Sussex, as early as 1628. Denzil Fleming, an officer of the Royal Navy, writing to Secretary Nicholas, August 11, states that Willoughby had laden a bark at Stopham, and was about to load another at Arundel, with timber for repair of the Victory at Woolwich, but, as the French men-of-war were very busy off that coast, he desired that some convoy might be procured for the same. From this time forward, frequent mention is made in the Calendar of State Papers (so far as published) of William Willoughby, one of the Purveyors of Timber for his Majesty's Navy. In April, 1636, he, together with John Taylor, sent in a proposition to the Board of Admiralty, for the raising of the Ann Royal, which, with all her ordnance and provisions, had recently sunk off the mouth of the Thames, and he is alluded to, immediately after, as one of the chief shipwrights engaged in the undertaking.

A few years previous to this event, viz., in May, 1632, Gov. Sir John Harvey wrote to the Virginia Commissioners, recommending that Capt. William Tucker,† Mr. Stone, and Maurice Thompson,‡ should contract for three or more years, for all the tobacco of the growth of Virginia. In pursuance of this advice, the latter gentlemen, together with Gregory Clements,‖ Robert South, and others, merchants of London, shipped from the colonies during the summer of 1634, a cargo of 155,000 pounds of tobacco, worth 15,500*l.*, on the Robert Bonaventure, Richard Gilson, master, but unfortunately the vessel was taken by a Dunkirker, Capt. Peter Norman. To recover the same some 500*l.* were now expended in prosecution of law in Flanders, but to no effect, and when by Jan. 1636–7, the amount, including the value of the vessel and the accrued interest, had increased to 18,000*l.*, the parties interested petitioned that Letters of Marque should be granted them to set forth the Discovery (300 tons, John Man, master), and the pinnace Despatch (100 tons, Samuel Lee, master), both of London, "to apprehend at sea ships and goods of the King of Spain or his subjects." The petition was granted April 4, 1637, and by subsequent papers it appears that Capt. Trenchfield (afterwards of the Navy) and Mr. Willoughby were interested in the Discovery, and that four prizes of very great value were soon taken.

Civil war having broken out, an ordinance was passed by Parliament, April 12, 1643, that the Committee for the Militia of London should raise regiments of volunteers, as auxiliaries to the trained bands of the city, for

---

* King's Pamphlets, Brit. Mus., &c.
† A commissioner and councillor of Virginia.
‡ A Virginia merchant, member of the Guinea Company, and Commissioner of the Somers Islands: in Sept., 1659, he declined his appointment by Parliament, as a Commissioner of the Customs.
‖ A merchant and M.P.; one of the King's judges, and executed after the Restoration; vide Heath's Chronicle, p. 197.

the better security and defence thereof and of the Parliament, with power to appoint officers and to order said regiments to such places as they shall see cause. Mr. Willoughby forthwith raised a company of volunteers, consisting of a hundred "well affected and stout youngsters," whom he exercised at Gravesend until they were expert in the use of arms, and on June 17 the H. of C. ordered that he continue in command of such soldiers as had enlisted under him, living within the Hamlets of the Tower, and that said soldiers be required, from time to time, to obey his command and not list under any other. Soon after this, "desirous to try what good service he could do to his King, the Parliament and his country," the Captain set forth from Gravesend towards Woolwich, where he found and seized seventy-five pieces of ordnance, in the carpenter's yard, called the wool-yard. "They had done more than they could justify," said a Mr. William Barnes, residing near Woolwich, which words having been reported to Capt. Willoughby, by some of his youngsters, he with forty of his men went to the house of Barnes, where they seized plate of the value of 1000 pounds, together with some popish books and priests' garments.

Information having been received, about July 1, of divers persons from Oxford, and other parts of the King's army, having crossed to and fro with their coaches, horses and arms, over the ferry at Greenwich, it was ordered by Parliament that Capt. W. should stop the passage of any vehicle to that ferry, by cutting a ditch on the west or river-side of the Thames, and that the Dept. Lieutenants of Kent and Middlesex should station a guard there to stop all horses, arms, ammunition and suspected persons, and to search such as they shall think fit, that endeavor to pass that way.

Nov. 22, it was ordered by the Com. of the Militia of the City of London, sitting at Guildhall, of whom Capt. W. was the head, that the ordnance in the blockhouse at Gravesend should be removed to Tilbury Fort, in which was to be placed a strong garrison of men that might be confided in; and three ships or more, of a convenient burden, were to be appointed to sail up and down, and scour the river above and below Gravesend. The following day, upon some fresh alarm, it was ordered that Greenwich Castle and the blockhouses at Gravesend and Blackheath should be secured.

During the succeeding year, Capt. Willoughby, with the rank of Colonel, at the head of a regiment known as the Regiment of Auxiliaries of the Hamlets of the Tower, was ordered, together with two troops of horse commanded by Cols. Heriott Washbourne and Underwood, to join Major-General Richard Brown, at Abingdon, Berks. This place, situated some fifty-six miles westward from London, was but seven miles south of the royalist stronghold at Oxford, and proved a great check upon all movements in that quarter. In October, 1645, the Committee of the Three Counties having reported that the forces, above specified, could then be spared, the Committee of the Militia of London suggested to the House of Lords (Oct. 10), that directions be given for their speedy return to the metropolis, and for the payment of their arrears. Col. Willoughby, however, appears to have been still stationed at Abingdon towards the close of December, when the Commons passed an order for the payment of 200*l.*, on account, to his regiment.

On the 3d of April, 1646, he was one of the officers authorized by the House of Lords to execute martial law within the cities of London and Westminster and the lines of communication, and soon after composed one of a court martial for the trial of William Murray, Esq., as a spy.

During the succeeding year, information having been received, in July, of a design to seize upon Tilbury-fort, on the Thames river, the officers of the Trinity House were impowered by the House of Commons to take the care and custody thereof and of the Block-house at Gravesend, and to secure them for the Parliament. Ten months later, news reached the House of the formidable disturbance in Kent, immediately followed by the revolt of a large portion of the fleet, and the deposition of the Vice-Admiral, Col. Thomas Rainsborough, whereupon it was resolved that the orders of restraint be taken off, as to the forces of horse and foot, stationed at the Mews, Whitehall, and the Tower, for guards of the Parliament, and that they be sent for the suppression of tumult into the county of Kent. Moreover, the Lord General Fairfax, who was also at the time Constable of the Tower, was requested to send reinforcements, and if necessary to go in person. June 16, 1648, a Council of War was held at Warwick House, to consider measures for reducing the revolted ships, at which meeting, besides the Earl of Warwick, who had been reinstated in his position of Lord High Admiral, there were present, Capts. Tweedy, Peter Pett and Andrewes, Col. Willoughby, Capts. Bowen and Penrose, Mr. Smith, and Capts. Swanley, Ben. Crandley, Lymery and Phineas Pett. It was resolved "That as great a fleet as the Parliament shall think fit be provided, with all possible expedition, for the safety of the kingdom and the reducing of the revolters. That a letter be written, by the Lord High Admiral, to the Trinity House, to employ their best endeavors, for the manning of the ships of such a fleet, with cordial and well-affected men. That the Parliament be pleased to make a promise, by an ordinance, to those seamen, both Officers and Mariners, of a gratuity, suitable to the faithful and good service they shall do in this business."

On the 27th of the succeeding month, the Committee of both Houses at Derby House, reported a letter of July 20th, from Tilbury, and also a petition of Col. William Willoughby. Upon the reading of the latter before the House of Commons, it was ordered that the Colonel's accounts should be audited by the city-auditor, "and that he have the public faith of the kingdom for what shall appear to be due and owing to him," also that 800*l.* due, upon account, to the garrison at Tilbury, with interest at 8 per cent., be charged upon the excise, in course, and paid to said Col. William Willoughby, or his assigns. From this we may infer, that the Colonel had, at this critical juncture, been placed temporarily in command of the fort at Tilbury, opposite Gravesend.

Jan. 8, 1647-8, the Committee of both Houses appointed Col. Robert Tichborne,* Col. William Willoughby, Maurice Thompson, gent., and several others, as a Committee for the Militia of the Tower Hamlets, said ordinance to be in force for two years from Dec. 20, 1647. Soon after, in recognition of their services, he, together with Mr. Thomas Smith and Mr. Peter Pett, were recommended to the Naval Committee, by the merchants of London, as persons fit and able to be employed as Commissioners for the Navy, and it was particularly requested that Col. Willoughby should personally attend at Portsmouth, and receive in recompense the fee of a commissioner at large. He was accordingly appointed by the House of Commons, Feb. 16, 1648-9, Master Attendant for Portsmouth, and a Commissioner of the Navy.

---

* At the time Lieutenant of the Tower under the Lord General, and an Alderman of the City; subsequently Lord Mayor; he was a prisoner of state, after the Restoration, and died July, 1682, in the Tower.

On Oct. 25, 1650, Gen. Deane, one of the Generals of the Fleet, wrote to Vice-Admiral Penn of the Irish Squadron, to repair forthwith, with the new frigate Fairfax, then commanded by him, into Portsmouth, there to careen and fit out said ship with all things wanted, " which," continues the General, " I have written to Col. Willoughby to get in readiness against you come." This was preparatory to Penn's service in the Mediterranean. But the Colonel's term of usefulness in this department was of short continuance. July 11, 1651, it was reported to the House by Mr. Bond, from the Council of State, that Col. Willoughby was lately dead,* and that they recommended Capt. Robert Moulton, senior, in his place ; whereupon Moulton was appointed. At the same time it was referred to the Council of State to make payments to Col. Willoughby " of his monies ; which with great willingness and good affection, he laid out for defence of the river of Thames, in the time of the insurrections of Kent and Essex ; and of other monies due to him from the State."

The Colonel's widow, Elizabeth Willoughby, left a will, dated London, May, 1662, mentioning her late son William (ob. s. p.); the six children of her son Francis, of whom Sarah was then the only daughter ; and her sisters, Mrs. Jane Hammond of Virginia, and Anna, wife of William Griffin of Portsmouth. Mrs. Hammond's son Lawrence was the same person who, as Capt. Lawrence Hammond, was located in Charlestown, Mass. Colony, whose third wife was Margaret, widow of Dept. Gov. Francis Willoughby (his cousin), and whose eldest son was Francis Hammond.

The name Hammond, or more correctly Hannam and Hanham,† may be found on the rolls of the Parliamentary Navy in 1659, in the person of Capt. Willoughby Hannam, of the " Kentish," who, retained in the service after the Restoration, was killed in action against the Dutch, May 28, 1672, being then in command of a seventy-four gun ship, the " Triumph." In the body of the church of St. Margaret Pattens, London, is a flat stone to Willoughby Hannam and his sister Frances, 1683–4, and Berry's Kent Genealogies gives the descendants of this Capt. Hannam,‡ through his son Jonathan, born at Andover, 1670, and died at Crondall, Hants, April 30, 1754.

The original will of Mrs. Willoughby, sent out from England, was identified by her son Francis, 23 : (12): 1662, at Charlestown, and filed 2: 2: 1663. A seal, attached to the signature, bears a chevron engrailed between three boars' heads.

Concerning the son Francis Willoughby, much of interest may be found in Frothingham's History of Charlestown. Coming to New-England as we have stated, in 1638, with his wife Mary and infant son Jonathan, he was admitted an inhabitant Aug. 22, and joined the church during the following year (Oct. 10), from which time forward, till his death, he " was almost constantly engaged in the public service," and is always respectfully alluded to in the colonial records. He was a prominent merchant and did much for the improvement of the town. From a petition of 1641 we learn that he and others had invested a great part of their estates in " building warehouses and framing wharves," to facilitate the landing of goods, " not only from about home, but from further parts," praying that the Court would " appoint a certain rate of wharfage, porterage, and housing of goods." His wharves were on each side of the Ferry-ways, where he owned considerable

---

* The Colonel left a will, a copy of which has not yet been received.
† From Hanham, a small place, situated near Bristol, co. Gloucester.
‡ Berry has given the name incorrectly as Capt. Jonathan Hannam.

property, and his ship-yard on the site of the Fitchburg railroad depot (or in Warren Avenue), where in 1641 he was engaged in building a ship, to encourage which enterprise, the town gave him liberty " to take timber from the common," and without " being obliged to cut up the tops of the trees." He was a selectman 1640–47; representative 1649–50; assistant 1650 and '51,[1] and set out, during the latter year, for England, doubtless to arrange the estate of his late father. Not long before his departure (in May, 1650), he was appointed one of a committee to draw up, within the next six months, a code of maritime laws for the colony.

In June, 1652, war having been declared against Holland, Francis Willoughby, Edward Winslow[2] and Edward Hopkins[3] petitioned that they might be permitted to send a ship, with store of powder, shot and swords, to New-England, and to give notice to the colonies of the differences between the Commonwealth and the United Provinces. The Committee for Foreign Affairs, in recommending that liberty be granted for the same, also suggested " that it be declared by the Council of State that, as the colonies may expect all fitting encouragement and assistance from hence, so they should demean themselves against the Dutch, as declared enemies to the Commonwealth." License was accordingly given, July 29, for the John Adventure, Richard Thurston, master, to proceed to Boston, with one ton of shot and fifty-six barrels of powder, in consort with the other ships bound the same way, and the receipt of this ammunition was acknowledged by the Commissioners of the United Colonies, in a letter of Sept. 24, 1653, to Mr. Winslow.[4]

Sir Henry Vane, jr., was now president of the Council of State, in which body was vested all the power formerly belonging to the office of the Lord Admiral; whether Sir Henry favored the New-Englanders, over whom he had formerly ruled as Governor, cannot be precisely asserted, but several of the colonists obtained, about this time, excellent positions in the navy. Sept. 28, 1652, the President reported from the Council of State, that they " having taken into consideration the necessity of settling some fit person to be a commissioner at Portsmouth, in the room of Capt. Robert Moulton, lately deceased; and having received very good satisfaction of the fidelity and good ability of Capt. Francis Willoughby, son to the late Colonel Willoughby, late commissioner there, for that trust: do humbly present him to the Parliament as a fit and able man for the management of the State's affairs in that place, if the Parliament shall so think fit." Whereupon Capt. Willoughby was appointed one of the Commissioners at Portsmouth, in the place of Capt. Moulton, deceased, and with " like commission, power, authority, salary and other profits and commodities, as the said Capt. Moulton had, or was to receive or enjoy." On 8th March following Parliament " resolved that there be a Master of Attendant allowed for Portsmouth, distinct from the Commissioner of the Navy, with same salary as other Masters of Attendant have," whence it would appear that Capt. Willoughby did not hold both these offices, which had been enjoyed by his father.

From the recently published Memoir of Gen. Deane (see REGISTER, xxv. 299), we learn that the first intelligence of " the three days' battle off Port-

---

[1] Whitmore's Civil List gives 1650–55.

[2] Ex-Gov. of Plymouth Colony; sent out 1646 as Agent for Mass. Bay Colony.

[3] Ex-Gov. of Connecticut Colony; appointed 1652 a Com. of Navy; chosen 1656 M.P. from Clifton, co. Devon; died, London, 1657, and appointed Mr. Francis Willoughby an overseer of his will.

[4] Plymouth Records, x. 104.

land," in which that officer, together with Generals Blake and Monk, were engaged against the Dutch, was received in London by the Commissioners of Admiralty through a letter from Capt. Willoughby, dated Feb. 19, 1652–3.

Almost six years after this event, on the calling of a parliament by the Protector Richard, one of the members chosen for Portsmouth was Francis Willoughby, Esq. This parliament having met Jan. 27, 1658–9, was dissolved by the short lived authority, through which it had been convened, on 22d April following, to be succeeded in a fortnight by the restoration of that fragment of the old Long Parliament, called the Rump, which had not met since its forcible dissolution by Cromwell, April 20, 1653. But their present session was not of long continuance ; Gen. Lambert, acting for the army, excluded them from the House, Oct. 13, and a council of officers, appointing among themselves what was called a Committee of Safety, to manage affairs, proposed even to call a "new and free parliament" by their own authority. Early in November, General Monk, who commanded the forces in Scotland, and many of his officers expressed their dissatisfaction with these proceedings and declared for the old parliament. The first active steps for the restoration of that body, however, were taken by Sir Arthur Haselrig, Col. Morley, and Col. Walton, who, adopting the views of Monk, occupied, with their regiments, the important town of Portsmouth, on Dec. 4th, and with the consent of the Governor, Col. Nathaniel Whetham, immediately issued orders for more forces to come to their assistance, and despatched letters to the General in Scotland justifying their proceedings. Col. Rich, sent on from London, by the army-faction, to dispossess them, entered the town with his regiment and united interest with the party in occupation. This latter officer was an intimate friend of Lawson, who had been restored to his position of Vice-Admiral on May 26, and the fleet, having been invited to join them, despatched a messenger to Portsmouth, assuring Haselrig that they would do nothing in opposition to his party, and soon after sent a letter (Dec. 13) to the Lord Mayor, Aldermen, and Common Council of London, calling upon them to "use their utmost" for the removal of that restraint and force now put upon the parliament.

Saturday, Dec. 17, Vice-Admiral Lawson, having left the Downs, sailed into the river Thames with the "James" and the rest of the fleet, "declaring their resolutions to endeavor the restoring of the parliament to the exercise of their authority, they judging them the only means to restore peace and settlement into these distressed nations." Accordingly on Monday, Dec. 26, the old parliament met again, and the next day ordered that Messrs. Scott, Weaver, and Col. Martin "prepare letters of thanks and acknowledgments of the fidelity and good service of Gen. Monk, Vice-Admiral Lawson, and the Commissioners at Portsmouth: and that Mr. Speaker do sign and seal the said letters with the seal of the Parliament." Jan. 9, 1659–60, Lawson was heartily thanked at the bar of the house, "for his constant fidelity, and the great and eminent service done by him since the late interruption of parliament." On Saturday, Feb. 21 (17 days after Monk had reached London), those members who had been excluded by Col. Pride in 1648, again took their seats in the house, and the Long Parliament, which had first met in 1640, dissolved by its own act, made a final exit March 16, 1660, and on May 29 King Charles made his public entry into London.

When, early in 1662, it was deemed advisable by the general court of

Massachusetts to congratulate the king upon his restoration, and to send out an agent to act for the general interests of the colony, a letter was written to Herbert Pelham, Esq., Mr. Nehemiah Bourne, Mr. Francis Willoughby, Mr. Richard Hutchinson[1] and others, desiring that they would supply the Commissioners,[2] upon their arrival, with such funds as they might require on account of the colony.

Soon after this Mr. Willoughby left England, taking with him a third wife, Margaret, whom he had there married; he appears to have been again present in the Colony by May, 1662, and sat as an assistant at the general court, held Oct. 20, 1663; was again chosen the succeeding year; became deputy governor, May, 1665, and so continued until his decease. In Sept. 1666, the deputy governor was appointed head of a committee for procuring two masts to be sent out to England and presented "to His Majesty, by Sir William Warren and Capt. John Taylor (one of the commissioners for the navy), as a testimony of loyalty and affection from ye country." About this same time the necessity of proper laws, for regulating maritime affairs and admiralty cases, was again agitated, and information was given to the court, "that divers unskilfull persons, pretending to be shipwrights, doe build shipps and other vessels in seuerall parts of the country, which are defective, both for matter and forme, to the great prejudice of merchants and ouners, and the danger of many mens liues at sea;" whereupon the court was moved "to nominate and appoint Francis Willoughby Esq., Jno. Leverett Esq., Capt. George Corwin, Mr. Humphrey Davy, and Capt. Edward Johnson to be a Committee to consider, draw up, and present to this Court, at their next session, such directions, orders, and laws as may be necessary and expedjent in the premises."

Three years thereafter (Oct. 12, 1669), he was granted 100 acres "in any place that may not prejudice a plantation," for his public service, as well at home as in England.

The original will of the deputy governor does not appear on file. This will, drawn up June 4, 1670, and witnessed by Capt. Lawrence Hammond and Lawrence Dowse, was proved April 10, 1671, six days after the testator's decease. He states therein that the legacies left to his children, Jonathan, Sarah and Nehemiah, by their grandfather Willoughby, had been paid, and desires that his mother's will, which had not yet been carried out, might be made good. To his wife, who had brought a considerable estate with her, he bequeathed all household goods, plate and jewels, which had formerly belonged to her, or which had been given to her before or since marriage. To his eldest son Jonathan 10l. and some wearing apparel, and to each of his living children 5l., for that said son "hath cost me much money both in breeding up and several other ways, to the value of near a treble portion already, and for other serious and deliberate considerations, which I am not willing here to mention, it being a grief of soul to me that he should run out an estate so unprofitably as he hath done to his present suffering, &c. &c." After deducting all legacies and debts the testator leaves $\frac{14}{32}$ of the residue of his estate to his wife; $\frac{3}{32}$ to his son Nehemiah, including what had already been paid in 1669: to the other children, when of age, $\frac{3}{32}$ to son William; $\frac{5}{32}$ to son Francis; $\frac{4}{32}$ to daughter Susannah, and $\frac{3}{32}$ to child still unborn. To eldest daughter Campfield, as a token of love 10l., she having already received a liberal portion; to aunt Hammond, if alive 5*l.*; to cousin Lawrence Hammond 40*l.*, "provided he deal respectively with my wife and assist her about settling my estate." To cousin March liberty, during her widowhood, to live in and make use of my house in which she now dwells, rent-free. To the use of the school in Charlestown my three hundred acres of land, given me by the said town, but never laid out, lying beyond Woburn. After several other legacies to friends, his pastor and domestics, he observes: "Now for as much as the College hath been a Society that I have had much affection to, and desires for the prosperity of, having made it my work to solicit the Country in generall, & perticular persons to take care thereof in order to the advantage of posteritie, It might be expected that I should manifest myselfe to be cordial in some more than the ordinary beneficence: But my estate being very uncertaine, as it is abroad in other mens hands, & so not knowing what the Lord may doe with it: And a vessel being lost that I had bequeathed to that use: But chiefly considering the backwardness and indisposition that is in the Country to consider their owne interest with reference to posterity; and finding particular persons holding their owne and disclaiming any motion for good that hath been made that way, being at a loss to know what the mind of God therein may be, and unwilling to injure my family, the state of my concernments lying as aforesaid : I find not any inclination to doe what my heart and soul is free for; Desiring the Lord to pardon & forgive that backwardness and indisposition which seemes to appear in the generality of persons to so worthy a worke as it is."

He forbids the giving of scarfs or ribbons to any persons except magistrates, and those who officiate at his funeral, and instead thereof leaves 20*l.* to the town towards commencing the purchase of a stock of arms, to furnish poor men on exercise-days, and to be in readiness against any sudden emergency. His wife he appoints executrix, and his loving friends, Mr. Thomas Danforth, Mr. Richard Russel, Mr. Humphrey Davie, and cousin Lawrence Hammond as overseers of his last will and testament, "earnestly entreating them that as they did ever manifest any affection and respect for me, that they would manifest the like to my wife in all that assistance that she shall stand in need of, she being a stranger in the country, and not knowing whom to apply for help in case of need." He also desires his wife, by the affection she bears him, " to take a little care of his son William, in case he will be ruled by her ; but if he or his own mother's relations shall desire otherwise, or carry themselves uncivilly towards her, I leave her at liberty, being unwilling to put her under any snare or inconvenience."

The Rev. Simon Bradstreet of New-London, says: "he desired to be buried one foot deep and to have ye top of his grave plain, only covered with ye tops of ye grasse."[1]

The widow Margaret Willoughby married, Feb. 8, 1675, Capt. Lawrence Hammond, of Charlestown, the cousin of her late husband ; she was his third wife (though he had no children by this marriage), and died Feb. 2, 1683. Her will, signed Aug. 21, 1680, and proved April 12, 1683, leaves one-half of the property, left her by her former husband, to her present husband Capt. Hammond, the balance to her only child Susannah Willoughby ; to her sister Elizabeth Lock 100*l.* due testator out of rents in England ; the residue of her estate in Old and New-England to her daughter aforesaid, committing her and her portion to the care and protection of her father-in-law Capt. Hammond.

---

[1] New-England Hist. and Gen. Register, ix. 65.

Issue by first wife Mary :—

   i. JONATHAN, b. about 1635 in England; Harv. Coll. 1651–54, but did not graduate ; preached in Wethersfield from Sept. 1664, to May, 1666, and afterwards, for a short time, in Haddam, Conn. Mentioned in his brother William's will, 1677. By wife Grizzel he had a dau. *Mary*, b. May 8, 1664, and prob. other children.

Issue by second wife Sarah (Taylor?) :—

   ii. SARAH, bapt. June 13, 1641 ; m. —— Campfield (or Canfield) ; prob. Samuel, bapt. Oct. 19, 1645, eldest son of Matthew C. of New-Haven.

   iii. HANNAH, b. May 17 ; d. Sept. 4, 1643.

2. iv. NEHEMIAH, b. June 8 or 18, 1644.

   v. JERINNAH, b. July 29, 1647 ; d. young.

   vi. WILLIAM, b. about 1652. His will, dated Sept. 1, 1677, was filed Dec. 7, 1694, in Midd. Probate Co.; the house and land left him by his uncle William Willoughby, he bequeaths to his brother Nehemiah, together with the 100*l.* or more, now in his mother's hands ; of the estate now falling to him by the decease of his brother Francis Willoughby, he leaves one-half to his sister Susannah, and one-half to Capt. Hammond's children, and the legacy left by his grandfather Taylor, to be divided equally between his sister Campfield and his brother Jonathan, as a token of love : to cousin Elizabeth Moore 10*l.* ; books, monies and wearing apparel to eldest son of his brother and executor Nehemiah. Savage states that he died of small-pox Aug. 28, 1678.

Issue by third wife Margaret :—

   vii. FRANCIS, d. (says Savage) June 15, 1678, of small-pox, but is mentioned as deceased in William's will, 1677.

   viii. NATHANIEL, d. 1663 (Frothingham).

   ix. SUSANNAH, b. Aug. 19, bapt. 21, 1664 ; m. 1683, Nathaniel Lynde, b. Nov. 22, 1659, son of Judge Simon L. by wife Hannah Newdigate, and grandson of Enoch L. of London, by wife Eliz. Digby, said to be related to the family of John, Earl of Bristol. Mr. Nath'l Lynde removed to Saybrook, Conn., and d. Oct. 5, 1729; among his children was Elizabeth, b. Dec. 2, 1694, m. Judge Richard Lord of Lyme.

  2. NEHEMIAH[3] WILLOUGHBY, merchant of Salem, married Jan. 2, 1672, Abigail, dau. of Henry Bartholomew, bapt. Oct. 6, 1650, died Sept. 2, 1702; constable 1679; allowed 1690 to sell wine, &c. out doors ; died Nov. 6, 1702. Issue :—

   i. FRANCIS, b. Sept. 28, 1672 ; bapt. Feb. 16, 1672–3 ; deputy and representative 1713 ; requested to provide King's Arms for the Court House, June 26, 1716 ; was prob. of Boston 1734, when one of the name was appointed on committee for markets. Issue :—
     William,[5] bapt. at Salem, July 28, 1705 ; Harv. Coll. 1726 ; d. 1735.
     Bethia,[5] bapt. at S., March 27, 1709.

   ii. NEHEMIAH.

   iii. ELIZABETH, b. June 22, bapt. 28, 1674, at Charlestown.

   iv. MARY, b. Sept. 1, 1676 ; m. May 10, 1710, Col. Thomas Barton of Salem, b. July 17, 1680 ; selectman, town-clerk, physician and apothecary ; Lt. Col. of the Reg't ; he d. April 28, 1751 ; she d. about Jan. 1758. Issue :—
     John,[5] b. Dec. 5, 1711 : Harv. College 1730 ; merchant of Salem ; d. unm. Dec. 21, 1774.
     Mary,[5] m. June 27, 1734, Bazaleel Toppan (son of the Rev. Christ'r T. of Newbury) ; Harv. Coll. 1722 ; physician ; d. 1762. Had children Anna[6] and Mary[6] ; the latter m. Col. Benj. Pickman,

b. 1741, Harv. Coll. 1759 ; lived on Essex St., Salem, in a house
which had come to Nehemiah Willoughby from his father-in-law
H. Bartholomew.

v.   ABIGAIL, b. April 4, 1679, at S. ; m. Capt. Joshua Pickman (son of
     Benj. P.) ; mariner of S. ; she d. Aug. 24, 1710 ; he d. Jan. 24, 1750,
     aged 69.
vi. SARAH, b. July, 1684, at S.
vii. ELIZABETH, b. June 10, 1687, at S.
viii. JOHN, b. Dec. 11, 1688, at S.

ABSTRACTS OF THE EARLIEST WILLS ON RECORD, OR ON THE FILES IN THE COUNTY OF SUFFOLK, MASSACHUSETTS.

Prepared by WILLIAM B. TRASK, Esq., of Boston.

[Continued from vol. xx. page 242.]

THIS series of abstracts was commenced by the late SAMUEL G. DRAKE, A.M., in
the first number of the REGISTER edited by him (January, 1848, vol. ii. p. 102),
and was continued by Mr. D. to July, 1851 (vol. v. p. |297). The writer began
his abstracts of wills, inventories, &c., with the will of James Bate, of Dorchester, printed on the last named page. The volume of the REGISTER for 1853 (vii.)
contains more than thirty-one pages devoted to unrecorded wills and inventories,
being upwards of a hundred in number, which were taken from the Suffolk files.
The abstracts in all the other volumes before and after the above date, with, it may
be, one or two exceptions, are from the records, but occasionally corrected by the
files.   An attempt was made in the year above mentioned to copy these papers from
the files, chronologically, but they were then in a very disordered state, a difference
occurring, sometimes, of a century or so in the same bundle. Often the wills and
inventories belonging to one estate were separated from each other, as though they
had no family connection. Not unfrequently they were wrongly labelled, and the
names written on the backs in some cases were as far from the real names given on
the documents inside as can well be imagined. Under these circumstances it was
considered too great a labor to carry out the plan as contemplated, consequently it
was only in part fulfilled. But recently these files, down to a late date, have been
carefully arranged, and the good work is still in progress. The papers have been
placed in tin boxes, sometimes a hundred or more files in a box, suitably enveloped,
labelled and numbered. Indices and dockets have been made, evidently with great
care, and the volumes containing them have been substantially bound. The facilities, therefore, now afforded for consulting these documents are of the best kind,
creditable alike to the city and county, and to those who arranged and carried out
the work.

We have accordingly recommenced giving abstracts, and in some instances copies
of the entire papers from these early files, omitted in 1853, being matter not on
record, unless so stated.

OLIVER MELLOWES.[1]—Inventory of the outward Estate of Mr Olyvar
Mellowes deceased, taken ye 12th day of ye 9th Month Called November
1638.

Elizabeth Mellowes was granted administration 5th 10th 1638.

---

[1] Oliver Mellowes and wife Elizabeth admitted to the Church in Boston, July 20, 1634.
He was made freeman on the 3d of Sept. following; was one of the 59 Boston men who
were disarmed in 1637, as "opinionists," or supporters of Wheelwright. See Court
Records, i. 211.
His widow, Elizabeth, m. Thomas Makepeace of Dorchester. She was his second wife.
On the Records of the First Church, Boston, according to the "*Makepeace Family*," page
11, is the following entry.—" The 25th day of ye 5th Mon. 1641, Mrs. Elizabeth Makepeace,
lately called Mrs. Elizabeth Mellowes, but now ye wife of Mr. Makepeace, of Dorchester,
was granted l're of Recommendation thether."

Mentions dwelling house, garding, & ground about it, 50℔ ; 6 acres of planting ground on the necke, 25℔ ; 5 acres of wood land & 3 acres of marsh att Hogg island, 4℔ ; Lott att Mount Woollystone conteyning 80 Acres, 20℔. Whole amount of inventory 190.19ˢ. Signed by Atherton Haughe, Tho Leueritt, Will Colbron. More in Corne 20℔. Deposed by said Elizabeth, 17th, 12th mo. 1638. before vs, Jo: Winthrop Gouʳ, Increase Nowell. (File No. 9, Suffolk Wills.)

JOHN LOVERING.[1]—Will. October the 4, 1638, that John loaeren of water towne being sicke in boody did mak his will as folloeth. first I giue to my wif Ann lovern all my hoole Estat of goods and all that I haue and my mynd is that thar shall be payd ought of my Estat After my wifes death twenty poundes to the Church of watertowne to Remayn for a stoak and one hundered pounds to my brother in England which hath childeren.

 witnes
  Edward Howe,
  Margret How.

The 24th of the 9ᵗʰ mᵒ 1638 Edward & Margaret How appeared before mee Incr: Nowell & tooke their oaths that this is a true Coppey of the will of John Loveren.   witnes my hand,   pʳ Increase Nowell.

(File No. 13. The above is a copy of the paper entire.)

JUDITH SMEAD.[2]—An Inventory of the goods of the weadow Smead deseassed, taken the 18ᵗʰ day of the 3 mounth 1639. " My selfe had as folloeth "—(various utensils, household goods, produce, &c., mentioned), " I haue had for Commones of Mʳ Joanes, £4. ; of goodman Bird for the house & lot & Corne, £30 ; for Necke of land of Mr Joanes, £5.5." The names introduced, to whom various household articles were given, are those of John Pope, Sumner, Gibson, goodman Tomkins,[3] Mʳ Payne, Brother Knight,[4] sister vrsilah, Johnson, Joanes, goodman Juets[5] wife ; vyolette coat

[1] John Lovering, of Watertown, was made freeman, May 25, 1636; according to Savage was from Dedham, Co. Essex, Eng.; a selectman in 1636 and 7, a grantee of 9 lots in Watertown, all large in proportion to most others. His homestall, of 40 acres, was bounded S. by the river; E. by E. Child; W. by J. Benjamin; N. by highway. After Mr. Lovering's death, his widow, Anna, became the wife of the Rev. Edmund Browne, the first minister of Sudbury. She was probably a sister of John Barnard, Sen., of Watertown. He is doubtless the Loverell of Watertown, who was allowed by the General Court, in 1637-8, to sell in W. " wine and strong water made in the country, and no other strong water is to bee sould.'" See the testimony of Elizabeth Child and others, REGISTER, iii. 79, in regard to the will and effects of " John Lovran," or " Loveran," as he is there and elsewhere called.—*Bond's Watertown, Barry's Framingham, Court Records.*

See also abstracts of papers on file at East Cambridge, relative to Thomas Loverin, of Watertown, in the REGISTER for October, 1864, *ante* xviii. 338.

[2] Judith Smead joined the church in Dorchester about the year 1636; had 20 acres of land granted her below the burying place in D. in 1638. It is stated by Savage, that she was a sister to Israel Stoughton. Although she died in or before the year 1639, her estate was not settled until March, 1657-8. Israel Stoughton, Administrator. See REGISTER, ix. 344.

[3] Ralph Tompkins, of Dorchester, freeman May 2, 1638, removed to Salem some nine or ten years afterwards. Inventory of his estate taken there, Nov. 12, 1666.

[4] John Knight, in September, 1634, with eight or nine others, had a grant of land from the town of Dorchester of 3 acres each upon the Neponset river. Also in November of the same year, " John Knite " had 6 acres allotted him, with 12 others, for " their small and great lotts at Naponset betwixt the Indian feild and the mill," Stoughton's mill. See REGISTER, xxi. 274, 276.

In 1642 he was proprietor of lands in Watertown, and in 1651-2, with his wife Mary, sold to Thomas Underwood, late of Dorchester, ten parcels of land in Watertown. See *Bond's Watertown*, 328.

[5] Joseph Jewett, of Dorchester, had wife Mary ; removed to Rowley ; was freeman May 22, 1639, representative 1651-4 and '60 ; died Feb. 26, 1660. His second wife was Ann, widow of Bozoan Allen, whom he married in May, 1653.

to goodman Oldreges;[1] Swift, bro. Kinslie,[2] Mr. Newman,[3] White, sister Clarke, Oliver Purchase, Butler, Thomas Bird, brother Clarke, Mr. Mathers maide, Mr Palsgraue, John Dorman for stockines and shoos, clothes to his master, to goe forth with him, £13.06.08; payd goodman Pope with the boy,[4] £32; payed towards clothing of Mary, £1.10.03; payed John Scudder, 10ˢ; payed for bloodding, 1ˢ; payed for other charges of wine & cake, £1. Articles to the amount of £8.15.10 are given as "Things I know not who had as they are still in being." "debts payed by me on my sisters Account," &c. (File No. 15.)

RICHARD CRUSE.[5]—This is a true a cont or in ventory of the estate of Richard Cruse [which consisted chiefly of wearing apparel. Mentions, also, one cheste, one bybel, &c.] Amt. £1. 4. Signed by Simmon Rogers, the marke of Richard ✕ grigley. 29. 2. 1640. (File No. 18.)

ROBERT HUNT.[6]—Will. The last will and Testament of Robert Hunt, late of Sudbury in the County of Hampton,[7] Yeoman, &c. As followeth. Imprimis I Comit and comend my Soule into the hands of Allmighty God my Creato͏ͬ, And my body to bee buryed in a deacent and comely maner.

Itm. I doe by this my last will and Testament make Constitute and ordeine Susana my deare and welbeloved wife, my sole executor For possessing inioying and improueing of all my Estate Temporallse Lands Howses Tenements Chatells debts or goods moueable or immoueable For the sol vse benifit and Subsistance of her my sd wiffe and all my Children to bee at her disposall dureing the time of her widdowhoode or single estate.

Itm. my will is That if the sd Susan my wiffe shall not Continue her widdows estate but Marry and therby allter her condicon That then my Estate be deuided equally into Fowre parts the one of wᶜʰ parts thus deuided shall belong vnto her my sd wiffe as her proper estate and Legacy and the other Three parts of my sd Estate to bee deuided equally among my Children then liuieng vnmaryed or vnder age.

[1] George Aldrich, or Aldridge, had wife Catherine; freeman Dec. 7, 1636; was afterwards of Braintree, and in 1663 became one of the first settlers of Mendon.

[2] John Kinsley, or Kingsley, was in Dorchester before the arrival of Richard Mather; had a grant of land in 1635; was one of the seven signers of the covenant in 1636, when the church was newly organized and Mr. Mather became pastor. Mr. Kinsley married Alice, widow of Richard Jones, of Dorchester. The latter died in 1641.

[3] The celebrated Rev. Samuel Newman, author of the Concordance, subsequently of Weymouth, then of Rehoboth, where he died July 5, 1663, aged 61 years. See abstract of his will, REGISTER, vi. 96.

[4] This was William Smead, her son, who is spoken of in John Pope's will (12 : 2 : 1646), as "my Littell boy" to whom Mr. Pope leaves his "Lomes, and such Tackling as do belong vnto them, which is to the vallew of 3lb. provided he be willing to dwell with my wife after his time is out, also provided he be willing to Learn my Trad, and that there be a comfortable Agreement mad betweene the[m] Afterward. See REGISTER, vii. 229.

[5] The name of Cruse may be found in Paver's list of Matches or Alliances, Yorkshire pedigrees, REGISTER, xi. 265. See Burke's Encyclopedia of Heraldry for description of Coats of Arms of the Devonshire and other Cruse families.

[6] Robert Hunt, of Sudbury, was admitted an inhabitant of Charlestown, 1638. An inventory of Mrs. Susan Hunt, of Soodberie, probably his widow, taken 24 : 9 : 1642, is given in REGISTER, vii. 32.

[7] John Hunt, of Sudburowe, Nort hamptonshire, England, husbandman. Will dated Sept. 1, 1623; proved Oct. 6, 1623. Sister Alice, wife of Thomas Hunt, of Islip. Sister Helen, wife of John Fowler. Sons-in-law James Hornby, Thomas Carrington and Thomas Foster. Brother-in-law Robert Simpson. (See Hunt genealogy, by Thomas B. Wyman, pages 5, 137.) *Sudborough, Sudborow,* or as it is called in Domesday Book, *Sutburge,* is in the Hundred of Huxlow or Huxloe, sometimes Hocheslaw, and Hochesland, in Northamptonshire, England. It is 4¼ miles northwest from Thrapstone. The church is dedicated to All Saints. (See Lewis's *Topographical Dictionary of England.*)

Itm. I doe will and declare that if any of my sd Children shall in the meane time (dureing the widdowhoode or single estate of my sd wiffe) ateine to the age of Twenty and one yeares or shall hapen to Marry That then at the time of theire age of Twenty and one yeares or vppon theire day of marriage which of them first shall happen: my estate: that is to say Three parts of the aforesd Fowre be equally deuided by estemacōn among the Children then liueing and that a part proportionable thervnto bee giuen in preasent possession vnto that Child as his or her property dowry and portion and For their proper vse and benifit.

Itm. I doe will and ordeine my trusty and well beloued Friends [blank] Sedgwick and [blank] Lyne of Charles Towne in New England my ouerseers For the due performance and execution of this my last will and Testament giueing them Full power and authoryty as I my selfe to ouerveiue and see the well ordering and manageing and improueing of all my afforsd estate to preuent the vnlawfull Embezelling or makeing of it away from the vse and benifit of my wife and Children: allsoe vppon the seuerall times seasons and occations aboue specifyed to deuide and alot vnto eatch person theire seuerall porsions, as allsoe if my sd wife shall depart this preasent life or allter her Condicon by mariage to take soe many of my Children as are liueing vnder age and so dispose of them seueraly wth their portions as feofeers in trust, and my will is that what soeuer Charge or paines they are at shalbe made good vnto them by my estate to theire Full satisfacon: and this doe I confirme by my hand and seale the second day of October in the yeare of Lord one Thousand Six Hundred and Forty.

Witnessed by   pr me ROBERT HUNT.
Ro. Fordham
John Tinker   (File No. 20.   The above Will given entire.)
Thomas Bacon

SAMUEL HOLLY.—An abstract of the will of Samuel Holly is printed in the REGISTER, ii. 385, from the Record, page 30. He gives to his son one "Black Stuffe suit," instead of blue, as mentioned in the REGISTER. Samuell Hollye makes his mark, and the name of Renolt bvsh, between the names of John Jackson and Edward Jackson, is given as a witness to the original will. From the inventory we learn that he died "in ye bounds of Cambridge." On the back of the instrument are the names of Frances Gould, Will Almey, David Williams, Jo. Barcher.   (File No. 26.)

DANIEL SHEPERDSON.[1]—Inventory of the Howsing, Lands, Goods,[1] Cattell and Chattells that belonged vnto Daniell Shepherdson, deceased in Charltowne, which inventory was taken the 25th of the 3d Moneth 1647. Amt £49. 17. 00.

Witnesses and prisers.
John Greene
Faithfull Rouse[2]
Other articles enumerated to which John Greene deposed 27 : 3 : 1647.
INCREASE NOWELL, Sec.
(File No. 28.)

---

[1] Abstract of his Will in REGISTER, vii. 32.
[2] Faithfull Rouse and his wife Suretrust joined the church in Charlestown, the wife in 1642, and the husband the year after. He died May 18, 1664, aged 75.

LETTERS FROM THE GERRISH MANUSCRIPTS.

Communicated by Mrs. ISABELLA JAMES, of Cambridge, Mass.

THE following letters are copied from the originals, found among the Gerrish manuscripts, and will, doubtless, be interesting to many of the readers of the REGISTER, some of whom I trust will be able to throw light upon the historical animal who was the subject of the correspondence. In the present age of steam it is well to put on record the fact of a "Province Horse;" what were his duties and emoluments? was every member of the Provincial Council or of the Assembly furnished with a beast to ride upon, or was there only one Province Horse as the definite article might lead us to suppose?

The first letter was written by Col. Timothy Gerrish to Deacon Buckram, and was a copy made by him on the back of the other original letters, and therefore without address or date.

I.—THE PROVINCE HORSE.

Sir I rec^d your Letter bearing Date Last August 24th & you Say there is no Doubt but ye Court will see that I am p^d for Keeping ye Province horse, Above there is the acco^t of the Keeping ye horse the Court has ordred me to Deliver ye horse to S^r. W^m. Pepperrell Baronet but has ordered me no pay for Keeping So I Can Look to nobody but you who Delivered me ye horse & Desire you'd order me the money or I Shall order you to York Court in april next to answer the Above acco^t. & am your Hum^ble Servt. Kittery Jan^ry¹ 18th 1752 T. G.

To S^r. Willm. Pepperrell B^t. In Kittery. Camb. Sep^t. 18. 1752.

Sir ‖ Deacon Buckram [sic] when I was at Concord last Thursday acquainted me, That he had received a Letter from Col^o. Gerrish of ye 31 of August last, purporting, That if he did not hear from him in a short time about the Province horse he should put him to trouble for the keeping of him.—Now as what the Deacon did was in behalf of the Government, and the General Court is not sitting, I pray that you would desire the Col^o. to be easy about the matter till the Court meets; when I doubt not but some further order will be taken about the horse.

It is at the Deacon's desire that I write this; whereby I take the opportunity to salute you and your good lady; and to assure you that I am
your very respectful friend and
humble Servant
To Sr Wm Pepperrell B^t. FRA: FOXCROFT.

To The Honourable Timothy Gerrish Esq. Kittery Sept 22nd 1752
Kinsman Gerrish
this Letter came to me as you will See from our Friend Foxcroft, with best respects to your Self & my Dear Kinswoman
Yor. obed^t Humble Servant
Wm PEPPERRELL.

[To be continued.]

¹ This date was probably that when the letter was filed; it must have been written Aug. 31.

GENEALOGY OF THE FO(R)STER FAMILY DESCENDANTS OF REGINALD FO(R)STER, OF IPSWICH, MASS.

By Edward Jacob Forster, M.D., of Charlestown, Mass.

BY a tradition which exists in different branches of the family, Reginald Foster, the first of the name, is reputed to have come to this country from Exeter, Devonshire, England, and to have crossed the water in one of the ships embargoed by King Charles the First: but of this, nothing certain is as yet known.

He brought with him his wife, Judith, five sons and two daughters, and settled in Ipswich, Essex Co., Massachusetts, about the year 1638, and was one of the earliest inhabitants of that town. He lived near the "East Bridge," which stood where the stone bridge now is. It is supposed that the remains of what is known as the "old Foster house," may have been the site of his residence. This seems probable, for 6 April, 1641, there was "granted Reginald Foster, eight acres of meadow in the west meadow, if any remain there ungranted, in consideration of a little hovel that stood at the new bridge, which was taken away for the accommodating of the passage there," and "4th 11 mo., 1646," he with others "promise carting voluntary toward the East Bridge beside the rate a day work a piece."

Of his life we know very little; the following facts, gleaned from town and county records, indicate however that he was an active citizen.

The danger from Indians in these early times was such that in the year 1645 a law was passed requiring the "youth from ten to sixteen years to be exercised with small guns, half pikes, bows and arrows," and also that "every town is to have a guard set a half hour after sunset, to consist of a pikeman and musketeer, and to prepare for any sudden attack from the Indians." Our ancestor, on the 19 December, 1645, subscribed with others his proportion of 3sh. towards the sum of £24. 7sh. "to pay their leader Maior Dennison," who then commanded the military forces of Essex and Norfolk Counties.

He bought of Ralph Dix, of Ipswich, 8 March, 1647–8, "all his six acre lott he" (Dix) "bought of Wm White, lying in the common field on the north side of the river, bounded on land of Thomas Smyth, Humphrey Broadstreet and Robert Lord."

We find no mention of him again until 1652, when it was "Granted Thomas Clark and Reginal Foster, that when they shall have cut through a passage from this river into Chebacco River of ten feet wide and soe deepe as a lighter may pass through laden, and to make a ford and footebridge over, that then the town have given unto them £10 towards said passage."

On 3 June of the same year he was a witness to the will of William Averill, of Ipswich.

He bought of Roger Preston, 11 March, 1657-8, for £50, his dwelling house, house lot, barn and other buildings, also another house lot, with gardens, orchards, &c., which Preston bought of Robert Wallis, situated on the north side of the river, and one planting lot of three acres, on the north side of Town Hill, bounded on land of widow Rose Whipple, Andrew Hodges, John Morse and Thomas Treadwell. The houses were on "the High Street," probably at the east end—and in the vicinity of the ancient dwelling house of Rev. Mr. Norton, which yet stands. He had also a house lot near the "meeting-house green." On 29 September, 1663, he was an appraiser of the estate of Robert Roberts. Reginald Fo[r]ster was married when he came to this country, his wife being Judith ————. She died in Ipswich, Oct. 1664.

He married again, Sept. 1665, Sarah, widow of John Martin, of Ipswich. She survived Reginald, and 21 Sept. 1682, she became the second wife of William White, of Haverhill. She died 22 Feb. 1682–3. Reginald brought with him the following children:

    i.   Mary,[2] b. 16—; m. Francis Peabody.
    ii. Sarah,[2] b. 1620; m. William Story.
1. iii. Abraham,[2] b. 1622.
2. iv. Isaac,[2] b. 1630.
3. v. William,[2] b. 1633.
4. vi. Jacob,[2] b. 1635.
5. vii. Reginald,[2] b. 1636.

The exact date of Reginald's death is unknown. His will was proved 9 June, 1681.

1. Abraham[2] (*Reginald[1]*) was a yeoman, lived in Ipswich, where he died 15 Jan. 1711, aged about 89 years.

There is no will or administration of his estate, as he distributed it among his family by deed, 21 Dec. 1698 (Essex Deeds, lib. 13, p. 206).

He married Lydia, daughter of Caleb and Martha Burbank, of Rowley. Their children were:

 6. i.   Ephriam,[3] b. 9 Oct. 1657.
 7. ii. Abraham,[3] b. 14 Oct. 1659.
     iii. James,[3] b. 12 June, 1662; died before 1698, not mentioned in division of father's estate.
 8. iv. Isaac,[3] b. 1668; d. 13 Feb. 1717, s. p.
     v. A still child,[3] 27 Dec. 1668.
 9. vi. Benjamin,[3] b. 1670.
10. vii. Ebenezer,[3] b. 15 July, 1672.
     viii. Mehitable,[3] b. 12 Oct. 1675; m. Ebenezer Averill.
11. ix. Caleb,[3] b. 9 Nov. 1677.
     x. Ruth,[3] m. Jeremiah Pearley, of Boxford.

2. Isaac[2] (*Reginald[1]*) lived in Ipswich, near Topsfield, at the east end of "Symond's Farm," the town line dividing the farm. He married, 5 May, 1658, Mary Jackson. She died 27 Nov. 1677. He married again, 16 March, 1679–80, Martha Hale, who survived him. His children were:

     i.   Jonathan,[3] b. 9 Jan. 1658–9; d. young, not mentioned in father's will.
     ii. Mehitable,[3] b. 19 Sept. 1660; d. February, 1660–1.
12. iii. Jacob,[3] b. 9 Feb. 1662–3.
     iv. Benjamin,[3] b. June, 1665; d. 1700; adm. on estate granted to brother Daniel, 20 Nov. 1700.
     v. Elizabeth,[3] b. 20 April, 1667.
     vi. Mary,[3] b. 26 June, 1669; m. Robert Grant, 27 Feb. 168–.
13. vii. Daniel,[3] b. 14 Nov. 1670.
     viii. Martha,[3] b. 1 Aug. 1672; m. Thompson Wood, 8 Dec. 1691.
     ix. Ruth,[3] b. 20 Feb. 1673–4; m. —— Groue.
     x. Prudence,[3] b. 23 May, 1675; m. Joseph Borman, 17 Feb. 1696–7.
     xi. Hannah,[3] b. 24 Oct. 1676.
14. xii. Eleazer,[3] b. April, 1684.
     xiii. Sarah,[3] b. 19 March, 1687.

3. William[2] (*Reginald[1]*) was a yeoman; he first lived in Ipswich. In 1661 he was received as an inhabitant of Rowley, settling in that part

of the town known as Rowley Village, and afterwards incorporated as the town of Boxford. Before removing, he purchased of Joseph Jewett, of Rowley, for £11. 13s. 4d. a seventy-second part of the village lands of that place. Mr. Jewett died before the deed was passed, but 30 May, 1661, one was received from his executors. About the year 1666-7, the village lands were laid out by John Pickard and Ezekiel Northend. Wm. Foster, his brother-in-law Francis Peabody, Joseph Bixbie and Abraham Reddington received 800 acres, bounded north by land of Messrs. Dorman, Cummins and Stiles, west by Andover line, south by Wade's Brook, &c., and east by various other lots. This grant contained upland, swamp and meadow. 27 Feb. 1706-7, he deeded to his son Samuel one-half of his right in this property.

With his sons William and Jonathan, and John Kimball, all of Boxford, he bought, 3 April, 1695, 300 acres of land of Robert Eames, "lying between Five Mile Pond and Moses Tyler's house on both sides Ipswich road."

By deed, bearing date 25 Aug. 1710, he gave "to his son David, of Haverhill, all that right which falleth to us in lands, orchards, &c., which our Hon'd Father Wm. Jackson, formerly of Rowley dec'd did give to his son John Jackson and John Jackson's son John, William Jackson's grandson, and in case his grandson John died childless, then * * * * the estate mentioned in said deed * * * to return to our father's three daughters or their children. William Jackson's grandson John dying childless, said lands are divided among said daughters, viz.: Elizabeth How, Mary Foster my wife and Deborah Trumbull; which land in my right I give to my son David."

Mr. Foster was quite a prominent citizen of Rowley, frequently serving on committees in matters of importance. In 1675, he with Joseph Peabody and John Kimball were appointed collectors of taxes. In 1677 and 1680, John Peabody and he were appointed on part of the village to enforce the strict observance of the Sabbath, "and to have special inspection of those families nearest their house on either side of them," in compliance with a law passed by the general court, 23 May, 1677.

The following is a copy of a paper found among the court files:

"Theas few Liens may Sertify anney gentilmen whome it may Consern that the Town of Boxford have with the Consent of the Selectmen of Boxford chosen William Foster, Sener, to bee thaier ordenary Keepper for this year '93 and doe desier that hee may have a Lisenc for the aboue said purpos this 13th of June 1693   as a test

(sd)   John Pebody
                        Clark."

He was one of the petitioners for the incorporation of Boxford. The petition was granted 5 June, 1685. Subsequently he was a member of the committee on the part of Rowley Village to agree upon "a parting line betwixt the town of Rowley and the village." While of Ipswich he married, 15 May, 1661, Mary, daughter of William and Joanna Jackson, of Rowley; she was born 8 Feb. 1639. Their children were all born in Rowley, and were, viz.:

   i.   MARY,[3] b. 16 March, 1661-2; m. 20 Nov. 1682, Samuel Kilburn, of
          Rowley.
   ii. JUDITH,[3] b. 19 June, 1664; m. 13 April, 1693, John Platts, of Rowley.
   iii. HANNAH,[3] m. March, 1709-10, Theophilus Rix, of Wenham.

15. iv.   JONATHAN,[3] b. 6 March, 1667-8.
16. v.   WILLIAM,[3] b. 1670.
17. vi.   TIMOTHY,[3] b. 1672.
18. vii. DAVID,[3] b. 9 May, 1679.
19. viii. SAMUEL,[3] b. 20 Feb. 1681.
    ix.   JOSEPH,[3] b. 168-.

In his will he gives his five sons,—Jonathan, William, Timothy, David and Samuel,—all his salt marsh he had of his father Foster lying in Ipswich, which is to be enjoyed by his wife Mary and son Joseph during her widowhood, his "son Samuel to keep son Joseph at his house to look out for him." Jonathan and Samuel were appointed executors.

4. JACOB[2] *(Reginald[1])*, born in England about 1635, was a resident of Ipswich, in which place he died 9 July, 1710. He was deacon of the first church. He married first, 12 Jan. 1658-9, Martha Kinsman, who died 15 Oct. 1666; he married secondly, Abigail, daughter of Robert and Mary (Wait) Lord, 26 Feb. 1666-7. She survived him, dying 4 June, 1729.

The grave of Deacon Foster is marked by a stone rudely carved; the inscription is,—"Here lies Dec'n Jacob Foster, who died July ye 9th 1710, in ye 75 yr of His Age."

Deacon Foster lived in the first house built by his father Reginald. It stood on the south side of the Ipswich river, near the stone bridge; and on a portion of what is now the Heard Estate. The house lots as they were granted from the bridge, were given as follows:—1. to John Proctor. His house, built in 1635, yet stands; and is now owned by the venerable Capt. Samuel Baker. 2. Thomas Wells, probably a physician, as he had "*phissic books.*" In 1677 mention is made of "the house that Thomas Wells built." 3. Samuel Younglove. The house he doubtless built was taken down in 1862. 4. The Foster lot. An old "Foster House" remained on this lot till within the recollection of the present generation. Its last Foster occupant was an aged woman, known as "Molly Foster."

The house was called in Ipswich "the old Foster house," as long as it stood. It was given by Reginald Foster at his death to Deacon Jacob, his son, and the Deacon lived in it. The deacon also owned another house, which he sold to Abraham Perkins,—son of John, and grandson of Elder John Perkins. For in the will of Hannah (Bemsley) Perkins, widow of Abraham, she bequeaths the house her husband bought of "Deacon Foster, dec'd," to three of her grandsons. His children were:

i.   JUDITH,[3] b. 20 Oct. 1659; d. 27 Jan. 1659-60.
ii.   JOHN,[3] b. 1660; d. 1660.
iii. JACOB,[3] b. 15 May, 1662; d. June, 1662.
iv.   MARY,[3] d. 11 Jan. 1666-7.
v.   SARAH,[3] b. 3 Aug. 1665; m. John Caldwell.
20. vi.   ABRAHAM,[3] b. 4 Dec. 1667.
21. vii. JACOB,[3] b. 25 March, 1670.
    viii. AMOS,[3] b. 15 Aug. 1672; d. 12 Oct. 1672.
    ix.   ABIGAIL,[3] b. 3 July, 1674.
    x.   NATHANIEL,[3] b. 7 Oct. 1676; d. previous to 1710.
    xi.   SAMUEL,[3] b. 10 Sept. 1678;   "   "   "
22. xii. JOSEPH,[3] b. 14 Sept. 1680.
23. xiii. JAMES,[3] b. 12 Nov. 1682.
    xiv. MARY,[3] b. 25 Dec. 1684, not mentioned in father's will.

5. REGINALD[2] *(Reginald[1])*, of Chebacco, Ipswich, married Elizabeth, daughter of John Dane. He died 28 Dec. 1707, leaving an estate of about £350. His will was dated 11 July, 1704, and proved 10 Jan. 1708. His children were:

    i.   ELIZABETH,[3] b. 1653; m. Simon Wood, 8 Aug. 1674.
    ii. JUDITH,[3] b. 20 Jan. 1659–60.
24. iii. ISAAC,[3] b. 1656.
    iv. SARAH.[3]
    v. MARY,[3] b. 18 June, 1662.
25. vi. JOHN,[3] b. 15 July, 1664.
  vii. REBECCA,[3] b. 25 Feb. 1667; d. 1 July, 1684.
 viii. NAOMI,[3] b. 6 May, 1669.
    ix. RUTH,[3] b. 19 Dec. 1671; d. 1 Jan. 1677.
    x. ELEANOR,[3] b. 14 June, 1673.
    xi. HANNAH,[3] b. 5 Oct. 1675.
26. xii. NATHANIEL, b. 19 Sept. 1678.

Daniel Warner in his "Record" mentions the above children and no more, saying his "aunt Foster had," &c.—*N. E. H. G. Register*, vol. xv. p. 50.

6. EPHRAIM[3] *(Abraham,[2] Reginald[1])*, b. 9 Oct. 1657; d. at Andover, 21 Sept. 1746. He was a blacksmith. His first wife was Hannah Eames, who died 8 July, 1731. His second was Mary West, of Bradford, probably widow of John West, to whom he was published 25 Nov. 1732, and married 3 Jan. 1732–3. His children were:

    i. ROSE,[4] b. 9 May, 1679; d. 25 Feb. 1692–3.
    ii. HANNAH,[4] b. 28 May, 1682; d. young.
   iii. HANNAH,[4] b. 25 May, 1684; m. Timothy Styles, of Boxford.
   iv. JEMIMA,[4] b. 25 Feb. 1686; m. Ezekiel Ladd.
27. v. EPHRAIM,[4] b. 12 March, 1687–8.
28. vi. JOHN,[4] b. 26 March, 1690.
  vii. GIDEON,[4] b. 13 May, 1692; d. 25 June, 1707.
29. viii. DAVID,[4] b. 18 April, 1694.
30. ix. MOSES,[4] b. 27 Sept. 1696.
31. x. AARON,[4] b. 21 April, 1699.
32. xi. JOSHUA,[4] b. 13 March, 1702.
  xii. RUTH,[4] b. 1703; m. Jacob Abbott, of Brookfield.

7. ABRAHAM[3] *(Abraham,[2] Reginald[1])*, b. at Ipswich, 14 Oct. 1659; d. 23 May, 1741. He m. Mary, dau. of Robert Robinson, of Newbury, 15 Nov. 1693. His children were:—

33. i. ABRAHAM,[4] b. 12 June, 1696; bapt. at Topsfield, 12 July.
34. ii. NATHAN,[4] b. 17 May, 1700.
35. iii. DANIEL,[4] b. 13 April, 1705; bapt. at Topsfield, 15 April.

8. ISAAC[3] *(Abraham,[2] Reginald[1])*, b. at Ipswich, 16—; d. 13 Feb. 1717. Made his will "upon going out upon his country's service."

Upon a chart sent me by Moses Foster, cashier National Bank, Andover, I find the following: "had one son Ebenezer, who settled at Rowley," but I think this must be wrong.

9. BENJAMIN[3] *(Abraham,[2] Reginald[1])* was born in Ipswich, 1670; removed to Topsfield, then to Boxford, finally to Lunenburg, where he died 12 Sept. 1735. He was a 'weaver' by trade. While of Boxford, he sold "to Thos. Potter ½ of one of the 2 rights granted to the heirs of Abraham Foster by his father Rennold, in Bush hill & Turner's 8[ths], so that the ½ of one I have sold depended from my grandfather Renold, to my father Abraham, and from him to me." 29 May, 1727.—(Essex Deeds, v. p. 50.) His wife's name was Ann. He had the following children:

36. i. BENJAMIN,[4] b. 25 Nov. 1700; bapt. 27 Nov.
37. ii. AMOS,[4] b. 28 April, 1702; bapt. 10 May.
  iii. DEBORAH,[4] b. 7 May, 1704.
  iv. KEZIA,[4] b. 4 May, 1707.

38. v.   GIDEON,[4] b. 10 Oct. 1709.
    vi. JEMIMA,[4] b. 24 12 [Feb.] 1711–12; d. young.

The above were born in Ipswich.

39. vii. ISAAC,[4] b. 3 Dec. 1722; bapt. Dec. 1722.
    viii. JEMIMA,[4] bapt. Dec. 1725.

These two were born in Boxford.

Widow Ann Foster, Kezia and Isaac were cautioned at Billerica, 1739.

10.   EBENEZER[3] *(Abraham,[2] Reginald[1])* was born in Ipswich, 15 July, 1672; here moved to Rowley, where he married, 23 Jan. 1705–6, Mary Borman. He was a husbandman. His will, dated 5 June, 1717, was proved 14 April, 1718. Caleb and Isaac, his brothers, were executors. Mary, his wife, died 19 June, 1716. Their children were:

    i.   JEMIMA,[4] b. and bapt. 6 Feb. 1706–7; d. 12 March, 1706–7.
    ii. RUTH,[4] b. 23 Jan. 1709–10; bapt. 5 Feb. 1709–10.
40. iii. MOSES,[4] b. 5 Oct. 1713.

11.   CALEB[3] *(Abraham,[2] Reginald[1])* was born in Ipswich, 9 Nov. 1677. He was published on 26 April, 1702, and married on the 9 June, 1702, to Mary Sherwin, of Ipswich. He died 25 Jan. 1766. Their children were:

    i.   LYDIA,[4] b. 14 May, 1703; bapt. 16 May; pub. Nathan Dresser.
41. ii.   JONATHAN,[4] b. 30 Nov. 1704; bapt. 3 Dec.
    iii. SARAH,[4] b. 3 7 [Sept.] 1706; bapt. 8 Sept.
42. iv.   CALEB,[4] b. 5 June, 1708.
43. v.   STEPHEN,[4] b. 24 April, 1710; bapt. 30 April.
    vi.   MARY,[4] bapt. 30 Dec. 1711.
    vii. SARAH,[4] bapt. 11 Sept. 1715.
    viii. PHILEMON,[4] b. 2 June, 1713; bapt. 6 June; d. previous 1766.
    ix.   JOHN,[4] bapt. 10 Nov. 1717; d. previous 1766.

In deeding, in 1766, his property to his sons, as he does not mention Philemon or John, it is to be presumed that they died before that date.

12.   JACOB[3] *(Isaac,[2] Reginald[1])* was born in Ipswich, 9 Feb. 1662; removed to Topsfield as early as 1686, where all his children were baptized. In 1718 he removed to Lebanon, Conn. He married first, Sarah, daughter of Isaiah Wood, 12 Sept. 1688, who died 27 Sept. 1697; secondly, Mary Edwards, 20 May, 1700. Jacob and his wife Mary were dismissed the church at Topsfield, 29 Jan. 1718, and admitted to the church at Lebanon, 6 July, 1718. His children were:

44. i.   BENJAMIN,[4] bapt. 6 Oct. 1689.
    ii.   MARY,[4] b. 13 May, bapt. 17 May, 1691.
    iii. ISAAC,[4] b. 13 March, bapt. 16 March, 1701; d. 27 Dec. 1703.
45. iv.   JOHN,[4] b. 11 Sept., bapt. 13 Sept. 1702.
    v.   EZEKIEL,[4] bapt. 31 Dec. 1704; d. 20 Oct. 1727, Lebanon, Conn.
    vi.   MARTHA,[4] bapt. 24 —, 1709.
46. vii. DAVID,[4] bapt. 29 April, 1711.
47. viii. JONATHAN,[4] b. 3 June, 1711.

13.   DANIEL[3] *(Isaac,[2] Reginald[1])* was born in Ipswich, 14 Nov. 1670; resided in Topsfield, where his children were born, until 1718, when he removed to Lebanon, Conn., where in company with his brother Jacob and with his wife Mary were admitted to church there at the same time. His will, dated 4 May, 1746, was proved 19 Nov. 1753. He married, first, Katherine Freese, of Topsfield, 2 March, 1693, who died 3 March, 1694–5; secondly, Mary, daughter of Samuel and Mary (Seaver) Dresser, of Rowley, 4 Dec. 1696. His children were:

     i.   KATHERINE,[4] b. 21 Aug., bapt. 23 Aug. 1696.
     ii. MARY,[4] b. 24 Feb. 1697; d. 23 Jan. 1698–9.
     iii. HEPSIBAH,[4] b. 7 May, 1700.
     iv. MEHITABLE,[4] b. 16 Oct., bapt. 19 Oct. 1701; m. Daniel Dennison at Lebanon, Conn.
       v. PHINEAS,[4] b. 19 July, bapt. 25 July, 1703.
     vi. HANNAH,[4] b. 29 April, bapt. 6 May, 1705; d. young.
49. vii. JEREMIAH,[4] b. 16 June, 1707; bapt. 15 Jan. 1707–8.
     viii. HANNAH,[4] bapt. 5 Jan. 1709; unm. 1746.
50. ix. ASA,[4] b. 15, 11 1710 [15 Jan. 1710–11]; bapt. 21 Jan. 1710–11.

14. ELEAZER[3] (*Isaac,*[2] *Reginald*[1]) was born in Ipswich, 6 April, 1684. He died there 15 Nov. 1771. He was a weaver. He was published to Eliza Fiske, 6 Dec. 1703, who died 19 Feb. 1758. Their children were:—

     i. ELIZABETH,[4] bapt. 17 Feb. 1705.
51. ii. HABIJAH, or ABIJAH,[4] bapt. Jan. 1707–8.
52. iii. JOHN,[4] b. 20 May, 1714.

15. JONATHAN[3] (*William,*[2] *Reginald*[1]) was born in Boxford, 6 March, 1667–8; died there 21 May, 1730. No will or settlement of estate on record. He married Abigail, daughter of John and Sarah Kimball, 14 Dec. 16—. She was born 29 April, 1677. They were admitted to the church, 21 Sept. 1702–3. Their children were:

53. i. JONATHAN,[4] b. 15 Sept. 16—.
     ii. ABIGAIL,[4] b. 22 Nov. 1697; m. Jacob Tyler, of Andover.
54. iii. ZEBADIAH,[4] b. 28 Sept. 1702.

16. WILLIAM[3] (*William,*[2] *Reginald*[1]) was born in Rowley Village, afterwards Boxford, 1670; removed to Andover, 1697–8, and died there 29 Aug. 1755, in his 86th year. He was a weaver, and in his will he gave to his son Asa his "Weaver's loom." He was at first a member of the North Parish in Andover, but in 1711 he was one of thirty-five who were dismissed to form the South Church. He married, first, Sarah, daughter of John and Sarah Kimball, of Boxford, 6 July, 169–. She was born 19 Sept. 1669; died 6 Nov. 1729. Secondly, Margaret Gould, 13 Nov. 1744, who survived him. His children were:

     i. SARAH,[4] b. 20 April, 169–, in Boxford; bapt. 15 July, 1693, in Topsfield; m. Nehemiah Abbot.
     ii. MARY,[4] b. 2 Jan. 1698, in Boxford; m. Timothy Abbot.
55. iii. JOHN,[4] b. 27 Sept. 1701, in Andover.
     iv HANNAH,[4] m. John Lovejoy.
     v. LYDIA,[4] b. 1707; m. David Blunt.
56. vi. ASA,[4] b 16 June, 1710.

An account of his real estate transactions can be found in "One Line of the Descendants of William Foster," by Perley Derby, p. 20.

17. TIMOTHY[3] (*William,*[2] *Reginald*[1]) was born in Boxford, 1672. He married, first, Mary, daughter of Ephraim and Martha Dorman. He received from his father-in-law, 4 Sept. 1718, 100 acres of land for the benefit of his children by Mary, she being then deceased; said land being formerly in Coxhall, now Swansfield, Me. He married, secondly, Ruth ———. His children were:

57. i. JEREMIAH,[4] b. 4 May, 1701.
58. ii. DAVID,[4] b. 17 Aug. bapt. 20 Aug. 1704.
59. iii. AMOS,[4] bapt. 1 Feb. 1713.
     iv. MARY,[4] b. 21 June, 1718; d. young.
     v. REBECCA,[4] bapt. June, 1710; m. Solomon Gould.
     vi. MARY,[4] b. June, 1720.

18. DAVID³ (*William,² Reginald¹*) was born in Boxford, 9 May, 1679. He removed to Haverhill after the birth of his second child, where he was living in 1725. He married there Mary Black. There is no will or settlement of his estate on record. He was a joiner and yeoman. His children were:

 60. i ABIAL,⁴ b. 2 May, 1702.
 61. ii. PHINEAS,⁴ b. 5 June, 1704.
 62. iii. SIMON,⁴ b. 17 June, 1707.
   iv. HANNAH,⁴ b. 29 Oct. 1709.
   v. LYDIA,⁴ b. 28 Feb. 1712.
   vi. GRACE,⁴ b. 20 May, 1714.
   vii. DORCAS,⁴ b. 1 April, 1717.

19. SAMUEL³ (*William,² Reginald¹*) was b. in Boxford, 20 Feb. 1681–2 ; died there 30 August, 1747. He married Mary Macoon, of Cambridge, 2 Sept. 1703. She died 6 Dec. 1740. Their children were:

   i. SAMUEL,⁴ bapt. 27 Jan. 1705 ; d. young.
 63. ii. THOMAS,⁴ bapt. 23 May, 1708.
   iii. MERCY,⁴ b. 23 Oct., bapt. 30 Oct. 1710.
 64. iv. WILLIAM,⁴ b. 22 July ; bapt. 2 Aug. 1711.
   v. MARY,⁴ b. 5 May ; bapt. 5 July, 1719.
   vi. SAMUEL,⁴ bapt. Jan. 1721–2 ; d. 15 Feb. 1748.

20. ABRAHAM³ ((*Jacob,² Reginald¹*) was born in Ipswich, 4 Dec. 1667, where he died 25 Dec. 1720–1. Administration on his estate was granted his widow, 27 Jan. 1720–1. He was a carpenter. His wife was Abigail ———. She died 8 Oct. 1732. Their children were :

 65. i. JEREMIAH.⁴
   ii. ABRAHAM,⁴ b. 11 April ; d. 20 May, 1702.
   iii. NATHANIEL,⁴ b. 11 (2), 1706 ; d. young.
 66. iv. ABRAHAM,⁴ b. 5 (6), 1716.
 67. v. NATHANIEL,⁴ b. 9 Aug. 1719.
   vi. JUDITH,⁴ b. 15 March, 1713 ; d. unm. before 1735.
   vii. ABIGAIL,⁴ m. Daniel Safford.
   viii. MARY,⁴ b. 15 May, 1715.
   ix. SARAH,⁴ m. John Rust.

21. JACOB³ (*Jacob,² Reginald¹*) was born in Ipswich, 25 March, 1670, and died there 6 March, 1758. He was a blacksmith. He was thrice married : first to Mary, dau. of John and Sarah Caldwell, 5 March, 1697. She was born 26 Feb. 1672 ; d. 2 April, 1709. Secondly to Martha Graves, to whom he was published 10 Dec. 1709. Thirdly to Mary Willis, to whom he was published 14 Oct. 1742. His children were :

   i. JACOB,⁴ b. 9 May, 1697 ; d. young.
 68. ii. WILLIAM,⁴ b. 11 May, 1699.
   iii. MARY,⁴ b. 19 March, 1700 ; m. Jacob Louden.
   iv. ABIGAIL,⁴ b. 27 Sept. 1703 ; m. William Holland.
   v. ISRAEL,⁴ b. 3 March, 1706–7 ; not mentioned in father's will.
 69. vi. NATHANIEL,⁴ b. 14 Dec. 1712.
   vii. ANNE,⁴ b. April, 1715 ; m. Robert Mitchell.
   viii. MARTHA,⁴ m. Richard Harris.

22. JOSEPH³ (*Jacob,² Reginald¹*) was born in Ipswich, 14 Sept. 1680, in which place he died 22 Feb. 1755. He was a cordwainer. He attended the South Meeting-House, owning one half of a gallery pew. His estate was valued at £215 11 7. He married first, Elizabeth Goodwin, 23 Jan. 1704. Secondly, Mary Cressy, of Salem, to whom he was published 20 July, 1712. Thirdly, Sarah, dau. of Nicholas and Mary (Linforth)

Brown, to whom he was published 30 (11) 1714. She was born in Haver-hill 3 March, 1685–6, d. May, 1761. His children were :

    i.   ELIZA,[4] b. 23 (12), 1706 ; not mentioned in father's will.
    ii. SAMUEL,[4] b. 16 April, 1709 ; d. 5 Sept. 1730.
70. iii. JOSEPH,[4] b. 14 Feb. 1714.
71. iv. JAMES,[4] b. 4 March, 1716.
72. v. NATHAN,[4] b. 19 Feb. 1717–8.
    vi. SARAH,[4] bapt. 13 Jan. 1722 ; d. 24 March, 1722.
73. vii. ISAAC.[4]
    viii. SARAH,[4] bapt. 23 Feb. 1723 ; d. 30 April, 1729.
74. ix. JACOB,[4] b. and bapt. 27 March, 1726.
    x. EBENEZER,[4] bapt. 6 Nov. 1720 ; not mentioned in father's will.
75. xi. ABRAHAM,[4] bapt. 27 Oct. 1728.

23. JAMES[3] (*Jacob,*[2] *Reginald*[1]) was born in Ipswich, 12 Nov. 1682. His will, dated 20 April, and proved 6 May, 1751, gives the use of his estate, valued at £165 : 17: 6, to his wife Anna during her life, afterwards to the children of his brothers Jacob, Abraham and Joseph, and brother-in-law John Caldwell. He married Anna Cross 15 May, 1706–7, but left no issue. His widow was published to Benjamin Fowler, of Rowley, 23 July, 1756.

24. ISAAC[3] (*Reginald,*[3] *Reginald*[1]) was born in Ipswich, 1656. He was styled "corporal." Administration on his estate was granted to son Jonathan, 15 Dec. 1741. (Essex Probate Records, vol. xxiii. p. 41. Estate £124.15.) Jonathan was appointed administrator of the estate of his mother, Abigail, 30 Oct. 1749. (Essex Probate Records, vol. xxix. p. 28). The children of Isaac were :

    i.   HANNAH,[4] b. 16 Feb. 1681.
76. ii. JONATHAN.[4]
77. iii. ISAAC.[4]
78. iv. JACOB.[4]
    v. ABIGAIL.[4]
    vi. FREEBORN,[4] bapt. 28 Jan. 1727–8 ; m. Isaac Balch.

25. JOHN[3] (*Reginald,*[2] *Reginald*[1]) was born in Ipswich, 15 July, 1664, where he died 9 Dec. 1736. He was styled "Sergeant." He lived in Chebacco Village. His wife was Mary ———. Their children were :

79. i.   JEREMIAH,[4] b. 1691.
80. ii. MOSES,[4] b. 1697.
81. iii. JOHN.[4]
    iv. JOSHUA,[4] d. unm., a mariner.
    v. MARTHA,[4] m. Jonathan Burnam.
    vi. ELIZABETH,[4] m. Daniel Smith.

26. NATHANIEL[3] (*Reginald,*[2] *Reginald*[1]) was born in Ipswich, 19 Sept. 1678, and lived in Chebacco Parish. His will, dated 9 Dec. 1756, was proved 21 June, 1762. He married Joanna Marshall, 19 April, 1704. She died 27 May, 1762. Their children were :

    i.   DINAH,[4] b. 17—, d. 23 July, 1781, aged about 78 years.
    ii. SARAH,[4] b. 18 March, 1706 ; m. William Holmes,
    iii. HANNAH,[4] b. 27 April, 1710 ; d. 5 Aug. 1794, unm.
    iv. MARY,[4] b. 18 Aug. 1713 ; d. 24 Sept. 1773, unm.
    v. JEMIMA,[4] b. 29 May, 1721 ; d. 22 July, 1797.
82. vi. NATHANIEL.[4]

27. EPHRAIM[4] (*Ephraim,*[3] *Abraham,*[2] *Reginald*[1]) was born in Andover, 12 March, 1687–8. He died there 8 April, 1738. His wife was Abigail,

dau. of Joseph Poor, of Newbury, to whom he was published 16 Jan. 1715–16.   She died 28 Aug. 1747, having married, after Mr. Foster's death, Lieut. Nathaniel Frie.   Their children were :

    i.   JEDIDIAH,[5] b. 7 Oct. 1718 ; d. young.
    ii. SALLY,[5] d. young.
    iii. HANNAH,[5] b. 3 April, 1725 ; d. 7 March, 1725–6.
    iv. JEDIDIAH,[5] b. 10 Oct. 1726.
    v. NAOMI.[5]
    vi. HANNAH,[5] b. 23 March, 1730 ; d. 18 Dec. 1736.

28. JOHN[4] (*Ephraim,[3] Abraham,[2] Reginald[1]*) was born in Andover, 26 March, 1690.   His will was proved 7 Dec. 1778.   He married first, Rebecca Roe, of Boxford, 7 Jan. 1714–15.   Secondly, Dorcas, dau. of Luke Hovey, to whom he was published 17 Sept. 1732.   His children were :

    i.   JOHN,[5] b. 17 Feb. 1716.
    ii. JEMIMA,[5] b. 19 May, 1717 ; d. 24 Jan. 1736–7.
    iii. STEPHEN,[5] b. 14 Aug. 1720.
    iv. NATHAN,[5] b. 4 July, bapt. 7 July, 1734.
    v. REBECCA,[5] b. 20 Nov. 1735 ; d. 18 Jan. 1736–7.
    vi. JEMIMA,[5] b. 22 Nov. 1741 ; d. young.

29. DAVID[4] (*Ephraim,[3] Abraham,[2] Reginald[1]*) was born in Andover, 18 April, 1694; died there 22 June, 1759.   He was a deacon of the church.   He was thrice married: first to Elizabeth Abbott, 25 Nov. 1714. She died 1 Dec. 1715.   Secondly, to Lydia Farnum, 29 Aug. 1716.   She died 21 March, 1745–6.   Thirdly, to Judith Norton, of Salisbury, to whom he was published 17 Sept. 1748.   After his death she married Nehemiah Carleton, of Bradford, to whom she was published 14 June, 1760.   His children were :

    i.   EBENEZER,[5] b. 23 Nov. 1715.
    ii. DAVID,[5] b. 20 Dec. 1717 ; d. 22 Dec. 1736.
    iii. LYDIA,[5] b. 31 July, 1720 ; d. 24 Aug. 1736.
    iv. MEHITABEL,[5] b. 21 May, 1730 ; m. Nathan Andrews.
    v. REBECCA,[5] b. 25 July, bapt. 30 July, 1732.
    vi. ELIZABETH,[5] m. Benjamin Stiles, of Boxford.
    vii. RUTH,[5] m. Benjamin Porter, Jr.
    viii. DAVID,[5] d. young.
    ix. GIDEON.[5]

30. MOSES[4] (*Ephraim,[3] Abraham,[2] Reginald[1]*) was born in Andover, 27 Sept. 1696.   He removed to New-Hampshire, living in Suncook and Pembroke, Merrimack Co.   He was in the latter place as early as 1746. His will, dated 12 March, was proved 7 Dec. 1766, at Exeter, N. H.   He married Elizabeth Rodgers, of Boxford, to whom he was published 27 Nov. 1719.   She died 2 Oct. 1729.   He then married Mary Gray, 26 Nov. 1730. His children were:

    i.   ASA,[5] b. 15 April, 1721.
    ii. MOSES,[5] b. 25 March, 1723 ; d. young.
    iii. DANIEL,[5] b. 7 Jan. 1726.
    iv. MOSES,[5] b. 26 March, 1728.
    v. EPHRAIM,[5] b. 30 Aug. 1731 ; d. young.
    vi. HENRY,[5] b. 23 July, 1733 ; d. 16 Jan. 1736–7.
    vii. MARY,[5] b. 21 March, 1736 ; d. 29 Jan. 1736–7.
    viii. MARY,[5] b. 27 Dec. 1737 ; m. ——— Conner.
    ix. ELIZABETH,[5] b. 3 March, 1740.
    x. HENRY,[5] b. 8 March, 1742.
    xi. CALEB.[5]
    xii. SARAH,[5] m. Francis Carr.

31. AARON[4] (*Ephraim,*[3] *Abraham,*[2] *Reginald*[1]) was born in Andover, 21 April, 1699. Settled in Bolton. He married Martha Smith, 13 March, 1721–2. His children were:

    i.   PENELOPE,[5] b. 6 Jan. 1723; d. 29 Aug. 1724.
    ii. MARTHA,[5] b. 12 March, 1725; d. 7 July, 1735.
    iii. ELIJAH,[5] b. 11 March, 1727.
    iv. ISRAEL,[5] b. 17 July, 1729.
    v.   ELEANOR.[5]
    vi. PENELOPE,[5] b. 30 Jan. 1732.

32. JOSHUA[4] (*Ephraim,*[3] *Abraham,*[2] *Reginald*[1]) was born in Andover, 13 March, 1702. He married first, Mary Barker, 7 May, 1730. Secondly, Mary Town, 17 Aug. 1769. His children were:

    i.   JOSHUA,[5] b. 19 May, 1731.
    ii.   NATHAN,[5] b. 11 Aug. 1733; d. 20 Oct. 1752.
    iii. ISAAC,[5] b. 25 May, 1736; d. 7 Sept. 1738.
    iv. HANNAH.[5] b. 9 April, 1739; m. Phineas Tyler, of Andover.
    v.   MARY,[5] b. 23 Nov. 1741; d. 10 Dec. 1747.
    vi.   ISAAC,[5] b. 10 Feb. 1745; d. 12 Jan. 1747–8.
    vii. SUSAN,[5] b. 17 Nov. 1747; m. Samuel ——.
    viii. MARY,[5] b. 22 March, 1750; m. Bradstreet Tyler, of Boxford, 13 April, 1769, in Atkinson, N. H.; having been published in Andover 29 March, 1769, and forbidden by her father.

33. ABRAHAM[4] (*Abraham,*[3] *Abraham,*[2] *Reginald*[1]) was born in Ipswich, 12 June, 1696. He was a carpenter. Administration on his estate was granted to his son Thomas, 29 June, 1767. He was published at Topsfield, 5 April, 1718, to Sarah Dunnell. She was admitted to the church at Topsfield, 2 July, 1732. Their children were:

    i.   ABRAHAM,[5] b. 4 May, 1719.
    ii. SARAH,[5] b. 4 May, 1721; m. —— Adams.
    iii. THOMAS,[5] b. 11 Aug. 1724.
    iv. HANNAH,[5] b. 18 Sept. 1726; d. 1802, unm.
    v.   AMOS,[5] bapt. 22 Dec. 1728.
    vi. RUTH,[5] bapt. 17 March, 1734; d. 1806, unm.
    vii. ABIGAIL,[5] bapt. 3 April, 1737.

34. NATHAN[4] (*Abraham,*[3] *Abraham,*[2] *Reginald*[1]) was born in Ipswich, 17 May, 1700.

This may be the Nathan who settled in Stafford, Conn., about 1720, and was the ancestor of the Hon. Lafayette S. Foster, of Norwich, Conn. At present there is no proof of the identity of these two Nathans.

35. DANIEL[4] (*Abraham,*[3] *Abraham,*[2] *Reginald*[1]) was born in Ipswich, 13 April, 1705. He was living in Rowley in 1724, and in Ipswich as late as 1746–7. He married first, Hannah Black, of Rowley, to whom he was published 1 Jan. 1724. Secondly, to Elizabeth Davis, of Rowley, 16 May, 1733. His children were:

    i.   ISAAC,[5] b. 19 Feb. 1725.
    ii. MERCY,[5] b. 14 Aug. 1727.
    iii. DANIEL,[5] b. 28 Aug. 1729.
    iv. HANNAH,[5] b. 20 Sept. 1731.
    v.   ELIZABETH,[5] b. March, 1733–4.

36. BENJAMIN[4] (*Benjamin,*[3] *Abraham,*[2] *Reginald*[1]) was born in Ipswich, 25 Nov. 1700; died there 19 Dec. 1775, of asthma. He was a physician. Felt, in his History of Ipswich, says of him: " He had been in the practice of his profession over fifty years, was a distinguished botanist, a

skilful and successful physician." He married Sarah Low, a widow, 22 June, 1761.

Benjamin Foster, Boxford, and Lydia Burbank, were first published 30 Aug. 1730. This may have been the first marriage of Benjamin.

37. AMOS[4] (*Benjamin,[3] Abraham,[2] Reginald[1]*) was born in Ipswich, 28 April, 1702; bapt. 10 May, 1702. Removed to Boxford with his father, thence to Tewksbury, where he was in 1730. His will was proved 17 June, 1754. He married Elizabeth Kittredge, of Haverhill, 8 Oct. 1725. His children were:

i. JAMES.[5]
ii. JONATHAN.[5]
iii. AMOS.[5]
iv. MARY.[5]

38. GIDEON[4] (*Benjamin,[3] Abraham,[2] Reginald[1]*) was born in Ipswich, 10 Oct. 1709; resided in Danvers; died ———, 1772. He was a mason. He married, first, Lydia Goldthwait, 10 Feb. 1731–2; she was born 7 May, 1710. Secondly, Deborah ———. His children were:

i. LYDIA,[5] b. 22 May, 1733; d. 23 May, 1741.
ii. GIDEON,[5] b. 23 May, 1741; d. 13 June, 1741.
iii. LYDIA,[5] b. 12 April, 1747; m. Abel Osborn.
iv. GIDEON,[5] b. 13 Feb. 1748–9.
v. BENJAMIN,[5] b. 12 June, 1750.

39. ISAAC[4] (*Benjamin,[3] Abraham,[2] Reginald[1]*) was born in Boxford, 3 Dec. 1722, probably removed to Lunenburg with his father.

40. MOSES[4] (*Ebenezer,[3] Abraham,[2] Reginald[1]*) was born in Rowley, 5 Oct. 1713, removed to Arundel (now Cape Porpoise), York Co., Maine, where he was living in 1735. He was married at Ipswich, to Hannah Andrews, of Boxford, 10 March, 1736–7.

41. JONATHAN[4] (*Caleb,[3] Abraham,[2] Reginald[1]*) was born in Ipswich, 30 Nov. 1704; died there May, 1779. He married, first, Jemima Cummings, 1 Jan. 1733–4. Secondly, Dorcas Porter, 17 Dec. 1751, at Topsfield. His children were:

i. AFFE,[5] b. 4 Dec. 1734.
ii. PHILEMON,[5] b. 11 June, 1737.
iii. APPHIA,[5] b. 16 Jan. 1739.
iv. JEMIMA,[5] b. 1 April, 1742.
v. OLIVE,[5] b. 20 Aug. 1744.
vi. JONATHAN,[5] b. 16 Sept. 1753.
vii. MOSES,[5] b. 3 April, 1755.
viii. DORCAS,[5] b. 18 Dec. 1756.
ix. MARY,[5] b. 10 June, 1759.
x. CALEB,[5] b. 8 Dec. 1760.
xi. MERCY,[5] b. 20 Jan. 1764.
xii. SALOME,[5] b. 4 Nov. 1766.

42. CALEB[4] (*Caleb,[3] Abraham,[2] Reginald[1]*) was born in Ipswich, 5 June, 1708. He was married at Rowley, to Priscilla Baxter, 4 Nov. 1729. Caleb Foster, Jr. and wife Priscilla, make deed to Thomas Foster, Ipswich, 14 Jan. 1763; this is the latest we find any account of him. There is no record of any children.

43. STEPHEN[4] (*Caleb,[3] Abraham,[2] Reginald[1]*) was born in Ipswich, 24 April, 1710, lived in Topsfield, where he died 15 Jan. 1781. There is no settlement of his estate on record. He married Rebecca, daughter of Deacon Jacob and Rebecca (Barker) Peabody, 21 April, 1737. She was born in Topsfield, 3 Feb. 1715; died 23 March, 1790. His children were:

    i. Stephen,[5] b. 13 July, 1741.
    ii. Nathaniel,[5] b. 9 Jan. 1743–4; d. 23 Jan. 1743–4.
    iii. Abigail,[5] b. 25 Feb. 1746; m. Philemon Perkins.
    iv. Jacob,[5] b. 26 July, 1749; d. 28 Jan. 1770, "a young man."

44. Benjamin[4] (*Jacob,[3] Isaac,[2] Reginald[1]*) was baptized in Ipswich, 6 Oct. 1689. He removed to Lebanon, Conn.

45. John[4] (*Jacob,[3] Isaac,[2] Reginald[1]*) was born in Ipswich, 13 Sept· 1702. Removed to Lebanon, Conn., where he owned covenant 23 Feb. 1729· He married Hannah Thorp, 26 Aug. 1724. She owned covenant 3 Dec. 1727·

46. David[4] (*Jacob,[3] Isaac,[2] Reginald[1]*) was baptized in Topsfield, 29 April, 1711. Removed to Lebanon, Conn. He married Althea ———. His children were:

    i. Reuben,[5] b. 3 April, 1733.
    ii. Elijah,[5] b. 26 Feb. 1734–5.
    iii. Eliab,[5] b. 18 April, 1737.
    iv. Lucy,[5] b. 14 Sept. 1740.

47. Jonathan[4] (*Jacob,[3] Isaac,[2] Reginald[1]*) was born in Topsfield, 3 June, 1711. Removed to Lebanon, Conn.

48. Phineas[4] (*Daniel,[2] Isaac,[2] Reginald[1]*) was born in Topsfield, 16 July, 1703. Removed to Lebanon, Conn., where he married Lydia Hill, 1 May, 1735. He had:

    i. Phebe,[5] b. 5 April, 1736.

49.* Jeremiah[4] (*Daniel,[3] Isaac,[2] Reginald[1]*) was born in Topsfield, 19 June, 1707. Removed to Lebanon, Conn. He married there Mary Skinner. His children were:

    i. Samuel,[5] b. 13 Feb. 1731–2; d. 23 Feb. 1731–2.
    ii. Mary,[5] b. 3 July, 1733.
    iii. Jeremiah,[5] b. 9 May, 1735.
    iv. Nathaniel,[5] b. 27 Feb. 1738.

50. Asa[4] (*Daniel,[3] Isaac,[2] Reginald[1]*) was born in Topsfield, 15 (11), 1710. Removed to Lebanon, Conn. He married Hannah ———. His children were:

    i. Mary,[5] b. 20 May, 1745; d. 25 June, 1751.
    ii. Samuel,[5] b. and d. 5 April, 1747.
    iii. Daniel,[5] b. 26 Feb. 1747–8.
    iv. Asa,[5] b. 22 April, 1750.
    v. Mary,[5] b. 24 Sept. 1753.
    vi. William,[5] b. 24 Oct. 1755.
    vii. Hannah,[5] b. 5 May, 1757.

51. Habijah[4] or Abijah[4] (*Eleazer,[3] Isaac,[2] Reginald[1]*) was baptized in Ipswich, Jan. 1707–8. Removed to New Ipswich, N. H., probably being sent there by the grantees about 1734. His was the first family that went there, and he must be considered as the first settler. In 1736 he was in Ipswich, but he soon returned, for his son Ebenezer was the first child born in New Ipswich. In 1758 or 9, with his son Ebenezer, enlisted in the army against the French and Indians. While encamped near Crownpoint both father and son died of small-pox. He married Mary Knowlton, of Ipswich, 13 Dec. 1733. During the revival of 1786, she joined the Rev. Mr. Farrell's church. His children were:

    i. Mary,[5] b. in Ipswich, Aug. 1736.
    ii. Ebenezer,[5] b. in N. Ipswich, about 1739; d. 1759.

iii. ELIZABETH,[5] b. in N. Ipswich about 1741 ; m. { John Fletcher. / William Hodgkins.

iv. SAMUEL.[5]

v. DANIEL.[5]

vi. EPHRAIM.[5]

vii. HEPSEY,[5] b. 1759 ; m. Isaac Appleton.

52. JOHN[4] (*Eleazer,*[3] *Isaac,*[2] *Reginald*[1]) was born in Ipswich, 20 May, 1714; was probably a weaver, for that was his father's occupation, and Essex Deeds 83, 105, 1 Dec. 1741, Eleazer Foster, Ipswich, weaver, sells to John Foster, weaver, ¼ acre land bounded on that of John Manning.

53. JONATHAN[4] (*Jonathan,*[3] *William,*[2] *Reginald*[1]) was born in Boxford, 15 Sept. 16—; baptized 1693. He married Hannah, daughter of William and Hannah (Hale) Peabody. She was born Aug. 1693. His children were:

i. OLIVER,[5] b. 17 Aug. 1719, at Boxford.

ii. HANNAH,[5] b. 15 Dec. 1721, at Boxford.

iii. JONATHAN,[5] b. 11 Oct. 1727, at Haverhill.

iv. WILLIAM,[5] b. 9 Nov. 1729, at Haverhill.

v. RICHARD,[5] b. 20 Feb. 1732–3, at Boxford.

Jonathan Foster, of Boxford, sold land in Chester, N. H., in 1762. Witnesses, Oliver and Richard Foster. Exeter Deeds.

54. ZEBADIAH[4] (*Jonathan,*[3] *William,*[2] *Reginald*[1]) was born in Boxford, 28 Sept. 1702. He and his wife were admitted to the church there, 28 Jan. 1728. He was living in 1771. He married Margaret Tyler, to whom he was published 12 Jan. 1723–4. His children were:

i. MARGARET,[5] b. 13 July, 1724.

ii. LYDIA,[5] b. 24 Feb. 1725–6.

iii. ANNE,[5] b. 13 May, 1728 ; d. 9 April, 1748.

iv. ZEBADIAH,[5] b. 14 Dec. 1730 ; d. 8 Nov. 1734.

v. ABNER,[5] b. 23 April, 1733.

vi. ZEBADIAH,[5] b. 25 Aug. 1735.

vii. DUDLEY,[5] b. 21 Feb. 1737.

viii. ABIGAIL,[5] b. 25 June, 1740 ; m. Nathan Kimball, Jr., of Boxford.

ix. LUCY,[5] b. 25 March, 1747.

55. JOHN[4] (*William,*[3] *William,*[2] *Reginald*[1]) was born in Andover, 27 Sept. 1701 ; died there 17 June, 1773. He was a yeoman, and possessed considerable land. In the history of Andover he is styled captain. He appears to have been a man of some influence, and with his brother Asa was appointed on a committee to instruct the representative at the General Court to enter a protest against the Stamp Act. Again in 1768 the two brothers were on a committee to frame resolutions to induce the inhabitants to "ignore extravagance, idleness and vice, and to promote manufactures, industry, economy and good morals in the town, and discountenance importation and the use of foreign superfluities." He married Mary Osgood, 13 Jan. 1724–5. She died 6 April, 1772. His children were:

i. WILLIAM,[5] b. 24 Sept. 1727 ; d. 8 April, 1729.

ii. JOHN,[5] b. 22 March, 1729 ; d. 7 April, 1729.

iii. WILLIAM,[5] b. 4 March, 1730.

iv. A son.[5] b. and d. 13 Jan. 1732.

v. JOHN,[5] b. 14 Feb. 1733.

vi. MARY,[5] b. 12 Jan. 1735 ; d. 7 Dec. 1763.

vii. ISAAC,[5] b. 28 April, 1737.

viii. GIDEON,[5] b. 21 Aug. 1739.

ix. OBADIAH,[5] b. 25 May, 1741.

x. SOLOMON,[5] b. 14 April, 1743.

xi. OSGOOD,[5] b. 10 Nov., d. 15 Nov. 1745.

56. Asa,[4] Captain (*William,*[3] *William,*[2] *Reginald*[1]) was born in Andover, 16 June, 1710. He died there 17 July, 1787, leaving an estate valued at £830 16s. 7d. He owned 160 acres of land in Canterbury, N. H., besides large tracts of upland, meadow, &c., in Andover. 8 March, 1776, he was appointed one of the members of a committee of the town, on Correspondence, Inspection and Safety. He married first, Elizabeth, dau. of John Abbot, 26 Oct. 1732. She was born 1712, died 4 July, 1758. Secondly, Lucy Rogers, of Ipswich, to whom he was published 10 Dec. 1763. She died 17 Oct. 1787. His children were:

   i.   Asa,[5] b. 29 Aug. 1733.
   ii. Abiel,[5] b. 8 Aug. 1735.
   iii. Daniel,[5] b. 25 Sept. 1737.
   iv. David,[5] b. 7 May, 1740; d. 14 Oct. 1740, at Canterbury, N. H.
   v. David,[5] b. 24 Dec. 1741.
   vi. Elizabeth,[5] b. 14 April, 1744; m. Gen. Nathaniel Lovejoy.
   vii. Jonathan,[5] b. 28 July, 1747.
  viii. Sarah,[5] b. 15 Feb. 1750; m. —— Bradley.
   ix. Lucy,[5] b. 1 Feb. 1765; d. 1 Nov. 1845.

57. Jeremiah[4] (*Timothy,*[3] *William,*[2] *Reginald*[1]) was born in Boxford, 4 May, 1701; died 15 Aug. 1785. He was styled lieutenant. He married first, Abigail Wood, to whom he was published 31 Oct. 1731. She d. 27 July, 1750. He married second, Bridget Pemberton, a widow, 14 Aug. 1755, in Andover. His children were:

   i.   Jeremiah,[5] b. 11 Nov. 1732.
   ii. Ezra,[5] b. 22 Oct. 1734.
   iii. Huldah,[5] b. 12 Jan. 1736; m. Amos Gould.
   iv. Moses,[5] b. 9 March, 1738–9.
   v. Ruth,[5] b. 15 Sept. 1741.
   vi. Hannah,[5] b. 14 Sept. 1742; d. young.
   vii. Hannah,[5] b. 4 Sept. 1744; m. Deacon Moses Peabody.
  viii. Phebe,[5] bapt. 12 July, 1747; d. 9 April, 1749.
   ix. Rachael,[5] b. 25 Oct. 1749.
   x. David,[5] b. 23 Aug. 1756.
   xi. Abigail,[5] b. 27 Aug. 1758.
   xii. Sarah,[5] b. 2 Sept. 1760.
  xiii. Joshua,[5] b. 20 Oct. 1762.

58. David[4] (*Timothy,*[3] *William,*[2] *Reginald*[1]) was born in Boxford, 17 Aug. 1704. He was perhaps the David Foster, of Pomfret, who married Elizabeth Dow, of Haverhill, 16 Oct. 1749.

59. Amos[4] (*Timothy,*[3] *William,*[2] *Reginald*[1]), was bapt. in Boxford, 1 Feb. 1713. Lived in Ashuelot and Keene, N. H. His will was proved 25 March, 1761. He married Mary Dorman, 22 Dec. 1751. She died before 1761. He left no issue.

60. Abial[4] (*David,*[3] *William,*[2] *Reginald*[1]), was born in Boxford, 2 May, 1702. Lived in Haverhill. He married first, Ruth Clement, 11 July, 1728. She died 4 Feb. 1740–1. Secondly, Hannah Russell, 26 Nov. 1741. She died 30 March, 1803. His children were:

   i.   Elizah,[5] b. 9 June, 1729; d. 15 July, 1736.
   ii. Sarah,[5] b. 12 Sept. 1731; d. 5 July, 1736.
   iii. Ruth,[5] b. 26 Jan. 1733.
   iv. Merriam,[5] b. 13 Feb. 1735–6; d. 22 April, 1737.
   v. Samuel,[5] b. 16 Feb. 1737–8.
   vi. Moses,[5] b. } 27 Jan. 1739–40; { d. 16 March, 1739–40.
   vii. Joshua,[5] b. }
  viii. Abigail,[5] b. 6 April, 1745.

61. PHINEAS[4] (*David,*[3] *William,*[2] *Reginald*[1]) was born in Boxford, 5 June, 1704, and we have no further knowledge of him.

62. SIMON[4] (*David,*[3] *William,*[2] *Reginald*[1]), was born in Haverhill, 17 June, 1707. Of him we know nothing except that in 1725 he was a soldier.

63. THOMAS[4] (*Samuel,*[3] *William,*[2] *Reginald*[1]) was bapt. in Boxford, 23 May, 1708. He married Alice Pearly, 14 July, 1731. He had:

    i. JOHN,[5] bapt. July, 1732.

Allis Foster, supposed to be the widow of Thomas, was published in Boxford, 25 Aug. 1734, to Benjamin Rogers.

64. WILLIAM[4] (*Samuel,*[3] *William,*[2] *Reginald*[1]) was born in Boxford, 22 July, 1711. He removed to Newbury between March, 1756, and Jan. 1758, and was living there in 1763. There is no settlement of his estate to be found. He married first, ——, who was the mother of his son William, as per Essex Deeds, vol. 105, p. 74. Secondly, to Mary Clarke, of York, Me., to whom he was published 7 Feb. 1747. He was a tailor, yeoman and innholder. His children were:

    i. WILLIAM.[5]
    ii. HANNAH.[5] b. 27 May, 1749.
    iii. SAMUEL,[5] b. 22 Nov. 1750.

65. JEREMIAH[4] (*Abraham,*[3] *Jacob,*[2] *Reginald*[1]) was born in Ipswich about 1700. Removed to Harvard, Mass. He married Rebecca Metcalf, to whom he was published 21 June, 1735. His children were:

    i. JEREMIAH,[5] bapt. 8 Aug. 1736.
    ii. ABIGAIL,[5] bapt. 17 Feb. 1737-8.
    iii. JEREMY,[5] bapt. 6 Jan. 1739-40, "son of Jeremy."
    iv. SAMUEL,[5] bapt. 8 Jan. 1741-2, "   "

26 May, 1743. Jere'h Foster and Rich'd Harris of Ipswich bought of Benj. Morse of Harvard, Worcester co. 112 acres land situated in Stow on west side of the river, bounding on Lancaster and Lunenburg lines.

13 Jan. 1759. Jere'h Foster and wife Rebecca, of Dorchester Canada, Worcester Co. to Josiah Haynes of Sudbury Middlesex Co.—[*Middlesex Deeds.*]

66. ABRAHAM[4] (*Abraham,*[3] *Jacob,*[2] *Reginald*[1]) was born in Ipswich, 5 (6) 1716. Mark Haskell was appointed his guardian, 3 April, 1733, he then being seventeen years old. He was a joiner, and resided in Boston and Charlestown, and died before 1750. He married Elizabeth Davis, of Charlestown, 5 Nov. 1742. She died 19 Jan. 1775. Their children were:

    i. ELIZABETH,[5] bapt. 18 Nov. 1744, at Charlestown; m. John Rogers, 27 May, 1762.
    ii. ABRAHAM,[5] bapt. 2 Dec. 1744, at Charlestown.

67. NATHANIEL[4] (*Abraham,*[3] *Jacob,*[2] *Reginald*[1]) was born in Ipswich, 9 Aug. 1719, removed to Salem, where he pursued the occupation of a tailor, and died October, 1808. He married Sarah, daughter of George and Bethiah (Peters) Daland, of Salem, 6 May, 1741. She was bapt. 1st church, Salem, 12 July, 1724; died August, 1796. Their children were:—

    i. NATHANIEL,[5] bapt. 1st church, 7 Nov. 1742.
    ii. SARAH,[5] "   "   "   13 Jan. 1744-5.
    iii. ABRAHAM,[5] "   "   "   1 March, 1746-7.
    iv. ABIGAIL,[5] "   "   "   26 March, 1749.
    v. GEORGE,[5] "   "   "   13 Jan. 1750-1.

vi. JOSEPH,⁵ bapt. 1st church, 11 Nov. 1753.
vii. SAMUEL,⁵   "   "   "   6 Nov. 1757.
viii. JOHN,⁵   "   "   "   11 May, 1760 ; d. young.
ix. JOHN,⁵   "   "   "   2 May, 1762.
x. ——,⁵   "   "   "   April, 1764.

68. WILLIAM⁴ *(Jacob,³ Jacob,² Reginald¹)* was born in Ipswich, 11 May, 1699. Administration was granted on his estate to Isaac Dodge, who gave bonds with Nathan Foster, 1 Jan. 1776. 30 April, 1760, Wm. Foster, cordwainer, and wife Elizabeth, sell to Isaac Dodge, miller, 1 upland right in Jeffrey Neck. He married Elizabeth Clark, to whom he was published 7 Sept. 1734. She died February, 1767. His children were:

i. WILLIAM,⁵ bapt. 17 Aug. 1735.
ii. ELIZABETH,⁵ b. 19 March, 1737, living 1776, unm.
iii. SARAH,⁵ bapt. 12 May, 1740, pub. Nath'l Hodgkins.
iv. MARY,⁵ bapt. 25 July, 1742 ; m. —— Kimball.
v. HANNAH,⁵ bapt. 2 Feb. 1745 ; d. before 1776.
vi. ABIGAIL,⁵ bapt. 20 March, 1747 ; d. young.
vii. ABIGAIL,⁵ bapt. 18 March, 1749.
viii. REBECCA,⁵ bapt. 1753.

69. NATHANIEL⁴ *(Jacob,³ Jacob,² Reginald¹)* was born in Ipswich, 14 Dec. 1712, where he died 16 Aug. 1747. He was a blacksmith. He married Elizabeth Leatherland, to whom he was published 29 Nov. 1735. His children were:

i. ELIZABETH,⁵ b. 5 Feb. 1736 ; pub. to Richard Sutton.
ii. NATHAN,⁵ b. 20 June, 1737.
iii. MARTHA,⁵ b. 6 May, 1739 ; d. young.
iv. MARTHA,⁵ ⎫ b. 13 April, 1740.
v. MARY,⁵ ⎭
vi. SARAH,⁵ bapt. 1 Aug. 1742.
vii. NATHANIEL,⁵ bapt. 22 Dec. 1745 ; d. 23 Aug. 1747.

His widow Elizabeth was married to Benjamin Brown, 3d, previous to 1758.

70. JOSEPH⁴ *(Joseph,³ Jacob,² Reginald¹)* was born in Ipswich, 14 Feb. 1714. Removed to Beverly, where he died 27 Feb. 1767. He was deacon of the first church, overseer, selectman and town clerk. He married in Ipswich Hannah Trask, 12 Nov. 1735. She died 11 Aug. 1778. His children were :

i. THOMAS,⁵ b. 18 Oct. 1736 ; d. 26 July, 1794.
ii. JOSEPH,⁵ b. 25 Dec. 1739 ; d. young.
iii. MARY,⁵ b. 18 Jan. 1741 ; m. Henry Herrick, 1765.
iv. HANNAH,⁵ b. 4 March, 1743–4 ; m. first, Jonathan Ellingwood, 1767 ; second, Nehemiah Smith, 1774.
v. DANIEL,⁵ b. 14 Feb. 1745–6.
vi. ELIZABETH,⁵ b. 7 April, 1748.
vii. SARAH,⁵ b. 29 Dec. 1750.
viii. EZRA-TRASK,⁵ b. 29 Sept. 1752.
ix. JOSEPH,⁵ b. 1753.
x. MERCY,⁵ b. 9 Dec. 1754 ; d. 1 Dec. 1755.
xi. JEREMIAH,⁵ b. 21 April, 1756.
xii. LYDIA,⁵ b. 8 March, 1757.
xiii. JAMES,⁵ b. 31 Aug. 1759.

71. JAMES⁴ *(Joseph,³ Jacob,² Reginald¹)* was born in Ipswich, 4 March, 1716. Removed to Boston, where two of his children were born. Returned to Ipswich, being admitted in 1766 to the south church at Chebacco, from the Brattle-Street Church, Boston. His wife was Sarah Hart, to

whom he was published in Ipswich, 25 June, 1746. She was living in 1803. He was postmaster of Ipswich, being succeeded by Daniel Noyes, 23 June, 1775. He gave a deed, 10 Oct. 1807, being then 91 years of age. His will, dated 29 May, 1786, was *disproved* 9 Dec. 1807, as one of the witnesses, Mary Foster, had no recollection of being present at the signing, and the others, Sarah Lowater and Nathan Foster, were deceased. Administration was afterwards granted Nathaniel Lord 3d, 2 Nov. 1807. The will mentions wife Sarah, *only* son James, and *only* daughter Sarah. His children were :

    i.   SARAH,[5] b. in B., 25 Dec. 1747.
    ii. JAMES,[5] b. in B., 30 Aug. 1749.
   iii. JOHN,[5] bapt. in I., 29 March, 1752.
   iv. JOSEPH,[5] bapt. in I., 3 June, 1753.

72. NATHAN[4] (*Joseph,[3] Jacob,[2] Reginald[1]*) was born in Ipswich, 19 Feb. 1717–18 ; died Oct. 1795. He married Mary, daughter of Nathaniel and Sarah Hart, 27 Dec. 1743. She was born 20 Jan. 1718 ; died 10 April, 1778. Their children were:

    i.   MARY,[5] b. — Nov. 1744 ; d. unm. March, 1828.
    ii. SAMUEL,[5] b. 23 Oct. 1746.
   iii. JAMES,[5] b. 18 Dec. 1747.
   iv. NATHANIEL,[5] b. 30 Nov. 1752.
    v. WILLIAM-HART,[5] bapt. 24 July, 1757 ; d. young.

73. ISAAC[4] (*Joseph,[3] Jacob,[2] Reginald[1]*) was born in Ipswich, 17—. Removed to Billerica. His will was made in 1783. He was married by Mr. Samuel Ruggles to Sarah Brown, of Boxford, 8 Nov. 1744. His children were :

    i.   ISAAC,[5] b. 8 March, 1745–6.
    ii. JACOB,[5] b. 20 Dec. 1747.
   iii. SARAH,[5] b. 4 March, 1749 ; d. 4 April, 1750.
   iv. JOSEPH,[5] b. 21 March, 1750.
    v. SARAH,[5] b. 29 May, 1753 ; d. before 1783.
   vi. JOHN,[5] b. 28 June, 1755.
  vii. SAMUEL,[5] b. 31 March, 1758.
 viii. ABIGAIL,[5] b. 21 Feb. 1761 ; d. before 1783.

74. JACOB[4] (*Joseph,[3] Jacob,[2] Reginald[1]*) was born in Ipswich, 27 March, 1726. Removed to Billerica, where he died. His will, dated 4 Aug. 1760, was proved 19 Oct. 1761. In it he bequeaths to " my said sone three of my books viz :—Bailey's Dictionary, Salmon's geographier & Historical Grammar and modern gazetteer." He married Sarah Kimball, to whom he was published 25 Aug. 1750. His children were :

    i.   TIMOTHY.[5]
    ii. SARAH.[5]

He may have had others, but if so they were deceased before 1760.

75. ABRAHAM[4] (*Joseph,[3] Jacob,[1] Reginald[1]*) was baptized in Ipswich, 27 Oct. 1728. Removed to Boston, where he settled. He was a cabinet-maker. His wife was Susannah Sumner. He had six children.

Oct. 1761, he bought of Jno. Downe, for £230.14.4, parcel of land, house and buildings on Fish Street, in the North End of Boston. 16 Aug. 1773, Abraham Foster and wife Susannah mortgaged this estate to John White for £133.

Administration on the estate of Abraham Foster, cabinet-maker, was granted to Joseph Foster, Boston, goldsmith, who gave bonds with James

Foster, Jr., and Nathaniel Foster, gent., 9 Aug. 1796. His personal estate was valued at $2579.70. Real estate, house and land on Fish St., $2333.33. The marriage of *Ephraim* Foster, Boston, and Susannah Sumner, 1 Nov. 1753, is recorded in Boston. It was probably a mistake for *Abraham.*

76. JONATHAN[4] (*Isaac,*[3] *Reginald,*[2] *Reginald*[1]) was born in Ipswich; removed to Lincoln, and was there 1 Nov. 1764, for at that time, with wife Elizabeth, he sold two wood-lots to Jeremiah Burnham and son Jeremiah of Ipswich.

Again, 19 April, 1765, they sold to Moses Foster of Ipswich ⅓ of wood-lot in Chebacco. He married Elizabeth Storey, 5 July, 1733. His children were:

   i. JONATHAN,[5] b. 23 April, 1734.
   ii. MARTHA,[5] baptized 20 July, 1735; m. Aaron Burnham, 26 Oct. 1756.
   iii. JOSHUA,[5] baptized 18 Feb. 1736–7.
   iv. ELIZABETH,[5] b. 11 Dec. 1738; m. Nathan Page, of Newbury, 19 April, 1758.
   v. ABIGAIL,[5] baptized 22 Feb. 1740–1.
   vi. ISAAC,[5] b. 10 Feb. 1742–3.
   vii. EUNICE,[5] baptized 22 Aug. 1744.
   viii. JACOB,[5] b. 15 July, 1746.
   ix. SUSANNA,[5] b. 6 March, 1749–50.

77. ISAAC[4] (*Isaac,*[3] *Reginald,*[2] *Reginald*[1]) was born in Ipswich. He married twice: first, ——; secondly, Rachel ——. Removed to Holliston, where he was 16 Jan. 1756. Administration on his estate was granted Timothy Townsend, of Holliston, 24 Jan. 1764. His children were:

   i. STEPHEN.[5]
   ii. HANNAH.[5]
   iii. SARAH.[5]
   iv. ABIGAIL.[5]

78. JACOB[4] (*Isaac,*[3] *Reginald,*[2] *Reginald*[1]) was born in Ipswich about 1675. He removed to Holliston, Mass. On various deeds, &c., he is styled "captain," although of what I have failed to discover. On other documents his name appears as "Jacob Foster, Gentleman." He was married 10 April, 1728, by the Rev. Daniel Baker, to Mary, daughter of William and Hannah (Bullard) Sheffield, of H. Their children were:

   i. MARY,[5] b. 3 Nov. 1729; m. Moses Twitchell.
   ii. JACOB,[5] b. 10 March, 1732; m. Hepzibah Prentice.
   iii. WILLIAM,[5] b. 29 April, 1734.
   iv. SHEFFIELD,[5] b. 10 Oct. 1738.
   v. HANNAH,[5] b. 14 May, 1740.
   vi. ISAAC,[5] b. 27 Sept. 1741; d. 3 Dec. 1741.
   vii. ISAAC,[5] b. 18 March, 1743–4.
   viii. ABIGAIL,[5] b. 5 Feb. 1749–50.
   ix. REBECCA,[5] b. 7 Dec. 1753.

79. JEREMIAH[4] (*John,*[3] *Reginald,*[2] *Reginald*[1]) was born in Ipswich, 1691; died 25 March, 1769. He was a mariner. He married Dorothy, daughter of Nathaniel and Joanna Rust. She died 14 May, 1745. His children were:

   i. JEREMIAH.[5]
   ii. MOSES.[5]
   iii. JOHN.[5]
   iv. JOANNA,[5] bapt. 12 June, 1726.
   v. EPHRAIM,[5] bapt. 7 July, 1728.
   vi. JOSEPH,[5] bapt. 19 July, 1730.

    vii. MARTHA,[5] bapt. 30 July, 1732.
   viii. DOROTHY,[5] pub. Jno. Emerson, 19 Oct. 1754.
    ix. BENJAMIN,[5] b. 5 Jan. 1734-5.
     x. MARY,[5] m. John Emerson, 12 Jan. 1756.
    xi. ELIZABETH,[5] bapt. 5 Dec. 1736.
   xii. JOSHUA,[5] bapt. 16 Sept. 1739.
  xiii. MIRIAM,[5] bapt. 11 Oct. 1741.

80. MOSES[4] (*John,*[3] *Reginald,*[2] *Reginald*[1]) was born in Ipswich, 1697. He was a husbandman. His will was dated 28 March, 1782. He died at Chebacco, Ipswich, 27 Sept. 1785. He married first, Mary, daughter of Nathaniel Rust. She died 2 May, 1732, in her 30th year. Secondly, Mary Blodgett, 18 Jan. 1732-3. Thirdly, Ann Varney, a widow, who died 21 Feb. 1787, in her 87th year. His children were:

     i. MIRIAM,[5] bapt. 14 Aug. 1726.
    ii. ZEBULON,[5] bapt. 22 Sept. 1728.
   iii. MOSES.[5]
    iv. AARON,[5] b. 1723.

81. JOHN[4] (*John,*[3] *Reginald,*[2] *Reginald*[1]) was born in Ipswich. He married Mehitable Burnham, 27 Dec. 1732. Administration was granted on his estate to widow Mehitable, 28 Oct. 1766; it was valued at £196. His children were:

     i. JACOB,[5] bapt. 14 July, 1734; d. young.
    ii. MARY,[5] bapt. 3 Dec. 1738.
   iii. LUCY,[5] bapt. 3 May, 1741. d. young.
   iv. JOHN,[5] bapt. 29 May, 1743.
    v. LUCY,[5] bapt. 27 Oct. 1745.
   vi. JOANNA,[5] bapt. 19 June, 1748.
   vii. ELIZABETH,[5] bapt. 9 Sept. 1750.
  viii. SARAH,[5] bapt. 15 April, 1753.
    ix. JACOB,[5] bapt. 5 Oct. 1755.

82. NATHANIEL[4] (*Nathaniel,*[3] *Reginald,*[2] *Reginald*[1]), was born in Ipswich, 17—. He removed to Newbury, being dismissed from the church at Chebacco to the third church there, 20 May, 1744. He was a shipwright. 5 Nov. 1762, he deeded 10 rods of land and a house to his son Nathaniel, Jr., shipwright. He married Mary, daughter of Thorndike Low, to whom he was published 26 Nov. 1726. They were both admitted to the church at Chebacco in Jan. 1727-8. Their children were:

     i. MARY.[5]
    ii. DEBORAH,[5] bapt. 16 April, 1729.
   iii. ISAAC,[5] bapt. 19 July, 1730.
   iv. NATHANIEL,[5] bapt. 19 March, 1731-2.

NOTES AND QUERIES.

LIEUT. LOW AND THE SCHOONER FAME.—In Eaton's "History of Thomaston, Me.," vol. i. p. 304, it is stated that : " Among other vessels fitted out as privateers was the Schooner Fame, originally a Chesapeake Bay craft captured by the British and by them used as a privateer, and sometimes as a vessel of burthen. In the latter capacity, freighted with a cargo of sugar and molasses, probably destined for the American market, she had been at sea some time on her way, in company with a fleet from the British Provinces to Castine, under the command of a British subject as captain, and a Lieut. Lowe, an American, not known as such, as he was shipped in Nova Scotia."

Lieut. Jonathan Low was the said officer, and his name was afterwards changed to James Willis Low, by an act of legislature, for reasons. Capt. James W. Low was the third son of Capt. David Low, of Ipswich, who married Hannah Haskell, of Gloucester, and was a descendant of the first Lows of Ipswich. Capt. David Low was a lieutenant of an Ipswich company in the battle of Bunker Hill, and a captain after in the war of the revolution. He died at sea on a voyage from the West Indies, as master of the vessel, leaving five sons and two daughters, one of whom is now (1875) living.

Capt. James W. Low commanded several vessels from Boston,—the Gen. Jackson and Chance in Mr. Roberts's employ; the Concordia and Cabot in Mr. Thomas Lamb's employ. He was for many years an inspector for insurance offices in New York; and lived in Brooklyn. He left one son and a daughter; the son, James, commanded a company of infantry from New-Jersey in the war of the rebellion, and is now living. Capt. James W. Low died Aug. 23, 1865, aged 76 years.

Billerica, Mass.   Charles A. Ranlett.

Dignitaries of Easton.— "Capt. John Phillips departed this life ye 14th day of November in ye year 1760 he being the first Captain that ever bore a commission in ye town of Easton."

"Edward Hayward Esq departed this life ye 22d of May in ye yeare 1760 the first Esq that ever was in ye town of Easton he died in the 71st year of his age."

The above items are copied from the town records of Easton, Mass.

                                                     A. M. Alger.

Philbrook.— Wanted, the parentage of Penelope Philbrook, b. 1751, and m. 1768, Job Chapman, of Greenland. Her brother, Eliphalet, settled at Wakefield Corner, N. H., about 1770, and her sister is supposed to have married a Wingate, at the same place. She is thought to have been a daughter of Benjamin, youngest son of Elias and Rhoda, both of whom d. 1747. Elias was son of John[3] (John,[2] Thomas[1]).

Kingston, N. H.   Jacob Chapman.

Henry Blague.—[In answer to a query in the April number of the Register, vol. xxix. p. 112.]—The name of Blague was sometimes written Blake. Among the Boston records of births are these entries :

"Martha daughter of Henry Blake and Elizabeth his wife was born November 2, 1655."

"Joseph son of Henry Blake and Elizabeth his wife was born September 2, 1660."

That this Henry Blake was no other than Henry Blague, the brickmaker, is proved by the fact that the latter had a wife Elizabeth, and also a son Joseph and daughter Martha. In proof of these facts, the following items are cited :

Nathaniel Blague, son of Henry, mentions in his will his *sister Martha Squire.*

Nov. 16, 1681, Elizabeth Blague, widow, and *Joseph Blague, her son,* convey lands to William Norton, in consideration of £28. The said Joseph accepted this sum in satisfaction of £30 that should have been paid unto him by his mother, as guardian, out of the estate of his *father Henry Blague.*

After this date (1681) no mention of Joseph Blague is to be found on Boston records. Soon after a Joseph Blague appears in Saybrook, Conn. Was he the Boston Joseph, the son of Henry? It seems quite certain to me that he was.

                                                     Arthur M. Alger.

Willoughby.—Susannah, daughter of Deputy Governor Francis Willoughby, m. Mr. Nathaniel Lynde, brother of the first chief-justice of the name. Her descendants retain the genealogy as far as Col. William Willoughby, of Portsmouth, England, father of Gov. Francis. Can any further information be obtained of the Willoughby family? Are there any living descendants of other children of Deputy Gov. Francis Willoughby? Please inform Judge C. J. McCurdy, Lyme, Conn.

To Restore Faded Writing.—A correspondent of the *Sunday Dispatch,* Philadelphia, Dec. 6, 1874, in reply to a previous correspondent who had asked how faded writing could be restored, advises him to "wash a word or two with a camel's-hair pencil dipped into an infusion of powdered nutgalls. If the ink is not restored, then wash a few more words with a weak solution of copperas. Ink, such as was used by our great-grandfathers, was a tanno-gallate of iron. If it be the gallate that has disappeared, the nutgalls will restore it. If it be the iron that has faded away, the copperas. In either case, the experiment costs nothing, and is worth trying; but if both have evaporated, he will have small luck."

PEIRCE.—Jacob Peirce purchased land of Daniel Stone in Watertown, Mass., March 28, 1698.

Joseph Peirce and wife Elizabeth Peirce deeded land to their son Joseph Peirce in Watertown, Mass., March 29, 1709.

Jacob Peirce, of Weston, administered on the estate of his honored father, Joseph Peirce, lately of Watertown, in 1715: had brother Joseph Peirce. Witness, John Peirce, wife Hannah Peirce.

Daniel Stone, of Lexington, conveys to Joseph Peirce lands in Lexington, Dec. 6, 1714.

Daniel Esterbrooks conveys lands to Joseph Peirce, March 9, 1709.

Joseph Peirce and wife Hannah convey lands in Weston to son George Peirce, Nov. 13, 1719.

George Peirce had a son Simon Peirce, and probably William. His daughter was Mary Wheeler.

Copied from old wills, deeds and accounts, once in possession of the Peirce family, now in possession of Rev. G. T. Ridlon, Genealogist, Harrison, Maine. Other information relating to the Peirces provided if applied for.

Harrison, Maine.   G. T. RIDLON.

TALCOTT GENEALOGY.—S. V. Talcott, Esq., of Albany, N. Y., has his genealogy of the Talcotts nearly ready for the press. He will give short biographical notes of many of the name, and of some collaterals; besides copies of the wills of the early generations. The name as far as he can learn is extinct in England, and is not numerous in this country.

In the REGISTER for July, 1867 (*ante*, xxi. 216), Mr. Talcott states that Dorothy, wife of John Talcott, who came over in 1632, was a daughter of Mark Mott, D.D., of Braintree. He writes, under date of June 9, 1875: "I have ascertained that this cannot be the case, as his daughter, Dorothy, was born Jan. 28, 1620; too young to be the wife of John Talcott, whose third child was born in 1635.

"Col. Andrew Talcott found on searching the manuscripts relating to the county of Essex, England, in the British Museum, that Mark Mott, eldest son of Thomas Mott and Alice Meade of Bocking in Essex, lived in Braintree, married Frances Gutter, and had : *Francis*, m. Frances Forward ; *Thomas*, m. dau. of John Brand ; *Mark*, D.D., rector of Rayne ; *Dorothy*, who probably m. John Talcott.

"This Mark Mott was the owner of Sheme Hall, Lexden hundred, and was a witness to the will of John Talcott, father of John the settler who died in 1604."

WOOSTER (vol. xxix. p. 318).—The late Hon. Henry C. Deming, in his oration upon the life and services of Gen. David Wooster, delivered at Danbury, Ct., April 27, 1854, says, David Wooster was born at Stratford on the second of March, 1710–11, old style, the son of Abraham and Mary Wooster, and the youngest of six children. —*Oration*, p. 6.

Some inquiry has been made in the old town recently for the maiden name of Abraham's wife, but so far without success.

The dividing line between Stratford and Huntington (once a part of Stratford) runs through the farm once in possession of the Wooster family.

The following list of the children of Abraham and Mary Wooster, obtained from the late Edward C. Herrick, Esq., of New-Haven, and to whom Mr. Deming acknowledged himself indebted for much information concerning the General and his family, may be of interest : —

Ruth, b. Sept. 26, 1700.	Sarah, b. April 2, 1705.	Hannah, b. Feb. 23, 1709.
Joseph, b. Jan. 16, 1702.	Mary, b. April 3, 1707.	David, b. March 2, 1710–11.

QUINNIPIAC.

[Since the above was sent us, the following memorandum, from the same source, has been received :— "Abraham Wooster and Mary Walker were married on the 22d of November, 1697."]

HAYES.—In connection with the sketch of the life of Dr. Ezra Green, of Dover, N. H., in the April REGISTER, 1875, is a note regarding "Hayes," which needs correction. See pp. 180-1.

JOHN[1] HAYES.—This paragraph is copied quite accurately from my notes in the REGISTER, except that it fixes exactly the number of children, which is not certain. It should be added that he was married 28 June, 1686; and the vague date of birth of the first child is not reliable.

But the second paragraph, that concerning John,[2] top of p. 181, is essentially erroneous.

It says that John[2] married "Mrs. Tomson." In fact, he married, first, 29 Dec., 1704, Tamsen, daughter of Ezekiel and Elizabeth Wentworth, and widow of James Chesley; 2d, Mary (Roberts), widow of Samuel Wingate.

A worse error is, that the eight children here given to John[2] were not his, but were those of his brother Peter.[2] John[2] had eleven children, but a totally different list. The list of eight children (and one other not given), should remain on the page, but instead of reading — "2. John,[2]" &c., strike out those first three lines on p. 181, and substitute:

"2. PETER[2] (*John*[1]), lived at Tole-End in Dover. He married Sarah, daughter of John Wingate, and granddaughter of the emigrant John. They had (at least) nine children, viz.:"

That my record is correct is further sustained by the record of *baptisms* of Dover church:

1721, Sept. 3. Peter Hayes, Ann and Reuben his children.
1722, July 1. Joseph, son of Peter Hayes.
1724, July 5. Benjamin, son of Peter Hayes. [Birth, p. 181, should be 1723-4, instead of "1723."]
1726, June 12. Mehitabel, dau. of Peter Hayes.
1728, Oct. 27. John, son of Peter Hayes.
1735, Aug. 10. Lydia, dau. of Peter Hayes.
1737, Oct. 2. Ichabod, son of Peter Hayes.
1741, Sept. 27. Elijah, son of Peter Hayes.

This gives one more child, and reverses the order of the last two.

A few references to the article may be allowed.

Page 173, it is said that Dr. Belknap settled at Dover on a salary of £150. It was £100 salary; he had £150 as a slight allowance towards a house. Nor was it because the salary was "inadequate," that he finally left, but because he could not obtain the payment of even that.

Page 174, it is said that Dr. Green was "deacon of the 'First Congregational Orthodox Society' in Dover." The quotation-marks to the title are in the article. He was deacon of the *church*, and probably an officer of the society also; but the name of the church is simply,—"The First Church in Dover;" that of the society, —"The First Parish in Dover."

Page 175, last line, it is said that Dr. Green was "chairman of the State convention for the adoption of the constitution of the United States. His vote gave a majority in its favor." John Sullivan was *president* of the convention. The vote was not so close. The following letter of Sullivan is worth inserting:

Concord [*N. H.*], *June* 21, 1788.

SIR,

I have the honour to inform your Excellency, by favour of Mr. [Sampson] Reed, who is obliging enough to forward this letter, that the Convention of this State have, this moment, adopted the new Constitution. Yeas, 57; nays, 46. The amendments recommended, nearly the same as in your State.

With every sentiment of respectful attachment, I have the honor to be,

Yeas, 57   Your Excellency's
Nays, 46   most obedient servant,
—   JOHN SULLIVAN.
Majority, 11
His Excellency Gov. Hancock.

But no corrections are needed in the estimate of Dr. Green's character and services. I am glad to see the sketch in print, and with it the likeness of the venerable citizen whom I used to see in my boyhood.   A. H. QUINT.

HISTORY AND GENEALOGY OF THE REVOLUTIONARY WAR.—The revolutionary war is an era in the history of this country, corresponding to that which was inaugurated in England, during the reigns of Alfred the Great and William the Conqueror. During the latter period the names of all families were collected and recorded in the "Doomsday Book," which in connection with subsequent collections, has become valuable for historic and family references, having been protected with sacred care by the sovereigns and officials of Great Britain.

The operation of the several acts of Congress granting pensions to soldiers of the revolutionary war and their widows, caused a vast amount of information to be embodied in the declarations of claimants, comprising their military services, naming the battles in which they participated and embracing their personal and family histories, prior to and subsequent to the war, together with dates of birth, residence, dates of marriage, names of and births of children. There are many narratives in these applications and proofs, of particular expeditions and campaigns, of absorbing interest and historical importance, which should be better preserved than they have been in the past or can possibly be in the future, under the present limited arrangements.

More or less of these records have been misplaced or lost from the files of the Pension Bureau, and the necessity for their future preservation is evident. Provision should be at once made by Congress to cause the same to be compiled, and, in some condensed form, given to the public, perhaps in the nature of a biographical dictionary or other archive of the department. The calls upon the Pension Bureau for copies of papers filed by ancestors, and for various kinds of information, usually sought by compilers of family genealogies and town histories, are increasing year by year. Clerks necessarily must soon be employed for this specific duty, or otherwise the requests of parties for such information cannot well be complied with. This matter is well worthy the attention of our American historians, who should aid in the effort to secure for it the speedy attention of Congress.—*United States Pension Record,* November, 1874.

QUAKERS IN KITTERY, ME., IN 1737. [Copied for the REGISTER by J. S. H. Fogg, M.D., from the original document in his possession.]

"Kittery, May 6, 1737.—A List of Quakers allowed by the Selectmen this year Vizt :

Andrew Neal	Jabez Jenkins	Samuel Hill sen[r]
John Neal	Francis Allin	Michell Kinnard
Andrew Neal Jr :	Francis Allin Jr :	Samuel Johnson
Thomas Weed	W[m] Fry	Nicholas Morrell
Daniel Furbush Senr :	W[m] Fry Jr :	Edward Whitehouse
Peter Wittum	Benj : Fry	John Fry
James Ferris	Jos : Fry	James Whittham.
John Morrell sen[r] :		

[Signed by]

Nathan Bartlet,   Thomas Hutchings,
John Rogers,   Joseph Gunnison,
Richd : Gowell,   Tobias Leighton,
                                    Selectmen of Kittery.

MARRIAGES IN 1773.—The following items are from an interleaved almanac of 1773, belonging to William Parsons :—

Jan. 11.	Samuel Osgood & Betty Sanborn,	married.
12.	Dudley Hutchinson & Sarah Bachelder,	"
Feb. 17.	John Sandborn & Hannah Eastman,	"
M'ch 10.	David Glidden & Susanna Glidden,	"
Ap. 21.	Barzilla Hinds & Lucy Seavy	"
July 15.	Ambrose Hindes & Sarah Mudget,	"
Sep. 8.	Mr Porter ordained at New Durham.	
Dec. 7.	Simeon Lovering & Sarah Sanborn, married, both of Chichester.	

Mr. Parsons probably lived in Gilmanton, N. H.   J. COLBURN.

HAWLEY.—The father of the Rev. Stephen Hawley, of Bethany, Conn., long since deceased, is understood to have been Stephen Hawley, of Milford, Conn. Wanted, the name and residence of the Rev. Stephen Hawley's grandfather?
Buffalo, N. Y.   E. S. HAWLEY.

HISTORY OF SOUTHINGTON, CONN.—The Rev. Heman R. Timlow, pastor of the First Congregational Church of that place, has prepared a volume entitled "Ecclesiastical and other Sketches of Southington, Conn.," which is now in press and will probably appear about the same time as this number. It will make an 8vo volume of between 700 and 800 pages, illustrated with engravings. It will contain the church records for the first century and genealogies of the early families. The edition will be limited by the subscription list. Price, $5. Address Dr. F. A. Hart, Southington, Conn.

SPOONER GENEALOGY.—The Hon. Thomas Spooner, of Reading, Ohio, has his book entitled "William Spooner and his Descendants," upon which he has been engaged for sixteen years (*ante*, xxv. 394), in such a state of forwardness that its early publication can be assured, provided enough copies are subscribed for to pay the cost of publication.

The work will contain about 4,000 families and 15,000 individuals, and will make two large 8vo volumes of about 700 pages each. It will be printed in the best style of the art, and delivered, in cloth, to subscribers at $15 the set. There must be 350 copies subscribed for to ensure its publication. This will not leave any remuneration for the labor of compilation, nor even the repayment of the sum (fully $5,000) expended in obtaining the materials.

CENTENARIANISM.—I have undertaken to investigate all alleged cases of centenarianism of which I can obtain information, and I desire here to state the evidence in the case of Mrs. Anah Goss, who died at Amherst, N. H., on the 19th of last March, aged (as I have reason to believe) 105 years, 1 month and 18 days. If any error can be detected, I desire that it may be exposed. I have the entire family records of Mrs. Goss and of her parents, the former from the family Bible, and the latter from the town records of Lunenburg, Mass., where Mrs. Goss was born Feb. 1, 1770. She was the daughter of Stephen and Jemima Bathrick. While she spelled her name Anah, it was recorded at her birth *Anar*. She was married to Ephraim Goss, July 14, 1786, she being then but 16 years old. Her first child was born April 30, 1787. This fact of her early marriage goes far to corroborate the record of her birth, for if she was less than 105 years old at her death she must have been so much less than 16 at her marriage. Her history throughout can be exactly traced, and I feel satisfied as to her age. I have other cases in hand, upon which I shall be glad to report when the evidence is conclusive, and in the meantime shall be thankful for information from any source. Mr. Thoms found but four genuine cases of centenarianism on record in England after the most thorough investigation. According to the U. S. census of 1870, there were then over 3,500 centenarians living in this country, of whom perhaps a score could have been shown to be genuine. Upon the occasion of our centennial it will be a matter of interest to know who our native-born centenarians really are. I would gladly cöoperate with any who may be interested in this line of inquiry.

No. 13 *Laight St., New York.*　　　　　　　EDWIN F. BACON,
　　　　　　　　　　　　　　　　　　　　Office of *Herald of Health.*

WALLER.—The undersigned would be happy to correspond with any one that can give him any information in regard to the early history and genealogy of the Wallers of Virginia. Address all communications to

Portsmouth, Ohio.　　　　　　　WILLIAM WALLER, Attorney-at-Law.

EXTRACTS FROM THE DIARY OF SAMUEL LANE, OF HAMPTON, N. H. : —
1737. April 10.—"Cold storm of snow and rain,—about 48 hours, which killed many sheep.—It is a terrible time for want of hay, as well as many sorts of provision.

" June 13.—English corn begins to ear out. Training day.
" 25th.—Indian corn begins to spindle out. July 12.—Some barley is cut.
" 21.—Thunder fell in Smith's pasture."
Mem. December, 1737.—" We had an exceedingly hard winter, & a backward spring. Hay exceeding scarce, (some sold for 8ˢ old tenor, a hundred. Creatures were very poor & abundance died. When the cry for hay was a little over, there came a worse for corn, & almost as bad for meat. Many people in our out towns were almost ready to *faint*, for want of food,—Many in a day, coming about & begging people to sell them a peck, half peck, and some a quart of corn, not sticking at any price.

" But a comfortable crop of English grain put a stop to this melancholly cry. We had a comfortable crop of hay, and more than a common crop of Indian corn. And much pork is fatted by Beech nuts. It has been very healthy, Sixteen persons died in Hampton."

Remark. It seems that *potatoes* were not then much used as an article of food; for Mr. Lane does not notice them in his annual record of the crops, for some 30 or 40 years from this date.

Mr. Lane was born in Hampton, Oct. 6, 1718.

Kingston, N. H.   J. CHAPMAN.

FAWNE CLEMENTS.—[Copied from Notarial Records, Essex co., by H. F. WATERS.] —This is to certifye all & every p'son that I who hereto Subscribe having lived in New England upward of fforty years at my fflirst Coming into yᵉ Country I had knowledge of one known & called by yᵉ name of Mr. —— ffawne who fformerly as I heard lived at Ipswich in New England and after that at Haverhill in New England where I knew him who had there two daughters living with him whereof one of them by name Elizabeth is yet alive & now yᵉ wife of Robert Clement of sᵈ Haverhill which sᵈ Elizabeth was allwayes Accounted & called by yᵉ name of Elizabeth ffawne before her marriage so farr as ever I knew & was all along in sᵈ Mʳ ffawnes time in this Countrey owned by him to be his own Naturrall Daughter she being yᵉ eldest of yᵉ two & hath lived ffull or neare fforty years in Haverhill where now she is living in yᵉ Same Towne with me, where I am minister of yᵉ place. Witness my hand this Nineteenth day of August in yᵉ year of our Lord God 1681.

JOHN WARD.

Memorial of Fawn Clements son of Mʳˢ. Elizᵃ. Clements who was a daughter of Mʳ. John & Elizabeth Fawn wᶜʰ Elizᵃ. Clements was Neece to one Mʳ. Luke alias Look Fawn a Stationer in Paul's Church yard at yᵉ Sign of yᵉ Parrot who died a little before yᵉ fire; and gave yᵉ sᵈ Mʳˢ. Elizabeth Clements £300. And left it in yᵉ hands of Mʳ. John Cressit in Charter house yard in London Mʳ. Edward Clements at yᵉ Sign of yᵉ Lamb in Abchurch lane Mʳ. Edward Henning Mercht. in London & Mʳ. Jerrat Marshal in London. Recorded Sepʳ. 15ᵗʰ 1716.

MORGAN.—[Memorandum found among the papers of the late Capt. JOSEPH WATERS, of Salem, born 1758, died 1833.]—John, Joseph & Miles Morgan saild from Bristol England & arrived at Boston N. E. April 1636. They resided at Roxbury a short time. Joseph went to Plymouth Colony & after removed to Connecticut. John, the elder brother, disgusted at the bigotry superstition & persecutions then so prevalent in Massachusetts that he went to Virginia and there settled. Miles the youngest joined Wᵐ. Pincheon Esqʳ. on his enterprize to Springfield. Morgan married Prudence Gilbert of Beverly. This family of Gilberts were passengers in the same vessel with Morgan and there formed acquaintance.

Mary daughter of Miles & Prudence Morgan was born 12ᵗʰ mo. 14ᵗʰ day 1644. Jonathan born 9ᵗʰ mo. 16ᵗʰ day 1646. David born 7ᵗʰ mo. 23ᵈ 1648. Pelatiah born 5ᵗʰ mo. 17ᵗʰ day 1650. Isaac born 3ᵈ mo. 12ᵗʰ day 1652. Lydia 2ⁿᵈ mo. 8 day 1654. Hannah born 2ⁿᵈ mo. 11ᵗʰ day 1656. Mary born 5ᵗʰ mo. 18ᵗʰ day 1658. Prudence wife of Miles Morgan died 11ᵗʰ mo. 14ᵗʰ day 1660.——Miles Morgan & Elizabeth Bliss were married Feby 15ᵗʰ 1669. Nathaniel their son was born June 14ᵗʰ 1671. ——Miles Morgan died May 28ᵗʰ 1699 aged 84 years.   H. F. WATERS.

COMER—DYNN.—[Copied from Notarial Records of co. Essex, by H. F. WATERS.]— Evidences for Eliz. Comer alias Eliz. Dynn recorded June 18, 1716.

Anno Regni Regis Georgii nunc Magnæ Britaniæ &c Secundo.

The Depositions of Daniel Webb of Salem in yᵉ County of Essex Marriner aged sixty four yeares & Daniel Caten formerly of Bandonbridge in Ireland now of Salem aforesᵈ in yᵉ Countey & province aforesᵈ Taylor aged about Sixty one yeares on their solemn oathes doe testify & say that they formerly well knew & were acquainted with mʳ John Dyn of Kingsale in yᵉ Kingdom of Ireland Merchᵗ or shopkeeper decᵈ. who dwelt nigh yᵉ water gate & that Elizabeth Comer wife of Richard Comer of providence within his Majᵗⁱᵉˢ. Coloney of Rhode Island Taylor is yᵉ reputed Daughter of yᵉ aforenamed John Dyn of Kingsale aforesᵈ. Deceased who has been Dead thirty odd yeares yᵉ Deponent Webb further adds that being Master of yᵉ Ketch Tryall of Salem brought over yᵉ aforenamed Elizabeth Comer whose maiden name was then Elizabeth Dynn in or about yᵉ year 1679 a passenger to New England from Kingsale & that yᵉ year before viz in yᵉ year 1678 this Deponent tooke William Dynn son of yᵉ sᵈ John Dynn an apprentice & brought him to New England as such

& both yᵉ Deponents on yʳ Oathes say that yₑ said Elizabeth Comer alias Dynn is yᵉ very person aliue & well at yᵉ taking these affidavits being present at yᵉ Caption.

They further add that William Dynn before named is departed this life severall yeares since & that he hath no survyving Issue to yᵉ best of these deponents knowledge being next neighbours & that he had Two Sons viz John Dynn & William Dynn who are both departed this life before they were maried which was all yₑ children yᵉ said William Dynn left as these deponents know of. Daniel Webb & Daniel Caten personaly appeared before me yᵉ Subscriber one of His Majᵗⁱᵉˢ Justices of yᵉ peace for yᵉ Countey of Essex & made oath to yᵉ truth of yᵉ foregoing affidavit.

Salem June 18. 1716
Sworne Coram Stephen Sewall
Justice as aforesᵈ.

HUGUENOT CHURCH IN BOSTON.—In Drake's "History of Boston," the following statement is found:—"*The Records of the French Church are supposed to be in existence, but their possessor is unknown.*" The Rev. Charles W. Baird, of Rye, N. Y., is engaged in the preparation of a history of the Huguenot Emigration to America. and has already gathered much valuable information on the subject. At his request we make the inquiry, whether any clue to the discovery of the records of the French congregation founded in Boston in 1686 or 1687 exists. Mr. Baird would also be glad to receive any other details regarding the Huguenot colony here, and the families that composed it.

MARRIAGE CERTIFICATE OF ISAAC WALDRON. [From family papers. Communicated by Walter Lloyd Jeffries.]

"March 1ˢᵗ 1674.

"These are to Certifie all whom it may Concerne that Isaac Waldron of the parrish of Sᵗ Bedast in ffoster lane, London, and Priscilla Byfeilde of east Sheene in the county of Surry were married in the Tabernacle of Sᵗ Bennett grace church on the 25ᵗʰ day of february 1674 by me

Wittnes Richard King   John Cliffe Rector of Sᵗ
Clerke and Register of   Ben: Grace Church."
Sᵗ Bennett grace church."

POOLE AND WEBBER. — "Know all men by these pʳsents yᵗ I, Thomas Webber of Boston marriner engage my selfe to pay mis Elizabeth Poole or her assignes in London yᵉ sû of fiue pounds sterl. yᵉ danger of yᵉ seas excepted, & is for & in consideration of one thousand of mʳchantable wᵗᵉ oake pipe staues here recᵈ of Mʳ Wᵐ Davis. In wittnes whereof I haue subscribed to two bills of this tenure & date yᵉ one of wᶜʰ being p'formed yᵉ other to stand voyd.   p' Mee
Boston 30ᵗʰ (10) 50."   Thos: Webber

The original of the above document has been loaned us by Walter Lloyd Jeffries of Boston.   EDITOR.

JEDIDIAH PREBLE was a private and enlisted in a company by Major John Storer in 1744, in the attack upon Louisburg by Sir Wm. Pepperrell.

Pepperrell writes Storer, from Kittery, Feb. 20, 1744: "If Mr Preble can get his sloop reddy, I know nothing against his sloop being improved, provid'd it is agreeable to yᵉ other field officers."   G. H. PREBLE.

HALL, LANGDON, &c.—In the memoir of Col. Joshua W. Peirce, REGISTER, 1874, p. 369, it is said: "From this family of Halls are descended the Marches of Greenland, and Gov. John Langdon, of Portsmouth." An error in one part.

The Hall ancestor of the March and Peirce families was John Hall, of Dover Combination, 1640, known later as *Sergeant* John Hall. The descent was,—*John*,[1] JOSEPH,[2] *Elizabeth*[3] (married Joshua Peirce), Sarah[3] (married Clement Jackson), and *daughter*[3] (married Israel March).

The Hall ancestor of Gov. Langdon was Ralph Hall, of Exeter Combination 1639, of Dover 1650, known as *Lieut.* Ralph Hall. The descent was,—*Ralph*,[1] *Kinsley*[2] (the judge), *Josiah*,[3] *Mary*[4] (married John Langdon), *John*[5] Langdon, the Governor.

Between these two families, no relationship is known.

The John Hall appearing on Dover records prior to 1650 was the *Sergeant.* In 1650, suddenly three Johns appear, entered as "John Hall," "John Hall, jun.," and "Sergeant John Hall." The first disappears at once. The second was the deacon. In 1650, Ralph, hitherto of Exeter, appears in Dover. Tradition, entirely unsupported however, makes Lieut. Ralph and Deacon John to be brothers, and sons of the John first named of the three in 1650.

I take this occasion to ask for light. A *Ralph Hall* bought land " on Mistick side," in 1646. Several conveyances for him and wife Mary are on record. The last is, 25, 1, 1649, of land which " did Antiently belong unto *John Hall* & Richard Kettle." I believe that nothing shows the Exeter Ralph to have been in Exeter after 1645, and he appears in Dover in 1650, with wife Mary. These questions : 1st. Are the Ralph and Mary of "mistick-side" and "of Charlestown" (by deeds), the same as Ralph and Mary of Exeter 1639–1646, and of Dover 1650 ? 2d. How did the land which did "Antiently belong to John Hall," come into Ralph's hands? 3d. What became of this John of Charlestown? I take him to be the one, of Charlestown, who, in 1633, had lot No. 48 on Mistick side.   A. H. QUINT.

BILL OF MATTHEW ALLYN. — I find the following bill, without date, amongst the papers left by Maj. Elijah Williams, son of the Rev. John Williams, first minister of Deerfield : —

" Brother John Williams of Deerfield Ditter

to yᵉ suruay [s. x.] laying out 300 accers of land at Stafford	£0	06	0
My own time chayne barers & expence which suruay was last	0	12	0
pᵈ to yᵉ Secutary for recording the graunts of Corurt [or Couirt?] Suruays & Coppyes	0	4	0
To recording the Suruay	0	1	6
To Mr Kimberly for writeing yᵉ pattin			
to executeing the pattin 12	0	12	0
to recording yᵉ pattin	0	04	0
My tim & trobel in yᵉ latter suruay is not included			

Mathᵂ Allyn."

Can any of your correspondents identify the parties named in this paper ?
Deerfield, Mass.   GEORGE SHELDON.

JOHN HILL, GUILFORD, CONN., 1646.—The undersigned is now collecting material for a genealogy of the descendants of the above mentioned John Hill, and would respectfully request all persons who may be interested in the work to forward to him whatever information they are able to furnish.   EDWIN A. HILL.
255 Fourth Ave., New-York.

HASKITT. [Copied from Notarial Records of co. Essex, by H. F. WATERS.] Elizabeth Haskitt's Oath & Certificate Entred May 30ᵗʰ, '98.

Mʳˢ. Elizabeth Haskitt widow formerly the wife of Stephen Haskitt of Salem personaly appeared (before me) yᵉ subscriber & made Oath that she hath six children liuing (viz) one sonne whose name is Elias Haskitt aged about Twenty Eight yeares & fiue Daughters Elizabeth* Mary Sarah Hannah & Martha all which she had by her husband yᵉ abouesaid mʳ Stephen Haskitt & Were his Children by him begotten of her body in Lawfull Wedlock being married to him by Doctor Ceauell in Exiter in yᵉ Kingdome of England & whose sd husband serued his time with one mʳ Thomas Oburne a chandler and sope boyler in sᵈ place & was yᵉ reputed Sonne of —— Haskit of Henstredge (so called) in Summersetshire in sᵈ Kingdome of England & haue often heard my sᵈ husband say that he had but one brother whose name was Elias Hasket & that he liued in said Towne of Henstredge.   ELIZABETH HASKITT.

Sworne Salem May yᵉ 30ᵗʰ 1698 before me John Hathorne One of yᵉ Councill & Justice pe & Q. in yᵉ County of Essex in his Majᵗⁱᵉˢ province of yᵉ Massachusets Bay in New England.

HAYFIELD, HAFFIELD, HAFFELL. [Abstract from Mass. Archives and co. Essex Court Papers, by H. F. WATERS.]

Richard Hayfield of " Sudbury, Old England," married, it seems, first, Judith, secondly, Martha, by each of whom he had issue. He came over to Ipswich with

---

* This Elizabeth Haskett m. 1st, William Dynn, June 6, 1684, and m. 2d, Roger Derby, as his second wife ; as has been ascertained by Mr. E. S. Waters, now of Chicago.   W.

his second wife and her children and with the two surviving children of his first wife, viz.:—Mary and Sarah, of whom the former m. *Josiah Cobbet* and the latter m. John Ilsley. Of the issue of his second wife, Ruth m. Thomas White (son of John White of Lancaster), Martha m. Richard Coye, who, with his bro: Matthew and, I think, his sister Mary, was brought over in 1638 from Boston, Lincolnshire, England, by Mr. Whittingham. From evidence on file I am led to suspect that the old home of the Coyes was not very far from Boston. Rachel Haffield m. Laurence Clinton, who won his way into her good graces by his physical beauty and his boasting professions of riches and high connections.

COTTON.—I am anxious to trace the genealogy of John Cotton, who was born July 17, 1712, and died Nov. 5, 1778. He was married at Portsmouth, N. H., Dec. 15, 1742, by Mr. Fitch, to Mary Cutt, who was born 1716 and died Sept. 4, 1799. They had eleven children, of whom five died in infancy. The eldest surviving son was Solomon, born Aug. 21, 1748, died April 15, 1812, married Sept. 20, 1770, by Mr. Odlin, to Mary Green, who died Aug. 11, 1819, aged 65. These dates are from records in a family bible. I shall be grateful for any assistance.

Hendersonville P. O., North Carolina.   S. CLINTON CORTLAND.

AXTELL.—I communicated to the REGISTER for April, 1868, some "Notes on the Axtell Family of Mass.," referring only to those of Sudbury and Marlborough. I have since found persons of the same surname, and all the same male Christian names in Bristol County in the first half of the last century. At Taunton is the will of Daniel Axtell, of Dighton, 1735-6, which mentions his wife Thankful, sons Daniel, William, Henry, Samuel, Ebenezer, and Thomas, dau. Elizabeth, wife of Thomas Burt, daus. Rebecca, Hannah and Thankful. The son Daniel, of Berkeley, made his will 1761, mentioning wife Phebe, only son Daniel, daus. Thankful and Elizabeth.

I write this now to ask if any relationship is known to exist between the two families, and shall be glad to receive information from any person connected with either of them or interested in their history.—I am myself descended from the first Thomas of Sudbury, and wish to learn all I can concerning all of the name here.— Is it possible that Daniel Axtell returned from South Carolina, and settled at Dighton? W. S. APPLETON.

MRS. ABIGAIL LOVERING.—Amid the many centennial celebrations of *events* in these days, let us notice a *personal* centennial. On September 1, 1875, Mrs. Abigail Lovering celebrated her 100th birthday at the house of her son-in-law, Wm. Wardwell, Esq., at Oxford, in the State of Maine, where she has resided for the last few years. Her descendants (of which are still living 7 children, 45 grandchildren [oyes], 100 gr. grandchildren [besoyes], and 9 gr. gr. grandchildren [tresoyes], in all 161) are widely scattered, but twenty of them gathered to celebrate the interesting anniversary, and a large number of friends and neighbors joined with them in the congratulations and festivities of the occasion. Mrs. L. was in good health and spirits, receiving the congratulations with a thankful heart for the prolonged extension of her days, and enjoying fully the presence of her descendants and friends.

On the 9th of October I called upon her at her residence, and met a good-looking old lady (in appearance not over 85 years of age) neatly attired, sitting in her rocking chair knitting a pair of mittens for a gr. grandchild (a pair of stockings very nicely knit by her since she became a centenarian is now in my possession). Her intellectual faculties were bright and active, and her memory quite clear. From her I derived much information of which I was in search. She uses spectacles when reading, and by their aid reads with ease. During the summer she has walked and ridden about without difficulty, getting into a carriage as quickly and easily, apparently, as she did fifty years ago. I had, at intervals, quite a long conversation with her in relation to genealogical and other matters, and throughout she exhibited a wonderful clearness, notwithstanding it required, at times, a good degree of thought and consideration to arrive at the facts.

Mrs. L. belongs to a long-lived race, and has a brother now living at Woburn, Mass., aged 91 years. Her maiden name was Flagg, and she was born at Woburn, Sept. 1, 1775, married in April, 1797, to David Lovering (born at Hollis, 1771, died 1858), and about 1800 moved to Poland, Maine. Her genealogy is traced from Thomas Flagg, who came over with Richard Carver 1637, and settled at Watertown 1641,—and is as follows:

1. THOMAS FLAGG, of Watertown, b. about 1615.
2. GERSHOM, eldest son of Thomas, b. April 16, 1641.
3. GERSHOM, second son of Gershom, b. March 10, 1668-9.
4. ZACHARIAH, "   "   "   "   2d, b. June 20, 1700.
5. JOHN, fourth son of Zachariah, b. Aug. 29, 1746.
6. ABIGAIL, b. Sept. 1, 1775.

JOHN FLAGG m. 1st, Hannah Tidd, and had one son *Joseph;* m. 2d, Abigail Thompson, and had *John* (who m. ——— Fowle) ; *Josiah,* who d. young ; ABIGAIL (the centenarian); *William* (b. July 7, 1784, now living at Woburn); and *Hannah,* (who m. ——— Loomis).

Mrs. Lovering had ten children :

i.   MARY, b. 1798 ; m. Levi Maxfield, of Woburn.
ii.   JOSEPH, b. 1799 ; m. Harriet Brooks, of Alexander, Me.
iii. ELIZA, b. 1801 (d. 1835); m. Elijah Caldwell, of Greenwood, Me.
iv.   ABIGAIL, b. 1802 ; m. William Wardwell, of Oxford, Me.
v.   JOANNA, b. 1805 ; m William Rowe, of New Gloucester, Me.
vi.   GARDNER, b. 1807 ; d. young.
vii. BELINDA, b. 1810 (d. 1847); m. Daniel Stone, of Otisfield, Me.
viii. HANNAH, b. 1812 ; m. Francis Hill, of Stoneham.
ix.   PRESCOTT, b. 1814 ; m. 1st, ——— Hutchinson, 2d, Widow Delphina Tubbs.
x.   JOSIAH, b. 1818 ; m. 1st, Deborah Jordan, 2d, Sarah Abbott, of Albany, Me.

Of the gr. gr. grandchildren of Mrs. L. 3 are gr. grandchildren of Mrs. Maxfield, 2 of Mrs. Caldwell, and 4 of Mrs. Wardwell.

Since visiting Mrs. L. I have called upon her brother William, at Woburn, whom I found bright, cheerful and *youthful* (for his years), surrounded by his books, from which he read to me fluently without glasses, and from whom I received a cordial greeting as bearer of tidings from his aged sister.

These instances of longevity it seemed to me must be regarded as exceptions to the rule " yet is their strength but labor and sorrow," and surely the " grasshopper " has not yet become a " burden."

Boston, Mass.   ———   B. A. G. FULLER.

MARYLAND—LETTERS OF JESUIT MISSIONARIES.—Father White's Journal, edited by the Rev. Dr. Dalrymple, and published by the Maryland Historical Society in 1874 [REGISTER, xxviii. 358], contained a translation of sundry letters of Jesuit missionaries in Maryland, 1635-1677, and a portion of the Latin text of these letters. Since then the residue of the Latin text has been found, and will be published by the Society above named.

NECROLOGY OF THE NEW-ENGLAND HISTORIC, GENEALOGICAL SOCIETY.

Prepared by the Rev. SAMUEL CUTLER, Historiographer of the Society.

FREDERIC WILLIAM SAWYER, Esq., a resident member of this Society, was born in Saco, Maine, April 22, 1810. He died at his residence, 433 Beacon Street, Boston, Sept. 6, 1875, aged 65 years, 4 months and 14 days. His father was William Sawyer, who was born July 28, 1776, and married Margery Scamman, daughter of Deacon Samuel Scamman, of Saco. His grandfather William Sawyer married Mary Warren, and settled very early on the Buxton road, where it unites with the Heath road, about four miles from Saco village.

In a MS. autobiography, the subject of our notice says, " My grandfather used to tell me that when he located on that estate, about 1775, there was no house north of him, between there and Canada. Bears, wolves and catamounts were quite plenty in the woods near by ; especially in what has always been called ' The Great Heath,' an interminable quagmire extending for miles north and east of the Heath Road " In connection with the bears and wolves, he also speaks of the outlying neighborhoods of the Buxton road, inhabited by the queerest set of Yankee inhabitants ever met with in New-England. " They were outlandish enough to need an interpreter to understand their gibberish : then came along an inspired set of them, who spoke in tongues ; after them came a saint, one Cochrane, a sort of *avant courier* of Joseph Smith, who had the whole Heath and Loudon villages after him. He was more of a Mormon than the Mormon Elder himself, and for years dominated all through that region."

William and Margery (Scamman) Sawyer, the parents of Frederic William Sawyer, Esq., at their marriage settled on a farm, in 1803. Beside their son Frederic, they had two daughters, Sarah Frost, born Nov. 6, 1804, and Harriet, born Sept. 12, 1806.

William Sawyer, the father, early made voyages in vessels between Saco and the West Indies. In February, 1812, James Maxwell, of Biddeford, owner of the brig Cataract, loaded her with timber, and despatched her on a voyage to the West Indies, under the command of Capt. Sawyer. The vessel arrived at her destined port, but after leaving was never heard from.

Mr. Sawyer has left, in manuscript, his childish impressions of the long and agonizing waiting of his mother for her husband's return, and the speculations and gossip of their neighbors, as they told of mischances by flood and piracy, by war and imprisonment ; of the months of waiting and watching for his father's return. "Nothing in life," he says, "is so undying as hope." And circumstances which he narrates, encouraged hope until long after the close of the war in 1814–15.

Mr. Sawyer as a child lived with his mother on the old farm, surrounded on three sides by Cutts woods. In his narrative, he says : "By going about one mile through the woods to the right, I could reach the river (Saco) near the boom, where I could attend a public school a few months in the summer, or I could attend the primary school at Saco village, two miles distant, the year round. I chose, except for one summer, to walk the two miles. Winters, I either spent at my uncle James Curry's house on the Ferry road, afterwards owned by Josiah Calef, or at my grandfather's on the Buxton road. The school-house there was on the corner where the Buxton and Heath Roads intersected."

"I have always thought that my youthful experience beside the deep and lonely forest, where I encountered so often great numbers of beasts, birds and fishes, to amuse and interest me, has given me a much more lively enjoyment of my vacation in the country, than is usual among men bred in villages and cities. I love the woods, and all their wild fruits, flowers and inhabitants. The croak of the raven, the drumming of the patridge, 'the tapping of the woodpecker,' and the bark of the raccoon and fox, are all delightful sounds to me. There is no sound in nature more delightful than the low moaning of the woods, the rustle of the leaves, or the ripple of the distant sheltered brook or waterfall."

Again he writes : "My early home was near the sea, Old Orchard Beach being but a mile, or so, from Capt. Curry's where I spent so many years of my schooldays, and less than four miles from my own home. As may well be supposed, under the circumstances, my earliest thoughts were connected with the ever changing, uncertain sea. It always had a strange, sad, mysterious charm for me. I have always loved the sad sea wave. From my earliest days I have loved to wander alone by its sounding shore, and listen to its deep breathings. It seemed to have something it wanted to say to me, but lost heart and failed utterance just when it began to murmur on the shore."

The school days of Mr. Sawyer closed in the winter of 1824–5. From that date he was for five years a clerk in the store of his uncle James Sawyer, at Damariscotta Mills, New Castle, Me. Thence he went to Portland, Me., and was in a dry goods store about one year ; after that, in the dry goods store of J. M. Hayes, of Saco, a year or two. He then commenced business in Saco, on his own account, which he continued until 1837. He then went to Bangor, to take charge of some timber land he had, and while cutting and selling his timber, he commenced the study of law in the office of Blake & McCrellis.

"In the spring of 1838," he says, "I came to Boston, and entered myself a student in the office of Fletcher & Sewall, then at 14 State Street. Mr. Fletcher was then in Congress. Daniel Webster, Jeremiah Mason, Samuel Hoar, Rufus Choate, Samuel Hubbard, Franklin Dexter, William H. Gardner, Richard Fletcher, William D. Sohier, Benjamin Rand, Charles G. Loring, C. P. Curtis and H. H. Fuller, were then in full practice at the bar. B. R. Curtis was then sitting round watching the course of proceedings, and Sidney Bartlett was trying his hand as junior counsel."

Mr. Sawyer completed his studies with Hubbard & Watts, 20 Court Street. While there, he wrote and published the "Merchants and Ship Masters' Guide," which has passed through six editions of 750 copies, and is still a standard work. He was admitted to the bar, August 1, 1840. He occupied as his office, Room No. 1, Tudor's Building, No. 20 Court Street, 1840–1871, 31 years. He had, for a long time, a large admiralty practice, and a pretty large general practice.

In 1847, he published his "Plea for Amusements," which met with favorable notice; and in 1860, "Hits and Hints," a book of happy conception, and very readable matter. Under the signatures "Canty Carl," and "Carl," he was for many years a contributor to the Transcript. The Editor, in a notice of his death, speaks "of his unobtrusive good sense, his pleasant and witty way of putting things, his sympathy with the suffering and unfortunate, his advocacy of justice, mercy and charity, his love of children, his friendliness towards, and promotion of innocuous amusement, and his quick and active desire always alert to benefit his fellow creatures." He was joyfully benevolent in his disposition, free from all moroseness and harshness as he smilingly endeavored, in a zealous but modest way, to use his talents so as to make the world, or the circles in which he directly moved, the better and the happier also for his believing and cordial life. It is pleasant to learn that his faith to the last was serene and hopeful, and that he fell asleep quietly, as became the calm close of a well-spent day."

He married, Sept. 18, 1849, Caroline Beal, daughter of Benjamin and Mary (Swift) Burgess, of Sandwich, born March 1, 1821. They had : 1. Ella B., born August 15, 1850, died August 15, 1863. 2. Frederic C., born July 20, 1853. 3. Rufus F., born May 8, 1860. The widow and two sons survive.

Mr. Sawyer was instrumental in establishing the Pawner's Bank, and was its first President. He was for some years a member of the American Statistical Association, and its Librarian from Jan., 1849, to Jan., 1854. He was admitted a resident member of this Society, April 30, 1864. To it, he donated, under date of Aug. 15, 1875, his office book-case, with nearly a hundred volumes of Law Books, consisting of Digests, Reports, &c.

The Hon. DAY OTIS KELLOGG, a member of this society, and a contributor to the REGISTER, was born in Galway, Saratoga county, N. Y., Aug. 7, 1796, and died Aug. 9, 1874, aged 78 years and 2 days, at Fairfield, Conn.; whither he had gone from his home in Brooklyn, L. I., hoping to be benefited by the change of air, amid scenes familiar to him in earlier life.

The branch of the Kellogg family from which the subject of our memoir descended had its origin, as was ascertained by him, during a residence of three years as U. S. Consul in Glasgow, Scotland, among the headlands and braes of Fifeshire. The name has a Celtic formation, and through all its transformations of Killock, Killoch, and Kellogg, he found the two roots, "Kill" and "Loch," meaning a lake cemetery, and thus pointing to the origin of the family name.

The American branch of the Kellogg family Mr. Kellogg first found located among the Puritans in Barnstable county, Mass., about the middle of the 17th century. Thence it removed to the Connecticut Valley, spreading itself along that river into Vermont and Connecticut. One branch however followed the westward course of empire, and Mr. Kellogg's immediate ancestors were settled in Berkshire county, Mass. Both his parents were born in the same county, and in the valley of the Housatonic, though they met and were married in Saratoga county, N. Y. Charles Kellogg his father was born in Sheffield, Oct. 3, 1773.[1] His mother, Mary Ann, the daughter of David Otis, was born in Richmond, not far from Lenox, and belonged to a branch of the Otis family of Barnstable, Mass.

In 1797, the spring after his birth, his parents set out to seek a pioneer's home in what was then considered the "far west." After twice changing their location, each time pitching their tent in the unsubdued wilderness, they, in 1799, found themselves in possession of a farm perfectly wild, but of sufficient size to satisfy their ambition. The location was Sempronius (now Niles), where they resided forty years.

Sharing the vicissitudes of his father's fortunes, Day Otis Kellogg obtained such schooling as the new country afforded, together with eighteen months instruction in Saratoga village until he was twelve years of age. After this he had the benefits of one winter's tuition in a district school, but otherwise his time was given to work on his father's farm and as a clerk in his store until he was nineteen. One of his

---

[1] See "Genealogical Items of the Kellogg Family," REGISTER for July, 1858, and April, 1860.

younger companions during these years was Millard Fillmore, who was for a part of the time an apprentice in a clothier's shop to Alvan Kellogg, a cousin of the subject of this sketch, and a man who subsequently made his way to the legislature of New-York from Cortland county. These two comrades were smitten with a thirst for learning, and early adopted habits of reading which neither ever abandoned. Mr. Kellogg's associations led him directly into mercantile life, and his studies, therefore, except so far as they were directed to commercial economy, were not professional but literary. He eagerly pursued historical and geographical reading, and familiarized himself with the English classics of the 17th and 18th centuries.

While boyhood was passing away in Sempronius, the Galway homestead was being deserted by his father's brothers, whom a more luxurious fortune enticed to the valley of the Hudson. In the beginning of this century, a ferry, which is still maintained at the head of navigation on the Hudson, gave name to the present location of Troy. It was then called Ashley's ferry, and the site of the city was then divided among three farms. In 1801 a village charter was obtained for Troy, and here two brothers, Asa and Warren Kellogg, settled a few years later in mercantile pursuits. They had established themselves as leading wholesale merchants of that section, when in 1815 their nephew, Day Otis Kellogg, came to be their apprentice. Having served his time with them after the custom of those days, the emancipated clerk started to set up for himself, and, with an instinct like his father's, sought a home on the frontier. A visit to Ohio discovered no prospect of sufficient promise to detain him there, and he came back to join his father in merchandizing at Kelloggsville, where he remained accumulating some property for two years. His ambition exceeding his opportunities, he then removed to Owasco, a village midway between Auburn and his father's house, where he opened a country store and engaged in a flouring mill enterprise.

In 1827 Mr. Asa Kellogg retired from the mercantile house in Troy, of which he was the senior member, and his two younger brothers, Warren and Alexander C., continued the business, inviting their nephew, Day Otis, to join them the following year. The invitation was accepted, and a few years later, on the retirement of Mr. A. C. Kellogg, the firm took the style of Kellogg & Co., which name it retained until the dissolution of the house in New-York in the year 1855, to which city it removed four years previously. For more than ten years Mr. D. O. Kellogg was the senior member of the firm, three of his younger brothers being associated with him from time to time. It passed through the convulsions and prostrations of 1837 without impeachment of its credit, and when it dissolved Mr. Kellogg remarked that, during an existence of over fifty years, it had never suffered from any cause the protest of a single one of its notes.

We find our space will oblige us greatly to curtail what has been prepared for publication, including matter of great interest in the public life of Mr. Kellogg, by his son the Rev. Day Otis Kellogg, Jr., and can only enumerate some of the leading facts.

The most active and successful years of Mr. Kellogg's life were passed in Troy, N.Y. About the year 1827 he became active in the political movements of the day. He joined the new National Republicans, and warmly advocated the election of the State Electoral College by a general state ticket. His position connected him at once with the newly rising Whig party, with which the personal friends of his boyhood became identified, and with which all his own political success was won. He sustained the policy of internal improvement. He followed Clay's theories of tariff, and strongly opposed Jackson's attitude towards the United States Bank.

In the years 1836 and '37 he resided in the Island of Santa Cruz for the benefit of his health. He prepared, for publication, works valuable to the traveller, the invalid, and the public, relating to the soil, productions, and climate of the Island.

On his return he was elected to the assembly, and took his seat in the lower house in 1839, being made chairman of the Committee on Banks and Insurance Companies. In 1849 the city of Troy organized its Board of Education, of which he was made a member by the Common Council of the City, and first President by the action of the Board itself.

In the following year Mr. Kellogg was chosen by the Whigs Mayor of Troy, and his was the last administration of that party in the city. He did not complete his term of office, for, on the accession of Mr. Fillmore to the presidential chair in 1850, he was appointed to the consulship at Glasgow, Scotland, to which port he sailed in November of that year. Tendering his resignation to Mr. Pierce in 1853 on that gentleman's inauguration, Mr. Kellogg returned to New-York, where his business connections were then established, and took up a permanent residence in Brooklyn. For some years subsequently he engaged in mercantile pursuits, but gave up active life some years before his decease.

Mr. Kellogg's public spirit, and his desire to promote the interests of the city of Troy, led him at the cost of much time, and no small detriment to his private interests, to engage largely in efforts for more rapid transportation by railroads centring in that city. We have not room to speak of these in detail.

In his religious life Mr. Kellogg was connected from early manhood to his death with the Protestant Episcopal Church. He was ever ready to engage in religious enterprises for his fellow-men, and has said in his later years that nothing gave him more pleasure to recall than his connection with the Bible Society.

Beyond all the tributes to his judgment and character which the positions he occupied afford, those who knew Mr. Kellogg well, will prize more the modesty, the quiet dignity and courtesy which won their respect, the ingenuous truthfulness which sustained every confidence put in him, the stability and purity of his christian principles, which commanded men's esteem, and confirmed him in their love.

Mr. Kellogg was thrice married.

1. In 1825, to Ann Eliza, daughter of David and Ann Dickenson Smith, of Lansingburg, N. Y. She died Aug. 11, 1829, leaving two sons, Burr T. and Charles D. of New-York city.

2. In 1831, to Mary Ann, daughter of Ebenezer and Mary S. Hinman Dimon, of Fairfield, Conn. She died May 7, 1840, leaving three sons, George D., died 1865, Theodore D., and Day Otis, Jr.

3. In Sept. 1841, to Harriet Walter, daughter of John and Harriet Walter Odin, of Boston, Mass., who, with their adopted daughter, Lula Desbrisay Kellogg, a relative of her mother's, survive him. Mr. Odin was a prominent and worthy merchant of Boston, and Mrs. Odin was a daughter of the Rev. William Walter, D.D., of Boston.

Mr. Kellogg published a history of Troy and its resources, a pamphlet of 48 pages; a genealogical account of the Kellogg family, two numbers 1858 and 1860, 8 pages each. Besides these, he contributed a series of articles to the Troy papers on internal improvements, over the signature of Hancock; a serial life of Millard Fillmore to the New-York Commercial Advertiser, and a number of addresses and discussions of current themes to the newspapers of the day, and especially to "Hunt's Merchants' Magazine."

He was admitted a resident member of this society, Aug. 20, 1856.

Prepared by the Rev. DORUS CLARKE, D.D., late Historiographer of the Society.

Capt. CHARLES AUGUSTUS RANLETT, JR.—The subject of this sketch was born in Charlestown, Mass., Sept. 21, 1836, and died in Brooklyn, N. Y., Feb. 6, 1874, aged 37 years. His early life was not particularly eventful. A vigorous constitution carried him through the ordinary ills incident to childhood, and he attended the public schools from a very early age, with little interruption, until he launched out upon his career as a mariner. A natural, probably inherited, taste for a nautical life was encouraged, no doubt, by a voyage to New Orleans and Europe, at an early age, with his parents and a younger brother.

As a boy, he developed a strong disposition for adventure. Fearless almost to rashness, he was recognized as a leader among his young comrades, and was never known to show the least spark of pusillanimity in any situation in which he was placed. This bold and hardy spirit was held in check by the wise government of a mother, whom he ever, both as a boy and as a man, obeyed and revered with unwavering devotion. To her wise management and counsels he always attributed whatever success he attained in after years. Though a good scholar, he chafed under the restraint of school discipline, and it was thought best to give vent to his inclination for the seas. He did not leave school, however, until he had laid the basis of a good common-school education, with some knowledge of the classics, which was always useful to him in his reading and study of later years. To the good influence of the day-school were added those of the Sunday-school in forming his character. He was guided at home by a Christian mother, and to the time of his departure from home was a regular attendant at the First Baptist Church and Sunday-school in Charlestown. His after life was an exemplification of the purifying influence of the religious teaching he then and there received. A regular attendance upon Divine Service when in port, and the frequent observance of the Sabbath at sea, when compatible with the duties of proper navigation of the ship, were evidences of his regard for the " day to keep it holy."

At the age of fourteen, it happened that the great California excitement commenced. Vessels of beautiful model were being launched from our ship-yards, and spreading their white wings for the race to San Francisco. What wonder that the young man, with his intense nautical tastes, should spend much of his time in wandering about among the vessels that lay at the wharves, and pining for a day when he could begin a " life on the ocean wave." Yet for all his longing to go, he never would think of it without his mother's consent. This was at length reluctantly secured. At this time, 1851, his father was about to proceed to England, to take command of the Clipper Ship " Surprise," and it was arranged that Charles should sail as boy on board the ship " Samuel Russell," then loading at New-York for China, under Capt. Limeburner, who afterwards commanded the " Great Republic." So our sailor-boy bid farewell to home, and joyfully embarked upon the element he ever after loved so well. Capt. Limeburner always spoke of him as a good boy, faithful to his duty, anxious to learn navigation, and was sorry to lose him, when, in China, he joined his father, and was made third mate of the " Surprise," a position for which Capt. L. considered him competent, despite his brief experience.

And now he took up his home on board the ship with which, save for one passage, he was ever after identified. In 1856, being in China at the time the clipper ship " Panama" was about to sail for New-York, he was urged, by Capt. Cave, to take the position of chief officer of his ship, Capt. C. being ill, and feeling it important to have a reliable mate. He accepted, and during the greater part of the passage home was virtually in command of the ship, the Captain being confined to his room by sickness. He arrived in New-York in 86 days from Shanghae, then the shortest passage ever made between the two ports, and only twice beaten afterwards, by his father in the " Surprise" and by the " Swordfish." Capt. Cave was very loth to lose him when he decided to return to the " Surprise," and always spoke of him in the highest terms both as a man and a sailor. Hereafter, his career as a mariner was as mate and master of the ship " Surprise," in the employ of A. A. Low & Brothers, of New-York. Long service as mate of the ship, well fitted him for the command, which he received in 1860, when his father gave way for him and took another ship. From that time, he trod the quarter deck of the " Surprise" during a period of thirteen years, sailing her skilfully and successfully, having the confidence of his owners and the respect of all with whom he came in contact; making invariably the shortest passages to or from China, until the ship became world-renowned for her speed, and was admitted to be the Queen of the China fleet. The degree of affection he felt for the ship can only be understood by those who, like him, have made their home for years upon one vessel, and been carried safely through the perils of the deep hundreds of thousands of miles. Until his marriage, he ever spoke of the ship as his wife, and never was tired of decorating her and making her shine " alow and aloft." No ship ever entered the port of New-York from a foreign voyage in finer order—and her departure was a gala occasion with his multitude of friends of either sex, who always accompanied him down the bay, nor left until all sail was made for the distant haven.

Capt. Ranlett married, August 4, 1870, Miss Isabella, daughter of Luther Faulkner, Esq., of Billerica, who survives.

He was admitted to this society as a resident member, Nov. 8, 1866. He was also a member of the New-York Marine Society, and of the Clinton Commandery of Knights Templars of that city.

JOHN STRATTON WRIGHT, Esq., a life member and benefactor, was born at Plainfield, N. H., June 30, 1788, and died at Brookline, Mass., June 29, 1874, after a short illness, having gone to his counting-room in Boston as usual the previous Tuesday. He was son of Dr. Eben Wright, an eminent physician, born 1755, died 1798, and Martha Wellman. His grandfather, Samuel Wright, was descended from one of the earliest settlers of New-England, Deacon Samuel Wright, of Springfield, 1639. (See REGISTER, iv. 355–8.)

Mr. Wright, when quite young, started in business at Thetford, Vermont, being associated with the late George Peabody, the philanthropic banker. In 1824, he came to Boston, where he was engaged several years in the management of one of the city banks. In 1832, he commenced business in the dry goods line, and for more than half a century occupied a high position among the merchants of Boston. He possessed the highest qualifications for success in business, with the finest sense of integrity and honorable dealing, prompt and attentive in his business, and rarely absent from his counting-room. He always desired to die " in the harness," and his wish was gratified.

He married Mary Russell, daughter of Dr. Samuel Wellman, of Piermont, N. H. Children : *Charles*, died young ; Dr. *John H., Joseph B., Eben., Mary E.* He was admitted a resident member of this society, Dec. 30, 1871.

The Rev. THOMAS DEWITT, D.D., a corresponding member, born in Kingston, co. Ulster, N. Y., Sept. 13, 1791 ; died May 18, 1874, in New-York city. He was the son of Thomas DeWitt, born May 3, 1741, died Sept. 9, 1809 ; a Revolutionary officer, and lineally descended from one of the early settlers from Holland 1654, and Elsie Hasbrouck, born March, 1750, died June 28, 1833 ; descended from one of a band of French Huguenot Refugees, who for a short time resided in Holland, then came to America and settled in co. Ulster, N. Y. He was graduated from the Theological Seminary, New Brunswick, N. J. In 1812, was ordained at Poughkeepsie, a minister of the Dutch Reformed Church. In 1827, he was called to the Collegiate Reformed Dutch Church, in New-York, and remained their pastor until his death.

Dr. DeWitt was one of the most active and learned of the ministers of his church, and was the promoter of every good object for the advancement of religion and learning, and in all the charitable and educational movements of the church he was an earnest co-worker. He had so thorough a knowledge of the Dutch language, that when occasion required he preached in that language. He was one of the founders of the Board of Education of his church, and held responsible positions as a manager of various institutions of learning and religious and benevolent societies. He was a trustee of Rutgers College for more than thirty years ; also one of the superintendents of the Theological Seminary at New-Brunswick ; a trustee of Columbia College, of the American Tract Society, and of the Leake and Watts Asylum ; president of the City Mission, of the Tract Society, and of the New-York Historical Society. His kindly deportment and unpretentious yet dignified intercourse with his fellow-men caused him to be universally beloved. He was admitted a member of this society, January 15, 1858.

JOHN GOUGH NICHOLS, F.S.A., a corresponding member, was born at his father's residence, Red Lion Passage, Fleet street, London, May 22, 1806, and died at Holmwood Park, near Dorking, in Surrey, England, November 14, 1873. He was the representative of a family which, while carrying on successfully the business of printing, has for three generations, more or less, distinguished itself in the sphere of literature and archæological research. His grandfather, John Nichols, F.S.A., was the well-known author of the " Literary Anecdotes of the Eighteenth Century," the compiler of " The History of Leicestershire," and, for forty-eight years, the editor of the " Gentleman's Magazine." His father, John Bowyer Nichols, F.S.A., was from an early age the coadjutor of his father in editing the " Gentleman's Magazine," and completed many of his works.

In 1811, the subject of this notice was placed at a school at Islington, where Benjamin Disraeli was his school-fellow. In 1814, he was sent to Lewisham, where he remained until 1816, and in 1817 was placed at Merchant Taylor's, from which, in the summer of 1824, he left school to join in the business and literary labors of his father and grandfather, to whom, before his school-days were over, he was a useful assistant. Journals kept by him during his school-days, are still in existence, and indicate the bent of his mind. He makes notes on churches, and copies inscriptions and epitaphs. His first literary work, after leaving school, was to help in the compilation of the " Progresses of King James the First," the latest work of his father, which he completed after his father's death. He took an active part in the editorial management of " The Gentleman's Magazine," until 1856 (when the proprietorship was relinquished by the Messrs. Nichols), contributing to its pages many essays of considerable historical value. In 1829, he published his first separate work, a collection of " Autographs of Royal, Noble, Learned, and Remarkable Personages," accompanied by Biographical Memoirs, which show extensive research and historical knowledge in its young author. In 1831, he published a volume on " London Pageants," which was received with considerable favor. In 1833, the Messrs. Nichols commenced the publication, in quarterly parts, of the " Collectanea Topographica et Genealogica." Of this work, which was completed in eight volumes in 1843, Mr. John Gough Nichols was one of the original editors, and latterly the sole editor. In 1835, he was elected a Fellow of the Society of Antiquaries, of which he was an active and useful member until the time of his death. In 1838, he published " A Description of the Frescoes discovered in 1804, in the Guild

Chapel, at Stratford-on-Avon, and of the Records relating thereto." In the same year he suggested, and in conjunction with other friends, established the Camden Society, the objects of which were announced to be " to perpetuate and render accessible whatever is valuable, but at present little known, amongst the materials for the Civil, Ecclesiastical, or Literary History of the United Kingdom." This society rapidly achieved a triumph beyond the hopes of its projectors. He edited many of the volumes issued by that society. In 1844, he became an original member of the Archæological Association.

In 1849, he published the " Pilgrimages of Walsingham and Canterbury," by Erasmus, an original translation. The termination of Mr. Nichols's connection with the management of " The Gentleman's Magazine," had been rendered necessary by the state of his health, but it was with great reluctance that he renounced it, and in little more than a year we find him planning the establishment of another periodical, which ultimately took the form of the " Herald and Genealogist," which met with great favor, but other engagements and uncertain health interfered seriously with the regularity of the publication. Its pages were always open to American correspondents, and he had the opportunity of making known in this country many valuable American contributions to genealogical literature. In 1869, he attempted the publication of " The Register and Magazine of Biography," devoted wholly to contemporary biography and the record of family events, though he did not edit it ; but, receiving no pecuniary support, it was abandoned after six months trial. Mr. Nichols joined the London and Middlesex Archæological Association, on its first establishment in 1855, and was elected a member of its Council in 1857, and a Vice-President in 1865, which offices he retained until his death. The Transactions of this society also bear witness to his untiring industry and extensive knowledge.

John Gough Nichols married, July 22, 1843, Lucy, eldest daughter of Frederick Lewis, Esq., Commander R. N., by whom he had one son: John Bruce Nichols, born Nov. 18, 1848, whose name was joined, in 1873, to those of his father and uncle as " Printers of the Votes and Proceedings of the House of Commons." He also had two daughters. Throughout the summer of 1873, his friends had observed with regret a decided falling off in his health and strength, but he still bestowed an immense amount of labor upon his different undertakings. A few days before his death, he read a proof of a new edition of Mr. Evelyn Shirley's " Stemmata Shirleiana." The summer before his death, he prepared for this society biographical sketches of his friends, Sir Thomas Phillipps, baronet, and Sir Frederick Madden, members of this society, who had been associated with him in establishing the " Collectanea Topographica et Genealogica ;" which was published in the REGISTER, xxvii. 428–30.

He was admitted a member of this institution, July 23, 1864.

Prepared by WILLIAM B. TRASK, Esq., former Historiographer of the Society.

THOMAS WATERMAN, a resident member, died in Boston, Feb. 26, 1875, in his 84th year. He was a descendant in the 7th generation from *Robert*[1] *Waterman*, of Marshfield, through *Thomas*,[2] *Thomas*,[3] *Thomas*,[4] *Silas*[5] and *Thomas*[6] his father. Mr. Waterman contributed to the REGISTER for April, 1869 (*ante*, xxiii. 204–5), an article on " The Descendants of Robert Waterman, of Marshfield," in which further particulars of his ancestors will be found.

The subject of this notice was the eldest of nine children of Thomas[6] and Susannah (Cleveland) Waterman, and was born in Lebanon, N. H., Sept. 14, 1791. He remained at the old homestead with his parents until he was 18 years of age, working on the farm in the summer season, and attending the village school in the winter. He then left his home and engaged in the service of Peter R. Field, at his store in West Lebanon, where he remained till he was twenty-one years of age. The following year he taught in one of the District schools of his native town. In 1812, Master Waterman first exercised his right of suffrage (taking the Freeman's oath as was the custom then, before voting), and the first time was the last that he voted at the polls in Lebanon, as he left the state of New-Hampshire soon after, and resided in Hartford, Vt., now White River Junction, during the next five years, occupying a situation in the store of Justin and Elias Lyman. In December, 1817, he left the Lymans, came to Boston, and obtained employment as a clerk in the store of Stearns & Danforth, on India Street. In September, 1819, Mr. Waterman commenced business in Concord, N. H., with Sampson Bullard, under the firm of Bullard & Waterman. In five years time he relinquished the business to the senior partner, and returned to Boston, where he engaged in the West India goods trade, until the month of January, 1829. The September following found him occupying the position of discount clerk in the Bank of the United States, in Boston, where he remained until the charter expired in 1836, when the affairs of that bank were closed. The state of Pennsylvania having granted a charter for a bank of the same name, an agency was established in Boston. Sàmuel Frothingham, Esq., former cashier of the old Bank, was appointed Agent, and made Mr. Waterman his confidential clerk. He remained in this position until April, 1841, when the agency was discontinued. A branch of the Treasury Department of the United States was subsequently formed in Boston, Mr. Frothingham was made its Treasurer, and he, again, selected Mr. Waterman for his clerk. In the summer of 1841, Congress repealed the act authorizing the sub-treasury, as it was called, and the Boston business closed. In December, 1841, Mr. W. was chosen book-keeper in the Traders' Bank, now the Traders' National Bank of this city, where he remained until the infirmities of age precluded him from any active service.

Mr. Waterman married Joanna Towle, a native of North-Hampton, N. H., Jan. 12, 1832. She died April 22, 1864, aged 61 years, 12 days. They had five children, three daughters and two sons, of whom a daughter and a son, the oldest and the youngest, survive. The son, Thomas, fitted for college at the Public Latin School in Boston, graduated at Harvard College in 1864, studied medicine, and is now a practising physician in Boston.

Mr. Waterman was for fifty-three years a member of Mount Lebanon Lodge of Free and Accepted Masons, and for forty-four years its honored and respected secretary. He was connected for thirty-three years with the St. Andrew's Royal Arch Chapter ; associated fifty-seven years with the Boston Royal Council of Select and Royal Masters, and thirty years a member of the Grand Royal Arch Chapter of Massachusetts. He was an honorary member of the Zetland Lodge, of which Dr. Thomas Waterman, son of the deceased, was Master. In 1859, Mr. Waterman published biographical sketches of distinguished members of St. Andrew's Royal Arch Chapter, Boston, which was instituted in 1769. The By-Laws of the Chapter are contained in the volume, of 130 pages, 12 mo. ; but about two-thirds of the book is occupied with Mr. Waterman's sketches. These are prepared with great care, from reliable sources, and are without doubt very correct, as our friend was a cautious man, sparing neither time nor labor in his endeavor to make such things right. He added, also, a list of all the officers and members of the Chapter, from the time of its organization, a period of ninety years.

Mr. Waterman issued a second edition of the above work in 1866 (pp. 168), adding to it twelve biographies, bringing his list of officers and members down to the date of publication.

The rites of burial according to the Masonic ritual were performed at his funeral, which took place from the South Congregational Church, Union Park, March 2, mid a large concourse of friends and members of the Masonic fraternity, with which he had been connected more than sixty-one years, organizations of the latter bringing beautiful and costly floral tributes, consisting of camelias, tea-roses, violets, white and red carnations and other choice flowers. Rev. Dr. Blagden, and Rev. Jacob M. Manning, D.D., pastors of the deceased, officiated. The remains were conveyed to Mount Auburn, and were interred in his family lot, No. 1021, on Fir Avenue.

Mr. Waterman was one of the most honest, conscientious and faithful of men. He had the entire confidence, love and respect of every one who knew him. He was a gentleman of true antiquarian tastes, and had collected a valuable library of historical and miscellaneous books. He was made a resident member of our society, Feb. 18, 1852.

The Rev. THOMAS SMYTH, D.D., died in Charleston, South Carolina, August 20, 1873, aged 65. He was born in Belfast, Ireland, July 14, 1808, of Scotch and English ancestry. His father participated in what is called "the Rebellion of 1798," and suffered a long and painful imprisonment therefor. His mother, whose maiden name was Magee, was a woman of superior attainments. He always spoke of her with the greatest affection and reverential love. When Thomas was about 17 years of age, his father failed in business, and the young man felt the necessity of giving up his studies, that he might aid his parents in providing for their support. A kind friend offered him a situation in his counting-house. While hesitating whether or not to accept, his mother said to him, " Thomas, if you want to pursue your studies, go on ; I will work myself, if necessary, to secure your expenses." Alluding to her great kindness and affection for him, he thus writes in his diary: "Most blessed mother, could my thanks now reach thee, in thy bright throne above, I should here, amid these falling tears, pour forth the grateful acknowledgments of thy long cherished son. I love to think of thee, my mother, of thy illimitable, inexhaustible love." Encouraged in such a practical and efficient manner by this kind parent, he entered upon his studies with renewed energy. Reading was his great delight, the possession of books his ardent desire. His thirst for books, to use his own language, "became rapacious" "and he frequently overspent his supplies in procuring them, and had to deny himself for two or three months, in the dead of winter, almost the necessaries of life." It seems somewhat singular that he should have used the following language to young ministers "to beware of a passion for books, or a blind chase after a large library. It is, as a general thing, vain and useless. It is often impoverishing and infatuating. It becomes as insatiate as the grave, crying ' Give ! give ! ' I feel that I was an exception to the rule, a sacrifice, willingly offered up for the public good. I felt a special call to collect a large library, not for myself, but for my brethren's sake, and for posterity. This has been a part of my life work." He had at one time about 20,000 volumes. His books, by letter he informed me, cost him about 30,000 dollars. "I studied Bibliography," he says, "in order to collect a large, systematic, Presbyterian, Theological and Literary Library, as an armory for our Ministers and Churches in Charleston, similar to that of Dr. Williams in London. As it increased, I labored to adapt it for a Theological seminary, in which I hoped it ultimately would find a providential location. He retained a working portion ; the residue, some 15.000 choice books, went to the Theological Seminary, Columbia, S. C., where they are known as the "Smyth Library."

" In all his travels in America and Europe, he was in quest of books, often spending whole days in stores and antiquarian stalls ; and, for years, consuming the greater part of his salary in the purchase of books."

To return to his early life. He was the youngest of six sons. His constitution was so frail, "that no one expected him to live beyond the period of childhood,"[1] but he had an indomitable will and an earnest desire to become a scholar, seconded by his heroic mother, as we have before stated, who had a desire that he should be a minister. Notwithstanding his feebleness, he entered the first Institute at Belfast, at the age of 19, where he won prizes in every branch of study. " His superior scholarship was acknowledged by his entire class of nearly a hundred students, who, by their unanimous suffrage, awarded to him the highest prize." He had for his private instructor there, the famous tragedian, Sheridan Knowles, and there "he began to develop those powers of elocution, which afterward gave him a place among the princes of pulpit oratory."

His father was for many years an Elder in the Presbyterian Church of which Dr. Samuel Hanna was pastor. In this church he was brought up. His theological studies were prosecuted at Highbury College, in London. Here to obtain books "he would undergo the most painful self-denials, sacrificing his comfort, in the severest inclemency of winter, bartering his very food and fuel for his coveted treasures." " In addition to his theological studies, he attended a course of scientific lectures in London, read the higher classics, and roamed at will through the tomes of learned antiquity. But all this was too much for his physical endurance. He seemed sinking into a decline, and all his bright hopes for the future were apparently to be overthrown. At this critical moment his parents were preparing to remove to America, where the most of their children had preceded them. He sailed with them for New-York in August, 1830, and soon after his arrival joined his eldest brother in Patterson, N. J. Here he connected himself with the Presbyterian church, entered the senior class at Princeton seminary, and before graduating received an invitation to the 2d Presbyterian church in Charleston, S. C., and in Nov. 1831 he entered upon his labors there. Six months afterwards he had a unanimous call to become their pastor, which he accepted, giving them the preference over several other calls. He was installed by the Charleston Union Presbytery, Dec. 29, 1834. In 1832 he married the eldest daughter of James Adger, of Charleston, by whom he had nine children, six of whom—three sons and three daughters—survive their father. One of his sons is a ruling elder in the church, another is a deacon. In 1848 he was attacked with partial paralysis. In 1853 he had a second attack. Two months after

---

[1] His father said of him, "there is no cure for him but a plaister of earth."

the last stroke of paralysis, " a disastrous fire swept away the choicest portion of his collection of books, which he called his working library, together with valuable manuscripts upon which he had bestowed several years of laborious study." This loss he was never able to repair. " It was a sore trial to him and a serious loss to the world." He was a life-long sufferer, yet he labored on in his sphere of duty. In his graphic way he thus describes pain. " I have often thought I could write a natural history of pain. I have known her from childhood. We have walked arm in arm, dwelt in the same house, occupants of the same bed. She is like the chamelion, of every hue, and like Proteus, of every shape. She is sometimes as quick as light, and again, like an Alexandrian line, ' drags her slow length along.' Sometimes, she is as the forked •lightning coursing in tortuous torture through every limb and fibre of the body, and dissolving the pent-up and collected clouds of bitterness into flooding tears ; and sometimes she is that lightning in its negative form, of quiet, dull monotony, or occasional playful flashes, just enough to rouse the attention and excite the fancy. Sometimes she languishes into the faint tones of an infant, talking in its sleep, or like the bubbling groan of some strong swimmer in his agony, or like a strong man in the whirlwind of his passion, she puts on an angel's might, and mystery of power." He was a cheerful, happy sufferer. His great will "inspired him with untiring industry and unflagging energy." He often remarked that the will can conquer pain, and command the shattered nerves to hold their peace. On one occasion, when the night was dark and inclement, and his whole frame writhing with agony, he assumed a posture of defiance, and emphasizing his words with his crutch, while his chamber rung with his echo, he rose with determination, declaring that he would not " stand it any longer." Pushing out into the dismal darkness, against the earnest remon-strances of the members of his household, he returned, after several hours of gymnastic exercise, and exclaimed, with an air of triumph, "I told you so. Any man may subdue pain, if he only has the will to do it."

After ministering to his flock for 39 years, his increasing infirmities caused him to ask a dismission in Nov. 1870, which was reluctantly given. He was unanimously elected their *Pastor Emeritus.* The life, character and labors of Dr. Smyth, who received his degree of D.D. in 1843 from New-Jersey College at Princeton, are given in a discourse of 63 octavo pages, preached by his successor, the Rev. G. R. Brackett, entitled—"The Christian Warrior Crowned." This is contained in a volume " In Memoriam," of 186 pages, which, with a copy of an autobiographical letter of the compiler, dated Charleston, S. C., Nov. 10, 1866, is in the Library of this Society. From these we have gleaned the material for this notice.

Dr. Smyth was a well known author, having published, as he says, " some 70 " works. The names of 20 appear in Allibone's Dictionary. He was made a corres-ponding member of this society, June 26, 1855, and from 1856 to 1863 held the office of honorary vice-president for South Carolina.

The Rev. CURTIS CUTLER died in Cambridge, Oct. 13, 1874, aged 68. He was the third son and child of Nathaniel and Anna (Child) Cutler, and a descendant in the seventh generation from *James* [1] and *Anna Cutler* who settled early in Watertown, but afterward removed to Cambridge Farms, now Lexington ; through *James* [2] (their eldest son, born 1635, married Lydia Moore Wright, widow of Samuel Wright and daughter of John Moore, of Sudbury), *Thomas,* [3] *David,* [4] *Thomas,* [5] and *Nathaniel,* [6] above named, his father.

Curtis Cutler was born in Lexington, Mass., Jan. 1, 1806, graduated at Harvard College in 1829, studied theology at Cambridge, settled in the ministry at Gardner, in Worcester County, Mass., Oct. 30, 1833, where he remained six years ; was in-stalled at Peterboro', N. H., colleague with the Rev. Abiel Abbot, D.D., Jan. 30, 1840 ; resigned his pastorate, May, 1848, and removed to Lexington. While at Peterboro' he was associated with the Rev. Dr. Leonard, of Dublin, and the Reve-rends Mr. Whitwell of Wilton and A. A. Livermore, then of Keene, in the com-pilation of the volume of hymns known as the " Cheshire Collection." In 1850, in consequence of an increasing bronchial affection, he left the ministry and entered the counting-room of William Underwood & Co., merchants in Boston. In 1854-5, having removed to Lexington, he represented that town in the Massachusetts Legis-lature. In 1855 he took up his abode in Cambridge, which place was ever after his home. He had children : Sarah M., born in Gardner, Mass., April 14, 1838. Anna C., born in Peterborough, N. H., March 12, 1845. Mr. Cutler took a deep interest in his family history and contributed largely toward the Cutler genealogy, furnish-ing the Rev. Abner Morse with much of the matter contained in chapter fourth of his work on the Cutler family. He was a subscriber to the REGISTER, and had a true regard for its welfare. He was a quiet, modest, agreeable man, of a character lovely and pure. " Family and friends, classmates and all associates join in loving remembrance and honor of him." One who knew him long and well, as a friend and neighbor, writes of him : " He was always the kindly gentleman, cheerful and uncomplaining. He was an elder brother to his children. His was a real *home*, one of the pleasantest I was ever in, rich in love and good-will. The world will scarcely miss him, yet it is greatly the gainer for his life."

He was admitted to this society, as a resident member, Dec. 22, 1858.

Prepared by the Hon. JAMES D. GREEN, A.M., of Cambridge, Mass.

WALTER COOPER GREEN, Esq., the youngest of thirteen children of Dr. Ezra and Susannah Hayes Green, was born in Dover, N. H., July 1, 1799 ; and died in Boston, Mass., April 25, 1875, at the age of 75 yrs. 9 mos. and 24 days, and soon after the completion of the memoir of the private life and character of his venerated father ;—which was printed in the REGISTER for the month in which he died (*ante*, xxix. 173–81), to which reference may be had for ancestral details.

It is believed that his father, Dr. Ezra Green, intended to give Walter a collegiate education, and, for that purpose, sent him to Exeter Academy, where he was in 1815, and where he remained about two or three years ; when, that intention having been relinquished for the practice of the law, we find him in the office of one of the members of the New Hampshire bar, in his native town. Here he prosecuted his studies with most commendable diligence, for two or three years. From Dover he came to Boston, and entered the office of Judge Prescott, where he continued about two years, and then in 1823 opened an office for the practice himself. The prospect, however, seemed not encouraging, nor was the idea he entertained of the practice of the profession one congenial to his feelings ; and he readily embraced an opportunity that soon presented of joining his brother Charles, who had been doing a profitable business in Liverpool, Eng., and was now established as a commission merchant in New-York. This was about the year 1825 ; and, for a period of years, they prospered in their business ; but misfortunes overtook them, and failure was the consequence. Walter then went into business on his own account, as a metal broker, and, as I am informed, with more than common success.

In the mean time he had formed a matrimonial connection with Miss Almira Hammond, b. Dec. 13, 1809, youngest daughter of Samuel and Sarah Hammond, of Boston. This was in Sept. 1838. She died in 1847, a little less than ten years after her marriage, leaving two children, a daughter and a son, named respectively Sarah and Walter Hammond. The former married Henry Blake, son of George Baty Blake, who recently died in Brookline. They have two children, Harry and Alice.

Walter Hammond, son of the subject of this sketch, after his mother's death passed several years,—seven, as I am informed,—in Cambridge, in the family of Rev. Dr. Palfrey,—Mrs. Palfrey being his aunt, and, with her daughters, supplying the place of a mother. He attended school here ; was a playmate of one of my own children ; and next was placed at school in Vevay, in Switzerland, on the border of the Lake of Geneva, where he remained about two years. Not long after his return, at the age of 14 years, he had the scarlet fever, from which he had but recently recovered, when, on going to New-York, he was seized with the small-pox,—from what exposure was never known,—and lived but a few days, dying Nov. 26, 1857. The body was brought to Cambridge, and buried at Mt. Auburn, on Thanksgiving Day. In the words of a loving relative, to whom I am indebted for this account, " he was a beautiful boy, and his early death was the cause of a great sorrow to his father ; " and, I may add, more especially, since now, at the decease of the only surviving male member, now in his 93d year, the name (Green) will become extinct in that branch of the family.

Walter C. Green I have known from childhood. We were own cousins, nearly of the same age, and frequent playmates in the interchanging visits of the members of the two families. Our fathers, the only children of their parents, bore a strong personal resemblance to each other,—so much indeed that one was not unfrequently mistaken for the other. Both served in the Revolutionary War ; the older, Dr. Ezra, as Surgeon in the N. H. Regiment, during the siege of Boston, and afterwards under Arnold at Montreal and Ticonderoga. The younger, Bernard, my father, served as one of the minute-men engaged in the Concord and Lexington fight, and as one of the Coast Guard on the Chelsea shore of the Mystic River, on the 17th of June, in full view of the battle of Bunker Hill. Later in the war, the older was serving with Paul Jones in the battle of the Ranger with the Drake, and the younger, Bernard, was serving under Washington, in the battle of White Plains. After the war, the former, Dr. Ezra Green, relinquishing the practice of his profession, devoted himself to mercantile pursuits; the latter, Bernard, spent the rest of his days in the cultivation of the ancestral acres, which thus continued in the family for five generations, or upwards of 200 years,—he, the younger, dying first, July 15, 1834, at the age of 82½ years, and Dr. Ezra living till July 25, 1847, when he departed this life at the age of 101 years and 28 days.

With such intimate relations between the families it could not well be otherwise than that Walter, the subject of this sketch, and myself, nearly of the same age, should have a common sympathy, and be well acquainted with each other. Though, from the nature of our respective pursuits, we seldom met for a considerable period during our middle age, we occasionally corresponded; and, though circumstances did not admit of our visiting Europe in company, he availed himself subsequently of an opportunity, and leisurely made the tour of England and Scotland, France and Germany, Switzerland and Italy. On this trip it was that his exposure to the damp atmosphere of London, as he believed, was the cause of a cold, which resulted in the loss of voice, or power to emit a vocal sound, or to speak otherwise than in what may be called an *audible whisper.* His last sickness was contracted, as I understood him, when on a visit to Brattleboro', Vt., in the summer of 1874, from which he returned to his residence in Boston, and betook himself to his apartments,—to leave them but once or twice again. He sent me a letter, desiring to see me. I found him on his couch,—feeble, emaciated, expectorating, speaking with difficulty; but perfectly cheerful, and much interested in the proposed design of printing a memoir of his father in connection with the diary which his father kept when serving under Paul Jones on board the Ranger, and which Commodore Preble had then taken in hand for publication. He desired to confer with me on the subject. Several subsequent calls I made, and, for a time, he appeared to improve; but the appearance was illusive. The change for the better was of short duration. It is not improbable that the excitement attending the preparation of the memoir of his father proved too great for his years and enfeebled health, which may account, moreover, for deficiencies and inaccuracies the reader may detect in the narrative. and they are not a few. His system was evidently breaking up; of which he soon became aware, and began to make such dispositions as to his affairs as his feelings prompted, and passed away on Sunday, April 25th, last, in the 76th year of his age, and the very month in which his memoir of the Private Life and Character of his father appeared in the REGISTER.

His life had been comparatively uneventful. Having known him from youth, I think I can say—that he was an upright, sincere, honest and honorable man;—without a stain on his reputation, from his youth up; not ambitious of distinction; firm and decided in his opinions, political and religious; strong in his domestic attachments, and finding his greatest satisfaction in the company of his intimate friends, enjoying with them his *otium cum dignitate,*—and showing the rich treasures of Italian art, and especially the many magnificent paintings with which his apartments were adorned.

Prepared by the Hon. CHARLES F. SWIFT, of Yarmouth Port, Mass.

AMOS OTIS, Esq., departed this life, at his home in Yarmouth Port, on the morning of October 19, 1875. He was born in Barnstable, Aug. 17, 1801, making his age 74 years, 2 months and 2 days. His health had been failing for nearly a year, but until two or three weeks past, he attended in some measure to his usual duties.

Mr. Otis came from that historic Cape Cod stock which has given so many illustrious and useful men to the service of their native county and the state. He was himself one of the most remarkable and useful men of his generation, and in some respects it will be difficult, if not impossible, to fill his place.

Mr. Otis's early life was spent on the farm of his father, Amos Otis. Being of a studious turn of mind, he early devoted his leisure to books. He fitted for college under the instruction of the late Dr. Danforth P. Wight, but the condition of his father's fortune and other causes compelled him to forego his desire for a liberal education.

For more than fifteen years he was engaged in teaching, and was a very successful instructor of youth.

In May, 1836, he became cashier of the then "Barnstable Bank," at Yarmouth

Port, and continued in that position, as cashier of that institution and its successor, the " First National Bank of Yarmouth," for nearly forty years.

He was also the first secretary and treasurer of the Barnstable County Mutual Fire Insurance Co., incorporated in March, 1833, in which office he continued to the time of his last sickness.

Mr. Otis never held political office, the duties of his business professions engrossing the greater part of his active life. He, however, served for several years on the school committee of Yarmouth, and was frequently appointed on committees of the town, where familiarity with the ancient records and usages were required.

He was also for several years one of the directors of the Cape Cod Branch Railroad, and a trustee of the Yarmouth Public Library at the time of his decease. His fidelity and industry in these positions were remarkable. He investigated carefully every question presented, and was never satisfied unless he had given to them his personal attention and weighed their merits for himself.

He was a remarkably prolific writer, as well as a diligent student. He contributed hundreds of columns to the Cape Cod newspapers, upon a great variety of subjects, the preponderance being upon practical matters. Our local history he has made his study for the last fifty years, and in that department his labors have been invaluable. No man living or dead has done so much to elucidate the character, motives and acts of the men who settled on Cape Cod, and of their heroic successors; and no one ever had a more just appreciation of their character and achievements. He believed in them thoroughly, although not insensible to their faults. His facts were largely drawn from original sources, and his studies were pursued with a zeal and enthusiasm which were prompted by a thorough love of his subject. He has left a vast accumulation of material, which will be invaluable to future investigators in this field of study. It had long been his desire to leave a complete history of his native town, but other cares and the infirmities of age prevented his accomplishing his purpose, beyond a series of sketches of the families of the town, published some 15 years ago,—articles so full of information and clothed in such an agreeable style that our regret is deepened as we read them, that their author should not have completed his work. Beside these he has contributed to the various historical periodicals of the country articles on his favorite subject.

Mr. Otis has also written much on agriculture, horticulture, arboriculture and kindred themes. To his industrious pen the people of Barnstable county are largely indebted for the interest first aroused there on the subject of railroad facilities. He compiled column upon column of statistics, and never wearied until the steam-whistle was heard on Cape Cod. Among his political writings, the " Letters from Skipper Jack to my old friend that prints the Yarmouth Register," were immensely popular some twenty years ago.

Mr. Otis was the oldest surviving member of the Fraternal Lodge of Free Masons, and was for twenty-one years in early life the Secretary of the Lodge. He was a firm believer in the sublime principles of the order, and exemplified by his life the truths of Masonry. During the fierce anti-masonic excitement in this country, he never faltered nor disguised his sentiments, and held his position as an officer of the Lodge until the storm blew over. He never failed, when it was possible to attend the festivals of the order, and always appeared to greatly enjoy these social occasions. He was admitted to this Society July 21, 1847.

Mr. Otis was a man of deep religious feelings. He was for a large portion of his life a member of the East Parish (Unitarian) in Barnstable, but of late years became deeply interested in the doctrines of the New Jerusalem church, with which he formally connected himself within a few weeks. But he was no mere sectarian or bigot, and attached no undue importance to forms and creeds.

His liberality and public spirit were marked features of his character, and his private charities were numerous and discriminating. He never failed to aid, to the best of his abilities, a good cause, nor to help a fellow-man in trouble or distress.

Mr. Otis married, Aug. 15, 1830, Mary, daughter of Mr. Adino Hinckley, of Barnstable, whom he survived about four and one-half years. He leaves two sons, Henry and George.

Mr. Otis's memory will be kept alive in the hearts of his townsmen, so long as the noble elms which border their streets, many of which were planted by his own hands, remain to bear witness to his taste, foresight, and public spirit; and he will take his place in that long list of Cape Cod worthies, to the memory of whom he has been so tender and just, and whose character he has done so much to rescue from oblivion and neglect.

Prepared by JOHN WARD DEAN, of Boston.

JOSHUA GREEN, M.D., of Groton, Mass., died June 5, 1875, at the residence of his son-in-law, Dr. Charles Y. Swan, in Morristown, N. J., aged 77. He was a son of Joshua and Mary (Mosley) Green, and was born in Wendell, Mass., October 8, 1797. He was a descendant in the 7th generation from *Percival*[1] *Green*, of Cambridge, through *John*,[2] *Joseph*,[3] *Joseph*,[4] *Joshua*,[5] and *Joshua*,[6] his father. A genealogical account of this family in the REGISTER for April, 1861 (xv. 105–9), gives further particulars of his ancestors.

He fitted for college at New Salem, Westfield and Milton academies, and was graduated at Harvard College in the class of 1818. He studied medicine with Dr. John C. Warren, and, immediately after taking his medical degree, in 1821, was appointed apothecary at the Massachusetts General Hospital, the first year that it was opened for the reception of patients. At that time the apothecary, in addition to his ordinary duties, performed those of house physician and house surgeon. He began the practice of medicine in Sunderland, Mass., in 1823, and remained there till 1825, when he removed to Groton. He retired from the active practice of his profession forty years ago.

In 1836 and 1837, he represented the town of Groton in the Massachusetts legislature. For many years he was a trustee of the Lawrence Academy and secretary or president of the board.

In the summer of 1832 he had an attack of pulmonary hemorrhage, which rendered it necessary for him to pass the succeeding winter in Cuba. The trip seemed to restore him to perfect health. For some years before his death he suffered from paralysis, from which disease he died.

He married, Jan. 5, 1824, Eliza Lawrence, daughter of Major Samuel and Susannah Lawrence, of Groton. See her obituary, *ante* xxviii. 486, and tabular pedigree of Lawrence, x. 297. They had six children, namely: 1, *William Lawrence*, d. young; 2, *William Lawrence*, merchant, deceased; 3, *Henry Atkinson*, merchant, of Boston; 4, *Samuel Abbott*, M.D., city physician of Boston; 5, *Elizabeth Lawrence*, m. first, John Kendall (Dart. Coll. 1853); m. second, Charles Young Swan, M.D.; 6, *Joshua*, d. young.

He was admitted to this society as a corresponding member, August 18, 1849. He was much interested in antiquarian and genealogical studies, and was a diligent collector of books and manuscripts illustrating them. He was a subscriber to the REGISTER from its first publication.

SOCIETIES AND THEIR PROCEEDINGS.

NEW-ENGLAND HISTORIC, GENEALOGICAL SOCIETY.

Boston, Massachusetts, Wednesday, May 5, 1875. A stated meeting was held at the Society's House, 18 Somerset Street, at three o'clock this afternoon, the Hon. Marshall P. Wilder, the president, in the chair.

The president announced the death of the Hon. Hampden Cutts, of Brattleboro', Vt., vice-president for that state, and appointed the Rev. Edmund F. Slafter, J. Wingate Thornton and Gen. John S. Tyler, a committee to prepare resolutions.

The Hon. George Washington Warren, president of the Bunker Hill Monument Association, then read a very interesting paper on "The Celebrations of the Seventeenth of June in 1825 and 1843." Thanks were voted to Judge Warren for his paper.

Francis C. Whiston, who was toastmaster at the celebration in 1825, followed with reminiscences, and exhibited the masonic apron worn by Lafayette when laying the corner-stone of Bunker Hill Monument, and also the remarks of Lafayette and Webster at the banquet, in their own autograph, which were presented to Mr. Whiston by those illustrious personages. Remarks were also made by the Rev. Lucius R. Paige, D.D., the Rev. Samuel Cutler, Frederic Kidder, the Rev. Increase N. Tarbox, D.D., Joseph W. Tucker, the Hon. Marshall P. Wilder, John P. Payson and the Rev. Samuel Lee.

John W. Dean, the librarian, reported that during the last month 78 volumes, 221 pamphlets, 118 manuscripts, and several other articles had been presented to the society. Special mention was made of the donations of John S. H. Fogg, M.D., of South Boston, the Hon. Joseph W. Porter of Burlington, Maine, the Rev. Richard S. Edes of Bolton, Mass., the Vermont State Library, Henry A. Page of Boston, Benjamin S. Ewell, LL.D., of Williamsburg, Va., Lewis Rice of Boston, Joseph W. Tucker of Boston, and a lady aged 84 years who did not give her name.

The Rev. Samuel Cutler, the historiographer, read a biographical sketch of Thomas Waterman, prepared by William B. Trask.

The president announced the erection, since the last meeting, of an elegant memorial tablet in the vestibule of the society's house, the gift of the talented American sculptor, Martin Milmore, a member of the society, now residing in Rome, Italy.

June 2.—The monthly meeting was held this afternoon, president Wilder in the chair.

The Rev. Charles C. Beaman, of Cambridge, read an interesting paper on "The Burnt District of Boston as it was Sixty Years Ago."

After remarks and reminiscences by William M. Cornell, M.D., William H. Montague, the Rev. Lucius R. Eastman, Samuel G. Drake, Frederic Kidder, Isaac Child, the Rev. Dorus Clarke, D.D., Benjamin B. Davis, Joseph W. Tucker, the Hon. George C. Richardson and the president, thanks were voted to the Rev. Mr. Beaman.

The librarian reported 78 volumes, 187 pamphlets, 177 manuscripts and various other articles as donations during the past month. Special mention was made of the donations of Mrs. Grace Le Baron (Locke) Upham of Boston, Commodore Preble, U. S. N., of Philadelphia, the Rev. C. D. Bradlee of Boston, William B. Lapham, M.D., of Augusta, Me., Miss Eliza S. Quincy of Boston, the Rev. Lucius R. Paige of Cambridgeport, David M. Balfour of Charlestown, the Hon. Richard A. Wheeler of Stonington, Ct., Nahum Capen of Dorchester, Abner C. Goodell, Jr., of Salem, and Samuel Adams Drake of Boston.

The corresponding secretary reported letters accepting membership from the Hon. John Boyd of West Winsted, Ct., Howland Holmes, M.D., of Lexington, the Rev. Charles L. Hutchins of Medford, William B. Durant of Boston, William L. Weston of Danvers, and Francis S. Drake of Boston. The corresponding secretary then read a letter from Brevet Major General Henry W. Benham, U. S. A., accompanying press copies of his manuscript narrative or report of events that he knew of in a portion of the campaigns where he had commands in the recent War of the Rebellion. He also read an invitation extended to the society from the executive committee of the Bunker Hill Monument Association to attend on the 17th inst. the commemorative services of the one hundredth anniversary of the Battle of Bunker Hill, and offered the following resolutions, which, after brief remarks by several of the members, were unanimously adopted:

Resolved, That the thanks of the society be tendered to the Bunker Hill Monument Association for their invitation to participate with them in the celebration of the First Centennial Anniversary of the Battle of Bunker Hill, and that the same be cordially accepted.

Resolved, That the following-named gentlemen be a committee to make such arrangements as they may deem expedient: The president, Hon. Marshall P. Wilder; the vice-president, Hon. George C. Richardson; Charles O. Whitmore, John Cummings, and the Hon. Thomas C. Amory.

The Rev. Increase N. Tarbox, D.D., in behalf of the committee appointed at a previous meeting, offered the following resolutions, which were adopted, viz.:

Resolved, That in the death of Hon. William A. Buckingham, LL.D., vice-president of this society for the State of Connecticut,* we have lost one of our most worthy and honored officers. A native of Lebanon, Conn., the same town that in the last century gave Governor Jonathan Trumbull to the State and to the country for eminent public services during the war of the revolution, by a singular course of providence, Governor Buckingham was able to perform something like the same eminent service for his State and country during the recent War of the Rebellion. As governor of Connecticut for eight consecutive years, from 1858 to 1866, as senator of the United States until his death, as a man widely known in the world of business, as one holding many important trusts both in civil and ecclesiastical connections, as the generous promoter of all good causes by munificent gifts and charities, it is seldom that a man passes away who leaves behind a nobler record in Church and State than that of William Alfred Buckingham.

* A memoir of Gov. Buckingham is printed in this number of the REGISTER, pp. 9 to 15.

Resolved, That this testimony of our respect and love be transmitted to his family, with whom we deeply sympathize in their bereavement.

The Rev. Edmund F. Slafter, chairman of the committee appointed for the purpose, offered the following resolutions, which were adopted:

Resolved, That we hereby place upon record the profound sense of our loss in the death of the Hon. Hampden Cutts, A.M., a vice-president of the society for the State of Vermont, whose career as a public lecturer, a sound lawyer and graceful advocate, an able and impartial Judge, an accomplished student of English literature and of New-England history, whose warm heart and genial manners added grace to his dignified bearing, commands our cordial and sincere respect.

Resolved, That we tender to the family of our late esteemed associate our hearty sympathy in their great bereavement, and that the recording secretary be requested to inform them of the action of the Society, and to transmit to them a copy of these resolutions.

The Rev. Samuel Cutler, the historiographer, read biographical sketches of the following deceased members, namely: the Hon. Hampden Cutts, of Brattleboro', Vt.; the Hon. Albert Fearing, of Hingham; and Francis Bush, Jr., of Boston.

Thanks were voted to Gen. Benham and the several donors mentioned by the librarian.

The Hon. Hiland Hall, LL.D., of North Bennington, Vt., was unanimously chosen vice-president of the society for that state, in place of the Hon. Hampden Cutts, deceased.

September 1.—The society met, for the first time after the summer recess, this afternoon at three o'clock, president Wilder in the chair.

The president announced the death, since the last meeting of the society, of two of the three[1] surviving ex-presidents of the society, namely, Samuel Gardner Drake, A.M., one of the founders of the society and president in 1858, who died June 14 in his 77th year, and Winslow Lewis, M.D., president from 1861 to 1866, who died August 3, aged 76. In accordance with a custom of the society, he had appointed committees to prepare resolutions of respect to their memory, the committee on Mr. Drake being Frederic Kidder, William B. Trask and John A. Lewis, and that on Dr. Lewis being the Hon. Charles L. Woodbury, Col. Almon D. Hodges and the Rev. C. D. Bradlee.

Reference was also made to the deaths of other prominent members of the society.

Frederic Kidder and the Hon. Charles L. Woodbury, chairmen of the committees appointed to prepare resolutions on the deaths of Mr. Drake and Dr. Lewis, made their reports, and in order to give several persons who were necessarily absent an opportunity to speak upon the subject, on motion of the Rev. Dr. Clarke, the resolutions were laid on the table till the October meeting, which was to be regarded as a memorial day.

Edward Rupert Humphreys, LL.D., of Boston, read a valuable and instructive paper entitled ": Lessons from the Words and Works of Oxford Worthies," it being supplementary to that read at the February meeting. Thanks were voted to Dr. Humphreys for his paper.

The librarian reported 141 volumes, 328 pamphlets, and various other articles as donations during the last month. Special mention was made of the donations of George H. Moore, LL.D., Mrs. John K. Wiggin, Commodore Preble, U. S. N., Jehiel C. Hart of Plainville, Ct., Mrs. Harriet A. de Salis of London, Eng., John B. Newcomb of Elgin, Ill., Mrs. Caroline H. Dall, the Hon. James D. Green of Cambridge, Isaac C. Bates of Paris, France, the Rev. Joseph F. Tuttle, D.D., of Crawfordsville, Ind., Cortlandt Parker of Newark, N. J., James S. Buck of Milwaukee, Wis., and Benjamin B. Davis of Brookline.

Thanks were voted to the several donors, and particularly to George H. Moore, LL.D., of New York, for his donation—a set of the Journals of the House of Lords, 1509 to 1764, thirty folio volumes, and the Journal of the House of Commons sixty-six volumes, and six volumes of Parliamentary Reports.

The president, as chairman of the committee on participating in the Centennial Celebration of the Battle of Bunker Hill, on the 17th of last June, reported that a delegation of twenty-six members [*ante*, xxix. 490] joined the procession in carriages and listened to the oration at Bunker Hill. He also, in behalf of several of those members, presented to the society the banner painted for that occasion and borne in the procession.

[1] Col. Almon D. Hodges, president in 1859 and 1860, is now the only surviving ex-president.

THE RHODE ISLAND HISTORICAL SOCIETY.

Providence, Tuesday, Oct. 4, 1875.—A quarterly meeting was held this evening at the cabinet on Waterman street, the Hon. Zachariah Allen, LL.D., vice-president, in the chair.

The librarian, the Rev. Edwin M. Stone, reported numerous and valuable donations.

Henry L. Greene of Riverpoint, Warwick, R.I., read an instructive paper on "The Original Settlers of Warwick."

Marcus D. Gilman, of Montpelier, Vt., secretary of the Vermont Historical Society, made an interesting statement of the condition and prospects of that society.

Nov. 9.—A meeting was held this evening, vice-president Allen in the chair.

The librarian read a very interesting paper on "The Life and Revolutionary Services of Lieut-Col. Samuel Ward," prepared by Col. John Ward of New York. Samuel Ward was a son of Gov. Samuel and Mrs. Anne (Ray) Ward, and was born in Westerly, R. I., Nov. 17, 1756, graduated at Rhode Island College, now Brown University, in 1771, and served in the Revolutionary army, attaining the rank of lieutenant colonel. In 1781, he retired from the army and engaged in business as a merchant in Warwick. He became a member of the society of the Cincinnati in 1784. He made several voyages abroad, and died in the city of New York, Aug. 16, 1832. He was a ripe classical scholar, and a gentleman of winning urbanity of manner and of unblemished honor.

Nov. 23.—A meeting was held this evening, the Hon. Samuel G. Arnold, the president, in the chair.

Prof. J. Lewis Diman, D.D., of Brown University, read a paper on "Religious Progress in America during the Last Century."

Remarks on the subject were made by the Hon. Zachariah Allen and President Arnold.

An invitation was read and accepted from the Rhode Island Soldiers' and Sailors' Historical Society, to attend a meeting Dec. 1st to hear a paper from Col. J. Albert Monroe on "The Rhode Island Artillery at Bull Run."

Nov. 30.—A meeting was held this evening, President Arnold in the chair.

The Hon. Henry B. Anthony read a paper entitled, "Reminiscences of the Thirty-Sixth Congress." This congress, the last before the war and the last in the administration of President Buchanan, was the first in which Mr. Anthony served as United States senator.

THE NEW-LONDON COUNTY HISTORICAL SOCIETY.

New-London, Ct., Thursday, Dec. 2, 1875.—The annual meeting was held this day in the City-Hall Building, the president, Hon. Lafayette S. Foster, in the chair.

The Hon. William H. Potter, of Mystic River, Ct., chairman of a committee previously appointed to report on the true site of the old Pequot fort, presented a written report, in which the committee unanimously agree, fixing the site and giving satisfactory reasons for the same. A committee, consisting of the Hon. William H. Potter, the Hon. Richard A. Wheeler, and Daniel Lee, was appointed to examine plans and models for a suitable monument to be placed upon the site of that fort as a memorial of one of the most decisive events in the history of Connecticut.

The annual election of officers then took place, and the following gentlemen were elected to the respective offices, namely:

President.—Lafayette S. Foster.

Vice-Presidents.—Charles J. McCurdy, Ashbel Woodward, F. B. Loomis.

Advisory Committee.—Thomas P. Field, Hiram P. Arms, Henry P. Haven, William H. Potter, John T. Wait, Thomas L. Shipman, Ralph Wheeler, Richard A. Wheeler, J. P. C. Mather, David A. Wells, Joseph G. Lamb, John W. Crary, George W. Goddard, Henry I. Gallup, James Griswold, Ledyard Bill, Daniel Lee..

Secretary.—William H. Starr.

Treasurer.—William H. Rowe.

Judge Foster, the president, made some remarks on the life of the Hon. George Pratt, of Norwich, a former member of the board of directors, lately deceased, and offered resolutions of respect to his memory which were unanimously adopted.

The meeting then adjourned to the First Congregational conference house, where the Rev. E. B. Huntington, of South Coventry, Ct., read a paper on "Lieut. Thomas Leffingwell, a prominent Pioneer in the Settlement of New-London County."

Remarks by the Rev. Dr. Field and the Hon. David A. Wells followed, after which thanks were voted to the Rev. Mr. Huntington.

After adjournment, the members, by invitation of the Hon. Henry P. Haven, partook of a bountiful collation at the Crocker House, and after dinner repaired in a body to the society's new rooms in the National Union Bank building, and expressed approbation of their improved accommodations.

The Historical Society of Delaware.

Wilmington, Dec. 7, 1875.—The literary annual meeting of this Society was held this evening at its rooms in the Masonic Temple, the president, the Hon. D. M. Bates, in the chair.

Joseph R. Walter, the secretary, read the necrology of the year, briefly sketching the lives of eight deceased members, viz., the Hon. Willard Hall, Ziba Ferris, the Hon. John M. Read of Philadelphia, John Stockton Littell of Philadelphia, Samuel G. Drake of Boston, James C. Douglass, Samuel Wollaston and Samuel Canby.

The Hon. Isaac D. Jones then read a paper entitled "An Historical Sketch of Delaware in connection with Maryland, Virginia, New-Jersey, and Pennsylvania, in Colonial Times, under Royal and other Grants." As one of the Maryland Commissioners to settle the boundary dispute with Virginia, Mr. Jones has familiarized himself with the early history of the colonies, and his paper was as exhaustive as it could well be made. It will be printed, we understand, in connection with Mr. Jones's argument in the boundary-line case. Thanks were voted for the paper.

Mayor Whiteley, of Wilmington, in behalf of Gen. R. H. Kirkwood Whiteley, who was present, presented to the Society some relics of Gen. Whiteley's grandfather, Capt. Robert Kirkwood, who was killed at St. Clair's Defeat, in 1791, consisting of the sash he wore the day on which he was killed, and his journals of the Northern and Southern campaigns. In presenting these donations, the mayor briefly recalled the leading facts in Capt. Kirkwood's military service. Thanks were voted for the donations.

BOOK-NOTICES.

An Inquiry into the Authenticity of Documents concerning a Discovery in North America claimed to have been made by Verrazzano. Read before the New-York Historical Society, Tuesday, Oct. 4, 1864. By Buckingham Smith. With a Map. New-York: Printed by John F. Trow, 1864. [8vo. pp. 31. 250 copies printed.]

Verrazano the Navigator, or Notes on Giovanni da Varrazano, and on a Planisphere of 1529, illustrating his American Voyage in 1524. With a reduced copy of the Map. A Paper read before the American Geographical Society of New-York, Nov. 28, 1871. With a Map. By J. C. Brevoort, a Member of the Society. New-York, 1874. [8vo. pp. 159. 250 copies printed.]

The Voyage of Verrazzano: A Chapter in the Early History of Maritime Discovery in America. With five Maps. By Henry C. Murphy. New-York, 1875. [8vo. pp. 198.]

These tracts, under somewhat varying titles, all relate to the same subject, and treat of the genuineness and authenticity of the narrative of an alleged voyage made upon the American coast by Verrazzano, a Florentine navigator under the authority and patronage of the king of France, in 1524. The narrative in question was first printed in Italian in a collection of voyages by Giovanni Ramusio in 1556, and Verrazzano himself is the reputed author. There is also a manuscript copy of the narrative, differing from it in language and matter, but of the same general tenor, preserved in the Magliabechian library in Florence. As this copy is fuller than that printed by Ramusio, it is supposed that the latter is a version made from this with liberal changes and revisions. Both copies are in the form of a letter addressed by Verrazzano to Francis I., and describe a voyage to America, making his landfall on the shores of the Carolinas, and sailing along the whole northern coast of the United States and a part of the British provinces, describing with more or less minuteness the character of the country, the appearance of the native inhabitants, their manners and customs, with the products of the soil. For more than three hundred years this letter has been regarded as genuine and its statements as authentic, and consequently has been incorporated into all the histories relating to the discoveries on our Atlantic coast.

The late Mr. Buckingham Smith discovered, in the archives of Spain and Portugal, certain documents which led him to entertain grave doubts as to the authenticity of the Verrazzano narrative, and the reasons of his doubts are briefly stated in his paper, the title of which we have given above. It is proper to state that Mr. Smith afterward obtained additional documents in Spain, which he intended to publish in farther elucidation and confirmation of his views, but his death intervened and the work was never accomplished.

Mr. Brevoort gives us in his paper a memoir of Verrazzano, with some account of his family, his career as a corsair, his alleged voyage to America and his occupations afterward. He furnishes translations of the most important passages of the Verrazzano letter, with explanations and illustrations of their meaning. He believes in the genuineness of the voyage to America, and displays much learning, ingenuity and skill in disposing of the contradictions and inconsistencies of the narrative and the circumstances attending its publication.

Mr. Murphy, in a more elaborate discussion of the subject, denies the genuineness of the letter and the truth of its statements. He believes it to be a fabrication, introduced by Ramusio into his collection without proper scrutiny, and with an entire misapprehension of its origin and character. Mr. Murphy has in preparation a work on the earliest explorations of the coast which have led to the settlement of the United State by Europeans. He comes, therefore, to this discussion with a broad and thorough knowledge of the whole field of history in any way connected with the period of the alleged Verrazzano voyage. We know of no one better qualified to conduct this interesting investigation. His style is at once simple, clear and direct. His facts are well marshalled, and his logic is irresistible. It would be quite impossible in the space which we can give to this subject, to present Mr. Murphy's views in detail or with any degree of fulness. For a thorough examination of the whole subject we must refer the student of our early history to the work itself. It must suffice for our present purpose to state a few of the leading objections, which may be urged against the genuineness and authenticity of the Verrazzano narrative.

We may remark in the outset that there is no evidence that the original letter, alleged to have been addressed by Verrazzano in 1524 to Francis I., ever existed. This letter purports to have been an official document, a report made by a servant of the government relating to a great and successful enterprise, undertaken by command of the king for the emolument and glory of France. If the voyage had been a failure, the letter might have been treated with neglect. But it was eminently successful. It added by discovery to the domain of France a territory stretching from the Carolinas to the British provinces, including the bulk of the present soil of the United States. It is incredible that a prince of the ability and enterprise of Francis I. should have allowed a document describing such a discovery to be forgotten or lost: a discovery the glory of which in all coming time was to be attributed to the sagacity and energy of the king himself. Not only the original document has not been known to be at any time in the archives of France, but it was never alluded to by the king himself or by his council; nor is there a word or syllable in the history of France, covering that period, recognizing this letter or alluding to it in the remotest manner.

• But there is no evidence, in the history of the time, that the alleged voyage to which the letter refers ever took place. The letter claims that the Dauphine, the ship in which the voyage was made, manned with fifty men, had returned to Dieppe on the 8th July, 1524. The news, which the fifty men composing the expedition brought home of the discovery of a vast territory on the American coast, must have made a profound sensation in the maritime town of Dieppe. The principal officers of the expedition could not have been indifferent or silent touching the honor of the discovery, which they in some sense shared with Verrazzano himself. It was a subject in which every intelligent, prominent or patriotic man in France was personally interested. It must have been the theme of conversation and correspondence in every part of the kingdom. If such a voyage had taken place, it would have been proclaimed officially by the king as an event gratifying to every subject in the kingdom, and important to be widely known, that all other nations might understand that the territory discovered by Verazzano under his authority henceforth belonged to the sovereignty of France. There was every reason for proclaiming the result of the voyage to the world, and no motive whatever for holding it in silence. But not one of the fifty men alleged to have been engaged in the expedition, either by letter or report, public or private, left a syllable behind him to show that he was in any way connected with this great achievement. Francis I. issued no instrument, patent or charter authorizing the voyage, he made no announcement of it to his ministers or to the councils of the nation, he sent out no expedition, or even projected one, for the purpose of following up or securing the great advantages which such a discovery would have conferred upon France. The history of France, covering the whole period from 1524 to 1556, when the letter was published by Ramusio, is utterly silent as to this voyage of discovery by Verrazzano. But if this voyage and discovery were actually made, why were Cartier and Roberval sent out by the same sovereign, Francis I., to discover lands in the colder and more sterile north, when he already possessed, by his recent discovery, a vast empire in the more productive and genial regions of the south? The commissions under which Cartier and Roberval sailed, and the report brought back by Cartier, make no allusion or reference whatever to a previous and successful voyage to the same coast, made a few years before by Verrazzano, under the same sovereign and for the similar purpose of extending his dominion and aggrandizing France.

The map of the world, entitled *Mappe monde peinte sur parchemin par ordre de Henry II., roi de France,* issued between 1543 and 1547, does not indicate that the author of it had any knowledge of the voyage of Verrazzano, and yet this author was a Frenchman, living at the time of Francis I. and at the period when the alleged voyage was made, whose business it was to be thoroughly informed, and who therefore could not have failed to know of all discoveries made by his own nation, and, as it were, under his own observation, on the American coast.

It is quite impossible, on any rational theory, to account for these singular omissions, if these discoveries of Verrazzano were actually made.

But the letter or narrative of the voyage itself contains internal evidence against its authenticity.

Agreeably to the statement of the letter, Verrazzano sailed only in the *day time*, and with great *watchfulness*, but nevertheless did not not find any harbor into which he could enter, for the distance of eight hundred miles, viz., from the coast of the Carolinas to the mouth of the Hudson river. Such a statement as this is incredible. To say nothing of the less important ones, to admit that he could not find the magnificent harbor of Chesapeake Bay is tantamount to an acknowledgment that he was never on that part of the coast at all.

The letter informs us that on the coast of North Carolina, early in the month of April, they repeatedly tasted the native grapes and found them sweet and pleasant. It is to be observed that the grape in that latitude does not flower before May, and does not ripen before July. This statement must therefore be regarded as utterly false, unless we accept the theory, which has not been advanced, that they were cultivated by the savages in green-houses and by artificial heat.

In the manuscript letter, the complexion of the Indians in North Carolina is said to be "black, not much different from Ethiopians." There has never been any conflict of testimony as to the color of the natives on the Atlantic coast. They were of a tawny or yellowish brown color, and by no misapprehension could they be described as black like Ethiopians. Ramusio, in his printed version, changes the words so that they read "brownish, not much unlike Saracens," but this only renders the fabrication more apparent, and plainly shows that he regarded the original representation as obviously untrue, and that it required revision.

The omissions of the letter are very remarkable, if it was written by an eyewitness and founded in truth. Some of the most striking and characteristic articles in use among the Indians are not mentioned. Wampum was used by them for the two-fold purpose of an ornament of dress and a medium of exchange. The use of tobacco and the pipe was universal. The pipe which they offered to the stranger was their token of friendship and hospitality. Neither of these are alluded to in any form. But the most remarkable omission of all is the bark canoe. This was peculiar to northern tribes, and was perhaps the most extraordinary and interesting of all the Indian fabrications. For lightness and speed it was unsurpassed by anything of the sort then known in Europe. Hundreds of them must have been seen in the great bay where Verrazzano is alleged to have spent fifteen days. The grace of its movement and the beauty of its form must have attracted the attention and admiration of all European visitors. As he does not mention it, we cannot believe that he had ever seen it, or been on the coast where it was in universal use.

After leaving what may have been Hudson's river, the writer says, "we sailed eighty leagues *towards the east*, as the coast stretched in that direction, and *always in sight of it.*" At this distance he passed by an island ten leagues from the main land, and of the size of the island of Rhodes, or nearly three times as large as Martha's Vineyard, which is the largest island on the coast, and not three leagues from the main land. As there is no island in this region of the size and position of the one described, or even approximating to it, it is obvious that the whole story of the island is a pure fiction. Fifteen leagues distant from this fictitious island he finds a commodious harbor, where he spends fifteen days, and then proceeding still in an easterly course, he sailed a hundred and fifty leagues further, always keeping the land in sight. It is too obvious to need any comment, that if he sailed two hundred and forty-five leagues in an easterly direction from the Hudson river or New-York harbor, as he declares he did, he must have lost sight of land off Cape Cod, and would not have seen it again till he had reached the shores of Nova Scotia. It is plainly obvious that to keep in sight of land, it would have been necessary for him to turn to the west at Cape Cod, and coast along the great bay that stretches from that point to Cape Sable.

Mr. Murphy shows, on the evidence of Peter Martyr, that at the time Verrazzano is alleged to have returned from his voyage of discovery on the coast of America, on the 8th of July, 1524, he was actually engaged in an expedition as a corsair, and that he had just captured a Portuguese ship returning from India with a large and valuable cargo. It will be necessary to concede that he was endowed with ubiquity, or else to deny one of the statements of his whereabouts at that time. Under all the circumstances it is not difficult to determine which horn of the dilemma to accept.

These are some of the very many irreconcilable difficulties in the way of receiving the Verrazzano narrative as genuine and authentic.

Several other interesting matters are discussed by Mr. Murphy, such as the discourse of the Dieppe captain referred to by some writers in support of the claims of Verrazzano, and the map supposed to have been constructed by Verrazzano's brother.

It is Mr. Murphy's belief that the fictitious narrative of this expedition is founded on the voyage of Gomez, made in 1525, touching our coast at the Carolinas and continuing northwardly as far as Cape Breton. The treatment of this part of the subject is interesting and curious, and will repay a careful perusal. The motive for perpetrating this fraud upon the world is referred by Mr. Murphy to the ambition and pride of Florence. All the evidence in favor of the story is traceable to Florence. But there is no reason to believe that Verrazzano himself was in any way accessory to the imposture. The discussion closes with some account of the adventurous life and ignominious death of Verrazzano, the latter resting upon documents of undoubted authority introduced into the appendix of the volume.

The conclusion to which this discussion leads us we confess is not agreeable. It is painful to see any monument of the past defaced or broken down. It is painful to know that what has stood, as a central fact for more than three hundred years, must be withdrawn from the sum of our history. This narrative does not stand alone. It has diffused itself and entered into our historical associations. It has tinged our estimates, colored our philosophy and shaped our deductions. It must remain, moreover, in the web into which it has been woven. And it will, therefore, henceforth be the embarrassing duty of the student and reader of the earliest chapter of our history, to draw a black line over all that has been taken, directly or indirectly, from the voyage of Verrazzano.

Com. by the Rev. Edmund F. Slafter.

*History of the State of Rhode-Island and Providence Plantations. From
the Settlement of the State, 1636, to the Adoption of the Federal Constitu-
tion, 1790.* By SAMUEL GREENE ARNOLD. In two volumes. Second
Edition. New-York: D. Appleton & Company, 549 and 551 Broadway.
London: 16 Little Britain. 1874. [8vo. pp. xi. and 574; iv. and 592.
A. Williams & Co., Boston.]

The first edition of this work appeared in 1860, and, as the first elaborate history
of Rhode-Island, it attracted the notice of those historical students who were not
engrossed by the exciting public events which in the next ensuing year, and for several years thereafter, naturally engaged the public attention. Since the close of
the civil war the work has received more general and more careful notice; and it is
but simple justice to say that it has steadily grown in repute. Hence we are not
surprised to learn that a new edition has been issued to meet the demands of an enlarged circle of readers and students.

In respect to the materials made use of by the author, it may be sufficient to say
that he has had the benefit, whatever that may have been, of the previous attempts
to write the history of the State: by Callender in 1739; by Hopkins in 1762; by the
Hon. Theodore Foster, and by Henry Bull, at a later date; and the benefit, also,
of the historical writings, journals, society collections, and memoirs that have appeared from the first settlement of Rhode-Island to the present time bearing upon
his subject. In addition to these, he has had access to original sources of information, not open to any of his predecessors and only within a few years available to
his contemporaries,—the records and documents in the State Paper Offices in London
and Paris, and at the Hague. Indeed, it is only after a careful study and honest use
of these materials that anything like a complete and candid history of New-England
can be written. It is from these sources that the most important data have been
drawn upon which our later and most creditable histories are based. What has
already come to light has greatly modified the opinions and conclusions of historical students. To such an extent has this enlightenment and modification gone,
even upon the partial opening of the public archives referred to, that it may well be believed that in some important particulars our present histories are only provisional.

In regard to the manner in which the author has dealt with some of those subjects upon which our historians have most widely differed,—the character of Roger
Williams, and his controversies with ecclesiastical and civil authority in Massachusetts, and the many points upon which in the later history of the two colonies differences more or less grave took their rise,—it must be conceded that the author
exhibits great research, and a disposition to impartial judgment.

There are prejudices and biases, inheritable and inherited, as strong as any which
we style theological, religious. or political,—local prejudices and biases, inherited
from antagonistic communities. Of these we see no evidence in this work.

                                                          A. H. HOYT.

*The History of Democracy: or, Political Progress, historically illustrated,
from the earliest to the latest periods.* By NAHUM CAPEN, LL.D., author
of "The Republic of the United States of America; its Duties to itself,
and its responsible Relations to other Countries," &c. &c. With Portraits
of Distinguished Men. Vol. I. Hartford: American Publishing Company. 1874. [Royal 8vo. pp. xix. and 677.]

This "History of Democracy" is not the history of the democratic party as such;
nor is it written in the interest of any party, in any country, in any age, except it
be in the interest of that minority in all civilized countries,—sometimes large and
influential, sometimes small and feeble,—which, now honestly and soberly, at other
times as honestly but tumultuously, struggles for civil and religious freedom. Our
reading does not furnish us with satisfactory evidence that a pure "democracy," as
a form of civil government, has ever been successfully administered by a numerous
population occupying a country which reaches through different zones, and devoted
to occupations and interests more or less antagonistic or competitive. For a small,
compact population,—homogeneous in origin, in religion, and in the pursuits of
life,—the case may be different; although the experiment has yet to be tried upon a
scale sufficiently large to warrant absolute affirmation in its favor.

The author evidently means the "history of civil and religious liberty," for they cannot be separated; "liberty" in its highest, fullest, and best sense, without regard to forms of government. The theme is as vast as it is noble and inspiring. Its full and accurate study is the study of history in its largest scope and minutest detail; for (in the eloquent language of the author), it "comprehends all the great intents of the world. It embraces thought, labor, inventive genius and skill,—industry, in its beneficent rewards and necessities; commerce, in its enlarging enterprise and influences; science, with its keen and patient discernments of the natural laws; the arts, in their beautifying refinements; society and nations, under the conditions of success or failure, peace or war; government, with its collective power and authorized agencies; the theories of human agency, the unnumbered ways and methods of doing the same things,—which are the perpetual sources of inquiry, discussion. experiment and action. The record of this vast activity, of its meaning and uses, is history. Every subject in its simple elements has its basis in principle, and its record in progress. In all this diversity, truth demonstrates harmony." These sentences give the key to the plan, scope and purpose of this "History of Democracy,"—the record of the progressing development of the ideas and principles which shall culminate eventually in a wise, just and enlightened government of "the people, by the people, and for the people."

The author traces the progress of these principles from the earliest times. The work shows vast reading and research, and that the writer has a rare faculty of analysis and discrimination. He is never misled by appearances or professions: everything is tested by the issue.

One might, perhaps, expect that a work of this kind would be dull and wearisome; on the contrary, the author's language glows with a subdued enthusiasm that carries the reader along with him without abatement of interest. It is a philosophic production, highly creditable to the scholarship of the country.

In saying this we do not forget that the author alone is responsible for his conclusions; and that his greatest service to us must be, and is, in bringing together an array of facts and instances sufficiently comprehensive to accurately illustrate the development of the forces operating in the direction of man's elevation.

The volume is handsomely printed, and is illustrated with fourteen portraits of men distinguished for their labor in behalf of liberty.   A. H. H.

The Freeman Genealogy, in three Parts, viz.: I. *Memorials of Edmund Freeman of Sandwich, and his Descendants;* II. *Memorial of Samuel Freeman of Watertown, and his Descendants;* III. *Notes, Historical and Genealogical, of Families of the Name of Freeman, distinct from Parts* I. *and* II., *or whose connection is not clearly ascertained.* "An old man was seated upon a monument, and busily employed in deepening with his chisel the letters of the inscription. . . . . Motives of the most sincere though fanciful devotion induced him to dedicate years to perform this tribute to the memory of the deceased. He considered himself as fulfilling a sacred duty, while renewing to the eyes of posterity the decaying emblems of their forefathers."—*Sir Walter Scott's mention of a "stroll" into a deserted "burial ground."* Private. Boston. 1875.

Of this the first part is before us. The title-page tells the story of its contents, but Old Mortality's devotion was hardly on a level with that of the venerable Frederick Freeman, whose "History of Cape Cod" is itself a monument of filial reverence, conscientious toil, and admirable narrative. The reverential son of Dr. Nathaniel Freeman, the compeer of Otis and Warren, and Samuel Adams, in the assertion and vindication of our national independence, and trained in that school, Mr. Freeman was the fit man to be the historian of that land of sturdy patriots.

Mr. Edmond Freeman, his progenitor, was *primus inter pares* by position, energy and sagacity. He is rightly called the founder of Sandwich, the first successful attempt at the settlement of the cape. His brother-in-law, John Beauchamp, was a merchant "adventurer" in the Plymouth colony, and, of course, we find him a strong parliamentarian in 1642, "merchant of London" in the Amsterdam trade. —*Husband's Coll.*, 1642, p. 343. Another brother, William Coddington, one of Mr. Cotton's parishioners at Boston in Lincolnshire, was one of the "antinomian" victims, and so, one of the purchasers of Rhode Island, and its governor. His daughter Alice was the wife of the colonial treasurer of Plymouth colony, Mr. William Paddy, a merchant of large estate, influence and usefulness. This singular surname was borne by an eminent contemporary physician, Sir William Paddy, whose picture was in the library of the College of Physicians.—*Evelyn's Diary*, i. 369. A son Edmond married Rebecca, daughter of Gov. Thomas Prence and granddaughter of Elder Wm. Brewster. A favorite daughter, Elizabeth, married John Ellis of Sandwich, who was probably of the family of John Ellis of Robinson's congregation at Leyden.—*Hist. Mag.*, 1859, 359—363.

Mr. Freeman makes his arrangement and reference by Italic and Roman numerals, one of the best plans yet devised for genealogical statement. The paper, type and impression are all that could be desired.

Communicated by J. Wingate Thornton, Esq.

New History of the Battle of Bunker Hill, June 17, 1775, its Purpose, Conduct and Result. By WILLIAM W. WHEILDON. Reprinted from "The Boston Daily Herald," Revised and Enlarged. Second Edition. Boston: Lee & Sheppard. New York: Lee, Sheppard & Dillingham. 1875. [8vo. pp. 56.]

Bunker Hill: the Story told in Letters from the Battle Field by British Officers engaged. With an Introduction and Sketch of the Battle. By SAMUEL ADAMS DRAKE, Author of "Old Landmarks of Boston," "Historic Fields and Mansions of Middlesex," "Nooks and Corners of the New-England Coast," &c. Boston: Nichols & Hall. 1875. [8vo. pp. 76.]

General Israel Putnam the Commander at Bunker Hill. By SAMUEL ADAMS DRAKE. [To accompany Drake's "Bunker Hill."] Nichols & Hall. Boston. 1875. [8vo. pp. 24.]

Colonel William Prescott, the Commander in the Battle of Bunker's Hill. Honor to whom Honor is Due. A Monograph. By FRANCIS J. PARKER. Boston: A. Williams & Co., 283 Washington Street. 1875. [8vo. pp. 21.]

These are some of the publications which the centenary of the battle of Bunker Hill has brought out. The work of Mr. Wheildon is a clear and impartial account of the battle, newly and carefully compiled from all sources, both American and British. It is illustrated by a facsimile of a contemporary map of Charlestown (in flames) and Boston.

Mr. Drake, in his first work, has brought together the principal English accounts of the battle, which had not before been done; and he has appended a succinct narrative, based on the reports of both sides. The book is illustrated by a facsimile of a rude view of the battle, which appeared in 1781 in George Cockings's poem, "The American War." In his second publication, Mr. Drake produces strong reasons in support of the opinion that Gen. Putnam was the commander of the entire field of operations on the 17th of June, 1775. Mr. Parker, who appears as the advocate of Col. Prescott, contends that as Prescott "commanded at the redoubt, the key of the position, to obtain possession of which was the sole object of the battle," he "was the superior military commander in the action." Mr. Wheildon comes to the conclusion that there were two distinct engagements, one at the redoubt, commanded by Col. Prescott, and the other at the rail-fence, commanded by Gen. Putnam. Others say that the battle was fought without a commander; and there are facts which give plausibility to this view of the case.

The question of the command of the American forces in this battle will probably never be settled to the satisfaction of all parties. The newspaper press last summer contained several arguments upon it, among which may be named two series of articles by the Rev. Increase N. Tarbox, D.D., in favor of Gen. Putnam, one in the *New York Herald*, June 12 and 14, and the other in the *Boston Journal*, June 10, 11 and 14, 1875; and an article by the Rev. George E. Ellis, D.D., in favor of Col. Prescott, in the *Boston Daily Advertiser*, June 22, 1875. It is admitted by all that Col. Prescott was the commander at the redoubt, and did heroic service there.   J. W. DEAN.

The History of Raymond, N. H. By JOSEPH FULLONTON. * * * Dover, N. H.: Printed at the Morning Star Job Printing House. 1875. [8vo. pp. 407. For sale in Raymond, by the author; in Boston, by D. H. Brown, 25 and 28 Cornhill.]

For many years, the Rev. Mr. Fullonton, a retired clergyman, has been diligently collecting the materials for this book. Those who know how slight must have been the aid, if any, received by him, and how scattered are the sources from which alone he could draw; and, especially, those who have undertaken similar works, will readily and duly appreciate this book, the fruit of long, patient, and, we fear, unremunerative labor. We see little to criticize, and much to praise in this volume. In fact, we are so thankful for such books, and really owe so great a debt to the public benefactors who bring them out, that we have no heart to criticize anything in them, unless it be an error in an important matter.

It was remarked in this periodical a few years ago that a railroad was needed in sundry parts of New-Hampshire to wake up the people. Whether that honest burst of impatience had any basis is not for us to say, but it is an interesting and suggestive fact that town histories are multiplying along the lines of railway.

So far as we have the means of knowing, this book is accurate. It is well printed, and contains several portraits and other illustrations.   A. H. H.

The Genealogist. Edited by GEORGE W. MARSHALL, LL.D., Fellow of the Society of Antiquaries. London: Mitchell & Hughes, 24 Wardour St. No. I. July, 1875. No. II. October, 1875.

In March, 1874, a few months after the death of John Gough Nichols, F.S.A.,—a sketch of whose life appears in this number (*ante*, pp. 118–19),—the Herald and Genealogist (*ante*, xx. 385) which he had established, and, for upwards of eleven years, had edited with marked ability, was brought to a close. The discontinuance of this work caused many expressions of regret among genealogists. They will therefore gladly welcome The Genealogist, a new periodical devoted to genealogy and kindred subjects, which was commenced last summer in London. The prospectus of this work and the contents of the first two numbers, were printed on the cover of the October number of the REGISTER, to which the reader is referred for information as to the scope of this magazine. The work is under the editorial charge of Dr. Marshall, F.S.A., who edited, for the Harleian Society, LeNeve's Catalogue of Knights, and who is known as a talented antiquary. The magazine is edited with ability; and it gives us pleasure to learn that it meets with a favorable reception in England. We hope it will have many subscribers in this country. The price is six shillings a year, or 1s. 6d. a number.   J. W. D.

The Maine Genealogist and Biographer. A Quarterly Journal. "None of us liveth to himself and no man dieth to himself."—*Paul.* Augusta, Me.: Printed for the Society by Sprague, Owen & Nash. [No. I.] September, 1875. [No. II.] December, 1875. [8vo. pp. 32 each.]

These are the first numbers of a new periodical to be issued quarterly under the auspices of a newly formed society, the "Maine Genealogical and Biographical Society." We wish them both success,—the periodical and the society; and we have no doubt, from the character of the gentlemen engaged in the enterprise, that they will deserve it. The work will consist of matter relating to the State of Maine, such as genealogical and biographical sketches, notes and queries, obituaries, &c. &c., and will be furnished at $1.50 a year. Numbers will be sent to any address for 40 cents each. The contributors to these numbers are the Hon. James W. North, president of the society; William B. Lapham, M.D., the secretary; Rev. G. T. Ridlon, Samuel L. Boardman, Lemuel Perham, the Hon. Joseph W. Porter, and Col. F. W. Galbraith. Dr. Lapham, we presume, is the editor of the work, and all communications are to be addressed to him.   J. W. D.

(1) *Address delivered before the Essex Institute, October 5, 1874, at the Centennial Anniversary of the Meeting of the Provincial Assembly in Salem, October 5, 1774.* By ABNER C. GOODELL, Jr. Salem: Published by the Essex Institute. 1874. [Royal Octavo, pp. 60.]

(2) *Memorial Services at the Centennial Anniversary of Leslie's Expedition to Salem, Sunday, February 26, 1775, on Friday, February 26, 1875, by the City Authorities of Salem.* Salem, Mass. 1875. [Quarto, pp. 91.]

(3) *Proceedings at the Centennial Celebration of the Battle of Lexington, April 19, 1875.* Lexington: Published by the Town. Boston: Lockwood, Brooks & Co. 1875. [Royal Octavo, pp. 170. Price, $2.50.]

(4) *Celebration of the Centennial Anniversary of the Battle of Bunker Hill, with an Appendix containing a Survey of the Literature of the Battle, its Antecedents and Results.* Boston; Printed by order of the City Council. M DCCC LXXV. [Royal Octavo, pp. 174.]

(5) *Proceedings of the Bunker Hill Monument Association at the Annual Meeting, June 23, 1875, with the Oration of* Hon. CHARLES DEVENS, Jr., *and an Account of the Centennial Celebration, June 17, 1875.* Boston: Bunker Hill Monument Association. M DCCC LXXV. [Octavo, pp. 217.]

(6) *Centennial Orations commemorative of the Opening Events of the American Revolution.* With other Proceedings. 1874–1875. Boston: 18 Somerset Street. 1875. [Octavo, pp. 178. Rubricated Title-page.]

In the July number of the REGISTER we noticed the oration of Mr. Henry Armitt Brown, delivered in Carpenters' Hall, Philadelphia, September 5, 1874. Since that notice was written, we have received the publications whose titles are given above. They sufficiently explain themselves, perhaps; yet, it may be proper to state that Number 2 in the list contains the oration of the Hon. George B. Loring; Number 3, the oration of Richard H. Dana, Jr., LL.D.; and that both Numbers 4 and 5 contain Mr. Justice Devens's oration at Bunker Hill.

Number 6 is a reprint from the October number of the REGISTER of six orations, viz.: of Abner C. Goodell, Jr., Esq., in Salem, Mass., Oct. 5, 1874; of Richard H. Dana, Jr., LL.D., in Lexington, April 19, 1875; of George William Curtis, LL.D., in Concord, April 19, 1875; of the Hon. Charles Devens, Jr., at Bunker Hill, June 17, 1875; of Andrew P. Peabody, D.D., LL.D., in Cambridge, Mass., July 3, 1875; and of the Hon. Henry Armitt Brown, in Philadelphia, Sept. 5, 1874.

In addition to the orations, a very full and revised account of the other proceedings at the several centennial commemorations, above named, is given. In the appendix will be found an account of " General Israel Putnam's Ride to Concord," upon which he started as soon as news of the fighting in Lexington and Concord had reached him; and the text of his letters from the last named place, on the 21st of April, to Colonel Ebenezer Williams, of Pomfret, Connecticut; also, the full text of " An Account of the Battle of Bunker Hill, by an Eye-witness," being the letter of Peter Brown, a soldier in that battle, to his mother, Mrs. Sarah Brown, then of Newport, R. I. This letter is dated " Cambridge, June 25, 1775." This volume is accompanied by a portrait of General Joseph Warren, the most distinguished of the martyrs of the 17th of June. The price of the volume in muslin covers is $2.00; in paper covers, $1.50. The edition is limited to 250 copies.

Librarians, collectors of rare books, and historical students will appreciate the convenience of having these learned, eloquent, and patriotic discourses gathered into a single volume. A. H. H.

General Sullivan not a Pensioner of Luzerne (Minister of France at Philadelphia 1778–83). With a Report of New-Hampshire Historical Society, vindicating him from the Charges made by George Bancroft. Second Edition. Boston: A. Williams & Co. 1875. [8vo. pp. 73. Price 25cts.]

This is an able vindication of a Revolutionary patriot of whom the state of New-Hampshire is justly proud. This interesting pamphlet arrives as we are going to press, and we have space to give this brief announcement only.

DEATHS.

Astor, William B., in New York city, Nov. 24, aged 81, said to have been the wealthiest person in the United States. He was born in that city, March, 1794, and was the son of John Jacob Astor, who died in 1848, the founder of the Astor Library, to which institution he was himself a liberal benefactor. He attended the public schools in boyhood, and afterwards studied in Heidelberg and travelled over Europe. Returning to New-York, he engaged in business with his father. While in active commercial business, he was engaged chiefly in the fur and tea trades, but for many years he has devoted himself to collecting the rents and dividends on his invested capital and making reinvestments, a vast business of itself. He married a daughter of Gen. John Armstrong, secretary of war under President Madison, by whom he had six children, three sons and three daughters.

Brown, John Carter, in Providence, R.I., June 10, 1875, aged 76. He was the second son of the Hon. Nicholas Brown, the distinguished benefactor of Brown University, from whom that institution received its name. He received his education at that university, where he graduated in 1816. Soon after, he entered upon the pursuit of business in connection with the house of Brown & Ives, of which firm in 1832 he became a partner. On the death of his father in 1841, he inherited a large estate, and became more fully identified with business affairs. He travelled much in all parts of the United States, and resided in Europe at different times, for several years. He early began to take an interest in collecting rare and curious books, a pursuit on which he bestowed great attention and care, and in the prosecution of which he made large expenditures. The private library which he left was one of the most valuable in this country. By far the most conspicuous portion of it was his collection of books relating to North and South America, of which a catalogue was privately printed in 1865, in four royal octavo volumes, and a second edition of the first volume in 1875.

In 1828, he was chosen a trustee, and in 1842 a fellow of Brown University, and he was ever after connected with the management of its affairs. He bestowed upon the university many munificent gifts of different kinds.

Butler, Miss Clarissa, of Groton, died in Boston, Dec. 22, 1875, aged 61. She was a daughter of Caleb and Clarissa (Varnum) Butler, and was born in Groton, July 14, 1814 (*ante*, ⅺi. 353). Her father, Caleb Butler, was the author of the History of Groton, and contributed to the 2d and 3d volumes of the Register, a genealogy of the Butler Family.

Miss Butler will be greatly missed by her neighbors and townfolks, as she occupied a position of remarkable usefulness. For the last forty years she has been closely connected with the local charities and the questions of public education, and she has been so capable in whatever duties she has undertaken that it will be difficult for any one to fill her place. She inherited her father's antiquarian taste, and was more familiar with the history of the town than any other person. At one time she was the preceptress of the Lawrence Academy, and of late years she has served as a member of the school committee, where her opinions were always justly treated with great deference. She took an active interest in the Groton public library, and made her influence felt in various directions for the benefit of her town's-people. Her loss will be felt in many different walks of life. Apart, however, from her cultivation and strength of mind, she will be remembered best for her conscientious and Christian life.

Cooke, McLaurin Furber, M.D., in Chelsea, Mass., Nov. 11, of consumption, aged 54. He was a son of Thomas and Nancy Cooke, and was born in Newington, N. H., Jan. 5, 1821. In early life he removed to Farmington. He graduated at Dart. Coll. in 1847, and at the Medical School in 1855. He commenced the practice of his profession, but relinquished it for schoolteaching. He taught in Gilmanton and Greenland, N. H., Hartford, Ct., Somerville, Mass., and Charlestown. He was sub-master of the Eliot school, Boston, for several years, and in 1866 was elected master of the Hancock school, which position he held till failing health obliged him to retire from active labor. He m. in 1855 Mary Elizabeth, dau. of Edward B. Moore, M.D., of Boston, and leaves one daughter, the wife of George L. Gould, of Chelsea.

Edwards, the Hon. Jonathan, in New Haven, Conn., Aug. 23, 1875. He was born in Hartford, Conn., Sept. 27, 1798. His father was Jonathan Walter Edwards, of Hartford (a graduate of Yale in 1789), a lawyer and a member of the Connecticut bar. Jonathan Walter Edwards was the only son of the Rev. Jonathan Edwards, president of Union College, who was the son of the eminent theologian and scholar, commonly known as President Edwards, the author of " Edwards on the Will," a work said by Daniel Webster to be " the greatest achievement of the human intellect." Jonathan Edwards, the subject of this notice, was educated at the Grammar School in Hartford and at Yale College, graduating at Yale in 1819. Soon after he entered the office of Zephaniah Swift, the author of Swift's Digest and Chief Justice of the Supreme Court of Connecticut, and was admitted to the bar of that State in 1824. For several years afterwards, Mr. Edwards was a practising attorney in Hartford; and during part of that time was the editor of the Connecticut Mirror, when Gideon Welles, ex-Secretary of the United States Navy, and George D. Prentice, afterwards so widely known as the editor of the Louisville Journal, were editors of the Hartford Times and the New-England Review. In 1834, Mr. Edwards was appointed by the legislature of the State judge of probate for the district of Hartford.

In 1837, Mr. Edwards was married to Maria Champion, born in Colchester, Ct., then a resident of Troy, N. Y., and soon after took up his residence in that city. For a number of years he was president and acting superintendent of the Troy and Greenbush Railroad. His knowledge of railroads, his enterprise and energy, rendered him valuable not only to the road with which he was connected, but to the railroad interests generally of the locality.

In the fall of 1853, Mr. Edwards accepted the whig nomination for the New York assembly, and was elected. In that year the project of bridging the Hudson was before the legislature. Troy, as usual, opposed the measure, and in the opposition Mr. Edwards was very effective. The following spring, Mr. Edwards was chosen mayor of the city. He devoted an unusual amount of time to the office, and his vigilance and efficiency were felt in every department of the city government. The following fall he was prevailed upon to accept a renomination to the Assembly, and was elected; serving throughout with great general acceptance.

In 1858, he was elected supervisor from the eighth ward, though the ward was politically hostile to him. He was reëlected in the spring of 1859. He took a prominent part in the proceedings of the board, and, with the city representatives, succeeded in securing what was deemed a more equitable and just apportionment of taxes. Owing to the death of his wife, Mr. Edwards terminated his residence in Troy in the spring of 1867, since which time he has been a resident of New Haven, with his only son, Jonathan Edwards, M.D., a graduate of Yale in 1863.

Mr. Edwards prepared during the later years of his life, in connection with his son, a careful and full genealogical history of his branch of the Edwards family.

KIDDER.—Mrs. Harriet Maria, in Melrose, Dec. 22, aged 58. She was a daughter of Jonathan and Lois (Mixer) Hagar, of Cambridgeport, where she was born Oct. 26, 1817 (See *Bond's Watertown,* p. 269). She married Jan. 12, 1841, Frederic Kidder, Esq., author of the History of New Ipswich and other historical works, and a prominent member of the New-England Historic, Genealogical Society. She took much interest in her husband's historical studies, and in the society.

Mrs. Kidder was beloved by all who felt the charm of her manner; and in few cases, it is believed, has such Christian fortitude, as a lingering illness exacted, such sweetness of character as she constantly displayed, left their fragrant memory in the hearts of friends and kindred.

PARK, Mrs. Laura Hall, in Brooklyn, N. Y., June 21. She was the wife of the Hon. Trenor W. Park, and a daughter of the Hon. Hiland Hall, of North Bennington, Vt. She was a lady of most estimable character, with rare graces of heart and culture which won the friendship of those who made her acquaintance. Her benevolence was proverbial.

WENTWORTH, Joseph Fuller, in Lee, Oneida Co., New York, 13 August, 1875; born at Windsor, Mass., 24 November, 1792, son of *Sylvanus*,[5] in line of *William*,[4] *Sylvanus*,[3] *Paul*,[2] *William*.[1]

J. WENTWORTH.

THE

HISTORICAL AND GENEALOGICAL REGISTER.

APRIL, 1876.

THE LOWNDES FAMILY OF SOUTH CAROLINA.*

A GENEALOGICAL SKETCH.

BY GEORGE B. CHASE, A.M.

AMONG the leading families of the State of South Carolina, in by-gone days, there was hardly one that exercised so strong an influence throughout its colonial dependence, and the first half century of its existence as one of the United States, as that of Lowndes of Charleston, and of Colleton County where were its first plantations,—a junior branch of an old and very numerous English family which attained its highest honors in the mother country during the reign of Queen Anne.

For well nigh a century from the year 1725, when Mr. Thomas Lowndes of Overton, in the county of Cheshire, and a descendant of the "*anciente familye* of Loundes of Legh Hall," was busily engaged in schemes for the settlement of South Carolina, of which he held the patent of Provost Marshal, and was in active correspondence with the Board of Trade, at White-hall,—down to the period of the Missouri Compromise in 1820, and the lamented death, two years later, of William Lowndes of Charleston, then nominated, after ten years of eminent service in Congress, as a candidate for the Presidency of the United States,—the strenuous character of their race had maintained a continual representation of their name in the service of the colony and state.

When Crowfield, the family residence on the Ashley river, was burned with all its contents, soon after the Revolution, the library, together with its books, portraits and papers, including a pedigree and all the early correspondence with their relatives in England and the West Indies, were utterly destroyed. As the generation then living, according to tradition, were very familiar with the history of their line, and as little importance was then attached to a continuance of that intercourse which had been rudely severed by the outbreak of the War of Independence, no steps were taken to make any record of the history of the Carolina family, and so it happened after the lapse of two generations of planters, who were thoroughly content with their lot in life, and, "*incuriosi suorum,*" were unaware of the importance to their descendants of a full family record, that, when there arose among them, a few years since, the natural spirit of inquiry into their antecedents, and a desire to establish anew their traditional connection with England, there was no where in Carolina any paper or record of the family descent, or even of the family correspondence in the last century. Beyond an old seal and a few pieces of English porcelain dinner service sent from England to Rawlins Lowndes, subsequently President of South Carolina, soon after his second marriage in 1750, and decorated with his arms, there was no clue to which branch of the name in England the Carolina planters had been related.

Several years since, Major Rawlins Lowndes, formerly of the Army, and now of Hopeland, near Staatsburgh on Hudson, authorized the inquiry which, conducted by the writer in the West Indies and in England, resulted, after many unforeseen delays, in perfecting anew proofs of that pedigree which had been consumed at the burning of Crowfield nearly a hundred years before.

A comparison of the arms upon the seal and dinner service with that of Lowndes of Bostock House and Hassall Hall, in Burke's History of the Commoners, showed them to be identical, save with the proper difference when borne by a younger son, but the genealogy of the Bostock line, as recorded by Burke, although it showed a representation in the American Colonies at a late period, contained no mention of any possible ancestor of Charles Lowndes of St. Kitts, the founder of the Carolina family.

A correspondence was thereupon instituted with the clergy in the island of St. Christopher, usually called St. Kitts, as it was known from the printed notes of his grandson, the late Hon. Thomas Lowndes, that Mr. Charles Lowndes had come with his family from that island. After an interval of some months, an answer was received from the late Rev. Ebenezer Elliott, then rector of Christ Church, Nicola town, and St. Mary's, Cayou, St. Kitts, giving a record of all births, marriages, and deaths under the Lowndes name before the removal to Carolina. A diligent search was commenced in the record office at London, and a careful examination was made of all the wills which seemed to bear upon the family of either Mr. Thomas Lowndes, of Overton, the first Provost Marshal of Carolina under the king, or that of the Bostock line. Wills were transcribed, parish registers were searched, and the present representative of the Bostock family in England, now merged in the female line, Miss Sophia Kirkby Reddall, of Congleton, niece and heiress of the last Mr. Lowndes of Hassall, caused an examination of the family papers in her own possession to be made by her solicitor.

It became at length evident, although not till the end of a long and wearisome inquiry, which was carried on at intervals for upwards of five years, that there were material errors and omissions in the English pedigrees, the result of an imperfect and probably hasty examination of the papers of the late Mr. William Lowndes of Hassall, the last representative of his name, before they were submitted to Mr. Burke's compilers for their perusal and use in the preparation of his most comprehensive book, "The History of the Commoners of Great Britain."

As Mr. Thomas Lowndes, Provost Marshal of Carolina in 1725, was of the Overton family, an especial search was also made in the will offices and among the church records of the various parishes in Cheshire where the family name was found, for a proof of his pedigree and with the hope of bringing to light the presumed relationship between this gentleman and Charles Lowndes, whose son Rawlins had, as early as 1741, succeeded to the provost marshalship, with the approval of the assignee of the patent. The wills of all persons recorded under the name of Lowndes at the probate office in Chester were carefully examined, and full extracts were taken from the parish registers of Sandbach, Middlewich and Astbury, but while the family of Mr. Thomas Lowndes of Overton, and afterwards of Westminster — although never himself, after his appointment, in the new world — was clearly ascertained, there was no trace of Charles Lowndes, nor any one of his name.

In the autumn of 1872, the writer, who was then in London, procured some additional lists of wills registered at Doctors' Commons, under the name of Lowndes, with copies of the names of all persons mentioned in them. Among them he read the name of Charles Lowndes as found in the will of Frances Lowndes of Covent Garden. A copy of the will was immediately procured. While it was, at once, evident that, although her name nowhere appeared in the history of the Hassall family, she could have belonged to no other, and that her place in the record could be marked out with absolute precision, it was also apparent that the omission of her name was not the only one of her generation, and that further additions to the family genealogy would probably be found.

In the summer of 1874, by the kindness of Miss Reddall, a copy of the will of William Weld of Weld House and Hassall Hall, who died in 1705,* in which the name of Charles Lowndes the elder occurs, was furnished the writer, and from Mr. William H. Turner were received abstracts of certain deeds relative to the Lowndes property at Congleton.

From these various papers, the following genealogical sketch has been prepared, imperfect as it must always remain from the destruction of so many records in the disorganized condition of South Carolina during the last fifteen years. The genealogy, however, establishes perfectly the connection which was known by tradition to have existed between the old family of Cheshire and the officers of the crown in the province of South Carolina a century and a quarter ago.

WILLIAM[1] LOWNDES,† a descendant of a younger son of the family of Lowndes, of Overton, in Smallwood, and itself a branch of the ancient family of Lowndes of Legh Hall, near Middlewich, bought, in the reign of Queen Elizabeth, Bostock House in Little Hassall, in the parish of Sandbach, all in the county Palatine of Chester, from the family of Bostock of Moreton Say in the county of Salop. He married Ellen, daughter of ——, and had issue:

 i. ELLEN,[2] bapt. Sept. 25, 1580.
 ii. JOAN,[2] bapt. Oct. 21, 1582.
 iii. WILLIAM,[2] bapt. June 9, 1585, who died in childhood.
2. iv. RICHARD,[2] who succeeded as heir.
 v. THOMAS,[2] bapt. March 15, 1590-1; buried May 8, 1591.

Mr. Lowndes died 4th June, 1590, and by his will, proved 9th October in the same year, appointed his wife, and his brothers Richard and Thomas, executors of his will.

2. RICHARD[2] LOWNDES, gent., of Bostock House, baptized 22d Jan. 1587-8; married 11th Aug. 1611, Elizabeth, daughter of —— Rawlins, and had issue:

 i. MARGERY,[3] bapt. Sept. 17, 1612.
 ii. ELIZABETH,[3] bapt. Oct. 22, 1613.
 iii. RICHARD,[3] bapt. April 19, 1615, who died in infancy.
 iv. ELLEN,[3] bapt. Feb. 27, 1617-18.

By his second wife, Margery, daughter of ——, Mr. Lowndes had one son:—

3. v. JOHN.[3]

---

* By the will of William Weld, his estates passed to his great nephew, Richard Lowndes, of Bostock House and Hassall Hall, son of Richard, and nephew of Charles Lowndes the elder. From the accession of Mr. Richard Lowndes to the Hassall property, Bostock House ceased to be the family residence. Ormerod, in his History of Cheshire, thus describes the estates of Bostock and Hassall Hall, as they appeared in 1818.

Of Bostock Hall, he says: "The hall, from which this estate derives its name, is a farm house, containing within its walls some portion of an ancient mansion, which was defended by a moat, of which a part is remaining, and was the property and occasional residence of the Bostocks of Moreton Say, co. Salop. Henry Bostock of that place, by an *Inq. p. m.* 23. Eliz., is found to hold (inter alia) lands in Hassall from the lord of Hulfield, in socage."

"The Hall of Hassall is a very respectable residence, finished with gables, and surrounded with antiquated gardens and offices. The situation is on an elevated knoll, where the neighboring country undulates agreeably, and the circumstances of the term interest of the possessor, "with impeachment of waste," have already ornamented it with pleasure grounds and hedge rows, with trees of growth and proportions strikingly distinguished from those of the adjacent townships."

† Burke's History of the Commoners.

On 4th Jan. 1651, Mrs. Margery Lowndes died, and Mr. Lowndes dying 20th April, 1652, was succeeded by his son,

3. JOHN[3] LOWNDES, gent., of Bostock House, baptized 24th April, 1625. He married Jane, daughter of John Welde, gent., of Weld House, in Newbold Astbury, and co-heir to her brother, William Weld, Esq., of Weld House and Hassall Hall.

By his wife Jane, Mr. Lowndes had ten children:

    i.   RICHARD,[4] bapt. at Sandbach, Oct. 13, 1645, who succeeded as heir.
    ii. JOHN,[4] bapt. at Sandbach, Nov. 8, 1646.
    iii. MARY,[4] bapt. at Sandbach, June 4, 1648; m. —— Savyle.
    iv. AUDREY,[4] bapt. at Sandbach, June 5, 1649; m. John Walker.
    v.   ELLEN,[4] bapt. at Sandbach, April 19, 1651; m. Robert Bennett.
    vi. CHRISTOPHER,[4] bapt. at Sandbach, Aug. 27, 1652.
    vii. EDWARD,[5] bapt. at Sandbach, Aug. 1, 1653.

Not long after the birth of his seventh child, Mr. Lowndes, as appears by the deeds of Congleton Borough, moved to Middlewich,* where, by an indenture dated 13th Oct. 1657, he made a feoffment to William Welde of Newbold Astbury and John Welde of London of certain premises which he held as heir of his father Richard Lowndes. It is probable that there were born to Mr. Lowndes, while a resident of Middlewich, his younger children, of whose existence the compilers of the family history appear to have been unaware; for, in addition to the children whose baptisms are recorded in the Sandbach records, Mr. Lowndes had:—

    viii. FRANCES.[4]
4. ix. CHARLES,[4] who was bapt. at Middlewich, Dec. 6, 1658, and was described
          in the parish register as " son of John Lownes."
    x.   WILLIAM.[4]

Mr. Lowndes made his will 18th May, 1667, and died the same day. He was buried two days later at Sandbach. His wife, who was co-executrix of his will, died 2d Feb. 1690, and was buried at Worthenbury in Flintshire.

Frances[4] Lowndes, of Covent Garden, made her will 29th March, 1690. She did not long survive, for the will was proved 11th April following. In her will she mentions her mother Jane, her brothers Richard[4] and Charles,[4] her sisters Mary,[4] Audrey[4] and Ellen,[4] and their husbands, who have not, hitherto, been anywhere recorded. She also mentions her sister-in-law Sarah, wife of Charles,[4] and their son Charles,[5] to whom she left a bequest of money which was to be paid him when he attained the age of twenty-one years. She also mentions her cousin, Ann Whittingham, the daughter of her mother's sister, Elizabeth Weld, who had married Thomas Whittingham, gent., of Brereton.

It is worthy of note in this place that the brother of Mrs. Jane Weld Lowndes, William Weld, of Weld House and Hassall Hall, who died at Hassall, and was buried at Sandbach, 23d April, 1705, bequeathed by will to his nephew Charles[4] Lowndes, the elder, an annuity of £5. No trace of

---

    * Middlewich and Sandbach are adjoining parishes, and the Lowndes family which had been settled in the neighborhood from the earliest dates had become wealthy, in the seventeenth century, from their success in the opening of salt mines on their property. Of these mines in Cheshire which have now been worked for several centuries, an English writer (Littell's Living Age, May 2, 1874, No. 1560, p. 319) says, in 1871 an enormous amount of salt was sent out of that country to foreign lands and the home market. "The demand increases, and the supply as yet shows no sign of failure, for the salt district occupies about twenty six square miles, of which not more than five have been hitherto worked. As a single square yard of surface is reckoned to cover one hundred and twenty tons of salt, it will be understood that the total quantity is amazing."

the three younger children of John[3] Lowndes had been found by Mr. Burke in the Hassall papers, nor was their existence known to the representatives of the family in England, until the discovery of the existence of Frances[4] and Charles[4] had led, at the request of the writer, to a re-examination of the early wills, and the discovery by Miss Reddall in the will of William Weld, of the tenth child, William[4] Lowndes, of whom, however, we have no other trace.

4.　CHARLES[4] LOWNDES, the elder, as he was known and described in the family papers, married Sarah, daughter of ———, and had one son,

5.　CHARLES[5] LOWNDES, the younger, the ancestor of all of the name of Lowndes in South Carolina, who emigrated in early life to St. Christopher's, or, as it is usually called, St. Kitts, the largest of the Leeward Islands. Soon after his arrival he married Ruth, daughter of Henry Rawlins and —— his wife.* By this marriage he connected himself with a numerous and influential family, long established in the island, for, as early as 1635, the name of Rawlins is found, and more than once among the list of passengers to St. Kitt's from England. Henry Rawlins was in the third generation of planters there, and although he had been at one time a heavy loser by the depredations of the French cruisers, as appears by a record of the year 1705 in the state paper office at London, showing that he had sustained damage on one such occasion, to the amount of £961. 15s. 3d., of which a third part was subsequently recovered, he was enabled to bequeath to his daughter a considerable estate, both real and personal. Mr. Lowndes, whose three children were born to him before the year 1723, embarrassed his property by free living and an unrestrained expenditure, as his grandchildren were informed by their father, and, in 1730, having resigned his position in the Council as representative of the parish of St. Peter, Basseterre, to which he had been elected in the previous year, sailed with his family for Charleston, South Carolina. He was soon after followed by his negroes and movable property, paying £25 duties upon his slaves, and £54. 8s. 8d. on his effects. He executed a mortgage, recorded in the registry of deeds at Charleston, on the 7th of March, 1731, to secure certain bills of exchange drawn by him on the 18th of February previous.†

Mr. Lowndes died in Charleston, March, 1736. His children were:

6. i.　WILLIAM.[6]
7. ii.　CHARLES.[6]
8. iii.　RAWLINS,[6] b. January, 1721.

6.　WILLIAM[5] LOWNDES, the eldest of these brothers, accompanied his mother on her return to St. Kitts after the death of her husband, whom she survived more than twenty-seven years, dying in Christ Church, Nichola Town, 25th July, 1763. She was buried there on the following day.

---

* Mr. Elliott was not able to find the record of Mr. Henry Rawlins's marriage. In a lawsuit, instituted in 1716, at St. Kitts, the papers of which are preserved among the colonial records at London, there is a deposition of one Robert Davis, showing that Henry Rawlins and Ruth Garner, widow, had seized a long time before upon land in Basseterre, to which Davis conceived he had a claim, and the deposition recites much of Mr. Rawlins's doings, but says nothing further of the widow Garner. The assumption is reasonable that Mr. Rawlins married the widow, and that Mrs. Charles Lowndes had thus received at baptism the name of Ruth from her mother who bore it.

† Among the acts passed in 1733 by the Colonial Legislature was one entitled, "An act to encourage Charles Lowndes, Esquire, to make a new machine to Pound and Beat Rice and to appropriate the benefit thereof to himself."

William Lowndes was married at Christ Church, April 7th, 1739, to Mary, daughter of Nicholas and Mary Taylor. Their children were:

    i. MARY,[7] bapt. June 1, 1740.
    ii. JOHN TAYLOR,[7] bapt. Aug. 1, 1744, named in the will of his uncle Charles Lowndes. John Taylor[7] Lowndes m. —— and had : —
        i. *John Lowndes.*[8] He m. ——, dau. of —— Bailey, of Domenica, and had,
        i. Henrietta,[9] m. Rev. Henry Newman, of Roseau, Domenica.
        ii. Grace,[9] m. —— Walsh, of Roseau, Domenica, and had issue.

Mr. John[8] Lowndes was Surveyor-general of Dominica. He died in 1812.

7. CHARLES[6] LOWNDES, at the time of his father's death, was about seventeen years of age. His portrait, taken not long before his death, represents a very tall man, with a countenance indicating great determination and fixity of purpose, traits which have been recognized in Carolina as characteristics of the race since Thomas Lowndes, as agent for the duke of Newcastle, had first visited the colony, as early as 1685. Charles[6] Lowndes finished his education under the care of Mr. Robert Hall, a lawyer of position and influence, and soon after established himself as a planter in Colleton County. In 1752, he was appointed Provost Marshal in immediate succession to his brother Rawlins,[6] and held the office several years. He married Sarah, daughter of —————— Parker, and had :

    i. CHARLES,[7] m. Jeannie Perry.*

Mr. Lowndes made his will 18th Jan. 1763, and died the same year. In his will, which was proved in the following May, he mentioned his brother Rawlins,[6] and his nephew John Taylor[7] Lowndes, of St. Kitts, and bequeathed his estate to his wife and son.

8. RAWLINS[6] LOWNDES, who was about fourteen years of age when his mother returned to St. Kitts, had been placed by her in the family of the resident provost marshal, Mr. Robert Hall, as his guardian. This gentleman, who possessed a large library, of which his ward was a diligent student, carefully directed, during the four remaining years of his most useful life, the education of his pupil in the study of the law. Such was the value of Mr. Hall's training, and such was the diligence of young Mr. Lowndes, that on the death of his guardian in January, 1740, it proved to be the well-nigh unanimous desire of the provincial bar that the position of Provost Marshal should be but temporarily filled, and the permanent appointment reserved till he came of age and be enabled to take the oath of office. Early in 1742, Mr. Lowndes received the appointment, which he held for ten years, when he was succeeded, as we have already seen, by his brother Charles.[6]

The office of Provost Marshal corresponded to that of High Sheriff, and had been granted to Mr. Thomas Lowndes, of Westminster, Gent., 27th Sept. 1725. A copy of his Patent, which contains a curious provision, is preserved at the Record Office, London.†

---

* The authority for this lady's name depends solely upon an old rhyme, for which the neighborhood rather than the family were responsible, handed down through the retentive memory of the late Hon. James L. Petigru :

    "H—ll of a wedding over the Ferry ;
    Charley Lowndes to Jeannie Perry."

The ferry, in the neighborhood of which this old fashioned jollification seems to have taken place, was Parker's Ferry, on the Edisto river.

† Plantations General, vol. 51, p. 63.
"1725, Sept. 27th, Patent for Mr. Tho: Lowndes to be Provost Marshall, Clerk of the Peace and Clerk of the Crown in South Carolina."
"KNOW all Men by these Presents, that We the true and absolute Lords Proprietors of Carolina, do hereby give and grant unto *Thomas Lowndes, Gent.*, his Heirs and Assigns

After Mr. Lowndes retired from office and commenced the active practice of the law, he was elected a member of the Legislature. He carried as zealous a spirit of fidelity to the discharge of his duties into this assembly as he did to the conduct of his cases at the bar. By his untiring industry and impressive speech, no less than by his intellectual power and that spirit of absolute independence by which he was best known among the public men of his time, Mr. Lowndes soon rose to be Speaker of the House. He was also Justice of the Quorum. He discharged upon a writ of *habeas corpus* Powell, a printer of Charleston, who had been imprisoned by the Governor and Council. In 1766, he received from the Crown the appointment of associate judge.

On the 13th of May, 1766, he delivered the first judicial opinion rendered in America upon the Stamp Act, declaring it against common rights and the Constitution, and refusing to enforce it in his court. His rapid success at *nisi prius*, and his superior influence with juries, excited the enmity of Chief Justice Gordon, who laid before the Governor and Council charges of misbehavior against him. He was, however, unanimously acquitted. In 1775, he was removed from the Bench under the prerogative of the Governor, owing to a letter of the Attorney General, Simpson, who was also Secretary to the Governor and Council, and thus in a position to have great influence with them. Simpson, who feared the impending troubles, shortly after returned to England. Mr. Lowndes's reputation as one of the Judges of the Province had, however, become so well known in England, that, on information of his removal by the Colonial Authority, the Home Government appointed Gordon to a situation in Jamaica, and directed the commission of Chief Justice of South Carolina to be issued in favor of Mr. Lowndes.

The Provincial Congress, as it was styled, called in defiance of the royal authority, met on the first of June, 1775. Henry Laurens was chosen President. A committee of safety was immediately appointed, which consisted of thirteen members who were vested with supreme power. Of this

the Office and Place, and Offices and Places of *Provost Marshall, Clerk of the Peace,* and *Clerk of the Crown* of and in the Province of South Carolina in America, for the several and respective natural lives of the said Thomas Lowndes and Hugh Watson of the Middle Temple, Gent., to execute the same by the said Thomas Lowndes, his heirs and assigns, or by his or their sufficient Deputy or Deputies. And we do hereby authorize and impower the said Thomas Lowndes, His Heirs and Assigns to demand and receive take and enjoy all Salaries, Wages, Fees, Allowances, Profits, Perquisites, Travelling Charges, Bill Mony, Benefits, Immunities, Privileges, Advantages and Emoluments anywise incident or appertaining to the said Offices or Places or any of them in as ample and beneficial manner as any former Provost Marshall or Marshalls, Clerk of the Peace, and Clerk of the Crown of any other Province or Colony in America, have or hath used, had received or enjoyed. And Lastly We do hereby revoke and make void all former commissions granted for all or any of the said Offices or Places by us or by our Predecessors, or by any Governor or Governors of the said Province of South Carolina. Witness our hands and the seal of the said Province this twenty-seventh Day of September, Anno Domini, 1725.

	[Signed]	Beaufort	Jon. Tyrrell
		Craven	Hen. Bertie
		Ja. Bertie	J. Colleton."

This patent was accompanied by the further grant to Thomas Lowndes of four baronies of land in the province, of twelve thousand acres each, by possession of which he became one of the original landgraves of the colony. When the government of Carolina was taken from the Lords Proprietors in 1729, Mr. Lowndes surrendered his patent, and in the following year received a renewal of it from the crown, under date 30th Nov. 1730. Hardly two months later, 11th Feb. 1731, Mr. Lowndes assigned it to George Morley, who soon after left England for Charleston, and assumed the duties of the office. In 1736, Morley returned to England, and on his nomination, Mr. Robert Hall was appointed to succeed him, and held the office, as we have seen, till his death. A temporary appointment was then given by the governor, Colonel Bull, to Mr. William Williamson, who held it till the 1st March, 1742–3, when Rawlins Lowndes received his commission.

committee Mr. Lowndes was chosen the third member, being preceded only
by Mr. Laurens and Mr. Charles Pinckney. That he was influential in
their debates may be seen in the following letter of Andrew Marvell to
William Henry Drayton, written at

" Charleston, Sunday, August 12th, 1775.

"I have twice pushed hard for the 'Resolution for attaching Estates in
case of Desertion,' but have not been lucky enough to get a second. The
matter, however, is not *rejected*, only postponed. Rawlins postponator declares the resolution not proper to proceed from the Committee of South
Carolina, and so arbitrary, that nothing but the Divan of Constantinople
could think of promulgating such a law."

He opposed the pretensions of the British Government, as violations of
the rights of English subjects, and he was the first to denounce on the floor
of the House the claim of taxation without parliamentary representation
as the chief grievance of all. Yet while there were none in their attitude more bold than he in Carolina, he did not till the last abandon the hope
of reconciliation with England. Either from his training as a lawyer, his
position as a judge, and his peculiar means of ascertaining the temper of the
friends of the Colonies in England, he had been led, as he stated later in
life, to the belief that the early measures of hostility would lead to reconciliation and to the retirement of the British Ministry from their unfortunate
position on colonial questions.

His opposition to all harsh acts at this time and to the declaration of independence in the Colony was consistent with his uniform policy to oppose all
measures that would tend to close the door to reconciliation, while there was
yet a hope of success. A fortnight later, the last Royal Governor, Lord
William Campbell, arrived to supersede Colonel William Bull. The Provincial Congress made him an address which he refused to receive, as he did
to recognize their existence. On the 16th of the following September, he
fled to the British ship-of-war Tamar, carrying the great seal of the
Colony. Six months later, on the twenty-fourth of March, 1776, South
Carolina declared her independence of the British Crown, and Mr. Rutledge was elected President of the State. Mr. Lowndes, who had been one
of the committee of eleven to devise a plan of government, was chosen a
member of the legislative council.

On the 10th of March, 1778, he succeeded to the Presidency of South
Carolina, and was so formally proclaimed at the State House on that day,
"under the discharge of the Artillery both from the Troops and Forts and
the discharge of small arms."[*] He gave his approval to the Constitution
of 1778, by which the power to reject a legislative act, the *veto* power, which
had been vested in the Executive, was relinquished, and a subject of earnest
contention in the State, since John Rutledge had rejected the first bill for a
reformed constitution, was thus settled in favor of the representatives of the
people.

After the treaty of alliance between France and the United States had
been concluded, the British Government sent the Earl of Carlisle, Governor
Johnstone, and Mr. Eden[†] to America, as commissioners authorized to offer

<hr>

[*] Letter of James Cannon to the Honorable George Boyle, Vice-President of the Commonwealth of Pennsylvania, 14th March, 1778.
[†] Ramsay, i. p. 293.

Congress a repeal of all those Acts of the Crown which had led the Colonies to declare their independence, and to threaten with the extreme penalties of war all those who should continue to prefer an alliance with France to a re-union with the mother country. The Commissioners, repelled by Congress, determined to address the people of each state, and sent a vessel under a flag into the port of Charleston, with their propositions separately addressed to the governor, the assembly, the military, the clergy, and the people of South Carolina. By order of President Lowndes, the vessel was detained in the roadstead, below the harbor, until the council was convened, and the chief men of each class of the people to whom these propositions were addressed, were assembled. When the letter of the Commissioners had been opened and read, a resolution was drawn up and unanimously voted requiring the flag-ship to immediately leave the waters of the State. President Lowndes accompanied the resolution with a stern reprimand of the attempt to violate the constitution of the country, by the offer to negotiate with the state in its separate capacity.

As soon as it was known, towards the end of the year 1778, that the British authorities intended to transfer the seat of active hostilities to the southern states, President Lowndes laid a general embargo, and prohibited the sailing of vessels from any port of the State.* He ordered all live stock from the islands and exposed parts of the coast, to be transported inland, and sent an address to the Legislature calling upon them to take the most energetic measures for successful resistance. In that message, he said, " Our inveterate and obdurate enemy, foiled in the northern states, and by the valor and good conduct of the inhabitants compelled to abandon their hope of conquest there, have turned their arms more immediately against the southern states, in hopes of better success. They are now in possession of Savannah, the capital of Georgia, from whence, if not prevented, an easy transition may be made into this country. This situation of danger, gentlemen, calls for your most serious consideration. Our whole force and strength should be exerted to stop the progress of the enemy."

President Lowndes gave to General Lincoln, who had been sent by Congress from the North to the command of the southern department, an earnest support, and exerted his official and private influence in vigilant and unremitted efforts for the defence of Charleston.

In 1779, Mr. Lowndes was succeeded in the Presidency by John Rutledge. He shared, however, in the defence of Charleston, and was personally a heavy sufferer by the enemy's depredations along the coast and rivers, as he was obliged on one occasion to drive into Charleston, in his carriage hauled by a yoke of oxen, his horses having all been carried off by a sudden raid.

On his retirement from the Presidency, he had been elected a member of the Senate from St. Bartholomew's, the parish he had before represented in the other House. Upon the declaration of peace, he was chosen to the Legislature as Representative from Charleston, and was continued in this position by reëlection until the removal of the seat of government to Columbia led him to decline further service.

The constitution of the United States, recommended by the general convention at Philadelphia, in 1787, was received by the legislature of South Carolina, and read before the House of Representatives on the 16th of

* Ramsay, i. p. 296.

January, 1788. It was debated for three days in Committee of the Whole—by Charles Pinckney, Gen. Charles Cotesworth Pinckney, John Rutledge, and Pierce Butler, who had been delegates to the Federal Convention,—by the Speaker, John Julius Pringle, by Robert Barnwell, Edward Rutledge, Dr. David Ramsay the historian, all men of signal ability, the reputation of whose talents has long survived them, and all in favor of the constitution, and by Rawlins Lowndes alone on behalf the minority in opposition to it.*

Among the discussions upon the adoption of the Constitution there is no debate more able, nor, in the light of history since, is there one more curious and interesting. Mr. Lowndes, who spoke four times, objected principally to the restrictions upon slavery, nor did he shrink as others did from saying so,—to the provisions which gave Congress power to regulate commerce, and to the centralization of power in the Federal Government. He concluded on the third day in these words:

"I desire to thank the House for their very great indulgence in permitting me, on behalf of those members who have desired that I should fully express my sentiments, to debate it at such length. The vast importance of the subject will plead my excuse. I thank the gentlemen on the other side of the question for the candid and fair manner in which they have answered my arguments. Popularity is what I have never courted, but, on this issue, I have spoken merely to point out those dangers to which my fellow citizens are exposed, dangers so evident, that, when I cease to exist, I wish for no other epitaph than to have inscribed on my tomb, 'Here lies the man who opposed the Constitution, because it was ruinous to the liberty of America.'"

When the question on the assembly of the convention to consider the Constitution was about to be put, Colonel James Mason, of Little River, by desire of the minority members of the House, rose and formally thanked Mr. Lowndes for his opposition.

The Convention assembled on the 12th of May. Mr. Charles Pinckney opened the debate on the 14th, and on the 23d the Constitution was adopted by a vote of one hundred and forty members in its favor, to seventy-three in opposition.

The debate in convention, however, attracted but little notice in the State, so thoroughly had the battle been fought in the legislature. The opponents of the Federal Constitution had lost by the refusal of Mr. Lowndes to stand for St. Bartholemews the leader of their party, nor could they furnish another to give dignity and interest to debate by a forcible presentation of such objections as had occurred to the ingenious and able reasoning of Mr. Lowndes.

Many years ago, one who remembered him well, contributed to a Southern journal his impressions of Mr. Lowndes's character and attainments to this effect.

Possessed of a strong judgment, a clear, logical, and discriminating mind, he enforced his opinions, unmindful of their popularity, with strength and freedom. In a debate, at Charleston, when the question of the right of his constituents to instruct their representatives was under discussion in the House, he opposed it with vehemence and great force, declaring it to be a pretension which required representatives to suppress their own judgment and substitute that of others, and which renders their oath to discharge their duty according to their best judgment, a mere form and in effect a sham.

Mr. Lowndes married, 15th of August, 1748, Amarinthia, daughter of Thomas Elliott, of Rantoules, Stone River. Mrs. Lowndes died 14th of

* Elliot's Debates, vol. iv. pp. 253–316.

January, 1750, and was buried by the side of her parents at the cemetery near Rantoules.

Mr. Lowndes married, 2d, December 23d, 1751, Mary, daughter of —— Cartwright, of Charleston.   By this lady he had:

    i.   AMARINTHIA,[7] b. July 29, 1754; m. Sept. 23, 1776, Roger-Parker Sanders, Esq., and after his death, married, second, —— Champney, Esq.
    ii. MARY,[7] b. Aug. 1755; d. unm.
    iii. RAWLINS,[7] b. November 5, 1757; d. in childhood.
    iv. HARRIET,[7] m. —— Brown, and had:
        i.   LOWNDES,[8] who m. Margaretta Livingston, dau. of Hon. John-R. Livingston, third son of Judge Robert-R. Livingston, of New-York.   By this marriage Mr. Lowndes Brown had:
           i. *Harriet-Lowndes,[9]* who m. August, 1855, Henry, Baron Solwyns, of the Belgian Diplomatic Service.
    v.   SARAH-RUTH,[7] b. 1764; m. —— Simmons; d. 1852.
9. vi. THOMAS,[7] b. January 22, 1766.
10. vii. JAMES,[7] b. ——, 1769.

Mr. Lowndes married, third, Sarah, daughter of —— Jones, of Georgia, and had:

11. viii. WILLIAM[7]-JONES, b. Feb. 1782.

By his success at the bar and by fortunate investments in land Mr. Lowndes left to his children large estates on the Ashley, Combahee, and Santee Rivers. He died in Charleston, 24 August, 1800, and was buried in St. Philip's Church.   A few months later, his widow, while driving with her son, was thrown from a chaise and instantly killed.

9. THOMAS[7] LOWNDES was educated in the city of Charleston, and at the family residence on the Ashley River.

A child of seven years at the outbreak of the Revolution, he was old enough to fix in his memory as they occurred the entire succession of events which led the colonies from unheeded petitions for redress to their Declaration of Independence, and through a weary and painful war to an absolute union of independent States.   He was already of age when he studied, as part of his preparation for the practice of law, those debates upon the new Constitution he may have heard in the old State House at Charleston, where his father had stood as the solitary speaker in opposition to an able and triumphant majority.   Inheriting strong powers of mind, he cultivated in his youth that taste for English literature and the study of constitutional law, which has always largely characterized the best minds in the Southern States.   Remaining unmarried till, for those days, the somewhat ripe age of thirty-two, he met as guests at his father's table in town and country a long succession of men from the North and the South who had made their names illustrious in the public service, either in peace or war.   He had been, too, an attentive listener to their interesting discussions upon the questions how best to build up a free Republic in the new world.   He was thus by study, by acquaintance and by family tradition, no less than by the almost inevitable tendencies of the profession he had chosen as the recognized path to public life, a politician, familiar with the whole subject of national legislation,—like so many other leaders of opinion under the old order of things in the Carolinas,—and he fitted himself with care for his turn of duty, when the time determined in his own mind should come.

In the autumn of 1800, a few months after his father's death, having already served in the Legislature of the State, he accepted from the Federal party the nomination of Representative from the Charleston District to

the Seventh Congress. He took his seat at the opening of the first session
on the 7th of December, 1801. On the next day he was appointed to the
Committee of Commerce and Manufactures, and was prominent from that
time in the discussions of the House. As early as Dec. 14th, almost in the
first week of business, he spoke upon the resolution of inquiry into the
conduct of Mr. Pickering when Secretary of State, and he took part in
" an animated debate,"—as the National Intelligencer of that day, more
mindful for the dignity of Congress than are the public journals of our own
time, described in language somewhat euphuistic a stormy scene, so often
repeated afterwards on any sectional issue,—which occurred over an amendment to the Apportionment Bill providing that Maryland should be entitled to
nine rather than eight representatives. The Intelligencer tells us that
" a debate of the utmost dilatoriness took place. Much personal recrim-
ination, chiefly on the charge of delay on the one side and precipitation on
the other, was exchanged, which we think it our duty entirely to suppress."

Mr. Lowndes on the 15th of March, 1802, opened the debate on the
French Spoliation Claims, speaking in favor of their recognition, and urging
prompt measures for their settlement. Little could he, or any statesman of
that day, foresee the uncertainties of legislation which the history of this
measure was in itself to illustrate. Reported formally to Congress again
and again by Committees, it finally passed both Houses only to become void
by the refusal of the Executive's approval. Again revived and apparently not
yet despaired of, these claims, now as old as the century, have already outlived
three generations of public men. At the end of the long debate, in April,
1802, in the Act providing for the redemption of the entire public debt of
the United States, Mr. Lowndes was in the minority of nineteen members,
all federals, who voted against the bill.*

Constant in attendance upon the House, he was earnest and assiduous in
committee, and though mingling often in debate, he was yet able to contribute
to the discussion something of value in fact and much of weight in judgment,
enforced as his sentiments always were by a natural eloquence, which had
been carefully cultivated under the sound opinions then entertained by all
educated men, who valued the study of oratory not as that of a graceful
accomplishment, but as the mastery of an essential influence and tested power
over the emotions and conduct of men.

In the intervals between the sessions, Mr. Lowndes, accompanied by his
family, visited the Northern States, and passed the summer in New England
and the neighborhood of Boston. He was warmly welcomed by his political associates, and received much hospitality from them. An intimate acquaintance with many northern families was thus established, which was
maintained with unvarying cordiality through life, and descended to his
children.

He resumed his seat at the Second Session, on the 13th of December, 1802. On the 22d of that month, he spoke in the discussion on the
circulation of gold coin, which, owing to the erroneous valuation put by the
statute upon the eagles and half eagles previously coined, below their metallic
worth, had led to their being everywhere hoarded. In the long debate on
the 6th of January, 1803, on the cession by Spain of Louisiana to France,
he was early upon the floor, urging with force the proposed call upon the
Executive for the precise facts of the transaction which had been withheld
from Congress.

* National Intelligencer, 14th April, 1802.

Mr. Lowndes was re-chosen to the Eighth Congress, and took his seat in the House on the 29th of October, 1803. He spoke, on the 6th and 8th of the following December, on the constitutional amendment relative to the method of election of President and Vice-President, in favor of postponement till after the ensuing election, and again on the 6th of January, 1804, in opposition to the proposed impeachment of Samuel Chase, a Justice of the Supreme Court, who was tried a few months later by the Senate, and acquitted.

At their session of this year, the Legislature of South Carolina had passed an act repealing all restrictions upon the importation of slaves. The subject early attracted the attention of Congress, and on Tuesday, 14th of February, as will be seen from the following extract from the debates, the following motion by Mr. Bard, of Pennsylvania, was taken into consideration in Committee of the Whole.

" Resolved, that a tax of ten dollars be imposed upon every slave imported into any part of the United States."

On motion of Mr. Jackson, it was agreed to add after the words United States, " or their territories."

Mr. Lowndes. " I will trespass a very short time upon the attention of the House at this stage of the business; but as I have objections to the resolution, it may be proper that I should state them now. I will do so briefly, reserving to myself the privilege of giving my opinion more at length when the bill is before the House, should the resolution be adopted, and a bill brought in. I am sorry, Mr. Speaker, to find that the conduct of the Legislature of South Carolina, in repealing its law prohibitory of the importation of negroes, has excited so much dissatisfaction and resentment as I find it has done with the greater part of this House. If gentlemen will take a dispassionate review of the circumstances under which the repeal was made, I think this dissatisfaction and resentment will be removed, and I should indulge the hope that this contemplated tax will not be imposed. Antecedent to the adoption of the constitution under which we now act, the Legislature of South Carolina passed an act prohibiting the importation of negroes from Africa, and sanctioned it by severe penalties,—I speak from recollection, but I believe not less than the forfeiture of the negro and a fine of one hundred pounds sterling for each brought into the State. This act has been in force until it was repealed by the Legislature at their last session. * * * * *

" The law was completely evaded, and for the last year or two, Africans were introduced into the country in numbers little short, I believe, of what they would have been had the trade been a legal one. Under the circumstances, Sir, it appears to me to have been the duty of the Legislature to repeal the law, and remove from the eyes of the people the spectacle of its authority daily violated.

" I beg, Sir, that from what I have said, it may not be inferred that I am friendly to a continuation of the slave trade. I wish the time had arrived when Congress could legislate conclusively upon the subject. I should then have the satisfaction of uniting with the gentleman from Pennsylvania who moved the resolution. Whenever it does arrive, should I then have a seat in this House, I assure him I will cordially support him in obtaining his object. But, Mr. Speaker, I cannot vote for this resolution, because I am sure it is not calculated to promote the object which it has in view. I am convinced that the tax of ten dollars will not prevent the introduction into the country of a single slave. * * * * The gentleman from Pennsylvania, and those who think with him, ought, above all others, to deprecate the passing of this resolution. It appears to me to be directly calculated to defeat their own object,—to give to what they wish to discountenance a legislative sanction, and, further, an interest to the government to permit this trade after it might constitutionally terminate it. When I say that I am myself unfriendly to it, I do not wish, Mr. Speaker, to be misunderstood; I do not mean to convey the idea that the people of the Southern States are universally opposed to it—I know the fact to be otherwise. Many of the people in the Southern States feel an interest in it, and will yield it with reluctance. Their interest will be strengthened by the immense accession of territory to the United States by the cession of Louisiana. * * * * * *

"My greatest objection to this tax is, Mr. Speaker, that it will fall exclusively upon the agriculture of the State of which I am one of the Representatives. However odious it may be to some gentlemen, and however desirous they may be of discountenancing it, I think it must be evident that this tax will not effect their object; that it will not be a discouragement to the trade, nor will the introduction of a single African into the country be prevented. The only result will be that it will produce a revenue to the government. I trust that no gentleman is desirous of establishing this tax with a view to revenue. The State of South Carolina contributes as largely to the revenue of the United States, for its population and wealth, as any state in the Union. To impose a tax falling exclusively on her agriculture would be the height of injustice, and I hope that the Representatives of the landed interest of the nation will resist every measure, however general in its appearance, a tendency of which is to lay a partial and unequal tax upon agriculture."

MR. BEDINGER. "The gentleman from South Carolina has so fully expressed the opinions I entertain, I shall say but little. Every one who knows my opinions on slavery, may think it strange that I shall give my vote against the resolution. There is no member on this floor more inimical to slavery than I am, yet I am of opinion that the effect of the present resolution, if adopted, will be injurious. I shall, therefore, vote against it."

When on Friday, February 17th, the third day of the debate, the House resumed the discussion of the bill, Mr. Lowndes rose, and after a rapid review of the subject, moved that its further consideration be postponed till the following December. By an amendment, the bill was set down for the second Monday in March, and thus the same end was accomplished, as the House did not sit on that day.

Upon the issue of this debate, Mr. Benton* remarks, "To prevent an erroneous impression being made upon the public by the above proceedings, it is proper to remark, that, during the whole discussion, not a single voice was raised in defence of the act of the Legislature of South Carolina, allowing the importation of slaves, but that, on the contrary, while by some of the speakers its immorality and impolicy were severely censured, by all its existence was deprecated. A large number of those who voted for the postponement, advocated it on the express and sole ground that it would give the Legislature of South Carolina an opportunity, which they believed would be embraced, to repeal the Act."

* Abridgment of Debates, iii. p. 142.

Just three years later, the question was definitely settled by Congress. On the 13th of February, 1807, the House passed the Senate bill, prohibiting the importation of slaves by a vote of one hundred and thirteen members in favor over five in opposition,—and this slender, indeed nominal, minority were members from both free and slave states, who dissented only upon matters of detail, so that, as Mr. Benton observes,* " the prohibition of the trade may be deemed unanimous."

Mr. Lowndes passed the summer at the North and in the neighborhood of Philadelphia. He did not reach Washington till the 6th of November following, after the second session of Congress had commenced, and had thus not been in his place when the Committees of the House were appointed; but, a fortnight later, on the announcement of the resignation of Mr. Samuel L. Mitchell, chairman of the Committee on Commerce, who had been appointed by the Legislature of New York a Senator of the United States, it was *Ordered*, "That Mr. Lowndes be appointed chairman of the Committee of Commerce and Manufactures," &c. &c. He thus returned to his old place on the Committee to which he had been first appointed on his entry to the House.

He spoke for the last time in Congress, on the 13th of December, against a bill to regulate and permit the clearance of private armed vessels. His speech, though brief, was marked by the same quick, ready and logical reasoning which had always characterized his appearance in debate. He left Washington on the 6th of March, 1805, and, failing to obtain his reëlection to Congress on the general overthrow of the Federal party in the South, retired to private life. He continued, however, a steadfast adherent to the principles of his party, and earnestly supported John Quincy Adams, when nominated for the presidency against Andrew Jackson. He often remarked, in allusion to the brilliant political career of his brother, William Lowndes, that coming as a Republican later into public life than himself, his brother differed from him in no essential principle of his political faith.

Mr. Lowndes never resumed the practice of the law. He devoted the remainder of his days to the education of his family, and care of his large estates, and especially the cultivation of his plantation Oakland, on the Combahee river. He passed a portion of each year at his residence in Charleston. He entertained both in town and country, with the cordial hospitality characteristic of the manners of the period, and his conspicuous social station. His house was the resort, as his father's had been before him, of distinguished citizens of the State. An occasional journey to the North, where two of his children had married, enabled him to continue those friendships which he had formed when in the public service.

Mr. Lowndes married on the 8th of March, 1798, Sarah Bond, daughter of Richard Ion, Esquire, of Springfield, St. James, Santee.

By this lady, who united great charm of manner to a handsome and distinguished presence, and whose portrait by Gilbert Stuart has been ranked among the most successful of all his pictures of women, as it was the favorite of the artist himself, Mr. Lowndes had :

i.   RAWLINS,[8] b. May 28, 1789; d. October, 1800.
ii. MARY-ION,[8] b. August 1, 1800; m. March 12, 1816, to Frederic Kinloch, of Charleston, and had issue :

* Abridgment of Debates, iii. p. 519.

      i. MARTHA-RUTLEDGE,[9] b. April 28, 1818; m. Matthew Singleton.
      ii. THOMAS-LOWNDES,[9] b. January 3, 1820; d. unm.
      iii. CLELAND,[9] b. October 6, 1823.
12. iii. RAWLINS,[8] b. September 1, 1801.
13. iv. THOMAS,[8] b. June 26, 1803, at New-Haven, Conn.
      v. JACOB-ION,[8] b. Sept. 19, 1804, at Philadelphia; d. February 7, 1829, unm.
14. vi. WILLIAM-PRICE,[8] b. Sept. 21, 1806.
15. vii. CHARLES-TIDYMAN,[8] b. June 28, 1808.
      viii. EDWARD-TILGHMAN,[8] b. January 15, 1810; d. July, 1837, and was buried in Georgetown, South Carolina.
      ix. HARRIETT,[8] b. January 18, 1812; m. February 3, 1831, the Hon. William Aiken, proprietor of Jehossee Island, Governor of South Carolina 1844–46, a member of Congress from 1851 to 1857, and has :
          i. HENRIETTA,[9] who m. Burnett Rhett, Esq., and has issue.
      x. CAROLINE-HUGER,[8] b. Sept. 25, 1813; d. Sept. 8, 1817.
16. xi. RICHARD-HENRY,[8] b. March 4, 1815.

Mr. Lowndes died in Charleston, on the 8th July, 1843. He had survived his wife less than three years, as Mrs. Lowndes had died 7th October, 1840.

10. JAMES[7] LOWNDES, m. Catherine Osborne, and by her had issue :

      i. THOMAS,[8] b. 1801; m. 1824, Elizabeth Wragg, dau. of William-Loughton Smith.
      ii. AMARINTHIA,[8] b. 1803; m, 1834, Lewis Morris, and had :
          i. ELIZABETH,[9] died unm.
          ii. LEWIS.[9]
          Mrs. Morris died 1843.
      iii. JAMES,[8] b. 1806; d. unm. 1838.
17. iv. EDWARD RUTLEDGE,[8] b. 1809; m. 1833, ——; d. 1853.
      v. JULIA,[8] b. 1811; m. 1830, W. Brisbane, and had :
          i. MARY,[9] m. —— Hickok.
          ii. JULIA,[9] m. R. Rhett.
          iii. RUTH,[9] m. Colden Tracy.
          iv. CATHERINE-OSBORNE,[9] m. Charles Davis.
          v. AMARINTHIA.[9]
          vi. WILLIAM.[9]
          vii. JAMES.[9]
          Mrs. Brisbane died 1847.
      vi. WILLIAM,[8] b. 1817; m. 1841, Mary Middleton, and had issue :
          i. HARRIET-KINLOCH.[9]
          ii. MARY-AMARINTHIA.[9]
          Mr. Lowndes died 1865.

Mr. Lowndes died 1839.

11. WILLIAM[7] LOWNDES, as he is usually styled, since he never used his second baptismal name, was taken by his mother, in his seventh year, to England, and placed at the school of Mr. John Savage, at Brompton Grove. The first glimpse of him in England, is obtained in a letter from Mr. Savage to Mr. Rawlins Lowndes, at Charleston, written in the month of December, 1790. The son's progress was spoken of in cordial approval, and as equal to his father's anticipations. This favorite report was, unhappily, soon followed by one of a different nature, which carried the news of a singular and most unfortunate occurrence to the little boy. After a fatiguing game with his playmates, one day during the heavy snows of the winter of 1791, he sat down to rest by a drift of snow and soon fell fast asleep. He was there left unnoticed by his companions, aud was not thought of by them till his unexplained absence, on their return to school, caused a search to be made

for him. He was brought back alive, yet so thoroughly benumbed with cold, that, despite the remedies which were at once given to him, he only escaped with life after a long and severe attack of inflammatory rheumatism. His health, on convalescence, was found to be so seriously affected, that a return to his home and the warm climate of Carolina was pronounced necessary by the physician of the school. Nor was this opinion ill founded, for, during the remainder of his boyhood, cut off from its sports, he struggled against a constitution permanently impaired.

On his return home, he was sent to a school in Charleston, long famous in the South,—the joint establishment of three divines—Dr. Simon Felix Gallagher, a Roman Catholic, Dr. Beust, a Presbyterian, and Dr. Purcell, an Episcopalian. Dr. Gallagher was a man of great ability and learning, and young Lowndes soon showed how quick, capacious, and retentive was his mind. His memory was such that he could repeat long passages of poetry after a single reading. His progress in his studies was most rapid, and seemed to his schoolmates, as they were wont to say in after life, and in warm remembrance of him, absolutely marvellous.* He remained under Dr. Gallagher's charge more than five years, when the teacher at length said of his pupil, that " his mind had drank up knowledge as the dry earth did the rain from heaven,—that he had learned all that his teacher could impart to him, and that he must thenceforth depend on his own guidance for further progress." The pupil was but fifteen. He joined at this time a youth's debating society, and was soon conspicuous for his fluency and readiness in debate. It was remembered of him, afterward, that all his written essays, while at school, had been deemed by the instructors remarkable for their merit. He had, too, some talent for versification, and translated the Odes of Horace into English verse.

His father watched with pride the rapid progress of this child of his old age. Guided by him, the son pursued his studies from an early period, to fit himself for a political career ; yet his peculiar desire for information, based, perhaps insensibly, upon an instinctive confidence in his own large capacity for knowledge, seems to have led him into wider paths of learning than were usually entered by those who aspired to political distinction. He had studied the writings of La Place as they appeared, and had attained sufficient proficiency in Greek to correspond years afterwards upon the principles of its pronunciation. He continued to read, under the influence and suggestion of Dr. Gallagher, until he entered the law office of De Saussure, at a later period Chancellor of the State.

Mr. Lowndes was, at this time, conspicuous in society, fond of gaiety, and had some tastes unusual in one of his studious mind. He was fond of horses, and eager in his desire to improve the breed in Carolina. He had, too, a strong infusion of military zeal, and, a few years later, on the formation of the Washington Light Infantry was chosen its first commander.† He was fairly entitled to the distinction; he was head and shoulders taller than his men. At the time of his marriage to Miss Pinckney in 1804, he was hardly more than twenty years of age. As soon as he felt able to practise, he was admitted to the Charleston Bar. He applied to Mr. Cogdell, then City Attorney, for permission to enter his office and assist him, without recom-

---

* Mr. Fraser to Mr. Ravenel.
† This company still exists, and enjoys a conspicuous and honorable position among the widely known militia organizations of the Union. Its visit to Boston at the celebration of the 17th of June, 1875, was a distinct feature in the occurrences of that day.

pense, in its duties.* This proposal was generously refused by Mr. Cogdell, who offered him in turn a partnership on equal terms. The offer was accepted, and in March, 1804, the two gentlemen commenced practice together as law partners. The firm, however, did not continue long, for at the end of the following September, a severe storm raged over the whole of the lower country, and did much damage to the plantations, especially to the rice harvest. When Mr. Lowndes learned that his own valuable plantation had been well nigh ruined by the rains and winds, he felt obliged to go to it at once and direct in person the slow work of restoration. In taking leave of his partner, he modestly regretted that he had been of so little service to him.

As he had never intended to pursue the practice of law as his profession in life, but rather to acquire the power to use it as a means to an end in the work of sound legislation, so he never returned to it. As early as 1806 he was engaged in the discussion of a subject, connected with international law, which bore directly upon the political questions of the day. England was then at war with France and her tributary states, and she had sought help in the great struggle by a grave violation of neutral rights. Her merchants, who had seen with alarm that the maritime trade of Europe was bestowing immense profits upon the commerce of America, made bitter and indignant complaint to Pitt. He speedily determined that neutral trade should cease. An interdict, by the issue of new orders in council, was put upon it, and American vessels with their cargoes were seized and confiscated. To support its action, the British ministry called at this time into its service able pamphleteers, and, among their productions, there was one of great influence and power, which attained a wide circulation, entitled "War in Disguise." It was ascribed at first by some to Canning, by others to James Stephens, a lawyer of great ability, who was, in fact, its author. It was an ingenious and eloquent attempt to show that neutral trade was in effect the maintenance of war against England, and of all the political productions of the time was the best designed and fitted to make quick mischief between two countries peopled by the same race. The claims of England were discussed by Mr. Lowndes in a series of thirteen papers, which appeared in the Charleston Courier over the signature of "A Planter," in the spring and summer of 1806. They were written with great clearness of language and force of reasoning; considered as the production of a very young man, they were not unworthy of the author's later high reputation. They indicated the tendency of his mind to political discussion, and, in a larger view, the turn of thought and sentiment which was nerving the South to overcome all resistance to a declaration of war with England. These papers procured for their writer an election to the general assembly of the State from the Parish of St. Bartholomews' in the autumn of 1806.

Mr. Lowndes began his political career under some light shadows of annoyance in social life, for he supported, with a few other young men of his class, the Republican Party and the political principles of Jefferson. The old Federal leaders of the day were the recognized heads of society, and they resented the defection of their juniors as a revolt from sound principles and just authority. Every social influence was brought to bear upon young men of such striking promise as William Lowndes, Langdon Cheves and Joseph Allston, and compel their return to the Federal fold. Deaf to the

---

* E. S. Thomas, "Reminiscences of sixty-five years," i. p. 104.

persuasion of their elders, these young gentlemen soon found that the principles they openly avowed caused them to be looked upon with aversion and distrust by the Federal authorities, and shut them out from much of the gaiety of town and country life. It was during the service of Mr. Lowndes in the Legislature, from 1806 to 1810, that the change was made in the basis of representation in the State, which lasted down to the abolition of slavery.

The constitutions of 1776 and 1778 had apportioned the representation arbitrarily, and upon the basis of wealth alone. As the upper country increased in population, a change became necessary, and, in 1809, the Legislature passed an act, providing that one half of the members of the lower house should be elected on the basis of population, and the other half on the basis of wealth.

The history of all measures of political reform has shown how difficult it is to take the first steps, and how easy the solution of the riddle afterwards appears when the details of the question have been matured, and its various issues turned into one comprehensive measure. It then becomes a matter of some interest to know who was the author of the system of representation which served its purpose so well in South Carolina for more than fifty years, and secured her, by the ability and character of her congressional reputation, and the honest and dignified administration of her domestic concerns, so great an influence among her sister states. The authorship of the amendment has been attributed by some to Col. Blanding, and by others to Mr. Lowndes. Both were on the committee who reported it, but the original manuscript, interlined and corrected, was in the hand-writing of Mr. Lowndes.*

The political nominations of 1810 were canvassed with an especial reference to the attitude of candidates upon the all important question of the apprehended war with Great Britain. Mr. Lowndes's views were already well known from his letters to the Charleston Courier in 1806. He had no confidence in the shifts and expedients, the Embargo and Non-intercourse Acts of a former administration. He regarded them rather as the illusory schemes of a philosopher, than as the measures of a clearsighted statesman. The commerce they were created to defend, they tended in reality to destroy. The encroachments of England on Neutral Rights had continued in face of such enactments to increase, and had culminated at last on the attack of a British man-of-war on an American frigate in our own waters, in the summer of 1807.

---

* The late Mr. Francis J. Grayson made the question of the authorship of this amendment a subject of careful study, and wrote upon it an elaborate note, in which he reviewed the various arguments from time to time put forth in Carolina on behalf of the friends of Mr. Lowndes and Col. Blanding. His conclusions were wholly in favor of the claims of the former, and one of his reasons is so entirely in accordance with the conditions of the measure at the time it was under debate, previous to its passage, as to deserve great weight.

Mr. Grayson was of opinion, that there was at that time a desire that Col. Blanding should be regarded as the head of the movement. It was important to conciliate the upper and middle country. It conduced "to this end that the measure should have the approbation of a judicious member from that quarter. Colonel Blanding was the man, less connected than any other with the conflicting parties of the State and commanding the confidence of all. He was willing to lend his aid to the proposed change, was put forward for that end, and gave his help in a mode that necessarily connected his name with it before the people."

The reason here given is one that in its very nature would have occasioned great reserve on the part of Mr. Lowndes and his friends, and such as would prevent not only any recognition of his connection with the movement, but would even lead its friends to obtain the leadership of one who represented as distinctively, as did Col. Blanding, the other sections of the state. Yet it was due to Mr. Lowndes and to his subsequent distinguished reputation that the evidence of his claims should be preserved, and the declaration of Judge Huger, his colleague in the Legislature, who spoke from personal knowledge, and declared to Mr. Grayson that Lowndes and not Blanding was the author, be authoritatively noted as it fell from his lips.

The pride of the American people had been then touched to the quick. In vain had Mr. Canning offered instant and ample apologies,—for it had been every where felt among the young, the bold, and the aspiring, that the very fact that such an occasion for apology should exist was in itself a disgrace. It was in this condition of the Southern mind that Mr. Lowndes received the nomination of the Republicans of the Beaufort and Colleton District, as Representative to the Twelfth Congress. He was elected in 1810, and took his seat in obedience to the executive proclamation, in the early assembly of the House, on the 4th of November, 1811. South Carolina has neither before nor since introduced to the national service three such able men as William Lowndes, John C. Calhoun, and Langdon Cheves, whom she sent to Washington at this time—as new and untried members.

It was not in the nature of Mr. Lowndes to rush into the arena of debate with that eager haste for distinction, so often seen, since it is so natural to men of an acquired local reputation. He was master of himself and felt he could bide the worthy subject and the proper time. He had been named by the Speaker, Mr. Clay, second on the Committee of Commerce and Manufactures, a position which at once gave him influence in those days in shaping the business of the session. He was earnest and diligent in the advancement of all the measures of preparation for war, and made his first speech, 4th of January, 1812, in the support of the bill to provide an additional military force, by an addition to the army of twenty-thousand men, and he immediately followed it with another in support of an increase of the naval establishment, voting on this question during the long debate upon it for every amendment in favor of an heavy increase to our vessels of war, more than once finding himself upon the record in company with the Federalists under the lead of Josiah Quincy, rather than with his own party.

The war spirit continued to increase in and out of Congress, despite the opinions of the older and more cautious politicians who were averse to it, and who had, in their opposition, the undivided support of the Executive and the Cabinet. Madison, indeed, viewed a declaration of war with no favor, and only gave at last to the deputation of his political supporters who, with Clay at their head, waited upon him in a body, and demanded it as the necessary condition of his renomination to the Presidency, a timid and reluctant assent.

When the House re-assembled on the 2nd of November, 1812, Mr. Lowndes, who had already been elected to the ensuing Congress, was appointed to the Committee of Military Affairs, on which he served throughout the session as a zealous supporter of the war. He received in consequence, on the assembling of the Thirteenth Congress, 13th of December, 1813, the appointment of Chairman of Committee on Naval Affairs, and on the 4th of January following, having reported a resolution of honors to the Navy, made in support of it a speech, brief, yet so eloquent and stirring that it was received and read with enthusiasm in every part of the country. Nor can this kindling address, so happily conceived and so forcibly delivered, be read to-day without emotion. It deserves, too, an especial attention from the extensive popularity it gave to its author. Mr. Lowndes spoke as follows:

"I should be inexcusable if I were long to detain the committee from the vote—I hope the unanimous vote—which they are prepared to give upon the resolutions. The victories to which they refer are, indeed, of unequal magnitude and importance; but the least important of them, if it had been obtained by the subjects of any government on the continent of Europe, would have been heard with admiration and rewarded with munificence. I refer to the action between the Enterprise and the Boxer, from which the public eye appears to be withdrawn by the greater magnitude and the confessedly superior splendor of a more recent victory. * * * Although Lieut. Burroughs was mortally wounded early in the action, yet the skill and gallantry with which he commenced it, leave no doubt that if he had been longer spared to the wishes and wants of his country, the same brilliant result would have been obtained under his command; while the ability, with which Lieut. McCall continued and completed the contest, assures to him as distinguished a fame as if he had carried the vessel into action. The loss of a commander, indeed, may fairly be considered as rendering a victory more honorable to a successor, because it must render it more difficult: it may be expected to confuse, though it may not depress.

" Of the victory of Lake Erie it is impossible for me to speak in terms which will convey any adequate conception of its importance, of the unrivalled excellence of the officers, and of the gratitude of the country.

" The documents referred to the committee sufficiently prove that superiority of force on the part of the enemy which would have insured their victory, if it were not the appropriate character of military genius to refute the calculations which rely on the superiority of force. Nor was the victory obtained over an unskilful and pusillanimous enemy. The English officers were brave and experienced, and the slaughter on board their vessels before they were surrendered, sufficiently attests the bravery of their seamen. They were skilful officers subdued by the ascendency of still superior skill. * * * * * * * * * *

" There was one characteristic of this action which seems to me so strongly to distinguish it, that I cannot forbear to ask the attention of the committee to it for a few moments. I know no instance in naval or military history, in which the success of the contest appeared so obviously to result from the personal act of the commander as in this. When the crew of Capt. Perry's vessel lay bleeding around him; when his ship was a defenceless hospital, if he had wanted—not courage, which in an American officer forms no distinction—but if he had wanted that fertility of resource which extracts from disaster the means of success and glory, I do not say, if he had surrendered his ship, but if he had obstinately defended her, if he had gone down wrapped in his flag; if he had pursued any other conduct than that which he did pursue, his associates might have emulated his desperate courage, but they must have shared his fate. The battle was lost.

" Now examine any other victory, however brilliant. If, in the battle of the Nile, Lord Nelson had fallen even by the first fire, does any man believe that it would have affected the result of the contest? In the battle of Trafalgar he did fall, and Victory never for a moment fluttered from what was then her chosen eyrie—the British mast. And, not only in this view was the victory of Capt. Perry unrivalled, but in the importance even of its immediate consequences. I know none in the modern history of naval warfare that can be compared with it. An important territory immediately rescued from the grasp of English power—uppermost, Canada conquered, or prepared for conquest; an ocean secured from the intrusion of every foreign flag; a frontier of a thousand miles relieved from the hostility of the most dreadful foe that civilized man has ever known! Nay, further, Capt. Perry and his gallant associates have not only given us victory in one quarter, but shown us how to obtain it in another yet more important.

How deep is now the impression on every mind that we want but ships to give our fleet on the Atlantic the success which has hitherto attended our single vessels! We want but ships. We want then but *time*. Never had a nation, when first obliged to engage in the defence of naval rights by naval means—never had such a nation the advantages or the success of ours. The naval glory of other States has risen by continued effort—by slow gradation; that of the United States, almost without a dawn, has burst upon the world in all the sudden splendor of a tropical day. To such men we can do no honor. All records of the present time must be lost,—history must be a fable or a blank,—or their fame is secure. To the naval character of the country our votes can do no honor, but we may secure ourselves from the imputation of insensibility to its merit—we can at least express our admiration and our gratitude."

The first measure of importance brought up at this session had been the new and stringent Embargo Act. It became a law on the 17th of December, and provided for a strict embargo until the 1st of January, 1815, unless hostilities ceased meanwhile. The news of the battle of Leipsic and Napoleon's retreat across the Rhine, which was made known just before new-year's day, 1814, caused an immediate agitation in favor of its repeal by all who were in favor of peace, and who dreaded the advent of English armies in Canada, when released from service in Europe by the fall of Napoleon then thought to be imminent. Lord Castlereagh had at the same time written to Monroe, then Secretary of State, to express the willingness of the British government to treat for peace. Nor was it long before the embargo act was found to injure the country, whose commerce it paralyzed, and not the enemy, who had accumulated provisions for a whole year in advance. On the 14th of April, such was the pressure of the peace party, acting in concert with leading members who supported Mr. Lowndes in his opposition to any restrictions upon commerce, that the Act was repealed hardly four months after its passage.

The bills which were passed under Mr. Lowndes's influence at this session were laws—in aid of the naval establishment and the general system of national defence; to authorize an increase of the marine corps, and the construction of floating batteries; to allow rank to be bestowed on naval officers for distinguished conduct; to provide for the appointment of flotilla officers, for bounties for prisoners captured on the high seas and brought into port, and for pensions for the widows and children of those who were slain in action.

Although the treaty between England and the United States had been signed on the 24th of December, 1814, the despatches of our Commissioners did not reach America, as is well known, till the 11th of the following February, more than a month after the battle of New-Orleans. As fast as the news of peace was made known, the sound of rejoicings everywhere filled the air, and the roads leading into the large cities were alive with people hurrying to behold illuminations or to listen to the congratulations of party leaders.

The war had never been popular, for the sufferings and hardships it entailed had caused the grievances which led to it to be so far overlooked, that there were very few to grumble at their relinquishment by President Madison, in the final instructions to the American Commissioners. The country, however, soon saw and clearly understood that the reëstablishment of peace in Europe had removed that intense strain upon the resources of England which had caused its government to wink at the impressment of seamen from vessels belonging to the United States and the consequent dishonor to their flag. The American army had got no great amount of glory by the war, but had rather given promise of future distinction by its gallantry at Chippewa and its steadiness at Lundy's Lane. The navy had carried off the honors of the struggle, and was the popular arm of the service. Congressmen and politicians who had labored for it and supported it acquired an undoubted hold upon the favor of the people. They were well nigh the only class of public men who did.

Nor was England less willing to negotiate; for there had been from the outset a large party in the mother country, who, like the Federalists of the North, welcomed the treaty as " the conclusion of a destructive war which wisdom and temper might have entirely prevented." *

The unwise project of invasion had been tried upon the northern and southern border of the union, and had failed through the victory of McDonough on Lake Champlain and Jackson at New-Orleans. While the defence of Canada and her supremacy upon the ocean were possible to England from the abundance and character of her resources, yet so distant was the scene of war, that she could only maintain hostilities at an enormous expenditure. Both countries desired peace so equally, that when peace was made, the contemporary historian wrote of the provisions of the treaty that " not the least notice was taken of any of the points at issue on the commencement of the war and which were the occasion of it; so that the continuance of peace must depend either upon the absence of those circumstances which produced the disputes, or upon a spirit of reciprocal moderation and conciliation, the desirable fruit of dear-bought experience." †

In place of the circumstances which led to the dispute, a wise spirit of conciliation has arisen among the educated statesmen of either country, which is gradually spreading among the people of both nations, leading to a study of their independent as well as their long common histories, and removing many of the misconceptions which had naturally sprung into existence, like baneful weeds in neglected ground, between two branches of the same race so long widely separated, and whose only intercourse had been on little other than cold or hostile terms.

While there were some among the public men who brought about the war, who suffered in popular opinion, it was the good fortune of Mr. Lowndes, from his diligence as chairman of the Naval Committee of the House, and his identification thereby, as it were, with the navy itself, to increase his reputation and strengthen the favor in which his name was held.

On the 4th of December, 1815, Mr. Lowndes was placed at the head of the Committee of Ways and Means. He served as its chairman for three years, and until he staid away from Washington, in November, 1818, in order to avoid reappointment, not taking his seat until the second week of the session.‡

He voted for the reëstablishment of the United States Bank when the measure was carried by the Republican adoption of the Federal argument that it was a necessary financial instrument of the government. Few questions have produced such violent controversy. The first bank had only received the approval of Washington, when the federal party was prepared to

* Annual Register, vol. 57, p. 123.
† Ibid, p. 124.
‡ Memoirs J. Q. Adams, iv. p. 174.

pass it over his veto.* The Republican party which had abolished it as unconstitutional, were subsequently led by the embarrassments of the government during the war, the disorder of the currency, and the difficulty of taxation, to reverse their opinions and to regard its restoration as indispensable. At a later period, Mr. Lowndes, who had constantly supported the bank, defended its refusal to redeem the notes of one branch at any other,—wherever the holder might choose to present them,—and reviewed the whole subject of banking and exchange after a long study of the subject in a speech which was widely reprinted by the public journals. During the whole period of his service upon the Ways and Means, he was most diligent in committee, constant in attendance in the House, and a participant in every important debate.

On the 16th of October, 1816, he was invited by Madison to become a member of his cabinet as Secretary of War, but declined the honor. In the following year he was again offered by President Monroe the War portfolio, but he preferred his position as the leader of the House, and it was given, on his second declination of it, to Calhoun. The President's letter to Mr. Lowndes upon this subject has been preserved. It is interesting, since it serves to clearly indicate the considerations which formerly governed the selection of the cabinet. It reads :

Confidential.   WASHINGTON, MAY 31, 1817.
DEAR SIR :
    Having manifested my desire to draw into the administration, citizens of distinguished merit from each great section of the Union, and Governour Shelby who was appointed Secretary of War from the State of Kentucky having declined the appointment, I consider myself at liberty to look to other parts for aid, from those best qualified to afford it. On you my attention has in consequence been fixed, and I beg you to be assured that your acceptance of that office will be highly gratifying to me from personal as well as public considerations. As I am about to leave the city and shall be absent some time, I will thank you to be so good as to transmit your answer to me under cover of Mr. Rush, who will forward it to me.
    I am, dear Sir, with great respect and esteem,
                        Your Obd't Sv't,
                            (signed)   JAMES MONROE.

Mr. Lowndes also refused the mission to France, and again, a year later, the choice of the special missions to Constantinople and St. Petersburgh, which President Monroe, after consultation with John Quincy Adams, then Secretary of State, had offered to him.†

In 1818, he spoke almost every week of the session upon a great variety of subjects, and never failed to command the undivided attention of the House. On the 30th of January, 1819, he reviewed the whole subject of the Seminole War, and the course pursued by General Jackson in Florida, in a long but close reasoned speech, taking the ground that if Congress were to suppress its disapprobation of the occupation of St. Marks and Pensacola, it would not serve to raise in any way the military character of General Jackson, but that it would impair its own character, its reputation and its dignity. He was chairman of the Committee on Coins and on Weights and

---

* Letter of James Madison to William Lowndes.
† Memoirs of J. Q. Adams, vol. v. p. 77.

Measures, and made upon these subjects numerous and elaborate notes, which show his thorough method of work in the preparation of reports to the House. He had, however, for a long time, over-tasked himself, and was obliged to leave Washington in the spring of 1819, suffering greatly from exhaustion. By the advice of his physicians he sought restoration to health in the entire relaxation of a sea voyage, and, on landing at Liverpool, received the thoughtful, cordial, and generous welcome of an English gentleman, from the historian of the Medici, Mr. Roscoe. Intent upon self-improvement and knowledge, he remained at Liverpool until he had studied and recorded in his note-book everything which struck his curious and active mind. He found in the docks, the system of labor, the workshops, the commercial regulations, both of statute and local enactment, subjects worthy of careful examination and study, to be afterwards made available in the committee rooms of the Capitol.

He met, on one occasion, at Liverpool, a gentleman with whom he had a long conversation, and, under the English custom of intercourse without introduction, they separated without receiving it. Mr. Lowndes had so impressed himself upon the other, that the latter went immediately to Mr. Roscoe and inquired who the stranger was, describing him as the tallest man he had ever seen, the most unassuming he had ever met, and, certainly, the man of the greatest intellect he had ever heard speak. " It is the great American Lowndes you have been talking with; come and dine with me to-morrow, and I will introduce you to him." [*]

The journey to London gave him an opportunity to observe the agriculture of the midland counties. He visited Newmarket, went through the stables, and wrote down in his note-book everything he could learn about the care and improvement of horse-flesh, which he thought could be usefully adopted on his own side of the Atlantic. At London, he took every opportunity to visit the House of Commons, making the acquaintance of the parliamentary leaders, and watching their conduct of public business. On his departure from London he went directly to Paris, and there dined with Humboldt at Mr. Gallatin's table. He constantly attended the Chamber of Deputies, listened to their debates, and noted in his diary the characteristics of the Chamber, comparing it with the House of Commons. He thought its parliamentary rules well planned, and the French method of arresting debate by a direct vote to close the discussion seemed to him an improvement upon our own rule of the previous question. He travelled through France and Northern Italy, and returned to London after a tour through Holland and Belgium. Remaining but a short time in England on his way home, he took his seat on the 8th of December, two days after the assembly of the Sixteenth Congress. He received on the same day the appointment of chairman of the Committee on Foreign Affairs. On the 22d of February, 1820, he introduced a resolution, which was unanimously adopted, to authorize the report of a bill to confer upon the family of Commodore Perry the same pension that they would have been entitled to receive had Perry fallen in the battle of Lake Erie, instead of surviving for a few short years to die of yellow fever at Port Spain. Mr. Lowndes's speech on this occasion was written out by him on the evening after its delivery, at the request of his friend the Hon. Nathaniel Silsbee, of Massachusetts. It is noticeable as the only speech of the long series, comprehending every question of the

---

[*] " Reminiscences and Sketches," by E. S. Thomas, i. p. 103. The author gives this anecdote on the authority of Mr. Roscoe himself.

time, which he delivered during his congressional career, that ever received any revision at his hands.* As soon as the question upon the resolution had been put after he resumed his seat, John Randolph of Roanoke arose, to offer another resolution, the basis of the subsequent act, which provided not only for the support of Perry's family, but also for the education of his children. His remarks, very characteristic of the man and strongly put, were prefaced by these opening words of compliment,—a thing rare at any time from him,—to Mr. Lowndes. "Mr. Speaker, I believe it will prove a very difficult undertaking for any member of this House to keep pace with the honorable gentleman from South Carolina in the race of honor and public utility. It is certainly not possible for me to do so, for I have already been anticipated in a proposition which I desired to make to-day, because it is one eminently fit to introduce on this anniversary so inspiring to patriotic emotions."

Mr. Lowndes spoke at this session on the Missouri Compromise, against Mr. Clay's resolutions on the Spanish treaty, and in opposition to the revision of the Tariff. When Mr. Clay resigned the speakership, at the opening of the second session in November, 1820, Mr. Lowndes became the candidate of his party against Mr. John W. Taylor, of New-York. At the close of the ballot on the second day of the session he lacked but one vote of an election. Fourteen votes had been diverted by the candidacy of Gen. Smith, of Maryland, "a man ruined in fortune and reputation, yet who commanded votes enough," as John Quincy Adams recorded in his diary on the evening of that day, "to defeat the election of Lowndes, a man of irreproachable character, amiable disposition and popular manners."

Mr. Taylor was chosen Speaker on the next ballot, and on the 23d of November, Mr. Lowndes, who had been appointed chairman of the select committee on the proposed constitution of Missouri, reported a bill for her admission to the Union. Its consideration was set down for the 6th of December, and the whole country awaited the debate with a deeper interest than it had given to any subject since the adoption of the constitution. It was the first great encounter on the question of slavery, and the South, more distinguished then in the superior weight and character of her delegations in the House, than at any other period of her long supremacy—if we accept the recorded opinion of him, then, too, illustrious in every branch of the public service, yet destined to attain his own most enviable honors years afterwards in that House as the worthiest champion of the North—the South, grasping the situation with the keenest comprehension of its magnitude, entrusted the presentation and management of her cause to Mr. Lowndes, the wisest since he was the most moderate of all her public men.

Of his speech, in opening the debate, there is left to us in the annals of Congress only an insufficient abstract. His opening sentences were lost to the official reporters of the House, as Mr. Benton tells us in his note upon the speech, by the movement of representatives from every part of the chamber, as they hurriedly changed their seats to get near the speaker, and catch every word that fell from his lips, "Mr. Lowndes being one of those so rare in every assembly around whom members clustered when he rose to speak, that not a word should be lost where every word was luminous with intelligence and captivating with candor. This clustering around him, always the case with Mr. Lowndes when he rose to speak, was

* Abridgment of Debates, vol. vii. p. 346.

more than usually eager on this occasion from the circumstances under which he spoke ;—the Union verging to dissolution, and his own condition verging to the grave." *

The debate lasted through the winter, and it was not till the 28th of February, 1821, that the State of Missouri was conditionally admitted to the Union, and the second Missouri question compromised like the first.†

During the greater portion of the winter Mr. Lowndes was confined to his residence by severe illness, the premonition of the end to come two years later. The management of the Missouri question, owing to his inability to attend the House, was entrusted by him to Mr. Clay, who frequently conferred with him in his chamber in regard to it. The compromise became thus the work, as it was the fortunate opportunity of Henry Clay. He availed himself of the weakness of the Northern position to undermine it, and dissension was, for a few years, allayed. Mr. Lowndes spoke but rarely after his recovery, once or twice when able to attend the House on some point in the Missouri debate, and once in favor of an inquiry into the Bankrupt Laws. He was under medical observation during the summer of 1821, and rallied somewhat before he returned to Washington, which was not until the 21st of December, nearly three weeks after the opening of the Seventeenth Congress, having once more kept away at the organization of the House to avoid the chairmanship of a committee. In the last week of December, at a caucus of the Legislature of South Carolina, he received its nomination for the Presidency. This movement of his native state was an entire surprise to him. His answer, which passed into a proverb, and was destined to be the speech by which he will be longest remembered, is best given in a letter to his wife, written at Washington, 6th January, 1822. " You have heard of the caucus nomination at Columbia. I hope you have not set your mind too strongly on being President's lady. While you wish only a larger fence for the poultry yard, and a pond for the ducks, I may be able to gratify you, but this business of making a President either of oneself or of another I have no cunning at. We live in a terrible confusion. I thought when I came here the question was a fact confined to two persons, Mr. Crawford and Mr. Adams. Now, we have all the secretaries and at least two who are not to be named. As to the answer which I have made to the notification, here it is : ' I have taken no step and never shall to draw the public attention upon me as a competitor for the Presidency. It is not in my opinion an office to be either solicited or declined.' "

Mr. Lowndes served at this session on the Committee on the Mint and the Coinage, and spoke for the last time in Congress on the 22d of March, 1822, on a resolution authorizing an exchange of government bonds.

He continued to decline in vigor, under the debilitating influence of disease and the method of treatment adopted in his case. The strength of the overworked statesman at length gave way entirely. He resigned in the autumn his seat in Congress, and sailed in October in the ship Moss, from Philadelphia. Accompanied by his wife and daughter, he hoped to find, in a longer absence from home, and in the choice of climate which Europe afforded, restoration of health. It was not thus to be. He grew rapidly worse, and died on the 27th of October, when he had been but nine days at sea. The news of his death, which occasioned universal concern and sorrow,

---

* Abridgment of Debates, vol vii. p. 12.
† Memoirs of J. Q. Adams, vol. v. p. 307.

did not reach the United States till the 11th of January, 1823. Ten days later, on the 21st of the month, the House of Representatives, of which, at his death, he was not a member, and in which James Hamilton, Jr. already sat as his successor, passed the same resolutions of respect to his memory, and of mourning for his loss, which they would have done had he fallen like the second Adams upon its floor. The eulogies upon him of Hamilton, and Archer, and Taylor are among the most beautiful of such efforts. Hamilton declared that his wisdom was equalled only by his moderation, that he had less self-love and more self-denial than any other man he had known. Archer described his character as one in which the qualities that win esteem were blended in the happiest way with those that command it. Taylor, of New-York, affirmed that the highest and best hopes of the country had looked to William Lowndes for their fulfilment, that the Chief Magistracy would have been illustrated by his virtues and talents. "During nine years," said Mr. Taylor, "I have served with him on many important committees, and he never failed to shed new light on all the subjects to which he applied his vigorous and discriminating mind. To manners the most unassuming, to patriotism the most disinterested, to morals the most pure, to attainments of the highest order in literature and science, he added the virtues of decision and prudence so happily combined, so harmoniously united, that we knew not which most to admire, the firmness with which he pursued his purpose, or the gentleness by which he disarmed opposition. You, Mr. Speaker," he concluded, "will remember his zeal in sustaining the cause of our country in the darkest days of our late war. You cannot have forgotten—who that heard him can ever forget the impression of his eloquence in announcing the resolutions of thanks to the gallant Perry for the victory on Lake Erie? Alas! Alas! the statesman has joined the hero,—never—never again shall his voice be heard in this Hall."

Said the National Intelligencer of the following day: "The tribute, which was yesterday paid to the memory of the lamented William Lowndes, is as honorable to the feeling of the House as it is to the memory of the deceased. The brief addresses, delivered on the occasion, were such as worthily became the speakers, and never perhaps was eulogy more justly or more disinterestedly bestowed."

For the period of one month, in accordance with their resolution, the House wore, as a badge of mourning, crape upon the left arm. This action, which had been without precedent in the annals of the House, has served as its example since that time, on the few occasions that the House has been called upon to pay especial honor to the memory of a great citizen who was not at the time of his death a member of their own body.

Not less deep and earnest than the tributes of the House were the later words of Mr. R. H. Wilde, subsequently Professor of the University of Louisiana, in his "Sketches of Members of the Fourteenth Congress."

"Preëminent, yet not more proudly than humbly preëminent among them was a gentleman from South Carolina, now no more: the purest, the calmest, the most philosophical of our country's modern statesmen, one no less remarkable for gentleness of manners and kindness of heart than for that passionless unclouded intellect which rendered him deserving, if ever man deserved it, of merely standing by and letting reason argue for him. The true patriot, incapable of all self-ambition, who shunned office and distinction, yet served his country faithfully because he loved her,—he, I mean, who consecrated by his example the noble precept so entirely his own, that the first station in the Republic was neither to be sought after nor declined, a sentiment so just and so happily expressed that it continues to be repeated because it cannot be improved."

Nor is the deliberate opinion of the graver historian less warm. Benton, who said of Mr. Lowndes, that his opinion had a weight never exceeded by that of any other American statesman, who wrote at a period when almost all who had ever served with him in Congress had passed away, and whose personal acquaintance with him had been but slight, since he commenced his own long career at the time that declining health had led to Mr. Lowndes's resignation, devotes to his character and influence one of the opening chapters of his work.

"All that I saw of him confirmed the impression of the exalted character which the public voice had ascribed to him. Virtue, modesty, benevolence, patriotism, were the qualities of his heart; a sound judgment, a mild, persuasive elocution were the attributes of his mind; his manners gentle, natural, cordial, and inexpressibly engaging. He was one of the galaxy, as it was well called, of the brilliant young men whom South Carolina sent to the House of Representatives at the beginning of the war of 1812,— Calhoun, Cheves, Lowndes,—and was soon the brightest star in that constellation. * * * He was the moderator as well as the leader of the House, and was followed by its sentiment in all cases in which inexorable party feeling or some powerful interest did not rule the action of the members, and even then he was courteously and deferentially treated. It was so the only time I ever heard him speak,—session of 1820–21, and on the inflammable subject of the admission of the State of Missouri. His death was a public and national calamity."*

When Mr. Clay was asked, towards the close of his long life, by Colonel John Lee, of Maryland, who, of all the public men he had known, was in his opinion the greatest, he replied that it was difficult to decide among the many whom he had been associated with, but, said he, " I think the wisest man I ever knew was William Lowndes."

Ex-President Van Buren, towards the end of that work which occupied his later years, and which he did not live to see published,† in speaking of the protective system, which had its origin in the prolific mind of Hamilton, says: " The enforcement of Hamilton's recommendations was reserved for the close of the war of 1812, a period of which I have already spoken as one which brought on the political stage a new class of Presidential aspirants, members of a succeeding generation and unknown to Revolutionary fame. Among the most prominent of these stood Crawford, Clay, Calhoun, Adams, Webster and Lowndes,—the latter, perhaps, the most likely to have succeeded, if his useful life had not been brought to a premature close."

Such are some of the opinions given of this most highly gifted man. He was a descendant, let it be here said, of the same family as was his distinguished namesake, William Lowndes, Secretary of the Treasury to Queen Anne. This statesman, the author of the British funding system, rose to influence of the first rank by service upon the Committee of Ways and Means in the House of Commons. By a curious and striking coincidence, a century later, the subject of our sketch, as chairman of a similar committee in the House of Representatives, earned the same designation in the annals of the

---

* Benton. " Thirty years View," vol. i. pp. 9, 10, 15.
† " Political Parties in the United States," pp. 415–16.

United States that the other had won as the " Ways and Means Lowndes " of the Parliamentary History of England, and thus, long ago, there sprang from the old manor house of Legh Hall in Cheshire, offshoots of that family, which had been even then long associated with its walls, that were destined to carry in after time their common name high into the councils of each of the great families of the English race.

To the student of the constitutional history of the United States, the life and character of William Lowndes, although it may be utterly forgotten among the people, will always have a peculiar interest from the numerous possibilities which associate themselves with it and which were extinguished at his death. He was called " an old statesman " by the press, and yet he was but forty when he died. He had never served the country but as a member of the lower House of Congress, rejecting in turn the summons of Madison and Munroe to their cabinets, and the offers of three foreign missions, yet it is safe to say that the Union has never, in this the first century of its independence, lost another statesman of his age who made so deep an impression upon its affection and judgment, and who left so enviable a fame. His last public act, as it might be called, such is the temper of the Republic towards all who have incurred her suspicion of unduly striving for the Presidency, and in such sharp contrast was his attitude to that assumed by his three great contemporaries, Webster, Clay, and Calhoun,—the dignified position he took in reference to his nomination,—won for him a feeling of personal admiration, even from his opponents, which was expressed long afterwards in conversation and private correspondence whenever his character and attainments were the subject of affectionate and interesting reminiscence.

The personal appearance of Mr. Lowndes was remarkable; for his stature exceeded six feet and six inches, and he was as slender as he was tall. Though loose limbed he managed his length easily. His features were large, while the face was thin, long and pale. He was habitually grave and thoughtful, and never relaxed into idle conversation or even social raillery, yet—*comitate condita gravitas*—he was neither solemn nor severe, and his smile, though rare, was said to be inexpressibly engaging. His habitual seriousness was relieved by the presence of his children, and he was always cheerful when they were with him or came to be tossed in his long arms. Present or absent, says Mr. Grayson, they were objects of tender solicitude. He found time to correspond with them even during the labors attendant upon a session of Congress, and watched their progress as evidenced by their letters. He urged them to be diligent by appeals to their filial affection rather than to their desire of emulation. His manners and address were full of dignity, and he was as invariably courteous in private life as he was in his public career. How distinctively he may be said to have earned his public reputation for these qualities we have already seen, yet it is well to notice the valuable opinion of the distinguished historian of the Abolition Party, the late Vice-President of the United States, who speaks of Mr. Lowndes " as one of the ablest and certainly one of the most courteous and moderate Southern statesmen."*

While sought in society by its most conspicuous members, and honored by the friendship of his elders in years and station, he was always a peculiar favorite of men and women younger than himself. He had from natural modesty rather than from cultivation that faculty of deferent attention to

---

* " Rise and Fall of the Slave Power," by Henry Wilson, i. p. 158.

others which wins in social intercourse at once confidence and regard. The late Mr. John Ravenel sometimes told the following anecdote in illustration of the attachment Mr. Lowndes inspired among young people:—Mr. Ravenel was the pupil of a Major Wilson, a surveyor, and had been sent by him into the neighborhood of El Dorado, the estate of General Thomas Pinckney. He was at once asked by the General to his house. A youth and a stranger, he felt and perhaps betrayed something of natural embarrassment incidental to his position in the company at General Pinckney's table, when a tall gentleman, who was entirely unknown to him, engaged his attention, and delighted him by the charm of his manner, and by his agreeable conversation. He soon learned that the tall gentleman was his host's son-in-law, and the leader of the congressional delegation of his State.[*] As he was considerate and attentive to others, he was modest in his own share of conversation; and, while insensibly guiding it, never took the exclusive control which would so often have been willingly accorded him. Conversation in his presence never became monologue. He was in no sense disputatious, and talked for the sake of truth and not for victory. Whether in the drawing-room, in committee, or in the House, he never became heated nor vehement, but turned an angry disputant by calm remark and gentle manner.

When once asked by a gentleman long noted for colloquial skill, what but failure would be the fate of the American Republic; what would be the condition of things when there came to be more than thirty states; how could faction be controlled, where could safeguards be found in a democracy to protect the liberties of the people, Mr. Lowndes, to whom it would have been easy as one hopeful of the Union to reply in "glittering generalities," quietly observed, "That the people of that future time would be so much better informed than he could be of the evils approaching and their remedies, that he was entirely content to leave the whole subject for them to examine and arrange."

Without despising popular opinion, he placed no great value either on its praise or its censure, and was entirely undisturbed by the occasional attacks of party journals. It was Mr. Rutledge who related of him the story that once, while on a journey with Mr. Lowndes through Pennsylvania, they stopped a short time at a village, and that a stranger to them in the hotel, who seemed to be a prominent character in the town, after listening to their conversation, came up to Mr. Lowndes and asked him as a favor to run his eye over a communication he had prepared for the country newspaper and give him the benefit of his corrections. Mr. Lowndes, on reading the article, found it to be an attack upon the administration and its leading supporters, and especially virulent upon himself. He corrected and returned the paper without intimating who he was, and then asked the writer what reason he had for abusing Mr. Lowndes. "None at all," was the reply, "but I don't believe any man ever possessed so many good qualities as are imputed to him by all parties."[†] From this slight incident we may infer his estimate of popular censure and applause.

His oratory was easy, unaffected, and refined in manner. It made a deep impression upon his audience by its contrast with the more florid style of the period in which he lived. In the State House at Columbia he was always heard with profound attention. His manner was calm and persuasive, his action subdued, his style clear and flowing, his voice good but not strong. He made no questionable rhetorical flights, but seemed to the

---

* Mr. F. J. Grayson.   † Ibid.

listener to be animated solely with the desire to ascertain and enforce the truth. He was remarkable in debate for a candor that never failed to see and acknowledge the strength of an opponent's argument. He would freely admit what an inferior mind would have striven only to elude, and would always concede all that his adversary's argument could demand. His practice in debate was to state at the outset, fully and clearly, the strong points of the speech to which he had risen to reply. Mr. Alfred Huger related that, on some occasions, Mr. Lowndes would put his adversary's argument with such force that his own friends would become alarmed lest he might fail to pull down what he had so firmly erected. The fear was needless, even on the occasion when John Randolph of Roanoke, who was opposed to him, had declared aloud on the floor of the House, as Mr. Lowndes went on, that the speaker had entrapped himself and would never answer his own argument. Mr. Randolph, however, at the end of the speech, admitted that he had been mistaken.

Fortunate as Mr. Lowndes was in his public career, he was not the less happy in his private relations. No censure ever assailed his domestic life, for he was known of all men to be pure.

Mr. Lowndes married, ———, 1802, Elizabeth-Brenton, daughter of General Thomas Pinckney.* By this lady, who died in July, 1857, Mr. Lowndes had :

    i. RAWLINS,[8] b. 1804 ; m. ———, 1827, Emma-Raymond Hornby, and died *s. p.* ———, 1834.

18. ii. THOMAS-PINCKNEY,[8] b. Oct. —, 1808.

    iii. REBECCA-MOTTE,[8] b. ———, 1810 ; m. June 16, 1829, to Edward-L. Rutledge, of the Navy, and has issue :

        i. HARRIOTT-HORRY,[9] m. ———, 1851, St. Julien-Ravenel, and has issue :

            i.   *Harriott-Rutledge,*[10] b. 1852.
            ii. *Anna-Eliza,*[10] b. 1853.
            iii. *John,*[10] b. 1856.
            iv. *Elizabeth-Rutledge,*[10] b. 1857.
            v. *Edward-Rutledge,*[10] b. 1859.
            vi. *St.-Julien,*[10] b. 1861.
            vii. *Frances-Gualdo,*[10] b. 1865.
            viii. *Francis-Gualdo,*[10] b. 1869.
            ix. *Helen-Lowndes,*[10] b. 1872.

        ii. ELIZABETH-PINCKNEY,[9] b. 1842 ; died in infancy.

12. RAWLINS[8] LOWNDES, now the senior representative of the family which has been the subject of this sketch, was educated at the United States Military Academy at West Point, which he entered August 31, 1816. He was graduated 1st July, 1820, and promoted in the Army to the rank of 2d Lieutenant, Corps of Cavalry. He was stationed at Fort Moultrie in the winter of 1820, and was on topographical duty in 1821, in the valley of the Missouri, at that time a pathless waste of prairie. He was appointed Aide-

---

* Thomas Pinckney was born in Charleston, 23d October, 1750. The child of wealthy parents, he received a thorough classical education in England. He was conspicuous at the outbreak of the Revolution, and on the assumption by Gates of the command of the Southern Army was appointed his aide. When the army was defeated at the battle near Camden, Major Pinckney, whose leg had been shattered by a musket ball, was taken prisoner. He succeeded General Moultrie as Governor of South Carolina in 1787. In 1792 he received the appointment of Minister Plenipotentiary to Great Britain, and in 1794 was sent with the same rank to Spain to treat in reference to the navigation of the Mississippi. In 1800 he was chosen Member of Congress. At the commencement of the second war with England, Dearborn, having received the appointment of Commander-in-Chief, and been assigned to the Northern Army, Pinckney was commissioned as Major General and placed in command of the Southern Department. At the end of the war he retired to his plantation, El Dorado, where he died on the 2d of November, 1828.

de-Camp, with the rank of Major, to Brevet-Major General Gaines, July 1, 1821, and remained on the staff of this officer till Dec. 31, 1830, when he resigned from the army, and returned to Carolina.

Here at his plantation, The Strip, on the North Santee River, for a period of thirty years, Major Lowndes resided during a portion of each year, returning to his town residence in New-York in the spring. In 1860, having purchased a small estate on the east bank of the Hudson, near to and between the old family seats of the Livingston family, into which he had married, he gave up his town residence, and, a few months later, in April, 1861, was forced to abandon his Carolina estate to swift destruction from neglect and the plunder of marauders, when the sea coast of the state became the scene of active war.

Since the year 1861, Major Lowndes has resided upon the Hudson River. He married, October 24, 1826, Gertrude-Laura, daughter of Maturin Livingston and Margaret Lewis his wife, only daughter and heiress of Morgan Lewis,* a Major General in the Army in the last war with England, son of Francis Lewis, a Signer of the Declaration of Independence, and by her has issue:

    i. JULIA-LIVINGSTON,[9] m. May 19, 1853, William-Augustus James, of Lynwood, near Rhinebeck-on-Hudson, and had issue:
        i. WILLIAM-LOWNDES,[10] b. June 1, 1855.
    Mrs. James died January 26, 1875.
    ii. MARY-LIVINGSTON,[9] m. January 31, 1855, John-Pyne March, son of the late Charles March, of Greenland, New-Hampshire. By her husband, who died November 25, 1873, she had issue:
        i. CHARLES,[10] b. September 23, 1856.
        ii. CLEMENT,[10] b. November 21, 1862.
    iii. GERTRUDE-LEWIS,[9] b. September 22, 1833; d. October 26, 1834.
    iv. ANNE,[9] m. George-B. Chase, of Boston [Harv. Coll. 1856], son of the late Theodore Chase, of Portsmouth, New-Hampshire, and afterwards of Boston, and has issue:
        i. STEPHEN,[10] b. January 30, 1863.
        ii. GERTRUDE-LOWNDES.[10]
    v. HARRIETT-LOWNDES,[9] m. April 27, 1859, Eugene Langdon, son of the late Walter Langdon, of Portsmouth, New-Hampshire, and has issue:

* Upon the east wall in St. James's Church, Hyde-Park-on-Hudson, N. Y., there is a mural tablet with this inscription:

To the Memory of
Major General MORGAN LEWIS,
Younger son of
Francis Lewis,
A Signer of the Declaration of Independence:
Born in New York, Oct. 16, 1754,
Died April 7, 1844.
In 1775, he enlisted as a volunteer in the army investing Boston.
In 1777, he served under General Gates, as Chief of his Staff,
and received the surrender of Burgoyne.
He conducted the retreat from Ticonderoga,
led the advance at Stone Arabia,
and was in active service till the close of the war.
In 1783, he commenced the practice of the Law,
and became Attorney General, Chief Justice, and
Governor of his Native State.
Under his administration the foundation was laid for our public school fund.
In 1812, as Major General, he served through the second war.
He was, for many years, Senior Warden of this Church,
and at the period of his death, was President of the Cincinnati,
and Grand Master of the Masons.
Warned by advancing years, with a mind unimpaired,
He retired from public life to the quiet of his family,
Where living and beloved, he went down to the grave
In a good old age, and in the fulness of honors.

i. MARION.[10]   ii. ANNE-LOWNDES.[10]

Mr. Langdon died Februrary 22, 1866. Mrs. Langdon m. second, November 2, 1872, Philip Schuyler, of New-York.

13. THOMAS[8] LOWNDES was graduated at Harvard College, 1824 ; m. February 12, 1828, Allen, daughter of Henry and Margaret Deas, of Charleston, by whom he had issue:

i. HENRY,[9] b. January 29, 1829.   ii. SARAH-ION.[9]

iii. THOMAS,[9] b. September 26, 1842 ; d. 18—.

Mr. Lowndes died July 8, 1833.

14. WILLIAM-PRICE[8] LOWNDES, educated at New-Haven, and afterwards at Columbia College, South Carolina ; m. October 30, 1833, Susan-Mary-Elizabeth, daughter of Maturin and Margaret (Lewis) Livingston, of Staatsburgh, New-York, who died in New-York, February 10, 1875. By her he had issue :

i. MARGARET,[9] m. June 6, 1865, Edward-Henry Costar, of the City of New-York, and has issue.

ii. FRANCIS-LEWIS,[9] b. August 8, 1837 ; now a Councillor-at-Law, of the City of New-York.

iii. WILLIAM,[9] b. August 1, 1843 ; m. May 22, 1875, Katherine-Grant, daughter of Daniel Ransom, of New-York.

15. CHARLES-TIDYMAN[8] LOWNDES, m. December 31, 1829, Sabina-Elliott, daughter of Daniel-Elliott and Isabella Huger, by whom he had issue :

i. DANIEL-HUGER,[9] b. February 27, 1832 ; d. August 1, 1832.

ii. DANIEL-HUGER,[9] b. June, 1833 ; d. January 9, 1835.

iii. MARY-HUGER,[9] m. Edward-Laight Cottenet, of New-York, and has issue.

iv. RAWLINS,[9] b. July 23, 1838 ; m. ———, Sarah, daughter of General John-S. Preston, of Virginia, now a resident on the family estate, Oaklands Parish of St. Bartholomew's, South Carolina.

v. SABINA-HUGER,[9] m. William-Harleston Huger, M.D., of Charleston.

vi. EMMA-HUGER.[9]

16. RICHARD-HENRY[8] LOWNDES, entered the Navy in 1831, served on the Brazils in the Lexington, as Aide to Com. A.-J. Dallas, in the Constellation, and as Aide to Com. Hull, in the Ohio, when flag-ship of the Mediterranean Squadron. Mr. Lowndes resigned in 1842. He m. Nov. 10, 1845, Susan-Middleton Parker, daughter of John and Emily (Rutledge) Parker, of Charleston, and has issue :

i. CAROLINE,[9] m. Nov. 10, 1870, Dominic-Lynch Pringle, son of the Hon. John-Julius and Jane [Lynch] Pringle, and by him has issue.

ii. RICHARD-ION,[9] b. Dec. 13, 1847 ; m. Nov. 15, 1870, Alice-Izard, dau. of Ralph-Izard and Charlotte-Georgina [Izard] Middleton, and has issue :

i. WILLIAM,[10] b. Aug. 10, 1872.

iii. EMILY-RUTLEDGE,[9] m. Nov. 7, 1874, Charles-Petigru Allston, son of the Hon. R.-F.-W. and Adele (Petigru) Allston, and by him has issue.

iv. WILLIAM-AIKEN,[9] b. April 20, 1856 ; d. April 23, 1863.

17. EDWARD-RUTLEDGE[8] LOWNDES, m., 1833, Mary-Lucia Guerard, and by her had issue :

i. JAMES,[9] b. Jan. 6, 1835 ; was graduated at South Carolina College, Dec. 1854, and afterward a student at Heidelburg. Councillor-at-Law ; served on the staff of the Confederate Army ; resumed the practice of the law as partner of the Hon A. G. Magrath, in Charleston, in 1866 ; now a member of the bar of the District of Columbia, and resides at Washington.

ii. EDWARD,[9] b. 1836 ; m. Celestina Fuller, and had :

i. EDWARD-RUTLEDGE.[10]   ii. RAWLINS.[10]   iii. ALICE.[10]

iii. MARY-LUCIA.[9]   iv. EMILY.[9]   v. ELIZABETH.[9]   vi. SOPHIA-PERCY.[9]

vii. JULIA,[9] m. William Hamilton. viii. MARY-RUTH.[9]
ix. CATHERINE-HAMILTON.[9]

Mr. Lowndes died 1853.

18. THOMAS-PINCKNEY[8] LOWNDES, m. ———, 1829, Margaret-M., daughter of William and Martha (Blake) Washington, of Charleston, and granddaughter of Colonel William Washington, of the Revolutionary Army. By whom he had:

    i. JANE-WASHINGTON,[9] m. May 18, 1854, Robert-William Hume, and has issue:
        i. MARY-MORSE,[10] b. 1858.
        ii. MARGARET-LOWNDES,[10] b. 1859.
        iii. WILLIAM-LOWNDES,[10] b. 1863.
        iv. JANE-WASHINGTON,[10] b. 1871.
    ii. WILLIAM,[9] b. 1832; d. at Heidelberg, Germany, 1856.
    iii. THOMAS-PINCKNEY,[9] b. Feb. 22, 1839; m. Nov. 9, 1865, Anne-Branford Frost, daughter of the Hon. Edward Frost, of South Carolina, and Harriet-Horry his wife, by whom Mr. Lowndes has issue:
        i. HARRIET-HORRY,[10] b. Oct. 1866.
        ii. MARGARET-WASHINGTON,[10] b. May, 1869.
        iii. WILLIAM,[10] b. Oct. 1871.
        iv. EDWARD-FROST,[10] b. March, 1874.

Mr. Lowndes died in 1838.

Bardsley, in his work on surnames, derives the name of Lowndes from the old English word of launde, which "signified a pretty and rich piece of grassy sward in the heart of a forest, what we should now call an open wood, in fact. Thus it is we term the space in our gardens within the surrounding shrubberies *lawns.*

"Chaucer says of Theseus on hunting bent—

    To the *launde* he rideth him ful right,
    There was the hart wont to have his flight.

"In the 'Morte Arthur,' too, we are told of hunting—

    At the hartes in these hye *laundes.*

"This is the source of more surnames than we might imagine.
"Hence are sprung our 'Launds,' 'Lands,' 'Lowndes,'"* etc.

In a list of ninety-nine wills of persons of this name proved, in the probate court at Chester, between the years 1586 and 1768, the writer found the names variously spelled, viz.: Lounds, Lownes, Lounde, Lowndes, Lound, Lounde, Lownds, Loundes. The first of the spellings here given occurs in the will of Roger Lounds of Sandbach, and the last, which has been the form in general use for now more than a century, is found in that of John Lowndes of Cranage.

ARMS OF RAWLINS LOWNDES, President of South Carolina in 1778. Quarterly of six.

LOWNDES.—Argent fretty azure, on a canton gules a lion's erased, or.
WELD.—Azure, a fesse nebule, between three crescents, ermine.
WETTENHALL.—Vert—a cross engrailed, ermine.
LIVERSAGE.—Argent, a chevron between three plough-shares erect, sable.
WHELOCK.—Argent, a chevron between three catherine wheels, sable.
RAWLINS.†

* "Our English Surnames," by Charles Wareing Bardsley, M.A.
† It has not been possible to ascertain with certainty the seal of the St. Kitts family of this name. In tropical climates wax impressions are rarely used, and can never be preserved. A wafer impression from the seal of Mr. Henry Rawlins is too faint to authorize any description of the arms of his family.

ADDRESS OF THE HON. MARSHALL P. WILDER.

Delivered at the Annual Meeting of the NEW-ENGLAND HISTORIC, GENEALOGICAL
SOCIETY, January 5, 1876.

GENTLEMEN OF THE SOCIETY:

I acknowledge most gratefully the honor conferred on me by the election which has just taken place, nor can I be unmindful of these oft-repeated expressions of your confidence and respect. But when I see around me so many who are entitled to this distinction, I feel, in deference to their long services and eminent qualifications, a delicacy in occupying the chair to their exclusion. But, gentlemen, we have been so long associated together, I shall not rudely sever the official relations which have existed between us, and which have been to me of a most honorable and agreeable character. Nothing, however, would induce me to accept of it again but your assurance that my services are useful, and your pledges of coöperation in the discharge of my duties.

By the reports of the various committees, it will be seen that the Society is in the same flourishing condition as of late years, and that although our income has not been increased the last year, it has been able to meet all its responsibilities by adhering, as before, strictly to the principle of limiting its expenses to its annual receipts. I should not forget to keep before the public the fact that all the duties performed by our officers and committees, with the exception of the Librarian and his assistant, are performed without compensation ; and I cannot disguise the fact that with the constant growth of the Society and the increase of its library, these duties are becoming more and more responsible and arduous ; and, while we would ever remember with a lively sense of gratitude those who contributed to erect this House and to found a library-fund, I trust the day is not far distant, when by bequests or donations the Society may be able to render some compensation for these services, and to place itself in a still higher sphere and on a wider plane of usefulness. Nor can I doubt that with the return of prosperous times, funds will be forthcoming from the numerous friends whose sympathy and interest have been so often manifested in our behalf. The contributions of books, pamphlets, manuscripts and curiosities have been numerous. Of books alone, there have been presented nearly thirteen hundred bound volumes, many of which are quite rare, making this addition to our library more valuable than that of any former years. In this connection I take great pleasure in stating that while writing the foregoing paragraph, I was informed that a lady lately deceased,—a warm friend of the Society, and a subscriber to the

Historical and Genealogical Register,—left by will a bequest of several thousand dollars for the endowment of our library. I reserve to the close of my remarks the formal announcement of the terms of the bequest.[1]

And now in these days of centennial celebrations, let us refer very briefly to the history of our own Society, and thus at the commencement of the second century of the republic, set up another milestone to mark our progress on the road of time. Thirty-one years ago last October, five gentlemen met in this city to counsel together how they could best promote a taste for antiquarian, historical and genealogical research. This resulted in the establishment and incorporation of the NEW-ENGLAND HISTORIC, GENEALOGICAL SOCIETY. Well does Mr. Slafter remark in his admirable discourse in 1870, at the Quarter-Centennial Celebration of this Society: "Our gratitude is due to these five gentlemen who entered into the primary organization, and to them must the honor be accorded of giving form to the idea and method of historical study inaugurated in this Society, and on which its whole fabric has been firmly and persistently reared."

In all new enterprises, the first thing to be done is to create a public sentiment favorable to the object, and this was one of the chief purposes of the founders of this Society. But this was a work of time, and strange as it may now seem, there was, as Mr. Slafter says, "a deep-seated prejudice lurking everywhere in the New-England mind against the cultivation in any degree of ancestral or family history. It was regarded as an infringement upon good taste to speak of our ancestors with any fervent interest, at least beyond the family circle." But thanks to an enlightened age, that false modesty and unnatural regard, has yielded to the higher and nobler sentiment of filial love and reverence for those who have made us what we are. Thus has been wrought out by the influence of this and kindred associations an entire change in the public mind, until the pride of honorable ancestry and a worthy life are referred to as the natural and generic influences of physical, intellectual and moral character.

But while we have these subjects of congratulation in the progress and prosperity of the Society, and the general interest it has awakened in behalf of the objects it seeks to promote, we have other considerations which move the fountains of sorrow and call for our

---

[1] At the close of his address, Mr Wilder read the following letter from Edward Russell, Esq., to Col. Albert H. Hoyt, dated Boston, Jan. 4, 1876:

I herewith send you the extract from the Will of my late wife, Mrs. Mary W. Russell, which relates to her bequest to the New-England Historic, Genealogical Society. It is as follows:

"I give, devise and bequeath to the New-England Historic, Genealogical Society, of Boston aforesaid, the sum of three thousand dollars ($3,000) to constitute a fund, the income of which to be used for the purchase of English county histories and genealogies for the library of said Society, the said three thousand dollars to be paid from the legacy belonging to me, of which Mrs. Cheever Newhall has the income during her natural life."

condolence and sympathy. In my last annual address I stated that the Society had been called during the previous year to mourn the loss of a larger number of those who had held official relations with us than in any year since its organization. Among them were six who had held the office of Vice-President or Honorary Vice-President of the Society. And now I have the sad duty to state that the death-reaper is still at work, and the loss of members the past year has been still greater than in any one year before. During this period we have been called to part with two ex-Presidents, Samuel Gardner Drake, A.M., and Winslow Lewis, M.D.; also with two Vice-Presidents, the Hon. William A. Buckingham, LL.D., of Connecticut, and the Hon. Hampden Cutts, A.M., of Vermont; and one Honorary Vice-President, the Hon. Increase A. Lapham, LL.D., of Wisconsin.

Nor can I stop here. Still another is to be added to the starred roll of worthies which graces our list of deceased members. I refer to our associate member, Henry Wilson, Vice-President of the United States, whose services and official relations with our Commonwealth and country have given to his name an immortality on earth, to whose mortal remains such distinguished honors have been paid as they passed through the capitals of other states to our own, there to receive the universal plaudit of "well done good and faithful servant." Mr. Wilson had won imperishable renown for his integrity of character as a statesman, his sympathy for the oppressed, and will ever be remembered as a blessing to his country and a benefactor to his race. As Moses went up to Nebo Mount there to close his pilgrimage on earth, so Henry Wilson went up to the capital of his nation, where he had labored so many years for the welfare of his country, there to close his mission, there to wrap the drapery of his couch about him and gently fall asleep.

The whole number of deaths for the year 1875, as will be seen by the report of the Historiographer, is thirty-eight. The united ages of these is twenty-seven hundred and forty years and nine months, being an average of seventy-two years, one month and fifteen days, an average of more than two years beyond the bounds of life allotted to man by the inspired Psalmist.

Special notice has been taken with appropriate resolutions and remarks in regard to the decease of Senator Buckingham, Mr. Cutts, Mr. Drake, Dr. Lewis, Dr. Lapham and Mr. Wilson. Memoirs of many of those who have died during the last year have also been read by the Historiographer, the Rev. Samuel Cutler, which, with biographies of members, have been published in the NEW-ENGLAND HISTORICAL AND GENEALOGICAL REGISTER, thus preserving a record of the lives of those who have left us for higher spheres.

Delegations from this Society, with the President and other officers, attended the funerals of Messrs. Drake, Lewis, Wilson, and of other members who had fallen on their way. Since the establishment of our Society in 1845, the number of deaths of members, honorary, corresponding and resident, has been about four hundred and fifty. These have all gone before us.

> " We a little longer wait,
> But how little none can know."

Let us remember, however, with gratitude, that the same Almighty Disposer of events who has removed these friends and co-workers, has spared us to labor together for the advancement of our cause and the benefit and brotherhood of mankind. But time is hurrying us on to our end. Soon the recording angel will inscribe our names with theirs on the roll of eternity, and our mission will be ended. Let us, then, buckle on the harness again, enter the field with more vigor and enterprise, and while we turn over the furrows of research and rake over the ashes of the past, let us see to it that no root of error creeps into our record, so that the harvest which shall be gathered of our sowing, shall enrich the garner of history and add to the general stock of knowledge.

Among the influences which have given prominence and popularity to our institution, there is no one which has, perhaps, operated more favorably to increase its usefulness than the publication of the NEW-ENGLAND HISTORICAL AND GENEALOGICAL REGISTER.

For the last twenty-nine years this has been regularly published. Its volumes constitute a treasury of thought and research, and are everywhere acknowledged as authority in matters pertaining to history and genealogy. With every issue they become more and more valuable, not only to the student, but to every one who takes an interest in the history of the towns and families of New-England, or the biographies of those who have made themselves worthy of remembrance in the annals of our country. Since the creation of the office of Historiographer in 1855, there have appeared in the pages of the Register, memoirs and biographies of nearly three hundred and fifty of our members. It is regarded as one of the great mediums of information on these subjects both at home and in foreign lands; and, as I have before stated, is a monument of the industry of its editors, successive publishing committees, and contributors. And here I desire to acknowledge our obligations to Col. Albert H. Hoyt, for his able, energetic and successful services as editor for the last eight years.

A peculiar interest attaches to the volume of last year. The double number for the month of October contains six national Centennial Orations, namely, those delivered at the Concord and Lexington celebrations on the 19th of April; at Bunker Hill on the 17th of June, and at Cambridge on the 3d of July; together with the addresses of Abner C. Goodell, Jr., our associate member, before the Essex Institute, on the centennial anniversary of the Meeting of the Provincial Legislature in Salem, Oct. 5, 1774, and the address of Henry Armitt Brown at Philadelphia, on the hundredth anniversary of the Meeting of the first Continental Congress, on Sept. 5, 1774. These have also been issued in a separate volume. Its publication confers a benefit on society and an honor on its editor and publishing committee.

What adds permanent value to the Register is the probability that it will continue to be the medium of treasuring up the local and family history of New-England long after its present representatives shall have passed away. It is, therefore, very desirable that every member of our Society should become a subscriber, and thus make its funds commensurate with the magnitude of its work. Its field of labor is constantly enlarging, and were its receipts ample, its operations would be greatly facilitated and its usefulness widely extended. With more patronage its pages could be increased and its contents become more and more interesting.

The question is often raised, "why we attach so much importance to the history of the past? Why all this poring over musty records—this everlasting study and research into the history and traditions of by-gone days? The world will move on, planets will revolve in their destined circuits, and civilized man will adapt himself to the age in which he lives." True, but how little should we have as an impulse to good deeds, or for our guidance in life, were it not for the history and traditions which have come down to us.

And then, there are agencies and forces which Providence has created for the furtherance of his grand designs of progress, and among these the most important are the examples of the great and good, of right and wrong, as expressed in the history of nations and of men. To gather up and preserve a record of all that can be useful, all that is worthy of imitation, either in the past or present time, and to transmit it unimpaired to future generations, is the object and purpose of our own and similar institutions.

Much of the progress of this wonderful age can be traced directly or indirectly to influences which have been transmitted from generations which have preceded us. Many of the wonders of our own time are but repetitions of what has occurred long before, lessons which are handed down for the benefit and government of mankind. The province of history is to treasure up not only the genealogy of men, but all that can be learned from traditions, books, pamphlets, addresses, orations, speeches,—all that can be learned of the lives of men and the customs and relics of former ages, whether they pertain to mind or matter; so that we can present on the living page, or portray on the canvas, all that can be known of the generations of our race, the forces of nature, the dominion of man, the wisdom of the ages, the flight of time.

History embraces not only the genealogies of men and the record of nations, but it secures for all time a record of those wonderful transitions from age to age, those mighty revolutions in the political and moral world, those startling developments of genius and modern research, and those momentous events which control the happiness, peace and perpetuity of the human family. History enlarges the mind, widens the range of human thought, connects the present with the past, holds out a light for the guidance of future generations, proclaiming as with a voice from heaven,—This is the way, walk ye therein.

But to bring these reflections closer home: How little we know in regard to the events which brought to the eyes of the world the discovery of this western continent! True, we have the records of the New Netherlander, the Jamestown, the Plymouth, the Massachusetts Bay, and the neighboring Colonists. How little we know, moreover, of the explorations of the Chinese and the Norsemen in regard to our own land, or even of the later voyages to this continent; and were it not for the research of the explorer and the record of historians, we should have grown but little wiser, and the world but little better for our existence upon it.

But over and above all these considerations, there is the love of country, kindred and home. There is an instinct implanted in the human breast which yearns to know something of by-gone days, something of the source from which we and the objects of our affection were derived; even the untutored Indian has his traditions of ancestry, hunting fields and tents. Thus strongly does the soul sympathise with these objects of its attachment. This sentiment animates the heart of childhood, and growing with our growth and strengthening with advancing years,

> " Maintains its hold with such unfailing sway,
> We feel it e'en in age and at our latest day."

If there is any one sentiment which strikes down deep into the soul, it is the love of family, parent and child,—a love which takes hold of the finest sensibilities of our nature, treasures up with undying affection the memories of the departed, and reaches forward with tender solicitude for the welfare of those that may succeed us. Not to revere the memory of an honorable ancestry, not to profit by the experience of the wise and good; not to treasure up the lessons of patriotism and virtue which have been left us, is to prove unmindful from whence we came, ungrateful for what we are, and regardless of the welfare of mankind. He that has no regard for the record of the past, no interest in the present, and no anxiety for the future, is scarcely to be named as a citizen of the world.

Few can look back to the history of their own lives, family and ancestry, and not discover the elements which have shaped their destiny. "Like produces like" in the moral as well as in the natural world. This is as true of nations as of individuals, as we have seen in the influence of the principles of our fathers upon us. Who can review the history of our American people since the landing of the pilgrim fathers, or even of thē republic for the century now closing upon us, and not perceive the workings of that over-ruling hand which has, through a God-fearing and fearless people, set up this nation as a burning and shining light before the world. And who so perverse as not to discover that the secret of its prosperity is to be found in the influence of those immutable principles of justice and truth, which are the very constituents in the government of God. Other nations had the means of progress long before the discovery of this country; but it was reserved for this blessed land to furnish a new and more perfect civilization than the world ever saw, and for these United States the most free and perfect form of government the world ever knew. Thus the great principle of human right, like the internal fires which make the earth tremble to its centre, is undermining the thrones of the old world, and teaching the sublime philosophy, that "all men are born equal,"—that fealty to conscience is better than submission to power, and that the right of man transcends "the divine right of kings." "This love of religious liberty," says Mr. Webster, "is able to look despotism in the face, and, with means apparently inadequate, to shake principalities and powers. Human invention has devised nothing, human pówer has compassed nothing, that can restrain it."

Among the prominent events of the last year were the several centennial celebrations of our own and other States commemorative of the opening events of the American Revolution. I refer to these that they may have a place in the records of this year's proceedings, standing as we do on the threshold of the second century of the republic, a year which will be ever memorable by the International Exposition at Philadelphia, and the assembling of representatives from our own and other nations of the world in honor of the occasion.

The first of these celebrations took place at Lexington and Concord simultaneously, on the ever-memorable 19th of April, and was signalized with appropriate ceremonies in the presence of the President of the United States, his cabinet and a vast concourse of citizens from all parts of our land. The second occurred in Boston, on the 17th of June, the anniversary of the Battle of Bunker Hill, and was celebrated with a larger procession, display and significance than has perhaps ever been witnessed in this city. The third and immediately succeeding was the observance of July 3, by the citizens of Cambridge, in remembrance of the day when Washington took command of the Continental Army in that place in 1775. In all these celebrations, with the exception of the latter, this Society has been represented by members who have participated in the ceremonies of the occasion. But as these facts, with the full history, have gone into the published proceedings in our REGISTER and the various public journals, no further comment is necessary at this time.

And now, my friends, as we are about entering on another century of our existence as a free nation, let us thank the Giver of all good that he has permitted us to witness the dawning of this glorious year, which is to commemorate the independence of a republic which we believe is to endure while patriotism, philanthropy and religion shall have a place in the hearts of men. When I look back on the history of our country, and the way in which the Lord hath led us, I feel that this land and this nation were designed by Him as examples of that divine providence which ultimately is to emancipate all the nations of the earth and make them " free indeed." When I reflect on that august scene in Independence Hall on the Fourth of July, Seventeen Hundred and Seventy-Six, I feel that no transaction for the welfare of mankind was so transcendant in importance, if we except the law given on Mount Sinai, as that sublime declaration that " all men are created equal."

Could Robinson and Brewster have had but a glimpse of this vast empire, stretching from ocean to ocean, to whose boundaries, population and influence no human power can assign a limit; could Hancock, Adams and those other patriot sires have looked forward with prophetic eye to the Grand Centennial, where on the very spot that gave it birth this Imperial Union should celebrate the grandest epoch in American history, — how would their souls have risen in gratitude to the Ruler of nations, that this republic and its free institutions were to stand as beacon lights for the guidance of the world; that our land was to be the asylum for the down-trodden and oppressed of earth; that our prosperity and power were to stand as the exponents of those great principles which must ever include justice to all, the majesty of law, the freedom of mankind, and the will of God.

True, we have passed through a terrible conflict by the estrangement of some of our brethren, — a conflict which we believe has worked out for this nation a salutary lesson, and is never to return. The cloud that overshadowed our national horizon was, indeed, dark and portentous, but it has retired, gilded by the bow of promise, and refulgent with brighter hopes and firmer faith in the stability and perpetuity of our beloved union. This union we believe will continue to live in the hearts of our people; and that with the lapse of years and the coming of new generations, all the differences and animosities between the North and South will be in the deep bosom of oblivion buried, and all shall rejoice in a nation regenerated, emancipated and sanctified by its afflictions. Our fathers and brothers have labored together for the preservation of the dearest rights of man; hand in hand they wrought out the august problem of self-government and constitutional authority, and shoulder to shoulder they fought to purchase the priceless blessings we enjoy. Let us, then, as brethren of the same household and heirs of this glorious hope, work out for the generations which are to succeed us, a still richer inheritance,—the inheritance of a Union that none can sever. And as we their children go up together from the various sections of this great land to worship at the shrine of American Liberty,—as we go up with other nations to compare the products of the world, to rejoice in the conquest of genius, the rewards of industry, and the blessings of our free institutions,—let us welcome to our shores the representatives of foreign lands, of whatever nation or tongue, as children of the same Heavenly Parent, and heirs to the same privileges we enjoy.

And while we commemorate by the celebrations of this year the grandest step in the history of modern times, while we celebrate the day that gave this nation birth, the first of that cycle of grand centennials, which we hope are in process of time to bless mankind, let us not forget from whose customs, laws and constitutions we have, primarily, derived so much of the spirit and virtue which characterize our institutions. Yes, let us remember, especially, Old England, our mother-land, between whom and her offspring we trust war shall never again rear its bloody crest, with whom the reign of peace has already begun by the arbitration of national differences, and through whom we hope to make the English tongue the messenger of peace and good-will to all mankind. And while we bring together in friendly competition the products of our soil, mines and manufactories, the skill, enterprise and energy of our countrymen, let us also exhibit the influence of our free schools, churches, literary and benevolent institutions, as evidence not only of well-directed industry, but of the blessings which naturally flow from the principles of our government.

Thus shall we show, not only our progress in art, science and government, but clearly demonstrate that the people of these United States were specially commissioned to aid in the advancement of a new civilization on this continent,—a civilization which has conferred on our country an enduring renown,—which will be ever cherished as among the most precious memorials of history, and which will be revered and honored, wherever and whenever the principles of our government shall be made known. How precious the blessings we enjoy! How touching the memorials which our fathers have left us of their patriotism, privations and virtues! Forever hallowed be the day on which the banner of American Freedom was unfurled to the world! Forever cherished in the heart of memory be the recollection of those patriots and martyrs who laid down their lives in defence of human rights! Forever sacred to time and to eternity be the record of those events which gave this nation to the world and these blessings to mankind!

The centennial celebrations which have taken place the past year, and are to be succeeded by others of similar character in various parts of our country, will not only strengthen the bonds of friendship between our own and other nations, but will add greatly to the knowledge of our revolutionary history and of our age, and will hand down to all future time lessons of wisdom, which shall influence the dynasties of the world, promote the welfare of our race, and bring about that millennial day, when all differences shall be settled without the sacrifice of blood, when the communion of christians shall be enjoyed without regard to sect,—

> " When man shall own no monarch
> But justice and his God."

These will be treasured up by our historical societies as among the most precious relics in their archives.   Their record will forever constitute the most valuable encyclopedias of the era they represent, portraying as they will, that spirit of civil and religious freedom which was inherent in the soul of man, far back of the landing of our fathers or the declaration of our independence.

Thus we shall commemorate the First Centennial of the American Republic.   On that day the great heart of this nation will thrill with joy and gratitude as never before.   On that day, from the Atlantic to the Pacific, the flag of our nation, luminous in every thread with the history of our land, not a star fallen or blotted from its union, shall be unfurled from hill top, tower and spire, the emblem of all that is great and good in the past, of all our dearest hopes in the future, the emblem of a free, happy and united people.   On that great day the voice of congregated thousands, like the sound of many waters, shall ascend to the God of nations that he would preserve this people from discord and disunion, and bind these States together in bonds of indissoluble friendship and brotherly love.   On that glorious day the pealing of bells, the booming of cannon, and the shouts of freemen shall echo through this blessed land ; and heaven responsive to earth shall join in the general jubilee of GOOD WILL TO MEN AND FREEDOM FOR THE WORLD !

A YANKEE PRIVATEERSMAN IN PRISON IN ENGLAND, 1777–1779.

Communicated by WILLIAM RICHARD CUTTER, of Lexington, Mass., with Notes.

THE following Journal of the experience of TIMOTHY CONNOR, one of the crew of the brigantine Rising States, taken the 15th of April, 1777, by the Terrible, of 74 guns, and committed to Forton prison the 14th of June, 1777, the first prisoners in that place, —with a roll of men's names, ship and stations, from what state, run, dead, &c.,—has come to light in a pile of my father's old papers. Barring grammatical and orthographical errors, the Journal is as follows :

FORTON GAOL, *June the 15th,* 1777.[1]

I now shall begin to keep a journal and recollect the particulars that have happened since we sailed from Boston; of which I shall take the following particulars, according to the best of my remembrance since I left Boston.

January the 26th, 1777, our brigantine sailed from Boston for Cape Cod, and arrived there the next day. I sailed from Boston the 31st of the same month, myself and eleven more in a fishing boat, in which place we stayed three weeks to get hands, and got a few ; then we weighed and sailed for Casco Bay for the same purpose. Night coming on, the wind hauled ahead. We were obliged to put our ship about. Stood for Cape Cod again, but a heavy snowstorm coming on, we fell to leeward, and were obliged to come to an anchor the outside the island,[2] the storm still continuing, till the next day in the afternoon, when we weighed and sailed for Nantucket.

All this time it snowed, hailed and rained very fast. We fell to leeward on the shoals. The ship struck two or three times, but did no damage. There we were beating for some time, but could not get into the harbor. Our captain called all hands on the quarter deck, to know their minds; whether we had rather beat there, or put the ship before it. It being very cold and blustering weather, we all agreed, as one, to bear away ; the wind being very fair to put to sea. Then, we put her before it, with a fine gale, which soon carried us off the coast of America. We had sixty-two men and boys on board.

February the 24th, we spied a sail on our weather bow, about three leagues distance, for which we made sail, and gave her chase ; and at four o'clock came up with her. She proved to be a topsail schooner, from Virginia, bound to Boston. She gave us an account of nine men of war cruising off the capes of Virginia, and had chased her the day before.[3] We still stood to the eastward, the gale still continuing, with snow and rain and hail, sometimes under close reefed topsails, till we had almost got up to the Western Islands.[4] The 1st of March, at eight in the morning, we had the

---

[1] This date was Sunday, the day following that of the author's committal to the prison at Forton, England, June 14, 1777. with his comrades—including himself, thirty-eight in all— of the crew of the brigantine Rising States, of Massachusetts; the first prisoners—as is stated in the roll appended—in that place. The location of "Forton Gaol" is stated further on in the Journal, under date of June 13-14, 1777—viz.: "about one mile out of town," near Portsmouth, England, the principal naval station of Great Britain on the southern coast. More strictly speaking, Forton is one mile northwest of Gosport, which is on the western side of Portsmouth harbor, and opposite to and separated about a mile from Portsmouth and Portsea by the narrow gut at the entrance. The Gosport Branch of the Southwestern Railway now passes through it. The fine anchorage known by the name of Spithead, lies about half way between Portsmouth and the Isle of Wight, but nearer to the latter.

Dr. Franklin, in his description of Portsmouth in 1726, speaks of its "fine harbor"; entrance "so narrow that you may throw a stone from fort to fort"; yet it is near "ten fathoms deep," and "bold close to"; town "strongly fortified." Gosport "lies opposite to Portsmouth, and is near as big, if not bigger." Spithead is "the place where the fleets commonly anchor, and is a very good riding place."

[2] Nantucket Island, perhaps.

[3] "His Majesty's ships stationed about Chesapeake and Delaware Bays have destroyed or taken, within the space of the two last months, above 70 sail of rebel ships and privateers."—Domestic Intelligence, America, New York, March 24, 1777, *Town and Country Magazine* (London) for 1777, p. 278.

[4] Western Islands, or Azores.

land all around us—Corvo, Flores and Pico—and, by Capt. Thompson's[1] reckoning, he was three degrees to the eastward of them all, and would be mad if any of his officers told him to the contrary. But so it proved, we run down by them all, and went to the northward of St. Mary's and Madeira, and very squally all the while we ran them down. Some days after we had passed these lands, we spoke with several vessels, both French and Spaniards; and as soon as we got in the latitude of the Bay of Biscay, we carried away our foretopmast with our master and mate on the topmast shrouds; both saved, but the master little bruised. We saved the topmast rigging and sails. The next day we got up a new topmast; still blowing very hard to the northward.

March 12th, we fell in with a bark from Whitehaven, bound to Jamaica, Sponsiby, master. We took her about twelve o'clock at night, and boarded her the next morning, when we put Mr. Fuller in her, as prizemaster, and Ingraham, as mate, and sufficient hands to work her. She was ordered into Port L'Orient, in France.

And now the wind got to the eastward, sometimes blowing very hard, and sometimes moderate. March 15th, we carried away our bowsprit home to the bow, with our spritsail, and spritsail-topsail jib and staysail all bent. It was about nine at night, when it was carried away; raining and blowing very hard, when all hands were hard at work in getting the rigging on board.

The next day, employed in splicing the bowsprit, and getting all the rigging out again, but could not carry our spritsails for fear of carrying our bowsprit away the second time.

Still in the Bay of Biscay, April the 3d, we fell in with a brigantine, Fleece, from Lisbon, bound to Cork, laden with wine and salt. We took her, and put on board of her, Mr. Dillaway, as prizemaster, and men sufficient to work her, and sent her for France. A few days after, fell in with another bark from London, bound to Quebec. She mounted sixteen carriage guns. We came up with her just after sundown. She fired a gun to leeward,—a signal for friendship,—but we gave them a broadside, and the cheers. They returned us the compliment, and thus commenced hostilities. Gun for gun was our play. All the damage they did us, was cutting away our foretopsail halliards, and two strands of our mainstay close to the nut. The wind blowing very hard, and a heavy sea which made a continual breach over us, that we could not sight our guns to advantage. The damage done them was by killing the master's mate and boatswain, and wounding one or two more; and a very heavy squall coming up, we lost sight of her in the night.[2]

Still continuing our cruise in the Channel of England, till the 12th of April, when we fell in with a sloop from Lisbon, bound to Southampton, having on board wine and fruit; we took her, and put Mr. Bulfinch on board her as prizemaster (being our first lieutenant), and men sufficient to work her into France. And we proceeded for France, as fast as possible, the wind being to the southward.

[1] James Thompson, captain, brigantine Rising States—see Roll. This officer commanded that vessel when she was taken by the Terrible, April 15, 1777, and was made prisoner and committed to Forton Prison, June 14, 1777, with his men. He effected his escape with others from prison, June 19, 1777, and got safely into France, whence he sent letters afterwards and contributions of money to his less fortunate shipmates. See entries in Journal, for April 15, June 13-14, 19, 23, Aug. 9, Oct. 31, 1777, and March 18, 1778, &c. *Vide* REGISTER, xxvi. 26.

[2] The escape of this vessel was probably instrumental in the capture of the Rising States by a seventy-four, April 15, following.

The next day, the wind shifted to the eastward. We spoke with several French vessels, all bearing for the coast of France. On the 15th of April, about sunrise, we spied a large ship to windward and another astern. This one astern began to make sail after us. We called all hands on deck, to do the same; and making all the sail we could, we found they gained on us; then we began to lighten our ship by throwing eight of our carriage guns overboard, and everything else we came across. When they came within gunshot, they began firing at us their nine-pounders from their forecastle. When some came over us, and some alongside, we knew that we were taken; and that we would not be behind hand in returning the compliment, we got out two of our own stern-chases, and began firing them at the ship. The captain of the ship, enraged at our small ship firing upon him (a seventy-four gun ship), ordered the gunner to get out three eighteen pounders forward, and sink us when we came alongside. But our having English prisoners on board, prevented its being put into execution. We had thirty-seven on board when we were taken, and nineteen prisoners; thus was our situation.

When we were taken, it was by His Majesty's Ship Terrible, of 74 guns, Sir Richard Bickerton, commander.[1] As soon as we had struck, they sent their cutter on board, and ordered Capt. Thompson into the boat, and pushed him off the quarter-deck, and used him very ill. Likewise, carried all of our people, prisoners and all, except Mr. Martin and three boys, who were ordered to stay on board till they arrived at Spithead. Our officers were ordered into the gun-room of the ship, and the men under the half-deck, on three-quarters of allowance, with marine sentinels over us.

The third day after we were taken, which was the 18th of April, the ship began to make the best of her way for Spithead, and standing into the Channel, we had near liked to been lost off the Rocks of Scilly.[2] Our brig being about one half a league ahead, made the first breach in the night, being close on board the rocks, and fired several signal guns, which were answered by our ship, and before we could put our ship about, the brigantine was afoul of our quarter, and carried away our ship's starboard quarter gallery; our ship struck twice, but did no other damage. When we had got clear of the rocks, we stretched away for the westward in Bristol Channel; and took us three days to beat out again, when we met with a gale of wind, and carried our maintopmast by the board, sails all standing, about nine o'clock at night, rained and blowed very hard. The next day, employed about getting up a new topmast, and the rigging overhead; and we almost starved, not allowed to go to any part of the ship without a sentinel. Sometimes we had nothing but burgout[3] and peas, without salt, butter or meat; only what we begged from some of the sailors, as it happened there were some of our own countrymen on board.

[To be continued.]

---

[1] The Ship Terrible, 74 guns, Sir R. Bickerton, captain, put into commission, Nov. 4, 1776, at Portsmouth. The Terrible, 74, mentioned as having taken American vessels, in a list of the line-of-battle ships cruising in the British Channel, July, 1777.—*Town and Country Magazine* (London), for 1776, pp. 611, 613; 1777, p. 389. The Terrible was of Keppel's fleet, in 1778, and was struck by lightning, April 23, 1779 — *vide* account in *Gentleman's Magazine*, for 1779, p. 215. The Terrible, 74 guns, was of Admiral Sir Samuel Hood's fleet, arrived at Sandy Hook from the West Indies, Aug. 1781. In the naval engagement, Sept. 5, 1781, between the British and French fleets, off the Chesapeake, the Terrible was so much damaged, as occasioned the taking out her guns, &c., and setting her on fire.—*Vide* Heath's *Memoirs* (Boston, Aug. 1798), pp. 304, 311; Bancroft, *Hist. U. S.* x. 515.

[2] *Vide* REGISTER, xxiv. 50, note.

[3] "Burgue," in original.

(Continued from vol. xxix. page 294.)

— Page 300 (*Concluded*). —

[1706]					
June	9	Mary D of John & Sarah Devereux	— —	Devereux.
		Sarah D of m^r Francis & Mary Bafset	— —	Bafset
		Mary D of Benjamin &	— —	Pierce
		Rachel D of Thomas &	— —	Harris
	16	Sarah D of Richard & Mary Boylftone	— —	Boylstone.

1706   Baptized   — Page 301 —

M	D			
July	21	Mary D of m^r Adam & m^{rs} Mary Bathe — —	Bathe.
Augst	25	Elizabeth D. of m^r Richard & m^{rs} Parnel Foster,	Foster.
		Thomas S. of m^r Tho: & m^{rs} Anna Ruck — —	Ruck
		James & } sons of James & Mary Austin —	Austin.
		Thomas }	
Septem^r:	8	Jfaac & } twins of John & Mehitabel Rand —	Rand.
		Rebekka }	
	15	Jofeph S. of Jofeph & Mary Phipps — —	Phipps.
	22	Samuel S. of Samuel & Hannah Wood — —	Wood.
		Elizabeth D of John & Elizabeth Rand — —	Rand.
		Martha D. of Elizabeth Read.	
	29	William S of Charles & Elizabeth Hunnewell	Huñewel
Octob^r		Sarah D. of John & Elizabeth Pierce — —	Pierce.
	13	Mary D. of Job & Mary Hilliard — —	Hilliard.
	27	Samuel S of Samuel & Sarah Huchifon — —	Huchifon.
Novem^r	10	James S of Elkana & Elizabeth Ofburn — —	Ofburn.
	17	Mary D. of Maj^r Henry & Mrs Anna Smith —	Smith.
Decem^r	1	Oliver S. of Oliver & Anna Atwood. —	Atwood.
	8	Samuel S. of Samuel & Hannah Trumble —	Trumble
		Mercy D of m^r Benj & m^{rs} Mercy Frothingham	Frothingham
	15	Eliz: D. of m^r Michael & m^{rs} Releif Gill —	Gill
	22	Samuel D of m^r Samuel & m^{rs} Hannah —	Frothingham
	29	Jonathan S. of Robert & Margarit Ward —	Ward
		Hannah D of William & Abigail Kettle —	Kettle.

1706|7   Baptized   — Page 302 —

M.	D.			
Jan.	5	Anna D. of Col: Henry & m^{rs} Anna Smith —	Smith
	12	John S. of William & Hannah Hurry —	Hurry.
	19	Sarah D. of m^r Samuel & m^{rs} Sarah Cutler —	Cutler
	26	Jofeph S. of Benjamin & Mary Kettle —	Kettle
Feb:	2	William S of m^r William & m^{rs} Abigail Smith	Smith
		Richard S of m^r Thomas & Lord —	Lord
	9	Mary D. of Nathaniel & Eliz: Howard —	Howard
		Deborah D. of Phillip & Deborah Cutler —	Cutler
	16	Thomas S of Caleb & Abigail Crofsewel —	Crofsewel
	23	Mary D. of Benjamin & Anna Lawrence —	Lawrence.
March	2	John S. of m^r Edward & m^{rs} —	Emerfon
		Elizabeth D of m^r Abrahā & m^{rs} Martha —	Hill.
	16	Mary W. of Miller Frost — — — —	Frost
	23	Timothy S. of Jonathan & Eliz: Sherman. —	Sherman.
		Rebekkah. D. of Elias & Abigail Stone. —	Stone
		Eliz: D of m^r Calvin & m^{rs} Katharine Galpin —	Galpin.
		Eliz: D of Edward & Mary Sheaffe — —	Sheaffe.
	30	Eliz: Dunklin — — — — — — —	Dunklin.
		Rebekkah D. of Jacob & Eliz: Hurd — —	Hurd.

17|07		— Page 302 *(Concluded)*. —	
April	6	Ephraim S of m^r Ephraim & m^{rs} Martha Breed	Breed
	13	Stephen. | John. | Samuel | William | Mary |	
		children of Stephen & Mercy Badger —	Badger
		Benjamin S of Benjamin & Lucy Phillips —	Phillips.
	20	John S of John & Sufannah Frothingham —	Frothingham
		Sarah D of John & Sarah Waters — — —	Waters.

17|07		Baptized — Page 303 —	
May	.4.	Mary Noffitur — — — — — — —	Noffiter
		Elizabeth ⎱ D^s of m^r John & m^{rs} Abigail —	Rainer
		Katharine ⎰	
		Miller S of Miller & Mary Froft — — —	Froft
	18	Katharine D of m^r Jonathan & m^{rs} Katharine Dows	Dows.
		John S of John & Hannah Damon — — —.	Dammon.
June	15	John S of John & Abiel Hovey. — — —	Hovey.
	29	Henry Pounden — — — — — — —	Pounden
		Mary Rofe — — — — — — —	Rofe.
July	6	Benjamin S of Benjamin Hurd — — —	Hurd
		William S of Robert & Ruth Wier — — —	Wier
Augs^t	3	Sarah Mirick — — — — — —	Mirick
		Anne D of Thomas & Esther Frothinghā. —	Frothingham.
	10	Sarah D. of Joseph & Sarah Rand. — — —	Rand.
	24	William | Thomas | Edward |	
		Sons of m^r William & Elener Wire. — —	Wire
	31	Hannah. D. of William & Hannah Teal — —	Teal.
Sept.	7	Stephen. S of Stephen & Ford — —	Ford
		Elizabeth. D. of Caleb & Anne Call — —	Call
	14	Henry S. of m^r Ifaac & Rebekka Fowl — —	Fowl.
		Eliz: D of m^r Nathaniel & Hannah Cary. —	Cary.
	28	Deborah Lee (adult) — — — — — —	Lee.
		Lydia D of m^r Eleazer & m^{rs} Lydia Phillips —	Phillips
Octo^r:	5	Eliz: D. of James & Patience Webber — —	Webber
	19	Abigail D of William & Perfis Rand — —	Rand

1707		Baptized — Page 304 —	
Novem^r	9	Isaac S. of Stephen & Mary Kidder — —	Kidder.
	16	Thomas S. of William & Sarah Melenden —	Melenden.
		Mary D. of Chriftopher & Mary Goodwin —	Goodwin.
		Mary D of & Mary Sanford —	Sanford.
		Elizabeth D of Thomas & Harris —	Harris
		Eleazer | Ifaac | Sufannah |	
		Children of m^r Eleazer & Sufannah —	Johnfon
Decem^r	7	Hannah D. of m^r Samuel & m^{rs} Hannah Froth-	
		ingham.	Frothinghā
	28	Lydia D. of Joseph & Mary Heath. — —	Heath.
17|07–8			
Jan	4	John S. of William & Hannah Stevens — —	Stevens
		Abigail D. of Samuel & Rachel Knight — —	Knight.
	25	Abigail D. of John & Hannah Newel — —	Newel.
		Andrew. S of m^r John & m^{rs} Sarah Foy. —	Foy
Feb.	15	Edward. S. of Samuel & Hannah Counts —	Counts.
		Anne. D of m^r Francis & m^{rs} Mary Baffit —	Baffit.
		Katharine. D. of m^r Eleazer & m^{rs} Sufannah. —	Johnson.
170|7.8			
March	7.	John S. of John & Mary Rofe — — —	Rofe.

— Page 304 (*Concluded*). —

		Nathaniel S of William & Mary Sheaff — —	Sheaf.
	14	William S. of William & Hannah Hurry —	Hurry.
		Thomas. S of Jofeph & Mary Wood — —	Wood
	21	Jofeph S. of Stephen & Mercy Badger — —	Badger.
April	11.	Benjamin. S. of Nathaniel & Hannah Frothingham.	Frothinghā
		Sarah D. of Jacob & Katherine Waters — —	Waters.
		Katharine D. of Jonathan & Katharine Kettle	Kettle.
		Mary. D of Samuel & Hannah Trumble. —	Trumble
	18	Benjamin S. of mᵣ Benj. & mᵣˢ Abigail Bunker	Bunker.
		John. S. of mᵣ Samuel & mᵣˢ Elizabeth Burr —	Burre

1708		Baptized — Page 305 —	
May	2	Daniel S. of John & Grace Eades — —	Eades
		Deborah. D. of Philip & Deborah Cutler —	Cutler.
	9	Joshuah S of mᵣ Joshuah & Sarah Scottow —	Scottow.
		William S. of mᵣ Wᵐ & Abigail Smith — —	Smith
	16	Mary Pollod (Adult pfon) — — — —	Pollod
June	13	Abigail D. of Thomas & Sarah White — —	White.
July	4	Mary D. of Nathaniel & Eliz Webber — —	Webber.
	11	Elizabeth. D. of Henry & Hannah Bodge —	Bodge.
	25	Dudley S. of Richard & Mary Boilston — —	Boilston
Augᵗ	1	Benjam̄ S of mᵣ Benj & Mercy H. Frothingham	Frothinghā
		Rebecca D of John & Mehitabel Rand. — —	Rand.
		Hannah D. of Thomas & Mary Fofdick —	Fofdick.
Sept.	5	Hannah D. of John & Sarah Edmunds — —	Edmunds
		Mary D. of John & Sufannah Toocker — —	Toocker
	26	mᵣ Jacob Waters — — — — — —	Waters
		Richard S. of mᵣ Thomas & Eliz: Lord — —	Lord.
		Jonathan S of mᵣ Jonathan & Fofdick	Fofdick.
Novembr	28	Jerahmeel S. of Benj: & Pierce — —	Pierce.
Decembr	19	James S. of James & Mary Auftin — —	Auftin.
170 8.9			
Jan	9	William S of mᵣ Zechariah & Dorcas Symms —	Symms.
	16	Joseph. S. of mᵣ Jonathan & mᵣˢ Kathariñ Dows.	Dows.
	23	John S. of Jacob & Elizabeth Hurd. — —	Hurd
		Jofeph S. of Stephen & Margarit Fofdick —	Fofdick.
		Jane. D. of Charles & Eliz. Huñewell —	Huñewell

1707.8 Month	Day	Baptized — Page 306 —	
Febr.	6	Nathaniel S. of Mᵣ Ebenezer & Rebekah Austin	Austin.
		Andrew. S. of Caleb & Abigail Crofsewell —	Crofsewell
	13	John S. of mᵣ Stephen & Mary Kidder — —	Kidder.
		Jofeph, & Samuel, Sufañah & Margarit, children ⎱	Mirick.
	20	of Jofeph & Sarah Mirick — — — — ⎰	
	27	Abigail D. of John & Eliz. Pierce — — —	Pierce.
March	6	Sarah D. of John & Abiel Hovey — — —	Hovey.
1708–9			
	13	Richard S. of Elias & Abigail Stone — —	Stone.
	20	Annah D. of mᵣ Nathaniel & Annah Addams. —	Addams.
1709			
April	10	John Foskit | Miriam Fofkit | Abigail Fofkit. |	Fofkit.
		Samuel S. of Samuel & Abigail Trumble —	Trumble
	17	Bets. S. of Oliver & Anna Atwood, — —	Atwood.
	24	Hannah D. of mᵣ Nathaniel & Hannah Cary —	Cary.

— Page 306 (*Concluded*). —

		Mary D. of m^r Abraham & Martha Hill	—	Hill.
May	1	Samuel S. of Mr Samuel & Sarah Cutler	—	Cutler
	8	James. S. of m^r James & Abigail Miller	—	Miller.
	15	Abigail. D. of Robert & Mercy Fofkit	—	Fofket.
	22	Sarah D. of m^r John & Sarah Waters	—	Waters
		Sarah D. of William & Perfis Rand	—	Rand.
		Elizabeth D. of Jonathan & Elizabeth Sherman	⸱	Sherman.
	29	Samuel S. of m^r Samuel & m^rs Eliz: Bur	—	Bur
Iune	26	Simon. S. of Simon & Mary Bradstreet.	—	Bradftreet.
		Rebeka, D. of m^r Ephraim & m^rs Martha Breed		Breed
July	3	Mary D. of Benj. & Mary Kettle	— —	Kettle.
	17	John. S. of John & Hannah Login	— —	Login.
		Hannah D. of Benj. & Lucy Phillips	— —	Phillips.
	13	Mary D. of Stephen & Ford	— —	Ford.

1709 M.	D.	Baptized — Page 307 —	
Augt	7	Nathaniel. S. of m^r Calvin & m^rs Katharine Galpin	Galpin.
	14	Thomas. S. of m^r Tho. & m^rs Sybill Greaves —	Greaves.
		Sarah. W. of m^r James & m^rs Sarah Fowl. —	Fowl.
	28	Ruth of Elkana & Elizabeth Ofburn. — —	Ofburn.
Sept.	10	Eliezer S. of Robert & Ruth Wire. — —	Wire.
		Rebekah D. of Ifaac & Rebekah Fowl. — —	Fowl.
		Abigail D. of Benjamin & Hurd — —	Hurd.
	18	Robert. S. of Robert & Katharine Cutler —	Cutler
		Nathaniel S. of Jofeph & Sarah Rand — —	Rand.
		Johanna D. of Chriftopher & Mary Goodwin.	Goodwin
		Rebekah D. of Jeremiah & Margaret Storer —	Storer.
	25	John S. of William & Hannah Teal. — —	Teal.
		Elizabeth D. of James & Elizabeth Capen. —	Capen.
		Abigail. D. of m^r Samuel & Frothingham.	Frothingham.
Octob^r	2	Margarit. D. of Edward & Mary Sheaf. — —	Sheaf.
		Elizabeth D. of James & Patience Webber —	Webber.
	9	Jofeph. S. of Miller & Mary Frost — —	Froft.
		Caleb. S. of m^r Caleb & Anne Call — —	Call
	16	Benjamin S. of m^r Benjamin & m Mercy Froth-ingham.	Frothingham
		Mary D of m^r Thomas & m^rs Mary Clark —	Clark
		Bethiah D. of Samuel & Huchifon —	Huchifon.
	23	Esther D. of William & Hannah Hurry — —	Hurry
Nove^{mr}.	13	Benjamin S. of John & Grace Eads — —	Eads.
	27	Sufannah D. of Nicholaus & Mabel Hoping —	Hopping
		Mary D. of Amos & Mary Story — — —	Story.
Decem^r	18	Enoch. S. of m^r John & Susannah Frothingham	Frothingham
Januar	1	Mary D. of m^r Richard & Mary Miller — —	Miller.
	8	Thomas. S. of m^r Nathaniel & Hannah Froth-ingham	Frothingham

1709 10 month	Day	Baptized — Page 308 —	
Jan.	22	Jacob S. of m^r Nathaniel & Elizabeth Howard	Howard
		Thomas S. of m^r Thomas & Eliz. Lord	Lord
Feb	5	James S. of m^r James & Elizabeth Capen —	Capen.
		Mary D. of Elifha & Mary Doubleday — —	Doubleday.
	12	Mary D. of m^r Michael & m^rs Relief Gill —	Gill.
	19	Hannah D. of m^r John & Sarah Edmunds —	Edmunds
March	5	Peter S. of m^r Francis & m^rs Mary Bafset —	Bafset.
		Samuel S. of Samuel & Knight — —	Knight

— Page 308 *(Concluded)*. —

	Katharin D. of mr John & mrs Anna Phillips	—		Phillips
	Hannah D. of Samuel & Hannah Wood	—	—	Wood
12	Mary D. of Stephen & Mercy Badger	—	—	Badger.
13	Mr Nathaniel Addams	—	—	Addams

1710 April	2	Andrew S. & Sarah D. } Twins } of mr John & mrs Sarah Foy		Foy
	9	Jofeph S. of Jofeph & Mary Heath	—	—	Heath
	16	Abigail D. of mr Jonathan & Katharine Kettle		Kettle.
		Richard S. of William & Sarah Melenden		Melenden.
	30	William S. of mr William & Abigail Kettle	—	Kettle.
May	7	William S. of mr William & Hannah Patten	—	Patten
		Hannah D. of mr William & Hannah Patten	—	Patten.
	14	Elizabeth D. of mr Richard & mrs Eliz. James		James.
		Mary D. of mr William & Mary Sheaff	—	Sheaff.
	21	Martha. D. of mr Jofiah & mrs Martha Montjoy		Montjoy.
June	4th	Mary D. of the Revd mr Thomas & mrs Mary Tuft.		Tuft.
		Jfabel Pouning (an adult perfon)	—	—	Powning
	11	George S. of mr George & Abigail Darling	—	Darling
July	9th	Edmund S. of John &	—	—	Rand
	16	William S. of mr William & Elener Wire	—	Wire.
	30	Mary D. of mr Wm & Mary Rowfe	—	—	Rowse.
Auguft	6	James. S. of James & Hannah Lowden	—	—	Lowden

1710		Baptized — Page 309 —			
Month	D				
October	15	Efther D. of mr Caleb & Anna Call	—	—	—	Call.
Novemr	5.	David S of Jofeph & Mary Wood	—	—	—	Wood
	19	Mr Henry Bodge	—	—	—	—	Bodge
		Elizabeth D. of mr Jonathan & M Katharine Dows		Dows.
		Timothy S. of mr Timothy &	Goodwin	—	Goodwin
		Mary D. of mr Henry & Hannah Bodge	—	—	Bodge
	26	Nicholaus S. of mr Eleazer & Sufannah Johnson		Johnson.
		Anna D. of mr Richard & Mary Boylftone		Boylftone.
Decemr	10	Abigail D. of mr Benj & Mrs Abigail Bunker	—	Bunker
		Patience D. of Charles & Eliz. Hunnewell	—	Huñewell.
	24	Timothy S. of mr Ebenezer & Rebekah Auftin		Auftin.
		Mary D. of mr William & Abigail Smith	—	Smith
	31	Benjamin S. of Caleb & Abigail Crofsewel	—	Crofsewel.
1710.11					
January	14	Samuel S. of mr Samuel &	Frothingham	Frothingham.
		John S. of mr John & mrs Sarah Waters	—	Waters.
	21	Abigail D. of mr Benj &	Pierce	—	Pierce.
		Sarah. D. of Mr Thomas & mrs Sybill Greaves		Greaves.
Feb.	11	Samuel S. of mr William & mrs Mercy Butrech.		Butreck
		Zechariah S. of mr John &	Johnfon	Johnson
	25	Abigail D. of Stephen & Margarit Fofdick	—	Fofdick
March	4	Sarah D. of mr Jacob & Elizabeth Hurd	—	Hurd.
	11	Sarah D. of mr John & mrs Anna Phillips	—	Phillips
	18	Rebekah D. of mr Samuel & mrs Elizabeth Burr.		Burr.
	25	Abraham S. of mr Samuel & mrs Sarah Cutler.		Cutler.
		Thomas of John & Hannah Login	—	—	Login
April	8	James S. of mr Samuel [?] &	Trumbal	Trumball
		Katharine D. of mr Nathaniel Webber	—	—	Webber

1711	D.	Baptized — Page 310 —	
M	D.		
April	29th	Benjamin. S. of Benjamin & Hurd —	Hurd
May	13	Johanna D. of Mr Nicholaus & Johanna Johnson	Johnfon
		Hannah D. of Jofeph & Sarah Mirick — —	Mirick
June	3	Sarah D. of William & Sarah Melenden — —	Melenden
		Rebeka D. of Elkanah & Elizabeth Ofburn —	Ofburn
	10th	Henry S. of mr Henry & Sarah Davis. — —	Davis
		James. S of mr James & Abiah Turner — —	Turner
		Martha & ⎫ D. of mr Thomas & Mary Harris — Mary ⎭	Harris
	17	Mercy D of Robert & Mercy Fofkit — —	Fofkitt.
	24	Jonathan S. of mr. Abraham & Martha Hill —	Hill.
		Margarit D. of Jeremiah & Storer	Storer.
July	15	Mr Elisha Doubleday — — — —	Doubleday.
	29	Thomas S of mr Vincent & mrs Hannah Carter.	Carter.
Auguft	19	Abigail. D. of mr John & mrs Abigail Rainer —	Rainer.
	26	Thomas. S of William & Perfis Rand — —	Rand
		Ebenezer S. of Jofeph & Sarah Rand — —	Rand.
Sept	2	Elizabeth D. of mr Thomas & Eliz. Lord —	Lord.
	9	Efther D. of William & Teal — —	Teal.
	23	Zechariah S. of Zechariah & Mildred Davis —	Davis
		Elizabeth ⎫ Crowch Adult perfons — — — & Mary ⎭	Crowch.
	30	Hannah D. of mr Richard & Mary Miller —	Miller
Octob	7	Samuel S. of Simon & Mary Bradftreet —	Bradftreet.
		Edward. S of Edward & Mary Sheaff —	Sheaff.

1711	D	Baptized — Page 311 —	
M	D		
Octor.	21	Mary D. of mr James & Mary Auftin — —	Auftin
		Thomas S of mr Benjamin & Balch —	Balch
Novr	4	Sarah D. of mr John & Eliz. Pierce — —	Pierce
		Sarah D. of mr John & Grace Edes — —	Edes.
	11	William S. of mr William & Hannah Hopping	Hopping
		Rebekah D. of mr Ephraim & Martha Breed —	Breed.
		Mary D of mr James & Fowl — —	Fowl.
	18	Benjamin S. of mr John & Sarah Foy — —	Foy.
	25	Mary D of mr Samuel & Mary Smith — —	Smith
Decemr	2	Mercy W. of William Rogers — — — —	Rogers
		Stephen S. of Miller & Mary Froft — — —	Froft.
	9	Mary D. of Mr Theophilus & Katharine Jvory	Jvory.
	23	Rebekah D of Mr Jonathan & Eliz: Sherman —	Sherman
1711–12			
Jan.	27	Ebenezer S. of Mr. William & Hannah Stevens	Stevens.
		Benjamin S. of Mr Benj. & Mary Kettle —	Kettel.
Feb	3	Abigail D. of Mr. Stephen & Mary Kidder —	Kidder.
		William S. of mr. William & Margarit Alley —	Alley.
	10	Benjamin S. of mr. William & Mary Sheaff. —	Sheaf.
	17	Mercy D. of mr. Benjamin & Mercy Frothingham	Frothingham
		Katharin D. of mr Robert & Katharin Cutler. —	Cutler.
	24	David. S. of mr. William & Elener Wire —	Wire
March	2	Hannah D. of mr James Capen junr & Eliz. his wife	Capen
		Abigail Mirick & her Sifter Annah Mirick (Adult perfons)	Mirick
		John. S of mr John & Johnfon — —	Johnfon
	16	Anne D. of Mr. Tho. Fofdick & Mary his wife	Fofdick
	23	Jofiah S. of Mr Ebenezer & Prudence Swan. —	Swan
		Ruth D. of Jofeph & Ruth Hopkins — —	Hopkins

BRIEF HISTORY OF THE REGISTER.[1]

From the Report of the Committee on Publication, by ALBERT H. HOYT, A.M.

SOON after the organization of this Society, its members took into formal consideration the feasibility of publishing a magazine to be "devoted to the printing of ancient documents, wills, genealogical and biographical sketches, and historical and antiquarian matter generally." The value of such a periodical and its pressing necessity, in view of the scattered and perishing condition of the larger part of such important materials of history, were sufficiently obvious.

It was not, however, until the autumn of the year 1846, that definite arrangements were concluded for the publication of such a work under the auspices of the Society. By this arrangement it was understood and agreed between the publisher and the Society that the "title and good will" of the magazine should forever remain in the Society, and that it should be published and edited under its general direction; but that the salary of the editor and all other costs and charges incident to the undertaking should be paid by the publisher. A member of the Society volunteered to publish the magazine, and an editor was chosen by the Society,—the Rev. William Cogswell, D.D.[2]

The first number was issued on the fifth day of February, 1847, under the title of "The New-England Historical and Genealogical Register." Under this title every volume of this Quarterly has been regularly issued without interruption; and with adequate support, we see no reason why it should not be continued for generations to come.

[1] A history of the REGISTER for the first seventeen years of its existence was written in 1863 by the present editor, and was printed as the preface to vol. xvii., which volume was edited by him.—ED.

[2] The following is a statement of the names of those who have edited volumes or parts of volumes of the REGISTER, their residences at time of election, and the numbers edited by them respectively:

The Rev. William Cogswell, D.D., of Boston,	Jan.	1847,	4 numbers.
Samuel G. Drake, A.M., of Boston,	"	1848,	5 "
William Thaddeus Harris, A.M., of Cambridge,	April,	1849,	3 "
Samuel G. Drake, A.M., of Boston,	Jan.	1850,	1 "
The Hon. Nathaniel B. Shurtleff, M.D., of Boston,	April,	1850,	3 "
Samuel G. Drake, A.M., of Boston,	Jan.	1851,	4 "
The Rev. Joseph B. Felt, LL.D., of Boston,	"	1852,	2 "
The Hon. Timothy Farrar, LL.D., of Boston,	July,	1852,	1 "
William B. Trask, of Dorchester,	Oct.	1852,	1 "
Samuel G. Drake, A.M., of Boston,	Jan.	1853,	24 "
William B. Trask, of Dorchester,			
William H. Whitmore, A.M., of Boston,	} Jan.	1859,	8 "
John Ward Dean, A.M., of Boston,			
Samuel G. Drake, A.M., of Boston,	Jan.	1861,	4 "
William B. Trask, of Dorchester,	"	1862,	1 "
The Rev. Elias Nason, A.M., of Exeter, N. H.	April,	1862,	1 "
The Hon. Charles Hudson, A.M., of Lexington,	July,	1862,	1 "
John Ward Dean, A.M., of Boston,	Oct.	1862,	5 "
William B. Trask, of Dorchester,	Jan.	1864,	2 "
John Ward Dean, A.M., of Boston,	July,	1864,	2 "
William B. Trask, of Dorchester,	Jan.	1865,	4 "
The Rev. Elias Nason, A.M., of Billerica,	"	1866,	8 "
Albert H. Hoyt, A.M., of Boston,	"	1868,	32 "
John Ward Dean, A.M., of Boston,	"	1876.	

From 1847 to 1864, inclusive, the Register had four different publishers.[1] In the summer of 1864 a few members of the Society, with its consent, formed themselves into an association, known as the Register Club, for the purpose of securing the continuance of the Quarterly, the members of which pledged themselves to bear the responsibility of the publication. The Society readily conceded to them the privilege of annually nominating the Committee on Publication, the latter choosing the editor. This Club existed for nine years, some members going out and other persons interested in the work coming in at the end of each year to lend their support. They so prudently administered this trust that, while saving themselves from loss and gradually enlarging and improving the publication, they were enabled out of the small surplus to place upon the shelves of the Society's library a considerable number of much-needed volumes and useful periodicals.[2]

The editor of the first volume was engaged at a salary of one thousand dollars. The first publisher, and for several years nominal editor, of the Register, Mr. Drake, kept a book-store, and issued publications of his own. He used the pages of the magazine as an advertising medium, and undoubtedly realized no inconsiderable returns from that source, as he did also from the sale of surplus portions of each issue of the Register. To him as editor the publisher of the volume for 1857 paid, we are informed, the sum of five hundred dollars as salary for that year. It is stated, also, that two hundred dollars were paid to Mr. William T. Harris for editorial service in

[1] The publishers have been as follows: Samuel G. Drake from 1847 to 1861, inclusive, except for the years 1852 and 1857; Thomas Prince, 1852; Charles B. Richardson, 1857; Joel Munsell, 1862, 1863, and 1864. Since the last date the successive volumes have borne the imprint of the Society. David Clapp & Son have been the printers since 1864.

[2] The names of those who were members of the "Register Club," and the years of their membership, are as follows:

Winslow Lewis, M.D., 1865, 1866, 1869, 1871.
William B. Towne, A.M., from 1865 to 1874, inclusive.
Frederic Kidder, from 1865 to 1874, inclusive.
Charles S. Fellows, 1865, 1866, 1867, 1868, 1869, 1870.
William B. Trask, from 1865 to 1874, inclusive.
William H. Whitmore, A.M., 1865, 1866, 1868, 1869.
William S. Appleton, A.M., 1865, 1868, 1870.
Samuel G. Drake, A.M., 1865, 1866, 1867, 1868, 1869, 1870, 1872.
John K. Wiggin, from 1865 to 1868, inclusive.
John Ward Dean, A.M., from 1865 to 1874, inclusive.
Jeremiah Colburn, A.M., from 1865 to 1874, inclusive.
John M. Bradbury, from 1865 to 1868, inclusive.
Deloraine P. Corey, from 1865 to 1874, inclusive.
Edward S. Rand, Jr., A.M., 1865, 1866, 1868.
The Hon. George W. Messinger, 1865.
The Rev. Alonzo H. Quint, D.D., 1865, 1866, 1870.
The Hon. Calvin Fletcher, 1865, 1866.
Col. Almon D. Hodges, 1865.
David Clapp, 1865.
The Rev. Henry M. Dexter, D.D., 1865.
Charles W. Tuttle, A.M., from 1866 to 1874, inclusive.
Brig.-Gen. Ebenezer W. Peirce, 1866.
William R. Deane, from 1866 to 1869, inclusive.
Francis French, 1866.
The Rev. Edmund F. Slafter, A.M., 1867, 1868, 1869, 1870, 1871, 1872, 1874.
The Rev. Elias Nason, A.M., 1868.
Albert H. Hoyt, A.M., from 1868 to 1874, inclusive.
The Hon. Marshall P. Wilder, from 1868 to 1874, inclusive.
H. H. Edes, from 1870 to 1874, inclusive.
The Rev. Dorus Clarke, D.D., 1871, 1872, 1873.
Thomas Waterman, 1871, 1872.
Commodore Geo. Henry Preble, U.S.N., from 1871 to 1874, inclusive.
John H. Sheppard, A.M., 1872, 1873.
The Rev. Lucius R. Paige, D.D., 1874.

1849. With these three exceptions, no editor of the Register, so far as we are aware, has ever received any compensation for his services.

The legal and equitable property in the title, subscription list, and good will of the Register has always been in the Society; and this has never been questioned by any one, so far as our knowledge extends, since that matter was settled by the timely and decisive action of the Committee on Publication and the Society in 1849.[1]

And here it is but just to say, that the Society and all friends of the Register are more indebted than is generally known to Mr. John Ward Dean and Mr. William B. Towne for prompt and most valuable services, at a critical period in the history of our Quarterly, in the autumn of 1861, when they saved it from premeditated death.[2] They have also rendered, since then, long-continued and unselfish service in its behalf.[3]

To Mr. Joel Munsell, of Albany, who volunteered, at a crisis in the existence of the Register, to undertake its publication, we are under great obligations. He bore the sole financial responsibility of its publication during the years 1862, 1863, and 1864, "without any idea of deriving profit

---

[1] The following are the names of those who have served on the Committee on Publication, and their places of residence at the time of their first election:

Charles Ewer, of Boston,	Mar. 1847, to	Jan. 1851
The Hon. Nathaniel B. Shurtleff, M.D., of Boston,	" 1847, to	" 1849
The Rev. Samuel H. Riddel, A.B., of Boston,	" 1847, to	" 1851
David Hamblen, of Boston,	Jan. 1849, to	Oct. 1855
William T. Harris, A.M., of Cambridge,	Feb. 1849, to	" 1849
The Rev. Joseph B. Felt, LL.D., of Boston,	Jan. 1850, to	July, 1852
The Hon. Nathaniel B. Shurtleff, M.D., of Boston,	" 1850, to	Jan. 1851
The Rev. Lucius R. Paige, D.D., of Cambridge,	" 1850, to	" 1851
Charles Deane, LL.D., of Boston,	" 1851, to	Oct. 1851
J. Wingate Thornton, A.M., of Boston,	" 1851, to	Mar. 1852
William T. Harris, A.M., of Cambridge,	" 1851, to	Oct. 1851
Frederic Kidder, of Boston,	Oct. 1851, to	" 1855
The Hon. Timothy Farrar, LL.D., of Boston,	Nov. 1851, to	Dec. 1854
William B. Trask, of Dorchester,	April, 1852, to	Dec. 1853
Charles Mayo, of Boston,	Oct. 1852, to	" 1853
The Rev. William Jenks, D.D., LL.D., of Boston,	" 1853, to	" 1858
Lyman Mason, A.M., of Boston,	" 1853, to	Dec. 1854
†John Ward Dean, A.M., of Boston,	Dec. 1854.	
William Reed Deane, of Brookline,	" 1854, to	Oct. 1856
Lemuel Shattuck, of Boston,	" 1854, to	" 1856
The Rev. Alonzo Hall Quint, D.D., of Jamaica Plain,	Oct. 1855, to	" 1856
James Spear Loring, of Boston,	" 1855, to	" 1856
The Hon. Francis Brinley, A.M., of Boston,	" 1856, to	" 1858
Charles H. Morse, of Cambridge,	" 1856, to	" 1858
William H. Whitmore, A.M., of Boston,	" 1856, to	Nov. 1861
The Hon. Timothy Farrar, LL.D., of Boston,	" 1857, to	Oct. 1858
William B. Trask, of Dorchester,	" 1858, to	" 1867
The Hon. Charles Hudson, A.M., of Lexington,	Nov. 1861, to	" 1863
The Rev. Elias Nason, A.M., of Exeter, N. H.	" 1861, to	" 1864
George Wingate Chase, of Haverhill,	" 1861, to	" 1862
William H. Whitmore, A.M., of Boston,	Oct. 1862, to	Nov. 1872
William S. Appleton, A.M., of Boston,	" 1863, to	" 1872
The Rev. Henry M. Dexter, D.D., of Roxbury,	" 1864, to	Oct. 1867
The Rev. Elias Nason, A.M., of Billerica,	" 1865, to	" 1868
†William B. Towne, A.M., of Brookline,	Nov. 1865.	
Frederic Kidder, of Boston,	Oct. 1867, to	Oct. 1868
†Albert H. Hoyt, A.M., of Boston,	" 1867.	
Charles W. Tuttle, A.M., of Boston,	Nov. 1872, to	Nov. 1873
Commodore Geo. Henry Preble, U.S.N., of Charlestown,	" 1872, to	Oct. 1874
†The Rev. Lucius R. Paige, D.D., of Cambridge,	" 1873.	
†H. H. Edes, of Boston,	" 1873.	
†Jeremiah Colburn, A.M., of Boston,	Oct. 1874.	

† Members of the Committee for 1876.

[2] See "Publisher's Preface" to vol. xv., for 1861.

[3] For ten years, 1865 to 1874, Mr. Towne managed the business affairs of the Register, gratuitously.

from it, but rather as a contribution to a cause in which he felt," and still feels, " a deep interest." Mr. William B. Trask also volunteered his services as editor of the first number of the volume for 1862. He has edited and assisted in editing fifteen other numbers, besides having been a contributor of valuable papers from the beginning. Mr. Frederic Kidder is also entitled to special mention, for having furnished means to one of the early publishers, and for other labors in the interest of the Register.

While the Quarterly was under the control of the Register Club, others, besides those already named, rendered important services in extending its circulation, among whom Charles W. Tuttle, Esq., and Commodore George Henry Preble, U.S.N., should be mentioned.

The Register Club having voluntarily dissolved in the autumn of 1874, the financial responsibility for the publication of the Quarterly was assumed by the Society, where it now rests; while its editorial conduct still remains in the hands of the editor chosen by the Committee on Publication.

It is gratifying to know that the magazine has a wider circulation at the present time than at any former period of its existence; and the Committee have good grounds for believing that it was never more highly appreciated. Still, as the history of all periodicals teaches, systematic, persistent and continuous efforts must be made to keep the Register before the public and secure its continued prosperity.

That this publication has accomplished all, and more than all, its projectors anticipated, and that it is worthy of continued support, will be evident to all who consider how large a number of valuable historical documents, and how much of family and town history it has drawn from private sources, and thus saved from destruction or oblivion. Not only this, but it has begotten what may properly be styled a habit in the community of collecting and preserving such materials. It has also fostered a widespread and honorable desire among the people generally to ascertain, compile and secure the data pertaining to family histories,—data obtained with difficulty always, even in respect of the later generations, but with still greater difficulty the further back the investigation is prosecuted. Advantage has thus been taken of the aid to be derived from aged people, whose clear recollections extended into the last century, and of family traditions.

When this Society was formed in 1844, only a few genealogies of American families had been published or printed. The first of which we have any knowledge is a pamphlet of twenty-four pages, printed in 1771. Between that date and the year 1813, only one more was printed; while during the ensuing thirty years twenty-two were produced. Prior, therefore, to the establishment of the Register in 1847, but thirty-two genealogies or family pedigrees had been printed; and these, for the most part, were very limited in extent and inferior in character, as compared with most of those published at the present day. Since the year 1847, or during the last thirty years, the number of genealogies, more or less extended and complete, that have been printed, is nearly six hundred; of which by far the larger number were produced in New-England. Of histories of New-England towns, published anterior to 1845, we have knowledge of only forty-one; since that date about one hundred and twenty have been published, and many more are in preparation. In other parts of the country also, genealogies and town-histories are rapidly multiplying. Of each of these classes of publications, no inconsiderable number were compiled by subscribers or readers of the Register.

In this magazine itself will be found the genealogies, or at least historical outlines, of about four hundred and fifty families of English origin; while the number of papers containing genealogies, ranging from one page or less to ten or more pages, is about one thousand. Besides these are hundreds of biographical and obituary sketches. Many of these articles embody the results of laborious and costly research.

Prior to the establishment of this Quarterly, the only book printed in this country that could afford much aid in the study of family history, was the "Genealogical Register of the First Settlers of New-England," by John Farmer, Esq., Corresponding Secretary of the New-Hampshire Historical Society,—a volume of 351 pages, published in 1829. This work was a great help to the early conductors of our magazine. From our Register Mr. Savage drew largely for materials for his invaluable Genealogical Dictionary, published in 1860–1862. He corrected many errors in our early volumes; while many mistakes into which he himself was led, have been pointed out, and his own work has been greatly supplemented, in our later volumes.

It may, therefore, be fairly assumed that this Quarterly has afforded no little aid and stimulus in all these praiseworthy and useful labors of historians and genealogists,—much more aid, apparently, than is sometimes acknowledged.

Moreover, the Register has been essentially serviceable to this Society, as its special organ, and as a potential agent in making its existence known and its objects respected. Other Societies, too, in New-England and beyond, that have done and are doing distinguished and valuable service for historical and archæological science, neither have received nor will receive, we are sure, any injury from the circulation of this periodical.

With the close of the last volume, the writer of this report resigned his place as editor, which he had held for eight years,—a longer period of continued service, it appears by the records, than has been rendered by any of his predecessors. His efforts have been to make the publication worthy of the patronage and confidence of historical students and experienced genealogists; to make it thorough and accurate; to introduce a larger proportion of historical matter; to elevate its literary character; to improve its typography and dress; to keep its pages free from personal and party animosities; and to extend its patronage. How far he has succeeded in these efforts is best known to the patrons of the work. To the gentlemen with whom he has been associated on the Publishing Committee, he returns hearty thanks for their unvarying kindness, support and encouragement. Not the least pleasant of his recollections of this long association will be the fact, that from first to last the Committee have been a unit in every vote or act affecting the interests of the Register.

The January number of the Register is already published. With this issue the Quarterly enters upon its thirtieth volume, under the editorial charge of Mr. John Ward Dean, the librarian. His experience, having been a member of the Committee on Publication continuously for upward of twenty-one years, and other ample qualifications, are a sufficient guaranty that the work will not suffer in his hands.

EXTRACTS FROM THE DIARY OF THE LATE HON. WILLIAM D. WILLIAMSON, OF BANGOR, MAINE,

WHILE A MEMBER OF THE SEVENTEENTH CONGRESS OF THE UNITED STATES.

Communicated by the Hon. JOSEPH WILLIAMSON.

Thurs. Nov. 29, 1821, left Bangor.

Nov. 30. Arrived at Augusta, having on the way seen a piece in the A. Advocate, and heard something said as to my franking letters as a member of Cong. while acting as Govr.

Dec. 1. Arrived at Portland in evening—wrote a letter to Mr. Ames to come and take upon himself the office of Chief Magistrate.

Dec. 3. Mond. Lay my determination of resigning the office of Governor before the Council. Objectors a little disappointed that I am so desirous and ready to leave the administration.

Dec. 5. Resign my office of Gov. to Mr. Ames, Spk. of the H. of Rep. Some doubts who ought to administer to him the oaths.

Thurs. Dec. 6. Left Portland at 5 A.M. breakfast at Saco. 2s. 6d. arrived at Boston at 1 in morning, having supped at Salem, 2s. 6d.—fare from Portland to Portsmouth $4.00, thence to Boston $4.00—whole charge of the day $9.40. Slep^t at Davenport's.

Friday, Dec. 7. From Boston to Providence 42 miles, fare, $3. Lodging and Break. at D's. 0.75. Expenses of this day, $4.14. From Prov. thro' Pomfret to Hartford, is 70. m. fare $4.90. Visited Mr. Messar.

N.B. Passed through Roxbury, Dedham, Walpole, Attlebury and Patuxet. Land on the road stony, hard—growth, oak, walnut, maple. Patuxet has cotton factories—buildings of stone.

Saturday, Dec. 8. Tarried at Blake's Stage-house. Bill for supper last night, board this day and breakfast tomorrow morning, $2.58, per his bill.

Sunday, Dec. 9. Left Prov. for N. London, distant 51 miles : stage fare $3.75. Dinner and sling at E. Greenwich 0.50.—had a dreary road through a poor country. We passed Cranston, Natic, Greenwich, Stonington to N. London. The Thames at N. London between one half and a mile wide. Boat will carry four stages at a time : 5 or 6 horses work it.

Monday, Dec. 10. From N. London to N. Haven 61 miles; arrived at 4, P.M. Fare, including board from N. London to N. York, $8.00. Rode up to N. Haven, took a view of the town, the Colleges all in a range, the Churches and the extensive burying-ground—monuments.

Monday, Dec. 10, con^d. From N. Haven to N. York, 90 miles. Changed Boats at N. Haven ; got under way at 7 P.M., arrived at N. York 5 next morning.

Tuesday, 11. Got the steward to carry my trunk to the Union Stage Coach tavern, in Courtland street—took a sling and breakfast, 0.56. Crossed the ferry and took the stage to Newark, 8 m. Elizabethtown, 6. Burlington 13 m., dined at 4 P.M., dinner only, .62. We passed Princeton in the evening, 10 miles from Trenton, and arrived at Trenton, 53 m. from N. Y. Fare from N. Y. to Phil^a. $5.00, distance, 84 m. Bill at Trenton, supper, brandy, lodging, glass of beer, 0.81. Left Trenton in the steamboat at 6, A.M. Wednesday.

Wednesday, Dec. 12.   Arrived at Phil^a. at 10, A.M.   Breakfast on board the steamboat.   Changed boats at Phil^a.   From Phil^a to Newcastle, 40 m. from N. Castle to Frenchtown, 16 m., thence to Baltimore 70 m., thence to W. City 38 or 40.   Fare from Phil^a. to Frenchtown, on the Chesapeak, including dinner on board, $3.50.   Passed Wilmington in plain sight, 3 m. from the water—the water very dirty.   Arrived at N. Castle at ½ past 3, P.M., took stage. and arrived at Frenchtown at 6, P.M.   Supper and fare to Baltimore, $3.50.   Left at ½ past 6, P.M. in the steamboat Phil^a for Baltimore.

Thursday, Dec. 13.   Arrived at Baltimore at 3, A.M.   Left Baltimore in the mail stage at 6, A.M., took breakfast after riding 12 m. $0.50. Reached Washington city at ½ past 12 at noon, fare $4.00, and went into the State House.   The House of Representatives had adjourned.

From Bangor to Boston, 240 miles.		Fare, $18.25
Thence to Providence,	42	3.00
Thence to N. London,	51	3.75
Thence to N. Haven,	61	
Thence to N. York,	90	8.00
Thence to Trenton,	53	
Thence to Phila.	31	5.00
Thence to Newcastle,	40	
Thence to Frenchtown,	16	3.50
Thence to Baltimore,	70	3.50
Thence to Washington,	40	4.00
	734	**$49.00**

RECAPITULATION.

I find the whole distance from Bangor and Washington as travelled by me 734 miles.   Some say it is only 468 to Boston from Washington—and 240 thence to Bangor=708.   My stage fare and boat fare, including 4 meals, was $49.00
   Luggage at N. York and Baltimore   50

I was on the road from Bangor to Portland, 2½ days, and from Portland to Washington 7½ days, resting and stopping only one day, viz., at Providence.

Expenses on road besides fare from Bangor to Portland,   2.50
From Portland to Washington,   12.50
                                                            _____
                                                            $64.50

At no place on the road were meals more than 50 cts. each, except at Burlington, N. Jersey, I paid for Dinner 0.62½.

Thurs. Dec. 13.   Went to the Capitol at ½ past one P.M.   H. of Rep. had adjourned early—saw one or two quondam friends—hunted for a seat—returned to Indian Queen Stage tavern.

Friday, Dec. 14.   Settled with the Ass^t P. M. Gen. and paid him $184.59 in full and took his receipt.   Funeral of Mr. Trimble, of Ohio. The Marine corps escorted the corpse to the Senate chamber, laid it in front of the Pres^ts chair, the Senators took the fore seats, the Rep^s. the hinder seats, the Pres^t of the Senate and Spk^r. of the House sat together in the Pres^ts' seat, the Chaplain in the Secy's place in front of the chair.   He gave an extemporaneous address of 20 minutes—in substance, "the occasion reminds us all of our own mortality.   Tho' we are prone to think less of death than of any other thing of moment, yet of all others it ought to fill our minds and hearts with the most concern."   He then made a short prayer.

The Senators, the Speaker of the House & the Rep⁵ from Ohio, wore white scarfs,—the others (members of the House) wore crape on the left arm. The coffin was cov⁴ with black velvet, a very large silver plate on its lid. Most of both Houses followed the corpse in hacks.

Friday, Dec. 14. In the first view one has in approaching Washington, his eye fixes on the Capitol, its two stupendous wings ; its two lofty domes. It is built of white granite, made more white by a washing. The area of many acres about it is enclosed with an iron banister picket fence, standing on a wall one & a half foot high, which wall is cap' with hewn stone 2½ feet wide, into which the iron pickets, 5 or 6 feet high are set. A very few houses near the Capitol, which stands on an eminence. The Capitol we pass, leaving it on the left hand, & enter Pennsylvania Avenue, running west from the Capitol, one mile to the President's house.

Half way down the Avenue is the Indian Queen tavern, where the stages leave the travellers unless requested to be left at some other particular place. Here one will have a room by himself, fire and candles at 12 or $14 per week. A bell for each room—the house is divided into sections—a servant to a section. Here a number of members, vulgarly called a "Mess," put up, and have a separate table.

As the House of Rep. was very full, I could not find a seat to my mind. Took one in the rear. The rule is, they who first attend, select their seats, to which, when so selected, the occupants have a prior right till they abandon.

Saturday, Dec. 15. Visited the Library, in the Capitol,—it contains about 10,000 vols. Members may take books 2–8ᵛᵒˢ or 12ᵐᵒˢ a week 4ᵗᵒˢ or folios, 3 weeks to their lodgings. Took seat—the Houses meet at 12—adjourn at 3 P.M. Sworn—each member is sworn according to the form in his own state. I lifted my hand—John Randolph sworn just before me—swore on the Bible, and kissed it. Prayers in the morning by the Chaplain, the Speaker then takes the chair, calls to order—the members sit with hats on or off at pleasure. The Speaker first calls, "Have the members from New Hampshire any petitions to present"—"Mass."—and all the states successively. A member rises, holds the petition in his hand, states its substance, moves to dispense with reading its details, and to have it referred to one of the Standing Committees, naming the Comᵉᵉ. A page takes it from the member, and lays it on the table, and the Speaker says it is now moved that the petition last presented be referred, &ᶜ.—and it is so referred. Next, he calls for reports of Standing Committees, then Special Comᵉᵉˢ, then motions, resolutions.

Several resolutions offered; one by Mr. Whitman to amend the constitution as to Electors, &ᶜ.

Sunday, Dec. 16. Attended public services in the Rep. Chamber,—a concourse of gent. and ladies. Only one exercise, beginning at 11, A.M. Chaplain of the Senate, Mr. P———, preached extempore from these words, "In Christ Jesus, neither circumcision availeth anything, or uncircumcision, but a new nature." He undertook to show the nature, necessity and evidences of Regeneration. A Methodist, he variously modulates his voice, and has much action. A small choir of singers.

The hacks stand about the tavern as on other days.

(To be continued.)

THE PROPRIETORS OF THE SUDBURY-CANADA GRANT, 1741.

Communicated by the Hon. Israel Washburn, Jr., LL.D., of Portland, Maine.

WHILE Mr. Washburn was preparing for publication his "Notes Historical, Descriptive and Personal of Livermore, Maine," which work was noticed in the Register, volume xxviii. page 483, there came into his hands, he writes, "two small memorandum books belonging to the family of Dea. Elijah Livermore, the founder of that town.   In one of them, a small leather-covered book, are sundry entries by different hands.   Among them is the following article, which refers evidently to the proprietors of the Sudbury-Canada Grant, ultimately located in Maine, embracing the present towns of Jay and Canton."   Mr. Washburn has printed in the above-named book (page 131), a journal of a person who went out to assist in the survey of Livermore in 1772, copied from this book. He has also furnished us with other extracts which will appear in future numbers of the Register.   EDITOR.

October yᵉ 26ᵗʰ 1741.

A Lift tax of Fifteen Shillings a man to be paid on every wright by the petitioners in the Expedition to Canada in 1690—who are as follows—(viz)

James Taylor	Richard Burt
John Flin	Danˡ Mackclafelin
John Jones	Joseph Merriam
John Green	Peter Grant
Thomas Gree	Samˡ Graves
Ephraim Twichell	Joseph Trumbull
Isaac Shefield	Samˡ Wright, Esqʳ
Pallmer Goulding	Ebenezer Rice
Joseph Johnson	John Coggin
James Moore	Josiah Coggin
Ebenezer Flagg	Samˡ Robins
Daniel Moore	Caleb Bridges
Joshua Kibbe	Ebenezer Newton
James Taylor	John Fay
Nathaniel Morss	Samˡ Lyzcom
Charles Richardson	Daniel Mixer
Frᵃ Mockett	Nathaniel Dike
Richard Ward	William Green
David Bruce	Thoˢ Weaks
Samˡ Graves	Daniel Wallker
Samˡ Stone	Daniel Wallker, Junʳ
Joseph Stone	John Woodward
Micha Stone	Ebenezer Corey
John Wasson	Edward Ward
Ebenezer Twichell	James Paterson

Amos Hide
Norman Clark
Ebenezer Corey, a secondwright
Noah Parker
Benjⁿ Parker
Joseph Bouthetot
John Clark
Richard Willde
Joseph Rutter
Jonathan Parker
Jacob Gibbs
Peter Bent
Randall Davis
John Jackson
James Taylor[1]
John Oslin
John Mixer
John Jones
John Green
Thomas Green
Ephraim Twichell
Isaac Shefild
Palmer Goolding
Joseph Johnson
James Moore
Ebenezer Flagg
Joshua Kibey
James Taylor
Nathaniel Morse
Charles Richardson
Francis Mockett
Richard Ward
John Brewer
Samuel Graves
Saml Stone
Joseph Stone
Micah Stone
John Wesson
Ebenezer Twichell
Richard Burt
Daniel Mackclafelin
Joseph Meriam
Peter Grant

Samuel Graves
Joseph Tremball
Saml Wright
Ebenezer Rice
John Cogin
Josiah Cogin
Saml Robins
Caleb Bridges
Abner Nuton
John Fay
Saml Lyscomb
Daniel Mixer
    Fletcher
Nathaniel Dike
William Green
Thomas Wakes
Daniel Walker
Daniel Walker, Junior
John Woodward
Ebenezer Corey, a firstwright
Edward Ward
James Paterson
Amos Hide
Norman Clark
Ebenezer Corey, a secondwright
Noah Parker
Benjⁿ Parker
Joseph Bouthetot
John Clark
Richard Willd
Samuel Parris

January 27th 1738
Received of Mr Parker
ye Colector the sum of 2-15.0
To convay to ye Tresuar pr me
    Josiah Richardson
The Tresuar is Capt Samuel
Stone, J^r of Sudbury
The Comitee are
Capt Samuel Stone
Capt Palmer Goolding
Seg^t Joseph Johnson
    Josiah Richardson

The names of the men admitted into the Sosiatey are as follows—who are to pay down the sum of Thirteen shillings:

Joseph Rutter
Jacob Gibbs
Jon^a Parker

Peter Bent
Randall Davis

[1] It will be observed that here commences a repetition of most of the preceding names. —Editor.

October yᵉ 3ʳᵈ 1741

A true list of the naimes of the persons are contained hearein that ware noted to pay five shillings a man one wright and to be payed to Mʳ Noah Parker their Colector and this list is comitted to him accordingly by order of yᵉ sd Sosiatey

Attest   Josiah Richardson
Clerk for sd Sosiatey.

September the first Tusday 1739

September yᵉ 14ᵗʰ 1741

The Reconing at Mʳ Mokets   £.   s.   d.
    was in the hole   2.   12.   0
    ondly yet due to sd Moket   3.   6

The meeting is adjorned to Monday yᵉ 26ᵗʰ day of October next at Twelve oth clock noon sd day

The adjornement is to the first Tusday of October next at Twelve of yᵉ clock noon sd day

1. 15. 0

Framingham, Octʳ 26, 1741

Recᵈ of Mr. Noah Parker the sum of three pounds four shillings & four pence being the expence of the Canada Petitionors &c.

Pr Francis Moquet

Framingham, Octʳ 26, 1741

Recᵈ of Mr. Noah Parker the sum of seven pounds of the Canada Petitionors Money

Pr Pal: Goulding

MARRIAGES IN WEST SPRINGFIELD, 1774–96.

Contributed by Lyman H. Bagg, A.M., of West Springfield.

[Continued from vol. xxix. page 152.]

THE Intentions of Marriage between John Allen of Wt Springfield & Rachel Hendrick of Northampton were entered and published July 3, 1779.

Lt. John Millar & Mrs. Lucretia Day both of West Springfield were joined together in Marriage July 8ᵗʰ, 1779.

The Intentions of Marriage between Jacob Chapin & Ruth Bedortha both of West Springfield were entered & published July 10ᵗʰ 1779. [M. July 29.]

The Intentions of Marriage between John Single & Widᵒ Margaret Forbes both of West Springfield were entered and published July 31ˢᵗ 1779.

The Intentions of Marriage between Jeremiah Stebbins of Wt Springfield & Elizabeth Brewster of Windham were entered July 31ˢᵗ 1779, & published the same Day.

Capt John Bryant & Miss Hannah Mason both late of Boston were joined together in Marriage Tuesday August 10ᵗʰ, 1779.

The Intentions of Marriage between Mr. Heman Day & Miss Lois Ely both of West Springfield were entered and published September 11, 1779.

The Intentions of Marriage between Thomas Burbank of Springfield & Elizabeth Higgins of West Springfield were entered and published October 9th 1779.[1]

The following persons were married on the [dates attached?] to their respective names by me Joseph Lathrop?

Darius Wright & Lovisa Taylor both of West Springfield Jan 16th 1783.

Dirick Van Horne & Rachel Bartlet both of West Springfield, Feb. 17th 1783.

Elisha Farnham & Thankfull Day both of West Springfield June 12th 1783.

Roger Cooley Jnr & Huldah Ely both of West Springfield August 7th 1783.

Simeon Ely Junr & Margaret Smith both of West Springfield August 21, 1783.

Captn Moses Field of Springfield & Mrs. Lydia Champion of West Springfield November 26th 1783.

Hezekiah Warriner Junr and Katherine Leonard both of West Springfield December 4th 1783.

Joseph Carrier & Irene Howard   ⎰ all of West Springfield
Joseph Howard & Eunice Carrier   ⎱ Decemr 17th 1783.

Stephen Miller & Sarah Taylor both of West Springfield February 20th 1784.

Samuel Alvard & Hannah Day both of West Springfield, May 13, 1784.

The Intention of Marriage between Pelatiah Ashley and Polly Jones both of West Springfield was entered January 21, and published the 24, 1796.

Paul Chapin of Springfield & Clarissa Killborne of West Springfield were joined in Marriage 30 June 1784.

Benjamin Brackett & Lois Tuttle both of West Springfield were joined in Marriage Sept. 30th 1784.

Captn Augustus Diggins of Enfield & Miss Sabra Stebbins of West Springfield were joined in Marriage Octo 1, 1784.

David Deane of Washington & Phebe Hitchcock of West Springfield were joined in Marriage 6th Decemr 1784.

The Intentions of Marriage between Gidn Jones Junr & Mrs. Lydia Woolcott both of West Springfield were entered July 9th & published the 10th 1785.

The Intention of Marriage between Mr. Isaac Morley Junr of West Springfield & Miss Beulah Harmon of Suffield was entered August 4th & published the 7th 1785.

The Intention of Marriage between Aaron White & Lucy Kellogg both of West Springfield were entered & published July 30th, 1785.

The Intentions of Marriage between [Seth? Ward?] of Wilmington in the State of Vermont; and Ruth Taylor of West Springfield, were entered August 23d & published the 28th 1785.

---

[1] The preceding records should have been printed after the heading on p. 146 of vol. xxix., but they were accidentally omitted.

The Intention of Marriage between Reuben Frost & Hannah Farnham both of West.Springfield was entered August 23ᵈ & published yᵉ 28ᵗʰ 1785.

The Intention of Marriage between Mr. Alexander Wolcott of Springfield & Miss Frances Burbank of West Springfield was entered August 30ᵗʰ & published Septemʳ. 4ᵗʰ, 1785.

The Intention of Marriage between John Pheland & Mary Lamb both of West Springfield was entered September 3ᵈ and published yᵉ 4ᵗʰ, 1785.

The Intention of Marriage between Elijah Bliss and Charlotte Bagg both of West Springfield was entered Septʳ. 10ᵗʰ and published the 13, 1785.

The Intention of Marriage between Oliver Leonard and Abiah Warriner both of West Springfield was entered Septemʳ 24, and published Octᵒ 1ˢᵗ 1785.

The Intention of Marriage between Lewis Smith of West Springfield & Eunice Judd of Northampton was entered September 26ᵗʰ & published Octᵒ 2, 1785.

The Intention of Marriage between Solomon Stebbins and Mahlah Day both of Wᵗ Springfield was entered Octᵒ 1, & published yᵉ 2ᵈ, 1785.

The Intention of Marriage between Ephraim Deane of Washington in the State of Connecticut and Abigail Hitchcock of West Springfield was entered November 16ᵗʰ and published the 22ᵈ 1785.

[To be continued.]

DOCUMENTS RELATING TO THE EXPEDITION TO PORT ROYAL, 1710.

Communicated by WALTER LLOYD JEFFRIES, A.B., of Boston.

THIS expedition, which completed the conquest of Acadia, sailed in September, 1710, and arrived before Port Royal towards the end of the month. After a short defence the garrison surrendered with the honors of war.

The good ship Despatch was owned by David Jeffries & Co., of Boston, and William and Sheldon Chambers, of London—the two firms being intimately connected in business.

The debtor side of the second document is missing. The third document is a copy, written evidently by the clerk of the council, the other papers being all originals.

[DOCUMENT No. I.]

[Page 1.]

The Honᵇˡᵉ ffrancis Nicholson Esqʳ to David Jeffries & Partnʳ Dr.

To the Hire of the Ship Dispatch Beamsly Perkins Comᵈʳ from yᵉ 12ᵗʰ: of Augᵗ to the 9ᵗʰ of October Is two months two days at £140 pʳ month being taken up for an Hospital to Port Royal   .   .   £290 .. ..
Sundrys delivered at Anna Polis Royal formerly Port Royal for the use of Her Majᵗⁱᵉˢ Fort there

To 14900 f^tt of Boards D^d Mr Veering
  7296 of Joyce D^d   Ditto
30 f^tt Plank   60 of Boards D^d **Mr. Hutchinson**
  40 of Joyce D^d   Ditto
  748 of Boards D^d   Ditto

23044 foot . . . . at 52s. p' m	59 17 10
600 red oak hhd. staves at 35s. p' m	1 1 0
1800 shingles . . . at 11s. 6d. p' m . . .	1 0 8
45 foot of oak plank at 4d.	15 0
20 fathom 3½ inch rope	2 0 0

Suma   £354 14 6

Three hundred fifty four ponds, fourteen shillings & Sixpence New-England mony, makes (at forty per Cent Exchange) Sterling mony, two hundred fifty three pounds, seven shillings & Sixpence; being the Exchange agreed upon p' ye Councill of War, with Mr John Boreland Her Maj^ties Agent here.

By Capt George Martin Commander of
Her Maj^ties Ships upon the Intended
Expedition.

You are hereby required and directed without Loss of time to order the fitting & Equipping of the Dispatch ffrigott for the receiving on board the Sick & Wounded men, according to yor agreement with the Councill of War; and I have ordered two Men to Oversee that the work be done as it should be, and for yor so doing this shall be yor order Dated at Boston this 12th of Aug^st 1710.   G. MARTIN.

  To Mr Jeffries
  or his Partner
        These.

[Page 2.]

At Her Maj^ties Councill of War for the
Expedition to Port Royal &c: held at
Boston In New England September
ye 12th 1710.

Pursuant to a vote of the Board the thirty first of July past, That it's necessary for ye Service a Ship be taken up to go in the said Expedition, as an Hospital for Her Maj^ties British forces, And it being reported that the Ship Dispatch ffrigott Capt Beamsly Perkins Commander is suitable for that occasion and proposals having been made to Mr David Jeffries Merchant, Agent for ye Owners of the said Ship. That the same hire be allowed for her as was paid by ye Government here for the Ship Marlborough Gally Capt Carnock, taken up for a storeship in the Last Years intended Expedition to Canada, which by the Record presented appears to be at the rate Ten shillings p' tun p' month in Consideration of her being Equipt wth Twenty Guns.

Resolved that the like sum of Ten shillings p' tun p' month be paid in New England to the Owners of the said Ship Dispatch ffrigott or their Agent for her hire, the time commencing on the twelfth Day of Aug^st Past, she being a ship of Greater Burthen & of the same force wth ye Marlborough above named.

And that she stand on the same foot as to her risque by ye Enemy, with the Establishment of the Massachusets Government for Ships & Vessells, by them taken up & hired for the Publick Service & no otherwise.

G. Martin   ffr Nicholson
Wall: Riddell   Sam : Vetch
Geo: Gordon   Robt Reading

[Page 3.]

Boston In New England 9ber 7th 1710.

My Lords.

    I desire that yor Lordships would be pleased to order payment thirty days after sight of this my first bill of Exchange, my second, third & fourth of the same tenor and date not being paid, unto Messrs William & Sheldon Chambers of London Merchants or their order, the sum of Two Hundred fifty three pounds, seven shillings & Six pence Sterling mony of Great Britain being for the hire of the Ship Dispatch ffrigott being taken up p' order of the Councill of War here for an Hospital Ship in the Expedition against Port Royal now Anna-Polis Royal; and for Lumber delivered at Port Royal for her Maj^{ties} Fort, according to the acco^{tt} herewith. I desire that yor Lordships would be pleased to order the payment according to the tenor of this bill & yor Lordships so doing will be for her Maj^{ties} Interest & Service, I am   My Lords

Yo^r Lordships most obedient humble serv^{tt}
FR. NICHOLSON.

To The Right Honble
the Lords Commissioners of the
Treasury, at the Treasury
Chamber at White Hall.

[DOCUMENT No. II.]

P' Contra . . . . C^r.

By Sundry Provisions rec^d out of Her Maj^{tys} Ship
  Dragon vizt

Bread 4728 : is 42c. ... qrs. 24lb. at 22s.	£46	8	10		
Pork 1310 pds. at 8d.	£43	13	4		
Pease 25 bushells at 6s.	£ 7	10	00		
Oatmeal 37 bushells at 6s.	£11	2	00		
Butter & Suet 26, at 6^s	£ 6	10	6		
	115	4	8		
Is Sterling mony allowing 40 pr C^t Exch of M^o				82	6	1
Ballance due				£164	6	1
				246	12	2

Boston, New England 18th July 1711.

Errors Excepted p'

[Reverse.]

Pursuant to an Order Directed to us from their Excell^{ces} Joseph Dudley Esqr Capt Genl & Governo^r of Her Maj^{tys} Province of Massachusets Bay in New England &c: And Francis Nicholson Esqr Genl of Her Maj^{tys} Forces on the late Expedition to Nova Scotia bearing date June 14th. We have examined the within Acco^{tt} & allow as a Just charge agreeable to y^r rates then given & after deduction made for ye Provisions from Her Maj^{tys} Fort & Ships Due to Ballance the Sum of one hundred Sixty four pounds, Six Shillings & one penny Sterling mony. Witness our hands at Boston June 21th 1711.

[DOCUMENT No. III.]

1711.   The Honble Francis Nicholson Esqr. Generall of Her Maj^{tys}
Forces for the Expedition to Nova Scotia.

D^r.   1711.   *Pr Contra. . . .* **C^r.**

To Hire of the Ship Dispatch taken up by Order of ye Council of Warr at Annapolis-Royal ye 9th 8ber 1710 to Transport the French Garrison to France & to remain in Her Majtys Service untill her return to Boston where she arrived the 18th June 1711, Is 9 months One Day at 12s. p' Tun p' Month the said Vessel measuring 284½ Tuns is Sterling . . . . £1542| 8|...

By : Ballance due | £1542| 8|...

Boston New England 18th July 1711.

Errors Excepted p'

[Reverse.]

Pursuant to an Order Directed to us from his Excell^{cy} Joseph Dudley Esqr Capt Genl & Govern^r in Chief of Her Maj^{tys} Province of the Massachusets Bay in New-England &c. & The Honble Francis Nicholson Esqr Genl of Her Maj^{tys} Forces in the Late Expedition to Nova Scotia We have Examined the within acco^{tt} & allow fifteen hundred and forty two pounds Eight shillings Sterling a Just Charge & due according to ye Resolve of ye Councill of Warr   Witness our hands at Boston July 21st 1711.

John George
Thos Steel
John Coleman
Wm Harris.

Copy.

[DOCUMENT No. IV.]

To All People unto whom this present bill of sale shall come Timothy Brett & Robert Gregory Gentlemen, Lieutenants of Her Maj.^{ties} Ship the Chester, Capt Thomas Mathews Commander, & now Riding at Anchor; in the Harbour of Boston in the County of Suffolk in New England,   Know Ye that we the said Timothy Brett & Robert Gregory, for & in consideration of the Sum of one hundred & Fifty pounds Currant mony of New England to us in hand at and before the Ensealing & delivery of these presents well & truly paid by Messrs David Jeffries & Charles Shepreeve of Boston aforesaid merchants Have given, granted, bargained & sold and by these presents do fully, freely and absolutely Give, Grant, Bargain, sell and confirm unto the said David Jeffries & Charles Shepreeve all that the whole Hull or Body of the Good Sloop named or called the [blank] of the Portage or Burthen of thirty five tuns or thereabout now at Anchor in the Harbour of Boston aforesaid being lately taken from the French by Her Maj^ties Forces under the Command of the Honble Francis Nicholson Esqr Generall for the late Expedition to Port Royal in Nova Scotia, & there condemned wth all & Every the Mast, Sails, Anchors, Cables, Boat, Oars, Ropes, Cords, Tackle, Apparell, Stores, Guns, Small Artillery Ammunition, Furniture, Bowspritt, Boom & Appurtenances whatsoever to the said Sloop belonging or in any wise appertaining To Have and To Hold the said Sloop [blank] and premisses with the appurtenances unto the said David Jeffries and Charles Shepreeve their Exec^rs Admin^rs & Assigns to his & their own sole & proper benefitt & behoof for Ever; And we the said Timothy Brett & Robert Gregory Do avouch our selves at the time of the Ensealing & delivery of these presents, to be the only true sole & Lawfull Owners of the said Sloop [blank] and premisses: Having in our selves, full power good right & lawfull authority to Grant, bargain, sell, and assure the same unto the said David Jeffries & Charles Shepreeve their heirs, Execut^ts Adm^ts and Assigns for Ever. And that free & Clear and clearly acquitted Exonerated & discharged of and from all and all manner of former and other Gifts, Grants, bargains, Sales, Titles, troubles, charges, Incumbrances and Demands whatsoever And lastly do covenant, promise, Grant & agree bind & oblige our selves, our heirs, Exec^rs Admin^rs from henceforth and for ever hereafter to Warrant & Defend the said Sloop [blank] and premisses wth the appurtenances unto the said David Jeffries & Charles Shepreeve their Heirs, Executors, Administrators & assigns against the Lawfull Claims & demands of all & Every person & Persons whomsoever, Perils of Seas, fire, Pirates & Enemies only Excepted In witness whereof we have hereunto sett our hands & Seals the twenty first day of December Anno Dom: 1710 Annoq Reginæ Annæ Mag: Britt: Nono.

Signed, Seal'd & Delivered
in the presence of us   T Brett   [seal.]
  David Jeffries jun^r   R Gregory   [seal.]
  John Francklyn.

> Recd the Day & Year above written of Messrs David Jeffries & Charles Shepreeve one hundred & fifty pounds in full for the above mentioned premisses.
>
>   P' R Gregory
>   T Brett.

A WRECK IN 1695–6 ON CAPE FEAR ISLAND.—A correspondent in Charleston, S. C., informs me that in the year 1695 or 1696, a vessel from New-England was wrecked on Cape Fear Island, and fifty-two of the passengers were removed therefrom by the Governor of South Carolina to the vicinity of Charleston. What was the name of this vessel, the port in New-England from which she sailed, and the names of the passengers?

Boston, Mass.   C. W. TUTTLE.

ABSTRACTS OF THE EARLIEST WILLS ON RECORD, OR ON THE FILES IN THE COUNTY OF SUFFOLK, MASSACHUSETTS.

Prepared by WILLIAM B. TRASK, Esq., of Boston.

[Continued from page 81.]

RICHARD BARBOUR.[1]—Inventory of the house, lands and goods of Richard Barbour deceased taken and apprised by Henry Chickering, Samuell Morse and Nathan Aldous,[2] 15. 1mo. 1644. The house and lands, £18. Amount of inventory, £30. 03. 09. See abstract of the Will of Richard Barbour, REGISTER, iii. 178.   (File No. 33.)

JEFFERY STAPELL.—A True Inuentory of the goods of Jeffery Stapell latte deseased valewed By Eaderd Batts [Bates] and John vppame,[3] in the fyrst month 1647. On house with 8 ackers of land. 12. 0. 0 ; wearinge aparell, Bedinge, Brass vesells, puttor, Iron, workinge Toolls, Earthen vesels, woodene things, goatts and a Callf, Debts Dew, swyne. Sume is, 34. 7. 2. Edward Bate, John vppame.   (File No. 58½.)

[Jeffrey Staples, or Staple, of Weymouth, had Martha, buried Feb. 17, 1640. *Savage.*]

THOMAS LECHFORD.—An in ventory of the goods of Tho : Leatchford,[4] deceased, valued by Robert hull and James Johnson according to theire best Judgment & Consience.

3 day	Impⁿ 4 paire sheetes one p'	01	10	00
3 mo.	2 paire	01	00	00
1648.	3 paire	00	16	00
	4 paire	0	10	00
	It. foure paire of pillow beares	0	13	06
	It 4 table cloathes	00	07	06
	It 14 table napkines	00	07	06
	It 6 old towels	00	01	04
	It two old cloathes	00	00	06
	It one glass	00	01	00
	It one Pillow	00	04	00
	It an old cloake badge & seuerall small things in it, but all valued at	00	06	00
	It A cap 8ˢ & a bible 6ˢ	0	14	00
	It A chest	00	02	06
		06	13	10

lettⁿ ad colligendum bona defuncti
are granted to Robᵗ Hull

ROBERT HULL
JAMES JOHNSON.

[1] Richard Barbour, or Barber, of Dedham, was freeman May 13, 1640. He was one of the 68 original proprietors of Lands in Dedham, to whom was granted 6. 12mo. 1642, "upland ground fit for improvement with the plough." He died June 18, 1644, leaving probably no near connections, as he gives his house, lands and goods in Dedham to his executors, Henry Brock and his son John Brock.

[2] Nathan Aldis, one of the first two deacons of the church in Dedham.

[3] John Upham removed from Weymouth to Malden about 1650.

[4] Incorrectly *Fratchford*, REGISTER, vii. 175.

Mr Samu: Wilbore did depose that when he married the widow of Tho: Lechford late of Boston scriv. deceased, he never received or had any of the Widow or other estate of the s^d Lechford no not so muche as his s^d wiues wearinge apparell, taken vpon Oath before the Court   Incr. Nowell, Sec^ry

2 (3) 48   (File No. 71.)

NOTE.—The Hon. J. Hammond Trumbull, of Hartford, Conn., who so ably edited and annotated an edition of Lechford's "Plaine Dealing: or, News from New-England," in 1867, has the following in his introduction to that work (page xviii.), relative to the wife of Lechford. "His wife is mentioned in 1639 and afterwards; and, as no evidence has been discovered of his marriage on this side of the water, we infer that she accompanied him from England; but he nowhere gives any information of her family, nor even introduces her Christian name. In July, 1640, he writes: 'I have not yet here an house of my owne to put my head in, or any stock going.' He lived in a house, or part of a house, hired of Nathaniel Micklethwaite of Boston, who was, I think, the agent or factor in New-England of Richard Hutchinson of London, and perhaps of Edward and William Hutchinson after their removal to Rhode Island. It appears that he paid his rent, until August, 1639, to Samuel Hutchinson, and subsequently to Mr. Micklethwaite, whose signature appears, on a page of the journal, to the lease of 'the chamber, etc.,' at £5 per year, from Sept. 1, 1639." He borrowed from Mr. Story, as we learn from the journal, in 1639, two and a half pounds "of the best suger," at 2 shillings a pound, received "of Mr. Keayne for a silver laced coate and a gold wrought cap, £2. 10s.," had also "of Mr. George Story" some holland for his wife's waistcoat, etc. He mentions his wife again in 1640, and also in 1641. He embarked from Boston for England, and sailed on the 3d of August of that year, in company with John Winthrop, Jr., Hugh Peters, Thomas Welde, William Hibbins and others. There were forty passengers, according to Gov. Winthrop, in all. The preface to his book was written from "Clements Inne, Jan. 17, 1641," that is 1641-2, and the work, itself, was printed in London in 1642. Rev. John Cotton, in his *Way of Congregational Churches cleared*, pt. 1, p. 71, says, "When he came to England, the Bishops were falling, so that he lost his friends, and hopes, both in Old England and New: yet put out his Book (such as it is) and soon after dyed." Such was the finale of "*the first Boston lawyer*." But some of his personal effects remained, and they are enumerated and prised in the above inventory, made by two prominent men in the colony.

Having recently seen this inventory of Lechford, among the files at the Suffolk Probate Office, I at once communicated to Mr. Trumbull the fact relative to Lechford's widow. In his reply, dated Jan. 26, 1876, he makes the following suggestion and remarks with regard to Lechford. "Probably he was too poor to pay his wife's passage, with himself, to England in 1641, and left her to follow him when he could provide means. He was in intimate relations with all the banished Wheelwright men, and the 'Antinomians' generally, and acted as the attorney of several of them for the care of the property they left in Boston."

As regards the marriage of Samuel Wilbor to the widow, it must have been prior to Nov. 29, 1645, for on that day, according to the records of the First Church in Boston, Elizabeth Wilbor was admitted to the church. She was his second wife, for it appears that he had previously married Ann, daughter of Thomas Bradford of Doncaster in the south part of the county of Yorkshire, as in his will of March 1, 1607, is shown, as Savage says. Wilbor was an esteemed merchant in Boston. He was disarmed and banished for his known sympathy with the opinions of Wheelwright. In company with Coddington and others, he purchased Aquidneck, afterwards returned to Taunton and Boston, where he had possessions. In his will, dated April 30, 1656, he states that he is " of tanton, in plimouth patten," but gives to his wife Elizabeth, "all ye moueable goods y^t is or shalbee in my house in Boston, where at present I doe inhabit at ye time of my decease." His property seems to have been in various other places, as in Dorchester, Braintree, Rhode Island, Bridgewater and Taunton. He died Sept. 29, 1656, and his will was proved the 6th of November following. An abstract of said will from the original record, Suffolk Probate office, Vol. i. page 281, is printed in the REGISTER, vi. 290. A copy was ordered to be made for the county of Plymouth. A brief abstract of it, from the Plymouth Probate records, was published in the REGISTER, v. 385.

HENRY PEASE.—The last Will & testam^t of Henery Pease Senior. This preasent writeing testifyeth that I, Henery Pease, being verey weake in bodey but in p'fect memorey, haue giuen and granted and by thes preasents doe giue and grant vnto my beloued wife her dwelleing in that p't of my dwelleing howse wch I now dwell in, vntill my two Sonns haue finished my howse wch standeth next the streette. I doe giue her also all the moueables in the said howse, wth the wood and garden stuff and hay. I doe giue her also my Kow and Swyne, wth fowre pownds of the 24^l wch is in the hands of Richard Tare [Thayer] of brantry. I doe also giue her my aforsaid howse next the streett (wch howse my 2 Sonns ar to finish for her so soone as conveniently may be) wth the ground therunto belonging, wch is all the ground betwixt Thomas Matsons[1] and Arthur Clarke,[2] wth all the convenyensyes & easm^{ts} therto belongeing, so long as shee liueth, and at her desece shee shall giue it to one or more of my posterity whom shee pleaseth & to noe other. I doe also giue her my aker of ground, be it more or lesse, lying at Blackstons poynt,[3] so long as shee liueth. I doe also herby giue and grant vnto my Sonn John Pease,[4] The South west p't of my dwelleing howse, wth halfe the ground now belongeing to the whole howse, for him and his heires foreuer. I doe giue him, also, Eight pounds and ten shillings of the 24^l wch is in the hands of Richard Tare, of Brantry. I doe also giue him halfe my aker of Grounde at Blackstons poynt, after my wifes desece. I doe giue him also one of my greate bibles. I doe further by thes presents giue and grant vnto my sonn, Henrey Pease, (when my wifes howse is finished) the North east end of my dwelleing howse, wth halfe the ground Now belonging to the whole howse, the ground is to be deuided by the Execitor and Supervisers. I doe also giue him Eyght pounds and ten shillings of the 24^l y^t is in the hands of Richard Tare, of [Brantry]. I doe also giue him halfe my aker of ground at Blackstons poynt, after my desece. I giue him also one of my greate bibles, as also all my wearing cloathes.

I doe also giue vnto my Daughter, Susana Jacklin, three pounds of the 24^l y^t is in the hands of Richard Tare, of Brantrey, and from her to her 2 Children, that is to say, forty shillings to the Sonn, and Twenty shillings to her daughter.

I doe Further make Thomas Matson Exec'tor, and Franses Dowse[5] and Robert Bradford[6] sup'visers. And to this last my last will & testam^t I haue sett my hand this 3 of August, 1648.

The mark **H** of
Henry Pease

Confermed in the presense
 of Arthur Clarke
  William Ludken[7]
Witnes my hand, henery Pease.

Testifyed by Arthur Clarke & Wm Ludkin, before the Court, that this was the last will & test. of Henry Pease, & that he was of a disposeing mind. Sworne 26(11)48 in Court. WILLIAM ASPINWALL, Recorder.

At a County Court sitting in Boston,
 by Adjournm^t 6° February A° 1683.
The Court being informed that the wife of the above named Testato^r

---

[1] Thomas Matson, a church member and freeman, was one of the disarmed men; a friend of Wheelwright. He moved to Braintree, where he had children born to him. He subsequently became a military officer; died after 1666.

[2] Arthur Clarke was of Hampton and Salem, removed to Boston in 1643, wife Sarah, children Sarah and Samuel; died probably in 1665.

[3] Blackstone's Point, Mr. Drake thinks, "was that afterwards called Barton's Point, now near the northern termination of Leveret street and the Depot of the Lowell Rail Road." See *Drake's Boston*, p. 97.

[4] Savage makes no mention of John and Henry Pease, sons of Henry, Sen., nor of his daughter, Susanna Jacklin. The latter was probably the wife of Edmund Jacklin of Boston, whose will was proved in Sept. 1681.

[5] Francis Dowse lived in Boston, afterward removed to Charlestown, had wife Catharine and several children.

[6] Robert Bradford was of Boston, had wife Martha and children, afterwards wife Margaret; will dated Nov. 16, 1677.

[7] William Ludkin, of Boston and Hingham, was a member of the artillery company.

dyed without makeing a will or disposeing of the house and ground within bequeathed to her for life, with power to give the same to one or more of his posterity as shee should please at her decease, Did therefore grant Power of Administration, de bonis non Administratis of the Testato[rs], unto his surviveing son, Henry Pease, And hee hath given Security to Administer the same according to law, and to bee accountable and responsable for the same and his Adm[con] thereof unto the Court for the County of Suffolke when lawfully required and called thereunto.

Attest p[r] Is[a] Addington, Clre

Administrator's Bond.—Know all men by these pnt[s] that wee Henry Pease, Obadiah Wakefield[1] Joyner, & Grimstone Bowd[2] Cordwainer, all of Boston in the County of Suffolke in New England, are holden and stand firmly bound & obliged unto M[r] John Hubbard, of Boston, Treasurer for the s[d] County, his successors in s[d] office or assignes, in the Sume of two hundred pounds currant money of New England, To the true payment of which Sume wee do binde and oblige our selves, our heirs Exec[rs] and Am[rs] jointly and severally, firmly by these presents. Sealed with our Seales. Dated in Boston the Seventh day of February Ann[o] Dom[l] 1683.

The Condicoñ of this present obliga[con] is such that whereas Henry Pease, formerly of Boston dece[d] did make and ordein his last will and Testam[t] and thereby gave a certain p[t] of his Estate unto his wife during her life, impowering her to make her will concerning the same and dispose thereof at her death to some of his posterity, but shee makeing no disposition thereof, Power of adm[con] de bonis non Administratris of the s[d] Henry Pease was grant[d] unto his surviving son Henry Pease to bee annexed to y[e] will of his said Father. If therefore the above bounden Henry Pease shall and do exhibit unto y[e] County Court for Suffolke a just and true Inventory upon oath of all such goods and Estate left by his s[d] Father as are yet unadministered, and shall well and truely Administer y[e] same according to law, And bee accountable and responsible for the same and his Adm[con] thereof unto y[e] Court for s[d] County of Suffolke when lawfully required & called thereunto, Then this above written obligation to bee void & of none Effect, Or else to abide and remain in full force and virtue.

HENRY PEASE.

Sealed and Deliu[rd]   OBEDIAH WAKEFEILD.
in y[e] presence of   GRIMSTONE BOWDE.
   Samuell Beighton[3]   (File No. 78.)
   Is[a] Addington Clre.

[The Will of Henry Pease is not on record. It is now printed in full from the files.]

THOMAS SATELL.—This to be the last will and Testament of my servant Thomas Satell lately deceased wth much comfort in the Lord. I John Wilson can & will (if called therevnto) Attest vpon my oath w[ch] he expressed to me, betweene him & me Alone, being not willing as he sayd that any

---

[1] Obadiah Wakefield is not mentioned by Savage. Mr. Drake in his Boston history, page 427, has this name on the list of 129 "Handy craftsmen," who petitioned, in 1677, for protection in their several callings.

[2] Not found in Savage, but among the inhabitants of Boston, 1687.—*Dunton's Letters,* p. 325.

[3] Samuel Beighton, of Boston, by wife Ann, had children. He died about 1692.

other should be privy thervnto saue my self vntill he was dead (save that he declared the same or most of it to his brother when he came to visitt him) having Expressed the same to me a former time but After he had spoken to him, he called for me again And declared the same over againe wth this addition, y^t my daughter Mary should have 20^s for a legacy as hauing been much beholding to her (so as is in his will expressed). The wch will of his, laying aside what I wrote before, I did presently sett downe in writing, (according as is in this paper on the other side) setting my name ther vnto. 18. 9. 1651.   JOHN WILSON.

[The above statement and the nuncupative will of Thomas Satell—an abstract of which is given in the REGISTER, iv. 286—are in the hand-writing of the first minister of Boston, who deposed in Court on the presentation of the will, at the date above given.]   (File No. 111.)

MARGERY ELLIOT.—To the Honnord County Court now sitting at Boston

The petition of Margery Elliott Relict of the late Jacob Elliot,[1]

Humbly sheweth

That wheareas yor petitioners late husband made his last will & testament bearing date 28 2m^o 1651 appointing Elder Willyam Colebron & James Penn to be ye overseers of the sayd will, but on due pervsall thereof finds y^t neither executor nor executrix is named therein yett the minde of the Testator in relation to his Eldest sonne & Eldest daughter is fully expressed ; And the rest of the children in relation to their portions left with the death of yor petitioner or alteration of her Condit$\bar{o}$n. And whereas yor petitioner by the Advise of the Elders aforesaid hath married two of hir daughters, & deliuered the some of fifty pounds apeece to their husbands in order to their portions, yor petitioner finding It lyes not in hir power or theirs to devide y^r estate, And y^t Its but necessary for the prevention of future troubles & Inconveniences y^t may arise betweene hir children that due order be observed In order wherevnto hir Request (hir children therevnto consenting & concurring) to this Honnord Court is that Administration to the estate of hir late husband be Graunted vnto yor petitioner and an order for the stateing of each of the childrens parts, y^r Eldest sonne & daughter being appointed by the said Testator & left at their libertys to make & take necessary exchange and satisfaction for their parts as the sayd Administrator & Elders and themselves shall agree for the same as also such part for hir self by ye said order Assigned to hir as this Court sees meet & just, y^t so when God Calls hir out of the world shee maye dispose thereof to such & all of hirs as shee judgeth meete & their neede may be, and that if what shee hath payd allready should exceed their parts due provission in the same order may be made for the Repayment of so much as this Court shall determine and yor petitioner shall pray, &c.

marke

MARGERIE   +   ELIOTT.

This petition of o^r honnored mother we whose names are vnder writt: doe declare y^t wee doe allow & approve thereof as just & necessary & w^t

---

[1] Jacob Elliot was an elder brother of the Rev. John Eliot, "the Apostle." An abstract of his will is printed in the REGISTER, iv. 53, proved 20. 9. 1651. His widow, Margery died Oct. 30, 1661.

order yʳ Honoʳᵈ shall make therein wee shall gladly rest in the same

Jacob Elliot[1]

Theophilus Frary for my selfe & wife [Hannah.]

Susanna Elliot

Mehetabel Elliot

Att a County Court held at Boston the 9ᵗʰ of May 1661. In Ansʳ to this petition the Court graunted yᵉ sayᵈ Margery Administration to the estate of the late Jacob Elliot to performe the Imperfect will as neere as she may: as this Court shall order.　　　　　　　EDW. RAWSON, Recorder.

Seth Perry of Boston, Taylor, & Mehittable, Daughter to yᵉ late Jacob Eliot & Margery his wife, now wife to yᵉ sᵈ Seth Perry, consideration, fifty pounds wᵗʰ such other somes as legacies given vnto yᵉ said Mehittable by hir late father Jacob Eliot & Margery his wife by wills now payd vnto vs by Jacob Eliot oʳ eldest brother & executor to yᵉ last will of yᵉ late Margery Eliot oʳ mother of all which wee acknowledge oʳselves fully satisfied, do discharge sᵈ Jacob Eliot, from all due vnto vs by virtue of yᵉ last will of yᵉ late Jacob Eliot & Margery oʳ father & Mother or by any other way or meaning wᵗsoeuer 14ᵗʰ 8ᵐᵒ 1662.　　　　　SETH PERRY.

MEHETABELL PERRY

Witness herevnto Willm Colbron
James Penn

[The above acquittance of Seth Perry was copied from the *Massachusetts Archives*, Book 15 B, page 94.]

Decembʳ 9, 1661.—An Inventorie of the remaining stock of Cattle & Land of Jacob Eliot senioʳ formerly deceased wᶜʰ was designed to pay the portions of severall children, some are allready pᵈ.

Thirteen Acres of Land about Roxbury Gate, £78; one old house, £08; five Cowes, one yearling, £23; Twenty sheep, £08; Mares & horses at Rehoboth, £38; Att Medefeild one Mare & half off a Colt, £14; one Mare at Sudbury, £12; debtes To the sᵈ stock Edwᵈ Adams of Medefeild, £05. 10s; Tho: Dexter Junioʳ, £13; Goodman Puffer, £5; Jacob Eliott, Junioʳ, £1. 10s; Mʳ Pettʳ Olivʳ, £8; Theoph. Frary, £44; Mares & colts at Brantrey with Francis Eliot, £22. Whole amount, £280.

(File No 113.)

WILLIAM FROTHINGHAM.—An Inventory of the estate of William Frothingham of Charlestown, who departed this life 18ᵗʰ of the 8ᵗʰ mᵒ 1651. Dwelling house & orchard & 7 acres of lande, more or lesse in the east feild, £71; 4 acres at Newtowne line, £08; 14½ acres beyond wenotomies & a house there, £30; 7 acres by goodman Lothrops house, £4; 6½ cow com͞ons, £13; 2 hay lots on misticke side, £4; 2 hay lots in the high Feild on this side, £6; 60 acres at Wooburn bounds, 2s. pʳ acre, £6; a bible & doctʳ Prestons worke, 15s. etc. etc. Whole amount of inventory, £308. 09s. 9d.

(File No. 119.)

[To be continued.]

---

[1] Jacob Eliot, son of Jacob, his brother-in-law Theophilus Frary, and Seth Perry, were three of the twenty-nine original members of the Third, or Old South Church in Boston, which was formed at Charlestown in May, 1669.

THE FOLSOM FAMILY.

By the Rev. NATHANIEL S. FOLSOM, of Boston, Mass., and the Rev. JACOB CHAPMAN, of Kingston, N. H.

ON the 26th of April, 1638, the ship " Diligent, of Ipswich," Eng., of 350 tons burden, John Martin, master, set sail from the mouth of the Thames for Massachusetts Bay, having on board nineteen families and six or eight single persons, in all one hundred and thirty-three. Twelve of these families, numbering eighty-four souls, were from old Hingham, the rest from the immediate vicinity; and they had all embarked for the purpose of joining a colony settled in Hingham, Mass., 1633–37 (consisting of ten families and five single persons, in all forty-nine), who had been their friends and neighbors in old Hingham. Among those now emigrating were John Foulsham of Hingham, then twenty-three or twenty-four years of age, and his young wife, to whom he had been married about a year and a half. They were attended by two servants. His wife's father and mother, Edward and Mary Clark Gilman, of Hingham, three younger brothers, Edward (not quite twenty-one years old), John and Moses; two younger sisters, Sarah, and Lydia (who married Daniel Cushing, 1645), and three servants of the family, were fellow-passengers. The rector of the parish, Rev. Robert Peck, with his family, consisting of wife, two children and two servants, also formed part of the company. The immediate occasion of their departure seems to have been trouble in ecclesiastical matters. Their rector, doubtless with the sympathy and aid of most of those constituting the emigrating party, had pulled down the rails of chancel and altar, and levelled the latter a foot below the church, as it remains to this day. Being prosecuted by Bishop Wren, he left the kingdom, together with his friends—who sold their estates at half their real value—promising to remain with them always.

In an account of the family, published forty or fifty years ago in the " Exeter News Letter," from which a large portion of names and dates in the present record has been taken, there is mentioned a tradition that " as several John Smiths were in the company, one of them who came from the town of Foulsham was, for the sake of being distinguished from the others, familiarly called ' John Foulsham,' and by this name, on his arrival in New-England, he chose to be known. So it became his and his posterity's name." Now there may be a real fact of a change or abridgment of name lying at the basis of the tradition. There is presumptive evidence, nay, fair proof of it, in an attestation given by the compiler of the Exeter News Letter Genealogy, of his inspection of a deed signed by John Foulsham, 1672, and recorded in vol. xi. p. 287, in the Registry of Deeds for the Co. of Rockingham, in which some property is conveyed by John Foulsham to his daughter, commencing thus :   " Whereas there is an Intent of marriage between George March, the son of Hugh March of Newbery and Mary Foulsham the daughter of John Foulsham, *alias* Smith, of Exeter."* Why the " alias " there, unless he had once borne the name " Smith," and now wished to make the bequest to his child forever indisputable ? Assuming this to

---

* A friend and kinsman, Nathaniel Shute, Esq., of Exeter, has kindly inspected this deed for us, and we give from his pen a more exact transcript in the text than the News Letter contains, together with the closing portion, here in this note.

" Know ye all men by these presents, that I the said John Foulsham in consideration of

have been his name when he embarked, the explanation given by the " News Letter" cannot be wholly accurate; for there is only one more " Smith" on the list of passengers, and his name was " Henry." There is, however, printed in the town records for 1639, as will be seen further on, the name of a " John Smith" associated with that of " John Foulsham." Where did he come from? In all probability he was one of the sons of the " Henry Smith" already mentioned; and two John Smiths—though there were not " several "—presented motive enough for distinguishing them in name if possible. But with full evidence that " Foulsham" had been for centuries a family name, as well as that of a parish, in Norfolk county; that it was written on monuments, in town records and in history, there does not seem any probability that " John Smith" on his voyage across the Atlantic would drop the name " Smith" and take that of " Foulsham" from the name of a parish in the neighborhood of Hingham. By the change he put himself among the " Foulshams." A better explanation of the adoption of the name " John Foulsham" by the husband of Mary Gilman—if we must accept the change—is that he took the surname because it was his mother's maiden name, and possibly was his own middle name, though middle names were very rare in England at that time. In dropping the last word, his father's surname, he did what many have done, and are doing down to this day. He was nevertheless a lineal descendant of the Foulshams,

the said marriage do Give, grant, Covenant Enfeoffe and fully clearly and absolutely doe give unto the said George and Mary one hundred acres of land lying and being in said Exeter and bounded," &c. &c.

" In witness whereof I the above-said John Foulsham have set my hand and seal the eighteenth of May Anno Domini 1672. 　　　　　　　JOHN FOULSHAM."

" In the presence of
　John Gilman,
　Anthony Somerby."

There is in existence in the Norfolk (formerly part of Essex County, and part of the Province of New-Hampshire) Records of Deeds, Book 2, leaf 291, a copy of still another deed, given by the first John Folsom—for the two following paragraphs from which we are indebted to the kindness of the family of the late Mr. Charles Folsom.

" John Ffulsham of Exiter [N. H.] in respect of y^t paternall love and affeccon and fatherly care and good will of my trustie and well beloved sone Peter Ffulsham of Exiter afores'd and for ye future good and benefit of him and his posterity," gives him

" 40 or 50 acres of land in Hingham in ye county of Norfolk [Eng.] near Norrald Comon and formerly cald by ye name of Ffulsham at ye Boxbushes;—bounded W. wth Norrald Comon, E. with great Langhames and little Langhams, N. with Hardingham Comon, S. E. with land of John Buck formerly and Edward Fflower formerly." " 10 April, 1673."

In possession of the same family is a fac-simile of an autograph of John Folsom, penned the year he died, and showing another way of spelling the name, as follows: "John Foullsam, 1681."

The definite location of the " land in Hingham" is worthy of notice. It may assist in gaining a correct conception of it, to consider that " Hingham was once the head town of a deanery, and contained 43 parishes." " Ffulsham" seems to have been one of these outlying parishes; and the deed proves that the first John Folsom had land there as well as in " Hackford-by-Hingham," as the latter place was sometimes called by way of distinction. The appellation " Ffulsham at the Box-bushes" suggests a site where the Box-shrub abounded, and was planted as an ornament of garden and lawn, perhaps an ancient home of his ancestors—the buildings long gone—one of the freeholds gained by purchase or gift in the parishes in which the manors of the noblemen were a moiety only. The De Marshalls and Morleys had " manors in Folesham" from 1202 to 1580. The De Poinings had " fees" there in 1324. (See for these various statements, " Blomefield's County of Norfolk," vol. 2.) It was also an " advowson" (i. e. with right attached of appointing to a church-living), a " demesne" (the nobleman's tenants being exempt from tolls and taxes). &c., and the names of the bordering parishes of Hardingham, Langham and Norrald (Northwold, where it is stated that " the site of a manor" had become " a pasture-close "), can be all identified. Perhaps the land had been kept so long because of the dear associations connected with it. He remembered the fragrance and greenness of its shrubbery. And now, eight years before his death, he will not alienate the ancestral possession from this family, but bestows it on one of his sons. The father's tribute to the good qualities of the son supplies valuable testimony of character in the absence of any other record.

worthy to be the founder of the Folsom family in America, and fit to transmit the vigorous pulsations of his ancestral blood to future generations.*

The party having landed at Boston, Mass., Aug. 10, 1638, immediately proceeded to their place of destination, about fourteen miles S. E. from Boston. An Adam Foulsham, probably a son of the Adam who died in 1627, and a cousin, if not brother, of John Foulsham, came from Hingham, Eng., to Hingham, Mass., in 1639, but returned to England and died 1670. Their rector remained about three years, when hearing that the bishops were deposed, he returned to England in 1641† (the date given by Daniel Cushing), resumed his rectory, and died 1656. Edward Gilman had with others obtained a grant of land eight miles square in a place now called Rehoboth, near the Rhode Island line, in 1641. In 1647 his name is recorded in Ipswich. Soon afterward he went to Exeter, N. H., where his sons were already established in business. John Folsom and wife, with their children, followed her father and mother to Exeter, probably not earlier than 1650; the first authentic record of their residence in that town being in the year 1655.

During the twelve or fifteen years' residence of John Foulsham in Hingham, Mass., he was not without tokens of the good will of the people.

---

* As to the original derivation of the name FOULSHAM, Hon. George Folsom, in one of the MSS. left by him, says "It arose, upon the adoption of surnames in England, from the town of Foulsham, a village in the county of Norfolk, England [six or eight miles north of Hingham], in which county the family was seated for many centuries, possessing estates in fifteen different places." Thus, John of Foulsham became John Foulsham.

The orthography and pronunciation of the name have varied in the family itself, as well as among others writing and pronouncing it. The first Anglo-American bearing the name spelt it "Foulsham." His son, Dea. John, wrote it "Fullsom" in 1709, and it is so signed in his last will, 1715. In one instance in the Hingham town records it is spelt "Fulsham," but always afterward "Foulsham." In the Exeter records it is uniformly written "Folsom" from the year 1659, with one exception in 1681, when the town clerk wrote "Foulshame." In the records of the First Parish, Haverhill, Mass., 1749–64, it is spelt "Foulsham," "Foulsam," "Folsham," and "Fulsom," on occasion of the baptism of children of "Josiah Foulsham." Originally it was doubtless spelt "Foulshame"—its etymological significance being the *Fowls home*, or breeding-place, or mart. The old syllabic division must have been Fouls-hame, the final syllable becoming shortened into "ham," with the first letter silent, pronounced like *um*, as may now often be noticed in words of that termination. A further shortening appears in 1504—how extensively practised is uncertain—in a Latin inscription on a monumental stone in the floor of the church of Repps, Norfolk co., which translated is, Pray for the soul of Mr. Thomas Folsham, Baccalaureate of the Chapel (Hist. of Norfolk Co., vol. xi. p. 182). This last mode of spelling appears on modern maps of England, designating the town. But everywhere it is now written *Folsom* by those bearing the name.

In regard to the pronunciation of this word, it is now generally pronounced by the family quite like *wholesome* (the writer has never known but one exception). And we suggest that this is a preservation of the old way of pronouncing the name; that in the first syllable "Fouls" the diphthong "ou" was sounded as in "souls, poultry," &c. Certain it is that this old spelling—fouls (or foules)—of our modern word "fowls," occurs in Chaucer—as in his "House of Fame," and in his "Legend of Nine Good Women":—

"As this foule when hit beheld."
"I hear the foules sing."

Our suggestion is, moreover, fully borne out by similar phenomena of pronunciation in modern times. We hear "bowling-alley" (once written *bouling*-alley, and the sphere or ball, *boule*) pronounced in two ways, with the first syllable like "ow" in *howl* and in the drinking-vessel *bowl*. "Johnson, Elphinstone and Perry declare for the former, i. e. as in *howl ;* Sheridan, Scott, Rennell and Smith pronounce it like *hole*. Garrick corrected Walker for pronouncing it like "howl."—(Early English Pronun., vol. i. p. 152.) Even the pronunciation of the word when written as Dea. John Folsom wrote it, "Fullsom," has authority in the old pronunciation of the word "Cowper," like that of *wound* (a hurt) as now heard, with the *ou* as in "group," or possibly nearer the sound of *o-oo*—the sound of the *ow* in "Cowper" as in *howl* being "given it only by those who do not know the family."

† In Mr. Blomefield's "County of Norfolk," vol. 2, p. 425, it is stated that he "came back to Hingham in the year 1646, after ten years voluntary banishment."

It is quoted from Daniel Cushing's Records in Sprague's Genealogy, Appendix, p. 50, that "there was given him by the Town four acres of Land butting upon the Playne eastward and upon the Common westward;" and the author of the Genealogy mentions that "the house standing upon this lot [1828] was built by Foulsham before Daniel Cushing was Town-clerk [1669]—the frame is of sawed oak-timber. My grandfather," the author adds, "bought it in 1744 of Daniel Beal—my father left it in 1800; the Spragues own it at present." This house was taken down in 1875, and some of its sawed oak manufactured into memorial chairs. Another record is quoted of the 30th of January, 1645, that "the seven or nine men chosen to order the prudential affairs of the town shall be chosen out of *the body of the Town,* as well non-Freemen as Freemen;" and the seven chosen were "Thomas Josselyn, George Marsh, Thomas Gill, John Tower, John Smith, John Foulsham, William Sprague." And again, "it is ordered & agreed upon by the town that Capt. Joshua Hubbard and John Foulsham shall have liberty of the two rivers, Rocky Meadow & Bound Brook Rivers, so far as the town hath property, to build & maintain a saw-mill or mills."

It is related in the Exeter News Genealogy that in 1645 there arose some "troublesome business," as Gov. Winthrop calls it in reference to himself personally; a man named Emes, who had been lieutenant of Hingham, having been appointed captain by the government, but rejected by the people, who elected Allen in his stead. Winthrop, then lieutenant-governor, insisted that Emes should be obeyed as commanding officer; the people insisted upon having Allen for their captain, and, "speaking evil of dignities," asked, "What have magistrates to do with us?" protesting also that they would die at the sword's point if they might not have the choice of their own officers. The result was a requisition on some of the leaders to give security for appearance at court, and on their refusal a commitment to prison. In turn, the friends of the imprisoned arraigned Winthrop for assumption of power and illegal imprisonment. The affair terminated in the acquittal of the deputy governor; and a fine of £155½ was imposed on about ninety persons, £20 of which John Foulsham was sentenced to pay. By some means he was finally exempted; for his name does not appear among the censured and fined.

After his removal to Exeter, the name of "Goodman Folsom" appears in 1659 on the list of "selectmen." He obtained a grant of land, 1660; his sons also all obtained similar grants in years following; he was a juryman, 1662. In July, 1665, being one of a committee representing Dover, Portsmouth, Exeter and Hampton, to consult on certain political grievances, he presented "a petition to the King's Majesty," for consideration by the committee, praying that they "might be governed by the laws of England," and expressing "joy that the King had sent over Commissioners into these parts," and "sorrow that the Commissioners were evilly entertained by the Bay Government." Connected with this, and showing further action in the matter, it is recorded in volume i. of the Provincial Papers of New Hampshire, p. 280, without date, but about 1665, that "testimonies of selectmen are made that John Foulsham, Sen., and three others, Abraham Corbitt, Robert Burnham and Edward Hilton, are principal actors in trying to procure hands to be taken off [i. e. to sign off] from the Bay Government." In 1776, he and his brother-in-law, Moses Gilman, disagreed about their boundary-lines, and the latter, in a passion, pulled up a parcel of fence that stood between their lands. "John Sen'r" instantly entered his complaint; the case was "respited" a few days at the request of Moses. Intercession on the part of mutual friends "persuading to peace meantime proved fruitless." John felt that an insult and a wrong had been committed, and he pressed the trial. The decision was slightly evasive of the question of real line of boundary. But so far as it went it was against Moses, who was required to bear the cost of complaint (16 shillings), and where, by pulling down the fence, he had made gaps and exposed his neighbor's crops to injury, he must put it up and keep it up, "until after next Indian harvest," when, of course, the matter in dispute might be opened again, and a more intelligent decision be given. Mr. Commissioner Dalton, however, "does advise to peace and love in the mean time, as their relation and duty requireth."

From facts like these, the descendants of the Anglo-American JOHN FOLSOM may learn what were some of the traits of character in their ancestor. He was enterprising, courageous, prominent in the communities in which he lived, a leader in public affairs, determined on simplicity in religious worship and equity in the state, a solid, independent, righteous and true man.

The earliest period in which the name appears in history, is the first half of the fourteenth century. There was a John Foulsham of Foulsham, prior of a Carmelite monastery in Norwich, and "præses provincialis" of all England. In all probability he belonged to a family of which the Folsoms are lineal descendants. He was D.D. of Cambridge, and, according to Pitt, is spoken of in John Bayle's Catalogue of Eminent Writers (p. 421), as follows: After an acquaintance with Aristotle's methods, and having got a smattering of the original scriptures [gustatis scripturarum corticibus], he became no mean proficient in controversial theology, knowing how, by means of syllogistic tricks, to turn white into black and men into donkeys. He died in the great plague at Norwich, 1348. Richard Foulsham, also of Foulsham, and probably the prior's brother, was much in the court of John XXII. at Rome (1316–34), with whom he corresponded, and some of his letters to whom were published.

The first traceable ancestor of John Foulsham is (1) ROGER Foulsham, of Necton, county of Norfolk, Eng., whose will is dated 1534. (2) WILLIAM, his son, married Agnes Smith, alias Foulsham, of Besthorpe, and was father of (3) ADAM, of Besthorpe, who married Emma ———, and whose will is dated 1565; he owned lands in Besthorpe, Wymondham (Windham), Bunwell, Hingham and Hackford. (4) Adam, his son, was baptized 1560; married Grace ———; had a home in Hingham and lands in Besthorpe; he died 1630. (5) ADAM, of Hingham, son of the latter, married Agnes ———, and died 1627. The facts in the preceding paragraph, and thus far in the present, are given on the authority of the MSS. of Hon. George Folsom, who visited England and explored every possible source of information. He next states that "Adam," the fourth in descent from "Roger," left a son named "John," i.e. the first Anglo-American John Foulsham. Those who shall accept the "*alias Smith*" can hardly consider him as the son of Adam the third, but of Adam's sister, who had married a Smith. Through her he was the grandson of the previous "Adam." From this first Anglo-American John Folsom, of Exeter, N. H., and his wife Mary Gilman Folsom, are descended, so far as we know, all the Folsoms in America — with the exception of one family, with which is connected a story curious enough to be given in a note below.*

* Mr. Abraham Folsom, of Boston, has related to the writer the following: That his younger brother, James Madison Folsom, who went to Savannah, Ga., 1829, and died before

1. John[1] Folsom, bapt. 1615, in Hingham, Eng. (a town about 14 miles W.S.W. of Norwich, and 97 N.E. of London, in the neighborhood of a small lake about a mile in circumference, and having a fine old stone church with a tower and chime of bells); m. Oct. 4, 1636, Mary, oldest child of Edward and Mary Clark Gilman; d. at Exeter, N. H., Dec. 27, 1681. His widow survived him eight or ten years. They had:

2. i.   John,[2] b. 1638 or '39; m. Nov. 10, 1675, Abigail, dau. of Abraham Perkins, of Hampton; d. 1715.
3. ii. Samuel,[2] b. 1641.*
   iii. Nathaniel,[2] b. 1644; m. 1674, Hannah Faxon, of Hingham; had a son Samuel, b. April 18, 1679. He gave a deed of land in Exeter, 1696.
   iv. Israel,[2] b. 1646; m. and had a son Israel; received "a Grant of Land" in 1664; nothing more is known of him.
4. v.   Peter,[2] b. 1649; has always borne the title of Lieut. Peter.
   vi. Mary,[2] b. 1651; m. 12 June, 1672, George Marsh, of Newbury.
5. vii. Ephraim,[2] b. 1654.

2. Dea. John[2] Folsom (*John[1]*) was a man of high standing and good property, active both in church and in political affairs. He is among the worthies of the first century of Exeter, of whom Judge Smith in his Centennial Address, July 4, 1838, says that "they filled acceptably the municipal and public offices conferred upon them." He was frequently sent to the General Assembly. In the first volume of Provincial Papers, already quoted with reference to his father, there is a deposition (pp. 554–7) from the son as constable, bearing date 1684, that he "had received a list of names in Exeter with fines annexed amounting to £50; that he was required by Gov. and Council to go and demand the sum; but the people refused to pay, saying the taxes should be raised by the General Assembly—which answer he gave to Gov. & Council: whereupon they took the scroll out of his hands and delivered it to Thos. Thurton, provost-marshal, and he was ordered by a warrant from the Secretary to aid the said Thurton." This summary treatment was honorable to him from such a government as that of Cranfield, and shows how "acceptably," at least to the people, if not to the party in power, he filled that special office of constable by forbearing to push the demand for oppressive and unconstitutional taxes and fines. The following

the rebellion, had two sons, Dr. Robert W., who fell in the Battle of the Wilderness, the colonel of his regiment, and James M., a young lawyer, and colonel on the staff of Gov. Brown. As Col. James was passing with a Georgia regiment through Sumter, S. C., a crowd of gentlemen and ladies had gathered at the depot to greet them—the ladies throwing bouquets to the officers and soldiers. Col. James caught one, and on his departure found in it a slip of paper, on which was written the name "Rosa Folsom." His curiosity being greatly excited, he wrote to know about the family, and received the following reply from the young lady's father: "We are descended from one who espoused the cause of liberty under Cromwell, but who died during the Protectorate. At the Restoration his estates were confiscated; and soon afterwards the sons embarked for America, and landed at Albemarle Sound [this must have been, if at all, at the settlement of the second colony at that place, 1667]. Two of the brothers married in America. Shortly after they simplified their name by spelling it 'Folsom.'" Col. James M. is the author of the "Heroes of Georgia," and is now clerk of the court of the county of Strafford, N. H.

* We have received a letter from Hon. Solomon Lincoln, of Hingham, containing an extract from Rev. Peter Hobart's diary, copied by his son, in which it is stated that the two oldest children of John Folsom were baptized—

Samuel, Oct. 3, 1641.
John, Oct. 11, 1641.

There is obscurity in this. No hint exists anywhere that they were twins. And the interval of *eight* days would prove that one of them could not have been baptized on a *Sunday*. Is it probable that John was born on the voyage, or amid the confusion of becoming established in their new home, so that his baptism was delayed until after the second child was born? Nothing definite fixes the birth of John. We have assumed that he was the oldest, without any explicit authority for it.

quotation from the same portion of the Provincial Papers will show the sort of "aid" he gave to the "provost-marshal," and that he could turn with wrath and contempt on the public foes, deacon though he was. Under date of Dec. 29, 1684, there is a deposition of this Thurton that "being sent to collect those fines, and one of 50 shillings on John Foulsham for neglecting the duty of his office as constable, Foulsham told him that if he came to levy execution at his house, he should meet him with a red-hot spit and scalding water; and bade him go, like a rogue as he was." The women of the Gilman family must also have some of the fame of this affair; for the provost-marshal adds, that "being at the house of Edward Gilman [son of the first Edward, and lost at sea about 1653] the wife of James Gilman [grandson of the first Edward, born 1659] told him she had provided a kettle of scalding water for him, if he should come." He thought it rather rough treatment, especially as no money had yet been demanded of them. In one instance in which Dea. John's wife had been slandered by his sister-in-law Hannah, wife of his brother Nathaniel, he was determined the offender should smart for it; and accordingly making complaint before Mr. Commissioner Dalton, he obtained sentence against her that she should "make acknowledgment at some public town-meeting."

Dea. Folsom had nine children, viz.:

    i.   ABIGAIL,[3] b. Dec. 23, 1676.
6. ii. JOHN,[3] b. 1685.
   iii. SARAH,[3] wife of —— Stevens.
   iv. MARY,[3] m. and left two children.
   v. LYDIA,[3] wife of —— Stockman.
   vi. MERCY,[3] m. Lieut. James Dudley, cooper, son of Stephen (Rev. *Samuel,*[2] of Exeter, Gov. *Thomas*[1] *Dudley*); had seven children, one of whom, John, of Raymond, was a judge of the supreme court of New-Hampshire.
7. vii. ABRAHAM,[3] m. Elizabeth ——, and died about 1740.
8. viii. JEREMIAH,[3] m. Elizabeth ——; built, in 1719, the brick house just south of Newmarket village, which stood till 1874; d. 1757.
9. ix. JONATHAN,[3] m. Anna, dau. of Nathaniel Ladd, Esq., whose wife Elizabeth was dau. of Hon. John Gilman. He died 1740, the father of twelve children. His wife administered on his estate.

3. SAMUEL[2] FOLSOM (*John*[1]) m. Dec. 22, 1663, Mary, dau. of Henry Robey; d. about 1700: had:

    i.   MARY,[3] b. Sept. 27, 1664; m. Ezekiel Ladd.
   ii. EBENEZER,[3] lived in Hampton in 1712; afterwards probably went to Stratham.
   iii. SAMUEL,[3] was administrator on his father's estate in 1702; removed to Hampton, near the Portsmouth line; purchased a place in Greenland, 1710; d. prior to 1723, without children.
   iv. RUTH,[3] m. March 4, 1692, Moses Norris.
   v. ISRAEL.[3]
   vi. DELIVERANCE,[3] united with the church in Greenland, 1723.

4. Lieut. PETER[2] FOLSOM (*John*[1]) m. May 6, 1678, Susanna Cousins, of Wells, Me.; d. 1717. Children:

    i.   ELIZABETH,[3] wife of Samuel Sanborn.
   ii. SUSANNA,[3] who m. Caleb, son of Moses Gilman and grandson of first Edward; they had two children, David and Caleb.
   iii. MARY,[3] m. Joseph Thing.
10. iv. BENJAMIN,[3] m. Rachel, dau. of James Gilman (son of Moses, who was born in Hingham, Eng., and grandson of the first Edward); d. about 1750.

11. v. PETER,[3] m. Catherine, dau. of Hon. John Gilman and granddaughter of the first Edward. He d. 1718. His widow married a second husband, Richard Calley, of Stratham.

12. vi. JOHN,[3] m. (1) Hannah, dau. of James Gilman ; (2) Mary Lyford.

5. EPHRAIM[2] FOLSOM (*John*[1]) m. Phaltiel Hall ; lived and died (killed by the Indians, 1709) in Newmarket, on a farm still owned and occupied by his descendants. Children :

   i. A daughter, who m. —— Robinson, of Exeter.
   ii. A daughter, m. —— York.
   iii. LYDIA,[3] m. —— Glidden.
   iv. ABIGAIL,[3] wife of Joseph Judkins.
   v. SARAH,[3] m. Thomas Young, Esq., of Newmarket ; children : (1) Joseph ; (2) Thomas, who had a son John.
   vi. EPHRAIM,[3] Jr., m. —— Taylor, whose children were—1. *Ephraim*, who m. Eunice Smart, and had Joseph ; John (who had Joshua, Mary wife of Richardson, Elizabeth wife of Sanborn, Rhoda wife of Sanborn, Eleanor wife of Smith). 2. *Andrew*, of Ossipee, m. Anna dau. of William Folsom, and had Ella wife of Brackett, of Wolfborough ; Andrew, who m. —— Hodgdon. 3. *William*, m. Mary, daughter of John Folsom, son of Lieut. Peter. He was of Newmarket, and died there about the first of the year 1787. Children : John (died of smallpox during the Revolutionary war, one of whose children, Susan, m. Lamson, of Exeter) ; Edward, of Gilmanton (one of whose sisters m. Abraham, son of Abraham, br. of Josiah, son of John, son of Dea. John), m. —— Burley, and had numerous descendants ; Jonathan, who m. Prudence Weeks, Dec. 7, 1786, and left no children ; Ephraim ; Benjamin, blind (living in 1848) ; Hannah ; Mary ; Elizabeth ; Rachel ; also one of the daughters m. —— Kimball, and had a son William.
   vii. WILLIAM,[3] m. (1) Hannah Gilman, of Exeter, and (2) Elizabeth, widow of Benjamin Sanborn. All of his children but Dudley are supposed to be by his first wife. He was twenty years successively a selectman of Newmarket, and died in 1755. He had—1. Maj. *David*,[4] of Epping ; m. Sarah, dau. of Thomas Gilman, of Exeter ; he is on State records as Second Major in the 19th Regiment, 1780 ; died 1791. His children were : (1) Thomas, who m. a dau. of Benjamin Watson, of Nottingham ; (2) Winthrop, who m. a dau. of Thomas Noble, of Lee, had children Noah and Nancy, and removed to New-York ; (3) James, who m. —— Blake, of Epping, and had Winthrop, of Dorchester, N. H. ; (4) Gilman, who m. Ruth Page (of his children, Gilman, b. April, 1796, m. a dau. of Col. Marvin, was in Cleveland, Ohio, 1864, and had two sons. Another, Ezekiel, b. Dec. 1798, m. a daughter of Rev. Ebenezer Fitch, D.D., president of Middlebury College, was for some years a business man in Cleveland. George P., a son of the latter, b. Dec. 1826, graduated at Williams College, studied theology at Auburn Theological Seminary, m. Lilia Frazer, is settled over a Presbyterian Church in Baraboo, Wis.) ; (5) Ezekiel, m. —— Norris, of Epping, and had Noah (m. a dau. of Josiah Smith) ; Moses and Gilman ; (6) David ; (7) Anna, wife of Moses Davis ; (8) Hannah, wife of Noah Dow ; (9) Sarah. The next children of William were : 2. *James*.[4] 3. *Dudley*,[4] who perished with cold in a gondola between Portsmouth and Newmarket. 4. *William*,[4] who administered on his father's estate. He m. Mary Low, of Stratham ; died Feb. 1809. Children : (1) Anna, m. Andrew Folsom, Ossipee. (2) Jacob, of Wolfborough, m. Elizabeth Smart, of Newmarket, June 4, 1787, and had Gilman, whose wife was Mary Rust ; John, who m. Hannah Blake ; Mary, wife of Joseph Edmunds ; Lydia, wife of Nathaniel Rust ; James, of Somersworth, whose wife was Sally Rust ; George, who m. Clarissa Lee ; Henry, of Somersworth, who m. Sally Leighton ; Charles, of Somersworth, who m. Sally Richards. (3) Mary. (4) Lydia. (5) Mehitabel, wife of Robert Smart and mother of Charlotte (wife of Thomas Pendergast, of Exeter), Robert and Jacob. (6) Hannah, wife of Joseph Cooley, of

Exeter, who removed to the West. (7) Betsey, wife of John Brackett, of Wolfborough. (8) Josiah, who m. Abigail Ham, of Durham, and occupied the farm owned by his great-grandfather in the seventeenth century. Of the children of Josiah and Abigail are—1. William, a physician, who m. a dau. of Hon. Smith Lamprey, of Kensington. 2. Mary. 3. Abigail. 4. Josiah. (9) Sally, wife of Joseph Tucker, of Wolfborough. There were also three daughters to William,[3] viz. : *Abigail, Mary* (wife of Dea. James Cram), and *Lydia* (wife of John Lyford).

6.   JOHN[3] FOLSOM (*John,*[2] *John*[1]) b. 1685 ; m. Sarah, dau. of Stephen[4](?) Dudley (b. 1688, m. July, 1708, which would make John at least twenty-four or five years older than his wife ; the dates of two sons of Stephen being given at 1721, 1724, but those of the other six children not being given) ; d. 1755.   They had (with other children):

13. i.   PETER,[4] b. 1718.
14. ii. ABRAHAM,[4] b. 1720.
15. iii. JOSIAH,[4] b. Sept. 25, 1725 ; not to be confounded with Josiah, seventh child of John[3] (Lt. *Peter*,[2] *John*[1]).

7.   ABRAHAM[3] FOLSOM (*John,*[2] *John*[1]) had :

i.   DANIEL,[4] married ; lived in Exeter.
ii. JONATHAN,[4] of Sheepscote, York co., Me. ; d. 1745.
iii. ABRAHAM,[4] joiner, of Exeter ; m. a dau. of William of Newmarket, and sister of Edward of Gilmanton.
iv. MARY,[4] m. James Rundlett ; was a widow in 1745.

8.   JEREMIAH[3] FOLSOM (*John,*[2] *John*[1]) had :

16. i.   NATHAN,[4] b. Newmarket, 1717 ; m. Elizabeth —— ; d. 1769.
17. ii. JEREMIAH,[4] Jr., b. July 25, 1719 ; m. March 28, 1742, Mary Hersey ; d. 1802.
     iii. ELIZABETH,[4] wife of Walter Bryant, Esq.
     iv. SUSANNA,[4] wife of John Mead, of Stratham ; children : *Benjamin*, of Newmarket; *John*, of Deerfield ; *Levi*, of Northwood, and *Jeremy*, of Newmarket.
     v.   ABIGAIL.[4]
     vi. SARAH,[4] wife of Jacob Low, of Stratham.
     vii. ANN,[4] wife of Joseph Young, of Stratham.
     viii. JOHN,[4] of Stratham, b. July 7, 1723 ; m. 1748, Sarah, dau. of Samuel Veasey.   Children : 1. *Samuel*, who died an infant.   2. *David*, b. May 20, 1750 ; m. Dorothy, dau. of the Rev. Wm. Johnson, of Newbury ; their children : (1) Hon. JOHN, of Chester ; (2) William ; (3) Mary, wife of —— Poor ; (4) Martha, wife of Thomas Brackett, and afterwards of Shadrach Robinson ; (5) Nancy, wife of John Adams. (6) Elizabeth, wife of Winthrop Hilton, of Newmarket.   By a second wife, Martha Wiggin, b. 1729, he had : 3. *Sarah*, b. 1758, m. 1777 to John Poor ; 4. *Martha*, b. 1760, wife of Thomas Bracket, and afterwards of Shadrach Robinson ; 5. *Anne*, b. 1762, m. 1788, John Adams, father of Rev. John-Folsom Adams of the Methodist church ; 6. *Elizabeth*, b. 1769, m. to Winthrop Hilton, of Newmarket.   John,[4] of Stratham, was a man of influence, often in office.   His son David,[5] father of Hon. John, ranked very high in general ability ; was one of the early settlers of Tamworth : is said to have been the first to make cut-nails by machinery.   He left in 1788, went to Harrisburg, Pa., died there, and his widow, returning to Exeter, m. —— Blanchard, of Chester.

9.   JONATHAN[3] FOLSOM (*John,*[2] *John*[1]) had :

i.   JOHN,[4] m. (1.) —— Hilton, of Newmarket, and their children were : *John;*[5] *Emma,*[5] wife of Winthrop Odlin ; m. (2) Abigail, dau. of Theophilus Smith (and sister of Theo. S., of Exeter, teacher), and their children were *Mary;*[5] *Elizabeth*[5] (the first and second wives of

John Shaw, Esq. of Pittsfield); *Theophilus,*[5] of Wheelock, Vt.; *James,*[5] of Cornville, Me.; *Ann Bradstreet,*[5] wife of Joshua Bangs, a preacher.

ii. MARY,[4] b. Feb. 17, 1722 ; m. Peter Folsom, son of Peter[3] and Catherine Gilman Folsom.

iii. JONATHAN,[4] b. 1724 ; of Newmarket, next of New Durham ; lost his leg by the bursting of a swivel in the rejoicings over the recent capture of Louisburg : was town clerk of New Durham several years. The most of his children removed to Western New-York.

18. iv. NATHANIEL,[4] b. 1726.

v. ANNA,[4] m. David Gilman (prob. son of Capt. John, son of Moses).

19. vi. SAMUEL,[4] b. Feb. 22, 1732 (same day with Gen. Washington).

20. vii. TRUEWORTHY[4] ("Treworgye," the maiden name of Hon. John Gilman's wife, b. about 1734, and mother of his children), m. Mary West, of Boston.

21. viii. JOSIAH,[4] b. Nov. 5, 1735; moved to Dover ; m. May 27, 1762, Elizabeth (b. April 23, 1742), dau. of Dr. Josiah Gilman, of Exeter, son of Judge Nicholas. Dr. Gilman, when past eighty, would mount his horse and canter off to answer calls from patients who often sent from far. In 1776 he was " appointed to examine and store whatever saltpetre was brought into town ;" held the office of clerk of the proprietors of Gilmanton for more than thirty years. His daughter Elizabeth's children, who passed much of their childhood at his home, cherished his memory with great veneration and love.

ix. SARAH,[4] wife of John Nelson, d. about 1800.

x. LYDIA,[4] wife of Moses Lougee.

xi. ELIZABETH,[4] wife of William Bowden. Their daughter m. —— Nealy, and was the grandmother of Col. Joseph Cilley, of Nottingham, and of Hon. Jonathan Cilley, of Thomaston, Me.

xii. ABIGAIL,[4] wife of Ebenezer Sinclair, who d. 1754. Her brother, Gen. Nathaniel, was guardian to her son Richard. A daughter m. William Hackett, brother of Col. Hackett.

10. BENJAMIN[3] FOLSOM (*Peter,*[2] *John*[1]) had :

i. THOMAS,[4] b. Dec. 2, 1737 ; m. his cousin Elizabeth Gilman (b. Sept. 13, 1739, d. Aug. 5, 1819, dau. of Nehemiah in the line of Moses, son of the first Edward ; a daughter of her brother Theophilus was grandmother of Gen. Lewis Cass) ; d. Dec. 9, 1794. Their children were: *Mary;*[5] *Benjamin;*[5] *Nehemiah*[5] (b. June 16, 1769, m. Betsey Taylor, d. 1836); *Rachel*[5] (b. Dec. 24, m. Nathaniel Neal of Tuftonborough); *Thomas,*[5] b. June 12, 1772, resided in Portsmouth, m. (1) Nancy, widow of Josiah Adams, Esq., of Newmarket, and their only child was Rev. *Albert-Adams Folsom,*[6] an able minister of the Universalist denomination and most excellent man, whose son is the present city treasurer of Springfield, Mass. The other children of Thomas are *Elizabeth;*[5] *Deborah*[5] (b. April 29, 1778, m. D. Thurston); *Lucretia;*[5] and (9) *Lydia,*[5] b. June 2, 1787, m. April, 1809, Jonathan Folsom, of Portsmouth.

ii. RACHEL,[4] m. March 20, 1760, James Sinclair, of Brentwood.

11. PETER[3] FOLSOM (*Peter,*[2] *John*[1]) had :

i. SUSANNA,[4] b. Sept. 27, 1704 ; m. in Kingston, 1739, Henry Morrill, of Exeter.

ii. ELIZABETH,[4] b. March 20, 1706 ; m. 1725, John Robinson.

iii. JOHN,[4] b. March 14, 1709 ; m. Hannah Sanborn. He was a house carpenter ; skilful with his tools, but not familiar with books. Tradition says he kept his accounts by notches made on a particular piece of timber with his broad axe.

22. iv. JAMES,[4] b. Oct. 16, 1711 ; m. June 18, 1735, Elizabeth, dau. of Capt. Jonathan Thing ; d. 1748.

23. v. PETER,[4] b. July 27, 1714 ; m. Mary, dau. of Jonathan (son of Dea. John) and sister of Gen. Nathaniel ; d. July 11, 1792. His wife was born Feb. 17, 1722 ; d. 1791.

vi. CATHERINE,[4] b. Jan. 24, 1716 ; m. Samuel Lamson.

12.   JOHN[3] (*Peter,*[2] *John*[1]), by his first wife had : *

i.   PETER,[4] who lived near Exeter line in what was called Piscassick (New-
     market). In his will, Feb. 1, 1756, John[3] (Lieut. *Peter,*[2] *John*[1]) gave
     "the mill, &c. to Joshua," and "the lands on the line of Newmar-
     ket and Exeter to his oldest son Peter," who paid taxes on them for
     many years.

24. ii. JOSHUA,[4] b. 1721 (1711 ?) ; a Quaker ; m. Abigail Mead ; d. at Epping,
     1793.

iii. ELIZABETH,[4] m. —— Thurston ; named in will of her father, 1756.

iv. MARY,[4] m. William, son of Ephraim Folsom.

By his second wife, Mary Lyford, he had :

v.   SARAH,[4] who m. Abraham Tilton, of Epping.

vi. SUSANNA,[4] wife of Nathaniel Bean, of Warner, and mother of Nathaniel
     Bean, Esq., of Warner. Exeter records say, b. May 10, 1718.

vii. JOSIAH,[4] b. July 27, 1725 (?) ; d. July 27, 1820.

13.   PETER[4] FOLSOM (*John,*[3] *John,*[2] *John*[1]) m. Hannah Morison ; removed to Gilmanton, where he died, Aug. 5, 1815, aged 97.   He had :

i.   Lieut. PETER,[5] who m. Betsey Calef ; moved to Gilmanton, and had *Ruth,*[6]
     James,[6] *Peter Lawrence.*[6]   Peter L.[6] was b. March 27, 1772 ; grad.
     D. C. 1796 ; taught the Academy in Fishkill, N. Y., one year ; was
     the first Principal of Gilmanton Academy, commencing 1797, and con-
     tinuing until 1804 ; m. widow Mary Lawrence, of Fishkill, Nov.
     1797 ; was merchant, magistrate, trustee of the Academy 1812–1836 ;
     d. Oct. 1, 1842, aged 70 ; his wife, Aug. 28, 1839. Lieut. Peter-F.
     had also *Benjamin,*[6] *Jonathan,*[6] *John,*[6] *Hannah*[6] (wife of William
     Peaslee), *Jeremiah,*[6] *Betsey-Smith*[6] ; and by a second wife, Elizabeth
     Bean, he had *James*[6] and *Lawrence.*[6]

ii. JOSIAH.[5]   iii. MARTHA.[5]

iv. ABRAHAM,[5] who lived in Epping ; had two sons, Abraham and John, who
     lived in Gilmanton.   v. JOHN.[5]

vi. BENJAMIN,[5] who went to Deerfield and lived there for a time ; next with
     four sons, *John-Dearborn,*[6] b. Dec. 28, 1762, (2) *Nathaniel,*[6] (3) *Peter-
     Sanborn,*[6] b. about 1766, (4) *Tristram,*[6] emigrated into Kennebec Co.,
     Me., when John D. was 12 years of age (these " Dearborns " and " San-
     bournes " being historic names in Exeter and neighborhood).   John-
     Dearborn was twice married ; used to carry the mail on horseback from
     East Machias to Cooper (some 20 miles) when quite an old man ; lived
     until past 90 ; left sons, one of whom, Benjamin,[7] aged about 84, lives
     in Rome, Me. ; two others, Elisha and Cyrus-G., with their married
     families, in Oconto, Wisconsin.   Peter-Sanborn[6] m. Betsey Philbrick,
     of Exeter, and had (youngest) *Benjamin,*[7] of Topsfield, Me., aged 71,
     and (oldest) *Titus-Philbrick,*[7] of East Machias, who married twice, d.
     1832, leaving an only child, PAUL-FOSTER,[8] b. Feb. 29, 1820, now among
     the well-known merchants of Boston, prominent in her religious activi-
     ties, an example of the success, which through great obstacles and dis-
     couragements in youth, may be reached by industry, capability and
     integrity.   One factor of that success, by no means a solitary instance
     of the kind, and yet deserving of special mention, was that for a short
     time he had a teacher in his native place who knew how to speak an

---

* In the closing portion of Mr. Kelley's Genealogy of Lieut. Peter,[2] and in the section
"vi. John"—in the two paragraphs commencing with "1" and "7"—there is a discrep-
ancy between him and Mr. Lancaster, author of the History of Gilmanton, in giving the
pedigree of *Peter L.*, of Dart. Coll. 1796, and in tracing the genealogy of *Josiah,* ancestor
of Dea. Josiah of Exeter, father of Charles Lane Folsom.   Mr. Kelley makes them descendants of the first John in the line of Lieut. Peter ; Mr. Lancaster puts them in the line
of Dea. John.   Now both in the Exeter Records and in the family tradition, this "Josiah" is declared to be "the son of John and Sarah [Dudley] Folsom."   And as Peter
L. was living when Mr. Lancaster's History was published, the genealogy given of Peter
L. in that book is doubtless correct.   Mr. K. has not a word to say of Dea. John's son John,
who m. Sarah Dudley.

encouraging word, and to stimulate to noble endeavor—and that teacher no other than Rev. Dr. Harris, now Professor in the Yale Divinity School. Paul Foster m. (1) *Maria G.*, dau. of Jesse Brown, who died March 5, 1852; (2) *Helen-S.-F.*, b. June 15, 1830, dau. of George-W. Livermore, Esq., of Cambridge. Their children are: *Martha-Maria*, b. Feb. 7, 1852; *Sarah-Helen*, b. Oct. 15, 1854; *Jennie-Sophia*, b. April 20, 1856; *Mary-Olivia*, b. Nov. 18, 1861; *George-Frank*, b. July 18, 1864; *Paul-Foster*, b. Sept. 23, 1865; *Eva*, b. Jan. 30, 1868; *Grosvenor*, b. Aug. 8, 1872.*

14. ABRAHAM[4] FOLSOM (*John*,[3] *John*,[2] *John*[1]) lived in Epping; had two sons:

 i. ABRAHAM,[5] b. April 29, 1744; d. July 6, 1811; m. in 1765, Hannah Folsom (b. March 29, 1744, dau. of William (*Ephraim*,[3] *Ephraim*,[2] *John*[1]), of Newmarket).

 ii. JOHN.[5] d. Nov. 5, 1820. (Both Abraham and John lived in Gilmanton.)

From Abraham and Hannah sprung four children, as follows:
JONATHAN,[6] b. Sept. 17, 1766; d. ——.
WILLIAM,[6] b. July 12, 1771; d. Nov. 20, 1801.
HANNAH,[6] b. March 17, 1775; d. ——.
ABRAHAM,[6] b. Oct. 8, 1777; d. Feb. 28, 1824.

This fourth and youngest child Abraham[6] m. Mary Libbey, April 12, 1806 (b. Sept. 28, 1789, d. May 12, 1865); children:
SALLY-T.,[7] b. Oct. 9, 1807; m. Charles-G. Forest, and has a dau. *Josie.*
GEORGE-C.,[7] b. July 12, 1810; d. Jan. 24, 1840, leaving two children—one a son, *Gustavus-Decatur*, who resides in Cleveland, Ohio, and is the only one living that bears the name Folsom in a direct line from Abraham.[6]
DECATUR-A.,[7] b. Feb. 5, 1814; d. May 18, 1834.
JOSEPH-L.,[7] b. May 19, 1816; d. at San Jose, Cal., July 19, 1855.
CHARLES-P.,[7] b. Jan. 30, 1819; d. Dec. 16, 1819.
FRANK-C.,[7] b. Nov. 30, 1821; d. Feb. 9, 1846.

The birth-place of JOSEPH L.[7] was Meredith, at the outlet of Lake Winnipiseogee.† The first thing resolved on, when the father had been taken away by an early death—the oldest child not seventeen, JOSEPH not eight, and the youngest not three—was to provide means for the education of the children; and to accomplish this, the estate was sold, and the family moved to Northfield. Through the kind offices of Hon. Frank Pierce, member of Congress, a cadetship was subsequently secured for JOSEPH at the Military Academy, West Point. He entered, June, 1836; graduated with honor, June, 1840; commissioned Brevet Second Lieut. 8th Infantry; Second Lieut. 5th Infantry, Nov. 3, 1840; served in Florida under command of General Worth against the Seminoles. At the end of the war, having been appointed Second Lieutenant, he served another year at his own request; then conducted a body of Indians to their new home in the West. Rejoining his regiment—the 5th Infantry, commanded by Brevet Brig. Gen. Brooks

---

* Of Benjamin,[5] son of Peter,[4] no record is known to exist which gives any trace of him after going to Deerfield. But in the group of families above mentioned, there is preserved an unvarying tradition of a grandfather or great-grandfather Benjamin, who having married in Exeter, went to Deerfield, and thence into Maine, under circumstances and with subsequent occurrences as above stated. A correspondence between Mr. Paul Foster F. and his kinsfolk, east and west, which was put into the present writer's hands, fully attests these facts—and the remarkable coincidences of periods of time, with the confirmation from the early historic Exeter and Newmarket and Hampton names of the "Dearbornes" and "Sanbournes" and "Philbricks," seem clearly to show the line of descent running direct from the first John through John,[2] John[3] and Peter[4] to the individuals of this group, so long seeking in vain for their exact genealogical place. The history of three thousand years and more is repeated. The missing "cup" is "found in Benjamin's sack," and "Joseph is made known to his brethren."

† For the substance of the facts here stated, see a Sketch of Capt. Joseph L. Folsom in the "History of San Francisco."

on the upper Mississippi—he served in various places in the North-West
until 1844, when he was ordered to the Academy at West Point as Instructor
in Infantry Tactics. Having continued there two years, and war being
ready to break out and at last actually begun with Mexico, he asked even
to the third time for permission to join his regiment in active service, but
was refused.

In the autumn of 1846, Col. Stevenson being about to leave for California
in command of the first regiment of New-York volunteers, and learning the
character of Lieut. FOLSOM, applied to have him sent as staff-officer in the
Quartermaster's department. Satisfactory arrangements having been made,
particularly in regard to his promotion first to the grade of 1st Lieutenant,
and soon after to that of Captain, and all the needful commissariat having
been provided by him, he sailed with the expedition, and after a five or six
months voyage arrived at Yerba Buena, in the beginning of the spring of
1847. Agreeably to orders from Gen. Kearney, he set about the work
of inspecting the Bay of San Francisco for the purpose of selecting a site
for the army stores; and Yerba Buena seemed to him to be the fittest place.
Accordingly that became the military depot, and that his station both during
the war and for a year after its close, receiving all funds, and making all
disbursements both for the military and civil government of California.

Capt. FOLSOM had the sagacity to perceive what San Francisco—the
name "Yerba Buena" having now been dropped for this by his own happy
thought and instant action—was to become. He invested in it the little
which he had—about fifteen hundred dollars; purchased, during leave of
absence on a visit to the East, all the interest of the heirs in the Leidesdorf
estate, returned after an absence of seven months, and was on duty again, a
year and a half longer. The discovery of gold aided in the rapid development and growth of the new city. It opened like one of the magnificent
flowers on that Pacific coast, not soon to wither and die, but to bloom in
perpetually renewing and multiplying beauty. No man indeed makes a
great city. Capt. FOLSOM did not make San Francisco. But it was a
great thing to have a man of his intelligence and culture and generous public
spirit one of its leading inspirers and moulders and builders. Nor will its
future glory and greatness be separable from his name. But not the fortune
of eleven millions to which his estate has already reached, and beyond which
it is destined to swell; not the magnificent street bearing his name, on which
stand some of his palatial edifices, and through which the breezes are wafted in
eternal freshness from the Pacific in one direction and the Sierras in the
other, will be his chief distinction. It is far greater to have one of the greatest
and bravest commanders of modern times, Major Gen. William T. Sherman,
place that name with honor in his "Memoirs," and record it on the imperishable tablets of the heart, entitling it "MY CLASSMATE AND INTIMATE
FRIEND."

In general address, Capt. FOLSOM is said to have exhibited a slight
formality, through the influence of his military education. But he was quiet
and gentlemanly in manners, unreserved and companionable with intimate
friends. Amid the civil and military duties that never in his hands bore
even the faintest suspicion of neglect, he found time for literary pursuits that
gave him no inferior place among educated minds. But he has left behind
him, for his friends and kinsfolk, what is better than all this—a stainless
character, an irreproachable integrity, a wakeful sense of honor, a conscience
void of offence in respect to the pursuit of any personal gain at the expense

of ruin to others, a reputation which under the drill and discipline of actual life, amid its marches and conflicts, meets the true soldierly ideal; overcomes in the warfare with evil, and, having done all, stands. Captain FOLSOM'S earthly labors were closed in life's prime, before he had reached the age of forty. His eyes saw not, his ears heard not, the opening of that conflict more momentous and terrible than any with Indian or Mexican, or whatever foreign foe. Who can doubt that, had he lived, he would have counted his millions but loss, nor lingered a day to present himself, as in youth, for the service and security of his country, for the perpetuity and enjoyment throughout the Republic of the blessings of the Union?

15. JOSIAH⁴ FOLSOM (*John,³ John,² John¹*), b. Sept. 25, 1725; d. 1820, aged 95; m. widow Martha Gould, dau. of Jeremiah Eastman, May 17, 1754, and had:

   i. JEMIMA,⁵ b. March 17, 1755; m. Peter Folsom.
   ii. MARTHA,⁵ b. Dec. 7, 1756; m. John Nelson, of Gilmanton; had John Nelson, Esq., of Haverhill, N. H., who grad. at Dartmouth, 1803, and died 1838, aged 60.
   iii. LYDIA,⁵ m. Jonathan Folsom, of Gilford, son of Peter.
   iv. MARY,⁵ b. 1763; m. 1784, James Folsom, and had ten children.
   v. JOSIAH,⁵ b. June 1, 1765; was deacon of the 1st church in Exeter; m. Sarah Lane, of Stratham. Their children were: (1) *Charles Lane,⁶* b. 1799; of Dart. Coll. 1820; teacher in the Academy, 1820–22; a superior scholar, in whose early death, 1829, great hopes were blasted; (2) *Josiah-H.⁶;* (3) *Mary,⁶* who m. W. Keyes; (4) *Martha,⁶* wife of Dr. Nichols; (5) *Sarah,⁶* wife of Dea. John-T. Gordon; (6) *Ann,⁶* wife of W. Palmer, of Boston; (7) *Lucy.⁶*
   vi. DUDLEY,⁵ b. Dec. 15, 1767; a physician, of Gorham, Me; m. Lucretia Swansey, of Gorham.
   vii. JOHN,⁵ b. 1770.
   viii. DEBORAH,⁵ b. May 12, 1772; m. James Lane, Esq., of Stratham.

16. NATHAN⁴ FOLSOM (*Jeremiah,³ John,² John¹*) had:

   i. ELIZABETH,⁵ m. (1) —— Hilton; (2) David Gilman.
   ii. ASA,⁵ b. Sept. 24, 1757, called Capt. Asa; inherited the homestead in Newmarket; m. (1) Sally Boardman, and had *Nathan Boardman,⁶ Betsey, Polly, Sally, Nancy* and *Hannah;* m. (2) Betsey Guild; (3) Mary Gove, and d. in Deerfield, July, 1843.
   iii. ABIGAIL,⁵ b. Aug. 6, 1760; m. (1) Israel Gilman, of Tamworth; (2) Capt. Shepherd, of Holderness.

17. Col. JEREMIAH⁴ FOLSOM (*Jeremiah,³ John,² John¹*) had:

   i. JEREMIAH,⁵ b. 1743; of Rochester; m. Nancy ——; d. at New Durham, leaving no child.
   ii. Col. JOHN,⁵ b. 1745; of Newmarket; m. 1767, Elizabeth, dau. of Col. Joseph Smith; d. 1820, leaving children: (1) *John,⁶* who had Mary, Eliza and John-Odlin; (2) *Joseph-S.,⁶* childless; (3) *Winthrop,⁶* who m. Nancy Tash, had Eliza and John-S.; (4) *Jeremiah,⁶* who m. Betsey Hersey, had Eliza and Nicholas; (5) *Betsey,⁶* w. of Elder Israel Chesley.
   iii. PETER,⁵ b. 1747; of Lee; afterwards moved into Maine; m. Sally Dam, at Harpswell; had ten children, one of whom, Elizabeth, was mother of James and Erastus Brooks, of New-York; d. at Harpswell.
   iv. SIMEON,⁵ b. April 7, 1749; m. Sarah Rust; d. at Exeter, 1810, leaving two sons: (1) *Jacob,⁶* who d. early; (2) Hon. SIMEON,⁶ b. in Newmarket, June 19, 1776, came to Exeter at the age of 18, let himself to perform in a year's time a stipulated amount of nail-making for a stipulated sum of money and board; then having done the work in half the time, spent the other six months in getting what education he could at the Academy. Thence he set up nail-making for himself; m. Mary, dau. of Capt. James Leavitt, of Exeter, 1800; opened a store for general

trade ; took an active part in politics ; was elected Senator to the State legislature, 1813 ; was made Master of the Masonic Lodge ; was chosen delegate to a convention at Portsmouth for sustaining Madison's measures in the war-crisis ; died suddenly while on business in Wolfboro', Aug. 23, 1816, and in the midst of a career becoming more and more distinguished.* He was the father of one daughter and seven sons— (1) *Sarah-Rust*, who m. Thomas Hardy, grad. Dart. Coll. 1807 ; first a teacher in Boston, afterwards of Dublin, N. H., and a representative of that town in the State legislature, and has four children : *Charles-Carroll*, Capt. *Washington-Webster, Laura-Cordelia* (m. Wm. Vinton), *Mary-L.* (m. John Pinkham) ; (2) *Isaac-Lord*, b. 1801, m. Lydia Titcomb, died suddenly like his father, in the fulness of apparent health and fine personal development, leaving a son, *Charles-Edward*, (m. and has a family) ; (3) *Jacob*, of Bridgewater, b. 1803, m. Eliza Newell, has two children, *George-William, Mary-E.* ; (4) ABRAHAM, b. 1805, commenced life (the present writer well remembers) an enthusiastic young artist ; then tried the union of the practical with the ideal, and sought to adorn the homes of men by spreading his painted canvass on the floors of their halls ; m. Abigail Smith Pierce, of Dover, Sept. 5, 1832 ; has three daughters, *Lydia-Ellen, Mary-Leavitt, Grace-Osborne*, and two sons, *Simeon-Peirce* (d.), and *Abraham-Wilbur* associated in the firm still bearing the name of the father and " sons ;" has won his place among the honored manufacturers and merchants of Boston, through events most adverse ; stands with tradesmen and workers who have made their names more noble as those of men deeply interested in the problems of modern thought, and earnestly devoted to the humanities of the age ; (5) Maj. *George-P.*, who m. Sarah Cross, and has four children : *Simeon-B., George-L., Nathaniel-C., Abraham ;* (6) *James-Madison*, who went to Savannah, Ga., m. Mary-Caroline Haupter, died and left two sons, Col. *Robert* (d.), Col. *James-M.*, and one daughter, *Maria-D.;* (7) *Simeon*, died 1824 ; (8) *Josiah-Bartlett*, who m. Olive B. Pierce, and has six children : *Mary-Olive, James-L., Alice-O., Andrew-Peirce, Rebecca-White, Anna.*

v.　JOSEPH,[5] b. 1751 ; m. dau. of Rev. Jonathan Cushing, of Dover, and died at Rochester, leaving children Peter and Nancy.

vi.　LEVI,[5] b. July 12, 1753 ; m. 1776, Joanna, dau. of Dr. John Weeks, of Hampton. He removed to Tamworth, N. H., and had nine children. His dau. Elizabeth-S. was the wife of Samuel Chapman, of Tamworth, and mother of Rev. Jacob Chapman, one of the authors of the Genealogy of the Folsom Family.†

vii.　ENOCH,[5] b. 1755 ; m. —— Foss ; had no child.

viii.　JACOB,[5] b. 1758 ; d. about 1777, in the army, unmarried.

ix.　MARY,[5] b. 1761 ; m. Peter Hersey ; had five children, and d. Aug. 31, 1839.

x.　SAMUEL,[5] b. 1765 ; d. unm., about 1787.

18.　Gen. NATHANIEL[4] FOLSOM (*Jonathan,*[3] *John,*[2] *John*[1]) received a military commission quite early in life. In the expedition against Crown Point, 1755, then in possession of the French, one of the ten companies,

---

* Mr. F.'s Sunday suit was a snuff-colored dress-coat, with covered cloth buttons, light fawn-colored small clothes and white-top boots, light vest, ruffled shirt and standing collar, white cravat, square gold watch key with black ribbon, hair worn with a queue and combed back from the forehead. Add to this a stature full six feet and well proportioned, light blue eyes, dark hair, pale complexion, small white teeth, and manly address.

† Mr. Chapman through many difficulties fitted for college at the Exeter Academy ; grad. at Dartmouth 1835, and at Andover Theological Seminary 1838 ; was Principal of the Academy at Lyndon, Vt., one year, and at Bridgeton, Me., two years ; m. (1) Mary C., dau. of Hon. Nathaniel Howe, of Bridgeton ; was Principal of Meyerstown Academy, Lebanon Co., Penn., remaining in this vicinity nearly ten years, during four of which he was Professor in Franklin College, Lancaster, and during two, Principal of Harrisburg Academy—preaching often, and to some ten different denominations ; in 1852, became pastor of the church in Marshall, Clarke Co., Ill., serving there twelve years, including one in which he was Professor of Languages in Terre Haute Female College ; returned to New-England, where he was pastor of the Congregational Church in Deerfield, N. H., six years ; m. (2) Mary E., dau. of Charles Lane, Esq., of Stratham ; is now pastor of the Congregational Church in Kingston, N. H.

which New-Hampshire was required to raise, consisted of men from Exeter and neighboring towns, and was put in command of Capt. Nathaniel Folsom of Exeter, who proceeded through the woods to Albany, and thence to Fort Edward, where the New-Hampshire Rangers were posted. On the 8th of September, the enemy attacked the Americans in camp at Fort George, but were repulsed, and their commander, Baron Dieskau, was mortally wounded and taken prisoner. In the course of the day Capt. Folsom with his company of 80 men was despatched in the direction of Lake George, who having met the retreating forces of the French, Canadians, and Indians about 4 o'clock in the afternoon, posted his men behind the trees, and kept up a brisk firing of musketry until night, with great loss to the enemy, while of the Americans only six fell, and their commander brought off safely all his wounded, with several prisoners and a large quantity of baggage. The engagements of the day, thus closed by Capt. Folsom, "served more than anything else," it is said, "to revive the spirit of the colonies." He became Major in 1767, and soon Colonel; was for several years a member of the N. H. House of Representatives and a prominent member of the liberal party. He was chosen, together with Major Gen. John Sullivan, to represent New-Hampshire in the first General Congress, which met at Philadelphia, Sept. 5, 1774; was appointed delegate from New-Hampshire to meet other New-England delegates at Providence, R. I., in respect to sending supplies to the army; served as Brigadier General during the siege of Boston, until relieved by Sullivan. In 1775 he was commissioned Major General; in 1776 was appointed one of the four Justices of the Court of Common Pleas for Rockingham County; in 1777 and 1779 was again chosen member of Congress. In the first year of his return to Washington, he writes to his friend Hon. Meshach Weare, President of the Council of New-Hampshire, that "the 8th Article of the Confederation gave him great uneasiness," as the South obtained by it an exemption from taxation for its negroes, who in reality constituted one third of its wealth, and thus caused the free States to bear a larger share of the burden of the charges of the war than was equitable. In 1778 he was chosen Councillor, and was temporary President of the Convention that framed the Constitution of New-Hampshire in 1783.

Gen. Folsom m. first, (Mary?) Smith, by whom he had six children; (2) Mrs. Fisher, of Newburyport (formerly Mary Sprague of Boston), by whom he had a daughter:

   i. NATHANIEL,[5] merchant, of Portsmouth, who m. (1) Mary Studley, Nov. 26, 1771; (2) Olive Husk Rindge, Aug. 24, 1789. The children by his 1st wife were *Mary*,[6] wife of Thomas-W. Rindge; *Elizabeth*,[6] b. Jan. 4, 1774, m. (1) to Joseph Noble; (2) to Joseph Lowe—of whose children, Elizabeth-Studley Noble m. Major Cobbs, U. S. Army, and is mother of Capt. Cobbs, ship-master, of Boston; Olivia-Folsom Noble, m. Calvin Willard, of Worcester, (since d.); and Mary-Folsom Noble, m. Feb. 22, 1826, Capt. John-Sherburne Sleeper, and has a family of married children. Capt. Sleeper, after retirement from sea-life, edited the Exeter News Letter; next, for about a year, one of the Lowell papers; then became chief editor and soon one of the proprietors of the Boston Journal, conducting that paper ably from 1833 to 1853, making it lively, vigorous, instructive, effective in promoting the political and moral welfare of city and state, pure and high-toned, read by its many readers with pleasure as savoring of the freshness of the sea; *Dorothy*,[6] third daughter of Nathaniel,[5] b. March 21, 1775; m. Col. Nathaniel Gilman of Exeter, one of whose 11 children, Mary-Olivia, m. Commodore John-Collins Long, U. S. Navy. Of the second marriage was born Capt. *Nathaniel*,[6] ship-master, of Portsmouth, m. to Hannah Sheafe, dau. of William Sheafe; *Sarah-Ann*,[6] wife of Rev. George-E. Adams, D.D., for some years a teacher of the Academy in Portsmouth, afterward a greatly beloved and respected pastor of the Cong. church in Brunswick, Me.; *Arthur*,[6] b. 1795, who held office many years as Consul and Commercial Agent in Jeremie, Hayti (where he married and had children), was then removed in 1868 for sympathy with the revolutionary leaders, but appointed Consul General on Saget's obtaining the presidency, in which office he d. Nov. 21, 1870, in Orange County, N. Y., soon after his return from a visit to Europe.

ii. MARY,[5] b. 1751; m. (1), 1774, Caleb-G. Adams; (2) was the 2d wife of Gov. John-Taylor Gilman; d. Oct. 15, 1812.

iii. DEBORAH,[5] b. 1753; m. 1776, Gov. John-Taylor Gilman, and was the mother of his five children: d. Feb. 20, 1791. .Of these children, *John-Taylor*,[6] b. 1779, Dart. Coll. 1796, d. in Char'eston, S. C., Feb. 21, 1808, unmarried. *Ann-Taylor*,[6] m. 1807, Hon. Nicholas Emery of Portland, Judge of the Supreme Court of Maine. *Dorothy*,[6] m. Rev. Ichabod Nichols, D.D., one of the purest and noblest of men, and among the highest in his profession, whose two sons are George Henry (H. C. 1833, M.D. Penn. 1836), of Boston, and Rev. John T. Gilman, (H. C. 1836), of Saco, Me. *Mary*,[6] m. Joseph-Green Cogswell, LL.D., who was associated with Hon. George Bancroft in the Round Hill School, Northampton, Ms., and was afterward Superintendent of the Astor Library. *Elizabeth-Taylor*[6] (b. Aug. 14, 1788, d. Apr. 3, 1860), m. June 1, 1815, Hon. Charles-S. Daveis, an eminent lawyer of Portland, one of whose daughters is wife of Rev. David Greene-Haskins, of Cambridge.

iv. JONATHAN,[5] lost at sea.

v. ANNA,[5] b. 1762; m. Gen. Nathaniel Giddings, and had five children.

vi. DOROTHY,[5] m. Samuel Blodgett, and was mother of Mrs. West, of Baltimore.

vii. RUTH-WEARE,[5] b. May 30, 1780, whose home for many years was at Judge Emery's, where she died, May 21, 1854.

19. Col. SAMUEL[4] FOLSOM (*Jonathan*,[3] *John*,[2] *John*[1]) m. (1) Anna Thing, (2) April 30, 1780, Elizabeth (b. Jan. 13, 1750, d. Sept. 1805), dau. of Noah Emery, Esq.; d. May 22, 1790. Col. Folsom was "Lieut. Col. of the Exeter corps of Independent Cadets, commanded by Col. John Phillips." When John Langdon of Portsmouth pledged his private property for the support of an expedition under Gen. Stark against Burgoyne, President Weare, chairman of the Committee of Safety, delegated Col. Folsom to visit Gen. Stark, to convey to him money for present expenses, to see what articles were immediately needed, and "advise with all persons in the service of the State of New-Hampshire on such things as he thought needful to forward the business they are engaged in."

"Two years afterwards Col. F. was selected by the General Court to present to Col. Joseph Cilley, in behalf of the State, a pair of pistols which had been the property of Col. Stephen Holland, the tory absentee."

"Col. Folsom kept a public house, as his widow continued to do many years after his death. And it was at his house that General Washington stopped and partook of a collation when he visited Exeter in his Eastern tour in the autumn of 1789." (For these particulars, see "Exeter in 1776," prepared by the Hon. Charles H. Bell for the Ladies' Centennial Levee held in Exeter, Feb. 22, 1876.) Children (all by second marriage):

i. NANCY,[5] m. Joseph Tilton, Esq., of Exeter; d. childless, March 10, 1837.

ii. SAMUEL,[5] b. June 7, 1783.

iii. ELIZABETH,[5] b. 1785; m. (1) Noah Emery, Esq., 1811 (d. 1812); m. (2) Rev. Isaac Hurd, D.D., of the 2d church of Exeter. He was a favorite with the students of the Academy, not simply because his sermons were invariably short, but because he was a most amiable, scholarly, accomplished man—short in stature, but the largest and finest in culture of any clergyman whom they knew. Dr. Hurd d. 1856; his wife, 187-. They left one child, *Francis P.* (H. C. 1839, M.D. Penn. 1845), of Reading, Mass.

iv. JOANNA,[5] b. 1787; m. 1810, Samuel-B. Stevens; lived in Exeter; had several children, of whom was *Elizabeth*, wife of William Augustus Norton, A.M., Prof. of Civil Engineering in Yale College; also *Samuel*, who left a family now residing in New-York City.

20. TRUEWORTHY[4] FOLSOM (*Jonathan,*[2] *John,*[2] *John*[1]), not so "well to do" in the world as his brothers, the Colonel and the General, but superior to them both in humor and wit; m. Mary West, of Boston, by whom he had:

i. JOHN-WEST,[5] who came to the place where his mother was found by his father, learned the printers' trade, and became established as printer and bookseller. One of his books is entitled "Aphorisms of Wisdom . . . . . from the works of various writers upon Divine Subjects. Boston: Printed and Sold by John W. Folsom, No. 30 Union St. M.DCC.XCIV." 214 pp. 12mo. The Aphorisms are taken chiefly from Swedenborg, a list and description of whose writings are given in an Appendix. He also printed and published, in 1795, "Doctrines of the New Jerusalem Church, concerning the Sacred Scriptures"—together with numerous minor works. Mr. F. was master of the Columbian Lodge, 1799–1801; the first secretary of the Mass. Charitable Mechanic Association, continuing in office 5 years; member of the Board of Health for Boston, 1803; a Justice of the Peace, 1817–22; d. 1823, aged 66 or 8.

ii. SAMUEL.[5]

iii. MARY,[5] m. to Benjamin Silsbee, 1786.

iv. ANN,[5] m. to Dudley Kimball, 1789.

v. ELIZABETH,[5] m. to Thomas Swazey, 1787.

21. JOSIAH[4] FOLSOM (*Jonathan,*[3] *John,*[2] *John*[1]) succeeded no better than his brother Trueworthy in getting worldly gear. His home in Dover, on the rising-ground southwardly from the village, had a fine outward look over fields and village, and toward river and sky and distant hills, but it was very humble, one-storied, unpainted, and the income of its owner from making wigs and perukes, in which he was really an artist, quite meagre. He had indeed rich stores of anecdote and of results of observation obtained in his yearly trips into the Canadas, making him one of the most entertaining men of his day; but this did not bring worldly comforts into his household, nor procure advantages for his children. And so his boys, knowing well that for any good start in business, or position in society, they must depend solely on their personal efforts, and desiring, each of them, to build for himself as good a household as he could, early left the cabin-home, one by one, and went forth into the great world. "And God was with the lads." There were four of them, and three sisters.

i. JOSIAH-GILMAN,[5] b. 1763; lived, and, Dec. 31, 1837, d. in Portsmouth. He was a nail-cutter, chair-maker, and at the same time carried on a retail trade in West India goods. By a first marriage he had one son, *Josiah*, who went to Pittsburg, Pa., and two daughters, *Mary* and *Eliza*. He married (2) Sarah Hull, of Durham (b. Feb. 6, 1775, d. Sept. 1829, in whom the best qualities of womanhood were contained in a noble form), by whom he had (1) *Sarah*, m. Jan. 1, 1828, to her cousin J.-Gilman Folsom, a promising young merchant of Portsmouth, in partnership with his uncle Nathaniel, taken away by fever on return from a business trip to the West, 1835, leaving two children—a dau. m. to Ferdinand Bosher, of Manchester, and Gilman, of Worcester; (2) *Lydia*, m. to John Oxford, of Portsmouth, and having two children; (3) *William-Cutter*, house-builder, m. in Maryland; d. in Vicksburg, Miss., leaving two active sons, one now of Manchester, N. H., the other of Worcester, Mass.

ii. ELIZABETH,[5] b. 1765; d. 183–.

iii. NANCY,[5] b. 1767; d. 1791.

iv. SAMUEL,[5] b. Jan. 30, 1770; went to Marietta, O., 1789, where he met his kinsman, not quite four years his senior, Benjamin Ives Gilman, whom he had known in Exeter and by whom he was perhaps led to go West; engaged with him in the purchase of peltry and furs; m. in Gallia co., 1802, Catherine Smith, formerly of Londonderry, N. H.; bought and settled on a farm of 217 acres in the French Grant, Scioto co., 1805; built vessels and sent them down the Ohio river; d. 1813, leaving four children : *James-Smith*, merch. (who owns and lives on the homestead), *Samuel, Melissa, Mary* (now widow of a minister who d. 1865). All were married, and their descendants, numbering 26, are engaged in the industries of life, are miners, millers, merchants, farmers, ironfounders and agents. Two of the sons of Mary, Charles-W. and James-H., living, with their mother, in Prairie City, Ill., edit and manage the "Prairie City Herald."

v. ABIGAIL,[5] b. April 13, 1772, made her home with her youngest brother until she married (1816 or '17), Dea. Skates, of Milton, where she died. She was as dear an aunt as ever blessed human household. It was fascinating to see her measure the hands of young misses for nice deer-skin gloves, never failing to fit them; and she knew how to fit the circumstances of life to young souls. She was a prominent member of the Rev. Dr. Buckminster's church.

vi. JONATHAN,[5] b. June 12, 1779; m. Oct. 20, 1802, in Gilford (where he at first lived), Sarah Rowe (b. May 27, 1778, d. May 9, 1846); moved across the Bridge and settled on a large farm (now in Laconia) running down to the Bay, carrying on also his trade as house-carpenter; d. June 22, 1872, aged 93—a man very tall and large; thoughtful, intelligent, righteous and good, beloved not less by his nephews and nieces than by his own family. Of his children, *Jeremiah*, b. May 8, 1803, m. twice and had three children; *Sarah-H.*, b. Jan. 20, 1805, m. Edmund Davis, Nov. 5, 1826, well known with his sons for their iron castings in Dover and Portsmouth, N. H., North Andover and Lawrence, Mass., two of them and a daughter being married and having children (one in Lawrence and the other in Sagamore, Michigan); *Josiah-Gilman*, b. Nov. 29, 1806 (see under JOSIAH[5]); *Mary*, m. L. B. Smith, of Exeter, and has three children; *Eliza*, m. Geo. W. Evans, but has no children; *Adeline*, m. Judge Jonathan Chase, of Conway, both of whom are dead, and left a son, now member of Dart. Coll.; *Albert-Gallatin*, b. Oct. 12, 1816, one of the influential citizens of Laconia, m. to Olive B. Robinson, Jan. 5, 1843, and has two living and married daughters.

vii. NATHANIEL,[5] Jr., b. in Dover, Feb. 13, 1782; d. March 12, 1866; m. April 15, 1805, his second cousin Mary (b. Dec. 24, 1786, d. Oct. 3, 1853), second dau. of Theophilus Smith, farmer, of Stratham (d. 1824), the oldest son of Theophilus Smith, of Exeter (H. C. 1761, m. Sarah, third dau. of Dr. Josiah Gilman and sister of the mother of Nathaniel, Jr.; was father of a large family, the most of whom were married, had families, and lived and died in Exeter—the mother of Mr. Nathaniel Shute of Exeter being one of his daughters; was teacher, one of the proprietors of Gilmanton, their clerk one year, their moderator and treasurer seven years, their selectman ten years; was the *fifth* Theophilus Smith and oldest son in uninterrupted descent from the first that settled in Winniconnet, a part of Stratham, 1630,—that same uninterrupted descent now embracing the *ninth* Theophilus Smith and oldest or only son, Theophilus Gilman Smith, Esq., of Boston, who grad. at H. C. 1871, just 110 years after the fifth*). The lad Nathaniel,

---

* The following anecdote was told the writer some time since 1862, by Mrs. Odiorne, sister of Mr. William Charles Gilman, and living at that time in a house built on the old foundations of the one formerly occupied by Dr. Josiah Gilman, just east of Dr. Gorham's. Before William Charles entered the Academy at Exeter, he was a pupil of Mr. Theophilus Smith, at that time teacher of a large private school. One of the exercises, occasionally, was a spelling-match, in which two leaders "chose sides," and the whole school, being evenly divided, stood arrayed one side against the other. Every one who missed a word was obliged to sit down; and thus the battle went on until, on one of these occasions, only William Charles, the youngest and littlest boy in the school, was left standing. His teacher, placing him upon the table, then required the whole school, one by one, to go and bow down to

youngest child of his parents, began to earn money at eleven years of age, giving it all to his parents for their support; went to Portsmouth at 12 or 13, to learn the baking-business with Col. Woodward (a man of high consideration and ample means, the father of Mrs. John Haven); walked home weekly on Saturday, often bare-footed, carrying his small pecuniary stipend to his parents; set up in business at the age of nineteen, and engaged a popular colored man, *Pomp Spring*, to carry bread around and sell at a public stand, giving him one-half the net-proceeds; bought, before he was 21, the house and lot in the rear of the Old North Church, for which he paid Col. Jonathan Warner in silver all but one hundred dollars, and received his deed, the Colonel declining to take a note for the remainder, and saying that he would trust him; took his father and mother and sister Abigail very soon to live with him, the old folks now made comfortable and happy as they had not been for years, until they died, the mother Aug. 3, 1812, aged 72, blessing God, to her latest breath, for her youngest-born; the father, Feb. 4, 1816, aged 81. When the latter was past the meridian of life, stout in person, broad-chested, muscular, his sky became darkened by mental alienation. The attacks were temporary, and the son had always the most perfect control of him. They became less and less frequent, with longer intervals of sanity, in which he was a great factor in a merry household. The last few years of his life were serene and lovely, with not a solitary flash bursting as from clouds in distant horizon. His sleeping-chamber in the new house built by his son, was that of his grandson also, and had an outlook from its windows upon the not far distant ocean open between two head-lands, where, though with dim eyes, he could see, or think he saw, the vessels appearing and disappearing from behind them. Meantime and afterward, his youngest-born, Nathaniel, went on prospering, left his trade, became merchant, ship-owner in 1816, and real-estate holder (not always nor all to his advantage), retired from business on a small income about 1836; lived a life calm and happy, principally with his youngest daughter and her family, with several other married children around him, until in his eighty-fifth year he died. In early manhood he was a member of the Royal Arch Chapter of Masons; member of the Mechanics Charitable Association, and Mechanic Fire Society. The red buckets of the latter hung in his entry. In the terrible night of the fire of Dec. 22, 1813, followed by another fire on the 12th of January, 1814, he came home once, girt about with his blanket, all begrimed with smoke, wet through and through with the water, and from the next day after the last fire, suffered a long and most painful confinement to his chamber—the first and only sickness he ever had until his death. He was the most even-tempered and the best man the writer has ever known. She who was his only wife was also his true helpmeet, "rising while it was yet night to give meat to her household," "stretching out her hands to the poor," "shewing hospitality," eminently religious, a great reader and thinker as her father and mother were before her, seeking to stimulate her children to honorable endeavors in life. They had eight children: (1) *Nathaniel-*

---

him. The father was justly displeased on being informed of it, and feared that Mr. Smith would spoil the boy. But that young lad, who was also the cousin and early companion of Charles Folsom, maintained in subsequent life, both as a business man and a Christian, the same preëminence among his fellows, and was as unassuming as he was preëminent.

Theophilus, son of the teacher, did not do much of the work of farming personally, except in planting and in haying time. He used to visit Portsmouth almost every Saturday, carrying his butter and cheese and lamb, in his wagon or sleigh, to market, and take up his oldest grandson with him about once a month. He loved to roam the woods in pursuit of game, and by the banks of the stream running into the Winniconnet for trout and perch, taking his grandson along with him. He was a reading man, familiar with works as Plutarch's Lives, Josephus, and Rollins's Ancient History. The works of Chillingworth, Reeve's Apologies of Justin Martyr, Tertullian, and Minutius Felix, once his, have been since his death in the possession of the writer. He used to tell me, that in a fit of anger at being severely punished by his father for what was but an accident, but caused serious injury to his next older brother, he abandoned his preparation for entering Harvard. He never repented of it but once, and that was for the whole of his after life.

Smith,* b. March 12, 1806 ; bap. the 27th of the next April, by Dr. Buckminster ; m. Oct. 30, 1832, Ann Wendell, dau. of Hon. Hunking Penhallow, of Portsmouth, and Harriet Scot (children : Justin-Nathaniel, b. Aug. 8, 1833, d. April 20, 1851 ; Edward-Penhallow, b. June 28,1835, fell in the first battle at Yuca, Miss., in the late war; Sarah-Brainerd, b. Aug. 21,1836, d. June 1, 1839 ; Paris-Hill, b. Jan. 12, 1840, of Washington, D. C., who is married and has two sons and one daughter ; Charles-Follen, b. April 3, 1842, H. C. 1862, M.D. 1870, of Boston, Secretary of the State Board of Health ; Harriet-Elizabeth, Anna-Smith, Ellen Minot, the last three all teachers—the youngest being one of the teachers in the Boston Girls' High School) ; (2) *Mary-Gilman,* b. Sept. 2, 1811, d. Feb. 12, 1819 ; (3) *Ann-Elizabeth,* b. Aug. 15, 1814, m. in 1833, Jeremiah Mathes, merchant of Portsmouth, d. March 16, 1862, leaving four sons (two of whom, Edwin N. of D. C. 1854, and Capt. George, are dead) and two daughters (the father also d. March, 1866) ; (4) *Sarah-Jane,* b. Sept. 28, 1817, d. March 10, 1836 ; (5) *Samuel-Gilman,* accountant, b. Dec. 6, 1820, m. Mary Ann Seavy, by whom he has one son, Eugene of San Francisco, and one daughter ; (6) *John-Henry,* house-builder, b. Aug. 18, 1822, m. Lucy Jane Trundy, by whom he has had two sons and one daughter (d. young) ; (7) *James-William,* accountant, b. July 15, 1824, m. and has a son ; (8) *Mary-Frances,* twin sister of the latter, m. Nathan F. Mathes, merchant, of Portsmouth, and has two daughters, Frances-Abby, teacher in the Bradford Female Academy ; and Ella, m. C. Morris Tredick, of Portsmouth, who has one daughter, Helen.

22. JAMES[4] FOLSOM (*Peter,*[3] *Peter,*[2] *John*[1]) m. June 18, 1735, Elizabeth Thing, dau. of Capt. Jonathan Thing. They had one child :

JAMES,[5] b. June 27, 1737, who m. Elizabeth, dau. of Thomas Webster, Dec. 1763. Of their seven children was

i. JAMES,[6] b. 1765 ; m. to Sarah (b. 1766, d. 1805), dau. of Capt. Josiah Gilman, and grand-dau. of Rev. Nicholas, the brother of Dr. Josiah. The children of James[6] by Sarah were : Sophia, b. 1787, wife of Daniel Rundlett; *Joseph-G.,* b. 1788 ; *Sarah-G.,* b. 1790, wife of Silas Gould ; *Henry,* b. 1792 ; *Charles,* b. 1794, d. 1872 ; *Anna-G.,* b. 1797, wife of J. C. Gerrish ; *Mary-G.,* b. 1799 ; *George-W.,* b. 1803 ; also, by a second wife, *Harriet, Stephen* and *James.* Out of these eleven children,

CHARLES[7] attained special distinction. Having graduated at Harvard, 1813, he began in the autumn of 1814 to study divinity, but was obliged to relinquish it from ill health, and in the spring of 1816 he accepted the offer to go out in the 74 gun-ship '' Washington'' as chaplain and as the midshipmen's teacher in mathematics. In 1817, he was appointed *Chargé d'Affaires* at Tunis, where he continued until 1819. One of these young lads obtained permission to accompany him and continue his studies under him. Almost half a century passed, and there visited Boston a naval officer of renown, whose first visit, after the public honors of reception, was to Mr. Folsom in Cambridge. It was Vice-Admiral Farragut, now a veteran of national fame, who wanted to see his old teacher. On leaving New-England, the Admiral sent him a magnificent vase, with beautiful engravings from sketches drawn by

---

* Nathaniel-Smith, grad. Dart. Coll. 1828, Andover Theological Seminary 1831; was missionary at the South and West, 1831–33 ; Prof. in the Lit. Department of Lane Seminary, 1833–4; Prof. of Biblical Literature (with his classmates Clement Long, Prof. of Intellectual and Moral Philosophy, and Jarvis Gregg. Prof. of Sacred Rhetoric) in the Western Reserve Coll., Hudson, Ohio, 1834–36 ; pastor of the Congregational Church in Francestown, N. H., 1836–38 ; of the High Street Church, Providence, R. I., 1838–40 ; and of the Church of the First Parish, Haverhill, Mass., 1840–47 ; minister-at-large in Charlestown, in connection with Dr. G. E. Ellis's society, and also editor of the Christian Register, 1847–49 : Prof. of Biblical Literature in the Meadville Theological School, 1849–61 ; since then a private teacher. He is the author of a '' Commentary on Daniel, 1842,'' 12 mo. pp. 231 ; of the '' Four Gospels, translated from the Greek text of Tischendorf, with various readings, and with Critical and Expository Notes, Boston, A. Williams & Co., 1869,'' 12 mo. pp. 486; also of articles in various religious periodicals.

his own hand, as an acknowledgment of indebtedness to " the young Yankee pastor " for good influences, helping him to do whatever he had done for his country and the world.   Returning from the Mediterranean, Mr. Folsom became Tutor in Harvard, 1821–23 : Librarian of the Coll., 1823–26 ; Librarian of the Boston Athenæum, 1845–56.   He performed many important literary labors ; sent forth an excellent school edition of Cicero's Orations ; and it is especially to his praise that authors like Quincy and Norton and Sparks and Palfrey and Prescott and Parsons —both Dr. Parsons and Dr. Palfrey contributing beautiful memorial sketches of him—put their manuscripts or proofs into his hands, and cordially acknowledged their great indebtedness to his valuable services. The most fragrant of the memories still blooming from his dust, is that " his kindness was warm, constant and unselfish.   No one ever knew him refuse a favor which it was in his power to grant, or think first of himself, when the question was whether he should benefit himself or another."

On the 19th of October, 1824, he m. Susanna Sarah, daughter of Rev. Joseph McKean, Prof. of Rhetoric and Oratory in Harvard.   His wife, three sons (Col. Charles-W., H. C. 1845, Civil Engineer ; Norton, M.D., Harv., Surgeon 45th colored troops, Resident Physician Mass. Gen. Hospital ; Rev. George-McKean, H. C. 1857, Supervisor of Public Schools), and one daughter, survive him.   Two of the sons are married.

ii.   THOMAS,[6] b. May 11, 1769 ; m. Ednah Ela ; resided in Kennebunk and Portland ; had children : Louisa, Charles, Clarissa, also

GEORGE,[7] of Harvard College 1822, LL.D. of Vermont University 1860, an eminent author of several annalistic, antiquarian and historic papers and works, member of the N. Y. Senate 1844–47, U. S. minister to Holland 1850–53.   He was born in Kennebunk, May 23, 1802 ; m. Margaret Cornelia, dau. of Benjamin Winthrop, 1839 ; d. at Rome, Italy, 1870, leaving one son *George-W.* of New-York, who m. Miss Fuller, and two daughters *Margaret* and *Helen-Stuyvesant*—the latter a member of the sisterhood at Cluer, Eng., who in a brief sketch has wrought a beautiful tribute to her father's domestic virtues, his love of literary men and pursuits, his abundant and elegant hospitality, genial temper, courtesy and kindness to high and low, exhibiting in particular that trait which obtained for him when a lad the name of " Gentle Georgie," but which was not less conspicuous in the man than in the child.

iii.   NATHANIEL,[6] b. April 2, 1771 ; m. Mary Bond ; d. in Hallowell, Me., whose children were : *Thomas-Oliver*, M.D., Harv. 1825 ; d. 1827 ; *Mary, Elizabeth,* and *Clarissa.*

iv.   PETER,[6] b. Feb. 22, 1775, Kennebunk ; m. Susan Jenkins ; d. June, 1817.

v.   MARY,[6] b. July 12, 1776, wife of Nathaniel Jefferds, Kennebunk.

vi.   JOHN,[6] b. Nov. 5, 1777 ; m. Hannah Swasey, of whom was born *John-Fulford,*[7] bookbinder, of Boston.   The latter's wife, Caroline, was dau. of Mary Rogers (b. Jan. 10, 1780, dau. of Capt. Benjamin Rogers of Newburyport) and John Shaw, son of Rev. Jeremiah Shaw, of Moultonborough, N. H. (H. C. 1767 ; first supplied as missionary at the Isles of Shoals, 1773–75, when most of the people became dispersed through fear of being captured by the British ; was ordained, Nov. 17, 1779, pastor of the Congregational church in Moultonborough then quite on the frontier, where he continued until 1816, when he resigned, but supplied the pulpit six years longer.   He d. 1834, in the 88th year of his age, " a man of a quiet turn of mind and of good judgment," drawing to public worship people who used to walk, or ride on horseback, 10 miles each way—one old man of Centre Harbor saying that he could not recollect of more than one or two instances in which the weather or bad travelling kept him away ; and an intelligent farmer of Tamworth being accustomed to say, in the hearing of his son, Rev. Mr. Chapman, who told the present writer, " When I want a fervent prayer, I like to hear Parson Hidden ; when I want a sermon, I like to hear Parson Shaw ").   From this parentage sprung :

ALBERT-ALONZO,[8] whose name and fame are inseparable from the Boston and Providence Rail-Road, of which he has been several years Superintendent, having developed naturally from quite early life into pre-eminent fitness for the duties of his office. He has named some of his iron steeds after characters which are an embodiment of the most genial thoughts of one of the greatest of the writers of fiction in modern times. We cannot help thinking that with Mr. F. this intercourse with works of the imagination is no unusual mode of relaxation, and that like many other efficient men he owes to it much of the ease and heartiness and success with which he wields his large responsibilities, and not simply to his industry and fidelity and ability.

Mr. F. is Senior Warden of the Columbian Lodge. He married, April 11, 1861, Julia Elizabeth, dau. of Francis B. Winter, of Boston. Their children are : *Frank-B.-W.*, b. Feb. 6, 1862; *Chandler-R.*, b. Dec. 1, 1865 ; *Mary-Winter*, b. Sept. 30, 1867.

23. PETER[4] FOLSOM (*Peter*,[3] *Peter*,[2] *John*[1]) m. Mary, b. 1722, d. Oct. 1791, dau. of Jonathan[3] Folsom (*John*,[2] *John*[1]). This is the first intermarriage between the lines of Dea. John and Lieut. Peter—the great-grandson of the first John in the line of the latter marrying the great-granddau. in the line of the former. They had ten children :

i. MARY,[5] b. Aug. 31, 1744 ; m. Samuel Clark, of Gilmanton, July 4, 1762, and was mother of *Elder Peter Clark.*

ii. CATHERINE,[5] m. ―――― Wadleigh.

iii. ANNA (or Nancy), b. Jan. 1749 ; m. Feb. 1771, Joseph Young, Esq., of Gilmanton, whose dau. MARY was mother of Hon. *W. H. Y. Hackett*, of Portsmouth.

iv. PETER,[5] b. June 24, 1750 ; m. Jemima, b. March 7, 1755, dau. of Josiah Folsom (grandson of Dea. John). They lived in Gilmanton, and both died in 1832 ; had JEMIMA, LYDIA, PETER, JOSIAH, NATHANIEL, POLLY, SAMUEL and MARTHA.

v. ELIZABETH,[5] m. Lieut. Jonathan Perkins of Gilmanton, officer in the Revolutionary army.

vi. NICHOLAS,[5] b. at Exeter, April 29, 1752 ; m. Dorothy, dau. of Joseph Leavitt, of Exeter ; moved to Gilmanton, about 1787 ; d. June 20, 1847. They had Capt. *Nicholas*, b. Aug. 9, 1785, father of *Nicholas-Leavitt Folsom*, M.D., b. Dec. 20, 1815, of Portsmouth, also of *Peter*, *Joseph*, *Dudley*, *Jonathan*, *Thomas*, *Polly*, *Dolly*, *Love-Leavitt*, *James* and *Lydia.*

vii. JONATHAN,[5] of Gilford, b. at Exeter, 1753 ; m. (1) Lydia, dau. of Josiah, grandson of Dea. John ; m. (2) Sarah Green of Stratham, who was his administratrix 1814. He had four sons : *Jonathan*,[6] *Peter*,[6] *Samuel*,[6] *Benjamin*,[6] and a dau. *Sarah*.[6] The first of these, Jonathan,[6] b. 1785, m. Lydia (see under Benj.[3]), d. 1825. He was an eminent contractor and builder : built the sea-wall at the Isles of Shoals, to form a haven for imperilled vessels, and only proved the futility of saying to the furious sea just there, Hitherto shalt thou come and no further ! He built the enduring works of the large stone wharf on the western side of the Portsmouth Navy-Yard, the first Seventy-Four-House, vast and nobly-proportioned, and timber-houses. The Stone Church in Portsmouth, which for use as a house of worship and kindred religious exercises, for simple beauty and quiet grandeur, has not been surpassed, nor is likely to be, he began to build, saw its walls rise with exultation, but died of exposure and overwork a year before its completion. He left four children : *Dea. Thomas*, of Exeter, b. 1810; *Mary-Elizabeth*, b. 1812 ; *Hiram*, b. 1814; *Charles*, b. 1816.

PETER,[6] brother of Jonathan,[6] m. Hannah Hook, and had eight children, among whom is *Peter-William*, b. 1813, of Boston (Roxbury District), married, and having a son and daughter.

viii. JAMES,[5] b. July 22, 1756 ; m. Dec. 2, 1784, Mary, dau. of Josiah Folsom (grandson of Dea. John) ; had eleven children, of whom *Lydia*, m. Nathaniel Nelson, of Gilmanton ; *Martha*, m. Dudley Nelson, of Gilmanton ; *Lavinia*, m. Samuel Nelson, of Salem, Mass. ; *Sarah-R.*, m. Joseph Safford, of Danvers, Mass. ; *Frances*, m. Benjamin Gordon ;

Nancy-Y., m. Daniel Melcher ; *Mary*, was unm. The sons were *James*, *Josiah*, *Peter-G.* of Danvers, *Nicholas D.*

ix.　SAMUEL,[5] b. Nov. 3, 1761 ; went to Deerfield, 1792 ; m. (1) Anna Shepherd of Deerfield, (?) by whom he had, with three other children, *Peter*, b. Oct. 31, 1789, who m. (1) Nancy Smith, and is father of *Peter*, b. Aug. 16, 1817, now of Bloomington, Ill., m. to Cordelia Soule, and the father of five children. By a second wife, Nancy Smith, Samuel had two more children ; then is said to have moved to Cornville, Me., where several of his children also live.

NATHANIEL,[5] m. —— James, lived in Gilmanton.

24.　JOSHUA[4] FOLSOM (*John*,[3] *Lieut. Peter*,[2] *John*[1]), b. 1711(?), was a Quaker or Friend, of Epping, a public speaker in the Society of Friends, who died 1793 or '4. His children were : 1. *Thomas*, b. 1746, and d. without children. 2. *John*, b. 1755, m. Mary Fowler, lived and died in Sandwich. 3. *Joshua.* 4. *Mary*, wife of —— Fry. 5. *Abigail.* 6. *Benjamin*, who had Mead, Thomas and John. 7. *Samuel*, who died soon after his father, leaving children, Joshua, Mary, Huldah and Betty. 8. *Betty*, who died before her father. He has a very large number of descendants. In correspondence with *Henry-Page Folsom*, Esq., of Circleville, O. (who, besides the particulars of his own genealogy, gave information concerning the *descendants of Samuel* Folsom, son of Josiah (Jonathan[3] &c.), when the senior writer had been long and utterly baffled in trying to find their whereabouts), Mr. Chapman learned that a branch of Joshua has flourished there for a long time. H. P. F., b. 1854, is son of Charles and nephew of Henry Folsom[7] (now Henry Page, a lawyer, b. Circleville, O., 1821), son of Joshua,[6] Joshua,[5] Joshua[4] (the Quaker). His mother's family lived in Philadelphia, and belonged to the Society of Friends.

Some years ago, a farmer of Wayland, Mass., bearing the name of "Folsom," a lineal descendant of the Quaker, and, in common with his whole family, cherishing a remarkable veneration for him, but at that time unable to trace his pedigree further back, related to the writer in substance the following story, which was put on record without delay and is now simply transcribed.

Joshua was the proprietor of 2,000 acres of land, still in the possession of his descendants. He was a miller. The people of the town, in those Revolutionary times, called him *a Tory*, because being a Friend he could not go with them in their war measures ; and they combined to spill all his grain into the water. Mr. Cilley, of Nottingham or Deerfield, hearing of this, and being an executor of an estate which the miller owed for rye, immediately proceeded to secure, if possible, the payment before the catastrophe. "In which will you take your pay," said the miller, "in silver or in rye"? "In rye, if agreeable, because it is every day rising." The miller measured out the same number of bushels that he received. "Why, Sir," exclaimed the amazed executor, "rye is worth twice as much as when you bought, and you ought to give me only one-half the amount." "No matter, I choose to return what I received." "Is that your principle ?" responded Mr. C., "why they call you a Tory, and say you are opposed to independence." "No, I am not! I want the country to be free, but I don't want to go to war about it." Mr. C. then added, "they are going to throw all your grain into the water to-night. But they shall pass over my dead body first"! And off he rode, got the people together and told them the story. The plot was abandoned. The Quaker Joshua became the most famed hero in the region for his kindness to the widow and fatherless. We may still see those pitiful, determined eyes, through the dust of the mill, and hear that calm Christian voice amid the clatter uttering its " Yea " and " Nay," avoiding in reply " whatsoever is more than these," because it " cometh of evil," and feel that he did what was wisest and best.

NOTE.—The preceding article originated from a conversation between the two gentlemen named at the beginning, and from the known intention of the Rev. Mr. Chapman to prepare a book embracing a complete genealogy of the Folsom Family. The latter was advised to furnish an article for the Historical and Genealogical Register, with a view to obtain the coöperation of all interested in the object. It was accordingly furnished, confined strictly to " the first four generations " and within the " six printed pages " to which such articles are in general limited. It was then submitted to the senior writer's revision, who could not take it in hand until January of the present year. On consultation with friends it was thought advisable to introduce historical and biographical sketches—the additional expense being cheerfully borne by them. And then as it became known that a multitude of the Folsoms of the present generation would not be helped at all by a paper within the specified limits, it was deemed expedient to include all the names given in Mr. Kelley's Genealogy published many years ago in the " Exeter News Letter " (of which very few copies are in existence), in as full and perfect a form as possible. And so the paper grew in the senior writer's hands until it has swelled to more than four times the " six pages," embracing a large amount of new names and dates within the scope of the generations assigned to himself by Mr. Kelley as well as beyond them.

The kindness of postmasters and postmistresses is gratefully acknowledged, especially in the instance of finding a married sister of Capt. Folsom, of California, who, through her daughter, furnished a very full family-record, going back far enough to be easily connected with names found in Mr. Lancaster's History of Gilmanton, in direct descent from the first John Folsom. Nor could important portions of the article have been written without the valuable aid of Mr. John Ward Dean, the Librarian of the Historic Genealogical Society, and Editor of its periodical, in putting just the needed books before the writer for personal research; also of the Librarian of the Congregational Library. A constant correspondence has also been maintained with Rev. Mr. Chapman, who has already a more extensive collection of names, dates, &c., of the Folsoms than any other person in the country.

In taking his final leave, the senior writer earnestly asks the descendants of John Folsom to communicate names, dates (going back the farthest they can), occupations, biographical sketches, &c., to the Rev. Jacob Chapman, Kingston, N. H. Let them do this before the oldest generation now living shall pass away. Especially let efforts be made like that of Mr. Paul Foster Folsom (mentioned in note, p. 218), and the work of putting the various groups in lineal connection with the first John Folsom will be more practicable; whereas in their present state many of the names now in the hands of Mr. Chapman are utterly untraceable. And let every family pledge itself to purchase his book when completed. We trust he will be able to produce a companion-volume to the " Gilman Genealogy," that model of its class in form and method and general execution. If in five or in seven years from the present time he shall have published such a work, he will not fail to win the gratitude of his kinsmen, and to find a welcome also from many beyond them.					N. S. F.

NOTES ON AMERICAN HISTORY.

[Continued from vol. xix. page 300.]

By the Rev. EDWARD D. NEILL, President of Macalester College, Minneapolis, Minnesota.

No. VII.

SPEECH OF SIR WILLIAM BERKELEY TO THE VIRGINIA ASSEMBLY, 1651.

NEITHER in Sabin's valuable catalogue of books on America, nor in the " Manual " of Lowndes is mention made of a pamphlet which I once examined in the library of the University of Dublin. It is the speech of the Royalist Governor of Virginia, occasioned by the Parliament of England passing an ordinance in 1650, which declared that Virginia having originated from the authority, wealth and population of England was dependent upon and subject to the legislation of Parliament.

The title of the pamphlet is—

THE SPEECH

of the Honourable

WILLIAM

BERKELEY

Governour and Capt: Generall of *Virginea,*
to the *Burgesses* in the *Grand*
Assembly at *James Towne* on the
17 of *March* 165½.

TOGETHER WITH A

DECLARATION

Of the whole Country, occasioned upon the
Sight of a printed paper from England
Intituled An Act, &c.

━━━━━━━

HAGH.

Printed by Samuel Broun, *English*
Bookseller, 1651.

The opening sentences evince the "perfervidam vim," for which
the old Royalist was distinguished. We give them in the hope that
at no distant day the whole may be reprinted.

Gentlemen, you perceave by the *Declaration,* that the men of *Westminster*
have set out, which I beleeve you have all seene, how they meane to deale
with you hereafter, who in the time of their wooing and courting you proposed not hard conditions to be performed on your parts, & on their owne
nothing but a benigne acceptance of your duties to them.

Indeed me thinks, they might have proposed something to us, which might
have strengthened us to beare their heavy chaines they are making ready
for us, though it were but an assurance that we shall eat the bread for
which our owne Oxen plow, and with our own sweat we reape; but this
assurance (it seemes) were a franchise beyond the Condition they have *re-*

solved on the Question we ought to be in. For the reason they talk so *Magisterially* to us, is this; we are forsooth their worships' slaves, bought with their money and by consequence we ought not to buy or sell but with those they shall authorize with a few trifles to cozen us of all for which we toile and labour. If the whole current of their reasoning were not as ridiculous as their actions have been Tyrannical and bloudy, we might wonder with what browes they could sustain such impatient assertions. For if you looke into it, the strength of their argument runs onely thus: we have laid violent hands on your Land-Lord, posses'd his Manner house, where you used to pay your rents, therefore now tender your respects to the same house you once reverenced.

I call my Conscience to witness, I lie not, I cannot in all the Declaration perceave a stronger argument for what they would impose on us than this which I have now told you. They talke indeed of money laid out on this Country in its infancy. I will not say how little, nor how Centuply repaid, but will onely aske was it theirs? Surely, Gentlemen, we are more slaves by nature, than their power can make us, if we suffer ourselves to be shaken with these paper bulletts & those on my life are the heaviest they either can or will send us.

Notwithstanding this confident assertion, in September, 1651, Sir William Berkeley surrendered the government to Parliament Commissioners, and the best men of Virginia, among others Col. Richard Lee, the ancestor of Richard Henry Lee, who in the Continental Congress offered the resolution that the colonies ought to be free, became most faithful and useful to the interests of parliament.

NOTES AND QUERIES.

EDUCATION AT THE CENTENNIAL.—The Bureau of Education in the Department of the Interior at Washington has undertaken a very elaborate series of inquiries to obtain information relating to educational institutions for exhibition at the Centennial. General Eaton, the Commissioner of Education, who also represents the Department of the Interior in whatever is to be shown under the auspices of government from that department, has sub-divided the duties among several gentlemen of experience in their several lines of inquiry, and the researches will embrace every grade of instruction, from the primary school to the college and professional seminary. The inquiries concerning universities, colleges, professional schools and special schools of science, have been placed in charge of Dr. Franklin B. Hough, of Lowville, N. Y., who is personally visiting as many of them as time will admit. In January last he informed us that he had already visited over a hundred of these institutions, and from nearly every one had received cordial assurances of coöperation. Many more have expressed their approval of the plan proposed, and there is reason to expect that nearly all will comply with the request.

The plan consists in a representation of maps of College grounds, on a scale of 100 feet to the inch; plans of buildings, showing internal arrangements, on a scale of 24 feet to the inch, and drawings or photographic views of buildings, on sheets of paper 10 by 12 inches. The portraits of founders, benefactors and professors will also be collected, as fully as possible, and by preference, on paper 8 by 10 inches in size.

The institutions are also requested to forward series of catalogues, circulars, commemorative addresses, and, in short, whatever may have been printed by, or relating to them. The design is to make the library of the Educational Bureau at Washington as full as possible, in its special department, and when these collections, made for the Centennial, are finally placed in that repository, it will become a most valuable collection of information in its special line of research.

A feature in these collections deserves especial commendation. It is proposed to prepare a card list of the names of all graduates of American Colleges, in one alphabetical series. To this end, a special circular has been issued, for the purpose of collecting triennial or other general catalogues, and many colleges, in the absence of such, are sending manuscript lists, as well as lists to supplement the last edition, and bring the series down to date. It is not certainly known that this list will be printed, but its existence in a public library, accessible to the student of history and biography, will be highly appreciated by every person who has ever tried to find such data and failed for want of catalogues for reference. It cannot probably be made complete, as some records have been irretrievably lost ; but anything like an approximation to fulness will be valuable, and when once made, a little attention on the part of the office will enable it to keep its list complete to date.

The inquiries relating to colleges, &c., are embodied in a series of eight circulars, that have been issued to each of these institutions. If any have failed to receive them, they should notify the office of the fact, in order that another set may be forwarded. Persons having old copies of college catalogues, and especially triennials, would confer a public favor by sending them to the Bureau of Education at Washington. If they prove to be duplicates there, they will find their way into some other library, in the course of exchange, and thus aid in completing some collection that will benefit the locality.

Dr. Franklin—Isaiah Thomas.—In 1824, Josiah Flagg, of Lancaster (a relative of Dr. Franklin, and also employed by him as clerk in 1785-6), presented to Isaiah Thomas, as President of the American Antiquarian Society, certain books, &c., which had been given to him by his " great'uncle," Dr. F.—being a quarto volume of " Experiments and Observations on Electricity," and pamphlets— " Maritime Observations," and " Stilling the Waves at Sea."

In making this gift, he related this circumstance. " One day in his (Dr. F.'s) library, I opened an elegant folio Bible and said, ' This, sir, is a splendid edition.' ' Yes,' said he, ' it was printed by Baskerville, the greatest printer in England ; and our countryman, Mr. Thomas, of Worcester, is the Baskerville of America.' "

This tribute to Mr. Thomas seems to me worthy of publication and preservation.

Boston, Mass. B. A. G. Fuller.

[The Hon. Benjamin F. Thomas, in the life of Isaiah Thomas, his grandfather, prefixed to the new edition of the " History of Printing " (vol. i. p. lxxvii.), quotes, from the letter of a relative of Franklin, this anecdote ; but he does not give the name of the relative.—Ed.]

Indian Deserter, 1708. (*Communicated by Frederic Kidder, Esq.*)—

Boston Aug. 2ᵈ 1708

Sir, I am directed by his Exᶜʸ to aquaint you that the Indian deserter whom you sent by Moulton and Atkinson was safely conducted hither is committed to prison, Your care therein is well accepted, the charge must be added to your account of other expenses. I am sir your humble Servt

To Col. Thomas Noyes   Isa. Addington.
    Newbury.   Sec'y.

Barrett.—Can any of your readers give me information as to the ancestry of Samuel Barrett, or his wife Sarah Manning? They were married March 8, 1693-4. He was a merchant, living on Hanover st. His will was proved Aug. 7, 1733. So far as I can find out, he was the father of fifteen children.

Boston, Mass. J. L. Hale.

Gibbons.—Rachel Edgecomb, Patience Annable, Rebecca Wakefield, Hannah Mace and Elizabeth Sharp, supposed to be children of James Gibbons of Saco, as his property was divided between them in 1730.

Harrison, Me. G. T. Ridlon.

AGES OF HARVARD COLLEGE GRADUATES.—The document of which the following is a copy is evidently intended to give the ages of certain graduates of Harvard College at the time of their graduation. The manuscript, which belongs to the New-England Historic, Genealogical Society appears to have been written near the beginning of the present century.

Christopher Gore was	17 ys.	10 ms.	in July,	1776
Judge Sam¹ Sewall	18 :	7	do.	1776
Judge Thomas Dawes	20 :	0	do.	1777
Rufus King	22 :	4	do.	1777
Doctʳ W. Spooner	18 :	4	do.	1778
Judge John Davis	20 :	6	do.	1781
Dudley Atkins Tyng	20 :	10	do.	1781
Harrison G. Otis	17 :	9	do.	1783
Arnold Welles	18 :	10	do.	1780
John Welles	17 :	9	do.	1782
Artemas Ward	21 :	6	do.	1783
Wᵐ Eustis	19 :	1	do.	1772
Perez Morton	20 :	8	do.	1771
Revᵈ Doctʳ J. Eliot	17 :	2	do.	1772
Levi Lincoln	19 :	2	do.	1772
Theophilus Parsons	19 :	5	do.	1769
William Tudor	19 :	3	do.	1769
John C. Jones	18 :	1	do.	1768
Benj. Hichborn	22 :	5	do.	1768
Sir Wᵐ Pepperell	19 :	5	do.	1766
Govʳ Caleb Strong	19 :	6	do.	1764
Sampson Salter Blowers	25 :	4	do.	1763
Timʸ Pickering	18 :	0	do.	1763
Elbridge Gerry	18 :	0	do.	1762
Elisha Hutchinson	18 :	6	do.	1762
Thomas Palmer	18 :	0	do.	1761
Daniel Leonard	20 :	0	do.	1760
Ebenʳ Hancock	18 :	9	do.	1760
Doctʳ Sam¹ Danforth	18 :	0	do.	1758
Thomas Hutchinson	17 :	9	do.	1758
John Pitts	19 :	6	do.	1757
Henry Hill	19 :	6	do.	1756
Govʳ John Wentworth	18 :	0	do.	1755
Presdᵗ John Adams	19 :	9	do.	1755
Doctʳ Isaac Rand	18 :	3	do.	1761
Oliver Wendell	19 :	3	do.	1753
Lᵗ Govʳ Thoˢ Oliver	19 :	6	do.	1753
Dʳ Mather Byles	16 :	6	do.	1751

WITHINGTON.—The undersigned is collecting material for a genealogy of the descendants of *Elder* Henry Withington, of Dorchester, Mass., and would be happy to correspond with any who can give him any information in regard to the early history and genealogy of such descendants.

No. 33 Nassau St., New York City.   CHARLES S. WITHINGTON.

STARR.—I wish to know the date of the death of John Starr, who was born in Middletown, Ct., 1761, and died at Catskill, N. Y., somewhere between 1800 and 1820; also of his wife Bathsheba (Cotton) Starr, who died in Newark, N. J., between 1815 and 1830.   Address,   WILLIAM H. STARR.

14 South Canal St., Chicago, Ill.

LILLINGTON OF CAROLINA. (*Communicated by H. F. Waters, Esq., of Salem.*)— " I, Alexander Lillington of Albemare County in the province of Carolina, planter, & now pʳesent in Salem in new England, being the husband of Sara James the daughter of Thomas James, late of the sᵈ Carolina deceased : but formerly of Salem in new England which sᵈ Sara is the only surviving child and rightfull heire of yᵉ sᵈ Tho: James:" &c. &c. This deed was signed and sealed 3ᵈ August, 1675.— *Essex Co. Deeds, B. 4 P. 379.*

Pell.—The following is copied from a manuscript found among the papers of my late grandfather, the Hon. Cyrus King (obt. 1817), who for twenty years practised law at Saco, Me. I forward it to you, hoping that it may be of value to some of your readers ; at the same time desiring to record my thanks for various similar "scraps" recorded in your valuable Register.

"The Genealogy of John Pell, now living & residing in the town of York, Commonwealth of Massachusetts.

"Edward Pell and Elizabeth his wife were born in Great Britain, at the West of England, and married together in the year 1684 ; and afterwards came to Boston New England, and had possessions, and settled there, and died in the year 1700.

"Capt. Edward Pell, son of Edward and Elizabeth Pell, was born in Boston, New England, in the year 1687, whose occupation was a painter, and died at Boston in the year 1736.

"Revᵈ Mr. Edward Pell (only surviving son of Capt. Edward Pell) son to Edward, and Sarah Pell, his wife, was born in Boston, New England, in the year 1711, and died at Harwich, in the County of Barnstable in the year 1752.

"Edward Pell, son to the Revᵈ Mr. Edward Pell and Jerusha his wife, was born at York in the Province of Maine, in the year 1739 and died in the year 1792.

"John Pell son to the Revᵈ Mr. Edward Pell and Jerusha his wife, was born at Rochester in the County of Plymouth in the year 1744, now living. The only surviving son of the Revᵈ Mr. Edward Pell deceased.

"York Ms., May 3, 1809.   Err's excepted per me John Pell."

The *original* date is erased, but was, so far as I can make out, "April, 1805." From endorsements, the document was probably prepared for the purpose of examining the title of the then possessors of land in Boston which had belonged to "Capt. Edward Pell."

Boston, Mass.   J. L. Hale.

––––––

Capt. James Parker, of Groton.—It will be an assistance to the descendants of Capt. Parker to fill the blank in their genealogy with the surname of his second wife, not given in any printed account. After the death of his first wife, Elizabeth Long, who long continued with him till about the golden period of wedded life, he married Eunice Carter, formerly Brooks, the widow of Samuel Carter, son of Rev. Thomas Carter, of Woburn. This fact is developed by a clause in the will of Sarah Mousal, her relative, widow of John Mousal, Jr., in 1702. Soon after this date, Capt. Parker having died in 1701, she became the third wife of John Kendall and was surviving him in 1706. Revisions may be made in the Register xvii. 51. Shattuck Genealogy 375. Savage I. 260, 341; II. 9, 250. Groton History 421. On this last page, it may be well to note in the margin that Elizabeth, 1st ch. of James Parker, married —— Gary. Joshua 8th married Abigail (Shattuck) Morse, widow of Jonathan Morse. Joseph Parker of the next group was son of Joseph of Chelmsford, m. Nov. 19, 1684, 2d w. pr. Shattuck Hannah Blood, who m. second Robert Blood, whose first wife was Elizabeth Willard. Hannah survived till 1716. Adm. on her estate to Thomas Estabrooks and Hannah Chandler. Revise Robert Blood on Shattuck 369. Jeremiah Shattuck m. Sarah Parker, b. 1705, dau. of Nathaniel, not Sarah dau. of Capt. James by Eunice, b. 1697.

Charlestown, Mass.   Thomas B. Wyman.

––––––

Boston Schools, 1713–15. (*Communicated by J. S. H. Fogg, M.D., of Boston.*)—

Boston 8—15—1713.   *To the Selectmen*

Gent¹men

These are to certifie you, that I find keeping of the free school grows too hard for me,—and therefore am determined to hold it no longer than this year, which ends in the beginning of the next Aprill, and is the 30th year of my keeping school. So remain   Yoʳ humble Servant

                                                     John Cole.

––––––

Roland Young, of Kittery, names sons—Joseph, Beniah, Jonathan, Matthew ; and daughters—Mary, Susanna, Elizabeth, Sarah and Mercy. His wife was Elizabeth. Was not the above Matthew the same person as Matthias Young of York, York Co., Maine, whose daughter Susanna married to Ichabod Austin?

Harrison, Me.   G. T. Ridlon.

THE OLD ELM ON BOSTON COMMON.—During a severe gale on the evening of the 16th of February, 1876, the ancient elm tree on the common was broken off near the ground and laid prostrate. On Bonner's Map of 1722 it has the appearance of a full-grown tree. In 1792 it was spoken of as "an ancient tree." In 1831 it was badly damaged during a severe storm, and shorn of some of its limbs, and again in 1860, and 1869, several limbs were broken off, one measuring three and a half feet in circumference.

The city engineer, Mr. Chesbrough, measured it in 1854-5, and gave it the following dimensions: "Height 72½ feet; height of first branch from the ground, 16½ feet; girth, one foot above the ground, 22½ feet; four feet above the ground, 17 feet; average diameter of greatest extent of branches, 101 feet."

In a history of this tree by Dr. John Collins Warren, then president of the Boston Society of Natural History, published in 1855, he says, "As it was certainly the Great Tree in 1729 and 1722, we may indulge the belief that it sprang up previous to the settlement of Boston; that it cast its protecting shade over the heads of our earliest American ancestors; and that even the native inhabitant of the soil enjoyed the protection of its wide-spreading branches."

The whole population of the city and its vicinity were sensibly affected by the fall of this venerable tree. It had grown into the affections of old and young. From the moment it fell, for several days, from morn till night, until every vestige of it was removed, a constant current of people might be seen winding their way to the spot where it lay, to look upon it for the last time. We presume that a thousand persons could have been counted at any hour of the day standing about it.

A section of one of the branches of this tree, 4 inches thick and measuring 22 inches in diameter, was presented to the New-England Historic, Genealogical Society, March 13, 1876, by the Hon. Samuel C. Cobb, mayor of Boston, and John T. Clark, Esq., alderman, both members of the society.

———

FIRE IN BOSTON, 1762.—(*Communicated by J. S. H. Fogg, M.D., of Boston.*)

To the Honorable his Majestys Justices of the Peace, and the Gentlemen the Selectmen of the Town of Boston:

William Price of Boston Humbly Shews That in the morning of the 11th of June last, a Fire broke out in William's Court so called which burnt all the Houses in said Court, and it was then apprehended from the Violence of the Flames in said Court, that the Dwelling houses and Buildings adjoyning & near to Cornhill, were in great danger of taking Fire & being consumed :—In order to prevent so threatning a Desolation, & for the stopping & preventing the further spreading of the same Fire, The Honᵇˡᵉ Judge Hutchinson, Colonel Joseph Jackson & Capt: Thomas Marshall gave directions for the pulling down a House or Building belonging to your Petitioner of 47 feet in length & 16 feet in width & two storys high, of the Value of about one hundred Pounds lawful money,—That the said Fire did stop before it came to the same House or Building: and as Provision is made by an Act of this Province now in force intitled, An Act for Building with Stone or Brick in the Town of Boston and preventing Fire; That every owner of such House or Houses pulled down as aforesaid shall receive reasonable satisfaction and be paid for the same by the rest of the Inhabitants whose Houses shall not be Burnt to be raised & Levyed as in said Act is directed.

Your Petitioner humbly Prays that Your Honors would be pleased to order him reasonable satisfaction & that he may be paid for said House or Building pulled down as aforesaid or otherwise Relieve him herein as in Your goodness shall seem meet—And as in Duty Bound will Ever Pray &c.

Boston, Nov. 1762.   WILLIAM PRICE.

———

RUSSELL AND ROSE.—Mr. John Russell is said, in Newell's "Church Gathering of Cambridge," to have been "a prominent citizen" there "in 1634—was Town Clerk in 1645—Constable in 1648—removed soon after to Wethersfield, Conn." Can any one give information as to his place of birth or residence in England?

"Robert Rose embarked at Ipswich, co. Suffolk, England, April, 1634, in the ship Francis, John Cutting, Master. Information is earnestly desired as to his place of birth and residence in England?   M. R.

North Branford, Conn.

COMMODORE PREBLE'S HISTORY OF THE AMERICAN FLAG.—The author of this valuable book, noticed in the REGISTER, xxvii. 106, has in preparation a second edition, which will be an extension and improvement of the first. He will be glad to receive from any source incidents, corrections or suggestions that will render his work more perfect. Such communications may be addressed to him at 18 Somerset street, Boston.

In Potter's American Monthly for February, 1876, we find an article by Commodore Preble in relation to a plagiarism from his book, from which we make an extract :—

"In Appleton's Journal, No. 354, Jan. 1, 1876, there is an article entitled, ' Centennial Sketches, I.— *Our National Flag,*' signed and purporting to be written by C. H. Woodman, which is entirely derived, and in part copied verbatim from my History of our Flag (a copyright book published in 1872), as any one having the book, and comparing it with the article can see. It is annoying to have the labors and researches of *over twenty-four years,* collected and published at a pecuniary sacrifice, thus appropriated by a magazine writer without a word of acknowledgment of the source of his information.

"Several of the anecdotes given in the article referred to, viz., Washington's Christening Robe, The Flag of Fort Schuyler, The Standard of the 1st City Troop, The Flag by Copley, The Chinese name for the Flag, Our Flag in the French Convention, &c. &c., were never connected in the history of our flag until I grouped them in it, giving credit to my sources of information."

SALE OF THE PRIVATE LIBRARY OF THE LATE SAMUEL G. DRAKE, THE HISTORIAN.— It having been decided to offer this library at public sale, a catalogue has been prepared and printed. The catalogue is issued in two parts, and embraces nearly 10,500 titles—representing 15,000 bound volumes and 30,000 pamphlets. The sale of the First Part will commence on Tuesday, May 2d, and of the Second Part on Tuesday, June 6th, unless some institution or individual purchases, which we hope may be the case, the entire library. The expected sale is exciting a general interest throughout the country.

The library is generally too well known among collectors to need especial comment. It is the fruit of many years of exhaustive search in the United States and in Europe for whatever relates to American History, Biography, Poetry, Theology or Education. It is especially rich in Indian Annals, in the chronicles of early voyages to America, and in the printed accounts of travels within the American continent ; in books and tracts bearing early American imprints ; in Magazine and Newspaper Literature ; and in rare and valuable MSS., Portraits and Maps. A fuller description will be found in the introductory pages of the catalogue.

Both catalogues will be mailed, by Samuel Adams Drake, Adm'r, 17 Bromfield Street, Boston, on receipt of one dollar.

THE NOBLE FAMILY.—The Hon. Lucius M. Boltwood, of Hartford, Conn., has nearly ready a history and genealogy of this family, which will be put to press as soon as a sufficient number of subscribers can be obtained to defray the expense of printing. The proposed volume will make from 400 to 500 octavo pages, and will be printed on good paper and bound in cloth, and will be sent by mail, postage paid, for $5 a copy. It will contain more than five thousand descendants of Thomas Noble, an early settler of Springfield and Westfield, Mass., and as full records of other families of the name in the United States as the compiler could obtain.

AUTOGRAPH LETTERS AND PORTRAIT OF WASHINGTON.—On the evening of the 22d of February, the anniversary of the birth of Washington, the Old Settlers of Hennepin County, Minn., held their annual meeting at Minneapolis. The Rev. Edward D. Neill, president of Macalester College, gave an interesting "talk" on the above subject, which is reported in the St. Paul Pioneer Press of February 23. The portrait which he spoke about was painted from a silhouette by Folwell, and was shown to his auditors by the Rev. Mr. Neill.

WATSON.—Can any of your readers inform me where Jonathan Watson came from who was in Dover, N. H., in 1675 ? Who was his father, and who were his children ? *Institute and Public Library, Portland, Me.* S. M. WATSON.

BILL CONTRACTED IN 1686 BY PRESIDENT DUDLEY'S GOVERNMENT OF NEW-ENGLAND. —(*From the Jeffries Manuscripts*, communicated by WALTER L. JEFFRIES.)

His Excellency ye Governor & the Honour'
Councill are Drs:

	vizt.		
To Arrears due from ye Late Prst & Councill			
To ye cutting of ye Seale of ye Prst & Councill	0	15	00
To ye cutting of ye Kings Arms	0	15	00
To an order for a Thanksgiving Dec 1686	0	12	06
To an order for ye Price of Grain	0	10	00
To an order for ye Rates of peny p' pound	0	12	06
	3	05	00

Errors Excepted | pr Rd Pierce
Decembr | 2d 1687 | Received ye full Contents | of this Acct

p' Rd PIERCE.

Indorsed, " pierce £3. 5.—

[Richard Pierce was a printer in Boston. Thomas (History of Printing, vol. i. 1st ed. p. 282; 2d ed. p. 89) suggests that he may have been from London where there was a printer of that name in 1679; and states that he was probably the fifth person who carried on the printing business in Boston. He married, Aug. 27, 1680, Sarah, dau. of the Rev. Seaborn Cotton, and continued in business in Boston as late as 1695. See Dunton's " Letters from New-England," p. 76. He printed, Sept. 25, 1690, for Benjamin Harris, " Perfect Occurrences both Foreign and Domestick," the first newspaper printed in New-England. Only one number was issued, which is reprinted entire in the " Historical Magazine," 1st series, vol. i. p. 238.—ED.]

AXTELL—PRATT (*ante*, p. 111).—William,[3] son of Thomas[2] Pratt. of Weymouth, who was "slayne by the Indians" April 19, 1676, was born in 1659. He married Elizabeth Baker, of Dorchester, Oct. 26, 1680, by whom he had but one child, as far as I can find, Thankful, born 1683. In a Diary written by him, lately found, and now in possession of his descendant, Hon. J. E. Crane, of Bridgewater, he states that " in 1690 he moved to Dorchester, in 1695 he went with the Dorchester Colony to Ashley river in South Carolina (to promote religion on the southern plantations), where he arrived Dec. 20th, " and he and Increase Sumner were kindly entertained by Lady Axtell ; in 1697 he was ordained a Ruling Elder of the Church of Christ," and " May 12, 1702, my daughter Thankful was married to Daniel Axtell." He soon after returned to Weymouth, and from thence, in 1705, removed to Bridgewater, and soon again removed to Easton. I believe he was a Presbyterian in his form of religion. He died in 1713, and was buried in the old burying-ground in Easton, the inscription on his grave-stone being as follows : " HERE–LISE–THE–BODY–OF–ELDER–WILLIAM–PRATT –AGED–54–IN–THE–YEA–1713––IANVARY–THE–13."

Daniel Axtell, probably the son of " Lady Axtell," came with his father-in-law or about the same time he returned, and settled in that part of Bridgewater which afterward became Abington. He bought one half of the Briggs grant, which was given to the children of Clement Briggs, " old comer," by Plymouth Colony in 1664. In 1712, Jan. 30, he sold his farm in Abington to Samuel[3] Porter (ancestor of the writer), from Weymouth, and removed to Taunton, that part which afterward became Dighton or Berkeley. JOSEPH W. PORTER.
Burlington, Me.

COOK.—Information wanted respecting the ancestry of *Sarah Cook*, of Boston, who was published Jan. 20, 1728, to Robert Haskins, of Boston? And also of *Israel Cook*, of Boston, who married, Jan. 11, 1745, Mrs. Hannah Upham, of Malden? Israel Cook is said to have been born Oct. 29, 1710.
Hartford, Conn. LUCIUS M. BOLTWOOD.

FLOWER.—According to Savage, Lamrock Flower was living at Hartford in 1686, and died in 1716, leaving eight children : Lydia, b. 1687, Lamrock 1689, Elizabeth 1693, John 1695, Mary 1697, Francis 1700, Ann 1703, Joseph 1706. I wish to know the history of all of these except the last named, and especially the names of the parents and wife of the first mentioned Lamrock.
West Springfield, Mass. L. H. BAGG.

A REMARKABLE CHURCH CHOIR—FIFTY-FIVE YEARS OF HARMONY.—It is well known that churches in the country towns depend for their music on volunteer choirs. The Congregational Church of Atkinson, N. H., affords a remarkable instance of such service on the part of one family by the name of Noyes. It consisted of ten children, six sons and four daughters, all of whom were at different times members of the choir. In 1870, the four sisters and one brother—Mrs. Jane Noyes Gilbert,* Mrs. Tamar Noyes Bartlett,† Mrs. Eliza W. Noyes,* Mrs. Mary Noyes,† Mr. Albert Noyes*— who had continued to reside in the town, had sung in the choir together for 45 years, and the oldest sister for 55 years. The husband of the oldest sister, Dea. Franklin Gilbert, has also been a member of the choir for 55 years, and for 25 years acted as leader. All this service was of excellent quality, and gratuitous.

An organ was purchased a few years ago by subscription, for the church, which has always been played without pay by one of the society.

Boston, Mass. W. C. TODD.

ROOT.—Joshua Root, of Westfield (23 Nov. 1682—28 Sept. 1730), was one of the original proprietors of Lower Housatonic (the present Sheffield and Great Barrington), probably settled in the latter place about 1725-6, and is the first white person known to be buried there. By his wife, *Margaret* ———, he had nine children (1713-1728), who are numbered 2852-2860 in the Root Genealogy. I wish to know the family name of his wife, her parents' names, and the dates of her birth, marriage and death.

West Springfield, Mass. L. H. BAGG.

MRS. GOSS, THE CENTENARIAN.—Among the Notes and Queries of the Register for January, I notice an article on Centenarianism, which refers to the age of Mrs. Anar Goss, who died at Amherst, N. H., March 19, 1875, aged 105 years, 1 month, 18 days.

From an abstract of the town records of the town of Lunenburg, made while I was clerk of that town, I find the following, confirmatory of the statement of Mr. Bacon, which, if of any value, is at your service.

Stephen Bathrick and Jemima Dodge were married at Lunenburg, Aug. 17, 1769. Their children were: Anar, born Feb. 1, 1770; Stephen, b. Aug. 30, 1771; Daniel, b. June 3, 1773; Sally, b. July 27, 1775.

Lawrence, Mass. JOHN R. ROLLINS.

"BASON OF ALCHIMY."—These words occur in the attesting clause of Thomas Cammock's deed of Black Point Patent to Henry Jocelyn (Coll. Maine His. Soc., iii. 230). Are they the title of a book? If not, to what do they refer?

A. H. HOYT.

RECORDS OF FALMOUTH, ME.—The records of this *town*, previous to 1690, were captured by the Indians, or deposited and never returned. Can any one inform me relative to them? S. P. MAYBERRY.

Cape Elizabeth, Me.

EDWARD WIGGLESWORTH. (*Communicated by J. S. H. Fogg, M.D., of Boston.*)

Boston Jan: 7. 1714-15.

GENTLEMEN:

This may certifye you that Mr: Edward Wiglesworth has continued to assist me in keeping the Gramar School another quarter, even to this day.

Yᵣ humble Servt:
NATHˡ WILLIAMS.

To the Selectmen for the Town of Boston.

---

* Deceased.   † Reside in Atkinson.

NECROLOGY OF THE NEW-ENGLAND HISTORIC, GENEALOGICAL SOCIETY.

Prepared by the Rev. SAMUEL CUTLER, Historiographer of the Society.

The Hon. WILLIAM PRESCOTT, M.D., a corresponding member, was born in Sanbornton, N. H., Dec. 29, 1788, and died at his home in Concord, N. H., Oct. 18, 1875, aged four-score and six years, nine months, twenty days. He was a descendant, in the sixth generation, of James Prescott, an emigrant from England, who settled in Hampton, N. H., in 1665.

Dr. Prescott has so fully and ably made known the leading events of his life, and his family connections, in the "Prescott Memorial," a voluminous work of between six and seven hundred octavo pages ; and to which he devoted some thirty years in collecting, arranging materials, writing and publishing, that it does not seem necessary, in this sketch, to do more than refer to this monument of his persevering industry, his scholarly attainments, his professional success, his diversity of talent, his manly and Christian virtues.

Referring, therefore, to this "Memorial" for an account of his interest in, and connection with numerous educational, medical, historical, scientific, and representative bodies, we would simply point to him as one of those self-made men, the architects—under God—of their own characters and fortunes, who, with high aspirings, determine to do, what, under seemingly adverse and discouraging circumstances, they think can be done.

The parents of Dr. Prescott were respectable, but poor. At the age of sixteen he was indentured to serve the residue of his minority with a farmer. Up to this time no attention had been paid to his education. During his five years of apprenticeship he was allowed two months each winter to attend the district school. The few books he used were purchased by the proceeds of chestnuts, gathered by him during hours usually devoted to rest. Thus he struggled on during his five years. Arrived at his majority, he placed himself under the instruction of a clergyman in a neighboring town, who, in a short time, gave him a certificate authorizing him to instruct in a common school. Under another clergyman he studied mathematics, including the theory of navigation and land surveying ; and this was all the assistance he ever received, until in 1811, he commenced the study of his profession with Dr. George Kittredge of Epping. He graduated at the Dartmouth Medical School in 1815, and commenced the practice of his profession at Gilmanton, where he remained eighteen years. In December, 1832, he removed to Lynn, Mass., where he soon found ample employment for his professional services. In September, 1845, he removed from Lynn to Concord, N. H., where in 1852–53 he relinquished active professional labor for the purpose of devoting himself to those literary, scientific, genealogical and antiquarian studies, for which he had a marked talent and a decided taste.

While at Gilmanton, he represented that town in the New-Hampshire Legislature in 1825, 1826, 1830 and 1831, when he declined being any longer a candidate. In 1827 he was elected a senator by the sixth district.

In religion and politics, Dr. Prescott ever cherished a greater regard to principle than to denomination or party. In the former, though for a long life connected with the Methodist denomination, he discarded sectarian bigotry, and thought it the duty of every man to follow his conscientious convictions. In politics he was a republican, and in every war, foreign and domestic, firmly decided for his country. In social life he was a gentleman of the old school, and possessed that modesty which characterizes scientists of genius. His daily walk was the embodiment of Christian and manly virtues. And so, when the great change came, he met it with peace and serenity. His long life had been one of distinguished usefulness to his fellow-men and to the world,

He married, June 22, 1819, Cynthia Parish, who died Dec. 20, 1856, aged 62 years, 3 months, 10 days, by whom he had four children, of whom two lived to maturity, namely : William C., of New-York, and Laura M. the first wife of Amos Hadley, Esq., of Concord, N. H.

He was admitted a member Sept. 17, 1847.

FRANCIS DANE, Esq., of Boston, a life-member and benefactor, was born in Hamilton, Mass., Aug. 6, 1819; died in Hamilton, July 30, 1875, aged 55.

The subject of this sketch was the son of John and Fanny (Quarles) Dane. His father was born Jan. 12, 1782; died June 16, 1829, leaving a family of eleven children—six boys and five girls. His estate, which was a farm less than a hundred acres, when divided gave to each of the children four hundred and twenty-nine dollars. Mrs. Dane, by her executive ability and prudential management of the property, brought up her large family.[1]

At the time of his father's death, Francis was between nine and ten years old. He worked for one or two seasons on a farm; he tried the trade of a mason, but he did not find in these pursuits the proper opening for his abilities. It was in the year 1834, when about fifteen years old, he began his career as a manufacturer of shoes, on the small capital of twenty dollars which his mother gave him. His first effort was successful, and encouraged by his mother he went on in the business.

In the spring of 1840 he removed to South Danvers, the facilities for the shoe business being better there than at Hamilton. By his sterling business qualities he established a reputation as a successful manufacturer. In 1857 he began business on Kilby Street, Boston, and in 1860 became a resident.

On his removal to Boston his resources were so ample he was able greatly to extend his business, and, by his wise management, his means increased rapidly. Those who knew him well bear testimony, "that as a merchant he was energetic, prompt, honorable, sagacious, persistent, successful; that as a financier he was almost unequalled."

Intellectually Mr. Dane was endowed with qualities which gave promise of success. To a retentive memory was joined great clearness of perception, prompt decision, and energetic action. He began business in a small way and with good habits. He adapted himself to his necessities, not entering upon risks he could not measure, or obligations he could not meet. He was a man of great integrity. "He always," said one, "met all his obligations; his word was as good as his bond, and could always be relied upon." He was generous in his charities, answering readily to the calls made upon him as a merchant; in the parish to which he belonged in Boston; the church in Hamilton; and to those in his large circle of kindred who needed aid.

Oct. 10, 1842, Mr. Dane married Miss Zerviah Brown, of Hamilton, born Feb. 1, 1819, who survives him.

He was admitted a member of this Society, Dec. 31, 1873.

DAVID SNOW, Esq., of Boston, a life-member and benefactor, was born in Orleans, Mass., Nov. 30, 1799; died in Boston, Jan. 12, 1876, aged 76.

Mr. Snow was the descendant in direct line from Nicholas Snow, who came from England in 1623, and settled in Nausitt, now Eastham, Mass., in 1644. His father was David Snow, born in Orleans, Oct. 1775. His mother's maiden name was Lutia Higgins, born in Orleans, 1774. From Nicholas Snow and Richard Higgins, who came in the same vessel from England and settled in Nausitt in 1644, have descended all who bear the names of Snow and Higgins, in Barnstable county.

David Snow, the subject of our sketch, married Betsy Fish, of Barnstable, Jan. 1, 1824. Their children are: 1, *Sarah H.*, b. Sept. 30, 1824; 2, *Elizabeth A.*, b. March 25, 1826; 3, *David*, b. Dec. 10, 1827; 4, *Addie*, b. Aug. 31, 1832; 5, *Henry C.*, b. Jan. 20, 1835. Several other children died in infancy.

In 1799, when Mr. Snow was only three weeks old, his father, who was a sailor, was lost at sea, leaving his widowed mother very poor. His education was necessarily very limited. He went to the public school in Orleans, and one quarter to the Sandwich Academy. Speaking of his early life he says: "I was thrown upon the world a fatherless boy, exposed to all its vices and dangers, but by assiduity, economy and perseverance, I escaped the maelstrom where so many are lost, and remain to this present time, June 12, 1870, to praise God from whom all blessings come."

Having accumulated about six thousand dollars, the result of twelve years hard toil, he removed to Boston in 1833, and commenced the fish business on City Wharf. He was successful from the beginning. He afterwards formed a partnership with

[1] For the Genealogy of the Dane family, see Appendix by Perley Derby, Esq., of Salem, Mass., to a Sermon in Memory of Francis Dane, by the Rev. S. J. Spalding, D.D., Aug. 8, 1875, and the REGISTER, *ante* viii. 148.

the late Isaac Rich, and their firm became extensively known as very enterprising, fortunate, and progressively enlarging their means. Their business increased so rapidly they were induced to go into navigation, and built some very fine ships. They also owned a line of packets to New Orleans. After the opening of the war of the rebellion, Mr. Snow disposed of his shipping and turned his attention to real estate in Boston, of which, at the time of his death, he was a large owner. In 1855 he was chosen a director in the Bank of North America. In 1860 he was instrumental in organizing the Bank of the Republic, of which he was elected President, and filled that position until his death.

Mr. Snow was well known in the Methodist denomination, having been a prominent and active member for many years.

He was admitted a member of this Society, June 11, 1870.

Gen. JOHN STEELE TYLER, of Boston, a life member and benefactor, born in Guilford, Vt., Sept. 29, 1796 ; died in Boston, Jan. 20, 1876, aged 79 years.

Gen. Tyler was among the oldest of the active citizens of Boston, where he has resided since, at the age of fourteen years, he entered upon his business life as a clerk in a dry goods store. His ancestors were identified with the early history of Boston. His paternal great-grandfather, William Tyler, b. 1687, d. 1758, whose portrait, by Smibert, was presented to this Society by Gen. Tyler, Nov. 4, 1874 (*ante* xxix. 119), was a prominent merchant; and his grandfather, Royal Tyler, was a member of the Provincial Council in the days of Gov. Bernard, and was a firm supporter of Colonial rights. Judge Royal Tyler, the father of Gen. Tyler, was a gentleman of fine literary attainments. He was born in Boston in 1756, graduated at Harvard Coll. in 1776, and died in Brattleboro', Vt., in 1826. In 1794, he married Mary Hunt Palmer, a granddaughter of Gen. Joseph Palmer of Revolutionary fame, and daughter of Joseph P. Palmer. She died July 8, 1866, at the advanced age of ninety-one years.

Gen. John S. Tyler, when about fifteen years old, entered the counting-room of Abiel Winship, who was engaged in the North West Coast trade; and to his daughter, Mary Wheeler, he was married in 1820. She died in October, 1871, leaving but one daughter, Mrs. Lucinda Baldwin Cutter, wife of George Henry Cutter, the faithful companion and support of her father, who survives him. After Mr. Winship's death, Gen. Tyler was clerk with Col. Amos Binney, and later was associated with his son, Amos Binney, Jr., under the firm of Tyler & Binney, on Long Wharf. In 1829, Gen. Tyler engaged in the adjustment of averages of losses by Insurance Companies, which he has since successfully continued.

Gen. Tyler has for two generations been prominently known from his connection with public bodies. He began his military life as a member of the Boston Light Infantry, in 1816. Through many subordinate offices he attained the rank of Major-General of M. V. M. For four years he was commander of the Ancient and Honorable Artillery Company, and the senior member at his death. He was for many years identified with the institution of Masonry. He was an active member of the DeMolay Encampment of Knights Templar. He held many civil offices, was a member of the Constitutional Convention in 1853 : of the Common Council 1859-60-62 ; Alderman 1863-65-66 ; Trustee of the Public Library two years ; member of the Legislature four years. His knowledge of military tactics, and his executive ability, often led to his selection as marshal of civic and other processions, and to preside on public occasions. Inheriting from his father, and his uncle Col. John S. Tyler, a love for the drama, he was at one time associated as amateur manager of the Tremont Theatre, and, for several years, a director of the Boston Theatre. In politics he was an old Whig, but, early in its history, identified himself with the Republican party.

He was admitted a member of this Society, May 7, 1858.

The Rev. WILLIAM TYLER, A.M., a corresponding member, was the son of Ebenezer and Mary (French) Tyler, and was born at Attleboro', Jan. 7, 1789, and died at Auburndale, Mass., Sept. 27, 1875, aged 86 years.

He was descended in the sixth generation from *Job[1] Tyler* and wife Mary, of Andover, probably from England, through *Samuel,[2]* b. Andover, May 24, 1655, wife Hannah ; *Ebenezer,[3]* b. Mendon, April 28, 1685, m. Catherine Bray ; *John,[4]* b. Attleboro', Jan. 18, 1724, m. Anna Blackinton ; and *Ebenezer,[5]* his father, b. Attleboro', Sept. 8, 1760, m. 1. Mary French ; m. 2. Rachel (Dean) Fobes, Sept. 5, 1805.

Mr. Tyler was a graduate of Brown University, in the class of 1809. After several years spent in business with his father, who was largely engaged in the manufacture of cotton goods, in Pawtucket (then in Mass., now in) R. I., he determined to give himself to the work of the ministry. He was a pupil of the Rev. Dr. Nathaniel Emmons, and learned to imitate him in fearless utterance, and epigrammatic style. He was licensed to preach in 1818; was settled as colleague of Rev. Simeon Williams, over the Congregational Church in South Weymouth, Mass., where he remained as sole pastor about thirteen years.

At a meeting of the Norfolk Conference of Congregational Churches, at South Weymouth, since his decease, resolutions of sorrow at the tidings of his death, and of respect for his memory, as one of the founders of the Conference, "an able and devoted minister of Christ, one of the first and most active laborers in the cause of temperance, and in all moral reforms, one whose teachings and influence were blessed to the edification of our churches," were passed.

In August, 1832, Mr. Tyler was installed as pastor of the Congregational Church, in South Hadley Falls. Here he remained for seven years. In 1839, he removed to Amherst. He ministered to the churches in this region, for some time, under a commission from the Massachusetts Home Missionary Society. He was instrumental in the erection of a new church edifice in Pelham, and in the establishment of a Congregational Church in New Salem.

In 1847, he removed from Amherst to Northampton, where he became proprietor and editor of the Northampton Courier, which position he held about two years. His sympathies and efforts were for the Free Soil party. In 1852, he removed to Pawtucket, Mass., which town he represented in the Massachusetts Constitutional Convention of 1853.

In the fall of 1863, Mr. Tyler removed to Auburndale, " adding," says his pastor, " to the fruits of his active ministry, the honors of a good parishioner." " Reading and observation, and thought, had made him well versed in history, in politics, and in poetry ; and he made good use of his resources to enforce and adorn his speech." He was an earnest friend of education, using freely his influence and his means for its promotion. He was much interested in the Mt. Holyoke Seminary, was one of its first trustees, and a valued friend and adviser of its honored founder. He was a good man, a man of faith and of prayer. He was social and hospitable, of a progressive, hopeful spirit, zealous in reformatory movements, not afraid of new things, and when the last change came to him he was not afraid of that. He had long before left all to Christ, and declared it " sweet to lie passive in his hands, and know no will but his."

The Rev. William Tyler m. 1st, Betsy Balcom, July 1, 1813; 2d, Nancy W. Newell, Nov. 29, 1825. By his first wife he had : 1, *William Ebenezer*, b. April 20, 1822. By his second wife : 2, *Elizabeth Balcom*, b. Sept. 8, 1826 ; 3, *Annie Newell*, b. Feb. 1, 1828 ; 4, *Henry Erastus*, b. Nov. 29, 1829 ; 5, *Evarts Cornelius*, b. Feb. 10, 1832 ; 6, *Edmund Whiting*, b. May 28, 1834 ; 7, *John Augustus*, b. April 21, 1837, d. Sept. 22, 1837 ; 8, *Arthur Frederic*, b. Nov. 3, 1838, d. Sept. 15, 1846 ; 9, *Francis Maurice*, b. May 27, 1845.

He was admitted a member, July 4, 1845.

JAMES MADISON BEEBE, Esq., a life member and benefactor, was born in Pittsfield, Mass., March 18, 1809, and died at his residence, Beacon Street, Boston, Nov. 9, 1875, aged 66.

Mr. Beebe was the son of Levi and Sarah (Pierson) Beebe, of Pittsfield, Mass. His father was a farmer. His early education was in the schools of his native town, and the Academy at Stockbridge, of which the Rev. Jared Curtis was, during his pupilage, the Preceptor. At the age of 16, in the year 1825, he came to Boston to seek employment. On reaching the city he began, where many of our most successful merchants begin, as the younger clerk, or boy, in a dry goods store. After about three years of faithful service, in which he manifested great energy of character, and adaptation to the business, he was entrusted with the entire management of a branch of the store. In 1830, and on his twenty-first birth-day, he opened a retail store on Hanover Street. Soon after he formed a business connection with Mr. John Hathaway—his former employer—which continued five years. The firm was known as J. M. Beebe & Co.

From 1835 to 1850 Mr. Beebe had united with him several partners, the steady, but large increase in his business demanding the oversight of many minds, though his, as afterward in his more extended engagements, was the leading mind.

In 1850 the store in Hanover Street, where during 20 years Mr. Beebe had built up a very large business, being inadequate to the wants of the firm, a removal was made into the granite store on Kilby Street, built by Mr. Charles Codman, it being at that time unequalled in size by any in the city.

After occupying the store on Kilby Street some ten years, the business was removed to Franklin Street; and in 1861 there was another removal to the magnificent warehouse erected by Mr. Beebe, on Winthrop Square, where the firm continued until 1866 when he retired from active business, with a large fortune, and the firm was dissolved.

For many years Mr. Beebe was a director on the Boston & Albany Railroad, which position he filled in the most efficient and satisfactory manner. He was also for a long period a director in the Webster Bank; and, in 1853, a member of the State Convention to revise the Constitution of Massachusetts.

In early life he wisely married Miss Esther Brown, of Pittsfield, Mass., by whom he had four sons and three daughters. She, with three sons and three daughters, survives him.

In contemplating the successful business career of Mr. Beebe, we find personal qualities which well fitted him for his chosen occupation. Under a kind Providence, his success, as a merchant, was the result of a combination of characteristics, physical, mental, and moral. In his boyhood, and as a young man, we have reason to believe that principles were formed which contributed to his success. In the morning the seed was sown; a most important guide to be followed by those entering upon the activities of life. Persevering industry, prudence in entering upon, and faithfulness in fulfilling his engagements, patience and promptness in dealing with his customers, were among the characteristics of Mr. Beebe. These, supplemented by good health, and regular habits; a sound mind in a vigorous body; enabled him to do an amount of work accomplished by comparatively few of his compeers.

Of the early cotemporaries of Mr. Beebe but few remain. The familiar names— the Lawrences and Hows, the Almys, Blakes, Clarkes, Fosters, Edwards, Stoddard, and others,—who thirty or forty years ago were so well known in the domestic and foreign dry goods trade of Boston, have, with but here or there an exception, passed from the now enlarged business of the city, which since that period has increased its population from between sixty and seventy thousand inhabitants, to its present three hundred and forty-two thousand. May we not recall their business probity as an incentive to their successors to maintain the high standard of Boston merchants, as among the honorable of the land?

He was admitted to the Society, Aug. 18, 1863.

Prepared by the Rev. DORUS CLARKE, D.D., late Historiographer.

SOLOMON ROBINSON SPAULDING, Esq., a life member and benefactor, born May 31, 1805, at Putney, Vt., died Aug. 31, 1874, at Saratoga Springs, N. Y., aged 69. He was the son of Beniah[5] (Joseph,[4] Joseph,[3] Joseph,[2] Edward[1]), born July 5, 1766, died Sept. 16, 1832, and Hannah Robinson, born Aug. 9, 1770, died Nov. 29, 1850. His early education was limited, owing to pecuniary embarrassments of his father, who had intended to give him a collegiate education. When sixteen he conceived the idea of seeking his fortune in Boston, and gaining his parents' consent, although it seemed to them extreme folly, he started for Boston with twelve dollars and a half in his purse. He obtained a situation, and soon won the confidence of his employers by his fidelity and integrity. After three years he obtained a vacation to visit his home; soon after his return he was thrown out of employment by the failure of his employer, and he obtained a situation as book-keeper and salesman with a firm in the hide and leather business. From this time the circumstances date which have so frequently given him the name of father of the hide and leather trade of Boston.

In 1847, Mr. Spaulding went to Europe, and was the first in his trade to import hides, leather and skins to any large extent. The same year he obtained the charter of the Exchange Bank, now the National Exchange Bank of Boston, and has been a director in the institution since its organization. In 1853 he started a line of steamships between Boston, Norfolk and Baltimore, which proved a success. Prior to the Rebellion, the Company conferred the honor of naming one of its steamships the "S. R. Spaulding." This vessel was a transport and flag-ship doing signal service during the war, and her name became familiar along the coast.

He was one of the vice-presidents of the Boston Board of Trade for several years.

He married Ann Maria Kingsbury, May 23, 1833, and had four children: 1, *Edward*, merchant, of Boston; 2, *Francis E.*, d. 1866; 3, *Anna*; 4, *Emma F.*

He was admitted into this Society, June 4, 1870.

Prepared by the late Frederic W. Sawyer, Esq., of Boston.

The Hon. Francis Bassett, of Boston, a member of the Suffolk bar and a life member of this Society, died at his winter residence in Boylston street, May 25, 1875. He was born in that part of Yarmouth, now Dennis, Sept. 9, 1786, and had reached the ripe age of eighty-eight years. He was descended from William Bassett, who came from England in 1621 in the ship Fortune, and who settled first in Plymouth, then removed to Duxbury, and finally settled in Bridgewater, where he left numerous descendants. Mr. Bassett was descended from the oldest son William, who settled in Sandwich, Mass. The subject of this notice was left an orphan at the tender age of three years, his father, William Bassett, who was born June 22, 1750, having died in September, 1789, and his mother, Betsey Howes, having died while he was yet an infant.

His father and mother were both citizens of Yarmouth, now Dennis, and his uncle, Elisha Bassett, who took charge of him, educated him, and subsequently sent him to Harvard College, was also of Dennis, though he afterward removed to Ashland. The old family home of this branch of the Bassett family was still in the Bassett family at the decease of this honored descendant at his death. For a great number of years he had been in the habit of passing his summers at the old place.

After leaving College he studied law with Timothy Bigelow, at his office in Boston, and was admitted to the bar in 1814.

Mr. Bassett was a man of good presence, of a genial happy temperament, possessed of a well cultivated mind, and having the prestige of a Cape Cod name and origin soon drew around him a very respectable clientage. He was in the Massachusetts Legislature in 1818, 1819, and 1820, and again in 1824, 1828, and 1829. He had the satisfaction of serving his alma mater eleven years on the Board of Overseers of Harvard College.

In 1830 he was appointed Clerk of the United States Circuit Court for the second Circuit, and of the United States District Court of Massachusetts, under Judges Story and Sprague. In 1845, having acquired a competence, he resigned and went to Europe. Since that time he has been a man of elegant leisure, fond of books, interested in history and genealogy. He took a commendable interest in the preparation and publication of Mr. Freeman's History of Cape Cod.

In 1858 he married Frances Cutter Langdon, daughter of Jacob Cutter of Portsmouth, and widow of Woodbury Langdon, who survives him. Mr. Bassett was the cotemporary at the Boston bar of Mr. Webster, Judges Shaw, Wildes, Putnam and Hubbard, Story and Sprague, and of Harrison Gray Otis, Richard Fletcher, Benjamin Rand, and Henry H. Fuller. He took a lively interest in his early associates at the bar, and contributed an interesting article of reminiscences concerning some of them to the Register for October, 1871 (*ante*, xxv. 370–5).

Mr. Bassett owned at his death the estate on which he was born, at Dennis, and which had been in the Bassett family about two hundred years.

He was admitted to this Society, April 19, 1869.

Prepared by Samuel H. Russell, Esq.

George Williams Pratt, A.M., a resident member, who died at his residence in Louisburg square, on the 13th of January last, was born in Boston the 27th of May, 1802. He was the son of William and Mary (Williams) Pratt, his father a native of Derby, England, having come to America in 1783, and married his wife from Salem. William Pratt engaged in business in Boston, under the style of Boott & Pratt, names permanently associated with the most valuable industrial enterprises in New-England.

Our deceased friend and associate began life with every advantage of birth, education and fortune that could be desired in his day, to which was added the blessing of unimpaired health and vigor of body and mind through a long life. He graduated from Harvard in the class of 1821, with Josiah Quincy and Ralph Waldo Emerson. After leaving college he engaged in commerce, beginning with the unattractive duties which were supposed to be necessary to a mercantile education. From that time, with the exception of a trip to Europe in 1825, including a visit to his uncle Samuel Williams, an eminent London banker, there were few days when his manly figure and pleasant smile were not to be seen on the Exchange. In later years, till retired from active business, he was a broker, having been one of the original founders of the Boston Stock Exchange, an institution for usefulness and fair dealing second to no other business association in the city.

Attentive, and interested in all matters that concerned the welfare of his native city, it was in developing his taste for the beautiful in art and nature that the character of our deceased friend presented a most attractive side to public recognition. Always a devoted son, a tender and affectionate brother, of spotless purity in the domestic walks of life, peaceful, courteous, hospitable, kind, he found time and opportunity to illustrate and embellish its routine with what was useful, beautiful and enduring. He was one of the founders of Mount Auburn, which has been the model of all later American rural cemeteries. An earnest member of the Horticultural Society, which has recognized his industry and assiduity in horticulture, and especially his introduction of the Dahlia into New-England. He was also a member of the Natural History Society, and one of the founders of the Boston Numismatic Society. For many years he was a constant attendant and vestryman in the King's Chapel, where he devoted himself with untiring pains and attention to the cultivation of church music, and the preservation and restoration of the antiquities of that venerable church. Mr. Pratt was one of the first to introduce and encourage the pleasing custom of decorating the altar and chancel with flowers and rare plants on church festivals, now so universally followed by all denominations that many may be surprised to hear of its recent origin. The gardens and hot-houses of "Oakley," his patrimonial estate in Watertown, were laid under contribution whenever they could adorn the church or gratify his friends.

From these beneficent pursuits our friend was suddenly snatched by a disease which terminated his life after two months of suffering, which he bore with cheerful resignation. Mr. Pratt married, the 3rd of May, 1831, Mary White, daughter of Joseph White, Jr., Esq., of Salem, who survives him. Of their four sons, two survive. The oldest son, George William Pratt, Jr., died in Florence, Italy, 25th May, 1865, from exposure and hardship endured in the army of Italian Independence, under Garabaldi. A touching tribute to his worth and services was printed in "La Nazione," of Florence. The second son, William, served in our own army, in the 24th Reg. of Mass. Vols., and was promoted to a staff appointment under Gen. Stevenson. A third son, Robert M., also survives him, while the fourth, Joseph, died in infancy.

Mr. Pratt was admitted as a member, June 8, 1870.

SOCIETIES AND THEIR PROCEEDINGS.

New-England Historic, Genealogical Society.

Boston, Wednesday, October 6, 1875.—A quarterly meeting was held at the Society's House, 18 Somerset street, this afternoon at three o'clock, the president, the Hon. Marshall P. Wilder, in the chair.

David G. Haskins, Jr., the recording secretary, read the record of the previous meeting, which was approved.

The president announced the death, since the last meeting, of Hon. Increase A. Lapham of Milwaukee, Wis., an honorary vice-president of this society for that State, and appointed a committee, consisting of Cyrus Woodman of Cambridge, William B. Towne of Milford, N. H., and Rev. Samuel Cutler of Boston, to prepare resolutions to be reported to the next meeting.

The resolutions of respect to the memory of the late Samuel G. Drake,* the historian, an ex-president of the society, reported at the last meeting, were taken from the table. Remarks were made by Frederic Kidder, William B. Trask, John A. Lewis, Rev. Edmund F. Slafter, Rev. Dorus Clarke, D.D., William Allen, Abraham A. Dame, Hon. James D. Green, and the president, after which the resolutions were adopted, as follows :

Resolved, That in the sudden departure of the late Samuel Gardner Drake we mourn the loss of one of the founders of this society, to whose energy, perseverance and true love of historical pursuits we are more than to any other person indebted for its strength and progress during the first decade of its existence, and who continued to be its unwearied friend and supporter to the end of his life.

---

* Mr. Drake died at his residence in Rockville Place, Boston Highlands, Monday, June 14, 1875, aged 76. A memoir of him by the late John H. Sheppard, with a portrait, was published in the REGISTER, vol. xvii. pp. 197–211.

Resolved, That his early, constant and untiring researches into the history and antiquities of New-England and the genealogies of its families, his patiently-acquired and accurate knowledge of the aborigines of the country, the industry and thoroughness he so abundantly manifested in garnering up and having ready for use the minute and scattered materials and details of history, as his volume of the " History of Boston," "The Book of the Indians,'' and other published works fully show, the sympathy and kind encouragement he ever extended to others in the incipiency and progress of kindred pursuits, place him among the foremost of our countrymen in his particular departments of literature, and entitle his name to our high esteem and gratitude.

Resolved, That as the editor, and for many years the publisher, of the New-England Historical and Genealogical Register, in its earliest and struggling efforts to excite and influence to the study and publication of local and family histories, he has performed a work the value of which cannot be over-estimated.

Resolved, That as members of this society, and many of us long personal friends of Mr. Drake, we desire to express and put on record the loss we, as well as all students of history, have sustained in his death.

The resolution on the late Winslow Lewis. M.D.,* also an ex-president, reported at the same meeting, were then taken up. Remarks were made by Sereno D. Nickerson, J. Wingate Thornton, Abraham A. Dame, Hon. Charles L. Woodbury, Rev. Edmund F. Slafter, Frederic Kidder, Hon. Marshall P. Wilder, William B. Trask, Howland Holmes, M.D., and William H. Montague, and the resolution was adopted as follows :

Resolved, That the members of this society deplore the loss from their ranks of Dr. Winslow Lewis of Boston, for five years their president and who had been their associate almost from its foundation. Skilful in antiquarian research and ardent in its pursuit, untiring and unshrinking in every labor and every work that tended to advance this society in its means, its accumulations and its influence, his exertions well entitle him to an honored place in the front rank of those veterans who have borne the brunt in the ordeals it has undergone in reaching its present flourishing condition, and his memory will be cherished and venerated by those who follow with unequal steps in the path he illuminated. The character of our brother was robust in the stern virtues of the race from which he descended ; strong, consistent, scorning wrong measures and bigotry, comprehensive in his views, vigorous in the tone of his thought, and having that large toleration for the free thought of others which sat like a jewel on his firm faith, radiant with the great Master's example. There was a yearning for kindly relations about our deceased friend which, with the frankness of his manners, his courtesy and willingness in all work of charity or benevolence, gave benignity and winning grace to the sincerity of his friendship. He was not only esteemed for his abilities, his professional preëminence and the excellence of his learning in his varied pursuits, for the easy and genial flow of his wit, the sparkle of his conversation and the cheerfulness he diffused around him ; the heart of our dear brother surpassed all these. This Society, in token of its love, admiration and grief, direct these resolutions to be spread upon the records, and request the president to communicate to the afflicted widow of the deceased a copy, with a further expression of our profound sympathy for her affliction and our earnest hope that her strength may be found equal to this overwhelming calamity, and that she may long be spared to her loving children and friends.

J. Wingate Thornton, who was not present when the resolutions upon Mr. Drake were passed, here added his testimony to his worth.

A report from Charles W. Tuttle, chairman of a committee to nominate a Publishing Committee for 1875–6, was read. The members nominated were unanimously elected, namely, Colonel Albert H. Hoyt, John Ward Dean, William B. Towne, Rev. Lucius R. Paige, D.D., Harry H. Edes and Jeremiah Colburn.

John Ward Dean, the librarian, reported that during the month of September there had been presented to the society 111 books, twenty-nine pamphlets, two manuscripts, two broadsides, and a file of newspapers for three months. Special mention was made of the donations of Mrs. F. W. Sawyer of Boston, Mrs. John Carter Brown of Providence, Sampson, Davenport & Co. of Boston, and Osgood Field of London.

The Rev. Edmund F. Slafter, corresponding secretary, read letters accepting mem-

---

* Dr. Lewis died at Grantville, Mass., Aug. 3, 1875, aged 76. A memoir of him by John H. Sheppard, with a portrait, was published in the REGISTER, vol. xvii. pp. 1–13.

bership, from David M. Parker, M.D. of Boston, Henry E. Waite of West Newton, William H. Wilder of Brookline, William T. Lambert of Charlestown, Phineas Bates, Jr. of Boston, Justin Allen of Topsfield, Nathaniel C. Towle of Brookline, Sidney Brooks of Harwich and Rev. A. B. Muzzey of Cambridge as resident members; and from Robert A. Brock of Richmond, Va., David Ravenal of Charleston, S. C., and G. Delaplaine Scull of Hounslow Heath, England, as corresponding members.

The corresponding secretary also read a letter, dated June 7, 1875, from Hon. Hiland Hall of North Bennington, Vt., accepting the office of vice-president for that State, to which he had been elected, and expressing great interest in the objects and works of the society.

Boston, Nov. 3.—A monthly meeting was held this afternoon, president Wilder in the chair.

William B. Towne, in behalf of the committee appointed at the last meeting, reported the following resolutions:

Resolved, That in the death of the Hon. Increase Allen Lapham, LL.D., not only this Society, of which for more than ten years he was an honorary vice-president, but the community, has to mourn the loss of one of those self-made men, who, without the advantages of an early and classical education, raised himself by great and persevering industry, and a natural taste for scientific studies, to a high place in the estimation of those best qualified to judge of his labors and his attainments. For forty years an inhabitant of Wisconsin, his loss will be specially felt in that State, whose resources have been so remarkably developed by his historical, botanical, geological, and mineralogical investigations and publications. And beyond Wisconsin, and our own Continent, even in Europe, where for several years Dr. Lapham has occupied a high rank among scientists, his memory will be kindly cherished.

After remarks by Mr. Towne, the resolutions, on motion of Rev. Dr. Clarke, were unanimously adopted.

Rev. Samuel Cutler then read a paper upon The Life and Scientific Labors of Dr. Lapham.

Biographical sketches of several deceased members were then read, namely Frederic W. Sawyer of Boston, Isaac C. Bates of Paris, France, Walter C. Green of Boston, Amos Otis of Yarmouthport, the Hon. Francis Bassett and the Hon. Isaac Emery of Boston; the Rev. William Tyler of Auburndale, William Prescott, M.D. of Concord, N. H., Joshua Green, M.D. of Groton, and the Hon. Horace Binney, LL.D. of Philadelphia. The sketch of Mr. Bates was prepared and read by Hamilton A. Hill, that of Mr. Green by the Hon. James D. Green, and that of Mr. Otis by the Hon. Charles F. Swift. The other sketches were read by the historiographer, the Rev. Mr. Cutler, and all were prepared by him except that of Mr. Bassett by the late F. W. Sawyer, that of Dr. Green by J. W. Dean, and that of Mr. Binney by C. J. F. Binney.

The Rev. Edmund F. Slafter, the corresponding secretary, reported letters accepting resident membership from John D. Ames of Fall River, and Cheever Newhall, J. Russell Bradford and Arthur M. Alger of Boston; corresponding membership from James Macpherson Lemoine of Quebec; and honorary membership from Rear Admiral Joseph Smith, U.S.N., of Washington. He also reported other correspondence.

The librarian reported as donations during October, 81 volumes, 358 pamphlets, 26 manuscripts and a number of other articles. Special mention was made of the donations of the Rev. Dr. George R. Entler, of Franklin, N. Y., Commodore George H. Preble, U.S.N., the Literary and Historical Society of Quebec, the Hon. Henry C. Murphy of Brooklyn, J. Wingate Thornton, the Hon. Robert B. Forbes, William Allen of East Bridgewater, Charles Randolph of Chicago, Stanislas Drapeau of Ottawa, Can., Alexander Beal and the Rev. Edwin M. Stone.

The president read a letter from Miss Harriet B. Derby, accompanying a donation of two miniatures painted for her mother, the late Mrs. E. Hasket Derby, one a portrait of the Rev. John Clarke, D.D. of Boston, the other a portrait of the Rev. John Prince, LL.D. of Salem.

Mr. Hill in behalf of Mrs. Isaac C. Bates presented the voluminous genealogical collections left by her husband relating to the Bates and Henshaw families, including the result of his thorough researches in England.

Col. Albert H. Hoyt, the Rev. Edmund F. Slafter, William B. Towne, William B. Trask and Jeremiah Colburn were chosen a committee to nominate candidates for the annual election in January.

Boston, Dec. 1.—A stated meeting was held this afternoon, president Wilder in the chair.

The president announced the death of five prominent members since the last meeting, namely, the Hon. Henry Wilson, the Hon. Amasa Walker, the Hon. Theron Metcalf, James M. Beebe and Andrew T. Hall. As chairman of a committee appointed for the purpose, he reported the following resolutions on the death of Mr. Wilson:

Resolved, That in the death of Henry Wilson, for many years Senator in Congress from Massachusetts and at the time of his death Vice-President of the United States, who had long been a resident member of this society, we lament the loss of one whose name will stand on the roll of those who have most adorned our country's history as a legislator, a philanthropist, and a distinguished friend of temperance; whose example of persistent and energetic self-culture will incite our generous youth; whose kindliness of temper, sympathy with humanity, integrity and moral courage gave special value to his prolonged public services, and whose career was fitly crowned by Christian faith and hope.

Resolved, That these resolutions be entered upon the records and a copy thereof be sent to the relatives of the deceased.

Remarks upon the resolutions and the character of Mr. Wilson were made by the Rev. Elias Nason, Frederic Kidder, the Rev. Dorus Clarke, D.D., and the president, after which the resolutions were unanimously adopted.

The Rev. Elias Nason then read a paper on the Ancient Psalmody of America, which was listened to with deep interest. Remarks upon the subject were made by the Rev. Lucius R. Eastman and President Wilder.

Samuel J. Bridge, for many years a resident of California, related an interesting narrative connected with the life of Dr. Marsh of that state.

The librarian reported as donations in November, 213 volumes, 43 pamphlets and various other articles. Special mention was made of the bequest of the late John Wells Parker, and the donations of Mrs. Anna B. F. Crane, from the library of the late Judge Farrar, her father; the Hon. Robert S. Hale, LL.D., of Elizabethtown, N. Y., William B. Lapham, M.D., of Augusta, Me., State Historical Society of Wisconsin, Paymaster Henry M. Denniston, U.S.N., the Hon. John S. Sleeper, William B. Trask, William C. Fowler, LL.D., of Durham, Ct., the Hon. Edward S. Davis, William G. Brooks and the Hon. Silas N. Martin of Wilmington, N. C.

The corresponding secretary reported the acceptance of resident membership by the following gentlemen: the Hon. John P. Putnam, William C. Waters, Walter Hastings, Henry W. Holland, Beverley O. Kinnear, M.D., the Rev. Charles C. Beaman, all of Boston; the Rev. Grindall Reynolds of Concord, Benjamin A. Chace of Fall River, and Samuel E. Tinkham of Malden.

The historiographer read biographical sketches of four deceased members, the Hon. Amasa Walker, LL.D., James Madison Beebe, the Hon. Theron Metcalf and Andrew T. Hall.

Col. Albert H. Hoyt offered the following resolutions, which were unanimously adopted.

Resolved, That this society takes a hearty interest in the success of the International Exhibition to be held in Philadelphia in the centenary of American Independence, and that it will gladly aid in every practicable way this laudable enterprise.

Resolved, That the Board of Directors be, and they are hereby authorized to take measures to carry the foregoing resolution into effect.

THE RHODE ISLAND HISTORICAL SOCIETY.

Providence, Tuesday, Dec. 21, 1875.—A stated meeting was held this evening, the president, the Hon. Samuel G. Arnold, in the chair.

After the report of the Rev. Edwin M. Stone, the librarian, President Arnold introduced Henry C. Dorr, of New-York, who read a valuable paper on the "Ancient Town Council of Providence," a subject upon which Mr. Dorr has previously read papers before the society. At the close of the reading, the Hon. Zachariah Allen, who was a member of the Town Council for seven years, about a half a century ago, gave some interesting reminiscences. Thanks were voted to Mr. Dorr on motion of the Hon. John R. Bartlett.

January 11, 1876.—A meeting was held this evening. Rev. Mr. Stone, the librarian, announced valuable donations.

The president introduced the Hon. Abraham Payne, of Providence, who read his "Reminiscences of Rhode Island Lawyers," this being his second paper upon the subject. Thanks were voted to Mr. Payne, who intimated that he should have more to say on this subject, and also something on the "Dorr War."

January 18.—The annual meeting was held this evening, president Arnold in the chair.

Richmond P. Everett, the treasurer, made his annual report, which showed a balance of $894.35 in favor of the society. The annual reports of the cabinet keepers of the Northern and Southern Departments were also presented. The former, the Rev. Mr. Stone, reported 2649 contributions. During the year the progress of the society had been steady. Three thousand Rhode Island pamphlets historical, political, judicial, military, financial, scientific, medical, educational, and upon various other topics have been collated, classified and bound, making 2000 volumes in all. Seven thousand manuscripts have been examined, arranged in chronological order in twenty volumes and placed in the hands of the binder. No more important work has ever been done since the society was founded than putting these manuscripts in an available form; and they will be of incalculable advantage to the students of Rhode Island history for the light they throw upon the business and social life among us. These are the first instalments of still more valuable treasures yet to be brought to light from the archives of the society. Among the collection of Rhode Island pamphlets, an interesting document was discovered, concerning which no public notice has been given. It is a printed pamphlet, written by Roger Williams, and entitled, "An answer to a letter sent from Mr. Coddington, of Rhode Island, to Gov. Leverett, of Boston, in what concerns R. W., of Providence." The original title-page is gone, and it is impossible to learn where it was printed, or in what year it was issued. From the general tenor of it, however, the evidence is strong that it appeared subsequent to the discussion between Roger Williams and the disciples of George Fox, at Newport.

The officers for the ensuing year were then elected, as follows:

President—Hon. Samuel G. Arnold.
Vice-Presidents—Hon. Zachariah Allen, Hon. Francis Brinley, of Newport.
Secretary—Hon. Amos Perry.
Treasurer—Richmond P. Everett.
Librarian and Cabinet Keeper, Northern Department—Rev. E. M. Stone.
Cabinet Keeper, Southern Department—Benj. B. Howland, of Newport.
Committee on Nominations—William G. Williams, George L. Collins, Albert V. Jenckes.
Committee on Lectures and Reading of Papers—William Gammell, Charles W. Parsons, Amos Perry.
Committee on Publications—John R. Bartlett, J. Lewis Diman, Edwin M. Stone.
Committee on Grounds and Buildings—Isaac H. Southwick, Joseph R. Brown, Albert Dailey.
Auditing Committee—Henry T. Beckwith, Walter Blodgett.

On motion of Hon. Amos Perry, a committee was appointed to take charge of the genealogical matters which have been brought to the attention of the Society by Dr. Henry E. Turner, of Newport. The subject was spoken of favorably by Messrs. Perry, Allen, Paine and others, the intention being to save from oblivion the early records of the cemeteries in the State. The committee was appointed as follows: Henry E. Turner, Zachariah Allen and Amos Perry. Dr. Channing gave notice of an amendment to the constitution, providing for the election of a genealogical committee as one of the standing committees of the Society.

The Committee on Publications were authorized to have 500 copies of the records printed, including papers, reports and a necrology of the members deceased during the year.

An annual tax of $3 was assessed.

Isaac H. Southwick, for the Committee on Grounds and Buildings, reported that $250 had been expended for repairs. On motion of Mayor Doyle, the Committee on Grounds and Buildings were directed to enlarge the room of the Cabinet by having the inner doors removed back.

On motion of Henry T. Beckwith, an offer of a member to have printed at his own expense, the papers by Henry C. Dorr of New-York, was accepted, with the usual understanding that the Society does not hold itself responsible for any of the ideas advanced by the authors of papers read at its meetings.

Hon. Zachariah Allen read an historical sketch of the family of Capt. Gallup, slain in the great Swamp Battle in 1675, written by Mrs. Carolina Gallup Read of New-York, who also offered to send to the society the orderly book of General Sylvanus Read, on General Sullivan's staff in Rhode Island in the revolutionary war; also two banners. The paper had been intended to have been read on the occasion of the bi-centennial of the swamp fight last December. Mr. Allen was requested to return the thanks of the society to Mrs. Read and to accept her generous offer.

NEW-LONDON COUNTY HISTORICAL SOCIETY.

New-London, Conn., Feb. 22.—A meeting was held this day, the Hon. Henry P. Haven, in the absence of the president, in the chair.

The Hon. Richard A. Wheeler, of Stonington, read a paper upon The Pequots, which presented in a concise form the history of the tribe from the earliest known accounts down to the present time. It was replete with descriptions of heroic, barbarous and treacherous deeds and their penalties.

The committee appointed at the last meeting reported a design for a monument to mark the site of the Pequot fort. It is designed to be of the Doric order, seven feet square at the base and thirty-two feet high, including an ideal statue of Capt. John Mason. The die is to be inlaid with bronze tablatures, on each side, with proper bas-relief and inscriptions. The whole is to be of granite, and it is estimated that it will not cost more than five thousand dollars.

The society accepted the design, and empowered the same committee, namely, Hon. William H. Potter, Judge Wheeler and Daniel Lee to obtain funds, contract, call a meeting of consultation, and go before the legislature if need be. The Hon. L. S. Foster, the Hon. Henry P. Haven, Henry Bill and Capt. William Clift were added to the committee. Remarks were made by Judge Wheeler, Mr. Haven, Drs. Daggett and Arms, Messrs. Lee, Potter, Horace Clift, Judge Mather and others.

THE VIRGINIA HISTORICAL SOCIETY.

Richmond, February, 1876.—At a meeting of the executive committee of this Society, the Hon. A. M. Keiley in the chair, William A. Maury, in behalf of the committee appointed at the January meeting, to examine the manuscript compilation of the letters of the three Colonels Byrd of Westover, and others, recently presented to the Society, reported that a careful examination had shown its interest and value. Thanks were voted to the donor, Miss Elizabeth Byrd Nicholas, by whom these letters were first brought together, and who had prefixed to them an interesting introduction. It was also voted to publish the manuscripts. A photographer is now taking pictures to illustrate the work, namely, a view of the Westover mansion, copies of the portraits which formerly adorned its walls, now preserved at the seats of Upper and Lower Brandon, and pictures of other objects of interest.

R. A. Brock, the corresponding secretary, reported the donations, among which were many books and pamphlets, an antique snuffer's tray, an heirloom of the Hedgeman family of Virginia, presented by Mrs. Susan H. Rawlings, of Richmond, and a valuable historical record, being the manuscript proceedings of the Southern Rights' Association from its organization, Dec. 7, 1850, to April 6, 1860, from its final secretary, J. Bell Bigger, whose predecessors were William F. Ritchie, John M. Daniel, R. R. Duval and Roger A. Pryor.

The corresponding secretary read a very interesting letter from the Hon. H. B. Grigsby, LL.D., the president of the Society, conveying information regarding the library of old William and Mary College in 1776 and 1800, and the number and character of the volumes bequeathed to it by Commissary Blair, its first president, who died in 1743.

He also read an extract from a letter from the Rev. E. A. Dalrymple, D.D., of Baltimore, Md., who tenders a donation of $100 to the proposed fund for the erection of a Society hall, as suggested by Mr. Grigsby. Dr. Dalrymple also writes: "Is the Governor Wood, whose papers you have secured, the Wood under whose auspices or by whom a map of Virginia was made many years ago? If it be, tradition says he made a collection of all the Pamunkey and Mattaponi Indian words that were known in his day. I heard of this vocabulary over thirty years ago, and also that the Hon. Andrew Stevenson, when a young lawyer, was his executor. I communicated with Mr. Stevenson at the time I first heard of the matter, and he sent me word that he also had heard about that vocabulary, and did not doubt but that it would be found among Wood's papers, which he thought were at some place in King William county, Va."

Mr. Brock thought that John Wood, the somewhat notorious author of "The Administration of John Adams—1802," was most probably the Wood alluded to. He was a Scotchman of considerable linguistic and mathematical attainments, who taught school for a number of years in this and the neighboring city of Petersburg. He prepared maps of several counties in the State, and possibly one of the entire State, though his accuracy must have been questionable, as he was known never to have visited the localities delineated. Among other works, he was the author of "A New Theory of the Diurnal Motion of the Earth," published at Richmond in 1809. He died in this city in May, 1822. Governor Wood also died here June 16, 1813, and his remains were interred in Shockoe Hill cemetery.

Mr. Brock was requested to prepare a circular-letter making an appeal in behalf of the Society and soliciting subscriptions to its hall fund.

We are glad to see that Mr. Brock, who succeeds the late Colonel Wynne, as corresponding secretary and librarian of the Society, is prosecuting its interests with zeal. We hope he will find a large number of persons ready to coöperate with him in labor and pecuniary contributions.

BOOK-NOTICES.

The History of Printing in America, with a Biography of Printers, and an Account of Newspapers. In two Volumes. By ISAIAH THOMAS, LL.D., Printer, late President of the American Antiquarian Society, Member of the American Philosophical Society, and of the Massachusetts and New-York Historical Societies. Second Edition. With the Author's Corrections and Additions, and a Catalogue of American Publications previous to the Revolution of 1776. Published under the supervision of a special Committee of the American Antiquarian Society. Albany, N. Y.: Joel Munsell, Printer. 1874. [8vo. Vol. I. pp. lxxxvii. and 423; Vol. II. pp. viii. and 666+47.]

The first edition of Dr. Isaiah Thomas's "great and distinctive enterprise," The History of Printing in America, was published in the early part of the summer of 1810. The author of that work was born in 1749, and put to learning the noble "art preservative of all arts," at an age when boys generally are in the schools struggling with the rudiments of knowledge. He continued at the trade and business of printer and publisher until 1802. Then, in the fulness of his intellectual strength, with a deserved reputation for ability, integrity and patriotic devotion to the rights of man, with an ample estate, the fruit of incessant industry and sagacious enterprise, he retired from active business; but not to idleness, nor to a misuse of talents and resources acquired in a half-century of toil and study. He soon set himself to the task of gathering the material for a history of printers and printing in America.

Dr. Thomas possessed more than ordinary intelligence and intellectual force even for men of his own craft. His habits of industry, accuracy and method were extraordinary. Difficulties and impediments served only to arouse all his powers. What the obstacles were that stood in the way in 1802 of the prosecution of such an undertaking, we at this day cannot properly estimate. In the first place, there did not exist anywhere in all America what we now regard as a well equipped working-library, public or private. The Prince collection, the libraries in Harvard and Yale colleges, and the library of the Massachusetts Historical Society, constituted the entire resources of that kind in New-England. The first named has not materially increased in volume since that day; but the enlargement and enrichment of the other three since 1802, especially in their collections of American publications prior to the revolution of 1776, have been very great. The Boston Athenæum, now one of the best working-libraries in this country, did not exist even in name till 1807. The nucleus of the present superb library of the American Antiquarian Society, prior to its incorporation in 1812 was the property of Dr. Thomas. The large and inestimably valuable collections of early American books now in our public libraries, or in the possession of other historical societies and of private individuals, were then scattered among a multitude of owners in this and foreign lands. The rich collections now existing in other parts of the United States, with few exceptions, had hardly been so much as dreamed of.

Books of reference of any kind were few in number. There were no dictionaries of American biography,—those of Eliot and Allen not having been published till 1809. The only two publications of New-England origin that could fairly claim to take rank with purely historical works of that day, were Belknap's History of New-Hampshire, Trumbull's History of Connecticut, and the first two volumes of Hutchinson's History of the Colony of Massachusetts-Bay,—the third volume did not appear till 1828. Moreover, the great mass of the books and pamphlets previously published in New-England, or in America, whether historical or biographical, were essentially fragmentary and superficial, loose and inaccurate, to a degree that rendered them, for the most part, either but little better than blind guides, or of very slight value for such inquiries as Dr. Thomas was engaged in.

It was under such unfavorable circumstances that this history was constructed. In about eight years from the outset of his labors, the author gave the results to the public in two volumes, including in the aggregate ten hundred and sixty-three octavo pages. The work was received into great favor at once. It certainly had the merit of being the fruit of long, pains-taking and industrious research in an interesting and important field of history hitherto unexplored. The intrinsic merits of the work, coupled with the fact that it was the only publication upon the subject, gave to it the place of authority. This place it has kept unquestioned to the present time.

From 1810 to his death in 1831, Dr. Thomas seems to have never lost sight of the subject; he looked upon his history as susceptible of enlargement and correction. He made considerable progress in collecting materials for a second edition; and at his decease left a partially revised copy of his history. These were included in his bequests to the American Antiquarian Society.

It was his expressed wish, we are informed, that if he did not live long enough to prepare a second edition, some "friend" would use his materials for that purpose. It was altogether fitting and desirable, therefore, that his intentions should be fulfilled by that Society, of which he was the founder, for a long time the first president, and a generous benefactor in his life-time as well as by his testamentary gifts. Surely he could not have been succeeded by a "friend" dearer to his heart, or by one that would more faithfully observe the conditions and intentions of his munificent endowments.

For many years the History of Printing has been classed among the rare books, and large prices have been paid for such copies as now and then have found their way into the market. These facts clearly indicated a continued demand for the work. This demand the Society wisely recognized, and some years ago they took steps to bring out a new edition in pursuance of the author's plans. Very justly the Society also resolved to incorporate this history with their own series of archæological publications, "as a memorial of their honored founder."

This duty was intrusted to a special committee, of which the chairman was Mr. Samuel F. Haven, the librarian of the Society since the year 1838, whose industry, precise learning, thorough research, and distinguished labors as author and editor, have conferred honor upon the Society and greatly enlarged its capacity for usefulness. His associates on the committee were Mr. Nathaniel Paine, the treasurer of the Society, who has been a very active member for several years, and has given ample evidence of his careful and intelligent habits of investigation by valuable historical and bibliographical monographs; and Mr. Joel Munsell, who is entitled to the advanced post of honor in that small class of persons in America who have successfully combined the labors of author, printer, and publisher of historical and biographical works. All the members of the committee have contributed to the undertaking, but the chief labor has been borne by the chairman. The results are before us in two octavo volumes, whose outward style and dress is in fit keeping with the character and importance of the work.

On comparing this with the former edition, it will be observed that the preliminary account of the history of printing in the Old World has been omitted. For the time when it was prepared, and the state of knowledge on the subject then accessible, this part of the original work was reasonably full and accurate; but to have enlarged and modified it sufficiently to embody the later and far more ample information would have necessitated a third volume. Although meritorious, it was not an essential or important part of the original work. Besides, since then, more elaborate and accurate publications on the subject have appeared. In the room of this omitted part, we have a full and satisfactory biography of the author, by his grandson, the Hon. Benjamin F. Thomas. Some articles of less importance have also been left out. In all other respects, we believe, the text of the history is given as it was left in the copy revised by Dr. Thomas, except where it has been enlarged or modified by the committee in pursuance of his evident but incompleted designs.

In elucidation and correction of the text, notes have been supplied by Mr. Haven, Mr. Munsell and Mr. Bartlett. Mr. H. G. Jones, of Philadelphia, has also furnished notes, respecting paper-making, &c., in Pennsylvania.

In the appendix to the first volume of the new edition, we have a learned and valuable contribution on the bibliography of Spanish America, from the Hon. John R. Bartlett, of Providence, who has given special attention to the subject.

By far the most important portion of the new matter is the catalogue of publications in the English colonies of America previous to the revolution of 1776. This list, printed in brevier type, covers three hundred and fifty-eight pages of the second volume. In pursuance of Dr. Thomas's expressed intention, the preparation of the catalogue was undertaken by the late Samuel F. Haven, Jr., M.D., before the outbreak of the late civil war. Availing himself of some materials collected by Dr. Thomas, Dr. Haven had pushed his own inquiries and researches far and wide, and, with that zeal and patient toil that few can appreciate, had collected materials sufficient, as we learn, to make a volume, on brevier type, of four or five hundred pages. This accomplished and deeply lamented young man subsequently lost his life by a mortal wound received from the enemy's battery in the battle of Fredericksburg, while he was on active duty as surgeon of the 15th Massachusetts regiment. This catalogue, which will perpetuate the memory of his historical zeal, and endure as a monument of the son's honorable lineage and inherited tastes, was thus left to be completed by his father; a pathetic instance of a sort of fortune that comes to but few parents. In this case a degree of solace may be afforded by the reflection that the sacrifice was made in behalf of that which in the estimation of many great souls has been held dearer even than life. *Dulce et decorum est pro patriâ mori.*

This catalogue, revised and enlarged by the chairman of the committee, is the first and, so far as we know, the only attempt at a complete list of the major and minor issues of the American press prior to the year 1776. It should be borne in mind, however, that it is not intended for what is technically called a bibliographical catalogue. From a careful reading of the preface to the new edition, in which the important labors of the committee are very modestly stated, and from an examination of the catalogue itself, it will be seen that no such thing was attempted, and could not be, unless the titles in all cases could be taken from the publications themselves. Apparently, the effort has been, so far as practicable, to give such titles as would serve to identify the work, more or less full as the case might require, or the means might be at hand. So that, though all the editions are not specifically mentioned, and though the titles may not correspond in all cases with those in the library of a collection, yet they will be found, we think, to be substantially correct and sufficiently full for the purpose intended.

From such examination as we have been able to make,—and this has been somewhat minute on certain parts,—we are confident that this catalogue will be found to be very nearly exhaustive, and accurate to an unusual and admirable degree. Entire accuracy and absolute completeness could not have been secured without a personal examination by the editor of every publication extant. This manifestly was impossible.

Such a list as this suggests many thoughts which, had we space, we should be glad to state at length. For instance, it is interesting to observe how large a proportion of the publications up to the year 1700 were theological, or, to be more precise, doctrinal, as distinguished from ethical, and to note how few of the writers seem to have left any distinctive, permanent mark upon the public mind. It is interesting also to see in how few instances the exceptionally strong intellectual abilities of fathers were transmitted to their sons and grandsons, so far as the latter are represented in the list of authors. It is no less interesting to observe how the fecundity of the press was increased or diminished by important public events. The periods of greatest religious activity, or of theological disputation, are easily discernible by a glance at this catalogue. The same may be said of those periods when domestic difficulties or foreign interferences occupied the public attention. It is note-worthy also, how plainly the growing lists of titles, and the character of the publications, after the year 1700, indicate that rising and broadening tide of political feeling which culminated in the War for Independence. To this war the author of the "History of Printing in America" was accessory before the fact, and aiding and abetting during the fact, by his voice and pen. It is a happy and perhaps a designed coincidence that the second and greatly improved edition of that history comes forth in the centenary of the Republic. A. H. HOYT.

Bibliotheca Americana. A Catalogue of Books relating to North and South America in the Library of the late John Carter Brown, of Providence, R. I., with Notes. By JOHN RUSSELL BARTLETT. Providence. 1875.

The Historia Americana described by this catalogue was collected by the late John Carter Brown during a period of not less than forty years, under circumstances favorable for making it the most valuable collection of the kind in the world, which we believe it now to be. By the will of Mr. Brown it was devised to his widow, and the process of accumulation, we are happy to learn, is still going on with the same persistent zeal and energy as in the past, under the direction of the learned and accomplished bibliographer, the Hon. John Russell Bartlett. Mrs. Brown is fortunate in being able to place it in the charge of one so eminently qualified for the work, especially as he is conversant with this particular collection, and knows well its fulness and its needs ; for rich as it is, it will undoubtedly rise to a still higher degree of opulence under his wise counsel and direction.

The work consists of four volumes, royal octavo, covering in all seventeen hundred and seventy-five pages. It is divided into three parts, and the titles are entered in chronological order. The first part includes all works printed before 1601, the second part those between 1601 and 1700, and the third those between 1701 and 1800. The number of titles increases in the several parts with the progress of time. The first part includes six hundred titles, the second eleven hundred and fifty-four, while the third contains four thousand, one hundred and seventy-three. Each volume has an illuminated title-page with the family arms and crest.

The first part, which supersedes a former one printed ten years ago, contains, as we have seen, a smaller number of titles than the others, but a much larger proportion of exceedingly rare, and, commercially speaking, valuable works.

It is to be observed that the whole collection is made up, with scarcely an exception, of original editions. Mr. Brown was never satisfied with reprints. It is this that gives to it its extraordinary value in a historical as well as a commercial point of view. Historical tracts, printed in very limited editions, three hundred years ago, are obtained with the utmost difficulty. Few of them, escaping the casualties and dissolving power of time, actually exist. Those that have found their way into the great libraries of Europe, or of this country, happily cannot be withdrawn. When one of a half dozen existing copies of a work, by any chance, is thrown upon the market, it is only those of a princely fortune, who can afford the purchase No obstacle of this sort interfered at any time with Mr. Brown's purpose. His aim therefore to secure original editions, his ample means of competition and the opportunities which arise during a long period of time for obtaining scarce books, have combined to secure a library of Americana, unsurpassed in richness and rarity.

The first part, comprising books printed anterior to 1601, is not merely a catalogue, but a bibliography. Not only are the full titles given by a complete transcript of the title-pages, with a description of the size, number and character of the leaves and often of the type, but of all the more important and extensive works, there are added analyses of their subjects, revealing to the reader their contents in detail. Annotations by Mr. Bartlett, with occasional opinions and conclusions of other bibliographers, are richly scattered through the whole, with frequent epitomised discussions of grave historical questions. The full titles of works in foreign languages are translated, in many cases, into English, a very great convenience, to say the least. The work is embellished by a large number of portraits, vignettes, printer's marks, maps and title-pages in fac-simile, with quaint emblems and mottoes, significant of the customs and manners of the time, and in many ways of historical value. In this feature Mr. Bartlett has exceeded all that have gone before him. In the catalogue of the library of the Duke of Sussex, issued in a princely style, there are fac-similes of the illuminations of certain Hebrew and Caldee manuscripts, and likewise of early typography. Brunet's invaluable Bibliography is illustrated with a limited number of printer's marks. These, interesting in themselves, are chiefly useful in sometimes establishing the date at which certain very ancient volumes were printed. But neither these, nor any other catalogues with which we are acquainted, have illustrations extending to portraits, and especially to complete title-pages and maps. Dibden's Decameron forms no exception, for it is neither a catalogue nor a bibliography, but a general and superficial talk about libraries and books, and book-sales, illustrated with exquisite steel engravings, eminently adapted to the bibliomanian market. While Mr. Bartlett has not omitted the "printer's marks" he has added other illustrations of far greater importance and historical value.

The first three titles in the catalogue are of volumes printed before the discovery of America. They are all cosmographies, and constitute a suitable preface to what follows. They exhibit the world as it was known on the eve of the addition to it of a new continent, and one of these works at least, the *Imago Mundi* of Cardinal D'Ailly, was a favorite text-book of Columbus, and from it he doubtless derived the inspiration and the knowledge that led to his great achievement.

Many of the volumes in the collection, though properly included in the list of Americana, treat of the new continent only incidentally, some of them adding merely a chapter, or even a few sentences or lines, but nevertheless they enter into the warp and woof of our history, and sometimes contain a fact or an allusion, or a date, on which grave conclusions are made to turn.

The original editions of the Columbiana and Vespuciana are numerous in this collection. Of the famous letter of Columbus printed in 1493, immediately after his first voyage, Mrs. Brown has four out of the six editions of that year, all of which are exceedingly rare. This is a larger number than is found in any library, public or private, in this country or Europe. She has also the two other editions in fac-simile.

Besides the long list of historical works relating to America, printed in the sixteenth century, treating of the numerous expeditions to our shores, such as that of Ribault and of Menendez, of Gilbert and Frobisher, and Raleigh and Jacques Cartier, of which we have not space to speak more particularly, there are the great Historical Collections, rare and of inexpressible value to the historical student, beginning with the *Præsi nouamente retrouati* of 1507, followed by that of Simon Grynæus, 1532; of Ramusio, 1554; of Richard Eden, 1555; of Richard Hakluyt, 1582; of Theodore De Bry, 1590, and of Levinus Hulsius, near the end of the century, with his elaborate work in twenty-six quarto volumes. Mr. Bartlett has added great value to the catalogue by giving copious analyses of these collections, excepting those which had already been satisfactorily treated by other bibliographers.

An interesting feature of the work is the introduction of several early maps in fac-simile, which are worthy of a particular notice. That of Stobnicza, of 1512, taken from a copy in the Imperial Library at Vienna, is the first on which America is represented as a distinct continent extending as far north as 50°. In its sombre incompleteness it brings to mind the period of chaotic uncertainty when the earth was void and without form. The map of the world by Peter Apian, of 1520, cuts away the isthmus and separates America into two distinct continents, denominating the northern *ulteriora terra incognita*, an appropriate appellation at that period of undeveloped geographical knowledge. It is distinguished as the earliest engraved map of the new world yet known, on which the name, America, is inscribed. America is however found on a manuscript map, supposed to have been made as early as 1514, and now in a collection belonging to the Queen at Windsor Castle. There are several other maps represented in fac-simile, but we will only mention the very rare and interesting one by Sir Humphrey Gilbert, of 1576, on which are laid down Florida, Labrador, Baccalaos, New France, Hochelaga and Canada, the latter represented as an island by itself. This map was constructed to illustrate his discourse on a passage to Cataia, and it consequently delineates an open sea stretching from Labrador due west across the continent to the Pacific ocean. It was made before his celebrated voyage to our northern coast, and even before the first voyage of

Frobisher, and his information must have been obtained both from the French voyagers, Cartier, and perhaps Alfonse, and from the " Charts of Sebastian Cabota," as he calls them in the " Discourse " which this map was made to illustrate. These charts Sir Humphrey informs us were at that time " to be seene in the Queens Maiesties priuie Gallerie at Whitehall."

These maps are all so excessively rare, that their reproduction in this catalogue will bring them within the reach of many historical students, who would otherwise have been unable to consult them.

We have thus far only spoken of the first Part of the catalogue. The second and third Parts are not illustrated, and the annotations are less frequent and elaborate, although the titles are given in full with brief bibliographical descriptions.

It is hardly necessary to inform our readers that a collection, containing so many exceedingly rare works as this, is carefully preserved. By the courtesy of the late Mr. Brown we have several times visited the Library for historical investigation. The apartment is spacious, chaste and rich. The minor appointments are simple, and the binding of the volumes harmonizes in richness with the preciousness of their contents. When the old binding is strong and whole, bronzed with the sober rust of age, it is retained as better than new. When rebinding is necessary it is done by Bedford and other distinguished binders, and is always plainly rich and chastely beautiful.

The prevailing idea of Mr. Brown appears to have been not to gratify his pride in a collection that should be uniquely rare, but to make one that should be practically useful, to meet as fully as possible the demand of historical investigation in one of its important branches. He was in no sense a bibliotaphist. He did not aim to conceal knowledge but to diffuse it. The mere collector of rare books, who withdraws them from the use of scholars, is a nuisance. He commits a crime against the republic of letters and the rights of mankind. He takes that which not enriches him, but makes the scholar poor indeed. Mr. Brown made this collection in the interest of history, and it has always been, and we fancy it will continue to be in the future, accessible to scholars who are desirous of examining any rare volume for the honest and legitimate purpose of critical study.

Com. by the Rev. Edmund F. Slafter.

History of the Civil War in America. By the Comte de PARIS. Translated, with the approval of the author, by LOUIS F. TASISTRO. Edited by Henry COPPEE, LL.D. Vol. I. Philadelphia : Jos. H. Coates & Co. 1875. [800, pp. 640 ; Cloth, $3.50 ; Sheep, Library Style, $4.50 ; Half Turkey Morocco, $6.00.]

No sooner had the Confederate armies disbanded than the press teemed with histories of the late civil war. Most of these were essentially political, and all were so far partial that they consisted substantially of little more than a diffuse restatement of events as given in the newspapers of the day by army correspondents, or in the official reports of Federal officers. They were incomplete, inaccurate and one-sided, and, for the most, were but the hasty compilations of impecunious journeymen writers, who had no part or lot in the war. They occupied the ground, and, hence, deterred more competent men from undertaking the work.

The best publications of the kind that have appeared from an American source are the histories of single campaigns. Some of these, written by actors in the war, merit the highest confidence from their fulness, accuracy and impartiality.

As to a history of the war, written by an American, such as should command the general approval of candid and well-informed soldiers and civilians on both sides of the controversy, we do not expect to see any serious attempt made until at a time yet distant when the passions, prejudices, jealousies and vain ambitions of soldiers and politicians shall have sunk to rest,—certainly not until the vast and documentary material, still in a measure scattered and incomplete, shall have been collected and digested. It could not have been anticipated that a foreigner would essay this difficult and responsible task. Upon the announcement of such a history from the Count of Paris, the unexpectedness of the source and the character of the writer greatly stimulated public curiosity to learn what he had to offer upon so sensitive a theme ; and his work, so far as it has appeared, has met with an eager public appetite.

The Count of Paris, the author of the work under notice, has had the benefit of a military education and some experience. It is well known that he served for some time on the personal staff of General McClellan. Still it might well be conjectured that he would fail in respect to the fulness, accuracy and candor of his narratives, in the grasp and correct appreciation of the causes of the war, and of the peculiar and extraordinary conditions,—geographical, political and financial,—under which it was carried on. This volume, however, discloses no evidence of failure in any of these respects.

It is stated that the work will be completed in eight volumes in the French language ; two of which are included in the volume before us. It is not possible, therefore, to pass a final judgment upon the work as a whole, since we have but an instalment of it at present ; and, inasmuch as the volumes that are to follow will cover the chief part of the war, including those operations by land and sea, and those partly military, partly political, questions about which there has been the greatest controversy and heat, the most difficult part of the author's labors is yet to come.

The work, so far as it is published, offers but slight occasions for criticism. The author claims to have entered upon his work with due preparation, with a desire to be strictly accurate and impartial, and with the purpose rather of instructing the European public than Transatlantic readers. In his introductory note, he says : " I hope that my readers will acknowledge that I have tried to make Europe understand the magnitude of the strife which divided the New World, the extent of the sacrifices borne by the American people, and the heroism displayed by both sides on the bloody field of battle. I should be proud to have my share in raising the monument which is to perpetuate that heroism and the glory of the American soldier, without distinction between the blue and the gray coats."

The object of this work being essentially a military history, the author, unlike any of his predecessors, begins in a philosophical manner with the origin of the American Army. The first book is devoted to a preliminary sketch of the volunteers of the eighteenth century, of the war of 1812, and the standing army of 1815, of the regular army and of West Point Academy, of the army of occupation in Mexico, the army of invasion in Mexico, and of the American army among the Indians. The second book is devoted to Secession :—slavery, the Confederate volunteers, the presidential election of 1860, Fort Sumter, and the Federal volunteers. In book third, the author gives an elaborate and admirably written account of the rivers and railways of the country, which played so important a part in the war ; the battle of Bull Run ; the preparation for the strife and the organization of the army by Gen. McClellan ; the impatience of the public, stimulated by the intrigues and fears of politicians, and aggravated by the incompetence and ill-regulated temper of the war department ; and an instructive chapter on the *matériel* of war. The next two books give an account of the battles of Lexington, Ball's Bluff, Port Royal, Donelson and Pea Ridge, Shiloh and Roanoke, and the fight between the Monitor and the Virginia in Hampton Roads. The last chapter in this volume especially deserves, on many accounts, a careful study. The causes of General McClellan's failure in the Peninsular Campaign are here outlined in a way that challenge a respectful attention.

The narrative is brought down to the month of April, 1862, and the volume closes with these pregnant sentences : " The government at Washington, by its want of skill, from the outset compromised the success of the decisive campaign for which the patriotic people of the north had begrudged it neither men nor money. In the next volume the reader will see how dearly this error cost."

The volume is elegantly printed, and furnished with several excellent maps engraved from the originals, and printed in three colors.

The translator has done his part of the work of the American edition in an acceptable manner generally. If the remaining volumes shall be written with the ability, research and care that characterize this, the honor and merit of having furnished us with the best history of the Civil War in America will be readily conceded to the grandson of King Louis Philippe.   A. H. H.

Potter's American Monthly : an Illustrated Magazine of History, Literature, Science and Art, Vols. IV. and V. 1875. Philadelphia : John E. Potter & Company. [Sm. 4to. pp. 950.]

Sixteen numbers of Potter's American Monthly, the successor of the American Historical Record (*ante*, xxvi. 222 ; xxviii. 230 ; xxix. 126), have been issued. The first twelve make a volume of nearly one thousand pages, whose title is given above. Its columns abound in articles—most of them illustrated—which will interest people of historical, biographical and antiquarian tastes. With these, to meet the taste of a large class of readers, some lighter literature is interspersed.

Dr. Lossing, who edited the Record during the whole period that this periodical was published under that title, though he vacated the editorial chair when the change was made, still retains a connection with the work, being a principal contributor to its pages. His series of articles on The Historic Buildings of America, and Washington's Orderly Book, annotated by him, are contributions to our historical literature that will be appreciated by scholars. Other contributors have enriched the pages of this work with valuable articles. Mr. Morris, the editor, has performed his labor with good judgment and taste.   J. W. Dean.

A History of the City of St. Paul and of the County of Ramsey, Minnesota. By J. Fletcher Williams, Secretary of the Minnesota Historical Society; Cor. Sec. of the Old Settlers Association of Minnesota; Sec. of the Ramsey County Pioneer Association, &c. &c. [Collections of the Minnesota Historical Society: Vol. IV.] Saint Paul: Published by the Society. 1876. [8vo. pp. 475.]

The first building erected by a white man within the limits of the city of St. Paul was commenced early in June, 1838; and now, three-eighths of a century later, there is a population of upwards of thirty-three thousand persons, a valuation of nearly thirty million dollars, and structures that vie in elegance and durability with those of our Atlantic cities. This elegant book, which would do credit to the press of Boston or New-York, is an evidence of the growth of the city in taste and in the arts.

In the Register for April, 1873 (xxvii. 216), we have given an account of the Minnesota Historical Society, organized in 1849, of whose collections this work forms the fourth volume, and have glanced at the rapid progress of that state in population and wealth. The author of this book has been an efficient officer of the society for nine years, and to his enterprise and industry we think is mainly due the high position which it has attained.

Mr. Williams informs us in his preface that it is ten years since he first began te collect materials illustrating the history of St. Paul; "and it was fortunate," he adds, "that I began the work then. I secured, in writing, the minute statements of some of the earliest pioneers of our city, who have since gone to their reward, and which, if not recorded by me then, would have probably been lost. Among these were" some of "the earliest residents here, who took a prominent part in the pre-territorial period of our history. Coming to St. Paul at quite an early day myself, it was my good fortune to be well acquainted with nearly all the early settlers — scores of them since deceased — and being in an occupation which enabled me to do so, I was accustomed to secure from them, and write up for publication, little sketches, historical and biographical, about the early days and early men of St. Paul."

The author has made a good use of the materials thus collected, and those obtained from books and manuscripts relating to the west, and has produced a book that older cities would be proud of. Biography holds a prominent place in it, and most of the sketches are illustrated by portraits. What would we, in Boston, give for the portraits and the minute details of the lives of our early settlers?   J. W. D.

Proceedings of the Grand Lodge of the most Ancient and Honorable Fraternity of Free and Accepted Masons of the Commonwealth of Massachusetts: Special Communication August 6, 1875, and Quarterly Communication September 8, 1875. Boston: Press of Rockwell & Churchill. 1875. [8vo. pp. 386.]

A large portion of this number of the proceedings of the Grand Lodge of Massachusetts is filled with tributes to the memory of Winslow Lewis, M.D., a past Grand Master of this Lodge. A memorial of Dr. Lewis, prepared by a committee of which Col. John T. Heard was chairman, occupies 250 pages. In this report is printed entire the proceedings of the New-England Historic, Genealogical Society, of which Dr. Lewis was for five years president, comprising the resolutions and the remarks of Messrs. Nickerson, Dame, Woodbury, Slafter, Kidder, Trask, Holmes, Montague and Wilder; also the memoir of Dr. Lewis by John H. Sheppard, which made the leading article in the REGISTER for January, 1863.

Much historical and biographical matter is preserved in the printed proceedings of this institution. In the issue containing its doings for December, 1873, is printed a communication from Col. Heard, showing " the non-sectarian religious character of Freemasons by adducing as evidence the denominational proclivities" of the chaplains of the Grand Lodge from 1796 to 1873, of which he furnished a list of 64 clergymen of seven different denominations, who had served in that capacity, adding biographical sketches, more or less full, of the whole. The sketches, some of which are accompanied with portraits, fill 230 octavo pages, and show great research in the author; for many of the chaplains, though prominent in their day, had but brief obituaries printed at their death, and the materials for their lives had to be collected from widely scattered sources.   J. W. D.

Essays: Historical, Literary, Educational. By WILLIAM CHAUNCEY FOWLER, LL.D.   Printed by the Case, Lockwood & Brainard Co. Hartford. 1875. [8vo. pp. vi. and 298.]

Dr. Fowler is too well known to the readers of the REGISTER and to the literary public to need any introduction. The thirteen essays from his pen are upon the following topics : The origin of the Theological School in Yale College ; the appointment of Nathaniel William Taylor to the chair of the Dwight Professorship of Didactic Theology in Yale College ; report on an ecclesiastical history of Connecticut ; English universities ; obituary notice of Prof. Alexander Metcalf Fisher ; memoir of Rufus Woodward ; review of Silliman's chemistry ; review of Thompson's sermons ; the cultivation of the taste ; reading as a means of culture ; educational influence of libraries ; eloquence ; clergy and common schools. A considerable number of these essays, as we are informed, were originally published in various literary, educational and theological journals, and are now first collected. They contain much important information, acute criticism, and philosophical investigation on a variety of subjects, and chiefly upon subjects of permanent interest. They undoubtedly exercised no little influence through the medium of the publications in which they first appeared, but it was wise to collect them into one volume, and thus place them within the reach of a larger class of readers. We regret that Dr. Fowler did not also include his admirable papers on " Local Law in Massachusetts and Connecticut historically considered " (See REGISTER, xxiv. 33–42, 137—146 ; xxv. 274— 284, 345–51 ; xxvi. 55–60, 284-293). The latter papers somewhat enlarged have been republished in a separate volume, and deserve the attention of the students of our political history.   A. H. H.

A History of the Origin of the Appellation Keystone State, as applied to the Commonwealth of Pennsylvania ; together with Extracts from many authorities relative to the adoption of the Declaration of Independence by the Continental Congress, July 4th, 1776. To which is appended the New Constitution of Pennsylvania, with an Alphabetical Contents. Philadelphia: Claxton, Remsen & Haffelfinger, Nos. 624, 626 and 628 Market street. 1874. [12mo. pp. 190.]

From the year 1870 to the year 1874 several of the newspapers of Pennsylvania diligently and fervidly discussed the question of the origin of the term " Key-Stone State " as applied to that commonwealth. By some it was asserted that the phrase took its origin in the fact, that the bridge built over Rock Creek to connect Pennsylvania with Georgetown, soon after the city of Washington was laid out, contained an arch, the stones of which, named after the States, were so arranged that the one representing Pennsylvania formed the key. By others, and more plausibly, is was claimed that the appellation had its origin in the circumstance that in the voting by colonies in the Continental Congress, July, 1776, upon the question of adopting the Declaration of Independence, there was a tie, until the vote of John Morton of Pennsylvania brought the majority of the delegation of that colony into the support of the Declaration.

This volume reproduces the literature of the controversy above referred to ; but it is probable that nothing less than an " amendment " of the Federal Constitution will ever settle the question.   A. H. H.

The Valentines in America, 1644 *to* 1874. By T. W. VALENTINE, Member of the Long-Island Historical Society. New-York: Clark & Maynard, Publishers, 5 Barclay Street. [8vo. pp. 247.]

The Rawson Family. A Revised Memoir of Edward Rawson, Secretary of the Colony of Massachusetts Bay, from 1650 *to* 1686 *; with Genealogical Notices of his Descendants, including Nine Generations.* By E. B. CRANE. [Motto.] Worcester: Published by the Family. 1875. [8vo. pp. 334. Price $2.75.]

Genealogy of the Odiorne Family. With Notices of other Families connected therewith.. By JAMES CREIGHTON ODIORNE, M.A., Nosce parentes, nosce seipsum. Boston: Printed by Rand, Avery & Co. 1875. [8vo. pp. 222.]

The Bulkeley Family; or the Descendants of Rev. Peter Bulkeley, who settled at Concord, Mass., in 1636. *Compiled at the Request of Joseph E. Bulkeley.* By Rev. F. W. CHAPMAN. ...... Hartford: The Case, Lockwood & Brainard Co., Printers. 1875. [8vo. pp. 289.]

John Stoddard of Wethersfield, Conn., and his Descendants. 1642–1872. *A Genealogy* By D. WILLIAMS PATTERSON. Honour thy Father and thy Mother. Author's Edition. Printed for Private Circulation. 1873. [8vo. pp. 96.]

A Genealogy of the Descendants of Peter Vilas. Compiled by C. H. VILAS. [Motto.] Madison, Wis.: Published by the Editor. 1875. [8vo. pp. 221.]

An Account of Percival and Ellen Green and of Some of their Descendants· By SAMUEL ABBOTT GREEN. ...... Groton, Mass. 1876. [8vo· pp. 67.]

Genealogy of the Tenney Family, more particularly of the Family of Daniel Tenney and Sylvia Kent, his wife, late of La Porte, Lorain County, Ohio. From 1634 *and* 1638 *to* 1875. Compiled by HORACE A. TENNEY. Madison, Wis.: M. J. Cantwell, Printer. 1875. [8vo. pp. 76.]

Genealogy of the Warren Family, from Richard, who came in the Mayflower in 1620, *to* 1872. Albany, N. Y.: J. Munsell, State Street. 1874. [8vo. pp. 7.]

A Short and General Account of the Family of People by the name of Booge, being so far as known the only Family of that name in the United States. [8vo. pp. 7.]

History of the Cutter Family of New-England. Supplement. 1871–1874. Boston: Printed by David Clapp & Son. 1875. [8vo. pp. 55 (364–420.) Price of Supplement, 75 cts; of History with Supplement, $3.]

Third Supplement of the Notices of the Ellises of England, Scotland and Ireland, from the Conquest to the Present Time, including the Families of Alis, Fitz-Elys, Helles, etc. By WILLIAM SMITH ELLIS, Esq., of the Middle Temple. [Arms and Motto.] London: Published by J. R. Smith, 36 Soho Square. 1875. [8vo. pp. 56 (93–148). Price, Half a Crown.]

The Valentines in this country belong to various stocks, concerning which Mr. Valentine of Brooklyn, N. Y., in the book the title of which is first given above, has collected much valuable and interesting material. The genealogies of several of the families are given from their first settlement in this country.

Of Secretary Edward Rawson, a portrait and memoir were given in the REGISTER for July, 1849 (iii. 201–8), and genealogical notices of his descendants, with a portrait of Rebecca Rawson in the next number (iii. 297–330). The latter article was principally condensed from the Rawson Genealogy, which was noticed in the same volume (p. 105), the materials for which were chiefly gathered by Reuben Rawson Dodge, though his name does not appear on the title-page. Mr. Dodge has continued for a quarter of a century to collect materials for the genealogy of his mother's family, which materials we learn from the preface of Mr. Crane's book have been used in its compilation; but still Mr. Dodge's name does not appear on the title-page as a joint author. We do not think an acknowledgment of indebtedness in the book itself is sufficient in such a case. We are pleased, as are many others who know the difficulties under which he has pursued his genealogical researches, to see a portrait and biographical sketch of Mr. Dodge in the book. Mr. Crane has done his work in a creditable manner.

Mr. Odiorne, the author of the third book, was an early contributor to the REGISTER, having prepared the valuable lists of Boston Ministers in our first volume. He is very thorough in his research, and careful and methodical in his compilations, and has produced a work of a high order of merit. The other families referred to in the title, are Stedman, Creighton, Brackett, Meacham and Warren.

The Rev. Mr. Chapman, author of The Bulkeley Family, was a vice-president of the New-England Historic, Genealogical Society from 1859 to 1865, and is the author of The Chapman, Pratt, Trowbridge, Buckingham and Coit Families, all valuable works, which have been noticed in the REGISTER. The present work has the same excellent characteristics as these. We are sorry to learn that Mr. Chapman has been compelled by ill health to suspend his genealogical labors. He was engaged on the Griswold, Bushnell, Robbins and Hooker families, the first of which is nearly done, the second in very good shape, and the others in different stages of progress. The book is for sale by the author's son, Henry A. Chapman, 12 Canton Street, Hartford, Conn. Price, $5 per express, or $5.24 by mail.

Dr. Patterson, of Newark Valley, N. Y., the author of the Stoddard Genealogy, is a genealogist of high standing, and his work is a very thorough and satisfactory one. It was so far completed in 1863 that proposals were then issued for publishing it. "As the people were then engaged in a greater undertaking, the subscriptions," the author informs us, "reached only one fourth of the sum needed" to defray the bare cost of printing. No doubt the work is more perfect than it would have been had it been printed then.

The Vilas genealogy relates to a family of comparative recent origin in this country, the emigrant Peter Vilas having been born in England, Feb. 24, 1704. His son Noah was an early settler of Alstead, N. H. Their descendants are now scattered in different parts of the Union.

Dr. Green, the author of the next work, prepared in 1861 an article for the REGISTER on Percival and Ellen Green and their descendants, which was printed in the April number of that year. He has added much new matter to it, rearranged it and issued it in this form. A copious appendix of about forty pages, consisting of documents, wills, etc., some of which contain matter of much historic interest, adds much to the value of the work.

The Tenney genealogy contains one line of the descendants of Thomas Tenney who emigrated in 1638, from Rowley in Yorkshire to Rowley in Massachusetts. It also contains a brief genealogy of the Kent family, descendants of John and Sarah (Woodman) Kent of Newbury. Quite full biographical sketches of the several members of the family of Daniel and Sylvia (Kent) Tenney are given.

The Warren pamphlet contains only one line of the descendants of the Mayflower "pilgrim."

The pamphlet on the Booge family is by D. Williams Patterson, author of the work on the Stoddard family, noticed above. It is reprinted from the New-York Genealogical and Biographical Record for April, 1872.

The History of the Cutter Family was published in 1871, and was noticed in the REGISTER for July of that year (xxv. 306). The Supplement now issued brings the work down to the present time.

The Notices of the Ellises and the first and second supplements to that work, were noticed together in July, 1872, in this periodical (*ante*, xxvi. 346). The Third Supplement, now issued, is filled with interesting genealogical matter. Mr. Ellis is the author of "The Antiquities of Heraldry," a valuable work published in London, in 1869.

Portraits, views and other engravings add to the attractions of most of the volumes noticed in this article.   J. W. D.

History of the Town of Rindge, New-Hampshire, from the date of the Rowley Canada or Massachusetts Charter to the Present Time, 1736–1874, with a Genealogical Register of the Rindge Families. By EZRA S. STEARNS. [Motto.] Boston: Press of George H. Ellis. 1875. [8vo. pp. 788.]

This is an excellent book in every respect — literary, artistic and mechanical. If we were asked to select a model for a town history, we know of no book that we should recommend in preference to this. The town has done nobly; and it has had the good fortune to secure the services of one who not only has a just and clear idea of what a town history should be, but also has the ability to reduce his ideas to practice. Mr. Stearns is a practised writer, the master of an agreeable and effective style, besides being a persevering collector of facts and a careful scrutinizer of them.

After an introductory chapter devoted to the hills, water-courses, lakes, fish, animals, arboreal products, scenery, &c., of this locality, the author gives a history of the Canada Expedition of 1690, which occasioned the first grant of this township. To defray the expenses of this expedition, Massachusetts issued the first paper money circulated in New-England. This money depreciated, and, as a tardy compensation to the soldiers for their loss, they or their heirs, nearly half a century later, were granted several townships of land which were named from the localities to which the soldiers chiefly belonged, Dorchester Canada (Ashburnham), Ipswich Canada (Winchendon), Rowley Canada (Rindge), &c.; the last-named being the subject of the book under review. The grant, however, was soon rendered void by the new line run, in 1741, between the two provinces, which transferred Rowley Canada from Massachusetts to New-Hampshire. A second grant was obtained, in 1749, from the Masonian proprietors, as one of the Monadnock townships, this being numbered one. These transactions are fully detailed by Mr. Stearns. The town was incorporated by the province of New-Hampshire in 1768.

The arrangement of the book is mainly chronological, though certain topics are treated separately, as schools, sacred music, manufactures, &c. The author furnishes a graphic narrative of the events in that town, which for a time held a frontier position, and was the witness to many exciting scenes. He paints a faithful picture of the life passed there, thus furnishing a valuable contribution to the history of the people of New-England.

The revolutionary history of the town is unusually complete, containing the names of the soldiers, the duration and character of their services, list of casualties, and a general account of the home experiences of the inhabitants of the town.

This agricultural and far from wealthy town, though incorporated but little over a century ago, and having had at no time a population much in excess of one thousand, has furnished to New-England and the nation some of their most enterprising and talented citizens. It was the birthplace of at least two persons whose influence has extended beyond the nation :—the Rev. Edward Payson, D.D., of Portland, Me., the eloquent and pious divine, whose fervent utterances are household words; and the Hon. Marshall P. Wilder, president of the New-England Historic, Genealogical Society, who has won an enviable reputation in literature, politics and the science of agriculture. Of the latter gentleman, one of the most competent European authorities declares that "by his careful researches and experiments" he has "laid the horticulturists of all nations under heavy obligations."

The genealogical portion of the work fills 357 pages — nearly half the book. It shows thorough research, and must have cost the author a vast amount of labor. It is clearly arranged, the plan being similar to that used by Dr. Bond in his Genealogies and History of Watertown, and the dates are full and precise. The ancestry of not a few of the settlers of Rindge are briefly carried back to the earliest families of their name in New-England. These genealogies contain much valuable information not previously published, and will be of exceeding interest to many persons of the same family names whose ancestors have not been residents of this town.

The book is elegantly printed, and is illustrated with a view of the second meeting-house, built in 1796, and steel portraits of the Hon. Marshall P. Wilder, the Rev. Amos W. Burnham, D.D., Col. Ezekiel Jewett, Dr. Ira Russell, Samuel Burnham, A.M., Samuel L. Wilder, Thomas Ingalls, Joshua Converse, Eliphalet Hale and Harry Hale, Esquires, the Hon. Erastus Rugg and Thomas Sherwin, A.M.

The author (E. S. Stearns, Rindge, N. H.) will send the book by express on receipt of $4, or for $4.60 if sent by mail. Natives of Rindge, and all others whose interest in the town leads them to wish to assist in meeting the expense of publication, are advised to send for several copies. J. W. D.

The Town of Hingham in the late Civil War, with Sketches of its Soldiers and Sailors, also the Address and other Exercises at the Dedication of the Soldiers' and Sailors' Monument. Prepared by FEARING BURR and GEORGE LINCOLN. Published by order of the Town. 1876. [8vo. pp. 455.]

This is a very handsome volume from the press of Rand, Avery & Co., of Boston, and is a noble tribute, by the town of Hingham, to the memory of its soldiers and sailors who lost their lives in the war of the Rebellion. It comprises nineteen chapters, and an Appendix, with two indexes. The volume contains very full and interesting accounts of the action of the town and its citizens, including the ladies, during the war,—a detailed and carefully prepared record of the services and sacrifices of its soldiers and sailors,—and well-written biographical sketches of those who gave their lives to their country.

The whole matter is methodically arranged by the compilers, and shows excellent taste and a warm and patriotic interest in their work. The chapter giving a history of the Lincoln Light Infantry is well written and especially interesting.

The committee who performed the agreeable duty of erecting the monument to the soldiers and sailors in the Hingham Cemetery, were authorized by the town to publish an account of its dedication, including the address of Solomon Lincoln, with a record of its soldiers and sailors. The Monument Committee delegated their authority to prepare the work to Mr. Burr and Mr. Lincoln, two very competent persons for the task.

The volume is embellished by a view of the graceful monument, engraved portraits of Abraham Lincoln and John Albion Andrew, with a sketch of the life of the former by Arthur Lincoln, and of the latter by John Davis Long.

We regard the work as a very important contribution to the history of Hingham, —an honor to the town and to the committee who prepared it.

Communicated by the Hon. Solomon Lincoln.

Transcripts of Original Documents in the English Archives relating to the Early History of the State of New-Hampshire. Edited by JOHN SCRIBNER JENNESS. New-York: Privately Printed. 1876. [Royal 8vo. pp. 161.]

Nothing is more certain than that our standard local histories, written near the close of the last century, must be laid aside as defective; that the venerable names of Hutchinson, Belknap, Trumbull and others, must no longer be our guides to the history of past times. This is lamentable and inevitable. The narratives of these historical writers cannot be relied on when we know that only part of the documentary history of the period, they essayed to write, was before them. Down to the epoch of our national independence, the Provinces and Colonies were politically and commercially united with the mother country. In consequence of this the records of public transactions found appropriate lodgment in two places, namely, in our domestic archives and in the English archives. The documentary evidence of a single transaction being thus divided, necessitates an examination of both archives in order to gain a full and accurate view of it. Our early writers had neither the means nor the leisure to go abroad for this purpose; they contented themselves with what they could find at home. The histories of Dr. Palfrey and of Mr. Bancroft, which are supplanting our older histories, derive their great merit from the respective writers' examination of the foreign archives, and thereby obtaining a full view of characters and events.

What was true of our early historians is true to-day of many persons whose inclinations and fitness qualify them for historical research, but whose means and leisure do not authorize their going abroad for this purpose. This fact has been recognized by one of our State Governments. New-York, with an enlightened liberality that does her the highest honor, has collected from foreign archives all that bears, in any way, on her past history, and placed the same before her citizens in printed volumes. When other states have done likewise they may expect to have their history fully and thoroughly written.

It should seem to be the appropriate function of our national government to gather from foreign archives whatever relates to the history of the States, or even North America. One would think that our national vanity would not only prompt such action, but would execute it. The mere drippings of an Indian Bureau, or of a fat trading-post, diverted to this object for a year or two, would defray the charge, and do honor to the intelligence and enterprise of the nation. Our ministers and consuls ought to have knowledge enough to qualify them to direct an examination of the archives of the government to which they are accredited. England has distinguished herself by the zeal and the liberality which she has shown in this worthy undertaking. The materials for her history from the earliest times are now within the realm, or fast coming in.

But private enterprise and liberality have now begun to do what the public should. Here is a printed volume of 161 pages, large octavo, containing documents copied from originals in the English archives, relating to New-Hampshire, during the first sixty years of that settlement, not more than two or three of which have ever been in print ; and except a few in manuscript in the hands of the writer, not one was ever before on this side of the Atlantic. How this volume would have gladdened the eyes and heart of the venerable Dr. Belknap, the historian of that state ! It is quite impossible in this brief notice to give a just idea of the real contents of this volume. Every document is of a public character, relating directly or indirectly to public men and events of this early period. All, or nearly all, the official correspondence of Lieut.-Governor Cranfield is here, and a rich development it is. The map in this volume, giving a view of the maritime parts of Maine and New-Hampshire, supposed to have been made as early as 1655, is of great interest and value. This map, found in the English archives, seems to have escaped the notice of all our historical investigators, and to have been unnoticed for more than two centuries. It is a precious document, and is calculated to throw much light on the progress of settlement in those parts. The recent discovery and recovery, by Mr. Thornton, of the Trelawney Papers, strengthens the probability that Gorges and Mason's papers, so much wanted, may yet be found. Their recovery would throw a flood of light over the early settlements of Maine and New-Hampshire.

Mr. Jenness, the editor of this volume, is already known as the author of a Historical Sketch of the Isles of Shoals, a work of acknowledged merit. His interest in the history of New-Hampshire, and his appreciation of materials required for writing history, led him to make this collection of documents, and to print them, at his own expense. He could hardly have done a wiser thing, or one more certain to gain for him the gratitude of all historical students, now and hereafter. Hutchinson made a collection of similar state papers, chiefly relating to Massachusetts, and printed them more than a hundred years ago. This collection is more widely known than his history, excellent as it is ; and it is destined to outlive that great work, the labor of so many years. No future discovery and no lapse of time can possibly lessen the value of such a collection of historical documents as Mr. Jenness has made and given to the public. C. W. TUTTLE.

History of the First Church in Springfield. An Address delivered June 22, 1875. With an Appendix. By HENRY MORRIS. With Portraits and Illustrations. Published by Request. Springfield, Mass.: Whitney & Adams. 1875. [12mo. pp. 60.]

1636–1875. *Early History of Springfield.* An Address delivered October 16, 1875, on the Two Hundredth Anniversary of the Burning of the Town by the Indians. By HENRY MORRIS. With an Appendix. Springfield, Mass.: F. W. Morris, Publisher. 1876. [12mo. pp. 85.]

Account of the Centennial Celebration of the Town of West Springfield, Mass., Wednesday, March 25th, 1874, with the Historical Address of Thomas E. Vermilye, D.D., LL.D., the Poem of Mrs. Ellen P. Champion, and other Facts and Speeches. Compiled by J. N. BAGG. Published by Vote of the Town. 1874. [8vo. pp. 144.]

Springfield was organized as a town, May 14, 1636, and West Springfield was set off from it and incorporated Feb. 23, 1774 ; but no complete history of either town has been published. We are glad, therefore, to see the present contributions to the history of towns so rich in historical associations as these.

The late Hon. Oliver B. Morris, who died in 1871 (*ante*, xxiv. 337), on the 25th of May, 1836, delivered at Springfield an address commemorative of the 200th anniversary of the settlement of that town, which address, though never printed, we learn is still preserved in manuscript; and the late Hon. Charles Stearns (*ante*, xiii. 187; xiv. 192), is said to have made at the time of his death, in 1860, considerable progress on a work entitled, "Historical Collections relative to Springfield." Of printed historical literature, we may refer to the Century Sermon of the Rev. Robert Breck, pastor of the First Church, preached Oct. 16, 1775, and printed at Hartford in 1784; the address of the Hon. George Bliss, March 24, 1828, on the opening of the town-hall, at Springfield, containing sketches of the early history of the town, which was printed the same year; the 20 pages which Holland, in the second volume of his "History of Western Massachusetts," devotes to Springfield, and the 8 pages which Barber devotes to it in his "Historical Collections" of Massachusetts.

In West Springfield the Rev. Joseph Lathrop, D.D., preached a Century Sermon, August 25, 1796, and the Rev. William B. Sprague, D.D., on the annual thanksgiving, Dec. 2, 1824, preached a historical discourse, both of which were printed. Holland and Barber also give something about the town.

The above are the principal historical productions relative to the two towns. Large portions of their records, however, have been printed in the REGISTER (*ante*, ix. 170; xviii. 82, 142; xix. 61, 249; xxix. 54, 146, 283; xxx. 50, 194).

Judge Morris, the author of the first two books whose titles we give, is a son of the Hon. Oliver B. Morris, and has had the benefit of the historical collections made by his father; while his own tastes and studies qualify him for the work he undertakes. In the history of the first, and for a long time the only church in Springfield, much of the history of the town necessarily appears. We have in the two books, with their appendixes of documents, &c., a succinct account of the early and many of the later events in the town.

The book on the Centennial Celebration at West Springfield, besides the address of the Rev. Dr. Vermilye and the poem of Mrs. Champion, contains the speeches and letters, in whole or part, at the Centennial Dinner; and an appendix of 50 pages, which, besides copies of documents, furnishes lists of the various officers of the town, with their terms of service, from its incorporation in 1774 to the present time: genealogies of the families of Ashley, Bagg, Bliss, Champion, Chapin, Cooley, Day, Ely, Lathrop, Parsons, Rogers, Smith, Stebbins, Wade, and White; reminiscences of old people, and other interesting matters. The three books are illustrated by portraits and other engravings. The portraits engraved by Thomas Chubbuck, of Springfield, will compare favorably with those by any of our artists.

J. W. D.

Cyclopædia of American Literature: Embracing Personal and Critical Notices of Authors and Selections from their Writings, from the Earliest Period to the Present Day; with Portraits, Autographs, and other Illustrations. By EVERT A. DUYCKINCK and GEORGE L. DUYCKINCK. Edited to Date by M. LAIRD SIMONS. In Two Volumes. Philadelphia, New York and London: T. Ellwood Zell. 1875. 4to. Vol. I. pp. xxii. and 990; Vol. II. pp. xiv. and 1054.

The Cyclopædia of American Literature has already been noticed in the REGISTER (xx. 189); but, had not this been the case, the work has been too long before the public to need a formal introduction now. The twenty years which have passed since its first issue have each added to its reputation, and it is now recognized as a standard work, indispensable to the library of every person of culture.

The preparation of the book was undertaken at the suggestion of the well known New-York publisher, Charles Scribner,—to whom we suppose the public is indebted for the magazine which bears his name,—and was intended to do for the literature of America what the Cyclopædia of English Literature, by Chambers, had done for that of the mother country. The first edition appeared in the latter part of the year 1855.

Ten years later, in 1865, Evert A. Duyckinck, the senior author of the work,—his brother George L. Duyckinck, the junior author, having died in 1863,—superintended the revision of the plates of the original work and prepared a Supplement. The whole was issued in that year in two volumes. This edition was noticed in the REGISTER, as before stated.

A few years ago, Mr. Scribner, who owned the plates and copyright, died; and in 1872, they passed into the hands of William Rutter & Co., of Philadelphia. Mr. Duyckinck was solicited to undertake a second revision, but his engagements would not permit him to do so. The work was then, with the approval, we think, of Mr. Duyckinck, placed in the hands of M. Laird Simons, of Philadelphia, whose name appears on the title-page as editor of this edition.

Mr. Simons has brought together the matter relating to the same author in the original work and in the supplement ; and has arranged the whole chronologically, adding to the sketches when necessary and introducing new ones, thus bringing the work down to the present time. This labor,—which has been greatly increased by the decision of the publishers to use the old plates, properly revised, as far as practicable,—has been performed in a very satisfactory manner. Mr. Simons deserves great praise for the taste, judgment, skill and industry shown in this work. The additions of Mr. Simons are properly and clearly indicated.

We are told in the preface of Mr. Simons that Mr. Duyckinck has given " advice in the preparation of this edition, approved the list of new authors introduced, and generously looked over the plate-proofs ;" and that he has " cordially endorsed the method of its execution, which sought to give a clear narrative of what American authors have done to the year 1873, without censorious or laudatory criticism."

The previous editions have appeared in two royal octavo volumes. This edition is elegantly printed in quarto form, and is published by subscription in fifty-two numbers at fifty cents each. The numbers are each illustrated by a fine steel portrait.

The index is a model one, very full and minute, besides which an excellent table of contents is given. Both have been thoroughly revised. These add much to the value of the work as a book of reference.   J. W. D.

Coasting Voyages in the Gulf of Maine, made in the Year 1604, 5 *and* 6, *by Samuel Champlain ; A Paper read at the Winter Meeting of the Maine Historical Society in Portland, Feb.* 18, 1875. By Gen. JOHN MARSHALL BROWN, of Falmouth. Bath : Printed by E. Upton & Son. 1875. [8vo. pp. 24.]

Gen. Brown, in this paper, details the explorations of Champlain on the coasts of Maine, in the years named in the title, and identifies some important places which that navigator visited. He clears up points that were obscure in our historical writers from their relying not on the 1613 edition of Champlain's voyages, but upon the patch-work edition of that work published in 1632, and upon Lescarbot who was " not particularly friendly to Champlain."

American State Universities, their Origin and Progress. A History of Congressional University Land-Grants. A Particular Account of the Rise and Development of the University of Michigan, and Hints towards the Future of the American University System. By ANDREW TEN BROOK. Cincinnati: Robert Clarke & Co. 1875. [8vo. pp. viii. and 410.]

The contents of this interesting and instructive volume consist of a sketch of the early progress of higher education in the Atlantic States ; the state of culture in the West at the commencement of the land-grant policy, and subsequently ; congressional land-grants for universities ; Michigan's early condition as to culture and education ; early organization for higher education in Michigan and their contemporary events ; grant of the present university fund and its administration by the board of trustees ; organization of the school system and administration of the endowment fund ; the branches—rise of union schools ; preparations for the opening of the university at Ann Arbor and the actual organization of its working forces ; review of the period from 1844 to 1852 ; President Tappan's administration ; President Haven's administration, and thence to the present time ; conclusion of the history of the University of Michigan ; the prospective university, &c.

Michigan University has had an eventful and unique history, which affords abundant materials for study for all who are interested in Higher Education, and especially for those who advocate or are opposed to colleges or universities under State control.

Professor Ten Brook is amply qualified by his long connection with Michigan University to write its history, and it is presumed that he has given the facts fully and impartially. The record, upon the whole, is not favorable to the project of a State University.

The chapter which will most profit the reader, is that in which the author discusses the "prospective university."

The work is a valuable contribution to the literature and history of the subject, and will, no doubt, be widely read. **A. H. H.**

Genealogical History of Deacon Stephen Hart and his Descendants, 1632–1875. *With an Introduction of miscellaneous Harts and their Progenitors, as far as known; to which is added a list of all the Clergy of the name found, all the Physicians, all the Lawyers, the Authors, and Soldiers.* By ALFRED ANDREWS, New-Britain, Conn., member of Connecticut and Wisconsin Historical Societies, author of "History of New-Britain, Conn.," "Andrews' Memorial," and "Pedigree of the Harts." Published by Austin Hart, Esq., New-Britain, Conn. Hartford: The Case, Lockwood & Brainard Co., Printers. 1875. [8vo. pp. 606. To be had of the Compiler at his residence. Price, $4.00.]

This handsomely printed volume contains the American genealogy of an influential and numerous family, which includes a large number of men and women of eminence and merit in letters and in the several professions. The American progenitor, Stephen Hart, was born in Braintree, Essex, England, about the year 1605, and is supposed to have settled first in Braintree, Mass., about 1632. He was a deacon of Mr. Hooker's church in (Newtown) Cambridge, and it is probable he settled there as early as 1632. In 1635 he removed to Hartford, Conn., with Mr. Hooker's company; was a proprietor there in 1639, and became one of the eighty-four proprietors of Farmington, Conn., in 1672. He was one of the "pillars" of the church in the latter place, and held important offices in the colony.

The collection of the materials of this work was begun by Deacon Simeon Hart, of Farmington, who died in 1853. The work was still further prosecuted by the late Rev. William S. Porter, of Farmington (and later of New-Haven), and, after his death, was taken up by Mr. Alfred Andrews, assisted by Mr. Gad Andrews, of Southington. The experience of the Messrs. Andrews in genealogical investigations enabled them to use the materials, already secured by themselves and others, to the best advantage in still more extended researches. The result is the admirable compilation before us. It is a plain, straight-forward and condensed compilation of names and dates, with a fair proportion of biography.

The Introduction contains an interesting catalogue of the names of the English and American authors and other prominent members of the family, and a list of those of the name who have served in the wars in this country. The index of names is constructed upon the novel and convenient plan of arranging the christian names of the heads of families (male or female) in alphabetical order, and the figures indicating the page of the volume where they are to be found, with the names of their parents and grandparents, in parallel columns.

The volume is illustrated with portraits of Deacon Simeon Hart, Mrs. Emma Hart Willard, Mrs. Almira Hart Lincoln Phelps, Prof. John S. Hart, LL.D., Lewis Austin Hart, Austin Hart, Esq., Hon. Alphonso Hart, and Benjamin Franklin Hart, M.D. **A. H. H.**

The Report of the Council of the American Antiquarian Society, made October 21, 1875, *at Worcester.* By SAMUEL A. GREEN, M.D. Worcester: Charles Hamilton, Printer, Palladium Office. 1876. [8vo. pp. 19.]

The meetings of the Antiquarian Society are held semi-annually. At each of these meetings the Council makes a report upon the condition of the society, which contains notices of deceased members and a statement of what its members have done for literature during the preceding half year. The report at the annual meeting in 1875 was written by Dr. Green, of Boston, and is a very able document. It closes with some eloquent remarks suggested by the centenary of the opening of the revolution. **J. W. D.**

The History of Maine, from the Earliest Discovery of the Region by the Northmen until the Present Time. ...... By JOHN S. C. ABBOTT. ...... Illustrated. Boston: Published by B. B. Russell, 55 Cornhill. Portland: John Russell. 1875. [8vo. pp. 556.]

An Illustrated History of the State of Wisconsin, being a Complete Civil, Political and Military History of the State from its First Exploration down to 1875. ...... By CHARLES R. TUTTLE. ...... Published by B. B. Russell, Boston, Mass. Madison, Wis.: B. B. Russell & Co. 1875. [8vo. pp. 800.]

These two volumes, issued by the same publisher, are histories of two of the states of our union, one at the east and the other at the west; the former being among the earliest settled, and the latter among the latest. We understand that Mr. Russell has in preparation, by competent writers, the histories of New-York and Pennsylvania, uniform with these.

Mr. Abbott, the author of the History of Maine, is well known as a writer. His Memoirs of Napoleon and his histories of the French Revolution and the Civil War in America, published by the Harpers, as well as other works of his, have had a wide sale. He was born in Maine and educated at her principal college, and this work, we may well believe, has been "a labor of love." It is not his object "to search out discoveries which have hitherto eluded the scrutiny of antiquarians or to settle disputed questions which have arisen in reference to minute details in early days;" but to "give a faithful and graphic record of the wondrous past," that "will be read with interest at every fireside." The work includes "a narrative of the voyages and explorations of the early adventurers, the manners and customs of the Indian tribes, the hardships of the first settlers, the conflicts with the savages, and the gradual advancement of the State to its present aspect of opulence, culture and refinement."

Mr. Tuttle, the author of the history of Wisconsin, has written several "Illustrated Histories," namely, of the States of Indiana and Michigan, and of the Border Wars of Two Centuries. He has here brought together a great amount of historical information relating to Wisconsin. Particular attention is paid to the biography of her public men, many of the memoirs being accompanied by portraits. The author gives a "Cyclopædia of Legislation during the administration of each governor, from the organization of the territorial government down to Governor Taylor," whose term of office expired last January; also "historical and descriptive sketches of each county in the state, separately embracing interesting narratives of pioneer life, including an account of the commercial, agricultural and educational growth of Wisconsin." J. W. D.

The Battle-Field of Bunker Hill: with a Relation of the Action by William Prescott, and Illustrative Documents. A Paper communicated to the Massachusetts Historical Society, June 10, 1875, with Additions. By RICHARD FROTHINGHAM. Boston: Printed for the Author. 1876. [Pamphlet, 8vo. pp. 46.]

The centennial of the battle of Bunker Hill, so called, caused the public attention to be freshly and particularly directed to the details of the history of that event. The attention of not a few historical students has also been called to the same subject. Consequently, we have the benefit of several interesting and able publications, more or less elaborate and valuable, from their pens. Some of these are mainly devoted to a re-statement of the claims of different officers to the rightful honor or title of commander in that battle. So far, however, we do not see anything that materially adds to or modifies the history of the battle as it was given in "The History of the Siege of Boston," by the same author.

At the meeting of the Massachusetts Historical Society, held on the 10th of June last, Mr. Frothingham exhibited all the maps, drawings, pictures, &c., of Charlestown, and of the scene of the battle, which he had been able to collect,—a large number,—which he explained. He called special attention to the "Plan of the Action," by "Lieutenant Page of the Engineers, who acted as aide-de-camp to General Howe" in that action, the ground-plan of which was from an actual survey by

Captain Montresor, subsequently an aide-de-camp to General Howe. This plan was obtained by Mr. Frothingham some thirty years ago in England. It was re-produced in the "Siege of Boston," but seems to have failed to have such weight as it deserves. The author shows, from a variety of sources, how the main features of this plan are confirmed by evidence drawn from British and American actors in the battle, and from other contemporary sources. If it is conceded, as we think it must be now, that this plan is correct, or even substantially correct, its bearing upon some of the contested questions that have grown out of the battle will be quickly recognized by all who are familiar with the literature of the subject.

We have here also, for the first time in print, the account of the battle by Judge William Prescott, the son of Colonel Prescott. It is quite different from what, in a late account of the battle, is called "The Prescott Manuscript." It is accompanied by an important letter written by Judge Prescott to the late Col. Samuel Swett.

In addition to these papers, the author prints the following letters : from James Warren to John Adams (June 20, 1775), James Warren to Samuel Adams (June 21), Lieut. Samuel B. Webb to Silas Deane (July 11), Extracts from the Diary of Col. Eph. Storrs, of Mansfield, Conn. (from June 1 to June 17, inclusive), William Williams, of Lebanon, Conn., to Roger Sherman and others, delegates in Congress (June 20), Loammi Baldwin to Mary Baldwin (June 18), from J. R. Adan (Boston, Dec. 21, 1841), and a copy of a letter from Brig. Gen. Jones, Colonel of the 52d Regiment (Boston, June 19, 1775).

The text is illustrated with views of Charlestown, taken in 1743 and 1775, and with a heliotype fac-simile of General Lafayette's speech at his reception on Bunker Hill in 1824.

This is a valuable addition to our centennial literature.   A. H. H.

Bibliotheca Munselliana. A Catalogue of the Books and Pamphlets issued from the Press of Joel Munsell, from the year 1828 to 1870. Albany : Privately Printed. 1872. [8vo. pp. 191.]

No. 93. First Printed 1784. Webster's Almanac or the Albany Almanac for the Year of our Lord 1876. ...... By JOEL MUNSELL. *Astronomical Calculations for the Latitude and Longitude of Albany,* by FRANK MUNSELL. ...... Albany, N. Y.: J. Munsell, State Street. 1876. [12mo. pp. 36.]

The New-England Primer Improved For the more easy Attaining the True Reading of English. To which is Added The Assembly of Divines, and Mr. Cotton's Catechism. Albany : Joel Munsell. 1875. [24mo. pp. 80.]

The first title is that of a bibliographical list of the works printed by our American Aldus, whose unselfish labors for the preservation of the historical literature of our country, have long been conspicuous. Mr. Munsell did not commence business for himself till 1834 ; but, in 1828, while a clerk in a bookstore, he published for three months a semi-monthly paper called the "Albany Minerva." In the present volume he gives the titles of the works printed by him, the size, number of pages in each volume, and frequently the number of copies in the edition. Occasionally he inserts memoranda about the author or the book, so interesting that we regret that they are not more frequent. At this time, when associations and individuals are making up their records as contributions to the centennial literature, we would suggest to Mr. Munsell that he continue his bibliography to the present time, and prefix to it reminiscences of his printer-life.

Webster's Almanac for 1876 is the thirty-third published by Mr. Munsell, and the thirty-fifth printed by him. In 1844, the publishers of this almanac, which had then been printed 60 years, finding the circulation gradually decreasing, concluded to abandon the publication. "I made them," says Mr. Munsell, "the proposition to continue it as long as I should live, although its sale might entirely cease, so that I should need but a single copy for myself ; and to pay them a royalty for the title of a certain number of copies each year during their lives. ...... I found an immediate sale for about twenty thousand copies."

The edition of the New-England Primer whose title is given, is an exact reprint of the 1777 edition printed at Boston by Edward Draper; with a preface by Mr. Munsell. The first edition of the Primer was printed as early as 1690, but though a call for information concerning early editions was made in the REGISTER for 1849 (*ante*, iii. 211), none earlier than 1761 (*ante*, x. 184) has been reported as extant. There must have been numerous and large editions printed before this, and it is difficult to believe that they have all disappeared. Will our readers hunt in the by-places for a copy of an earlier date?   J. W. D.

The Descendants of Joseph Loomis, who came from Braintree, England, in the year 1638, *and Settled in Windsor, Connecticut, in* 1639. By ELIAS LOOMIS, LL.D., Professor of Natural Philosophy and Astronomy in Yale College. Second Edition, revised and enlarged. New-Haven: Tuttle, Morehouse and Taylor, 221 State Street. 1875. [8vo. pp. 611. To be had of the Compiler. Price, $5.00.]

In announcing this work on the cover of the REGISTER for July, 1875, we gave a pretty full statement of its contents. It is proper, however, to say here that this enlarged edition of the Loomis Genealogy contains the record of 8,686 persons, all having the family name, whose descent is traced from Joseph Loomis, of Windsor, besides a list of 4,682 persons who have intermarried with them, or a total of 13,368 names. The work has full and convenient indexes, is printed on superfine paper, and is illustrated with three portraits, viz.: of Rev. Hubbel Loomis (in his 96th year), James C. Loomis, and Prof. Loomis, the compiler. The edition is limited to 200 copies.

The reputation of Prof. Loomis is a sufficient guaranty of the accuracy and thoroughness of this work.   A. H. H.

Life and Public Services of Henry Wilson, late Vice-President of the United States. By Rev. ELIAS NASON, author of "Life of Charles Sumner," "Gazetteer of Massachusetts," etc. etc., and Hon. THOMAS RUSSELL, late Collector, Port of Boston. . . . . . . Boston: Published by B. B. Russell, 55 Cornhill. Philadelphia: Quaker City Publishing House. San Francisco: A. L. Bancroft. Portland: John Russell. 1876. [12mo. pp. 452.]

In 1872, on the first appearance of this work, we noticed it in the REGISTER (*ante*, xxvi. 451). Since then Mr. Wilson has been elected to the second office in the gift of the people of the United States, from which office in November last he was removed by death.

The Rev. Mr. Nason, since the death of Mr. Wilson, has completed the biography of his friend and former parishioner; and we have now a reliable and well-written narrative of the whole life of one of the most devoted philanthropists and far-seeing statesmen which this country has produced. "So far," says his biographer, "as a living sympathy with man as man, so far as a life unselfishly devoted to the sons of toil and suffering, so far as the daily exemplification of the ennobling principles of Christianity, may be regarded, he has made a record that will hold its brightness when the memories of men more brilliant in exterior graces shall have passed into oblivion."   J. W. D.

History of the Chippewa Valley, a Faithful Record of all Important Events, Incidents and Circumstances that have transpired in the Valley of the Chippewa from its Earliest Settlement by White People, Indian Treaties, Organization of the Territory and State; also of the Counties embracing the Valley, Senatorial Assembly and Congressional Districts, &c. Also a brief Biographical Sketch of the most Prominent Persons in the Settlement of the Valley. By THOMAS E. RANDALL. 1875. Free Press Print, Eau Claire, Wis. [8vo. pp. 207.]

This work was first published in the Eau Claire Free Press, where it met with so favorable a reception that it has been reprinted in a more permanent form. The title-page furnishes a good idea of the contents of the volume.   J. W. D.

Documents and Records relating to the State of New-Hampshire during the Period of the American Revolution, from 1776 to 1783; including the Constitution of New-Hampshire, 1776; New-Hampshire Declaration for Independence; the "Association Test," with Names of Signers, &c.; Declaration of American Independence, July 4, 1776; the Articles of Confederation, 1778. Published by Authority of the Legislature of New-Hampshire. Volume VIII. Compiled and Edited by NATHANIEL BOUTON, D.D., Corresponding Secretary of the New-Hampshire Historical Society. Concord, N. H.: Edward A. Jenks, State Printer. 1874. [8vo. pp. xxviii. and 1006.]

We have so often called attention to the series of State Papers which are being issued under the wise liberality and prudent forecast of the legislature of New-Hampshire, that but little further notice of this volume seems called for than to give the title-page in full. It will be seen, however, that this volume is a continuation of documents and papers relating to New-Hampshire after it assumed government and took the name of *Colony* and then of *State* of New-Hampshire. The colonial period lasted for about one year. The Constitution adopted by the people of this State in 1776, was the first that was adopted by any colony or state in the Union.

Not the least valuable portion of the present volume is that which gives the names of those who subscribed and of those who for various reasons refused to subscribe to the "Association Test," or Declaration of Independence of New-Hampshire, adopted in "Committee of Safety," April 12, 1776. The language of the Test is as follows: *We, the Subscribers, do hereby solemnly engage, and promise, that we will, to the utmost of our Power, at the Risque of our Lives and Fortunes, with Arms, oppose the Hostile Proceedings of the British Fleets and Armies against the United American Colonies.* 8,199 persons signed this test or declaration, and 773 refused to sign. The aggregate is understood to represent very nearly the total number of male inhabitants of the colony above the age of twenty-one years in 1776. Another volume in continuation is promised. **A. H. H.**

A History of the Character and Achievements of Christopher Columbus. By AARON GOODRICH. * * * With numerous Illustrations and an Appendix. New-York: D. Appleton and Company, 549 and 551 Broadway. 1874. [8vo. pp. viii. and 403. *A. Williams & Co., Boston.*]

The author of this work, who resides in St. Paul, Minn., and is, we believe, an active member of the historical society of that State, undertakes "to sink the so-called Christopher Columbus to his just level in the estimation of posterity, and raise to theirs those of his contemporaries whose fame was sacrificed to create the fictitious glory with which he has been endowed."—(Preface, vii.) To this end, by great research and study, he has brought together the substance of all that can be found in original documents and papers,—by no means neglecting the writings of Columbus and his sons,—that tend to show that the former was a knave and an impostor, and that he is entitled to little credit for his alleged discoveries. To Americus Vespucius the author ascribes the highest praise, both for his discoveries and his private virtues. The weight of authority at the present day ascribes the greatest credit to Vespucius.

Introductory to the History of Columbus, is an essay upon the learning of the ancients. Much curious and instructive matter is here brought together.

The work is handsomely printed, and illustrated with engravings, among which are several portraits of Columbus. **A. H. H.**

1824–1874. God's Work in the World the last Fifty Years. A Discourse preached at Franklin, Indiana, November 29, 1874. By JOSEPH F. TUTTLE, D.D., President of Wabash College. [12mo. pp. 33.]

In this discourse President Tuttle dwells upon the wonderful changes that half a century has made in the world, particularly in the western portion of the United States, and eloquently enforces the duties of the present generation.

The Isles of Shoals. An Historical Sketch. By JOHN SCRIBNER JENNESS. Second Edition, Enlarged and Revised. New-York: Published by Hurd and Houghton. Cambridge: The Riverside Press. 1875. [12mo. pp. 214.]

The first edition of this work appeared in 1873 and the second in 1875, two years after. The first edition was noticed in the REGISTER, vol. xxix. pp. 213. A second edition following so soon after the first is proof enough of its worth and popularity. The text has now been revised and corrected, 32 pages have been added to it, and it has been issued in the same attractive style. It is now so complete that hardly anything further can be desired.

Only two writers have preceded Mr. Jenness in this field of historical inquiry. About the year 1800, the Rev. Jedediah Morse, D.D., the geographer and historian, wrote " A Description and Historical Account of the Isles of Shoals," which was printed in the seventh volume of the Massachusetts Historical Collections. This seemed so complete that for more than seventy years no one ventured to look further into their history. In 1870, Charles W. Tuttle, Esq., of this city, having discovered an original document of great value, emanating from the Shoals in 1653, prepared a brief historical sketch of these islands previous to that date. This sketch showed that there was much early information preserved concerning the Shoals which Dr. Morse had not touched on. Among other things, Mr. Tuttle broached an entirely new theory of the origin of their name, supposing them so named from their number, rather than from the depth of water there. The sketch and the document above referred to were printed in the REGISTER for April, 1871. They attracted much attention at the time and revived an interest in the history of the Isles. Mr. Jenness has copied largely from this article.

The two sketches being printed in the collections of historical societies were not easily accessible to the public, and an increasing interest in the history of these isles demanded a popular account of them. The author has succeeded in supplying this want. His style is clear and vigorous, and he makes the dullest historical facts interesting by picturesque grouping. He has brought out too many new matters to be noticed here. The appendix is large, consisting of valuable historical documents, many of which, if not all, are here printed for the first time. There is a fac-simile of Capt. John Smith's famous map of New-England and a useful map of the Shoals, reduced from the Coast Survey chart. A table of contents or an index would greatly facilitate the finding of matters in the work. If the volume were much larger this would be a serious defect.   J. W. D.

An Outline History of the United States, for Public and other Schools; from the Earliest Period to the Present Time. By BENSON J. LOSSING, LL.D., Author of the Field Books of "The Revolution," "The War of 1812," and the " Civil War;" the "Home of Washington," "Life and Times of Schuyler," etc. Copiously illustrated by Maps and other Engravings. New York: Sheldon & Company, No. 677 Broadway. 1875. [12mo. pp. 399.]

This is one of a series of school histories of the United States by Dr. Lossing, which promises to be a great aid in teaching the youth of our country its history. The other books in this series are The " Primary United States History," and " Common School History," the first being intended for the youngest children and the latter for the more advanced scholars. Several new features are introduced for the purpose of making the study attractive and impressing upon the mind of the scholar the most important facts and characteristics of our country's history.
                                                                J. W. D.

Why is History so little Read? An Address to Parents, Teachers and Members of Fashionable Society. BY A STUDENT OF HISTORY. Printed by Walter F. Wheaton, New Bedford, Mass. 1876. [8vo. pp. 27.]

This pamphlet has been written to create a greater interest in history among the people. The author's case is another instance of " the pursuit of knowledge under difficulties," and he wishes to draw the attention of young men, as well as of parents, to the value of historical studies, which he himself prizes so highly.
                                                                J. W. D.

A History of Northfield, Massachusetts, for 150 years, with an Account of the prior Occupation of the Territory by the Squakheags: and with Family Genealogies. By J. H. TEMPLE and GEORGE SHELDON. Albany, N.Y.: Joel Munsell, 82 State st. 1875. [8vo. pp. vi. 636.]

Reminiscences of Men and Things in Northfield as I knew them from 1812 to 1825. [8vo. pp. 26.]

When we first learned that the two gentlemen above mentioned were actively engaged in collecting materials for the History of Northfield, and that the work when completed was to be printed and published by Mr. Munsell, a well known son of that town, we made up our mind, *instanter*, that we were to have as good a history of the place as could well be produced; and we have not been disappointed. In fact, it has exceeded our early expectations in many of its details. It is noteworthy how much new matter is brought before the public in these compact pages, drawn from the most reliable sources, such as the church, town and county records, the state archives, old family papers and original narratives, besides the well formed traditionary accounts and statements of aged people whose memories extend far back into the past. Localities and points bearing upon the topography of the town, the region adjoining, the history of the early settlers, Indian village sites, and the like, have been with commendable industry and by personal visits examined, to verify or make clear historical facts. Especially was this true in regard to the aborigines, their manners, customs, religion, etc. Every paragraph and page throughout the work teems with interest. Old Squakheag was a frontier town. The perils and privations of such an isolated settlement were extreme. On the North was a wild territory, now the State of Vermont. Deerfield, the nearest English plantation, was at a distance of some sixteen miles; the communication difficult and dangerous. Hadley was nearly twice as far away, while Brookfield, Lancaster and Groton, like oases in the wilderness world, were two and three score miles beyond their reach. But there those noble pioneers, chiefly from Northampton, the Lymans, Hutchinsons, Mudges, Merrys, Dickinsons, Janeses, Smeades, and their compeers, settled. The preparatory movements to that end were made in 1671. In the spring of 1673 they built their small thatched huts, one for their Elder, Wm. Janes, their minister, in the midst, and raised a stockade and fort around their clustered homes, as a refuge in case of attack by the "barbarous enemy." Allotments of land were made, grain planted, cattle raised, and prosperity seemed prospectively their portion. But, alas, the Indians, who for some two or three years had appeared friendly towards them, who had freely bartered, begged and borrowed, began to show their latent savage propensities. Brookfield they destroyed, on the second of August, 1675, and the thirst for blood soon became insatiate. We have not space for the details of the horrid measures and movements that followed. Ignorant of the destruction that had happened at Deerfield the day before, by the hands of the foe, the Squakheag people were engaged in their usual avocations on the morning of the fatal September second, scattered about in the meadow and on the lots where the duties of the day had called them. The Indians fell upon them, killed those who were unable to reach the fort, destroyed their grain and cattle, and laid the houses in ashes. Sixteen families were left within the enclosure, in a desolate condition. Capt. Beers of Hadley, who marched with his company to relieve them, was killed on the way thither, with many of his men. Help came, however, at last, to the Squakheag garrison, through Major Treat. After the evacuation the Indians burned the fort and the houses that remained, and the entire village was exterminated. Preliminary steps were taken in 1682 for a re-settlement of Squakheag, the results of which, and its continued history, are related in chapters four and five. Then came what was called "Father Ralle's War," which was opened in 1722, the year before the incorporation of the town. The latter event took place just fifty years after its first settlement. An interval of peace followed, then came the Old French and Indian war, the last French and Indian war, and the war of the Revolution. To illustrate these portions, public documents, muster rolls, memorials, and petitions, many of them entire, as also letters of Sir Edmund Andros, John Schuyler, Capt. Benjamin Wright, Col. Israel Williams, Seth Field and others are given. The letters, diaries and journals of John Pynchon, John Stoddard and Elias Alexander are of special interest. The Short Narrative of the Rev. Benjamin Doolittle, the second minister of Northfield, is inserted, copied from the rare tract printed in Boston in 1750.

The book contains several wood-cut illustrations, views of churches, plans of allotments of land, and steel portraits of the Rev. Thomas Mason and Joel Munsell, Esq. The latter, we emphatically say, is an excellent likeness.

Evidently, Mr. Munsell has spared neither time, labor or expense in his laudable efforts to produce a book worthy of himself, his profession and his native town, without regard to remuneration.

The Family Genealogies take up near 200 pages. These are followed by the tombstone inscriptions from the old cemetery in Northfield, copied by Mary T. Stratton, including all that could be decyphered by her. There are two indices, one to the historical portion of the book, the other to the genealogies.

The second work whose title is given above, is by Joel Munsell, Esq., who records some of his early recollections of individuals, places, events, &c., suggested by the History of Northfield. References are made to the pages of that History in about fifty short articles, such as the Council Rock, Great Swamp, Belden Inscription, Deacon Janes and his Mill, Deposition of Elihu Lyman, the Tornado, Timothy Swan, the Great Bridge, the Artillery, &c. &c. These supplementary paragraphs to Mr. Munsell's work are entertaining and instructive, some of them being illustrated by diagrams. There are also views of the Dickinson Monument, Old Meeting House, and the House in which General Baum died. W. B. TRASK.

The Public Records of the Colony of Connecticut, from May, 1744, *to November,* 1750, *inclusive. Transcribed and Edited in accordance with a Resolution of the General Assembly.* By CHARLES J. HOADLY, State Librarian. Hartford: Press of the Case, Lockwood & Brainard Co. 1876. [8vo. pp. 621.]

The present volume, the ninth, of the Records of Connecticut, is transcribed with the same care and edited with the same ability as the previous volumes noticed in these pages. It contains the remainder of the seventh volume of the manuscript records from page 222, together with the first 51 pages of the eighth volume, closing with the session of November, 1750, which chose Roger Wolcott as governor in place of Jonathan Law who had died early in that month.

The appendix contains the "Proceedings of the English Privy Council on the appeals of Samuel Clark against Thomas Tousey and others, relative to the law governing the descent and distribution of intestate estates, 1737–1745, and also Queries from the Board of Trade, with the Answers thereto, 1748–9."

Mr. Hoadly informs us that for "the time covered by this publication neither the Journals of the Governor and Council, of the Committees of War, nor of either branch of the General Assembly, save that of the lower house at the May session, 1744, are now in the State archives." J. W. D.

A Collection of upwards of Thirty Thousand Names of German, Swiss, Dutch, French and other Immigrants in Pennsylvania, from 1727 *to* 1776, *with a statement of the names of Ships, whence they sailed, and the date of their arrival at Philadelphia. Chronologically Arranged, together with the necessary Historical and other Notes, also an Appendix containing Lists of more than one thousand German and French in New-York prior to* 1712. By Prof. I. DANIEL RUPP, author of several Historical Works. Second Revised and Enlarged Edition, with German Translation. Philadelphia: Ig. Cohler, 202 North Fourth street. 1876. [12mo. pp. x. and 495. *A. Williams & Co., Boston.* Price, $2.50.]

The title-page of this volume is so full as to preclude the necessity of extended explanations. It is proper to say that the first edition was issued in 1856, but is now out of print, and cannot be had at any price. Within the last five years, we are informed, from five dollars to seven dollars have been paid for second-hand copies. The collection was made up from the lists of immigrants on file in the secretary's office in Harrisburg; and, as will be seen, the whole has been revised and enlarged.

The volume is embellished with well-executed wood-cuts of the buildings erected and to be erected in Philadelphia for the Exposition in 1876.

A. H. H.

Historical Discourse commemorative of the Centennial Anniversary of the Congregational Church, Plymouth, N. H. Preached Dec. 24th and 31st, 1865, by HENRY A. HAZEN, Pastor. With Introduction and Notes relating to the Early History of the Town. Boston: Congregational Publishing Society, Congregational House. 1875. [Pamphlet, 8vo. pp. 38.]

This discourse, though prepared and preached in 1865, has been enlarged and, at the request of friends, has recently been published. This valuable discourse gives not only the history of the religious society named, but a good deal of important matter bearing upon the early history of Plymouth, and of the northern and western part of New Hampshire. The reverend author has an established reputation for thoroughness, and this is a sufficient guaranty of the character of this historical production.   A. H. H.

Manual of Education: a Brief History of the Rhode Island Institute of Instruction, including a Synopsis of annual and other Meetings, Lists of Officers and Members, together with the Constitution and Charter. By EDWIN MARTIN STONE. Providence: Providence Press Company, Printers. 1875. [8vo. pp. 144.]

The Rhode Island Institute of Instruction, incorporated in 1863, has exerted an important influence in the educational interests of that State, and its history is worth preserving.   A. H. H.

Ohio Annals. Historic Events in the Tuscarawas and Muskingum Valleys and in other Portions of the State of Ohio. ...... Edited by C. H. MITCHENER, of the New Philadelphia (Ohio) Bar. Dayton, Ohio: Thomas W. Odell. 1876. [8vo. pp. viii.+358.]

This Centennial contribution to the history of the country commences with the adventures of the early pioneers of Ohio, particularly of Christian Frederick Post, John Heckewelder, David Zeisberger and Gen. Rufus Putnam. Putnam and Heckewelder, the author considers the founders of the State. The book also records the local history of the early settlements; traces the " growth of Ohio in population, political power, wealth and intelligence;" and gives the " legends and traditions of the Kophs, Mound Builders, Red and White Men." The author deserves much credit for his production. It is printed on tinted paper, and makes a handsome book. The work will be sent, postpaid, by the publisher or by the author, for $3.50 a copy. Three copies will be sent for $10, or 5 copies for $15.   J. W. D.

Memorial Services of Commemoration Day, held in Canton, May 29, 1875, *under the auspices of Revere Encampment, Post* 94, *Grand Army of the Republic.* Boston: William Bense, Printer. 1876. [8vo. pp. 19.]

The orator on this occasion was D. T. V. Huntoon, Esq., of Canton. He stepped aside from the ordinary topics of commemoration day to dwell upon the events of a century ago, and particularly of the part which Stoughton, which then included Canton, took in the Revolution, introducing sketches of the lives of two of Stoughton's revolutionary patriots, Col. Benjamin Tupper and Capt. Ezra Badlam. These contributions to centennial literature, when prepared with the care and ability shown in this oration, are valuable additions to local history.   J. W. D.

The names we bear: a Descriptive Compendium of Biblical, Classical, and Common Names, compiled so as to aid Memory, in an Etymological Narrative Form, and a Copious Index. By H. A. LONG, with Preface by Rev. JAMES McCANN, D.D. * * * Boston: A. Williams, 283 Washington street. 1875. [8vo. pp. iv. and 244.]

Mr. Long, after fourteen years of great research, presents to the world in the most compact form, the origin and meaning of about six thousand personal names. Dr. McCann vouches for the author's competency to such an undertaking, and for his habits of careful and thorough investigation.

The object of the work is not to give a philosophy of language, of which the names we bear are a portion, but to present as large a statement of facts as is possible. The work is valuable and cannot fail to be useful.   A. H. H.

DEATHS.

DEAN, Mary Morse, in Charlestown district, Boston, March 13, aged 68. She was the daughter of Charles and Patience (Kingsbury) Dean, and was born in Wiscasset, Maine, Nov. 5, 1807.

DEVOTION, Col. John Louis, in Norwich, Conn., Feb. 8, aged 59. He was a son of Jonathan[6] Devotion, of Windham, Conn., by his second wife, Mrs. Clarissa (House) Tyler, and was born in Windham, May 31, 1816. From a genealogy of this family, by William L. Weaver, in the Willimantic Journal, March 2d, 9th and 16th, 1865, we learn that he was the seventh in descent from *Edward*[1] *Devotion*, who settled at Muddy River, now Brookline, Mass., as early as 1645, through *John*[2] of Suffolk, Conn., Rev. *Ebenezer*[3] (H. C. 1707) of Suffield, Rev. *Ebenezer*[4] (Y. C. 1732) of Windham, Hon. *Ebenezer*[5] (Y. C. 1759) of Windham, and *Jonathan*,[6] above-named, his father.

He was first a clerk in a drug store, and afterwards carried on that business with William S. Tyler, under the firm of Tyler & Devotion. In 1849 he went to California, but soon returned. In 1855 he entered the Shetucket Bank, became its cashier, and retained the position till his death. He was also secretary and treasurer of the Norwich City Gas Co., secretary of the New London Mutual Fire Insurance Co., and director of that and other institutions. In 1855, and at a subsequent date, he held the office of city clerk of Norwich. He was prominent as a Mason and Odd Fellow, a man of integrity and liberal views, and the advocate of all progressive movements. He had a taste for historical and genealogical studies, and was a subscriber to the REGISTER. An obituary sketch was printed in the Norwich Morning Bulletin, Feb. 9, 1876. He married, May 4, 1854, Mrs. Adeline H. (Kinney) White.

HOBART, Peter, in Boston, March 10, aged 93 years, 23 days. He was born Feb. 16, 1783, in Hanover, Mass., where his father, Dr. Peter Hobart, a graduate of Harvard College in the class of 1775, was a physician. He was a descendant in the seventh generation from *Edmund*[1] *Hobart*, of Hingham, the father of Rev. Peter Hobart of that town, through, *Edmund*,[2] *Samuel*,[3] *Peter*,[4] *Peter*,[5] and Dr. *Peter*,[6] above-named, his father. He was in active business, in Boston, as a carpenter and builder, for forty-five

years, and was one of those unobtrusive citizens whose works are the best monuments of their virtues. For many years till his death he was an officer of the Evangelical Church of the Advent. His son, Peter[8] Hobart, Jr., a member of the New-England Historic, Genealogical Society, is the father of Henry L.[9] Hobart, also a member of this society (*ante*, xxviii. 209), who died July 23, 1873. A memoir of Mr. Hobart and his ancestors, by the Hon. Solomon Lincoln, was printed in the Hingham Journal, March 24, 1876.

JONES, Henry Hall, in Boston, March 10, aged 73 years, 11 months and 26 days. He was formerly a merchant of Boston.

PORTER, Mrs. Rhoda Keith, in Burlington, Maine, Nov. 30, 1875, wife of the Hon. Joseph W. Porter and daughter of the late Rev. Jonas Perkins, of Braintree, Mass., in the 50th year of her age. She was the fifth in descent from Rev. James Keith, the first minister of Bridgewater, ordained February, 1664, and the fourth from Mark Perkins, who settled in Bridgewater from Ipswich in 1741.

ROBINSON, William Stevens, in Malden, Mass., March 11, aged 57. He was born in Concord, Mass., Dec. 7, 1818, and learned the printer's trade in the office of the *Norfolk County Advertiser*, edited and published by his older brother, Elbridge G. Robinson. He is best known as an editor and newspaper writer, having edited various papers in Boston and Lowell, has contributed to many others. In 1857 he commenced writing weekly letters for the *Springfield Republican*, under the signature of " Warrington," which *nom de plume* he took from the character of that name in Thackeray's " Pendennis."

He was one of the founders of the Free-Soil party, and an active leader of the Republican party which succeeded it. He represented Lowell in the Massachusetts House of Representatives, 1852-3, and was clerk of that body from 1862 to 1872. In 1853 he was secretary of the Massachusetts Constitutional Convention. His Legislative Manual, recently published, is considered a standard work.

WENTWORTH, Mark, in line of Mark,[4] Ezekiel,[3] Ephraim,[2] Elder William,[1] died at Wakefield, N.H., Jan. 31, 1875, aged 85 years.

Painted by J.S.Copley.   AET. 46.   Engd by H.B.Hall.

Samuel Adams

From the Original Painting in Faneuil Hall.

SAMUEL ADAMS.

By the Rev. INCREASE N. TARBOX, D.D., of Boston.

IN 1775, Thomas Gage, royal governor of Massachusetts and commander-in-chief of his majesty's forces in these parts, issued his proclamation, offering pardon to all rebels, if they would return to their allegiance, excepting Samuel Adams and John Hancock. These two recusants Gov. Gage describes as men "whose offences are of too flagitious a nature to admit of any other consideration than that of condign punishment." Here is one of those instances, where, "in the course of human events," the ring-leaders, in what a human government calls the greatest of crimes, come at length to be regarded as among the chief benefactors of mankind. In this proscription, however, Gov. Gage included two men quite unlike in character. John Hancock was a popular and showy man during his long public career, and as president of the Continental Congress placed that magnificent signature of his at the head of the Declaration. His name will not soon be forgotten. Both these men were afterwards governors of Massachusetts, Hancock for eleven years, and Adams for three. But in strength of intellect, in purity of private and public character, in extent of services, Hancock could bear no comparison with Adams.

It is one of the curious accidents of human history, that in the earlier years of the present century the name of Samuel Adams seemed to be in a great measure retired from public observation and familiar recognition. This fact is due, perhaps, to the coming forward of other men of his family name, who filled such conspicuous positions as for a time to eclipse this stern old organizer of the Revolution. John Adams, second cousin of Samuel, was made President of the United States in 1797, and his illustrious son, John Quincy Adams, was elected to the same high office in 1825. Samuel Adams died in 1803. No longer mingling in the thought and conversation of men as a living actor, he was in a measure forgotten in the new generation, and among the newer men of his own kindred. Readers now past middle life, in recurring to their early memories, will probably bear witness that practically they did not hear much or know much about Samuel Adams. Of John Adams and John Quincy Adams their recollections are fresh and full. Yet we shall not be deemed extravagant when we say, that for solid worth, for great virtues, for breadth of influence, for organizing power, Samuel Adams holds a higher place in our national history than any other man of his name, and some would add, of any name.

He was born in Purchase Street, Boston, on the 16th of September, 1722, O.S. His father, also Samuel Adams, was deacon of the Old South Church. Boston was then a place of only a few thousand inhabitants, and his home looked out upon the waters and islands of the bay in quite a country fashion. The Adamses who have borne so distinguished a part in our colonial and national history were descendants of Henry Adams, of Braintree, who came to these shores in the early years, bringing with him a large family. John Adams, who was of the fifth generation from Henry the founder, erected a granite monument to the memory of his ancestor, with an inscription which begins thus: "In memory of Henry Adams, who took his flight from the Dragon persecution in Devonshire in England, and alighted with eight sons, near Mount Wollaston."

Deacon Samuel Adams was a man of various business; active in affairs civil and ecclesiastical, a strict old-fashioned Puritan, not afraid to comment freely on what was passing around him, and struggling against the financial adversities of his times. Gordon states that as early as 1724, Samuel Adams, senior, "with about twenty others, one or two from the north end of the town, where all ship-building was carried on, used to meet, make a *caucus*, and lay their plans for introducing certain persons into places of trust and power." It has been suggested that this association may have been called the "Calker's Club," from being composed largely of ship-building mechanics, and that the word *caucus*, now in such common use, may have been derived from the name of the club.

Samuel Adams, the subject of this sketch, was therefore early introduced into the realm of politics from the conversations to which he listened in his father's house. But in the thoughts and plans of his father, he was destined to the ministry. It should be stated that, before his birth, his father, with thirteen others, had organized the New South Church in Summer Street, at the Church Green, of which Samuel Checkley was the first regular pastor, ordained in 1719, though the house had been dedicated two years before. This was the place where the boy first went to meeting and received his early religious instructions. From his childhood up, and through his whole life, he "walked in the ways of his fathers," keeping strictly to the old Calvinistic faith and order, and when he knew his father's wishes and the plans for his own future, he seemed to have no aversion to them, but entered upon his course of study with eagerness and good courage. His standing in college was highly commendable, and his special love was for classical studies.

It may be worthy of passing notice, that Jonathan Trumbull, governor of Connecticut through the whole revolutionary period, and whose public services during that long struggle were so eminent, was also educated for the ministry, and had actually begun the business of preaching before he was turned aside to civil cares. In some of the old papers of his earlier administration, he is not unfrequently called Rev. Jonathan Trumbull.

Samuel Adams entered Harvard College in 1736, with the expectation, as we have said, that he was to be a minister. He was then but fourteen years of age. At that period, and down to more than thirty years later, the names of students on the catalogue were arranged, not alphabetically as now; not according to any good or evil, brightness or dulness in the students themselves, but according to the honors and distinctions, the wealth and standing of the families from which they came. The class of 1740 at Harvard numbered twenty-two. In that list the name of Samuel Adams is the fifth. This shows a high valuation of his family. The standing and reputation of the father must have been exceedingly good to have secured for the son this prominent place on the roll. The first name in that list is Thomas Prince, son of Rev. Thomas Prince, then pastor of the Old South, whose life is so closely linked with Boston history, especially in connection with the "Prince Library." This son, of the same name, graduating in 1740, died in 1748. The second name on the list is Benjamin Stevens. He was the son of Rev. Joseph Stevens, then deceased, but beforetime a minister in Charlestown and one of the Fellows of the College. This Benjamin Stevens was afterwards Doctor of Divinity, and the life-long pastor at Kittery, Me. But the eighteenth name on that roll of twenty-two was Samuel Langdon, afterwards president of the College, and the man who made that prayer on Cambridge Common in the evening of June 16, 1775. It not unfrequently happened both at Harvard and Yale, while this arrangement of names prevailed, that the democratic principle broke up this decorous order of the old families, and the last became first and the first last.

It is most interesting to notice the signs of character—the prevailing bent of thought, which will often be exhibited by the young, while they themselves are entirely unconscious that they are making any such revelation. A young man, choosing the theme for his oration on graduating day, will only be conscious himself of having had many subjects before his mind, and of an inward difficulty in deciding which one to take; but when he comes to deliver his oration, it may be found the very motto or text of his life. This fact was most strikingly exemplified in the case of Samuel Adams, not on his graduating day, but three years after, when he gave his oration for the Master's degree. In the presence of college authorities, and government dignitaries, agents of England, he discussed the question " Whether it be lawful to resist the supreme magistrate, if the Commonwealth cannot otherwise be preserved." He took the affirmative of that question. Those who heard him may have smiled inwardly at a young man of twenty-one boldly arguing what to some of them was little better than treason ; but they probably regarded it only as the audacious spirit of youth, putting itself forth in crude ideas, to be tamed into sobriety and good sense as the years passed on. But the theme that day debated was the theme of his life. He never rested till the " supreme magistrate " was successfully resisted and the " Commonwealth preserved."

In the very year of his graduation, and probably in the very month, Whitefield came to Boston on his second voyage to America, drawing after him crowds of people, and stirring their souls by the marvellous power of his eloquence. Young Adams was deeply interested in these religious themes. But his "irresistible love of political subjects," and the general condition of his father's affairs, turned him away from the ministry. He gave some attention to law studies, and also endeavored to help his father, who had fallen upon evil times, as to business.

We cannot dwell with any minuteness upon the events of his life for the twenty-five years which intervened between his graduation and the enactment of the Stamp Act in 1765. Indeed, all that can be said about his whole life, in this article, must of necessity be brief and detached. But fortunately the historical student now has the opportunity of gaining full and accurate knowledge upon this subject. " The Life and Public Services of Samuel Adams," in three volumes, by William V. Wells, published in 1865, supplies a want long felt. One may there find, *in extenso*, what this man was and what he did.

It has been somewhat common to name Mr. Adams "the father of the Revolution ; " and doubtless he merits that designation as fully as any man. But there is something misleading in such forms of expression. There were many kindred minds working alongside of his. There were other centres of life and activity besides Boston, and when we cast words into these set and convenient forms, they often do something more than justice for one man and less than justice for others. It is like attempting to find the source of a great river, and giving the chief glory to one particular rivulet which may happen to start a little farther up on the hills, but which is not the originating cause of forty other rivulets that spring among those same hills and mingle their waters in the plains below. It is undoubtedly true that Samuel Adams was one of the earliest, boldest, and most systematic organizers of opposition to British rule on these shores. He wrought patiently at that problem for long years. He studied it day and night. He marshalled the hosts of opposition, and set the forces in battle array. Gov. Gage knew his man when he exempted him from British clemency in 1775. But there were other men in Massachusetts, and men in the other colonies, who wrought at the same problem, and would have wrought if he had not; and the grand outbreak could not have been very long deferred. The sense of justice, the instincts of righteousness, were in the people. The voters in the little town-meetings on the hills, in Massachusetts and in the other colonies, comprehended the principles underlying this strife. All this is not to detract from Mr. Adams, for vain would have been his labors if he had stood alone in this great contest with the mother country. He was a calm, bold, able leader. He shaped and compacted this opposition of the people, and gave it head and front against the enemy.

But to go back a moment to the period between 1740 and 1765. In business matters Mr. Adams was by no means prosperous. The times were hard for organizing successful enterprises. The whole currency of the country was in such a dilapidated and uncertain state as to baffle one's plans and expectations. His father dying in 1748, left a complicated estate to be settled, and involved the son in long and vexatious suits. It is safe to say that Samuel Adams's business life was not a success. This was partly owing to causes beyond his control, but also to his incapacity for business, by reason of his thorough absorption in public questions. The glory of the man was, that as he could not serve *himself* and the *public* at the same time, he left himself and turned to the public. It is to his credit that all his life long he was a man without any considerable worldly estate, living in extreme simplicity, and yet in a home cultivated and attractive, ruled by religion, and made cheerful by intelligence and household virtues.

He was first married in 1749, to Elizabeth Checkley, the daughter of his minister, he being then twenty-seven and she twenty-four. She died in 1757, leaving him only two children that survived their mother, three having died previously. In 1764 he was again married to Elizabeth Wells, the daughter of a Boston merchant. Mr. Adams lived in Purchase Street, where his father had lived before him, remaining there until 1774, when his own active opposition to England and the coming in of British troops made it needful that he should seek some other place of residence. His biographer quotes from Bancroft (vol. v. p. 194) sentences that fittingly describe the man in these years, and the manner of his domestic life:

"He was a tender husband, an affectionate parent, and relaxing from severer cares, he could vividly enjoy the delights of conversation with friends; but the walls of his modest mansion never witnessed dissipation or levity or frivolous amusements, or anything inconsistent with the discipline of the man whose incessant prayer was that 'Boston might become a Christian Sparta.'   *   *   *   *

" He was at this time near forty-two years of age, poor, and so contented with poverty that men censured him as 'wanting wisdom to estimate riches at their just value.'

" But he was frugal and temperate; and his prudent and industrious wife, endowed with the best qualities of a New-England woman, knew how to work with her own hands, so that the small resources, which men of the least opulent class would have deemed a very imperfect support, were sufficient for his simple wants. Yet such was the union of dignity with economy, that whoever visited him saw around him every circumstance of propriety. Above all he combined with poverty a stern and incorruptible integrity."

By the year 1750 he became a frequent contributor to the newspapers, on the one great theme which lay near his heart. His articles attracted much attention, and men began to turn towards him as a wise, strong, able leader. He had a skilful way of warring against English tyranny and yet keeping himself within the enclosures of law. Year by year he held fast to the one predominant idea. It grew upon him, and he grew wiser and stronger in the management of it. His biographer quotes from John Adams a passage which will show us how active was his agency through all those troubled years. He says :

" Samuel Adams, to my certain knowledge, from 1758 to 1775, that is for seventeen years, made it his constant rule to watch the rise of every brilliant genius, to seek his acquaintance, to court his friendship, to cultivate his natural feelings in favor of his country, to warn him against the hostile designs of Great Britain, and to fix his affections and his reflections on the side of his native country. I could enumerate a list, but I will confine myself to a few. John Hancock, afterwards president of the Congress and governor of the State ; Dr. Joseph Warren, afterwards Major-General of the militia of Massachusetts and the martyr of Bunker Hill ; Benjamin Church, the poet and orator, once a pretended, if not a real patriot, but afterwards a monument of the frailty of human nature ; Josiah Quincy, the Boston Cicero, the great orator in the body meetings, the author of the Observations on the Boston Port Bill, and of many publications in the newspapers."

And the biographer suggests that " to this list John Adams might with propriety have added his own name." He was thirteen years younger than his cousin Samuel, and when he came upon the stage of public action his kinsman was exerting this large and magnetic influence over men. If he had been thus engaged in personal management for selfish ends, as politicians sometimes are, his conduct would have been simply contemptible. But he was a patriot true and undefiled, and in all his immense labors he wrought for his country, that it might be delivered from the yoke of bondage and stand free and independent.

In 1764 slavery had not been abolished in Massachusetts, and in that year a female slave, named "Surry," was given as a present to his wife. When told of the gift, his reply was, "A slave cannot live in my house. If she comes she must be free." He liberated her at once, but she lived and died as one of his family.

In 1765, the year of the passage of the Stamp Act, he became a member of the Colonial Assembly of Massachusetts, and at once began to instruct his associates in the art of fighting a royal governor in a strictly constitutional way. Those were years of adroit fencing. We have no room for long details, but the strife waxed warmer and warmer, and Sam. Adams had become clearly the Massachusetts leader of the people. His pen and tongue were perpetually busy. He was carefully organizing the revolution which must soon break. He was not to be driven from his great purpose. Some one wrote from England, inquiring why Mr. Adams "was not taken off from the opposition by an office." To which Gov. Hutchinson replied, "Such is the obstinacy and inflexible disposition of the man that he never can be conciliated by any office or gift whatever." Gov. Hutchinson also bears his testimony to what has already been suggested, that Mr. Adams was one of the most artful and cunning men he ever knew in "robbing men of their characters"—in "calumniating governors and other servants of the crown," which being interpreted probably means that he himself had been made to appear most mean and ridiculous by this artful leader of the people, but that it was done in such a legal and constitutional way that there was no help for it and no relief from it.

In 1774 Mr. Adams became a member of the Continental Congress at Philadelphia, and was present at its first session. The delegates, fifty-three in number, first convened Sept. 5, at the City Tavern, and moved thence to Carpenters' Hall, where their sessions were held. John Adams, also a delegate, has given us a graphic description of that scene, when the question came up whether the meeting should be opened with prayer, and what followed. Art has since glorified the occasion, but John Adams's word-painting makes a vivid picture. The passage may of course be found in his published works, but in Wells's Life, &c. (vol. ii. p. 223), it is quoted, and reads as follows :

"When the Congress first met, Mr. Cushing made a motion that it should be opened with prayer. It was opposed by Mr. Jay of New-York and Mr. Rutledge of South Carolina, because we were so divided in religious sentiments—some Episcopalians, some Quakers, some Anabaptists, some Presbyterians, and some Congregationalists—that we could not join in the same act of worship. Mr. Samuel Adams arose and said 'he was no bigot, and could hear a prayer from a gentleman of piety and virtue, who was at the same time a friend to his country. He was a stranger in Philadelphia, but had heard that Mr. Duché (Dushay they pronounce it) deserved that character, and therefore he moved that Mr. Duché, an Episcopal clergyman, might be desired to read prayers to the Congress to-morrow morning.' The motion was seconded, and passed in the affirmative. Mr. Randolph, our President, waited on Mr. Duché, and received for answer, that if his health would permit, he certainly would. Accordingly next morning he appeared with his clerk and in his pontificals, and read several prayers in the established form, and then read the Collect for the 7th of September, which was the Thirty-fifth Psalm.   *   *   *

" After this, Mr. Duché, unexpectedly to everybody, struck out into an extemporary prayer, which filled the bosom of every one present. I must confess I never heard a better prayer or one so well pronounced. Episcopalian as he is, Dr. Cooper himself never prayed with fuch fervor, such ardor, such earnestness and pathos, and in language so elegant and sublime, for America, for the Congress, for the Province of Massachusetts Bay, and especially the town of Boston. It had an excellent effect upon everybody here."

It is difficult in a brief article like this to give any just and adequate idea of Mr. Adams's services in the Continental Congress. For, first of all, it must be borne in mind, that he, perhaps more than any other one man, called that body itself into existence. Up to that time we were simply a collection of provinces under British supremacy. It was no small task to do the work preliminary to this first meeting of Congress in Philadelphia in 1774. There was an immense inertia to be overcome, to say nothing of active opposition. And because Mr. Adams had exerted so large an agency in the convening of this body, he went to Philadelphia to attend its first session, with a set purpose not to obtrude himself upon its deliberations, but to keep rather in the back-ground, until such time as he should be drawn naturally into an active participation in its debates. He was a member of the Congress for seven years, from 1774 to 1781. If his heart rejoiced when he heard the noise of the guns on the 19th of April, 1775, if he called that a "fine day," not with reference to the weather or the outward aspects of nature, but because he saw in it the "beginning of the end," towards which all his thoughts and labors were directed; how much more did his heart rejoice, when on the 4th of July, 1776, he saw that Congress, man by man, giving their votes for that Declaration which sundered our connection with the mother country, and launched us upon an independent national existence ! But even then, with all his far-sightedness, how little could he know what he and his compatriots were doing when they set their hands to that great instrument ! How vague must have been the conception of any man in that day as to the consequences of this transaction in the coming years of human history ! Could he and his fellow-workers have seen what we are permitted to see, now at the end of a century, as to the reach and compass of that act, there would have been imparted such a joy as was not given them to know. For to every man, in his own time, the future lies dark and full of strange uncertainties. " We walk by faith, not by sight."

After the war was over and our independence was established, the next great care was the framing of constitutions for the several states, and for the nation itself. In this work, both as it regards the federal constitution and that of his own state, Mr. Adams took a large and important part. In the balancing of these great interests he was what might be called a "state-rights" man, though in his day that term would not imply all that is meant by it in our modern use. But he was apprehensive lest too much power should be given over to the central government, and not enough left with the states. On that point it has been found, practically, that the opinions of men are apt to vary with circumstances, and that the true balance can only be exactly determined by long years of experience. And when the constitution was formed, it was certainly well that some were found exceedingly jealous for the honor and dignity of the several states.

Dr. William Allen, who published the first edition of his Biographical Dictionary in 1809, has given considerable space to Samuel Adams. He (Dr. Allen) was born in 1784, and was nineteen years of age when Mr. Adams died. Moreover, being at Harvard College during the last years of Gov. Adams's life (that was then his title), he had opportunities to see and know what kind of a man he was, and to hear what living men said of him. A few sentences from him may be fitly given in this article.

" His ingenuity, wit and profound argument are spoken of with the highest respect by those who were cotemporary with him. * * * This was an eventful time. But Mr. Adams possessed a courage which no dangers could shake. He was undismayed by the prospect which struck terror into the hearts of many. * * * The leading traits in the character of Mr. Adams were an unconquerable love of liberty, firmness, decision; * * a man of incorruptible integrity. * * On the christian Sabbath he constantly went to the temple, and the morning and evening devotions in his family proved that his religion attended him in his seasons of retirement from the world. * * *

" He was poor. While occupied abroad in the most important and responsible public duties, the partner of his cares supported the family at at home by her industry. Though his resources were small, yet such were the economy and dignity of his house, that those who visited him found nothing mean or unbecoming his station. His country, to whose interests he devoted his life, permitted him to remain poor ; but there was not wanting a few friends who showed him their regard. In this honorable poverty he continued to a very late period of his life ; and had not a decent competency fallen into his hands by the very afflicting event of the death of an only son, he must have depended for subsistence upon the kindness of his friends or the charity of the public."

He died Oct. 2, 1803, after a life of public service reaching over half a century. After long employment in the affairs of Boston, and the State of Massachusetts, he was for quite a number of years, from 1774 onward, a member of the Continental Congress; a member of the Convention for framing the Constitution of the United States; from 1789 to 1794, Lieut-Governor of Massachusetts; and from 1794 to 1797, Governor—when, through age and infirmities, he withdrew in a great measure from this active career, and the last six years of his life were passed mainly in the retirement of his home. He died in his eighty-second year.

HOLLIS, NEW–HAMPSHIRE, IN THE WAR OF THE REVOLUTION.

By the Hon. SAMUEL T. WORCESTER, A.M., of Nashua, N. H.

Extracts from the Revolutionary Records and Documents of the Town.—Votes and Resolutions of its Town Meetings.—Number of Soldiers in the several years of the War.—Their Wages in different years, and how paid.

WRITTEN history as well as tradition, the provincial and early state records, alike with the records of very many of the older towns in New-Hampshire, bear ample testimony to the unanimity, courage and sacrifices of the people of the then province in the cause of our national independence.   There is abundant evidence that the like spirit and patriotism animated the population of most of the other New-Hampshire towns, as were manifested in the town meetings and doings of the people of Hollis, though, as is believed, but in very few other towns were the revolutionary records and documents so well kept and preserved. *Ab uno disce omnes.* In what we have to say of Hollis, it is far from our wish to make any invidious distinction between the doings of the people of that town and what was done in the same cause and the same years in other New-Hampshire towns, but rather to exhibit this sketch of Hollis as an example and illustration of the results of the predominant public sentiment in all parts of the province.

The town of Hollis (spelled *Holles* in all the older town records, as well as in the town charter) was on the south line of the province, about 45 miles N. W. of Boston, and 22 from Concord, Mass. According to the provincial census taken in September, 1775, it then contained 1255 inhabitants, of whom 174 were males between the ages of 16 and 50; 60 soldiers then in the army, not counting 10 or 11 who had previously died of disease or been killed in the service.   Like many other towns in New-Hampshire between the Merrimack and Connecticut rivers, Hollis was originally chartered by the General Court of Massachusetts, and was included in the parish known as West Dunstable, and most of its early settlers, before the revolution, were from Chelmsford, Groton, and other Massachusetts towns between the province line and Boston.

VOTES AND RESOLUTIONS OF THE TOWN MEETINGS THE FIRST YEAR OF THE WAR.

We copy verbatim from the Records of the Hollis Town Meetings the first year of the war, the following votes and resolutions, as expressive of the popular sentiment and of the earnestness of its citizens in the cause of national liberty. Did our limits permit, it could be readily shown that the votes and resolutions of the following years, and the other doings of the people of the town, were animated with the same spirit to the end of the conflict. The records of these proceedings and votes of the people speak for themselves, and tell their own story in plain, blunt, honest Anglo-Saxon, and need no comment of mine to make them more intelligible or to add force or point to their significance.

In the records of a special town meeting held Nov. 7, 1774, more than five months before the battle of Lexington, we find the first recorded allusion to the impending political troubles and the forthcoming conflict in arms. This meeting was called to choose delegates to a "county congress" for Hillsborough county, to be holden the next day (Nov. 8) at Amherst, and was the first of three Hollis town meetings called for the like purpose. After having made choice of "Dea. Stephen Jewett," "Ensign Stephen Ames" and "Lieut. Reuben Dow," to represent the town at that congress, the following preamble and resolution, with three other resolutions of the like tenor, were adopted by the meeting:

" PREAMBLE.—We the inhabitants of the town of Holles having taken into our most serious consideration the precarious and most alarming affairs of our land at the present day do firmly enter into the following resolutions:

1st. "That we will at all times endeavor to maintain our liberty and privileges, both civil and sacred, even at the risque of our lives and fortunes, and will not only disapprove, but wholly despise all such persons as we have just and solid reasons to think even wish us in any measure to be deprived of them."

This year (1774) it appears from the tax lists that the sum of £27. 16s. 3d. "Lawful money" was assessed upon the inhabitants for ammunition for the town, as a part of the annual tax.

The next special town meeting was held Dec. 30, 1774, to choose delegates to the provincial congress at Exeter, called to advise in respect to a continental congress. At this meeting, as appears from the record of it, the following votes were passed:

1st. "Voted to send a delegate to Exeter to meet the delegates of this province to consult on a Continental congress, and John Hale, Esq., was chosen said delegate."

2d. "Voted that we do cordially accede to the just statement of the rights and grievances of the British colonies and the measures adopted and recommended by the Continental congress for the restoration and establishment of the former, and for the redress of the latter."

3d. "Voted that Col. John Hale, Dea. Stephen Jewett, Dea. John Boynton, Ensign Stephen Ames, Dea. Enoch Noyes, Ensign Noah Worcester, Daniel Kendrick, Jeremiah Ames, William Brown and William Nevins or the major part of them, be a committee in behalf of the town to observe the conduct of all persons touching the association agreement."

4th. "Voted to raise £16. 13s. 8d. as a donation to the poor of Boston."

There are still to be found among the revolutionary documents of Hollis, three original rolls of military companies made in the year 1775. The two oldest of these rolls are dated January 26, 1775; and the third, June 7, of the same year,—ten days before the battle of Bunker Hill. The heading of one of the two oldest rolls is—"*A List of the Company of Militia in Holles under the command of Capt. Joshua Wright, made January 26th, 1775.*" Of this company, Reuben Dow was lieutenant, and Noah Worcester ensign. Besides commissioned officers, this roll contains the names of 4 sergeants, 1 corporal, 1 drummer, 1 fifer, and 214 rank and file,—in all 224; and it is supposed to have embraced all the able-bodied male inhabitants of the town, between the ages of 16 and 60.

The caption of the second roll is—"*The Alarm List made Jan. ye 26th, 1775.*" On this list are 100 names, and it is supposed to include the names of all such able-bodied men of the town as by the province law were exempt from military duty, either on account of age or from some other cause specified in the law. For the purpose of exhibiting the character of this roll as a curiosity of the times, we copy from it the first twenty-four names, with the several titles prefixed or appended to each of them, and in the order in which they appear upon this roll :

Capt Leonard Whiting	Ensign Daniel Merrill
Benjamin Whiting Esq	Ensign Jonas Flagg
Richard Cutts Shannon Esq	Ensign Benjamin Parker
Samuel Cummings Esq	Rev. Daniel Emerson
Daniel Emerson Jun Esq	Dea Samuel Goodhue
Lieut Benjamin Farley	Dea Nathaniel Jewett
Lt. Samuel Farley	Dea Enoch Noyes
Lt David Farnsworth	Dea John Boynton
Lt Amos Eastman	Dea Stephen Jewett
Lt. Robert Colburn	William Cummings Sch. Master
Lt. Samuel Gridley	John Hale Physician
Ensign Stephen Ames,	Samuel *Hosley* do.

The title of the third of these rolls is as follows : "*The List of the present Militia Company of Holles, exclusive of the 'Minute Men' and all that have gone into the Army, June ye 7th, 1775.*"

Of this company Noah Worcester was captain, Daniel Kendrick lieutenant, and Jacob Jewett ensign, and including these officers this roll contains 122 names—102 less than the company roll made on the previous 26th of January.

In the record of the annual town meeting, March 6, 1775, no reference is made in any way to the coming conflict; but on the 3d of April following, a special town meeting was called for the choice of delegates to a second county congress, to be held at Amherst on the 5th of that month, "and to see what method should be taken to raise money for the continental congress at Philadelphia." After choosing and instructing the delegates to the county congress, the meeting, as shown by the record,

"Also Voted that all persons who shall pay money by subscription to send *now* to the Continental Congress shall have the same deducted out of their Province Rates."

The next special town meeting was held April 23, 1775, upon the receipt of the following letter from Col. John Wentworth, written the day after the battle of Lexington, to the selectmen of Hollis, in behalf of the New-Hampshire Committee of Safety, and which forms a part of the record of the meeting:

"*Gentlemen:* This moment melancholy intelligence has been received of hostilities being commenced between the troops under the command of General Gage and our brethren of the Massachusetts Bay. The importance of our exerting ourselves at this critical moment has caused the provincial committee to meet at Exeter, and you are requested instantly to choose and hasten forward a delegate or delegates to join the committee and aid them in consulting measures necessary for our safety."

J. WENTWORTH,
In behalf of the Committee of Safety."

"Province of New Hampshire, } Special town meeting, April 23, 1775.
Hillsborough County, SS.   }

"Pursuant to the above notice and request, the inhabitants of the town of Holles being met unanimously voted, that Samuel Hobart, Esq., be and hereby is appointed to represent this town at Exeter, with other delegates, that are or shall be appointed by the several towns of this Province for the purpose above mentioned.

NOAH WORCESTER, Town Clerk."

The following is a copy of the full record of a town meeting, April 28, 1775, called to raise soldiers for the army, nine days after the battle of Lexington:

"Province of New Hampshire, } Special meeting April 28, 1775.
Hillsborough County, SS.   }   Col. John Hale, Moderator.

"At a meeting of the town of Holles called on a sudden emergency in the day of our public distress.

"1st. Voted, that we will pay two commissioned officers, four non-commissioned officers, and thirty-four rank and file, making in the whole forty good and able men to join the army in Cambridge, paying said officers and men the same wages the Massachusetts men receive, and will also victual the same till such time as the resolution of the General Court or the Congress of the Province of New Hampshire shall be known respecting the raising of a standing army the ensuing summer.

"2nd.   Voted, that the selectmen provide necessaries for sundry poor families where the men are gone into the army till further orders, and the amount be deducted out of their wages.

"3d.   Voted, that what grain was raised for the poor of Boston shall be one half sent to the army, and the other half to be distributed to the above families."

The sequel of the doings of the town furnishes abundant evidence that this vote of the 28th of April was no empty boast, and that the patriotic pledges then made were amply and faithfully redeemed.

The extracts presented below are copied from the doings of a town meeting, May 11, 1775, called to choose delegates to the Provincial Congress at Exeter.

"Voted and chose Col. John Hale and Dea. Enoch Noyes Delegates to the Provincial Congress to meet at Exeter on the 17th of May inst.   Also, Voted and instructed our delegates to join the other Governments in raising and paying their proportions in men and money in the Defence of the Liberties of these Colonies."

We present next below, a full copy of the record of the third town meeting, held May 18, 1775, to appoint and instruct delegates to a third and last county congress.

"Province of New Hampshire,　⎫　Speci'l town meeting, May 18, 1775.
　Hillsborough County, SS.　⎭　　Ensign Noah Worcester, moderator.

"At a meeting of the inhabitants of the town of Holles, May the 18th, in the Day of our public distress, occasioned by a letter from Mr. Daniel Campbell and Mr. Jonathan Martin, a committee for calling a congress for this county, which congress was called for the following purpose:

"1.   To go into some measures for the better security of the internal policy of the county to prevent declining into a state of nature.

"2.   To see if the Congress will appoint a Committee of Correspondence to wait on or join the Congress of Massachusetts Bay."

"3.   To enforce a strict adherence to the Association Agreement of the Continental Congress.

"Mr. William Nevins, Mr. Jeremiah Ames and Lieut. Sam'l Farley chosen delegates for the congress which is to be holden at Amherst on the 24th of May next.   As to the article in the letter of Messrs. Campbell and Martin respecting the sending a committee to the Massachusetts congress,

"Voted unanimously that as we have a Provincial congress now sitting which will doubtless send to them—therefore it appears to us not best for this county to take it upon them to send such a committee."

It is shown by the town records that the style "*Province of New-Hampshire*" was used in the margin of all warrants for town meetings till after the battle of Bunker Hill (June 17, 1775).   After that date, to July 4, 1776, the word *"Colony"* was used in those warrants in place of "Province," and after the declaration of independence the word "State" took the place of "Colony."

The following is a copy of the record of the last Hollis town meeting in 1775, and shows, among other things, how the right to vote of soldiers absent in the army was settled by our ancestors one hundred years ago :

"Colony of New Hampshire,   } Special meeting, Dec. 12, 1775.
   Hillsborough County, SS.   }   Col. John Hale, Moderator.

"Voted and chose Ensign Stephen Ames a delegate to the Congress or Assembly at Exeter for a year.

"SOLDIERS VOTES.—A dispute arose respecting some votes which were brought in writing of persons gone into the army, which being put to vote they were allowed as if the men were present themselves."

SOLDIERS FURNISHED FROM HOLLIS THE FIRST YEAR OF THE WAR.

Late at night of the 18th of April, the detachment of British troops under command of Lieut. Col. Smith, crossed from Boston common to East Cambridge on their march to Lexington and Concord.   The distance from Cambridge to Hollis by the roads then travelled was 42 miles.   The news of this expedition was at once spread through the country by mounted express.   According to the well-established tradition, it was brought to Hollis early in the morning of the 19th by Dea. John Boynton, who lived near the province line, and was a member of the Hollis committee of observation, who came riding through the town at the top of his horse's speed, and calling out to his townsmen as he passed, "The red-coats are coming and killing our men."   Riding at full speed and out of breath (as tradition tells the story), Dea. B. announced his message at the door of Capt. W., another member of the committee, living near the middle of the town, who had just risen from an early breakfast, and was then standing at his glass with his face well lathered, and in the act of shaving.   The latter, without stopping to finish his work, with his face still whitened for the razor, at once dropped that instrument, hurried to his stable, mounted his horse, and in that plight assisted in spreading the alarm.   Other mounted messengers were soon despatched to the several parts of the town to convey the news, and in the afternoon of the same day ninety-two minute-men were rallied and met on the Hollis common with their muskets, each with his powder-horn, one pound of powder and twenty bullets.

Having made choice of Reuben Dow as Captain, John Goss, Lieutenant, and John Cummings, Ensign, this company on the evening of the same day, or before day-break the next morning, was on its march from Hollis to Cambridge.   The names of all the officers of this company, as well as of the privates, copied from an original company roll, showing the time of service of each of them, with their daily wages and pay for travel, is to be found in the October number of the N. E. HIST. and GEN. REGISTER for 1873, pp. 382–83. Thirty-nine privates of this company, as appears from this roll, after an absence of from six to twelve days returned home. The remainder, with but few exceptions, stayed at Cambridge and enlisted in other companies organized to serve for eight months. Much the largest part of the Hollis men who remained at Cambridge reënlisted in a new company commanded by Capt. Dow, which was afterwards mustered into the Massachusetts regiment of Col. Wm. Prescott, who lived at the time near the line of the adjoining town of Pepperell, a part of his farm being in Hollis, and who was a neighbor of Capt. Dow. Thomas Colburn and Ebenezer Youngman, two of this company of ninety-two, enlisted in the company of Capt. Moore, of Groton, in the same regiment, and were both killed at Bunker Hill. Others of them enlisted in the company of Capt. Spalding, of Nottingham West, in the New-Hampshire regiment under Col. Reed, and others in a company under Capt. Towne, of Amherst, N. H., in a Massachusetts regiment commanded by Col. Hutchinson.

The company of Capt. Dow, inclusive of its officers, consisted of 59 men, that number making a full company under the Massachusetts Act for organizing the troops of that province. It is shown by an original roll and return of this company, now in the office of the secretary of state in Boston, exhibiting the names of the wounded and dead, as well as of the living, that all of the 59 were from Hollis, and that it was the only company in Col. Prescott's regiment in which it appears from the rolls that all the men were from a single town. A copy of this roll may be found in the October number of the REGISTER for 1873, pp. 384–85, from which it appears that six of the men had been killed at Bunker Hill, one on the 19th of June after the battle, and that two had died of sickness on the 29th of May previous.

The original commission of Capt. Dow, dated at Watertown, May 19, 1775, with the autograph signature of Gen. Joseph Warren, as president pro tem. of the Massachusetts Congress, is still preserved by the Dow family of Hollis, a copy of which appears below.

"The Congress of the Colony of Massachusetts Bay.

"To Reuben Dow, Gentleman,—We, reposing especial trust and confidence in your courage and good conduct, do by these presents constitute and appoint you, the said Reuben Dow, to be Captain in the —— Company in the Regiment of Foot commanded by William Prescott, Esq., Colonel, raised by the Congress aforesaid for the defence of said Colony. You are therefore carefully and diligently to discharge the duty of Captain in leading, ordering and exercising the said Company in arms, both the inferior officers and soldiers, and to keep them in good order and discipline; and they are hereby commanded to obey you as their Captain, and you are yourself to observe and follow such orders and instructions as you shall from time to time receive from the General and Commander in Chief of the Forces raised in the Colony aforesaid for the defence of the same, or any other of your superior officers according to military rules and discipline in war in pursuance of the trust reposed in you.

Per order of the Congress,   JOSEPH WARREN, President, P. T. Watertown, the 19th of May, 1775.

SAMUEL FREEMAN, Secretary, P. T."

DESCRIPTIVE LIST OF THIS COMPANY.

From an original descriptive roll (still preserved) of Capt. Dow's company, showing the ages, height and complexion of fifty of his men, it appears that Jonathan Powers, the oldest of them, was 60 years of age, and that the youngest was Peter Cummings, a son of the ensign, John Cummings, who was but 13. The next youngest was the fifer, Noah Worcester, Jr., long afterwards known as Noah Worcester, D.D., and as one of the originators of the Massachusetts and American Peace Societies, who was but 16 the November previous. The next youngest was Phineas Nevins, killed in the battle, who was 17. Five of the others were but 19. The two oldest next to Powers were each 48; and the average age of the rest of the men was about 25 years.

Fourteen of the fifty men were of "dark" complexion; the remaining thirty-six being described as "light." The three tallest of the men were 6 ft. in height. The shortest was the boy Peter Cummings, who was but 5 ft. Of the rest, one was 5 ft. 4 in. in height; four, 5 ft. 5 in.; eighteen, 5 ft. 6 in.; six, 5 ft. 7 in.; three, 5 ft. 8 in.; six, 5 ft. 9 in.; six, 5 ft. 10 in., and two, 5 ft. 11 in.

CASUALTIES.

The two first deaths in this company were those of James Fisk and Jeremiah Shattuck, both of whom died of sickness on the 29th of May. The names of those killed at Bunker Hill were Phineas Nevins, aged 17; Jacob Boynton, 19; Isaac Hobart, 19; Peter Poor, 21; Thomas Wheat, 24; and Nathan Blood, 28. Caleb Eastman, aged 23, was killed at Cambridge two days after the battle by the bursting of his gun. Fisk, Shattuck, Wheat and Blood were married and left families. The rest of the killed were unmarried. It is stated in Frothingham's Siege of Boston that the whole loss in killed in Col. Prescott's regiment in the battle was 42—the aggregate loss in killed of the two New-Hampshire regiments engaged was 20. The loss of Hollis in the battle, including the two men killed in Capt. Moore's company, was 8, equal to two-fifths of the loss in killed of the two New-Hampshire regiments, and nearly one-fifth of that of the regiment of Col. P.

LOSS OF EQUIPMENTS IN THE BATTLE.

It is shown by the original rolls of Capt. Dow's company that his men furnished all their own equipments, except cartridge-boxes, which were furnished by Nathaniel Prentice, a Massachusetts quartermaster, and for which they were charged 1s. 8d. each. In the fall of the year next after, an account was taken of the loss of equipments at Bunker Hill, with a view to compensation. From this account it appears that twenty-five of the men lost their knapsacks, valued at from 1s. 4d. to 1s. 8d. each; twenty-four, their tump-lines,* 1s. 4d. each; nine, their guns, appraised from 16s. to £2. 4s. each; two, their bayonets; three, their cartridge-boxes; and one, his sword.

THE NEW-HAMPSHIRE REINFORCEMENTS.

Early in December, 1775, the New-Hampshire Committee of Safety made a call for New-Hampshire volunteers to reinforce the army at Cambridge, to supply the place of the Connecticut troops who had refused to remain longer in the service. Under this call, New-Hampshire with patriotic promptness is said to have sent to Cambridge 31 companies of 63 men each, or some more than 2000 in all. The 26th company of this force was commanded by Capt. Noah Worcester, of Hollis. No roll of the company is known now to exist, but it appears from Hollis revolutionary documents that it is supposed to have contained the names of 45 Hollis soldiers.

NUMBER OF HOLLIS SOLDIERS THE FIRST YEAR OF THE WAR.

Minute men who went to Cambridge, April 19,	92
Men in Captain Dow's Company,	59
Men who enlisted in other companies for 8 months,	20
In Capt. Worcester's company,	45
Making in all,	216

Deducting from this last number 58 of the 92 minute-men who went to Cambridge, April 19, and who afterwards enlisted a second time, it will be seen that 158 different soldiers went from Hollis the first year of the war; a number equal to more than one in eight of the whole population.

WAGES OF SOLDIERS IN 1775, AND HOW PAID.

We find but very little in the common histories of the revolution touching the wages of the brave men by whose privations and valor our independence was won. I have examined several original Hollis documents, still preserved, that throw much light upon this subject

---

* Tump-line (as defined in Worcester's Quarto Dic.) was "a strap to be placed across the forehead to assist a man in carrying a pack on his back."

in respect to the Hollis soldiers. Among these documents there are, 1st, the pay-roll of the company of 92 minute-men of April 19; 2d, a pay-roll of Capt. Dow's company, dated in August, 1775, after the men had been in the service 3 months and twenty days; 3d, a document called the "Great Return," made out and certified by the selectmen of Hollis, after the war was ended, showing the names of most of the Hollis soldiers, and the bounties and wages paid to each of them by the town.

By the pay-roll of the 92 minute-men, it is shown that those of them who reënlisted at Cambridge in other companies were credited with six days' service. For these six days, the private soldiers were paid 8s. 6d. each, equal to 1s. 5d., or some less than 24 cents per day in federal money. The wages of a corporal for the six days were 9s. 4d.; of a sergeant, 10s. 3d.; of the 2d lieutenant, 15s.; of the 1st lieutenant, 17s. 1 1-2d.; of the captain, £1. 5s. 7 1-2d.; being somewhat less than 4s. 4d. per day, or about 80 cents in federal money. The private soldiers who went home without reënlisting were paid the same daily wages, with 84d. or 7s. for travel, being at the rate of 1d. a mile each way.

It appears from the pay-roll of Capt. Dow's company that the private soldiers were paid £2, equal to $6.67 per month, or near 24 cents per day; the wages of the corporals, drummers and fifers were each £2. 5s. per month; of the sergeants, £2. 10s.; of the 2d lieutenant, £3; of the 1st lieutenant, £4; and of the captain, £6 per month.

From the following copy of an original receipt, now in the office of the Secretary of State in Boston, it appears that the soldiers in Capt. Dow's company received the military coat voted by the Massachusetts Congress in the spring of 1775, to "eight-months' men" as a bounty.

"CAMBRIDGE, Nov. 20, 1775.

"*To the Honorable Committee of Supplies:* This may certify that we who have hereunto subscribed our names do declare that we being under officers and soldiers enlisted under Captain Reuben Dow of Holles, in Col. William Prescott's regiment, have received each of us a coat according to a vote of the late Congress held at Watertown, and provided by the committee of supplies, we say received of Lieutenant John Goss of said company."

This receipt has appended to it the names of 47 members of this company, being all the non-commissioned officers and privates of the company, except the nine who had been previously killed or died of sickness.

It appears from the document before referred to, known as the "Great Return," made by the selectmen of Hollis, that in 1775 the town paid for its soldiers the following sums:

	£	*s.*	*d.*
For the 92 minute-men in April	93.	07.	07
For the men enlisted for eight months	792.	00.	00
For men enlisted in Capt. Worcester's company	115.	10.	00
Making in all paid that year	£1000.	17.	07

STORY OF A HOLLIS WOMAN. — CAPTURE AND SURRENDER OF A HOLLIS TORY.

Among the citizens of Hollis in 1775, were four known as tories, whose sympathies were strongly with the royal government. These four were Benjamin Whiting, the first sheriff of Hillsborough county; his brother, Capt. Leonard Whiting; and Samuel and Thomas Cummings, two of the sons of Samuel Cummings, Sen., the first town-clerk of Hollis. We copy the following notices of the two Whitings from Sabine's "Loyalists of the American Revolution," vol. ii. p. 422.

"*Whiting, Benjamin*, Sheriff of Hillsborough County, N. H. He was proscribed and banished and his property confiscated."

"*Whiting, Leonard*, of Hollis, N. H. A noted Tory. In 1775, Whiting was the bearer of despatches from Canada to the British in Boston, and was arrested in Groton, Mass., under the following circumstances. After the departure of Col. Prescott's Regiment of 'Minute Men,' Mrs. David Wright, of Pepperell, Mrs. Job Shattuck, of Groton, and the neighboring women, collected at what is now Jewett's bridge, over the Nashua river, between Pepperell and Groton, clothed in their absent husbands' apparel, and armed with muskets, pitchforks, and such other weapons as they could find, and having elected Mrs. Wright their commander, resolutely determined that no foe to freedom, foreign or domestic, should pass that bridge. Rumors were then rife that the Regulars were approaching, and frightful stories of slaughter flew rapidly from place to place and from house to house. Soon there appeared Mr. Leonard Whiting (the subject of this notice), on horseback, supposed to be treasonably engaged in carrying intelligence to the enemy. Whiting, by direction of Mrs. Wright in her assumed character of Sergeant of the Bridge Guard, was seized, taken from his horse, searched, and detained a prisoner. Despatches were found in his boots, which were sent to the Committee of Safety, and Whiting himself was committed to the custody of the Committee of Observation of Groton."

The maiden name of Mrs. David Wright was Prudence Cummings, a sister of Samuel and Thomas Cummings, two of the Hollis tories before mentioned, and also of Benjamin Cummings, a younger brother, who was in the company of Capt. Dow at Bunker Hill, and was afterwards a soldier in the continental army. It appears from the Hollis Records of Births and Marriages, that Prudence Cummings was born at the parish of West Dunstable, now Hollis, Nov. 26, 1740, and that she was married to David Wright, of Pepperell, Dec. 28, 1761.

NOTES ON AMERICAN HISTORY.

[Continued from page 233.]

By the Rev. EDWARD D. NEILL, President of Macalester College, Minneapolis, Minnesota.

No. VIII.

WASHINGTON'S LETTER ON THE APPOINTMENT OF JOHN PARKE, POET, ASSISTANT QUARTER-MASTER.

THE following letter of Washington, never before printed, is of interest, in view of the time and place of its being written, the camp at Cambridge, a few weeks after his assuming the command of the army; and also because of the persons to which it was addressed, Cæsar Rodney and Thomas McKean, delegates to Congress from Delaware; and the person alluded to, Mr. Parke, an early contributor to American literature. Rodney and McKean had always been friendly to the independence of the colonies. They were both members of the Stamp-Act Congress which had assembled, in 1765, at New-York, and of the Congress which had convened on the 5th of September, 1774, in Carpenters' Hall, Philadelphia.

John Adams, in an account of a dinner he took at the house of Miers Fisher, a young Quaker lawyer, of Philadelphia, two days after the Congress of 1774 assembled, writes:

"We had a large collection of lawyers. Mr. Andrew Allen, the Prothonotary, a Mr. Morris, the Attorney General, Mr. McKean, Mr. Reed, and Mr. Rodney, and besides these, Governor Hopkins, and Governor Ward. We had much conversation upon the practice of the law in different provinces. But at last we got swallowed up in politics."

The Mr. Parke, who brought a letter from Rodney and McKean to Washington, was John Parke, one of the early poets of Pennsylvania, and in 1768 a student at the College of Philadelphia.

In looking over the "General Orders" of the Commander at Cambridge, we find under date of August 16, 1775, the following: "John Parke Esq. is appointed an Assistant Quarter Master General. He is to be obeyed as such."

The next year, when the army was in New-York city, on June 29th, he was appointed Lt.-Colonel of artificers. He appears to have been with Washington at Valley Forge and other points.

Mr. Fisher, in an article read before the Pennsylvania Historical Society many years ago, gives an interesting account of his literary career.

Oswald, one of his old army companions, after the war, became a bookseller in the Coffee House in Philadelphia, and in 1786 published an octavo of 334 pages from the pen of John Parke, with the following title:

" *The Lyric Works of Horace translated into English Verse, to which are added a number of Original Poems. By a Native of America.*"

To the usual inscriptions of the Odes of Horace, he added the names of his companions in the army, his friends and teachers.

The Rev. James Davidson, one of the professors in the College of Philadelphia (now the University of Pennsylvania) was an accomplished Latin scholar, and Parke in imagination presses into the service the ship that brought Virgil to Athens, to transport Davidson from England to America.

To the 38th Ode, Book 1st, "*Ad puerum*," Parke adds the inscription, "To my waiter, Jabez Trapp, soldier."

The last Ode of the 3d Book, in which the poet predicts immortal fame from his verses, commencing with the line,

" Exegi monumentum ære perennius,"

he inscribes "To L't Colonel Ebenezer Oswald of the American Artillery," now become his publisher.

The 14th of the same Book, which celebrates the return of Augustus from Spain, is paraphrased, and made to refer to the return of General Washington from Virginia. The opening verses are as follows :

" Rejoice, Columbia ! for thy Son,
  As great Alcides did of yore,
  With laurels crown'd and fame in battles won,
  Returns victorious from Virginia's shore !
  Cornwallis vanquished and our Country saved,
  The grateful tribute of our joy demands.
    On every heart his name's engraved
    Long as the United Empire stands.

" Chaste Martha shall embrace her spouse,
  So long detained by war's alarms ;
  And to the righteous Heaven prefer her vows
  For giving back her hero to her arms.
  Her widowed daughter, beautiful in tears,
  Shall grace the scene and swell the thankful train,
    While aged matrons, bent with years,
    Shall crown the supplicated fane."

The reference in the second verse is to Mrs. Washington's daughter-in-law, Eleanor Calvert, the widow of her son John Parke Custis, who was aid-de-camp to Washington at Yorktown, and died a few weeks after the surrender of Cornwallis.

There has been no alteration in the spelling of

WASHINGTON'S LETTER.

Camp at Cambridge, Aug. 30th 1775.

Gentⁿ

    I endeavoured to pay the best attention in my power to your recommendation of Mr. Parke, by making him an assistant Quartermaster General, an office indispensably necessary in discharge of that important and troublesome business. I wish it was in my power to provide for more of the young Gentlemen, who, at their own expence have travelled and now continue here, from Pennsylvania and elsewhere; but the Congress seems to have put it out of their own power to do this, leaving by their instructions to me, the ultimate appointment of all officers as high as a Colonel to the Government in which the Regiments originated, the obvious consequence of which is, that every commission will be monopolized by these four New England Governments; the good policy and justice of which, I submit to your better judgment, but should give it as my own opinion, that as the whole Troops are now taken into the pay of the United Colonies, the Congress (which I presume will either by themselves, or a Committee of their own Body always be sitting) ought to reserve the filling up of all vacancies themselves, in order that Volunteers from every Government may have an equal chance of preferment instead of confining all offices to a few Governments to the total exclusion of the rest. I have dropt these thoughts by way of hints wh^{ch} you may improve or reject as they shall appear to have or want weight.

For the occurrences of the Camp, the State of the Army &c. I refer to my Publick Letters addressed to Mr. Hancock, and with great respect, and gratitude for y^r good wishes contained in your Letter

I remain Gentl^n

Y'r most obed't H'ble

Servt

G^o WASHINGTON.

LETTERS OF CAPT. THOMAS MIGHILL, OF ROWLEY, MASS.

Communicated by the Hon. WILLIAM D. NORTHEND, A.M., of Salem, Mass.
Copied from the originals in his possession.

THOMAS Mighill, the writer of the following letters, was the captain of the first Rowley company in the Revolutionary war. He was deacon of the first church in Rowley, from 1769 to the time of his death, Aug. 26, 1807. He was also town clerk twenty-five years, was representative to the General Court from 1783 to 1793 inclusive, and a member of the Massachusetts Convention which ratified the Federal Constitution. He voted against its ratification. The vote stood 187 yeas and 168 nays. He resided in the house now owned by the widow of William Moody in Rowley.

His wife was Sarah Northend, daughter of Capt. John Northend, who earlier was captain of the first foot company of Rowley. Tradition says that she loaded a wagon, at Rowley, with provisions, and drove it alone to our troops near Boston, a distance of about thirty miles, where she distributed its contents among the soldiers. It is probably true, and the first of these letters is suggestive of it.

I.

Camp N   Feb. 21. 1776

To my dear wife and children
          I am in prity good Health. I did expect to have been at Rowley
before this day, and it is a great disappointment to me for I want to see you
vere much. I asked the Gen¹ but he told me he did not know as he could
give me leave to go I do not expect to have leave untill we make an
atack on Boston which I suppose will be in a fortnit or three week if the
weather be good for working and what will be ye Issue Heaven only know-
eth give my kind respect to my friends.
          I whould have you save what provisions you have to part with for the
Poor and especially those in the army if you want money I expect soon to
send sum to you but as for my Coming have not too much dependance for
if I should not the disappointment will be the greater. Thomas Pee has in-
listed with me he ran away and enlisted three times since and Has spent
his wages and is in debt now 20 Dollars now sick at the Hospatal. I remain your true friend till Death
                                                  THOMAS MIGHILL.

          If you have an opertunity send me two
Shirts if redy put fine cloth to the sleaves.

II.

Norwich April 6. 1776

To my Dear wife and Children
          I imbrace this opertunity to let you know where I am We arived at
Norwich this day except David Story he being unwell we left him on the
road but I am in hopes he will be well so as to follow after us I am in
good Health we are to march on the morrow to New London then I expect
we shall go by Water to New York I have not time to write only to let you
know how I do
          remember me to all friends wishing peace with Godlyness to be and
abound among you From your friend and affectionate Husband and
Father   THOMAS MIGHILL.
          [Addressed, "To Capt. Thoˢ Mighill | of Rowley |
                    In | the Bay Coliny."]

III.

New York July 17ᵗʰ 1776.

          I wrote you last month and Sent you Sum money by the Post but had
no return to let me know weather you had recd the Same or know how
you did. I have Sent by the Same Post Twenty three Pounds four Shil-
ings L M be so kind as to write me by the Post that I may hear how you
do for it is a Verey Dark day I have not time to let you know how the
affairs stand. I was out last night and have but a few minits to write
the men that was in the Conspirecy are Still in confinement it is expected
my Drumʳ Green will be condem'd two large Ships and 3 tenders went
by our Batreys on the 12 Instant. a great maney Cannon was discharged
on both Sides we are informed by Deserters we kiled and wounded a Considerable number of theirs but not one of ours we had 6 men killd by our

own Cannon they went up Hudsons River about 30 miles it is Thought there is 120 Ships about 10000 thousand men enemy they lay all within Sight of our incampment we are upward of 40000 men the camp disorder prevails in the armey very much but a few dies Lord How has Sent a Flag with a letter to George Washing Esq' But we know no Such a man the letter was Sent back again and a nother Came Subscribed George Washington Esq' &c. &c. &c. as I am informed it fared the Same fate as the former I hear there is one come this day but we have so many fals reports that we know not what to beleve a number of Ships is gorn out this day it is thought they are gorn to stop up our paseg on the other side of Long Island remember me to all friends   To my Dear wife and children

THOMAS MIGHILL.

P. S. I recd a letter from son Gage
[Addressed : "To Capt. | Tho' Mighill | of Rowley |
New England | Post Paid."]

LETTERS OF SIGNERS OF THE DECLARATION OF INDEPENDENCE, MILITARY MEN, AND OTHERS, DURING THE REVOLUTIONARY WAR.

Communicated by JOHN S. H. FOGG, M.D., of South Boston, Mass.

THE following letters,[1] selected from my collection of autographs, will give an idea of the state of affairs in Philadelphia and in the various military camps, at various times during the Revolution. The letters of Robert Howe, Joseph Reed and Joseph Warren, show much of the spirit that pervaded the people from one extreme of the colonies to the other, in the period immediately preceding it. Those of John Adams, Elbridge Gerry and John Langdon give some idea of the extent to which the thought of an independent government had taken possession of the public mind.   The letter of Gen. Gage seems almost prophetic, though written ten years before the Declaration of Independence.

Thomas Gage to Robert Monckton.

New York 28 Sept. 1765.

Dear Sir,
       As the Government of Berwick will keep you in England, and on that Account more agreeable to you, than that of New York, I beg Leave to congratulate you on His Majestys' Appointing you to Succeed the late General Guise. Though I can assure you it is a great Disappointment to the People in general of this Province, who testify their Regret in losing you.

       The sooner S' Henry Moore arrives the better, tho' he will find his hands full, and will enter upon Government in most troublesome and boisterous Times. *The Provinces never declared their Sentiments of Independency so*

---

[1] Only a portion of the lettters furnished by Dr. Fogg appear in this number of the REGISTER.—ED.

openly before. *And they state their Grievances, (if in reality they have any) in such a way, that I do not see how it will be possible to relieve them.* They push Matters so closely to the Point, that the Subject seems to be, whether they are Independent States, or Colonys dependent on Great Britain.

Sir Henry Seaton is arrived, as is also Lieut Lyons, and you may be assured Sir, that I shall always receive very great Pleasure, in serving any Persons recommended by you, as far as I have Power.

Capt: Sheriffe certainly merits the Character you are pleased to give of him. He is very obliging and assiduous.

I hope you have perfectly recovered of your late Indisposition, and that you will enjoy a Series of Health.

I am with very great Regard,
Dear Sir,
Your most obedient
humble Servant
THO' GAGE.

Genl: Monkton.

[Endorsed: " Genl. Gage To Genl. Monkton | 28 Sept 1765."
" Provinces never declared their sentiments of | Independency
so openly before."]

From Robert Howe.[1]

Wilmington 30th of March 1773.

Dear Sir,

The zeal, capacity and Eloquence you displayed as a Representative of the People upon some constitutional questions of the greatest importance to America while I was in Virginia, gave you a just Claim to my attention and Approbation as a Brother Member of a sister Colony, and did you honour as a Patriot determined to support the Rights and Liberties of your Country uninfluenced by fear favour or affection.

It is to this opinion of you sir, You owe the liberty I now take of introducing to your notice and civilities Mr: Josiah Quincy of Boston, who Breathing the spirit of Liberty has abilities and Resolution to defend it, and so can not but be an acceptable Acquaintance to one of your disposition. I shall therefore make no Apology for the trouble I give you in this letter, indeed I flatter myself I shall give pleasure to each of you by making you acquainted with one another.

I must beg of you sir to make my compliments to Mr: Councillor Lee and to all your Relations to whom I have the pleasure to be known and permit me to add that should any of your acquaintance come to this Country a line from you will entitle them to the attention of

Dr. Sir   Your most ob. Servt:
R. HOWE.

---

[1] There is no superscription to this letter. I think it must have been addressed to one of the Lees of Virginia.

Josiah Quincy, as appears from his Memoir, travelled in North Carolina in 1773. He thus writes : " *March* 30, spent the night at Mr. Harnett's —the Samuel Adams of North Carolina, except in point of fortune. *Robert Howe,* Esq., Harnett, and myself, made the social triumvirate of the evening. The plan of continental correspondence highly relished, much wished, and resolved upon as proper to be pursued."

This letter, as will be seen, bears the same date, and was probably written on the very evening that Quincy and Howe were at Harnett's house.   J. S. H. F.

Joseph Reed to John Hancock.

Dear Sir,

I am sorry to be obliged to renew an Acquaintance from which I had so much Pleasure on so melancholy an Occasion as the State of your Publick Affairs at present affords: Being obliged to attend a sick Relation in the Country I was not able to meet the Committee appointed to transmit an Answer to the Letters received by Express; but I could not excuse myself from giving you such farther Information as may enable you to form a proper Idea of the Temper & Disposition of the Inhabitants of Philad^a. A general Indignation is expressed by all Ranks of People at your singular & barbarous Situation. But it has always happened in the publick Affairs of that City that some Time must be given to animate the Mass of the People. The Quakers who form a very respectable & numerous Body of our Citizens are always timid and cautious—There are also some private & partial Interests in the City that endeavour to damp the rising Spirit of Liberty & Opposition, particularly a Number of Gentlemen interested in the new Colony on the Ohio which has been obstructed by the Commotions of America—Under these circumstances we Thought ourselves exceedingly happy to commence an Opposition even on general Ground which I hope will every Day extend & e'er long bring about the desirable Union in a general suspension of all Trade to Great Brittain, & the West India Islands, until some adequate Relief is afforded. But in Order to bring about so salutary a Measure I apprehend it will be expected that those Towns in the Province of Massachusetts Bay, who are not under the immediate Pressure of this cruel Act will stand forth in Behalf of their Brethren & lead the Way in this great but necessary Sacrifice for the Salvation of our common Liberty—Could this be extended to the Port Towns of New Hampshire & Connecticut I think that it would succeed in Philad^a; but unhappily the Evasions of the last Non-Importation Agreement to the Northward have diffused such Jealousies, that nothing but a most vigorous & general Opposition (to which Interest must for a Time give Way) can restore the Confidence necessary to carry any seasonable & proper Measure into Execution.—The Trade of Philad^a during the Non-Importation Agreem^t was so much injured by the unfair & interested Conduct of some of the neighboring Colonies that in my Opinion it will be very difficult to prevail upon the Inhabitants to relinquish their Trade unless they are convinced that the Suspension will be very general & therefore effectual. The present Views of the Friends of Boston are gradually to warm & animate the People both from the Press & otherwise, to make them consider it as a common Cause & unite as a Band of Brothers. To have pressed an immediate Closure with the Proposal of your Town of the 13th May would in all Probability have been opposed & perhaps defeated. But you may depend upon it that your Friends are many, warm and spirited. Mr: Dickinson spoke fully at the Meeting & pathetically recommended your Cause as the Cause of all. Indeed as far as can be judged from the Sentiments expressed on that Occasion you need not doubt but Philad^a will be brought to concur in any Measure which may be generally adopted thro' the Colonies to relieve you from your present Distress & defeat the wicked Design of a corrupt & infamous Minister.

I am sure you will pardon this hasty Scrawl. It is the Effusion of a Mind deeply affected with your present Calamity & tremblingly alive in the

Cause of Liberty.—But you will consider it as only containing the sentiments of a private obscure Person and therefore to be weigh'd only as such.

I pray God to direct you to wholesome & proper Measures & hope the humiliating & base Submission required by the Act of Parliament will not be made but in the last Extremity : Those who give up essential Liberty for temporary Safety deserve neither Liberty nor Safety says a great Author. I am with much Respect

& Esteem Dr Sir,

Your most obed: Hble

Trenton 30 Miles from Philad^a May 22, 1774.

Servt.

Jos : **Reed.**

John Adams to Joseph Palmer.

Philadelphia September 26. 1774.

Dr. Sir.

Yesterday I had the pleasure of receiving yours of the fourteenth Instant, for which I am very much obliged to you. I receive a greater Pleasure from the Letters of my Friends, than ever, and every Line we receive is of Use to us.

Before this reaches you the Sense of the Congress concerning your Wisdom, Fortitude and Temperance, in the Massachusetts in general and the County of Suffolk in particular, will be public in our Country.—It is the universal Sense here that the Mass. Acts, and Murder Act ought not to be Submitted to a Moment. But then, when you ask the Question what is to be done ? they answer Stand Still, bear, with Patience, if you come to a Rupture with the Troops all is lost.—Resuming the first Charter, Absolute Indepen'cy &c are Ideas which Startle People here.

It Seems to be the general opinion here that it is practicable for Us, in the Massachusetts to live wholly without a Legislature and Courts of Justice as long as will be necessary to obtain Relief.—If it is practicable, the general Opinion is, that We ought to bear it.—The Commencement of Hostilities is exceedingly dreaded here. It is thought that an Attack upon the Troops, even tho it should prove successfull and triumphant, would certainly involve the whole Continent in a War.—It is generally thought here that the Ministry would rejoice at a Rupture in Boston, because that would furnish him with an Excuse to the People at home, and unite them with him in an opinion of the Necessity of pushing Hostilities, against Us.

On the Contrary, the Delegates here and other Persons from all Parts, are universally, very Sanguine, that if Boston and the Massachusetts can possibly Steer a middle Course between Obedience to the Acts, and open Hostilities with the Troops, the Exertions of the Colonies, will procure a total Change of Measures and full Redress for Us.

However my Friend, I cannot, at this Distance pretend to judge. We must leave all to your Superior Wisdom.

What you propose, Sir, of holding out some Proposal which Shall Shew our Willingness to pay for our Protection at Sea, is a Subject, often mentioned in private Conversation here. Many Gentlemen have pursued the Thought, and digested their Plans : But what is to be the Fate of them I ca'nt say.

It is my opinion, Sir, that we do our full Proportion towards the Protection of the Empire, and towards the Support of the Naval Power.—To the Support of the Standing Army, We ought never to contribute voluntarily.

A Gentleman, put into my Hands a Plan, a few Days ago, for offering to raise 200.000 £ St. annually and to appropriate it to the maintenance of a Ship of War.

But is this not Surrendering our Liberty?

I have not Time however to discuss these Questions at present—I hope to have the Pleasure of considering these Things in private Conversation— mean Time, I pray God to direct assist and protect you, and all our Friends, amidst the Dangers that Surround you.

Am glad to hear Mr: Cranch is about taking Refuge at Braintree. I wish every living Creature, except the Tories, was well provided for in the Country. My Respects to all your worthy Family. I remain, with great Respect

Your Friend & humb. Servt.

To Joseph Palmer Esq. JOHN ADAMS.
Germantown.

Joseph Warren to Joseph Palmer,

Boston January 14, 1775.

Dear Sir,

I hope your Health is by this Time perfectly recovered. Mr Gridley (as an Engineer) is (I apprehend) much wanted, we have an Opportunity of obliging him which will I believe secure him to us in Case of Necessity.

The Furnace owned by him and Mr. Quincy is held as Security for £250 L Money. Mr: Pitts has this Money and is willing to lend it if the Security is good. He confides in [your] Judgement, begs you would visit the Furnace, know what it is worth as it now Stands, and what the Place would be worth if Fire should destroy the Buildings.

If you can settle this Matter I think you will do the Cause an essential Service—I need not urge you to undertake this Affair. Your Zeal in the Cause of your Country is a sufficient Stimulus.

I am Sir your most obed\.

Mr: Palmer. Sert: JOS WARREN

[Addressed: " Mr: Joseph Palmer | German Town."]

Endorsed in the handwriting of Gen. Joseph Palmer : " Doct\ Warren | Jan\. 14 1775 "]

Daniel Moulton to the Selectmen of Kittery, Me.

York Apr\. 26 1775.

Gentlemen,

As the Times are Difficult & Hazzardous And we know not but our Enemies Troops or some of them, at least may Land here and Attack us, I am concerned about the County Records of Deeds, and have concluded in my own Mind, upon the first Intelligence of Danger to pack them up in Chests, under Lock and have them ready at a Minits Notice to convey them to some remote place of Safety.

Sho\ be glad of your & the Justices of your Town's Advice & Direction in the matter as Soon as possable, That if to be removed, say when, where &c.

I am, your Distress'd Friend & fellow Sufferer.

DAN[1]. MOULTON.

[Addressed : " To the Gentlemen | Selectmen | of the Town of | Kittery."]

George Washington to Joseph Palmer.

Cambridge Aug[t] 22[d] 1775.

Sir,

In answer to your favour of yesterday I must inform you, that I have often been told of the advantages of Point Alderton with respect to its command of the shipping going in and out of Boston Harbour; and that it has, before now, been the object of my particular enquiries——That I find the Acc[ts] differ, exceedingly, in regard to the distance of the Ship Channel, —& that, there is a passage on the other side of the light House Island for all Vessells except Ships of the first Rate.

My knowledge of this matter would not have rested upon enquiries only, if I had found myself at any one time since I came to this place, in a condition to have taken such a Post.—But it becomes my duty to consider, not only what place is advantageous, but what number of Men are necessary to defend it—how they can be supported in case of an attack—how they may Retreat if they cannot be supported—& what stock of Ammunition we are provided with for the purpose of self defence, or annoyance of the Enemy.—In respect to the first, I conceive our defence must be proportioned to the attack of Gen[l] Gage's whole force (leaving him just enough to man his Lines on Charles Town Neck & Roxbury) and with regard to the Second, and most important object, we have only 184 Barr[ls] of Powder in all, which is not sufficient to give 30 Musket Cartridges a Man, and scarce enough to serve the Artillery in any brisk action a single day.

Would it be prudent then in me, under these circumstances, to take a Post 30 miles distant from this place when we already have a Line of Circumvalation at least Ten Miles in extent, any part of which may be attacked (if the Enemy will keep their own Council) without our having one hours previous Notice of it ?——Or is it prudent to attempt a Measure which necessarily would bring on a consumption of all the Ammunition we have ; thereby leaving the Army at the Mercy of the Enemy, or to disperse ; and the Country to be Ravaged, and laid waste at discretion?——To you Sir who is a well wisher to the cause, and can reason upon the effects of such a Conduct, I may open Myself with freedom, because no improper discoveries will be made of our Situation ; but I cannot expose my weakness to the Enemy (tho I believe they are pretty well informed of every thing that passes) by telling this, and that man who are daily pointing out this—that—and t'other place, of all the motives that govern my actions, notwithstanding I know what will be the consequence of not doing it—namely, that I shall be accused of inattention to the publick Service—& perhaps with want of Spirit to prosecute it.—But this shall have no effect upon my Conduct. I will steadily (as far as my judgement will assist me) pursue such measures as I think most conducive to the Interest of the cause, and rest satisfied under any Obloquy that shall be thrown, conscious of having discharged my Duty to the best of my abilities.

I am much obliged to you however, as I shall be to every Gentleman, for pointing out any measure which is thought conducive to the publick good, and chearfully follow any advice which is not inconsistent with, but corrispondant to, the general Plan in view, & practicable under such particular circumstances as govern in cases of the like kind.—In respect to point Alderton, I was no longer ago than Monday last, talking to Gen¹ Thomas on this head, and proposing to send Col° Putnam down to take the distances &c, but considered it could answer no end but to alarm, & make the Enemy more vigilant, unless we were in a condition to possess the Post to effect. I thought it as well to postpone the matter a while.

                        I am Sir
                                Yʳ Very Hᵇˡᵉ Servᵗ
                                            G. WASHINGTON.

[Addressed: "To | the Honᵇˡᵉ | J. Palmer | Watertown."]

Samuel Adams to James Warren.

                                        Philadᵃ. Nov: 14. 1775.

Dear Sir.
    I wrote to you a few days ago by Fessenden and then promised to write you again by Dr Morgan who is so obliging as to take the Care of this Letter. The Dr. though not yet arrived to the Age of forty has long sustained the Character of learned and is very eminent in the Profession of Physick and Surgery, and I dare say will fill the place to which he is appointed with Dignity.
    You will find him to be an agreeable Acquaintance.
    I have not time to write you a long Letter and indeed if I had I ought not to do it, for I believe my last effectually tired your Patience.
    I will only tell you that an Account is just come from Virginia, that Dunmore had Landed a Number of Men in Hampton whereupon a Scuffle ensued, with the Loss of fifty on his Side, besides the sinking of one of his Tenders—We wait with Impatience for a Confirmation of this Story—
                            I am in haste
                                Your affectionate Friend
                                            S. ADAMS.

[Addressed: "To | The Honᵇˡ. James Warren Esq | at | Watertown"
"Favored by | Dr: Morgan."]

John Langdon to Josiah Bartlett.

Col: Bartlett.   Portsm°: Feby: 26. 1776.
        Dear Sʳ.
    Things are pretty much in the same Situation as they were, at my last writing you,—not one word about *independence*, am ready to think he's gone out of Town, and those gentlemen who kept him Company while in Town, seem rather ashamed of them Selves—Inclosed you have a Draught of our harbor, or rather, a sketch, by which you have a Tolerable view of the Channel, and the place where the Ship is built,—after makeing what use of it you please, you may present it to my Friend Mr: Wharton, by which he may see what a safe Harbour he sends his flower to.—I have got no Draught of the Ship as yet.—but, we are going on with one of our own Drawing, by the Dimentions which I bro't down. pray Bring me down every Necessary from the Committee. do'nt Cramp my Genius, and the ship shall be Launched

soon—my kind Regards to all, and Believe me to be with Respect—Your Friend & H^{bl}: Servt.

J^{No}. LANGDON.

[Addressed: "Honl: Josiah Bartlett Esq: | Member of Congress | Philadelphia."]

Portion of an imperfect Letter of Samuel Adams to Joseph Palmer.

Some Advantages arose to our Colony by the Congress adopting the Army raised in New England the last Spring; but among other Circumstances attending it, this was one, namely, that it being now a Continental Army, the Gentlemen of all the Colonies had a Right to and put in for a Share in behalf of their Friends in filling up the various Offices. By this Means, it was thought, that military Knowledge & Experience as well as the military Spirit would spread through the Colonies; and besides, that they would all consider themselves the more interested in the Success of our Army, and in providing for its Support. But then there was less Room for Persons belonging to the Colonies which had first raised the Army, who were well worthy of Notice. Many of our Friends were discontented who did not advert to this as the true Cause why they were not promoted. * * * * *

I heartily congratulate you upon the sudden and important Change of our Affairs, in the Removal of the Barbarians from the Capital. We owe our grateful Acknowledgements to him, who is, as he is frequently stiled in Sacred Writ, "The Lord of Hosts." We have not yet been informed with Certainty what Course the Enemy have steered.—I hope we shall be upon our Guard against future Attempts. Will not Care be immediately taken to fortify the Harbour, and thereby prevent the Entrance of Ships of War ever hereafter?—But I am called off and must conclude abruptly.

Adieu my Friend, and be assured that I am affectionately

<table>
<tr><td>To</td><td>Yours,</td><td>S. ADAMS.</td></tr>
<tr><td>Genl: Palmer.</td><td></td><td>Phila. Apr. 1776.</td></tr>
</table>

John Adams to Joseph Palmer.

Philadelphia April 12. 1776.

Sir,

We begin to make some little Figure here in the Naval Way. Capt: Barry was fitted out here a few days ago in a sixteen Gun Brig, and put to Sea by the Roebuck Man of War which lies in Delaware River, and after he got without the Capes fell in with a Tender belonging to the Liverpool Man of War, and took her after an Engagement of two Glasses—She had 8 Carriage Guns and a Number of Swivells. One Thing remarkable is that four of her Guns are marked Liverpool, which shows that Guns are not very plenty with them otherwise the Liverpool would not have Spared any Part of hers.

I long to hear what Fortifications are preparing for Boston Harbour.—I cant but Think that Row Gallies would be of excellent Use. They might dodge about behind the Islands in that Harbour and into Shoal Water, in such a Manner, that the Weight of their Metal, and the Certainty of their Shoot, and the Place, between Wind & Water, at which They would be levell'd, would render them terrible to large Ships. Fire, carried upon Rafts and in Small Vessells, I should think would be very troublesome to these Gentry. I cannot bear the Thought of their ever getting into Boston again, or into that Harbour.—I would willingly contribute my share, that indeed would be but little, towards any Expense, nay I would willingly go and work myself upon the Fortifications if that was necessary.

Where will the Cloud burst next? Are they gone to Halifax? Will they divide their Force? Can they do that with Safety? Will they attempt Quebec? or will they come to New York? or will they come to Philadelphia, or go farther South, to Virginia, or one of the Carolinas? or, which I Sometimes suspect is more probable than any other Supposition, will they linger out the Summer in Halifax, like Lord Loudoun and themselves, fighting Mock Battles and acting Grubstreet Plays? I should dread this, more than their whole Force applied to any Part of the Continent.

I really think this would be the best Game they can play with such a Hand as they have, for upon my Word I am almost enough elated to boast that We have high, low, & Jack in our Hands, and we must be bad Gamesters indeed if We loose the Game.

You and the rest of my Friends are so busy I presume in purifying Boston of Small Pox, and another Infection which is much more malignant, I mean Toryism, and I hope in fortifying the Harbour, that I have reconciled myself, to that State of Ignorance, in which I still remain of all the Particulars, discovered in Boston.

Am very desirous of knowing if I could, what Quantities of Salt Petre come in, and what Progress is made in the Manufacture of it, and of Cannon & Musquitts, and especially the Powder Mills—have you Persons who understand the Art of making Powder?

Your friend
JOHN ADAMS.

Joseph Palmer Esq.

William Floyd to John McKesson.

Phila: May 9. 1776.

Dear Sr.

I have this morning Rec^d. a letter from Thomas Everit acquainting that he was offering to his Creditors the payment of one half Down provided he Could have letter of licence for two years and half, if there is no better Chance and the Creditors in General agree to it, I believe you had as good Do it in my behalf. But I leave the matter wholly with you to Conduct it as you would your own, and I shall be Content—two Men of War yesterday came up the River with some tenders and prize vessels with them between Wilmington and Chester, they were met by 13 Roegalleys of this place when a Battle Ensued which lasted most all the afternoon, with very heavy fireing on Both Sides. I have not heard the Galleys have suffered any Damage, the Roe Buck which is the largest Ship was Obliged to Stop the Bullet holes Round her Side and at highwater Ran aground: while the men of War was Engaged, our vessel the Wasp went out of Wilmington River and Retook one of the prize vessels, the provence Ship mounting 16 or 18 guns full maned is gone to the Assistance of the Galleys. We have no news this morning from them But expect every moment to hear.

The preparations which are making By our Enemies on the other side the water from the Intelligence we have, appears to be Very Considerable, which makes it Necessary that all the Collonies should be in a Situation best Calculated to Exert its whole Strength. I think it Cannot be long before our provencial Congress will think it Necessary to take up Some more

Stable form of Government than what is now Exercised in that provence. the two Carolinas have Done it, and Virginia I expect will soon Do the Same. As to Commissioners Coming to treat of peace we have little or no hopes of it therefore we ought to be in a Situation to preserve our Liberties another way—   my Compliments

to all friends. I am S^r your

Most Obe^t.

W^m. FLOYD.

[Addressed : " To | John McKesson Esquire | at | New York " " Free W Floyd "]

Elbridge Gerry to Joseph Palmer.

Philadelphia May 31. 1776.

Dear Sir,

The Conviction which ye late Measures of Administration have brot to ye Minds of doubting Persons has such an Effect, that I think ye Colonies cannot long remain an independent depending People, but that they will declare themselves as their Interest & Safety have long required, entirely separated from ye prostituted Government of G Britain. Upon this Subject I have wrote to our Friend Col: Orne & beg leave to refer you thereto— The principal object of our attention at this important Time I think should be ye Manufacturing Arms, Lead & Cloathing, & obtaining Flints, for I suppose since ye Measures adopted by North Carolina and Virginia that there cannot remain a Doubt with our Assembly of ye propriety of declaring for Independency and therefore that our Tho'ts will be mostly directed to ye Means for supporting it. Powder & Cannon are so successfully manufactured that if ye Spirit continues & with sufficient Encouragement for ye Manufacturer I think We may be sure of full Supplies.—With respect to Arms then, is it not necessary that each Assembly should give such Encouragement as will effectually answer ye purpose ? I was of opinion last fall that twelve Dollars should be given for all that should be brot to the Commissary in Consequence of ye Resolve then issued by ye Court, but since that was not ye opinion of ye Members in General & We are now greatly in Want of this Article would it not be a good plan to exempt from ye Duties of War all Manufacturers of fire Arms, to give a premium to them for each Apprentice which they shall take & Journeyman that they shall employ, & thirteen or fourteen Dollars for all that shall be delivered agreeable to ye former Resolve in twelve Months. Surely when ye Success of our Measures so much depends on obtaining the Article We shall not hesitate to give such Encouragement as will obtain it with as good Success as We have heretofore ye Article of Saltpetre.

The Lead you have before attended to and I hope you will pursue ye plan of carrying on ye Works at North Hampton. If a Manufacturer is Wanted I apprehend the Colony of Virginia will spare Us one. They sent to Europe for several & are now successfully carrying on ye Works in that Colony. Pray my Dear Sir pursue these objects as of ye greatest Importance.

Flints I think must be imported, & Cloathing may be manufactured if ye Inhabitants are timely apprized thereof. Would it not be well to recommend to them at large to exert themselves for obtaining by their manufactures a Sufficiency of Woolen and Linnen for ye ensuing Year, & also for ye Assembly to cause a Sufficient Number of Blankets, Coats &c to be made for ye Soldiers agreeable to ye Method pursued ye last Year? The Men must be well fed, cloathed, armed, and payed or You can never oblige them to do their Duty.

Our Friends Major Hawley ye Speaker, Genl. Orne & Mr: Sullivan I think will assist & promote these Measures, if you think it convenient to suggest ye Same.

I hope that one or more Cannon Forges will be encouraged in our Colony, and with Respect to Cloathing think that after this Year our Trade will plentifully supply us.—I remain Sir with sincere Regard for your Self and all our Friends   Your most obed^t &

Very humb^e Servt.
ELBRIDGE GERRY.

P. S. If Manufacturers can be obtained without sending to Virginia It will save much Time & Expence, as ye Works are far beyond ye Alleghany Mountains.

[Addressed : " Hon^l Joseph Palmer Esq: | at | Boston | Massachusetts Bay "
" On ye Service of ye united | Colonies | E. Gerry."]

J. Rutledge to the President of the Provincial Council of North Carolina.

Sir,

The Bearer, Mr. Page, who is sent, Express, to your Colony & Virginia, & to the Cont^l Congress, by Genl Lee, and myself, can give you the particulars of the Action of the 28th Instant, between the British Fleet, & our Fort on Sullivan's Island, of which he was an Eye-Witness—I therefore refer you to him, & have only to request, & entreat, that you will let us have, what powder you can possibly spare, having expended a large Quantity in that Action, our Stock being small, that Article being essential, & understanding that a very large Quantity is lately arrived in your Colony. I have no doubt that you will, most readily, serve Us, and the common Cause, in this Matter & with the utmost Expedition. Sending it in Waggons, will certainly, be expensive, but, that is now an Object of no Consequence. The Consumption by Cannon, is amazing—therefore, pray Sir, let us have what you can, for the Scene seems fixed here.

I am Sir
Yr. obed: & very hble: Servt
J. RUTLEDGE,
Chas Town   So. Carolina,
June 30, 1776.

To the Honble the Presid^t of
the Provincial Council of
North Carolina.

John Witherspoon to the President of the New-Jersey Convention.

Philadelphia July 3^d 1776.

Sir,

This afternoon Mr: Philip Livingston of New York told me that one of our Delegates at Burlington desired him to tell me that Mr: Franklin was carried no farther than Hackinsack and refused to go any farther. I spoke to Mr: Hancock of our number after, who gave me the enclosed Letter to you & expressed great Surprise that the Guard we sent with him had not proceeded straightway to Gov: Trumbull.   Possibly you may have already taken order in this Matter: if not I hope it will be done immediately.

The Congress this Day read your Letter and ordered a Battallion to March to Monmouth and have also directed that the Militia of three Counties of Pennsylvania intended for part of the flying Camp should rendezvous at Brunswick and be there as soon as possible.

I am Sir, Your most obd^t
humble servant
JNO: WITHERSPOON.

[Addressed: "The Honble the President of | the Convention of New Jersey at | Burlington."
" Public Service."]

Abraham Clark to Samuel Tucker.

Philadelphia July 9th 1776.

Sir,
   Your Letter of the 6th Inst: wherein you mention the want of Ammunition was yesterday before Congress.   Upon Motion of your Delegates four Tons were Ordered to be sent immediately, on Continental Acc^t for the use of the Militia who March out to guard the Province untill the Flying Camp is formed, or for the use of the flying Camp if not expended before they take the field.   I have the Pleasure to Assure you Congress pay particular Attention to the Defence of New Jersey, and hitherto have denied us nothing which we have Asked for that Purpose—they look upon our Province in great danger of being ravaged by the Enemy, and it is hoped you will not esteem it so far free from danger as to make your Continuing together unnecessary.   It is indeed a busy Season, but we have a busy Enemy near us, and from the best intelligence Lord Howe is hourly expected to Arrive with 20.000 Troops—these with what have Already Arrived will make a formidable Army, and requires the utmost exertion of the Middle Colonies to Oppose them.   I expect the Militia of Phil^a will begin to March to day—and from Acc^{ts} the Colony of Connecticut, are sending forward the strength of the Colony.   I am

Sir, Your most Obedient
Hum: serv^t

Samuel Tucker Esq: ABRA CLARK.

[Addressed: "To—The Honorable | Samuel Tucker Esqr | President of the New Jersey | Congress | at | Trenton."
" Free | Abra Clark."]

From Francis Hopkinson.

Philadelphia 23 July 1776.

Sir,
   I beg leave to submit to the Consideration of your House the Propriety of passing an Ordnance for the Regulation of *Elections* in our Province.   What I have principally in View is the collecting of Votes by *Ballot* only, and providing effectual Means for the Prevention of Fraud in Elections.   This is undoubtedly the most equitable Way of ascertaining

the Choice of the People, and I am confident would be very acceptable to our Constituents. Elections are now of greater Importance, if possible, than heretofore: because by your late excellent Constitution the Source of all Government originates with the People at large. I thought it my Duty to suggest this Hint, and hope it will be deemed worthy the attention of the House.

I have, further to request that the House would be so good as to furnish their Delegates with printed Copies of your new Constitution, and with such other Ordinances & Regulations as you may pass, from Time to Time. We should likewise be glad of a Copy of that part of your Minutes which ascertains what Number of Delegates shall represent the Province in Congress. I am told you have made one Delegate sufficient for this Purpose: but as I have no good Authority for this Opinion and was the other Day the only Member from Jersey attending in Congress, I was in great Doubt as to the Propriety of giving my Vote.

With great Respect to the Honble. Convention
I am Sir,
Your very humble Servant
FRAS. HOPKINSON.

From John Armstrong.

Charlestown 21ˢᵗ August 1776.

Sir:
General Lee now in Georgia, apprehending that Two Ton of Gun Powder additional to their present little Stock, will be necessary for the farther encouragement & Safety of that Colony, has desired I would in the first instance apply to President Rutledge for, and forward to him the Quantity mentioned above, and earnestly request your Honor, as I now do, That the said two Ton may be replaced by the Government of North Carolina, as by this conveyance I make the same requisition of Governor Henry, that the like quantity be forwarded from Virginia for the particular use of yʳ Government. The General informs me by what he calls the best authority that a large quantity hath lately arrived in Maryland & Virginia.

To this requisition Sir, which claims no other authority than the generous Zeal & good Sense of that body where you preside, I should fail to add, farther than that I am with great truth

Yʳ honorˢ Most Obedᵗ
humble Servant
JOHN ARMSTRONG
Bʳ General.

Silas Deane to Count de Vergennes.

Paris Nov: 20. 1776.

May it please your Excellency,
In pursuance of the Orders of the honorable Congress, to me expressed by Letters, bearing date, the 8ᵗʰ of July last and of the 7ᵗʰ of August following, I have the honor to deliver your Excellency, the enclosed Declaration of the independence of the United States of North America, and to inform you that by the first of said Letters, the Congress appears to have been unanimous in this important resolution: in the last their Committee say,

" The Congress has taken into consideration the heads of a Treaty to be proposed to France, but as they are not yet concluded upon, we cannot say more of them per this conveyance." They also say " In the different Colonies we have now near Eighty Thousand Men in the pay of Congress: The Declaration of Independence meets with universal Approbation, and the people seem everywhere animated still more by it in defence of their Country."

I will not detain your Excellency longer, than just to observe, that by the first Letter, dated July 8th which must have been intercepted, it appears that the Congress took measures, immediately after declaring their independancy, to have the same announced in Europe, and first of all to the Court of France: and that by the latter it appears, they were preparing such propositions for an Alliance as might be agreeable to your Court: but the variety of business before them, with the attention to the critical situation of the two opposite Armies must undoubtedly have for some Time retarded their Completing their Deliberations on so important a subject, and when compleated, the difficulty of transmitting the result may Acc[t] for the particulars not being arrived.

I have the honor of being with the greatest respect

Your Excellency's most Obed[t]
and very humble Servt:
S. DEANE.

To His Excellency,
    Compte de Vergennes.

From Richard Henry Lee.

Philadelphia May 26 1777.

Dear General,

I well know your attachment to Men of worth, and I am sure it will not be esteemed the less because it comes recommended by me. I therefore, with pleasure introduce to your acquaintance and civilities the Bearer Mr: Demmere a Gentleman of Georgia, who comes to the Army with a strong desire of becoming a part of it.

Brigadier Gen: Howe of Carolina recommends this Gentleman to me as a person of great spirit and zeal in the American cause, and one whose activity and influence has served it much.

Your pamphlets are ready and I will contrive them by the first safe conveyance.

I am, with great regard,

dear Sir, Your most affectionate and obedient
RICHARD HENRY LEE.

John Penn and Cornelius Harnett to Richard Caswell.

York Town Nov[r] 2nd 1777.

Sir:

By an express who was going to Williamsburg last week we Informed you of the report that General Burgoyne and his whole Army had surrendered themselves prisoners of War to General Gates. Yesterday Col[o]: Wilkinson arrived here, which enables us to enclose you a Copy of the Articles of Convention, which circumstance we hope will be followed by others of equal Importance soon.

General Clinton with 4 or 5000 from the City of York had got possession of Fort Montgomery and had passed so far up the N[o] River as to burn the little town of Kingston: they were within a few days of Albany. General Burgoyne had twelve days Provision, and in strong Ground well fortified; in such a situation the above was a most fortunate event for us.

General Gates is exerting himself against the rest of the British Soldiers in that Quarter; our Troops are in high spirits, having been successful in every engagement since the evacuation of Ticonderoga.

We have received no accounts from Genl: Washington since our last to you, which we expect will be delivered to you before this, as we wrote to George Wythe Esq. in Williamsburg requesting that he would Immediately send off our letter by an express & that your Excellency would take care to have the expense paid.

Inclosed is a Resolve of Congress appointing the eighteenth day of December for a General thanksgiving throughout the United States. In our last we sent a copy of all the money that has been paid for the Use of North Carolina, also several other resolves relating to the recruiting business.

We shall take care to give you the earliest account of whatever change may happen in our affairs. We have no newspapers to inclose for want of a press being established in this Town, however we expect one soon. We are with due Respect

Sir Your obed^t Servts.

We hope to get over the Confederation in
   a Fortnight, we shall transmit a Copy to
   your Excellancy as soon as that event
   happens without loss of time. J. Penn
J. Penn,
Corn^s Harnett.

C. Harnett.

[Addressed : " To His Excellency | Richd Caswell."]

William Whipple to Josiah Bartlett.

Portsmouth 12 July 1778.

My Dear Sir,
Your much esteemed Favour of the 20 ulti° is now before me. The evacuation of Philadelphia is an event I had been some weeks expecting to hear of. I hope (with you) that Congress may find some place more commodious than where you now are, but I think, was I with you I should not wish to go to Philad^a till the hot weather was over, nor then if a better place could be found, which in my Opinion is not very difficult; but that is a matter not for me to Judge of, nor is it of much importance where they set, so long as they continue to act with that firmness which is so conspicuous in their conduct towards the British Commissioners, a conduct that must do them Eternal Honor. No transaction of Congress ever gave more General satisfaction in this Quarter.

We had Yesterday some imperfect acco^t of a Battle fought on the 28th Ulti° in which it is said the Enemy left 300 on the field & our army took 100 Prisoners, our loss not ascertained. This Victory does not satisfy the *most* sanguine among us; others (with whom I place myself) think this with *better* will do. I hope we shall soon have a particular acc^t of all the movements, &c.

As I am happy in agreeing with you in Opinion in general I should be exceedingly Glad if there was a coincidence in our sentiments respecting Privateering. I agree with you that the privateers have much distressed the trade of our Enemies, but had there been no privateers, is it not probable there wo^d have been a much larger number of Public ships than has been fitted out? which might have distressed the Enemy nearly as much & furnished these States with necessaries on much better terms than they have been supplied by Privateers,—however I will not contend with you about the advantages or disadvantages that have been the consequence of that business; all I wish to convince you of is, that it is *now* attended with the most pernicious Consequences, which there would be no need of my undertaking, if you were only to pass three months in this, or any other town where the spirit for Privateering rages with such violence as it does here. No kind of Business can so effectually introduce Luxury, Extravagance, & every kind of Dissipation, that tend to the Destruction of the Morals of People. Those who are actually engaged in it soon lose every Idea of right & wrong, & for want of an opportunity of gratifying their insatiable avarice with the property of the Enemies of their Country will without the least compunction seize that of her Friends; thus far I am sure you wo^d agree with me had you the opportunity before mentioned of making your observations: but perhaps you may say these are evils attendant on this business to society in general. I will allow that to be the case, but then it must be allowed they will operate with more violence in this Country in its present unsettled state than in a country where all the Powers of Government can be vigorously exercised. But besides these there are many other mischiefs that attend this business peculiar to these states in our present circumstances. Some of the towns in this State have been obliged to give 400 Doll^s Bounty a Man to men to serve 3 or 4 months at Road Island exclusive of what's allowed by the State. This is wholly owing to privateering. The Farmer cannot hire a laborer for less than 30 or 40 Dol^s pr. Month, and in the Neighborhood of this town 3 or 4 Dol^s pr day and very difficult to be had at that; this naturally raises the price of Provision. Indian Corn is not to be purchased under 6 Dol^s pr Bushel. There is at this time 5 Privateers fitting out here which I suppose will take 400 men; these must be by far the greater part Countrymen, for the seamen are chiefly gone & most of them are in Hallifax Goal.—Besides all this You may depend no public ship will ever be maned while there is a Privateer fitting out; the reason is plain—those people who have the most influence with seamen think it their interest to discourage the Public service because by that they promote their own interest viz: Privateering—; in order to do this effectually, every officer in the public service (I mean in the Navy) is treated with general contempt. A man of any feeling cannot bear this; he therefore to avoid those indignities quits the service & is immediately courted to go a Privateering & highly caressed. By this means all the Officers that are worth employing will quit the service, and You'll have the Navy (if you think it worth while to keep up that show) officered by Tinkers, Shoemakers & Horse-Jockeys—and no Gentleman worth employing will accept a Commission. This you may depend will soon be the case unless Privateering is discouraged and the Business of the Marine in this department is more attended to & conducted with more regularity. In short it would be much better to set fire to the ships now in port than to pretend to fit them for sea, for as matters now are (if I am rightly informed, and my authority is very good) the public are at an amazing Expence to procure men for privateers, for if they, the public, get two men, one day, they are sure to loose four, the next, who take care to carry off with them the advanced pay &c.—I think I have given you a long chapter on Privateering, much longer than I intended when I began.   I have said the more on the subject as it is the last time I shall trouble you with my sentiments of that business.   And as I have got to the end of the sheet shall conclude this long scrawl with my best wishes for Your Health & Happiness & with the fullest assurance that I am

Your very affect. Friend &c.

To Col. Bartlett.   Wm WHIPPLE.

Horatio Gates to Jonathan Trumbull.

White plains 5th August. 1778.

Sir.

With great regret I part with Colonel Jonathan Trumbull, who does me the Favour to present you with this Letter—The ease, and Seeming indifference, with which Congress have submitted to the resignation of your Three Valuable Sons, I confess astonishes me—when such Men undertake the Public Service, they are entitled to every deference that can be Shewn.— We entered into this War to preserve our Freedom, & to establish that Republican Equality, without which, Freedom is but a Name,—in my Opinion, The British Fleet, & Army, will leave Our Coast the Moment they can do it with a good appearance of Safety—but Confederation is not Signed : & what with the Arts of the Wicked, The Arguments of The Designing, I fear it will never be Signed.   Wo then to America, for the last War will be worse than the First.—I fear every thing, but hope The Great Governor of Heaven, & Earth, will give Peace, & Freedom to The United States.   The Colonel, & I, have conversed Freely upon most matters, he will tell you my unreserved Sentiments upon these great Points.

Permit me Sir to return you my Sincere Thanks for the Great Assistance you have at all Times given me when I had the Honor to Command The Army in this Department : I shall most Gratefully remember them—with the most perfect Esteem for Yourself & Family believe me Sir

Your Excellency's
Most Obedient

His Excellency   humble Servant
   Governor Trumbull.   HORATIO GATES.

William Whipple to Josiah Bartlett.

Portsmouth Sept: 13. 1778.

My Dear Sir,

Since my last I am informed that Mr: Wentworth has returned home in a bad state of health and that your ill health will not permit your tarry long after him : however as the weather is growing cool I hope you will be able to tarry till you are relieved.   Who you will be relieved by, is impossible for me to say at present.   I received a letter Yesterday from the Committee informing me that I was appointed at the last session of the Genl. Court, and requiring an answer which they shall have in a day or two ; tho' I have not yet fully determined what my answer will be, but at present am inclined to think it will be in the Negative.   It certainly will be unless I can have assurance of better treatment than I have heretofore received.—Could I be made sensible that I could be essentially serviceable to My Country I think I co^d: with pleasure forego many private advantages, but no consideration can be a sufficient inducement to me to submit to abuse from that very Body who I am sacrificing my interest to save.—That I have

been treated very Scurrilously you are a witness.   Such treatment in future
I am determined to guard against.   I shall therefore wait on the Committee
tomorrow or next day : a conference with them will determine me, the result you shall have by the first oppor.

The Count D'Estaing is fitting his fleet at Boston from whence they are
obliged to send here for all their Masts & timbers : a considerable quantity
have been sent round & more going,—I suppose by the time this Fleet is
ready for sea it will be time for them to go to the West Indies, so we can
expect no great good from them.   We are told Byron has arrived at Sandy
Hook but there is no Acc. of his being followed by a Brest Fleet.—This
you will receive by Major Gardner, who has business with the Clothier
Gen: ; as you are acquainted with this Gentln: he needs no farther introduction from me.   You no doubt will render him any services he may need.
To him I must beg leave to refer you for any particulars this way, and by
his return I hope to be furnished with such occurrences as you may suppose
will afford any Gratification to Your

Very Affectionate Friend &
Most Humbl. Servt:
Wm. WHIPPLE.

Col: Bartlett.

John Penn to William Woodford.

Philad. Dec 6th. 1778.

Dear Sir,

Yesterday the Sentence against General Lee was confirmed, by a
great Majority, only two votes against approving : he has been Complaining
of every body, I suppose this will make him outrageous.

It is very uncertain whether the enemy will Evacuate New York this
winter, tho' many Gentln. think they will : a considerable number sailed
from New York to Augustine, to reinforce the Garrison there.   I expect
Congress will, in a few days agree on some plan for appreciating the Currency.   I have only time to add that I am very Respectfully

Dear Sir
Your obt servt.
J. PENN.

Genl: Woodford.

[Addressed : " To General Woodford | Fredericksburg | Virginia."
" Mr. Shannon will be so good as to | leave this letter at Fredericks-
burg | J. Penn."
" Favrd. by | Mr: Shannon "]

From Thomas Nelson, Jr.

Williamsburg Sept: 16. 1781.

Dear Sir.

The difficulty in procuring Vessels for the transportation of Flour is so
great that I fear our supplies will come in but slowly unless some aid can
be obtained from the French Fleet.   If an empty Transport or two could
be spared for this purpose we should find them of infinite advantage.   That
part of the Country whence we expect our immediate Supplies has been so
fully in possession of the Enemy that they have destroyed almost all the
Vessels.   I intended to have done myself the Honor of waiting on you but
am prevented by indisposition.   I am Dr. Sr:

Your obt. Servt
Tho. NELSON Jr:

KNOX'S DIARY DURING HIS TICONDEROGA EXPEDITION.

From the KNOX MANUSCRIPTS, by permission of the Directors of the NEW-ENGLAND HISTORIC, GENEALOGICAL SOCIETY.

A MONG the MSS. of Gen. Knox presented to the New-England Historic, Genealogical Society by his grandson Rear-Adm. Henry Knox Thatcher, U.S.N., is a leather covered pocket memorandum book which, it is not unlikely, formed a portion of the stock of Henry Knox, bookseller, at the time he so unceremoniously quitted Boston in disguise, and only just in season to participate in the memorable affair of Bunker's Hill.

This timeworn relic contains a fragment of a hasty diary kept by Knox during his expedition to Ticonderoga, the object of which was to transfer the serviceable portion of the cannon and other ordnance captured in that fortress to the camp of Washington where it was so greatly needed for the successful prosecution of the siege of Boston. It is perhaps needless to say that this project was his own, and that its prompt and skilful execution at once stamped him as a man fertile in expedients, enterprising, sagacious, persevering, and one not to be deterred by any obstacle however formidable. These qualities had from the first attracted the notice of Washington, and together with his amiable, warm-hearted and generous personal traits won for him the love and esteem of that great and good man, whose sincere friendship for him ended only with his life. It was at the suggestion of Washington that Congress appointed him to the command of the artillery, a position which he filled most admirably, and in which he earned the rank of major general. From 1785 to 1795 he was secretary of war.

An interesting episode of this expedition was the chance meeting of Knox with André, whose sad fate makes so conspicuous a chapter in our revolutionary annals. André was on his way to Lancaster, Pa., on parole, having been made a prisoner at St. John's. They passed the night together in a cabin at the foot of Lake George, and conversed as they reclined upon the floor until long past midnight. A strong feeling of mutual regard sprang up between them, and at parting on the following morning, each made himself known to the other. Their next meeting was under less auspicious circumstances, Knox, then a member of the tribunal sitting in judgment upon him, having the hard task of passing sentence of death upon this amiable and intelligent but unfortunate young officer.

Knox's younger brother William accompanied him and was of great service in the expedition. The vicissitudes attending it are depicted in the diary, and are also alluded to in his letters to Washington from which we make a few extracts :

"Fort George, Dec. 17, 1775. * * It is not easy to conceive the difficulties we have had in getting them (the Cannon) over the lake owing to the advanced season of the year and contrary winds. Three days ago it was very uncertain whether we should have gotten them until next spring; but now please God they must go. I have had made 42 exceeding strong sleds, and have provided 80 yoke of oxen to drag them as far as Springfield where I shall get fresh cattle to carry them to camp. The route will be from here to Kinderhook, from thence to Great Barrington and down to Springfield. * * I expect to begin to move them to Saratoga on Wednesday or Thursday next trusting that between this and then we shall have a fine fall of snow which will enable us to proceed further and make the carriage easy."

"Albany, Jan. 5, 1776. I was in hopes that we should have been able to have had the cannon at Cambridge by this time. The want of snow detained us some days, and now a cruel thaw hinders from crossing Hudson river which we are obliged to do four times from Lake George to this town. The first severe night will make the ice on the river sufficiently strong; till that happens the cannon and mortars must remain where they are. These inevitable delays pain me exceedingly as my mind is fully sensible of the importance of the greatest expedition in this case."

Knox's indomitable energy and perseverance were at length rewarded, and on the 24th of January, 1776, he had the satisfaction of reporting in person to the commander-in-chief who warmly congratulated him on the important service he had rendered the army and the country. What follows is well known. The cannon and mortars were speedily placed in position, and Dorchester Heights so effectually menaced the foe, that he beat a hasty retreat, and Boston was for all time, let us hope, freed from her invaders.

1775   DIARY.

Nov. 20. Went from Worcester to go to New York, reach'd Western that night 30 m.

21. From Western to Hartford 44 m.

22. From Hartford to New Haven 40.

23. From Newhaven to Fairfield 28.

24. From Fairfield to Kingsbridge 56 miles.

25. From Kingsbridge to New York 14. Stay'd at New York 26. 27.

28th. Left New York[1] the Tuesday following and reach'd Crotons ferry 39½ miles.

29. From Crotons ferry to Poughkeepsie 44½.

30. From Poughkeepsie to Livingstons Manor 40.

Dec. 1. From Poughkeepsie to Albany 40 miles.

2. Stay'd at Albany.

3. Rode from Albany to Saratoga 35.

4. Sat out about 10 o'Clock,[2] from Saratoga to Fort George, 30 [miles] which place we reach'd 2 o'Clock.

---

[1] In another place in this book are memoranda of expenses in New York and elsewhere. Among them, under date of New York, Nov. 27, 1775, he makes this entry: "Glad to leave N. York, it being very expensive."

[2] "Sat out about 10 o'clock," seems to be an interlineation to be inserted here; but it may be an addition to the last entry.

5. We sat sail from Fort George to go over the lake about 10 o'Clock & having an exceeding fine passage reach'd the landing place belonging to Ticonderoga about half past five, and immediately went up to the fort Ticonderoga, 3 miles, the length of the lake being 38 miles;

6th. Employ'd in getting the Cannon from the fort on board a Gundaloe in order to get them to the bridge.

7th. Employ'd in getting the Cannon from the bridge to the landing at Lake George.

8. Ditto & mortars.

9th. Employ'd in loading the Scow, Pettianger & a Battoe. At 3 o'Clock in the afternoon sat sail to go down the lake in the Pettianger, the Scow in coming after us run aground we being about a mile ahead with fair wind to go down but unfair to help the Scow, the wind dying away we with the utmost difficulty reach'd Sabbath Day Point about 9 o'Clock in the evening— went ashore & warm'd ourselves by an exceeding good fire in an hut made by some *civil* Indians who were with their Ladies abed—they gave us some Venison, roasted after their manner which was very relishing—we warm'd

[Probably a leaf torn out.]

we had been there when one of the Battoes which had set out nearly the same time the same day that we had, allur'd by the view of the fire likewise came on shore, & the crew of which inform'd us that the Scow had run on a sunken rock but not in such a manner as to be irretrievable; that they had broken all the ropes which they had in endevoring to rouse her off, but was ineffectual; that they had sent up to the Fort for more ropes, & hands & intended in the morning to make another trial—& doubted not but that they would succeed. The crew of the Battoe after having sufficiently refresh'd themselves told me that, as they were not very deeply loaded, they intended to push for Fort George. I jump'd into the Boat & order'd my man to bring my baggage & we would go with them. Accordingly we sat out it being eleven o'Clock with a light breeze ahead the men row'd briskly, but we had not been out above an hour when the wind sprung up very fresh & directly against us. The men after rowing exceedingly hard for about four hours seem'd desirous of going ashore, to make a fire to warm themselves. I readily consented knowing them to be exceedingly weary. They made an Excessive fire having on perhaps one or two Cords of wood at a time there being very large quantities of dry wood ready cut. We warm'd ourselves sufficiently & took a Comfortable nap, laying with our feet to the fire. About half an hour before day break that is about a quarter after six we sat out and in six hours & a quarter of excessive hard pulling against a fresh head breeze we reach'd Fort George. On Monday the 11th I sent an Express to Squire Palmer of Stillwater to prepare a number of Sleds & oxen to drag the Cannon presuming that we should get there, & on Wednesday the 13th he came up & agreed to provide the necessary number of sleds & oxen & they to be ready by the first snow. On the 12th being very uneasy at not hearing of our little fleet we dispatch'd an Express boat about 2 o'Clock, but in the afternoon we receiv'd advice that on the morning of the 10th the Scow had gotten from off the rock on which she had run & with great difficulty had reach'd Sabbath Day Point—& on the same Night the wind being exceeding high the sea had beat in her in such a manner that she had sunk—this news was

[Leaves torn out]

on foot about 6 miles in the midst of an exceeding fine Snow— when Judge

Dewer [?] procur'd me a sleigh to go to Stillwater—after crossing the ferry we got with Considerable difficulty to Arch. McNeals Saratoga where we din'd & sat off about three o'Clock it still snowing exceeding fast & it being very deep after the utmost efforts of the horses we reach'd Ensign's about 8 Miles beyond Saratoga where we lodg'd.

26. In the morning the snow being nearly two feet deep we with great trouble reach'd about two miles we then procur'd Saddles & went to Stillwater, where we got a Sleigh to go to Albany, but the roads not being broken prevented our getting farther than New City, about 9 miles above Albany, where we lodg'd. In the morning we sat out & got about 2 miles, when our horses tir'd and refus'd to go any farther. I was then oblig'd to undertake a very fatiguing march of about 2 miles in snow three feet deep thro' the woods, there being no beaten path. Got to Squire Fisher's who politely gave me a fine breakfast & provided me with horses which served me as far as Col. Schuyler's, where I got a sleigh to carry me to Albany, which I reach'd about two o'Clock, almost perish'd with the Cold. In the afternoon waited on Gen'l Schuyler & spent the evening with him.

27. Sent off for Mr. Palmer to Come immediately down to Albany.

28th. Mr Palmer Came Down, & after a considerable degree of conversation between him & General Schuyler about the price the Genl offering 18s. 9d. & Palmer asking 24s. p' day for 2 Yoke of Oxen. The treaty broke off abruptly & Mr Palmer was dismiss'd. By reports from all parts the snow is too deep for the Cannon to set out, even if the Sleds were ready.

29th. General Schuyler agree'd with. Sent out his Waggon Master & other people to all parts of the Country to immediately send up their slays with horses suitable, we allowing them 12s. p' day for each pair of horses or £7 p' Ton for 62 miles.

The 31st, the Waggon master return'd the Names of persons in the different parts of the Country who had gone up to the lake with their horses in the whole amounting to near 124 pairs with Slays, which I'm afraid are not strong enough for the heavy Cannon, if I can Judge from the sample shown me by Genl Schuyler.

January 1st to the 4th employ'd in getting holes cut in the different crossing places in the river in order to Strengthen the Ice. This day the 4th arrived a brass 24 pounder & a small mortar. I this day sent a Letter to Genl Washington, one to Brig Genl Gates, also one to Capt Baylor and one to my lovely Lucy.

In the afternoon much alarm'd by hearing that one of the heaviest Cannon had fallen in to the river at Half Moon Ferry. This Genl Schuyler came & inform'd me just as I was going to sit down to Dinner. I immediately sent out for a Slay & went up to the Half Moon where I reach'd at Dusk, & not hearing of the others & fearing that they would meet the same fate, I sent off an express to Sloss's ferry, about 7 miles Distant, with a letter to Mr. Schuyler, informing him of my excessive surprize at the Careless manner in which he carried the Cannon over, without taking those precautions which by his Instructions he was bound to have done & by no means to attempt crossing where he was untill I came. The express return'd & inform'd that they had all got safely over. I then sent off another express to Mr Swartz to cross at Sloss's, as the Ice was so much stronger there than at Half Moon, the usual place of crossing.

5th. I went up the Mohawk river about seven miles, & then crossed over, on very weak Ice indeed for horses, & ran down along side the river untill we came to the falls, so famous in this part of the Continent & known by the name of the Cohoos falls. Those stupendous falls, inferior to none except the Grand one of Niagara, are form'd by the whole body of the Mohawk River falling at one pitch from a perpendicular of eighty feet. It is the most superb & affecting sight I ever saw. The river is about 4 or 500 Yards wide. The time I saw it was about 9 o'Clock in the morning, when the beams of the sun reflected on the whole Icy Scene around. Vast Icicles of twenty feet long and three or four feet thick hung in pendents from the neighboring rocks, which were form'd from the rain & melted snow falling from the neighboring heights, & a very severe frost coming up which arrested the Water in its fall, this ornamented the scene in a very particular manner. The water falling from such a height gave the water the look of milk. It look'd like one vast torrent of milk pouring from a stupendous height. Its fall occasion'd a very thick mist to arise, which look'd like a shower of rain, & I was told that in Summer time a perpetual rainbow was to be seen here. After having gaz'd & wonder'd for a long time I return'd to Albany, about 12 miles, from admiring the stupendous Works of nature & not a little humbl'd by thoughts of my own insignificance.

Sunday Jan. 7th. Albany. The Cannon, which the night before last came over at Sloss's ferry, we attempted to get over the ferry here, which we effected excepting the last, which fell into the River notwithstanding the precautions we took, & in its fall broke all the Ice for 14 feet around it. This was a misfortune as it retarded the dispatch which I wish'd to use in this business. We push'd the 10 Sleds on, which got over safe & then I went to getting the drown'd Cannon out, which we partly effected, but by reason of the nights coming could not do it entirely.

8th. Went on the Ice about 8 o'Clock in the morning & proceeded so cautiously that before night we got over three sleds & were so lucky as to get the Cannon out of the River, owing to the assistance the good people of the City of Albany gave, in return for which we christen'd her—The Albany.

The 9th. Got several spare slays also some spare string of horses, in case of any accident. After taking my leave of General Schuyler & some other of my friends in Albany, I sat out from there about twelve o'Clock & went as far as Claverac, about 9 Miles beyond Kinderhook. I first saw all the Cannon set out from the ferry opposite Albany.

10th. Reach'd No. 1, after having climb'd mountains from which we might almost have seen all the Kingdoms of the Earth.

11th. Went 12 miles thro' the Green Woods to Blanford. It appear'd to me almost a miracle that people with heavy loads should be able to get up & down such Hills as are here, with any thing of heavy loads. 11th. At Blanford we overtook the first division who had tarried here untill we came up, and refus'd going any further, on acco[tt] that there was no snow beyond five or six miles further in which space there was the tremendous Glasgow or Westfield mountain to go down. But after about three hours persuasion, I hiring two teams of oxen, they agreed to go.

MEMORANDA.[1]

	On board the Scow.		Pettianger.
6	18 pounders	1	barrell flints
3	13 Inch Mortars	1	brass 24 pounder
1	Barrell flints	2	Do Mortars 8 or 9 Inch

[1] See Drake's *Memorials of the Massachusetts Society of the Cincinnati*, pp. 544–5, for a more perfect inventory of Cannon, &c., brought from Ticonderoga.

1	Iron d° 9 Inch		*Mortars.*
23	Boxes Lead	1	$8\frac{1}{2}$
6	Royall Cohorns	1	$7\frac{1}{2}$ one Trunnion wanting
2	field peices 6 pound	1	$6\frac{1}{2}$ Iron
6	d° 4 d°	3	13 do
		1	10 do
42	Cannon of different Sizes	1	$10\frac{1}{4}$
16	Mortars Howitzers		

Howitzers.

Cohorns.

2	$5\frac{7}{10}$	} Brass	1	8
4	$4\frac{1}{2}$		1	$8\frac{1}{4}$

RECEIPTS.

Fort George Dec. 16. 1775

Rec^d of Henry Knox twenty six dollars which Capt John Johnson paid to different Carters for the use of their Cattle, in dragging Cannon from The Fort of Ticonderoga to the North Landing of Lake George

£10.8   Wm BROWN Junr Lieut

Blanford Jany 13. 1776

Rec^d of Henry Knox eighteen shillings lawful money for Carrying a Cannon weighing 24C. 3 from this Town to Westfield being 11 Miles

18s.   SOLOMON BROWN

DID THE AMERICAN COLONISTS DESIRE INDEPENDENCE?

LETTERS OF JOHN JAY AND JOHN ADAMS TO GEORGE A. OTIS.

Communicated by JEREMIAH COLBURN, A.M., of Boston.

THE following letters from John Jay and Ex-President John Adams to the translator of Botta's "History of the American Revolution" are copied from the originals in my possession. The letter of Mr. Jay is entirely autograph; but only the signature in that of Mr. Adams is in his handwriting.

These letters will be read with interest; for they give important information as to the state of feeling previous to the Revolution in the British American Colonies in regard to independence of the English crown.

Letter of John Jay.

Bedford, West Chester County, State of New York, 13th Jany 1821.
Sir

I have rec^d your Letter of the 23^d ult—expressing a Desire that Botta's History and your Translation of it, may have my approbation—And also that I would mention to you the most authentic of the Documents which are before the Public, relative to the negociations at Paris in 1782.

Having as yet rec^d and read *only* the *first* volume of the History, I cannot form, and consequently cannot express, an opinion of the whole work.

As to the *first* volume—there are in it certain assertions, Representations, and Suggestions, of which there are some which I believe to be *erroneous*, and others which I suspect to be inaccurate. Being too feeble either to write or to read much at a Time without Fatigue; I forbear to enumerate them. I will nevertheless, for your satisfaction, select and notice one of the most important—vizt.

That anterior to the Revolution, there existed in the Colonies a Desire of Independence.

The following extracts respect this Topic :—

Page 10. "The Love of the Sovereign and their ancient country, which the first colonists fnight have retained in their new Establishments, gradually diminished in the Hearts of their Descendants."

P. 11. "The greater part of the Colonists had heard nothing of Great Britain, excepting that it was a distant Kingdom, from which their ancestors had been barbarously expelled."

P. 12. "As the means of Constraint became almost illusory in the Hands of the Government, there must have arisen and gradually increased in the minds of the Americans, the Hope and with it the Desire to shake off the Yoke of English superiority." "The Colonists supported *impatiently* the superiority of the British Government."

P. 15. "Such was the State of the English colonies in America, such the *opinions* and *Dispositions* of those who inhabited them, about the *middle* of the Eighteenth century." "It was impossible that they should have remained ignorant of what they were capable ; and that the progressive Developement of national Pride should not have rendered the British Yoke *intolerable*."

P. 33. "Already those who were the most zealous for Liberty, or the most ambitious, had formed in the secret of their hearts the Resolution to shake off the Yoke of England whenever a favorable occasion should present. This Design was encouraged by the recent cession of Canada."

P. 199. "The Colonists looked upon (the Congress of 1774) as a convention of men who in some mode or other, were to deliver their country from the Perils that menaced it. The greater part believed that their ability &^c would enable them to obtain from the Government, a Removal of the Evils that oppressed them, and the Re-establishment of the ancient order of Things. Some others cherished the Belief, that they would find means to conduct the American nation to that Independence, which was the *first* and most ardent of their aspirations or rather the sole Object of that intense passion, which stung and tormented them, night and Day."

P. 314. "Both (Putnam and Ward) had declared themselves too openly in favor of Independence. The congress desired indeed to procure it, but withall in a propitious Time."

P. 388. Thus ceased, as we have related, the Royal Authority in the different Provinces. It was replaced progressively by that of the People ; that is by congresses or conventions extraordinary, that were formed in each Colony. But this was deemed insufficient by those, who *directed* the affairs of America—*their real* Object being *Independence*."

Explicit Professions and Assurances of Allegiance and Loyalty to the Sovereign (especially since the accession of King William) and of affection for the mother Country, abound in the Journals of the colonial Legislatures, and of the congresses and conventions, from early Periods to the second Petition of congress in 1775.

If those Professions and Assurances were sincere, they afford Evidence more than sufficient to invalidate the charge of our desiring and aiming at Independence.

If, on the other hand, those Professions and Assurances were factitious and deceptive, they present to the world an unprecedented Instance of long-continued, concurrent, and detestable Duplicity in the colonies. Our country does not deserve this odious and disgusting Imputation. During the course of my Life, and until after the second Petition of congress (in 1775), I never did hear any American, of any class, or of any Description, express a wish for the Independence of the colonies.

Few Americans had more or better means and Opportunities of becoming acquainted with the Sentiments and Disposition of the colonists relative to public affairs than the late Doct^r Franklin. In a letter to his son, dated the 22 March, 1775, he relates a conversation which he had with Lord Chatham in the preceding month of August. His Lordship having mentioned an opinion prevailing in England, that America aimed at setting up for itself as an independent State, the Doct^r thus expressed himself.

" I assured him, that having more than once travelled almost from one End of the continent to the other, and kept a great variety of company, eating, drinking and conversing with them freely, I never had heard, in any Conversation, from any Person, drunk or sober, the least Expression of a wish for a Separation ; or a Hint that such a Thing would be advantageous to America."

It does not appear to me necessary to enlarge further on this subject. It has always been, and still is, my Opinion and Belief, that our country was prompted and impelled to Independence by necessity and not by choice. They who know how we were *then* circumstanced, know from whence that necessity resulted.

It would indeed be extraordinary if a Foreigner, remote (like Mr Botta) from the best Sources of authentic Information, should in writing such a History, commit no mistakes. That Gentleman doubtless believed his narrations to be true. But it is not improbable that he sometimes selected his materials with too little apprehension of Error ; and that some of his Informers were too little scrupulous. This Remark derives a degree of Weight from the following Passage in the History, vizt :

General Montgomery " left a Wife, the Object of all his Tenderness, with several children, still Infants—a spectacle for their country, at once of Pity and Admiration. The State, from Gratitude towards their Father, distinguish^d them with every mark of Kindness and Protection."

I have been acquainted with General Montgomery's Widow from my Youth. The fact is, she never had a child.

In making the Translation, attention has doubtless been paid to the Rule that a Translator should convey into his Translation with Perspicuity and Precision, the Ideas of his Author, and no others; and express them, not literally, but in well adapted classical Language. How far your Translation is exactly correct, I am an incompetent Judge ; for, not understanding the Language of the original, I cannot examine and compare the Translation with it. Of the style and manner of the Translation, I think well.

Which are the most authentic Documents before the Public, relative to the negociations at Paris in 1782? is a question which I am not in capacity to answer. Many years have elapsed since I have read any of them ; and others have since been published, which I have not seen. Without a previous and careful Examination of each of them, it would be rash and unfair to give a Preference to either.

On receiving your *first* Letter, I conjectured that you was of the respectable Family of *your name* in Massachusetts ; and that conjecture appears from your *last* to have been well founded. If in going from Philadelphia to Boston, you should not find it inconvenient to take the Road through this Town, you will meet with a welcome Reception from

Sir your ob^t Servt

George Alexander Otis Esqr. John Jay.

The 2^d Vol. was brought here this Evening.

[Addressed : " George Alexander Otis, Esqr | Philadelphia."]

Letter of John Adams.

Montezillo, February 9th 1821.

Dear Sir

I thank you for your favour of the 29 January, and your Translation of Botta. I have not yet read it for I received it but yesterday, and reading is to me so laborious, and painful an occupation, that it requires a long time. But I cannot refrain from expressing the pleasure I have received from the reasoning of Mr. Jay, upon the passage from Botta—"That anteriour to the Revolution there existed in the Colonies a desire of Independence." There is great ambiguity in the expression, there existed in the Colonies a desire of Independence—it is true there always existed in the Colonies a desire of Independence of Parliament, in the articles of internal Taxation, and Internal policy ; and a very general if not a universal opinion, that they were Constitutionally entitled to it, and as general a determination if possible, to maintain, and defend it—but there never existed a desire of Independence of the Crown, or of general regulations of Commerce, for the equal and impartial benefit of all parts of the Empire.—It is true there might be times and circumstances in which an Individual, or few Individuals, might entertain and express a wish that America was Independent in all respects, but these were " rari nantes in gurgite vasto." For example in one thousand seven hundred and fifty six, seven, and eight, the conduct of the British Generals Shirley, Braddock, Loudon, Webb and Abercromby was so absurd, disastrous, and distructive, that a very general opinion prevailed that the War was conducted by a mixture of Ignorance, Treachery and Cowardice, and some persons wished we had nothing to do with Great Britain for ever. Of this number I distinctly remember, I was myself one, fully believing that we were able to defend ourselves against the French and Indians, without any assistance or embarrassment from Great Britain. In fifty eight and fifty nine, when Amherst and Wolfe changed the fortune of the War, by a more able and faithful conduct of it, I again rejoiced in the name of Britain, and should have rejoiced in it, to this day, had not the King and Parliament committed high Treason and Rebellion against America as soon as they had conquered Canada, and made Peace with France. That there existed a general desire of Independence of the Crown in any part of

America before the Revolution, is as far from the truth, as the Zenith is from the Nadir. That the encroaching disposition of Great Britain was early foreseen by many wise men, in all the States, would one day attempt to enslave them, by an unlimited submission to Parliament, and rule them with a rod of Iron ; that this attempt would produce resistance on the part of America, and an awful struggle was also foreseen but dreaded and deprecated as the greatest Calamity that could befal them. For my own part, there was not a moment during the Revolution, when I would not have given every thing I possessed for a restoration to the State of things before the Contest began, provided we could have had any sufficient security for its continuance. I always dreaded the Revolution as fraught with ruin, to me and my family, and indeed it has been but little better. I could entertain you with many little trifling anecdotes which though familiar and vulgar, would indicate the temper, feelings, and forebodings among the people, that I cannot write.

I see at the end of the Biography, of the Author, that Botta has written the Biography of John Adams.—I never saw, or heard of it before, but if he means me, it must be a curious mess, for he can certainly have no authentic information on the very insignificant subject.

I am Sir, Your obliged friend

George Alexander Otis, Esqre   and humble servant,

JOHN ADAMS.

BIOGRAPHICAL SKETCH OF JOSEPH P. MARTIN, OF PROSPECT, MAINE, A REVOLUTIONARY SOLDIER.

By the Hon. JOSEPH WILLIAMSON, A.M., of Belfast, Me.

JOSEPH P. MARTIN, Esq., a revolutionary soldier, died in Prospect, now Stockton, Maine, May 2, 1850, aged 90 years. He was the son of a Congregational clergyman in western Massachusetts,[1] but at the age of seven years went to reside with his maternal grandparents, in New Haven County, Conn. In the spring of 1776, when only sixteen years of age, he enlisted in the army of the revolution ; and excepting the interval of a few months, continued in active service until the close of the war. He shared largely in the hardships and perils of that eventful struggle. He was in several bloody battles, and witnessed the siege of Yorktown, and the surrender of Cornwallis. In 1830, he published a duodecimo volume entitled "A Narrative of the Adventures, Dangers and Sufferings of a Revolutionary Soldier,"[2] in which he gave an account of the various campaigns of the war. It is to be regretted that before sending this book to the press, he had not placed it in the hands of some judicious friend for revisal. But with all its defects, it gives a lively view of the privations and sufferings of the common soldiery in the mighty conflict for liberty and independence. One can hardly

---

[1] Mr. Martin says in his Narrative that his father entered Yale College between 1750 and 1755, and that he was settled in the county of Berkshire. Here the narrator was born, Nov. 21, 1760. Query : was his father the Rev. Ebenezer Martin, Y. C. 1756, who at that time was the minister of Becket, Berkshire county, Mass. ?—ED.

[2] Hallowell, Maine : Printed by Glazier, Masters & Co., pp. 213. A copy is in the library of the New-England Historic, Genealogical Society, presented by the author of this article. —ED.

fail, from its perusal, to feel that he owes a vast debt of gratitude to the men of 1776, whose treasure, toil and blood secured for us so goodly a heritage. The year following the close of the war, Mr. Martin settled in what is now the town of Stockton, then a sparsely settled plantation. Here he remained until the close of his life, a period of sixty-six years. In securing an act of incorporation for his adopted town, in reducing the place to system and order as a civil community, he bore a prominent part. He held various stations of trust, being repeatedly selectman, representative to the state legislature, and for over a quarter of a century town clerk. His readiness as a scribe, and his intelligence, rendered him highly useful in those early days. He possessed more than ordinary capacities, and had a fondness for intellectual pursuits,—a taste for drawing, for poetry and for composition. Had he enjoyed a thorough mental training, he would probably have enrolled his name among the poets of America. With all his disadvantages, some pieces which he produced indicate that the elements of pure poetry formed a part of his nature. Intellectual pursuits contributed largely to the comfort of his old age. Within the last four years of his life his sight became so impaired that he was unable to read, and deeply did he feel the privation. His history furnishes a strong argument for cultivating the taste and the habit of reading, however humble may be one's condition. It not only augmented his powers of usefulness while in the active part of life, but when age and infirmity came on, it furnished resources for profit and entertainment. This aged man had acquired a fund of knowledge, which, with his lively, social disposition, and ready wit, made him a highly entertaining and instructive companion.

In his religious opinions, Mr. Martin adopted the views of the Puritan fathers of New-England, and held them with a firm grasp. In 1818, he made a public profession of religion, and united with the Congregational church, of which he remained an honored member until his death. At his funeral a large concourse of people of various political and religious faith showed how deep was the respect felt for the aged veteran.

DOCUMENTS AND LETTERS BY ACTORS IN THE AMERICAN REVOLUTION.

Communicated by JEREMIAH COLBURN, A.M., of Boston.

From the originals in his Collection of Autographs.

Gen. Sir Robert Pigot.

GEN. Pigot was commander of the thirty-eighth regiment at the battle of Bunker Hill. He was thanked in general orders for the prominent part he took in the engagement. His regiment had nine officers among the killed and wounded.

> " Here the firm animating PIGOT fought,
> His warlike flame the gallant leaders caught;
> The privates felt its force, from man to man
> T' excell in fight an emulation ran."
> *Cocking's Poem, London,* 1781.

Mr. Wheeler,

Will you be so good as to let my Landlord or his Brother know if you can find an Opportunity that I do not intend to be his Tenant any longer after the year expires, as I am obliged to reside on this side the water & can have but little Use & no Enjoyment of his House. If he has no Objection my Serv.ᵗ shall continue in it & a Sentry kept at the gate till he can provide a Tenant, or will send any one to take care of it

I am Sir
yr. very Huml. Servᵗ.
Rᵗ. PIGOT.

Bunker's Hill
    24 July [1775]

Gen. John Thomas.

He was born in Marshfield, Mass., 1725, and died in Chamblee, Canada, June 2, 1776.

" By the way, I must do justice to Thomas; he is a good officer, and is esteemed. We have no trouble with his camp; it is always in good order, and things are conducted with dignity and spirit in the military style."—*James Warren to Samuel Adams, June 21, 1775.*

Roxbury Febʸ 17ᵗʰ 1776.

Recᵈ. of Capᵗ Amos Turner two pounds Nine Shillings & Eight pence half penny which being the Balance of Wages Due from Said Capᵗ Turner to Mʳ Calvin Garnet a Private in said Turner's Company

Jɴᵒ Thomas

John Glover, Brigadier General.

He joined the army at Cambridge in 1775 with 1000 men from Marblehead, was in the advance of the army which crossed the Delaware on the night of the 25th of December, 1776. "·I think I may tell you without flattery, that I know of no man better qualified than you to conduct a brigade."—*Washington to Glover, April 26, 1777.*

Sir,

I recᵈ yours by your boy respecting the swivils Borrowᵈ for the Use of yᵉ American Navey. Doubtless you remember when I recᵈ yʳ Guns, it was agreed that if they should be Lost, I was to see you paid four pounds for the pair, agreeable to that I maid my return to General Washington I therefore Cannot of my self pay a greater Prise. I think if I mistake not I gave you a Receipt for that amount which if you will receive, I will Desier Capᵗ Wᵐ Bartlett to pay.

I am Sir yours &c.
JOHN GLOVER.

Beverly Febʸ. 29. 1776.

[Addressed: "To Capᵗ John White Junʳ | In Salem"]

Col. James Lockwood.

He was aid to Maj.-General David Wooster.

Camp. before Quebec, April 25th, 1776.

Dear Sir

I have just received your favour of yesterday & say in answer—The Genl [Wooster] thinks it will be better that Mr Lizott should be sent by Water than through the Country—with regard to the two Vessels Capt Tenyck who takes command of Peppers Schooner has Orders to take up all suspected Vessels & boats & those two, have been mentioned to him, he will stop at Point au Tremble, the Genl therefore desires you to direct him, at any rate to secure those Vessels, he will receive proper information from you concerning them—remember me affectionately to your family & believe me your most obed^t Servt

Capt McNeil—   JA^s LOCKWOOD

[Addressed: "To Capⁿ Hector McNeil | at | Point au Tremble "]

Maj.-General David Wooster.

He was born in Stratford, Conn., 1710, and died May 2, 1777, from wounds received in an engagement with British troops at Danbury, Conn., 27th April, 1777.

Camp Before Quebec, April 26th 1776

Dear Sir,

I am much obliged to you for the information you give me in yours of yesterday which I have received & say in answer—I shall write Genl Arnold concerning the Acadien & also to arrest Palmer—

I have Ordered four Bar^{ls} Pork to be sent you from here should be glad you would send two of them to Capⁿ Scott if you can possibly procure flour at Point au Tremble I hope in a few days to be able to replace Cash for it. I am informed that Mr Cole with a large sum was left at Crownpoint & was every hour expected at Montreal.

With regard to the Gaspee please to procure a Pilot & put some hands on board of her from Capⁿ Church's party & send her to Jackes Cartier with Orders to be left ashore there—Let Matherman follow his Capt. The Articles for the Maria with a Gunner were sent from this place yesterday, I have sent for Capⁿ Goforth from three Rivers a very good man, to take charge of her—Prince, Pepper's Mate I shall send after immediately— Give me leave to congratulate you upon the Good News from Boston & believe me most affectionately your very

hble Servt

My Comp^{ts} to your family   DAVID WOOSTER.

Capt Mc Neil

[Superscribed: "On the Service of the United Colonies"
Addressed: "To Capⁿ Hector McNeil | at | Point au Tremble "]

Col. Elias Dayton.

In 1759 he was in the army under General Wolfe at Quebec. He joined the American army in 1775, and was in the battles of Brandywine, Germantown, Monmouth, Springfield, and at the Siege of Yorktown.

Fort Stanwix July 18th 1776.

Dr Sir

The bearer —— Schuyler has just returned from a scout to Oswego where he says everything is as yet quiet he saw a horse & a number of Cows there which he says can be easily brought off if General Schuyler Approves of the scheme I will send proper persons with Schuyler to effect it if the Cows are left a little longer without doubt our enemy's will possess them— I expect tomorrow to dismiss two scouts towards Oswegotse hope to be allways so much upon our guard as to prevent being surprised by our barbarous enemies what do you think of seting fire to Fort Ontario

E. D.

Maj.-Gen. William Heath.

He was born in Roxbury, Mass., March 2, 1737; and died there Jan. 24, 1814. In early life entered into military duties, in 1761 and 1771–4 was a member of the legislature; was a member of the committees of Safety and Correspondence and a delegate to the Provincial Congress in 1774–5. He joined the army in 1775, and continued till the close of the war.

Head Q^{rs}. Boston, 1st September 1776.

Sir,

You will immediately repair to and take the Command of Castle Island.

I am Sir
your obed^t serv^t

Lt Col^l Revere   W. HEATH, M. Genl

John Gooch.

New Jersey. Fort Constitution, Sept. 23. 1776.

Sir

The many favors Received from you will ever hold a gratfull place in my heart, and I flatter myself a Letter will not prove disagreeable as I look on myself obliged in gratitude to let you hear from me, as I know you must be anctious for the certainty of events of which you can have at that distance but a confused account, as I was on the spot will endeavor to give you as Concise & Just account as possible; on the 15th Inst we evacuated New York & took all stores of every kind out of the City, and took Possession of hights of Haerlem eight miles from the City, the Enimy incamp'd about two miles from us; on the 16th the Eninimy advanced and took Possession of a hight on our Right Flank ab^t half a mile Distance with about 3000 men, a Party from our Brigade of 150 men who turned out as Volunteers under the command of Lieut. Col^o Crary of the Regm^t I belong to were ordered out if possible to dispossess them, in about 20 minits the Engagement began with as terrible a fire as ever I heard, when Orders came for the whole Brigage imediately to march to support the first detachment, the Brigade Consisted of ab^t 900 men, we immediately formed in front of the Enimy and march'd up in good order through their fire, which was incessant till within 70 yards when we Engaged them in that situation we engaged them for one hour and eight minits, when the

Enimy Broke & Ran, we persued them to the next hights, when we were ordered to Retreat   Our lose does not exceed in killed and wounded twenty five men, the lose of the Enimy was very considerable but cannot be ascertaind, as we observed them to carry of their dead and wounded the whole time of the Engagement, they left a Number of killed and wounded on the Field of Battle & a great number of small Armes, the great Superiority of Numbers and every other advantage the Enemy had, when considered makes the Victory Glorious, and tho' but over a part of their Army yet the Consequences of it are attended with advantages very great, as they imediately quited the hights all round us and have not been troublesome sinse, our people behaved with the greatest Spirit, and the New England men have gained the first Lawrells.   I received a slight wound in the Anckle at the first of the Engagement but never quited the Field during the Engagement. I'm now Ready to give them the second part whenever they have an appetite, as I'm convinced whenever stir from their Ships we shall drubb them.

Every thing here is very dear Rum 16s. l. my: p^r Galls and every thing in proportion.   I expect to see you in Jany if heaven spares me when perhaps may fall on a sceme that you may think advantageous as it will be impossible for me to stay in the Army for eight pounds p^r month   should esteem myself very in having a line, my Best Respects to your Lady & Family.

I am with a due sense of obligations
Your oblig'd & most obd^t Servant
JOHN GOOCH.

[Addressed: " To Thomas Fayerweather Esq | Merch^t | In | Boston "]

William White.

Fort Washington October 5th 1776.

Mr. Comasery Cuts S^r pleyse to Let the Baiere have the Rum for Twenty seven men on fortugue
WILLIAM WHITE Liu^t

Robert Morris, Philip Livingston, Richard H. Lee, William Whipple and Francis Lewis.

In Secret Committee
of Congress.   Philad^d. Decr. 4th. 1776.
Gent^n.

A Committee of Congress was appointed the 25th Septr. to procure Cloathing in all the States on this Continent for the use of our Army and we find they wrote to you on the 10th Octr. requesting the favour of you to employ proper persons to purchase what cou'd be obtained in your State to this letter they have not rec'd any answer and the Congress being very anxious and impatient to have this important business duely attended to & executed have directed us to send one or more trusty persons into the Eastern States to collect what has been bought & to make such further purchases of suitable articles as they can accomplish.   We have engaged Messrs Ab^m Livingston & Wm Turnbull bearers hereof to go upon this Service.   You will be pleased to direct them to the persons who have made purchases on Continental acc't by order, & let the Goods be delivered to these Gent^m or their order.   We have also by direction of Congress authorized them to make further purchases & must beg the favour of your advice and assistance to them in the prosecution of that business, or that you will desire your Committee to give them such assistance.

We have judged it dangerous to send a large amount of money with them at this time on acc't of the situation of our Enemy neither cou'd we judge what sum might be sufficient, therefore we request you will order them to be supplyed out of your Public Treasury if needfull, their drafts on this Committee for the amount shall be Paid & if desired the money shall be sent by express. Your Zeal to serve the general cause on all occasions makes us satisfied of your concurrence with our desires & we remain with the utmost respect

Gent'ⁿ.
Your most Obed't & most
h'ble Serv'ᵗˢ.

Robᵗ. Morris.
Phil. Livingston.
Richard Henry Lee.
Wᵐ Whipple.
Fra: Lewis.

To
    The Honᵇˡᵉ. Assembly of
      Massachusets Bay.

Gen. George Clinton.

In October, 1777, Forts Montgomery and Clinton, on the Hudson river, were bravely defended by Gen. Clinton and his brother Gen. James Clinton—the latter being badly wounded. He was the first governor of the State of New-York, holding the office for eighteen years, being active in both civil and military offices during the war.

March 3ᵈ 1777

Sir
    You are not upon any Pretence whatever unless obliged by the stress of weather to land upon Long Island nor to suffer any of your Men so to do—nor are you or any of your men in such Case to plunder or distress any of the Inhabitants whatever their political Principles or characters may bee and these Instructions you are to follow at your Peril.

To Capᵗ Wᵐ Smith Scudder

Maj.-General William Heath, Capt. Thomas Jackson and Major Jonathan Pollard.

An Abstract for Six Weeks Pay from the first Day of January 1777 for a Detachment of Men under the Command of Capᵗ Lᵗ. Thomas Jackson of the Artillery

1 Sergant	.	.	a 60s.	.	.	£. 4. 4. 0
1 Corporal	.	.	a 55s.	.	.	3. 17. 0
1 Bombardiar	.	.	a 55s.	.	.	3. 17. 0
1 Gunner	.	.	a 55s.	.	.	3. 17. 0
14 Matrosses	.	.	a 50s.	.	.	49. 0 0
						64. 15. 0

To Travelling Money Due for 18
Men from Peekskill to Boston Beign   }   16. 10. 0
220 Miles a 20 Miles for 1 Days Travelling
the Whole Amount   .   .   .   .   .   £. 81. 5. 0

Thomas Jackson Capᵗ. Lᵗ. Artillery

Roxbury, March 13th 1777.
Received of Major-General Heath the above abstract in full
Tho⁸ JACKSON Capt Lt Artillery

To Ebenezer Hancock Esq. Deputy Paymaster General to
The Forces of the United States of America

Sir
Pay to Major Jonathan Pollard Two Hundred and Seventy Dollars ⅚
as a refund of the within, for which this shall be your Sufficient Warrant
Given at Head Quarters
Boston March 29th 1777

W. HEATH, M.G.

Received the above for Major-General Heath,

JON⁸ POLLARD A Dᶜ

Gen. Joseph Spencer.

He held the rank of Major in the colonial army in 1756. He was
appointed Brigadier-General in the continental army, June 22,
1775, and Major-General Aug. 9, 1776. In 1777 he was in command
of the forces on Rhode Island. He resigned June, 1778, and was
elected a delegate to Congress the same year. He died at East-
Haddam, Conn., January, 1789, aged 75 years.

Providence 10th Decʳ. 1777
Sir
According to agreement with Mʳ Adams when here I wrote to him to
be here to pay the Troops the beginning of this Week and according to his
desire ordered the Officers to be here ready with their abstracts, and not
until yesterday did I know but that the Cash would be ready. Yesterday
Sundry Officers came for their pay, and then I Rec'd a Letter from Mʳ
Adams informing that he had no Cash to bring which is a very unhappy
disappointment to the Troops and happening at the present Juncture is very
prejudicial to me in my Command at this place and indeed I am in absolute
need of Three or Four Thousand pounds of Cash to provide for the necessary subsistance of the Army—I think, Sir, out of what Cash you have I
ought to have my part. I must depend on some. I shall soon be at Boston
on other business as well as this, when I shall wait on you relative to this
matter.

I am Sir your Humble Servt
Ebenʳ Hancock Esq.   Jo⁸ SPENCER M.G.
[Addressed: "On publick Service" "Ebenʳ Hancock Esq | Dʸ Pay
Master Genˡ | to the Eastern Department | Boston "]

Col. Jonathan Trumbull.

In 1775–8 he was paymaster of the northern department of the
army, and in 1780 first aide-de-camp to Washington, with whom
he remained until the close of the war. This letter is franked by
his father, "Brother Jonathan," the friend of Washington.

Lebanon 19th Janʸ. 1778
Sir
The Draft from Continental Treasury Board in my Favor on your
office for 200,000 Dollars which was protested by you on the 10th of last

Month has been to Congress, & is now returned to me again, with Instructions "to hold it in my Custody, untill there shall be Cash in the Massachusetts Loan Office for supplying the Amount which the Treasury Board are assured will, by partial Payments, be compleated at no very distant Period." You will be so good Sir, as to inform me pr this Messenger, what Prospect there is of the money being obtained—to prevent Trouble & Expence I shall be glad to be furnished with the whole Sum att one Payment if possible, if that cannot be soon compleated, our necessities will oblige me to call for a partial Payment whenever you inform of any considerable Part being ready. Our Department has already suffered very Deeply by the Disappointments occasioned by M[r] Hancock's unaccountable Delay—or non Information of the first Draft which was Dated 16th Oct°—On which, if it had been forwarded agreable to the Expectations of Congress I am told the Money might have been received—the money for supply of this Failure, has not yet been furnished at my office—the Distress of many for Want of it is great —great Part of which falls on the Militia of your State—who are at this Day unpaid for their Services in Gen[l] Gates army last Fall

I send this pr special Messinger who will wait your Reply.

I am   Sir
Your most humble Servant

Nathan[l] Appleton Esq   Jon[a] Trumbull Jun[r]. P. M. G.
Northern Department

[Superscribed, "Public Service"
   franked "Jonathan Trumbull"
  Addressed: "Nathaniel Appleton Esq | Commissioner of Loan Office |
   State of Massachusetts Bay"]

Lord Stirling (William Alexander).

He was born New-York city in 1726, and died Albany, Jan. 15, 1783. He was a Colonel in 1775, and was made a Brigadier-General by Congress, March, 1776. He distinguished himself in various battles during the Revolution.

Aquakanock Octob[r] 5. 1778.

Dr Sir

I must desire that you will immediately march with your whole force including militia up to the Heights near Second River, a detachment of the Enemy is on the heights near Arant Schylers, you will Do your best to Anoy them in Case they should Attempt to pass the River below us. Let me hear from you as often as possible

I am

Colonel Dayton.   your most Humble Serv[t]
  Elizabeth Town   STIRLING
let the River be examined to see if they have any boats in it.

  [Addressed: "To Co[l] Dayton | Elizabeth Town"]

Gen. Rufus Putnam.

He was born in Sutton, Mass., April 9, 1738, and died at Marietta, Ohio, May 4, 1824. In 1775 he joined the army of the Revolution as a Lieut. Colonel in the regiment of Col. David Brewer. He served with distinction as an engineer and commander until the close of the war.

Coller   Barrack February y[e] 20th. 1779.

Sir.

I send you six men to chop logs you will Quarter them and Imploy them as you think propper if a Sawyer is wanted I can furnish one.

Yours.

To Cap[t] Flowers

R Putnam Col[o]

P. S.   The Mens Names
are
    Jonathan Harwood
    Enoch Fuller
    Isaac Train
    John Church
    John Cummins
    John Ayres.
[Addressed: "To Cap[t] Flowers"]

Richard Henry Lee.

Philadelphia March 29. 1779.

Dear Sir,

I am honored with your favor of the 19th. and thank you for it.   I always thought too well of your wisdom and justice to suppose you could be influenced by the most groundless, ill designing, and improbable calumnies that ever were devised by wicked minds.   From the most intimate confidential correspondence and from the best information, I have abundant reason to be satisfied that both my brothers in Europe are as firmly attached to the independence and happiness of America as any men that breathe the vital air.   I should detest them if I thought otherways, or had any reason to think of them than as I have above expressed.   A strict adherance to duty, active Services for their Country, and opposition to public peculation has drawn this calumny on them.   Mr Ford being such a man as you describe, and having with him authentic documents to prove that he had been confided in by one of these States might well impose upon D[r]. Lee who was an utter stranger to any misconduct that he had been guilty of here.   I will answer for it, that he wont remain an hour in his employment after the Doctor knows his character.   I shall be greatly concerned indeed if we have been so unfortunate as to have lost the military Stores that you expected.   But since D[r] Lee does not mention anything in his letters to me about having shipped them, and not having seen any mention of such capture in the N. York papers, I yet hope they may be safe.   T'is true the number of privateers that avarice and enmity have equipped from N. York & Bermuda to cruise on our trade is very great indeed.   I think by their list they amount to more than eighty.   Some Frigates are ordered to clear our Coast of these Rovers, and I hope they will be successful.   But this destination of our Frigates ought not to be made public.   I wish with all my heart we had any important intelligence to communicate to you.   I know of none, unless what I have before written, that we have very good reason to know that our enemies have no prospect of aid of any kind from any European Power to assist them in their war against us.   Holland seems much disposed to us, at least Amsterdam is securely with us, and that is a Powerful Part of their Union.   The King of the two Siclies has opened his Ports to us, and the English themselves Publish that Spain has notified to the Court of

London that they will join France if the former does not acknowledge the Independence of America and make peace. But such is the distructive obstinacy and wickedness of our enemies, that they appear determined to try another Campaign, and therefore our efforts should be exerted to reenforce our Army with all possible dispatch.

The malice of our foes must recoil upon their own heads, if we are but wise and take the necessary precautions.

I am, dear Sir, yours with much
Affection and Sincerity
RICHARD HENRY LEE.

[Addressed & franked : "Honorable John Page, esquire | at Williamsburg, in | Virginia."
"R. H. Lee "]

Gen. Mordecai Gist.

He was born in Baltimore, Md., 1743, and was appointed major of a battalion of Maryland regulars, in July, 1776, attached to the brigade under the command of Lord Stirling. In 1777 he was promoted to colonel, and was engaged in the battle of Germantown. In 1779 Congress appointed him a brigadier general, and he served with distinction throughout the war.

Camp Butter Milk Falls.
24 July 1779.

Dear Sir.

It is now two Weeks since my arrival from the S. Ward during which time my horses have had no Forrage of any kind whatever, which with the fatigue of a long Journey has operated so forcibly on the frame & Spirit of those Honest Creatures, that you might from appearances, venture to swear they have suffered all the pains of transmutation; pray my Dear Sir remedy this evil or enable the bearer my Brigade * * * * * the request of Mrs Alexander I have to inform you that she with her family & Miss Buchanan are in perfect health & beg their compliments to you

With due Respect
I am Sir
y^r mo Hum Servt
M. GIST.

William Eustis, LL.D.

He was born Cambridge, Mass., June 10, 1753, and died in Boston, Feb. 6, 1825. He entered the army as a regimental surgeon in 1775, and served during the Revolution. He was a member of Congress 1800–5 and 1820–3 ; Secretary of War, 1809–12 ; Minister to Holland in 1815 ; and Governor of Massachusetts in 1824–5, dying while in office.

Dear Craigie

There is so favorable an opportunity by Doctor Foster to remind you of your promise last Winter that I cannot suffer it to pass unimproved. For God's Sake (if not for the sake of your friends) let us have the pleasure to hear from you. Acquaint us what methods you pursue in Philadelphia rather what steps Congress imagine we shall very shortly be obliged to take. Is it not astonishing that regardless of the decent applications from the medical dep^t they use us with a neglect which would weary the patience of Job? Do they imagine us stocks and stones? and are we not human nature?

I do assure you, my good friend our ill treatment is not seldom mentioned by officers of the line & its only palliative is that we have the honor to taste that inattention which the Saviours of this Country have long experienced:

I have not time to write Doctor Browne by this opportunity and will thank you to inform him that after signing one copy of the Paper I have transmitted it to Doctor Warren in Boston: and another to Dr. Turner in Norwich to be sent on by him to Dr. Adams &c at Providence: mentioning the necessity of their loosing not a post, but of forwarding them to Dr Browne in Ph: as soon as possible. To Doctors Foster & Ledyard I have likewise given a copy which I imagine Doctor Foster is to take on with him to Philadelphia.

One good effect will at least be produced by this which from its nature must be our last representation to Congress. January will either give us some compensation for five the most valuable years in life expended in the service of the country, or it will send us home with a most useful lesson: and which alternative will conduce most to our advantages as individuals, I am utterly at a loss to determine

Adieu, my dear friend and believe me with affection y^r friend & servant

WILLIAM EUSTIS.

22 October At Robinsons House

And^r Craigie Esq.   [1779 near West Point]

Gen. Joseph Reed.

He was born Trenton, N. J., Aug 27, 1741, and died Philadelphia, March 5, 1785. A lawyer by profession, he took an active part in the early movements in favor of independence. He was a member of the Committee of Correspondence, President of the first Pennsylvania Convention in 1775, and delegate to Congress. At the solicitation of Washington, in 1775, he accompainied him to Cambridge as his first Secretary and Aide-de-Camp. In 1777 he was appointed Chief Justice of Pennsylvania, and by Congress a Brigadier General—both of which he declined. He served as a volunteer at the battles of Brandywine, White Marsh, Germantown and Monmouth. He was a member of Congress in 1778, and a signer of the Confederation. He held many other important positions, and aided many philanthropic movements.

Jan 7. 1780.

Dear General

I received your Letter last Evening giving me Expectation of meeting you this Day: But not hearing from you, I have sent again to know whether I may expect you & when & whether any Persons on the Part of the Troop will make known their Complaints, which will most certainly be redressed on every reasonable Point, & when any Doubt arises the Construction to be in Favour of the Soldiers. The Proposals made by them on the 4th Inst. seem to form a reasonable Ground of Accomodation. The 4th Article has been hastily drawn, their own Experience will convince them of the Necessity of some Alteration. It will be necessary also to distinguish those who have freely enlisted for the War, otherwise all Contract is at an End. & when they are requesting an Allowance for Depreciation agreable to Contract, they certainly will not vindicate a Breach of Contract. We will also agree upon some equitable Mode of determining who are so enlisted which may be done by three Persons agreed on for that Purpose. But this will not exclude those from a Gratuity proportioned to their service. They may depend upon every just & reasonable allowance & I hope they have too much Honour & Spirit to tarnish their former good conduct by asking unreasonable Things, or those which are impracticable. Their honourable & patriotick Conduct this morning will be ever remembered & suitably rewarded if nothing unfavorable to their Country should happen. Should they refuse to serve their Country at this time it will be an eternal Reproach to the State to which they belong & to which they have done so much Honour by their Bravery & they must acknowledge that when they compare the Conduct of the State to them with that of most of the States, they have been better provided than others. Those who after being discharged choose to reinlist will be kindly received but they will be at their own Liberty to do so or not. If they choose to engage again they will be allowed Furlows to see their Friends when the Circumstances of the Army will admit—The Arrears of Pay, Depreciations, Cloathing &c. I mentioned in my former letter these will be taken care of immediately. Should they take any rash step after this all the world will condemn them, & they will condemn themselves: for America will not be lost, if they decline their Asistance to save her.

I am Dear Sir
Your Obed Hble Ser[t]
JO[s] REED

Gen. David Cobb.

He was born in Attleborough, Mass., Sept. 14, 1748, and died April 17, 1830. He graduated at Harvard College, 1766, and practised medicine in Boston and Taunton for several years. He was a member of the Provincial Congress in 1775 from Taunton, having as colleague Robert Treat Paine, afterwards a signer of the Declaration of Independence. He entered the army in 1777, and was appointed by Washington one of his Aides-de-Camp in June, 1781, in whose family he remained till the close of the war. He was appointed by Gov. Hancock a judge of the Court of Common Pleas, and Major-General of the militia, in which positions he showed much ability and determination of character. In 1789 he was Speaker of the House of Representatives, and in 1793 elected member of Congress, Senator in 1795, and in 1809 Lieut.-Governor of the State. [See REGISTER, viii. 5.]

Boston April 25th. 1780.
Dear Col[o].

I got to this Town, from Taunton last Evening, & to my very great disappointment found M[r] Lovell here, with my *great* Letter in possession, that I wrote you a month ago, I was damn'd mad in seeing him & more so, when I was inform'd that he had not sent my Letter, as it contains matters that you'd be fond of knowing—As I have just got to Town, can't be able to inform you any particulars relating to cloathing, small stores &c. but shall write you next post what scituation they are in—

Mr Lovell's detention was occasioned by the lameness of his Horse, the poor fellow had bo't him and that cost him ¼ part of his Depreciation & in three days after he was Kick'd in such a manner that he has not been out of the stable these three weeks—we Gent^n. Officers are not able to purchase Horses every month—Lovell feels anxious about his being detain'd, but his scituation cou'd not be prevented.

Your Friend

Col. Jackson.   DAVID COBB

[Addressed: "Col Henry Jackson | Headquarters"]

A YANKEE PRIVATEERSMAN IN PRISON IN ENGLAND, 1777-1779.

Communicated by WILLIAM RICHARD CUTTER, of Lexington, Mass., with Notes.

[Continued from page 177.]

[1777.] We arrived at Spithead, the 30th of April; and it is common when a ship comes in from sea, for small boats to come off and supply the ship's crew with such necessaries as they stand in need of, where we sold what trifle of clothes we had, to get supplied with provisions.

In a few days after our arrival, our officers were sent on shore to be examined at Portsmouth. Sir Richard[1] ordered them a dinner, with a bottle of wine and some beer to drink. The next, they were sent on board again. The wind blowing so hard the night before, they could not get off again the same day, but were obliged to lay on board the brigantine on the sails; and for three weeks after, we had news constantly of our being sent on shore to prison. And on the 13th of June, all our officers were sent on shore, and the next day the remainder of the men were sent on shore at Portsmouth, there to be examined at the Royal Hospital.[2]

From thence, were conducted under a very strong guard to Forton Prison, which is about one mile out of town; and for twenty-four hours after we got to prison, we had nothing to eat but boiled cabbage, which was part of the officers' allowance. We had a little bread that our captain bought for us.

Sunday, 15th, we had three quarters of a pound of beef allowed us and some cabbage; one pound of bread, one quart of small beer for twenty-four hours. The cabbage is only every other day. So we continued, nobody being there but our own ship's company (and great numbers of people coming from all quarters to see the Yankees, or rather Rebels), till the 19th, at night, our people made a large hole through the wall of the prison, and eleven made their escape. Two were three days afterwards retaken, and

---

[1] Sir Richard Bickerton, captain, Terrible, 74, their captor. See Note, *ante*, p. 177.

[2] June 13, 1777. "This morning a guard of soldiers came over from Portsmouth to defend the prison at Forton, part of the prisoners being this day landed and conveyed to this place."—*London Chronicle*, for 1777, p. 570.

brought back again—which were the gunner Woodward,[1] and B. Lambert.[2] The next day at ten o'clock, they found out where they got away, and soon after searched all our hammocks and beds; took all our chests from us, and put them in another apartment under a lock and key; and threatened to put us in irons if we did the like again.

The people in general used to come in great numbers on Sundays. We were only allowed the forenoon to walk the yard, and were locked up at two o'clock, but for what reason we knew not; and of week days, till the sun was an half an hour high.

June the 23d, Woodward and Lambert were brought back to Forton again; and left the captain and Fritz,[3] the night before, very much fatigued. Woodward and Lambert were put into the Black Hole on six ounces of beef, half a pound of bread, one pint of small beer for 24 hours. There they were to have continued for forty days. In a few days after, I was taken out of my bed at eleven o'clock at night, on suspicion of going to break out, by some secret intelligence, and was kept there till the next day, when nothing being proved against me I was released.

The Black Hole is a place where you are by yourselves, and not allowed to come out, or even to speak to us.

Thus they were kept thirty-five days upon that short allowance. About this time two men broke out of the hospital, and Mr. Martin was nurse there.[4] They were taken the same afternoon, and put in the Black Hole, and Mr. Martin likewise, where they stayed about eight days, when the same two, by means of making a hole up through the floor, made their escape the second time and got clear off. Mr. Martin, Woodward and Lambert all stayed behind.

July the 30th, four more broke out at twelve o'clock in the day. One got off clear, and the other three were retaken and brought back and put into the Black Hole, viz., Christopher Clark,[5] William Tryon,[6] and John Cockran, boatswain of the Yankee from Boston.[7] There they were kept for

[1] James Woodward, gunner of the Rising States, Boston—see Roll and List of Officers appended—committed to Forton Prison, June 14, 1777—escaped with eleven of his ship's company from prison, June 19, 1777; retaken three days afterwards, and recommitted to prison, June 23, 1777; confined in the Black Hole thirty-five days on short allowance for his offence.

[2] Benjamin Lambert, one of the crew of the Rising States, from Massachusetts—see Roll—the companion of Gunner Woodward, committed, escaped, retaken, recommitted and confined in the Black Hole likewise; remained there thirty-five days on short allowance for his offence.

[3] Henry Fritze, captain of marines, brigantine Rising States—see Roll—committed to Forton Prison, June 14, 1777; effected his escape with Capt. Thompson and others, June 19, 1777.

[4] Mr. Martin—probably the same, already mentioned in this Journal, under date of April 15, 1777. Josiah Martin, one of the crew of the Rising States—see Roll—was committed to Forton Prison with the rest, June 14, 1777. Mr. Martin is also mentioned in this Journal, under the dates of August 15, 16, and September 9, 1778.

[5] Christopher Clark, carpenter, Rising States, Boston—see Roll and List of Officers appended—committed to Forton Prison, June 14, 1777.

[6] William Tryon—William Tryan, lieutenant, of the Notredame, belonging to South Carolina, is named in the List of Officers appended to this Journal—*John* Trion, prizemaster, and six companions, were committed to Forton Prison, July 15, 1777—see Roll—fifteen days previous to this attempted escape. Mr. Tryon again attempted his escape, March 7, 1778; and succeeded in a final attempt, July 23, 1778—see entry in Journal, under date of July 24, 1778. The Notredame.—Cooper, *Naval Hist. U. S.*, i. 77; Lee's *Memoirs of the War*, p. 76, note, &c.

[7] John Cockron, boatswain of the Yankee, from Boston, was committed to Forton Prison, June 26, 1777—see Roll—David Hall, gunner of the Yankee, Boston, being his companion. John Cockran broke out of Forton Prison, Dec. 2, 1777, and got safely home to Boston, by way of France, before May 24, 1778—see item in Journal, under date of July 11, 1778, &c. The Yankee, sloop, armed vessel of Massachusetts, 1776, and career—*vide* REGISTER, xxvi. 29, and Drake's *Historic Fields and Mansions of Middlesex*, under the subject of Dr. Downer.

forty days half starved; allowed neither bed nor bedding to lie on, but the soft side of a good plank.

August the 9th, this day came on shore forty-nine American prisoners. Amongst them were three captains of armed vessels, viz., Capt. Courter of the Oliver Cromwell,[1] Capt. Harris of the *Miscator*,[2] and Capt. Hill of the Montgomery.[3] The Agent made his business to make them deliver up their money by the point of the bayonet. There is no such thing as refusing.

August 9th, Mr. Lunt[4] received a letter from France, from Capt. Thompson, with some money for all of us. About this time, there came ten more prisoners, mostly French, from the Princess Amelia guard ship, lying at Spithead; among them a French gentleman that was with General Lee when he was taken, and a French engineer that was taken in Fort Washington.[5]

October 10th, one of the French made his escape over the pales, but was taken and brought back the same morning, and was committed to the Black Hole; a place for all that try to make their escape. All that get away from this place, and are taken again, stay forty days.

October the 12th, George Chamberlin[6] jumped over the pales and was taken again, and sent to the Black Hole.

---

[1] Hammon Corter, captain, of the Oliver Cromwell, privateer—according to Roll appended—was committed to Forton Prison (Oct. 13), 1777; twelve of his crew likewise. The Oliver Cromwell, armed vessel of Massachusetts, 1776—captured by the British sloop-of-war Beaver, May 11, 1777.—*Vide* REGISTER, xxvi. 23.

[2] John Harris, captain, *Miscator* or *Muscetor*, belonging to Virginia—see Roll and List of Officers appended—committed to Forton Prison, with seven of his officers, Aug. 8, 1777 —according to Roll. The name of his vessel (Musquito?) is here given as spelt in the original.

[3] Benjamin Hill, captain, from Massachusetts, of the Montgomery, belonging to Philadelphia—see Roll—committed to Forton Prison, Aug. 8, 1777; taken by the Levant frigate, March 8, previous.

[4] Joseph Lunt, lieutenant, Rising States, Boston—see Roll and List of Officers appended —committed to Forton Prison, June 14, 1777. He appears never to have attempted his escape, but abided by the fortunes of his imprisoned shipmates until their eventual release.

[5] Mr. "Babatrang," gentleman, committed to Forton Prison, Aug. 26, 1777—see Roll— is probably the "French gentleman" with General Lee when he was taken. Mons. "Bubotrong," a "French gentleman," was one of ten "officers" who effected their escape from Forton Prison, July 23-24, 1778. His companion, the French engineer—"Indianeer," in the original—who was taken in Fort Washington, was probably the Mr. "Webber," colonel, committed to Forton Prison, Aug. 26, 1777—see Roll—styled also in this Journal, "Wybert" and "Vibert." Aug. 24, 1778, Mr. "Wybert" received a letter from Mr. "Bubottrong"—escaped, July 23, 1778—in France. Mr. "Webber," colonel, is specified in the Roll as "exchanged." In the Journal, under date of Dec. 11, 1778, Mons. "Vibert," stated to be "the French engineer that was taken at Fort Washington," is alluded to as exchanged out of prison "yesterday" (Dec. 10, 1778), and sent to France. Lt. Col. Weibert or De Weibert, of the corps of American engineers, volunteered as a coadjutor of Paul Jones in 1779, and held a command on the Bon Homme Richard in the action with the Serapis, Sept. 23, 1779.—Sherburne's *Life of Jones*, pp. 104, 113, 120, 165, 174, 177, 187, 194.

Fort Washington on the Hudson was stormed by the British, under Howe, and carried, Nov. 16, 1776. According to Howe's returns, published in the London Gazette, Extra-ordinary (*Town and Country Magazine*, Supplement for the year 1776, pp. 684, 686, &c.), two thousand seven hundred Americans surrendered prisoners; of commissioned officers, four colonels, four lieutenant-colonels, five majors, &c.; of the staff—one engineer (probably Weibert himself) is enumerated.

General Charles Lee was taken prisoner at Baskingridge, N. J., Dec. 13, 1776, by a scouting party of the British cavalry, under Lt. Col. Harcourt. "It is a certainty that General Lee is taken prisoner by Colonel Harcourt, at the head of forty light dragoons, and is now trying by a court-martial for desertion. He was secured by stratagem," &c.—*Town and Country Magazine* (London) for February, 1777, p. 109. In the same magazine, for January, 1777 (p. 54), intelligence is given, under date of Nov. 30, 1776, of "General Lee dubious of the courage of the Provincial troops," having sent "some proposals to General Howe, the particulars we are not acquainted with." Lee, previous to his capture, appears to have surrounded himself with French officers of more or less competency.

[6] George Chamberlin, lieutenant *Muscetor* from Virginia—see Roll—committed to Forton Prison, Aug. 8, 1777.

October the 13th, this day twenty-two more prisoners were sent on shore, Capt. John Nicholson of the Hornet,[1] and Capt. Welch,[2] and all their officers and men. About this time two men made their escape over the pales, and got clear off, and never were heard of afterwards.

October the 22d, this day we had the news of General Burgoyne's defeat by a letter from France, but it was not believed in England for a great while afterwards.[3]

---

[1] From Philadelphia—see Roll. Capt. John Nicholson, of the Hornet (of the Revolutionary navy)—thus committed to Forton Prison, Oct. 13, 1777—a brother of Commodores James and Samuel Nicholson, U. S. N.

[2] John Welch, captain—committed to Forton Prison, Oct. 13, 1777—see Roll.

[3] Perhaps the news of those earlier reverses, which led to his speedy capitulation in October. The editor of the *Town and Country Magazine*, in his comments on the news for August, 1777, at London, writes:—

"This month, pregnant with the most important intelligence, has not, as the partizans of the Americans foretold, only brought forth a mouse. General Howe's success against the Rebels (which will be found in the subjoined news) was only the fore-runner of that very capital stroke of General Burgoyne, the taking of the important post Ticonderoga : an event that has sealed the fate of this campaign entirely to our advantage, if no other operations were to take place ; but there is the greatest reason to believe that this will accelerate far more advantageous pursuits. Mr. Washington may now be said literally to be situated between two fires ; and the ardour that distinguished the troops under General Burgoyne at Ticonderoga, of which he made so very easy a conquest, cannot fail striking a terror into troops in a much less defensive state. The success of our cruizers has been remarkable, as all the ports of our West India Islands can testify, as well as our own. The retaking of the Fox frigate, and the capture of the Hancock privateer, have struck a great damp upon the spirits of the American privateers. Moreover, the ill success of the agents of the Congress at Paris, and the orders sent to the different ports of France to suffer no American vessels to remain there above 48 hours, must convince the Americans that they have given too much faith to the assurances of Messieurs Franklin and Deane, whose interest it is to support the flagging spirits of the Colonists with ideal alliances, and assistances that never probably will exist. The nominal patriots, whether from the heat of the weather, or the warm reception their friends met with at Ticonderoga, have their visages most amazingly relaxed, and it is generally believed, they will not be again braced up, even by Christmas. Upon the whole, there is the strongest reason to believe that the unfortunate war in America will come to a speedy conclusion ; this at least is the hearty wish of every man who has the good of his *own* country at heart, and must sincerely lament the shedding of English blood."

The comments for September are in much the same tenor ; likewise October. In October, however, is the acknowledgment—" As to the operations of the American campaign, we are still left in the dark, as no authentic intelligence has been published since the account from General Burgoyne of the taking of Ticonderoga. Various are the speculations of the politicians upon this occasion : the ministerial party declare that government has received no advices officially, and therefore they cannot with propriety lay them before the public. The opponents to administration insinuate that dispatches have been received at Lord Germaine's office ; but they are of such a nature that government think it prudent to conceal them. In the meanwhile the news-papers daily amuse us with accounts from various parts of the American Continent : at one time General Burgoyne has reached Albany, and routed Washington : at another, the American general has beat Burgoyne *à plate couture*. In this state of contradiction it is almost impossible to form any just idea of the real situation of affairs in America. All that can be concluded is, that ere now some important stroke must have been struck, or else the campaign must be at an end. A few days will, it is expected, clear up this matter, and either dissipate the fears of the one party, or cherish the hopes of the other."

In November, 1777, the comments are as follows :—" The session of parliament has been opened with a speech from the throne, from which we have reason to expect that the great powers of Europe are well disposed towards a state of pacification, and that we have grounds to believe that our arms in America have been successful. Nevertheless lord North, in the House of Commons, upon the motion for the address, acknowledged he was totally in the dark with regard to the late operations in America. Hence we may conclude that no dispatches have been received officially from general Howe or general Burgoyne ; though, from repeated accounts from various parts of America, it is generally believed that Sir William Howe has obtained a victory over Mr. Washington, and is actually in possession of Philadelphia. A very short space of time must determine these points, and set us right with regard to the real situation of general Burgoyne. The opposition have, as might be expected, availed themselves of the ignorance of the ministry in this respect, and attacked lord Germaine and lord North with uncommon severity in the debates that have occurred upon the subject. Lord Chatham took the lead in the upper house, and in a long winded speech, pompous and flowery, abused administration for adopting measures, which he him-

October 31st, we received another letter from France, together with twenty guineas from Capt. Thompson, to be divided amongst twenty of us. This night, seven of the prisoners made a bold push, and broke open the door, and made their escape. Six got clear off, and one was retaken and brought back the next day, and sentenced the Black Hole for forty days.

November 18th, William Humber, one of our men,[1] made an attempt to break out of the hospital, but was discovered, and was put into the Black Hole.

November 19th, this day five of the prisoners made their escape through a door in the storeroom, and four got off clear. The other was taken and brought back, and committed to the Black Hole. Amongst them were Richard Chapman and Thomas Clark, both belonging to our ship.[2]

December 2d, this afternoon thirty-five prisoners broke open the gate, and made their escape. Fourteen got off clear, and twenty-one were taken and brought back, and sent to the Black Hole. There were four there before, and the twenty-one brought back made twenty-five, cooped up in a very small room, half starved to death; and, the next day, two young boys were confined for hiding in their hammocks, to make a false muster, for twelve days.

December 11th, this morning three prisoners broke out of the hospital, and made their escape; but by reason of so many five pounders about, they were retaken and brought back before night, and confined in the damned Hole.

December 25th, now the people begin to use humanity throughout England. Since the defeat of Burgoyne,[3] things wear another face, and the humanity shown them by the Americans. They begin to use us better. There are subscription books opened in many parts of England for our relief as poor prisoners.[4]

---

self, when in power, thought eligible. Mr. Burke, Mr. Fox, and several others in the lower house, followed his lordship in many of his arguments; but with as little success with respect to the amendments they proposed: the address (the subject of these altercations) was carried in its original state by a great majority. The other principal object that has engaged the attention of the political world during the course of this month, has been the sentence passed upon Mr. Horne, on the 24th, in the King's-Bench, for publishing the libellous advertisement reflecting on the king's troops, and proposing a subscription in behalf of the rebels."

In December, 1777, after the news of the "remains of General Burgoyne's army had surrendered to the enemy on the 18th of October,". had been publicly announced in England, the tone of the editorial comments on the event was thus:—" The success of General Howe against Washington, and his taking Philadelphia, we are sorry to say, were but preludes to news of a very disagreeable nature; this must necessarily strike the reader, to be the capitulation of General Burgoyne with General Gates, which however honourable on the part of the former, must naturally be highly mortifying to a man of his spirit and courage, as well as to many officers under his command, whose uncommon bravery he has particularly noticed in his letter to Lord George Germaine," &c.

Dr. Franklin said the pride of England was never so humbled by anything, as by Gates's capitulation of Saratoga.—*Franklin to Gates*, June 2, 1779.

[1] Of the crew of the Rising States—see Roll—committed to Forton Prison, June 14, 1777. He effected his escape, Feb. 15, 1778.

[2] Of the crew of the Rising States—see Roll—committed to Forton Prison, June 14, 1777.

[3] At Saratoga, Oct. 17, 1777. The articles of convention between General Burgoyne and General Gates, are published in full, in *Town and Country Magazine*, December, 1777, pp. 619–24. *Ibid*, pp. 668, 684, &c.

[4] " At a meeting held about the latter end of December [1777], for the purpose of relieving the distresses of the American prisoners, a subscription was entered into for immediately supplying them with cloathing and other necessaries, when the sum of 3,815l. 17s. 6d. being subscribed, and that sum with the contribution in the country being more than sufficient for their present necessities, the subscription was this day closed."—*Gentleman's Magazine*, for 1778, p. 43.

[1778.] January the 13th, Mr. Wrenn[1] and Mr. Duckett[2] came and told us that the officers were to receive five shillings, and the men two per week; and we were to have such clothes (pushers) as we stand in need of, from Government; likewise from donations, both officers and men.

January 20th, this day Parliament sits after Christmas holidays. The same day the officers moved from our prison to their new apartment, and it leaves us more room.

January 23d, this day forty-eight more prisoners came on shore, four of them were Frenchmen, and thirteen officers with them; Capt. Murphy,[3] Capt. Oakman,[4] Capt. Chew,[5] Capt. Slacom,[6] &c. &c.

February 15th, this day William Humber and George Pease[7] made their escape over the pales and got clear off.

March 1st, great talks of an accommodation with this Country and the Americans, but not so easy as they expect.[8]

March 7th, this day sixteen prisoners broke out, but were all taken again; Mr. Tryon[9] and Manning[10] were among them, and all put into the Black Hole, but Manning, who by hiding escaped the Hole for the first night,

---

[1] Mr. Wrenn, or Wren, a name oft repeated in this Journal. He is styled "Rev. Mr." Wrenn, in Journal, under date of April 17, 1778. Thomas Wren, a dissenting clergyman of Portsmouth, devoted a great part of his time for several years to the relief of the prisoners in Forton Gaol, near Portsmouth; access to which was expressly granted him by the government. "When American prisoners were continually carried into Portsmouth during the late war, and many of them were in the most wretched condition, he was struck with compassion, and flew to their relief. He contributed most liberally to their necessities out of his own small fortune, and sought the assistance of his friends. One of his first objects was to procure, from his acquaintances in the metropolis and other places, a large supply of clothes, these being particularly wanted. After this, he set on foot that subscription for the relief of the prisoners, which extended so liberally through the kingdom. As he was the cause, so he was the distributor, of the bounties that were raised; and this work employed his constant attention for several years. The management of the affair not only required his daily visits to the captives, but engaged him in a very large correspondence, both at home and abroad."—*Gentleman's Magazine*, for November, 1787. "Dr. Franklin, who was in constant correspondence with him during the whole period of the Revolution, for it was through Mr. Wren that the allowance of eighteen pence a week each, granted by the envoys, was paid to the prisoners, had the liveliest sense of his worth. It was in consequence of Franklin's suggestion, that Congress, in 1783, sent him a vote of thanks, and that Princeton College conferred on him the degree of Doctor of Divinity."—Parton, *Life and Times of Benjamin Franklin*, ii. 322-23; Sparks, *Works of Franklin*, ix. 545.

[2] Mr. Duckett, a name oft repeated in this Journal; styled "Esq.," in Journal, under dates of May 26, July 15, Sept. 16, 1778, &c.; with Mr. Wrenn, evidently almoner to the prisoners.

[3] John Murphy, captain of the Swallow, belonging to Rhode-Island—see Roll and List of Officers appended—committed to Forton Prison, Jan. 23, 1778. He is mentioned in Journal, under entries of June 13, and 15, 1778, and effected his escape from prison, July 23, 1778—see entry in Journal, for July 24, 1778.

[4] Tobias Oakman, prizemaster—see Roll—committed to prison, Jan. 23, 1778.

[5] Benjamin Chew, lieutenant, Sturdy Beggar, Maryland—see List of Officers—prizemaster—see Roll; where the Sturdy Beggar is alluded to, as "out of Virginia"—committed to Forton Prison, Jan. 23, 1778. "Capt." Chew is several times alluded to in Journal, entries for June 15, 19, Sept. 7, 1778, &c., and effected his escape from prison, July 23, 1778—see entry in Journal, for July 24, 1778—and got to France. The Sturdy Beggar was destroyed in the Delaware, 1777. July 30, 1777, news was received in London, that four of the Leeward Island fleet were taken by the Sturdy Beggar privateer, one of which they gave up to the crew.—*Town and Country Magazine*, for 1777, p. 443.

[6] Gabriel Slacomb, or Slacom, prizemaster, Sturdy Beggar, Maryland—see Roll and List of Officers appended—committed to Forton Prison, Jan. 23, 1778. "Capt." Slacomb effected his escape from prison, July 23, 1778—see entry in Journal, for July 24, 1778.

[7] Of the crew of the Rising States—see Roll—committed to Forton Prison, June 14, 1777.

[8] In allusion perhaps to Lord North's conciliatory bills of February 17, previous—see note, under entry of Journal, for April 16, 1778.

[9] See note to Journal, under entry, dated July 30, 1777.

[10] Edward Manning, one of the crew of the Rising States—see Roll—committed to Forton Prison, June 14, 1777. For further adventures of Mr. Manning, see entries in Journal, under dates of April 20, 24, 26, 28, May 1, 6, 13, 17, 19, and June 6, 1778.

and the next morning had liberty to stay out to dinner. After dinner he made another trial and got clear off. After he got out he found a friend that both supplied him with money and clothes, and immediately set out for London ; and just as he got into the bounds of London the Pressgang came across him and pressed him, and carried him on board of the Nightingale tender off the Tower. I do not expect to see him again, as they are in great want of men.

March 14th, this day Mr. Hartly[1] and Mr. Thornton[2] came to see us, and told us that we should be exchanged very soon, and that he would do

---

[1] Mr. Hartly, member of parliament—alluded to again under entries of Journal, for April 7, June 23, July 10, and Dec. 20, 22, 1778, as taking a friendly interest in these American prisoners. Hartley, an informal agent to Franklin, at Paris, is mentioned by Bancroft, *Hist. U. S.* ix. 324, 485, 497. David Hartley, Esq., member of parliament for Kingston upon Hull, accompanied by other members of both houses, exhibited on Wimbledon Common, Nov. 11, 1776, his sixth and last experiment for demonstrating the certainty and utility of his invention for preventing the destruction of houses on fire. His method consisted in arming buildings with fire plates—see descriptions more at length, &c., in *Town and Country Magazine* (London), for 1775, p. 276; 1776, pp. 499, 555, 613, &c. After some experiments upon his method, on Sept. 4, 1776, the then lord mayor of London laid the foundation stone of a pillar—" one hundred and ten years after the Fire of London," on the " anniversary of that dreadful event "—in memory of " an invention for securing buildings against fire." A bill to enlarge Mr. Hartley's patent, for his invention of iron plates to prevent the fatal consequences of fires, received the royal assent by commission, March 3, 1777.—*Town and Country Magazine,* for 1777, p. 164. He took an active part in the parliamentary debates against the American measures ; was considered a liberal member of parliament, who had opposed all the measures of government in relation to the American war, but whose character was so high and honorable that he was confided in by both parties; a warm friend of Franklin, and the American cause, to the end of the Revolution, when as English commissioner, after a negotiation of two years, he signed the treaty of peace between England and America, Sept. 3, 1783. A faithful and cordial coöperator in behalf of Americans languishing in British prisons; agent for the prisoners of war. Franklin, Oct. 14, 1777, among other things, wrote to him from France, as follows :—" The prisoners now in your gaols, complain of very severe treatment, far from their friends and families, and winter coming on, in which they must suffer extremely, &c.; fed scantily on bad provisions, without warm lodging, clothes, or fire; not suffered to invite or receive visits from their friends, or even from the humane and charitable of their enemies. If you could have leisure to visit the gaols in which they are confined, and should be desirous of knowing the truth relative to the treatment they receive, I wish you would take the trouble of distributing among the most necessitous according to their wants, five or six hundred pounds, for which your drafts on me here shall be punctually honored. You could then be able to speak with some certainty to the point in Parliament, and this might be attended with good effects. If you cannot obtain permission for us to send a commissary, possibly you may find a trusty, humane, discreet person at Plymouth, and another at Portsmouth, who would undertake to communicate what relief we may be able to afford those unfortunate men, martyrs to the cause of liberty. Your King will not reward you for taking this trouble, but God will. I shall not mention the gratitude of America; you will have what is better, the applause of your own good conscience. Our captains have set at liberty above two hundred of your people, made prisoners by our armed vessels, and brought into France," &c. Franklin again writes, Feb. 12, 1778, " A thousand thanks for your so readily engaging in the means of relieving our poor captives, and the pains you have taken, and the advances you have made for that purpose. I received your kind letter of the 3d instant, and send you enclosed a bill of one hundred pounds. I much approve of Mr. Wren's prudent, as well as benevolent conduct in the disposition of the money, and wish him to continue doing what shall appear to him and to you to be right, &c. I beg you will present him, when you write, my respectful acknowledgment. * * * The subscription for the prisoners will have excellent effects in favor of England and Englishmen. If you have an opportunity, I wish you would express our respectful acknowledgments and thanks to your committee and contributors, whose benefactions will make our poor people as comfortable as their situation can permit." The subscriptions for the purpose of relieving American prisoners in Britain, ceased in England, by 1781. Franklin allowed to them at that period, a sixpence each per week during the summer. On May 3, 1782, Hartley announced to Franklin, that a general order was issued by his government, for the release of all American prisoners everywhere. Sparks says of Hartley, " He visited them often, collected money by subscription for their relief, interceded with the ministers in their behalf, and used his unremitted efforts at various times to procure their exchange." Hartley died 1813, aged 84.

[2] This gentleman is not again alluded to in the Journal. Major Thornton, afterwards private secretary of Arthur Lee, agent to visit American prisoners, by permission of Lord North, is evidently here meant.

all that lay in his power for us, and advised the officers to write a petition to Lord North, and another to Lord Sandwich, which was accordingly done, and sent them by Mr. Hartly, member of Parliament.

March 18th, this day we received letters from Capt. Thompson at Nantes, in France.[1] Last night, a very hot press through Portsmouth and Gosport. They pressed five hundred men, and sent them on board the guard ship at Spithead.[2]

March 21st, the news confirmed that the French Court has made an alliance with the United States of America, which has put this country into great consternation; and at this time, England has not but twenty-five thousand men in all England militia, and all which we have by the best accounts, and they dread a French war.[3] Admiral Mann is arrived at Spithead, from Gibraltar, with his fleet.[4]

1778, March 26th. Fine pleasant weather, but no certainty of our being exchanged. It is said we shall soon be exchanged, but cannot tell when. I am now going to begin with particulars.

March 27th. Nothing remarkable this day.

March 28th. Mr. Duckett came and told us the agreeable news of being sent home, which the Government has ordered; two ships to be got ready immediately to carry us home.

March 29th. Nothing strange. Cloudy weather.

March 30th. Still cloudy and rainy; daily expecting the transports to arrive at Spithead to carry us home in.

March 31st. This day great talks of an exchange of Ministry, and some say it is very certain.[5]

April 1st. Nothing worth speaking of this day.

April 2d. This day eleven prisoners came here from on board the Princess Amelia, all Americans, and three officers from the Southern States.[6] No news of the ships being come yet to carry us home, and we begin to grow in despair.

April 3d. This day clear weather and nothing strange.

April 4th. Very pleasant; nothing worth mentioning.

April 5th. Clear weather. Mr. Duckett came and told us it was certainly agreed on in Parliament of our exchange.

6th. This day cold and rainy; nothing remarkable.

7th. This day fine moderate weather. Mr. Duckett and Mr. Wrenn came and paid the officers eight shillings, and the men two; likewise told us that Mr. Hartly had waited upon Lord North to know a set time for our embarkation.

---

[1] See note to Journal, under entry, dated March 1, 1777.

[2] A like instance of the impressment of five hundred men for the men of war and transports, without respect of persons, that occurred in the streets of New York, May 20, 1757, is mentioned in Dr. A. R. Cutter's Journal of his Military Experience, 1756–1758, published in *Hist. Cutter Family* (Boston, 1871), p. 67.

[3] France concluded a treaty of amity with America, Feb. 6, 1778; officially announced to the British government, March 13, 1778, and communicated to both houses of parliament, March 17, 1778.

[4] Admiral Mann, commander in chief of his majesty's squadron in the Mediterranean. In February, 1777, letters from Gibraltar mentioned that Admiral Mann had quite cleared that part of the provincial privateers, as several frigates had been out a cruising, and had returned without meeting with anyone. In September, 1777, Admiral Duff was announced as appointed to relieve Admiral Mann, in the Mediterranean.—*Town and Country Magazine,* for 1777, pp. 109, 499, 556, &c.; *Ibid,* for 1776, 162, 276.

[5] See histories of the time.

[6] See Roll. "Southern States"—states south of New-England and New-York, were at this period often so designated.

8th. This day clear weather and nothing new stirring.

9th. This day a proclamation was read in Portsmouth for all deserters to come in, and they shall have his Majesty's free pardon.[1]

10th. Fine weather; nothing remarkable.

Saturday, 11th. Clear weather and nothing remarkable.

Sunday, 12th. Fine weather. Mr. Bailey was abused by some of the Frenchmen concerning their being taken.[2]

Monday, 13th. Clear weather; nothing new.

Tuesday, 14th. This day cloudy. Mr. Wrenn came and paid us the money, but brought no news of our going home.

Wednesday, 15th. Nothing remarkable this day.

Thursday, 16th. This day the Commissioners embarked at Spithead for America;[3] nothing new.

Friday, 17th. The first part of this day cloudy. Rev. Mr. Wrenn came here, but brought us no news of our exchange.

Saturday, 18th. Fine weather; nothing remarkable this day.

Sunday, 19th. This day we have the news of one of the English Islands being taken, &c. &c.

Monday, 20th. This day rain and hail. Mr. Manning was brought from on board the Princess Amelia, after being absent from us six weeks, and put into the Black Hole. He is not allowed to speak with us.

Tuesday, 21st. This day rainy and squally. Mr. Wrenn and Mr. Duckett came and paid us our wages; no news.

Wednesday, 22d. Clear weather and nothing new.

Thursday, 23d. Cold and cloudy. Yesterday the Commissioners sailed for America with a fair wind.

Friday, 24th. Clear weather. Mr. Manning was let out of the Black Hole for two hours to air himself.

Saturday, 25th. Fine weather. We hear the Boston Frigate[4] is arrived at Nantes with forty prisoners on board.

Sunday, 26th. Fine weather. Mr. Manning let out of the Black Hole for two hours to air himself; no news.

Monday, 27th. Nothing remarkable this day.

Tuesday, 28th. The first part of this day cloudy. Mr. Manning let out of the Black Hole for two hours.

Wednesday, 29th. Cloudy weather. Thomas, the turnkey,[5] informed me that he was down into Gosport last night, and he was told by one of the

---

[1] A similar proclamation to deserters from his majesty's service, issued by Howe, in New York, Sept. 30, 1776, is published in *Town and Country Magazine*, for that year, p. 615.

[2] Benjamin Bayley, prizemaster, Revenge, of the Continental Service, commanded a prize of that sloop, out of France—see Roll and List of Officers appended—committed to Forton Prison, Aug. 11, 1777—his crew mostly French. He—Capt. Benjamin Bayley—entered the British service on board of a man of war, near the close of the year 1778—see entries in Journal, for Dec. 17, 19, 1778, &c.

[3] Feb. 17, 1778, Lord North introduced two conciliatory bills, one declaring the intention of the parliament of Great Britain not to exercise the right of imposing taxes within the colonies of North America, and the other appointing commissioners to treat with America, whose propositions were rejected by Congress. These commissioners are again alluded to in this Journal, in entries for April 23, July 10, 23, 1778. Franklin's utterance on the above bills was as follows:—"England is in great consternation, and the minister, on the 17th instant, confessing that all his measures had been wrong, and that peace was necessary, proposed two bills for quieting America; but they are full of artifice and deceit, and will, I am confident, be treated accordingly by our country."

[4] Again alluded to in Journal, entries for Aug. 28, and Oct. 5, 1778. Of the American Navy, building at Boston, 1776.—*Cooper. Vide* REGISTER, xxv. 364.

[5] See entry for June 21, 1778.

watermen, that there were two ships arrived at Spithead, and he had been on board one of them, and was told by one of the men that they were to carry the American prisoners home to America; no more news.

Thursday, 30th. This day we have the news that General Howe was a prisoner (Godsend); likewise that Halifax was taken by the French, and our people were in possession of it.[1]

May 1st, Friday. Cloudy weather. This morning Manning was let out of the Black Hole, but by the Agent's orders he was put in again. Last night one of the commissioners from the Board of Admiralty came to Gosport, and is expected here every minute to view the prisons and to see what necessaries are wanting. The King and Queen are looked for at Portsmouth every day to view the fleet at Spithead;[2] likewise the Prince of Wales and Lord Sandwich. Various accounts about General Howe, but cannot find out the particulars.

Saturday, 2d. Cloudy weather. This day a rathole was found in our prison by means of one of the Frenchmen, who was well whipped for it. This day the King came to Portsmouth to view the fleet. (This day their Majesties arrived at Portsmouth, it being a wet, rainy day, &c.)

Sunday, 3d. Rainy and cloudy. Some of the officers wrote a petition to his Majesty to see if they could get a parole, but it did not go.

Monday, 4th. Clear weather. The King went off to Spithead to view the grand fleet, which is about forty sail of the line. He was saluted five or six times from all the shipping as he went from one ship to the other, and then retired on board the Princess Amelia to dinner.

Tuesday, 5th. This day Mr. Wrenn and Mr. Duckett came and paid us our money; no news of our going home.

Wednesday, 6th. Cloudy weather. This day Manning is let out of the Black Hole for two hours to air himself; no news.

Thursday, 7th. Cloudy weather. Mr. Wrenn came this afternoon and told us that there was a ship at Spithead, from France, with about forty prisoners on board to be exchanged for forty of us; but I can't tell how it will turn out.

May 12th, Tuesday. Nothing very remarkable all this time. This day Mr. Wrenn and Mr. Duckett came and paid us our money. Nothing to eat these two days but stinking beef. All the men in the prison, or at least best part of them, carried their beef back and threw it into the cook's window, and left and went without any.

Wednesday, 13th. This day the stinking beef was brought again for us, but by the Agent's orders it was sent back again, and we got a little cheese in the room of it. Manning still remains in the Black Hole yet.

Thursday, 14th. Last night General Burgoyne arrived at Spithead from America,[3] and this day came on shore at Portsmouth, and set out immediately for London; no news as yet.

Friday, 15th. This day Capt. McCullock[4] came on shore, and after being examined at Halsley Hospital,[5] was committed to prison with us. Mr. Wrenn and another gentleman came to see us, but could not get in.

[To be continued.]

---

[1] This like much of the news that they had was utterly without foundation.
[2] The Channel Fleet under Admiral Keppel.
[3] Burgoyne sailed for England on his parole.
[4] Edward McCullock, captain—see Roll.
[5] *Hasler* Hospital (?), the largest naval infirmary in Great Britain, outside of Gosport to the south.

SKETCH OF COL. JOHN ALLAN OF MAINE.

By GEORGE H. ALLAN, Esq., of New-York City.

COL. Allan was born in Edinburgh Castle, Scotland, Jan. 14, 1746. His father, Major William Allan, of the British army, with his wife and infant son, came to America with the military colony that founded Halifax, in 1749, and, taking up a tract of land in Nova Scotia after the dispersion of the Acadians in 1756, became a wealthy and prominent citizen of the Province. Four sons and three daughters were born after his removal to America. The former became distinguished as merchants and legislators, and the latter connected themselves by marriage with some of the best families of Nova Scotia. One of the daughters married Hon. Thomas Cochrane, President of the Provincial Council, a man of great influence and ability. Their eldest son, Thomas, became Chief Justice of Chester and Puisne Judge of Lower Canada. The second son, Joseph, was a commander in the English Navy; and the third, William, a Lieut. General in the British Army, and acquired great renown in India. The fourth son, Sir James Cochrane, became Chief Justice of Gibraltar in 1841, and was knighted in 1845. This venerable gentleman still worthily fills that honorable position, though he has attained the age of eighty-two years. One of the daughters married Dean Ramsay, of Edinburgh, and another married Bishop Inglis, of Nova Scotia, son of Rev. Charles Inglis, the loyalist Rector of Trinity Church, New-York, who left with the British army in 1783. Their son, Major-Gen. Sir John Inglis, K.C.B., was the gallant defender of Lucknow in 1857, and was knighted by the Queen for his distinguished services. Another son, Capt. Thomas C. Inglis, served with credit in the Crimea.

John Allan, the eldest son of Maj. William Allan, and the only one of his sons born in Scotland, was sent from Nova Scotia to Massachusetts in 1762, to complete his education. Here he mingled freely amongst the people, felt the grievances under which they labored, and warmly sympathized with them, and when he returned to Nova Scotia, he did not hesitate to advocate their cause, which brought him into some difficulty with his father. He married in 1767, and settling down as a farmer and Indian trader, became prosperous, and was elected to various positions of honor in the county of Cumberland, and also to a seat in the Parliament of Nova Scotia, which he held until the outbreak of the Revolution in 1775, watching, meanwhile, with earnest attention, the momentous events then occurring. The following letter from Dr. Isaac Winslow of Massachusetts will be found interesting:

Marshfield 5th April, 1775.

Sir,

Although I have not had the pleasure of hearing from you since I left Cumberland; yet I wish so well, both to Mr. Allan and his Family, that punctilio or Ceremony, shall not induce me to wait for a reply to the Letter I wrote you from Boston, on my arrival there, before I again enquire after your health and welfare; assuring you, that every thing which contributes to your happiness, will give me a very sensible pleasure. If the winter has been as pleasant with you as at the place of my present residence, it cannot have been disagreeable on account of the weather, and I presume the Colonel's tarrying among you has been one means of your passing the time more sociably, than had he come to New-England; though it has been a considerable disappointment to me and his friends here, and indeed I could have wished to have seen him on his own account as well as mine. We were very sorry for the account he gave me in his Letter of 25th Jan'ry, that Mrs. Allan had been so much and so frequently disordered with a pain in her head, and we hope that she has found Relief therefrom, long ere this, and that her health, with yours and your children's, may be confirmed is our very fervent wish.

Your present destination is ordered in Providence, in a Retired Situation, and that you have many disagreeables to Support under, is what I am very sensible of, from some persons in your vicinity. Yet you enjoy many Satisfactions, which I do assure are far from general in this Country; which is now totally reverse from that Pleasant and happy part of the World which you once knew it, in the days of your Youth. Instead of which, Discord and Contention seem to have spread their Banners, far and wide, and I am at times too ready to fear, that Desolation is at their heels, and just upon the eve of taking place amongst us. God only knows what great overtures may befall this Land within the Course of the ensuing Summer; but very great ones, we have sufficient Reason to apprehend. At Present we have neither Form nor Order amongst us. No Courts in the Province, either Legislative or Executive, Civil or Criminal, The Probate and Admiralty Excepted, which is a Situation we cannot long continue in without the utmost Confusion.

I am sometimes ready to wish myself at Cumberland again: But there is an overruling Providence; and we are taught in the Scriptures of Truth, that not a Sparrow falls to the Ground but by His permission; yet I may truly say, that, was I there with my Family, no very small Consideration would induce me, either to bring them, or come my Self into New England, until these distressing times are over.

Through the Goodness of Providence, my Family have enjoyed a good share of health through the Winter, and still continue to enjoy it, for which we cannot be sufficiently thankful, especially as the Small Pox and Malignant Fever at Boston has carried off a Considerable number of Persons within the Course of the Winter, some of whom we were nearly related to and connected with.

The Colonel informed me in his Last that Dolly had entered into the Matrimonial State. Be pleased, with my kind regards to tell her that I truly wish her every happiness which the Marriage State can afford. I hope She has a good Husband, because She is deserving of One, and I am Sure is Capable of making a very good Wife. Mrs. Winslow, our Daughter, and the Ladies of Mr. Thomas's Family (who are now with us) join me in Compliments of Congratulation to her.

Be pleased likewise to make our kind Regards to Mrs. Allan and Mr. Patton's Family, and accept the Same yourself. I shall allways be glad to hear from you and of your health and Prosperity, and am, with much Esteem, Dear Sir

Your most Obedient, Humble Servant,

I. WINSLOW, M.D.

John Allan Esqr.

In the summer of 1776, Col. Allan decided to leave his positions of honor and profit, and to take an active part with the Colonists in their resistance to tyranny. Having learned, while in his seat in Parliament, that the British authorities intended to encourage the Indians to act with them, and to harass and disturb the eastern settlements of Massachusetts, so as to annex those parts to Nova Scotia, he despatched couriers through all the villages of the River St. John and of the Micmac country, calling their deputies together for a conference. A large body assembled near Chediac on the 19th of September, and Col. Allan fully explained the causes of grievance between Great Britain and America. They heard him with gravity and attention, and after a consultation among themselves, a chief from Miramichi replied for the whole body. He expressed their sympathy for the Americans in the war now commenced, and promised, that if by their position they could not aid them, they would not injure or molest them. Being allied to the French in religion as well as in arms, and regarding the English as intruders in their country, they were more readily induced to favor the Americans. Col. Allan having accomplished his object, returned through the woods, and arriving at his own house on the 25th of September, learned that Col. Gorham, with a party of soldiers, had gone in pursuit of him, with orders to arrest him. He accordingly made preparation to leave Nova Scotia, and embarking on the 3d of October, 1776, with a small party of friends, made his final departure. He reached Passamaquoddy on the 11th, and Machias Bay on the 13th. Here he met Capt. Eddy and his party, on their way to attack Fort Cumberland. He endeavored to induce him to abandon his enterprise, but without effect. Capt. Eddy proceeded to Nova Scotia, attacked the fort Nov. 10th, and was defeated and driven out of the country.

Col. Allan remained in Machias several weeks, proceeding thence to Boston. Here he met the Governor and Council, and had interviews also with John Adams, James Otis and others, and acting upon their advice, he went to Baltimore to lay before Congress his plans for defending the Eastern frontier. He performed the entire journey on horseback, by way of Providence and Hartford, crossing the Hudson at Fishkill, and avoiding New-York, then in possession of the British. Having met Gen. Gates, he arrived at head quarters, and was presented to Gen. Washington, with whom he dined, Dec. 22d. He arrived at Baltimore on the 30th, and on the 4th of January, 1777, was received by Congress, who heard his statement with much interest. He was commissioned Colonel of Infantry and Superintendent of Eastern Indians, and, after a conference with, and full instructions from Hon. John Hancock, left Baltimore, Feb. 3d, for Boston, receiving on the way intelligence of Col. Eddy's disastrous repulse in Nova Scotia, and the destruction of his own property. His houses and buildings were burned, his crops destroyed, and his horses and cattle driven off, causing him altogether a loss of over $10,000. His wife and five little children were turned into the woods in bitter cold weather, and were obliged to creep up to the ruins of their late happy home, and satisfy their hunger with half-burned potatoes which they found among the ashes. They were afterwards imprisoned and harshly treated for several months, and the Council of Nova Scotia offered a reward of £100 for the arrest of the husband and father. Some months later, aided by the General Court, he succeeded in procuring the release of his family, as shown by the following document :

State of Massachusetts Bay
In House of Representatives, Sept. 16th 1777.

Resolved—that John Allan, Esqr be and he hereby is Permitted to write a letter to his Father and such other Persons in Nova Scotia, as he shall think proper, to procure his and other familys to be Conveyed from thence to some part of this State.
Sent up for Concurrence.
J. WARREN, Speaker.

In Council, Sept. 16th 1777.
Read and Concurred.   JOHN AVERY, Dep'y Sec'y.
Consented to by the Major Part of the Council.
 A True Copy.   Attest   JOHN AVERY, Dep'y Sec'y.

Indian Eastern Department
Head Quarters Machias, July 30th, 1780.
I do hereby Certifie that the foregoing is a True Extract from the Original Attested Resolve.
JA' AVERY, Sec'y to the Department.

In March, 1777, after his return from Baltimore, Col. Allan presented a memorial to the legislature of Massachusetts, asking power to erect two fortresses on the River St. John, and to raise six hundred men in Massachusetts and three hundred in Nova Scotia, for a formidable attempt on that province. The expedition was authorized, the coöperation of two armed vessels ordered, and the field officers were appointed June 7th. Col. Allan became the commander, succeeding Col. Little, who could not serve on account of ill health. Active preparations were commenced, and enlistments made; but from some cause, probably the scarcity of men and war material, the enterprise was abandoned. Greatly disappointed by this turn of events, Col. Allan commenced the organization of the Machias Agency for the Eastern Indians. Proceeding thence in June to the River St. John, he held conferences with the Indians, who placed themselves under his direction and guidance, and decided to act with him against the British forces. Gov. Francklin of Nova Scotia, having heard of their decision, brought a strong land and naval force, and used every endeavor to change their purpose and to arrest Col. Allan, but failed in both. The entire tribe of Indians left for Machias in a body, nearly five hundred in number, men, women and children, in one hundred and twenty-eight canoes, leaving their plantations, crops and most of their effects behind them, and traversing the rivers and lakes, reached Machias after a toilsome journey of twenty-eight days. Many of these dusky warriors remained true to the patriot cause throughout the war; and while there were bad men among them that needed continual watching, the majority of them were faithful and brave, and coöperating with the white troops, rendered material aid in the defence of the frontier.

From 1777 to 1783, Col. Allan continued at Machias, constantly attending to the duties of his department and subject to frequent alarms and rumors of attack. Whilst the importance of guarding the Eastern frontier was fully understood by the General Court of Massachusetts, but few troops could be furnished him, and but an inadequate amount of supplies. Not only was it necessary to keep the Indians in check and to restrain their savage propensities, but he had to counteract the seductions of the British agents, who constantly sought to bribe the Indians to desert the American cause. His life was repeatedly attempted by hostile savages in the pay of the British, and several times he escaped very narrowly. At one time when supplies failed, and it was necessary for him to make an urgent personal appeal to Congress, he left his two little boys as hostages amongst the Indians, where, during the winter, they suffered many hardships. When public supplies were exhausted, he freely used his own means, and he was often driven to the last extremity to sustain his post, as his letters to Hon. John Hancock abundantly testify.

Although no considerable battle occurred during his command, his spirited repulse of the British troops who made an attack upon Machias, in August, 1777, shows that the commander and his little band were always ready and anxious to do their duty. A full account of this action, and many other interesting particulars, and copies of original documents now in the archives of Massachusetts, will be found in a work compiled in 1867, by Frederic Kidder, Esq., entitled "Military Operations in Eastern Maine and Nova Scotia."

At the close of the war Col. Allan returned to Boston, resigned his commission, and honorably closed his accounts with the government, as the following certificate will show :

Boston, Sept. 24th, 1783.

To the Honorable the House of Representatives :
    The Committee appointed by the Honorable Court by their Resolve of 3d July, 1783, to settle the Accounts of Col. John Allan, Supt. of Indian Affairs in the Eastern Department & Commander of the Post at Machias, have attended that service.   They have carefully collected & examined all the Charges against him in Cash & Supplies received from the late Board of War & the Commissary General & they have also particularly examined all his Accounts & Returns for the expenditure of the Same with his Vouchers to support said Charges, & we find he has been particularly attentive to the business committed to his charge,   Very regular and correct in keeping his Books and Accounts & after critically examining the same & every Voucher, We find his Accounts right cast & well vouched, and that on a final settlement which we have made with him there remains a balance due to him of sixteen hundred & fourteen pounds nineteen shillings, Specie, for which we have given him a Certificate.

All of which is submitted.

£1614 : 19 : 0   THOMAS WALLEY, ⎫
                        PETER BOYER,   ⎬ Committee.
                        JOHN DEMING,   ⎭

After the close of the war he commenced mercantile business on Allan's Island in the Bay of Passamaquoddy, but it proving unsuccessful, he turned his attention to agriculture.   He was an active and public-spirited citizen, and took much interest in the political questions of the day.   Many revolutionary veterans settled near him in Washington County, prominent among whom were Gen. Lincoln, Col. Crane, of Crane's Artillery, and Major Trescott, the gallant companion of Lafayette.

In the year 1801, as a partial recompense for the great losses Col. Allan had sustained by joining with the revolted Colonies, Congress awarded him 1280 acres of land in Ohio, on a part of which the city of Columbus now stands, but which passed out of his hands with but little advantage to himself or his family.   He remained an invalid for several years, and died in 1805, aged 59 years.

His public services were great, and have never been properly understood or recognized.   During the war his prudence, sagacity and perfect knowledge of the Indian character enabled him not only to retain the affection and esteem of his savage wards, but to hold the frontier against the British ; and his task, though difficult and dangerous, was well performed.   Many of these Indians had come with him from the St. John River, and his personal influence over them retained them as allies of his white soldiers, in spite of repeated attempts on the part of British agents to win them over.   His position was one of great difficulty and sacrifice ; but having espoused the cause of the Colonies, he did not hesitate or falter, but bore up amidst many discouragements. His constant fear was, that in case the post at Machias were abandoned, additional trouble would arise as to the Eastern boundary. He occupied and held the ground, and it is mainly owing to his exertions that the Eastern boundary of the United States was fixed at the St. Croix river instead of the Kennebeck. Under date of July 16, 1779, while the British expedition against the Penobscot country was in progress, Col. Allan wrote to Gov. Hancock that the "British Government Expected to be Compelled to declare the Independency of the thirteen States, but were determined to keep Canada and Nova Scotia, and by this to Extend their line of Territory to Kennebeck River." Although the expedition proved disastrous to the Americans, the Machias post was held and occupied by Col. Allan and his brave compatriots, and this defence and occupancy being kept up through the war, secured the territory to the United States.

LETTER OF CAPT. JOHN PREBLE TO COL. JOHN ALLAN.

Communicated by FREDERIC KIDDER, Esq., of Boston.

THIS letter has been obtained since the preceding article on Col. Allan was in type. It shows what continuous efforts were necessary to manage the Indians and the great difficulty of obtaining supplies. For a brief memoir of Capt. Preble, who was a faithful aid to Col. Allan, see Kidder's "Eastern Maine and Nova Scotia," p. 92. Will some of our readers furnish us the locality from which the letter was written.—ED.

Head Quarters at

Dear Sir   Odcobbahommuck May 9th 178[0].

Nuel Wallis dident acquaint me he was bound to machias or I Should have Wrote you.

The Barrer Joseph Pislot has teas[d] me this two day to go by him acquaint you Nothing material has hapned Since I Wrote, acquamobbish has been gone three days for St. Johns, I ordered him to gitt all the Intelligence Possible & if he could find out where them Indians that was at St. Johns is Gone & what their design is.

Newlar, John Nule & others is Gone in to the Country to Bring what they left in a fright at the mohawk, John Francis Gave the Allarm at Wauwague by Saying he had seen four. Expresses was Sent through the Indians and they all precippitately Retreated to harber lateet [Lateer] taking some Boats to transport em.

Peer Newlar was to have set of yesterday to call the Indians in at the time you sot to Confer with them but hurt his Eye with a Stick which prevents his going yet.

They count every hour of time you are to meet them & Expect to live well they say while Waiting for you.

They had a Council the other day & warm Arguments arose for Part of them to go to S^t. Johns. Peer Tomma did him self Honour in Stopping them & they mutially Exchanged Wampom to tarry and see you. Their minds has been Verry Flucttuating. I hope the Vessells will git in Safe & that you wont fail of the time sot to meet them.

While I was Gone after Bowen they took the Corn & Lead left with Chaney & had it all divided on my Return.

Newlar desires you will Send down Some provition Which they will pay for what I Brought wont last them a Week, they do nothing but Eate I think, I argue with them till I am tired to use occonemy but to no Effect.

I have stopt^d. all persons from going to S^t. Johns to Return back for feare of the Small pox

I Called at M^rs. Currys for Littlefield Boy at My landing Suppose he Run of for I could find no thing of him altho Just before he was at Work sombody has advis^d. him to this I shall catch the young dog & send him up

I live at Newlars Camp for the most part of the time we all live verry agreable. Ambrois is not come in yett the Indians are douptfull somthing has hapned to him. With my Complements to your Good lady & all the Gentlemen Officers Remain

Sir

Your Devoted

Humble Ser^t.

JOHN PREBLE.

P. S. Some powder will be wanting before you Come please to Send me some paper this is the last I have.

[Addressed : "On Public Service | To | Col^o John Allan | att | Machias."
Endorsed : "May 9th | Rec^d 11th | 80 "]

MAJOR-GENERAL HENRY KNOX.

A LETTER FROM THE HON. HARRISON GRAY OTIS TO THE HON. CHAS. STEWART DAVEIS.

Communicated by DAVID GREENE HASKINS, Jr., A.M., of Cambridge.

THE writer of the following letter, the Hon. Harrison Gray Otis, nephew of the eminent patriot, James Otis, was born in Boston, Oct. 8, 1765, and graduated at Harvard College in 1783. He was a successful lawyer, and for many years took a distinguished part in public affairs. He was a leader of the federal party, and, in 1814, a prominent member of the Hartford Convention. He was speaker of the Massachusetts House of Representatives and president of the Senate, represented the state in both branches of Congress, and also filled the important offices of United States District Attorney, Judge of the Court of Common Pleas, and Mayor of Boston (*ante* iv. 143). He died in that city, Oct. 28, 1848.

The Hon. Charles Stewart Daveis, to whom the letter was addressed, was a native of Portland, Maine, where for many years he was an eminent lawyer. Mrs. Thatcher and Mrs. Holmes, the daughters of Gen. Knox, having placed in his hands their father's papers, he was at this time engaged in preparing a memoir of that distinguished soldier, which he designed should embrace also a history of the American Artillery in the Revolution. He entered upon the work with enthusiastic interest, and made unwearied and successful efforts to collect additional information relating to the subject. It was in response to a request for such information that this letter was written by one of Knox's few surviving friends.

The memoir was never completed. In the midst of his task, Mr. Daveis was stricken with paralysis in 1850, and, although he did not at once relinquish his undertaking, a few years later, unable in his feeble state of health to finish the work in time to satisfy the not unnatural impatience of the general's only surviving daughter, he returned the family papers, to be placed in other hands.

Providence however again frustrated the designs of the family, and the long-deferred task remained unaccomplished until 1873, when Francis S. Drake, at the request of the Massachusetts Society of the Cincinnati, wrote the life of Gen. Knox; in the preparation of which, it may be added, he made use of the collection of valuable material accumulated by Mr. Daveis, and now in possession of his grandson, the writer of this introductory note.

Boston, 3 Novem., 1845.

Dear Sir:

I acknowledge the receipt of your favor of the 27th ult. and its enclosures. I deeply lament that it is not in my power to make any valuable contribution to your materials for the biography of Gen. Knox. The rough draft of the contract between him and Mr. Bingham awakens some flitting reminiscences which I cannot hold " by legs or wings," and are therefore worth nothing. In 1792, the date of the contract, I knew nothing of the affairs of either of the parties. In 1805—the date of the Memo⁰.[1] of the

---

[1] The following is a copy of the memorandum referred to:

" Dec. 20 and 31, 1792. W. Bingham and H. Knox entered into certain contracts respecting Lands in the District of Maine amounting to about 2 millions four hundred thousand acres. By those contracts W. B. engages to make all the advances and secures to H. K. one third part of the residuary profits. These contracts are enrolled in the Rolls office for the state of Pennsylvania in letter of attorney book No. 4, page 140, &c., the 18th day of Feb. 1793, by Nath'l Irwin, M. R.

" In the latter end of the year 1795, or beginning of 96, Mr. Bingham sold to Messrs. Baring & Hope about 600,000 acres of the lands east of the Penobscot river at 40 or 44 cents p' acre.

" Prior to Mr. Bingham's becoming interested, these lands were held by H. K. and Wm. Duer, having been purchased for them of the state of Massachusetts and of individuals.

" Mr. Bingham paid William Duer fifty thousand Dollars for one moiety and reimbursed his advances. H. K. had also made certain advances, which are secured generally by the contract.

" H. K. feels confident that the heirs of Mr. Bingham will have this business adjusted on fair principles. The character of the parties secures this expectation to him. In the mean time, the contract is a most abundant security for the sums advanced to H. K."

The above memorandum is in the handwriting of Gen. Knox, who has made this endorsement on it: " Contract with Mr. Bingham. Copy given to H. G. Otis, the 22 April, 1805."

delivery to me of a copy—I was agent and attorney of Charles Hare,—Bingham's trustee and executor,—for *Kennebec lands.* I have no doubt upon the *internal* evidence of the mem° in connection with my habits of business and relationship to Hare, that I transmitted to him the copy given me. And I have as little doubt from what I know of him that he advised the heirs of Mr. Bingham—Lord Ashburton and others—of his having received it—though he was then subject to hallucinations which finally resulted in frenzy. I have also an obscure impression that Mr. Hare considered the General as a debtor to the estate. Probably he was in arrears for advances which he regarded as amply secured by land, and which the heirs did not view in the same light. If the particulars could be come at, and it should now appear that Bingham's heirs have derived more than value received, estimating lands at the prices at this day,—I think so well of those heirs that I believe they would now do most ample equity. But this would require a new Ashburton Treaty to be negotiated in England, with certain trouble and doubtful success. Respecting the public and private history of the great and lamented soldier, I can say nothing which is not known to others—nothing, however, which can shed much light upon either. I first became acquainted with him—if acquaintance it may be called—when I was about 9 years old. He then kept the "London book store," so called, in (now) Washington Street,[1] where Brewer & Co. now keep a large druggist establishment. It was a store of great display and attraction for young and old, and a fashionable morning lounge. I passed it every day, and have often seen him at his counter. I well remember the prevailing gossip concerning Harry Knox and Miss Flucker, whom he afterwards married. She was the daughter of Thomas Flucker, a high-toned loyalist of great family pretensions. She was distinguished as a young lady of high intellectual endowments, very fond of books, and especially of the books sold by Knox, to whose shelves she had frequent recourse, and on whose premises was kindled as the story went the "guiltless flame" which was destined to burn on the hymeneal altar, despite of "father and mother, and all of my kin." The opposition of her family to the connection was no secret in Boston. I learned it in my mother's family circle, she being herself of loyalist descent,[2] and moving in the same clique with the Fluckers at times. Henry Knox was at that time—just previous to the siege of Boston—an officer, perhaps in the Cadet Company ; but I rather think in the Boston Artillery, commanded by Adino Paddock. However that may be, he was a splendid figure in uniform. In April, 1775, I left Boston with my family for exile in the country; and I believe that Mrs. Knox's father and family left the country with the British army ; and whether the union of Mr. and Mrs. Knox took place prior to or soon after that event, I do not remember. In April, 1776, I came back to Boston, a schoolboy, and he went into the army. Of course, for many years his career was open to the public inspection of his

---

[1] Then number 92, now number 238 Washington street. When Knox kept here, the street was named Cornhill. Messrs. Brewer & Co. occupied these premises till 1859, when Messrs. Henry W. Dutton & Son, proprietors of the *Boston Daily Evening Transcript*, took a long lease of the estate and erected a new building on it for their own use. Here the *Transcript* was published till 1872, when it was removed to its present location. Soon after this, the *Boston Daily Globe* was commenced here; and the building is still used for the publication of that newspaper. The Blue Anchor Tavern, a famous inn, kept by George Monck in the seventeenth century, which John Dunton mentions in his "Letters from New England," stood on or near this spot.—ED.

[2] She was Elizabeth, dau. of Hon. Harrison Gray, Receiver General of Massachusetts, a loyalist, who died in England. See Sabine's "Loyalists of the American Revolution," 1. 488.—ED.

country. In the interval which elapsed between the epoch of the peace and the Congress of 1797, of which I was a member, I met Gen. Knox in society in Boston, where he occasionally resided for short periods, and partook of his splendid and exuberant hospitality in Philadelphia when that city was his domicil. During this period my acquaintance with him gradually ripened, but I could hardly claim an intimacy with him until after I terminated the first act in my political drama in 1801. From that date to the end of his life, my acquaintance with him was upon the most intimate and cordial footing. I had the honor of receiving him not unfrequently at my own house, and of meeting him in the society of our common friends. I also served with him in the legislature of Massachusetts, and enjoyed the gratification of a perfect communion of political opinions and efforts in that stormy period. He did not profess the talent of debate, but was unaffectedly diffident of his oratorical powers. He was nevertheless a fluent and effective speaker. He had the gift of natural eloquence ; his imagination was ardent, and his style sublimated perhaps to a fault. He often inscribed his notes upon the back of cards, a few of which he held in a lame hand and shuffled them over as if sorting them for a game of whist ; and no man commanded more attention and respect than were willingly yielded by his auditors as a homage to his unquestioned sincerity, magnanimity and grandeur of soul. But it was in familiar conversation with friends, and in the social, convivial and polished circles of society that he figured to the best advantage. Not that he was of the number who were expected " to set the table in a roar " ; not that he would have shone as a table-talker at the side of Coleridge or Lamb or Sydney Smith, or of Gouverneur Morris or Fisher Ames. His genius had not been brayed in the classic mortars. But his early vocation afforded the means which his natural taste improved, of amassing a large store from miscellaneous reading, and life in the camp had furnished him with a fund of anecdotes and made him a proficient in the knowledge of mankind. He was thus prepared by his own resources, and disposed by the delightful and playful amenity of his temperament, to fall in with the prevailing current of conversation, to touch gracefully the topics which happened to be started, to pass easily from " grave to gay," and catch the " Cynthia of the minute." These qualities, combined with a natural dignity of character, and his reputation as a patriot soldier, made him the " *desiré* "[1] and the ornament of all good company. It is natural to call upon one who knew him so well in the character of a private and accomplished gentleman, to furnish particulars of his occasional conversations and brilliant remarks. But it might be a sufficient excuse that he has been dead forty years, and that I am eighty years old. But I don't think this is necessary for you. The truth is, most men take no note of incidents in the conversation of friends, however piquant and racy they may have seemed upon utterance. Boswells are birds of a rarer plumage than Johnsons, which are sufficiently rare. When we can have frequent access to the purest streams, we take no pains to bottle and cork for future use ; " *labitur et labetur*," and away it goes with its bubblings and sparklings to the unfathomable lake of Lethe.

I will, however, venture to give you an anecdote of Gen. Knox's conversation at table with a most respectable, pious and orthodox lady, the wife of Lt. Gov. Phillips, in presence of a few friends, as it was associated with

---

[1] Louis le desiré.

what I know to have been his leading view of the condition of mankind in a future world. He was a Unitarian and liberal Christian, and consequently firm believer in the immortality of the soul. But he neither believed in the perfectibility of human nature under any condition of terrestrial existence, nor in the instantaneous transition of the soul to the supreme bliss of the celestial mansion upon its flight from the body. On the contrary, it was his creed that the souls of the good passed from one degree of bliss to another —from glory to glory, *towards* a supreme and endless beatitude. Conversing with this excellent person, he inquired if she really expected that upon " shuffling off this mortal coil," she should become *instantly* a partaker of the pleasures which eye hath not seen nor ear heard in their full extent. She answered that she humbly trusted such would be her destiny. " Talk not to me of humility, Madam," said he in a tone of subdued pleasantry and kindness; " you are the proudest lady I ever knew "—admitting, however, that if such an expectation could be authorized in any instance, she was entitled to indulge it.

I went in 1801 with Gen. Knox and a large party of both sexes to a then noted hotel in Milton, at the foot of the Blue Hills, to pass the day and see the total eclipse of the sun. I took with me a very fine telescope. When the company were about moving towards the crest of the mountain, he whispered me to stay on the spot with him and retain the telescope, observing very truly that it would be of no use to so large a party. I agreed, and we had the glass to ourselves. During the continuance of total darkness we surveyed the solemn scene in silence. But when the passing away of the shadow revealed the golden rim of the disk, apparently not wider than the moulding of a silver plate, and the sudden flash of light, like a repetition of the original fiat, made visible the beautiful panorama, Knox seemed to be seized with a universal spasm ; and with feelings too elevated for articulate utterance gave forth from his capacious bosom *a shout* which seemed to echo through the valley like his own artillery. This was followed by glowing expressions of awe and adoration.

As Knox's matrimonial connection was a love-match, and both parties possessed great good sense and were proud of each other, it was understood by their friends that their mutual attachment had never waned. It was, however, well known that they frequently differed in opinion upon the current trifles of the day, and that the " *iræ amantium*," though always followed by the " *integratio amoris*," were not infrequent, and that in those petty skirmishes our friend showed his generalship by a skilful retreat. On one occasion, at a very large dinner party at their own house, the cloths having been removed, the General ordered the servants to take away also the woolen cover, which Madam with an audible voice prohibited. He then instantly, addressing the whole circle, observed : " This subject of the undercloth is the only one on which Mrs. K. and I have differed since our marriage." The archness and good humor of this appeal to the company were irresistible, and produced, as was intended, a general merriment.

When this great and good man left the Federal cabinet, he became a victim to *anticipation.* Coming to the possession of large tracts of land in Maine, in right principally, I believe, of Mrs. Knox, he expected to accelerate, and to realize in a few years, not merely the growth and prosperity which Maine has now attained, but the high destination to which she may probably arrive in another half century. His own palace raised in the woods was a beau ideal in miniature only of the " castles in the air " which floated in his ardent imagination ; and his projects of improvement and civilization were worthy of Peter the Great, and would have required no inconsiderable portion of Peter's resources to be carried into effect. He regarded his lime kilns as mines of gold, and his standing timber as if cut and dried in the market of Boston. He therefore with the most sincere and honorable intentions, and nothing doubting his full ability to repay all advances, borrowed large sums not only of his friends, but I have reason to believe of the Jews. To this may be traced, I presume, the decay and ultimate ruin of his affairs ; of the details of which, documents in your hands will probably afford better evidence than I can furnish. I know of one instance where he was indebted to a large amount to a friend who highly valued and respected him, but who finally became impatient and irritated at the delay of payment, and sought an interview with him for the purpose of announcing his determination to proceed against him, forthwith, at law. The interview ended by an agreement to lend him a further sum. This was merely one example of his power over the minds of others, which, however, I believe was never exerted but with the most honorable intentions and profound conviction that his Pays d'Eldorado would pay all his debts and leave him an ample fortune.

In reference to his nomination to military command in Mr. Adams's administration, I was a member of congress at that time, and a visitor at his house upon the best terms. I was informed of Mr. Adams's intention to invite Washington to take command of the army before it was executed. I lived also in the house with Gen. Washington when he came to Philadelphia to organize his staff, &c. Hamilton was then in the same house. Of course I know nothing of their councils ; but it was understood by all the party, from the "voices" of the atmosphere, that Gen. W. had made it an indispensable condition that he should have the appointment of his *coadjutor*, and that Hamilton was the man of his choice. This certainly was the opinion of the cabinet. Mr. Adams, however, did not conceal his preference for Knox, nor his chagrin at being overruled ; and he imputed this not to the decided predilection of Washington, but to a cabal of his cabinet ministers. It is repugnant to one's knowledge of human nature not to infer that Gen. Knox was, as the report has always run, chagrined and wounded by this arrangement ; but I never knew him, at the time he was smarting under this fancied disparagement, to make a complaint, or manifest the slightest symptoms of discontent. And I doubt if any of his friends—except, perhaps, Mr. Adams and Gen. H. Jackson—ever heard a whisper from his noble, magnanimous soul of dissatisfaction or censure of this procedure.

Respecting Gen. Jackson's papers, I can afford no light, nor I fear a clue to the discovery of their place of deposit. His executors were Elisha Sigourney and Judah Hayes, both long since dead. I was their agent and counsel in the settlement of his estate—an affair of some difficulty, which was however overcome, and a perfect settlement effected. What became of the papers I know not ; but from the accurate habits of those executors, I have no doubt of their preservation, probably in the vaults of one of our banks.

I have thus thrown off at a heat all that occurs to my recollection, and more you will probably think than is worthy of being communicated. I am not able to copy or revise. I write with stiff fingers, and attempt merely to demonstrate my good will to the ladies of the General's family, to whom I pray you to present my respects. Should you wish for "more last words,"

and will do me the honor to call on me when you happen to be in Boston,
you will find me at your service.

I notice the postscript respecting " Harry Otis and Sally Foster."[1]   The
prediction contained in it was fulfilled, and followed by five and forty years
of conjugal happiness.   "*Hinc illæ lachrymæ.*"

   I am most respectfully and faithfully your obedient
               H. G. OTIS.

Mr. C. S. Daveis.

GENERAL STARK'S HORSE LOST AT BENNINGTON.

Remarks at a meeting of the NEW-ENGLAND HISTORIC, GENEALOGICAL SOCIETY, June 7,
1876, by Prof. JAMES D. BUTLER, LL.D., of Madison, Wisconsin.

IN listening to the curious researches regarding Paul Revere's Ride,
which Mr. Holland[2] has just read in our hearing, I have felt more than
ever that we are too neglectful of the historical fragments which fall in our
way.   We forget how many fictions of history trivial facts may enable us
to displace and rectify.   As members of this society, brethren, you will,
least of all men, if worthy of your position, need the exhortation to let
nothing be lost.   Since it cannot be foreseen which of your acquisitions shall
become most useful, you will become a snapper up of trifles, which most
neglect, as they do pins in their pathway, or poor relations.   You will then
scorn no key, for you know not what locks it may open; and no needle, for
you know not how much pointless thread it may utilize.

     " A spark from this or t'other caught,
      May kindle quick as thought
      A glorious bonfire up in you."

I once read in a Connecticut newspaper the following advertisement:

TWENTY DOLLARS REWARD.

Stolen from me, the subscriber, in the time of action, the 16th of August last, a
Brown Mare, five years old, had a star in her forehead.   Also a doe-skin seated sad-
dle, blue housing trimmed with white, and a curbed bridle.   It is earnestly requested of all committees of safety, and others in authority, to exert themselves to recover said thief and mare, so that he may be brought to justice and the mare brought
to me, and the person, whoever he be, shall receive the above reward for both, and
for the mare alone, one half that sum.   How scandalous, how disgraceful and ignominious must it appear to all friendly and generous souls, to have such sly, artful,
designing villains enter into the field of action in order to pillage, pilfer and plunder from their brethren when engaged in battle !

Bennington, 11th Sept. 1777.   JOHN STARK,
                    B.D.G.

This morsel, picked from the worm-holes of long-vanished days, seemed
worthy of a note, considered simply as a characteristic utterance of the hero
who broke Burgoyne's left wing.   The promise of ten dollars for a general's
horse was also significant.   The smallness of the reward showed how early
horses were cheap in Vermont, and how scarce money had become, since

---

[1] Harrison Gray Otis, the writer of this letter, married, May 31, 1790, Sarah, daughter of
William Foster.   She died Sept. 6, 1838, aged 66.—ED.

[2] At this meeting, Henry W. Holland, Esq., of Cambridge, read a paper entitled, " An
Account of William Dawes and his midnight ride with Paul Revere."

Stark was so far from offering, like king Richard, a kingdom for a horse. Who also could be blind to Stark's patriotism, oozing out even in a call to stop a thief, and flaying as with scalping-knife the tories of his time?

But a year afterward, being invited to address the Vermont legislature, when they received from Congress the cannon taken at Bennington, I looked up the reference in my savings bank of old odd-ends, quoted the advertisement in my speech, and found it a spice-island, a veritable oasis in the desert of details over which I was obliged to lead my legislative caravan. Through shaking my hearers with a laugh, it won a hearing for my history. At the end of a string of tame statistics, it resounded as, before the railroad era, we used to hear the snapper at the end of a stage-driver's whip-lash, when he enters the village with good news. Nor was this all. The same old scrap enabled me to correct a blunder into which Headley, Everett, Irving, Spencer, and, I believe, every other historian, had fallen. Thus Headley says, "Stark's horse sank under him;" Everett writes, "The General's horse was killed in the action." Irving's words are, "The veteran had a horse shot under him." They were all led to a false inference concerning this "sinking," "killing," and "shooting," by Stark's writing in the postscript of a letter these words: "I lost my horse in the action." How he lost him we have seen by his advertisement.

Nor is this half, for, on my writing Mr. Everett, he acknowledged the justice of this correction, and paid the reward offered for the horse, in the shape of books for the library of my parish. Seldom are debts for "dead horses" collected so successfully, especially when they had been a century outlawed. Had all the authors whose mistake I have rectified been as liberal as Everett, I should have made my fortune. Dr. Sparks subsequently made my finding the text for a discourse on the sources of historical errors. Mr. Everett also did at a war meeting in New-York. Thus a mouse brought forth a mountain, and Jonah swallowed a whale.

Who shall say that this antediluvian newspaper—from the dust of old oblivion raked—has not new uses yet to be revealed? Why, I am using it now, this minute. Often used, it is not yet used up, or a squeezed orange. My discovery in the paper from the Nutmeg State may also serve as a proof that we sometimes espy what we need in places where no one would anticipate that it could come to light. An Englishman fighting a duel with a Frenchman in a dark room, first received the fire of his antagonist, and then, as he escaped unwounded, not wishing to hit his adversary, shot his own pistol up the chimney. Notwithstanding, he brought down the Frenchman, who had no sooner discharged his piece, than he softly slipped up into the fireplace as into a niche of safety. The man of notes repeats the experience of that Briton, and brings down many a Frenchman from hiding places where no one would look for a prize. Far as was that Englishman from expecting to do execution when he snapped his revolver up a flue, so far was I on taking up the Connecticut Courant from hopes of exhuming such a historical gem as I now seem to have there detected. No matter how hackneyed a subject has become, it still abounds in good things not well applied, so that if you apply them fitly, men will call you "original." What says Irving? His words are, "Most of the traits that give individuality to Columbus in my biography of him, were gathered from slightly-mentioned facts in his journal, letters, &c., which had remained almost unnoticed by former writers." Brightest blazes are lit up by unexpected sparks.

BOSTON TOWN MEETING FOR GRANTING LEAVE TO ERECT FANEUIL HALL.

Communicated by JOHN S. H. FOGG, M.D., of South Boston, Mass.

THE following warrant is copied from the original document, which has been in my possession for fifteen years past. The date of the warrant, "4th of July," and the fact that the building has become the "Cradle of Liberty," may render it worthy of a place in the *Centenary Number* of the REGISTER.

To the Constables of the Town of Boston,
and every of them,   GREETING.

IN HIS MAJESTYS NAME You are Required forthwith to Warn all the Freeholders, and other Inhabitants of the Town of Boston, duly Qualified as the Law directs, to Convene at the Town House on Monday the Fourteenth of July current, at Nine O'Clock in the Morning, then and there to Consider the Petition of sundry of the Inhabitants, that the Town would give leave for the Erecting a Market House, on Dock Square, for the Towns Use and Service, at the Cost and Charge of Peter Faneuil Esquire—(who, as is represented in said Petition, has Generously Offered to Erect the same) and that the By-Law Establishing a Market, so far as it respects Buying Provisions out of the Market, may be Repealed, that so all Persons may be at Liberty at all times to Buy in any part of the Town: And also to Do, what may be thought proper to be done thereon—

To agree upon, conclude and finish such other Matters and things as were under Consideration at Other Meetings, and continued to be further debated at this: And also such other Matters as may be proper for their consideration at this Meeting.

Hereof fail not, and make a Return of this Warrant and Your Doings thereon, unto my self, before the said Time of Meeting.

Dated, in Boston the fourth Day of July, Anno Domini 1740. In the fourteenth year of His Majesty's Reign.

By order of the Select Men
SAMUEL GERRISH Town Clerk.

Boston July 10th 1740

By vertu of this warrant we have wornd the in habitunts of the town of boston to meet accordin to time and place within mentioned.

JOSIAH WATERS	THOMAS EYRE
SAMll HOLLAND	SAMUEL HASTINGS
LAW LUTWYCHE	Wm CROWELL
ANDREW SYMMES	JOHN DECOSTER
JOHN REILLEN	STEPHn WINTER
ROBT DUNCAN	STEPHEN ROGERS

LETTER OF SAMUEL PAINE UPON AFFAIRS AT BOSTON IN OCTOBER, 1775.

Communicated by NATHANIEL PAINE, Esq., of Worcester, Mass.

THE following letter, written by Samuel Paine, one of the loyalists of the Revolution, is copied from the original in possession of the Paine family at Worcester.

The writer was a son of Timothy Paine of Worcester, one of the Mandamus Councillors in 1774, and was born at Worcester, August 23, 1753. He graduated at Harvard University in the class of 1771, and like his father and brother was a warm adherent of the royal government. The Paines, and the Chandlers to whom they were allied by marriage, had long held offices under the crown, and therefore felt it for their interest as well as believed it their duty to remain loyal to the king. Soon after the appointment of Timothy Paine as one of the Mandamus Councillors, he was waited upon by a large concourse of people from Worcester and vicinity (stated by the Boston Post of Sept. 1774, to be near 3000), and was requested to resign his office, which he did in the presence of a committee appointed to receive his resignation.

In September, 1774, the Worcester County Convention voted to take notice of Samuel Paine, the assistant clerk, for sending out *venires*, and a committee was sent to remonstrate with him. Mr. Paine stated to this committee, that he had done nothing but what he felt it his duty to do, and as an officer was bound to comply with the Act of Parliament. This was not considered satisfactory, and early in 1775 he was sent under guard to Cambridge or Watertown to be examined by the Congress for this and other causes of displeasure to the town. He soon after escaped and went into Boston, where he was at the time of the battle of Bunker Hill, which he witnessed from Beacon Hill, and wrote an account of it to his brother in England five days after.[1] He was in Boston till its evacuation by the British in 1776, going with the army to Halifax, where he remained a short time, and then went to England. He lived there many years, and had an annual pension from the British government of £84.

He returned to Worcester in 1805, residing at "The Oaks," the family mansion (which is still standing), till his death in 1807. Mr. Paine was a man of fashion and elegance in his day, and is said to have resembled in manners and person the Prince of Wales, afterwards George IV. A portrait of him by Earle of London is in the possession of a branch of the family at Worcester.

---

[1] This account was printed in the Historical Magazine, 2d Series, vol. iii. p. 440.

Mr. Paine was a personal friend of Sir John Wentworth, the last royal governor of New-Hampshire, as is indicated by the following brief note (now in the possession of the writer) addressed to him by Sir John :

A Good Voyage,

God Almighty bless you my dear sir—be assured and account upon the best esteem of my heart,—Command it and return in honor and happiness speedily to your unfeigned friend   J. WENTWORTH.
     Jany 11—1786.

The brother to whom the following letter is addressed was William, who was born in Worcester, June 5, 1750. He was a pupil of John Adams, who kept school in Worcester while reading law in the office of Hon. James Putnam. John Adams, in his diary, alludes to a visit in Worcester, and speaks of meeting "Dr. Billy Paine," whom he calls "a very civil, agreeable and sensible young gentleman."

William Paine graduated at Harvard University in the class of 1768, and studied medicine with Dr. E. A. Holyoke, of Salem, and commenced practice in Worcester in 1771.

Dr. Paine, with his uncle, Hon. James Putnam, prepared in June, 1774, a remonstrance in behalf of the friends of the royal government against the treasonable actions of the whigs of Worcester and elsewhere, which was presented to the town. Its acceptance was refused, but the town clerk, who was a friend to the king, besides being a relative of Dr. Paine, copied the obnoxious protest into the town records. At a town meeting in August it was voted "That the Clerk do, in presence of the town, obliterate, erase, or otherwise deface, the said recorded protest, and the names thereto, so that it may become utterly illegible and unintelligible."

An examination of the records shows that this vote was most effectively carried out ; the work of a pen not being enough to satisfactorily deface it, the town clerk was made to dip his finger in the ink and draw it over the lines there written.[1]

Dr. Paine soon after went to England, returning, however, in May, 1775 ; but finding the country in a most excited state, and himself denounced as a tory, he at once reëmbarked for London. In November, 1775, he received a commission as surgeon in the British army, and joined the forces in America, serving in New-York and Rhode-Island. In 1782 he was appointed by Sir Guy Carleton surgeon-general of the army, and was afterwards stationed at Halifax.

In 1784 land was granted him by the British government on an island in the Bay of Passamaquoddy. He remained there for a short time, and then went to St. John, where he was elected a member of the New-Brunswick Assembly, and clerk of that body. He was

---

[1] The town clerk was Clark Chandler.

also commissioned by Sir John Wentworth as deputy surveyor general of the king's forests in America. His commission as such is now in the possession of the American Antiquarian Society.

Dr. Paine returned to Worcester in 1793, where he lived for many years one of its most respected and honored citizens. He was the first Vice-President of the American Antiquarian Society, and in 1815 delivered an address before it in King's Chapel, Boston. He received the degree of M.D. in 1775 from Marischal College, Aberdeen, and in 1818 an honorary degree from Harvard University. He died in Worcester, 1833, on the anniversary of the battle of Lexington

Boston, Oct. 2nd 1775.

Dear Brother,

This makes the 4th Letter I have wrote Since I have been here. I Rec'd Yours pr the Prince George Inclosed to Mrs. Putnam, & since found a very Safe Opportunity to Send your Other Letters to Worcester Via Newport. It is with Pleasure I acquaint you, that the State of the Town is materially altered for the better since my last & altho' we Remain in the Same Land Blockaded Situation, by the Rebel Army, yet such is the abundance of Provisions & Prizes daily taken & arriving here, that Boston Instead of being Starved, is like this Winter to be the Emporium of America for Plenty & Pleasure. The Town vastly Stronger, Growing very Healthy and the Army in Good Spirits. The Cerberus Man of War, which carried you the News of Charlestown Battle, is Returned here after a Short Passage. She brings us very pleasing Accounts, such as have put new Life into Every Body; Genrl Gage goes home in the Pallas a Transport Ship, and Genl Howe is advanced to the Chief Command, a Man almost adored by the Army and one that with the Spirit of a Wolfe possesses the genius of a Marlborough. I cannot give you any particulars from the Country, altho' I had the Pleasure a few Days ago of hearing from our Family. They were then Well and made out to live tolerably comfortable, tho' all the Torys are Confined to the Town & forbid any Intercourse one with the other. I Wish to God, our Friends were all here out of the Hands of such Villain's—My Dear Brother, We are frequently Serenaded here with 13 Inch Mortars and 24 Pounders, Yet such is the Effect of Use, that we mind but little of them. The Rebels have advanced so much upon us as to be able to throw their Shot, beyond the Hay Market & to Injure the South part of the Town. Several have been killed by them, & they have done Mischief at the Lines. Poor Capt. Pawlett of the Duke of Bolton's Family had the Misfortune while at Breakfast Stand'g in the Guard Room on the Neck, to have his Leg Entirely carried off by an 18 Pound Ball from the Rebels. These are Govr Hutchinson's Countrymen that would not fight, are they?

Fight they will and like the Devil, for this is their last Gasp, if the present Army should be routed, & Genl. Howe able to hold any Post at a Distance from here, in the Country, there is an End to them: but at present they are fortified from Mystic River to Dorchester Neck, with a Continued Line of Intrenchments, Redoubts &c—with an Army of 20,000 men. In short our Hopes here are very sanguine while Government may pursue Vigorous Measures.

I find the Intentions of the Ministry are to keep this Garrison Secure this winter by a Numerous Garrison, make some New Proposal and in Case not Immediately Complied with, that next Spring will open a most Vigorous Campaign so that by next Fall and not before, I hope you may arrive here in perfect safety, & visit your Connections once more—(So much for 2nd Oct^r.)

Oct. Monday &

For My Own Part I am Quite Reconciled to the Hardness of my Fortune, & thanks be to God, who has Restored me to better Health than I have ever known : I am perfectly well notwithstanding the Liv^{ng}, which upon the whole I think more Healthy than former Luxurious. I sail to Morrow upon a Short Cruize, (to touch at New York) being Entred on board a Letter of Marque, as an Adventurer Commissioned, to Distress the Trade of the Province, and bring all American Vessels into this Port. My Money is Exhausted, but I am in Good Spirits. I hope you may never have Reason to lament a Generosity of Mind, Profuse to a Fault, I am sure, Prudence becomes us in a very Particular Manner, a Dependance upon Court Favour is wretched. Pray write me every Opportunity, it will yield me the sincerest Satisfaction. Pray write to Friends at Worcester directed to my Care. I wish it was in my Power to acquaint you with many Things, that I know would be agreeable but Our Intelligence is very Scarce ; If I can Obtain a Worcester News-Paper I shall! Mr Rogers, Clerk to Col Berry is the bearer of this on Board the Prince George he will be able to give you much Satisfaction.

This Town is almost deserted by its Ancient Inhabitants & the People of Boston, like the Jews, are Scattered over the Face of the Earth! Just Punishment of God !

Brother Tim^o. lives pretty unmolested at Mendon, is obliged to take Paper Money.

You mention in yours to me about your Sudden Return, I never blamed you for going back, but I thought you might have tarried till Callahan went, and then your Friends would have seen you & perhaps Concert^d. better. for my own Part I Rode thro' thick and thin to See you but Unluckily you was Gone.

It is Surprising but some People cannot help shewing a Timidity of Mind at Ev'y Danger. I must Confess I should Esteem it a Great Unhappiness to be of your disposition : I beg you would not think of Returning to America till matters are Settled. I cannot think the Safety or the Happiness of your Friends or Family depend on it—Make yourself Easy Happy & Resigned, & know that there is a God, that must & will do Right.

Oct. 3rd.—Nothing Material transpires this day. We are Ev'ry Moment Expect'g Some Capital Blow, by the Unusual & vigorous Preparations here. Four New Regiments are Rais'g and to be Rais'd in America one of which, Col. Ruggles is to have the Comand of, & with the Appointment of the Officers perhaps I may stand a Very Good Chance for a Commission and it will be a pretty affair, as all the Officers will Continue upon half Pay, when disbanded they are to be upon the British Establishment.

We have Rec'd some very good news from Canada & in a short Time we may Expect Something Extraordinary. Gen. Carleton has Mustered a very Considerable Army, was building Boats in order to Cross the Lakes, & there had been a Skirmish between the Indians & Rebels in which the Indians Killed Several, and Cut of the Head of the Comanding Officer and brought it to Montreal.

What a Medley of a Letter I have wrote but I write to a Friend & Brother.

I hope my Example will influence you to devote some hours of your Leisure in giving me particular details of ev^ry thing remarkable and particularly of your expectations, designs & intentions. It will give me a sincere pleasure. I hope your Good fortune, will procure something to your advantage.

We have here Earls, Lords & Baronets, I assure you Names that sound Grand, a Play House for the Entertainment of the Town, is to be opened in Faneuil Hall, at the Head of which it is Reported is the Honble John Burgoyne Esqre. so that it bids fair to be an Agreeable Winter here.

Wishing you all happiness, I beg leave to Subscribe myself your true & Sincere Friend   SAM^el PAINE.

Pray send me next time some London Papers.

Wednesday.

Oct 9th. I Inclose you Some Addresses, to his Excll^s Gen Gage who this day sails for London with his Retinue and a Vast Number of Passengers. I tho't Mr. Rogers would have been the bearer of this, but his Business will not permit him to go in these vessels. Noth^g new has turn^d up. I can tell you for Certain, Shepherd your Partner will not Remit any Thing Home to London in payment for his debts, he is a Major upon the Rebel Establishment, and as great a Rebel as any one in *America.*

I sent him your Letter, but it will have no effect.   P.

DONATIONS TO THE PEOPLE OF BOSTON SUFFERING UNDER THE PORT-BILL.

Communicated by ALBERT H. HOYT, A.M., of Boston.

THE statute of the 14th of George III., commonly styled the "Boston Port-Bill" (entitled "An Act to discontinue, in such manner, and for such time, as are therein mentioned, the landing and discharging, the lading or shipping of goods, wares, merchandise, at the town, and within the harbour of Boston, in the Province of Massachusetts Bay"), was, as is well known, rapidly forced through the British Parliament, in the month of March, 1774. It was expressly designed to punish the people of Boston for their "unlawful resistance" to the tax on importations of tea, and to coerce the Province into submission to the authority of the Crown and the laws of Parliament. "If you pass this Act with tolerable unanimity," said Lord Mansfield, "Boston will submit, and all will end in a victory, without carnage." If Boston and Massachusetts are compelled to submit, so argued the advocates of this measure, all the other colonies will submit.

The Act went into effect at twelve o'clock on the first of June, 1774, and before the middle of August, all trade, foreign and coastwise, was cut off. Business of nearly every sort was soon paralyzed, and great suffering ensued.

The history of the distress of the people of Boston, caused by this Act of Parliament, has been written so often and so fully detailed that its repetition here and now would be superfluous.

The tidings of these sufferings penetrated every village, town, and hamlet throughout the colonies, and prompted generous offers of relief. The Committee of Donations kept records of their receipts and disbursements, which are still preserved in the archives of the city. By the courtesy of Samuel F. McCleary, Esq., the city clerk, whose ancestors were among the victims of the Boston Port-Bill, we have been permitted to make abstracts of these records.

Beyond their special historic interest, these records have a value as showing the character of the principal productions of the several colonies at that time, and the extent to which they were able to part with their surplus stores.

The book from which the following abstracts were taken has the following introductory certificate :

Boston, July 18, 1778.

I certify that this Book contains a True Copy of the Account of all the Donations Received by the Committee appointed by the Town of Boston, to receive the Generous Benefactions of the Sister Colonies, for the Relief and Support of the Inhabitants of the Towns of Boston and Charlestown, suffering by the operation of that Cruel Act of the British Parliament, commonly called the Boston Port Bill.

By order of the Committee of Donations,

ALEXʳ HODGDON, Clerk.

Donations received from the Province of the Massachusetts Bay.

1774.

July 5.   Wrentham   19¼ bush. Rye, 11¾ Corn
  "   Groton   21   "   "   20½   "
    7.   Pepperrell 24   "   "   17½   "
   20.   Charlemont 2 bbls. flour
   22.   Shrewsbury £6 : 2s : 6
  "   Beverly   14 : 2 : 1
   30.   Lenox   3 : 17 : 0½
Aug. 2.   Marblehead 224 quintals of fish, 53 gals. oil, £39 : 5 : 3.
    3.   Brookfield 8½ rye, 10 corn.
Sept. 8.   Old York, fr. Joshᵃ & Samˡ Sewall, £2 : 16 : 0
  "   Concord, fr. John Beaton, £3 : 0 : 0
   27.   Chelmsford, 40 rye
Oct. 10.   Berwick, 26 sheep, 6 oxen.
   20.   Middleborough 51 Rye, 30 Corn
   24.   Old York 106 potatoes, 57 sheep, 4 qtls. fish, 23 cords of wood,
        £1 : 4s.
   26.   Newbury Falls fr. Samuel Moody, schoolmaster, £7 : 0 : 0
Nov. 26.   Petersham fr. Silvanus How, 11 quarters mutton
  "   Belchertown, fr. Joshᵃ Boydell & Wᵐ Clark, 2 bshls. wheat
  "   Rehoboth, 88 sheep, £14 : 8 : 9
   30.   Pittsfield (Joseph Easton 12s.) £6 : 12 : 0
  "   Medfield, 132 lbs pork, 402 lbs. cheese, 22 cart loads wood.
Dec. 4.   No. Yarmouth, 43 cords of wood

14. Union Fire Club at Salem (consisting of 19 members) £40 : 0 : 0
28. Cambridge, fr. David Hoar, ten lbs. Balm & ten lbs. Sage.
" Unknown £1 : 16 : 0

1775
Jan. 2. Salem, Deaⁿ Whitaker's parish, £24 : 16 : 8
3. Rutland Dist. Co. of Worcester, fr. Col° Nathan Sparhaw, 593 lbs. beef.
" Dorchester, fr. Capt. Lem^l Robertson, 160 lbs. beef
" Braintree, 25 Carcasses.
4. Welfleet, £40
" Eastham, South, £3. 13. 6
" Billerica, 48½ rye, 2½ corn, £5. 7. 0¾
" Westford, 34½ rye, 6 corn
9. Salem, Rev. Mr. Dimon's parish, £87. 1.
10. Lexington, 61 cart loads of wood (with the Flagg), £3. 11. 6
12. Reading, First and Third parishes, 1 bush. rye, 7 lbs. pork, 26 cart loads of wood, £1. 8.
14. Salem, Rev. Mr. Dimon's parish, £3. 19
" Dorchester, 25 cords wood, 3 pr. men's and 2 pr. boy's shoes.
" Stoughton, 17 loads of wood.
18. Temple, 40 bush. rye.
20. West Springfield, 23 hogs.
21. Barnstable, West, £7. 9. 4—including 16 shillings collected of the Marshpee Indians.
23. Do. East, £12. 10. 8.
" Salem, No. Society—Rev. Mr. Barnard, £45.
" Manchester, £28. 0. 7½
24. Rehoboth, 59 lbs. flax (James Allyne, 8 ; Joseph Allyne, 24 ; Josiah Cushing, 12 ; Abner Allyne, 12 ; Jacob Cushing, 3 ; Saml Allyne, 12.)
" Salem, Rev^d Mr. Barnard & Dunbar's Society, £114 : 9. 0½
28. Attleborough, £33. 10. 7½
30. Falmouth, Casco Bay, 51½ cords wood.
" Cape Elizabeth, 44½ cords wood.
31. Danvers, £13. 13. 6
" Welfleet, £7. 10. 8
Feb. 2. Yarmouth, East precinct, £7. 4. 4.
3. Newburyport, £202. 10. 2
" Kittery, £41. 3. 5
" Middleton, £22. 9. 1.
" Rehoboth, Rev. Ephm. Hoit's, £6. 0. 2.
  do Rev. Robert Rogerson's, £2. 6. 3.
4. Berwick, South, £11. 6. 8.
"   do North, £2. 2
" Eastham, 52½ bush. corn, £0. 8.
6. Biddeford, Joseph Morrill, £0. 12.
" Southborough, £5. 0. 9
" Newbury, Rev. John Tucker's, £46. 4. 2
"   do Rev. Moses Parson's, £10. 16. 4.
"   do Rev. Oliver Noble's, £9. 0. 6
" Truro, £11. 16. 2½
" Scarborough, £11. 4. 3

7. George Town, First, £22. 14. 4
" Sturbridge, Capt. Eben^r. Crafts, £0. 12.
" " Joseph Peirce, £0. 5. 4
" do Nathl Walker, Jr. £0. 3.
" Beverly, £31. 9. 10 and goods estimated at £41. 10. 4.=
    £73. 0. 2
8. Brookfield, 9 bush. rye.
" Greenwich, 10 bush. rye, 2½ corn.
9, Sandisfield, £7. 10.
" Wells, £9. 1: 1.
" Mendon, 268 lbs. cheese, 50 flax.
" Marlborough, by Joseph Howe, who subscribed 40 shillings
    toward purch'sg, 334 lbs. beef.
" Paxton, 11 bush. rye, 9 corn, 2½ malt.
" Wells, 26¾ cords wood.
15. Brookfield, 19 bush. corn.
" Northborough 6½ bush. wheat, 51½ rye, 15½ corn, 61 lbs. pork,
    36 lbs. cheese, 6½ malt, £10. 19. 4.
" Milton, 24 cords wood.
" Littleton, 26¼ bush. rye, (collected by Mr. R. Harris, who gave
    the carting of 6¼, and Messrs Bennett & Jno Wood who gave
    the carting of 20 bushels), 1 check Handkerchief, ½ lb. pink
    flowers, £4. 3. 0½
16. Brookline, Joseph Winchester & others, 9 bush. corn, 18½ pota-
    toes, 2 fat sheep, 1 cord wood, 48 cabbages, £25. 7. 6½
" Shrewsbury, Second, 51 bush. rye, 2 corn.
17. Cambridge, 4 bush. rye, 33½ corn, 2 bu. potatoes, 17 loads
    wood, 1 bush. turnips, £31. 4. 6½
" Concord, 87½ bush. rye, 31 corn, £11. 4. 6½
" Lunenburgh, 2 bush. wheat, 82 rye, 2 corn.
" Lincoln, 29½ corn, 19 cords wood, 2 pr. boy's shoes, £1. 15. 5¼
" Dracut, 45¼ bush. rye, £3. 17. 1
" Acton, 38 " " 3½ corn, 32 lbs. pork, £3. 17. 4
20. A Gent^n unknown, £1. 14. 8
" Chilmark, £6. 10.
    Brookline, Rev. Joseph Jackson, £2.
21. Roxbury, Second, 2 bush. rye, 1 corn, 40 lbs. cheese, 13¾ cords
    wood, £15. 12.
" Roxbury, Third, 18 bush. potatoes, 51 lbs. pork, 5½ cords wood,
    72 cabbages, 1 bush. turnips, £20. 4. 7.
" Brookline, Maj. W^m. Thompson, 1 load wood, 2 cwt. rice.
22. Bolton, 28 bush. rye, 5 corn.
" Sandwich, £19. 0. 3
24. Malden, Rev. Mr. Willis' parish, 2 loads wood, 1 pr. women's
    shoes, 1 ton of hay, £3. 1.
    Malden, Rev. Mr. Thacher's parish, £9. 13.
    Lancaster, Second parish, 40 bush. rye, 38 corn, 96 lbs. cheese,
    £0. 12. 0
25. Sturbridge, 9 bush. corn, 2 bbls. flour, 5 cwt. flour, 3 bush.
    malt, 1 bbl. salt beef, 4 bbls. rye flour, £4. 13
" Dedham, 47½ cords wood.
27. Plympton, £4. 16.

28. Medway, East parish, 53½ lbs. cheese, £7. 2
  "   Sturbridge, fr. Nath¹ & Josiah Walker, 15 shillings
  "   Danvers, North parish, 8 pr. men's shoes, 2 pr. boy's shoes,
        8½ yds check, 1 pr. moose-skin breeches, 2 skeins thread,
        £26. 15. 4
March 6. Nantucket, Rev. Bezal. Shaw's par. £26. 16. 9.
   8. Marblehead, fr. Com^{ttee} of Inspection, one per cent. on Sales of
        sundry cargoes imported since Dec. 1, 1774, contrary to Re-
        solve of Con. Congress,=£120.
  10. Bradford, 17 prs. men's & 18 prs. women's shoes, £18. 14. 10.
  "   Duxbury, 21 cords wood.
  "   Roxbury, fr. Maj. Nath¹. Ruggles, 1 bbl. salt beef.
  "   Boston, fr. Stephen Bruce, 1 bbl. salt beef.
  "   Gloucester, £117. 0. 4
  13. Eastham, North parish, £7. 16.
  "   Brookfield, 30 bush. rye, 14 corn, 224 lbs. cheese, ½ bush. beans.
  15. Plymouth, fr. Nath¹. Goodwin, 20 bush. corn.
  "   Marshpee, fr. Rev. Gideon Hawley, 18 shillings
  17. Yarmouth (Cape Cod) West par. £5. 6. 8
  20. George Town, First par. £6. 0. 3
  "   do   fr. Capt. Wm Rogers, £2. 8.
  "   Old Hadley, 8 cwt. rye flour, £2. 13. 4
  "   Scituate, 1st par. £5. 6. 8
  21. Hatfield, £12. 15. 3
  22. Plymouth, fr. Com^{ttee} of Inspection, one per-cent. on sales of
        sundries imported since Dec. 1, 1774, contrary to resolve of
        Con. Congress.=£31. 5. 6½
  "   Brookfield, 2^d precinct, 12 shillings.
  "   Berkley, £8. 1. 7.
  "   Bridgewater, East par. 344 lbs. flax, 3 lbs. sheeps' wool, 9 lbs.
        tobacco, 2 iron shovels, 1 foot spinning wheel, £6. 15. 9¼
  "   Tisbury, £12.
        Falmouth (Casco Bay) 2^d par. 30⅞ cords wood.
        Scituate, South par. £6. 15. 11½
        Gorhamtown, 8⅞ cords wood.
  25. Falmouth (Co. Barnstable), £5. 16
  "   Fr. a Gent^n unknown, £0. 19. 8
  27. Salem, fr. Com^{ttee} of Inspection as above, £109. 9. 5½
  "   Duxbury, £4. 8.
  "   Marlborough, 24 bush. rye, 5½ corn, 80 lbs. cheese, 1 pr. men's
        shoes, 1½ bush. malt, £32. 18. 2
  29. Dartmouth (Acushnet River), £50. 17. 3
  "   Norton, £7. 2. 10.
April 9. Christian Town (Marthas Vineyard), fr. the Indians, £2 : 1
  10. Fr. persons unknown (supposed to be the Friends Society at
        Nantucket) £90. 9.
  11. Hanover, fr. a lady unknown, £2. 8
  14. Monson, 5 bush. rye, 1 bbl. & 2 cwt. 9 lbs. flour, 17 lbs. tobacco,
        12 lbs. butter, 2 prs. stockings, 8 cwt. 1 qr. 14 lbs. rye flour
  "   Sherburne, 2 bush. potatoes
  "   Shrewsbury, 1 bush rye.

1776
March   Weston, £13. 7. 11
1777
Jan. 28.   Brimfield, £9. 0. 4
Mar. 15.   Newton, £22. 16. 6
    "   Boston (Sarah Hutchinson 12s.; Ellis Gray, Esq., 13s. 4d.),
             £1. 5. 4.
July   Stockbridge, £9.
             Woodbury, 1st Soc. £8. 8. 4.
             Boston, (Nathaniel Peirce, 10 cords wood @ 36s. is £18; Jona-
             than Amory, 1 hh^d Sugar, 13 cwt. 3 qurs. 23 lbs. Net, @ £8
             per cwt. is £111. 12. 10; Saml Blodgett 35 bushels Indian
             meal @ 5s. is £8. 15.) £138. 7. 10
Dec. 17.   Sandisfield, fr. Matthew Williams, £1. 4.
             Arundel, £21. 8. 8¾

A SUMMARY of DONATIONS received by the COMMITTEE appointed by the TOWN of
BOSTON, to receive the GENEROUS BENEFACTIONS of the SISTER COLONIES, for
the Relief and Support of the Inhabitants of the Towns of BOSTON and CHARLES-
TOWN Suffering by the Operation of that CRUEL ACT of the BRITISH PARLIA-
MENT commonly called the BOSTON PORT BILL.

MASSACHUSETTS BAY.—10½ bush. wheat; 833 bush. rye; 399¾ corn; 5
    bbls. 11 cwt. 9 lbs. com. flour; 13½ bush. malt; 224 lbs. rice; ½ bush.
    beans; 173 sheep; 6 oxen; 23 hogs; 111 qurs. mutton; 8 bbls. 16
    cwt. 1 qur. 14 lbs. rye flour; 283 lbs. pork; 3 bbls. 1087 lbs. beef;
    228 quint. fish; 53 galls. oil; 12 lbs. butter; 1199½ lbs. cheese; 366¼
    cords & 165 cart loads of wood; 453 lbs. flax; 3 lbs sheeps wool; 1
    ton hay; 26 lbs. tobacco; 29 pr. men's, 19 women's, & 6 boy's shoes; 2
    prs. stockings; 146½ bush. potatoes; 120 cabbages; 2 bush. turnips;
    10 lbs. balm; 10 lbs. sage; ½ lb. pink flowers; 8¼ yds. check; 1 check
    handkerchief; 1 pr. moose-skin breeches; 1 foot spinning wheel; 2
    iron shovels, and cash £2213. 8. 0¼
CONNECTICUT.—448¾ bush. wheat; 5108¾ rye; 1051¾ corn; 85 bush.
    ship stuffs; 2 bbls. 4 cwt. com. flour; 16 bush. beans; 10 bush. beans;
    1841 sheep; "83 oxen, including a cow;" 15½ bbls. 27 cwt. 14 lbs.
    rye flour; 5 bbls. pork; 1 bbl. beef; 540 lbs. cheese; 8 pr. men's,
    1 women's, 2 prs. children's shoes; and cash £251. 4. 5.
PENNSYLVANIA.—105 bbls. and 249 cwt. 2 qrs. 18 lbs. ship stuffs; 36
    bbls. and 68 cwt. 3 qrs. 15 lbs. superfine, and 1035 bbls. 2122 cwt. 15
    lbs. com. flour; 2 bbls. 2 cwt. 21 lbs. ship bread; 107 bbls. 215 cwt. 3
    qrs. 17 lbs. rye flour; 3 tons nail rod iron; 3 tons bar iron; and
    cash, £435. 17. 18.
SOUTH CAROLINA.—712½ casks & 370,463 lbs. rice, and cash, £1403.
    12. 3¾. Of the rice 580 casks & 259,814 lbs. were sold in New-York,
    realizing £1304. 19. 0¾.
MARYLAND.—235 bushs. rye; 9329½ bush. corn; 57 bbls. & 114 cwt. com.
    flour; 21 bbls. 26 cwt. 1 qr. ship-bread; 20 bbls. 35 cwt. rye flour;
    2 bbls. pork; and £245.
NORTH CAROLINA.—2296½ bush. corn; 34 bbls. 68 cwt. com. flour; 10
    casks & 5,300 lbs. rice; 1 hogshead & 10 bush. peas; 1 hogshead, 61
    bbls. 80 cwt. ship-bread; 147 bbls. pork, and £1. 13. 6.
NEW-HAMPSHIRE.—30 bush. peas; 174 sheep; 15 oxen; and cash
    £370. 14. 10.

VIRGINIA.—4011 bush. wheat; 4595½ bush. corn; 27 bbls. & 54 cwt. ship stuff; 197 bbls. & 394 cwt. com. flour; 119½ bush. peas; 54 bbls. 67 cwt. & 2 qurs. ship bread; 30 bbls. pork; 6 firkins & 360 lbs butter; and cash £447. 5. 10.

CANADA.—1056½ bush. wheat; 2 bbls. 4 cwt. com. flour; and cash £100. 4.

RHODE ISLAND.—825 sheep; 13 oxen; 1 pr. men's shoes; and cash £363. 5. 3½

NEW JERSEY.—1140 bush. rye; 50 bbls. 87 cwt. 2 qrs. rye flour; and cash £594. 6. 2

NEW YORK.—44 bush. wheat, and 6 of rye; 394 bbls. & 714 cwt. 3 qrs. 2 lbs. com. flour; 5 hogsheads & 30 cwt. Indian meal; 24 tierces & 50 cwt. 2 qrs. 3 lbs. ship bread; 22 bbls. 34 cwt. 3 qrs. 9 lbs. rye flour; 10½ bbls. pork; 28 firkins & 1669 lbs. butter; 1 pipe & 123 galls. brandy; 3 tons nail rod iron; 1 ton bar iron.

GEORGIA.—Nett proceeds of sale in New York of 63 casks of rice=cash, £162. 0. 3¾.

ISLANDS IN WEST INDIES.—2 cwt. 2 qrs. cocoa, and cash, £22. 16.

ISLAND OF GREAT BRITAIN.—£154. 6. 8.

Totals :—Wheat, 5570¾ bushels.
         Rye,   7322¾   "
         Corn, 17,673½ "
         Ship-Stuffs, 85 " 132 bbls. 303 cwt. 2 qrs. 18 lbs.
         Flour, 1762 bbls. 3499 cwt. 6 qrs. 41 lbs.
         Indian Meal, 5 hhds. 30 cwt.
         Malt, 13½ bushels.
         Rice, 722½ casks, 375,987 lbs.
         Beans, 16½ bushels.
         Peas, 1 hhd. 169½ bushels.
         Ship Bread, 1 hhd. 24 tierces, 138 bbls., 226 cwt. 1 qr. 24 lbs.
         Sheep, 3013.
         Oxen, 117.
         Hogs, 23.
         Mutton, 111 qrs.
         Rye Flour, 222½ bbls. 416 cwt. 3 qrs. 8 lbs.
         Pork, 194½ bbls. & 283 lbs.
         Beef, 4 bbls. & 1087 lbs.
         Fish, 228 quintals.
         Oil, 53 galls.
         Butter, 34 firkins, & 2041 lbs.
         Cheese, 1739½ lbs.
         Wood, 366¼ cords.
            " 165 cart loads.
         Flax, 453 lbs.
         Sheeps Wool, 3 lbs.
         Hay, 1 ton.
         Tobacco, 26 lbs.
         Brandy, 1 pipe, & 123 galls.
         Shoes, men's 38 prs.; women's 20 ; children's 8.
         Stockings, 2 pairs.
         Potatoes, 146¼ bush.
         Cabbages, 120.

Turnips, 2 bush.
Balm, 10 lbs.
Sage, 10 lbs.
Pink Flowers, ½ lb.
Check, 8½ yrds.
Check Hdkfs. 1.
Mooseskin Breeches, 1 pr.
Foot Spinning Wheels, 1.
Iron Shoves, 2.
Nailrod Iron, 6 tons.
Bar Iron,   4 tons.
Cocoa, 2 cwt. 2 qrs.

Cash: From the Colonies, &c.,		£6765. 15. 0¼
A balance received from a committee of the General Court appointed to take care of the donations sent after the town of Boston was shut up and before the committee of donations could meet at Watertown		218. 17. 5
From Hon.John Hancock, rec'd from sundry gentlemen while in Congress in 1777 2500 dollars		750.

£7734. 12. 5¼

RECORD OF THE BOSTON COMMITTEE OF CORRES-PONDENCE, INSPECTION AND SAFETY, MAY TO NOVEMBER, 1776.

Copied by permission of SAMUEL F. McCLEARY, Esq., City Clerk, from the original record-book in the archives of the City of Boston, Mass.

THE records, of which the following is a copy, were recently found by Mr. McCleary, the city clerk, among the documents in his custody. We are not aware that any portion of them has been previously printed, or that they have in any way been used by writers on general or local history. Few of the records of the various committees of safety have been printed, if they have been preserved; and these records of a Committee which commenced its sessions in Boston soon after Gen. Washington and his army left here, and of which we have the doings for six months, will have a special interest, as they cover a period in the history of Boston concerning which little has been written.

We think it will add to their value to prefix to them the resolve of the General Court of Massachusetts under which the committee was chosen. It is as follows:

In the House of Representatives, February 13th, 1776.

Whereas, it appears to this Court that it will be greatly conducive to the safety and Welfare of this and the other Colonies at a time of common danger, that a Committee be chosen in each Town, and one only, for the special business of attending to the political and general Interest of the Colonies, while the attention of the other Officers is employed about the particular concerns of their respective Towns, in order to this and to prevent the confusion and mischiefs which may arise by the multiplying of Committees, diversely denominated, for purposes nearly the same.

Resolved, That the several Towns in the Colony be and hereby are directed and empowered at their Annual Town Meeting in March, to choose by written Votes of such as are qualified by law to Vote for Representatives, or in Town Affairs, such a number of the Freeholders, Inhabitants of said Towns respectively as they shall think proper, whose Principles are known to be friendly to the Rights and Liberties of America, to serve as a Committee of Correspondence, Inspection and Safety, for the year then next ensuing; And any either of them for Unfaithfulness in their office to remove and others choose in their room at any other Town Meeting legally assembled for that purpose—whose Business shall be to communicate with despatch any matters of importance to the Public that may come to their knowledge to the Committees of the same denomination of any other Town, County or Colony, which it may particularly concern, or to the General Assembly of this Colony, or in their Recess to the Council, and also to Inspect whether there are any Inhabitants of or Residents in their respective Towns who violate the Association of the Continental Congress or any other the Resolves, Directions or Recommendations of said Congress, or Acts or Resolves of the General Court and preceding Congresses of this Colony respecting the present struggle with Great Britain, and if any such be found that they proceed with them in such manner as the Resolves of the Continental Congress, or the Laws or Resolves of this Colony do or shall direct.

That they make known to the General Court or to the Council all gross breaches of trust in any Officers or Servants of this Colony that may come under their Observation—that they use their utmost influence to promote peace and harmony in their respective Towns, as also faithfully to execute any Orders or Resolves of this Court which may be to them directed from time to time during their continuance in office ; And in order to enable said Committee to proceed in a uniform and judicious discharge of the duty assigned them, it is further

Resolved, That said Committees be duly furnished with all the Resolves of the Continental Congress, which have been or may hereafter be published, that has [*sic*] any relation to their Office ; And that Captain Brown of Watertown be a Committee, during the recess of this Court, to procure and cause the same to be printed and sent to the Town Clerks of the several Towns in this Colony for the use and direction of said Committees, &c., and that he Cause this Resolve to be printed in hand Bills immediately and sent to the several Towns in this Colony.

Sent up for Concurrence.

J. Warren, Spk^{er}.

In Council Feby 13th 1776.
Read and concurred.

Perez Morton, D. Sec^y.

Consented to.

B. Greenleaf,	W. Spooner,	B. Lincoln,
T. Cushing,	Caleb Cushing,	Eldad Taylor,
John Taylor,	Jabez Fisher,	Michael Farley,
S. Holten,	John Whetcomb,	Moses Gill,
J. Palmer,	Jed^h Foster,	B. White.

The above Resolve is copied from the original in the archives of the Commonwealth of Massachusetts, as it was engrossed and signed by the respective officers of the two houses and a majority of the council, whose autograph signatures it bears. It has been carefully compared with the original by the well-known antiquary, David Pulsifer, A.M., of the Secretary of State's office. The abbreviations, except in the signatures, have been spelled in full, and the punctuation has been corrected.—Ed.

RECORD.

1776.
May 7.

The Committee of Correspondence, Inspection and Safety met at the Selectmen's Chamber, when the following attested Copy of the Appointment of said Committee was laid before them by the Town Clerk, Viz.

At a meeting of the Freeholders, and other Inhabitants of the Town of Boston, duly qualified and legally warned, in publick Town Meeting Assembled at the Old Brick Meeting House on Fryday the 29 Day of March Anno Domini 1776 and continued by Adjournment to the 1ˢᵗ of May following.

Commᵉᵉ of Correspondence, &c. appointed.

In pursuance of a *Resolve* of the General Court passed the 13ᵈ day of February last, wherein the several Towns in this Colony are directed and impowered, at their Annual Town Meeting in March, to choose by written Votes of such as are qualified by Law to vote for Representatives or in Town Affairs, such a number of the Inhabitants, Freeholders of said Town respectively, as they shall think proper, whose Principles are known to be friendly to the Rights and Liberties of America ; to serve as a Committee of Correspondence, Inspection and Safety, for the year then next ensuing, for purposes in said Resolve expressed & set forth—the Inhabitants were directed to bring in their Votes for a Committee of Correspondence &c. and the said Votes being brought in and sorted, it appeared that The Honᵇˡᵉ. Samuel Adams Esq. The Honᵇˡᵉ. John Hancock Esq. Joseph Greanleaf Esq. (resigns) Nathaniel Appleton Esq. Oliver Wendell Esq. Mʳ. William Dennie. Richard Boynton Esq. Capᵗ. William Mackey [Page 2] Nathaniel Barber Esq. John Bradford Esq. Mr. William Powell. Caleb Davis Esq. William Cooper. Mʳ. John Sweetser. John Brown Esq. John Pitts Esq. Mr. Edward Church. Capᵗ. Isaac Phillips. Thomas Crafts Esq. Capᵗ. Edward Proctor. Capᵗ. John Pulling. Major Paul Revere. Mr Peter Boyer. Major Abiel Ruddock. Mr Thomas Hitchburne. Perez Morton Esq. Benjamin Hitchburne Esq. were chose a Committee of Correspondence, Inspection and Safety for the Year ensuing.

The Resolve of the General Assembly of this Colony of the 13ᵗʰ of February last, directing and impowering the several Towns, in this Colony, to choose Committees of Correspondence &c—was read—whereupon

Commᵉᵉ to collect Resolves of Congress &c.

Voted that Collᵒ Nathaniel Barber, Benjamin Hitchburne Esq. Perez Moreton Esq. be a Committee to Collect all such Resolves of the Continental Congress, and Resolutions or Acts of the General Assembly of this Colony, pointing out the Duty and powers or having [Page 3] any reference to this Committee ; the same to be copied in a Book to be procured and kept for this especial purpose.

Commᵉᵉ to meet at Tuesdays.

On a Motion made Voted, that this Committee meet every Tuesday at 4 O'Clock, at the Selectmen's Chamber for transacting and ordering the business assigned them.

Commᵉᵉ to collect names &c. of Tories.

Voted, that Capᵗ William Mackey, Capᵗ John Pulling, Mr. William Powell, Majʳ Paul Revere, Mr. Thomas Hitchburne, Caleb Davis, Esq., Capᵗ Isaac Phillips be and hereby are appointed a Sub Committee to Collect the Names of all Persons who have

1776.
May 7.

in any manner acted against or opposed the Rights and Liberties of this Country or who have signed or voted any Address to General Gage approving his errand to this Colony, or his Administration since the dissolution of the General Court at Salem in 1774.—or to Governor Hutchinson after the arrival of General Gage or to General How, or who have signed or promoted any Association for Joining or assisting the Enemies of this Continent; and of such as have fled from this Colony to or with the British Army, Fleet or else where together with their respective Crimes and Evidences or Depositions, which may be procured to prove the same agreable to a Resolve of the General Court of this Colony bearing date April 19. 1776.

21.   At a meeting of the Committee of Correspondence, Inspection &c. at the Selectmen's Chamber May 21ᵗ. Joseph Greenleaff Esq. in the Chair.

Mr. Cooper appointed clerk.   [Page 4] This Committee in order for the better dispatch of the business that may come before them, and that a regular Record might be Kept thereof; unanimously made choice of Mr William Cooper, Town Clerk, to be Clerk to this Committee.

Order of Council on James Seward.   The following Order of Council on the Petition of James Seward of Boston, passed the 27th of April last, was laid before the Committee Viz.

" Read and Ordered that the Restrictions under which the said Seward now is, be so far removed that he be permitted to pass to Boston, and be set intirely at liberty, if the Committee of Inspection of that Town shall think it not incompatible with the public Safety "—and the same being considered, the Question was put— viz. Whether it appeared to this Committee to be incompatible with the public Safety that the said Seward be set at liberty— Passed in the Negative.

28.   At a Meeting of the Committee of Correspondence, Inspection & Safety at the Selectmen's Chamber May 28—Collᵒ Crafts in the Chair.

Commᵉᵉ to collect Resolves of Court &c.   Mr. Gray, Mʳ. Cooper, and Mr. Moreton, appointed a Committee, to procure such Resolves of the General Court and the Continental Congress, as relate to this Committee.

Counterfit Bill.   Mʳ. Kettle delivered to Major Barber of this Committee a Counterfitted Bill of the Colony of New Hampshire, of nine Shillings, which the Widow Barret took of a Soldier, who received it of one Clark.

Information of Bohea Tea being sold &c.   Information given the Committee that Captain Drinkwater of North Yarmouth and Mʳ. Ebenezer Hog of Hamstead, had bought Bohea Tea of Mʳ. Pierce a Shopkeeper in this Town whose Servant demanded & received of the said Person, at the rate of Eight Shillings per Pound, for the same.

Commᵉᵉ to confer with Commᵉᵉ of Sequestration.   [Page 5] The Committee took into consideration the Resolve of the General Court, relative to the taking possession of the Estates of the known Enemies to the Rights of America, whereupon Major Barber, Benjamin Hitchburne, Esq., Deacon Davis, Mʳ. Ellis Gray, Mʳ. Thomas Hitchburne, Colᵒ Crafts, Capᵗ. Mackay were appointed a Committee to confer with the Committee of the General Court, called the Committee of Sequestration, relative to their respective powers and duty, as enjoined by said Resolve.

1776.
June 18.

At a Meeting of the Committee of Correspondence, Inspection & Safety at the Selectmen's Chamber, June 18—The following return has been made to this Committee of the number of Men, now in this Town—Viz.

Number of men in Town.

Ward No. 1	25	Elias Parkman.
2	35	Elias Thomas.
3	60	James Gutteridge.
4	42	Caleb Champney.
5	32	John Hinckley.
6	42	John Newall.
7	90	Edward Langdon.
8	60	William How.
9	86	Jacob Williams.
10	132	John Fayrservice.
11	112	John Bartlet.
12	174	Hopestill Foster.

25

At a meeting of the Committee of Correspondence, Inspection & Safety at the Selectmen's Chamber June 25.

Capt. Moor to have a permit for Sayling.

Capt. William Moor of Waterford in the Kingdom of Ireland [Page 6] lately cast away at Newfoundland, and brought into Boston by the Phenix Man of War, prays a permit to Embarque on board the first Vessel for England, Ireland, Scotland or the West Indies—The Committee being satisfied of his good character from the declaration of several Gentlemen of this Town who had been long acquainted with him, it was Voted that his request be granted, and that he have a permit for embarking, on board such Vessel as the Committee may approve of.

Mr Knox's Certificate.

Mr. Adam Knox of this Town having applied to this Committee, for a Certificate of his friendly behavior, with respect to the Rights of his Country—the following was given him signed by nine of the Committee—Viz.

This may Certify whom it may concern, that Mr. Adam Knox who has been long improved in this Town as a Pilot, has ever appeared to us as a Person friendly to the Rights and Liberties of Americans.

Capt. Prince's Certificate.

Capt Job Prince Jr having a Vessel at Alexandria in Virginia, and being about to set out for said Place, applyed to the Committee for a Certificate of his political character—whereupon, the following signed by eight of the Committee was delivered him—Viz.

Capt. Job Prince jr. Master of a Sloop now at Virginia being soon to set out for that Colony, this may Certify, that from the acquaintance we have had with him, he appears to us to be a Person who has a friendly regard to the Rights and Liberties of Americans.

Application for removing Prisoners out of this Town.

The Committee taking into consideration, the dangers to which this Town and Colony are exposed, by the residence of so many Prisoners of War in a Sea Port Town and their being permitted to go at large.

Voted that Capt. James Mackay, [Page 7] Capt. Edward Proctor, Majr Abiel Ruddock be a Committee, to wait upon the Committee of the General Assembly, who have the disposition of the

1776.
June 25.
Prisoners of War brought into this Colony, and to request, that such of them as now reside in this Town, be immediately ordered, to some Town or Towns in the Inland parts of this Province.

July 15.
At a Meeting of the Committee of Correspondence Inspection & Safety at the Selectmen's Chamber July 15. Mʳ. Brown in the Chair.

Mr. J. Warden complained of to the Comᵐᵉ of Enquiry.
The Committee having information, that Mr. James Warden a Scotchman, who had lately gone from hence to Hallifax, was returned from thence and is now in Town.

Voted, that a Representation and Complaint be made of the said Warden to the Court of Enquiry, now setting in this Town, for the tryal of Persons who have appeared inimical to the Rights of this Country.

16th.
At a meeting of the Committee of Correspondence, Inspection & Safety, at the Selectmen's Chamber July 16ᵗʰ Mʳ. Brown in the Chair.

Information given the Committee, that Mʳ George Bright can Evidence with respect to the behavior of Dr. Rand—and James Sherman and Thomas Atkins, with respect to Dʳ. Danforth.

Information relative to Connor's vessel.
Information given the Committee, that Mr. Connors Vessel, Capᵗ. Mʳ. Daniel Master, was a Tender to a Man of War & purchased by the said Connor when this Town was shut up, for about 200 Dollars—whereupon Voted, that the Committee of Sequestration be made acquainted with this Information.

Town vote.
The following attested Copy of a Vote of the Town of Boston at their late Meeting, was laid before the Committee [Page 8] by the Town Clerk—Viz—

At a Meeting of the Freeholders & other Inhabitants of the Town of Boston at the Old Brick Meeting House, May 27, 1776.

Mr. Gray chosen one of the Comᵐᵉ of Correspondence &c.
The Town brought in their Votes for one to serve on the Committee of Correspondence, Inspection & Safety, in the room of Joseph Greanleaff Esq., who has lately resigned, and upon sorting the Votes it appeared, that—Mʳ. Ellis Gray was chosen one of the Committee of Correspondence, Inspection and Safety, for the year ensuing. *See page* 51.

Comᵐᵉ to apply to Council for removal of Prisoners &c.
The Committee having examined into the grounds of several Reports relative to the conduct of a number of the Prisoners of War in this Town—Voted, that a Sub Committee be appointed to wait on the Honᵇˡᵉ the Council of this Colony, and to Represent, That this Committee are fully satisfied, that a design has been formed to carry off some of the Commanders of Vessels, taken, and Officers of the Army, who are Prisoners, also to pray that orders may [be] taken, that all such Persons may be speedily removed from this Town to some place or places of Safety in the Country—and that,—John Brown Esq. Mʳ. Cooper and Mʳ. Gray be a Committee for the purpose aforesaid.

Mʳ. Barber not to give a Pass for McDaniel's vessel.
Collᵒ. Barber appointed by this Committee and the General Court, to act as Naval Officer, in giving Passes for Vessels leaving this Harbour, was desired not to grant one for Mr Conners Vessel, Capᵗ MᶜDaniel Commander.

The List of Persons inimical to their Country on the files of this Committee, having been read & considered,

1776.
July 16.
Comm^ee to make Representation to Court of Enquiry.

Voted, that Mr Brown, Mr Cooper, and Mr Gray be a sub Committee to prepare and Report to this Committee a Representation to be laid before the Court of Enquiry [Page 9] respecting Persons whose Residence in this Town is thought to be incompatible with the public peace and safety.

At a Meeting of the Committee of Correspondence, Inspection & Safety, at the Selectmen's Chamber July 17, Mr Brown in the Chair—

Representation to the Honble Board as to Capt. Holmes &c.

The Sub Committee appointed for that purpose Reported to this Committee the following draft of a Representation to be made to the Honble the Council of this Colony which was read and approved of, and is as follows, viz—

The Committee of Correspondence, Inspection & Safety for the Town of Boston being truly alarmed at the danger this Country was exposed to, from such Information as might be carried to the British Fleet and Army—beg leave to Represent to the Honble Board: that at ye time a Fleet of the Enemies Ships appeared for several days on our coast, a complaint was lodged with them that a certain Capt Homes, and a number of Persons with him all of them taken in the actual service of our Foes, were about departing for the British West Indies, in a Schooner purchased by said Holmes for that purpose, in consequence of which this Committee did order her Sails into custody, and have ever since detained them. And although the said Fleet has since disappeared yet the probability that the Foreign Troops are now near and the very evident danger that might arise from the Enemies being acquainted with the present melancholy situation of this Town, where so many of its own Inhabitants, of our Friends from the Country and of the Army are under Innoculation for the Small Pox—Knowing that one Person in the same predicament with Capt Holmes did depart, and in violation of the fairest professions and most solemn engagements went directly to our Enemies Head Quarters, and then delivered them all possible information, and even the private letters that had been intrusted to his honor, and tho' this Committee is disposed to entertain [Page 10] the most favorable opinion of Capt Holmes' integrity, and do most sincerely compassionate his very unhappy situation, yet as they know of no satisfactory security he can give, that he will not go and do likewise we do earnestly request of your Honors a Revocation of the Order in Council for his departure, or at least that it may be suspended: 'till a happier situation of this Town, shall make it less dangerous for him to leave it—

Information against one Cammell.

Mess^r Edes, Daws & Nathaniel Fitz appeared and informed this Committee, that they had heard one Cammell a Scotchman and Mate of one of the Prizes brought into this Harbour, express himself as follows viz "Dam any one that says anything against the King, who is one of the best of Princes—I know of 500 Tories in the Town, and 5000, in & out who are ready to take up Arms against you, in case of an attack, and with an Oath added he wished to God they would come for you are in a fine Situation with the Small Pox to receive them—that General How ought to be damned for leaving any Inhabitants in Boston when he went

1776.
June 16.

off, or leaving the Town safe"—that they had also heard him at different times express himself insolently with respect to the Committees & Selectmen of the Town, and the Officers of this Army, and had made use of many expressions equally injurious with those mentioned above.

Warr{t} to apprehend one Cammell.

In consequence of the foregoing information, the following Warrant was issued by the Committee for the apprehending and confining the said Cammell Viz—

Suffolk, S—

The Government and People of ye State of Massachusetts Bay—to George Thomas one of the Constables of the Town of Boston. —Greeting—

In consequence of the Information annexed, you [Page 11] are Commanded to apprehend, Donald Campbell Mariner and him to commit to the Goal in Boston, and the Keeper of our said Goal is commanded to receive the Body of the aforesaid Donald Campbell and him to detain in close custody, without the use of Fire or Candle, Pen Ink & Paper or conversing with any Person whomsoever, untill the further Order of this Committee or the Honble Council of this Colony—

By Order of the Committee of Correspondence, Inspection & Safety for the Town of Boston this 16 of July 1776.

JOHN BROWN Chairman.

17th

Adjourned to 3 O'Clock P.M. Council Chamber.

3 O'Clock P.M. Met according to Adjournment.

Donald Campbell apprehended.

Donald Campbell against whom a Warrant was issued, being apprehended was brought before the Committee

Voted, that Mr Constable Thomas be directed fully to execute the Warrant delivered him, by committing Donald Campbell, and that a Representation be made thereof to the Honourable the Council of this State—

Capt Bradford informed of it.

Capt Proctor is desired to wait upon Capt John Bradford the Continental Agent who has the care of their Prisoner, and to acquaint him with the proceedure against Donald Campbell, that his orders may be given for the supplying him with necessary Provisions during his confinement—

Adjourned to tomorrow morning 10 O'Clock A.M:—Council Chamber.—

[Page 12] At a Meeting of the Committee of Correspondence, Inspection and Safety. June 28—

Mr Brown in the Chair

Comm{ee} to write Circular Letters relative to Fishing Boats.

The Committee having discovered by an intercepted Letter from Hallifax, that our Enemies are endeavouring to gain intelligence of the situation of our affairs; and as Fishing Boats & small Vessels, being suffered to depart without Permits, may be one channel thro' which intelligence may be Conveyed to the Enemies Ships Cruising in our Bay

Voted, that Mr Boyer, Mr Mourton, and Mr Hitchbourne be a Committee to prepare draughts of Letters to be sent to the Committees of Correspondence, &c. of the Towns of Cape Ann, and the other Sea Ports; and to propose a method to regulate the Fishing Boats of this Town.

1776.
June 17.
The Letters brought by Cap[t] Hinckley from Hallifax have[g] been examined by the Committee, the same were sealed, and put into the Post Office—Cap[t] Hinckley appeared and was interrogated—

The following Advertisement from this Committee signed by John Brown Esq. Chairman, was sent for a place in the several News Papers—Viz—

*Advertise-
m[t] relative
to Persons
coming
from
Hallifax.*

Whereas the keeping up a Correspondence with our inveterate Enemies, particularly the Fleet and Army now employed against the UNITED STATES or those open & avowed opposers of our rights, who have forfeited all title to our confidence and protection, by seeking refuge under the power which has been long engaged in the destruction of this Country is in direct violation of the Laws of this State, and may be attended with the most fatal consequences to the public Safety—All Persons therefore who may arrive in this Town from Hallifax, or any port or place in possession of, or infested by our said Enemies, are hereby directed to leave their names [Page 13] with all the letters they bring with them and a memorandum of the places of their abode, with some member of this Committee, or at the Office of Nathaniel Barber Esq. as soon as may be after their arrival here—A non-compliance with this requisition will be deemed evidence of an unfriendly design in such person or persons against the interest of the UNITED STATES, and they will be proceeded against accordingly.

17   At a Meeting of the Committee of Correspondence, Inspection & Safety, June 29, [*sic*] M[r] Brown in the Chair.

The Sub Committee appointed on the yesterday Reported the following draught of a Letter to be sent the Committee of Correspondence of Newbury Port, which was accepted and ordered to be sent viz.

Gentlemen

*Letter to
y[e] Comm[ee]
of New-
buryport.*

The Committee of Correspondence &c of this Town find by an intercepted letter from Hallifax, that our Enemies there, have requested intelligence through the Channel of your Port; whether they have heretofore received advice by this way or not, we are unable to say, but at this time of general danger, when so much depend, on our withholding from our Enemies any information of our particular situation, we need not suggest to you the necessity of a most vigilant and careful attention to this matter— The Committee of this Town have thought it necessary for the common safety, to order that no Boat or Vessel on any pretence whatever be suffered to leave the Town without a special permission under the hand of an officer whom they have appointed for that purpose; and have confined the Fishing Boats within the limits of one League from the shore. We have wrote to the other Committees of the Sea Port Towns [Page 14] requesting them to take a similar order, and we are confident that you Gentlemen will not be last in doing so essential a Service to your Country.

*Letter,
Circular to
36 Towns.*

The Sub Committee Reported, the following Circular Letter to be sent to the Committees of Correspondence &c. of the Towns of— Chelsea, Lynn, Salem, Marblehead, Beverly, Ipswich, Manchester,

1776.
June 17. Gloucester, Newbury, Newburyport, Almsbury, Salisbury, Haverhill, Bradford, Kittery, Falmouth, York, Braintree, Dorchester, Hingham, Weymouth, Kingston, Situate, Marshfield, Duxbury, Plymouth, Barnstable, Sandwich, Weymouth, Eastham, Wellfleet, Billings Gate, Truro, Chatham, Province Town, Wells, Saco, Arundell and Scarborough—Viz—

Boston June 29. 1776

Circular
Letter. Gentlemen

The Committee of Correspondence &c. for this Town from being informed and induced to believe that a Communication has been kept up from time to time between our Enemies Ships, and some of our small Fishing Boats: have thought it necessary for the common safety, to order that no Boat or Vessel on any pretence whatever, be suffered to leave the Town, without especial permission in writing under the hand of an Officer, whom they have appointed for that purpose—They have confined the Fishing Boats within the limits of one League from the Shore. We need not suggest to you the necessity of a similar order taking place in every Sea Port Town through the Colony, especially as this is a time, when much depends on our withholding every kind of intelligence from our Enemies; and of consequence, the utmost vigilance and caution are necessary to effect it—

By Order of the Committee

JOHN BROWN Chairman

[Page 15] In the Letter sent to the Committee of Correspondence &c of the Town of Gloucester there was the following addition to the Circular Letter—Viz—

Addition
to yᵉ Cir-
cular Let-
ter sent to
Cape Ann. We must beg leave to add, that the unhappy Persons left by our Enemies at George's Island, sick of the Small Pox have made information, that a Boat from your place came to, and gave Commodore Banks intelligence of our design the day before we took possession of the lower Harbour by which means it is apprehended we lost the glorious opportunity of securing many of their Ships. We are therefore to ask that you would make the proper enquiry into this report, that the Delinquents, if any such there be, may suffer such exemplary and condign punishment as Traitors to their Country justly deserve.

[To be continued.]

NOTES AND QUERIES.

CHARACTER OF WASHINGTON.—In the biographical sketch of John Allan (*ante*, p. 358), it is stated that Gen. Lincoln, Col. Crane, Maj. Trescott, and other revolutionary veterans, settled near him in Washington County, in the District of Maine. As one result of conversations held with some of these officers, Col. Allan left among his papers an unfinished manuscript without date, but bearing evidence of having been written about 1785, of which nearly the whole is given below:

"That he was a hero, Christian Philosopher and Patriot, none doubts. * * * That a disposition, naturally Philosophic, led him to an exact rule of taciturnity and reserve, which hid such imperfections as he possessed ; and not being loquacious and free in conversation, it gave him an opportunity of studying man and manners, and digesting every minute circumstance ; whereby he became acquainted with things real and their consequences. When ready to put his determination into action, every avenue was so guarded as to secure success, to a moral certainty. If disappointed, the same taciturnity was strictly observed, without betraying the least motion of his mind. This of course gave respectability to himself and Council, and created an awe and reverence of all around him, and compelled them to give implicit confidence and obedience to every thing he suggested or directed. To give permanence and success to this system, he was remarkably abstemious and cautious in his mode of living. In company he threw off this reserve before very few, perhaps not any ; thereby rendering his maxims invulnerable against the attempts of all. Very economical and exact in all his transactions with men, both in his social and commercial intercourse. Austere in his manners, but mixed with mildness, so as to keep all within a certain distance. Severe in his resentments, often keeping the nearest friend a long time in suspense as to what he thought. Uniform and exact in domestic affairs, to that length as to give uneasiness, observing the strictness of a rigid military rule, but always an encourager of morals, industry and prudence. Thus by a resolution and perseverance rarely to be found, he became so fortified, and established a habit of industry, secrecy, prudence and stability—overruling and governing his own passions—so as not to expose his own objects and plans until properly matured ; by which he became enabled to fulfil all those great achievements, heroic and patriotic deeds so conspicuous through life, and finally was so great an instrument in securing and defending the Liberty and Independence of his Country, and establishing us in that permanent Situation, and dignity among the nations which we now enjoy. Yet there is no doubt but a great share of ambition was a leading trait in his character, the particulars of which, with his military conduct, we pass over for want of sufficient information, and ability to comment on so an illustrious part of his life. [Appended at a later date is this sentence :] Towards the close of his days, attachments seemed to grow stronger, and gradually became conspicuous, for when he seemed to form an attachment, he paid implicit obedience to every advice, and of such would support and vindicate his favorites with zeal, and obstinacy, even when every one else knew their counsel to be erroneous."

This document is endorsed by Col. Allan : " Character of George Washington as collected from several persons who were personally acquainted and domestically connected."

Geo. H. Allan.

Thompson and Mitchell.—Daniel Thompson, of Woburn, was killed on the 19th of April, 1775. Is it known where he fell ?

I have a mourning ring marked " Mary Mitchel obit August 4. 1763 Æ. 81." Who was she ? Perhaps of Nantucket.

Cambridge, Mass.

C. Woodman.

American Chronicles of the Times.—" The first Book of the American Chronicles of the Times. [In four chapters of eight pages each.] Boston : Printed and sold by John Boyle, in Marlborough Street. 1775. Where may be had compleat sets of these Chronicles."

The above copy contains 32 pages. Was that the extent of the work ?

18 Somerset St., Boston.

J. Colburn.

Warrant for a Meeting of the Town of York, Me., to act on Colonial Independence.—We have been furnished by J. S. H. Fogg, M.D., with the following warrant copied from the original in his possession.—Ed.

York ss. To the Freeholders and other Inhabitants of the Town of York within the said County qualified to Vote in Town-Meetings Greeting.

You are hereby Notified to assemble yourselves at the Town House in York aforesaid on Wednesday the 5th Day of June next at four of the Clock in the after-noon then and there (if you see fit)—

To advise your Representative at the Gener¹. Court that if the Honᵇˡᵉ. Congress shoᵈ for the Safety of the Colonies declare them Independent of the Kingdom of Great Britain you will Solemnly engage with your Lives & Fortunes to Support them in the Measure. Hereof fail not, Dated in York aforesaid the 27th of May 1776.

By order of the Select Men

Danˡ. Moulton Town Cler.

POST FROM BOSTON TO TICONDEROGA, 1776.—The following memorandum is copied from a leaf in an old blank book in my possession. It is in the handwriting of Capt. Thomas³ Brastow (*ante*, xiii. 249), who was born in Wrentham, Nov. 13, 1740, and was in the Battle of Quebec, on the Plains of Abraham, in 1759, at the age of 17. He was an officer in the Revolutionary War.

"Dec 16 1776
        I began to ride post from Boston to Tyconderoga under the direction of Mr. Perry [?] the chairman of the Corts Committee apointed for that purpose."

It is a tradition in the family that he furnished his own horses, for which he received no pay. After the revolution he was a sheriff for the county of Suffolk for several years, and died in 1799.
Burlington, Maine.   JOSEPH W. PORTER.

THE UNIFORM OF THE NAVY, 1776, 1777.—The Uniform of the Continental Navy, as ordered by the Marine Committee, Sept. 5, 1776, is given in vol. ii, page 181, of the 5th series of Force's "American Archives," and can be found reprinted on page 164 of my History of Our Flag. I have lately seen a MS. copy of the same in the first vol. of the Paul Jones papers now in the Congressional Library in Washington. In the same collection I found the following Uniform for the Navy *agreed upon* by the Captains of the American Fleet in March, 1777, and which I have never seen in print, and believe has never been printed.

Full Dress for Post Captains.—Dark blue coats, white linings, white cuffs, and narrow white lappells, the whole length of the waist. The coats full trimmed, with gold lace or embroidered button holes. The buttons at equal distance asunder on the lappells to button on the upper part of the shoulder, three buttons on each pocket flap, three on each cuff, stand up blue collars. White waistcoats, breeches and stockings, dress swords, plain hats, black cockades and gold buttons and loops. Gold epaulett on the right shoulder, the figure of a rattlesnake embroidered on the strap of the epauletts, with the motto, "don't tread on me." The waistcoat trimmed with gold lace, yellow flat buttons, with the impression of the rattlesnake and motto, "don't tread on me" on each of them.

Undress for Post Captains.—The same as dress coats, with this difference, that the undress coats have frock backs and turn down white collars.

Dress for Lieutenants.—The same as for Post Captains, excepting the lace or embroidery, the epauletts; and that instead of the rattlesnake, they wear buttons with the impression of an anchor.

Undress for Lieutenants.—The same as for Post Captains, excepting the lace or embroidery, the epauletts, the buttons, and that the coats be made short, or such as are usually called coatees.

Dress and Undress for Masters and Midshipmen.—The same as for Lieutenants, excepting the lappells, and that they wear turn down collars on their dress and undress coats.

The dress and undress of Commodores of ships and vessels under twenty guns, the same as for Post Captains, excepting the epauletts.

	(Signed)	John Manly	Joseph Olney
		Hector McNeil	John Roche
		Dudley Saltonstall	John Paul Jones
		E. Hinman	
		Hector McNeill for Capt. Wm. Thompson	
		Joseph Olney for Capt. Abra. Whipple.	

[Endorsed : "Uniform dress for the Navy agreed to at Boston by the major part of the Captains March 1777."]

The rattlesnake emblem and motto on the epaulets and buttons and the substitution of white for the red facings of the uniform of 1776 are its chief peculiarities.
GEO. HENRY PREBLE.

OPENING OF THE INTERNATIONAL EXHIBITION AT PHILADELPHIA.—The Centennial World's Fair was opened on the 10th of last May, with appropriate services, in the presence of Gen. Ulysses S. Grant, president of the United States, Dom Pedro, the emperor of Brazil, and other distinguished personages. The ceremonies began a little before eleven o'clock with a *pot-pourri* of national airs from the orchestra, followed by the "Centennial Inauguration March," composed for the occasion by Richard Wagner. The Rev. Matthew Simpson, bishop of the Methodist Episcopal

Church, then made a fervent and appropriate prayer; after which the "Centennial Hymn," written for this occasion by John G. Whittier and set to music by John K. Paine, was sung. John Welch, president of the board of finance, in a brief speech, then presented the exhibition buildings to the centennial commission, which Gen. Joseph R. Hawley, president of the commission, accepted. A cantata written for the occasion by Sidney Lanier, set to music by Dudley Buck, was next sung; after which Gen. Hawley in a clear and distinct voice delivered an address presenting the exhibition to the President of the United States. To this president Grant replied in a brief speech. When he had finished his address with the words, "I declare the International Exhibition now open," a sign was given from the platform and the United States flag was raised in the main building. Then the chorus sang the "Hallelujah," bells and organs joining in the melody.

———

CENTENARIANS.—*Hannah Elden*, daughter of Capt. John Elden and his wife Ruth Sands, was born in Saco, Maine, April 13, 1769; married to Samuel Andrews, of Hillsborough, N. H., and with her husband settled in Lovell, Maine. She died August 29, 1871, aged 102 years, 4 months and 16 days, and was buried on the farm of her son in Lovell. Her parents were married Dec. 17, 1747, and had a daughter Martha, born Oct. 14, 1748. Hannah was the 10th and youngest child. She was blind for *twenty years* previous to her death. She was granddaughter of John Elden, of Saco, who married Martha Knight, and died in 1746. Her record of birth upon the town books, and in the ancient family bible now with her son, agree. I have seen her likeness taken when she was past one hundred.

John Redlon, son of Matthias and Rachel (Edgcomb) Redlon, was born in Saco, Maine, November 11, 1769; married Hannah Holmes, of Kennebunk, Me., and settled in Hollis, then Little Falls Plantation, about 1780. He died in Waynesfield, Auglaize co., Ohio, in September, 1866, aged 106 years and 2 months. He was never sick the day of his death. When one hundred years old sat in a chair, and killed birds in his orchard with his gun. Once lived in Vermont. Emigrated to Ohio in 1800. A beautiful silk embroidered banner was presented to him by the women of St. Mary's, Ohio, on his 106th birthday, with the following letters in gold:

JOHN REDLEY, A SOLDIER OF THE
REVOLUTION,
AGED 106 YEARS.

He enlisted at Buxton, Me., in the spring of 1773, for 3 years, under Capt. John Elden, joining the army at Peekskill, N. Y., and attached to the 10th Mass. Regt. Col. Tupper going to West Point. About a year after, a re-arrangement transferred him to the 1st Reg. Mass., Col. Vose. He was discharged in the autumn of 1780 at New York City. Record of his birth in an account book once his father's, with those of his brothers and sisters. His sister Mary was born June 2, 1758, and a twin brother and sister—Abraham and Judy—September 21, 1763. He was a grandson of Magnus Riddell who came from Scotland, and settling in Maine, changed his name to Magnus Readlan, and Redlon. He was followed to his grave by a company of 1812 ex-soldiers, and two major generals on white horses—buried under arms.

Sarah Young, of Biddeford, Maine, was married to Ebenezer Redlon, then of Biddeford, August 8, 1751. Two of her children—Anna and Ebenezer—were baptized February 29, 1756. She died December 26, 1856, in Buxton, Maine. Her husband was a soldier in the Revolution, and died in the army. She was the mother of eleven children, and her descendants numbered 273 at her death. It will be seen that she must have been considerably more than one hundred years old by comparing the date of her marriage and the baptism with that of her death. I have not found the record of her birth, but think it may be found in the town records of York, Me.

Harrison, Me.   G. T. RIDLON.

———

MARBLEHEAD CENTENNIAL.—The one hundredth anniversary of the death of the brave Capt. James Mugford, of revolutionary fame, was celebrated in Marblehead, May 17, 1876, by the dedication of a monument to his memory. The Hon. George B. Loring delivered an oration, and there were other interesting ceremonies. The buildings in the town were extensively decorated.

BOOK-NOTICES.

Life of Israel Putnam (*" Old Put"*), *Major General in the Continental Army.* By INCREASE N. TARBOX. With Map and Illustrations. Boston: Lockwood, Brooks and Company. 1876. [8vo. pp. 389.]

Israel Putnam was one of the most popular generals in the American revolution, and it is well, in this centennial year, that a new life of him should be brought out. The Rev. Dr. Tarbox, to whom we are indebted for this memoir, is the author of the two series of articles, mentioned in the January REGISTER (*ante*, p. 137), as published last year, one in the *New-York Herald* and the other in the *Boston Journal*, in favor of Gen. Putnam as the commander at the battle of Bunker Hill. A large portion of the present work is devoted to this question. It is only the controversy which has been raised that renders this necessary ; for Gen. Putnam has a brilliant reputation independent of his services at Bunker Hill.

Though a great deal has been written on both sides of the question, Dr. Tarbox has been able to add much to the strength of the argument in favor of Putnam. Not only does he refuse to believe that Col. Prescott was the commander of the action of the 17th June, but he doubts whether he possessed some of the essential qualities of a commander. He allows him, however, patriotism and personal bravery. He thinks it singular that Col. Prescott, with military experience, family prestige and influential connections, was not, after an action that stirred the pulses of the whole people, recommended for immediate promotion by a general so discerning, so free from prejudice and so well informed of all the facts in the case as Washington, if Prescott was the man that our modern orators represent him to have been. Instead of this, he remained in the army to witness the rise above him of many of inferior rank who fought at Bunker Hill. He, himself, never rose above the rank which he then held.

What the true explanation of these facts is, we leave for others to decide ; but we are loth to think of Prescott otherwise than as an efficient as well as an heroic officer. We doubt, however, whether those who claim for him the command of all the forces in that action are doing a service to his memory. It may well be queried whether Col. Prescott, if he considered himself the commander, did his entire duty. It was his duty as such to post the new troops that arrived on the ground ; certainly, to inform himself of what the troops outside of the redoubt were doing, and to direct their movements. It appears by his letter to John Adams, two months after the battle, that even then he had a very imperfect knowledge of what the " party of Hampshire " and other troops at his left did. We judge from this letter that he thought the force in the redoubt inadequate to defend it. Why then did he not ascertain whether troops could be spared from other parts of the field, and order them here ? But there is no evidence that he did either ; or, in fact, that he gave any order to the troops outside of the redoubt. The most probable inference is that he did not then claim the right to do so.

The largest portion of the troops engaged on the American side were stationed outside of the redoubt, and the severest fighting was done by them. Over these troops Gen. Putnam appears to have exercised an influence, if not the command, in directing their station and their movements during the fight. By them, at least, he seems to have been recognized as the ranking officer.

Besides the controversy as to the command at Bunker Hill, the question has been raised whether Putnam's conduct there and at the battle of Long Island is deserving of praise or censure. The attack on his conduct in the first action, which was first made in 1818 by Gen. Dearborn, was ably answered the same year by Judge John Lowell in a series of articles in the *Columbian Centinel*, and by Daniel Webster in an article in the *North American Review*. Dr. Tarbox quotes freely from these articles. Some of the criticisms upon Putnam's conduct at Long Island have been replied to in the pages of the REGISTER (*ante*, xxii. 101 ; xxiv. 337). A lengthy newspaper correspondence upon his merits as a soldier, between Henry B. Dawson, his opponent, and A. Clifford Griswold, his advocate, which was reprinted by Mr. Dawson in a volume, was noticed in this periodical in July, 1860 (*ante*, xiv. 279).

Dr. Tarbox has evidently spared no labor in preparing this book. Besides making use of the new matter on the subject printed since the previous lives of Putnam were published, he has sought information from relatives of the family, at the same time making thorough research into contemporary literature, especially the newspapers of that day.

The author wields a vigorous pen, and presents, in an attractive manner, the romantic incidents in the life of his hero and in the family from which he sprung. The book is sure to have a wide sale, as the publishers have brought it out in a beautiful dress, one that is worthy of the interesting narrative it enshrines.

J. W. DEAN.

Potter's American Monthly. An Illustrated Magazine of History, Literature, Science and Art. John E. Potter and Company, Philadelphia. [Sm. 4to.]

In our April number we noticed this valuable periodical, the successor of Lossing's *American Historical Record.* We recur to it at this time to state that the numbers for this, the centennial year, are replete with centennial and revolutionary matters. Each number has several pages of "Centennial Exposition Memoranda," and the May number was a special "Centennial Exposition Number," illustrated by plans of the grounds, views of the buildings, &c. Every number contains views of historic buildings, portraits of revolutionary patriots, and fac-similes of their handwriting, or historical articles upon these subjects. J. W. D.

Proceedings at the Centennial Celebration of Concord Fight, April 19, 1875. [Device.] Concord, Mass.: Published by the Town. 1876. [Royal 8vo. pp. 176.]

Cambridge in the "Centennial." Proceedings, July 3, 1875, in celebration of the Centennial Anniversary of Washington's taking Command of the Continental Army on Cambridge Common. [Seal of Cambridge.] Cambridge: Printed by Order of the City Council. 1875. [8vo. pp. 127.]

An Oration delivered at Charlestown, June 17, 1875, in Commemoration of the Centennial Anniversary of the Battle of Bunker Hill. By CHARLES DEVENS, Jr. Boston: Privately Printed. 1876. [8vo. pp. 56.]

The oration at the Concord celebration was by George W. Curtis, and that at the Cambridge celebration was by Prof. Andrew P. Peabody. These orations are already familiar to our readers, for they were printed in the REGISTER for October, 1875. We are glad to see that the authorities of Concord and Cambridge have issued full reports of their proceedings, in such beautiful volumes. They are worthy of a place by the side of the other volumes noticed in our January number, issued by other bodies that commemorated opening events in the American revolution.

Gen. Devens's oration has been printed in the REGISTER, in the "Centennial Orations," and in the volumes printed for the city of Boston and the Bunker Hill Monument Association. The author has, we believe, carefully revised it, and has had a small edition printed for private distribution. J. W. D.

Town Papers. Documents and Records relating to Towns in New-Hampshire; with an Appendix embracing the Constitutional Conventions of 1778–1779; and of 1781–1783; and the State Constitution of 1784. Published by authority of the Legislature of New-Hampshire. Volume IX. Compiled and edited by NATHANIEL BOUTON, D.D., Corresponding Secretary of the New-Hampshire Historical Society. Concord, N. H.: Charles C. Pearson, State Printer. 1875. [8vo. pp. xli.+939.]

This large and compact volume contains much valuable information about the early history of the towns of New-Hampshire which has never before been printed. Not the least of its value will be found in the lists of names of the first inhabitants of these towns attached to petitions and other documents on file in the State archives. This volume also comprises, as will be observed, the era of the American Revolution.

Among other documents, the editor gives the text of the early Constitutions submitted to the people; also a summary of the arguments against the authenticity of the Wheelwright Deed, but not of the arguments in its favor. Another interesting paper is the editor's discussion of the question as to the date when slaves as property ceased to be recognized by the laws of New-Hampshire.

It is proposed to add another volume to this series, and this we hope will be done.
In this connection we cannot refrain from suggesting, that the change in the
general title of this series of volumes was unfortunate. The eighth and last published volume of the New-Hampshire Historical Society's Collections has "Provincial
Papers" for its sub-title. This is also the general title of the first seven volumes of
the papers and documents issued by the State, but the eighth volume is entitled
"State Papers," and the ninth, "Town Papers." One general title for the entire
series,—such as "State Papers,"—would have been better. Whoever shall attempt
to cite these volumes will readily experience the inconvenience of having so many
general titles for one series.   A. H. HOYT.

*Record of the Year. A Reference Scrap Book; being the Monthly Record
of Every Important Event of any nature worth Preserving. Together
with a Careful Selection of the Choicest Current Miscellany.* Edited by
FRANK MOORE. New York: G. W. Carleton & Co., Publishers. London: S. Low & Co. 1876. [8vo. Price 50 cts. a number or $6 a year.]

This is a monthly periodical, the object of which is clearly expressed in the above
title. It was commenced in April last, and two numbers are now before us. The
April number gives the prominent events in January, 1876, and the noteworthy
articles and fugitive pieces which then appeared. The May number preserves those
for February. The selection is made with judgment, as might be expected from the
ample experience of the editor.   J. W. D.

*March 17th, 1876, Celebration of the Centennial Anniversary of the Evacua-
tion of Boston by the British Army, March 17, 1776. Reception of the
Washington Medal. Oration delivered in Music Hall and a Chronicle of
the Siege of Boston.* By GEORGE E. ELLIS. [Seal of Boston.] Boston:
Printed by Order of the City Council, 1876. [Royal 8vo. pp. 199.]

In his inaugural address, Jan. 3, 1876, the Hon. Samuel C. Cobb, mayor of Boston,
recommended that the centenary of the evacuation of Boston, which would occur on
the 17th of March following, should be appropriately celebrated. The city council
gave a ready response to his proposal, and appropriated five thousand dollars for the
celebration. The mayor invited the Rev. George E Ellis, D.D., to deliver an
oration, and the Rev. Jacob M. Manning, D.D., to act as chaplain on the occasion.

A better selection for the orator could not have been made. The oration, printed
in the volume before us, is one of the best historical addresses that we have ever
read. The orator draws a vivid picture of the town of Boston at the commencement
of the revolution; ably portrays the character of Washington; and graphically describes the siege of Boston which resulted in driving out the British forces.

As an appendix to his oration, the Rev. Dr. Ellis has added a "Chronicle of the
Siege," filled with valuable matter relating to that event, which must have cost him
great labor to collect and prepare for publication. It makes about half the book,
and contains articles upon various interesting topics, besides many important documents, such as the proclamations of the day, extracts from contemporary periodicals,
books, diaries, &c. &c. A copy of Henry Pelham's "Plan of Boston in New-England
with its Environs," and the military works constructed in 1775-6; a reproduction
of views of several historic buildings as they appeared in the last century, and other
fac-similes, add much to the value of the volume. It is a worthy companion to
Frothingham's invaluable "Siege of Boston."

The volume also contains an account of the reception by the city of the gold medal
struck for Gen. Washington, by order of Congress, to commemorate the evacuation
of Boston. This medal Dr. Ellis made the text of his oration.   J. W. D.

*Worcester in the War of the Revolution: embracing the Acts of the Town
from 1765 to 1783 inclusive. With an Appendix.* By ALBERT A.
LOVELL. Worcester, Mass.: Printed by Tyler & Seagrave, 442 Main
Street, Spy Building, opposite City Hall. 1876. [8vo. pp. 128.]

Mr. Lovell's neatly-printed volume is a valuable contribution to local history, and
bears evidence that much time has been given to its compilation.

The author has brought into a compact and readable form much valuable information in regard to the town of Worcester, which has been heretofore widely separated, and most of it very difficult of access.

The matter contained in this volume was originally prepared and collected to gratify the author's personal taste for historical study, and without the thought of publishing it. Citizens of Worcester, and all others interested in the preservation of local historical information, should be grateful to Mr. Lovell for concluding to give the benefit of his researches to the public.

The volume is illustrated with a heliotype view of the Old South Church at Worcester as it appeared in 1776, with a floor plan showing the owners of pews in 1763. It was from the west porch of this pre-revolutionary edifice that Isaiah Thomas, the editor of the " Massachusetts Spy," read the Declaration of Independence on Sunday, the 14th day of July, 1776, he having intercepted it on its way to Boston. This was the first time it had been publicly read in New-England. It was also printed in the " Spy " before its appearance in any Boston newspaper.

Several interesting documents are given, which illustrate the spirit of the people of Worcester at an important epoch in its history, and are indications of public opinion there during the revolutionary period.

In an Appendix is a list of the members of Capt. Timothy Bigelow's company, which marched from Worcester on the 19th of April, 1775 ; a list of the town officers from 1774 to 1783 ; the jury list for 1776, and the names of Worcester men who were in the continental service.

The volume closes with two pages of quaint advertisements selected from the " Massachusetts Spy " of one hundred years ago.

Only a small edition has been printed, a limited number of which have been placed on sale at the bookstore of Putnam & Davis in Worcester, at $1.50 each.

N. PAINE.

The Journal of Claude Blanchard, Commissary of the French Auxiliary Army sent to the United States during the American Revolution, 1780–1783. Translated from a French Manuscript by WILLIAM DUANE, and edited by THOMAS BALCH. Albany: J. Munsell. 1876. [fcp. 4to. pp. xvi+207.]

The student of American history has reason to thank Mr. Balch for the opportunity of becoming acquainted with the very interesting journal of Claude Blanchard, chief commissary of Rochambeau's army in America during the revolutionary war. With the military operations of that army, Americans are tolerably familiar, but his description of prominent men and places, the glimpses he gives us of the personal characteristics of some of those gallant Frenchmen who afterward became famous in the wars of the French revolution,—Custine, Berthier, Lameth and others, give the book a more than ordinary interest and amply repay perusal.

Claude Blanchard was a native of Angers, and with the celebrated Carnot represented Arras in the Legislative Assembly of France. He was afterward chief commissary to the army of the Sambre and Meuse, then to the army of the Interior, and lastly to the Hotel des Invalides where he died in 1802.

Mr. Balch, who has already given us a history of the Expeditionary corps of Rochambeau, promises soon to issue at Paris a volume now ready, containing notices of the French regiments and fleets, and of the officers who served in our war for independence,—a contribution to our revolutionary lore which will be cordially welcomed. He has also, as he tells us in his preface, obtained the narratives and journals of several other French officers who served here, and is about publishing those of the Prince de Broglie and Gen. de Menonville. It is to be hoped that Mr. Balch's labors in this almost uncultivated field will meet with the encouragement they so abundantly deserve.

Mr. Blanchard's visit to Boston in July, 1780, shortly after his arrival in America, is thus described :

" On the the 27th I set out for Boston and arrived there at nine o'clock. I got down at M. Adolph's, who received me very well and offered me a room which I accepted. I had myself taken immediately to the house of Mr. Bowdoin, the president of the Boston committee, to whom I handed M. de Rochambeau's letter and another which had been entrusted to me by M. de Corny, who was acquainted with him and had been very intimate with him when he was in Boston.

" I had a Frenchman with me, as an interpreter, called the Chevalier de Luz. who called himself an officer. Mr. Bowdoin caused the committee to be assembled, agreeable to the general's letter ; and in the evening he sent me an answer which I immediately forwarded to M. de Rochambeau ; it was favorable and orders had been given for the militia to repair immediately to Rhode Island. On the 28th, I saw Mr. Bowdoin again, in company with M. de Capellis who had arrived. He invited us to come in the evening to take tea at his house. We went there; the tea was served by his daughter, Mrs. Temple, a beautiful woman, whose husband was a tory, that is to say opposed to the revolution; he had even left America and gone to England. Mr. Bowdoin has a very handsome house; he is a wealthy man and respected in his country; he is descended from a French refugee and his name proclaims it. He received us politely and had a very noble bearing. I ought not to forget that he told me that I resembled Franklin when he was young. On the same day we went to Mr. Hancock's, but he was sick and we were not able to see him. This Mr. Hancock is one of the authors of the revolution, as also is the doctor [Cooper] with whom we breakfasted on the 29th: he is a minister who seemed to me to be a man of intelligence, eloquent and enthusiastic. He has much influence over the inhabitants of Boston, who are devout and presbyterians, imbued, generally, with the principles of Cromwell's partisans, from whom they are descended. Therefore, they are more attached to independence than any other class of people in America; and it was they who began the revolution. During my stay in Boston, I dined at the house of a young American lady, where M. de Capellis lodged. At Newport we had seen her sister and her brother-in-law, Mr. Carter, an Anglo-American, who had come to supply provisions to our army. It is a great contrast to our manners to see a young lady (she was twenty at the most) lodging and entertaining a young man. I shall certainly have occasion to explain the cause of this singularity. The city of Boston seemed to me as large as Orleans, not so broad, perhaps, but longer. It is, otherwise, well built and displays an indescribable cleanliness which is pleasing; most of the houses are of wood; some are of stone and brick. The people seemed to be in easy circumstances. Nevertheless the shops were poorly stocked with goods, and everything was very dear, which resulted from the war. Their bookstores had hardly anything but prayer-books; an English and French dictionary cost me eight louis d'or. I saw on the signs of two shops the name of Blanchard, written like my own, one Caleb Blanchard, the other John."

F. S. DRAKE.

Memoir of the Life of Josiah Quincy, Junior, of Massachusetts: 1744–1775. By his son, JOSIAH QUINCY. [Quincy Arms.] Third Edition. Edited by Eliza Susan Quincy. Boston: Little, Brown and Company. 1875. [8vo. pp. 431.]

Josiah Quincy, Junior, was one of the most resolute and talented of the band of patriots, led by Samuel Adams, who in the period immediately preceding the commencement of actual hostilities, resisted the encroachments of England upon the rights which they and their fellow colonists held that they had inherited from their fathers. "The unanimous consent of his contemporaries," says his biographer, writing half a century after his death, "has associated his name in an imperishable union with that of Otis, Adams, Hancock, Warren and other distinguished men, whose talents and intrepidity influenced the events which led to the declaration of Independence. This honor has been granted to him notwithstanding his political path was, in every period of its short extent, interrupted by intense professional labors, and was terminated by death at the early age of thirty-one years. The particular features of a life and character capable, under such circumstances, of attaining so great a distinction, are objects of curiosity and interest. Those who recollect him speak of his eloquence, his genius, and his capacity for intellectual labor; of the inextinguishable zeal and absorbing ardor of his exertions, whether directed to political or professional objects; of the entireness with which he threw his soul into every cause in which he was engaged; of the intrepidity of his spirit, and of his indignant sense of the wrongs of his country. It is certain that he made a deep impression on his contemporaries. Those who remember the political debates in Faneuil Hall, consequent on the Stamp Act, the Boston Massacre, and the Boston Port-Bill, have yet a vivid recollection of the pathos of his eloquence, the boldness of his invectives, and the impressive vehemence with which he arraigned the measures of the British ministry, inflaming the zeal and animating the resentment of an oppressed people."

It is fortunate for us that his son, the author of this biography, inherited with the family papers, the talents and patriotism of his father. Consequently, we have a very faithful picture of his life, mostly in his own words, as the memoir consists largely of his letters and extracts from his diary. The book has now been published more than half a century, and both it and the author, who died at a patriarchal age about twelve years ago, have won a reputation to which no words of ours can add.

Miss Quincy, the editor of this edition, dates her preface, April 26, 1875, the one hundredth anniversary of the death of her grandfather, the subject of this memoir,—who died just one week after the battle of Lexington ;—and her father dates the preface of the first edition on the fiftieth anniversary. The second edition was published in the spring of 1874, one century after the publication of Mr. Quincy's "Observations on the Boston Port-Bill."

The tastes and studies of the editor,—whose intimate knowledge of New-England history, and particularly of the biography and genealogy of the prominent families of Boston in revolutionary times, render her an authority in such matters,—qualify her to edit the work in an acceptable manner. Comparatively few additions to her father's work were necessary; but time and her own researches had brought materials to light which deserved to be incorporated in the memoir, and these have been introduced in a judicious way, partly into the text and partly as notes. She has given a full list of her additions to the book.

The volume is handsomely printed by John Wilson and Son, of Cambridge.
                                                                    J. W. D.

Exeter in 1776. *Sketches of an old New Hampshire town as it was a hundred years ago. Prepared for the Ladies' Centennial Levee held in Exeter, Feb.* 22, 1876. Exeter: News-Letter Press. 1876. [8vo. pp. 39.]

This pamphlet gives a graphic description of the appearance of Exeter one hundred years ago, the history of the buildings then standing, and sketches of the prominent men in military and civil life who then flourished. A production like this, the materials of which are necessarily gathered from scattered sources, must cost the author much labor; and it is wonderful that so perfect a picture of a town which has changed so much as Exeter has could be reproduced. The author of this work is the Hon. Charles H. Bell, of Exeter, N. H., president of the New-Hampshire Historical Society.   J. W. D.

Sergeant William Jasper. An Address delivered before the Georgia Historical Society in Savannah, Georgia, on the 3rd of January, 1876. By CHARLES C. JONES, Jr. [Motto and device.] Albany: J. Munsell. 1876. [8vo. pp. 36.]

It is not often that a subaltern wins a place on the pages of history; but the daring deeds of Sergeant Jasper are among the best known achievements of the Revolution. Mr. Jones has given an interesting narrative of them and of the military operations in which Jasper took part.   J. W. D.

Washington, Bowdoin and Franklin, as portrayed in Occasional Addresses. By ROBERT C. WINTHROP. With a Few Brief Pieces on Kindred Topics and with Notes and Illustrations. Boston: Little, Brown and Company. 1876. [8vo. pp. 186.]

The four principal orations in this beautiful volume are: 1, On laying the corner stone of the National Monument to Washington, July 4, 1848; 2, The Life and Services of James Bowdoin, delivered before the Maine Historical Society, Sept. 5, 1849; 3, Archimides and Franklin, delivered before the Massachusetts Charitable Mechanic Association, Nov. 29, 1853; 4, At the Inauguration of the Statue of Franklin at Boston, Sept. 17, 1856.

All of these productions have long taken their place in the permanent literature of the country; and though most, if not all, of the remaining addresses and other pieces in the volume have before appeared in print, Mr. Winthrop has acted wisely in bringing them together at this time as his contribution to our centennial literature. A view of the National Monument at Washington, D. C., and fac-similes of a number of important letters and documents, add to the value of the volume.
                                                                    J. W. D.

_____

ERRATA.—Page 232, line 10, *for* 1651-2 *read* 1651-0.
"   237, "   2-3, " 16th of February *read* 15th of February.
"   300, "   16, " Ebenezer *read* Eleazer.

Chas. H. Morse

OCTOBER, 1876.

CHARLES W. MOORE.

By WILLIAM W. WHEILDON, Esq., of Concord, Mass.

CHARLES WHITLOCK MOORE, the distinguished advocate of freemasonry, was the son of John Moore, of Boston, and was born in this place, March 29, 1801. His father was a native of London, England, and, at one time, held a position in the household of king George III. In 1799 he came to this country and opened a music store in Boston. He is spoken of as a genial gentleman, courtly in manner and with fine tastes. He died here, March 24, 1803, aged fifty-four years, leaving a widow and two children, a son and daughter, with slender means for their support. Mrs. Moore had excellent mental qualities which her children inherited. Her maiden name was Elizabeth Corey, and she was one of several daughters of a farmer of moderate circumstances in the town of Groton, Mass. Two of the other daughters were married and lived in Boston, and another was the wife of a farmer in Malden. After the death of Mr. Moore, she was married to William Wheildon, a silver-plater and worker in silver, from Birmingham, England, with whom the son of her former husband worked at his shop in Bromfield Street, until he was apprenticed to Young & Minns, of the *Boston Palladium*, in 1818-19. By Mr. Wheildon she had two children, one of whom died in infancy. She outlived her husband, and performed her duty very faithfully to her children, and especially to her eldest son after he became engaged in business. The daughter married Daniel Prowse, a fellow-workman in the *Palladium* office with her brother, who was likewise a prominent mason.

Charles showed a marked capacity and force of character, and eventually won, by his own exertions, a conspicuous position in life, which he uniformly held. On leaving the *Palladium* office, he went to Haverhill, in November, 1820, and worked on the *Essex Patriot*, published by Nathaniel Greene. He worked partly on the newspaper, but most of the time on the Concordance of the Bible, published by Wells & Lilly, of Boston. Charles G. Greene—since editor of the *Boston Post*—a brother of Nathaniel, was at this time at school at Exeter, N. H., and was occasionally in the printing office. He relates a characteristic anecdote of Mr. Moore. While they were boys together in that office, an unfair and ungenerous attack was made upon the narrator by one who was his superior in age and position. Mr. Moore came to the rescue and most vigorously defended his fellow-apprentice and room-mate. From that time until Mr. Moore's death, a most friendly feeling subsisted between them. This little incident would indicate that even at that early age Mr. Moore was possessed of that love of justice and that sturdy zeal in the defence of right which he afterwards manifested in so marked a manner.

From Haverhill Mr. Moore came to Boston with Mr. Greene, in 1821, and worked on the *American Statesman*, a semi-weekly democratic paper, edited by Judge Orne and Nathaniel Greene—which paper is still published in connection with the *Boston Post*.

He continued in the *Statesman* office until April, 1822, when he went to Hallowell, Maine. It will illustrate the modes of travel of that day, and at the same time show his employment, to quote a passage from one of his letters to his half-brother, after his arrival at Hallowell : "I arrived here after two days' and one night's ride ; rode over one hundred and twenty miles without rest ; got almost beat out ; soon got over with it ; well and satisfied at present ; printing the laws of the state ; fine country and very agreeable people."

In February, 1822, the month before he attained his majority, he was proposed for the degrees of masonry in Massachusetts Lodge, one of the three oldest lodges in Boston, and would have been received into the order on the evening of his coming of age, had he not, before that evening arrived, been called temporarily to the state of Maine. Here, in the following May, he was admitted in Kennebec Lodge at Hallowell, with the consent and approbation of the lodge in which he had been originally proposed.

He returned to Boston within a brief period, and on the 10th of October, in the same year, became a member of St. Andrew's Lodge, wherein he continued in active association to the day of his death. Within six months from the time of his affiliation with the lodge he was appointed to an office therein, and from that time during the remainder of his life he continued to hold official relations and stations in some one or more of the various branches of the fraternity.

In 1822 he began business in Boston with Daniel Prowse, and for a time printed the *Independent Bostonian*. Three years later he commenced the publication of the *Masonic Mirror*. In an address in 1872, on the fiftieth anniversary of his membership of St. Andrew's Lodge, he gives this account of the *Mirror* and subsequent publications with which he was connected: "In 1825 I established what was not only the first masonic newspaper in Boston, but in the world—the '*Masonic Mirror*'—in which, to the best of my ability, I fought the battle of masonry against anti-masonry from that year up to 1834, and sustained it subsequently till 1841, in the masonic department of another paper. In November of the latter year I started the '*Freemason's Magazine*' as an *exclusively* masonic publication, and the only one then in the world based on that principle. It was very generally predicted that such a work, purely masonic, could not long be sustained, and friends, almost as much as foes, anticipated its early decay and downfall; but with gratitude alike to that Providence who has spared and those brethren who have sustained me, I am able to say that it has been continued to this day—still a purely masonic magazine—a career unequalled in duration by any similar work. During the above period my pen has been earnestly employed in the elucidation and defence of the great principles of our order, its history, antiquities, jurisprudence, and all that is of interest and value to sound masonry. From this summary of facts it will be seen that I am the oldest masonic editor living."

In 1826 the anti-masonic excitement broke out in the western part of New-York, and speedily spread itself over all the neighboring states. In 1830 and 1831, it raged with violence in Massachusetts. As the editor and publisher of a masonic journal, he was necessarily required to meet the head and front of the attacking parties. A less able, bold or devoted individual would have succumbed and yielded to the violence of the storm. It was fortunate for the institution that its champion then was a man of ability, of a physical and moral courage that recognized no such word as intimidation, and whose love for masonry led him to suffer the stings of outrageous wrong rather than abandon the defence of a cause in which his heart was enlisted. But it was not merely in public prints that Mr. Moore fought the battles of the order. In 1841 the anti-masonic excitement was at its height. In December of that year he wrote the famous "Declaration of the Freemasons of Boston and vicinity," which was signed by nearly six thousand names. It was issued under the sanction of the Boston Encampment of Knights Templars, Dec. 31, 1831, under the impression that means and measures of defence by the institution had been too long delayed. It contained in few but emphatic words the fundamental axioms and principles of the institution, and is regarded by the fraternity to-day in the same light as the declaration of independence is by the country. At the anniversary festival of St. John the Evangelist, in December, 1872—when a new edition of the Declaration was printed, copies of which are now carefully preserved by the members —the subject was alluded to by Brother Moore; whereupon the Grand Master requested the surviving signers who were present to rise. Twelve were present, of whom Marshall P. Wilder, A. A. Dame, E. M. P. Wells, George G. Smith, E. B. Foster, and possibly one or two others, are still living.

In 1828, Mr. Moore—in connection with Edwin Sevey as partner—commenced the publication of a monthly magazine entitled *The Amaranth or Masonic Garland*, which was continued two years— the *Mirror* having been suspended for want of patronage. In April, 1829, on the commencement of the second volume of the *Amaranth*, while the anti-masonic excitement was raging throughout the state, an appeal was made for encouragement in the revival of the *Mirror*, which was shortly after accomplished. The *Mirror* was continued until 1834, when it was transferred to the *Bunker-Hill Aurora*, published at Charlestown—which, although its editor was not connected with the masonic fraternity, had become prominent and efficient in its defence of the institution and the fraternity on general principles. A masonic department was added to the *Aurora*, which was specially under the charge of Mr. Moore. It is no more than justice to say, in this connection, that during the whole of this struggle to support the *Amaranth* and the *Mirror*, and the cause of the institution to which they were devoted, Mr. Moore and his partner, her son-in-law, received the greatest assistance from the labors and efforts of his mother.

Mr. Moore's masonic life may be briefly epitomized as follows: In 1825, he became a Royal Arch Mason in St. Andrew's Chapter; in 1830, Knight Templar in the Boston Encampment; in 1837, its Grand Commander; afterwards Grand Commander of the DeMolay Encampment; he was Grand High Priest of Grand Chapter, and Grand Lecturer; in 1841, Grand Commander of the Grand Encampment of Massachusetts and Rhode-Island; in 1832, he received the Royal and Select Masters' Degrees; in 1844, the 33d degree of the Scottish Rite, and held numerous other offices in the highest orders of the fraternity, and was Secretary of the Board of Trustees of the Charity Fund for sixteen years. "In short," says one of the brethren, "he has filled nearly every office in a lodge, chapter and encampment, holding each several years. He has rarely failed to occupy less than three or four, and frequently five or six official stations at the same time." In addition to all this he was chosen Recording Grand Secretary of the Grand Lodge in 1833, and held the office for thirty-four years, until 1867. This office, take it altogether, was, so far as the institution was concerned, the most important position in his masonic life. It gave him a post which not only enabled him, in its early years, to complete his masonic education, but also to make the most practical use of his knowledge. He was, in this position, the right hand of all the Grand Masters, from 1833 to 1867, and, in fact, he held the same relation to subsequent Grand Masters, while in the office of Corresponding Grand Secretary, and for one year, Deputy Grand Master. On all masonic questions of the day, whether at home or abroad, Mr. Moore was regarded as of the highest authority; and it is not too much to say, that his knowledge and experience were daily called into requisition. He was emphatically, what his friends often called him, "a walking encyclopedia of masonry." We ought not to omit to mention, in this connection, that Mr. Moore, at an early day and for years, availed himself of the instruction, especially in the ritual and higher degrees of the order, of the profound knowledge, large experience and extensive teachings of the late R. W. BENJAMIN GLEASON, for a number of years, commencing in 1805 under Grand Master ISAIAH THOMAS, the commissioned instructor of all the subordinate lodges—and we may say also of the Grand Lodge itself—in the commonwealth: one of the fathers of modern masonry in Massachusetts. Under his instruction, also, Mr. Moore, whose education in the public schools of Boston was of a very restricted and limited character, made himself acquainted with the French language. One of his most admirable labors, not strictly pertaining to the Constitution or Ritual of Freemasonry, is the appropriate and strictly historic decoration of the present halls of the Grand Lodge, which not only illustrate his taste and judgment, but his thorough knowledge of the history of the order.

Copies of the serials published by Mr. Moore are now in the library of the Grand Lodge, and embrace his labors in behalf of the masonic institution for forty-five years. To the report of the committee on the library in 1867, after the fire which destroyed their building and library, there is appended the following note:

"It is to be especially mentioned that these are the whole of all the varied serials published by that most erudite mason, R. W. Charles W. Moore, embracing the labors of forty-five years. Among these, either in folio or quarto, is the Masonic Mirror, which contains the best historical account of the anti-masonic excitement extant; in fact, there is no other copy known. It is priceless. These volumes will long remain as a proud monument of its accomplished editor."

While connected with the *Aurora* Mr. Moore contemplated the commencement of a new masonic periodical for the defence of the institution and the maintenance of the principles of the order, which in 1841 he accomplished and commenced the *Freemason's Monthly Magazine*, which he continued for thirty-two years, until the day of his death. It was conducted for this whole period with great intelligence and ability and a perfect knowledge of the history, character and principles of the order, in all its branches and all its degrees. He not only wrote the "Declaration," mentioned above, but also the "Memorial," to the legislature, in 1833, when the charter of the Grand Lodge was surrendered to the Commonwealth, in order that it might be relieved from the *espionage* of anti-masonic politicians. These historical documents, "and the triumphant acquittal on a charge of libel, in the same year, of the author of these celebrated documents, were the three blows which killed anti-masonry in Massachusetts, and redeemed the Masonic Institution from seven years of obloquy and unparalleled opposition."

During his connection with the *Bunker-Hill Aurora*, Mr. Moore, having a family of his own, went to Charlestown to reside, and was several times elected a member of the school committee, and was also, under the city charter, chosen president of the Common Council.

Mr. Moore's characteristics as a writer were perspicuity and force. He was the author of the "Masonic Trestle Board," and of a number of public addresses and other pamphlets. In 1829 he published Lawrie's "History of Freemasonry," with notes and additions. Col. John T. Heard, in his "History of Columbian Lodge," states that Mr. Moore "has probably written more on the subject of masonry than any other man, living or dead." The published volumes by Mr. Moore [may be enumerated as follows: Boston Masonic Mirror, commencing Nov. 27, 1824, by Moore & Prowse, folio, Vol. 1; The Masonic Mirror and Mechanics' Intelligencer, from Dec. 31, 1825, to Dec. 31, 1826, quarto, Vol. 2; same to Dec. 31, 1827, Vol. 3. The Amaranth or Masonic Garland, April 28, 1828, octavo, Vol. 1; same to Sept. 1829, 6 months, Vol. 2. The Boston Masonic Mirror, new series, from July 4, 1829, Moore & Sevey, to June, 1832, when it was purchased and connected with the Bunker-Hill Aurora. The Freemason's Monthly Magazine, by Charles W. Moore, No. 1, Vol. 1, Nov. 1, 1841, to Dec. 1873, twenty-two volumes octavo.

On the 10th of October, 1872, the golden anniversary of his admission to the Lodge of St. Andrew, that lodge of which he was so prominent a member, celebrated the event with appropriate services. The proceedings on this occasion were printed the same year in a beautiful volume, entitled, "A Memorial of the Half-Century Membership of R. W. Charles W. Moore in the St. Andrews Lodge." The Grand Lodge held a special communication on the occasion, and were present in due form. The large Masonic Hall was elegantly decorated with a profusion of flowers, and the bust of Brother Moore, by Millmore, was wreathed with *immortelles.* There was a very large gathering of ladies and gentlemen, and numerous letters from distinguished masons in other parts of the country received. Under the munificent liberality of St. Andrew's Lodge, it was the most brilliant masonic occasion ever held in Boston. An address, in which he gave interesting reminiscences of his masonic life, was delivered by Mr. Moore. From this address we have already copied passages. Extracts from a few of the other speeches on this occasion are given below.

The Hon. Marshall P. Wilder remarked: "I have known him for fifty years. I saw him the tall young man—in those days of terrible excitement which he has depicted this evening. I saw him standing there almost alone, head and shoulders above most of us, to receive those shafts of malignity scarcely less fierce than the shafts of lightning. As I remember him under these circumstances I have loved him ever since, and shall love him while I live. Long may he continue to be an ornament to our institution, to receive the love and esteem of his brethren, and when his sun shall finally go down, may it go down shining in all its brightness, and may his last days be his best days."

The late Winslow Lewis, M.D., his life-long associate, said: "The great historic friendships of the past, which have been the themes of both sacred and profane writers, are ennobling and touching; but David and Jonathan, Damon and Pythias, and many other noble friendships of which we have record, afford no better illustration of the power of attached hearts, than is found in, as it were, the wedded fraternal lives of brother Moore and myself. Of temperaments quite diverse, still there has been no jarring. Like the Voltaic pile, the movement and the effect have been produced by the contact of two elements, of opposite qualities, and have resulted in the life-giving, soul-inspiring vitalization of our long-continued assimilation."

Many other friends made eloquent and appropriate speeches; a beautiful ode was written for the occasion by Henry G. Clark, M.D.; and the late John H. Sheppard, Esq., whose memoir is printed in the REGISTER for October, 1873, contributed a poetical *jeu d'esprit* on his friend.

Mr. Moore's eldest son, Marcus Aurelius Moore, who served during the war of the Rebellion, died after his return to his family in Waltham, and was buried with masonic honors at Mount Auburn.

Mr. Moore's eminent and indefatigable services to the masonic institution were officially recognized at the regular annual meeting of the Grand Lodge in December, 1873. During his illness, on the 10th of December, the following resolution was passed:

"IN GRAND LODGE, ANNUAL COMMUNICATION,
December 10, A.L. 5873.

"Whereas, R. W. Bro. Charles W. Moore, for more than forty years, without interruption, has been a member of our Grand Lodge; its staunchest friend during the days of adversity and peril; and whereas our Brother has devoted his life to the interests of Freemasonry in all its branches, and especially to those of this Grand Lodge,—therefore

"*Resolved*, That the Grand Lodge of Massachusetts do now promote our R. W. Brother, Charles Whitlock Moore, to the rank of Honorary Past Grand Master, and that hereafter he be recognized and respected accordingly."

This resolution was communicated to him by his loving friend, Dr. Winslow Lewis, who reported that "with grateful emotion he expressed his benediction to his brethren, and added that this tribute was worth living for and worth dying for." "It smoothed his pillow," Dr. Lewis added, "and sweetened the bitter cup of that libation of which we must all sooner or later partake."

He died at his residence in West Concord Street, Boston, Dec. 12, 1873, aged 72, and was interred at Mount Auburn on the 16th of that month. At the adjourned meeting of the Grand Lodge on the 30th of December, Grand Master Nickerson announced his decease, and made a brief address on the occasion, in which he gave a short and very imperfect sketch of his life. Resolutions of respect for his memory and gratitude for his services were passed, in which "the purity of his character, the sincerity of his motives," "the correctness of his views, the firmness of his purpose, the zeal of his labors and the strength of his attachment" are spoken of. They add that "the whole course of his life makes him a bright example of the good citizen, the true man and the consistent christian."

The death of Mr. Moore was also noticed in a very respectful and impressive manner, with addresses and resolutions of the most eulogistic description, by St. Andrew's Lodge (which had previously secured a marble bust of him), and in fact by each of the masonic bodies with which he held connection, and also by the Charles W. Moore Lodge, of Fitchburg.

Mr. Moore was twice married: first, to Miss Charlotte Tolman, of Dorchester (*ante*, xiv. 256), by whom he had seven children, two sons and five daughters; the eldest son and one daughter have died. Second, to Miss Catherine Hews, of Cambridge, daughter of the late John Hews, also a prominent mason, by whom he had three daughters. The widow, with one son and six daughters, survive.

NOTE.—The short time which has been allowed the author in the preparation of this memoir, must be his excuse for any inaccuracies that may be discovered, or any incompleteness in the arrangement of the materials, which was not wholly under his control.

THE FIELDS OF NEW-JERSEY.

Communicated by OSGOOD FIELD, Esq., of London, England.

ALTHOUGH it has been supposed that the Fields of New-Jersey, or rather that some branches of them, are descended from the Flushing family, as far as the writer is aware no positive proof of this has hitherto been forthcoming.

Several circumstances have been known tending to show an early connection between the Long-Island Fields and that State; but they do not afford the evidence of this relationship which the genealogist should require.

Savage says in his Dictionary, that Robert Field, of Newtown—a patentee of Flushing in 1645—had a son John, who removed to Boundbrook, New-Jersey. I do not know on what authority this statement is made. In it the writer confuses the emigrant with his son Robert of Newtown, while the John referred to was probably the son of Anthony and grandson of the first settler. Accuracy cannot always be expected in a work of so extensive a character; however, that portion of the notice which is more intimately connected with the subject of this article, is partly confirmed by the record at Albany of a grant by Gov. Andros to John Field of a patent for land on Delaware Bay, called "Field's Hope." The date does not appear, but it must have been between 1674 and 1681, the extent of Andros's term.

I may add that the latest notices I find of John Field at Flushing are in the valuation of estates there in 1683 and the patent of 1685. His name does not appear among the witnesses to marriages there in the family commencing in 1689; nor is he mentioned in the list of inhabitants of the town in 1698. It is not improbable that he removed to New-Jersey before these dates, and he may be the same individual as the one named in the family record of an old bible, noticed in the REGISTER for April, 1868, who had a son born in 1689.

Among the papers preserved at the old Bowne house in Flushing, are three letters from B. Field to Samuel Bowne of that town, dated at Chesterfield, N. J., respectively 1700, 1701 and 1702, relating to purchases of land at Salem and elsewhere in that neighborhood, in which they both were interested. The writer's christian name was doubtless Benjamin, as I know of no other member of the family, then living, with the same initials.

One of them commences "dear friend," and before the signatures of all are the words "thy friend," from which I infer that they were not written by Benjamin Field, the son of Anthony, who married Samuel Bowne's sister Hannah, as other expressions would probably have been used in addressing one so nearly connected with the writer. We may suppose that Bowne's correspondent was residing at Chesterfield from the fact of all these being written there at considerable intervals of time, and also because it appears from one that the writer's wife was with him, and we know that the Benjamin spoken of remained at Flushing and died there in 1732.

There were two other members of the Long-Island Fields of the same name, who attained their majority before 1700—one the son of the emigrant who is named in the Flushing patent of 1665–6, and the other a grandson of Robert of Newtown.

The first of these Benjamins must have been nearly 60 years of age at the date of these letters, and they are apparently written by a younger man. In the one dated 26th 5th month, 1701, the writer says, "remember duty to my mother." The emigrant left a widow Charity,[1] who was living in 1672–3, but who probably died long before 1701; while we know that his son Robert's widow was then living, as it is stated in the marriage record of his son Nathaniel that it took place "9th day 5th month 1701," "at the house of his mother Susannah ffield, widdow."

For these reasons I am disposed to ascribe the authorship of these letters to Benjamin, son of Robert Field of Newtown, to whom his father deeded land there in 1690, and who probably removed to New-Jersey between that date and 1700.

It is pleasant to turn from the uncertain inferences derived from the foregoing statements to a piece of undoubted evidence.

The New-Jersey family, of which the late Hon. Richard Stockton Field was a distinguished member, have had in their possession for generations an old triangular seal of steel, or iron, believed by them to have belonged originally to Robert Field, the emigrant. It has on one side the initials R. F.; on another, a shield with a chevron between three garbs, which are the arms of the Fields of Yorkshire and Flushing, and on the third the crest granted to a member of the family in 1558; an arm, issuing from clouds, supporting a sphere.

The possession of this relic by the family induced me to apply to Judge Field's daughter for any information she might have of their ancestry, and I am indebted to this lady for the following copy of entries in their old family Bible, which—in connection with what is stated below—conclusively prove their descent from the Flushing Fields:

"Robert Field, son to Benjamin and Experience Allen, was born the 6th of January, 1694.

Mary Field, daughter to Samuel and Susanna Taylor, was born the 31st March, 1700.

Robert Field, son to the above Robert and Mary Field, was born the 9th of May, 1723.

Susannah Field, daughter to Robert and Mary Field, was born 25th October, 1725.

Mary Field, daughter to Robert and Mary, was born the 21st February, 1730.

Samuel Field, son to the above Robert and Mary, was born February, 1736.

[Two other children, names torn off.]

Robert Field, son to Robert and Mary, married Mary, daughter of Oswald and Lydia Pease.

Children of the above.

Lydia,	born	10th of Oct.	1766.
Mary,	"	" " "	1767.
Robert,	"	July 10th,	1769.
Grace,	"	Oct. 10th,	1770.
Susan,	"	April 20th,	1772.
Samuel,	"	July 14th,	1773.
Robert,	"	April 5th,	1775."

---

[1] She describes herself as "widow" in a document she signed Feb. 12, 1672–3, disclaiming any right to "my soue Anthony ffield's Lott."

All the children of Robert Field and Mary Pease died in infancy, except the last named, Robert, who married in 1797, Abby, daughter of Richard Stockton, and died in 1810, leaving five children, the fourth of whom was the Hon. R. S. Field.

Among my extracts from the old records of the Society of Friends at Flushing, I find the following : " Benjamin Field and *Experience Allen* declare intentions of marriage, 29th 6th month, 1692." Probably the marriage took place elsewhere, as I found no record of it in the Flushing registers.

This Benjamin, who is now shown to be the ancestor of a New-Jersey family, could not have been Anthony's son, whose wife Hannah Bowne was married to him in 1691 and survived till 1707.

There were two other members of the family of the name on Long Island at an early date, as already stated. I do not think that this one was the emigrant's son, who was at least 48 years of age in 1692, and probably several years older, as his brothers Robert[1] and Anthony had attained their majority in 1653, when their father conveyed land to them.

Apparently he was dead, or had left the neighborhood some little time before this marriage ; for, according to the Flushing records, two and only two of the name witnessed the marriage of Robert Field, Jr., of Newtown, in 1689, and of Samuel Titus[2]—a near connection—in 1691, and the signature of but one is appended to the entry of that of Benjamin Field and Hannah Bowne in the last named year.

As neither styles himself senior or junior, I infer that they were about the same age, and therefore the two cousins, who were grandsons of the emigrant, both of whom are known to have been residing on Long Island about this time. For a generation after these dates only one Benjamin signs these records.

The conclusions I derive from all these facts are, that Benjamin Field,[3] son of Robert of Newtown, was the husband of Experience Allen and the writer of these letters, and that he removed to New-Jersey shortly after his marriage, where he left descendants, as the old Bible clearly shows.

9 Fenchurch St., E. C. London.

---

[1] At the old Bowne house in Flushing is an official copy by John Clements, the town clerk, of a deed of land there by Robert Field to his sons Robert and Anthony, dated 12 Feb. 1653. The REGISTER for July, 1864, contained a notice of a pamphlet by the Rev. Henry M. Field, giving an account of the family, which, in the number for April, 1868, was shown to be erroneous. It is stated in this pamphlet that the brothers Robert and Anthony were born respectively in 1636 and 1638. This deed—whose existence has been known to me only recently—proves that the dates of birth assigned therein to the emigrant's sons are at least six years too late.

[2] Samuel Titus, born in 1658, was a son of Edmund and brother of Phebe, the wife of Robert Field, Jr., of Newtown.

[3] His sister Susannah and " Isaac Merrit of *Burlington in West Jersey* " declared intentions of marriage in 1699.

NOTES ON AMERICAN HISTORY.

By the Rev. EDWARD D. NEILL, President of Macalester College, Minneapolis, Minnesota.

[Continued from page 301.]

No. IX.

ENGLISH MAIDS FOR VIRGINIA PLANTERS.

AMONG the most important measures, inaugurated after Sir Edwin Sandys became the presiding officer of the London Company, was the transportation of virtuous young women to Virginia.

On the 3d of November, O. S., 1619, Sandys at the usual weekly meeting of the Company suggested "that a fit hundred might be sent of women, maids young and uncorrupt to make wives to the inhabitants."

At the regular quarterly meeting held on Wednesday the 17th of the same month he again alluded to the subject. "He understood that the people thither transported, though seated there in their persons for some four years, are not settled in their minds to make it their place of rest and continuance; but having gotten some wealth to return again to England. For the remedying of that mischief and of the establishing a perpetuity of the plantation he advised to send them over one hundred young maids to become wives, that wives, children and families might make them less movable, and settle them together with their posterity in that soil."

First Shipment of Maids.

The first shipment to the number of ninety was made by the "Jonathan" and "London Merchant," vessels which arrived in May, 1620, at Jamestown.

In a circular of the London Company dated July 18, 1620, they declare their intention to send more young women like "the ninety which have been lately sent."

Shipment per "Marmaduke."

In August, 1621, the Marmaduke left the Thames for Virginia with a letter to the Governor, from which we extract the following:

"We send you in this ship one widow and eleven maids for wives for the people in Virginia."

A choice Lot.

"There hath been especial care had in the choice of them for there hath not any one of them been received but upon good commendations, as by a note herewith sent you may perceive."

To be cared for.

"We pray you all therefore in general to take them into your care, and most especially we recommend them to you Mr. Pountes, that at their first landing they may be housed, lodged, and provided for of diet till they be married, for such was the haste of sending them away, we had no means to put provisions aboard, which defect shall be supplied by the Magazine ship. In case they cannot be presently married, we desire they may be put to several householders that have wives, till they can be provided of husbands."

More to come.

"There are near fifty more which are shortly to come, sent by the Earl of Southampton, and certain worthy gentlemen, who taking into their consideration, that the Plantation can never flourish till families be planted, and the respect of wives and children fix the people in the soil, therefore have given this fair beginning."

Price of a Wife.

"For the reimbursing of whose charges, it is ordered that every man who marries one of them gives 120lb weight of best leaf tobacco, and in case any of them die, that proportion must be advanced to make it up, upon those who survive."

Marriage to be Free.

"We pray you to be fathers to them in this business, not enforcing them to marry against their wills; neither send we them to be servants but in case of extremities, for we would have their condition as much better as multitudes may be allured thereby to come unto you. And you may assure such men as marry these women, that the first servants sent over by the Company shall be consigned to them, it being our intent to preserve families and proper married men, before single persons."

The Marmaduke Maids Married.

With the help of an old Virginia muster roll, we have found out that four of the twelve that came in the Murmaduke were married, and alive in 1624.

Maiden.		Husband.	His arrival.	
Adria	married	Tho's Harris	Ship Prosperous, May,	1610
Anna	"	Tho's Doughty	" Marigold,	1619
Katharine	"	Rob't Fisher	" Elizabeth,	1611
Ann	"	Nich. Bayly	" Jonathan,	1620

Consignment by the " Warwick" and " Tiger."

On Sept. 11, 1621, the London Company again write:

"By this ship [Warwick] and pinnace called the Tiger we also send as many maids and young women as will make up the number of fifty, with those twelve formerly sent in the Marmaduke, which we hope shall be received with the same Christian piety and charity as they were sent from hence."

Price of a Wife raised.

"The providing for them at their first landing and disposing of them in marriage we leave to your care and wisdom to take that order as may most conduce to their good and the satisfaction of the Adventurers for the charges disbursed in setting them forth, which coming to £12 and upwards, they require 150lbs of the best leaf tobacco for each of them. This increase of thirty pounds weight since those sent in the Marmaduke they have resolved to make, finding the great shrinkage and other losses upon the tobacco from Virginia will not bear less."

Extraordinary Care in Selection.

"We have used extraordinary care and diligence in the choice of them, and have received none of whom we have not had good testimony of their honest life and carriage, which together with their names, we send enclosed for the satisfaction of such as shall marry them."

Marriage of "Warwick" Maids.

The following maids were living as wives in 1624, who came in the Warwick.

Maiden.		Husband.		His arrival.	
Margaret	married	Hezekiah Raughton	in	Bona Nova,	1620
Sarah	"	Edward Fisher	"	Jonathan,	"
Ann	"	John Stoaks			
Ellen	"	Michal Batt	"	Hercules,	1610
Elizabeth	"	Tho's Gates	"	Swan,	1609
Bridget	"	John Wilkins	"	Marigold,	1618
Ann	"	John Jackson	"	Warwick.	

"Tiger" Maids.

The following who came in the Tiger were alive in 1624.

Maid.		Husband.		His arrival.	
Joan	married	Humphrey Kent	in	"George,"	1619
Joan	"	Tho's Palmer	"		

At a quarterly meeting of the London Company on Nov. 21, 1621, it was mentioned that care had been taken to provide the planters in Virginia with "young, handsome and honestly educated maids," whereof sixty were already sent.

No. X.

The Mayflower People.

The action of the passengers of the Mayflower in forming a social compact before landing at Plymouth Rock seems to have been in strict accordance with the policy of the London Company under whose patent the ship sailed.

On June 9, 1619, O. S., John Whincop's patent was duly sealed by the Company, but this which had cost the Puritans so much labor and money was not used. Several months after, the Leyden people became interested in a new project. On Feb. 2, 1619–20, at a meeting at the house of Sir Edwin Sandys in Aldersgate, he stated to the Company that a grant had been made to John Peirce and his associates. At the same quarterly meeting it was expressly ordered that leaders of particular plantations, associating unto them divers of the gravest and discreetest of their companies, shall have liberty to make orders, ordinances, and constitutions for the better ordering and directing of their business and servants, provided they be not repugnant to the Laws of England.

Five hundred pounds sterling had been presented to the Company for the education of Indian children, and it had been proposed by Sir John Wolstenholme, that John Peirce and his associates might have the training of some of these children, but on the 16th of February a Committee reported "that for divers reasons they think it inconvenient. First, because after their arrival they will be long in settling themselves : As also, that the Indians are not acquainted with them, and so they may stay four or five years before they have account that any good is done."

Under the Peirce patent the Mayflower sailed in September, 1620. She did not return to England until May, 1621. The next month John Peirce and associates took out a new patent from the "Council of New England." In view of this action on July 16th, at a meeting of the London Company, "It was moved seeing that Mr. John Peirce had taken a patent of Sir Ferdinando Gorges, and thereupon seated his company within the limits of the Northern Plantations as by some was supposed, whereby he seemed to relinquish the benefit of the patent he took of this Company, that therefore the said patent might be called in, unless it might appear he would begin to plant within the limits of the Southern Colony."

From this minute it would seem as if Peirce had some understanding with Gorges, in view of the profits from fishing, of settling the Leyden people beyond the confines of the territory of the London Company, although he did not until June 1, 1621, receive a patent from the "Council of New England."

No. XI.

Transportation of Homeless London Children.

Sir George Bowles or Bolles, the Lord Mayor of London, and the Aldermen thereof in 1617, "fearing lest the overflowing multitude of inhabitants should, like too much blood, infect the whole city with plague and poverty," devised as a remedy, the transportation to Virginia of their overflowing multitude, and in 1618–19 one hundred children were sent to Virginia.

The next year, 1619, the Mayor Sir William Cockaine resolved to ease the city of many that were ready to starve, and conferred with the Virginia Company. The following memorial from the Company was presented to the Mayor and Aldermen.

"The Treasurer and Company of Virginia assembled in their great and general Court, the 17th of November, 1619, have taken into consideration, the continual great forwardness of this honourable City, in advancing the plantation of Virginia, and particularly in furnishing one hundred children this last year, which by the goodness of God have safely arrived (save such as died on the way) and are well pleased we doubt not, for this benefit, for which your bountiful assistance we in the name of the whole Plantation, do yield unto you deserved thanks.

"And forasmuch as we have resolved to send this next spring very large supplies for the strength and increasing of the Colony styled by the name of the London Colony, and find that the sending of these children to be apprenticed hath been very grateful to the people, we pray your Lordship and the rest, to renew the like favours and furnish us again with one hundred more for the next spring.

"Our desire is, that we may have them of twelve years old and upward, with allowance of £3 apiece for their transportation, and 40s. apiece for their apparel as was formerly granted. They shall be apprenticed, the boys till they come to 21 years of age; the girls till like age, or till they be married. * * * And so we leave this motion to your honourable and grave consideration."

The City co-operated in procuring the second company of children, but some were unwilling to leave London, as the following letter of Sir Edwin Sandys, the presiding officer of the Company, written in January, 1620, N. S., to Sir Robert Naunton, one of the King's Secretaries, indicates.

"The City of London have appointed one hundred children from the superfluous multitude to be transported to Virginia, there to be bound apprentices upon very beneficial conditions. They have also granted £500 for their passage and outfit. Some of the ill-disposed, who under severe masters in Virginia may be brought to goodness, and of whom the City is especially desirous to be disburdened, declare their unwillingness to go. The City wanting authority to deliver, and the Virginia Company to transport these children against their will, desire higher authority to get over the difficulty."

The necessary authority was granted, and the second company of children duly shipped.

In April, 1622, it was proposed to send a third company, but no data can be found to show that they sailed.

No. XII.

Ships arriving at Jamestown, from the Settlement of Virginia until the Revocation of Charter of London Company.

It must always be regretted that the London Company did not keep a proper ship and passenger register. The good Nicholas

Ferrar, Dep. Gov. of the Company, on Oct. 23, 1622, alluded to the errors of management in the transportation of persons and goods. He alluded to ships now going from London and other parts, and that "there was no note or register kept of the names of persons transported whereby himself and other officers were not able to give any satisfaction to the persons that did daily and hourly enquire after their friends gone to Virginia."

The following list of vessels, made up from various sources, although not complete, approaches to accuracy, and is submitted for correction.

Ships which arrived at Jamestown.

1607—1624.

YEAR.	Mo.	SHIP.			REMARKS.
1607	April	Susan Constant[1]	100 Tons	Capt.	Chris. Newport, 71 passengers
"	"	God Speed	40 "	"	Bart. Gosnold, 52 "
"	"	Discovery	20 "	"	John Ratcliffe, 20 "
1607–8	Jan'y	John and Francis[2]		"	Newport, 50 colonists
1608	April	Phœnix[3]		"	Nelson, 70 "
"	Oct.	Mary Margaret		"	Newport, 60 "
1609	July	Discovery[4]		"	Robt Tindal, Factor Sam. Argall
"	Aug.	Diamond		"	Ratcliffe, Gates & Somers Fleet
"	"	Falcon		"	Martin, Nelson Master
"	"	Blessing		"	Archer, Adams "
"	"	Unity		"	Martin, Pett "
"	"	Swallow[5]		"	Moore
"	"	Virginia[6]		"	Davies, Built in 1607 at Sagadahoc
1610	May	Deliverance 70 tons[7]	⎱	Built at Bermudas, and brought	
"	"	Patience 30	⎰	Gates and Somers with 100 colonists	
"	June	Delaware		Lord Delaware's fleet	
"	"	Blessing		" " "	
"	"	Hercules		" " "	
"	Oct.	Dainty		Brought 12 men, 1 woman, 2 or 3 horses	
1611	April	Hercules		" 30 colonists	
"	May	Elizabeth		Dale's fleet	
"	"	Mary and James		" "	
"	"	Prosperous		" "	
"	Aug.	Star[8]		Gates "	
"	"	Swan		" "	
"	"	Trial		" "	
"	"	Three Carvills		" "	

[1] The Susan Constant, Capt. Newport, left Jamestown for England with mineral and forest specimens on 22 June, 1607, and arrived in the Thames in less than five weeks.

[2] Loaded with iron ore, sassafras, cedar posts, and walnut wood, sailed from Jamestown 10th of April, and on 20th of May reached England. The iron ore seems to have been smelted, and 17 tons sold to East India Co. at £4 per ton.

[3] Capt. Nelson returned to England in July, 1608.

[4] Discovery brought no passengers nor supplies, but was intended for private trade.

[5] Twenty-eight or thirty were sent in ship Swallow to trade for corn with the Indians. They stole away with what was the best ship, and some became pirates. Others returned to England and told the tragical story of a man at Jamestown so pinched with hunger as to eat his dead wife.—See *Purchas*, vol. iv. p. 1757.

[6] This vessel was built at Sagadahoc by the Popham colonists in 1607. Disheartened by Popham's death they set sail for England in a ship from Exeter, "and in the new pynnace the Virginia."—*Hakluyt Pub.*, vol. vi. p. 180.

[7] The Deliverance was built by Richard Frobisher.—See *New-Eng. Hist. and Gen. Reg.*, vol. xxviii. p. 317, for a sketch of this shipwright.

[8] In the autumn of 1611 the Star, of 300 tons, sailed from Jamestown for England with forty fair and large pines for masts.—*Hakluyt Pub.*, vol. vi. p. 130.

1612	——	John and Francis	A small ship
"	——	Sarah	"　　"　　"
"	Sept.	Treasurer	Capt. Argall, 50 men
1613		Elizabeth	Brought thirteen persons
1614		"	Second trip
1615		John and Francis	Brought twenty persons
"		Treasurer	"　　　　"　　　　"
1616	Oct.	Susan	Came in October laden with supplies
1617	May	George[1]	Gov. Argall and Rev. Mr. Keith, passengers
		Pinnace	Owned by Capt. Martin
1618	April	George	
		Diana	
"		Sampson	
"	Aug.	Neptune	Lord Delaware died on the voyage; among the passengers Wm. Ferrar who settled Ferrar's Island
		Treasurer	Capt. Elfred, Gov. Argall part owner
1619	March	Wm. and Thomas[2]	Probably the vessel in which Blackwell and other puritans sailed
"	April	Eleanor	Swift pinnace in which Argall secretly escaped
"	"	Gift	Gov. Yeardley passenger. 14 persons died on the voyage
"	May	George	
"		Duty	
"		Prosperous	
"		Marigold	
"		Edwin	
"	June	Trial	
"	Aug.	Privateer[3]	Commissioned by Duke of Savoy, consort of Treasurer, brought "20 negars"
"	Nov.	Bona Nova[4]	Of 200 tons. Brought Rev. Jonas Stockton, son and 120 colonists

[1] In April when the George arrived the number of men, women and children in Virginia was about 400, "and but one plough was going in all the country."—*Sir Edwin Sandys to Virginia Company.*

[2] The "William and Thomas" was without doubt the vessel in which the first body of Puritans embarked under Blackwell, formerly an Elder in the Amsterdam Church.

In Bradford's History, Cushman the Agent of the Leyden people writes under date of London, May 8, 1619, as follows: "Captain Argol is come home this week, * * * came away before Sir Geo. Yeardley came there. * * * He saith Mr. Blackwell's ship came not there till March, but going towards winter they had north-west winds which carried them to the southward beyond their course. And the master of the ship and some six of the mariners dying, it seemed they could not find the Bay till after long seeking and beating about. Mr. Blackwell is dead, and Mr. Maggner the captain; yea, there are dead he saith 130 persons one and other in that ship; it is said there were in all 180 persons in the ship, so as they were packed together like herrings. They had amongst them the flux, and also the want of fresh water, so as it is here rather wondered at that so many are alive, than that so many are dead. The merchants here say it was Mr. Blackwell's fault to pack so many in the ship."

[3] The Treasurer with a commission as privateer from the Duke of Savoy against the Spaniards left Virginia on a cruise to the West Indies, where she consorted with the Flemish ship, and captured a Spanish vessel with some negroes. The Flemish ship brought twenty negroes to Virginia in August, 1619, the first introduced.

On February 16, 1623-4, there had been but a small increase.

At Fleur Dieu Hundred 11 negroes

" James City	3	"
" James Island	1	"
" Plantation opposite	1	"
" Warasquoyak	4	"
" Elizabeth City	1	"

21

[4] The Bona Nova with the seven ships that follow in the list brought out 871 persons. *Hist. Virginia Co. of London*, p. 181.

1620	May	Duty	Of 70 tons, Capt. Damyron, brought 50 Bridewell vagabonds
"	"	Jonathan[1]	Of 350 tons. Brought maids for planters' wives
"	"	Trial	Of 200 tons, Capt. Edmonds, 60 kine, 40 persons
"		Falcon	Of 150 tons, Capt. Jones, 4 mares, 52 kine, 36 persons
"		London Merchant	Of 300 tons, Capt. Shaw, 200 persons
"		Swan	" 100 " brought 71 persons
"	Nov.	Francis Bona Ventura[2]	" 240 " " 151 " Rev. David Sandis passengers
1621	Jan'y	Supply	
"		Abigail	
"		Adam	
"		Margaret and John	
"		Bona Nova[3]	
		Charles	
"	Oct.	George	Gov. Wyatt, Rev. Haut Wyatt, Dr. Pott, George Sandys, poet, passengers
		Eleanor	
		Sea Flower	Rev. W. Bennett, passenger
		Concord	
		Duty	
	Nov.	Marmaduke	Capt. John Dennis, brought for wives, 1 widow and 11 maids
		Flying Hart[4]	Capt. Cornelius Johnson, a Dutchman, brought cattle of Daniel Gookin from Ireland
	Dec.	Temperance	
		Warwick	This ship and the Tiger brought 38 maids for wives
		Tiger[5]	Captured by Turks and released

[1] The Jonathan was a supply ship, and was among the first to bring maids for wives. On Nov. 3, 1619, Sir Edwin Sandys at a meeting of Virginia Company "wished that a fit hundred might be sent of women, maids young and uncorrupt to make wives to the inhabitants." The girls were sent from time to time, but not in one ship.

[2] On Dec. 16, 1620, Sir Edwin Sandys reported to the Virginia Company "that they had received certificate of the safe arrival of all their ships sent the last Spring, as namely, the Francis Bona Ventura with all save one, the Trial and Falcon with all their passengers, the London Merchant with all theirs, the Duty with all theirs no save one. And so likewise the Swan of Barnstable. But the Jonathan, in her tedious passage, had lost sixteen of two hundred. So by this last supply they had landed in Virginia, near the number of 800 persons, for which great blessing, he rendered unto the Almighty all possible thanks."

[3] The ships sent out by the London Company in 1621 were nine in number: the George, Sea Flower, Bona Nova, Concord, Marmaduke, Warwick, Tiger, etc. Upon the return of the "George" in 1622, the Company invited the Rev. Patrick Copland to preach a Thanksgiving Sermon in view of the safe arrival of all their ships at Jamestown. Upon the 18th of April, Copland in accordance with the request preached at Bow Church. Alluding to the vessels he uses these words: "The fittest season of the year for a speedy passage being now far better known than before, and by that means, the passage itself made almost in so many weeks as formerly it was wont to be made in months, which I conceive to be, through the blessing of God, the main cause of the safe arrival of your last fleet of nine sail of ships that not one (but one, in whose room there was another borne) of eight hundred which were transported out of England and Ireland should miscarry by the way."

[4] The Flying Hart brought Daniel Gookin of Ireland, with fifty men of his own, thirty other passengers, and a number of cattle. The London Company writing to the authorities of Virginia under date of Aug. 12, 1621, allude to Gookin. They say: "Let him have very good tobacco for his cows now at his first voyage, for if he make a good return, it may be the occasion of a trade with you from those parts, whereby you may be abundantly supplied, not only with cattle, but with most of those commodities you want at better and easier rate." Clarke seems to have been the pilot of the ship.

[5] The Tiger was captured by the Turks and released. Copland in his sermon alludes to it in these quaint words:

"When God brought some of the ships of your former fleets to Virginia in safety, here God's providence was seen and felt privately by some; and this was a deliverance written as it were on *quarto*, on a lesser paper and letter.

"But now, when God brought all of your nine ships, and all your people in them, in

1622	April	Bona Nova[1]	200 Tons. Capt. John Hudleston
"	"	Discovery[2]	Capt. Thos. Jones
"	July	Charity	Came by way of Plymouth in New England
"		God's Gift	
"		Darling	
		Furtherance	Nathaniel Basse, Passenger
"		Abigail	Catherine, wife of Rev. W. Bennett, Passenger
"		Southampton	
"		James	Rev. Greville Pooley, Passenger
1623	April	Providence[3]	Capt. Clarke, chartered by Daniel Gookin
"		Margaret and John	
"		Sea Flower	
"	July	Samuel	
"		True Love	
"	Aug.	Ann	
"	Oct.	George	
1624		Prosperous	
		Jacob	
		Susan	
		Due Return	Capt. Wm. Peirce

THE GARRISON FAMILY OF MASSACHUSETTS.

Communicated by WENDELL P. GARRISON, Esq., of Orange, N. J.

JOSEPH GARRISON, included by Sabine among his "American Loyalists" (I., 464, ed. 1864), is styled "of Massachusetts." There appears to be no doubt that he went from Massachusetts to Nova Scotia, and as little that he was not technically a "Loyalist." The Loyalist emigration does not antedate the evacuation of Boston, while Mr. Sabine admits that "notes from the family record, furnished me by two of his grandsons,

safety and health to Virginia, yea, and that ship Tiger of yours, which had fallen into the hands of the Turkish men-of-war, through tempests and contrary winds she not being able to bear sail, and by that means driven out of her course, some hundreds of miles, * * * * * * * * * When this your Tiger had fallen into the hands of those merciless Turks who had taken from them most of their victuals, and all of their serviceable sails, tackling and anchors, and had not left them so much as an hour-glass, or compass to steer their course, thereby utterly disabling them from going from them; when I say God had ransomed her out of their hands, by another sail which they espied, and brought her likewise safely to Virginia, with all her people, two English boys only excepted, for which the Turks gave them two others, a French youth and an Irish, was not here the presence of God printed as it were in *folio*, on royal crown paper, and capital letters."

[1] Capt. Hudlestone arrived at Jamestown sixteen days after the first great massacre of the whites by Indians. In June, 1622, he was fishing off the coast of Maine, and sent a boat to the Puritans of Plymouth Rock with a letter containing the sad news. He said, "I will so far inform you that myself with many good friends in the Southern Colony of Virginia have received such a blow, that 400 persons large will not make good our losses."—See *Bradford*.

[2] For Sketch of Capt. Jones, see vol. xxviii. p. 314.

[3] Clarke had been captured by the Spaniards in 1612. On June 20, 1620, Cushman writing to his pastor Robinson at Leyden said, "We have hired another pilot here, one Mr. Clarke who went last year to Virginia with a ship of kine."

On Feb. 13, 1621-22, the Presiding Officer of the London Company acquainted them "that one Mr. John Clarke being taken from Virginia long since by a Spanish ship that came to disarm that plantation, forasmuch as he hath since that time done the Company good service in many voyages to Virginia and of late went into Ireland for the transportation of cattle to Virginia, he was an humble suitor that he might be admitted a free brother of the Company."

Soon after he arrived in the "Providence" he died.

show that he (J. G.) was in Nova Scotia as early, certainly, as 1773." On the other hand, the so-called "Refugees" were those who anticipated the breaking of the storm that overhung the Colonies, and took their departure for the Provinces at least as early as 1776. On this point I have met two traditions among Joseph Garrison's grandchildren: (1) that he was a non-fighting man, and came as a Refugee to Nova Scotia at the time of the Declaration of Independence; (2) that he was a Quaker who came with the Refugees—with Woodwards and other Garrisons—from Staten Island, N. Y., after the peace (though then, it would seem, he should be termed a "Loyalist"). The latter tradition has a curious bearing on the possible descent of some of the American Garrisons from a Staten-Island Hollander (*Gerrit* Van Wagener), which can only be alluded to here. That Joseph Garrison was a born Englishman is the belief of his oldest surviving grandchild (Mrs. Wood). The earliest intelligence I get of him is, that in the old church at Rowley (Essex Co., Mass.) he fell in love at first sight with his future wife, Mary Palmer, to whom he had hitherto been a perfect stranger. Possibly, let me remark, it might have been in the neighboring church at Byfield, to which she was admitted a member October 10, 1762. They were married Aug. 14, 1764, but whether in the colony or in the province has not yet been ascertained. In the spring of that year her father, Daniel Palmer, with other Rowley and Byfield and Ipswich men and their families, removed to Sunbury Co., N. S., settling on the River St. John at a place then called Maugerville, and now Upper Sheffield or Taylortown (N. B.). Was Mary left behind to marry Joseph Garrison? How soon did they follow the emigrants to their new home? These colonists were, of course, neither Refugees as yet nor Loyalists. Daniel Palmer was an intrepid man and a staunch adherent subsequently to the cause of the Colonies (see Kidder's "Eastern Maine and Nova Scotia in the Revolution," pp. 61–72; and for D. P.'s connection by marriage the genealogy of the "Stickney Family," No. 29 and p. 166[1]). Joseph Garrison, if he was on the spot at the time, may have declined to join in the heroic effort, in which his father-in-law was conspicuous, to involve the isolated settlement in the fate of the Colonies. His name does not appear in these transactions nor in the list of the pioneers to the St. John. It seems probable, therefore, that his marriage took place in Massachusetts.

That he came late to the St. John, when the best land had been pre-occupied, would appear from his choosing a tract twenty miles away from the Maugerville settlement, viz., in the neighborhood of the subdued Fort Jemseg. Here he founded his homestead, occupied by his children till within a little more than a quarter of a century ago, and here probably he died, three months before the birth of his youngest child, say February, 1783. His wife survived him and married, without issue, a Mr. Angus, who in 1806 was already deceased.

————

1. JOSEPH[1] GARRISON, b. Aug. 14, 1734; m. Aug. 14, 1764, Mary, dau. of Daniel and Elizabeth (Wheeler) Palmer (b. in Byfield, Mass., Jan. 19, 1741, d. on the Jemseg Feb. 14, 1822); d. February, 1783. They had:

    i. HANNAH, b. July 16, 1765, named perhaps for her great-aunt, Hannah Palmer. According to Sabine, she "married John Lunt, lived at Eastport, Maine, some years, removed to the Penobscot, and died there

————

[1] While Kidder gives 1766 as the date of the settlement of Maugerville, Stickney (p. 166) makes the Essex Co. emigration thither begin as early as 1760. It probably did not take place in force till 1763–4. The second Rowley emigration is assigned to the latter year.

about the year 1843.'' Two of her daughters are said to have visited New Brunswick some years ago.

ii.   ELIZABETH (" Betsey "), b. July 18, 1767, named for her grandmother or aunt. She "married William Simpson (who went insane about 1805), and died at Kingston, N. B., in 1815 " (*Sabine*).

2. iii.   JOSEPH, b. April 26, 1769 (1770, according to *his* family record, but this is probably an error); m. Aug. 14, 1794, Rebecca (" Becky ") Murray; d. on Deer Island, N. B., Oct. 16, 1819.

3. iv.   DANIEL, b. April 6, 1771; m. 1799 (?), Deborah, seventh dau. of Capt. Christopher and Jemima (Eaton) Cross—he of Salisbury, she of Newburyport, Mass.; d. Oct. 10, 1803.

4. v.   ABIJAH, b. June 18, 1773; m. Dec. 12, 1796 (?), Fanny Lloyd; d. *post* 1814.

vi.   SARAH, b. May 8, 1776, named for her aunt Palmer. She married Joseph Clark, and in 1848 was still living on the River St. John, near Fredericton.

5. vii.   NATHAN, b. July 9, 1778; m., spring of 1802, Rebecca, fourth dau. of Ozias Ansley; d. Feb. 17, 1817.

viii.   SILAS, b. Sept. 16, 1780; m. about 1810 Eleanor (Standstreet) Linthwait, widow of William Linthwait (she d. at Jemseg, 1849); d. about June 1, 1849. They had no children. He was all his life a farmer on the Jemseg, occupying the homestead.

ix.   WILLIAM, b. May 6, 1783, a posthumous child; d. Feb. 14, 1837, on the St. John. He was a cripple from birth; was a schoolmaster, and never married.

2. JOSEPH[2] GARRISON (*Joseph[1]*) was survived by his wife Becky Murray (b. Dec. 24, 1778; d. Aug. 6, 1839), who afterwards married Jonathan Titus. Joseph was a farmer at Chocolate Cove, Deer Island, N. B. His children were:

i.   CHARLES W., b. Sept. 3, 1795; m. Nov. 9, 1835, Ann B. (" Nancy "), dau. of Abijah Palmer, who (b. Mar. 12, 1815) survived him, and m. Mar. 11, 1852, Jonathan Titus, and was still living in 1873; d. on the Jemseg, March 4, 1850. A cripple from his birth, he was a schoolmaster. He had one child, a daughter.

ii.   ELIZA J. S. (" Betsey "), b. Dec. 1, 1797; m. her kinsman, Henry Allen Palmer, up the River St. John. They had four sons and three daughters.

iii.   J. MURRAY, b. June 2, 1801; m. Dec. 25, 1823, Ann Heney, who survived him and was still living in 1873. They had seven sons and one daughter.

3. DANIEL[2] GARRISON (*Joseph[1]*) was named for his grandfather or uncle Palmer. Sabine says of him that he was drowned in the River St. John about the year 1798; but the true date has been given above. He was lost overboard from his "wood-boat." His wife, Deborah Cross, was born 1780 (?), died 1834 (?). They had two children:

i.   JOSEPH, b. August, 1800; d. November, 1818.

ii.   MARY, b. October 4, 1801; m. April 15, 1822, William Wood (he died Dec. 8, 1848), and is still living. They had seven daughters and four sons.

4. ABIJAH[2] GARRISON (*Joseph[1]*) was named for his uncle Palmer. He lived a while in the city of St. John, but removed (*post* July, 1801) to Newburyport, Mass. He was a sea-captain, in the West-India and coasting trade. The time and place of his death have not been ascertained. By his wife, Frances Maria Lloyd, dau. of Andrew and Catherine (Lawless) Lloyd, b. 1776 on Deer Island, N. B., d. 1823 in Baltimore, he had:

(?) i.   CAROLINE, b. 1797 (?); died young (*post* 1801) in Newburyport, from eating poisonous flowers in a garden.

(?) ii.   MARY ANN, b. 1799 (?); died in infancy.

iii.   JAMES HOLLEY, b. in St. John, July 10, 1801. He followed the sea, and died of a cancerous affection in Cambridgeport, Mass., 1841 (?). He was never married.

iv. WILLIAM LLOYD, b. in Newburyport, Dec. 10 (or 12, by the town records),
1804 ; m. Sept. 4, 1834, Helen Eliza, dau. of George and Sally (Thur-
ber) Benson (b. Feb. 23, 1811, d. Jan. 25, 1876). They have had five
sons and two daughters.

v. MARIA ELIZABETH, born in Newburyport, 1806 (?): died of yellow fever
in Baltimore, Sept. 21, 1822.

5. NATHAN[2] GARRISON (*Joseph*[1]) was named after his uncle Palmer.
His wife survived him, and married, Mar. 20, 1820, Valentine Troop, of
Granville, N. S., by whom she had several children, both sons and daughters:
he died 1848, in his 63d year; she died July 11, 1849. The children of
Nathan and Rebecca were:

i. GEORGE ANSLEY, b. Mar. 3, 1803. For many years notary public and
custom-house broker and forwarding merchant at St. John ; m. July
8, 1826, Charlotte Louisa, fourth dau. of Peter Lugrin (she d. Sept.
30, 1866). They had seven children, four sons and three daughters,
all of whom died in infancy except one, the oldest son, who survives
with his father (now residing in Washington, D. C.).

ii. EDWIN WILLIAM, born Aug. 12, 1804. He acquired by his own efforts a
classical education, and entered Waterville College (Maine) about 1827,
to fit for the (Baptist) ministry ; m. 1838 at Sedgwick, Me., Sophia
Dodge ; d. about 1844, survived by his wife. They had no children.

iii. ANDREW, b. Nov. 14, 1805. He was sheriff's clerk (about 1826), and
afterwards deputy-sheriff in St. John until he left the Province; for
the latter part of the time also an editor. He removed to the United
States in 1837, and settled at Sauk Prairie, Wisconsin; but setting out
for California during the gold fever, in the spring of 1850, he died of
cholera on the way, about 150 miles from Salt Lake City. He married,
in 1831, his cousin, Ann Ansley, and had no issue. She m., 1860,
James Taylor, Ph.D., an Englishman, residing in Cincinnati ; was still
living there in 1873.

GLEANINGS.

By WILLIAM H. WHITMORE, Esq., of Boston, Mass.

[Continued from vol. **xxviii.** p. 243.]

69.

CAPT. JOHN AYRES.

IN the REGISTER, xvii. 309, I published an article on the families of
Ayres and Ayer, correcting an article in this work, xv. 331–2. I have
also since printed a genealogy of the descendants of Capt. John Ayres of
Ipswich and Brookfield. Recently I have been shown a document now in
the library of the N. E. Historic, Genealogical Society, bearing date 28
Feb. 1650–1. It is an agreement for an exchange of lands between Robert
Whitman and Robert Lord, both of Ips-
wich. The witnesses are John Aires
and Robert Lord, Jr., and I give a copy
of the autograph of the former.

As a suggestion merely to those interested in the names of Ayer and
Ayres, I will note that in " Notes and Queries," 2d Ser. vol. xii. p. 26, it is
stated that March 27, 1654, at Frampton in Lincolnshire, there were chosen
for head-boroughs John Ayre, Thomas Appleby, Richard Coney, Thomas
Nicholls, William Eldred and Humphrey Hall.

I also add the two following advertisements from early newspapers :

Boston News Letter, Oct. 7, 1725. "For the sake of many Poor Afflicted Persons it has been thought Advisable to let it be known ; That if any Persons are troubled with the Sciatica or Hip-Gout, there is a Cere cloth, which has done many notable Cures for that Malady, and rarely fail'd of Success. It also gives Ease in the Gout it self ; and commonly cures the Tooth-ache : Indeed it is rarely applied unto any Pain, but it gives Relief. They that need it may be supplied at the House of Mr. Nathaniel Ayres, in Salem street, at the North End, Boston."

News Letter, June 23, 1726. "Several lots of very good Wood Land in Brook-field, To be Sold. Inquire of Mr. Nathaniel Ayres, Anchor-Smith in Salem Street, Boston, or of Mr. William Ayres in said Brookfield."

70.

FARRARS AND BREWERS OF ESSEX COUNTY, MASS.

In tracing some matters relating to persons of my own name, I was able to trace out two families not recorded in SAVAGE, but of course meriting a place in our lists. These were those of FARRAR and BREWER, of which families little had been said in print, and even that erroneously.

I will first give the document earliest in date and mentioning both families.

The record is as follows. The original is in the handwriting of Robert Lord, of Ipswich, and is one of the returns made to the County Clerk. It is in the court files at Salem, book vii. leaf 48, and the paper is now illegible in some parts, as the transcript shows. A portion is as follows :[1]

" Francis Jordon & Jane Willson maried 6 (9) 1635.

> Sarah Jordon born 8 (9) 1636.
> Hanah Jordon born 14 March 163–.
> Mary Jordon born 7 Apr. 163–.
> Mary Jordon dyed August 16—.
> Mary Jordon born 16 May 1641.
> Lydia Jordon born 14 Feb : 1643.
> Deborah Jordon born 4 December 164–."

George Farough.[2]

" Georg Farough & An Whitmore maryed 16 (11) 1643.

> Mary Farough borne January 6, 164–.
> Martha Farough borne 25 Feb : 164–.
> Febye Farough borne May 165–."

" Thomas Stace & Susanna Wooster m. 4 (8) 1653."
(Children recorded, &c.)

" Thomas Harris & Martha Lake maried the 15 of November 1647.

> Thomas 8 August 48.
> Martha 8 Jan'y 50.
> John 7 Jany 52.
> Elizth 8 Feb. 54.
> Margrett 6 Aug 57.
> Mary Last Jany 59.
> William 12 Dec. 6–."

" John Brewer & Mary Whitmore maryed 23 (8) 1647.

> Mary Brewer borne the 23 of September 1648.
> John Brewer borne the 6 of October 1653.
> Sara Brewer borne the 27 of March 1655."

---

[1] I am indebted to Henry F. Waters, Esq., of Salem, for this copy for publication. I have marked the portions copied literally.

[2] The original uses a " ff," but that is simply the old form of writing a capital F.

It is needless to say that Farrow and Farrar are but different forms of the same name, and that the latter has become the usual mode of spelling. GEORGE FARROW was of Ipswich, where he married Ann Whitmore in 1643-4, and had three daughters as above recorded. Savage's account is all wrong, as he mistook a word and put a son George, Jr., in place of Phebe, and so misplaced his facts.

GEORGE FARROW is credited on the Treasurer's books for killing wolves in 1648 and 1650, on several occasions. We may, perhaps, fairly conclude that he was not an old man, and that he was born about 1615-20, his wife being born in 1618, as we shall show. The volume cited is in the library of the N. E. Hist. Genealogical Society at Boston. In Ipswich Deeds, vol. i. p. 549, he is mentioned as a "weaver." In 1658, his wife Ann is mentioned in a deposition as being 40 years old.[1] In Essex Deeds (iii. 107), as Mr. Waters informs me, there is a deed dated Dec. 1, 1668, of George Farrow of Ipswich and Ann his wife, exchanging his house and seventy acres of land in Ipswich, with William Symonds, of Wells, gent., for a house and lands in Wells: witnessed by Wm. Bennett and Thomas Estman.

Farrow doubtless moved to Wells (Maine) soon, where he was killed by Indians, 27 Sept., 1676, " as he was too carelessly venturing to his House without any Company," as HUBBARD narrates in his History (Drake's ed., ii. 183).

The records of York county, at Alfred, give only the following item: " At a Court of Associates houlden at Wells 12th December, 1676—This Court ordereth John Wells with Phoeby Farrow to take care of the widdow & estate of George Farrow deceased."

BOURNE (Hist. of Wells, p. 146) says Farrow left a widow and three sisters. SAVAGE says that it was the presumed son, George, Jr., who was killed; that he left three daughters, and that William Symonds and Joseph Storer were administrators. Both are doubtless wrong in part. There was only one George Farrow, and he had no son, but did have three daughters.

Now it appears by a deed on record at Alfred, Me. (York co. Deeds, iv. 4, 5), that 3 Nov. 1682, John Smyth, Sen., of Cape Nuttacke (now Neddock), planter, and Mary his wife, sold to William Sayer of Wells, part " of that tract or parcell of upland and sault marsh and fresh, which fell to my wife MARY, by the death of her natural father, *George Farrow*," containing eighty acres of upland and eight acres of meadow, &c. &c. Both John and Mary make a mark, and the deed is acknowledged before Sam[l] Wheelwright, same day, and recorded March 9, 1683-4.

From documents still on record in York county, Me., it seems that John Smith, Sen., was of Casco under Cleeve's government, and that in 1653 his wife was Joan, sister apparently of Edward Wanton (? Wanerton, see Hist. Saco, p. 43 ?).

---

[1] The deposition is as follows :—

CLERK'S OFFICE, Essex co. Court Papers, iv. 90.

The deposition of Ann farro ye wife of georg Faro aged 40 yeres or there abouts This deponent sayth she bought a p'cell of grene cotton of mr. Robert Payne and sayd mr. Payne told this deponent that the price of y[t] was three shillings eight pence by the yard, wch price this deponent thought was to much for such cotton y[t] being as she judgeth a thin cotton and wanting of yard wide, this deponent further sayth she bought another pcell of red cotton at foure shillings eight pence ye yard as mr Payne told her was the price of yt and further this deponent sayth not.

Sworne in Court held at Ipswich | the 29th of Sept. 1658   Robert Lord cleric. |

In 1657 he was of Cape Nuddock, or Neddock, where he had lands granted in 1658.

In 1674, John Smith, Sen., with consent of his wife Joan, deeds land to his son John, Jr., mentioning, also, land of James Jackson. In the same year James Jackson had land granted to him "lying next to his father John Smith."

As already mentioned, in 1682 John Smith, Sen., had taken a second wife, Mary, daughter of George and Mary (Whitmore) Farrow. In 1684, he confirms to his son John, land given by him "and Joane my former wife, his mother."

June 23, 1685, John Smith, Sen., makes a deposition, being aged about 73 years, stating that about 40 years before he was marshal under Mr. George Cleaves. March 1, 1685-6, he sells land to Samuel Banks, and Mary acknowledged same 14 June, 1686.

Finally, 3 Feb. 1687-8, John Smith of York made a settlement with "Mary Smith, wife of my late deceased father John Smith," giving her a piece of land in lieu of all claims for dower.

I am informed by Nathaniel G. Marshall, Esq., town clerk of York, that about 1713, John Smith, late of York and then of Gloucester, Mass., as executor of his father John S., had the lands re-granted and the boundaries defined.

Now it seems by Essex county records, the administration was granted 18 May, 1713, to Susanna, widow of John Smith, of Gloucester, mariner;[1] that they had children John, Abigail, Rebecca, Susanna and Joseph.

Here I leave this line, having no Whitmore blood in it. As yet I find no trace of any children of Mary (Farrow) Smith, and it is unlikely that she had any. Still, as she was born in 1645, she may have re-married after Smith's death.

Mr. Marshall says that 12 Oct. 1722, John Smith's heirs sold his land to Samuel Bankes of York, but the deed cannot be found.

Possibly the widow Mary (Farrow) came to Gloucester with her step-son; and it is to be noted that I have not traced Phebe, her sister.

John Brewer, of Ipswich.

Savage says that John Brewer was of Cambridge and had John in 1642; then went to Sudbury probably, and as a farther surmise gives him as wife Mary Whitmore of Essex county. This is clearly wrong, as doubtless this John of Cambridge was father of John of Sudbury who married about 1668. At all events our Ipswich John Brewer is clearly traced, and there is no sign of his having had two wives or of his living in Cambridge. It is more rational to believe that there were two contemporaries of the name. We have already mentioned his wife and children on the old Essex records; it seems that his will, dated 14 June, 1684, presented 30 Sept. following, is in Essex Wills, iv. 100-4. He is termed John Brewer, Sen., of Ipswich,

---

[1] The Gloucester records have the children of John Smith, Jr., and Susanna, as follows:

John, b. 2 Nov. 1702; d. 25 June, 1719, aged 16½ years.
Abigail, b. 25 Aug. 1704.
Rebecca, b. 25 Dec. 1706.
Joseph, b. 20 March, 1709.
Susanna, b. 6 Nov. 1711.

Susanna, widow, aged about 46 years, died 2 March, 1725.

and mentions wife Mary, *father Brewer* of Hamton, grandchild Edward Chapman, other gr. ch. John Chapman; residuary legatees, son John Bruer and dau. Mary Chapman. Overseers, brother Thomas Lull and Simeon Stace; wife Mary, executrix.

Oct. 2, 1684, widow Mary, who, being incapable, renounced executorship, made an agreement with "son John Brewer," and Simon Chapman, "said Simon being the husband of said Bruer's daughter, deceased." Mary (Whitmore) Brewer, widow of John, 1st, died 10 Dec. 1684.

The inventory of J. B., "who deceased the 22 June, 1684,"[1] mentions as one item, "Bermoody basket, 1s."

It is thus not only shown that John Brewer, Sen., of Ipswich, was not the Sudbury man, but it is made evident that he had a father living in Hampton. Mr. Joseph Dow of that town has given me some facts which enable me to make a probable pedigree. Our Boston records (see REGISTER, xi. 202) say that "William Lane was married to Mary Brewer, the daughter of Thomas Brewer of Roxbury, 21 : 6 : 56 :" i. e., Aug. 21, 1656. Now, 29 Nov. 1657, at Hampton, N. H., were married Sarah Brewer and Thomas Webster; and at Hampton the record says "ould goodman Brewer dyed 23 March 1690" (the year being 1689–90, as other entries show).

The son of Mary (Brewer) Lane married at Boston, 21 June, 1680, Sarah Webster of Hampton, dau. of Sarah (Brewer) Webster. If Mrs. Lane and Mrs. Webster were sisters, these children would be first cousins; and the fact that Mrs. Webster lived at Hampton would account for her father's removing to that town. This view was urged in the REGISTER, ix. 160, and is in every respect most probable.

We have, then :—

1. THOMAS[1] BREWER of Roxbury, said to have been at Ipswich in 1642 (perhaps a brother of Daniel B. of same), who died "old" in 1690, at Hampton, with children John, Sen., of Ipswich, Sarah Webster and Mary Lane.

2. JOHN[2] BREWER, Sen., of Ipswich, m. Mary (Whitmore) and had:—
    i.   MARY, b. 23 Sept. 1648 ; m. Simon Chapman.
3. ii. JOHN, b. 6 Oct. 1653.
    iii. SARAH, b. 27 March, 1655 ; prob. d. unm.

In the next generation :—

3. JOHN[3] BREWER, Jr., of Ipswich, and Susanna Warner, were married at Ipswich, January, 1674, as the court records show. He was chosen clerk of the writs (or town clerk) of Ipswich, 27 Nov. 1683. Susanna, wife of John Brewer, died Nov. 20, 1688. (Town records.)

He married, secondly, 3 June, 1689, Martha, dau. of Abraham Perkins, and had :—

    i.   HANNAH,[4] } b. 19 Feb. 1689 ; d. young.
    ii. MARTHA,[4] }
4. iii. JOHN,[4] b. 1692 ; aged 5 years in 1697.
5. iv. MARY,[4] b. 1695 ; " 2 " " "
    v. MARTHA,[4] b. June, 1697 ; aged 4 months in 1697 ; d. young.

Oct. 4, 1697, his widow Martha was made administratrix ; her bond, as guardian of the three children, gives their names and ages. She afterwards made return as administratrix, 8 Oct. 1701, as Martha Brewer, *alias* Ingols (Essex Wills, vii. 101). She was also appointed guardian to John Brewer,

---

[1] The town record says he died 23d June.

minor, son of John B. of Ipswich, and mentions that his sister Martha was deceased.

Jan. 18, 1702–3, Abraham Perkins of Ipswich was made guardian of the children of John Brewer, viz.: John, aged about 10 years, and Mary, about 8 years. He was unquestionably their uncle, and their mother had married secondly —— Ingols.

These two grandchildren of Mary (Whitmore) Brewer both married; and there were also living their cousins, the children of Mary Chapman, two being mentioned in the will of John Brewer, Sen., viz.: Edward and John Chapman.

4. JOHN[4] BREWER, 3d, of Ipswich, was a mariner. Nov. 9, 1717 (Essex Deeds, vol. xxxii.), he with wife Abigail sell a half right in common land to Robert Calfe, clothier. Mentions his father John Brewer.

Again (Essex Wills, xi. 101), 14 Dec. 1714, Ephraim Smith and Mary his wife, dau. of John Brewer of Ipswich, having received £20 from his brother John Brewer, mariner, acquitted the estate.

JOHN[4] and Abigail Brewer had at Ipswich—

    i. ABIGAIL,[5] bapt. 19 Nov. 1721.

His wife d. 27 Sept. 1723, and I cannot trace this line farther.

5. MARY[4] BREWER, as just shown, married Ephraim Smith.

Administration was granted 9 Feb., 1720, on the estate of Ephraim Smith to his widow Mary. I have not been able to trace this line farther.

DEATHS IN STRATHAM, N. H., COMMENCING AUGUST 20, 1741.

Transcribed from a Record kept by Dea. *Samuel Lane,* and communicated by CHARLES C. HARDY, Esq., of Dover, N. H.

SAMUEL LANE was born in Hampton, N. H., Oct. 6, 1718; from which place he removed to Stratham, N. H., June 11, 1741, and remained there till his death, which took place Dec. 29, 1806. He was selectman and town clerk several years; a land surveyor, employed by the governors under the crown and after the revolution; deacon of the church thirty-five years until chosen elder, in which office he continued during the remainder of his life.

His house was near the burying-ground, and he kept the palls— a large one, and one smaller devoted to children—which it was then the custom to use. This fact adds very much to the value of his record, as a death occurring in Stratham could hardly have escaped his notice.

The original record, which is now in the possession of his grandson, Dea. EDMUND J. LANE,[1] of Dover, comes down to the year 1806.

---

[1] See REGISTER for April, 1873, *ante,* xxvii. 179–80.

1741.
Aug. 20. Nicholas Clarks child died in this Town.
Aug. 22. Nicholas Clarks wife died.
Octob. 16. Patience Leavit died.
Nov. 5. goody Avery died.
Nov. 30. Ebenezer Barkers child died.
Dec. 25. Caleb Rolings' wife died.
Dec. 28. Ens[n] Joseph Merrils wife died.

In this year since I came into Town have died 7 persons.

1742.
Jan. 9, 1741-2. Nicholas Clark died.
Jan. 10. John Larys child died.
Jan. 12. Joseph Merril Jun[r] died.
Jan. 21. Setchel Rundlets wife died.
Jau. 23. Mrs. Jones died.
Feb[r] 1. Benj[n] Cottons child died.
Feb[r] 16. the Rev[d] mr Rusts negro woman died.
Feb[r] 19. John Davis child died.
March 4. Enoch Merrils child died.
March 16. John Pipers young child died.
March 20. John Pipers wife died.
March 31. Abigael Keneson died.
Apr. 17. Justice Leavits dau[r] Milleson [torn]
April 26. Andrew Wiggin Jun[r] wife died.
May 26. Abr[m] Tiltons child died.
June 17. John Stockbridges child died.
July 3. widow Mary Lad died.
Aug. 1. Joseph Merrill Jun[r] child died.
Aug. 18. Thomas Chases child died.
Aug. 22. William Chases child died.
Aug. 26. William Chases other child died.
Aug. 30. Benj[n] Morris' child died.
Sept. 1. Joseph Palmers Son died.
Sept. 2. Joseph Palmers child died.
Sept. 3. Joseph Palmers child died.
Sept. 2. William Chases child died.
Sept. 4. Benj[n] Jewets daughter died.
Sept. 5. Samuel Veazeys child died.
Sept. 9. David Stevens child died.
Sept. 10. David Stevens Servant girl died.
Sept. 10. William Chases child died.
Sept. 10. Benj[n] Norris' child died.
Sept. 17. mr Noah Barkers Son died.
Sept. 17. mr Richard Youngs child died.
Sept. 17. Jona[n] Chases Jun[r] child died.
[torn]t. 17. mr David Robinson Jun[r] child died.
[torn] Caleb Rolings' child died.
Sept. 18. Jona[n] Chases Jun[r] child died.
Sept. 19. mrs Abbits child died.
Sept. 19. mr Richard Calleys child died.
Sept. 20. Richard Calleys child died.
Sept. 21. Richard Calleys child died.
Sept. 22. Widow Wadleys Son died.
Sept. 22. mr Joseph Merril Shoemaker dau[r] died.

Sept. 25.   Solomon Smiths child died.
Sept. 25.   Solomon Smith another child died.
Sept. 26.   Richard Calleys boy died.
Sept. 27.   Jona^n Sibleys child died.
Sept. 28.   Tuftin Wiggins child died.
Sept. 28.   Walter Wiggins child died.
Sept. 29.   Walter Wiggins child died.
Sept. 30.   Walter Wiggins child died.
Sept. 30.   Walter Wiggins apprentice girl died.
Oct.   2.   mr Benjamin Jewets son died.
Oct.   3.   Jonathan Rolings child died.
Oct.   5.   Walter Wiggins Son died.
Oct.   5.   Tuftin Wiggin child died.
Oct.   5.   mrs Abbits child died.
Oct.   5.   Jonathan Rolings^s child died.
Oct.   7.   Richard Calleys child died.
Oct.   8.   Joseph Masons Junr child died.
Oct.   7.   mr Joseph Merrils shoemaker child died.
Oct.   9.   Joseph Masons Junr child died.
Oct.   9.   Abraham Tiltons child died.
Oct.   11.   Jona^n Sibleys child died.
Oct.   11.   Richard Calleys child died.
Oct.   15.   Jonathan Sibleys child died.
Oct.   15.   Tuftin Wiggins^s child died.
Oct.   23.   mrs Abbots child died.
Oct.   27.   John Hills child died.
Nov.   2.   Jona^n Rolings child died.
Nov.   3.   John Hills child died.
Nov.   4.   John Hills child died.
Nov.   7.   Richard Palmers child died.
Nov.   8.   Abraham Stockbridges child died.
Nov.   8.   Abraham Stockbridge another child died.
Nov.   12.   John Hills child died.
Nov.   13.   John Stockbridges child died.
Nov.   14.   widow Hannah Merrils child died.
Nov.   20.   Abraham Stockbridges child died.
Nov.   27.   Moses Thirstons child died.
Nov.   27.   John Jones child died.
Nov.   28.   John Speeds Son George died.
Nov.   29.   John Speeds child died.
Nov.   30.   John Jones child died.
Dec.   1.   Abraham Stockbridges Son abr^m Died.
Dec.   2.   John Speeds child died.
Dec.   3.   Abraham Stockbridges Son Jacob Died.
Dec.   9.   Jonathan Rolings^s daughter Died.
Dec.   15.   Abr^m Stockbridges child died.
Dec.   19.   John Speeds child died.
Dec.   19.   Enoch Merrils child died.
Dec.   20.   Samuel Veazeys child died.
Dec.   31.   Moses Thirstons child died.
Dec.   31.   Samuel Veazeys child died.

in the year past have Died 95 persons.   Since Aug. 18, 77.[1]

[To be continued.]

[1] Tradition says that most of these died from a disease then called "putrid sore throat," said to be very much like the diphtheria of the present time.

EXTRACTS FROM THE DIARY OF THE LATE HON. WILLIAM D. WILLIAMSON, OF BANGOR, MAINE,

WHILE A MEMBER OF THE SEVENTEENTH CONGRESS OF THE UNITED STATES.

Communicated by the Hon. JOSEPH WILLIAMSON, of Belfast, Me.

[Concluded from page 191.]

[1821.] Monday, Dec. 17. Visited with Hon. Mark L. Hill, in hack, the Pres^t. of U. S.—waited in audience-room—introduced. He is an old man, dressed in black—breeches,—boots,—hair turned up, talks a little thick, motions with his hands when talking,—sociable, sedate,—about 5 feet 10 or 11 in. tall, rather spare. He has two daughters.

MR. CALHOUN, SEC'Y WAR.

He is a tall man, of about 40 years, quick spoken, light complexion, little florid, expressive, unwrinkled. He appeared to be a pleasant, sociable man, and clear headed.

MR. THOMPSON, SEC'Y NAVY.

He may be 50 years old—more port and consequence than Calhoun, and a shorter man,—pretty free to talk,—not so much so as the Pres^t or Sec'y War. He stands high,—has been Ch. Jus. S. Court, N. Y.

MR. CRAWFORD.

He is tall, about 45 years old, full of talk, wears a skull-cap,—is well proportioned.

This day spent in passing resolutions requiring standing com^{ees} to consider and report on various subjects, which each resolution names; raising some special com^{ees} for the consideration of special subjects,—calling on the Pres^t. &^{c}. for information. A considerable debate as to what com^{ees} certain subjects ought to be referred. Gov. Wright, of Maryland, Mr. Eustis, of Mass., and Randolph, of V^a., spoke some. A very bad house for debate—the echo or reverberation such, one can neither hear or speak with ease.

A message from the Pres^t. of the U. States. The Doorkeeper announces "A Message." The Pres^t's Sec'y then says, "I have a Message in writing which I am directed to present to the House of Rep."

Tuesday, Dec. 18. Debate in the House as to the Bonds or security to be given by agents entrusted with money to pay pensioners. Several spoke.

Weds. 19 Dec. A few petitions,—debate as to sureties of agents authorized to pay invalid pensioners,—as to adjourning over Christmas,—ayes 134, noes 30.

Thurs. Dec. 20. Local matters; little business.

Friday, Dec. 21. Reports unfavorable to individual claims,—argument as to staves taken by the army under Gen. Wilkinson for fuel. Visited the room of Paintings. " Surrender of Cornwallis "—emblem of the Treaty of Ghent.

Saturday, Dec. 22. No session. Remarks. Lots on Pen^a. avenue would sell for $1 a square foot; on other streets from 25 to 50 cts. a foot. Good fountains of water, which water the city. Mr. Monroe embarrassed till he was Pres^t., now free from debt.

Sund. Dec. 23. A meeting at Rep. Chamber,—one discourse. Mr. Sparks preached, "Having the form of Godliness, and denying the power thereof."

Mond. Dec. 24. Routine of business—Petitions, &c.

Tues. Dec. 25. Christmas; no meeting of Cong. House adjourned.

Weds. Dec. 26. Dined at the Presidents—fine furniture—house furnished by uncle Sam's money.

Thurs. Dec. 27. Routine of business—little done.

Friday, Dec. 28. Adjourned over to Monday.

Sunday, Dec. 30. Heard Dr. Morse from Matthew, " Forgive us our debts, as we forgive our debtors." Not a very full hall—the Rep. followed their Unitarian, Mr. Sparks, to hear him. Gen. Macomb called on me.

Mond. Dec. 31. Routine of business as usual. Adjourned to Wednesday.

Tuesday, Jan. 1, 1822. Went to the fort. All, without invitation or distinction, visited the Pres^t.—Members, Heads of Dept^s., Foreign Ministers, officers in the army and navy—& ladies—a great jam,—a band of music in the entry room—interchange of compliments,—Prest. and lady continually on their feet,—9 Indian chiefs from Missouri. The F. Envoy very richly dressed,—introduced to Mrs. Monroe.

Mr. Neuville & Channing at dinner, had a misunderstanding as to the slave trade.

Wednesday, Jan. 2. General routine, &c.

Thursday, Jan. 3^d. Debate on the appropriation bill, particularly as to the Indian Dep^t.

Friday, 4 Jan. Same subject resumed. Randolph, Smith (Md.), Tracy, Loundes, Ross, Reed (Ga.) spoke. Mr. Morse is taking a drawing of the Rep. Chamber. Drew lots for 2 portraits to a state—lot fell to Mr. Lincoln and self. It is said Mr. Crawford and Calhoun don't speak to each other except on business, and Gen. Jackson says Crawford is a damned rascal. Sec'y of the Senate comes to the house with such bills as the Senate has passed; stands just within the bar in the alley, says the Senate has passed the following bills: reads the titles, and says " in which the Senate requests the concurrance of the House." When Congress is in session, the flag is flying on the top of the Capitol; when the House goes into a Com^e of the whole, the Mace.

Sat^y. Jan. 5. Read in my room; very cold.

Sund. Jan. 6. Heard Mr. Houghton, 1. Pet. 2, 21—a full house,—poor singing,—deacon 2 lines at a time. Boys this Sabbath and every Sabbath seen skating without molestation.

Monday, Jan. 7. Presented petition of Jarvis and others for a term of Dist. Court at Union River. Debate as to the money to be raised for the Indian Department. Night, a party at Mr. Adams' house, music and dancing, card parties and back-gammon. Ladies dress, some with white plumes, some with roses, some with wreaths, on head, white, black, crimson. Mrs. De Neuville had a gilt comb in her hair: narrow wreath: bosom dressed low, bare neck; gown, brown silk velvet. Mrs. Adams had on a simple head-dress, a light silk, and light white gauze over.

Tues. Jan. 8. Debate on the Indian appropriation—dec^d out of order in making a motion. Went to Mr. Calhoun's in the evening.

Wed. Jan. 9. Debate on the appropriation bill. Smith Dwight spoke, and Buchanan. Galleries pretty full.

Thurs. Jan. 10. Debate continued. Mr. Randolph, Todd & Baldwin spoke. Presented petition for " Military Road." Families getting their ice.

Friday, Jan. 11.   Debate on Resolution, calling for information, &c. Adj^d over Sat^y to Mond.

Monday, Jan. 14.   Debate as to the Maryland Resolutions to divide the Public Lands among the States for the purpose of schooling. Labor,—a female slave gets $5 per mo., a male $10, if they be good,—worth $300, the price Launcelot paid for his wife.

Tues. Jan. 15.   Cold : clear—debate on several subjects.

Thurs. Jan. 17.   Debate on the ratio of Rep. postponed to a week from Monday.   Resolutions as to the Boundary and Batteries.

Friday, Jan. 18.   Debate till late on the claim of Handerson at Monday Point—allowed in Com^e of the W.

Sat'y, Jan. 19.   No session.   Talk with Gen. Macomb as to the Battery and military road.

Sunday, Jan. 20.   Heard Mr. Sparks.

Mond. Jan. 21.   Bankrupt bill—speech of Sargent, Penn^a.

Tues. Jan. 22.   Debate on Bankrupt bill by Mr. Sargent.

Weds. Jan. 23.   Very windy.   Mr. Stevenson's (of Va.) speech on Bankrupt bill.

Thurs. Jan. 24.   Debate as to receiving resolves from State Legislatures —decision of the Chair.   Did not go into Com^e of the whole.

Friday, Jan. 25.   Very clear and cold.   Gen Smyths speech on Bank^t. Bill.

Mond. Jan. 28.   Debate on the app^n bill, yeas 83, nays 90, on the ratio of 7 to 42,000.

Tues. Jan. 29.   Debate as to the printing of doc^{t}s, &c. as to Jackson and the Florida business.

Wed. Jan. 30 to Sat. Feb. 2.   Debate on the Ratio or Appropriation bill.

Sund. Feb. 3.   Heard Hayward preach an Arminian discourse in the Capitol, and Dr. Lawry in the afternoon.

Tuesd. Feb. 5.   App't or Ratio Bill settled, at 4 P.M.   Took "the previous question" the first time this winter.

Wed. Feb. 6.   Bill passed making appropriation for the naval service— pressed on account of the depredations on our commerce in the West Ind. seas.

Thurs. & Friday, Feb. 7 & 8.   Debates on the Bankrupt bill.   *Remark.* It is said there are 30 members of the H. of Rep. born in Connecticut.

Sat. Feb. 9.   Indian war dance before the President's house—a great concourse of people : 13 Indian chiefs from Missouri, who have been about here two months (one squaw).   They had a little drum as large as an 8 qt. milk pail, on which one beat, while the others danced, whooped, made gestures of killing their enemies.   They were painted red, blue and black about their eyes and cheeks,—heads shaved, except one lock,—naked down to their hips.

Sund. Feb. 10.   Heard Mr. Thacher, from N. Haven, in Capitol.

Mond. Feb. 11.   Debate on Bankrupt bill to Feb. 21.

Tues. March 19.   People began to plough gardens ; warm ; sit without fire.

Board bill Dec. 19 to May 8th 141 days, at $1.50 per day, $211.50.

ABSTRACTS OF THE EARLIEST WILLS ON RECORD, OR
ON THE FILES IN THE COUNTY OF SUFFOLK,
MASSACHUSETTS.

Prepared by WILLIAM B. TRASK, Esq., of Boston.

[Continued from page 206.]

Capt. WILLIAM TYNG.[1]—Inventory of the Goods and Chattells of Capt
William Tyng, made 25. 3. 1653. See REGISTER, vol. viii. p. 62. Houses,
warehouses, etc. cattle at the Farme at Brantree called Salters Farme, at
Goodman Mattocks, at George Speres Farme; 600 Akers of land at Rock-
stones Farme, 48 Akers land at Brantree, and Marsh in the possession of
John Gurney; 80 Akers of land at Monoctecott, £16; 30 Akers at Win-
chester's Neck, 4; 26 Akers vpon the Plaine, £13; 20 Akers of Marsh in
Knight Neck, £40. Whole am^t of lands, cattle, furniture, etc. 2774–14–04.
Appraised by Natha: Duncan, Anthony Stoddard, Wm. Dauis. Plate
afterwards mentioned.

Bookes, in folio.—Bookes of Martyrs in 3 volumes, Books of Statutes at
Large, The Survey of London, Speeds Chronicle, Camdens Brittania, Ains-
worth on Moses and Psalmes, Mr Harris[2] Workes, Dr Sibs Saints Cordiall,
Marchants Accompts, Gecords Herball.[3]

In Quarto.—A Concordance, Prestones Workes 2 of them, Dr Vsher
against Jesuitt, Barriffe, The Soules implantation, Treatise of Magistracy
Two, Childe of light in darknes, goodwin; Enonimous Tresure, Apeale to
Parliament, Janua Linguarum, Ans. to Mr Dauenport, Parralells Censures
observations, Dod & cleauer on Sacraments, defence of the Wach-Word,
Sibbs on faith, Mr Barnard against Seperatists, the Discouerer, Ecclesiastical cannons. Complainte euill doers, Interest States & kingdomes, Bloody
Tenent, Forbes 4 sermons, Axe at the roote, Popish Idollatry, Experience
of light & health, Circkle of Comerse, Mary Pope, Edward Renolds, Min-
ester against briges; Doctrine of the Saboth, the still destroyer; a Vindication of m^r Burrowes, a Duch Worke, An apollogy of Brownists, Doc-
trinall & Morrall instructions, Reformations obseruations, Censure on Anabaptists Answer, abridgm^t of Camden, Tolloration Justifyed, Burrowes
gospell Conversation, Moses Choice, Gospell Worship, Churches Resurrec-
tion Cott, Childrens Baptisme, 7 vialls 3 Congregationall churches, Singin
Psalemes.

---

[1] Capt. Tyng died Jan. 18, 1652. " leaving larger estate," says Savage, " than any in the
country of that day." This is the earliest extended list of books to be found among the
estates in the Suffolk Probate Office. One of a prior date, that of John Benjamin, of Watertown, 12 (4) 1645, contains about twenty volumes.

[2] Probably Robert.

[3] Doubtless " The Herball or Generall Historie of Plantes, Gathered by John Gerarde of
London." The first edition was imprinted by John Norton, London, in 1597, pages 1392.
The address to the reader is, " From my House in Holborn within the Suburbs of London,
this first of December, 1597." The second edition was printed by Adam Islip, Joice Norton and Richard Whitaker, London, Anno 1633. To the Reader—" From my house on
Snow-hill, Octob. 22, 1633, Thomas Johnson," who, it appears, edited this edition ; pages
1630, besides the indices. Both these volumes are in folio, illustrated with many hundred
wood-cuts. It is " ornamented with a more numerous set of figures," says Pulteney,
" than had ever accompanied any work of the kind in this kingdom." A second
edition of this rare work is in the library of the Mass. Horticultural Society. Allibone
mentions two other editions as having been published, one in 1636, fol., and another in 1744,
8vo.

In Octavo.—Excellency of a gratious spirit, office of executors, pentisia Indicaria, christians Engagement, Imposts & customes, Concordance, logick & Rethoricke, Christians dayly Walke, duch testaments & psalmes, An arrow against Idollotry ; 16 Ciceroas orations.   (File, No. 128.)

JOSEPH MORSE.—Thomas Boyden, late of Boston, now of meadfeild, co. Suffolk, in New England, yeoman : bond £300, together with the house, vpland & meadow now in my possession, lately the Inheritance of Joseph Morse, late of Meadfeild, wth all libe^{r}tyes, etc. to the same belonging, to pay unto Edward Rawson, Recorder, or his successo^{r}s, the some of one hundred & eighty pounds, etc.
Oct. 18, 1661.

The Condicōn of this obligation is such, that if the aboue bounden Thomas Boyden shall by himselfe, or his heires, executors, etc. keepe and mainteine the seuerall children of ye late Joseph Morse & Hannah his now wife during the time of theire Nonage or Unmarried Condicōn, or till they choose theire Guardians, teaching or Causing ye sonnes of the said Morse to write & Read and at theire seuerall marriages or days of Age, shall pay unto each of the said Morse his children, the seuerall portions to them Assigned by the County Court at Boston In January last & by the Generall Court Approved of as in s^{d} County Courts order so Allowed by the Generall Court in May 1661, Then this obligation to be voyd, etc.

THOMAS BOYDEN.

In the presence of vs 27 June 1665.
    John Ferniside   (File, No. 149.)
    peren rawson

See abstract of the inventory of the estate of Joseph Morse, REGISTER, viii. 277.

JOHN HARBOR, Senior.[1]—I, Jno Harbor Senr of Braintrie in New England, yeoman, doe acknowledge myself bound to Edward Rawson Recorder for ye County of Suffolk, in the some of fiuety pounds, etc.   Boston, Aug. 10. 1654.

The Condicōn of this obligation is such that if the said Jno Harbor Senr etc. pay or cause to be paid the seuerall portions determined by the magists. to be paid to the seuerall children of Benjamin Scott according to the times p^{r}fixed in ye determinacōn, then this obligation to be voyd, else to stand, etc.

JOHN HARBOR.

Signed Sealed & deliu^{r}d in p^{r}sence of vs,
    Edward Rawson Jvn:
    William needom.

A Trew Invitori of the Goods And Chattells of the Widow Scott, the late wife of Benjamen Scott, of brantri, deceased, and now the Wife of John Harber, of brantri, married 21 7 month 47.
    Amount of inventory, £86. 14^{s}.   Debts 3. 6. 0.
                    Steuen kinsley, Samuel bas, William needom.

Power of Administration to ye estate of Benjamin Scott is granted to Jno Harbor and Hannah his wife, late wife to Benjamin Scott, in behalf of hirself & the children.   EDW. RAWSON, Record^{r}.
    13 July 1654.
present ye Gou^{r}n^{r}, m^{r} Nowell, m^{r} Hibbins, Capt Gookin & Capt Atherton.

---

[1] Neither John Harbor, senior, nor John Harbor, junior, are mentioned by Mr. Savage.

Present y⁰ Gou'ner, m' Nowell, Cap' Atherton & Recorder. The magistrates on the 10ᵗʰ of August determined y⁰ estate should be thus divided, the wife to have one third p'te viz. twenty five pounds, Benjamine the Eldest sonne fowerteene pounds, the other [illegible] children seven pounds apeece : to be paid vnto them at the day of marriage or at their ages of fowerteene yeeres, the sᵈ Jnᵒ Harbor givinge in securitye to pay the said persons accordingly, education of the children being allowed for.   EDWARD RAWSON.

(File, 150.)

THE SECOND FOOT COMPANY OF NEWBURY, MASS.

Copied from the original document in the possession of FREDERIC KIDDER, Esq., of Melrose.

Newbury: janu: 15th 1710–11.

A list of y⁰ second foot Company in Newbury under y⁰ comand of Cap' Hugh March :

Cop¹¹ Joseph Brown
Corp¹¹ Abel Merrill
Corp¹¹ Nicholas Noyes
    Abial Kelley
    Abraham Merril ju.
    Abel Hale
    Ezra Rolf
    Ebenezer Knoulton
    Daniell Cheney
    Joseph Lowl
    Joseph Pilsberry
    John Chass
    John Emery sen'
    Jonathan Kelly
    Jonathan Hoag
    John Emery jun'
    John Carr
    Jonathan Chass
    Joseph Richerdson jun'
    John Swett ju.
    Moses Richerdson
    Daniell Morrison jun'
    Sam¹¹ Bartlet jun'
    Charls Chase
    Daniell Bartlett
    Isaac Chass
    Joshua Baily

Thomas Halle
Sam¹¹ Sayer
Solomon Holman
Isaac Annis
Joseph Chass
James Brown
Joseph Hills
Benjamin Hills
Nathaniel Hills
Daniell Chass
Daniell Morrison sen'
Thomas Steeples
Thomas Williams
Thomas Chass jun'
Moses Chass jun'
Thomas Noyes
Richard Bartlet jun'
Daniell Richerdson
Thomas ffollinsbe
Nathaniell Morril
James Chass
Nathaniell Greenlief
Caleb Pilberry
Enoch Little
Richerd Palmer
James Lowl
Hananiah Ordway

54   Taken by mee

TRISTRAM GREENLEAF Clark.

MEMORANDA FROM THE REV. WILLIAM COOPER'S[1] INTERLEAVED ALMANACS.

Copied by the late THADDEUS WILLIAM HARRIS, M.D., Librarian of Harvard University, and communicated by his successor, JOHN LANGDON SIBLEY, A.M., of Cambridge, Mass.

1715.

Feb. 6 (1714–5). Dyed Mr. Grindal Rawson, Pastor of y⁰ ch. in Mendon, aged 56.

Mar. 19. Dyed y⁰ truly Honble Isaac Addington, Esq. Ætat. suæ 71.

Mar. 23. I attended Mr Addington's funerall.

Mar. 23. A melancholy Relation of a barbarous murder committed at Rhoad Island, by one Jeremiah Meacham, a man of ab^t 40 years of age, born at Salem Village, but had liv'd in y^t colony ab^t 20 years : who one evening kill'd his wife with whom he had liv'd well, and had children ; and also his wife's sister ; both without any known reason or provocation, but by a diabolical impulse. He first cut them with his hatchet, and then his wife's throat with a penknife. A man coming to them he also dangerously wounded ; and then set fire to his house, and cut his own throat ; but the fire being extinguished, and his wound not mortal, he was apprehended & committed.

May 1. I preach'd at Mr Colman's P.M. from 1 Epist. John 2. 8, lat. part, the first time I preach'd publickly.

May 12. My mother was married to Mr. Stoddard.

May 20. Dyed Mr Peter Daille, Pastor of y⁰ Congregation of French Refugees in this place ; aged ab^t 70.

June 9. Margaret Callogharne, an Irish young woman, was here executed for the murder of her bastard child.

July 4. The Ch. meet today at 12 a Clock, and soon came to these two Votes. first, Y^t it was judg'd for y⁰ glory of God and y⁰ edification of that Ch. to have another settled in y⁰ Pastoral Office among them, and that they w^d soon proceed to y⁰ Election of one : 2^d, y^t the 1s^t Tuesday in August be kept by them as a day of Prayer to seek God's direction and blessing therein. N. B. Y⁰ meeting was of Church and Congregation together.

Aug. 7. Mrs Ann Colman was this day rec^d to y⁰ communion : the first y^t has been so of y⁰ children y^t were baptized in y⁰ church.

Aug. 16. Mr Colmans Congregation meet to proceed in y⁰ election of a Pastor, and it was found that in 66 votes y^r were 60 for myself.

Sept. 26. Dyed here the Revd Mr Thomas Bridge, in the 59th year of his age, and y⁰ 11 of his pastoral office to y⁰ 1st Ch. of X in this place. His birth and education were in England. He was a man of much piety, devotion, love, humility, meekness, &c. and of great fidelity in y⁰ discharge of his office. He dyed of lethargical or apoplectick disease.

Sept. 29. I attended his funeral wth a multitude of people. It being the public Lecture-day, a Sermon was preach'd on y⁰ occasion by Mr Colman.

October 31. Dyed here, Elisha Cooke, Esq., one of y⁰ Council, aged 77.

---

[1] The Rev. William Cooper graduated H. C. 1712, was ordained colleague of the Rev. B^r. Colman of Brattle-Street Society, Boston, May 23, 1716, and continued there till his death, Dec. 13, 1743, aged 49.—*Note by Dr. Harris.*

The same day, dyed at Newtown Thomas Oliver, Esq., who also was one of the Council, and a man of great piety and integrity.

November 16. Dyed at Piscataqua Ichabod Plaisted, Esq., one of the Council for this Province, in ye 52 year of his age.

Nov. 17. The Annual Thanksgiving.

Nov. 26. Dyed between 10 and 11 in ye morning ye virtuous wife of my cousin J. Ellis, in ye 27th year of her age.

Also dyed this 26th day, Mr Joseph Green, Pastor of ye Church in Salem village, aged 40 years, a very worthy man, and much lamented.

1716.

Jany 28. I was bearer to Ebenezer Mountford, A.M., who dyed ye 24th, having completed his 30th year.

Feb. 23. Dyed at Salem, Wm Browne, Esq., in the 78th year of his age : He was for many years one of his maj^s Council.

March 21. Dyed at Haverill of a violent Feaver, ye Revd Mr Joshua Gardiner, Pastor of ye ch. there, aged 27 years.

April 25. This day a new Ch. was gathered at Marblehead, and the Rev. Mr Edward Holyoke was ordain'd ye Pastor of it.

May 2. I went to Newtowne to visit Mr Howel who last Saturday removed there for ye benefit of ye air having been in a long languishing ; when I came I found him dying—he expired about an hour and a half after I came to him, aged 34.

May 23. I was ordained to the work of the ministry, &c. &c. Mr. Colman preach'd.

July 10. Dyed Mrs Elizabeth Hirst, ye virtuous consort of Grove Hirst, Esq., and daughter to ye Honble Judge Sewall, in ye 35th year of her age.

July 18. The Revd Mt John Barnard was ord^nd Colleague Pastor wth Mr Cheever over ye congregation in Marblehead.

Aug. 23 was observed as a day of Publick Thanksgiving for ye success of his maj^s arms ag^st ye Rebellion.

This day dyed Mr Henry Bromfield, son to Edwd Bromfield Esq. in ye 17th year of his age, and ye 3^d of his being at ye Colledge ; a youth of good hopes and design'd for ye work of ye ministry.

Sept. 20. Dyed Ebenezer Cornish in ye 21st year of his age. He was a very hopefull young man, had been of our communion above a year, and made a gracious end, &c.

Dec. 6. The annual Publick Thanksgiving.

1723.

Jany 30. At Madam Steel's (?) funeral.

Feb. 3. Baptized *Jonathan* Deming.
    "   *Josiah* Marshall.
  17.   "   *Hannah* Davis.
   "   "   *Ebenezer* Heath.
   "   "   *John* Millecan.
   "   "   *Eliz*^th Cotting.

Feb. 24. Baptiz^d *Mary* Boilstone.

Mar. 6. Attended the funerals of Mr Joseph Howard and Mrs Eliz^a Tyley.

Mar. 13. Mr David Stoddard buried.

" 14. General Fast.

" 16. Dyed Mr Benj^a Gibson, chaplain at ye Eastward. H. C. 1719.

" 17. Dyed ab^t 3 this morning, good old Mrs Dasset, very sudden.

April 7.   Baptiz^d *Ann* Thomas.
   " *Benjamin* Leveridge.
   At the burial of Burnel's child.
" 10. At the funeral of Mrs Eliz^a Pierce.
" 14. Baptiz^d *Nathaniel* Jackson.
   " *Hannah* Sprague.
" 15. At the funeral of Mr Jno Frizell.
" 19. At the funeral of Capt Bulkleys child.
" 21. At the funeral of Coll Dyer.
May 23. At the burial of Amaritta.
" 30. At the funeral of Mad^m Bridget Usher.
June 2. Baptiz^d *Ebenezer* Chubb.
" 4. At the burial of Mrs Dyers child.
" 9. Baptiz^d *John* Periway.
" 11. At the ordination at Watertown.
" 12. At the burial of Thorns child.
" 16. Baptiz^d *Simeon* Stoddard.
   " *Thomas* Armstrong.
" 18. At the burial of Mr Langdon.
" 28. Mehetabel born ab^t 10 in the forenoon.
" 30. Baptiz^d *Eliz^a* Stoddard.
   " *Mehetabel* Cooper.
   " *Sarah* Marshall.
   " *Aaron* Willis.
July 14. Mrs Stoddards child buried.
" 29. At the burial of Capt. Thomas's child.
Aug. 13. At the burial of S. Willis's child.
" 23. Dyed the Rev^d and renowned Dr. I. Mather, Ætat. 85.
" 28. At the funeral of Mr Shannon, aged 68.
" 29. At the funeral of Dr. Mather.
Sept. 1. Baptiz^d *Rebecca* Marshall.
In the evening at the funeral of the only son of Mr Jonas Clark.
Sept. 2. At the funeral of Mrs Story, daut^r to Mrs Tomlison.
" 5. At the funeral of Mr Nath. Stoddard's child.
" 8. At the burial of Mr Hail's child.
" 14. At the funeral of the desirable wife of cous. Jonath. Sewall.
" 23. At the burial of Mr Wass's father.
Oct. 4. Baptiz^d *Eliza* Hall.
" 11. At the burial of Mr Dorothy.
" 20. Baptiz^d *Mary* Steel.
" 27. " *Eliz^a* Maycock.
Nov. 3. At the burial of Mr James Oliver's child.
" 5. At the burial of Mrs Kelsey.
" 28. Publick Thanksgiving.
Dec. 1. Baptiz^d *Catherine* Greenleaf.
   " *Eliza* Rogers.
" 13. At the burial of Mr Maycock's child.
" 18. At Mr Gee's ordination.
" 22. Baptiz^d *Ann* Fowle.
" 29. " *Abijah* Estes, ætat. 17.
   " *John* Norman.
1724.
Jany 8. At the funeral of Dr Davis's eldest child.

Jan. 16. At the funeral of old Mrs Foye.
Feb. 2. Baptiz^d *Thomas* Fayrweather.
" 5. At Charlestown, at the ordination of Mr Abbot.
" 9. Baptiz^d *Thomas* Uran.
   " *Benjamin* Lenox.
" 16. " *Peregrine* White, ætat. 64.
   " *Marjora* Taylor.
" 23. " *Jane* Payne.
   " *Ann* Marks.
Mar. 26. Publick Fast.
Apr. 5. Baptiz^d *Mary* Waters.
" 14. Mr Basset ordain'd—he preach'd. **Mr. Colman gave an acc^t** of the call of Mr Basset frm. Carolina.
Apr. 26. Baptiz^d *Nanny* Coit.
   " *Joseph* Storer.
   " *Eliz^a* McDonald.
" 27. Attend Mrs Noyes's funeral.
May 2. Mr Basset sail'd for Carolina.
   At the funeral of old Mrs Leg.
" 3. President Leverett died very suddenly.
" 6. At the President's funeral.
" 17. Baptiz^d *Eliz^a* Dudley.
   " *Zechariah* Hubbart.
   " *John* Addison.
   " *Elizabeth* and *Sarah* } Leveridge (twins).
" 20. At the funeral of M^r An. Tyler's child.
" 24. Preach'd to some Pirates under sentence of death.
" 31. At the funeral of Mr Hall's mother.
June 2. At the burial of Mrs Greenleaf's brother.
" 11. At the funeral of Mr Proctor.
" 14. At the burial of old Mrs Weyman.
" 18. At the funeral of Mrs Tully.
" 28. Baptiz^d *Samuel* Hayley.
July 14. At the burial of Mr Sprague's child.
" 20. This evening was buried Mad^m Faneuill and Capt Fowle's child.
" 21. Fyfield's child buried.
" 22. Went to Watertown to ordination of Mr Storer.
" 24. At the funeral of Mrs Greenwood.
Aug. 2. Baptiz^d *Mary* Cotting.
   " *Benjamin* Warden.
   At the burial of Mr Gibbens.
" 4. Deacon Parker's child buried.
" 9. Baptiz^d *Marianna* Hail.
" 13. At the burial of Arnold's child.
" 16. Sister Hannah Sewall died at $\frac{1}{2}$ an hour after 10 **A.M.**
   Baptiz^d *John* Smith.
   " *Robert* Larmon.
   " *Sarah* Lee.
" 18. Sister Hannah Sewall buried.
" 19. This morning early died brother Sewall of Brooklin his child.
" 23. Baptiz^d *Sarah* Tyley.
   " *Prudence* Fitch.

Aug. 23. Baptiz^d *Sarah* Rogers.
" 25. At the burial of Stokes's child.
" 28. At the funeral of Capt Pemberton's child.
" 30. Baptiz^d *Dorcas* Davenport.
In the evening at the funeral of Mr. Jn° Rogers.
Sept. 4. At the burial of Mr Vinteno's child.
" 10. At the burial of Mrs Hutchins.
" 13. At the burial of Mr Storer's child.
" 15. Died our dear Mehitabel very quietly, a few minutes after 5 a clock, P.M.
Sept. 17. Mehit. buried.
" 22. At the burial of neighbour Thorn's child.
" 24. At the burial of Mr Cunningham's child, glazier.
" 29. At the burial of Mr Brocas's son.
" 30. At the burial of Capt Norris's daut^r.
Oct. 4. Baptiz^d *Joshua* Thomas.
" 5. At the burial of Mrs Jones.
" 18. Baptiz^d *Susanna* Rand.
    " *Mary* Newman.
" 20. At the burial of Capt Parnell.
" 23. At the burial of Mr Carey.
" 29. Preach'd the Lecture for my brother Sewall, he being sick.
Nov. 5. Publick Thanksgiving.
Thomas's child buried.
" 10. Mr Royall of Dorchester buried.
" 25. Went to Medford to the ordination of Mr Turrell. Mr Colman preach'^d.
" 30. Mrs Star's child buried.
Dec. 6. Baptiz^d *William* Maycock.
Mr Meinzey buried.
" 8. At the funeral of Mr Hall's child.
" 13. Baptiz^d *Sarah* Edwards.
1725.
Jan. 6. Scipio Hirst died—buried 7th. [Negro?]
" 10. Died Mr Walter of Roxbury the younger.
" 15. At the funeral of Mr Knight.
" 18. At the funeral of Mr N. Green, jun^r.
Feb. 6. At the burial of Mr Payne's child.
" 13. Y^r fell a considerable snow this afternoon, and in the night. Capt Lovell sent out wth a party of men to search the woods, came in the night upon ten Indians, kill'd and scalp'd them.
Feb. 14. Baptiz^d *Rooksby* Marshall.
Mar. 2. At the burial of Mr Arnoll.
" 3. Mr Spragues apprentice buried—name Bucknam.
" 9. At the burial of Mr Jarvis Ballard and Joseph Turner.
" 28. Samuel born, a quarter past seven in the evening.
" 29. At the funeral of Mr Wm Webster.
Apr. 1. General Fast.
" 4. Baptiz^d *Samuel* Cooper.
    " *Thomas* Lazenby.
" 11. " *John* Boen. [Bowen?]
" 14. At the funeral of Capt Dekaes.
" 16. At Mr Edmund Quincy's wedding. Mr Colman married him.

Apr. 18. Baptiz^d *James* Oliver.

"   "   *Ebenezer* Blackman.

"   25.   "   *Lydia* Hall.

"   "   *Eliz^a* Allen.

"   "   *Sarah* Millecan.

May 2. At the burial of a young man, Hubbart, at Mr Bulfinch's.

"   7. At the burial of Mr Deming. Ætat. 73.

"   9. At the burial of Mr John Edwards Junr in the evening.

"   13. At the burial of Mr Marshall.

"   24. Deacon Gibson carried me to Medford to see Coll. Aford.

"   27. At the burial of our old and good neighbour, Mrs Pain.

June 11. At the burial of Mr Harris a young man by Mrs Jacob's.

"   17. At the burial of Capt. Perkins.

"   20. Baptiz^d *John* Edwards.

"   27.   "   *Mary* Storer.

July 13. Died ab^t noon my brother Francklyn, æt. 33.

"   15. Mr Francklyn's burial.

Aug. 3. At the funeral of Capt Pollard ætat. 60, and of Mrs Willard,
            wife to Mr Secretary Willard, ætat. 35.

Aug. 5. At the funeral of Mad^m K. Winthrop, ætat. 61.

"   8. Baptiz^d *Sarah* Davis.

"   "   *Eliz^a* Scott.

"   "   *Mehitable* Fullerton.

"   17. A fast at the old chh. on Mr Wadsworth's Remove.

"   18. At the burial of Dr. Davis's child.

"   22. Baptiz^d *Eliz^a* Heath.

        At the burial of Addison's child.

"   24. Mr Oliver's child buried.

"   29. Baptiz^d *Benj^a* Welch.

"   "   *Sarah* Sprague.

Sept. 11. At the funeral of Andrew Tyler's child.

"   22. Began to remove to the house in Sudbury Street, late brother
            Francklyn's. (Lodg'd there 24th.)

Sept. 22. At the burial of Mr Storey.

"   26. Mr Professor Wigglesworth preach'd for me A.M.

"   27. At the burials of Mr Cowell's two children (twins) and of M^{rs}
            Pots's kinswoman.

Sept. 30. At the funeral of Mr. Pitts's daũtr Mary.

Oct. 3. Baptiz^d *Henry* Lowder.

"   "   *Alexander* Star.

"   "   *Lucy* Boilstone.

"   "   *Katherine* Beney.

"   10.   "   *John* Fyfield.

"   "   *Thomas* Fletcher.

"   "   *Thomas* Patten (Scotch).

"   12. At the burial of Mrs Doyle.

"   14. At the burial of Capt Hubbart's child.

"   17. Baptiz'd *Margarett* Sewall.

        Died this evening at Salem, our uncle Sewall, ætat. 69.

"   21. I went to the funeral wth my father and brother Sewall.

"   24. Baptiz'd *Timothy* Fitch.

        Mr Fitch of P—h preach'd for us both parts.

"   28. Publick Thanksgiving.

Nov. 29. Mrs Gibbens buried.

"   30. Mrs Pulsifer's son buried.

Dec. 8. Mrs Anne Pollard buried in the 105th year of her age.

"   21. At the funeral of Mr Eaton.

"   22. At the funeral of Mrs Robie.

"   26. Baptiz'd *William* Archer (adult).

"   *Thomas* Simpson (Scotch).

[To be continued.]

RECORD OF THE BOSTON COMMITTEE OF CORRES-
PONDENCE, INSPECTION AND SAFETY,
MAY TO NOVEMBER, 1776.

Copied by permission of SAMUEL F. McCLEARY, Esq., City Clerk, from the original
record-book in the archives of the City of Boston, Mass.

[Continued from page 389.]

1776.
July 17.

The Sub Committee also Reported the following Recommendation to the Committee for fortifying of Boston Harbour, which
was accepted and is as follows—Viz—

Recom-
mendⁿ to
Comm^{ee}
on Fortifi-
cation.

It is recommended to the Committee for fortifying the Harbour
of Boston, that they give orders to their respective Officers, on the
different Stations in this Harbour that they stop all Vessels and
Boats that may be passing from the Town below the Forts on
Dorchester Point, and Noddles Island; and that no one on any
pretence whatever be permitted to pass the Centinels below those
Posts, from Sun to Sun without their permission, or a special
permission from his Honor General Ward, or in writing from
Nathaniel Barber Esq. who is appointed by this Committee for
that purpose—And it is further recommended to said Committee,
that they give it in order to their said officers, on their respective
Stations in this Harbour to stop all Vessels (except Vessels of
War) and Fishing Boats that may be passing from [Page 16]
this Town, below the said Posts on Dorchester Point and Noddles
Island, between Sunrise and Sunset, and no one be suffered to go
down the Harbour on any pretence whatever without express
permission in writing from—

Recom-
mendⁿ to
Comm^{ee}
for Forti-
fying.

And it is further recommended to said Committee that at the
present and in any future times of peril or danger they at their
discretion stop all Boats & Vessels from which they apprehend
the public Safety to be endangered, any Pass, Permission or
Certificate to the contrary not withstanding.[1]

---

[1] It will be noticed by our readers that commencing with page 12 of the original record-
book (page 387, line 40, of the REGISTER), and ending here, the proceedings of this committee for June 28 and 29 are recorded, though the date of the previous record is July 17
and that of the next is July 18. The marginal dates against these entries are July 17.
Probably the minutes of the proceedings on these two days were accidentally omitted in
their proper place, and the omission being discovered on this day, they were then recorded.
No minute that the record is out of its place is found, however.

There is a typographical error in the date at the heads of the margins on pages 387, 388
and 389 of the REGISTER. The date should be July 17 and not June 17.—ED.

1776.
July 18.

At a Meeting of the Committee of Correspondence, Inspection &c. at the Council chamber July 18th Mr Webb was sent for and examined relative to the behavior of Nathaniel Cary, while the Town was shut up.

Voted that this Meeting be Adjourned to 6 O'Clock then to meet at the Selectmens chamber.

6 O'Clock P.M: met according to Adjournment. Pursuant to a Resolve of the general Court passed the 4 of July Instant, directing this Committee "to file Informations against any Persons suspected of being unfriendly to the Rights & Liberties of America before the major part of the Justices of the Court of Enquiry"— the following Information was given into said Court—Viz^t.—

The Committee of Correspondence Inspection & Safety for the Town of Boston—

Informa-
tion to the
Court of
Enquiry.

Represent to the Justices of the Court of Enquiry that Benjamin Phillips of Boston Wharfinger & Isaac Rand of the same Town Physician, are Persons that have discovered a fixt enmity to the Rights of this Country, and who are justly suspected of the most Criminal disposition to aid [Page 17] and assist the Enemies of the united Colonies of America in their attempt to enslave us, which in the opinion of this Committee renders it incompatible with the public Safety for such Persons to remain in this Town—

The names of a number of Persons, who are Evidences against the forementioned Persons were also given into the Court of Enquiry—

Voted, that this Meeting be Adjourned to tomorrow 6 o'clock—

19.

At a Meeting of the Committee of Correspondence, Inspection & Safety July 19—

Voted, that Coll^o Barber be desired to suspend the delivery of a Pass for Capt McDaniels Vessel.

Motion
as to y^e
Prayers
of the
Church.

A motion made, that a Sub Committee be appointed to wait upon the Ministers of the Church of England and to acquaint them, that this Committee apprehend, that their continuing to pray in public Assembly for the King of Great Britain our Enemie in the forms prescribed in the Book of Common Prayer may be attended with dangerous consequences to the peace of this Town— the Question being accordingly put—Passed in the Negative—

20th.

At a Meeting of the Committee of Correspondence Inspection & Safety July 20—

Court of
Enquiry
Informed
of &c.

The following Representation was made the Court of Enquiry, respecting a number of Persons Addressers to General Gage Viz^t.

To the Honble the Justices of the Court of Enquiry.

The Committee of Correspondence &c. for the Town of Boston in obedience to a late Resolve of the General Court, Represent to said Justices and give them to [Page 18] understand, that John Erving, Stephen Greanleaff, John Timmins, James Perkins, Thomas Amory, Ralph Inman, Richard Green, Daniel Hubbard,

13 Names
returned
to the
Court of
Inquiry.

Nathaniel Cary, John Hunt Tertius, all of Boston Merchants, Joseph Turel Clerk, James Lloyd Physician both of Boston, and Nathaniel Brindley Husbandman late of Frammingham and now residing in Boston aforesaid appear to us, to be enimical to the Rights & Privileges of the *United States of America*, they have aided, assisted abetted & comforted the Enemies of the said states in their attempts to inslave them, and have by a writing under their hand, in the highest terms approved of the conduct of the perfidious General Gage after he had insulted, abused, plundered & murdered many of the good & peacable Inhabitants of this Colony. For these reasons and from their frequent meetings, we apprehend their being suffered to go at large, more especially at this truly important crisis, incompatible with the peace of the Town and the public Safety. We therefore suggest to your Honors consideration the necessity of their being apprehended, disarmed, Committed, Rusticated or laid under other further restrictions as to your Honors may appear fitting and proper.

JOHN BROWN, Chairman.

Act read for draughting every 25 men. The Committee took into consideration the late act of the general assembly for draughting every twenty-fifth man out of the Training Band and Alarm Lists for the Northern or Cannada Department—the Militia of this Town not being settled, and the duty of the Field Officers as pointed out in said act for mustering and draughting the men as aforesaid falling to this Committee It was Voted [Page 19] that the further consideration of this matter be taken up in the afternoon.

Voted, that this Meeting be adjourned to 4 O'Clock in the afternoon.

At a Meeting of the Committee of Correspondence Inspection & Safety at the Council chamber 4 O'Clock P.M.

Mr Brown in the Chair

Votes relative to draughting every 25 men. The consideration of what would be the most suitable method of proceedure in discharging the duty enjoined by the General Court, was again taken up—whereupon

Voted, that twelve Persons be appointed one for each Ward, in order to take Lists of the Several Persons in their respective Wards, capable of bearing Arms—

Twelve Persons were accordingly appointed for the service aforesaid, and the following Order was given to each of those Persons. Viz^t—

Boston, July 20, 1776.

M^r ——

Order to take Lists of men in ye Wards. You are hereby impowered and directed forthwith to return to this Committee the names of every Person in Ward N^o.— who is capable of bearing Arms between Sixteen and Sixty-five years of Age

By Order of the Comm^{ee} of Correspondence &c.

JOHN BROWN, Chairman.

Notification for ye Militia to appear on ye Common. The following notification ordered to be printed and posted up in the most public places in the Town—Viz^t—

The Inhabitants of the Town of Boston both on the Alarm and Train Band Lists are hereby notified and directed, in Obedience to an Order of the great & general Court for that purpose to appear on Boston Common [Page 20] on Monday next the 22^d July Instant at 10 o'clock Beforenoon, if fair Weather, if not the next fair Day. Those who have Arms and Accoutrements are to appear therewith. Hereof they are not to fail, upon the penalty of Ten Pound, to be paid in twenty-four Hours after demand.

1776.
July 20. By Order of the Committee of Correspondence, Inspection &
Safety this 20 of July 1776.   JOHN BROWN, Chairman.

A number of Sergeants and Drummers were engaged to parade
the Town, and read the foregoing Order at the head of the most
public Streets.

The following Gentlemen were appointed to head and direct the
Inhabitants of the several Wards, that are to be mustered the next
Monday—Viz^t—

Persons to head yᵉ several Wards.	Capt Adams	for Ward	No. 1
	Maj^r Grenough	do.	2
	Capt Proctor	do.	3
	Capt Shaw	do.	4
	Mr Stoddard	do.	5
	Capt Barrett	do.	6
	Edward Carns	do.	7
	Capt Marston	do.	8
	Capt Spear	do.	9
	Capt Stimpson	do.	10
	Capt Dyer	do.	11
	Capt May	do.	12

The following Order was also sent to each of the forenamed
gentlemen—Viz^t—

Sir—

The Committee of Correspondence Inspection &c. desire you
will take charge of Company Ward No. — for next Monday, and
take two Persons to your assistance Viz^t, ——— & ———

By Order of the Committee.

JOHN BROWN, Chairman.

[To be continued.]

SAMUEL ALLEN, OF WINDSOR, CT., AND SOME OF HIS DESCENDANTS.

Communicated by WILLARD S. ALLEN, Esq., East Boston, Mass.

SAMUEL[1] ALLEN came from Braintree, Essex County, England. He
was born about the year 1588, in the reign of Queen Elizabeth. He
came to Cambridge, Mass., in 1632; was brother of Col. Matthew Allyn,
of Cambridge, Mass., afterwards of Windsor, Ct., and Dea. Thomas Allyn,
of Middletown, Ct. He removed to Connecticut in 1635, and settled in
Windsor. He was a juryman March 5, 1644, and was by occupation a
farmer. From the Windsor, Ct., land records we have the following:

"January 27, 1640, Samuel Allen hath granted from the Plantation at Windsor,
Ct. 1st. An house lott being six acres, three roods, ten poles, bounded from the
rivulet [Farmington River] to the West, by Rodger Ludlow on the South; by
Thomas Marshall on the North; and run in length to the West into a highway laid
out unto some part of the lot of the said Rodger Ludlow and him the said Samuel
Allen. 2nd. In Plymouth meadow Four acres, bounded by Bray Rossiter on the
North; and a rivulet that runs into the great [Connecticut] River on the South.
3d. Toward Hartford Nineteen acres more or less and runs in length to the Great
River to the West one hundred and thirty and four rods and is bounded by John
Witchfield on the North, and by Thomas Marshfield on the South. 4th. Over the
Great River next to the same fifteen rods in breadth, in the length to the East three
miles; bounded by Joseph Lummus on the South; John Hurd on the North.''

The fourth division was undoubtedly within the present limits of South Windsor. Samuel Allen was a man of public spirit, and was honored by his fellow citizens with positions of trust. He died at Windsor, Ct., and was buried April 28, 1648, aged 60 years, leaving a widow and six children. His widow, Ann Allen, removed to Northampton, Mass., where she m. second, William Hurlbut. Ann (Allen) Hurlbut died Northampton, Mass., Nov. 13, 1687.

Windsor, 8th September, 1648.

An Inventory of the estate of Samuel Allen, late of Windsor, deceased:

	£.	s.	d.
Impr: the housing and home lottes 11£ : It. 4 acres of meadow 7£.	18	00	0
It: 15 acres over the Great River	15	00	0
It: 15 acres of upland	4	10	0
It: In goods one bed with furniture	5	00	0
It: two beds more, &c.	2	14	0
It: One pillow becre, one table cloath & napkins		10	8
It: his wearing aparrell	5	05	0
It: Iron pots 2l. 5s : in brass 1l. 10s ; in pewter 1l.	4	15	0
It: in hogsheads, payles, tubbs and earthenware		19	0
It: 2 spinning wheels		07	0
It: in crooks, Grid iron, fire pan and tongs		13	0
It: his working tooles 2l. 2s.	2	02	0
It: a muskitt and sworde 13s.		13	0
It: a table and forme, and other lumber		10	0
It: in cattle, one cowe, one heifer, one yearling	12	00	0
It: two swynes	4	00	0

£76 18 8

Henry Clark.
David Wilton.

The children of Samuel and Ann Allen were:

i.   Samuel,[2] b. 1634; m. Nov. 29, 1659, Hannah Woodford, dau. of Thomas and Mary (Blott) Woodford. Was a freeman in 1683. He had a grant of land from the Town of Northampton, Mass., Dec. 17, 1657. He d. in Northampton, Mass., Oct. 18, 1718 or 1719. They had, among other children :

Samuel,[3] b. in Northampton, Mass., July 6, 1675 ; m. in 1699, Sarah Rust, dau. of Israel Rust. She was b. May 29, 1675. He d. in Northampton, Mass., March 29, 1739 ; was a Deacon in Rev. Jonathan Edwards's church in Northampton, Mass. They had, among other children :

Joseph,[4] b. in Northampton, Mass., April 5, 1712 ; m. Nov. 22, 1783, Elizabeth Parsons, dau. of Noah and Minwell (Edwards) Parsons. She was b. in Northampton, Mass., March 25, 1716 ; d. in Northampton, Mass., Jan. 9, 1800. He d. in Northampton, Dec. 30, 1779. They had, among other children : ·

Rev. Thomas,[5] b. in Northampton, Mass., Jan. 17, 1743 ; m. Feb. 18, 1768, Elizabeth Lee, dau. of Rev. Jonathan and Elizabeth (Metcalf) Lee. She was b. Sept. 4, 1747 ; d. in Pittsfield, Mass., March 31, 1830. He d. in Pittsfield, Mass., Feb. 10, 1810. First minister of Pittsfield. Ordained April 18, 1764. Harvard, 1762. They had, among other children :

Rev. William,[6] b. in Pittsfield, Mass., Jan. 2, 1784; m. first, Jan. 28, 1813, Maria Mallaville Wheelock, only dau. of John and Maria (Suhn) Wheelock. She was born Feb. 3, 1788 ; d. in Brunswick, Me., June 3, 1828. He m. second, Dec. 2, 1831, Sarah Johnson Breed, dau. of John McLaren and Rebecca (Walker) Breed. She was b. Jan. 11, 1789 ; d. Feb. 25, 1848. He d. in Northampton, Mass., July 16, 1868. Had eight children. He was the author of the American Biographical Dictionary.

    ii. NEHEMIAH,[2] m. Sept. 21, 1664, Sarah Woodford, dau. of Thomas and Mary (Blott) Woodford. She was b. in Hartford, Ct., Sept. 2, 1649; d. in Northampton, Mass., March 31, 1712–13. He d. in Northampton, 1684. [She m. second, in Northampton, Sept. 1, 1687, Richard Burk. She m. third, in Northampton, July 11, 1706, Judah Wright.] He settled in Salisbury, Ct. They had, among other children :

        Samuel,[3] b. in Northampton, Mass., Jan. 3, 1666 ; m. Mercy Wright, dau. of Samuel and Elizabeth (Burt) Wright. She was b. in Northampton, Mass., March 14, 1669 ; d. in Litchfield, Ct., Feb. 5, 1728. They had, among other children :

        Joseph,[4] b. in Deerfield, Mass., Oct. 14, 1708 ; m. in Woodbury, Ct., March 11, 1736–37, Mary Baker, dau. of John Baker. He d. in Cornwall, Ct., April 4, 1755. They had, among other children :

        Gen. *Ethan*,[5] of Revolutionary fame, b. in Litchfield (?), Ct., Jan. 10, 1737 ; m. first, in Woodbury, Ct., by Rev. Daniel Brinsmade, of (Judea Parish) Woodbury, Ct., June 23, 1762, Mary Bronson, dau. of Richard Bronson. She d. in Sunderland, Vt., 1783 ; buried in Arlington, Vt. He m. second, in Westminster, Vt., Feb. 9, 1784, Mrs. Frances Buchanan. She was b. April 4, 1760. He d. in Burlington, Vt., Feb. 12, 1789. He had five children by first wife and two by second. Gen. Allen paid Rev. Mr. Brinsmade four shillings as a marriage fee.

2. iii. JOHN.[2]
    iv. REBECCA.[2]   v. MARY.[2]
    vi. OBADIAH,[2] d. in Middletown, Ct., April 7, 1723 ; m. first, Oct. 23, 1669, Elizabeth Sanford, of Milford, Ct. He m. second, Mary (Savage) Whetmore, widow of John Whetmore and dau. of John Savage. She d. in Middletown, Oct. 20, 1723.

        He was adopted by his uncle, Deacon Thomas Allyn, of Middletown, soon after the decease of his father, where he resided, and after his uncle's death (Oct. 16, 1688) inherited most of his estate. He was admitted to the first Church, Middletown, by certificate from the church in Windsor, Ct., May 2, 1669, but owned the covenant Nov. 9, 1668, and was chosen Deacon May 31, 1704.

2. JOHN[2] (*Samuel*[1]), m. Dec. 8, 1669, Mary Hannum, dau. of William and Honor Hannum. She was b. April 5, 1650. He was killed by the Indians at the battle of Bloody Brook, Deerfield, Mass., Sept. 18, 1675.
    Children :

    3. i.   JOHN, b. Sept. 30, 1670.
    4. ii.   SAMUEL, b. Feb. 5, 1673.
       iii. HANNAH, b. Northampton, Mass., May, 1675 ; bapt. June 20, 1675.

3. JOHN[3] (*John*,[2] *Samuel*[1]), b. Northampton, Mass., Sept. 30, 1670 ; m. first, May 3, 1694, Bridget Booth, dau. of Simeon and Rebecca Booth. She was b. in Enfield, Ct., 1670 ; d. at Enfield, Sept. 5, 1714. He m. second, Elizabeth Gardner, of Gardner's Island. She d. in Enfield, Feb. 27, 1759, and he d. there, Nov. 3, 1739. He removed from Deerfield. Mass., to King Street, Enfield, Ct., to escape the Indians, about 1690, Farmer; lived in Enfield on the old Abiel Pease place.

    Children, all born in Enfield, Ct., by wife Bridget, were :

      i.   MARY, b. Feb. 26, 1696 ; d. in Enfield, Ct., Aug. 16, 1778, unmarried.
      ii. ELIZABETH, b. April 21, 1698 ; m. Nov. 20, 1717, Samuel Ellsworth, of East Windsor, Ct., son of Josiah and Martha (Taylor) Ellsworth, Jr. He b. July 18, 1697. Lived in East Windsor. Had five sons.
    5. iii. AZARIAH, b. May 14, 1701.
      iv. JOHN, b. Sept. 13, 1703 ; drowned in the Connecticut River at Enfield about 1721.
      v.   ISRAEL, b. March 18, 1705 ; d. in Enfield, March 24, 1712.
      vi. PATIENCE, b. May 22, 1709 ; m. first, a Mr. Bement of Suffield ; m. second, a Mr. Pease. She d. in Suffield, Ct.
    6. vii. EBENEZER, b. Feb. 10, 1711–12.

4. SAMUEL³ (*John,² Samuel¹*), b. in Northampton, Mass., Feb. 5, 1673 ;
m. there, 1700, Hannah Burrough. She was b. 1675. He d. Enfield, Ct.,
1735. Removed from Northampton, Mass., to King Street, Enfield, Ct., to
escape from the Indians, about 1700. Farmer; lived in Enfield where
Chauncy Allen now resides.

Children, all born in Enfield, Ct., were :

7. i.   SAMUEL, b. 1702.
8. ii.   JOSEPH, b. July 30, 1704.
   iii. HANNAH, b. Nov. 13, 1706.
9. iv.   JOHN, b. 1712.

5. AZARIAH⁴ (*John,³ John,² Samuel¹*), b. in Enfield, Ct., May 14, 1701 ;
m. in Longmeadow, Mass., Dec. 3, 1727, Martha Burt. She was born in
Longmeadow, 1706; died in Enfield, Oct. 12, 1782. He died in Enfield,
April 3, 1787. Farmer.

Children, all born in Enfield, Ct., were :

i.   MARTHA, b. Dec. 25, 1728; m. first, in Enfield, Aug. 12, 1749, David
      Chapin 2nd of New Hartford, Ct. ; m. second, in New Hartford, about
      1772, Joseph Merrills.
ii.   REBECCA, b. Nov. 13, 1730; m. first, Oct. 17, 1751, Maj. Benjamin
      Parsons, of Somers, Ct. He was b. in Enfield, Jan. 24, 1724 ; d.
      April 8, 1818. She m. second, Thomas Hale, of Enfield. She d.
      June 10, 1793. Had eight children.
iii. MOSES, b. Oct. 12, 1732 ; d. in Enfield, Sept. 30, 1741.
iv.   JEMIMA, b. July 15, 1734 ; d. in Enfield, Sept. 14, 1741.
v.   ABIGAIL, b. April 21, 1736 ; d. in Enfield, Sept. 13, 1738.
vi.   EUNICE, b. March 30, 1738 ; m. in Enfield, April 24, 1755, Nathaniel
      Pease, of Enfield, son of Samuel and Elizabeth (Warner) Pease.
      He was b. in Enfield, Sept. 29, 1728 ; d. Norfolk, Ct., March 28, 1818.
      She d. in Norfolk, March 21, 1807. Resided at Norfolk. They had
      thirteen children.
vii. ABIGAIL, b. July 5, 1740; d. in Enfield, Oct. 15, 1741.
viii. SUBMIT, b. May 14, 1742 ; m. Elisha Brown, of Canton, Ct. He d.
      in Canton, March 27, 1824. She d. in Canton, May 30, 1807. They
      resided at Canton (Collinsville), Ct. Had five children.
ix.   JEMIMA, b. Aug. 21, 1744 ; d. in Enfield, Oct. 14, 1767.
10. x. MOSES, b. May 14, 1746 ; d. in Enfield, Sept. 26, 1826.

6. EBENEZER⁴ (*John,³ John,² Samuel¹*), b. in Enfield, Ct., Feb. 10,
1711–12; m. Feb. 7, 1751, Rebecca Bartlett, of Stafford, Ct., dau. of Samuel and Rebecca (Kibbe) Bartlett. She was b. in Stafford, Nov. 26, 1729 ;
d. in Enfield, Sept. 15, 1817. He d. in Enfield, June 25, 1795. Farmer.

Children, all born in Enfield, Ct., were :

11. i.   EBENEZER, b. Oct. 31, 1751.
12. ii.   ISRAEL, b. Nov. 5, 1753.
13. iii. JONATHAN, b. June 22, 1755.
    iv.   REBECCA, b. March 31, 1757 ; m. in Enfield, Nov. 10, 1774, Eli Parsons,
          son of Lieut. Thomas and Mary (Parsons) Parsons. He was b. in
          Enfield, Jan. 23, 1756 ; d. in Enfield, Nov. 20, 1785. She d. in
          Enfield, May 12, 1785. Had eight children.
    v.   ABIGAIL, b. Dec. 17, 1758 ; m. Ezra Osborn, of East Windsor, son of
          Zebedee and Abigail (Osborn) Osborn. Had eight children.
    vi.   EUNICE, b. Feb. 21, 1761 ; m. Daniel Austin, Jr. of Longmeadow, Mass.,
          son of Daniel Austin. Had four children.
    vii. DORCAS, b. Dec. 17, 1762 ; m. Justus Munn, of Saybrook, Ct. Resided
          in East Windsor. He was a Revolutionary pensioner. Had one child.
14. viii. ELIJAH, b. April 21, 1765.
15. ix.   SOLOMON, b. Sept. 16, 1767.

    x. SARAH, b. May 8, 1770; m. Trustrum Fenton, of Willington, Ct. He d. in East Windsor, Jan. 15, 1846. She d. in Coventry, Ct., Jan. 15, 1846. Resided in East Windsor. Had six children.

    xi. RUTH, b. May 1, 1772; m. Jesse Eaton, of Tolland. She d. in Tolland, Ct., March 10, 1852. Had one child. Resided in Tolland.

  7. SAMUEL[4] (*Samuel,[3] John,[2] Samuel[1]*), b. in Enfield, Ct., 1702; m. Jan. 27, 1728, Elizabeth Booth, dau. of Zachariah and Mary (Harmon) Booth. She was b. in Enfield, Aug. 19, 1705; d. East Windsor, Ct., Sept. 10, 1751. He d. at the same place, Dec. 20, 1771. He lived in East Windsor, on the old Landlord Allen place.

Children, all born in East Windsor, Ct., were:

    i. SAMUEL, b. June 13, 1729; d. Jan. 20, 1759.
    ii. ELIZABETH, b. March 28, 1731.
16. iii. ABEL, b. Aug. 14, 1733.
    iv. TABITHY, b. April 13, 1736; m. Feb. or March, 1781, Abner Chapin, of Somers, Ct. She d. April 29, 1790. One child.
    v. LOVE, b. July 13, 1738.
    vi. PELETIAH.
17. vii. ZACHARIAH, b. Oct. 31, 1742.
    viii. SARAH, m. Jonah Pasco.
    ix. AMZI.

  8. JOSEPH[4] (*Samuel,[3] John,[2] Samuel[1]*), b. in Enfield, Ct., July 30, 1704; m. 1723, Mary Hewlet. She d. East Windsor, Ct., June 28, 1782, aged 78 years. He d. at the same place, June 11, 1777. He was a farmer, and in connection with his brother Samuel, manufactured tar and pitch. He settled in East Windsor, near the Enfield line, where Jabez S. Allen now resides. The old house in which he lived must have been erected about the year 1732–33, as the original deed to him is dated March 5, 1732–33. It stood about 30 or 40 feet west of the present house.

Children:

    i. HANNAH, b. in Enfield, Ct., 1724; m. Jan. 30, 1746, Caleb Booth, Jr., son of Caleb and Mary (Gleason) Booth. He was b. in East Windsor, Ct., June 14, 1723; d. there Sept. 29, 1772. She d. in East Windsor, Nov. 22, 1779. Had eight children.
18. ii. JOSEPH, b. Sept. 4, 1727.
19. iii. NOAH, b. May 15, 1730.
20. iv. DAVID, b. Nov. 22, 1734.
21. v. SAMUEL, b. June 8, 1736.
22. vi. HEZEKIAH, b. Oct. 8, 1739.
    vii. MARY, b. in East Windsor; m. Matthew Thompson. She d. in Enfield, Ct. He died in same place, Sept. 30, 1787, in the 68th year of his age. Two children, Mary and Matthew.
    viii. DORCAS, b. in East Windsor, Ct., June 10, 1742; m. in East Windsor, Henry Wolcott, son of Simon Wolcott. He was b. in East Windsor; d. in East Windsor, Oct. 24, 1813, aged 84. She d. in East Windsor, May 9, 1822. Had five children. Lived in East Windsor, where Mr. Filley now resides.

  9. JOHN[4] (*Samuel,[3] John,[2] Samuel[1]*), b. in Enfield, Ct., 1712; m. in Enfield, April 3, 1737, Elizabeth Pease, dau. of Samuel and Elizabeth (Warner) Pease. She was b. in Enfield, 1716. He d. in Enfield, 1791. Farmer. He lived in King Street, Enfield. He bought of Hannah Allen (relict of Samuel[3] Allen), Samuel Allen and Joseph Allen, house and home lot with 45 acres; also 20 acres in the south field, so called, all in Enfield, by deed dated April 2, 1735, for £600, and recorded with Hampden Deeds, Springfield, Mass., Book H, p. 327.

Children :

23. i. John, b. in Enfield, Feb. 17, 1739-40.
　　ii. Hannah, b. in Enfield, April 6, 1744 ; m. Elijah Hawkins.

10. Moses⁵ (*Azariah,⁴ John,³ John,² Samuel¹*), b. in Enfield, Ct., May 14, 1746 ; m. in Warehouse Point, Ct., May 1, 1766, Mary Adams, dau. of Thomas and Mary (Hammond) [Vallet] Adams. She was b. in East Windsor, Ct., Sept. 21, 1745 ; d. in Enfield, Oct. 9, 1805. He m. second, in Enfield, Feb. 16, 1807, Mrs. Mary Pease, widow of James Pease, of Enfield, and dau. of Thomas and Mercy (Hall) Pease. She was b. in Enfield, and died there, Feb. 6, 1814. He died in Enfield, Sept. 26, 1826. Farmer. Lived in Enfield.

Children, all born in Enfield, Ct., by wife Mary Adams, were :

i. Mary, b. Feb. 3, 1767 ; m. in Enfield, June 15, 1786, Samuel Allen, Jr. (see 21, ii.), of East Windsor, son of Samuel and Elizabeth (Wells) Allen. He was born in East Windsor, June 16, 1764 ; d. in East Windsor, Oct. 11, 1841. She d. in East Windsor, May 21, 1823. Resided in East Windsor.
ii. Moses, b. Feb. 10, 1769.
iii. George, b. Oct. 24, 1770.
iv. Anson, b. July 20, 1772.
v. Isaiah, b. July 8, 1774.
vi. Jemima, b. Aug. 16, 1776 ; d. in Enfield, July 22, 1820 ; unm.
vii. Rubie, b. May 14, 1778 ; m. in Enfield, Nov. 10, 1795, Erastus Eldridge, of Ellington, Ct. He was b. in Willington, Ct., April 3, 1775 ; d. in Springfield, Mass., May 6, 1820. She d. in Enfield, Ct., Sept. 15, 1844. He worked in the U. S. Armory, Springfield, Mass. Had ten children.
viii. Luther, b. June 11, 1780.
ix. Son nameless, b. Oct. 27, 1782 ; d. in Enfield, Oct. 31, 1782.
x. Esther, b. Aug. 26, 1783 ; d. in Enfield, Nov. 15, 1783.
xi. Esther, b. Sept. 24, 1785 ; m. in Enfield, March 7, 1806, Oren Cleveland, of East Windsor, son of Rufus and Mary (Chamberlin) Cleveland. He was b. in East Windsor, May 3, 1785. She d. in Huntsburg, Ohio, May 31, 1869. He living in Cleveland, Ohio. Had eleven children.
xii. Sabra, b. Jan. 18, 1788 ; m. in Enfield, Dec. 17, 1805, Sylvanus Olmstead, of Enfield, son of Simeon and Roxalana (Abbe) Olmstead. He was b. in Enfield, July 16, 1783 ; d. in Enfield, Feb. 6, 1826. She d. in Enfield, June 1, 1865. Had five children.

11. Ebenezer⁵ (*Ebenezer,⁴ John,³ John,² Samuel¹*), b. in Enfield, Ct., Oct. 31, 1751 ; m. first, in East Windsor, Ct., April 9, 1773, Chloe Osborn, dau. of Zebedee Osborn. She was b. in East Windsor, April 22, 1755 ; d. at East Windsor, June 17, 1788. He m. second, April 2, 1789, Elizabeth Pease, of Enfield, dau. of Hezekiah Pease. She was b. in Enfield, Sept. 10, 1759 ; d. East Windsor. He d. East Windsor, Feb. 15, 1725. Farmer. Lived in East Windsor.

Children, all born in East Windsor, Ct., by his wife Chloe, were :

i. Chloe, b. Nov. 19, 1773 ; m. in East Windsor, Nov. 17, 1798, Ammi Ellsworth, son of Job and Mary (Trumbull) Ellsworth. He was b. in East Windsor, Oct. 24, 1767 ; d. in Sodus, Wayne co., N. Y. She d. in Sodus. Had seven children.
ii. Ebenezer, b. July 31, 1775.
iii. Huldah, b. Feb. 16, 1778 ; m. in East Windsor, Feb. 20, 1826, Capt. Job Ellsworth, son of Job and Mary (Trumbull) Ellsworth. He was b. in East-Windsor, Aug. 26, 1765 ; d. in East Windsor, March 21, 1849. She d. there, March 12, 1858. No children.

iv.   LEVI, b. March 4, 1780.
v.   JOHN, b. Feb. 20, 1782.
vi.   JAMES OSBORN, b. July 14, 1785.
vii. CHESTER, b. Oct. 28, 1787.

Children by wife ELIZABETH, were:

viii. BETSEY, b. Nov. 8, 1789; m. in East Windsor, Nov. 25, 1813, Lemuel
      Charter, of Ellington, Ct. He died in Wilmington, Will co., Ill.
      She also d. in Wilmington. Had nine children.
ix.   REBECCA BARTLETT, b. June 10, 1792; m. in East Windsor, Feb. 17,
      1817, Eleazer Blood, of Weston, Mass. She d. in Suffield, Ct. Had
      no children.
x.   SABRA, b. July 27, 1796; m. in East Windsor, Oct. 2, 1817, Levi
      Webster, of Stafford, Ct., son of Daniel and Mehitable (Simonds)
      Webster. He was b. in Stafford, Ct., Aug. 17, 1799; d. in East
      Windsor, Jan. 4, 1844. She d. in East Windsor, Feb. 20, 1865.
      Had ten children.

12.   ISRAEL[5] (*Ebenezer,[4] John,[3] John,[2] Samuel[1]*), b. in Enfield, Ct., Nov.
5, 1753; m. 1778, Martha French, of East Windsor, Ct., dau. of John and
Lydia (Phelps) French. She was b. in East Windsor, and d. there Sept.
20, 1826. He d. in East Windsor, Sept. 26, 1828. Farmer. Lived in
East Windsor.

Children, all born in East Windsor, Ct., were:

i.   ISRAEL, b. July 6, 1779.
ii.   MARTHA, b. Nov. 18, 1780; m. in East Windsor, July 30, 1799, Elam
      Allen (see 21, v.), son of Samuel and Elizabeth (Wells) Allen.
      He was born in East Windsor, July 29, 1774; d. in East Windsor,
      Jan. 3, 1853. She d. in East Windsor, Oct. 25, 1852.
iii. LYDIA, b. Dec. 1, 1782; d. in East Windsor, in 4th year.
iv.   GAIUS, b. Jan. 16, 1784; d. in East Windsor, Dec. 23, 1787.
v.   LYDIA PHELPS, b. Oct. 12, 1787; m. in East Windsor, April 18, 1815,
      Matthew Read, son of Matthew and Dorothy (Bardin) Read. He d.
      in Albany, N. Y. She d. in East Windsor, Jan. 10, 1870. Had four
      children.
vi.   GAIUS, b. June 29, 1790.
vii. JOSIAH, b. Aug. 13, 1792: d. in East Windsor, Aug. 2, 1828; unm.
viii. MARY, b. Jan. 10, 1795; d. in Alton, Ill., Aug. 3, 1833; unm.
ix.   MICHAEL, b. May 18, 1797; drowned in East Windsor, July 4, 1813.
x.   CLARISSA, b. March 19, 1800; m. in East Windsor, Nov. 16, 1819,
      Whitting Cooley, of Longmeadow, Mass., son of Whitting Cooley.
      He d. in Longmeadow. She d. in Shipton, province of Ontario,
      May 10, 1854. No children.

13.   JONATHAN[5] (*Ebenezer,[4] John,[3] John,[2] Samuel[1]*), b. in Enfield, Ct.,
June 22, 1755; m. Sarah Adams, dau. of Thomas and Mary (Hammond)
[Vallet] Adams of (Warehouse Point) East Windsor, Ct. She was b. in
East Windsor, April 16, 1753; d. in Springfield, Mass., Jan. 2, 1844. He
d. in Enfield, Aug. 22, 1803. Farmer. Resided in Enfield.

Children, all born in Enfield, Ct., were:

i.   JONATHAN, b. Oct. 27, 1776.
ii.   [OBA] DIAH, b. Aug. 6, 1783.
iii. SALLY, b. Jan. 9, 1786; m. in Enfield, March 1, 1801, Rufus Bush, Jr.,
      son of Rufus and Huldah (Alden) Bush. Had three children.
iv.   DAVID, b. Sept. 18, 1793; d. in Enfield, Feb. 13, 1834. His wife d. in
      Enfield, Dec. 16, 1834. Children: George, Selden and Gates.

14.   ELIJAH[5] (*Ebenezer,[4] John,[3] John,[2] Samuel[1]*), b. in Enfield, Ct., April
21, 1765; m. Jemima Pease, dau. of Moses and Jemima (Booth) Pease,
of Enfield. She was b. in Enfield, April 8, 1762; d. in Chardon, Geauga
Co., Ohio, June 28, 1853. He d. there, May 1, 1853. Farmer. Moved
to New Connecticut, Ohio, in 1818.

Children :
i.   ALVIN, b. in Enfield, Ct., Feb. 26, 1789 ; m. Nov. 2, 1817, Eliza Buck. She d. May 2, 1874. Farmer. Had ten children, two daughters living.
ii. ORRIN, b. in Enfield, Feb. 2, 1791 ; m. Betsey Summers. She died in Chardon, Ohio, Oct. 1855. He left home, April 1, 1834. Shoemaker. Two sons living, one married.
iii. JEMIMA, b. in Enfield, May 4, 1794 ; m. Timothy Tainter. Farmer. Had three children.
iv. ELIJAH PEASE, b. in Sandisfield, Mass., Oct. 12, 1796.
v.   ELECTRA, b. in Enfield, Feb. 7, 1800 ; m. Henry Campbell. He d. in Kirtland, Ohio, April 4, 1856. Farmer. Had eight children.
vi. HULDAH, b. in Enfield, Oct. 5, 1803 ; m. June 12, 1830, Ralza Spencer. He was b. July 8, 1798. Had five children.
vii. ORPHA, b. in Enfield, May, 1807. Unmarried. Living in Chardon, O.

15. Capt. SOLOMON[5] (*Ebenezer,*[4] *John,*[3] *John,*[2] *Samuel*[1]), b. in Enfield, Sept. 16, 1767 ; m. first, in East Windsor, Ct., Jan. 30, 1794, Miriam Allen, dau. of David and Miriam (Parsons) Allen (see No. 20, v.). She was b. in Enfield, June 10, 1768, and d. there Dec. 8, 1794. He m. second, Jan. 26, 1797, Lucy Terry, dau. of Joseph and Lucy (Terry) Terry. She was b. in Enfield, Oct. 24, 1769, and d. there Dec. 9, 1849. He d. in Enfield, May 27, 1813. Farmer. Lived in Enfield.

Children, all born in Enfield, Ct., by wife Miriam, were :
i.   Daughter, b. Nov. 20, 1794 ; d. in Enfield, Nov. 20, 1794.
Children by wife LUCY, were :
ii. MARIAM, b. Nov. 30, 1797. Unmarried.
iii. LUCY, b. Sept. 3, 1799 ; m. in Enfield, Jan. 31, 1823, Lyman Terry, son of Peter and Terza (Colley) Terry.
iv. SOLOMON, b. Aug. 19, 1801.
v.   MARIA THERESA, b. Nov. 22, 1803 ; m. Charles McClallan, son of William and Lucretia (Phelps) McClallan. He was b. in Lancaster, Mass., Aug. 11, 1803. Resides in Chicopee, Mass.
vi. SALANEA, b. Feb. 13, 1806 ; d. in Enfield, March 4, 1809.

16. ABEL[5] (*Samuel,*[4] *Samuel,*[3] *John,*[2] *Samuel*[1]), b. in East Windsor, Ct., Aug. 14, 1733 ; m. Jan. 1, 1756, Elizabeth Chapin, of Enfield, Ct.
Children :
i.   ABEL, b. Nov. 15, 1756.
ii. PHINEAS, b. Oct. 31, 1758.

17. ZACHARIAH[5] (*Samuel,*[4] *Samuel,*[3] *John,*[2] *Samuel*[1]), b. in East Windsor, Oct. 31, 1742 ; m. first, in Windsor, Ct., Oct. 31, 1765, Huldah Parsons, dau. of Lieut. Thomas and Mary (Parsons) Parsons. She was b. in Enfield, Ct., Nov. 30, 1742; d. in East Windsor, April 2, 1784. He m. second, Hannah Baker, of Hadley, Mass. She d. in East Windsor, Dec. 28, 1841, aged 91. He d. in East Windsor, Nov. 17, 1831. Tanner and currier by trade ; served his apprenticeship with his father-in-law. Kept a public house for more than 40 years. He was called "Landlord Allen." Resided in East Windsor, on the old stage road from Springfield, Mass., to Hartford, Ct.
Children :
i.   HULDAH, b. in East Windsor, Ct., ; m. in Enfield, Ct., July 20, 1788, Joel Holkins, Jr., son of Joel Holkins, of Enfield. He was b. in Enfield and d. in East Windsor. She d. in East Windsor, April, 1835. Resided in East Windsor. Manufacturer of gin. Had eleven children.
ii. ZACHARIAH, b. Feb. 23, 1770.
iii. SARAH, m. Ezekiel Osborn. Had five children.

18. JOSEPH[5] (*Joseph,[4] Samuel,[3] John,[2] Samuel[1]*), b. in Enfield, Ct., Sept. 4, 1727; m. Jan. 17, 1750, Lois Burnham, dau. of Capt. Michael and Lois (Wise) Burnham. She was bapt. in East Hartford, Ct., Feb. 23, 1728; d. in East Windsor, Ct., Dec. 6, 1805. He d. in East Windsor, Oct. 8, 1808. Resided in East Windsor. Farmer. Held office under King Geo. III. He was drafted during the revolutionary war, but sent his son Joseph as a substitute. He was sometimes called Sergeant Joseph.

Children, all born in East Windsor, Ct., were:

i. LOIS, b. Sept. 13, 1751; m. in East Windsor, Sept. 26, 1771, Simeon Barber, son of Jonathan and Rachel (Gaylord) Barber. He was b. in East Windsor, May 12, 1741; d. in East Windsor, Oct. 7, 1808. She d. there, July 29, 1814. Had five children.

ii. JOSEPH, b. Aug. 21, 1753; d. in East Windsor, Oct. 12, 1757.

iii. AZENETH, b. Feb. 17, 1756; m. first, Edward Chapin, son of Dea. Edward and Eunice (Colton) Chapin. He was b. in Chicopee, Mass., Sept. 3, 1755, and d. there, June 22, 1795. She m. second, in Chicopee, Jan. 20, 1801, Eldad Parsons, Esq., son of Nathan and Amy (Gould) Parsons, of Belchertown, Mass. He was b. in Belchertown, Aug. 29, 1755, and died there July 10, 1823. She died at Belchertown, June 11, 1821. Had four children.

iv. EUNICE, b. March 18, 1758; m. James Burnham, son of Ezra Burnham, of East Hartford, Ct. He was b. in East Hartford, and d. in Granby, Mass., July 15, 1835, aged 74. She d. in Granby, Jan. 9, 1839. Resided in Granby. Had six children.

v. HANNAH, b. March 2, 1760; m. Roswell Prior, of East Windsor. He was b. in East Windsor, May 30, 1758; d. in Coventry, Ct. She d. in East Windsor in 1791 or 1792. Had three children.

vi. JOSEPH, b. March 23, 1762.

vii. BENJAMIN, b. June 19, 1764.

viii. ASHER, b. Sept. 22, 1766; m. in East Windsor, June 25, 1805, Chloe Moody, of South Hadley, Mass., dau. of Noah Moody. She was b. in South Hadley; d. in East Windsor, Feb. 14, 1850, æt. 84. He d. in East Windsor, Nov. 1, 1825. Resided in East Windsor. No children.

ix. ANNA, b. March 9, 1769; m. in East Windsor, Feb. 25, 1789, James Thompson, son of John Thompson. He was b. in East Windsor, Sept. 10, 1763; d. in Coventry, Ct., June 5, 1842. She d. in Rockville, Ct., Nov. 23, 1852. Had nine children.

x. HENRY, b. March 18, 1771.

19. Capt. NOAH[5] (*Joseph,[4] Samuel,[3] John,[2] Samuel[1]*), b. in East Windsor, Ct., May 15, 1730; m. in Somers, Ct., March 20, 1756, Anna Root. She was b. in Somers, and d. in East Windsor, Ct., Oct. 10, 1806, aged 78. He d. in East Windsor, Oct. 27, 1776. Farmer. Resided in East Windsor. He was in the revolutionary war.

Children, all born in East Windsor, Ct., were:

i. NOAH, b. Feb. 14, 1757.

ii. TIMOTHY, b. Nov. 25, 1759.

iii. ELIHU, b. Sept. 18, 1761. Lived in Sodus, Wayne Co., N. Y.

iv. JONATHAN, b. May 16, 1763; 4 children. Lived in Vermont.

v. ANNA, b. June 18, 1765; m. in East Windsor, Gideon Drake. Both d. in Westfield, Mass. Had twelve children.

vi. PETER, b. March 18, 1767; d. in East Windsor, Sept. 22, 1793; unm.

vii. DANIEL, b. Jan. 31, 1770.

20. DAVID[5] (*Joseph,[4] Samuel,[3] John,[2] Samuel[1]*), b. in East Windsor, Ct., Nov. 22, 1734; m. first, in East Windsor, Feb. 27, 1753, Mary Bancroft, dau. of Nathaniel and Ann (Wolcott) Bancroft. She was b. in East Windsor, 1731, and d. there Jan. 14, 1754. He m. second, in Somers, Ct., Nov. 11,

1754, Miriam Parsons, dau. of Luke and Sarah (Osborn) Parsons. She was b. in Somers, Ct., March 6, 1729–30; d. in East Windsor, July 2, 1805. He d. in East Windsor, April 9, 1789. Farmer. Lived in East Windsor.

Children, all born in East Windsor, Ct., by wife Mary, were:

  i.   NATHANIEL, b. Jan. 2, 1754.

Children by wife MIRIAM, were:

  ii. Dr. DAVID, b. Aug. 13, 1755.
  iii. LUKE, b. July 9, 1757.
  iv. MOSES, b. July 9, 1757; d. in East Windsor.
  v. SOLOMON, b. March 10, 1766.
  vi. MIRIAM, b. June 10, 1768; m. in East Windsor, Jan. 30, 1794, Solomon Allen (see No. 15), son of Ebenezer and Rebecca (Bartlett) Allen. He was b. in Enfield, Ct., Sept. 16, 1767, and d. there May 27, 1813. She d. in Enfield, Dec. 8, 1794. Had five children.

  21. SAMUEL[5] (*Joseph,[4] Samuel,[3] John,[2] Samuel[1]*), b. East Windsor, Ct., June 8, 1736; m. first, Elizabeth Wells, dau. of Capt. Hezekiah and Sarah (Trumbull) Wells. She was b. in East Windsor, June 5, 1740, and died there, May 11, 1778. He m. second, Sarah Booth, dau. of Joseph and Sarah (Chandler) Booth. She was b. in Enfield, Dec. 1, 1743; died in East Windsor, July 27, 1800. He m. third, Lucy (Alden) Markham, widow of Darius Markham, and dau. of Rev. Noah and Mary (Vaughan) Alden. She was b. in Longmeadow, Mass., July 2, 1749; d. in East Windsor, Feb. 3, 1837. He d. in East Windsor, Oct. 10, 1816. Farmer. Lived in East Windsor, near the Enfield line, where his grandson Jabez Samuel Allen now resides.

Children, all born in East Windsor, Ct., by wife Elizabeth, were:

  i.   ELIZABETH, b. April 8, 1763; m. in East Windsor, April 29, 1784, Jonathan Pasco, Esq., son of James and Abigail (Booth) Pasco. He was b. in East Windsor, Sept. 29, 1760, and d. there, Aug. 4, 1844. She d. East Windsor, Oct. 2, 1838. Had eleven children.
  ii. SAMUEL, b. June 16, 1764; m. first, Mary Allen (10, i.); m. second, Mrs. Azubah Moody.
  iii. MABEL, b. March 30, 1768; m. May 21, 1786, Simeon Pease, son of Israel and Ann (Bartlett) Pease. He was b. in Enfield, Ct., Feb. 7, 1758, and d. there 1847. Had twelve children.
  iv. JOSHUA, b. May 18, 1771; m. Abigail Bartlett.
  v. ELAM, b. July 29, 1774; m. Martha Allen.
  vi. SABRA, b. July 29, 1774; m. in East Windsor, Jan. 23, 1794, John McKnight Thompson, son of James and Elizabeth (McKnight) Thompson. He was b. in East Windsor, Jan. 8, 1768, and d. there, Feb. 22, 1841. She d. at East Windsor, Mar. 28, 1858. Had ten children.

Children by wife SARAH, were:

24. vii. CHESTER, b. June 13, 1780.
  viii. JABEZ, b. Jan. 22, 1783; d. in East Windsor, March 9, 1783.
  ix. JABEZ, b. Jan. 25, 1786; m. Lucy Markham.
  x. SARAH, b. Aug. 1, 1789; m. in East Windsor, Feb. 6, 1811, Roswell Phelps, son of David and Ann (Pease) Phelps. He was b. in Enfield, Ct., May 9, 1788, and d. in Wilbraham, Mass., Aug. 25, 1870. She d. in Wilbraham, Oct. 4, 1851. Had four children.

  22. HEZEKIAH[5] (*Joseph,[4] Samuel,[3] John,[2] Samuel[1]*), b. Oct. 8, 1739; m. Dec. 13, 1768, Abigail Bartlett, dau. of Samuel and Rebecca (Kibbie) Bartlett, of Stafford, Ct. She was b. in Stafford, and died in East Windsor, Jan. 25, 1825, aged 84. He d. in East Windsor, June 14, 1807. Farmer. Lived in East Windsor.

Children, all born in East Windsor, Ct., were :

i.   ABIGAIL, b. Oct. 28, 1769 ; m. Elam Pease, son of Joel and Lois (Warner) Pease. He was b. in East Windsor, Aug. 13, 1776 ; d. at
     Farmington,.Ill., July, 1842. She d. at East Windsor, Feb. 4, 1851.
     Shoemaker. Had three children.
ii. MARY, b. Sept. 18, 1773 ; m. Dec. 15, 1796, Grove Barber, son of Oliver and Ann (Root) Barber. He was b. in East Windsor, July 19,
     1769. She d. in East Windsor, July 18, 1859. Had one child.
iii. HEZEKIAH, b. Sept. 7, 1777.
iv. JOEL, b. June 28, 1781.
v.   EUNICE, b. Dec. 9, 1783 ; m. Luther Billings, son of Samuel Billings.
     She d. at Hyde Park, Vt., Aug. 1858. Lived in Somers, Ct.

23. JOHN[5] (*John,[4] Samuel,[3] John,[2] Samuel[1]*), b. Feb. 17, 1739–40 ; m.
Mehitable Rumerrill, dau. of John and Abigail (Chandler) Rumerrill. · She
was b. in Enfield, Ct., April 6, 1739. She m. second, Joel Hawkins. Farmer. Lived in Enfield.

Children, all born in Enfield, Ct., were:

i.   JOHN, b. Jan. 24, 1762. Killed at Horse Neck, at the age of 16.
ii. MEHITABLE, b. May 10, 1763 ; m. in Enfield, Ct., Feb. 26, 1788,
     Nathaniel Collins.
iii. PETER, b. March 10, 1764.
iv. ISAAC, b. March 27, 1768.
v.   HANNAH, b. Feb. 2, 1770 ; m. Joel Webster.

24. CHESTER[6] (*Samuel,[5] Joseph,[4] Samuel,[3] John,[2] Samuel[1]*), b. June 13,
1780 ; m. in East Windsor, Ct., May 8, 1804, Margaret Shaw, dau. of
David and Mary (Terry) Shaw. She was b. in East Windsor, Oct. 10,
1780, and d. there, May 10, 1843. He d. in East Windsor, March 11, 1849.
Farmer. He lived on London Street, Enfield, Ct., until April, 1816, when
he removed to East Windsor.

Children :

i.   ORLANDO, b. in Enfield, Feb. 13, 1805 ; m. Elmina Slate.
ii.   MARY TERRY, b. in Enfield, Feb. 4, 1809, and d. there April 23, 1810.
25. iii. RALPH WILLARD, b. in Enfield, Feb. 16, 1812.
iv.   MARY TERRY, b. in Enfield, March 31, 1814 ; m. James Leander
         Shepard.
v.   JOSEPH, b. in East Windsor, July 3, 1818 ; m. Martha Ann Barton.
vi.   WILLIAM, b. in East Windsor, June 22, 1821 ; m. Adeline Cordelia
         Meacham.

25. Rev. RALPH WILLARD[7] (*Chester,[6] Samuel,[5] Joseph,[4] Samuel,[3] John,[2]
Samuel[1]*), b. Feb. 16, 1812 ; m. in Hingham, Mass., Aug. 10, 1835, Mary
Jones Tower, dau. of Moses and Mary (Binney) Tower. She was b. in
Hingham, Feb. 24, 1810. Methodist clergyman. Resides in Malden,
Mass.

Children :

i.   MARY JANE, b. in Southbridge, Mass., Sept. 16, 1836 ; m. Rev. Pliny
         Steele Boyd, Congregational clergyman, settled at Amesbury, Mass.
ii.   SARAH BINNEY, b. in Manchester, Ct., Jan. 4, 1838 ; d. there, Oct. 4,
         1838.
iii.   SARAH BINNEY, b. in Manchester, Ct., March 26, 1839 ; m. Heinrich
         Christian Beck.
26. iv. WILLARD SPENCER, b. in Eastford,.Ct., May 12, 1841.
v.   ANNA SOPHIA, b. in New-London, Ct., Nov. 3, 1842 ; d. in New-London,
         Oct. 3, 1843.
vi.   THOMAS JONES, b. in Norwich, Ct., Jan. 10, 1846. Resides in Malden,
         Mass.

vii. ELLA ANNA, b. in Providence, R. I., Sept. 5, 1847 ; m. Rev. Elisha
Benjamin Andrews, Baptist clergyman ; president Denison University, Granville, Ohio.
viii. CHARLES FABYAN, b. in Providence, R. I., Dec. 1, 1848. Resides in
Malden, Mass.

26. WILLARD SPENCER[8] (*Ralph Willard,*[7] *Chester,*[6] *Samuel,*[5] *Joseph,*[4]
Samuel,[3] *John,*[2] *Samuel*[1]), b. May 12, 1841 ; m. in Lynn, Mass., April 6
1870, Adaline Augusta Newhall, dau. of George and Elizabeth (Harrington) Newhall. She was b. in Lynn, Aug. 15, 1838. Clerk of the " Municipal Court of the East Boston District " of the city of Boston.

Children :
i. MARY ELIZABETH, b. in Boston, Mass., June 1, 1871 ; d. in Boston,
Oct. 27, 1871.
ii. MARY ADDIE, b. in Boston, Aug. 24, 1872.
iii. CHESTER WILLARD, b. in Boston, May 26, 1875.

The compiler desires to obtain further authentic information preliminary to a
more extended genealogy. He wishes to obtain particulars of the female as well as
male lines. Corrections of errors will be thankfully received.

BAPTISMS IN DOVER, N. H., 1717—1766.

COPY OF THE REV. JONATHAN CUSHING'S RECORD OF BAPTISMS IN DOVER, N. H.,
NOW A PART OF THE RECORDS OF THE " FIRST CHURCH."

Communicated by JOHN R. HAM, M.D., of Dover.

[Continued from vol. xxix. page 270.]*

1742.
Jan.   24. Zechariah Bunker & Deborah his Wife. Sarah Drew. Margery Tibbetts.
"   30. Elizabeth, Frances, Solomon, Ralph, Lois & Joseph, the
child[n] of Ralph Hall—in his own house.
"   31. Jonathan Young & Abigail his Wife, & their Child[n], viz. Isaac,
James, Abigail, Mary, Elizabeth & Mercy, all adults excepting Mercy. Joshua Perkins, Sobriety Young, Mary
Brock, William Ham & Venus—Col. Gerrish's negro.
Feb.   4. Shadrach, son of Shadrach Hodgdon.
"   14. Ichabod Tibbetts, Jerusha Hill & Lydia Twombly.
"   28. Daniel Jacobs & Wife Mary, & their Child[n] Dan[l] & Abi-
gail. Mary Evans & Chil[n] Benj[a], Joseph & Stephen
(Evans) & Elizabeth (Mooney). John Mills & John
Twombly.
March 7. Jane Layn & her Child[n] Samuel, Styles, Edmund, & John
Hussey Layn.

* The following entries were omitted or misprinted in the REGISTER for July, 1875 :
1725. Aug. 22. William Foss.
1729. Sept. 12. Hannah Cushing, in private, born 11th inst., died 12th.
       Oct. 26. Abigail, Dr. of John Carter.
1731. June 27. Ann, Dr. of John Bickford, baptized by Mr. Cushing, at Rochester.
1733. Dec. 16. Mary, wife of Wm. Twombly.
1734. Oct. 13. Esther, Dr. of Thomas Horn.
1736. Jan. 30. For *Israel*, read *Isaac*.
1741. May 31. For *Mary*, read *Mercy*.

March 8. Nathaniel Garland, on a sick bed, & Nath¹, his son.
" 9. Dodavah Ham, on a sick bed.
" 14. Eph^m Tibbetts & Child^n Ephraim, Judith, Adults, and Samuel
James Thomson. Mary Tuttle. Ann, D^r of John Wingate.
" 31. Eliz^a Hall. Mehetabel Daniel, Wife of Joseph Daniel, Junr.
& their Child^n Sam¹, Joseph, Pelatiah, Abigail & Obadiah.
Anna, D^r of Wm Demerritt. John, son of Thomas Rines.
April 4. Henry Bickford & Eliz^a his Wife. Jeremiah Tibbetts, William
Hayes, Sarah Pinkham, Dorothy Tibbetts, & Margery D^r of
John Gerrish.
" 11. Samuel Starbird & Rebecca his Wife. Hannah Hayes, &
her Dr Patience. Mercy Watson, & David Polley—
Mr Hanson's servant.
" 18. Israel Hodgdon, Wm Twombly & his Daugh^r Eleanor. Eliz^a
Pinkham, Mercy Evans, Mary Wife of John Horn, Junr
& their Child^n John & Ebenezer.
" 25. Alice, Wife of Eliezer Young, & their Child^n Solomon &
Lucy. Abigail, Wife of Mesheck Drew & their Dr Patience. Elizabeth Bunker. Benj^a, son of Wm Twombly,
jun^r.
May 9. Prince—negro serv't to Col. Gerrish.
" 23. Ebenezer, son of Moses Wingate.
June 11. Mary, D^r of William Brown, of Nottingham.
" 16. Joanna, D^r of Isaac Watson.
" 20. Abigail, D^r of Ichabod Hayes.
" 27. Nehemiah, son of Nehemiah Kimbal.
July 4. Ann, D^r of Ichabod Tibbetts.
" 11. Mary, D^r of John Horn. John, son of John Mills. Philip—
negro servant to Thomas Hanson.
July 25. Joseph, son of W^m. Hanson. Eliz^a, Wife of Joseph Roberts,
in their house, she being sick. Phebe, negro servant of
Vincent Torr.
Aug. 22. Abigail Starbird, Widow. Daniel, son of Joseph Hall, Junr.
Sept. 5. Benedictus, son of Vincent Torr.
" 26. Stephen, Son of Stephen Pinkham. Deborah, Dr of John
Meserve.
Oct. 7. Betty, Mary, Abigail & Lydia, Child^n of Joseph Roberts (on
their mother's acc^t, who was sick).

───────

1741. Persons who owned the Covenant.
Decr 30. Nath¹. Davis & Hannah his Wife. Joseph Rines.
1742.
Jan. 1. Eliphalet Hill & Abigail Hill.
" 2. William Buzzell & Wife. Eleanor Perkins, Widow.
" 3. Elihu Hayes.
" 10. Elizabeth Hobart & Judith Heard.
" 17. Dan¹, Hezekiah, Benj^a & Mehetabel Hayes.
" 24. Eliz^a Mills.
Feb. 28. Reuben Hayes.
April 4. Hannah Pinkham.
" 18. Abra Hayes.
May 16. Robert & John Hayes, tertius.
Sept. 26. John Meserve & Wife.

1742.   [Baptisms.]
Oct.   14. Baptized—David, son of David Daniel.
 "   17. John, Abigail, Hannah & Sarah, Child[n] of John Starbird.
 "   24. Eliphalet, son of Tristam Coffin. Jonathan, son of John
             Layton.
Nov.   21. Mary & Joseph, Child[n] of Joseph Dam.
 "   28. Lydia, D[r] of John Wood. Ann, D[r] of Samuel Hodge.
Dec[r] 19. Turner, Son of W[m]. Whitehouse.

[To be continued.]

ABSTRACTS OF THE EARLIEST WILLS FROM THE REC-
ORDS AND FILES AT EAST CAMBRIDGE, MASS.,
IN THE COUNTY OF MIDDLESEX.

Prepared by WILLIAM BLAKE TRASK, Esq., of Boston.

[Continued from vol. xix. page 44.]

ROBERT DANIELL.[1]—3d July, 1655. I, *Robert Daniel*, of Cambridge, in
New England, weake in body, yet of sound mind, make this my last will.
Funerall expences discharged. Vnto my wife *Reana*, besides y[t] part of th[e]
estate I received with herr vppon my marriage to her, w[ch] by covenant was
to returne vnto her againe at my decease, I give 40[s] a yeare dureing her
life, to be payed th' one half in fruite, v[zt] in Apples &c. and the other halfe
in foure bushels of wheate. My will is, that my household goodes be
Equally divided Amongst my five Children, v[zt] to each a fift part. Also,
that my Eldest dau. the now wife of *Thomas Fanning*, shall have her fift
part imediately after my decease, and the remainder to remaine with my
sonne *Samuel*, vntill his Brothers and sisters shall come of age, of Twenty
one yeares or Mariage, w[ch] shall first happen. To my Couson *Anna Newcomen*, a young Cow, and to Elder *Frost* 40[s]; to my dau. *Elizabeth*, the
wife of *Thomas Fanning*, £50, to be payd in Cattle & Corne, at or before
the first of May next; vnto my three youngest Children, £50 a peece, to
be payd when they shall come to the Age 21 yeares, or within one yeare
after their Marriage, w[ch] shall first happen, or before, if my Executo[rs] shall
desire the same. The remainder of my estate, I give the whole, whether
Reall or personall, vnto my sonne *Samuel*, whom I nominate my Executo[r] together with my sonne in law *Thomas Fanning*. And my Loveing
Friends *Richard Jacson* & *Thomas Danforth* I do hereby Ordayne Super-
visors, to see this my last will and testament faithfully executed, to whom
I do also in speciall comitt the care and dispose of my Children, both in their
minority and in the change of their Condiccon by Mariage. My will is,
that if any of the children decease before Mariage or Arivall to the Age of
21, then the portion of such deceased shalbe to such as survive, and be
equally divided Amongst them. My will is, that my Executors pay yeare-
ly, after my decease, vnto my sonne *Joseph*, and to my daus. *Sarah* and
Mary, £5 apeece, in Corne or cattle, beginning the first payment in Aprill
1657, the w[ch] payment of £5 a peece, Annually, shalbe in part of the afore
named £50 a peece. It is mine intent that the household goodes app[r]tayne-
ing to each of my Children shalbe in part of the £50 a peece. My will is,
that my dau. *Elizabeth* shall have liberty to choose in the first place her

---

[1] A genealogy of the Daniell family, descendants of this Robert Daniell, was printed in
the REGISTER, xxviii. 185–94. To the author of that article, M. G. Daniell, A.M., we are
indebted for the use of a wood-cut of Robert Daniell's autograph and seal.—ED.

part of the household-stuffe, the whole being first divided into five **Equall** parts. I further declare my mind, that the 40ˢ pʳ Annu., to my wife, shalbe payd yearly, the Apples at Such time as they are gathered, and the wheate about the last of September, and the Executo's are to deliver them at her house, shee sending her mare or a horse for the same. Also what *Thomas Fanning* hath already received is to be in part of his £50 legacy.

In the pʳsence off: *Jnᵒ Shepard, Thomas Danforth*.

At the County Court held at Cambridge, Oct. 2, 1655, *Jnᵒ Shepard & Thomas Danforth* attested.   *Thomas Danforth*, Recorder.

An Inventory of the estate whereof *Robert Daniell*, late Inhabitant at Cambridge died, Seised, the 6th of July 1655. Mentions " a bill of 7ˡᵇ due from *Martine Vnderwood*, of Water-Towne, £7 ; rent due from Tho: Fanning £1.; from *Jnᵒ Spring*, £1. 11ˢ; one greate bible, 8ˢ; a psalme booke 1ˢ 6ᵈ ; one booke, tit: yᵉ soules Conflict, 2ˢ 6ᵈ ; a booke of mʳ *Masons* worke, 1ˢ 8ᵈ ; a booke of mʳ *Rogers* workes, 1ˢ 4ᵈ ; a booke of mʳ *Giffords* workes, 6ᵈ ; a booke of mʳ *Mathers*, 6ᵈ ; a booke called yᵉ Garden of Spˡˡ flowers, 1ˢ; a debt in *Daniel Smiths* hand, 6ˢ; a debt due from *Lewis Jones*, 6ˢ; mansion house, orchard & yardes, & 26 aceʳˢ vnbroken land, 24 aceʳˢ broaken land, 2 accʳˢ fresh meadow, 4 accʳˢ salt meadow, 2 accʳˢ remote meadow, 4 accʳˢ at Chesters meadow, 65 accʳˢ remote diveident, 29 accʳˢ ½ beyond the greate plaine lying in 2 lotts, 7 accʳˢ remote meadow, the whole vallued at £160.

Whole amᵗ of inventory £359: 19: 11: Taken by *Edward Goffe, Edward Oakes, Samˡ Thatcher*.

Entered and recorded Oct: 2: 1655.

By *Tho: Danforth*, Recorder.

Book I. pages 61–70.

Among the articles enumerated are—Cruse Jugs, 1ˢ 6ᵈ ; a little porsnett,[1] 5ˢ; black suite of Rash, £1 ; 4 yds. of Lockerre, 9ˢ 4ᵈ ; 3 Lockrm[2] napkins, 2ˢ 3ᵈ ; a sleck stone,[3] 4ᵈ ; 2 Lattin[4] pans, 1ˢ 8ᵈ ; one Cowle,[5] 3ˢ; one great fatt,[6] 4ˢ; 2 milk kellars,[7] 1ˢ 8ᵈ ; 4 cheese motes, 4ˢ; a little kellar, 1ˢ; 2 frowes,[8] 4ˢ; one passer stocke,[9] 3 pods, 2ˢ; one fier steele, 1ˢ.

---

[1] Posnet, a little basin ; a porringer, skillet or saucepan.

[2] Lockram, a coarse sort of linen cloth.

[3] A smoothing stone.

[4] Sheet-tin, iron plate covered with tin.

[5] Cowle, a word used in Essex, Eng., for a tub ; whence *cowler*, a kind of brewing vessel, now pronounced cooler.—Phillips's *New World of Words*.

A *cowl-staff* is a staff to carry *tubs* or baskets by the handles. Shakespeare, in his *Merry Wives of Windsor*, Act iii. Sc. 3, says, "Take vp these cloathes heere quickly; wher's the *cowle-staffe*?"

[6] *Fatt*, or *vatt*, a great wooden vessel commonly used for the measuring of malt, which contains a quarter, or eight bushels ; also a large brewing vessel made use of by all brewers to run their wort in ; also a leaden pan or vessel for the making of salt at Droitwitch in Worcestershire—*Ib.*

[7] *Keel*, a vessel for liquors to stand and cool in. *Keeler*, a shallow tub.

[8] *Frower*, an edge-tool, used in cleaving lathes.

[9] *Passer stocke*, what is probably now called by cabinet-makers and others, *bit-stock*.

PASSENGERS AND VESSELS THAT ARRIVED IN AMERICA.

[Continued from page 43.]

UNDER this head we propose to print lists of passengers and memoranda of the arrival of vessels in America. Contributions to this series of articles are solicited from our friends.

No. III.

THE SUSAN AND ELLEN, 1638.

From the GENEALOGY OF THE LOOMIS FAMILY.

[The Loomis Genealogy, noticed in the REGISTER for April last (*ante*, p. 272), contains the following document, copied from the original in the possession of the Hon. J. Hammond Trumbull, LL.D., president of the Connecticut Historical Society. It is a draft (unsigned) of the deposition of Joseph Hills, afterwards of Malden, taken 30th July, 1639.—ED.]

Joseph Hills of Charlestowne, in New England, Woollen Draper, aged about 36 yeares sworne, saith upon his oath that he came to New England undertaker in the ship called the Susan & Ellen of London whereof was master Mr. Edward Payne, in the yeare of our Lord one thousand six hundred thirty and eight, the 14th yeare of the raigne of our Sou'aigne Lord the King that now is, and this d^{pt} knowes that divers goods and chattells, victualls & commodities of Joseph Loomis late of Brayntree in the County of Essex, Woolen-draper, wch were put up in three butts, two hogsheds, one halfe hogshed, one barrell, one tubb & three firkins, transported from Malden in the County of Essex to London in an Ipsw^{ch} Hye, were shipped in the said ship upon the eleventh day of Aprill in the yeare abovesayd, and this deponent cleared the said goods wth divers other goods of the said Joseph Loomis and other mens, in the Custome-house at London, as may appear by the Customers bookes, and this dep^t saith that the said goods were transported into New England in the said ship where she arrived on the seaventeenth day of July in the yeare aforesayd.

No. IV.

MORE EARLY PASSENGERS TO NEW-ENGLAND.

Communicated by HENRY F. WATERS, Esq., of Salem.

These p^{r}sents are to certifie unto whome it may concerne that wee Thomas Cromwell[1] & John Cromwell whoe have beene long inhabitants here in ye towne of Salem, in the county of Essex in new England, doe testifie that wee haue known Hugh Joanes[2] as one coming from England in the same ship with us in to the contry aboue thirty yeares agoe (& as wee un-

---

[1] Thomas Cromwell is supposed to have been a son of Giles Cromwell, of Newbury, and John to have been a grandson of the same, being son of Philip and nephew of Thomas.

H. F. W.

[2] Hugh Joanes m. 1st, Hannah Tomkins, June 26, 1660; she died May 10, 1672; he m. 2d, Mary Foster, 31st 10 mo. 1672. I suspect that these two wives were cousins, one a dau. of John, son of Ralph Tompkins, and the other a gr. dau. of the same Ralph by a dau. who m. John Foster.

H. F. W.

derstood abord Mr Strattons ship*) that he came from uincanton† and was servant to Mr Robert Gutch) & his sister & Elizabeth Due & Margarett White & James Abbot & John Vinning as wee understood came from the same plaice, & the same Hugh Joanes that came along with us into the country is now liuing.

Taken upon the corporall oathes of the s^d Thomas and John Cromwell in Court at Salem the 27: June 1682 & alsoe the said Hugh Joanes then p̄sonally appeered in court being in health.

Attestes   HILLIARD VEREN Cler:

[Essex Co: Deeds, B. 6, p. 168.]

No. V.

CAPT. DOBLE'S PASSENGERS, 1763.

Communicated by JOHN S. H. FOGG, M.D., of South Boston.

List of Capt. Doble's Passengers, who arrived [at Boston] from Newfound Land December, 1763.

Matthew Brimigum		Patrick Day
Lawrance Glinden		Dennis Dennavan
William Murry		John Woodlock
Morris Jack		Patrick Welch
William Ryan		William Lee
James Cowen		Simon Mulley—died at sea
Jonas Jackson		Valentine Connel
James Gorman		Patrick Murphy
Richard Sprusin		John Mejory
John Welch		Robert Page
Edmund Hearn—Hospital		Gilbert Steel
John Burk	Ditto	Nicholas Flernin
Martin Grady		Thomas Dunn
John Crole		John Murray
Patrick Ashing	Ditto	William Brown
Edmund Butler		George Barstow
Daniel Flerta		

ANCESTRY OF ADMIRAL PORTER.

Communicated by the Hon. JOSEPH W. PORTER, of Burlington, Maine.

ALEXANDER[1] PORTER, born in Massachusetts, May 5, 1727; wife, Margaret Henry.‡ The children of Alexander were:

DAVID PORTER, b. April 6, 1754, in Mass.		ALEXANDER,	Aug. 22, 1764.
ROBERT,	Oct. 13, 1755, "	JOHN,	Sept. 1, 1766.
NANCY,	Dec. 18, 1757, "	MARGARET,	Sept. 2, 1768.
SAMUEL,	Oct. 14, 1759, "		

Note.—The above is copied from hand-writing of David Porter, Sen., father of Commodore David Porter.

---

* Can any one furnish the name of this vessel and the date of her arrival ?—ED.

† I find that Wincanton is a market town and parish in Somerset co., England, 23 miles south of Bath.

‡ Margaret Henry was probably a second wife.—J. W. P.

H. F. W.

DAVID[2] PORTER, son of *Alexander,*[1] born 1754; died 1808; wife, Rebecca Gay. Their children were:

DAVID,[3] Jr., born in Boston, Feb. 1, 1780.	MARY.[3]
MARGARET.[3]	NANCY.[3]
REBECCA.[3]	JOHN,[3] Com. U. S. N., d. 1831.

Commodore DAVID[3] PORTER, son of *David,*[2] born in Boston, Feb. 1, 1780; died March 3, 1843. [A good biographical sketch of him will be found in Drake's "Dictionary of American Biography."—ED.] Wife, Evelina Anderson, m. March 10, 1808. Their children were:

WILLIAM D., Commodore U. S. Navy.	HAMBLETON.
ELIZABETH.	EVELINA.
DAVID D.	HENRY O.
THOMAS.	FLORENCE.
THEODORIC, Lieut. U. S. A.	IMOGEN.

Admiral DAVID[4] D., son of *David,*[3] born in Chester, Penn., June 8, 1813. [Drake gives a good biographical sketch.—ED.] Married Georgiana Patterson. Children:

GEORGIANA.	EVELINA.	DAVID ESSEX.
CARLISLE P.	THEODORIC.	ELIZABETH.
RICHARD B.	ELENA.	

QUERIES.—Who was the father of Alexander[1] Porter? and where were he and his son David[2] born?

NOTES AND QUERIES.

ROBERT CALEF, AUTHOR OF "MORE WONDERS OF THE INVISIBLE WORLD."—Matthew A. Stickney, Esq., of Salem, who is preparing a genealogy of the Calef family, has, in his investigations, found reasons for doubting the modern statements which assign the authorship of the above-named book to Robert Calef, Jr. The work itself purports to be by Robert Calef, not Robert Calef, Jr. This, though not conclusive, is strong presumptive evidence. Then the age of the son is against the theory of his being the author. In 1693, when the writer of that book witnessed the afflictions of Margaret Rule, the son was but nineteen years old, while the father was forty-five, a much more probable age. In 1700, when " More Wonders " was published, the son was about twenty-six years old and the father fifty-two. The father was a merchant of Boston, and an owner of property there. It was not till after the publication of the book that he removed to Roxbury, where he died, April 13, 1719, aged 71 ; and where his gravestone may still be seen, with the prefix of " Mr." to his name, in the old burial ground. See REGISTER, xiv. 52.

Mr. Stickney has promised, for a future number of the REGISTER, a full statement of the reasons for his opinion. Can our readers refer us to an earlier author than Whitman (History of the Ancient and Honorable Artillery Company, Boston, 1842, p. 253), who attributes the work to the son? Is there any evidence in early books or manuscripts that Calef, the author, was a young man?—ED.

CONGRESS OF AUTHORS AT PHILADELPHIA, JULY 1, 1876.—In the autumn of 1875, the Committee on the Restoration of Independence Hall, of which Col. Frank M. Etting was chairman, issued invitations to American historians, biographers and literati, to meet in Independence Hall, Philadelphia, to commemorate the one hundredth anniversary of the declaration of independence by Congress, which body passed, July 2, 1776, the resolution introduced by Richard Henry Lee, that the colonies " are, and of right ought to be, free and independent states." The 2d of July this year falling on Sunday, the meeting was held on Saturday, the 1st. The authors invited had each been requested to prepare a brief biographical sketch of some individual whose name is associated with Independence Hall in the early days of the republic, to be deposited among the archives of the national museum.

The ceremonies commenced with a prayer by the Rev. William White Bronson, after which the authors deposited their manuscripts on a table on a platform erected on the south side of the state-house. Upwards of 150 sketches were deposited, the authors not present having previously sent their manuscripts to Col. Etting. The guests then passed into Independence Square, where William S. Stokley, mayor of Philadelphia, introduced in a brief speech the president of the Historical Society of Pennsylvania, John William Wallace, who had been chosen to preside, and who responded in a well-timed speech. The Centennial Hymn by Whittier was next sung, and then William V. McKeen delivered an able and appropriate address. Addresses were also delivered by the Hon. Leverett Saltonstall of Massachusetts, Gov. Henry Lippitt of Rhode Island, the Hon. Benjamin H. Brewster of Pennsylvania, and Frank P. Stevens of Maryland. These were interspersed with patriotic songs and instrumental music.

We are obliged for want of space to postpone to another number the insertion of a list of authors and subjects.—Ed.

A Treacle fetch'd out of a Viper.—" Newly Published a small Book Entituled, A Treacle fetch'd out of a Viper. Sold by Benj. Eliot, under the West-end of the Town-House in Boston. Price Four-pence." The above was copied, long since, from the Boston News Letter, No. 155, April 7th, 1707.

A few years ago, when we had almost despaired of learning the name of the author or seeing the book, a copy was put into our hands by a considerate neighbor, who, knowing our proclivities, thought we might be willing to accept of it. It has the autograph of Ann Clap at the close of the last page. The book is a small 12mo., pp. 32. The title reads thus :—A Treacle fetch'd out of a Viper. | A Brief Essay | Upon | Falls into Sins ; | Directing, | How a RECOVERY out of such | FALLS, | May be attended with a REVENUE, | of Special | Service and Glory to God, | From the | Fallen Sinner. | Boston in N. E. Printed by B. Green, for | Benj. Eliot, at his Shop under the | West-End of the *Town House.* 1707. [Quotation from Homer on the title page omitted.] The writer of this would like the name of the author.

W. B. Trask.

Bequest of John M. Bradbury, Esq.—The late John M. Bradbury, Esq., of Ipswich, a life-member of this society, who died on the 21st of March last, left a liberal bequest to this society. The following is an extract from his will :

" To the New-England Historic, Genealogical Society, now located at No. 18 Somerset street, Boston, I give the sum of two thousand dollars, and also all my shares in the Austin City Water Company."

At the June meeting of the society, Charles W. Tuttle, Esq., in some remarks on introducing resolutions of respect to his memory, used this language : " This is the largest unconditional bequest yet made to this society : and it places the name of Mr. Bradbury among the worthiest of our benefactors."

In a future number of the Register a memoir of Mr. Bradbury, with a portrait, will appear.—Ed.

Standish, Palmer, Foster.—A correspondent writes us that her grandfather, Nathan Palmer, always claimed to be a descendant of Miles Standish ; and she wishes to obtain the connecting links, if this be so. Nathan Palmer was a son of Elihu and Lois (Foster) Palmer, and was born in Scotland parish in Windham, Ct., Aug. 6, 1769. He married in Canterbury, Ct., Jerusha Barstow (see Barry's Hanover, p. 218), and removed at once to Wilkesbarre, Luzerne co., Pa., where he practised law. He was for a number of years a member of the Pennsylvania senate. He died in Mt. Holly, N. J., in 1842. The descent was probably through his mother, Lois Foster.—Ed.

Bason of Alchimy [Register, April, 1876, p. 240]. " Alchimy " basons and spoons were common in those days. See Robert Day's Inventory (and the footnote) in Conn. Col. Records, i. 489. The name was variously corrupted,—to occamy, ockumy, ochimy, &c. Webster's Dictionary has two forms of the word, " ochimy " and " ockemy," and, under each, says " see *occamy,*" but unluckily there is no " occamy " to be seen in the book. Under " alchemy " the definition is given.

Hartford, Ct. J. H. Trumbull.

DEATHS OF AGED PERSONS BY THE NAME OF FELTON IN MASSACHUSETTS IN 1875. —Hon. *Oliver C.⁶ Felton*, in Brookfield, Jan. 21, 1875, aged 79 years, 4 months. He has been a Representative from Brookfield, also a State Senator, was many years a school teacher, and author of Felton's Grammar, published in 1842. He was son of Capt. Benjamin⁵ Felton (Joseph,⁴ Skelton,³ Nathaniel,² Nathaniel,¹ who came to Salem in 1633).

John Swinton⁶ Felton, in Salem, Feb. 1, 1875, aged 87 years, 4 months. He was son of David⁵ (not Daniel), a tailor (who made for George Peabody the first suit of clothes he had made by a tailor) (Samuel,⁴ Samuel,³ John,² Nathaniel¹).

Mrs. *Nancy Felton*, in Salem, March 7, 1875, aged 83 years, 3 months. Was widow of John Smith⁶ Felton, son of James⁵ (Francis,⁴ John,³ Nathaniel,² Nathaniel¹).

George⁶ Felton, in Marlborough, March 15, 1875, aged 78 years, 10 months; son of Joel⁵ (Jacob,⁴ Samuel,³ John,² Nathaniel¹).

Capt. *Benjamin⁶ Felton* died at Worcester, April 6, 1875, aged 82 years, 7 months; formerly of Barre, son of Skelton⁵ (Joseph,⁴ Skelton,³ Nathaniel,² Nathaniel¹).

Mrs. *Mary Felton*, in Hudson, May 18, 1875, aged 73 years, 1 month; was wife of Jacob Felton⁶ (Stephen,⁵ Jacob,⁴ Samuel,³ John,² Nathaniel¹).

Nathaniel Felton, in Barre, June 5, 1875, aged 72 years. He was son of Nathaniel, and probably a descendant of the first Nathaniel of Salem.

There was one Skelton Felton in the third generation, and two in the fifth. Probably they are descendants of the Rev. Samuel Skelton, an early minister of Salem.

Any information relating to the Felton Family will be thankfully received by

Marlborough, Mass.   CYRUS FELTON.

EASTMAN.—On page 230, vol. xxi. of the REGISTER, July, 1867, is : " 5. Thomas Eastman,² m. a dau. of George Corbis."

Thomas Eastman, above, married, Jan. 20, 1679, Deborah, daughter of George and Joanna (Davis) Corliss, of Haverhill, Mass., who was born June 6, 1655. He d. April 29, 1688. They had :

Jonathan, Jan. 8, 1680.

Sarah, June 9, 1683 ; d. March 15, 1696.

Joanna, —— —— —— ; d. Aug. 17, 1684.

Joanna, May 27, 1686.   A. W. CORLISS,

Camp McDowell, Arizona Ter.   Capt. 8th Inf., U.S.A.

WILLIS, KNOWLES.—[Essex Co. Deeds, B. iv. page 446.]—Edward Rawson, of Boston, agent and attorney to " the Reverend John Knowles, hearetofore of water-towne, in the county of midlesex in New England aforesaid, lately : & now in & about the citty of London Clerk, as by his the said John Knowles : letter of Atturney the one bearing date from Bristoll, the 23 february 1657 : the other from London august the 14th sixteene hundred seauenty two," &c. &c., conveys (31 Dec. 1673) to Isaac Hart " of Lynn or Lynn Village, now called Redding," the five hundred acres granted by the town of Lynn to Mr. Thomas Willis, and " which the said John Knowles then had & enjoyed by the gift of his father in law, the sd aboue mentioned Thomas Willis." This conveyance Mr. Rawson makes " in the names of the said John Knowles & Elizabeth his wife."   H. F. WATERS.

Salem, Mass.

QUERY ABOUT COPYING SEALS.—Can some of your readers accustomed to genealogical research inform me how to take the best possible impress of a nearly illegible seal ?   BENJ. W. HUNT.

Purdy's, Westchester Co., N. Y.

LANG.—Whom did John Lang of Portsmouth, N. H., marry? Savage says he married a daughter of William Brooking ; but he gives other husbands to the daughters. When did his wife die? What were the names of his children, and where were they born ? Was he the father of Nathaniel and Stephen L. who were born at Portsmouth? Jeffrey Lang (my great-grandfather), son of Nathaniel, was born Jan. 16, 1707.   EDWARD S. L. RICHARDSON.

Chicago, Ill.

THOMAS HUNT.—Can any of the readers of this tell me who the parents of Thomas Hunt were? He was in Stamford, Ct., in 1650; said to be a high churchman; died in Westchester Co., N. Y., in 1698. He was with Edward and Ralph Hunt at Newtown, Long Island, in 1661. His seal on will in the City Hall, N. York, seems to be illegible. Can any of your English readers answer whether Thomas and Edward Hunt, sons of Francis Hunt and Dorothy, daughter of Rowland Durant, emigrated to America? The ages of the American Thomas and Edward agree with those sons to Francis Hunt and grandsons to John Hunt of London, whose arms were granted 20 July, 1585.　　　　　　　　　　　　　　　　　　BENJ. W. HUNT.
Purdy's, Westchester Co., N. Y.

DOUGLAS.—A Genealogical History of the descendants of William Douglas, of Boston, 1640, is in preparation, and any information relating to the subject or to the numerous branches of the family which have sprung from him will be gratefully received. Communications may be addressed to　　　　CHAS. H. J. DOUGLAS.
50 Olive St., Providence, R. I.

MATERNAL ANCESTRY OF GEN. JAMES CUDWORTH, OF SCITUATE, N. E.—Mrs. Harriet A. de Salis, of London, England, has presented to the Historic, Genealogical Society, a manuscript " Pedigree of the Mali Catuli or Saxon Family of Machell, Lords of Crakenthorpe in Westmoreland, with the collateral branches of the Machels of Lincoln, Bucks, Essex, Surrey and London," which she has compiled from family deeds, charters, records, parish registers, wills, heralds' visitations, county histories, inquests post mortem, chancery suits, &c. &c. In this document will be found the maternal ancestry of Gen. James Cudworth, the emigrant ancestor of most if not all of the Cudworths of New-England. From it we learn that his grandfather, John[18] Machell, was a descendant in the eighteenth generation from *Ulf[1] Malus Catulus* or Ulf le Machell de Catulino, whose sons were *Gamul*,[2] Dom. de Kerlythorp, and *Halth[2] Malus Catulus* or Halth le Machel, temp. Hen. I., cir. 1100–1135, who, by wife Eva, was the ancestor of the family whose pedigree is given.

JOHN[18] MACHEL, of Tangley in Surrey, m. Jane, dau. of Sir Nicholas Woodroofe, knt., and had:

　i. MARY, nurse to Prince Henry, son of James I.; m. 1st, Ralph Cudworth, rector of Aller, Somerset, and chaplain to James I. (see REGISTER, xxi. 249), who d. 1624. They had: 1, *James* of Scituate in Plymouth colony; 2, *Ralph*, b. 1617, author of the Intellectual System of the Universe; and other children. [Mrs. de Salis we understand has the English pedigree of the Cudworths.] She m. 2d, John Stoughton, D.D., of London, who d. May 4, 1639.

ii. JOHN of Wendover, Bucks.	v. *Dau.* m. —— Gibbs.
iii. MATTHEW.	vi. *Dau.* m. —— Cave.
iv. NICHOLAS.	vii. *Dau.* m. —— Welsh.

PARMELEE (*ante*, xxviii. 207).—In reply to the query whether there was any knowledge of a Parmelee family that settled in Haddam or Lyme, I would say that my grandfather, John[6] Gridley, b. July, 1774, at Farmington, Ct., married about 1795 or 6 Rachel Cotton, dau. of John Cotton and wife Sarah Parmalee, perhaps dau. of Jehiel Parmalee, formerly of Farmington, Ct.
Jackson, Mich.　　　　　　　　　　　　　　　　WILLIAM SEWARD[8] GRIDLEY.

RICHARD PORTER.—The undersigned is preparing a genealogy of the descendants of Richard Porter, who settled in Weymouth, Mass., in 1635. Those of the name in Norfolk, Bristol, and Plymouth counties, are mostly his descendants, with many in New-York and the west. He will be grateful for any information connected with this family.　　　　　　　　　　　　　　　　JOSEPH W. PORTER.
Burlington, Maine.

BAKER.—Information is desired from any person having knowledge of genealogies or family or town records that form a connection with or include the name of PETER BAKER, who married *Mary* PETE about 1730, and had children, James, Mary, Catharine, Sarah and Martha, and is supposed to have been a resident of Rhode Island. But this is not positively known.　　　　　　Address　SANFORD BAKER.
Denver, Colorado.

WHITE, FISKE, BRABROOKE.—From a petition of Walter Fairefield (probably acting as attorney to John Bare, occupant of certain land in Wenham which formerly belonged to John White, of Lancaster), dated 24th September, 1695, I find it probable that Joan, the widow of the aforesaid John White, was afterwards married to Richard Brabrooke. From other papers in the office of the clerk of the courts at Salem, it would appear that Capt. Thomas Fiske's first wife (and mother of his children) was Joan, one of the daughters of John and Joan White. Capt. Fiske married, secondly, widow Martha Fitch, who was doubtless his kinswoman, being a daughter of David Fiske of Watertown.   H. F. WATERS.
Salem, Mass.

——

DE WOLF (sometimes written De Aulf).—The following items are from the records of the First Church of Lyme, Ct. :

Baptisms.—April 4, 1731, Stephen, s. of Benjamin De Wolf.
        " 17, 1731-2, Phebe, da.   "
        Aug. 5, 1733, Joannah Jane, da. of Lewis De Wolf.
        April 6, 1735, Elijah, s. of Benjamin De Wolf.
        Aug. 28, 1736-7, Esther, da.   "
        Oct. 23,   "   Edward, s. of Lewis De Wolf.
        Aug. 3, 1739-40, William, s. of Josiah De Wolf, Junr.
        June 7, 1741, Jos., s. of Rebeckah De Wolf.
        Sept. 6, 1741, Phebe, da. of Benjamin De Wolf.
        Nov. 13, 1743, Daniel, s. of Josiah De Wolf, Junr.
        Nov. 25, 1744, Benjamin, s. of Simeon De Wolf.

Aug. 3, 1739-40, Josiah De Wolf owned the covenant.
April 12, 1741, Josiah De Wolf, Junr.,   joined the church.
     "   "   Martha, wife of Josiah De Wolf   "
June   7, "   Josiah De Wolf   "
     "   "   Nathan De Wolf[1]   "
     "   "   Luce, wife of Benjamin De Wolf, Junr., joined the church.
July 26, "   Juda De Wolf   "
     "   "   Jabez De Wolf   "
Sept. 28, 1741-2, Margaret, wife of Benjamin De Wolf   "
Jan. 31, 1744-5, Simon De Wolf.

The following inscriptions are copied from grave-stones at Lyme :
    1. " Here lies the body of Mr. Daniel De Wolf,[2] A.M., who died Oct. 10, 1752, aged 26 years."
    2. " Here lies the body of Anna, wife of Josiah De Wolf, who died Dec. 1752, in the 63d year of her age."
Lyme, Ct.   E. M. SALISBURY.

——

YOUNG.—The communication of G. T. Ridlon, found on page 236 of the April number of the REGISTER, contains some errors. He says Susanna, the daughter of Matthias Young, married Ichabod Austin. Matthias Young was the fifth child of Matthew Young, and married Mercy Main, January 9, 1733 ; Susanna above-named was the first child of Matthew above-named, born Nov. 3, 1696 ; married Ichabod Austin, had one child Ichabod, born March 29, 1718. Austin died and she married Magnus Readlan, by whom she had : 1. ——, born May 26, 1722, and " died when 6 days old " ; 2. Ebenezer, born Feb. 13, 1724 ; 3. John, born March 31, 1726 ; 4. Matthias, born Sept. 19, 1728. Matthew was, as Mr. Ridlon states, one of the sons of Roland who lived in York, and was an adult July 3, 1653, as he had land granted him at that date. He had sons bearing the names mentioned by Mr. Ridlon, also a son *Roland*, which name has continued to this day. It is in all cases spelled *Rowland*.   NATHANIEL G. MARSHALL.
York, Maine.

——

DR. WILLIAM WARE died in Dighton, Mass., June 11, 1764, in the 67th year of his age. I wish to know whose son he was, and also the name of his wife.
Burlington, Maine.   J. W. PORTER.

————

[1] Graduated at Yale College in 1743.
[2] Graduated at Yale College in 1747.

BROOKS.—William Brooks came to Scituate in the ship Blessing, 1635, age 20 ; married widow Susanna Dunham ; had an only son Nathaniel, born 1646 ; married 1678, Elizabeth, daughter of Richard Curtis ; sons William and Nathaniel (descendants probably living at Scituate). Noah Brooks, of Scituate, married, 1770, Hannah Stetson (dau. of Ebenezer of Dighton), born June, 1754 ; Noah Brooks, of Boston, born at Scituate, married, Feb. 1812, Esther Stetson, dau. of Micah, of Scituate. Barker Brooks, of Castine, Me. (brother of last named Noah Brooks), born at Scituate. Wanted, information concerning genealogy of this family, to enable undersigned to trace direct his line from William Brooks first mentioned, to Barker Brooks last mentioned, and items concerning family history. Any thing on this subject is respectfully requested, and will be gratefully received by
Fort Walla Walla, Washington Territory.   F. K. UPHAM, U.S.A.

BENJAMIN BAGNALL (*ante*, xxvi. 202).—William R. Bagnall, of Malden, Mass., informed us, Jan. 1876, that he was a great-grandson of Benjamin Bagnall, the clockmaker, through his only son Robert, whose only son Thomas[3] married Mary R., daughter of John and Hannah (Waite) Tucker, and was father of our informant. He further informed us that his ancestor, Benjamin, above named, owned the estate in Washington street where the Boston Journal is now published, and that he sold the estate in 1745.   ED.

WIFE OF RALPH INMAN.—Can any of your readers give the name of Ralph Inman's first wife, who died in Boston about 1759 ? She was a sister of Hannah wife of John Rowe, and was the mother of Susannah (wife of Captain Linzee, R.N.), and George Inman, Captain in the 26th Foot, who succeeded to the command of Major André's company on the appointment of the latter to the Adjutant-Generalship of the British army.   CHARLES R. HILDEBURN.
Philadelphia, Pa.

THE GREAT SEAL OF MARYLAND.—The following joint resolutions were adopted by the Maryland General Assembly at its last session :
" Whereas, Senate Joint Resolution No. 9, ' In relation to the Great Seal of the State,' passed by the General Assembly at its session in 1874, instructing the Governor to have the Great Seal of the State so altered that it should conform to the arms of Lord Baltimore as represented on the title page of Bacon's Laws of Maryland, printed in 1765 by Jonas Green, was passed under the impression that the said representation was accurate ; and
" Whereas, Investigation has shown that said representation of the arms of Lord Baltimore is imperfect ; and
" Whereas, A complete and accurate description of the Seal of the Province is to be found in the Commission of Cecilius, Lord Baron of Baltimore, that accompanied the said Seal when sent to the Province in 1648 ; therefore,
" First. *Be it resolved by the General Assembly of Maryland*, That Senate Joint Resolution No. 9, ' In relation to the Great Seal of the State,' passed by the General Assembly at its session in 1874, be, and the same is hereby, rescinded.
" Second. *And be it further resolved*, That the Governor of the State is hereby authorized and empowered to have the Great Seal of the State altered so that it shall bear the arms of Maryland as represented upon the Seal furnished the Province in 1648 by Cecilius, Lord Baron of Baltimore ; which arms are described as follows, namely : Quarterly, first and fourth paly of six or and sable, a bend counter-changed ; second and third quarterly argent and gules, a cross bottony counter-changed ; *Crest* (which is placed upon a helmet showing five bars, over a Count-palatine's coronet), on a ducal coronet proper, two pennons, dexter or, the other sable ; staves gules : *Motto*, ' *Fatti maschii, parole femine ;*' *Supporters*, a plowman and a fisherman proper ; a *Mantle* doubled with ermine, surrounding the arms and supporters. Upon a border encircling the Seal shall be engraven this legend : ' *Scuto bonae voluntatis tuae coronasti nos.*' The diameter of the Seal shall be three inches."
It was deemed proper to return to the seal as sent to the province by Cecilius, lord Baltimore, in 1648. An effort to do so was made some years ago, but the crest was omitted and an eagle substituted.
The commission for the Great Seal is to be found in the second volume of Bozman's History of Maryland.   LEWIS H. STEINER.
Frederick, Md.

PRESIDENT FILLMORE.—Has the pedigree of the late President Fillmore been traced out? I am anxious to see it, and especially to know from what part of England his ancestors came. Any information would be acceptable.

Queen's College, Oxford, England.　　　　W. P. W. PHILLIMORE.

[A genealogy of the Fillmore family to which President Fillmore belonged, will be found in the REGISTER, xi. 61–6, 141–7. The earliest ancestor traced is John Fillmore or Phillmore, mariner, of Ipswich, Mass., who married Abigail Tilton, June 19, 1701. He purchased an estate in Beverly, Nov. 24, 1704, and died before 1711. His widow survived. He was probably the first of the name in this country. It is not known from what part of England he came.—ED.]

PHILLIMORE, FINNIMORE, FYNMORE.—I wish for any information respecting these families however spelt. The three names are identical, and are to be found very variously spelt—*Phinnimore, Philimor, Fillimore, Finemore, Finmore, &c.* Even *Venmore* and *Vennimore* occur. Perhaps some of the readers of the REGISTER can assist me with accounts of persons of these names who have emigrated to America.

I may add that the home of the Phillimore family from the xvi. century (and probably earlier) downwards was Cam in Gloucestershire.

Queen's College, Oxford.　　　　W. P. W. PHILLIMORE.

RESTORING OLD DEEDS.—For restoring old deeds, I have found it best to employ a strong solution of tannic acid brushed over the writing with a camel-hair pencil. Tincture of nutgalls as recommended in the REGISTER, xxx. 103, is objectionable, as it stains the document. The parchment ought to be stretched with drawing-pins, and afterwards put to press between blotting-paper. Sometimes the dose of tannic acid may have to be repeated. It will be found that thus pressing the parchment will take away all creases.　　　　W. P. W. PHILLIMORE.

Queen's College, Oxford.

STIFF.—I am collecting notes about this family, and therefore any information about it would be gladly received. The name appears in Wiltshire, England, in the xiii. century; and in Normandy as *Rigidus* in the xii. century. A branch in which I am especially interested has been situated at Cam, co. Gloucester, since the commencement of the xvii. century. In deeds about that date it is spelt, *Stiffe, Styph,* and *Stift.* It is now found chiefly in Gloucestershire, Kent and Suffolk. The name occurs in Sweden and even Hungary.　　　　W. P. W. PHILLIMORE.

Queen's College, Oxford.

BRIGHAM.—In looking over my father's papers I found the following record of births:

Timothy Brigham, born Feb. 27, 1736.[1]
Lydia Brigham, born Nov. 8, 1740.

Their children:

Eber, born Nov. 25, 1761.	Lewis, born January 4, 1774.
Percis, born January 16, 1764.	Nabby, born Dec. 29, 1775.
Samuel, born Dec. 14, 1765.	Luther, born April 4, 1778.
Kitty, born Dec. 11, 1767.	Polly, born April 15, 1781.
Lydia, born Dec. 26, 1769.	Betsey, born Oct. 22, 1783.
Sally, born January 30, 1772.	

The above Timothy Brigham was a cousin to John Brigham who settled in Acworth in 1805. John was a son of Stephen, grandson of Jedediah, great-grandson of Samuel, and gr.-gr.-grandson of Thomas Brigham who embarked at London for New-England in 1635.　　　　HENRY A. BROOKS.

Acworth, N. Hampshire.

ZACHARIAH JENKINS came within the bounds of the Friends' Meeting of Warwick, Greenwich and Kingston, R. I. in 1708. The following entry is found on the records of this meeting:

"Greenwich, y[e] 16th 6 mo. 1708. Zachariah Jenkins with family settling among us hath produced a certificate from the meeting he did belong to."

From the best information I can get on the subject he settled in North Kingston. I wish to learn where he came from and who his father was.

Wyoming, Luzerne Co., Pa.　　　　STEUBEN JENKINS.

[1] See Morse's Brigham Family, pp. 14 and 22.—ED.

"THE CONQUEST OF THE WILDERNESS."—Under this title the Rev. B. F. De Costa has prepared a work on "the maritime and colonial history of New-England from the Cabots to the Pilgrims of Leyden." We are informed that amongst the original papers to be included in the volume is the Journal of the Colony of Sagadahoc (1607), by one of the adventurers. This journal, hitherto supposed to have been lost, was discovered recently by Mr. De Costa. The work will also include new and interesting voyages to Maine in New-England, in 1568, 1579, 1580. It will also contain a translation of the North American portion of the Cosmographie of John Allfonsce. It will be published by Joel Munsell, of Albany.

THE WILLEY FAMILY.—In the small family burying-ground on the old Willey farm in North Conway, N. H. (now the property of Erastus B. Bigelow, Esq., of Boston), lie the remains of Captain Samuel Willey and his wife Polly (Lovejoy) Willey, and of such of their children as were recovered from the earth and rocks brought down by the slides in the Notch of the White Mountains on the night of August 28, 1826. On the stone that marks the grave is the following inscription :—

" To the memory of the Family which was at once destroyed by a slide from the white Mountains on the night of 28 August 1826

Samuel Willey, Æ	38
Polly Willey,	35
Eliza A. Willey,	12
Jeremiah Willey, .	11
Martha G. Willey,	10
Elbridge G. Willey,	7
Salley Willey,	3

" We gaze around, we read their monument, we sigh, and when we sigh, we sink."

Interesting details of this distressing calamity will be found in numerous publications, especially in the accounts given by Mr. J. B. Moore, and Prof. Thomas C. Upham, both of which are printed in the third volume of the Collections of the N. H. His. Society. In the latter account there are two erroneous dates given for the disaster, possibly typographical errors. In Mr. Moore's account the age of the youngest child is given as 5 years. This should be 3 years. In 1856 "Incidents of White Mountain Scenery," &c., was published by the Rev. Benjamin G. Willey, a brother, I believe, of Captain Samuel, above-named.

A. H. HOYT.

DOVER, NEW-HAMPSHIRE.—I have a printed book of 204 pages, duodecimo, in good condition, having the following title-page, viz. :—

The Shipwreck and Adventures of Monsieur Pierre Viaud, A Native of Bourdeaux and Captain of a Ship. Translated from the French by Mrs. Griffith. First American Edition. *Per varios casus, per tot discrimina rerum.*—Virg. Dover, N. H. Printed and Sold by Samuel Bragg, Jun. 1799.

Query, whether this is not the first BOOK printed in Dover?   C. W. TUTTLE.

FACSIMILES OF THE STAMPS OF 1765.—J. W. Scott & Co., 146 Fulton street, New-York, have reproduced, by the Woodbury process, facsimiles of the stamps for the American colonies issued under the act of 1765 of the British Parliament. The different stamps are each affixed to a card, on the back of which is a description of the several kinds of stamps. Price, 25 cents each.

WHO SIGNALLED PAUL REVERE?—The Rev. John Lee Watson, D.D., of Orange, N. J., has communicated to the *Boston Daily Advertiser* of July 20, an article in which he produces evidence to show that Capt. John Pulling and not Robert Newman hung out the lanterns on the 18th of April, 1775, on the steeple of the North Church, Boston, as signals to Paul Revere. We have not room in this number of the REGISTER for an abstract, but will print one in the January number. Rev. Henry F. Lane, of Malone, N. Y., a great-grandson of John Pulling, communicated to the *Boston Journal*, July 25, an article in confirmation of the Rev. Dr. Watson's position.

EARLY SETTLERS OF HARRISON, MAINE.—A small work with this title will soon be published by the Rev. G. T. Ridlon, of Harrison. Price, 50 cents. Orders solicited.

THE CORLISS FAMILY.—Capt. Augustus W. Corliss, U.S.A., has in press a genealogy of this family, including partial records of some of the families connected by intermarriage ; also notes on the Corlies family. The book will be ready this autumn. Price, five dollars. Address the author at Yarmouth, Me., P. O. Box 261.

TWELVES AND REED. — (*From Braintree, Mass., Records.*) — " Lieut. Robert Twelves who erected the South Church at Boston died March 9 1696–7 aged 77 or thereabouts."

" Mrs. Reed a Captive taken at Casco Bay and carried to Canada was redeemed and came to Braintree and died May 16 1691."	J. W. PORTER.
Burlington, Me.

EPHRAIM TIBBETTS.—Can any one give information relative to Ephraim Tibbetts, the " celebrated Indian fighter," sometime of Dover, New-Hampshire? Pedigrees of Tibbetts families desired by	G. T. RIDLON.
Harrison, Me.

MR. DRAKE'S LIBRARY AND OTHER LITERARY PROPERTY.—*Concluding Sale (ante,* p. 238).—The third and concluding sale of Mr. S. G. Drake's literary property is advertised by Bangs, Merwin & Co., New-York, for Sept. 25 and following days. Its special attractions are the large pamphlet collections which Mr. Drake had accumulated for his History of Boston, and upon American local history ; an extremely valuable list of manuscripts, autographs, portraits, and the remainders of editions of works which Mr. Drake controlled.

Among the manuscripts may be mentioned the original of Increase Mather's " Cases of Conscience ;" the Examination of Hugh Parsons by William Pynchon, at Springfield in 1651 ; a deed of King Philip, with valuable autograph endorsements : autograph letters of Governors Bradford, Prence, Winslow, Endicott, Coddington, William Penn, and others.

SOCIETIES AND THEIR PROCEEDINGS.

NEW-ENGLAND HISTORIC, GENEALOGICAL SOCIETY.

Boston, Massachusetts, Wednesday, January 5, 1876.—The annual meeting was held at the Society's House, this afternoon, at half-past two o'clock, the president, the Hon. Marshall P. Wilder, in the chair.

Col. Albert H. Hoyt, chairman of the nominating committee, reported a list of candidates for officers and committees. The Hon. George Cogswell and the Rev. Thomas R. Lambert, D.D., were appointed a committee to collect and count votes, who reported the candidates unanimously elected. The officers and committees for 1876, are :

President.—The Hon. Marshall P. Wilder, of Boston, Mass.

Vice-Presidents.—The Hon. Israel Washburn, Jr., LL.D., of Portland, Me. ; William B. Towne, A.M., of Milford, N. H. ; the Hon. Hiland Hall, LL.D., of Bennington, Vt. ; the Hon. George C. Richardson, of Boston, Mass. ; the Hon. John R. Bartlett, A.M., of Providence, R. I. ; the Hon. Henry P. Haven, of New-London, Conn.

Honorary Vice-Presidents.—The Hon. John A. Dix, LL.D., of New-York, N.Y. ; William A. Whitehead, A.M., of Newark, N. J. ; William Duane, Esq., of Philadelphia, Pa. ; the Rev. Edwin A. Dalrymple, D.D., of Baltimore, Md. ; the Hon. William A. Richardson, LL.D., of Washington, D. C. ; the Hon. Silas N. Martin, of Wilmington, N. C. ; the Hon. Thomas Spooner, of Reading, O. ; the Rev. Joseph F. Tuttle, D.D., of Crawfordsville, Ind. ; Lyman C. Draper, LL.D., of Madison, Wis. ; the Rev. William G. Eliot, D.D., LL.D., of St. Louis, Mis. ; the Rt. Rev. William I. Kip, D.D., LL.D., of San Francisco, Cal.

Corresponding Secretary.—The Rev. Edmund F. Slafter, A.M., of Boston, Mass.

Recording Secretary.—David Greene Haskins, Jr., A.M., of Cambridge, Mass.

Treasurer.—Benjamin Barstow Torrey, of Boston, Mass.

Historiographer.—The Rev. Samuel Cutler, of Boston, Mass.

Librarian.—John Ward Dean, A.M., of Boston, Mass.

Directors.—The Hon. George C. Richardson, Boston ; Charles W. Tuttle, A.M., Boston ; the Hon. John Cummings, Woburn ; John Foster, Boston ; the Hon. Charles Levi Woodbury, Boston.

Committee on Publication.—Albert H. Hoyt, A.M., Boston ; John Ward Dean, A.M., Boston ; William B. Towne, A.M., Milford, N. H. ; the Rev. Lucius R. Paige, D.D., Cambridge ; H. H. Edes, Boston ; Jeremiah Colburn, A.M., Boston.

Committee on the Library.—James F. Hunnewell, Boston ; Jeremiah Colburn, A.M., Boston ; Deloraine P. Corey, Malden ; Prof. Charles P. Otis, Ph. D., Boston ; George T. Littlefield, Boston.

Committee on Finance.—William B. Towne, A.M., Milford, N. H. ; Henry Edwards, Boston ; the Hon. Charles B. Hall, Boston ; Percival L. Everett, Boston ; the Hon. Edward S. Tobey, A.M., Boston.

Committee on Papers and Essays.—The Rev. Dorus Clarke, D.D., Boston ; Frederic Kidder, Melrose ; the Rev. I. N. Tarbox, D.D., Boston ; the Hon. William S. Gardner, A.M., Boston ; Albert B. Otis, A.M., Boston ; Abram E. Cutter, Boston.

Committee on Heraldry.—The Hon. Thomas C. Amory, A.M., Boston ; Abner C. Goodell, Jr., A.M., Salem ; Augustus T. Perkins, A.M., Boston ; William S. Appleton, A.M., Boston ; George B. Chase, A.M., Boston.

The Hon. Marshall P. Wilder, having been re-elected president, then delivered the address printed in the REGISTER for April, pp. 165–74. At the conclusion he read a letter from Edward Russell, Esq., of Boston, to Col. A. H. Hoyt, enclosing the following extract from the will of his late wife, Mrs. Mary W. Russell : " I give, devise and bequeath to the New-England Historic, Genealogical Society, of Boston aforesaid, the sum of three thousand dollars ($3,000) to constitute a fund, the income of which to be used for the purchase of English county histories and genealogies for the library of said Society, the said three thousand dollars to be paid from the legacy belonging to me, of which Mrs. Cheever Newhall has the income during her natural life." Col. Hoyt read a brief sketch of the life of Mrs. Russell, which is printed in the Necrology in this number of the REGISTER. Resolutions expressive of gratitude for the noble bequest were unanimously passed.

The Rev. Edmund F. Slafter, the corresponding secretary, reported that fifty-six resident members, eight corresponding members and one honorary member have been added to the society during the year. He also reported the usual historical correspondence.

The following annual reports were then presented :

Benjamin B. Torrey, the treasurer, reported the income for the year, $2,939.61, and the expenses $2,927.98, leaving a balance on hand of $11.63. The receipts for life membership were $270.00.

William B. Towne, chairman of the committee of finance, made the report of that committee. He also, in behalf of the committees on the Building Fund and the Librarian's Fund, reported that subscriptions amounting to $43,925.00 had been collected in behalf of the Building Fund, of which $43,875.34 had been expended for the lot and building No. 18 Somerset street, and for alterations, repairs and furniture, leaving a balance of $49.66 which had been carried to the Librarian's Fund ;—and that $12,692.50 had been collected for the latter fund, which with the balance from the Building Fund now amounts to $12,742.16, and has been safely invested.

The Rev. Samuel Cutler, the historiographer, reported that the deaths of 38 members had come to his knowledge during the year, and that biographical sketches of twenty-five members had been prepared.

John Ward Dean, the librarian, reported that 1,240 volumes and 1,679 pamphlets had been added to the library. The library now contains 13,557 volumes and 55,670 pamphlets.

James F. Hunnewell, chairman of the committee on the library, reported its condition and specialties.

The Rev. Dorus Clarke, D.D., chairman of the committee on papers and essays, reported that eight papers had been read before the society during the last year.

Col. Albert H. Hoyt, chairman of the committee on publication, made his annual report, a portion of which, containing a history of the REGISTER, is printed in this volume, pp. 184–8.

At the conclusion of this report, Charles W. Tuttle made some remarks upon the retirement of Col. Hoyt from the editorial chair of the REGISTER, which he had occupied for eight consecutive years, and offered the following resolutions :

Resolved, That the thanks of this Society be given to Col. Albert H. Hoyt for his long, able and efficient services as editor of the REGISTER, the official organ of this Society.

Resolved, That the Recording Secretary transmit to Col. Hoyt an attested copy of these resolutions.

Remarks expressing approval of the manner in which Col. Hoyt had conducted the REGISTER were made by William B. Towne, the Rev. Dorus Clarke, D.D., the Rev. Edmund F. Slafter, and William Lawton, after which the resolutions were unanimously adopted.

The Hon. Thomas C. Amory, chairman of the committee on heraldry, made the report of that committee.

The Hon. Charles B. Hall, for the trustees of the Towne Memorial Fund, reported that the fund now amounts to $3,755.23.

William B. Towne, for the trustees of the Barstow fund, reported that 224 volumes had been bound at an expense of $122.73. The fund is $1,000.00.

Col. Almon D. Hodges, for the trustees of the Bond Fund, reported $26.00 received for sales and $34.88 for interest. For the purchase of books $2.50 have been expended. The fund is now $534.25.

Col. Hodges, in behalf of the Cushman fund, reported that it now amounted to $59.66.

Charles Carlton Coffin called attention to the fact that some original manuscript papers and documents of great value, relating to the Revolutionary War, on deposit in the State House, Boston, are in a rapidly perishing condition, and moved the appointment of a committee to consider the expediency of asking the Legislature to order them to be printed. A committee was appointed, consisting of Messrs. Coffin, A. H. Hoyt, and J. Colburn.

RHODE-ISLAND HISTORICAL SOCIETY.

Providence, February 29.—A stated meeting was held this evening. The Hon. Seth Padelford was called to the chair.

The Rev. E. M. Stone, the librarian, reported the donations.

The Hon. William P. Sheffield read a paper on "The Early History of Block Island."

March 14.—A meeting was held this evening, the Hon. Zachariah Allen, vice-president, in the chair.

The librarian announced the donations, among which was a large piece of "Slate Rock," presented by the Tingley Marble Company, bearing the following inscription : "What Cheer Rock, landing-place of Roger Williams, A.D. 1636."

William Jones Hoppin, of New-York, then read the paper of the evening, giving a detailed history of the Continental frigate Providence, built at or near Fox Point. She was launched May 24, 1776, and was commanded by a native of this State.

Critical and complimentary remarks on the paper followed from Messrs. Stone, Allen and Perry. Reference was made to the history, yet to be written, of the Rhode Island Society of the Cincinnati, the documentary records of which are in the possession of Mr. Hoppin, who was appointed and urged to prepare a memorial of that lamented fraternity of patriotic citizens.

March 28.—A meeting was held this evening, vice-president Allen in the chair.

William J. Miller, of Bristol, read his third paper on Philip of Pokanoket and the Wampanoags. The first paper was read March 17, 1874 (*ante*, xxviii. 346), and the second, March 16, 1875 (*ante*, xxix. 332).

April 4.—A quarterly meeting was held this evening. Isaac H. Southwick was called to the chair.

The Hon. Amos Perry read a paper on the History of the Providence Marine Society, and gave a list of its officers (presidents, vice-presidents, treasurers and secretaries) from its organization in 1798 to the present time.

April 10.—A meeting in commemoration of the two hundredth anniversary of the burning of the town of Providence,[1] April 10, 1676, was held this evening, vice-president Allen in the chair.

The librarian announced the donations.

---

[1] A full narrative of this disaster, illustrated by engravings, with sketches of the events which preceded and followed it, prepared by the Rev. Edwin M. Stone, was printed in a supplement to the Providence Daily Journal for April 10, 1876.

Charles Gorton, of Providence,—a lineal descendant of Samuel Gorton, one of the first settlers of the state, and the author of Simplicitie's Defence,—exhibited a large collection of Indian relics. This is probably one of the most perfect private collections in the country. The Hon. Zachariah Allen then read a paper on Indian History. Mr. Allen said the object of his paper was to contrast the Jewish ecclesiastical policy with which the Puritans attempted to subdue and govern the Indians they found here in possession of the lands, with the policy of "peace on earth and good will to all men," and freedom to worship God according to the dictates of conscience, which was the Christian principle on which Roger Williams founded a State here—the first ever founded on absolute civil and religious freedom, and which has been maintained and has spread through all our land.

A general discussion of the subject followed. Brief addresses were made by Wm. J. Miller, of Bristol, Rev. C. A. Staples, the Hon. J. R. Bartlett, Amos Perry, Dr. C. W. Parsons and Samuel H. Wales, of this city, and Wm. P. Upham, of Salem.

MAINE HISTORICAL SOCIETY.

Portland, March 30.—The winter session of the society was held in the Common Council Room, City Hall, March 30, 1876.

In the absence of the President and Vice President, Hon. Charles T. Gilman, of Brunswick, was chosen to take the chair.

The secretary read a paper communicated by Judge John E. Godfrey, of Bangor, on Norumbega.

Joseph Williamson, Esq., of Belfast, read a paper on Brig. Gen. Waldo.

Gen. John M. Brown, of Portland, made statements concerning the papers committed to the custody of the society by Rev. Robert Trelawney, of Ham, near Plymouth, England, relating to the settlement and early history of Richmond Island and Scarboro'. Several of the letters embraced in these documents were read. Great interest is taken in these papers, which are to be soon published in a separate volume.

R. K. Sewall, of Wiscasset, read a paper on the Rock-heaps or Cairns in Maine.

Gen. Brown read a paper, illustrated by maps, on the river systems of Maine and the Indian carrying places.

Dr. Theodore H. Jewett, of So. Berwick, and George F. Talbot, of Portland, having referred to certain papers of value in the early history of the state, were requested to take measures to secure the originals, or copies, for the society.

In the evening Hon. Wm. Goold, of Windham, read an elaborate article on Fort Halifax on the Kennebec, illustrated by drawings.

The reading of these papers was followed by discussions of members. The meetings were attended by several gentlemen and ladies of the city.

A gun was presented by Samuel Jordan, Esq., of Deering, to the society, known to have been in the Jordan family 187 years. Mr. Goold, through whom the donation was made, with the gun communicated a paper containing an account of the Jordan family from their first settlement in this region. At the close of the evening meeting the members were invited by the Portland members of the society to a very pleasant entertainment at the Falmouth.   A. S. PACKARD, *Secretary.*

CONNECTICUT HISTORICAL SOCIETY.

Hartford, May 16.—At the annual meeting held this evening, officers were elected as follows: *President*, Dr. J. Hammond Trumbull; *Vice Presidents*, S. H. Huntington, Hartford County; Henry White, New Haven County; Ashbel Woodward, Learned Hebard, New London; Caleb S. Henry, Fairfield; William Cothren, Litchfield; John Johnston, Middlesex; Dwight Loomis, Tolland; *Recording Secretary*, L. E. Hunt; *Corresponding Secretary*, Charles J. Hoadly; *Treasurer*, J. F. Morris; *Auditor*, Rowland Swift.   A. WOODWARD.

VIRGINIA HISTORICAL SOCIETY.

Richmond, Friday, April 7.—A meeting of the executive committee was held this evening, William Green presiding.

A number of valuable donations were reported. The corresponding secretary, R. A. Brock, read letters from Col. Frank M. Etting, chief of the historical department of the centennial commission, relative to the representation of Virginia, historically and otherwise, in the great exhibition. Mr. Brock also read an interesting letter

from Col. Joseph L. Chester, of London, England, who among other things writes:
"I shall soon devote myself to an exhaustive history of the Washington family in
England, for which I have been collecting materials during the last fifteen years.
You are probably aware that I have destroyed the existing pedigree of the illustrious
president, and left him for the moment without an ancestor.[1] My great anxiety now
is to trace his true ancestry, and I hope to be successful; but the difficulty is greater
than would be naturally supposed."

May 5.—The executive committee met this evening, Judge B. R. Wellford in
the chair.

Valuable donations were reported.

The corresponding secretary read a letter from Col. Etting, relating to the portraits
which he had obtained for the historical department of the centennial exhibition.

A resolution was passed, authorizing the corresponding secretary to forward for
exhibition such portraits belonging to the Virginia Historical Society as may be
desirable for that purpose.

A resolution was also passed, authorizing William Wirt Henry to place in the
hands of Peter V. Daniel, Jr., an unpublished MS. history of Virginia by Edmund
Randolph (of whom Mr. Daniel is a grandson), with a request, if he deems it
advisable, to prepare the same for publication in connection with a new edition of
the able "Vindication of Edmund Randolph," which has now become quite a scarce
book.

July 14.—A regular monthly meeting was held this evening, William Green in
the chair.

The corresponding secretary read letters from Peter V. Daniel, Jr., agreeing to
prepare for publication the History of Virginia by his grandfather, Edmund Randolph, in connection with his new edition of the "Vindication" of that statesman;
and from Conway Robinson, of Washington, D.C., proffering a subscription of $100
towards the fund for a fire-proof building, and suggesting that subscriptions of $20
or $25 be solicited for that object. (The society announces that it would be grateful
for any sum less or greater than that amount.) Mr. Robinson also furnished
information concerning John Wood, tutor, and Gov. James Wood, mentioned in the
proceedings in February last (*ante*, p. 252).

The corresponding secretary also read a circular invitation to attend an international convention of archæologists at Philadelphia on the 4th of September next.
The society appointed William Wirt Henry and R. A. Brock delegates to this
convention.

Valuable donations were reported.

New-Jersey Historical Society.

Newark, May 18.—A regular meeting was held this day at 12 o'clock noon, the
Rev. Samuel M. Hamill, D.D., president, and Peter S. Duryee, vice-president,
presiding.

Col. Swords, the treasurer, reported that the legacy of $5000 from the late
Thomas C. Barron had been received and temporarily invested. The balance in the
treasury was $1,392.90.

The committee on the library reported important donations.

The committee on publication reported the issue of another number of the society's
"Proceedings." They drew attention to a resolution adopted in May, 1869,
authorizing the publication of "The Paris Papers"—the correspondence of John
Ferdinand Paris with the proprietors of East Jersey during the early part of the
eighteenth century—which had never been acted upon, and expressed a hope that
circumstances would soon warrant its being carried out. In this connection the
committee referred to the advantages flowing from the establishment of a publication
fund that would allow of publications at regular periods, such as had been established by several societies, and which had been suggested as long ago as 1860.

After a bountiful repast spread for the members in the society's document room,
president Hamill read a sketch of Lawrenceville, Mercer county.

A telegram from the Rev. George Sheldon, D.D., of Princeton, was received,
asking for the appointment of delegates to the Princeton centennial celebration on
the 29th of June. On motion of Mr. Whitehead the invitation was referred to the
executive committee.

---

[1] The paper of Col. Chester on this subject is printed in the REGISTER, vol. xxi. pp. 25-35.

NECROLOGY OF THE NEW-ENGLAND HISTORIC, GENEALOGICAL SOCIETY.

Prepared by the Rev. SAMUEL CUTLER, Historiographer of the Society.

The Hon. THERON METCALF, LL.D., an honorary member, was born in Franklin, Norfolk County, Mass., Oct. 16, 1784; he died at the Hotel Berkeley, Boston, Nov. 13, 1875, aged 91 years 28 days. His father, Hanan[6] Metcalf, was a son of Michael[5] (see REGISTER, vi. 177), who m. Hannah Adams, and was a descendant of Michael[1] Metcalf, of Dedham, through Michael,[2] who m. Mary Fairbanks; Eleazer,[3] and Michael[4] who m. Abiel Colburn.

Theron Metcalf was a graduate of Brown University, in the class of 1805, and received its highest honors. After leaving college, he pursued the study of the law at the law-school in Litchfield, Ct., and with James Richardson, at Dedham, Mass. In 1809 he began practice in that town. Under circumstances unfavorable, owing to the aversion of the people of Norfolk County to the profession, he soon established a reputation as a persistent, able, and profound lawyer. In 1813 the *Dedham Gazette* was established by Jabez Chickering, and Mr. Metcalf was its editor until 1819. In 1831, '32 and '33, he was a representative from the town of Dedham to the legislature of Massachusetts; and in 1833 was chairman of the Judiciary Committee.

He was the author of a Digest of Cases in the Massachusetts Supreme Court, 1816–23; of Courts of Common Law and Admiralty in the United States, and many other reports and legal works. He also edited the General Laws of Massachusetts, to 1822, 2 volumes; and contributed a series of able articles on the Law of Contracts to the American Jurist, which were afterward published in a volume.

In 1832 he delivered an address before the Phi Beta Kappa Society of Brown University. In 1844 he received from this, his Alma Mater, the honorary degree of LL.D., and a like honor from Harvard University in 1848.

In 1839 he was appointed, by Gov. Everett, reporter of the Supreme Court of Massachusetts, and took his seat at the March term, 1840. He published thirteen volumes, 1840–49, with signal ability.

In 1848 he was appointed, by Gov. Briggs, Associate Justice of the Supreme Court, of which Lemuel Shaw was chief, and Wilde, Dewey and Forbes were associates. He continued on the bench eighteen years, when he retired to private life, spending his time in a way most suited to his tastes.

It is the testimony of his professional associates on the bench and at the bar, that he was a man of great simplicity and geniality of character, of courtesy and kindness of manner, of fidelity in the discharge of every public duty, of indefatigable labor, tenacious memory, and deep affection for all that concerned the learning or administration of jurisprudence. They express the opinion that other generations of lawyers will recognize and admire, as they do, the rectitude of his judgment, the clearness and directness of his intellectual processes, the unusual terseness and purity of his style, and the entire trustworthiness of his statements.

He was admitted to membership, May 22, 1847.

The Hon. BEAMISH MURDOCH, D.C.L., a corresponding member, of Halifax, N. S., was born in Halifax, N. S., Aug. 1, 1800; died in Lunenburg, N. S., Feb. 9, 1876, aged 75 yrs. 6 ms. 8 ds. He was a descendant from the Rev. James Murdoch, a Presbyterian minister, from Donegal, Ireland, who married Abigail, daughter of Malachi Salter. His father, Andrew Murdoch, was born in Nova Scotia, 1777, and married Elizabeth Beamish, born in Halifax, N. S., 1777. She was the daughter of Thomas and Amelia (Mason) Beamish.

Mr. Murdoch received his early education as a pupil of the Halifax Grammar School from 1807 to 1814. He was admitted to the bar of Nova Scotia in 1822. For several years he was a successful practitioner in his profession, but in the meridian of manhood he almost wholly relinquished his legal pursuits, and turned his attention more exclusively to literature. Although unmarried, his habits and tastes were in the direction of domestic quietude, and companionship with literature. In 1825 he published a pamphlet of 48 pages, descriptive of the Miramichi fire and the destructive disasters connected with that terrible occurrence, and in 1831, an essay concerning imprisonment for debt. In 1832–34, he published, in four small octavo volumes, an "Epitome of the Laws of Nova Scotia." When in 1849, the centenary celebration of the settlement of Halifax took place, Mr. Murdoch was chosen to deliver an oration in reference to that event. In 1865–67, he published his last and most voluminous work, the "History of Nova Scotia, or Acadia," in three octavo volumes. In all these literary efforts, industry, deep research, and considerable amount of literary labor and ability were manifest.

As a legislator he represented his native town in the Assembly of Nova Scotia, from 1826 to 1830. Subsequently he was a member of a law-reform commission, and a member and secretary to the Provincial Board of Education for some years. He was Recorder of the city of Halifax from 1850 to 1860. In 1863 he was appointed Queen's Counsel for Nova Scotia. In 1867 he received from the University of King's College, N. S., the honorary degree of D.C.L. He also held the offices of Master in Chancery and Surrogate in the Vice Admiralty. He was a corresponding member of the Historical Society of Maine. In a ripe old age he passed away, and his memory will be cherished as a pleasing writer and an able contributor to the literature of Nova Scotia.

He was admitted to membership in this society, Feb. 14, 1868.

GEORGE GAINES BREWSTER, D.D.S., a corresponding member, admitted March 6, 1848, was the son of Samuel and Mary (Ham) Brewster, of Portsmouth, N. H. He was born in that place, April 5, 1797. and died there July 7, 1872, aged 75. He was descended from *John*[1] *Bruster* or *Brewster*, who settled at Portsmouth in the seventeenth century, and died in 1693, aged 66 ; through *John*,[2] died 1720 ; *Samuel*;[3] *David*,[4] born 1738, died 1818 ; and *Samuel*,[5] his father, b. 1768, died 1833. No connection has been traced between this family and that of Elder William Brewster, of Plymouth.

Dr. Brewster's early education was obtained in his native town. He studied medicine, and, in 1826, began its practice at Portsmouth, N. H., but confined his attention mostly to dentistry. The degree of Doctor of Dental Surgery was conferred on him, March 2, 1843, by the Baltimore College of Dental Surgery. He was a member of the American Society of Dental Surgeons, and in 1840 collaborator of the American Journal of Dental Science. He wrote much for the newspapers.

He commenced sitting as a county justice in cases of trials in the police courts of Portsmouth, in 1836, and was afterward appointed a notary public and justice of the peace and of the quorum throughout New-Hampshire.

In 1839 he married Mary Ann Berry, daughter of Thomas Berry, Esq., of Greenland, N. H. Their only child is George Howard[7] Brewster, of Boston, Mass., born July 12, 1840.

PHILIP HENRY STANHOPE, D.C.L., 5th Earl of Stanhope, an honorary member of the society since 1864, was born in Walmer, Kent, England, Jan. 30, 1805; died in London, Eng., Dec. 24, 1875, aged 70 yrs. 10 mos. 24 ds.

He was a descendant, in the fifth generation, from *James*, the first Earl of Stanhope, who was distinguished as a gallant British statesman, and soldier, in the early part of the eighteenth century. In April, 1717, he was made first lord of the treasury, and afterward raised to the peerage as Baron Stanhope of Elvaston, and Viscount Stanhope of Mahon.

Philip Henry Stanhope, the subject of this notice, was a graduate of Oxford in 1827, and in 1830, being then known by his courtesy title of Lord Mahon, entered parliament as member for Wootton Bassett, but was subsequently returned for Hertford. Being unseated on petition, he was reëlected in 1835, and continued to represent Hertford until 1852. In politics he was conservative, and held office during brief periods in the cabinets of the duke of Wellington, and Sir Robert Peel. As a legislator he is favorably known by the copy-right act of 1842, which he introduced, and carried. As a writer of English history and biography, he occupies an important place.

In Allibone's "Dictionary of Authors," vol. ii. p. 1203, and in Appleton's New American Cyclopedia, vol. xv. p. 31, may be found lists of his somewhat voluminous writings.

During the publication of his history of England he had a controversy with Jared Sparks, LL.D., on the accuracy and value of the latter's edition of the "Writings of George Washington." He subsequently exonerated Mr. Sparks from the charges of serious "omissions and additions" originally preferred against him, but continued to "differ widely from him on the privileges and duties pertaining to an editor."

In 1834 he received from the university of Oxford, the degree of D.C.L. From 1846 he was president of the London Society of Antiquaries. He succeeded to his title in 1855, after which he took a less active part in public life. He was appointed by the duke of Wellington his literary executor.

The Rt. Rev. HENRY WASHINGTON LEE, D.D., LL.D., an honorary vice-president and corresponding member; bishop of the Protestant Episcopal Church in the Diocese of Iowa; was born in Hamden, Conn., July 29, 1815, died in Davenport, Iowa, Sept. 26, 1874, aged 59 yrs. 1mo. 28 ds.

Bishop Lee was the son of Col. Roswell Lee, superintendent of the U. S. Armory at Springfield, Mass., and his ancestors, of English extraction, resided in New England for several generations. In the infancy of Bishop Lee his father removed from Hamden to Springfield. His education commenced in the common school, and was continued at the Westfield Academy. After leaving the Academy he became a teacher at New Bedford, also pursuing his studies for the ministry, and so successfully and efficiently, that he was ordained by Bishop Griswold, May 20, 1838, to the Diaconate in the P. E. Church. His first parish was in the home of his youth, organizing Christ Church, Springfield, and remaining its rector during nine years of successful labor, when he accepted a call to St. Luke's, Rochester, N. Y., which, under his efficient care, became the largest, as it is one of the oldest Episcopal parishes in the Diocese outside the city of New-York.

After seven years in the Presbyterate at Rochester, he was, at a convention held in Davenport, June 1, 1854, chosen the first Bishop of that new formed diocese. His consecration to that office took place in St. Luke's church, Rochester, Oct. 18, 1854. In 1855 he removed to Davenport, and began his earnest, judicious, and persevering labors, which have, under the blessing of God, resulted in the prosperous increase in the membership and resources of this branch of the church in Iowa. At the time of his removal to Iowa the great body of the people were poor in worldly goods. At the convention which elected him as Bishop only six clergymen,—missionaries,—and nine laymen, representing nine feeble parishes, were present. At his decease the number of clergy reported was thirty-seven, of parishes fifty-six.

Bishop Vail, of Kansas, in a sermon preached at the funeral of Bishop Lee, and who for almost forty years knew him, in the ministry, as one of his nearest and most cherished friends, in speaking of his relations to the questions which have always divided opinion in the Episcopal church, says: "He started in life with Bishop Griswold as his model after Christ his master. * * He was devoted, and he never varied in his devotion, to the views of christian doctrine which are known as the Evangelical, while his attachment to the Order and Liturgy of the Church was as strong and fervent as that of any. * * He was always tolerant and never an extremist as a partizan. His mind was too broad, his charity too warm, his judgment too cool, to allow him to be carried away upon any mere *issue.*" "As a *reasoner*, he was of clear and logical mind, and gifted with a remarkable share of that faculty or combination of faculties, good common sense. His views on almost all subjects were sensible and comprehensive. He was liberal toward opponents, but firm in his convictions. And in this way his influence was widely felt." * * * * "If I speak of his *moral nature*, my thoughts run in many circles to which he was tenderly endeared by those sweet, kindly, affectionate traits which characterized him—his family, which he so fondly loved, and in which he was so much beloved—his parish, each member identified with himself in his strong personal regards—his diocese, in which he knew almost all the people, as well as the clergy, treasuring all in his apostolic heart, and saying in unaffected sincerity: "Yea, and if I be offered upon the sacrifice and service of your faith, I joy and rejoice with you all." "As I close, *his christian character* rises before our contemplation in its completeness. We cannot survey nor describe it in its details. It was symmetrical, its foundation a simple faith in Christ as the only Saviour of lost sinners, and a coming unto him in true repentance, and in humble trust, obedience, and self-consecration; and upon this foundation the superstructure was lifted up of a holy life in all its developments. His pure character so stood out before our sight, even as his own princely presence among men: attracted, admired, and wondered at."

Bishop Lee married Lydia, daughter of the Hon. Marcus Morton, of Taunton, Mass., governor of Massachusetts in 1840 and 1843. She survives him, with two sons, Henry M. and William, and a daughter Caroline.

He was admitted to membership, Nov. 27, 1855.

NATHAN DURFEE, A.M., M.D., of Fall River, Mass., a life member, was born in Freetown, now Fall River, Mass.. June 18, 1799. He died at his residence, Fall River, April 6, 1876, aged 76 yrs. 9 mos. 18ds.

Dr. Durfee was a descendant, in the fifth generation, of Thomas Durfee, who lived and died in Portsmouth, R. I., and was the ancestor of the Durfees of Fall River and vicinity. Charles Durfee, the father of the Dr., was a man of prominence in 1803, when Fall River was set off from Freetown. He had six sons and three daughters.

Nathan, the eldest son, graduated at Brown University in 1824. He studied medicine, and received the degree of M.D. at Harvard University in 1836, but its practice was not suited to his tastes, and he did not long pursue it. He became identified with the manufacturing interests of Fall River. At the time of his death he was president of the Border-city mills, the Annawan and the Fall River manufactory, first vice president of the Five Cent Savings Bank, and Director in the Fall River Iron Works Company, the American Print Works, the Union Mill Company, and the Metacomet National Bank.

Dr. Durfee was one of the largest landholders in the county, and took great interest in agricultural pursuits. He was for some years president of the Bristol County Agricultural Society; was the originator of the Bristol County Central Society, was for many years its president, and contributed largely both of money and zeal to its management. He was a trustee of the State Agricultural College, and its treasurer until he recently resigned on account of his failing health. About his home, his spacious grounds and green-houses were kept in a high state of cultivation, and were open to the public to the gratification and delight of multitudes.

In the cause of education Dr. Durfee was largely interested. He was for many years a trustee of Bradford Academy, and that institution is largely indebted to him for his pecuniary assistance. He was an advocate of the cause of temperance, and during the active period of his life was a public and efficient worker in it.

But the distinguishing field of his zeal and liberality was the Church of Christ of which during his college term he became a member. The organization of the Central Congregational Church, Fall River, in 1842, and the recent erection of a new house of worship, were largely due to him. Through this church, as a channel, he made large contributions for foreign missions to the American Board of Commissioners.

He was twice married: 1, to the eldest sister of Holder Borden, who died in 1863; 2, to Mrs. Gladden, of Providence, who survives him. His children are Mary M., b. 1830, m. S. A. Chase. Hattie M., b. 1839, m. M. C. D. Borden. Holder B., b. 1841. Annie G., b. 1843.

He was admitted to membership, Nov. 8, 1869.

The Hon. WILLIAM BRADFORD REED, LL.D., of New-York, a corresponding member, born in Philadelphia, Penn., June 30, 1806, died in New-York, Feb. 18, 1876, aged 69 yrs. 7 mos. 18 ds.

He was the grandson of Joseph Reed, a statesman and lawyer of Revolutionary celebrity, a member of Congress, and who in 1778 signed the articles of confederation. In reply to an offer of Gov. Johnstone, one of the British peace commissioners, Reed is said to have answered, "I am not worth purchasing; but, such as I am, the king of Great Britain is not rich enough to do it."

William Bradford Reed was a graduate of the University of Pennsylvania, at the early age of sixteen. Having entered the legal profession, he became, in 1838, Attorney General of his native State. He also became prominent in literary labors, contributing valuable papers to periodical literature, and holding at one time the professorship of English literature and rhetoric in his alma mater. He published in 2 vols. 8vo., 1847, the Life and Correspondence of his grandfather, Joseph Reed. In 1853, the Life of his grandmother, Esther Reed, 8vo. 1 vol. Also a "Vindication of Joseph Reed," in reply to Mr. Bancroft's history, in several pamphlets. He edited the posthumous works of his brother Henry, and has published a large number of historical addresses, and political pamphlets.

He became interested in politics early in his professional career, and, in 1825, accompanied our legation to Mexico. In 1857 he was appointed, by President Buchanan, envoy-extraordinary and minister to China, where he proved himself a successful diplomatist, and negotiated the treaty ratified Jan. 26, 1860. A few years since he became a resident of New-York. He leaves two sons, and a daughter, the latter inheriting her father's literary ability.

Admitted a corresponding member, May 10, 1855.

Dr. Abijah Weld Draper, a resident member, died in West Roxbury, March 19, 1874, at the age of 66 years. He was born Jan. 25, 1808, in that town. He and his father were the only physicians in the old first parish (formerly second of Roxbury) for a period of more then seventy years. He was one of the few in the parish who were connecting links between the present generation and the past. He was baptized in infancy in the first church, and for almost thirty consecutive years was a parish officer. He was greatly interested in the history of the town, and particularly in that of the First Parish. The old families, their ancestors and descendants, their homesteads and acres, and the changes time had wrought in society around him, he had gathered from records and the memories of aged people, and they were woven together in his mind into one continuous narrative. Whatever interested him he prosecuted with earnestness and ardor. To the care of his patients, and to the old church of his parents and of his own childhood and life, he was eminently devoted. He was truly generous, and his sympathies were deep and strong for the sick and suffering. In a practice of thirty years he was faithful to all who sought his care. He saw valuable life and brothers and sisters in his patients, not wealth or distinction. By day and night, in cold and weariness, he obeyed the summons of the poorest, when he knew he should receive no compensation, as readily as that of the wealthy.

He was a public-spirited man, and was deeply interested in schools and in whatever pertained to the welfare and good order of society. He was especially anxious to preserve the ancestral standard of virtue, which his family name had long represented. He was an earnest Unitarian, but willing to consider new ideas, and accepted, as much as would be expected of a man of his years, the more liberal views of that denomination.

He was a representative in the Massachusetts legislature in the years 1857 and 1858, and was admitted a member of this society Aug. 13, 1856.

Biographical Sketch of a Benefactor.

Prepared by Albert H. Hoyt, A.M., of Boston,

Mrs. Mary Warren (Field) Russell was born in North Yarmouth, Me., on the 11th of August, 1822. She was the first child of James and Achsah (Whitcomb) Field of that town. Upon the death of her mother she was taken by her father's sister, Mrs. Enoch Baldwin, to her home in Dorchester; and from that time until her death, she resided in Dorchester and Boston. On the 8th of October, 1845, she was married, by the Rev. Charles Lowell, D.D., to Edward Russell, Esq., of this city, a member of this society.

Mrs. Russell possessed an active and vigorous mind; and while she failed in no respect in the complete discharge of her family and social duties, she was much occupied in the later years of her life with foreign travel and objects of art.

When her attention was called some years ago to the subject of genealogy, probably by the possession of Mr. Savage's Dictionary, she entered upon that study with enthusiasm; and but for her failing health would, it is believed, have contributed to the public, through the pages of the Register, much valuable and useful information gathered from her careful collection of manuscripts and published books. We are in fact indebted to her for an important paper in the 27th volume (July, 1873, pages 289–291), in which she corrected some errors in Bond's "Genealogies of the Families and Descendants of the Early Settlers of Watertown." In this article she supplies information, not previously published, in regard to Edward Russell, M.D. (H. C. 1759), born in Cambridge, 1736, died in North Yarmouth, 1785, her husband's grandfather, who married Hannah, daughter of Parker Clark, M.D., and wife Lydia, granddaughter of the Rev. Samuel Phillips, and their descendants.

In her own home and family Mrs. Russell was tenderly affectionate and helpful, while to a large circle of friends, and to many outside these relations, she was endeared by her amiable and benevolent character.

Her death occurred after a brief illness in Jacksonville, Florida, on the 28th of March, 1875, whither she had gone to attend an invalid son.

She leaves two children: Edward Baldwin (H. C. 1872), and Margaret Elizabeth, who married, first, Dec. 8, 1870, the Baron Vicco von Stralendorff of Mecklenburg-Schwerin (who died July 1, 1872); and secondly, in 1876, William Stuart Macfarlane, Esq., counsellor-at-law of this city.

Her bequest to this society is noticed in this number of the Register, *ante*, p. 470.

BOOK-NOTICES.

The Marriage, Baptismal, and Burial Registers of the Collegiate Church or Abbey of St. Peter's, Westminster. Edited and annotated by JOSEPH LEMUEL CHESTER, Fellow of the Royal Historical Society; Honorary or Corresponding Member of the Historical Societies of the States of Massachusetts, New-York, Pennsylvania, Virginia, Maryland, Maine, New-Hampshire, Rhode-Island, Connecticut, and Minnesota; the New-England Historic, Genealogical Society, etc. etc. (Private Edition.) London. 1876. [Royal 8vo. pp. xiii.+631.]

This royal octavo volume of 644 compact pages is a monument of prodigious labor and critical research, of patient investigation among scattered archives and obscure authorities. By immemorial abuse the parish registers of England have been held, not as public records for public benefit and rightful inquiry, but as a source of petty income for usually incompetent custodians who are blind to the archæological and historical value of the manuscripts which they reluctantly draw forth from their dank and mouldy chests. This injurious custom has for once been happily set aside, in a notable way characteristic of the liberal spirit of the chief dignitary of Westminster Abbey.

At his instance the entire extant registers of the venerable minster have been published to the world under the admirable supervision of Col. Chester, a man of unequalled fitness for the task. The editor says that: "From the inception of the design to the last moment of its completion he [Dean Stanley] has taken the liveliest interest in the work, and the editor desires to record permanently here his gratitude for the numerous courtesies, generous sympathy, and cordial encouragement, which he has received from him during the many years of his interesting labor."

The 104 pages of double-columned index are estimated to contain 16000 names, of which perhaps one-fourth are in the text, the rest in the editorial annotations. Col. Chester says that: "Anything like biographical sketches of the various persons named in the Abbey Registers would have swelled the work into half a dozen volumes, and it was deemed best that the editor should restrict his labours to their identification, giving, perhaps, any salient facts concerning them, and references by which their own history or that of their families could be pursued. The present volume is therefore designed for reference, rather than for popular perusal. Brief as many of the annotations are, however, they have often cost much time and labour, and there is many a line and half line which is the concentrated result of weeks of patient research. Those only who have been engaged in a similar undertaking can have the slightest conception of the amount of serious work embodied in the following pages."

The Register of marriages from 1607 to 1875 occupies 63 pages; for the same period, the baptisms, which averaged hardly more than one a year, take less than 33 pages. There is no record of baptisms for more than eight years, between 1629–1637, none for the five years between 1637–1642-3, and none for sixteen years between 1645–166½. Indeed the editor states that "from the manner in which the earliest volume of the Abbey registers was compiled, and from the too evident carelessness of some of the later officials, it is quite certain that many other persons have been buried in the Abbey and its cloisters of whose interment no record now exists. * * * One fact, however, should be noticed. It has always been customary to attribute the mutilation of parish registers, as well as the spoliation of monuments and sepulchral brasses, to the rough soldiers or the stern officials of the Commonwealth. Even if this were generally true, there is good reason to believe that part, at least, of the damage done to the Abbey registers was the work of some over zealous loyalist who had the custody of them, or access to them, immediately after the Restoration. Else, why do we fail to find in them, for instance, the name of a single member of the Protector's family? Yet Cromwell himself was buried in the Abbey, as were his mother, his sister, his daughter, his son-in-law, and his grandchild. Why do we also fail to find the names of Bradshaw, and Pym, and Strode, and Bond, and May, all of which appear in the royal warrant for disinterment in 1661, and of whose places of burial there must have been some record, as their coffins were readily found?"

And here we may add that this gross carelessness is not an isolated or peculiar instance ; as, for example, in the diocesan records of the See of Exeter is a hiatus of more than sixty years in the seventeenth century, by reason of which there will probably forever remain a painful uncertainty as to the apostolic ordination of many of the clergy, among whom may perhaps be numbered the Rev. Robert Jordan, one of the pioneers of the Anglican Church in Maine ; the only certainty being the uncertainty arising from the absence of official record.

With customary vigilance the editor says : " It will be noticed that, in accordance with the system of annotation adopted, as much care has been taken with the names of persons in humble positions as with those of their superiors. This seemed necessary in order that their very names, and their appearance in the Abbey Register, should not hereafter mislead inquiries as to their social rank."

" It may be well to add that the editor has a large collection from which he may eventually decide to print a list of such persons as were probably buried in the Abbey, but whose names do not appear in the registers, with the evidences, and also that, if his life is spared a few years longer, he intends to embody in a supplement such important information as he may acquire respecting the persons named in the present volume, and especially concerning the few still unidentified."

The editor produces the royal warrant for the disinterment of Cromwell and the statesmen of the Commonwealth, the friends of New-England, men whom the England of to-day honors.

There are some names of American interest in the Registers, as Downing, Thorndike, André. and last, not least, Sir Edmund Andros. Of this last character we cannot but think that Col. Chester has too readily accepted a favorable impression. It has been said of late that : " It will hardly be imputed to Andros as a fault that he took the view of the royal authority which prevailed at Court. As a subordinate, appointed to a certain position to carry out a certain policy, he had no choice but to obey or resign. In carrying out the commands of his master, he can only be blamed if his conduct was cruel or even harsh, in excess of his instructions." So much could also be said of his equals, Jeffreys and Scroggs ; but are their names therefore less worthy the everlasting infamy to which they are consigned?

J. WINGATE THORNTON.

As to Roger Williams and his 'banishment' from the Massachusetts Plantation ; with a few further words concerning the Baptists, the Quakers, and Religious Liberty : a Monograph. By HENRY MARTYN DEXTER, D.D. * * * Boston: Congregational Publishing Society. 1876. [4to. pp. 156.]

Whatever opinion any one may entertain of the chief point at issue in this volume, no scholar can fail to appreciate the amplitude and minuteness of the investigation embodied in these pages. Dr. Dexter has searched the records with a carefulness and completeness truly admirable. If there is any fragment of ancient and contemporary literature, bearing upon his subject, which he has not inspected and used, we know not where to look for it.

Moreover we think the calm judgment of historical students will bear the author out in the conclusions he has reached. The book is not a wholesale defence of the Puritans of the Massachusetts Bay in their action respecting Roger Williams. But one thing is very fully shown. It was not *religious persecution*, in any strict sense, that drove this man from the Bay. He was sent away as a disturber of the civil peace. If he had some ideas in religious matters, which were in advance of his times, it was not for those *ideas* that he was banished. It was for the use he made of them, in the way of disturbing men in their civil interests and relations, so that the very fabric of the infant society was threatened. The men of the Bay, looking back upon what they had done, from the year 1646, described a class of persons with whom they had had to deal, " whose conscience and religion seemed only to sett forth themselves and raise contentions in the country." It was their conduct, which " did provoke us to provide for our safety, by a law, that all such should take notice how unwelcome they should be unto us either coming or staying. But for such as differ from us only in judgment and live peaceably among us, such have no cause to complain."

It is the best practical commentary upon this whole matter, that when Roger Williams came to be at the head of a colony of his own, he stoutly and openly condemned in others the very conduct which the men of the Massachusetts Bay condemned in him. He grew wiser as he grew older, and the volume before us confesses, what many have seen and felt, that, after all, there was something very lovable in Roger Williams in spite of all his faults.   I. N. TARBOX.

Memoir of William Madison Peyton, of Roanoke, together with some of his Speeches in the House of Delegates of Virginia, and his Letters in Reference to Secession and the threatened Civil War in the United States. By JOHN LEWIS PEYTON. * * * London: John Wilson, Publisher, 93 Great Russell Street, W. C. 1873. [8vo. pp. 392.]

Over the Alleghanies and Across the Prairies. Personal Recollections of the Far West One and Twenty Years Ago. By JOHN LEWIS PEYTON. * * * London: Simpkin, Marshall & Co. Stationers'-Hall-Court. 1870. [12mo. pp. 377.]

Biographical Sketch of Anne Montgomery Peyton. By her son, J. L. PEYTON. * * * Guernsey: F. Clarke, Publisher, States Arcade, July 4, 1876. [8vo. pp. 32.]

Col. John L. Peyton, the author of these three works, is also the author of "The American Crisis or Pages from the Note-book of a State-agent during the Civil War," "The Adventures of my Grandfather," and other works whose titles will be found in Allibone's "Dictionary of Authors." He is a native of Augusta Co., Virginia, and, since 1861, has resided in Europe, for the first four years as the foreign agent of North Carolina.

The work whose title is first given above, is a memoir of the author's half-brother, Col. William M. Peyton, who studied at New-Jersey and Yale colleges, was qualified for the bar, and after a short practice quitted it for the life of a planter in Virginia. He took an active part in the politics of his state. He was a strong advocate of free schools and popular education, both before the people and as a member of the legislature. In 1861 he opposed secession, but after the authorities of his state decided adversely to his views, he united his fortunes with them. He died in 1868. The book is particularly valuable for the light it sheds upon life in Virginia before the war, and even before the introduction of railroads. It has an appendix of 73 pages, which will have a particular interest for the genealogist; 44 pages being devoted to a genealogy of the Peyton family, and a visit of the author to Isleham, Cambridgeshire, where his English ancestors were seated; 30 pages to a reprint of the Preston genealogy by Orlando Brown, described in Whitmore's "American Genealogist," p. 192; and the remainder to brief genealogies of the families of Lewis and Washington, the latter being compiled by John Washington.

"Over the Alleghanies" is an account of a tour, in 1848, through Maryland, West Virginia, Ohio, Kentucky, Missouri, Illinois and Michigan. It abounds in personal reminiscences of an interesting character.

The remaining book is a sketch of the life of the author's mother, who died in 1850. She was a daughter of Major John Lewis, and the second wife of the Hon. John H. Peyton. This pamphlet is reprinted from the *Guernsey Magazine;* but it was written as a portion of the Lewis memorial volume, on which the author is engaged, at the request of the trustees and faculty of Roanoke College, Salem, Virginia; and which is to be "published during the first Centennial year of the Republic of the United States of America." Appended is a genealogical table of her descendants, and an account of her heroic grandmother, Mrs. Anne (Montgomery) Lewis, honorably noticed in Howe's "Historical Collections of Virginia."

J. W. DEAN.

The Early Bar of Oneida; a Lecture delivered at the Request of the Members of the Bar of Oneida County, at the Court House in the City of Utica, October 18, 1875. By WILLIAM JOHNSON BACON, LL.D., late Justice of the Supreme Court of the State of New York. Utica, N. Y.: T. J. Griffiths, Printer. 1876. [8vo. pp. 48.]

These sketches of the early lawyers of Oneida County, including personal reminiscences of many of the most prominent ones, are very interesting and valuable. They are a worthy companion of "Recollections of Fifty Years Ago," by the author's father, the late Hon. Ezekiel Bacon, and "Notices of Men and Events connected with the Early History of Oneida County" by William Tracy.   J. W. D.

*The Olden Time; A Monthly Publication devoted to the Preservation of
Documents and other Authentic Information in relation to Early
Explorations and the Settlement and Improvement of the Country around
the Head of the Ohio.* * * * Edited by NEVILLE B. CRAIG, Esq.
Pittsburgh: Printed by Dumass & Co., Chronicle Building, 1846–8.
Cincinnati: Reprinted by Robert Clarke & Co. 1876. [2 vols. 8vo.
pp. 582 and 580.]

The antiquarian periodical of which this is a reprint was commenced by the late
Mr. Craig, author of the "History of Pittsburgh," in January, 1846, and was
conducted by him two years. The present reprint is edited by his daughter, Mrs.
E. G. Wallingford. "Familiar in his boyhood and early years with many of the
characters who appear upon these pages," she writes of her father, "in later life
his antiquarian tastes led him to spend much of his time in searching for and preserving everything relating to the country about the head-waters of the Ohio."
This publication contains "many documents that are both rare and of great
interest—in some instances the private journals of persons taking a prominent part
in those early events." Consisting as it does of such materials, it is no wonder
that for a long time it has been much sought after ; and, before its republication,
being rarely found, it commanded a high price. It has been held as high as forty-
five dollars for the set, and perhaps higher.　　　　　　　　　　　　　　J. W. D.

*The Ordinance of 1787, and Dr. Manasseh Cutler as Agent in its Forma-
tion.* By WILLIAM FREDERICK POOLE. Cambridge, Mass.: Welsh,
Bigelow and Company, University Press. 1876. [8vo. pp. 38.]

This is a reprint of an article in the North-American Review for April last. In
it Mr. Poole has revealed to us the secret history of the adoption of the ordinance
of 1787, which excluded slavery from the "territory north-west of the Ohio river,"
and which adopted other beneficent provisions, the benefit of which our western
states are now reaping. The author shows that this ordinance was the work of the
Rev. Manasseh Cutler, LL.D., of Ipswich, Massachusetts, and he details in an
interesting manner the masterly negotiations by which Dr. C. induced Congress and
particularly the southern members to adopt it. Our orators and writers of history
are all wrong in this portion of the history of the United States.　　　　　J. W. D.

A History of the Eastern Diocese. By CALVIN R. BATCHELDER. In three
volumes. Vol. I. Claremont, N. H.: The Claremont Manufacturing
Company, Church Printers. 1876. [8vo. pp. 572.]

This work is a history of the Protestant Episcopal Church in Maine, New-Hampshire, Vermont and Massachusetts. It includes also a sketch of the operations of
the Church of England, acting through the "Society for Propagating the Gospel,"
in colonial times. For the chief part of this period the materials were few and
widely scattered. About twenty years have been spent by the author in collecting
his data, and preparing them for the press. As far as he could do it, he has given a
full memoir of the Churches established in New-England, excepting Connecticut,
before the consecration of Bishop Griswold, and of the clergymen who served in them.
Of the parishes which were formed during the time of that Bishop, sketches are
given in the form of notes to his Addresses. Notice is also taken of those clergymen
now deceased, who were ordained by him ; and the work contains general chapters
relating to the history of the Church in the several States.

The contents of this volume are as follows :

Chapter I.—1. The colony of Popham and Gilbert on the coast of Maine—Saco—
Richmond's Island—Spurwink—Falmouth—Scarborough. 2. Frankfort and George-
town—St. John's Church. 3. St. Paul's Church, Falmouth—St. Stephen's Church,
Portland—St. Luke's Church, Portland. 4. St. Ann's Church, Pittstown—Christ
Church, Gardiner. 5. Trinity Church, Saco—Kittery. General view of the Church
in Maine prior to 1847.

Chapter II.—1. An Account of the Origin and Design of the Society for the
Propagation of the Gospel in Foreign Parts. The Charter. 2. The Organization
of the Society and its early proceedings. The missions of the Rev. George Keith,
the Rev. Patrick Gordon and the Rev. John Talbot. Report of the travels of Keith
and Talbot.

Chapter III.—1. The Church in Portsmouth—Queen's Chapel—St. John's Church. 2. The Church in Claremont—Union Church—Trinity Church. 3. Trinity Church, Cornish. 4. Trinity Church, Holderness. 5. —— Church, Haverhill. 6. General view of the Church in New-Hampshire.

Chapter IV.—1. Early conflicts and stages of the Church in Massachusetts. 2. King's Chapel, Boston. 3. Queen Ann's Chapel, Newbury—St. Paul's Church, Newburyport. 4. St. Michael's Church, Marblehead.

Chapter V.—1. Christ Church, Braintree—Quincy. 2. Christ Church, Boston. 3. St. Andrew's Church, Scituate—Hanover. 4. Trinity Church, Boston.

The reverend author is to be congratulated upon his success in bringing together so large a mass of historical and biographical information; upon the candid manner in which he has handled many vexed and vexatious topics; and upon his strict adherence to the wise plan of giving the authorities for his most important statements.

A work of this kind has long been needed, and we do not doubt that every one interested in the subject, especially every clergyman and historical student, will make haste to secure a copy of this small edition.   A. H. HOYT.

An Historical Address, Bi-Centennial and Centennial, delivered July 4, 1876, at Groton, Massachusetts, by Request of the Citizens. By SAMUEL ABBOTT GREEN, a Native of the Town. Groton: 1876. [8vo. pp. 86.]

The Centennial Fourth. Historical Address delivered in Melrose, Mass., July 4, 1876. By ELBRIDGE H. GOSS. *Also, the Proceedings of the Day.* Privately Printed. Melrose: 1876. [8vo. pp. 46.]

Celebration of the Centennial Anniversary of American Independence at Leicester, July 4, 1876. Worcester: Printed by Charles Hamilton. 1876. [8vo. pp. 36.]

The present year is the two hundredth anniversary of the destruction of Groton as well as the one hundredth anniversary of American Independence. The citizens of Groton commemorate both events on the 4th of July last, with an historical address by Dr. Green, of Boston. The address, which is ably written and exhaustive of the subject, is devoted chiefly to the Indian history of the town, though other matters are not neglected. It is surprising that the author has been able to collect so much historical matter not in Butler's "History of Groton." An appendix of 34 pages of important documents, most of which have never before been printed, add greatly to the value of the handsome pamphlet before us, of which it is enough to say that it is from the press of John Wilson & Son of Cambridge.

The town of Melrose was incorporated only twenty-six years ago, though its territory has been settled over two hundred years. Mr. Goss's address seems to touch upon every topic upon which it is desirable to preserve information concerning the town. Its show of literature for so young a town is highly creditable. The recommendation of Congress, by their joint resolution, approved by the president on the 13th of March last, advising the celebration of the centenary of our Independence by the delivery of historical addresses in towns and counties, has been followed in a commendable manner by Melrose. This pamphlet does credit to the printer, T. W. Ripley, of Boston.

The address at Leicester was delivered by John E. Russell. It treats chiefly of the revolutionary history of that town. This address and the remarks of the Rev. Samuel May, the Hon. Emory Washburn and others here printed are suggestive and instructive.   J. W. D.

Proceedings of the Dedication of Hodgson Hall by the Georgia Historical Society on the occasion of its Thirty-Seventh Anniversary, February 14, 1876. Savannah, Ga.: Printed for the Society. 1876. [8vo. pp. 29.]

Hodgson Hall is an elegant structure, erected for the use of the Georgia Historical Society, in commemoration of the distinguished oriental scholar, William Brown Hodgson, LL.D., an active member of that society. The building having been begun at the expense of his widow, Mrs. Margaret (Telfair) Hodgson, her sister, Miss Mary Telfair, who survived her, undertook to carry out her plan. Miss Telfair did not live to see the completion of the building, but she made provision to finish it. This pamphlet, which is embellished with a photographic view of the interior of the hall, contains interesting addresses at the dedication, by Gen. Henry R. Jackson, president of the society, and others.   J. W. D.

The Clapp Memorial.   Record of the Clapp Family in America, containing Sketches of the Original six Emigrants, and a Genealogy of their Descendants bearing the Name.   With a Supplement, and the Proceedings at Two Family Meetings. EBENEZER CLAPP, Compiler.   Boston: David Clapp & Son, Publishers.   1876.   [8vo. pp. 436+80.]

Memorial of the Thayer Name from the Massachusetts Colony of Weymouth and Braintree, embracing Genealogical and Biographical Sketches of Richard and Thomas Thayer and their Descendants from 1636 to 1874. By BEZALEEL THAYER.   [Motto.]   Oswego: R. J. Oliphant, Printer. 1874.   [8vo. pp. 708.]

Mr. William Diodate (of New Haven, from 1717 to 1751) and his Italian Ancestry, read before the New Haven Colony Historical Society, June 28, 1875. By EDWARD E. SALISBURY.   [Privately printed.   4to. pp. 39.]

The Kinsman Family.   Genealogical Record of the Descendants of Robert Kinsman, of Ipswich, Mass.   From 1634 to 1875. Compiled for FREDERICK KINSMAN, by LUCY W. STICKNEY.   Boston: Printed by Alfred Mudge & Son.   1876.   [8vo. pp. 258.]

A Genealogical History of that branch of the Alger Family which springs from Thomas Alger of Taunton and Bridgewater in Massachusetts. 1665– 1875.   By ARTHUR M. ALGER.   [Motto.]   Boston: Press of David Clapp & Son.   1876.   [8vo. pp. 60.]

Genealogy of the Roberdeau Family, including a Biography of General Daniel Roberdeau, of the Revolutionary Army, and the Continental Congress, and Signer of the Articles of Confederation. By ROBERDEAU BUCHANAN.   Printed for Private Distribution.   Washington: Joseph L. Pearson, Printer.   1876.   [Large 12mo. pp. 196.]

Genealogical Notes relating to the Family of Scull. Compiled by G. D. SCULL.   [Arms.]   Private Impression.   1876.   [4to. pp. 12.]

The Name of Perkins as found on the Essex County Records. * * * Printed at the Salem Press, Salem, Mass.   [1876.   8vo. pp. 105.]

Lowndes of South Carolina, an Historical and Genealogical Memoir. By GEORGE B. CHASE, A.M. Harv.   [Motto.]   Boston: A. Williams & Company.   1876.   [8vo. pp. 81.]

The Clapp genealogy contains the descendants of Edward, Thomas and Nicholas Clapp, brothers, and Roger Clapp, their cousin, who were among the early settlers of New-England: also of George Gilson Clapp, who settled in New-York in the latter part of the seventeenth century.   Between the last named and the others no relationship has been traced.   The work embraces records of over 1200 families bearing the name, including about 3800 descendants in the male line, unequally divided among the five branches.   The descendants of Roger and Thomas, though themselves about equal in numbers, are each much more numerous than those of either of the other three progenitors.   The great majority of persons of the name now living in the vicinity of Boston are descendants of Thomas or Nicholas.   The descendants of Roger are in Western Massachusetts, or scattered throughout other states; those of George Gilson Clapp live mostly in New-York state, in the Western states, and in Canada; and those of Edward are nearly extinct.   This is a very thorough and praiseworthy book.   The compiler has been collecting materials for more than thirty-five years; and with his collections have been incorporated those of Messrs. David Clapp, William B. Trask and David C. Clapp, who have aided in the compilation.   The work is well printed, is illustrated by numerous portraits, and is thoroughly indexed.

The Thayer volume is by the late Gen. Bezaleel Thayer, of Mexico, N. Y., who died June 20, 1875, in his 80th year.   Previous to its publication, the Thayer Memorial, by the late Elisha Thayer, M.D., of Dedham, published in 1835 (a portion only of which is devoted to the Thayers) and the Thayer genealogy in the appendix to the Vinton Family, furnished the fullest information in print. This work contains upwards of four thousand six hundred families. The records are full and precise, and the book has a good index. It is sold by George A. Davis, of Mexico, Oswego Co., N. Y., at $3 a copy in cloth, or $4.50 in extra binding, full gilt.

The Diodate volume, by Prof. Salisbury, of New-Haven, gives the result of a wonderfully successful research in tracing the ancestry of William Diodate, who settled in New-Haven, Ct., early in the last century. It traces his pedigree for twelve generations, through England into Italy, to Cornelio Diodati, who settled at Lucca in 1300. Theodore Diodati, the great-grandfather of William Diodate, was a native of Geneva, and a brother of Jean Diodati, the celebrated theological writer. He settled as a physician in England. His son Charles was the well known bosom friend of the poet Milton. Another son, John, was the grandfather of William Diodate, of New-Haven, who left no descendants bearing his surname, but whose descendants of other names are given in this book. The work is brought out in an elegant style.

The Kinsman genealogy is a well arranged and handsomely printed volume, with excellent indexes. Besides giving a full record of the American Kinsmans, an effort has been made to trace the English ancestry of Robert Kinsman. Extracts from English records, with a tabular pedigree prepared by Mrs. de Salis, of London, Eng., giving descendants of John Kynesman, 1337, are prefixed. In the pedigree there are two persons of suitable age, by the name of Robert—one in Wiltshire, and the other in Northamptonshire—one of which may have been our immigrant. The evidence preponderates in favor of the latter.

The Alger genealogy, though a thin volume, is the result of much and thorough research. The arrangement is excellent. The plan is very nearly that used in the REGISTER. The work has, what is too often omitted in small books, a good index.

The Roberdeau volume is devoted to the descendants of Isaac Roberdeau, a Huguenot, who fled from Rochelle, France, in 1685, to the island of St. Christopher. His son Daniel settled in Philadelphia, and took a prominent part in our Revolution. The genealogy of the Scottish family of Cunningham, into which Isaac Roberdeau married, is also traced, and some information about the Buchanans, Bostwicks, &c. is given. The book is carefully compiled, and has a good index and some useful statistical tables.

The notes on the Scull family are by G. Delaplaine Scull, Esq., now residing in London, Eng. The tract contains copies of visitations and notes from English records and other sources relating to this family, which was seated in Herefordshire as early as 1400. It shows commendable research.

The Perkins tract is by Augustus T. Perkins, Esq., of Boston, and is reprinted from the *Historical Collections of the Essex Institute.* It consists of a digest of matters on record in Essex county relating to this name.

The Lowndes genealogy is a reprint from the April number of the REGISTER, to which are added much genealogical matter relating to the English and Virginia families of Lowndes, and a valuable appendix of documents.   J. W. D.

Principia or Basis of Social Science; being a Survey of the Subject from the Moral and Theological, yet Liberal and Progressive Stand-point. By R. J. WRIGHT. Second Edition. Philadelphia: J. B. Lippincott & Co. 1876. [8vo. pp. 524.]

This book discusses the principles of social science, including government, theology, morals, business, &c. Much thought and labor have evidently been bestowed upon the book and new views of the subject have been obtained. We commend its perusal to our readers, and particularly to those whose tastes lead them in this direction.   J. W. D.

School is out. By D. C. COLESWORTHY. Boston: Barry and Colesworthy, 66 Cornhill. 1876. [8vo. pp. 500.]

This is, surely, an original work, not in design, only, but also in execution. The writer, being in a musing mood, places himself, in imagination, at the door of a Winnisimmet school just as the inmates are making their exit from the building. He takes the names of many individuals known to him, among the living and the dead, as the basis of his thoughts, or comparisons. He then images, in rhyme, the future course and character of the lads and lasses who are the subjects of his mental vision, as they pass before him. Two-thirds of the book are in this manner taken up, the remainder being devoted to notes, biographical and descriptive, chiefly of the former. The production, as a whole, is highly creditable to the industry, ingenuity and genius of the author. The rhythm is in general smooth, with a natural flow of words and ideas, the sentiments and expressions being often equal to those of our justly famed poets. The biographical sketches, to which much time and labor have been devoted, are very valuable.

It is issued from the Franklin press, in Rand, Avery & Co.'s best style, on heavy paper. A carefully prepared index of persons and subjects adds greatly to the merits of the volume. Eight pages, additional, at the close, are taken up with recommendatory notices, from various publications, of a former book, by the same author, called "The Year."

The work is appropriately dedicated to a personal friend of Mr. Colesworthy, now departed, the late General Samuel Fessenden, of Portland, Maine.   W. B. Trask.

Bi-Centennial Celebration at Sudbury, Mass., April 18, 1876. *Full Report of Exercises, including the Oration.* By Prof. Edward J. Young, of Harvard College. [Sudbury:] Published by the Trustees of Goodnow Library. 1876. [8vo. pp. 44.]

On Friday, April 21, 1676, the famous "Sudbury Fight" took place, at which Capt. Samuel Wadsworth and a large part of his command fell in a deadly encounter with a greatly superior force of Indians. (See Register, vii. 17, 221 ; xx. 135, 341.) On the 18th of April last, the town authorities of Sudbury commemorated with appropriate services the heroic deeds performed by Wadsworth and his men, within their bounds, nearly two centuries before. The oration by Prof. Young is devoted to the early history of Sudbury, the Indian troubles of that day, and our treatment of the Indians as it has been and as it should be.   J. W. D.

State and Territorial Libraries. By Henry A. Homes, LL.D., Librarian New-York State Library. [8vo. pp. 20.]

Historical Societies in the United States. [By the same author. 8vo. pp. 14.]

These pamphlets are reprints of chapters xii. and xiii. of a volume preparing under the direction of the national Bureau of Education, intended to comprise the most recent statistics illustrative of the intellectual condition of the United States. Reserving our space for a more extended notice of the volume when it shall appear, we content ourselves with saying now that Dr. Homes brings to his part of the task large experience and habits of accurate and industrious research. These two chapters, in which he has happily condensed a vast mass of statistics and wise suggestions, give a foretaste of the value and interest of the completed work.   A. H. H.

An American Shakespeare-Bibliography. By Karl Knortz. Boston: Schoenhof and Moeller, Publishers and Foreign Booksellers, 40 Winter St. London: Truebner & Co. Paris: A. Lemoigne. Leipzig: L. A. Kittler. [1876. 12mo. pp. 16.]

This compilation was made to aid the author in preparing an essay on the study of Shakspeare in America, and is printed at the solicitation of his literary friends in the hope of obtaining additional titles. Such an addition to American bibliography was much needed.   J. W. D.

The Chronicles of the Land of Columbia, commonly called America, from the Landing of the Pilgrim Fathers to the Second Reign of Ulysses the I., a Period of Two Hundred and Fifty-Two Years. * * * By the Prophet James. Book I. 1876. Published by F. W. Stearns, 114 Michigan St., Milwaukee, Wis. [8vo. pp. 112+vii.]

This volume is by James S. Buck, Esq., of Milwaukee, Wisconsin. The chronicles are written in Scripture style, or "in ancient form," to use the author's language. They give a "short account of the settlement of the country, the wars with the

Amalekites that formerly occupied the land, the introduction of slavery, the formation of the different political parties, in consequence of that, and the emigration to our shores from the realms across the waters ; the name of each chief ruler and his councillors, the war of the revolution, of eighteen hundred and twelve, and the great rebellion." Much of the history of the United States is preserved by Mr. Buck in this quaint form.   J. W. D.

Early Chicago. A Lecture, delivered before the Sunday Lecture Society, at McCormick Hall, on Sunday Afternoon, May 7th, 1876. By Hon. JOHN WENTWORTH. * * * Chicago : Fergus Printing Company. 1876. [12mo. pp. 56.]

This is the seventh number, and the only one we have seen, of a series of publications by the Fergus Printing Company, illustrating the history of Chicago. Mr. Wentworth removed to Chicago in 1836, the year before it was incorporated as a city, and has since resided there, receiving frequent honors from its people. For about a quarter of a century he edited a newspaper there. He has therefore had good opportunities to note the various changes in Chicago, in its rise from a small town to one of the largest cities of the union. His reminiscences are interesting and valuable.   J. W. D.

The Genealogist. Edited by GEORGE W. MARSHALL, LL.D., Fellow of the Society of Antiquaries. London : Golding and Lawrence, 18 Ivy Lane. No. 5, July, 1876. [8vo. Quarterly. Price, 1s. 6d. a number.]

Miscellanea Genealogica et Heraldica. New Series. Edited by JOSEPH JACKSON HOWARD, LL.D., F.S.A. No. LXIII. Aug. 1876. Hamilton, Adams & Co. Paternoster Row, London. [Royal 8vo. Monthly. Price, 6d. a number.]

The New York Genealogical and Biographical Record. Devoted to the Interest of American Genealogy and Biography. Issued Quarterly. Vol. vii. No. 3. [Seal.] July, 1876. Published for the Society, Mott Memorial Hall, No. 64 Madison Avenue, New York City. [Royal 8vo. Price, $2 per annum.]

The Maine Genealogist and Biographer. A Quarterly Journal. June, 1876. Augusta, Me.: Printed for the Society by Sprague, Owen & Nash. [8vo. Price, $1.50 a year.]

The regular and prompt appearance of these four genealogical periodicals, two of which are English and two American, shows the interest which is felt in this subject on both sides of the Atlantic. The present issue of the *Maine Genealogist and Biographer*, the youngest of these magazines, completes its first volume, and is furnished with a title-page and index.   J. W. D.

DEATHS.

COOLIDGE, Mrs. Ellen W., in Boston, Mass., April 21, aged 78. She was the wife of Joseph Coolidge (H. U. 1817), and a dau. of the Hon. Thomas Mann Randolph, of Virginia, by his wife Martha, dau. of President Thomas Jefferson, the author of the Declaration of Independence.—See *Bond's Watertown*, p. 181.

JEFFRIES, John, M.D., in Boston, July 16, aged 80. He was a son of John and Hannah (Hunt) Jeffries, and was born in Boston, March 23, 1796. He was the sixth in descent from David[1] Jeffries, of Castle Green, England, through his son David,[2] who came to Boston in

1677 and m. Sept. 15, 1686, Elizabeth, only child of John Usher, Lt. Gov. of New Hampshire, by his wife Elizabeth, dau. of Col. Peter Lidget ; David,[3] H. C. 1708, lost at sea Sept. 14, 1716, by w. Katharine, dau. of the Hon. John Eyre ; David,[4] H. C. 1732, town treasurer of Boston, d. Dec. 26, 1785, by wife Sarah, dau. of the Hon. George Jaffrey ; and John,[5] M.D., his father, H. C. 1763, surgeon major of the British forces in America, who made a balloon trip across the English channel in 1785, and of whom an interesting sketch is published in the *New England Medical Journal* for January, 1820.

He graduated at H. C. in 1815. In 1819 he received the degree of M.D. from that institution, and in 1825 from Brown University. On receiving his medical degree he was taken into partnership with his father, and thus very rapidly entered into a large and active practice in his native town. In 1826, he became a fellow of the Massachusetts Medical Society, of which subsequently he was a counsellor and censor. He was the first president of the Suffolk District Medical Society, and was an honorary member of the New York State Medical Society and the American Ophthalmological Society. He served the city of Boston on the board of Consulting Physicians, and was a member of the consulting board of the Massachusetts General Hospital and the City Hospital of Boston. In connection with Dr. Edward Reynolds, he established the Massachusetts Charitable Eye and Ear Infirmary, to which charity he devoted his time, his talents and his social and professional influence. A memoir of him is printed in the *Boston Medical and Surgical Journal*, Aug. 10, 1876.

He m in 1820, Anne Geyer, dau. of Rufus Greene and Anne (Geyer) Amory of Roxbury. They had eight children, six of whom, two daughters and four sons, survive him.

MERRILL, Mrs. Hannah, in North Conway, N. H., July 6, aged 98. She was the widow of Joshua Merrill (b. in Fryeburg, Me., April 19, 1775; d. in North Conway, Aug. 17, 1843), and a dau. of Richard Eastman, then of North Conway, where she was b. Feb. 25, 1778. She was a descendant in the 6th generation from *Roger*[1] *Eastman*, of Salisbury, Mass., through *Thomas*,[2] *Jonathan*[3] (see REGISTER, xxi. p. 230, line 6; xxx. p. 463, line 33) by w. Hannah Green; *Richard*[4] by w. Molly Lovejoy and *Richard*,[5] her father. Until a very recent period she retained her faculties to a remarkable degree.

The longevity of her family is noteworthy. Her grandfather, *Richard*[4] Eastman, died at the age of 95, and her father Richard[5] at 80. The latter, who d. in Lovell, Me., Dec. 1807, had eighteen children, all born in North Conway, of whom seven are now living. Mrs. Merrill attained the greatest age. One brother lived nearly to 98 and another to 88; one sister to 93 and two others to 87 years. Of those now living, two

brothers are 96 and 71 years, and five sisters are 88, 84, 81, 73 and 61 years old, respectively.

Her brother Jonathan, b. in 1770, was the first male child born in North Conway. The deceased was the oldest person in that town. She was one of the singers in the choir at the funeral services in memory of Gen. Washington early in the year 1800.

Her gr. grandmother Hannah (Green) Eastman was taken captive by the Indians and carried to Canada.

R. E. MERRILL.

ROWE, Mrs. Mary Hamutal (Wells), in Montague, Mass., June 23, aged 88. She was the widow of Daniel Rowe, and the youngest daughter of the late Dr. Henry Wells of Montague. Mrs. Rowe was born in M., April 28, 1788, the twelfth of the thirteen children of Dr. Wells, of whom she was the last survivor, *one hundred years*, within a few days, after the death of an older sister, which made the first break in the family circle. Her entire life was spent in her birth-place, the home of six generations of her father's family.

Mrs. Rowe was a descendant of Wm. Wells, of Norwich, Eng., the first settler of Southold, L. I., under the Rev. John Youngs, 1640, in the line of his oldest son William (1660–96), and *his* third son Henry (1690–1760), the grandfather, through his second son Obadiah (1760–1800), of Dr. Henry Wells of Montague (1742–1814). Her mother, Hannah Stout, of New-York (1747–1813), belonged to the Dutch family of that name who became residents of N. York city in the last years of the 17th century. A memoir of the late Dr. Henry Wells, by Dr. Alden, of Randolph, was published in the REGISTER, vol. i. p. 178; and a fuller biographical and genealogical memoir of the Wells family of Southold and Montague is nearly ready for the press.

C. W. HAYES.

THORNTON, Henry-Thornton, at Miss Tyler's school, in Brattleboro', Vt., June 9, in his 11th year, only son of John Wingate and Elizabeth Wallace (Bowles) Thornton, of Boston.

WALDRON, Henry, in Brooklyn, N. Y., May 10, 1876, aged 68. He was born in Portsmouth, N. H., Sept. 18, 1807, son of the Hon. Isaac Waldron and Mary (Jones) Wallis.

ERRATA.—(Continued from page 398.)—Vol. xxix. p. 319, l. 22, *after* namely, *insert* John the: Vol. xxx. p. 102, l. 5, *for* Emerson *read* Emerton, *and for* 1756 *read* 1736. Page 288, ls. 2-4, *read* a member of the Massachusetts Convention for ratifying the Constitution of the United States. Pages 387, 388 and 389, margin, l. 2, *for* June 17, *read* July 17. Page 392, l. 25, *for* 1769 *read* 1760; l. 27, *for* 106 years and 2 months, *read* 106 years lacking 2 months. Page 461, l. 32, *read* but about nineteen years old.

INDEX OF NAMES.

A

Abbe, 449
Abbott, 39, 87, 89, 92, 97, 112, 122, 262, 270, 427, 428, 438, 460, 483
Abercrombie, 329
Adams, 23, 24, 59–62, 93, 127, 135, 136, 156, 164, 164*a*, 164*b*, 164*c*, 164*e*, 164*f*, 172, 180, 182, 206, 215, 216, 222, 223, 235, 238, 253, 266, 271, 279–288, 299, 303, 304, 306, 307, 309, 310, 311, 326, 329, 330, 332, 337, 341, 355, 365, 370, 382, 393, 397, 415, 430, 444, 449, 450, 474, 487
Adan, 271
Addington, 204, 234, 435
Addison, 438, 440
Adger, 121
Adolph, 396
Aford, 440
Aiken, 11, 57, 58, 157, 164*k*
Ainsworth, 432
Aitcheson, 36
Albion, 265
Alden, 41, 450, 453, 489
Aldis, 201
Aldrich, 80
Alexander, 23, 275, 338, 340
Alfonse, 257
Alfred, King, 106
Alger, 33, 42, 103, 249, 484, 485
Allan, 353–360, 389, 390
Allen, 25, 58, 61, 79, 106, 110, 128, 164*k*, 194, 210, 247, 249–252, 254, 287, 299, 375, 408, 409, 420, 440, 444–455, 471, 472
Alley, 183
Alliénce, 257, 468
Allibone, 16, 121, 432, 475, 481
Allston, 159, 164*k*
Alron, 40
Alvard, 195
Ambler, 61
Ames, 189, 249, 289, 290, 292, 293, 363
Amherst, 329
Amory, 127, 377, 442, 470, 471, 488
Anderson, 461
André, 321, 466, 480
Andrew, 25, 71, 92, 94, 265
Andrews, 269, 392, 455

Andros, 275, 407, 480
Angelo, 24
Angus, 419
Annable, 234
Annis, 134
Ansley, 420, 421
Anthony, 129
Anthram, 42
Apian, 257
Apthorp, 18
Appleby, 421
Appleton, 96, 185, 186, 238, 273, 338, 382, 470, 475
Archer, 164*c*, 415, 441
Archimides, 398
Argall, 415, 416
Aristotle, 211
Armitage, 20, 42
Armitt, 138
Arms, 129, 252
Armstrong, 139, 315, 437
Arnold, 30, 31, 63, 64, 129, 134, 250, 333
Ashburton, 362
Ashing, 460
Ashley, 34, 55, 115, 142, 195, 267
Aspinwall, 203
Astor, 139
Atherton, 79, 433, 434
Atkins, 42, 385
Atkinson, 93, 126, 234
Atwood, 178, 180
Aubrey, 15, 16
Austin, 178, 180, 182, 185, 236, 269, 447, 465
Averill, 83, 84
Avery, 262, 265, 356, 427, 486
Ayres, 339, 421, 422
Axtell, 111, 239

B

Balaam, 63
Babatrang, 345
Bacon, 11, 81, 107, 240, 466, 481
Badger, 24, 33, 34, 179, 180, 182
Badlam, 277
Bafford, 61
Bagg, 50, 54, 55, 194, 196, 239, 240, 266, 267
Bagnall, 466
Bagot, 63
Bailey, 42, 100, 147, 351, 411, 434
Baird, 109
Baker, 40, 86, 101, 239, 446, 451, 464
Balch, 91, 183, 396

Balcom, 244
Baldwin, 23, 271, 430, 478
Balfour, 127
Ball, 50, 52, 55
Ballard, 439
Baltimore, 466
Bancroft, 22, 25, 26, 54, 138, 177, 223, 265, 272, 349, 452, 477
Bangs, 23, 216, 469
Banister, 42, 43
Banks, 389, 424
Barber, 51, 201, 267, 382, 383, 385, 441, 452, 454
Barcher, 81
Bard, 154
Bardin, 450
Bardsley, 164*l*
Bare, 465
Baring, 361
Barker, 54, 55, 93, 94, 427
Barlow, 64
Barnard, 79, 375, 432, 436
Barnes, 17, 33, 70
Barnwell, 151
Barrett, 234, 383, 444
Barron, 473
Barry, 37, 79, 310, 462, 485
Barstow, 460, 469
Bartholomew, 77, 78
Barton, 23, 24, 77, 454
Bartlett, 106, 113, 195, 221, 240, 250, 251, 255, 256, 257, 309, 310, 317, 319, 320, 332, 384, 434, 447, 450, 453, 469, 472
Baskerville, 234
Basse, 418
Bassett, 178, 179, 181, 246, 249, 438
Batchelder, 58, 106, 482
Bate, 78
Batelle, 47
Bates, 128, 130, 201, 249
Bathe, 178
Bathrick, 107, 240
Batt, 412
Baty, 103
Baum, 276
Baxter, 94
Bayle, 211
Baylor, 324
Beal, 114, 210, 249
Beaman, 250
Beamish, 474
Beamsley, 86, 196, 197
Bean, 217
Beaton, 374
Beauchamp, 135
Beaufort, 148

Beck, 454
Bedford, 258
Bedinger, 155
Bedortha, 194
Beebe, 244, 245, 250
Beers, 275
Beighton, 204
Benjamin, 79, 432
Belknap, 105, 254, 265, 266
Bell, 39, 61, 223, 252, 398
Bellows, 36, 37
Bement, 446
Benham, 127, 128
Bennett, 145, 376, 417, 423
Bennick, 59
Bense, 277
Benson, 421
Benst, 158
Bent, 193
Bentley, 22
Benton, 155, 156, 164*c*, 164*f*
Berkeley, 231–33
Bernard, 17
Berthier, 396
Bertie, 148
Berry, 72, 372, 474
Bickford, 61, 62, 455, 456
Bickerson, 177, 343
Bigelow, 246, 396, 468, 482
Bigger, 252
Bill, 129, 252
Billings, 22, 25, 454
Biluton, 41
Bingham, 36, 361, 362
Binney, 243, 249, 454
Bird, 79, 80
Birge, 31
Bixbie, 85
Black, 90, 93
Blackman, 440
Blackinson, 243
Blackwell, 416
Blagden, 120
Blague, 103
Blair, 252
Blake, 25, 42, 74, 103, 113, 123, 164*l*, 214, 245, 457
Blanchard, 41, 125, 396, 397
Blanding, 160
Bliss, 108, 196, 267
Blodgett, 102, 223, 251, 377
Blomefield, 208, 209
Blood, 236, 295, 450
Blott, 445, 446
Blowers, 235
Blunt, 89

Boardman, 137, 220
Bodge, 180, 182
Bodortha, 51, 52, 54, 55
Boilstone, 436, 440
Bolingbroke, 63
Boltwood, 238, 239
Bond, 28, 72, 79, 140, 156, 228, 264, 471, 478, 479, 487
Bonner, 237
Boody, 61
Booge, 262, 263
Boott, 246
Booth, 446, 448, 450, 453
Borden, 477
Boreland, 197
Borman, 84, 88
Bosher, 224
Bostock, 143–45
Bostwick, 485
Boswell. 363
Botta, 326, 328–30
Bourne, 75, 423
Bouthetot, 193
Bouton, 273, 394
Bowd, 204
Bowden, 216, 433
Bowdoin, 396–98
Bowen, 71, 439
Bowes, 36
Bowles, 413, 489
Bowne, 407, 409
Bowyer, 118
Boyd, 127, 454
Boydell, 374
Boyer, 358, 382, 387
Boyle, 149, 390
Boylston, 178, 180, 182, 436, 440
Boynton, 290, 293, 295, 382
Brabrooke, 465
Brackett, 122, 195, 214, 215, 263
Bradbury, 38, 185, 462
Braddock, 329
Bradford, 202, 203, 249, 382, 387, 416, 469, 477
Bradley, 97, 127, 128
Bradshaw, 479
Bradstreet, 42, 75, 76, 83, 93, 181, 183, 216
Bragg, 64, 468
Brainerd, 227, 261, 262, 269, 276
Branch, 63, 64
Brand, 104
Branford, 164*l*
Brastow, 391
Brattle, 41
Bray, 26, 27, 243
Breck, 46, 47, 48, 267
Breed, 179, 181, 183, 445
Breet, 40
Brenghil, 36
Brenton, 164*i*
Brentnall, 36
Brett, 199, 200
Brevoort, 130, 131
Brewer, 193, 338, 362, 422, 424–26
Brewster, 42, 136, 172, 194, 462, 475
Bridge, 250, 435
Briggs, 239, 474
Brigham, 467
Bright, 385
Brimigum, 460
Brindley, 442
Brinley, 186, 251
Brinsmade, 446
Brisbane, 157
Broadstreet, 83
Brocas, 439
Brock, 201, 249, 252, 253, 455, 472, 473

Bromfield, 436
Bronson, 446, 462
Brooking, 463
Brooks, 112, 138, 218, 220, 236, 249, 250, 393, 466, 467
Brown, 33, 70, 79, 91, 99, 100, 137, 138, 139, 152, 169, 212, 218, 232, 242, 245, 248, 251, 256, 257, 258, 268, 290, 326, 341, 381, 382, 385, 386, 387, 389, 397, 398, 434, 436, 443, 444, 447, 456, 460, 472, 481, 483
Bruce, 27, 119, 192, 377
Brunet, 257
Bryant, 194, 215
Brydges, 20, 192, 193
Buchanan, 129, 340, 430, 446, 477, 484, 485
Buck, 128, 208, 392, 451, 486, 487
Buckingham, 9–15, 127, 130, 131, 167, 263
Buckminster, 225, 227
Bucknam, 439
Buckram, 82
Bulfinch, 176, 440
Bulkeley, 262, 263, 437
Bull, 41, 134, 149
Bullard, 101, 119
Bumstead, 35
Bunker, 180, 182, 347, 455, 456
Burbank, 84, 94, 195, 196
Burgess, 114
Burgoyne, 164*j*, 223, 316, 317, 346, 347, 352, 366, 373
Burke, 32, 80, 143, 144, 146, 446, 460
Burkit, 38
Burley, 214
Burnel, 437
Burnett, 23, 157
Burnham, 61, 62, 91, 101, 102, 210, 264, 452
Burr, 116, 180, 181, 182, 265
Burroughs, 162, 432, 447
Burt, 111, 446, 447
Bush, 128, 450
Bushnell, 263
Butler, 80, 139, 151, 366, 460, 483
Butreck, 182
Buzzell, 61, 62, 456
Byfield, 109
Byles, 47, 235
Byrd, 253
Byron, 320

C
Cabot, 257, 468
Caldwell, 86, 90, 91, 112
Calef, 113, 217, 461
Calfe, 6, 426
Calhoun, 161, 164*f*, 164*g*, 429, 430
Califf, 113, 217
Calvert, 300
Call, 179, 181, 182
Callahan, 372
Callender, 41, 134
Calley, 39, 214, 427, 428
Callogharne, 435
Camden, 432
Cammock, 240
Campbell, 149, 292, 386, 387, 451
Campfield, 75, 77
Canby, 130
Canfield, 77
Canning, 159, 161

Cannon, 149
Cantwell, 262
Capen, 127, 134, 181, 183
Carkett, 40
Carleton, 92, 370, 372, 395, 471
Carnot, 396
Carns, 444
Carr, 31, 92, 434
Carrier, 195
Carrington, 80
Carroll, 22
Carter, 132, 139, 183, 236, 248, 256, 397, 455
Cartier, 257, 258, 333
Cartwright, 152
Carver, 111
Cary, 179, 180, 439, 442
Case, 261, 262, 269, 276
Cason, 28
Cass, 216
Caswell, 316, 317
Catherine II., Queen, 24
Catland, 61
Caton, 108, 109
Cave, 117, 464
Ceauell, 110
Ceracchi, 24
Chace, 250
Chambers, 196, 198
Champion, 140, 195, 266, 267
Champlain, 268, 345, 449
Champney, 384
Chandler, 23, 25, 236, 369, 370, 453, 454
Channing, 42, 251, 430
Chapin, 194, 195, 267, 447, 448, 451, 452
Chapman, 103, 108, 207, 221, 228, 230, 231, 262, 263, 347, 425, 426
Charles I., King, 83
Charles II., King, 74
Charter, 450
Chase, 15, 141, 154, 164*j*, 186, 225, 250, 427, 434, 470, 477, 484
Chatham, 328, 346
Chattwil, 64, 67
Chaucer, 164*l*, 209
Chauncey, 261, 447
Cheap, 40
Checkley, 280, 283
Cheever, 166, 249, 436, 470
Chency, 434
Chesborough, 237
Chesley, 59–62, 105, 220
Chester, 22, 27, 455, 458, 473, 479, 480
Cheves, 159, 161, 164*f*
Chew, 348
Chickering, 201, 474
Child, 79, 122, 127
Chillingworth, 226
Chittenden, 58
Choate, 113
Chubb, 437
Chubbuck, 267
Church, 18, 284, 333, 339, 382
Churchill, 260
Cilley, 216, 223, 230
Claghorn, 56
Clapp, 185, 262, 484
Clarendon, 21
Clarke, 19, 40, 42, 43, 80, 83, 98, 99, 116, 127, 181, 185, 193, 203, 207, 212, 229, 237, 245, 247, 249, 250, 262, 268, 276, 314, 344, 347, 370, 405, 418, 420, 427, 437, 445, 471, 478, 481, 482

Claxton, 261
Clay, 24, 115, 161, 164*c*, 164*f*, 164*g*
Cleaves, 424
Cleeve, 423
Clements, 69, 97, 108, 409
Clevinger, 24
Cleveland, 119, 449
Cliffe, 109
Clifford, 393
Clift, 252
Clinton, 58, 111, 117, 316, 336
Coats, 42, 258
Cobb, 42, 96, 223, 237, 342, 343, 395
Cobbett, 111
Cochraine, 113, 344, 354
Cockaine, 413
Cocking, 136, 331
Coddington, 135, 202, 251, 469
Codman, 245
Coffin, 37, 457, 471
Cogdell, 158, 159
Coggin, 192, 193
Cogswell, 184, 223, 469
Coit, 11, 263
Colbron, 79, 205, 206
Colburn, 106, 185, 186, 248, 249, 290, 294, 326, 331, 390, 470, 471, 474
Cole, 236, 333
Coleman, 199, 435, 436, 438, 439
Coleridge, 363
Colesworthy, 485, 486
Coley, 52, 451
Colleton, 148
Collins, 222, 237, 251
Colton, 452
Columbus, 23, 251, 273, 367
Comer, 108, 109
Coney, 421
Congden, 56
Connel, 460
Conner, 62, 92, 174, 385*l*
Constant, 415
Converse, 264
Conway, 473
Cook, 37, 40, 139, 239, 435
Cooley, 33, 34, 119, 214, 267, 450
Coolidge, 487
Cooper, 40, 51, 52, 123, 286, 351, 382, 383, 385, 386, 397, 435, 437, 439, 440
Copland, 417
Copley, 23, 238
Coppee, 258
Corbett, 210
Cordis, 36
Corey, 185, 192, 193, 399, 470
Corliss, 463, 469
Cornell, 127
Cornish, 436
Cornwallis, 330, 429
Cort, 438
Cortland, 111, 128
Corwin, 75
Costar, 164*k*
Cotesworth, 151
Cothren, 472
Cotton, 22, 37, 111, 135, 239, 437, 464
Cottenet, 164*k*
Cotting, 438
Coulton, 52
Courter, 345
Cousins, 213
Cowell, 440

Cowen, 460
Cownts, 179
Cowper, 209
Coxe, 15, 31
Crafts, 375, 382, 383
Craig, 482
Craigie, 340, 341
Cram, 215
Cranch, 307
Crandley, 71
Cranfield, 21, 212, 266
Crane, 239, 250, 262, 263, 358, 389
Crary, 129, 334
Cravath, 47
Craven, 148
Crawford, 164*d*, 164*f*, 429, 430
Creighton, 262, 263
Cresset, 108
Cressy, 90
Crocker, 22, 34
Crole, 460
Crommet, 60
Cromwell, 74, 345, 397, 459, 460, 479, 480
Crosby, 60
Cross, 221, 420
Crossewel, 178, 180, 182
Crowch, 183
Crowell, 368
Cruse, 80
Cudworth, 464
Cummings, 85, 94, 290, 293, 295, 298, 339, 470
Cunningham, 42, 46, 439, 485
Curtis, 113, 122, 127, 138, 244, 394, 466
Curry, 113, 360
Cushing, 38, 207, 209, 210, 221, 285, 381, 416, 455
Cushman, 418, 471
Custine, 396
Custis, 300
Cutler, 112, 122, 123, 126, 128, 167, 178, 180, 181, 182, 183, 241, 247, 249, 469, 470, 474, 482
Cutter, 174, 224, 243, 246, 262, 263, 343, 350, 470
Cutting, 237
Cutts, 111, 113, 126, 128, 167, 237

D

Daggett, 252
Dailey, 251
D'Ailly, 257
Daland, 98
Dale, 415, 435
Dall, 63, 128
Dallas, 164*k*
Dalling, 40
Dalrymple, 112, 252, 440, 469
Dalton, 211, 213
Dam, 220, 457
Dame, 247, 248, 260, 402
Dammon, 179
Damyron, 417
Dana, 44, 47, 138
Dane, 86, 242
Danforth, 76, 119, 124, 235, 385, 457, 458
Daniel, 252, 385, 456, 457, 458, 473
Darcey, 26
Darling, 182
Dassett, 436
Davenport, 46, 47, 248, 432, 439
Davidson, 300
Davis, 20, 23, 24, 46, 59,

60, 61, 62, 93, 98, 109, 127, 128, 146, 157, 183, 193, 214, 223, 225, 235, 250, 256, 361, 366, 382, 396, 415, 427, 432, 436, 437, 456, 463, 485
Davy, 75, 76
Dawes, 45, 47, 235, 366, 386
Dawson, 393
Day, 50, 51, 53, 114, 115, 116, 194, 195, 196, 267, 460, 462
Dayton, 333, 338
Dean, 26, 27, 72, 73, 126, 136, 184–186, 195, 196, 231, 243, 248, 249, 260, 271, 278, 315, 316, 346, 394, 499, 470, 481
Dearborn, 217, 218, 393
Deas, 164*k*
De Broglie, 396
De Bry, 257
De Capellis, 396, 397
Decatur, 218
De Corney, 396
De Costa, 468
Decoster, 368
D'Estaing, 320
Dekais, 439
Delaplaine, 249, 485
Delaware, 415, 416
Deloraine, 470
De Marshals, 208
Deming, 104, 358, 436, 440
De Merritt, 456
Dembo, 60
Demmere, 316
De Menonville, 396
Dennavan, 460
Dennie, 382
Dennis, 417
Dennison, 83, 89, 455
Denniston, 250
De Paris, 258
De Poining, 208
Derby, 89, 110, 242, 249
Desbrisay, 116
De Salis, 128, 464, 485
De Saune, 42
De Saussure, 158
Devens, 25, 138, 394
Devereux, 178
Devotion, 278
Dewer, 324
Dewey, 474
De Witt, 118
De Wolf, 465
Dexter, 24, 113, 186, 206, 480
Dibden, 257
Dickinson, 116, 275, 276, 305
Dieskau, Baron, 222
Digby, 77
Diggins, 195
Dike, 192, 193
Dillingham, 136
Dilloway, 176
Diman, 251
Dimon, 39, 116, 129, 375
Diodate, 484, 485
Disraeli, 118
Dix, 83, 469
Dobbs, 18
Doble, 460
Dodd, 432
Dodge, 99, 240, 263
Doe, 59, 62
Doolittle, 275
Doring, 63
Dorman, 80, 85, 89, 97
Dorothy, 437
Dorr, 250–252

Doubleday, 181, 183
Doughty, 411
Douglass, 27, 130, 464
Dow, 97, 179, 180, 182, 214, 289, 294, 296, 297, 425
Downe, 100
Downing, 50, 55, 59, 480
Downer, 48, 344
Dowse, 75, 208
Doyle, 251, 440
Drake, 29, 30, 78, 109, 124, 127, 128, 130, 136, 167, 184, 185, 203, 204, 238, 247, 248, 325, 344, 361, 397, 423, 452, 461, 469
Drapeau, 249
Draper, 272, 469, 478
Drayton, 149
Dresser, 88
Drew, 61, 62, 455, 456
Drinkwater, 383
Drisco, 62
Duane, 396, 469
Duché, 285, 286
Duckett, 348, 350, 351, 352
Dudley, 199, 213, 215, 217, 220, 229, 239, 438
Due, 460
Duer, 361
Duff, 350
Dumass, 482
Dun, 59, 460
Dunbar, 375
Duncan, 39, 378, 432
Dunham, 466
Dunklin, 178
Dunnell, 93
Dunster, 26, 27
Dunton, 204, 239, 362
Durant, 127, 464
Durfee 477
Durgin, 61, 62
Durrier, 42
Duryea, 473
Dutton, 362
Duval, 252
Duyckinck, 267, 268
Dwight, 11, 430
Dynn, 108–110

E

Eames, 85, 87
Earle, 25
Eastman, 106, 127, 220, 250, 290, 295, 463, 489
Easton, 374
Eaton, 36, 102, 223, 420, 441, 448
Eckley, 46
Eddy, 355, 356
Eden, 149, 257
Edes, 43, 49, 126, 180, 181, 183, 185, 186, 248, 386, 470
Edgcomb, 234
Edgcumbe, 63, 392
Edgerly, 61
Edmunds, 180, 181, 214, 417
Edwards, 64, 88, 139, 140, 245, 439, 440, 445, 470
Ela, 228
Elden, 392
Eldred, 421
Eldridge, 449
Elfred, 416
Eliot, 35, 60, 62, 142, 146, 151, 164*k*, 205, 206, 235, 254, 462, 469
Elizabeth, Queen, 444
Ellingwood, 99
Ellis, 23, 136, 227, 262-264, 377, 395, 486
Ellsworth, 446, 449

Ellwood, 267
Elphinstone, 209
Emerson, 102, 178, 246, 290
Emery, 223, 249, 434
Emes, 210
Emmons, 244
Endicott, 469
Entler, 249
Erving, 442
Esterbrook, 104, 236
Estes, 437
Estman, 423
Eton-Oh-Koam, 24
Etting, 461, 462, 472, 473
Eustis, 235, 340, 341, 429
Evans, 225, 455, 456
Eveleth, 64
Evelyn, 119, 136
Everett, 251, 311, 367, 470, 474
Everton, 41, 42
Ewell, 127
Ewer, 186
Excel, 50, 52
Eyre, 368, 487

F

Fabyan, 455
Fairbanks, 474
Fairfax, 71
Fairfield, 465
Faneuil, 368, 438
Fanning, 457, 458
Farley, 290, 292, 381
Farmer, 28, 29, 42, 187
Farnsworth, 290
Farnum, 92, 195, 196
Farragut, 227
Farrell, 95
Farrar, 184, 186, 250, 422-24
Furwell, 30
Faulkner, 117
Fawne, 108
Faxon, 212
Fay, 192, 193
Fayerweather, 335, 438
Fayrservice, 384
Fearing, 128, 265
Fellows, 185
Felt, 184, 186
Felton, 463
Fenton, 448
Fenwick, 25
Ferrar, 415, 416
Ferris, 106, 130
Ferry, 15, 55, 56
Fessenden, 309, 486
Feveryear, 35
Field, 119, 129, 130, 195, 248, 275, 406, 409, 478
Fifield, 40
Fillmore, 115, 116, 467
Filley, 448
Fish, 242
Fisher, 222, 261, 299, 324, 363, 381, 411, 412
Fiske, 89, 295, 465
Fitch, 34, 214, 438, 465
Fitz, 386
Flagg, 111, 112, 193, 234, 290
Flavel, 38
Fleming, 69
Flernin, 460
Flerta, 460
Fletcher, 96, 113, 185, 193, 246, 260, 440
Flin, 192
Flower, 208, 239
Floyd, 311, 312
Flucker, 362
Flushing, 406, 407
Fobes, 243

Fogg, 106, 127, 236, 237, 240, 303, 368, 390, 460
Follen, 227
Follet, 61
Follinsbe, 434
Folsom, 207-231
Footman, 59, 60
Forbes, 194, 249, 432, 474
Force, 391
Ford, 179, 181, 339
Fordham, 81
Forest, 218
Forward, 104
Fosdick, 180, 182, 183
Foskit, 180, 181, 183
Foster, 41, 80, 83-102, 129, 134, 178, 217, 218, 231, 245, 252, 340, 341, 366, 381, 384, 402, 459, 462, 470
Foss, 221, 455
Fowl, 179, 181, 183, 437, 438
Fowler, 50, 52, 80, 112, 230
Fox, 251, 346, 347, 471
Foxcroft, 82
Foy, 179, 182, 183, 438
Francis, 359
Francis I., King, 129, 131
Franklin, 24, 31, 175, 200, 233, 234, 269, 313, 328, 346-49, 351, 357, 398
Frary, 206
Fratchford, 201
Frazer, 158, 214
Freeman, 134, 136, 246, 295, 440
Freese, 88
French, 185, 243, 450
Frie, 92
Fritze, 344
Frizell, 437
Frobisher, 257, 258, 415
Frost, 38, 52, 53, 113, 164l, 178, 179, 181, 183, 196, 457
Frothingham, 25, 36, 72, 77, 120, 178-81, 206, 270, 271, 295
Fry, 106
Fulford, 228
Fuller, 112, 113, 140, 164k, 176, 228, 234, 241
Fullerton, 440
Fullonton, 137
Furber, 139
Furbush, 106
Furness, 25, 63, 64
Fyfield, 38, 440

G

Gage, 279, 283, 291, 303, 304, 308, 371, 373, 383, 442, 443
Gaines, 164j, 475
Galbraith, 137
Galpin, 178, 181
Gallagher, 158
Gallatin, 164b, 225
Gallup, 129, 252
Gally, 39
Gammell, 251
Gardner, 39, 112, 113, 128, 167, 247, 320, 436, 446, 470
Garibaldi, 247
Garland, 456
Garner, 146
Garnet, 332
Garrick, 209
Garrison, 23, 418-21
Gary, 236
Gates, 164j, 316, 317, 319,

324, 347, 355, 412, 415, 450
Gay, 461
Gaylord, 452
Gee, 437
George, 199
George III., King, 390, 452
George IV., King, 309
Gerarde, 432
Germaine, 346
Gerrish, 82, 227, 368, 455, 456
Gerry, 235, 303, 312, 313
Geyer, 488
Gibbons, 234, 438, 440
Gibbs, 193, 464
Gibson, 40, 79, 436
Gidding, 223
Gifford, 56, 458
Gilbert, 32, 108, 240, 257, 482
Giles, 1, 27, 32, 36
Gill, 39, 178, 181, 210, 381
Gilman, 207-9, 211-14, 216, 220, 222-24, 227, 231, 472
Gilson, 69, 129, 440, 484
Gist, 340
Glazier, 330
Gleason, 403, 448
Glidden, 106, 214
Glinden, 460
Glover, 27, 332
Goddard, 34, 129
Godfrey, 472
Goforth, 333
Goffe, 458
Gold, 33
Golding, 487
Goldthwait, 94
Gooch, 334, 335
Goodell, 127, 137, 138, 165, 470
Gooden, 60
Goodhue, 290
Goodnow, 486
Goodrich, 273
Goodwin, 90, 179, 181, 182, 377, 432
Gookin, 38, 417, 418, 433
Goold, 472
Goolding, 193
Gordon, 148, 198, 220, 229, 482
Gore, 235
Gorges, 266, 413
Gorham, 225, 355
Gorman, 460
Gorton, 472
Gosnold, 415
Goss, 107, 240, 293, 297, 483
Gouge, 40
Gough, 118, 119, 137
Gould, 81, 89, 97, 139, 220, 227, 452
Goulding, 192, 194
Gove, 220
Gowell, 106
Grady, 460
Grafton, 35
Grant, 84, 164k, 192, 193, 391, 392
Graves, 90, 192, 193
Gray, 23, 33, 92, 246, 360, 362, 366, 377, 383, 385, 386
Grayson, 160, 164g, 164h
Greaves, 181, 182
Gree, 192
Green, 25, 81, 105, 111, 123, 126, 128, 129, 133, 192, 193, 223, 229, 247, 249, 262, 263, 269, 302,

399, 400, 436, 437, 442, 462, 466, 472, 473, 483, 488
Greenleaf, 381, 382, 383, 385, 434, 437-39, 442
Greenwood, 22, 36, 37, 67, 438, 444
Gregg, 227
Gregory, 119, 200
Greiers, 62
Greville, 418
Grey, 68
Gridley, 37, 290, 307, 464
Griffin, 72
Griffith, 468, 481
Grigsby, 252
Grigley, 80
Grindall, 250
Griswold, 129, 263, 393, 476, 482
Grove, 84, 454
Grynæus, 257
Gualdo, 164i
Guerard, 164k
Guild, 220
Guise, 303
Gullag, 23
Gunnison, 106
Gurney, 432
Gutch, 460
Gutter, 104
Gutteridge, 384
Gypson, 62

H

Hackett, 216, 229
Hadley, 241
Haffel, 110
Haffelfinger, 261
Haffield, 110, 111
Hagar, 140
Hakluyt, 257, 415
Hale, 51-54, 84, 96, 234, 236, 250, 264, 289, 290-93, 434, 437, 447
Hall, 34, 109, 110, 127, 130, 136, 140, 147, 186, 214, 235, 249, 250, 278, 344, 421, 434, 437-40, 449, 455, 456, 469-71
Ham, 215, 455, 456, 475
Hamblen, 186
Hamill, 473
Hamilton, 24, 27, 164e, 164f, 164l, 249, 269, 365, 483, 487
Hammond, 26, 29, 32, 72, 75-77, 123, 202, 449, 450, 459, 472
Hampden, 126, 128, 167
Handerson, 431
Hancock, 17-19, 105, 116, 172, 235, 279, 284, 301, 305, 313, 337, 338, 342, 346, 356, 357, 359, 380, 382, 397
Hanna, 121
Hannam, 72
Hannum, 446
Hanson, 456
Harbor, 433, 434
Harcourt, 345
Harding, 22, 23, 25
Hardy, 221, 426
Hare, 362
Harleston, 164k
Harmon, 195, 448
Harnett, 304, 316, 317
Harrington, 455
Harris, 35, 36, 39, 90, 98, 178, 179, 183-86, 199, 218, 345, 376, 411, 435, 440
Harrison, 21, 246, 360, 362, 366, 432

Hart, 99, 100, 107, 128, 269, 463
Hartley, 349, 350
Harvey, 69
Harwood, 339
Hasbrouck, 118
Hasbury, 74
Haskell, 30, 64, 67, 98, 103
Haskins, 223, 239, 247, 469
Haskett, 110, 249
Hastings, 250, 368
Hassell, 143, 145, 146
Hathaway, 244
Hathorne, 110
Hatt, 44
Haughe, 79
Haupter, 221
Haven, 129, 130, 226, 252, 254, 255, 268, 469
Hawkins, 449, 454
Hawley, 106, 313, 377, 392
Hayes, 41, 105, 113, 123, 365, 456, 489
Hayfield, 110
Hayley, 438
Haynes, 40, 98
Hayward, 11, 103, 431
Hazen, 277
Head, 60
Headley, 367
Healy, 25
Heard, 86, 260, 261, 404, 456
Hearn, 460
Heath, 69, 177, 179, 182, 334, 336, 337, 436, 440
Hebard, 472
Heckewelder, 277
Hedgeman, 252
Hendrick, 194
Heney, 420
Henning, 108
Henry, 460, 472, 473
Henshaw, 249
Heriott, 70
Herrick, 37, 99, 104
Hersey, 215, 220, 221
Hewlet, 448
Hews, 406
Hibbens, 202, 433
Hichborn, 235, 382, 383, 387
Hickok, 157
Hicks, 59, 61
Hide, 193
Hidden, 228
Higgins, 195, 242
Higginson, 23
Hiland, 249
Hildeburn, 466
Hill, 25, 42, 60, 61, 62, 95, 106, 110, 112, 178, 181, 183, 227, 249, 345, 428, 429, 434, 455, 456, 459
Hilliard, 178
Hilton, 200, 215, 220
Hinckley, 125, 384, 388
Hinds, 106
Hinman, 116, 391
Hirst, 436, 439
Hitchcock, 195, 196
Hoadley, 276, 472
Hoag, 435
Hoar, 113, 375
Hobart, 212, 278, 291, 295, 456
Hodgdon, 214, 374, 455, 456
Hodges, 83, 128, 185, 457, 471
Hodgkins, 96, 99

Hodgson, 483
Hog, 383
Hogarth, 24
Holden, 20
Holder, 477
Holkins, 451
Holland, 90, 223, 250, 267, 366, 368
Holly, 81
Holman, 434
Holmes, 58, 91, 127, 248, 260, 361, 386, 392
Holyoke, 370, 436
Homer, 462
Homes, 486
Ho-Nee-Yeath-Tan-No-Rron, 24
Hondius, 28
Hone, 28
Hood, 177
Hook, 17, 229
Hooker, 55, 56, 263, 269
Hope, 361
Hopkins, 55, 73, 134, 183, 299
Hopkinson, 314, 315
Hoppin, 471
Hopping, 181, 183
Horace, 300
Hornby, 81, 164*i*
Horne, 347, 455, 456
Horry, 164*i*, 164*l*
Hosley, 290
Hough, 233
Houghton, 274, 430
Hovey, 37, 92, 179, 180
Howard, 178, 181, 195, 436, 475, 487
Howe, 79, 85, 221, 245, 271, 303, 304, 314, 316, 345–47, 351, 352, 371, 374, 375, 383, 384, 481
Howell, 42, 436
Howland, 127, 251
Hoyt, 26, 134, 166, 168, 184–86, 240, 248–50, 256, 373, 375, 395, 468–71, 478, 483
Hubbard, 113, 204, 210, 246, 423, 438, 440
Huckins, 59–61
Hudleston, 418
Hudson, 184, 186
Huger, 157, 164*i*, 164*k*
Huggins, 33
Hughes, 38, 137
Hull, 164*k*, 201, 224
Hulsius, 257
Humber, 347, 348
Humboldt, 164*b*
Hume, 164*l*
Humphrey, 75, 128, 257, 258, 421
Hunking, 227
Hunnewell, 178, 180, 182, 470
Hunt, 35, 80, 81, 116, 243, 442, 463, 464, 472, 487
Huntington, 41, 129, 130, 472
Huntoon, 277
Hurd, 36, 178–83, 223, 274, 445
Hurlbut, 445
Hurry, 178, 180, 181
Husband, 135
Husk, 222
Hutchinson, 30, 69, 75, 106, 112, 178, 181, 197, 202, 235, 237, 254, 265, 266, 275, 285, 371, 378, 383

I
Iddington, 204

Ilsley, 111
Indecot, 33
Ingalls, 49, 264
Inglis, 353
Ingols, 425, 426
Ingraham, 176
Inman, 442, 466
Ion, 156, 157, 164*k*
Irving, 367
Irwin, 42.
Islip, 432
Ives, 225
Ivory, 183
Izard, 164*k*

J
Jack, 460
Jacklin, 203
Jackson, 24, 42, 81, 84, 85, 103, 109, 115, 154, 156, 164, 164*a*, 193, 237, 336, 337, 343, 365, 376, 412, 424, 430, 431, 437, 457, 460, 483, 487
Jacobs, 440, 455
Jaffrey, 487
James I., King, 464
James, 82, 164*j*, 183, 230, 235, 236
Janes, 275, 276
Jarvis, 227, 430
Jasper, 32, 398
Jay, 285, 326, 329
Jefferd, 228
Jefferson, 159, 487
Jeffries, 20, 109, 196, 197, 199, 200, 239, 487
Jeffry, 463, 480
Jenckes, 251
Jenkins, 39–41, 60, 106, 228, 467
Jenks, 186, 251, 273
Jenness, 265, 266, 274
Jennison, 60
Jennys, 18, 19
Jewett, 79, 85, 264, 289–91, 298, 427, 428, 472
Joanes, 459, 460
Jocelyn, 240
John XXII., Pope, 211
Johnson, 75, 79, 106, 179, 182, 183, 192, 193, 201, 209, 215, 326, 363, 417, 432, 445, 481
Johnston, 149, 472, 477
Jones, 41, 42, 50, 62, 79, 80, 124, 130, 152, 192, 193, 195, 235, 255, 271, 278, 345, 391, 398, 417, 418, 427, 428, 439, 454, 458, 471, 489
Jordan, 41, 112, 422, 472, 480
Josephus, 226
Josselyn, 210
Judd, 196
Judkins, 25, 214
Juery, 40
Juet, 79

K
Kearney, 219
Keayne, 202
Keeler, 31
Keiley, 252
Keith, 278, 416, 482
Kellogg, 114–16, 195
Kelly, 217, 231, 434
Kelsey, 437
Kendall, 126, 236
Kendrick, 290, 291
Keneson, 427
Kent, 54, 59, 262, 263, 412
Keppel, 177

Kettle, 110, 178, 180–83, 383
Keyes, 220
Kibbe, 192, 447, 453
Kibey, 193
Kidder, 126–28, 140, 179, 180, 183, 185–187, 234, 247, 248, 250, 260, 470
Kilburn, 85, 195
Killcup, 42
Killying, 39
Kimball, 85, 89, 96, 100, 214, 224, 456
Kimberly, 110
King, 24, 25, 34, 41, 109, 235, 236
Kingsbury, 245, 278
Kingsley, 80, 433
Kinlock, 156, 157
Kinnard, 106
Kinnear, 250
Kinney, 24, 25, 278
Kinnicutt, 25
Kinsman, 86, 484, 485
Kip, 469
Kirby, 143
Kirk, 20, 21
Kirkland, 47, 130
Kittler, 486
Kittredge, 94, 241
Knight, 79, 179, 181, 392, 439
Knock, 60
Knortz, 486
Knowles, 121, 463
Knowlton, 95, 424
Knox, 10, 36, 321–26, 360–66, 384

L
Ladd, 87, 213, 427
La Fayette, 10, 93, 126, 129, 271
Laight, 164*k*
Laird, 267, 268
Lake, 422
Lamb, 129, 196, 363
Lambert, 74, 249, 344, 469
Lameth, 396
Lamphrey, 215
Lamson, 204, 216
Lancaster, 217, 231
Landell, 41
Lane, 107, 108, 217, 220, 221, 425, 426, 455, 468
Lang, 463
Langdon, 33–7, 109, 159, 161, 164*j*, 164*k*, 223, 246, 281
Langley, 62
Lanier, 392
Lapham, 127, 137, 167, 247, 249, 250
La Place, 158
Larmon, 438
Lary, 427
Lasky, 61
Lathrop, 195, 267
Laud, 26, 27
Laurens, 148, 149
Law, 276
Lawrence, 17, 18, 40, 75, 76, 126, 178, 217, 245, 487
Lawson, 74
Lawton, 471
Lazenby, 439
Leach, 47
Leathers, 61
Leatherland, 99
Leavitt, 220, 229, 427
Le Baron, 127
Lechford, 26, 201, 202
Ledyard, 341
Lee, 69, 126, 136, 164*f*, 179, 214, 233, 252, 304,

313, 316, 320, 335, 336, 339, 340, 344, 345, 349, 445, 460, 461, 476
Leffingwell, 129
Leg, 438
Leighton, 106, 214, 457
Lemoine, 249, 486
Le Neve, 137
Lenox, 438
Leonard, 34, 50, 51, 53, 54, 122, 195, 196, 235, 298
Lescarbot, 268
Leslie, 138
Leverett, 23, 75, 79, 251, 438, 462
Leveridge, 437, 438
Lewis, 164*j*, 164*k*, 167, 185, 405, 406, 481
Libbey, 218
Lidget, 487
Lillington, 235
Lilly, 400
Limeburne, 117
Lincoln, 13, 24, 25, 150, 212, 235, 265, 269, 278, 358, 381, 389, 430
Lindall, 22
Linforth, 90
Linthwait, 420
Linzee, 466
Lippincott, 485
Lippitt, 462
Littell, 130, 145
Little, 356, 397, 398, 434
Littlefield, 360, 470
Livermore, 122, 192, 218
Liversage, 164*l*
Livingston, 152, 164*j*, 164*k*, 313, 335, 336
Lizott, 333
Lloyd, 20, 25, 109, 196, 420, 425, 442
Lock, 76, 127
Lockwood, 138, 261, 262, 269, 276, 332, 333, 393
Lodge, 36
Lodwick, 17
Login, 181, 182
Long, 222, 227, 236, 265, 277
Loomis, 34, 112, 129, 272, 459, 472
Lord, 77, 83, 86, 100, 178, 180, 181, 183, 221, 421, 422, 423
Loring, 113, 138, 186, 392
Lossing, 260, 274
Lothrop, 30, 32, 206
Louden, 90, 319, 329
Lougee, 216
Loughton, 157
Louis Philippe, 259
Lovejoy, 89, 97, 468, 489
Lovell, 342, 343, 393, 395, 396, 439
Loverell, 79
Lovering, 79, 106, 111, 112
Lovett, 36
Low, 42, 94, 102, 103, 117, 214, 215, 222, 395
Lowater, 100
Lowden, 182
Lowder, 440
Lowndes, 141–64, 231, 430, 484, 485
Lowell, 434, 478
Lowthe, 32
Ludkin, 203
Ludlow, 444
Lugrin, 421
Luke, 108
Lull, 425
Lummus, 444
Lunt, 345, 419

Lutwyche, 368
Lyford, 214, 215, 217
Lyman, 50, 119, 194, 275, 276
Lymery, 71
Lynde, 77, 103
Lyndon, 31
Lynch, 164k
Lyne, 81
Lyons, 304
Lyzcombe, 192, 193

M

Macdonel, 61
Mace, 234
Machell, 464
Mackclafelin, 192, 193
Mackey, 382–384
Macomb, 430, 431
Macoon, 90
Macpherson, 249
Macumber, 41
Macy, 41
Madden, 119
Madison, 139, 161, 163, 164a, 164g, 211, 221, 244, 250, 481
Magee, 120
Maggner, 416
Magrath, 164k
Main, 465
Makepeace, 78
Mann, 69, 350, 487
Manning, 26, 27, 96, 120, 234, 348, 351, 352, 395
Manly, 391
Mansfield, 373
March, 76, 109, 164j, 207, 434
Marchant, 432
Markham, 68, 453
Marks, 438
Marlborough, 371
Marsh, 40, 210, 212, 250
Marshall, 41, 50, 52, 91, 108, 126, 127, 137, 165, 187, 237, 247, 248, 264, 268, 402, 404, 424, 437, 439, 440, 444, 465, 469, 470, 481, 487
Marshfield, 444
Martin, 79, 84, 117, 197, 198, 207, 250, 277, 292, 330, 331, 344, 415, 416, 469
Marston, 444
Martyn, 480
Martyr, 133
Marvell, 149
Marvin, 214
Mason, 41, 60, 113, 151, 186, 194, 266, 276, 428, 458, 474
Masters, 330
Mather, 22, 80, 129, 235, 252, 437, 458, 469
Matherman, 333
Mathews, 39, 199
Matoon, 62
Matson, 9, 203
Mattock, 432
Maury, 252
Maxfield, 112
Maxwell, 113
May, 23, 43–9, 444, 479, 483
Mayberry, 240
Maycock, 437, 439
Maynard, 262
Mayo, 186
Mazzuoli, 23
McCall, 162
McCallock, 352
McCann, 277
McClallan, 445

McCleary, 374, 380, 441
McClellan, 259
McCormick, 487
McCrellis, 113
McCurdy, 103, 129
McDaniel, 385, 442
McDonald, 438
McDonough, 164
McKean, 228, 229, 462
McKesson, 311, 312
McKnight, 453
McLaren, 445
McLauren, 139
McNeal, 324
McNeil, 333
Meacham, 33, 263, 435, 454
Meade, 40, 104, 215, 217, 230
Meder, 60
Meinzey, 439
Mejory, 460
Melcher, 230
Melendon, 179, 182, 183
Mellowes, 78
Menendez, 257
Merriam, 97, 192, 193
Merrick, 25
Merrill, 59, 290, 427, 428, 434, 447, 489
Merritt, 34, 409
Mervin, 469
Merry, 275
Meserve, 456
Messar, 189
Messinger, 185
Metcalf, 98, 250, 261, 445, 474
Micklethwaite, 202
Middleton, 67, 157, 164k
Mighill, 301–03
Millecan, 436, 440
Miller, 23, 52, 53, 55, 62, 181, 183, 194, 195, 471
Mills, 455, 456
Milmore, 127, 404
Milton, 25, 485
Minns, 399
Minwell, 445
Minot, 227
Miors, 41
Miramichi, 355
Mirick, 52, 179, 180, 183
Misharvey, 60
Mitchell, 39, 90, 137, 156, 390
Mitchener, 277
Mixer, 140, 192, 193
Mobeley, 42
Mockett, 192–94
Mœller, 486
Mouck, 362
Monckton, 303, 304
Monk, 74
Monroe, 129, 164a, 429, 430
Montague, 127, 248, 260
Montgomery, 317, 328, 336, 345, 481
Montresor, 271
Moody, 38, 301, 374, 452, 453
Mooney, 455
Moore, 77, 122, 128, 139, 192, 193, 294, 295, 303, 384, 395, 399–406, 415, 468
Morehouse, 272
Morgan, 53, 54, 108, 164j, 309
Morghen, 23
Morison, 217, 434
Morley, 74, 195, 208
Morney, 63, 64
Morrell, 106, 375

Morrill, 216
Morris, 40, 157, 260, 266, 267, 299, 335, 336, 363, 427, 472
Morse, 83, 98, 122, 164l, 186, 192, 193, 201, 236, 274, 278, 430, 433, 467
Morton, 235, 381–83, 476
Moses, 24
Mosher, 56
Mosley, 126
Mott, 104
Motte, 164i
Moulton, 38, 72, 73, 234, 307, 308, 390
Moultrie, 164i
Mountford, 436
Mountjoy, 182
Mousal, 235
Mudge, 275, 484
Mudget, 106
Mugford, 392
Mulley, 460
Munn, 447
Munroe, 164g
Munsell, 185, 186, 253–55, 262, 271, 272, 275, 276, 396, 398, 468
Murdock, 474, 475
Murphy, 130, 131, 133, 249, 348, 460
Murray, 70, 420, 460
Muzzey, 249

N

Napoleon I., 163
Nash, 106, 216, 487
Nason, 184–86, 250, 272
Naunton, 414
Neal, 106, 216
Nealy, 216
Neill, 231, 238, 299, 410
Nelson, 162, 216, 220, 229, 320, 415
Nerdom, 433
Nerne, 42
Neville, 430, 482
Nevins, 290, 292, 295
Newcomb, 42, 128
Newcomen, 457
Newdigate, 77
Newell, 179, 221, 237, 244, 384
Newhall, 249, 455, 470
Newman, 80, 147, 439, 468
Newmarch, 37, 38
Newport, 415
Newton, 192, 193
Nichols, 42, 118, 119, 136, 137, 220, 223, 421
Nicholas, 252
Nicholson, 196, 198, 199, 200, 346
Nickerson, 248, 260, 406
Noble, 214, 222, 238, 375
Nock, 62
Norman, 69, 437
North, 137, 346, 348–50
Northend, 85, 301
Norris, 213, 214, 427, 426
Norton, 38, 75, 84, 92, 103, 224, 228, 232
Norwich, 68
Nossiter, 179
Nowell, 79, 81, 202
Noyes, 100, 234, 240, 290, 292, 434, 438

O

Oakes, 458
Oakman, 348
Oburne, 110
O'Connor, 25
Odell, 277

Odin, 116
Odlin, 111, 215, 220
Odiorne, 225, 262, 263
Oldreges, 80
Oliphant, 484
Oliver, 206, 228, 235, 436, 437, 440
Olmstead, 31, 449
Olney, 391
Ordway, 434
O'Reilly, 25
Orne, 312, 313, 400
Osborn, 94, 157, 178, 181, 183, 221, 447, 449–51, 453
Osgood, 33, 96, 106, 248, 406
Oslin, 193
Oswald, 299, 300
Otis, 114–16, 124, 125, 135, 137, 239, 246, 249, 329, 330, 355, 360, 361, 366, 397, 470
Overing, 63, 64
Owen, 137, 487
Oxford, 224

P

Packard, 472
Paddock, 362
Paddy, 136
Padelford, 471
Page, 101, 127, 214, 230, 270, 313, 340, 460
Paige, 126, 185, 186, 248, 270
Paine, 22, 251, 254, 342, 369–73, 392, 396, 440, 459
Palfrey, 123, 228, 265
Palgrave, 80
Palmer, 220, 235, 243, 306 –09, 311–13, 323, 324, 333, 381, 412, 419–21, 427, 428, 434, 462
Papillon, 40
Paris, 473
Parish, 241
Park, 140, 299, 300
Parker, 38, 46, 128, 136, 147, 152, 164k, 193, 194, 236, 249, 250, 290
Parkman, 36, 37, 384, 438, 478
Parmelee, 464
Parris, 193
Parsons, 52, 106, 228, 235, 251, 267, 445, 447, 451–53, 472, 469
Parton, 348
Pasco, 448, 453
Patten, 182, 355, 440
Patterson, 192, 193, 262, 263, 461
Paver, 80
Pawlet, 371
Payne, 42, 79, 423, 438
Payson, 126
Paxton, 23
Peabody, 31, 84, 85, 94, 97, 117, 138, 394, 463
Peacock, 40
Pearley, 84, 98
Pearson, 394, 484
Pease, 202–04, 348, 408, 409, 446–48, 451, 453, 454
Peaslee, 217
Peck, 207
Pedro, Dom, 391
Pee, 302
Peel, 475
Peirce, 26, 104, 109, 413, 418
Pelham, 22, 75, 395

Pell, 236
Pemberton, 97, 439
Pendergast, 214
Penhallow, 227
Penn, 15-17, 28, 29, 32, 72, 205, 206, 316, 317, 320, 469
Penrose, 71
Penwell, 41
Pepper, 333
Pepperrell, 82, 109, 235
Pequit, 56
Percy, 164*k*
Periway, 437
Perkins, 59, 61, 86, 95, 196, 212, 229, 278, 425, 426, 440, 442, 455, 470, 484, 485
Perley, 89, 242
Perry, 30, 147, 162, 164*b*, 164*c*, 164*e*, 206, 209, 251, 391, 471, 472
Pete, 464
Peter the Great, 365
Peters, 98, 202
Petigru, 147, 164*k*
Pett, 71
Petty, 17, 40, 54
Pevah, 60
Peyton, 481
Pheland, 196
Phelps, 269, 450, 451, 453
Philbrick, 217, 218
Philbrook, 103
Philip, King, 469
Phillimore, 467
Phillips, 42, 103, 119, 179, 181, 182, 223, 363, 382, 442, 458, 478
Phips, 18, 178
Pickard, 85
Pickering, 153, 235
Pickman, 77, 78
Pierce, 115, 151, 178, 180, 182, 183, 185, 218, 221, 239, 375, 377, 383, 437
Pierson, 244
Pigot, 331, 332
Pilsbury, 62, 434
Pincheon, 108
Pinckney, 149, 151, 158, 164*h*, 164*i*, 164*l*
Pinkham, 221, 456
Piper, 427
Pislot, 359
Pitman, 35, 60, 62
Pitt, 159, 211, 382
Pitts, 235, 307, 440
Pius III., Pope, 23
Plaisted, 436
Platt, 44, 85
Plutarch, 226
Pollard, 180, 336, 337, 440, 441
Polley, 456
Poole, 109, 482
Pooley, 418
Poor, 92, 215, 295
Pope, 25, 27, 79, 80, 432
Popham, 415, 482
Porter, 9, 92, 94, 106, 127, 137, 239, 269, 278, 391, 460, 461, 464, 465, 469
Post, 277
Potemkin, 24
Pott, 417
Potter, 87, 129, 238, 252, 259, 393
Pounden, 179
Pountes, 411
Powell, 148, 382
Powers, 24, 295
Powning, 182
Pratt, 129, 239, 246, 247, 263

Preble, 17, 19, 20, 109, 124, 127, 128, 185-87, 238, 249, 359, 391
Prence, 136, 469
Prentice, 101, 296
Prescott, 112, 123, 136, 137, 228, 241, 270, 271, 294, 295, 297, 298, 393
Preshaw, 42
Preston, 83, 164*k*, 206, 432, 481
Price, 157, 164*k*, 237
Pride, 74
Prince, 23, 136, 249, 281, 333, 384, 469
Pringle, 151, 164*k*
Prior, 252, 452
Proctor, 35, 37, 42, 86, 382, 384, 387, 438, 444
Prowse, 399, 400
Puffer, 206
Pulling, 382, 468
Pulsifer, 381, 441
Pulteney, 432
Pumroy, 42
Purcell, 158
Purchase, 80
Putnam, 58, 136, 138, 246, 250, 277, 309, 327, 339, 370, 371, 393, 396
Pym, 479
Pynchon, 275, 469

Q

Quarles, 242
Quincy, 26, 127, 156, 161, 164*a*, 164*c*, 228, 246, 279, 280, 284, 304, 307, 397, 398, 439
Quint, 105, 110, 185, 186

R

Racine, 24
Rainer, 179, 183
Rainsborough, 71
Raleigh, 257
Ralle, 275
Ramsay, 149-51, 353
Ramusio, 130-32, 257
Rand, 113, 178-83, 185, 235, 246, 262, 265, 385, 439, 442, 486
Randall, 272
Randolph, 20, 21, 164*c*, 164*i*, 286, 429, 430, 473, 487
Ranlett, 103, 116, 117
Ransom, 164*k*, 206, 433, 435
Ratcliffe, 415
Raughton, 412
Ravenel, 158, 164*h*, 164*i*, 249
Rawlins, 142-44, 146, 147, 149, 151, 152, 156, 157, 164*i*, 164*k*, 164*l*, 252
Rawson, 23, 262, 263, 434, 463
Ray, 129
Rayment, 64
Raymond, 164*i*
Read, 130, 252, 294, 450
Reddall, 143, 146
Reddington, 85
Reed, 105, 186, 299, 303, 305, 306, 341, 342, 430, 477, 469
Reeve, 226
Redlon, 392
Reillen, 368
Remsen, 261
Rendal, 61
Rennolds, 60, 61, 87, 432
Revere, 334, 366, 382, 468
Rexford, 39

Reynolds, 250, 489
Rhett, 157
Ribault, 257
Rice, 127, 192, 193
Rich, 74, 243
Richard, King, 367
Richards, 214
Richardson, 31, 127, 185, 192-94, 434, 463, 469, 470, 474
Riddel, 186, 198, 392
Ridlon, 104, 137, 234, 236, 465, 468, 469
Rindge, 222
Rines, 456
Ripley, 11, 483
Ritchie, 252
Rix, 85
Roberdeau, 484, 485
Roberts, 84, 103, 105, 456
Robertson, 375
Roberval, 132
Robey, 213, 441
Robins, 192, 193, 263
Robinson, 59, 87, 136, 172, 214, 215, 245, 278, 418, 427, 473
Rochambeau, 10, 396
Roche, 391
Rockwell, 260
Rodney, 299
Roe, 92
Rogers, 23, 30, 41, 42, 54, 55, 80, 92, 97, 98, 106, 183, 228, 267, 372, 373, 377, 437, 439, 458
Rogerson, 375
Roland, 236, 465
Rolf, 434
Rollins, 226, 240, 427, 428
Rooke, 42
Root, 240, 452, 454
Roscoe, 164*b*
Rose, 179, 257
Ross, 37, 430
Rossiter, 444
Roswell, 453, 476
Rouse, 81
Row, 39, 112, 225, 484
Rowland, 31, 472
Rowse, 182
Royall, 40
Ruck, 178
Ruddock, 382, 384
Rugg, 264
Ruggles, 30, 100, 372, 377
Rule, 461
Rumerrill, 454
Rundlett, 215, 227, 427
Rupp, 276
Rush, 164*a*
Russell, 28,39, 41, 42, 76, 97, 117, 118, 166, 237, 246, 249, 256, 264, 270, 272, 470, 478, 483
Rust, 90, 101, 102, 214, 220, 221, 427, 445
Rutledge, 149, 150, 151, 157, 164*h*, 164*i*, 285, 313, 315
Rutter, 193, 268
Ryan, 460

S

Sabin, 44
Sabine, 236, 298, 262, 418-20
Safford, 90, 229
Sa-Ga-Yeath-Qua-Pieth-Ton, 24
Saget, 223
Saintlow, 68
Salmon, 100
Salisbury, 22, 24, 465, 484
Salter, 432, 462, 464, 474

Saltonstall, 391, 462
Sampson, 105, 248, 416
Sanborn, 106, 213, 214, 216-18
Sanders, 49, 152
Sanford, 179, 446
Sandwich, 350, 352
Sands, 392
Sandys, 410, 413, 414, 416, 417
Sargent, 431
Sattell, 204, 205
Savage, 26, 29, 67, 77, 79, 157, 187, 203, 204, 236, 239, 407, 422-24, 432,433, 446, 463, 478
Sawyer, 58, 112, 114, 246, 248, 249
Saxton, 35
Sayer, 423, 434
Savyle, 145
Scardino, 23
Scarft, 19
Scarner, 112, 113
Schoendorf, 486
Schuyler, 164*k*, 274, 275, 324, 325, 334, 338
Scott, 31, 40, 50, 54, 74, 135, 209, 227, 333, 433, 440, 468
Scottow, 180
Scribner, 265, 267, 274
Scroggs, 480
Scudder, 80, 336
Scull, 249, 484, 485
Seagrave, 395
Seaton, 304
Seaver, 88
Seavy, 106, 227, 402
Secomb, 41
Sedgwick, 81
Seiruin, 40
Selby, 42
Seldon, 450
Sewall, 34, 109, 113, 235, 374, 436-40, 472
Seward, 383, 464
Seylor, 41
Seymour, 31
Shad, 42
Shakespeare, 458, 486
Shandy, 46
Shannon, 290, 320, 437
Sharp, 234
Shattuck, 186, 236, 295, 298
Shaw, 216, 228, 246, 377, 417, 444, 454, 474
Sheaffe, 178, 181, 183, 219, 271, 385
Sheffield, 101, 192, 193, 471
Sheldon, 110, 196, 198, 274, 275, 473
Shepardson, 81
Shepherd, 220, 230, 373
Sheppard, 40, 136, 185, 247, 248, 261, 405, 454, 458
Shepreeve, 199, 200
Sherburn, 61, 222, 345
Sheriffe, 304
Sheridan, 209
Sherman, 178, 181, 183, 219, 271, 385
Sherwin, 88, 264
Shipman, 129
Shirley, 17, 63, 119, 329
Shute, 207, 225
Shurtleff, 184, 186
Sias, 61
Sibb, 432
Sibley, 26, 428, 435
Sigourney, 365
Silliman, 261

Silsbee, 164b, 224
Simonds, 450
Simons, 267, 268
Simmons, 33, 152
Simpkins, 481
Simpson, 41, 80, 148, 391, 420, 441
Sinclair, 216
Single, 194
Singleterry, 66
Singleton, 157
Skates, 225
Skelton, 463
Skinner, 37, 95
Skipworth, 68
Slacombe, 348
Slade, 56
Slafter, 126, 128, 133, 166, 185, 247–49, 258, 260, 460–71
Slate, 454
Sleeper, 222, 250
Sloss, 325
Small, 61, 62
Smart, 214
Smead, 79, 80, 275
Smibert, 243, 428, 430, 438, 458
Smith, 25, 42, 59, 60, 62, 71, 83, 91, 93, 99, 113, 116, 120–22, 130, 131, 157, 164c, 178, 180, 182, 183, 195, 196, 207–09, 211, 214, 215, 217, 220, 221, 222, 225, 227, 230, 249, 262, 267, 274, 293, 336, 363, 402, 423, 424
Snow, 242, 243
Snowman, 42
Sohier, 113
Sog, 56
Solwyns, 152
Somerby, 208
Somers, 415
Soule, 230
South, 79
Southward, 30
Southwick, 251, 471
Sparhawk, 375
Sparks, 24, 228, 348, 367, 430, 431, 475
Spalding, 242, 294
Spaulding, 245
Spear, 186, 432, 444
Speed, 428, 432
Spencer, 337, 367, 451, 454, 455
Sperry, 31
Spooner, 56, 57, 58, 107, 235, 381, 469
Sprague, 29–31, 137, 210, 222, 246, 267, 437–40, 487
Spring, 458
Sprusin, 460
Squire, 103
Stacy, 33, 422, 425
Standstreet, 420
Standish, 462
Stanhope, 475
Stanley, 479
Staples, 201, 472
Starbird, 456
Stark, 223, 366, 367
Starr, 129, 235, 439, 440
St. Clair, 130
Stearns, 119, 264, 267, 486
Stebbins, 33–5, 55, 194–96, 267
Stedman, 263
Steel, 199, 243, 436, 454
Staples, 434
Steiner, 466
Sternberg, Von, 36

Stetson, 466
Stevens, 159, 179, 183, 213, 224, 278, 281, 427, 462
Stevenson, 51, 52, 60–2, 219, 247, 253, 431
Stewart, 360, 361
Stickney, 419, 461, 484
Stiff, 467
Stiles, 29, 85, 87, 92
Stillman, 47
Stimpson, 444
Stirling, 338, 340
St. John, 63
St. Julia, 164i
St. Loo, 68
Stoaks, 412
Stockbridge, 427, 428
Stockman, 213
Stockton, 130, 408, 409, 416
Stokes, 439
Stoddard, 18, 19, 21, 245, 262, 263, 275, 432, 435, 437, 444
Stokley, 462
Stone, 69, 104, 112, 129, 178, 180, 192, 193, 249, 250, 251, 277, 471
Storer, 109, 181, 183, 423, 438–40
Storrs, 271
Story, 40, 84, 101, 181, 202, 246, 302, 437
Stoughton, 79, 464
Stout, 489
Stralendorff, 478
Stratton, 117, 276, 460
Strode, 479
Strong, 235
Stuart, 24, 46, 156
Studley, 222
Stuyvesant, 228
Swinton, 463
Swords, 473
Sykes, 54
Symmes, 35, 180, 368
Symonds, 84, 423
Sudborough, 80
Suhn, 445
Sullivan, 23, 105, 138, 222, 252, 312, 323
Sully, 22
Summers, 451
Sumner, 58, 79, 100, 101, 239, 272
Sutton, 99
Swan, 39, 126, 183, 276
Swanley, 71
Swansey, 220, 224, 228
Swartz, 324
Swett, 271, 434
Sweetser, 382
Swift, 80, 114, 124, 140, 249, 472

T

Taber, 57
Tailer, 50, 54
Taintor, 451
Talbot, 472, 482
Talcott, 104
Tappan, 268
Tarbox, 126, 127, 136, 279, 393, 470, 481
Tasistro, 258
Tash, 220
Tasker, 61
Taylor, 69, 75, 77, 108, 118, 147, 164c, 164e, 192, 193, 195, 206, 214, 216, 223, 270–72, 381, 408, 421, 438, 446
Teal, 179, 181, 183
Tee-Yee-Neen-Ho-Ga-Kron, 22

Telfair, 483
Temple, 44, 275, 397
Ten Brook, 268, 269
Tenney, 262, 263
Tenyck, 333
Terry, 451, 454
Thackeray, 278
Thatcher, 321, 361, 376, 431, 458
Thayer, 202, 203, 483, 484
Thing, 213, 216, 223, 227
Thomas, 22–26, 40, 159, 164b, 234, 239, 253–255, 309, 332, 354, 384, 387, 396, 403, 437, 439
Thompson, 69, 71, 84, 105, 112, 175, 177, 344, 345, 347, 350, 376, 390, 391, 429, 448, 452, 453, 456
Thoms, 107
Thorn, 40, 437, 439
Thornbeck, 42
Thorndike, 102
Thornton, 68, 126, 136, 186, 248, 249, 266, 349, 480, 489
Thorp, 95
Thurton, 212, 213
Thurston, 73, 216, 217, 421, 428
Thwing, 33
Tibbetts, 61, 455, 456, 469
Tichbourne, 71
Ticknor, 46, 47
Tidd, 112
Tidyman, 157, 164k
Tilghman, 157
Tilton, 217, 223, 427, 428, 466
Tilley, 59
Timlow, 107
Timmins, 442
Tindall, 415
Tinkham, 81, 250
Tingley, 471
Tischendorf, 227
Titcomb, 221
Titus, 409, 420
Tobey, 470
Todd, 240, 430
Tolman, 406
Tomkins, 79, 459
Tomlinson, 437
Tomma, 360
Tompson, 61
Toocker, 180
Toppan, 77
Torr, 456
Torry, 34, 469, 470
Tousey, 276
Tower, 210, 454
Towle, 120, 249
Towne, 93, 185, 186, 247–49, 294, 469–71
Townsend, 101
Tracy, 157, 430, 481
Train, 300
Trapp, 300
Trask, 78, 99, 119, 127, 128, 184–87, 201, 247, 248, 250, 260, 276, 432, 457, 462, 484
Treadwell, 83
Treat, 275, 342
Tredick, 227
Trelawney, 266, 472
Tremball, 193
Trenchfield, 69
Trescott, 358, 389
Trippe, 28, 56, 57
Troop, 421
Trow, 130
Trowbridge, 263
Truebner, 486

Trueworth, 216, 224
Trumbull, 10, 26, 85, 178, 180, 182, 190, 192, 202, 254, 265, 281, 314, 319, 337, 338, 449, 453, 459, 462, 472
Trundy, 227
Tryall, 16
Tryon, 344, 348
Tucker, 69, 126, 127, 215, 314, 375, 466
Tuckerman, 43, 46
Tudor, 113, 235
Tuft, 182
Tufton, 40
Tully, 438
Tupper, 277
Turnbull, 335
Turner, 16, 60, 87, 144, 183, 251, 332, 341, 439
Turrell, 439, 442
Tuttle, 20, 128, 185–87, 195, 200, 248, 266, 270, 272–74, 456, 462, 468–470
Tweedy, 71
Twelves, 469
Twitchell, 101, 192, 193
Twombly, 455, 456
Tyler, 85, 89, 93, 96, 126, 243, 244, 278, 395, 438, 440, 489
Tyley, 436
Tyng, 41, 235, 432
Tyrrell, 148

U

Underwood, 70, 79, 122, 458
Upham, 127, 201, 239, 466, 468, 472
Upton, 268
Uran, 438
Usher, 432, 437, 487

V

Vail, 476
Van Buren, 164f
Vanhorne, 50, 195
Valentine, 262
Vallet, 449, 450
Vane, 73
Vanharbergreen, 40
Van Wagner, 419
Varenne, 42
Varney, 102
Vassell, 42
Vaughan, 21, 453
Veasey, 215, 427, 428
Veering, 197
Venteman, 40
Vermilye, 266, 267
Veren, 460
Vermaes, 83
Vernam, 41
Vernon, 31
Verrazzano, 130–33
Vespucius, 273
Viand, 468
Vilas, 262, 263
Vincent, 32
Vinteno, 439
Vinton, 221, 485
Virgil, 30
Voltaire, 24
Vose, 392

W

Wade, 85, 267
Wadleigh, 229
Wadley, 427
Wadsworth, 35, 36, 440, 486
Wagner, 391
Wainwright, 42

Waite, 56, 86, 129, 249, 266
Wakefield, 41, 204, 234
Wakeham, 60
Wakes, 193
Walcott, 47
Walden, 21
Waldo, 246, 472
Waldron, 109, 489
Wales, 472
Wales, Prince of, 352
Walker, 24, 34, 42, 64, 104, 145, 192, 193, 209, 250, 375, 377, 445
Walkins, 64
Wallace, 462, 489
Wallis, 83, 113, 359
Waller, 107
Walley, 36, 37, 358
Wallingford, 482
Walsh, 147
Walter, 116, 130, 439
Walton, 74
Wanton, 423
Wanerton, 423
Ward, 25–27, 108, 126, 129, 178, 184–187, 192, 193, 195, 231, 235, 248, 299, 327, 441, 469, 470
Warden, 385, 438
Wardwell, 111, 112
Ware, 63, 465
Warner, 58, 62, 87, 226, 425, 447, 454
Warren, 46, 75, 112, 115, 126, 135, 138, 237, 262, 263, 271, 284, 294, 295, 303, 307, 309, 332, 341, 356, 381, 397, 478
Warriner, 195, 196
Warrington, 278
Washburn, 24, 25, 70, 192, 469, 483
Washington, 10, 15, 24, 25, 44, 124, 126, 164, 164l, 216, 221–23, 238, 274, 299–301, 303, 308, 309, 317, 321, 324, 332, 335, 338, 341, 342, 346, 347, 355, 358, 365, 380, 389, 390, 393–95, 398, 473, 475, 476, 481, 489
Wass, 437
Wasson, 192
Waterman, 119, 120, 127, 185
Waters, 64, 108, 110, 179–82, 235, 250, 368, 422, 423, 438, 459
Watson, 63, 148, 214, 238, 456, 468

Watts, 113
Weaks, 192, 214, 221
Weare, 222, 223
Weaver, 37, 74, 278
Webb, 108, 109, 271, 329, 442
Webber, 109, 179–82, 345
Webster, 24, 34, 113, 126, 140, 164f, 164g, 221, 227, 246, 271, 393, 425, 439, 450, 454, 462
Weed, 106
Weibert, 345
Welch, 346, 392, 440, 460, 464, 484
Weld, 143–146, 164l, 478
Wellford, 473
Wellington, 475, 476
Wellman, 117, 118
Wells, 86, 129, 130, 140, 235, 250, 282, 283, 285, 400, 402, 423, 449, 450, 453, 489
Wendall, 227, 235, 382, 418
Wenmouth, 42
Wentworth, 105, 140, 235, 278, 291, 318, 370, 371, 387
Wesson, 193
West, 46, 87, 216, 223, 224
Weston, 127
Wettenhall, 164l
Whalton, 42
Wharton, 36, 309
Wheat, 295
Wheaton, 274
Whedon, 31
Wheeler, 25, 104, 127, 129, 243, 252, 332, 419
Wheelock, 46, 47, 164l, 445
Wheelwright, 78, 202, 203, 394, 423
Wheildon, 136, 399
Whetham, 74
Whetlock, 399, 405
Whincop, 412
Whipple, 83, 307, 319, 320, 335, 336, 391
Whiston, 126
Whitaker, 375, 432
Whitcomb, 381, 478
White, 40, 52, 80, 83, 84, 100, 111, 112, 180, 193, 221, 247, 267, 278, 332, 335, 381, 438, 460, 462, 472
Whitefield, 282
Whitehead, 469, 473

Whitehouse, 106, 487
Whiting, 244, 290, 298, 450, 465
Whiteley, 130
Whitman, 194, 421, 461, 481
Whitmore, 73, 127, 184, 185, 421–23, 425, 426, 446
Whitney, 266
Whittham, 106
Whittier, 392, 462
Whittingham, 111, 145
Whitton, 42
Whitwell, 122
Wier, 179
Wiggin, 128, 185, 215, 427, 428
Wigglesworth, 240, 440
Wight, 25, 124
Wignall, 30
Wilbur, 202, 221
Wilde, 164e, 193, 202, 246, 474
Wilder, 126–28, 165, 173, 185, 247–50, 261, 264, 402, 404, 469, 470
Wilkins, 412
Wilkinson, 316, 429
Willard, 25, 222, 236, 269, 440, 454
Willey, 60–2, 468
William the Conqueror, 106
Williams, 10, 36, 47, 62, 63, 81, 110, 121, 134, 136, 138, 227, 240, 244, 246, 251, 260, 262, 263, 271, 273, 275, 276, 377, 434, 471, 472, 480, 481, 484
Williamson, 189, 191, 330, 429–31, 472
Willis, 37, 90, 103, 376, 437, 463
Willoughby, 67–78, 103, 164h, 167, 204, 205, 250, 272, 398, 422, 481, 483
Wilton, 445
Winchester, 376
Wincklemann, 36
Wingate, 103, 105, 126, 136, 186, 248, 249, 456, 480
Winship, 243
Winslow, 30, 73, 128, 167, 248, 260, 353, 355, 405, 469
Winter, 37, 229, 368
Winthrop, 22, 24, 62, 79,

202, 210, 214, 215, 220, 228, 398, 440
Wire, 181–83
Wirt, 473
Wise, 67, 452
Wiswall, 35, 36
Witchfield, 444
Witherspoon, 313, 314
Withington, 235
Wittum, 186
Wolcott, 276
Wolfe, 329, 333, 371
Wollaston, 130
Wolstenholme, 413
Wood, 17, 34, 84, 87, 88, 97, 178, 180, 182, 252, 253, 376, 419, 457, 473
Woodbury, 128, 246, 248, 260, 468, 470
Woodford, 320, 445, 446
Woodlock, 460
Woodman, 59, 238, 247, 263, 390
Woodroofe, 464
Woodward, 25, 42, 129, 192, 193, 226, 261, 344, 419, 420, 472
Woolcott, 195, 196, 448, 452
Wooster, 104, 332, 333, 422
Worcester, 288, 290–92, 295, 296, 298
Wormwood, 61
Worth, 218
Wragg, 157
Wren, 207, 348–352
Wright, 40, 42, 117, 122, 192, 193, 195, 275, 290, 298, 429, 446, 485
Wyatt, 417
Wybert, 345
Wyman, 236, 438
Wynne, 253
Wyshe, 27
Wythe, 317

Y

Yeardley, 416
York, 62, 214
Young, 126, 214, 215, 229, 236, 399, 427, 455, 456, 465, 486, 489
Younglove, 53, 86
Youngman, 294

Z

Zeisberger, 277
Zell, 267